INTERNATIONAL HISTORICAL STATISTICS

THE AMERICAS
1750 - 1993

FOURTH EDITION

INTERNATIONAL HISTORICAL STATISTICS

THE AMERICAS
1750-1993

FOURTH EDITION

(Brian R.)

B.R. MITCHELL

Published in the United Kingdom by
MACMILLAN REFERENCE LTD, 1998
25 Eccleston Place, London, SW1W 9NF
and Basingstoke

Companies and representatives throughout the world.

Distributed in the UK and Europe by
Macmillan Direct,
Brunel Road, Houndmills,
Basingstoke,
Hampshire, RG21 2XS, England

ISBN 0-333-726898

A catalogue record for this book is available from the British Library.

Published in the United States and Canada by
STOCKTON PRESS, 1998
345 Park Avenue South, 10th Floor
New York, NY 10010-1707, USA

ISBN 1-56159-235-8
ISBN 1-56159-233-1 (Three volume set)

While every care has been taken in compiling the information contained in this
publication, the publishers, compilers and copyright holders accept no responsibility
for any errors or omissions.

Typeset by Laser Words, Madras, India
Printed and bound in the UK by The Nuffield Press, Abingdon

CONTENTS

INTRODUCTION

Historical statistics are now recognized, as never before, as a major raw material of much economic history, especially of that concerned with economic growth and development. In response to this, national collections of historical statistics began to make their appearance from the late 1940s onwards. Towards the end of the 1960s, it seemed that the time was ripe for gathering together the main statistical series for all the major countries of the world, and a beginning was made with those of Europe, for which there was more material available than for most others.[1] This was followed by *International Historical Statistics: Africa and Asia*, and the first edition of the present work[2] which then included Australasia. This will be included with Africa and Asia in the forthcoming new edition. The objective of these books has been to provide economists and historians with a wide range of statistical data without the difficulty of identifying sources, of obtaining access to them, and the often considerable labour of extracting the figures from many different places and, one hopes, ensuring that they form part of comparable series.

In all these continent-wide compilations, the sources relied on have been, for the most part, official national and international abstracts of statistics, rather than detailed publications. As a result, there are more breaks in continuity than are strictly necessary, since compilers of abstracts are continually trying to improve coverage and presentation; and whilst older, long-running series may often still be put together from detailed sources, the process is time-consuming and sometimes requires access to publications which are not readily available outside their country of origin. However, I am assured by many who have used the earlier volumes that these breaks are not often of as much importance as they seem to the compiler.

Even more irritating, to the compiler at any rate, are the gaps which sometimes appear in series, especially when he knows that they are not the result of a failure on the part of officials to collect and publish the data, but of his own failure to find them. As I pointed out in introducing the original Africa and Asia volume, such gaps could eventually be filled; but there are sharply diminishing returns to search effort when one has collected perhaps 99 per cent of available material, and publication of a not wholly complete collection continues to seem better than a paralysing perfectionism. I shall, of course, be as grateful for any help which users of this work can give me in improving the coverage for the future as I am for that which has improved this present edition.

All the countries covered in this volume were at one time colonies of European powers. The quality and availability of their statistics seems to bear a fairly close relationship to that of their original mother country, at any rate until fairly recently. The former British colonies published a fairly large amount of data at a comparatively early date in the 19th century, or even earlier; and the few, and small, French colonies in these continents were rather similar in some respects. The former Spanish colonies, on the other hand, tended to produce statistical material about as irregularly as did Spain itself throughout much of the 19th century. Brazil, in contrast, has a better record in this respect than Portugal, and it has some of the earliest series for any South American country where the subject covered is one involving a high degree of government involvement.

It should not need to be said that there are pitfalls for the unwary user of statistics, and this is scarcely the place to attempt to summarize those traps of which any introductory textbook will warn. However, there are certain problems which are of particular prominence in historical statistics, to which attention may properly be drawn. It is glaringly obvious that the biggest single problem is lack of availability of the data we should like to have, even, in some cases, for quite recent periods. But there is a comparably important problem in the existence of data which *seem* to relate to the same things in different countries or at different times, but which do not in fact do so. Some sort of data are available in these cases, but not the precise sort which we want. Basically these problems are ones of definition—in some times and places exports include bullion, in others they do not; pig iron can include or exclude ferro-alloys; bank deposits may include inter-bank deposits, or they may not; and so on. Often there is nothing one can do about this lack of uniformity except indicate its existence and warn against glib comparisons. (One can find little comfort, however, in the fact that failure to observe such warnings is one of the main reasons why statistics have sometimes been held to be worse than 'damned lies'!) Kindred definitional difficulties are provided by changes in boundaries, though these are less important than for Europe. A list of them is given below.

Two other problems are peculiar to historical statistics. The first is, in a sense, a mechanical one. That is the variable and unknown efficiency of past collectors and compilers of statistics, and of their printers, and the impossibility of even being able to check on these qualities. This is something one simply has to live with, keeping

---

[1] B. R. Mitchell, *European Historical Statistics, 1750–1970* (London, 1975; second edition (extended to 1975), 1980; and third edition (extended to 1988), 1992).

[2] London, 1982 and 1984.

a vigilant eye on one's own credulity, and endeavouring to estimate margins of error so far as that is possible. Too often, users of historical statistics simply take best-estimate figures for their calculations, without working out the effects on their analysis of compounding margins of error.

The second peculiar problem concerns the purposes for which statistics were usually collected up to around the end of the 19th century, and, indeed, for which they often are still. William Robson rightly said that 'the most important methodological development of the present century' is 'the introduction of measurement in varying degrees in virtually every one of the social sciences',[3] and it is only with this development that there has come much collection and publication of statistical material for its own sake, as it were. Actually, it began to develop a little before the end of the 19th century in some countries; but still, it is generally true to say that most statistics prior to 1900 were by-products of taxation or military preparedness, or at any rate of desire for honesty in administration. Some early series, therefore, have to be viewed with a measure of scepticism, because there was a premium on avoiding inclusion in the data. Registration of one's true age, if one was a young man liable to military service, and the smuggling of dutiable imports are but two of the most obvious examples. But understatement is not the only error to which statistics have been liable. Population and wealth have sometimes been inflated to impress potential enemies, or for prestige, or to enhance the power of a ruling group. To all these difficulties there is no ready solution. All one can do is be careful, and keep a firm rein on credulity, without going to the other extreme of a stultifying total scepticism.

These few generalities are not intended as a critique of the usefulness of statistics in historical studies, but simply as a warning against their careless and casual use in comparisons over time and between different countries. It has been rightly said that 'numbers are useful when they attain a level of subtlety and precision beyond that of words'.[4] Let the user of this volume be in no doubt of the need to seek for subtlety and of the difficulties in the way of precision.

Some of the problems peculiar to each topic are mentioned briefly in the introduction to each of the separate sections; but it must be pointed out that these are not intended to be comprehensive critiques of the statistics presented. To do this properly would require at least another volume, and it is the intention here only to draw the user's attention to the main types of difficulty in using the statistics. The problems for each individual country are not generally dealt with, unless they are outstandingly important. However, most of them are readily apparent from a careful use of the notes and footnotes to the tables.

Whilst the general plan of the first edition has been followed in this one, there are various changes. Possibly the most obvious is the omission of the section on climate. This was done to save space, and in the light of the general opinion expressed by those who could be consulted that these were amongst the least useful tables. No other table has been omitted, though two or three have been compressed. Newly available material has been included in several tables, and two completely new ones have been added: one giving estimates of annual population and the other providing money supply data for the last four decades. Another considerable change has been the expansion of the detail provided in the balance of payments table.

Boundary Changes

Boundary changes of the kind following wars in Europe have not been unknown in both North and South America, though the extension of the frontier of settlement has been of greater importance in changing the area of most of the national units covered in this volume. These are less easy to identify with precision, and no attempt to do so is made here, since for most purposes such extensions are best conceived of as economic expansions rather than shifts in the locus of units of statistical record. The list that follows is therefore confined to changes of status or in borders:

NORTH AMERICA

Canada: The Dominion of Canada was established in 1867 from the former British colonies of Upper and Lower Canada (i.e. Ontario and Quebec), New Brunswick, Nova Scotia, Prince Edward Island, and British Columbia.

Costa Rica: Declared independent of Spain in 1821. Part of the Confederation of Central America 1824–38.

Cuba: Declared independent of Spain in 1898.

[3] W. A. Robson (ed.), *Man and the Social Sciences* (London, 1972).
[4] W. Paul Strassman, *Risk and Technological Innovation* (Ithaca, NY, 1959), p. 5.

Dominican Republic:	Declared independent of Spain in 1821, but held by Haiti from 1822 to 1844.
El Salvador:	Part of the Confederation of Central America to 1838, when it became independent.
Guatemala:	Declared independent of Spain in 1821. Part of the Confederation of Central America 1823–38.
Haiti:	Declared independent of France 1804 (having been Spanish to 1697). Occupied by the United States 1915–34.
Honduras:	Part of the Confederation of Central America to 1838, when it became independent.
Jamaica:	A Spanish colony, occupied by Britain in 1655 and formally ceded in 1670. Independent from 1962.
Mexico:	Declared independent of Spain in 1810 and acknowledged so in 1821. Texas became independent of it *de facto* in 1836, and, along with the northern provinces which now form Arizona, California, New Mexico, and parts of Colorado, Nevada and Utah, was ceded to the USA in 1845. Another small area, the Gadsden Purchase, was transferred in 1853.
Nicaragua:	Part of the Confederation of Central America to 1838, when it became independent.
Panama:	A province of Colombia to 1903, when it became independent.
Puerto Rico:	Acquired by the United States from Spain in 1899.
Trinidad and Tobago:	Trinidad was a Spanish colony until ceded to Britain in 1802. Tobago was joined to it administratively in 1899.
United States of America:	Declared independent from Britain in 1776, and acknowledged in 1783. Enlarged in 1803 by the Louisiana Purchase, in 1819 by Spain's cession of Florida and neighbouring areas, in 1845 by the Mexican cession, and in 1853 by the Gadsden Purchase. Alaska was acquired from Russia in 1867, and Hawaii from its native rulers in 1898. Both became States in 1960.

SOUTH AMERICA

Argentina:	The Spanish Viceroyalty of the River Plate formed an autonomous government in 1810 and became formally independent in 1816. No stable central government existed in the area which later became Argentina until 1862. Adjustments of boundaries with Bolivia, Chile, and Paraguay have taken place subsequently, but they have been more in the nature of initial demarcations in unsettled territory than of transfers of territory, with the exception of the transfer of Misiones from Paraguay in 1876.
Bolivia:	Part of the Viceroyalty of the River Plate (see Argentina), to 1825, when it became independent. It has since suffered three major losses of territory—its coastal region (essentially the present province of Antofagasta) to Chile in 1884, part of its Amazonian northern region (the present Acre territory) to Brazil in 1903, and a large part of the Gran Chaco to Paraguay in the early 1930s (formally ceded in 1938).
Brazil:	A Portuguese colony, declared a separate kingdom under a king of the Portuguese royal house in 1815, and an independent empire in 1822. (It became a republic in 1889.) Boundary changes have been more in the nature of initial delineations than of transfers of territory, though Acre was acquired from Bolivia in 1903, and there were some transfers from Paraguay in 1872.
Chile:	Declared independent of Spain in 1810, and acknowledged so in 1818. It gained Antofagasta from Bolivia and Tarapaca from Peru in 1883–4 following the War of the Pacific. Africa and Tacna were also taken, the latter being returned in 1929 and the former being confirmed as Chilean.
Colombia:	Became independent of Spain in 1819 as part of Gran Colombia—the former New Granada, including Ecuador, Venezuela, and present-day Panama. Ecuador and Venezuela became separate in 1830, whereafter Colombia was known as New Granada to 1863. The province of Panama became independent in 1903. Minor boundary adjustments have occurred with Peru and Venezuela.
Ecuador:	Seceded from Gran Colombia and became independent in 1830. Small parts of its former eastern province were ceded to Brazil in 1904 and to Colombia in 1916, but they were more in the nature of initial boundary delineation than of territorial transfers. A large part of the remainder of the province was ceded to Peru in 1942.
Guyana:	The Dutch Colonies of Demerara, Essequibo, and Berbice were captured by Britain in 1796 and formally ceded in 1814, whereafter they were known as British Guiana until independence in 1966. The designation Guyana is used throughout this book.

Paraguay: Part of the Spanish Viceroyalty of the River Plate (see Argentina) which established its inde-
                   pendence in 1814. Following the war of 1865–70, some territory north of the Apa river was
                   transferred to Brazil (in 1872) and Misiones and some of the southern Chaco was transferred
                   to Argentina in 1876. A large part of Gran Chaco was acquired from Bolivia in the early 1930s
                   (formally in 1938).
Peru: Declared independent of Spain in 1821, and acknowledged in 1824. Lost Tarapaca province
                   and Africa and Tacna to Chile in 1883, though the last was returned in 1929. A large part of
                   Ecuador's eastern province was gained in 1942.
Surinam: Alternatively known as Dutch Guiana prior to its independent in 1975.
Uruguay: Part of the Spanish Viceroyalty of the River Plate, it became independent in 1825 after a
                   confused period when Brazil had occupied it.
Venezuela: Seceded from Gran Colombia and became independent in 1830.

Currency Changes

A major source of difficulty in comparing some statistics over time is changes in currency units. To some extent
this has been finessed in this volume by presenting older series in terms of more recent units. However, this is
not always either possible or desirable. The following list of changes may be useful:

NORTH AMERICA

Costa Rica: The colón replaced the peso in 1900 at the official rate of 1 colón = 1 silver peso.
El Salvador: The colón replaced the peso in 1920 at the official rate of 1 colón = 1 peso.
Guatemala: The quetzal replaced the peso in 1924 at the rate of 1 quetzal = 60 paper pesos.
Honduras: The name 'peso' was changed to 'lempira' in the early 1930s.
Jamaica: The Jamaican dollar replaced the pound in 1969 at the rate of 2 dollars = 1 pound.
Nicaragua: The cordoba replaced the peso in 1912 at the rate of 1 cordoba = 12.5 pesos. In February
                   1988 a new cordoba was issued equal to 1,000 old cordobas. In 1990 the cordoba oro was
                   introduced as a unit of account, and in March 1991 this replaced the cordoba at the rate of 1
                   cordoba oro = 5 million cordobas.

SOUTH AMERICA

Argentina: A new peso worth 100 old pesos was issued in 1970. In 1983 this was replaced by the peso
                   argentino, worth 10,000 of the previous currency. This was replaced in turn in 1985 by the
                   australe, at the rate of 1 australe = 1,000 pesos argentinos. In 1992 the austral was replaced
                   by the peso at the rate of 1 peso = 10,000 australes.
Bolivia: The peso replaced the boliviano in 1963 at the rate of 1 peso = 1,000 bolivianos, but was in
                   turn replaced by the (new) boliviano at the rate of 1 boliviano = 1 million pesos.
Brazil: The name 'milreis' was replaced by 'cruzeiro' in 1942. A new cruzeiro, worth 1,000 old cruzeiros,
                   was issued in 1966. This was replaced by the cruzado in 1986 at the rate of 1 cruzado =
                   1,000 cruzeiros. In January 1989 a new cruzado, equal to 1,000 old cruzados, was issued
                   and in March 1990 its name was changed to cruzeiro. In August 1993 the cruzeiro real was
                   created, equal to 1,000 cruzeiros and in July 1994 this was replaced by the real at the rate of
                   1 real = 2,750 cruzeiros reales.
Chile: The escudo replaced the peso in 1959 at the rate of 1 escudo = 1,000 pesos. In 1975 a new
                   peso was issued at the rate of 1 peso = 1,000 escudos.
Paraguay: The guaranie replaced the peso in 1943 at the rate of 1 guaranie = 100 paper or 1.75 gold
                   pesos.
Peru: The inti replaced the sol in 1985 at the rate of 1 inti = 1,000 soles. In July 1991 a new sol was
                   introduced equal to 1 million intis.
Uruguay: A new peso worth 1,000 old pesos was issued in 1975. A further new peso was issued in
                   March 1993 at the rate of 1 new peso = 1,000 of the previous issue.

SOURCES

The main national sources used have been the official publications of the various governments. In order to avoid excessive repetition of these in the notes to the tables, there follows a list of those used in more than a very few of the tables in this book.

Argentina:
Anuario del Dirección General de estadística (1892–1914)
Anuario estadístico: comercio exterior (1915–47)
Anuario estadístico de la República Argentina (1946 ongoing)
Anuario geográfico Argentino (1941)
Boletín de estadística
Censo de Poblacion (1869, 1895, 1914, 1947, 1960, 1970)
Estadística agrícola (1902/4–1917/18)
Digesto de Hacienda (1900–1949)
Resumenes estadísticos retrospéctives, 1900–1959
In addition, the following unofficial publication was used extensively: Ernesto Torn-quist & Co. Ltd., *The Economic Development of the Argentine Republic in the Last Fifty Years* (Buenos Aires, 1919)

Barbados:
Abstract of Statistics (1956 ongoing)
Quarterly Digest of Statistics (1956 ongoing)

Bolivia:
Boletín estadístico (1901 ongoing)
Censo de Poblacion (1900, 1950, 1976)
Comercio exterior (1920 ongoing)
Extracto estadístico de Bolivia (1936)
Bolivia en cifras (1973 ongoing)

Brazil:
Anuário estatístico do Brasil (1908/12, 1936 ongoing)
Censo de população (1872, 1890, 1900, 1920, 1940, 1950, 1960, 1970)
In addition, the following unofficial publication was used: Armin K. Ludwig, *Brazil: A Handbook of Historical Statistics* (Boston, 1985)

British Colonies in general:
Blue Books for individual colonies and *Colonial Reports* (In Parliamentary Papers to 1921)
Tables of Revenue, Population and Commerce, etc. of the United Kingdom and its Dependencies (1820–52, in Parliamentary Papers)
Statistical Abstract for the Colonies (1850–1965 with slight variations in title. In Parliamentary Papers to 1947)
Statistical Tables relating to the Colonies (1854–1914 in Parliamentary Papers)

Canada:
The Canada Year Book (1905 ongoing)
Statistical Year-book of Canada (1886–1904)
In addition, the following unofficial publication was used extensively: M.C. Urquhart and K.A. Buckley (eds.), *Historical Statistics of Canada* (1st edition, Cambridge, 1965, and Second edition, Ottawa, 1983)

Chile:
Anuario estadístico (1848/58–1925; in sub-series by subject from 1911)
Censo de poblacion (1895, 1907, 1920, 1930, 1940, 1952, 1960, 1970)
Síntesis estadística (1928 ongoing)
Estadística Chilena (1928 ongoing)

Colombia:
Anales de economía y estadística (1938 ongoing)
Anuario estadístico (1905, 1915 ongoing)

Boletın mensual de estadística (1951 ongoing)
Censo de poblacion (1905, 1912, 1918, 1951, 1964, 1973)
Sintesis estadística de Colombia (1941)

Costa Rica: *Anuario estadístico* (1883–93, 1907–45, 1948 ongoing)
                 Informe (of the Direccion General de Estadística) (1897–1908, 1920–47)
                 Censo de poblacion (1927, 1950, 1963, 1973)

Cuba: *Anuario Azucarero de Cuba*
                 Anuario estadístico (1914, 1952–57)
                 Census of Cuba (US Department of War, 1899)
                 In addition, the following unofficial publications were used: The Cuban Economic
                 Research Project of the University of Miami, *A Study on Cuba* (Miami, 1965) and
                 Susan B. Schroeder, *Cuba: A Handbook of Historical Statistics* (Boston, 1982)

Dominican   *Anuario estadístico* (1936–54)
Republic: *21 Años de Estadísticas, 1936– 1956* (1956)

Ecuador: *Anuario de comercio exterior* (1957 ongoing)
                 Ecuador en cifras, 1938 a 1942 (1943)
                 El trimestre estadístico (1945–47)
                 Síntesis estadística (1955–62)

El Salvador: *Anuario estadístico* (1911–23, 1927 ongoing)

Guatemala: *Annales estadísticos* (1882–83)
                 Anuario or *Informe* (of the Dirección General de Estadística) (1882–9, 1891, 1893–4,
                 1898 & 1928).
                 Anuario estadístico (1975)
                 Censo de Poblacion (1921, 1940, 1950, 1964, 1973)
                 Guatemala en cifras (1955 ongoing)

Guyana: *Quarterly Statistical Digest* (1965 ongoing)

Haiti: *Bulletin Trimestriel de Statistique* (1951 ongoing)

Honduras: *Anuario estadístico* (1889, 1950 ongoing)
                 Censo de poblacion (1910, 1930, 1940, 1950, 1961, 1974)

Jamaica: *Digest* or *Abstract of Statistics* (1947 ongoing)

Mexico: *Anuario estadístico* (1893 ongoing)
                 Censo de poblacion (1895, 1910, 1921, 1930, 1940, 1950, 1960, 1970)
                 Statistics on the Mexican Economy (1977)

Nicaragua: *Anuario estadístico* (1930–47, 1964 ongoing)
                 Boletin Mensuel de estadístico (1930 ongoing)

Panama: *Extracto estadístico* (1941/3 ongoing)

Paraguay: *Anuario estadístico* (1886–7, 1914–17, 1940 ongoing)
                 Boletín estadístico (1957 ongoing)
                 Mensaje del Presidente (1882 ongoing)

Peru: *Anuario estadístico* (1944 ongoing)
                 Censo de poblacion (1940, 1961, 1972)
                 Extracto estadístico (1919–43)

Puerto Rico: *Monthly Statistical Report* (1943 ongoing)
Statistical Abstract (1949 ongoing)

Surinam: *Jaarcijfers* (1887–1922)

Trinidad and
Tobago: *Statistical Digest* (1951 ongoing)

United States: *Commerce and Navigation of the United States* (1822–1965)
Historical Statistics of the United States (Bicentennial edition, 1975)
Statistical Abstract (1887 ongoing)

Uruguay: *Anuario estadístico* (1884 ongoing)
Censo de poblacion (1963)
Síntesis estadística (1919–36)

Venezuela: *Anuario estadístico* (1872–1912, 1939 ongoing)
Censo de poblacion (1926, 1936, 1941, 1950, 1961, 1971)
In addition, the following unofficial publication was used: Miguel Izard, *Series estadísticas para la história de Venezuela* (Mérida, 1970)

In addition, certain gaps have been filled from the British *Statistical Abstract for Foreign Countries* (1872–1912, in Parliamentary Papers, where certain other foreign statistics were published occasionally from 1844 onwards), from British *Consular Reports* (in Parliamentary Papers), and from publications of the German Statistical Office, *Die Wirtschaft des Auslandes, 1900–1927* and *Statistisches Handbuch der Weltwirtschaft*.

The phrase 'ongoing' should not be taken to imply that publication has always been continuous.

ACKNOWLEDGEMENTS

In compiling a volume of this kind I have, inevitably, contracted a large number of debts for the help which I have been given by a great variety of people. It is impossible to mention every single one of them here, and I hope that those who are not named below will accept this general expression of my gratitude.

My major obligation must be to those librarians and their staffs who have put up with the persistent demands which I have made upon them. I would particularly like to thank Mr Finkell and Mr. Ross of the Marshall Library, Cambridge; Mrs Peppercorn of the Department of Applied Economics Library, Cambridge; Mr Vickery and Mr Noblett and their staff in the Official Publications Department of the Cambridge University Library; Mrs Hulass and her staff at the Woolwich Repository of the British Library, and the staff of the Benson Latin American Collection at the University of Texas at Austin.

The Central Statistical Offices of the Republics of Guatemala and Panama very kindly filled certain gaps in the data for their countries.

I have received advice and help in identifying sources, and in other aspects of my work, from several of my colleagues and others scattered around the world. In this connection, I would particularly like to thank Professor W.W. Rostow, Dr Gabriel Palma, Dr Brian Pollitt, Mrs Marie Ruiz, and Mr C. Short, together with my wife, Ann, who has helped me with the compilation in numerous ways. I would also like to take this opportunity to thank Mrs. Penelope Allport and all others at Macmillan who have been helpful and understanding in seeing the book through to publication. Thanks are also due to Andrew Whitelegg for his extensive research for this latest edition.

WEIGHTS & MEASURES: CONVERSION RATIOS

The following is not a complete guide to all weights and measures used during the period covered by this volume. It is simply a list of those conversion ratios used in compiling the tables given here.

1 long (or imperial) ton = 1.016047 metric tons
1 short ton = 0.9072 metric tons
1 acre = 0.404686 hectares
1 mile = 1.609344 kilometres
1 Imperial gallon = 0.0454596 hectolitres
1 US gallon = 0.037854 hectolitres
1 US barrel (oil) = 158.95 litres
1 Imperial bushel = 0.363677 hectolitres

SYMBOLS

··· = not available
- - = less than half the smallest digit used in the table
— = nil

A POPULATION AND VITAL STATISTICS

The principal sources of population data are official censuses, administrative enumerations, and registration records. The earliest of these in the Americas, at other than a very local level, date from around the beginning of the period covered in the work, and cover Spanish colonial territories which later became independent nations. Individual British colonies in North America also organized enumerations at such a comparatively early date, though the first census covering the United States was not taken until after independence. Such of this early material as has seemed at all reliable, even in a very approximate way, has been included in table 1. Similar material has also been included for the cities shown in table 4.

Apart from the United States, which began in 1790, reasonably regular censuses started around the middle of the nineteenth century in most of the countries covered here. There are many exceptions to this statement, however, particularly with regard to regularity. Indeed, Latin America generally has never come anywhere near the former British colonies in this respect, although Mexico and, with one exception, Brazil have had a decennial census in the twentieth century. Chile, Colombia, Cuba, Honduras, Panama and (from 1920) Venezuela have also been reasonably regular in this period. At the other extreme, Haiti had no census until 1950, Peru had none between 1876 and 1940, and Uruguay none between 1908 and 1963. Bolivia, Ecuador, Paraguay, and various Central American countries also had long periods without a full enumeration.

It is generally agreed by demographers that the almost universal tendency of censuses is to under-enumerate,[1] and the probability is that, as in the United States, this was usually more pronounced in earlier than later censuses. This should be borne in mind in using the statistics shown here, but, unfortunately, it is only in a few recent cases that one can estimate the likely margin of error even approximately. Perhaps it can be regarded as reasonable to assume that regular censuses, other than the first one or two of a series, are accurate to within less than ten per cent overall, and probably a good deal less than that in most cases. Isolated censuses are likely to have a higher margin of error, most especially in large countries.

Some kinds of information elicited in censuses are likely to be less accurate than others. Data about occupations present special difficulties, which are considered in the next chapter. But the age-distribution data shown in table 2, probably contain the largest margins of error of all. For in addition to accidental errors, this information is peculiarly liable to deliberate falsification by respondents. Moreover, the sort of ignorance of their precise age which appears to have been common amongst older Balkan peoples up to the 1920s is also likely to have affected the largely illiterate Indian population of many Latin American countries until fairly recently.

Regional population statistics are shown here in table 3 only for the larger countries, for which such data are likely to have fairly general interest. They are subject to all the general problems pertaining to censuses and there are, in addition, changes in boundaries which sometimes impair their comparability over time. Similar changes affect the cities, whose populations are shown in table 4, for as cities grow in population, so they tend to grow in space, taking in areas which, whilst not previously uninhabited, are clearly not part of a city. This presents no conceptual problem, and the general rule adopted here has been to show the statistics which apply to the city limits of the year to which they refer. A problem does arise, however, when suburban areas which became functionally part of a central city remain administratively separate from it, a very common situation in recent times in the United States. The solution normally adopted here has been to show two figures in such cases, one for the city proper and the other of the urban agglomeration, for all periods since 1930.

---

[1] See the discussion in the introduction to Chapter A of *Historical Statistics of the United States*, p. 1 (cited on p. xv above) and the sources mentioned there.

Demographers may find the vital statistics here among the least sophisticated that are nowadays available; but they have the merit, from the historical point of view, of being extant for much longer periods than the more refined series. But just as censuses tend to underestimate, so a proportion of vital events escapes the registrars' nets. This is particularly true of most Latin American countries where, in any case, civil registration usually began late and has continued to be incomplete. However, even in the United States, national vital statistics were not collected until well into the twentieth century, and as late as 1940 birth registration was estimated to be only 92.5 per cent complete. Generally speaking, the smaller a country and the more homogeneous its population the earlier it acquired useful vital statistics. Thus Chile and Uruguay were the leaders in Latin American registration, and Brazil had still not got an effective system in the 1980s. The principle adopted here in tables 5 and 6 has been to show such rates as are available which are believed to have reasonable continuity, even if they are understatements. Estimates of the *actual* rates of quinquennial periods,made by O. Andrew Collver, and given in an appendix (A6a) to table 6.

A variety of statistics on overseas migration is available for different countries, though it is of an extremely heterogeneous nature, making comparisons between countries often hazardous. A selection of this material is given in table 8, though much more is available in the sources noted there.

A1 NORTH AMERICA: POPULATION OF COUNTRIES (in thousands)

Abbreviations used throughout this table: **M** males; **F** females

ALASKA

Date	Total	M	F
1880	33	...	...
1890	32	19	13
1900	64	46	18
1910	64	46	18
1920	55	35	20
1929	59	36	24
1939	73	43	30
1950	129	79	49

Incorporated in U.S.A.

ANTIGUA

Date	Total	M	F
1851	37	18	20
1861	37	17	20
1871	35	16	19
1881	35	16	19
1891	37	17	20
1901	35	16	19
1911	32	14	18
1921	30	13	17
1946	42	19	23
1960	54	25	29
1970	66	31	34
1991	63	...	...

BAHAMAS

Date	Total	M	F
1851	28	13	14
1861	35	17	18
1871	39	19	20
1881	44	21	23
1891	48	23	25
1901	54	25	29
1911	56	25	31
1921	53	24	29
1931	60	28	32
1943	69	32	37
1953	85	39	46
1963	130	63	67
1970	175	87	88
1980	223	109	114
1990	255	125	130

BARBADOS

Date	Total	M	F
1851	136	62	74
1861	153	71	82
1871	162	73	89
1881	172	77	95
1891	183	82	101
1901	196	88	107
1911	172	71	102
1921	157	63	93
1946	194	86	107
1960	233	106	127
1970	235	110	125
1980	252	120	132
1990	257	...	...

BELIZE/BRITISH HONDURAS

Date	Total	M	F
1861	26	14	12
1871	25	13	12
1881	27	14	13
1891	31	16	15
1901	37	19	18
1911	40	20	20
1921	45	23	23
1931	51	26	26
1946	59	29	30
1960	90	44	46
1970	120	60	60
1980	143	72	71
1991	190	96	93

BERMUDA

Date	Total	M	F
1843	10	4	6
1851	11	5	6
1861	12	5	7
1871	12	5	7
1881	14	6	8
1891	15	7	8
1901	18	9	9
1911	19	9	10
1921	20	10	10
1931	28	14	14
1939	31	15	16
1950	37	18	19
1960	43[1]	21	21
1970	52	26	26
1980	55	27	28
1991	59	29	30

BRITISH VIRGIN ISLANDS

Date	Total	M	F
1841	6.7	3.1	3.6
1871	6.7	3.4	3.3
1881	5.3	2.6	2.7
1891	4.6	2.1	2.5
1901	4.9	2.3	2.7
1911	5.6	2.6	2.9
1921	5.1	2.3	2.7
1946	6.5	3.1	3.4
1960	7.3	3.6	3.8
1970	9.7	5.1	4.5
1980	11.0	5.6	5.4
1991	16.1	8.3	7.9

CANADA[2]

Date	Total	M	F
1851	2,436	1,250	1,186
1861	3,230	1,660	1,570
1871	3,689	1,869	1,820
1881	4,325	2,189	2,136
1891	4,833	2,460	2,373
1901	5,371	2,752	2,620
1911	7,207	3,822	3,385
1921	8,788	4,530	4,258
1931	10,377	5,373	5,002
1941	11,507[2]	5,901[2]	5,606[2]
1951	14,009	7,089	6,921
1956	16,081	8,152	7,929
1961	18,238	9,219	9,019
1966	20,015	10,054	9,961
1971	21,568	10,795	10,773
1981	24,343	12,068	12,275
1986	25,309	12,486	12,824
1991	27,296	13,454	13,842

CAYMAN ISLANDS

Date	Total	M	F
1891	4.3	...	...
1911	5.6	2.4	3.1
1921	5.3	2.2	3.0
1943	6.7	3.0	3.7
1960	7.6	3.1	4.5
1970	10.5	5.0	5.5
1979	16.7	8.1	8.6
1989	25.4	12.4	13.0

A1 NORTH AMERICA: Population of Countries (in thousands)

COSTA RICA[3]

Date	Total	M	F
1824	65	...	...
1836	78	...	...
1844	94[4]	...	...
1864	120	58	62
1875	153	...	...
1883	182	90	92
1892	243	122	121
1927	472	238	233
1950	801	400	401
1963	1,336	669	667
1973	1,872	939	933
1984	2,417	1,208	1,209

CUBA[5]

Date	Total	M	F
1774	172	101	71
1792	272	155	117
1817	572	...	...
1827	704	404	301
1841	1,008	584	424
1861	1,397	801	596
1877	1,522	846	664
1887	1,632	866	743
1899	1,573	758	815
1907	2,049	1,075	974
1919	2,889	1,531	1,358
1931	3,962	2,103	1,860
1943	4,779	2,499	2,280
1953	5,829	2,985	2,844
1970	8,569	4,393	4,176
1981	9,724	4,915	4,809

DOMINICA

Date	Total	M	F
1844	22	11	12
1861	25	12	13
1871	27	13	14
1881	28	13	15
1891	27	12	15
1901	29	13	16
1911	34	15	19
1921	37	17	20
1946	48	22	25
1960	60	28	32
1970	71	34	37
1981	74	37	37
1991	72	36	36

DOMINICAN REPUBLIC

Date	Total	M	F
1920	895	446	448
1935	1,479	751	729
1950	2,136	1,071	1,065
1960	3,047	1,536	1,511
1970	4,006	1,999	2,007
1981	5,648	2,832	2,816

EL SALVADOR[6]

Date	Total	M	F
1901	1,007	494	513
1930	1,434	717	718
1950	1,856	918	937
1961	2,511	1,237	1,274
1971	3,555	1,763	1,791
1992	5,048	2,423	2,625

GRENADA

Date	Total	M	F
1851	33	16	17
1861	32	15	16
1871	38	18	20
1881	42	20	22
1891	53	26	28
1901	63	30	33
1911	67	30	36
1921	66	29	37
1946	72	32	41
1960	89	41	48
1970	94	44	50
1981	89	43	46

GUADELOUPE[7]

Date	Total	M	F
1852	125	...	...
1861	138	...	...
1876	176	...	...
1901	182	...	...
1906	190	...	...
1911	212	...	...
1921	230	...	...
1926	243	...	...
1931	267	...	...
1936	304	...	...
1954	229	112	118
1961	283	138	145
1967	313	153	159
1974	324	...	...
1982	327	160	167
1990	387	...	...

GUATEMALA

Date	Total	M	F
1771	315	...	...
1848	706	...	...
1880	1,225	605	620
1893	1,364	677	687
1921	2,005	992	1,013
1940	3,283[8]	1,660	1,623
1950	2,791	1,411	1,380
1964	4,288	2,172	2,116
1973	5,160	2,589	2,571
1981	6,054	3,016	3,038

HAITI

Date	Total	M	F
1950[9]	3,097	1,505	1,592
1971	4,330	2,090	2,240
1982	5,054	2,448	2,605

HONDURAS

Date	Total	M	F
1791	96	...	...
1801	130	...	...
1881	307	151	157
1887	332	163	169
1895	399	196	203
1901	544	267	276
1905	500	244	256
1910	553	271	283
1916	606	300	306
1926	701	348	352
1930	854	424	430
1935	962	480	482
1940	1,108	556	552
1945	1,200	602	599
1950[10]	1,369	686	683
1961[10]	1,885	939	948
1974	2,657	1,317	1,340
1988	5,054	2,448	2,605

A1 NORTH AMERICA: Population of Countries (in thousands)

JAMAICA

Date	Total	M	F
1844	377	182	196
1861	441	214	228
1871	506	247	260
1881	581	283	298
1891	639	306	334
1901	756	366	390
1911	831	397	434
1921	858	402	456
1943	1,246	603	643
1953	1,487	727	760
1960	1,624	781	843
1970	1,849	901	948
1982	2,206	1,080	1,126
1991	2,366	1,178	1,221

MARTINIQUE[7]

Date	Total	M	F
1867	153	...	...
1876	164	...	...
1886	175	...	...
1894	189	...	...
1901	208	...	...
1905	182	...	...
1910	184	...	...
1921	244	...	...
1927	228	...	...
1931	235	...	...
1936	247	...	...
1954	239	115	124
1961	291	140	151
1967	320	155	165
1974	324	...	...
1982	327	158	168
1990	360	174	186

MEXICO[11]

Date	Total	M	F
1831	6,382	...	...
1873	9,210	...	...
1895	12,632	6,281	6,352
1900	13,607	6,752	6,855
1910	13,607	7,504	7,656
1921	14,335	7,004	7,331
1930	16,553	8,119	8,434
1940	19,654	9,696	9,958
1950	25,791	12,697	13,094
1960	34,923	17,415	17,508
1970	48,225	24,066	24,160
1980	66,847	33,039	33,808
1990	81,141	39,879	41,262

MONTSERRAT

Date	Total	M	F
1851	7.1	3.1	3.9
1861	7.6	3.4	4.2
1871	8.7	4.0	4.7
1881	10.0	5.0	5.0
1891	12.0	5.0	6.0
1901	12.0	6.0	7.0
1911	12.0	5.0	7.0
1921	12.0	5.0	7.0
1946	14.0	6.0	8.0
1960	12.0	5.0	7.0
1970	11.0	5.0	6.0
1980	12.0	6.0	6.0

NETHERLANDS ANTILLES

Date	Total	M	F
1930	76	38	39
1960	189	93	96
1971	218	107	112
1981 Aruba	60	29	31
1981 rest	172	83	89
1992	189	91	99

NEWFOUNDLAND

Date	Total	M	F
1836	75	...	...
1845	97	53	44
1857	124	64	58
1869	147	...	...
1874	161	83	78
1884[12]	193	99	94
1891[12]	198	101	97
1901[12]	217	111	106
1911[12]	239	122	116
1921	263	134	129
1935	290	149	141
1945	322	165	157

incorporated in Canada

NICARAGUA

Date	Total	M	F
1906	505	...	...
1920	638	312	327
1940[13]	983	477	506
1950	1,057	520	537
1963	1,536	758	778
1971	1,878	922	956

PANAMA[14]

Date	Total	M	F
1911[15]	291	150	141
1920[15]	446	228	218
1930	467	239	228
1940[15]	567	291	276
1950	805	410	396
1960	1,076	546	530
1970	1,428	724	704
1980[14]	1,831	928	903
1990	2,329	1,179	1,150

PANAMA CANAL ZONE

Date	Total	M	F
1912	63	45	18
1920	22	15	8
1930	39	26	13
1940	52	38	14
1950	53	31	22
1960	42	23	19
1970	44	24	20

included in Panama

PUERTO RICO

Date	Total	M	F
1765	45	...	...
1775	70	...	...
1800	155	...	...
1815	221	...	...
1832	330	...	...
1846	448	...	...
1860	583	296	287
1877	732	375	358
1887	799	399	400
1899	953	468	482
1910	1,118	557	561
1920	1,300	648	652
1930	1,544	772	772
1935	1,724	862	862
1940	1,869	938	931
1950	2,211	1,111	1,100
1960	2,350	1,163	1,187
1970	2,712	1,330	1,382
1980	3,197	1,557	1,640
1990	3,522	...	...

A1   NORTH AMERICA: Population of Countries (in thousands)

ST KITTS, NEVIS & ANGUILLA[39]

Date	Total	M	F
1861	34	16	18
1871	40	19	21
1881	44	21	24
1891	48	22	26
1901	46	20	26
1911	43	18	25
1921	38	15	23
1946	46	21	25
1960	57	26	31
1980[39]	43	21	22

STLUCIA

Date	Total	M	F
1851	24	12	13
1861	27	13	14
1871	32	16	16
1881	39	19	20
1891	42	20	24
1901	50	24	26
1911	49	22	26
1921	52	24	28
1946	70	33	37
1960	86	41	45
1970	101	48	53
1980	113	55	59
1991	136	66	70

ST VINCENT

Date	Total	M	F
1851	30	14	16
1861	32	15	17
1871	36	17	19
1881	41	19	22
1891	41	19	22
1901	48	…	…
1911	42	18	24
1921	44	19	25
1931	48	21	27
1946	62	28	34
1960	80	38	42
1970	87	41	46
1980	98	47	50
1991	106	53	53

TRINIDAD & TOBAGO

Date	Total	M	F
1851*	69	35	33
1851[†]	14	7	7
1861*	84	46	38
1861[†]	15	7	8
1871*	110	60	49
1871[†]	17	8	8
1881*	153	84	69
1881[†]	18	9	9
1891	218	117	101
1901	274	144	129
1911	334	174	159
1921	366	187	179
1931	413	207	206
1946	558	280	278
1960	828	412	416
1970	941	466	475
1980	1,080	540	540
1990	1,234	618	616

*Trinidad;   [†]Tobago

TURKS & CAICOS ISLANDS

Date	Total	M	F
1871	4.7	2.3	2.4
1881	4.7	2.2	2.5
1891	4.7	2.2	2.5
1901	5.3	2.4	2.9
1911	5.6	2.5	3.1
1921	5.5	2.5	3.1
1943	6.1	2.8	3.3
1954	5.1	2.1	3.0
1960	5.7	2.7	3.1
1970	5.6	2.7	2.9
1980	7.4	3.6	3.8
1990	12.4	6.3	6.1

USA[16]

Date	Total	M	F
1790	3,929	[1,615][17]	[1,557][17]
1800	5,308	[2,195][17]	[2,111][17]
1810	7,240	[2,988][17]	[2,874][17]
1820	9,638	4,897	4,742
1830	12,866	6,530	6,336
1840	17,069	8,689	8,381
1850	23,192	11,838	11,354
1860	31,443	16,085	15,358
1870	39,818[18]	19,494	19,065
1880	50,156	25,519	24,637
1890	62,948	32,237	30,711
1900	75,995	38,816	37,178
1910	91,972	47,332	44,640
1920	105,711	53,900	51,810
1930	122,775	62,137	60,638
1940	131,669	66,062	65,608
1950	150,697[16]	74,833[16]	75,864[16]
1960	179,323	88,331	90,992
1970	203,212	98,912	104,300
1980	226,546	110,053	116,493
1990	248,710	121,239	127,470

US/Danish VIRGIN ISLANDS

Date	Total	M	F
1850	40	…	…
1855	37	16	21
1860	38	…	…
1870	38	…	…
1880	34	15	19
1890	33	15	17
1901	31	14	16
1911	27	13	15
1917	26	12	14
1930	22	10	12
1940	25	12	13
1950	27	13	14
1960	32	16	16
1970	62	31	31
1980	97	46	50
1990	102	49	53

ERRATA

The details that should appear on page 7 of International Historical Statistics: The Americas (1750–1993) are shown below.

A1   SOUTH AMERICA: POPULATION OF COUNTRIES (in thousands)

ARGENTINA[19]

Date	Total	M	F
1869	1,737	892	845
1895	3,955	2,089	1,866
1914	7,885[20]	4,227	3,658
1947	15,894[20]	8,145	7,749
1960	20,759[21]	10,032	9,973
1970	23,390	11,617	11,773
1980	27,947	13,756	14,191
1991	32,615	15,938	16,678

BOLIVIA

Date	Total	M	F
1854	2,326[22] 1,544	...	...
1882	1,172[22] 1,098	...	...
1900	1,696[23]	819	814
1950	3,019[23]	1,326	1,378
1976	4,648	2,280	2,368
1992	6,421	3,171	3,249

BRAZIL[24]

Date	Total	M	F
1854	7,678	...	...
1872	9,930	5,124	4,807
1890	14,334	7,238	7,096
1900	17,438	8,901	8,538
1920	30,636	15,444	15,192
1940	41,165	20,614	20,622
1950	51,976	25,885	26,059
1960	70,119	35,011	35,108
1970	92,342	45,755	46,587
1980	121,149	60,299	60,850
1991	146,825	72,485	74,340

CHILE

Date	Total	M	F
1835	1,111[25]	...	...
1843	1,192[25]	...	...
1854	1,516[25]	713	726
1865	1,819	906	913
1875	2,076	1,034	1,042
1885	2,507	1,249	1,250
1895	2,804[25]	1,333	1,355
1907	3,229[25]	1,609	1,611
1920	3,824[25]	1,843	1,872
1930	4,391[25]	2,123	2,165
1940	5,094[25]	2,490	2,554
1952	6,207[25]	2,913	3,020
1960	7,374[26]	3,613	3,761
1970	8,885[26]	4,344	4,541
1982	11,330	5,553	5,776
1992	13,348	6,553	6,795

COLOMBIA

Date	Total	M	F
1770	807	...	...
1778	829	...	...
1782	1,047	...	...
1825	1,229	601	629
1835	1,686	810	876
1843	1,932	925	1,007
1851	2,244	1,089	1,155
1864	2,694	...	...
1870	2,392	...	...
1905	4,355	2,020	2,124
1912	5,072[27]	2,392	2,585
1918	5,855[27]	2,749	2,947
1938	8,702	4,313	4,389
1951[28]	11,548	5,742	5,806
1964	17,485	8,615	8,870
1973	22,552	11,004	11,548
1985	27,838	13,778	14,060

ECUADOR

Date	Total	M	F
1950	3,203	1,595	1,608
1962	4,476	2,236	2,240
1974	6,522	3,258	3,263
1982	8,061	4,021	4,040
1990	9,468	4,796	4,852

FALKLAND ISLANDS/MALVINAS

Date	Total	M	F
1850	0.4	0.3	0.1
1861	0.6	0.4	0.2
1871	0.8	0.5	0.2
1881	1.6	1.0	0.6
1891	1.8	1.1	0.7
1901	2.0	1.2	0.8
1911	3.3	2.4	0.9
1921	3.3	2.5	0.9
1931	3.1	2.1	1.0
1946	2.2	1.2	1.0
1953	2.2	1.2	1.0
1962	2.2	1.2	1.0
1972	2.0	1.1	0.9
1980	1.9	1.0	0.8
1991	2.1	1.1	1.0

FRENCH GUIANA[29]

Date	Total	M	F
1901	22	...	...
1907	24	...	...
1911	26	...	...
1915	26	...	...
1922	26	...	...
1928	20	...	...
1931	22	...	...
1936	24	...	...
1946	22	...	...
1954	28	11	12
1961	34	17	16
1967	44	24	20
1974	55	...	...
1982	73	38	35
1990	115	60	55

A1   SOUTH AMERICA: Population of Countries (in thousands)

GUYANA/BRITISH GUIANA

Date	Total	M	F
1841	98	50	48
1851	128	67	60
1861	148	80	68
1871	193	109	85
1881	252	140	112
1891	278	152	127
1911	296	154	142
1921	298	151	146
1931	311	155	156
1946[30]	376	183	187
1960	560	279	281
1970	700	348	352
1980	759	376	383

PARAGUAY

Date	Total	M	F
1886	264	...	...
1899	644	...	...
1936[31]	932	...	...
1950	1,408[32]	649	679
1962[31]	1,817	896	921
1972	2,358	1,169	1,189
1982	3,030	1,521	1,508
1992	4,153	2,086	2,067

PERU[33]

Date	Total	M	F
1795	1,232	...	...
1836	1,374	...	...
1850	2,001	...	...
1862	2,488	...	...
1876	2,699	...	...
1940	7,023[34]	3,068	3,140
1961	10,420[34]	4,926	4,981
1972	14,122[34]	6,785	6,754
1981	17,005	8,490	8,515
1993	22,048	10,956	11,092

SURINAM/DUTCH GUIANA

Date	Total	M	F
1921	119[35]	56	52
1950	184	92	92
1971	385	193	192
1980	352	173	179

URUGUAY

Date	Total	M	F
1852	132	...	...
1860	223	121	96
1900	916	475	441
1908	1,043	531	512
1963	2,596	1,290	1,305
1975	2,782	1,363	1,419
1985	2,955	1,439	1,516

VENEZUELA

Date	Total	M	F
1810	802	...	...
1825	707	...	...
1030	807	...	...
1844	1,219	...	...
1855	1,564	...	...
1873	1,784	[736][36]	[805][36]
1881	2,075	1,006	1,070
1891	2,324	1,137	1,186
1920	2,412[37]	1,136	1,229
1926	3,027[37]	1,415	1,476
1936	3,468[37]	1,652	1,712
1941	3,951[37]	1,909	1,942
1950	5,092[37]	2,552	2,482
1961[38]	7,524	3,824	3,700
1971	10,722	5,350	5,372
1981	14,517	7,259	7,258
1990	18,105	9,020	9,086

A1 Population of Countries

NOTES

1. SOURCES: UN, *Demographic Yearbooks*, national censuses, and the national publications on pp. xii–xv. Statistics for Colombia 1825–51 come from Miguel Urrutia and Mario Arrubla (eds.), *Compendio de Estadisticas Historicas de Colombia* (Bogota, 1970).
2. A few of the figures given are official estimates rather than the results of complete censuses, but all were published as being comparable to the latter.
3. Totals are sometimes larger than the sums of males and females, because of the inclusion of people whose sex was not distinguished.
4. For boundary changes see pp. xi–xii
5. It is not always clear exactly which definition of population the statistics refer to. So far as possible, the data for population actually present are given, with known exceptions referred to in footnotes.

FOOTNOTES

[1] *Dejure* population. A further 2 thousand should be added for under- enumeration and for residents temporarily abroad.
[2] In vol. 1 of the 1941 Census of Canada the following figures were given of total white population, based on earlier censuses: mean population (in thousands) of the decade centred on:

1701	17	1751	71	1801	362
1711	22	1761	90	1811	517
1721	32	1771	105	1821	750
1731	45	1781	150	1831	1,085
1741	59	1791	233	1841	1,654

Newfoundland is shown separately prior to its incorporation in Canada in 1949.
[3] Authoritative estimates of total population at earlier dates are as follows (in thousands): 1700–19; 1751–24; 1778–34; 1801–53.
[4] This figure has been adjusted for under-enumeration, the reported total being 80.
[5] Statistics to 1943 are of *de facto* population. Subsequently they are of *de jure* population.
[6] R. Barón Castro, *La Población de El Salvador* (Madrid, 1942) bases the following estimates (in thousands) on earlier defective censuses:

	Total	Males	Females
1807	165	80	85
1882	613	291	322
1892	704	350	354

[7] Data to 1936 are believed to be grossly over-enumerated.
[8] This figure is believed to be about one million too high.
[9] Excluding any adjustment for under-enumeration, which is believed to require an addition of 8.3%.
[10] Excluding any adjustment for under-enumeration, which is believed to require additions of 10% in 1950 and 5.3% in 1961.
[11] Authoritative estimates of total population at other dates are as follows:

1803	5,765	1831	6,382	1854	7,853
1820	6,204	1838	7,044	1862	8,816

[12] Excluding Labrador, the total population of which was as follows (in thousands):

1881	4	1901	4
1891	4	1911	4

[13] These figures are believed to be too high.
[14] Excluding the Canal Zone (q.v.) except in 1980. Statistics to 1930 are of *de jure* population. Subsequently they are of *de facto* population.
[15] Excluding tribal populations, which were enumerated as follows: 1911–47; 1940–56.
[16] Alaska and Hawaii are shown separately prior to their admission as states. The following estimates of total population are given in *Historical Statistics of the United States*:

1610	0.35	1660	75	1710	332	1760	1,594
1620	2.2	1670	112	1720	466	1770	2,148
1630	4.6	1680	152	1730	629	1780	2,780
1640	27.0	1690	210	1740	906		
1650	50.0	1700	251	1750	1,171		

[17] The sex breakdown is for the white population only in these years.
[18] The total includes adjustment for under-enumeration in Southern states.
[19] The 1869 census gave the following earlier estimates of total population:

1809	406	1829	634	1849	935
1819	527	1839	768	1859	1,304

[20] Excluding any adjustment for under-enumeration, which is believed to require additions of 1.5% in 1914 and 1% in 1947.

A1 Population of Countries

[21] This figure has been adjusted for under-enumeration, the reported total being 20,006.
[22] The first figure relates to the territory at the time of the census, the second to the reduced area at the time of the next census.
[23] These figures have been adjusted for under-enumeration, the reported totals being 1,634 in 1900 and 2,704 in 1950.
[24] Earlier estimates accepted by the compilers of the 1920 census are as follows (in thousands): 1808–2,419; 1823–3,961.
[25] These figures have been adjusted for under-enumeration and, in 1907 and 1920, for Arica department, which was not tabulated by sex. The reported totals were as follows:

1835	1,010	1843	1,084	1854	1,439
1895	2,696	1907	3,221	1920	3,715
1930	4,287	1940	5,044	1950	5,933

[26] Excluding adjustments for under-enumeration, which are believed to require additions of 5.4% in 1960 and 8.5% in 1970.
[27] Including tribal population which was not tabulated by sex, and numbered 94 in 1912 and 158 in 1918.
[28] Including an adjustment of 192 for under-enumeration.
[29] Statistics to 1946 are believed to be substantially over- enumerated. They exclude Inini, which had a population of 5,000 in 1946.
[30] Excluding 6,000 Amerindians of unknown sex.
[31] These figures are known to be incomplete.
[32] This figure has been adjusted for under-enumeration, the reported total being 1,341 (including 13 not tabulated by sex).
[33] Official estimates of total population for 1896 and 1927 were 3,462 thousand and 5,157 thousand respectively.
[34] These figures have been adjusted for under-enumeration, the reported totals being 6,208 in 1940; 9,907 in 1961 and 13,538 in 1972.
[35] Including 11,000 Indian and negro population of the interior who were not tabulated by sex.
[36] Excluding Amazonas, Mérida and Trujillo.
[37] Including jungle population who were not tabulated by sex.
[38] Excluding any adjustment for under-enumeration, which is believed to require an addition of 5.8%.
[39] Excluding Anguilla in 1980.

A2 NORTH AMERICA: POPULATION OF MAJOR COUNTRIES BY SEX AND AGE GROUPS (in thousands)

Abbreviations used throughout this table: **M** males **F** females

CANADA

	1851 M	1851 F	1861 M	1861 F	1871 M	1871 F	1881 M	1881 F	1891 M	1891 F	1901 M	1901 F	1911 M	1911 F
0–4	233	218	277	266	276	265	304	295	309	302	326	320	450	440
5–9	173	173	218	211	264	255	284	278	300	292	313	306	396	389
10–14	152	146	203	196	243	233	262	251	282	272	297	285	356	346
15–19	136	141	187	187	202	206	240	243	262	259	283	275	355	331
20–24	112	111	154	150	172	179	215	221	242	240	260	255	390	322
25–29	93	91	129	125	138	144	168	169	199	196	220	209	374	289
30–34	75	70	103	97	111	112	134	132	167	158	192	177	313	246
35–39	62	56	84	77	94	94	117	115	142	132	176	160	260	211
40–44	54	47	72	64	81	77	100	97	121	114	155	139	215	177
45–49	43	38	59	51	72	67	83	83	102	96	127	115	180	153
50–54	35	29	48	41	60	53	73	70	89	84	107	99	154	133
55–59	27	22	38	33	48	42	58	54	68	64	83	79	114	100
60–64	19	16	32	26	38	31	53	46	63	58	74	69	95	84
65–69	13	10	24	18	31	25	37	32	45	40	55	52	68	64
70–74							26	23	33	30	39	37	48	46
75–79	22	20	30	26	43	36	16	15	20	18	25	23	30	29
80 and over							14	13	17	16	20	20	24	25
Unknown	—	—	—	—	—	—	—	—	—	—	—	—	—	—

	1921 M	1921 F	1931 M	1931 F	1941 M	1941 F	1951 M	1951 F	1961 M	1961 F	1971 M	1971 F	1981 M	1981 F	1991 M	1991 F
0–4	534	525	543	531	535	518	879	843	1,154	1,102	930	887	914	869	990	945
5–9	529	521	573	560	529	517	714	684	1,064	1,016	1,152	1,102	912	865	956	909
10–14	462	452	543	531	556	545	575	556	948	908	1,181	1,129	985	936	949	901
15–19	405	400	526	514	565	555	532	526	729	704	1,074	1,040	1,182	1,133	943	896
20–24	352	361	464	448	518	514	538	551	587	597	942	948	1,174	1,170	1,015	977
25–29	349	340	410	376	488	479	553	578	614	595	801	783	1,084	1,093	1,172	1,169
30–34	344	310	368	341	432	412	513	530	644	627	661	645	1,021	1,017	1,207	1,222
35–39	343	291	359	329	396	363	504	496	631	640	645	619	822	808	1,112	1,133
40–44	287	241	348	298	349	328	446	423	560	559	641	622	675	663	1,023	1,031
45–49	238	199	322	264	333	303	388	356	516	500	613	626	635	621	810	807
50–54	196	167	268	221	316	276	340	322	443	420	519	534	622	622	652	656
55–59	149	133	199	168	275	232	293	278	362	244	472	482	568	612	598	610
60–64	127	113	157	138	219	189	264	242	293	291	382	395	462	517	562	599
65–69	91	82	121	110	163	145	228	205	240	247	296	324	391	454	482	572
70–74	61	57	89	83	111	106	160	155	196	206	206	252	281	352	354	461
75–79	36	36	50	49	67	68	94	94	134	140	140	186	180	252	250	363
80 and over	28	31	35	39	50	57	69	81	104	123	140	201	159	292	222	435
Unknown	—	—	—	—	—	—	—	—	—	—	—	—	—	—	—	—

A2 NORTH AMERICA: Population of Major Countries by Sex and Age Groups (in thousands)

COSTA RICA

	1864 M	1864 F	1883 M	1883 F	1892 M	1892 F	1927 M	1927 F	1950 M	1950 F	1963 M	1963 F	1973 M	1973 F	1990 M	1990 F
0-4	10	10	15	14	20	19	37	37	67	65	126	123	131	128	200	193
5-9	9	9	13	13	17	17	32	31	57	55	110	107	147	142	187	179
10-14	8	7	12	10	15	14	29	29	50	49	86	84	141	136	169	162
15-19	6	7	9	9	12	12	25	27	40	44	64	66	111	111	145	139
20-24	5	6	8	9	11	12	22	22	38	39	51	53	82	85	149	143
25-29	5	6	8	8	11	11	18	19	29	30	41	44	61	63	144	139
30-34	4	5	7	7	10	10	15	14	24	24	38	39	50	50	123	120
35-39	3	3	5	5	7	6	14	13	23	24	33	34	44	47	97	95
40-44	2	3	4	5	6	6	13	11	18	18	27	27	40	40	75	74
45-49	2	2	3	3	4	4	10	8	14	14	23	22	32	32	57	57
50-54	2	2	3	3	4	4	8	7	12	12	21	20	27	27	47	47
55-59	1	1	1	2	2	2	5	4	8	8	13	13	20	20	40	41
60-64	1	1	2	2	2	2	4	4	8	7	13	13	19	19	32	33
65-69	--	--	1	1	1	1	2	2	5	4	7	8	12	12	24	26
70-74	--	--	--	1	1	1	2	2	3	3	6	6	10	10	17	19
75-79	--	--	--	--	--	-- }	2	2 {	2	2 }	7	8 {	5	5	10	13
80 and over	--	--	--	--	1	1			2	2			6	6	8	11
Unknown	--	--	--	--	--	--	--	--	--	--	1	1	—	—	—	—

CUBA

	1899 M	1899 F	1907 M	1907 F	1919 M	1919 F	1943 M	1943 F	1953 M	1953 F	1970 M	1970 F	1981 M	1981 F	1991 M	1991 F
0-4			173	169	208	202	323	305	376	361	606	579	366	348	464	442
5-9	293	284	114	111	222	215	294	280	364	349	598	571	535	511	403	385
10-14			93	88	191	186	276	261	340	328	417	396	610	579	371	355
15-19	84	94	117	119	150	147	227	228	269	289	390	378	589	573	534	512
20-24	79	74	125	109	110	89	240	244	264	257	365	356	404	402	592	566
25-29	73	64	100	85	128	111	208	202	223	230	332	320	357	362	566	557
30-34	64	55	139	114	122	94	181	173	203	201	287	275	345	348	379	385
35-39	101	84			105	80	189	150	190	193	234	230	310	312	351	358
40-44			105	83	76	56	139	97	183	164	216	212	270	267	333	345
45-49	64	53			61	44	91	75	160	133	191	183	220	222	297	305
50-54			60	50	51	42	106	79	121	89	179	167	199	196	260	262
55-59	37	31			35	27	80	62	76	63	162	153	173	171	203	207
60-64							60	46	83	69	142	122	159	154	179	184
65-69							33	27	57	48	127	101	136	133	142	142
70-74	19	19	48	46	72	66	22	20	36	31	52	40	108	104	124	129
75-79							13	13	19	17	43	40	80	73	93	100
80 and over							15	17	18	21	50	52	55	54	89	95
Unknown	--	--	1	1	1	1	—	—	2	1	—	—	—	—	—	—

A2 NORTH AMERICA: Population of Major Countries by Sex and Age Groups (in thousands)

DOMINICAN REPUBLIC

	1920 M	1920 F
0-6	109	105
7-14	104	97
15-20	58	65
21-60	161	167
61 and over	15	14
Unknown	—	—

	1935 M	1935 F	1950 M	1950 F	1960 M	1960 F	1970 M	1970 F	1990 M	1990 F
0-4	124	121	189	186	283	277	344	337	501	481
5-9	124	120	151	147	247	241	330	326	465	450
10-14	102	94	142	135	203	190	285	282	416	403
15-19	74	79	102	124	133	153	212	236	391	379
20-24	64	70	105	109	121	135	156	173	372	359
25-29	59	58	78	79	104	109	117	128	330	317
30-34	45	41	60	60	95	93	104	106	266	256
35-39	42	37	60	55	78	74	102	104	210	200
40-44	33	29	48	43	66	58	91	82	168	161
45-49	23	20	37	31	52	45	63	58	132	128
50-54	18	18	31	29	47	42	58	50	110	107
55-59	10	9	21	15	29	22	35	29	89	88
60-64	13	12	20	19	32	29	38	34	76	74
65-69	6	5	10	9	14	12	20	18	48	47
70-74	6	7	8	10	14	13	20	20	35	36
75-79	3	3	4	4 }	18 {	19	8	8	22	23
80 and over	5	6	7	10			14	17	13	17
Unknown	—	—	- -	- -	—	—	—	—	—	—

EL SALVADOR

	1930 M	1930 F
0-4	104	103
5-7	62	60
8-14	130	118
15-17	40	45
18-22	78	85
23-29	81	86
30-39	96	94
40-49	58	57
50-59	37	39
60-69	21	20
70-79	6	8
80 and over	3	5
Unknown	—	—

	1950 M	1950 F	1961 M	1961 F	1971 M	1971 F	1991 M	1991 F
0-4	146	143	218	214	301	297	406	392
5-9	127	124	193	190	296	285	376	362
10-14	116	108	160	150	242	230	372	359
15-19	97	102	117	125	175	184	319	320
20-24	84	93	101	113	143	153	246	258
25-29	66	74	81	92	109	121	167	194
30-34	55	57	73	78	99	101	126	151
35-39	54	58	66	73	91	95	110	131
40-44	44	45	55	57	74	77	94	108
45-49	34	35	44	46	59	63	88	98
50-54	31	32	37	39	48	51	75	84
55-59	17	19	25	26	34	36	62	70
60-64	19	19	29	29	34	34	50	57
65-69	10	10	14	15	21	23	39	44
70-74	7	8	10	11	18	19	27	32
75-79	4	4	6	7	9	10	16	21
80 and over	5	7	7	9	9	13	10	16
Unknown	1	1	1	- -	- -	- -	- -	- -

A2　NORTH AMERICA: Population of Major Countries by Sex and Age Groups (in thousands)

GUATEMALA

	1893		1921	
	M	F	M	F
0–4	[271][1]		153	150
6–7			59	57
8–14	} [233][1] {		175	163
15–18	124		81	83
19–30	324		226	253
31–40	167		126	129
41–50			78	83
51–60	} 165 {		49	50
61 and over	100		45	45
Unknown	—		—	—

	1940		1950		1964		1973		1981		1991	
	M	F	M	F	M	F	M	F	M	F	M	F
0–4	260	253	240	230	379	370	440	431	535	522	838	806
5–9	250	237	195	185	335	323	395	383	456	445	721	695
10–14	227	204	173	156	281	262	348	330	386	371	623	602
15–19	168	174	150	156	219	219	275	286	314	335	518	501
20–24	142	135	135	142	175	177	231	239	262	286	420	411
25–29	120	127	110	110	148	150	169	178	205	222	345	340
30–34	102	104	85	78	137	133	141	141	175	176	280	279
35–39	94	95	78	78	121	120	131	137	145	153	233	233
40–44	79	77	57	61	96	90	116	113	124	122	183	185
45–49	63	60	53	51	75	68	93	91	102	104	147	148
50–54	44	46	42	43	59	60	75	72	92	91	125	126
55–59	33	33	31	28	43	41	52	48	65	63	110	112
60–64	34	34	28	26	45	42	49	46	61	55	89	92
65–69	19	17	15	13	25	23	28	28	36	35	65	66
70–74	9	11	8	9	16	16	22	22	25	25	40	43
75–79	5	6	5	5	10	9	12	12	16	16	24	26
80 and over	8	11	6	8	9	10	12	13	17	18	19	22
Unknown	1	2	—	—	- -	- -	—	—	—	—		

A2 NORTH AMERICA: Population of Major Countries by Sex and Age Groups
(in thousands)

HAITI

	1950		1971		1982		1991	
	M	F	M	F	M	F	M	F
0-4	186	189	301	303	357	373	511	500
5-9	199	201	295	300	329	343	444	438
10-14	203	194	295	290	289	289	390	387
15-19	154	154	230	245	252	260	354	351
20-24	121	146	159	188	213	244	303	306
25-29	125	152	135	168	173	220	257	268
30-34	85	104	106	132	137	149	207	226
35-39	108	122	120	146	128	141	171	191
40-44	81	77	106	107	110	122	139	158
45-49	68	65	95	91	107	104	117	133
50-54	51	48	70	65	93	84	99	112
55-59	28	29	48	46	59	56	82	94
60-64	34	37	45	49	62	62	65	74
65-69	19	22	31	37	38	40	50	58
70-74	18	22	25	31	36	38	35	43
75-79	8	10	12	17	21	26	22	26
80 and over	10	15	16	27	45	54	16	19
Unknown	6	5	- -	- -	—	—	—	—

HONDURAS

	1930		1940		1950		1961		1974		1990	
	M	F	M	F	M	F	M	F	M	F	M	F
0-4	71	69	95	94	110	106	181	176	246	240	446	429
5-9	62	61	76	73	91	87	157	151	216	209	389	376
10-14	51	48	69	64	84	78	121	114	187	180	330	320
15-19	47	47	60	69	70	69	89	95	140	149	299	290
20-24	40	43	50	52	61	63	76	82	108	120	243	238
25-29	31	35	40	44	50	51	62	68	79	88	191	191
30-34	27	30	35	35	41	42	55	56	68	70	151	151
35-39	23	23	30	30	38	39	47	49	62	66	121	121
40-44	20	20	27	26	32	32	37	37	51	53	98	97
45-49	15	14	20	19	27	27	31	31	43	44	80	80
50-54	11	13	16	16	23	25	25	26	34	35	66	67
55-59	9	9	12	12	17	18	18	18	24	25	54	55
60-64			11	11	16	16	18	18	23	22	43	44
65-69			6	6	10	10	10	9	14	14	32	34
70-74	17	18	4	4	6	7	6	6	11	11	24	25
75-79			5	5	5	5	4	4	6	6	15	16
80 and over					5	5	3	4	5	6	10	12
Unknown	2	2	1	1	—	—	1	- -	—	—	—	—

A2 NORTH AMERICA: Population of Major Countries by Sex and Age Groups (in thousands)

JAMAICA

	1881		1891		1911		1921	
	M	F	M	F	M	F	M	F
0–4	38	38	41	42	57	58	56	56
5–9	37	38	39	40	59	59	60	60
10–14	36	36	44	42	50	48	53	53
15–19	27	29	32	35	39	41	41	47
20–24	28	30	29	35	37	45	36	49
25–34	44	47	42	53	57	69	50	67
35–44	29	30	32	36	41	45	42	51
45–54	18	19	24	24	28	32	32	34
55–64	11	13	11	13	17	20	18	21
65–74	6	7	5	7	9	11	9	11
75 and over	5	6	5	7	4	6	5	7
Unknown	4	4	1	- -	- -	- -	- -	- -

	1943		1953		1960		1970		1982		1991	
	M	F	M	F	M	F	M	F	M	F	M	F
0–4	78	78	108	109	135	133	145	142	135	133	144	131
5–9	78	78	102	83	111	110	151	150	143	142	140	128
10–14	70	70	88	70	87	87	123	121	146	143	141	127
15–19	55	61	63	71	68	76	81	85	131	132	147	132
20–24	53	62	59	73	57	68	59	67	102	111	142	133
25–29	50	57	51	66	50	61	49	53	74	81	122	119
30–34	46	48	46	52	43	51	39	42	59	62	96	93
35–39	39	41	43	51	41	49	37	43	47	50	68	68
40–44	35	35	44	42	40	42	37	40	42	43	52	52
45–49	25	25	33	35	39	39	33	36	35	37	44	43
50–54	20	22	29	31	33	34	32	35	36	39	38	37
55–59	14	16	17	19	24	25	29	30	29	30	33	35
60–64	13	16	15	18	18	20	25	27	27	31	29	30
65–69	8	10	8	11	10	13	19	20	25	26	24	25
70–74	7	9	7	11	8	11	12	14	21	23	20	20
75–79	3	5	4	6	5	8	7	9	13	15	16	18
80 and over	4	7	4	8	5	10	7	13	11	19	16	23
Unknown	- -	- -	- -	1	—	—	—	—	—	—	—	—

A2 NORTH AMERICA: Population of Major Countries by Sex and Age Groups (in thousands)

MEXICO

	1895 M	1895 F	1900 M	1900 F	1910 M	1910 F	1921 M	1921 F	1930[1] M	1930[1] F
0–4	1,094	1,060	1,190	1,157	1,366	1,297	946	928	[1,527]	[1,483]
5–9	896	840	928	870	1,102	1,046	940	899	[911]	[883]
10–14	692	661	739	705	816	779	935	858	[882]	[804]
15–19	605	732	670	795	718	852	728	822	[792]	[892]
20–24	1,119	1,243	1,179	1,325	627	712	610	704	[735]	[842]
25–29					699	787	547	655	[687]	[773]
30–34	820	802	877	874	420	397	468	526	[543]	[581]
35–39					534	555	445	469	[501]	[529]
40–44					270	249	343	388	[380]	[427]
45–49	820	816	909	897	335	354	268	270	[314]	[321]
50–54					148	136	219	249	[255]	[289]
55–59					226	236	141	138	[163]	[162]
60–64					89	78				
65–69					89	84				
70–74	227	190	250	219	31	28	346	354	[427]	[455]
75–79					35	35				
80 and over					21	21				
Unknown	8	8	11	13	9	10	70	69	3	—

	1940 M	1940 F	1950 M	1950 F	1960 M	1960 F	1970 M	1970 F	1980 M	1980 F	1990 M	1990 F
0–4	1,448	1,416	2,000	1,970	2,936	2,840	4,152	4,016	4,699	4,649	5,902	5,684
5–9	1,441	1,387	1,865	1,809	2,706	2,611	3,935	3,788	5,173	5,111	5,607	5,410
10–14	1,247	1,156	1,600	1,510	2,234	2,124	3,271	3,125	4,575	4,520	5,266	5,092
15–19	970	1,027	1,249	1,384	1,739	1,796	2,491	2,563	3,767	3,890	5,439	5,301
20–24	740	808	1,067	1,233	1,405	1,542	1,930	2,102	2,972	3,182	4,608	4,537
25–29	752	839	982	1,038	1,196	1,309	1,575	1,685	2,325	2,479	3,790	3,793
30–34	634	684	699	733	1,009	1,043	1,285	1,311	1,886	1,952	3,070	3,120
35–39	671	701	748	798	959	962	1,235	1,276	1,665	1,742	2,458	2,530
40–44	450	488	587	622	674	687	959	974	1,360	1,385	1,842	1,932
45–49	363	395	535	539	610	623	830	807	1,135	1,181	1,590	1,693
50–54	284	317	405	423	527	536	590	602	913	951	1,271	1,382
55–59	206	220	261	267	405	395	502	510	733	733	1,029	1,134
60–64	205	215	265	289	372	373	451	467	542	573	810	901
65–69	111	115	165	169	203	211	345	357	417	458	603	707
70–74	79	84	114	127	161	172	242	246	339	366	393	484
75–79	44	45	63	66	91	97	120	133	229	252	280	368
80 and over	50	60	72	90	121	139	152	196	220	281	247	325
Unknown	3	2	21	26	65	49	—	—	93	100	...	...

A2   NORTH AMERICA: Population of Major Countries by Sex and Age Groups (in thousands)

NICARAGUA

	1920		1940		1950		1963		1971		1991	
	M	F	M	F	M	F	M	F	M	F	M	F
0–4	} 202		79	81	86	83	141	137	163	159	357	344
5–9			69	70	79	75	135	130	158	156	307	299
10–14	} 151		61	62	70	64	101	96	135	131	254	252
15–19			53	54	53	58	71	77	98	106	187	215
20–24	} 117		42	44	47	52	58	64	73	82	132	185
25–29			36	39	40	44	51	57	57	65	116	153
30–34	} 74		30	31	29	31	40	42	45	49	102	119
35–39			27	30	30	32	40	43	46	51	86	98
40–44	} 46		22	25	21	23	29	30	36	37	68	74
45–49			16	18	18	19	24	25	29	31	54	58
50–54	} 29		12	15	16	17	20	21	23	25	46	48
55–59			9	11	9	10	13	14	16	17	37	39
60–64			8	11	10	11	15	16	15	17	29	34
65–69	} 17		5	5	5	5	} 13	15	8	9	22	27
70–74			3	4	5				8	9	14	18
75–79			2	2	2	3	} 7	10	4	5	8	12
80 and over			2	3	3	4			5	6	5	9
Unknown	2		--	--	—	—	—	—	—	—	—	—

PANAMA

	1920	
	M	F
0–5	39	39
6–21	71	75
22–60	112	97
61 and over	6	6

	1930	
	M	F
0–6	46	45
7–15	53	49
16–20	23	26
21–30	39	40
31–40	32	29
41–50	22	18
51–60	11	9
61–70	5	4
71–80	2	2
81 and over	--	1
Unknown	7	4

	1940		1950		1960		1970		1980		1990	
	M	F	M	F	M	F	M	F	M	F	M	F
0–4	42	41	62	61	92	90	117	114	118	115	152	146
5–9	38	37	54	53	79	77	109	107	122	121	142	136
10–14	33	31	43	42	66	64	88	85	118	111	137	131
15–19	27	30	36	37	53	54	72	73	100	100	135	130
20–24	29	28	33	33	45	46	62	63	79	82	122	121
25–29	26	25	31	30	38	38	51	51	67	68	106	105
30–34	19	16	27	25	33	32	42	41	59	59	92	87
35–39	17	16	25	23	30	29	37	36	48	48	74	70
40–44	} 28	23	18	15	27	24	32	29	40	41	62	59
45–49			14	13	23	21	28	25	34	32	50	48
50–54	} 18	14	12	11	17	15	25	22	29	29	40	39
55–59			9	8	13	12	20	18	24	23	33	32
60–64	} 9	8	9	8	11	10	15	13	22	20	27	27
65–69			5	5	7	7	10	10	16	15	22	21
70–74	} 3	3	3	3	6	5	7	7	11	10	17	16
75–79			2	2	3	3	} 9	10	7	7	11	11
80 and over	1	2	2	2	3	4			6	8	8	9
Unknown	—	—	1	--	—	—	—	—	3	3	—	—

A2 NORTH AMERICA: Population of Major Countries by Sex and Age Groups (in thousands)

PUERTO RICO

	1899		1940		1950		1960		1970		1980		1990	
	M	F	M	F	M	F	M	F	M	F	M	F	M	F
0-4	77	74	142	138	185	181	180	175	161	157	173	167	156	142
5-9	73	71	128	124	161	157	166	162	171	167	168	162	166	152
10-14	65	59	114	113	139	132	162	159	170	165	172	166	175	168
15-19	43	50	99	107	109	111	123	124	144	148	168	169	172	158
20-24	42	47	102	104	91	102	80	92	108	126	129	143	137	149
25-29	39	45	72	76	76	82	62	74	85	98	111	125	118	136
30-34	31	33	52	51	67	65	59	68	73	83	107	122	110	133
35-39	24	23	51	51	67	66	62	69	68	77	91	103	104	130
40-44	22	22	44	42	48	43	53	54	62	67	78	88	109	129
45-49	13	13	36	33	40	36	54	52	59	63	68	77	95	111
50-54	16	17	31	26	37	35	40	35	53	53	61	69	82	100
55-59	8	7	19	16	25	22	34	31	49	47	57	62	72	83
60-64	8	10	18	18	26	23	29	29	41	41	51	54	63	74
65-69	4	3	12	13	16	17	25	24	33	33	46	49	57	65
70-74	3	4	8	9	11	11	16	15	22	22	32	34	43	51
75-79	1	1	9	12	14	17	10	11	14	15	22	24	68	84
80 and over	2	3					9	12	17	22	21	26		
Unknown	- -	- -	- -	1	—	—	—	—	—	—	—	—		

TRINIDAD AND TOBAGO

	1891		1901		1911		1921	
	M	F	M	F	M	F	M	F
0-4	13	13	16	17	21	20	21	21
5-9	12	12	16	15	19	19	22	22
10-14	11	10	14	13	17	16	20	19
15-19	8	9	12	12	14	15	16	18
20-24	11	11	15	14	17	18	17	19
25-29	13	10	15	13	18	16	15	16
30-34	11	8	13	10	15	12	14	14
35-39	10	7	12	9	13	11	14	12
40-44	9	6	10	7	12	9	14	10
45-49	6	4	7	5	9	6	10	8
50-54	5	4	6	4	7	5	8	6
55-59	2	2	3	2	4	3	4	4
60-64	3	2	3	3	4	3	4	4
65-69	1	1	1	1	2	2	2	2
70-74	1	1	1	1	1	1	2	2
75-79	- -	- -	1	1	1	1	1	1
80 and over	1	1	1	1	1	1	1	1
Unknown	- -	- -	- -	- -	—	—	—	—

A2   NORTH AMERICA: Population of Major Countries by Sex and Age Groups (in thousands)

TRINIDAD AND TOBAGO

	1931 M	1931 F	1946 M	1946 F	1960 M	1960 F	1970 M	1970 F	1980 M	1980 F	1990 M	1990 F
0–4	23	24	44	44	66	65	61	65	63	62	81	79
5–9	25	25	34	34	59	59	73	59	61	57	76	74
10–14	22	21	27	27	51	51	63	51	60	60	64	62
15–19	19	22	23	26	39	41	51	41	65	66	60	59
20–24	20	22	25	26	32	33	40	33	55	55	58	58
25–29	17	18	23	23	25	27	28	27	44	44	63	63
30–34	15	15	21	20	24	25	24	25	35	35	52	52
35–39	13	14	19	19	23	24	21	24	28	28	41	41
40–44	13	12	16	15	22	20	20	20	23	23	33	33
45–49	12	10	13	12	19	18	20	18	18	19	26	27
50–54	9	8	9	9	16	14	18	14	17	19	21	22
55–59	6	5	8	7	12	11	14	11	16	15	17	19
60–64	5	5	6	6	8	8	11	8	14	13	15	16
65–69	3	3	5	6	6	8	8	8	11	13	12	13
70–74	2	2	3	4	4	5	5	5	7	9	9	10
75–79	1	1	1	2	2	3	2	3	4	6	6	9
80 and over	1	2	1	2	2	3	2	3	3	5	4	7
Unknown	—	—	—	—	—	—	—	—	4	3	…	…

USA (whites)[2]

	1790 M	1790 F	1800 M	1800 F	1810 M	1810 F	1820 M	1820 F
0–9	} 802 {	…	764	715	1,035	981	1,345	1,281
10–15		…	353	324	468	448	613	605
16–25	} 813 {	…	393	401	548	562	776	781
26–44		…	432	412	572	544	766	737
45 and over		…	262	248	365	338	495	463

	1830 M	1830 F	1840 M	1840 F	1850 M	1850 F	1860 M	1860 F	1870 M	1870 F
0–4	973	922	1,271	1,203	1,472	1,424	2,091	2,026	2,399	2,321
5–9	782	751	1,024	987	1,372	1,332	1,789	1,739	2,104	2,048
10–14	670	639	880	837	1,226	1,177	1,590	1,523	2,103	2,033
15–19	573	596	756	792	1,041	1,088	1,401	1,452	1,731	1,780
20–24	} 956	918	1,322	1,253	1,869	1,758	2,497	2,420	1,592	1,643
25–29									1,328	1,353
30–34	} 593	556	866	779	1,289	1,128	1,867	1,636	1,132	1,133
35–39									1,048	999
40–44	} 368	356	537	502	840	749	1,224	1,058	882	834
45–49									752	655
50–54	} 229	224	315	305	499	460	740	659	655	550
55–59									425	370
60–64									359	328
65–69									227	213
70–74	} 211	210	279	281	411	408	597	586	155	153
75–79									78	81
80 and over									58	67
Unknown		5	—	6	—	7	3	14	11	751

A2 NORTH AMERICA: Population of Major Countries by Sex and Age Groups (in thousands)

USA (whites)[2] (contd)

	1880		1890		1900		1910		1920	
	M	F	M	F	M	F	M	F	M	F
0–4	2,949	2,851	3,351	3,229	4,011	3,908	4,729	4,594	5,261	5,113
5–9	2,756	2,686	3,277	3,196	3,862	3,776	4,285	4,190	5,099	4,988
10–14	2,483	2,398	3,044	2,948	3,519	3,440	4,006	3,912	4,735	4,634
15–19	2,150	2,202	2,819	2,856	3,258	3,258	3,999	3,969	4,142	4,172
20–24	2,219	2,183	2,741	2,708	3,145	3,190	4,071	3,915	4,019	4,167
25–29	1,838	1,704	2,407	2,240	2,943	2,820	3,792	3,465	4,094	4,047
30–34	1,548	1,431	2,201	1,944	2,619	2,385	3,297	2,970	3,776	3,563
35–39	1,353	1,295	1,831	1,608	2,360	2,100	3,024	2,708	3,665	3,300
40–44	1,112	1,079	1,496	1,370	2,055	1,797	2,537	2,243	2,987	2,768
45–49	962	900	1,271	1,178	1,652	1,454	2,162	1,899	2,779	2,409
50–54	856	772	1,083	1,008	1,396	1,238	1,916	1,639	2,294	2,024
55–59	610	545	793	738	1,040	981	1,364	1,200	1,741	1,565
60–64	516	461	686	637	826	795	1,077	993	1,462	1,310
65–69	342	316	479	446	610	587	792	758	999	926
70–74	225	219	333	308	412	397	519	512	656	643
75–79	126	129	183	178	240	238	307	314	391	410
80 and over	85	102	129	145	155	170	206	232	252	306
Unknown	—	—	145	94	98	47	94	40	78	45

	1930		1940		1950		1960[3]		1970		1980[3]		1990	
	M	F	M	F	M	F	M	F	M	F	M	F	M	F
0–4	5,158	4,984	4,701	4,528	7,244	6,940	8,849	8,509	7,374	7,049	6,484	6,150	7,004	6,645
5–9	5,662	5,500	4,745	4,584	5,915	5,681	8,202	7,885	8,633	8,264	6,685	6,348	6,991	6,626
10–14	5,415	5,279	5,259	5,094	4,945	4,750	7,457	7,182	9,034	8,647	7,408	7,052	6,607	6,247
15–19	5,132	5,116	5,616	5,448	4,686	4,645	5,837	5,771	8,291	8,079	8,634	8,328	6,846	6,497
20–24	4,747	4,866	5,114	5,227	5,003	5,176	4,646	4,825	6,941	7,341	8,683	8,605	7,388	7,136
25–29	4,324	4,385	4,892	5,012	5,350	5,575	4,722	4,834	5,850	5,962	8,005	7,980	8,385	8,254
30–34	4,117	4,094	4,573	4,633	5,081	5,276	5,218	5,371	4,925	5,042	7,300	7,345	8,700	8,652
35–39	4,225	4,053	4,254	4,262	4,956	5,103	5,447	5,694	4,784	4,936	5,831	5,930	8,054	8,027
40–44	3,773	3,494	3,905	3,941	4,574	4,617	5,117	5,306	5,194	5,412	4,850	4,976	7,227	7,279
45–49	3,327	3,054	3,843	3,690	4,080	4,089	4,828	4,957	5,258	5,587	4,639	4,818	5,737	5,049
50–54	2,836	2,610	3,452	3,229	3,756	3,779	4,286	4,408	4,833	5,169	4,918	5,240	4,657	4,847
55–59	2,240	2,080	2,790	2,637	3,351	3,345	3,729	3,898	4,311	4,696	4,853	5,385	4,331	4,638
60–64	1,800	1,697	2,232	2,184	2,829	2,823	3,122	3,429	3,647	4,157	4,173	4,803	4,335	4,876
65–69	1,330	1,278	1,737	1,762	2,225	2,364	2,684	3,055	2,808	3,491	3,482	4,331	7,069	8,957
70–74	937	908	1,183	1,031	1,514	1,669	2,018	2,373	2,108	2,875	2,552	3,543		
75–79	516	528	681	737	1,625	1,983	1,255	1,580	1,438	2,115	1,650	2,660	4,146	7,680
80 and over	340	404	481	581			950	1,388	1,292	2,204	1,538	3,193		
Unknown	43	35	—	—	—	—	—	—	23[11]					

A2 NORTH AMERICA: Population of Major Countries by Sex and Age Groups (in thousands)

USA (negroes)

	1820 M	1820 F	1830 M	1830 F	1840 M	1840 F	1850 M	1850 F
0–4	392[4]	370[4]	402	395	479	477	297	304
5–9							268	269
10–14							248	241
15–19	227[5]	231[5]	356[7]	357[7]	444[7]	447[7]	197	205
20–24							326	324
25–29	187[6]	180[6]	213[8]	218[8]	271[8]	282[8]		
30–34							201	207
35–39								
40–44			141[9]	136[9]	174[9]	170[9]		
45–49							127	131
50–54							77	74
55–59								
60–64	95	89	54	56	66	66		
65–69							69	70
70–74								
75–79								
80 and over								
Unknown	—	—	—	—	—	—	2	2

	1860 M	1860 F	1870 M	1870 F	1880 M	1880 F	1890 M	1890 F
0–4	355	364	397	395	…	…	530[10]	518[10]
5–9	318	320	332	328	…	…	549[10]	544[10]
10–14	307	294	329	316	…	…	526[10]	507[10]
15–19	245	256	252	269	…	…	422	449
20–24	394	389	232	266	…	…	350	381
25–29			175	204	…	…	272	288
30–34	247	253	131	154	…	…	203	207
35–39			123	136	…	…	344	364
40–44	162	162	102	115	…	…		
45–49			85	84	…	…	257	242
50–54	93	91	84	77	…	…	145	124
55–59			44	37	…	…		
60–64			48	44	…	…		
65–69			24	21	…	…	46	38
70–74	81	82	18	19	…	…	30	29
75–79			8	9	…	…	16	16
80 and over			10	12	…	…	17	22
Unknown	14	12	512				28	26

A2 NORTH AMERICA: Population of Major Countries by Sex and Age Groups (In thousands)

USA (negroes)(contd)

	1900 M	1900 F	1910 M	1910 F	1920 M	1920 F	1930 M	1930 F
0–4	604	611	629	634	569	575	611	619
5–9	600	602	619	627	631	635	680	689
10–14	549	543	578	577	616	621	623	628
15–19	474	508	508	552	513	570	596	655
20–24	459	510	482	549	487	568	554	650
25–29	361	377	422	459	424	485	501	571
30–34	262	262	332	336	332	366	417	448
35–39	233	241	320	313	384	390	430	460
40–44	179	188	230	226	276	284	339	348
45–49	168	158	200	186	321	231	323	307
50–54	155	136	179	147	228	171	278	227
55–59	97	82	115	95	129	101	174	135
60–64	86	76	101	85	112	88	133	109
65–69	56	47	68	56	76	61	83	72
70–74	36	36	41	38	47	44	51	48
75–79	20	20	23	21	27	25	29	30
80 and over	20	25	21	26	23	28	27	32
Unknown	25	24	17	14	14	10	7	7

	1940 M	1940 F	1950 M	1950 F	1960[3] M	1960[3] F	1970 M	1970 F	1980 M	1980 F	1990 M	1990 F
0–4	622	627	948	943	1,363	1,360	1,220	1,213	1,228	1,208	1,408	1,377
5–9	644	651	761	768	1,195	1,196	1,377	1,370	1,255	1,235	1,350	1,321
10–14	661	669	674	678	989	984	1,407	1,403	1,344	1,329	1,314	1,287
15–19	630	675	592	635	741	756	1,202	1,221	1,489	1,496	1,342	1,316
20–24	550	645	564	668	569	642	840	974	1,300	1,425	1,259	1,320
25–29	530	616	580	669	548	631	658	771	1,084	1,237	1,286	1,422
30–34	468	525	511	593	564	663	568	685	871	1,018	1,251	1,431
35–39	463	523	530	609	569	652	541	655	662	795	1,083	1,254
40–44	400	415	469	504	508	578	544	654	567	685	866	1,010
45 49	348	345	410	444	480	534	520	603	515	628	642	763
50–54	283	267	350	352	407	445	459	531	505	624	532	647
55–59	207	190	264	251	365	393	405	469	467	570	457	576
60–64	154	142	195	190	259	290	334	399	385	486	414	547
65–69	152	145	189	213	229	258	277	350	332	445	618	886
70–74	84	79	109	114	151	173	184	232	234	329		
75–79	41	42	113	127	94	109	110	145	153	235	348	657
80 and over	32	41			66	87	105	157	128	231		
Unknown	—	—	—	—	—	—	11	11	—	—	—	—

A2 SOUTH AMERICA: POPULATION OF MAJOR COUNTRIES BY SEX AND AGE GROUPS (in thousands)

ARGENTINA

	1869[2] M	1869[2] F	1895 M	1895 F	1914 M	1914 F	1947 M	1947 F	1960 M	1960 F	1970 M	1970 F	1980 M	1980 F	1990 M	1990 F
0–4	[159]	[157]	299	291	582	567	902	881	1,079	1,052	1,197	1,158	1,640	1,601	1,642	1,588
5–9	[137]	[128]	282	270	517	504	798	779	1,050	1,026	1,163	1,134	1,407	1,377	1,638	1,587
10–14	[106]	[98]	233	211	438	421	772	753	976	963	1,114	1,087	1,240	1,216	1,632	1,584
15–19	[90]	[101]	190	202	434	406	789	781	834	852	1,059	1,040	1,170	1,165	1,403	1,365
20–24	[170]	[155]	173	174	458	383	749	741	755	776	970	981	1,096	1,121	1,232	1,203
25–29			190	158	420	323	642	644	766	774	843	860	1,058	1,076	1,166	1,142
30–34	[111]	[96]	165	129	332	235	618	610	773	788	785	796	980	991	1,131	1,109
35–39			154	115	264	207	598	561	721	722	779	767	860	871	1,078	1,062
40–44	[67]	[58]	115	90	212	155	553	473	607	609	770	770	772	779	967	953
45–49			95	63	166	125	468	403	591	589	684	699	744	751	834	839
50–54	[35]	[31]	68	52	140	106	386	312	521	498	562	585	710	748	740	768
55–59			42	30	94	71	316	262	443	413	518	549	618	658	681	733
60–64	[15]	[14]	33	30	73	62	225	194	330	326	436	455	468	534	610	690
65–69			15	14	39	34	142	136	237	236	322	350	398	477	487	588
70–74	[3]	[3]	11	13	27	26	84	85	160	172	202	244	282	356	350	466
75–79			5	5	25	30	44	51	85	100	123	157	181	247	239	351
80 and over			6	10			32	47	56	82	91	142	131	224	172	292
Unknown	- -	- -	12	10	4	2	27	38	21	28	—	—	—	—	—	—

BOLIVIA

	1900 M	1900 F
0–6	108	106
7–13	104	101
14–17	61	63
18–25	106	107
26–30	91	91
31–40	124	125
41 and over	169	169
Unknown	55	54

	1950 M	1950 F	1976 M	1976 F	1990 M	1990 F
0–4	216	210	371	371	538	627
5–9	194	185	323	320	486	524
10–14	141	125	279	273	445	448
15–19	135	133	241	248	384	381
20–24	116	130	195	217	321	322
25–29	104	118	171	172	272	272
30–34	78	89	136	141	232	231
35–39	77	87	122	130	198	196
40–44	55	65	92	103	169	166
45–49	49	55	94	101	138	134
50–54	39	47	64	74	116	111
55–59	30	33	54	59	99	93
60–64	38	39	49	53	82	76
65–69	19	19	35	36	62	56
70–74	15	18	20	28	42	37
75–79	7	8	15	17	25	22
80 and over	14	16	21	24	15	13
Unknown	- -	- -	—	—	—	—

A2 SOUTH AMERICA: Population of Major Countries by Sex and Age Groups
(in thousands)

BRAZIL

	1872 M	1872 F	1890 M	1890 F	1900 M	1900 F	1920 M	1920 F
0–4	560	499	2,122		1,522	1,453	2,318	2,275
5–9	604	576	2,069		1,344	1,257	2,326	2,249
10–14	540	551	1,710		1,048	998	1,989	1,920
15–19	540	527	1,400		900	954	1,997	2,221
20–24	555	520	1,352		773	785	1,069	1,070
25–29	556	523	2,182		714	733	1,231	1,258
30–34	667	597	1,802		1,047	988	1,847	1,713
35–39								
40–44	465	436	1,233		710	637	1,263	1,138
45–49								
50–54	324	289	733		412	359	753	698
55–59								
60–64	202	184	430		187	168	408	393
65–69								
70–74							148	160
75–79	107	95	160		69	69		
80 and over	97	86	84		31	33	54	71
Unknown	6	5	59		75	55	39	27

	1940 M	1940 F	1950 M	1950 F	1960 M	1960 F	1970 M	1970 F	1980 M	1980 F	1990 M	1990 F
0–4	3,256	3,184	4,236	4,135	5,712	5,484	6,970	6,842	8,461	8,188	9,578	9,388
5–9	2,924	2,835	3,561	3,455	5,159	5,002	6,800	6,660	7,230	7,042	8,910	8,824
10–14	2,682	2,646	3,165	3,144	4,287	4,287	5,934	5,925	6,807	6,743	8,161	8,119
15–19	2,158	2,286	2,645	2,858	3,446	3,697	4,995	5,258	6,488	6,789	7,427	7,420
20–24	1,836	1,978	2,384	2,607	2,964	3,197	4,037	4,249	5,656	5,970	6,927	6,896
25–29	1,649	1,707	2,030	2,102	2,522	2,687	3,173	3,331	4,806	4,948	6,748	6,735
30–34	1,300	1,281	1,622	1,623	2,254	2,261	2,801	2,864	3,955	3,915	5,735	5,763
35–39	1,166	1,154	1,524	1,517	1,956	2,034	2,502	2,587	3,181	3,231	4,826	4,879
40–44	1,004	946	1,228	1,161	1,653	1,580	2,288	2,247	2,884	2,843	3,867	3,906
45–49	786	706	1,019	958	1,400	1,327	1,795	1,752	2,295	2,406	3,037	3,073
50–54	641	606	811	774	1,124	1,065	1,486	1,454	2,043	2,113	2,595	2,647
55–59	413	386	550	516	828	770	1,160	1,128	1,637	1,673	2,112	2,182
60–64	338	352	473	463	728	685	903	888	1,230	1,333	1,765	1,851
65–69	187	199	255	260	396	376	605	612	1,064	1,131	1,335	1,432
70–74	128	156	165	196	267	280	389	417			916	1,012
75–79	65	79	83	102	139	151	195	223	1,372	1,568	617	710
80 and over	68	104	81	127	123	167	204	281			436	539
Unknown	15	18	54	63	53	57	93	91	36	33	—	—

A2   SOUTH AMERICA: Population of Major Countries by Sex and Age Groups
(in thousands)

CHILE

	1895 M	1895 F	1907 M	1907 F	1920 M	1920 F	1930 M	1930 F
0–4	222	215	[256][12]	[249][12]	239	235	296	294
5–9	182	172	[171][12]	[164][12]	257	250	270	266
10–14	154	150	196	183	226	216	238	231
15–19	134	148	[204][12]	[218][12]	194	204	229	240
20–24	122	128	[104][12]	[104][12]	174	180	206	211
25–29	121	133	146	149	155	164	172	190
30–34	78	79	} 200	203 {	125	127	145	143
35–39	89	95			118	118	132	137
40–44	52	50	} 140	147 {	102	100	110	108
45–49	56	59			72	68	90	88
50–54	28	28	} 100	98 {	65	69	74	76
55–59	41	41			39	37	49	50
60–64	17	17	} 61	62 {	43	50	44	52
65–69	16	17			17	20	26	27
70–74	7	7	} 26	29 {	20	22	20	24
75–79	7	8			8	8	10	11
80 and over	6	8	13	17	12	17	12	18
Unknown	—	—	—	—	—	—	—	—

	1940 M	1940 F	1952 M	1952 F	1960 M	1960 F	1970 M	1970 F	1982 M	1982 F	1991 M	1991 F
0–4	314	308	392	387	555	550	567	556	662	642	757	731
5–9	322	313	392	387	492	489	624	620	605	587	705	682
10–14	307	302	327	323	421	415	560	555	592	575	618	598
15–19	256	256	281	291	355	370	447	467	613	600	620	604
20–24	219	238	274	299	288	311	371	398	585	576	623	610
25–29	204	223	212	234	252	275	302	324	488	483	620	613
30–34	177	175	185	195	247	260	249	267	416	420	548	549
35–39	155	166	179	197	200	215	247	267	367	376	464	469
40–44	137	132	163	159	178	185	223	233	302	312	376	387
45–49	109	107	127	133	157	167	172	185	247	259	315	333
50–54	86	88	114	116	138	141	149	163	222	237	248	270
55–59	68	66	79	82	103	109	127	141	180	199	209	238
60–64	55	63	69	78	86	97	106	117	140	162	174	210
65–69	33	34	44	49	61	68	80	92	109	135	129	167
70–74	23	29	31	38	38	46	54	64	78	104	92	130
75–79	12	14	15	19	23	29	31	39	47	69	59	91
80 and over	12	20	15	25	20	33	35	53	35	63	53	93
Unknown	—	—	13	8	—	—	—	—	—	—	—	—

A2 SOUTH AMERICA: Population of Major Countries by Sex and Age Groups (in thousands)

COLOMBIA

	1918 M	1918 F	1938 M	1938 F	1951 M	1951 F	1964 M	1964 F	1973 M	1973 F	1985 M	1985 F	1991 M	1991 F
0–4	412	418	672	666	951	922	1,562	1,523	1,796	1,736	1,717	1,653	2,121	2,039
5–9	356	351	630	617	794	769	1,419	1,382	1,748	1,704	1,751	1,694	2,019	1,944
10–14	319	312	547	522	684	658	1,148	1,121	1,598	1,596	1,639	1,587	1,962	1,902
15–19	242	282	421	472	545	605	836	930	1,283	1,370	1,582	1,673	1,760	1,725
20–24	234	257	406	415	532	551	671	746	987	1,074	1,440	1,560	1,745	1,742
25–29	219	242	334	358	409	447	550	616	743	815	1,152	1,265	1,543	1,575
30–34	179	203	265	266	342	337	500	530	604	659	938	969	1,261	1,325
35–39	159	172	266	264	318	334	443	481	539	594	813	852	1,033	1,109
40–44	131	150	199	205	248	240	360	359	470	502	619	605	813	871
45–49	92	100	154	150	194	197	291	301	387	407	515	529	611	645
50–54	81	98	137	142	183	176	262	256	319	332	456	464	474	511
55–59	50	54	79	77	110	106	167	164	247	253	346	348	385	428
60–64	58	66	88	98	107	117	164	176	192	199	288	291	315	356
65–69	28	30	40	41	62	63	92	97	138	144	195	205	255	290
70–74	23	28	34	43	46	57	68	81	92	101	150	155	176	207
75–79	13	14	16	17	24	27	39	44	54	61	89	95	115	140
80 and over	23	29	23	36	29	43	41	62	44	61	87	114	94	123
Unknown	133	143	3	2	—	—	—	—	—	—	—	—	—	—

ECUADOR

	1950 M	1950 F	1962 M	1962 F	1974 M	1974 F	1982 M	1982 F	1991 M	1991 F
0–4	271	263	386	376	517	516	613	596	784	756
5–9	231	224	355	344	496	485	560	548	717	695
10–14	193	178	285	269	445	430	519	510	658	639
15–19	158	160	214	221	349	354	441	440	594	580
20–24	140	148	183	195	285	296	385	395	533	521
25–29	119	126	157	168	218	226	302	317	453	444
30–34	94	96	136	134	180	180	250	253	376	372
35–39	91	95	116	122	157	164	198	204	315	314
40–44	68	73	97	95	140	139	172	169	249	250
45–49	55	59	77	78	110	110	131	138	195	198
50–54	56	53	69	68	96	94	125	123	161	165
55–59	34	34	45	44	68	67	87	87	127	133
60–64	33	37	48	49	68	71	83	84	101	106
65–69	18	19	24	24	41	42	53	54	76	83
70–74	15	19	20	23	38	40	46	47	55	62
75–79	7	9	} 24	} 29	17	19	} 56	} 66	35	42
80 and over	11	16			22	31			26	36
Unknown	- -	- -	—	—	—	—	—	—	—	—

A2   SOUTH AMERICA: Population of Major Countries by Sex and Age Groups (in thousands)

GUYANA*

	1911		1921		1931		1946		1960		1970		1980		1990	
	M	F	M	F	M	F	M	F	M	F	M	F	M	F	M	F
0–4	14	15	15	15	23	22	26	26	49	49	56	55	49	49	48	46
5–9	17	17	18	18	19	19	24	23	46	45	60	59	53	53	45	44
10–14	15	15	15	14	15	14	20	20	35	35	50	50	53	52	41	41
15–19	11	12	13	15	14	17	18	19	25	26	40	40	48	49	46	46
20–24	15	16	15	15	13	14	16	17	21	21	28	29	37	40	45	45
25–29	15	14	12	13	14	14	13	14	17	19	19	20	28	29	40	42
30–34	14	11	12	11	10	10	13	13	16	16	16	17	22	22	31	34
35–39	13	10	12	11	11	11	11	11	14	15	15	16	16	17	24	24
40–44	12	8	11	9	9	8	11	10	12	12	14	14	14	14	18	19
45–49	8	6	9	7	9	8	9	9	12	11	13	12	13	13	13	14
50–54	6	5	7	6	6	5	6	6	9	9	10	10	11	11	11	12
55–59	4	3	4	3	5	5	6	6	8	7	10	9	9	9	9	10
60–64	3	3	3	3	3	3	4	5	6	6	6	6	7	7	8	9
65–69	2	2	2	2	2	2	3	4	4	4	5	6	6	6	6	6
70–74	1	1	1	1	1	1	2	2	2	3	2	3	4	4	4	4
75–79	- -	1	1	1	1	1	1	1	1	2	1	2	2	2	3	3
80 and over	1	1	1	1	- -	1	1	1	1	2	1	2	3	3	2	3
Unknown	1	1	1	1	- -	- -	- -	- -	—	—	—	—	1	1	—	—

*Formerly British Guiana

PARAGUAY

	1950		1962		1972		1982		1991	
	M	F	M	F	M	F	M	F	M	F
0–4	111	107	159	153	187	181	236	228	342	328
5–9	100	96	148	142	183	177	202	194	301	291
10–14	86	81	119	114	168	159	192	184	259	249
15–19	63	66	91	94	131	132	168	167	228	220
20–24	58	64	69	76	93	98	146	146	207	199
25–29	47	52	52	58	72	77	118	116	187	180
30–34	37	40	53	56	63	65	93	89	166	159
35–39	32	39	44	48	51	56	75	76	149	139
40–44	25	29	38	41	52	53	67	65	100	95
45–49	21	24	29	34	41	44	48	51	74	72
50–54	18	21	27	29	37	38	51	51	61	60
55–59	15	17	18	21	27	29	37	37	45	49
60–64	15	16	17	20	23	26	30	33	37	42
65–69	10	11	11	12	15	19	22	25	29	35
70–74	6	8	9	11	12	14	17	19	21	24
75–79	3	4	6	8	7	8	10	13	12	15
80 and over	3	5	5	9	8	13	11	14	8	12
Unknown	—	—	- -	- -	—	—	—	—	—	—

A2   SOUTH AMERICA: Population of Major Countries by Sex and Age Groups (in thousands)

PERU

	1940		1961		1972		1981		1991	
	M	F	M	F	M	F	M	F	M	F
0-4	486	475	840	831	1,108	1,093	1,490	1,464	1,467	1,412
5-9	468	455	739	728	1,023	1,000	1,281	1,266	1,374	1,328
10-14	383	345	595	557	884	829	1,150	1,152	1,321	1,279
15-19	296	293	494	480	715	698	1,002	984	1,214	1,176
20-24	264	267	421	428	572	579	845	836	1,082	1,052
25-29	227	255	360	381	458	472	694	690	942	919
30-34	191	194	312	308	390	381	566	565	783	769
35-39	179	194	261	279	356	373	458	459	651	644
40-44	137	141	209	211	307	298	387	388	528	525
45-49	118	124	177	187	242	246	328	330	430	431
50-54	85	94	143	149	195	193	273	276	363	368
55-59	65	74	110	115	149	151	219	224	300	312
60-64	57	73	99	112	133	141	167	173	231	249
65-69	36	46	60	70	89	98	123	130	167	188
70-74	28	40	42	55	66	77	86	94	112	133
75-79	17	24	63	86	35	43	90	106	68	85
80 and over	30	43			48	66			39	56
Unknown	1	1	2	3	13	15	—	—		

SURINAM

	1950		1964		1991	
	M	F	M	F	M	F
0-4	14	14	27	26	27	28
5-9	11	12	27	27	25	25
10-14	10	10	21	20	19	22
15-19	9	9	15	15	22	24
20-24	7	7	11	12	27	25
25-29	6	6	10	11	22	25
30-34	4	5	9	10	16	18
35-39	4	4	8	8	11	12
40-44	4	4	7	7	8	10
45-49	3	4	5	5	7	8
50-54	4	3	5	4	7	7
55-59	3	3	4	4	6	7
60-64	3	2	3	3	5	5
65-69	2	2	3	3	3	4
70-74	1	1	2	2	2	2
75-79	- -	1	1	1	1	2
80 and over	- -	- -	1	1	1	2
Unknown	6	6	4	3	—	—

A2   SOUTH AMERICA: Population of Major Countries by Sex and Age Groups (in thousands)

URUGUAY

	1900 M	1900 F	1908 M	1908 F	1963 M	1963 F	1975 M	1975 F	1985 M	1985 F	1991 M	1991 F
0–4	68	67	85	83	131	123	129	126	131	126	133	126
5–9	66	65	68	66	124	120	121	120	140	135	132	126
10–14	61	59	63	63	114	109	129	124	131	126	141	136
15–19	52	56	57	62	103	104	117	119	116	114	135	130
20–24	45	44	52	53	97	96	100	104	113	114	116	115
25–29	38	35	44	46	91	95	92	96	106	110	111	114
30–34	} 56	48	33	29	100	101	87	89	95	99	106	111
35–39			31	30	93	95	85	90	87	92	96	99
40–44	} 44	33	22	18	85	84	90	92	82	86	88	92
45–49			22	20	73	76	88	90	78	83	82	87
50–54	} 25	18	16	12	73	69	79	81	80	85	76	83
55–59			15	12	61	56	66	67	77	83	77	84
60–64	} 3	10	8	6	50	52	60	66	65	72	71	81
65–69			6	6	37	41	47	52	50	60	58	68
70–74	} 5	4	3	3	27	30	35	41	40	52	41	52
75–79			2	3	15	20	21	30	26	38	29	44
80 and over	2	2	1	2	12	20	17	30	23	42	25	47
Unknown	1	- -	1	1	6	16	—	—	—	—	—	—

VENEZUELA

	1920 M	1920 F		1920 M	1920 F
0–7	231	240	29–35	127	104
7–14	227	245	36–42	104	83
15–21	193	160	43–45	31	29
22–28	177	147	46 and over	139	125

	1963 M	1963 F	1941 M	1941 F	1950 M	1950 F	1961 M	1961 F	1971 M	1971 F	1981 M	1981 F	1991 M	1991 F
0–4	240	234	292	286	433	415	698	676	879	857	1,089	1,052	1,412	1,356
5–9	241	230	267	256	353	335	591	572	825	809	975	948	1,317	1,268
10–14	215	197	246	227	299	276	458	444	733	721	911	899	1,183	1,141
15–19	164	185	191	212	244	252	340	339	602	618	829	826	1,040	1,007
20–24	159	174	183	191	236	238	312	307	468	494	715	731	961	934
25–29	136	149	154	167	202	198	283	268	339	360	609	625	869	850
30–34	104	114	124	127	170	157	265	238	293	295	488	492	746	732
35–39	98	102	106	109	156	145	211	195	269	270	359	363	643	634
40–44	80	88	94	97	125	115	174	157	242	227	300	295	531	523
45–49	65	60	80	72	98	87	146	135	193	181	252	249	396	395
50–54	52	59	58	61	83	82	113	106	155	149	221	216	304	308
55–59	33	32	38	38	52	50	84	83	116	117	166	166	251	257
60–64	} 29	{ 38	32	41	42	51	62	69	94	97	126	131	202	212
65–69			16	19	22	26	36	42	58	63	90	100	145	159
70–74	33 }	{ 49	10	16	15	23	22	29	41	48	62	73	96	112
75–79			6	8	8	11	13	18	20	26	} 66	93	57	74
80 and over			7	13	10	18	13	25	23	39			45	67
Unknown	2	2	4	3	5	3	—	—	—	—	—	—	—	—

A2 Population of Major Countries by Sex and Age Groups

NOTES

1. SOURCES: UN, *Demographic Yearbooks*, national censuses, and the national publications on pp. xiii–xv.
2. Notes 4 and 5 to table B1 also apply to this table.

FOOTNOTES

[1] Age groups are 0–6 and 7–14.
[2] Prior to 1980 this includes some Asians and other non-negroes.
[3] Including Alaska and Hawaii for the first time.
[4] Under 14 years old.
[5] 14–25.
[6] 26–44.
[7] 10–23.
[8] 24–35.
[9] 36–54.
[10] Estimates based on population under 15 and age distribution of negro and other races.
[11] All races are included with whites.
[12] Age groups are 0–5, 6–10, 11–15, etc.
[13] Age groups are 0–5, 6–9, 15–20, and 21–24.

A3   NORTH AMERICA: POPULATION OF MAJOR ADMINISTRATIVE DIVISIONS
(in thousands)

CANADA (provinces)

	1851	1861	1871	1881	1891	1901	1911
Alberta	...	...	...	...	...[1]	73	374
British Columbia	55[2]	52[2]	36	49	98	179	392
Manitoba	...	...[1]	25	62	153	255	461
New Brunswick	194	252	286	321	331	352	
Newfoundland[3]	...	...	...	...	...	...	...
North west Territories	6[2]	7[2]	48	56	99	20	7
Nova Scotia	277	331	388	441	450	460	492
Ontario	952	1,396	1,621	1,927	2,114	2,183	2,527
Prince Edward Island	63[4]	81	94	109	109	103	94
Quebec	890	1,112	1,192	1,359	1,489	1,649	2,006
Saskatchewan	...	...	...	...	...[1]	91	492
Yukon	...	...	...	...	...	27	9

	1921	1931	1941	1951	1961	1971	1981	1991
Alberta	588	732	796	940	1,332	1,628	2,238	2,600
British Columbia	525	694	818	1,165	1,629	2,185	2,744	3,376
Manitoba	610	700	730	777	922	988	1,026	1,113
New Brunswick	388	408	457	516	598	635	696	748
Newfoundland[3]	...	...	...	361	458	522	568	58
North west Territories	8	9	12	16	23	35	46	61
Nova Scotia	524	513	578	643	737	789	847	918
Ontario	2,924	3,432	3,788	4,598	6,236	7,703	8,625	10,471
Prince Edward Island	89	88	95	98	105	112	123	131
Quebec	2,361	2,875	3,332	4,056	5,259	6,028	6,438	7,081
Saskatchewan	758	922	896	832	925	926	968	1,007
Yukon	4	4	5	9	15	18	23	29

A3 NORTH AMERICA: Population of Major Administrative Divisions (in thousands)

MEXICO (states)

	1895	1900	1910	1921	1930	1940	1950	1960	1970	1980	1990
Aguascalientes	104	102	120	108	133	162	188	243	338	519	720
Baja California	} 42 {	8	10	24	48	79	227	520	870	1,178	1,660
Baja California Sur		40	42	39	47	51	61	82	128	215	318
Campeche	88	87	87	76	85	90	122	168	252	421	535
Coahuila	236	297	362	394	436	551	721	908	1,115	1,557	1,972
Colima	56	65	78	92	62	79	112	164	241	346	429
Chiapas	315	361	439	422	530	680	907	1,211	1,569	2,085	3,210
Chihuahua	267	328	406	402	492	624	846	1,227	1,613	2,005	2,442
Federal District	485	541	721	906	1,230	1,757	3,050	4,871	6,874	8,831	8,236
Durango	294	370	483	337	404	484	630	761	939	1,182	1,349
Guanajuato	1,047	1,062	1,082	860	988	1,046	1,329	1,736	2,270	3,006	3,982
Guerrero	418	479	594	567	642	733	919	1,187	1,597	2,110	2,620
Hidalgo	548	605	646	622	678	772	850	995	1,194	1,547	1,888
Jalisco	1,108	1,154	1,209	1,192	1,255	1,418	1,747	2,443	3,297	4,372	5,303
Mexico	837	934	989	885	990	1,146	1,393	1,898	3,833	7,564	9,816
Michoacán	890	936	992	940	1,048	1,182	1,423	1,852	2,324	2,869	3,548
Morelos	160	160	180	103	132	183	273	386	616	947	1,195
Nayarit	149	150	171	163	168	217	290	390	544	726	825
Nuevo León	309	328	365	336	418	541	740	1,079	1,695	2,513	3,099
Oaxaca	883	949	1,040	976	1,085	1,193	1,421	1,727	2,015	2,369	3,020
Puebla	980	1,021	1,102	1,025	1,150	1,295	1,626	1,974	2,508	3,348	4,126
Querétaro	227	232	245	220	234	245	286	355	486	740	1,051
Quintana Roo	—	—	9	11	11	19	27	50	88	226	493
San Luis Potosi	588	575	628	446	580	679	856	1,048	1,282	1,674	2,003
Sinaloa	259	297	324	341	396	493	636	838	1,267	1,850	2,204
Sonora	191	222	265	275	316	364	511	783	1,099	1,514	1,824
Tabasco	135	160	187	210	224	286	363	496	768	1,063	1,502
Tamaulipas	208	219	250	287	344	459	718	1,024	1,457	1,924	2,250
Tlaxcala	167	172	184	179	205	224	285	347	421	557	761
Veracruz	856	981	1,133	1,160	1,377	1,619	2,040	2,728	3,815	5,388	6,228
Yucatán	298	310	340	358	386	418	517	614	758	1,064	1,363
Zacatecas	453	462	477	379	459	565	665	818	952	1,137	1,276

A3 NORTH AMERICA: Population of Major Administrative Divisions (in thousands)

USA (states)

	1790	1800	1810	1820	1830	1840	1850	1860	1870	1880
New England	1,009	1,233	1,472	1,660	1,955	2,235	2,728	3,135	3,488	4,011
Connecticut[5]	238	251	262	275	298	310	371	460	537	623
Maine[6]	97	152	229	298	399	502	583	628	627	649
Massachusetts[7]	379	423	472	523	610	738	995	1,231	1,457	1,783
New Hampshire[8]	142	184	214	244	269	285	318	326	318	347
Rhode Island[9]	69	69	77	83	97	109	148	175	217	277
Vermont[10]	85	154	218	236	281	292	314	315	331	332
Middle Atlantic	959	1,403	2,015	2,700	3,588	4,526	5,899	7,459	8,811	10,497
New Jersey[11]	184	211	246	278	321	373	490	672	906	1,131
New York[12]	340	589	959	1,373	1,919	2,429	3,097	3,881	4,383	5,083
Pennsylvania	434	602	810	1,049	1,348	1,724	2,312	2,906	3,522	4,283
East North Central	...	51	272	793	1,470	2,925	4,523	6,927	9,125	11,207
Illinois	...	...	12[17]	55	157	476	851	1,712	2,540	3,078
Indiana	...	6[15]	24[15]	147	343	686	988	1,350	1,681	1,978
Michigan	...	...	5[18]	9[18]	32[18]	212	398	749	1,184	1,637
Ohio	...	45[16]	231	581	938	1,519	1,980	2,340	2,665	3,198
Wisconsin	...	...	...	...	...	31[19]	305	776	1,055	1,315
						...				
West North Central	...	...	20	67	140	427	880	2,170	3,857	6,157
Iowa	...	...	...	...	...	43[20]	192	675	1,194	1,625
Kansas	...	...	...	...	...	...	...	107	364	996
Minnesota	...	...	...	...	...	...	6	172	440	781
Missouri	...	...	20	67	140	384	682	1,182	1,721	2,168
Nebraska	...	...	...	...	...	...	...	29	123	452
North Dakota	...	...	...	...	...	...	...	5[21]	2	37
South Dakota	...	...	...	...	...	...	...		12	98
South Atlantic	1,852	2,286	2,675	3,062	3,646	3,925	4,679	5,365	5,854	7,597
Delaware	59	64	73	73	77	78	92	112	125	147
District of Columbia	...	8	15	23	30	34	52	75	132	178
Florida	...	...	...	...	35	54	87	140	188	269
Georgia	83	163	252	341	517	691	906	1,057	1,184	1,542
Maryland[13]	320	342	381	407	447	470	583	687	781	935
North Carolina	394	478	556	639	738	753	869	993	1,071	1,400
South Carolina	249	346	415	503	581	594	669	704	706	996
Virginia[14]	692	808	878	938	1,044	1,025	1,119	1,220	1,225	1,513
West Virginia	56	79	105	137	177	225	302	377	442	618

A3   NORTH AMERICA: Population of Major Administrative Divisions (in thousands)

USA (states) (contd)

	1790	1800	1810	1820	1830	1840	1850	1860	1870	1880
East South Central	109	335	709	1,190	1,816	2,575	3,363	4,021	4,404	5,585
Alabama	...	1[22]	9[22]	128	310	591	772	964	997	1,263
Kentucky	74	221	407	564	688	780	982	1,156	1,321	1,649
Mississippi	...	8[22]	31[22]	75	137	376	607	791	828	1,132
Tennessee	36	106	262	423	682	829	1,002	1,110	1,259	1,542
West South Central	...	...	78	168	246	450	940	1,748	2,030	3,334
Arkansas	...	...	1	14	30	98	210	435	484	803
Louisiana	...	...	77	153	216	352	518	708	727	940
Oklahoma	...	...	...	...	...	...	...	...	...	...
Texas	...	...	...	...	...	...	213	604	819	1,592
Mountain	...	...	...	...	...	...	73	175	315	653
Arizona	...	...	...	...	...	...	...	...	10	40
Colorado	...	...	...	...	...	...	...	34	40	194
Idaho	...	...	...	...	...	...	...	...	15	33
Montana	...	...	...	...	...	...	...	...	21	39
Nevada	...	...	...	...	...	...	...	7[23]	42	62
New Mexico	...	...	...	...	...	...	62	94[24]	92	120
Utah	...	...	...	...	...	...	11	40[25]	87	144
Wyoming	...	...	...	...	...	...	...	...	9	21
Pacific[26]	...	...	...	...	...	...	106	444	675	1,115
Alaska[26]	...	...	...	...	...	...	...	...	...	[33]
California	...	...	...	...	...	...	93	380	560	865
Hawaii[26]	...	...	...	...	...	...	...	...	...	...
Oregon	...	...	...	...	...	...	12	52	91	175
Washington	...	...	...	...	...	...	1[27]	12[28]	24	75

A3 NORTH AMERICA: Population of Major Administrative Divisions (in thousands)

USA (states) (contd)

	1890	1900	1910	1920	1930	1940	1950	1960	1970	1980	1990
New England	4,701	5,592	6,553	7,401	8,166	8,437	9,314	10,509	11,848	12,348	13,207
Connecticut[5]	746	908	1,115	1,381	1,607	1,709	2,007	2,535	3,032	3,108	3,287
Maine[6]	661	694	742	768	797	847	914	969	994	1,125	1,228
Massachusetts[7]	2,239	2,805	3,366	3,852	4,250	4,317	4,691	5,149	5,689	5,737	6,016
New Hampshire[8]	377	412	431	443	465	492	533	607	738	921	1,109
Rhode Island[9]	346	429	543	604	687	713	792	859	950	947	1,003
Vermont[10]	332	344	356	352	360	359	378	390	445	511	563
Middle Atlantic	12,706	15,455	19,316	22,261	26,261	27,539	30,164	34,168	37,263	36,787	37,604
New Jersey[11]	1,445	1,884	2,537	3,156	4,041	4,160	4,835	6,067	7,168	7,365	7,730
New York[12]	6,003	7,269	9,114	10,385	12,588	13,479	14,830	16,782	18,241	17,558	17,991
Pennsylvania	5,258	6,302	7,665	8,720	9,631	9,900	10,498	11,319	11,794	11,864	11,883
East North Central	13,478	15,986	18,251	21,476	25,297	26,626	30,399	36,225	40,262	41,682	42,009
Illinois	3,826	4,822	5,639	6,485	7,631	7,897	8,712	10,081	11,114	11,427	11,431
Indiana	2,192	2,516	2,701	2,930	3,239	3,428	3,934	4,662	5,194	5,490	5,544
Michigan	2,094	2,421	2,810	3,668	4,842	5,256	6,372	7,823	8,875	9,262	9,295
Ohio	3,672	4,158	4,767	5,759	6,647	6,908	7,947	9,706	10,652	10,798	10,847
Wisconsin	1,693	2,069	2,334	2,632	2,939	3,138	3,435	3,952	4,418	4,706	4,892
West North Central	8,932	10,347	11,638	12,544	13,297	13,517	14,061	15,394	16,327	17,183	17,660
Iowa	1,912	2,232	2,225	2,404	2,471	2,538	2,621	2,758	2,825	2,914	2,777
Kansas	1,428	1,470	1,691	1,769	1,881	1,801	1,905	2,179	2,249	2,364	2,478
Minnesota	1,310	1,751	2,076	2,387	2,564	2,792	2,982	3,414	3,805	4,076	4,376
Missouri	2,679	3,107	3,293	3,404	3,629	3,785	3,955	4,320	4,677	4,917	5,117
Nebraska	1,063	1,066	1,192	1,296	1,378	1,316	1,326	1,411	1,484	1,570	1,578
North Dakota	191	319	577	647	681	642	620	632	618	653	639
South Dakota	349	402	584	637	693	643	653	681	666	691	696
South Atlantic	8,858	10,443	12,195	13,990	15,794	17,823	21,182	25,972	30,678	36,959	43,571
Delaware	168	185	202	223	238	267	318	446	548	594	666
District of Columbia	230	279	331	438	487	663	802	764	757	638	607
Florida	391	529	753	968	1,468	1,897	2,771	4,952	6,789	9,746	12,938
Georgia	1,837	2,216	2,609	2,896	2,909	3,124	3,445	3,943	4,590	5,463	6,478
Maryland[13]	1,042	1,188	1,295	1,450	1,632	1,821	2,343	3,101	3,922	4,217	4,781
North Carolina	1,618	1,894	2,206	2,559	3,170	3,572	4,062	4,556	5,082	5,882	6,632
South Carolina	1,151	1,340	1,515	1,684	1,739	1,900	2,117	2,383	2,591	3,122	3,486
Virginia[14]	1,656	1,854	2,062	2,309	2,422	2,678	3,319	3,967	4,648	5,347	6,189
West Virginia	763	959	1,221	1,464	1,729	1,902	2,006	1,860	1,744	1,950	1,793

A3 NORTH AMERICA: Population of Major Administrative Divisions (in thousands)

USA (states) (contd)

	1890	1900	1910	1920	1930	1940	1950	1960	1970	1980	1990
East South Central	6,429	7,548	8,410	8,893	9,887	10,778	10,477	12,050	12,808	14,666	15,180
Alabama	1,513	1,829	2,138	2,348	2,646	2,833	3,062	3,567	3,444	3,894	4,040
Kentucky	1,859	2,147	2,290	2,417	2,615	2,846	2,945	3,038	3,219	3,661	3,687
Mississippi	1,290	1,551	1,797	1,791	2,010	2,184	2,179	2,178	2,217	2,521	2,575
Tennessee	1,768	2,021	2,185	2,338	2,617	2,916	3,292	3,567	3,924	4,591	4,877
West South Central	4,741	6,532	8,785	10,242	12,177	13,065	14,538	16,951	19,326	23,747	26,703
Arkansas	1,128	1,312	1,574	1,752	1,854	1,949	1,910	1,786	1,923	2,286	2,351
Louisiana	1,119	1,382	1,656	1,799	2,102	2,364	2,684	3,257	3,643	4,206	4,220
Oklahoma	259	790	1,657	2,028	2,396	2,336	2,233	2,328	2,559	3,025	3,146
Texas	2,236	3,049	3,897	4,663	5,825	6,415	7,711	9,580	11,197	14,229	16,986
Mountain	1,214	1,675	2,634	3,336	3,702	4,150	5,075	6,855	8,289	11,373	13,659
Arizona	88	123	204	334	436	499	750	1,302	1,772	2,718	3,665
Colorado	413	540	799	940	1,036	1,123	1,325	1,754	2,207	2,890	3,294
Idaho	89	162	326	432	445	525	589	667	713	944	1,007
Montana	143	243	376	549	538	559	591	675	694	787	799
Nevada	47	42	82	77	91	110	160	285	489	800	1,202
New Mexico	160	195	327	360	423	532	681	951	1,016	1,303	1,515
Utah	211	277	373	449	508	550	689	891	1,059	1,461	1,723
Wyoming	63	93	146	194	226	251	291	330	332	470	454
Pacific[26]	1,888	2,417	4,192	5,567	8,194	9,733	14,487	21,198	26,549	31,800	39,125
Alaska[26]	[32]	[64]	[64]	[55]	[59][29]	[73][30]	[129]	226	302	402	550
California	1,213	1,485	2,378	3,427	5,677	6,907	10,586	15,717	19,953	23,668	29,758
Hawaii[26]	…	[154]	[192]	[256]	[368]	[423]	[500]	633	770	965	1,108
Oregon	318	414	673	783	954	1,090	1,521	1,769	2,091	2,633	2,842
Washington	357	518	1,142	1,357	1,563	1,736	2,379	2,853	3,409	4,132	4,867

A3 SOUTH AMERICA: POPULATION OF MAJOR ADMINISTRATIVE DIVISIONS (in thousands)

ARGENTINA (provinces)

	1869	1895	1914	1947	1960	1970	1980	1991
Federal Capital	187	664	1,576	2,983	2,967	2,972	2,923	2,965
Buenos Aires	308	921	2,066	4,272	6,735	8,775	10,865	12,594
Catamarca	80	90	100	147	172	172	208	264
Chaco	45	10	46	431	535	567	701	840
Chubut	...[31]	4	23	59	142	190	263	357
Comodoro Rivadavia	...	...	...	52	...	...	...	...
Córdoba	211	351	735	1,498	1,760	2,060	2,408	2,767
Corrientes	129	240	347	525	543	564	661	796
Entre Ríos	134	292	425	787	804	812	908	1,020
Formosa	...[31]	5	19	114	178	234	296	398
Jujuy	40	50	77	167	240	302	410	512
La Pampa	21	26	101	109	158	172	208	260
La Rioja	49	70	80	111	128	136	164	221
Mendoza	65	116	278	588	826	973	1,196	1,412
Misiones	3	33	54	246	391	443	589	789
Neuquén	...	15	29	87	111	155	244	389
Río Negro	...[31]	9	42	134	193	263	383	507
Salta	89	118	141	291	413	510	663	866
San Juan	60	84	119	261	352	384	466	529
San Luis	53	81	116	166	174	183	214	286
Santa Cruz	...[31]	1	10	25	53	84	115	160
Santa Fé	89	397	900	1,703	1,865	2,136	2,466	2,798
Santiago del Estero	133	162	262	479	477	495	595	672
Tierra del Fuego	...[31]	- -	3	5	7	13	27	69
Tucumán	109	216	333	593	780	766	973	1,142

BOLIVIA (provinces)

	1900	1950	1976	1992
Beni	32	120	168	276
Chuquisaca	204	283	359	453
Cochabamba	328	490	721	1,110
El Litoral	41	...	...	...
La Paz	446	948	1,465	1,900
Oruro	86	210	310	340
Pando	32	20	34	38
Potosi	326	534	658	646
Santa Cruz	210	286	711	1,364
Tarija	103	127	187	291

A3   SOUTH AMERICA: Population of Major Administrative Divisions (in thousands)

BRAZIL (states)

	1872	1890	1900	1920	1940	1950	1960	1970	1980	1991
North	323	476	695	1,439	1,462	1,845	2,562	3,604	5,880	10,030
Rondônia	...	...	...	...	...	37	70	111	491	1,132
Acre	...	...	...	92	80	115	158	215	301	417
Amazonas	58	148	250	363	438	514	708	955	1,430	2,103
Roraima	...	...	...	...	...	18	28	41	79	217
Pará	275	328	445	984	945	1,123	1,529	2,167	3,403	4,950
Amapá	...	...	...	...	...	37	68	114	175	289
North-East	4,639	6,002	6,750	11,246	14,434	17,973	22,182	28,112	34,812	42,497
Maranhão	359	431	499	874	1,235	1,583	2,469	2,993	3,996	4,930
Piauí	202	268	334	609	817	1,046	1,242	1,681	2,139	2,582
Ceará	722	806	849	1,319	2,091	2,695	3,296	4,362	5,288	6,366
Rio Grande do Norte	234	268	274	537	768	968	1,146	1,550	1,898	2,415
Paraíba	376	457	491	961	1,422	1,713	2,001	2,383	2,770	3,201
Pernambuco	842	1,030	1,178	2,155	2,688	3,395	4,096	5,161	6,142	7,127
Alagoas	348	511	649	979	951	1,093	1,258	1,588	1,983	2,514
Fernando de Noronha	...	...	...	...	...	1	1	1	1	1
Sergipe	176	311	356	477	542	644	752	901	1,140	1,491
Bahia	1,380	1,920	2,118	3,334	3,918	4,835	5,920	7,493	9,454	11,867
South East	4,017	6,104	7,824	13,655	18,346	22,548	30,631	39,853	51,734	62,740
Minas Gerais	2,040	3,184	3,594	5,888	6,763	7,782	9,658	11,487	13,379	15,743
Espírito Santo	82	136	210	457	790	957	1,171	1,599	2,023	2,600
Rio de Janeiro	783	877	926	1,559	1,848	2,297	3,363	4,743 }	11,292	12,807
Guanabara	275	523	811	1,158	1,764	2,377	3,248	4,252 }		
São Paulo	837	1,385	2,282	4,592	7,180	9,134	12,809	17,772	25,041	31,588
South	721	1,431	1,796	3,537	5,735	7,841	11,753	16,496	19,031	22,129
Parana	127	249	327	686	1,236	2,116	4,268	6,930	7,629	8,448
Santa Catarina	160	284	320	669	1,178	1,561	2,118	2,902	3,628	4,541
Rio Grande do Sul	435	897	1,149	2,183	3,321	4,165	5,367	6,665	7,774	9,138
Centre West	221	320	373	759	1,259	1,737	2,943	5,073	7,545	9,427
Mato Grosso	60	93	118	247	432	522	890	1,597[32]	1,139	2,027
Mato Grosso do Sul	...	...	...	...	...	...	...	...	1,370	1,780
Goiás	160	228	255	512	826	1,215	1,913	2,939	3,860	4,018
Federal District	...	...	...	...	...	...	140	537	1,177	1,601

A3   SOUTH AMERICA: Population of Major Administrative Divisions (in thousands)

CHILE (provinces)

	1835	1843	1854	1865	1875	1885	1895	1907
Aconcagua	82	92	112	146	133	176	113	175
Antofagasta	—	—	—	2	2	34	44	113
Arauco	...	...	10	17	40	69	59	62
Atacama	28	25	51	77	69	64	60	64
Aysén	—	—	—	—	—	—	—	—
Bío-Bío	7	19	40	59	76	102	89	98
Cautín	—	—	—	—	6	38	78	140
Chiloé	44	49	50	59	65	73	78	89
Colchagua	102	91	116	142	148	156	158	159
Concepción	67	92	104	139	151	182	188	217
Coquimbo	72	78	111	146	158	176	161	175
Curicó	65	60	77	91	93	100	103	107
Linares	38	43	64	85	119	111	102	109
Llanquihue	9	19	26	38	48	63	78	105
Magallanes	—	—	- -	- -	1	1	5	17
Malleco	—	—	—	3	20	59	98	110
Maule	53	76	93	103	118	124	120	110
Ñuble	73	81	101	125	137	150	153	166
O'Higgins	...	...	65	80	77	89	85	93
Osorno	...	...	...	...	...	...	...	...
Santiago	218	208[32]	208	261	289	329	416	516
Tacna	—	—	—	—	—	30	24	29
Talca	61	71	79	101	110	133	129	132
Tarapacá	—	—	—	—	—	45	90	110
Valdivia	7	14	18	23	35	51	61	118
Valparaíso	80	76	116	143	179	203	221	281

	1920[33]	1930[33]	1940	1952	1960	1970
Aconcagua	160/422	464/103	118	128	140	161
Antofagasta	172	171/145	145	184	214	251
Arauco	60/—	—/61	66	72	89	99
Atacama	48	61	84	80	114	152
Aysén	—/2	10/9	17	25	37	51
Bío-Bío	107/166	181/114	127	138	167	193
Cautín	194/313	384/315	375	362	393	421
Chiloé	110/178	183/93	102	99	99	111
Colchagua	166/282	296/126	131	138	158	168
Concepción	247/291	329/268	308	410	538	638
Coquimbo	160/176	198	246	256	306	337
Curicó	108/—	—/75	81	89	107	114
Linares	119/—	—/123	135	147	170	189
Llanquíhue	137/—	—/92	117	130	166	198
Magallanes	29	38	49	55	73	89
Malleco	121/—	—/136	154	157	174	176
Maule	113/204	197/74	70	72	79	82
Ñuble	170/224	232	243	250	285	315
O'Higgins	119/—	—/171	200	223	259	307
Osorno	...	—/87	107	122	144	159
Santiago	685/718	968	1,269	1,749	2,430	3,218
Tacna	39/—	...	...	...	...	...
Talca	134/202	218/142	157	174	205	231
Tarapacá	101	113	104	103	123	175
Valdivia	175/187	236/149	192	231	255	275
Valparaíso	320/—	—/360	425	492	613	727

A3 SOUTH AMERICA: Population of Major Administrative Divisions (in thousands)

CHILE (contd) (regions)

	1970	1980	1990		1970	1980	1990		1970	1980	1990
Antofagasta	251	342	389	Coquimbo	337	420	486	O'Higgins	475	587	649
Araucania	597	698	795	Los Lagos	743	849	922	Santiago	3,218	4,318	5,236
Atacarma	152	183	197	Magellanes	89	132	159	Tarapaca	175	275	358
Aysen	51	66	80	Maulé	616	731	840	Valparaíso	888	1,210	1,382
Bío Bío	1,146	1,519	1,674								

COLOMBIA

	1835	1843	1851	1864	1871	1881
Departments						
Antioquia	158	190	243	303	366	470
Bolívar	178	192	206	217	247	280
Boyacá	289	332	380	456	483	702
Caucá	210	269	324	386	435	621
Cundinamarca	256	279	317	393	410	569
Magdalera	61	62	68	89	85	90
Panama	115	119	138	221	221	285
Santander	262	306	360	378	425	556
Tolima	157	183	208	220	231	306

COLOMBIA (contd)

	1905	1912	1918	1928	1938	1951	1964
Departments							
Antioquia	651	741	823	1,011	1,189	1,570	2,477
Atlántico	112	115	136	243	268	428	717
Bolívar	198	416	457	643	765	991	1,006
Boyacá	503	585	655	950	737	779	1,058
Caldas	246	341	428	624	770	1,068	1,456
Caucá	223	212	239	318	356	443	607
Chocó	48	83	91	85	111	131	182
Córdoba	—	—	—	—	—	—	586
Cundinamarca	631	718	812	1,057	1,175	1,624	2,820
Huila	154	158	183	207	217	294	416
La Guajira	1	53	23	33	53	52	147
Magdalena	125	150	211	302	342	457	789
Meta	6	28	34	19	52	67	166
Nariño	248	292	341	412	466	547	706
Norte de Santander	164	204	239	329	346	387	534
Santander	386	403	439	595	616	748	1,001
Tolima	218	282	329	445	548	712	841
Valle del Cauca	215	217	272	506	613	1,107	1,733
Comisarias and Intendencias							
Amazonas	—	—	…	2	6	8	13
Arauca	7	7	10	13	11	13	24
Caquetá	—	24	74	14	21	47	104
Casanare	—	—	—	—	—	22	—
Guianía	—	—	—	—	—	—	4
Putumayo	1	31	41	17	16	22	56
San Andrés & Providencia	4	5	6	6	7	6	17
Vaupes	—	6	6	9	8	9	13
Vichada	—	—	6	11	9	12	10

A3   SOUTH AMERICA: Population of Major Administrative Divisions (in thousands)

COLOMBIA (contd)

	1973	1985	1992		1973	1985	1992
Departments				*Departments (contd)*			
Antioquia	3,133	3,888	4,467	**Quindio**	337	378	414
Atlántico	1,017	1,429	1,703	**Risaralda**	475	625	735
Bogota	2,880	3,983	4,819[90]	**Santander**	1,191	1,438	1,642
Bolivar	908	1,198	1,451	**Sucre**	411	529	611
Boyaca	1,135	1,098	1,274	**Tolima**	956	1,052	1,193
Caldas	740	838	909	**Valle de Cauca**	2,353	2,847	3,335
Caquetá	64	214	309				
Cauca	735	796	933	*Comisarias and Intendencias*			
Cesar	394	585	799				
Choco	226	243	350	**Amazonas**	16	30	52
				Arauca	46	70	96
Córdoba	771	914	1,115	**Casanare**	35	110	176
Cundinamarca	1,184	1,382	1,658	**Guaviare**	14	35	63
Huila	496	648	777	**Guianía**	6	9	13
La Guajira	214	255	347				
Magdalena	625	769	979	**Putumayo**	67	120	221
				San Andrés & Providencia	23	36	41
Meta	258	412	564	**Vaupés**	9	19	34
Nariño	856	1,019	1,163	**Vichada**	12	14	19
Norte de Santander	730	884	1,007				

A3 SOUTH AMERICA: Population of Major Administrative Divisions (in thousands)

PERU (departments)

	1862	1876	1896[34]	1927[34]	1940	1961	1972	1981	1993
Amazonas	33	34	71	80	90	118	196	268	336
Ancash	264	285	429	480	465	589	727	854	955
Apurimac	117	119	177	280	281	338	308	343	381
Arequipa	136	157	229	360	271	411	531	738	916
Ayacucho	183	142	302	320	414	448	460	524	492
Cajamarca	177	213	442	450	568	749	916	1,083	1,259
Callao	19	34	48	75	84	214	316	454	639
Cuzco	234	243	439	700	565	614	713	874	1,028
Huancavelica	107	103	224	230	266	299	331	362	385
Huánuco	75	79	145	200	277	362	421	506	654
Iua	61	60	91	120	145	244	358	447	565
Junín	203	210	394	450	500	506	691	897	1,035
La Libertad	133	147	251	381	404	588	806	992	1,270
Lambayeque	52	87	124	140	200	347	515	709	920
Lima	207	226	298	550	849	2,319	3,485	4,993	6,386
Loreto	52	62	101	150	321	331	246	475	687
Madre de Dios	—	—	—	5	25	15	22	36	67
Moqueguce	27	29	42	40	36	58	75	103	128
Pasco	...	...	...	...	...	126	177	231	226
Piura	130	136	214	300	431	717	855	1,156	1,388
Puno	225	259	537	700	646	687	780	910	1,079
San Martin				65	121	163	224	332	552
Tacna	34	36	50	60	38	69	96	148	218
Tumbes	—	—	—	12	26	52	75	108	155
Ucayali...	...	...	...	...	...	...	[156]	220	314

A3   SOUTH AMERICA: Population of Major Administrative Divisions (in thousands)

VENEZUELA (states)

	1873	1881	1891	1920	1926	1936	1941	1950	1961	1971	1981	1990
Federal District	60	69	113	140	195	283	380	700	1,258	1,861	2,071	2,265
Amzoátegui	101	124	134	104	114	130	156	238	382	506	684	924
Apure	19	21	23	39	43	58	71	85	118	165	188	305
Aragua	94	105	95	96	106	130	138	193	313	543	892	1,194
Barinas	59	57	63	55	57	56	63	81	139	231	326	456
Bolívar	34	51	56	66	75	83	95	122	214	392	668	968
Carabobo	118	136	169	126	147	172	191	243	382	659	1,062	1,558
Cojedes	86	84	88	82	82	48	50	52	73	94	134	196
Falcón	100	114	139	128	179	215	33	258	340	408	504	632
Guárico	191	203	184	122	125	120	135	164	245	319	393	525
Lara	144	176	190	220	271	291	333	370	489	671	945	1,270
Mérida	68	78	89	123	150	179	193	210	271	347	459	675
Miranda	129	136	141	174	190	217	228	278	492	856	1,421	2,026
Monagas	48	56	75	62	68	93	123	176	246	298	389	503
Nueva Esparta	31	38	40	56	69	73	69	76	89	119	197	280
Portuguesa	80	96	96	53	59	72	87	121	204	297	425	625
Sucre	55	78	92	150	216	262	291	333	402	469	586	722
Táchira	69	84	102	147	173	216	246	308	399	511	660	839
Trujillo	109	131	147	179	219	243	264	285	327	381	434	520
Yaracuy	72	82	86	108	123	124	127	133	175	224	301	411
Zulia	59	107	151	119	223	291	346	524	920	1,299	1,674	2,387
Amazonas Territory	23	18	45	49	60	41	4	7	12	22	46	60
Delta Amacuro Territory	6	18	7	13	27	20	28	31	34	48	57	91
Federal Dependencies	—	—	—	—	—	- -	1	1	1	- -	1	2

A3 Population of Major Administrative Divisions

NOTES

1. SOURCES: As for table A1.
2. Notes 4 and 5 for table A1 also apply to this table.

FOOTNOTES

[1] Included in Northwest Territories.
[2] Kenneth Buckley, in M.C. Urquhart and K.A.H. Buckley, *Historical Statistics of Canada* (Cambridge, 1965), estimated that the Indian population in the western provinces and territories was under-enumerated by about 30,000 in 1851 and 40,000 in 1861.
[3] Newfoundland was incorporated in Canada in 1949.
[4] In 1848.
[5] Earlier censuses showed total population as follows: 1756–131; 1774–198; 1782–209.
[6] Earlier censuses showed total population as follows: 1764/5–22; 1776–48; 1784–50.
[7] Earlier censuses showed total population as follows: 1764/5–224; 1776–291; 1784–307.
[8] Earlier censuses showed total population as follows: 1767–53; 1773–73; 1775–81; 1786–96.
[9] Earlier censuses showed total population as follows: 1708–7; 1730–18; 1748–34; 1755–41; 1774–60; 1783–52.
[10] A census in 1771 showed total population as 5 thousand.
[11] Earlier censuses showed total population as follows: 1726–32; 1738–47; 1745–61; 1772–122; 1784–149.
[12] Earlier censuses showed total population as follows: 1698–18; 1703–21; 1723–41; 1731–50; 1737–60; 1746–62; 1749–73; 1756–97; 1771–163; 1786–239.
[13] Earlier censuses showed total population as follows: 1704–35; 1710–43; 1712–46; 1755–154; 1782–254.
[14] Data relate to the territory of the state after the separation of West Virginia in 1862. Earlier censuses of the whole colony showed the following total populations: 1624/5–1; 1634–5; 1699–58; 1701–58.
[15] Including portions later incorporated in other territories.
[16] Territory north-west of the Ohio River.
[17] Ilinois Territory.
[18] Michigan Territory as constituted at the time. Boundaries were changed in 1816, 1818, 1834 and 1836.
[19] Including that part of Minnesota north-east of the Mississippi River.
[20] Including that part of Minnesota lying west of the Mississippi River and a line drawn from its source northwards to the Canadian border.
[21] Dakota Territory.
[22] Data relate to those parts of the Mississippi territory which constitute the present state.
[23] Nevada Territory as organized in 1861.
[24] Including the area taken to form part of Arizona Territory in 1863.
[25] Excluding that part taken to form Colorado Territory in 1861.
[26] Alaska and Hawaii are not included in the regional population until 1960.
[27] Those parts of Oregon Territory later taken to form part of Washington Territory.
[28] Includes the population of Idaho and parts of Montana and Wyoming.
[29] 1929.
[30] 1939.
[31] The combined population of these Patagonian territories in 1869 was 24 thousand.
[32] This province was subsequently divided.
[33] The first figure is for the province as defined at the time of the census, the second is for its territory at the next census.
[34] Estimates rather than census figures.
[35] Included in Boyaca.

A4 NORTH AMERICA: POPULATION OF MAJOR CITIES (in thousands)

	c1750	1790	1800	1810	1820	1830	1840	1850	1860	1870	1880	1890
Akron (USA)	—	—	—	—	—	—	—	3	3	10	17	28
Albany (USA)	…	3	5	11	13	24	34	51	62	69	91	95
Albuquerque (USA)	—	—	—	—	—	—	—	—	—	—	—	4
Allentown (USA)	—	4	4	4	5	6	8	10	8	14	18	25
Anaheim (USA)	—	…	…	…	…	…	…	…	…	…	1	1
Atlanta (USA)	—	—	—	—	—	—	…	3	10	22	37	66
Austin (USA)	—	—	—	—	—	—	—	1	2	4	11	15
Baltimore (USA)	…	14	26	36	63	81	102	169	212	267	332	434
Birmingham (USA)	—	—	—	—	—	—	—	—	—	—	3	26
Boston (USA)	16'65	18	25	33	43	61	93	137	178	251	363	448
Buffalo (USA)	—	—	—	2	2	9	18	42	81	118	155	256
Calgary (Canada)	—	—	—	—	—	—	—	—	—	—	—	4
Charleston, SC (USA)	…	16	19	25	25	30	29	43	41	49	50	55
Charlotte (USA)	—	—	—	—	—	—	…	1	1	4	7	12
Chicago (USA)	—	…	…	…	—	—	4	30	109	299	503	1,100
Chihuahua (Mexico)	—	…	12'03	…	…	11	…	…	14	12	16'82	18'95
Cincinnati (USA)	—	…	…	3	10	25	46	115	161	216	255	297
Ciudad Juarez (Mexico)	—	…	…	…	…	…	…	2	—	—	—	7'93
Cleveland (USA)	—	—	—	…	…	1	6	17	43	93	160	261
Columbus, Ohio (USA)	—	—	—	—	…	2	6	18	19	31	52	88
Corpus Christi (USA)	—	—	—	—	—	—	—	—	…	3	4	4
Dallas (USA)	—	—	—	—	—	—	—	—	—	—	10	38
Dayton (USA)	—	—	—	…	1	3	6	11	20	30	39	61
Denver (USA)	—	—	—	—	—	—	—	—	—	5	36	107
Des Moines (USA)	—	—	—	—	—	—	—	1	4	12	22	50
Detroit (USA)	—	—	—	…	1	2	9	21	46	80	116	206
El Paso (USA)	—	—	—	—	—	—	—	—	—	—	1	10
Fall River (USA)	—	—	—	1	2	4	7	12	14	27	49	74

A4 NORTH AMERICA: Population of Major Cities (in thousands)

	c1750	1790	1800	1810	1820	1830	1840	1850	1860	1870	1880	1890
Fort Worth (USA)	—	—	—	—	—	—	—	—	—	—	7	23
Grand Rapids (USA)	—	—	—	—	—	—	—	3	8	17	32	60
Greensboro (USA)	...	...	...	...	...	...	...	...	...	...	2	3
Guadalajara (Mexico)	...	...	20[03]	...	47[23]	...	...	63[52]	71[62]	65	75[78]	95[93]
Guatemala City	...	...	...	...	...	...	...	37	...	45	51	72[93]
Hamilton (Canada)	...	...	—	—	...	...	3[136]	14	27	29	36	49
Hartford, Conn. (USA)	...	4	5	4	5	7	9	18	29	37	42	53
Havana (Cuba)	...	44	...	96	...	94[27]	135	...	...	...	...	198[87]
Houston (USA)	—	—	—	—	—	—	...	2	5	9	17	28
Indianapolis (USA)	—	—	—	—	—	—	3	8	19	48	75	105
Jacksonville (USA)	—	—	—	—	—	—	—	1	2	7	8	17
Jersey City (USA)	...	...	...	...	...	...	3	7	29	83	121	163
Kansas City, Mo. (USA)	—	—	—	—	—	—	—	—	4	32	56	133
Kingston (Jamaica)	...	...	...	...	...	...	...	...	27	34	39	49
León (Mexico)	...	6	...	...	...	...	...	17	...	...	...	48[93]
London (Canada)	—	—	—	—	—	—	—	7	12	18	28	32
Long Beach (USA)	—	—	—	—	—	—	—	—	—	—	—	1
Los Angeles (USA)	...	...	...	...	...	...	...	2	4	6	11	50
Louisville (USA)	—	—	—	1	4	10	21	43	68	101	124	161
Managua (Nicaragua)	...	...	...	...	...	...	...	...	...	8	12	18
Memphis (USA)	—	—	—	—	—	—	...	9	23	40	34	64
Mérida (Mexico)	...	...	10[03]	...	...	...	...	...	24[62]	30	35[78]	37[95]
Mexico City	...	131[93]	137[03]	168	180	...	205[38]	170[52]	200[62]	225	250	327[93]
Milwaukee (USA)	—	—	—	—	—	—	2	20	45	71	116	204
Minneapolis (USA)	—	—	—	—	—	—	—	...	3	13	47	165
Monterrey (Mexico)	...	...	11	...	...	...	...	14[52]	15[62]	14	40	43[93]
Montreal (Canada)	6[65]	18	...	...	32[25]	44	...	58	90	107	155	220

A4   NORTH AMERICA: Population of Major Cities (in thousands)

	c1750	1790	1800	1810	1820	1830	1840	1850	1860	1870	1880	1890
Nashville (USA)	—	...	...	...	...	6	7	10	17	26	43	76
Newark, NJ (USA)	—	...	...	...	7	11	17	39	72	115	137	182
New Orleans (USA)	3[69]	5[88]	8[97]	17	27	46	102	116	169	191	216	242
New York (USA)[1]	22[73]	33	60	96	131	218	349	696	1,175	1,478	1,912	2,507
Norfolk (USA)	...	...	7	...	8	10	11	14	15	19	22	35
Oakland (USA)	—	—	—	—	—	—	—	...	2	11	35	49
Oklahoma City (USA)	—	—	—	—	—	—	—	...	—	—	—	4
Omaha (USA)	—	—	—	—	—	—	—	—	2	16	30	140
Ottawa (Canada)	—	—	...	—	...	...	...	8	15	24	31	44
Panama City	...	...	...	...	17	...	...	...	18	...	20	...
Paterson, NJ (USA)	12[31]	...	...	...	1	...	8	11	20	34	51	78
Philadelphia (USA)	—	43	69	95	119	161	206	340	566	674	847	1,047
Phoenix (USA)	—	—	—	—	—	—	—	—	—	—	—	3
Pittsburgh (USA)[2]	—	—	2	5	7	18	31	68	78	139	235	344
Portland, Oreg. (USA)	—	—	—	—	—	—	—	1	3	8	18	46
Providence, RI (USA)	3	6	8	10	12	17	23	42	51	69	105	132
Puebla (Mexico)	9[65]	57[93]	68[03]	...	60	...	...	72[52]	75	65	73[82]	91[93]
Quebec (Canada)	—	14	...	...	22[25]	36	...	42	60	60	62	63
Richmond, Va. (USA)	—	4	6	10	12	16	20	28	38	51	64	81
Rochester (USA)	—	2	2	2	2	9	20	36	48	62	89	134
Sacramento (USA)	...	—	—	—	—	—	—	7	14	16	21	26
St Louis (USA)	—	—	—	—	4	7	16	78	161	311	351	452
St Paul, Minn. (USA)	—	—	—	—	—	—	—	1	10	20	41	133
St Petersburg (USA)	—	—	—	—	—	—	—	—	—	—	—	—
Salt Lake City (USA)	—	—	—	—	—	—	—	10	8	13	21	45
San Antonio (USA)	...	...	...	...	...	...	...	3	8	12	21	38
San Bernardino (USA)	—	—	—	—	—	—	—	—	1	3	2	4
San Diego (USA)	—	—	—	—	—	—	—	...	1	2	3	16
San Francisco (USA)	...	—	—	—	—	—	—	35[52]	57	149	234	299

A4 NORTH AMERICA: Population of Major Cities (in thousands)

	c1750	1790	1800	1810	1820	1830	1840	1850	1860	1870	1880	1890
San José (Costa Rica)	...	...	11	...	15[24]	...	20[44]	...	...	...	...	19[92]
San José (USA)	—	—	...	...	...	...	...	4	...	9	13	18
San Luis Potosí (Mexico)	...	...	...	...	...	...	...	...	11[57]	...	...	63[93]
San Salvador (El Salvador)	...	...	...	7[07]	13	...	...	17[55]	...	25[74]	35	31[87]
Santo Domingo (Dominican Rep.)	...	...	12	...	...	...	...	12	...	...	...	25
Seattle (USA)	—	...	...	...	...	...	...	...	...	...	4	43
Springfield, Mass. (USA)	—	2	2	3	4	7	11	12	15	27	33	44
Syracuse (USA)	...	...	...	...	...	...	7	22	28	43	52	88
Tampa (USA)	—	...	...	...	...	...	...	...	...	1	1	6
Tegucigalpa (Honduras)	—	...	...	...	...	...	...	8	...	...	12	13
Toledo (USA)	—	—	—	—	—	—	1	4	14	32	50	81
Toronto (Canada)	—	—	...	...	2[24]	4	13	31	45	59	96	181
Tucson (USA)	—	—	—	—	—	—	—	—	—	...	...	5
Vancouver (Canada)	—	—	—	—	—	—	—	—	—	—	—	14
Veracruz (Mexico)	...	...	16[03]	...	11	...	7[42]	8[52]	11[62]	10	15	19[93]
Washington, DC (USA)	—	—	3	8	13	18	23	40	61	109	178	230
Wichita (USA)	—	—	—	—	—	—	—	—	—	—	5	24
Windsor (Canada)	—	—	—	—	—	—	—	...	...	4	7	10
Winnipeg (Canada)	...	—	—	—	—	—	—	—	—	—	8	26
Worcester, Mass. (USA)	...	2	2	3	3	4	7	17	25	41	58	85
Yonkers (USA)	—	—	—	—	—	—	—	—	—	—	19	32
Youngstown (USA)	—	—	—	—	—	—	—	3	3	8	15	33

A4   **NORTH AMERICA: Population of Major Cities** (in thousands)

	1900	1910	1920	1930	1940	1940	1950	1950	1960	1960	1970	1970	1980	1980	1990	1990
Akron (USA)	43	69	208	255	245	339	275	410	290	605	275	679	237	660	223	...
Albany (USA)	94	100	113	127	131	466[3]	135	514[3]	130	715[3]	116	778[3]	102	836[3]	101	874
Albuquerque (USA)	6	11	15	27	35	69	97	146	201	276	245	316	333	420	384	480
Allentown (USA)	35	52	74	93	97	397[4]	107	438[4]	108	545[4]	110	594[4]	104	635[4]	105	686[29]
Anaheim (USA)	1	3	6	11	11	...	15	...	104	704[5]	166	1 421[5]	219	1,935[5]	266	...
Atlanta (USA)	90	155	201	270	302	518	331	672	487	1,169	495	1,596	425	2,138	394	2,833
Austin (USA)	22	30	35	53	88	111	132	161	187	232	254	323	346	537	465	781
Baltimore (USA)	509	558	734	805	859	1,083	950	1,337	939	1,804	905	2,071	787	2,200	736	2,382
Birmingham (USA)	38	133	179	260	268	460	326	559	341	747	301	767	284	884	266	907
Boston (USA)	561	671	748	781	771	2,178	801	2,370	697	2,688	641	2,899	563	2,806	574	4,171
Buffalo (USA)	352	424	507	573	576	958	580	1,089	533	1,307	463	1,349	358	1,243	328	1,189
Calgary (Canada)	4	44	63	84	89	...	129	139	250	279	403	417	593	...	710	—
Charleston, SC (USA)	56	59	68	62	71	121	70	165	279	279	...	336	...	430	60	506
Charlotte (USA)	18	34	46	83	101	152	134[4]	197[4]	202	446[6]	241	558[6]	315	971[6]	395	1,162
Chicago (USA)	1,699	2,185	2,702	3,376	3,397	4,826	3,621	5,495	3,550	6,221	3,367	6,978	3,005	6,060	2,783	8,065
Chihuahua (Mexico)	30	40	48	62	57	...	87	...	150	...	257	...	386	...	530	...
Cincinnati (USA)	326	364	401	451	456	787	504	904	503	1,268	453	1,385	385	1,401	364	1,744
Ciudad Juarez (Mexico)	8	11	19	43	49	...	123	...	262	...	407	...	544	...	798	...
Cleveland (USA)	382	561	797	900	878	1,267	915	1,466	876	1,909	751	2,064	574	1,899	505	2,759
Columbus, Ohio (USA)	126	182	237	291	306	389	376	503	471	845	540	1,018	565	1,244	632	1,377
Corpus Christi (USA)	5	8	11	28	57	93	108	165	168	267	205	285	232	326	257	349
Dallas (USA)	43	92	159	260	295	399	434	615	680	1,738[7]	844	2,378[7]	905	2,931[7]	1,006	3,885
Dayton (USA)	85	117	153	201	211	331	244	457	262	727	244	853	194	942	182	951
Denver (USA)	134	213	256	288	322	408	416	564	494	935[8]	515	1,239[8]	493	1,618[8]	467	1,848
Des Moines (USA)	62	86	126	143	160	196	178	226	209	287	201	314	191	368	193	392
Detroit (USA)	286	466	994	1,569	1,623	2,377	1,850	3,016	1,670	3,950	1,511	4,435	1,203	4,488	1,027	4,665
Edmonton (Canada)	4	31	59	79	94	98	160	173	281	338	438	496	532	657	616	839
El Paso (USA)	16	39	78	102	97	131	130	195	277	314	322	359	425	480	515	591
Fall River (USA)	105	119	120	115	115	135	112	137	100	...	97	...	93	...	...	...
Fort Lauderdale (USA)	...	...	...	9	18	...	36	...	84	334[9]	140	620[9]	153	1,018[9]	149	...[30]

A4 NORTH AMERICA: Population of Major Cities (in thousands)

	1900	1910	1920	1930	1940	1950	1950	1960	1960	1970	1970	1980	1980	1990	1990
Fort Worth (USA)	27	73	106	163	178	226	279	396		393		385		447	[7]
Gary (USA)	...	17	55	100	112	134	...	178	574[10]	175	633[10]	152	643[10]	116	[31]
Grand Rapids (USA)	88	113	138	169	164	177	288	177	462	198	539	182	602	189	688
Greensboro (USA)	10	16	20	54	59	74	337[11]	120	622[11]	144	724[11]	156	852[11]	183	942
Guadalajara (Mexico)	101	119	143	185	229	377	...	737	...	1,194	1,456	1,626	2,245	1,650	...
Guatemala City	74[98]	90	116	121[28]	186	284	...	439	...	769	...	754	...	1,675	...
Hamilton (Canada)	53	82	114	156	166	208	260	274	395	309	499	306	542	318	625
Hartford, Conn. (USA)	80	99	138	164	166	177	358	162	588	158	721	136	716	139	1,085
Havana (Cuba)	236	312	364[22]	581	660[43]	785[43]	1,218[53]	978	1,463	1,001[67]	1,557[67]	...	1,929	...	2,143
Houston (USA)	45	79	138	292	385	596	807	938	1,430	1,233	1,999	1,595	2,736	1,630	3,711
Indianapolis (USA)	169	234	314	364	387	427	552	476[12]	944	745[12]	1,111	701	1,167	731	1,249
Jacksonville (USA)	28	58	92	130	173	205	304	201[13]	530	529[13]	622	541	722	635	906[26]
Jersey City (USA)	206	268	298	317	301	299	...	276	611	261	608	224	557	228	...
Kansas City, Mo. (USA)	164	248	324	400	399	457	814	476	1,109	507	1,274	448	1,433	435	1,566
Kingston (Jamaica)	...	60	64	...	110	142[55]	338[55]	123	377	112	475	104	525	103	524[82]
León (Mexico)	59	58	54	99	86	123	...	210	...	365	...	593	...	867	...
London (Canada)	38	46	61	71	78	95	122	170	181	223	286	254	284	341	381
Long Beach (USA)	2	18	56	142	164	251	}	344	}	359	}	361	}	429	}
Los Angeles (USA)	102	319	577	1,238	1,504	1,970	4,368[14]	2,479	6,039[12]	2,816	7,042[14]	2,969	7,478	3,485	14,531
Louisville (USA)	205	224	235	308	319	369	577	391	754	361	867	299	957	269	952
Managua (Nicaragua)	30	39[06]	59	33[26]	63	109	...	235	...	399	...	615	...	682[85]	...
Memphis (USA)	102	131	162	253	293	396	482	498	727	624	834	646	913	610	981
Mérida (Mexico)	44	62	79	91	115	159	...	191	...	242	...	400	...	556	...
Mexicali (Mexico)	—	—	—	...	19	65	...	175	...	263	...	342	...	601	...
Mexico City	345	471	615	1,029	1,448	2,234	3,050	2,832	4,871	6,874	8,590	8,831	12,932	8,235	15,047
Miami (USA)	2	5	30	111	172	249	495	292	935	335	1,268	347	1,626	358	3,192
Milwaukee (USA)	285	374	457	578	587	637	871	741	1,279	717	1,404	636	1,397	628	1,607
Minneapolis (USA)	203	301	381	464	492	522	1,117[15]	483	1,598[15]	434	1,965[15]	371	2,137[15]	368	2,464
Monterrey (Mexico)	62	79	88	133	186	333	...	597	...	858	1,213	1,085	1,916	1,069	...
Montreal (Canada)	268	470	619	819	903	1,022	1,395	1,191	2,110	1,214	2,743	980	2,828	1,017	3,127

A4 NORTH AMERICA: Population of Major Cities (in thousands)

	1900	1910	1920	1930	1940	1940	1950	1950	1960	1960	1970	1970	1980	1980	1990	1990
Nashville (USA)	81	110	118	154	167	257	174	322	171[16]	597	448[16]	699	456	851	488	985[26]
Newark, NJ (USA)	246	347	415	442	430	...	439	...	405	1,833	382	2,057	329	1,879	275	...
New Orleans (USA)	287	339	387	459	495	552	570	685	628	907	593	1,046	558	1,256	496	1,238
New York (USA)	3,437	4,767	5,620	6,930	7,455	8,707	7,892	9,556	7,782	9,540	7,895	9,974	7,072	8,275	7,322	18,087
Norfolk (USA)	47	67	116	130	144	259[17]	214	446[17]	305	629[17]	308	733[17]	267	1,160[17]	261	1,396
Oakland (USA)	67	150	216	284	302	[18]	385	[18]	368	[18]	362	[18]	339	[18]	372	[18]
Oklahoma City (USA)	10	64	91	185	204	244	244	325	324	566	366	699	404	861	444	958
Omaha (USA)	103	124[19]	192[19]	214	224	325	251	366	302	458	347	543	313	585	335	618
Ottawa (Canada)	60	87	108	127	155	226	202	292	268	430	302	603	295	718	313	920
Panama City	...	38	67	74	112	...	128	...	273	...	349	...	386	...	584	...
Paterson, NJ (USA)	105	126	136	139	140	...	139	...	144	407[20]	145	461[20]	138	29	140	...
Philadelphia (USA)	1,294	1,549	1,824	1,951	1,931	3,200	2,072	3,671	2,003	4,343	1,949	4,824	1,688	4,717	1,585	5,899
Phoenix (USA)	6	11	29	48	65	186	107	332	439	664	582	969	790	1,509	983	2,122
Pittsburgh (USA)[2]	452	534	588	670	672	2,083	677	2,213	604	2,405	520	2,401	424	2,219	366	2,406
Port-au-Prince (Haiti)	70	105	...	100	115	...	134	...	240	...	459	494	450	763	690	1,255[92]
Portland, Oreg. (USA)	90	207	258	302	305	501	374	705	373	822	383	1,007	368	1,298	437	1,477
Providence, RI (USA)	176	224	238	253	254	677[21]	249	737[21]	207	821[21]	179	909[21]	157	926[21]	160	1,141
Puebla (Mexico)	94	96	96	123	138	...	211	...	289	...	402	...	773	...	1,057	...
Quebec (Canada)	69	78	95	131	151	225	164	275	172	358	186	481	166	576	167	645
Richmond, Va. (USA)	85	128	172	183	193	263	230	328	220	457	250	542	219	761	203	865
Rochester (USA)	163	218	296	328	325	438	332	488	319	801	296	962	242	971	231	1,002
Sacramento (USA)	29	45	66	86	85	170	138	277	192	626	254	804	276	1,100	369	1,481
St Louis (USA)	575	687	773	822	816	1,432	857	1,681	750	2,144	622	2,411	453	2,377	396	2,444
St Paul, Minn. (USA)	163	215	235	272	288	[15]	311	[15]	313	[15]	310	[15]	270	[15]	272	[32]
St Petersburg (USA)	2	4	14	40	61	[22]	97	[22]	181	[22]	216	[22]	239	[22]	238	[22]
Salt Lake City (USA)	54	93	118	140	150	212	182	275	189	576	176	705	163	960	159	1,072
San Antonio (USA)	53	97	161	232	254	338	408	500	588	736	654	888	786	1,072	935	1,302
San Bernardino (USA)	6	13	19	37	44	161[13]	63	282[23]	92	810[23]	104	1,141[23]	119	1,558[23]	164	[29]
San Diego (USA)	18	40	74	148	203	289	334	557	573	1,033	697	1,358	876	1,862	1,110	2,498
San Francisco (USA)	343	417	507	634	635	1,462[18]	775	2,241[18]	740	2,649[18]	716	3,107[18]	679	3,251[18]	723	6,253

A4 NORTH AMERICA: Population of Major Cities (in thousands)

City	1900	1910	1920	1930	1940	1940	1950	1950	1960	1960	1970	1970	1980	1980	1990	1990
San José (Costa Rica)	24	32	39	51[27]	68	...	87	140	174	331	215	395	275	451	315[94]	1,186[94]
San José (USA)	22	29	40	58	68	175	95	291	204	642	446	1,065	629	1,295	782	[33]
San Juan (Puerto Rico)	32	49	71	115	169	303	225	466	432	542	453	695	425	1,086	441	1,816[84]
San Luis Potosi (Mexico)	61	68	83	...	104	...	155	...	194	...	268	...	342	...	525	...
San Salvador (El Salvador)	59	...	80	96	110	...	162	...	248	...	337	...	425	...	442	...
Santiago de Cuba	43	45[07]	70[22]	102	118[43]	...	163[53]	...	213	...	278	...	347	...	425	
Santo Domingo (Dominican Rep.)	20	22	31	71[35]	117[45]	...	182	...	367	...	671	...	1,313	...		2,055
Seattle (USA)	81	237	315	366	368	505	468	733	557	1,107[24]	531	1,425[24]	494	1,607[24]	516	2,559
Springfield, Mass. (USA)	62	89	130	150	150	365[25]	162	407[25]	174	504[25]	164	542[25]	152	515[25]	156	529
Syracuse (USA)	108	137	172	209	206	295	221	342	216	564	197	637	170	643	163	659
Tampa (USA)	16	38	52	101	108	272[22]	125	409[22]	275	809[22]	278	1,089[22]	272	1,614[22]	280	2,067
Tegucigalpa (Honduras)	13	22	26	40	47	...	72	100	134	...	275[73]	302[73]	444	485	670	...
Tijuana (Mexico)	...	...	...	...	16		60	60	152		277		429		747	
Toledo (USA)	132	168	243	291	282	344	304	396	318	695	384	763	355	617	332	614
Toronto (Canada)	219	382	522	631	667	910	676	1,117	672	1,824	713	2,628	599	2,999	635	3,893
Torreón (Mexico)	14	34	51	66	88	...	147	...	203	...	251	...	328	...	464	...
Tucson (USA)	8	13	20	33	36	73	45	45	213	266	263	352	331	531	405	666
Tulsa (USA)	1	18	72	141	142	193	183	252	262	475	332	549	361	657	367	708
Vancouver (Canada)	27	100	163	247	275	377	345	562	385	790	426	1,082	414	1,268	471	1,602
Veracruz (Mexico)	29	49	54	72	76	...	107	...	154	...	230	...	285	...	328	[17]
Virginia Beach (USA)	...	...	...	...	...		5	[17]	8	[17]	172	[17]	262	[17]	393	
Washington, DC (USA)	279	331	438	487	663	968	802	1,464	764	2,097	757	2,910	638	3,251	606	3,923
Wichita (USA)	25	52	72	111	115	143	168	222	255	382	277	389	280	442	304	485
Windsor (Canada)	12	18	39	63	105	124	120	158	114	193	203	259	192	246	191	262
Winnipeg (Canada)	42	136	179	219	222	300	236	354	265	476	246	540	564	585	616	632
Worcester, Mass. (USA)	118	146	180	195	194	253	203	276	187	354	177	372	162	403	169	436
Yonkers (USA)	48	80	100	135	143	[26]	153	[26]	191	[26]	204	[26]	195	[26]	188	...
Youngstown (USA)	45	79	132	170	168	474[27]	168	528[27]	167	509[27]	140	537[27]	116	531[27]	95	492

A4 SOUTH AMERICA: POPULATION OF MAJOR CITIES (in thousands)

	c1750	1790	1800	1810	1820	1830	1840	1850	1860	1870	1880	1890
Arequipa (Peru)	…	24[95]	28[04]	…	25	…	…	25[48]	26[62]	…	29[76]	35
Asunción (Paraguay)	…	7	…	…	…	…	…	10	…	…	…	25[86]
Barquisimeto (Venezuela)	…	…	…	…	…	…	…	…	…	7[73]	29	31[88]
Barranquilla (Colombia)	…	…	…	…	…	…	…	6	…	12	…	…
Belém (Brazil)	…	…	12	…	…	12	…	…	…	62[72]	…	50
Bogotá (Colombia)	…	18[93]	24	…	…	…	40[43]	30	…	41	96[84]	…
Bucaramanga (Colombia)	…	…	…	…	…	…	6[43]	10	11[64]	11	…	…
Buenos Aires (Argentina)	11[44]	22[70]	40	46	55[22]	…	65[38]	99[55]	140[64]	187	…	433[87]
Cali (Colombia)	…	7[93]	…	…	…	…	…	11	…	13	…	…
Callao (Peru)	…	…	…	…	…	…	3	8	18[62]	15[66]	34[76]	35
Campinas (Brazil)	—	1	2	…	6	8	…	…	…	…	26[84]	34
Caracas (Venezuela)	19	…	31	…	…	…	…	…	…	49[73]	56	72
Cartagena (Colombia)	…	…	24	…	…	…	…	10	18[57]	9	…	…
Córdoba (Argentina)	…	6	12	…	10[25]	…	14	…	…	29	…	48[95]
Cúcuta (Colombia)	…	…	…	11[13]	13	…	…	6	…	9	…	…
Curitiba (Brazil)	…	3[80]	…	…	…	13	12[45]	…	…	13[72]	…	25
Duque de Caxias (Brazil)	…	…	…	…	…	…	…	…	…	…	…	…
Fortaleza (Brazil)	…	…	…	…	…	…	…	…	…	42[72]	…	41
Guyaquil (Ecuador)	…	…	14	…	…	…	14	…	…	…	36	45
La Paz (Bolivia)	…	…	…	…	…	…	…	…	20[57]	…	…	40
La Plata (Argentina)	—	—	—	—	—	—	—	—	—	1	2	…
Lima (Peru)	…	53[92]	…	…	65	60[27]	56[36]	70	94[57]	…	101[76]	…
Maceió (Brazil)	—	…	…	…	…	…	…	…	…	28[72]	…	31
Manaus (Brazil)	…	…	…	…	…	…	…	…	…	29[72]	…	39
Manizales (Colombia)	…	…	…	…	…	…	…	3	…	11	15[84]	…
Maracaibo (Venezuela)	…	…	22	…	…	…	…	…	…	22[73]	25	29
Maracay (Venezuela)	…	…	8	…	…	…	…	…	…	3[73]	4	4

A4 SOUTH AMERICA: Population of Major Cities (in thousands)

	c1750	1790	1800	1810	1820	1830	1840	1850	1860	1870	1880	1890
Mar del Plata (Argentina)	...	...	...	...	...	...	...	...	...	...	...	...
Medellin (Colombia)	...	9[85]	5	...	5[25]	...	9[43]	14	...	30	37[84]	...
Mendoza (Argentina)	...	...	10	...	...	12[26]	...	...	12	8	12	29[95]
Montevideo (Uruguay)	...	...	14	...	...	15	31[43]	34	58	105[72]	164	215
Natal (Brazil)	...	...	...	...	...	...	...	...	...	20[72]	...	14
Niterói (Brazil)	...	...	...	...	...	...	...	...	...	48[72]	...	34
Pôrto Alegre (Brazil)	...	...	4	...	...	...	...	...	...	44[72]	...	52
Quito (Ecuador)	...	28[80]	...	...	...	...	...	...	36[57]	...	...	50
Recife (Brazil)	...	...	15	25	...	41[28]	72	...	90[62]	97[72]	...	112
Rio de Janeiro (Brazil)	29	...	43	50[07]	113	125	141	166	198	275[72]	360	523
Rosario (Argentina)	...	...	0.4	...	...	...	2	3	10[58]	23	...	51[87]
Salvador (Brazil)	34	...	46	100	115	130[35]	140	150[52]	...	129[72]	...	174
San Juan (Argentina)	...	6[77]	...	4[12]	...	8[26]	...	...	9	8	...	10[95]
Santiago (Chile)	...	...	45	...	...	...	...	...	...	115[65]	130[75]	189[85]
Santa Fé (Argentina)	...	...	4[97]	5	7[17]	...	...	...	6[58]	11	...	14[87]
Santos (Brazil)	...	...	6	...	...	5[28]	6[36]	...	...	10[72]	...	13
São Paolo (Brazil)	...	8	...	...	20	...	12[36]	15[55]	...	31[72]	...	65
Trujillo (Peru)	...	...	...	...	5[18]	...	...	...	8[62]	...	8[76]	8
Tucumán (Argentina)	9[63]	...	4	4[12]	...	10[26]	...	17[45]	...	17	...	...
Valencia (Venezuela)	...	...	7	...	...	...	...	...	...	16[73]	...	28
Valparaíso (Chile)	...	...	6	...	...	...	...	52[54]	...	70[65]	98[75]	105[85]

A4 SOUTH AMERICA: Population of Major Cities (in thousands)

	1900	1910	1920	1930	1940	1950	1950	1960	1960	1970	1970	1980	1980	1990	1990
Arequipa (Peru)	35	40	44[17]	46	61	97	…	135	…	302[72]	…	498	…	624	637[92]
Asunción (Paraguay)	…	80	…	90	120	207	219	305	…	399	…	457[82]	…	502[92]	745
Barquisimeto (Venezuela)	…	…	24	23[26]	54	105	…	200	…	331	…	497	…	602	…
Barranquilla (Colombia)	40[05]	49[12]	65[18]	140[28]	152[38]	280	…	521[64]	…	662[73]	727[73]	…	917[85]	…	1,018[92]
Belém (Brazil)	97	271	236	279[29]	206	255	…	402	…	633	…	933	…	1,244	1,620[91]
Belo Horizonte (Brazil)	13	35	55	109[29]	211	353	…	693	…	1,235	…	1,781	2,279	2,017	4,620[91]
Bogotá (Colombia)	100[05]	121[12]	144[18]	235[28]	330[38]	648	…	813[64]	…	2,855[73]	…	4,177	…	4,921[92]	…
Brasília (Brazil)	—	—	—	—	—	—	…	142	…	537	…	1,177	…	1,598	…
Bucaramanga (Colombia)	20[05]	20[12]	25[18]	44[28]	51[38]	112	…	251	…	292[73]	341[73]	…	352[85]	…	349
Buenos Aires (Argentina)	664[95]	1,576[14]	1,663	2,149	2,705	2,981[47]	4,722[47]	2,967	6,739	2,972	8,353	2,923	9,948	2,960	10,086
Cali (Colombia)	31[05]	28[12]	46[18]	123[28]	102[38]	284	…	251[64]	…	898[73]	923[73]	…	1,369[85]	…	1,624
Callao (Peru)	29[98]	…	53	64	69	88	…	156	…	297	…	443	…	515	…
Campinas (Brazil)	45[02]	…	116	135[26]	130	102	…	180	…	329	…	665	…	846	…
Caracas (Venezuela)	…	87[15]	92	…	269	495	694	788	1,336	1,663	2,175	1,817	2,944	1,828	2,784
Cartagena (Colombia)	10[05]	37[12]	51[18]	92[28]	85[38]	129	…	198[64]	…	293[73]	…	…	531[85]	…	688
Córdoba (Argentina)	48[95]	135[14]	140	253	274	370[47]	…	586	…	782	799	971	983	1,148	1,197
Cúcuta (Colombia)	15[05]	20[12]	29[18]	49[28]	57[38]	70	95	147[64]	175[64]	220[73]	228[73]	…	384[85]	…	450
Curitiba (Brazil)	50	61	79	100[29]	141	181	…	361	…	609	…	1,025	1,093	1,313	2,319[91]
Duque de Caxias (Brazil)	…	…	…	…	…	74	…	176	…	257	…	576	…	665	…
Fortaleza (Brazil)	48	66	79	99[29]	180	270	…	515	…	858	…	1,308	1,340	1,765	2,357[91]
Gioânia (Brazil)	—	—	—	27	48	53	…	151	…	381	…	718	723	920	…
Guayaquil (Equador)	60	85	94	120	147[38]	259	…	511	…	861[72]	…	1,199[82]	…	1,508	…
La Paz (Bolivia)	53	80	107[18]	147[29]	301[42]	321	…	353[62]	…	538	…	813	…	711	…
La Plata (Argentina)	45[95]	90[14]	151[22]	166[28]	200	207[47]	…	337	…	391	506	459	566	520	640
Lima (Peru)	130[03]	141[08]	176	281	521	835	…	1,262	1,436	2,834	…	4,165	4,669	5,706[93]	6,414
Maceió (Brazil)	36	61	74	104[29]	90	121	…	168	…	264	…	399	…	628	…
Manaus (Brazil)	50	77	76	84[29]	106	140	…	175	…	312	…	633	…	1,010	…
Manizales (Colombia)	25[05]	35[12]	43[18]	81[28]	86[38]	89	126	187[64]	222[64]	200[73]	207[73]	…	283[85]	…	327[92]
Maracaibo (Venezuela)	…	…	47	75[26]	122	236	…	421	…	652	…	889	…	1,207	1,363
Maracay (Venezuela)	…	…	7	11[26]	33	65	…	135	…	255	…	440	…	354	799

A4 SOUTH AMERICA: Population of Major Cities (in thousands)

	1900	1910	1920	1930	1940	1940	1950	1950	1960	1960	1970	1970	1980	1980	1990	1990
Mar del Plata (Argentina)	5['95]	28['14]	...	50	55['38]	...	115['47]	...	211	...	302	...	415	...	519	...
Medellin (Colombia)	55['05]	71['12]	79['18]	120['28]	168['38]	...	358	...	777['64]	...	1,071['73]	1,417['73]	...	1,452['85]	...	1,581['92]
Mendoza (Argentina)	28['95]	59['14]	...	59	102['42]	...	97['47]	212['47]	109	...	124	471	119	606	121	773
Montevideo (Uruguay)	268	328	385	482	770	...	784	...	1,159['63]	...	1,230['75]	...	1,252['85]	...	1,360	...
Natal (Brazil)	16	27	31	51	55	...	103	...	160	...	264	...	417	...	606	...
Niterói (Brazil)	53	80	85	108['29]	142	...	186	...	243	...	324	...	397	...	435	...
Nova Iguaçu (Brazil)	...	...	...	...	21	...	59	...	135	...	331	728	1,095	...	1,293	...
Osasco (Brazil)	...	...	...	...	...	...	43	...	116	...	283	...	475	...	566	...
Pôrto Alegre (Brazil)	73	130	180	273['29]	272	...	394	...	641	...	886	...	1,125	2,133	1,263	3,758['91]
Quito (Ecuador)	40	70	81	92	128['38]	...	210	–	355	...	565['72]	...	866['82]	...	1,100	...
Recife (Brazil)	113	193	239	341['29]	348	...	525	...	797	...	1,061	...	1,204	2,307	1,296	2,921['91]
Rio de Janeiro (Brazil)	811	870	1,158	1,469['29]	1,764	...	2,377	...	3,307	...	4,252	...	5,091	9,619	5,473	10,389['91]
Rosario (Argentina)	92['95]	223['14]	250	481	517	...	468['47]	...	591	672	699	811	794	957	894	1,095
Salvador (Brazil)	206	319	283	330['29]	290	...	417	...	656	...	1,007	...	1,502	1,563	2,072	3,135['91]
San Juan (Argentina)	10['95]	21['14]	...	17	80	...	82['47]	...	107	...	113	223	118	292	119	353
Santiago (Chile)	256['95]	333['07]	507	696	640	952	665	1,348	1,169	1,900	3,274	3,351	3,853	3,899	4,385	5,180['92]
Santa André (Brazil)	...	...	...	...	62	...	98	...	232	...	419	...	553	...	615	...
Santa Fé (Argentina)	22['95]	60['14]	84	121	149	...	169['47]	...	209	...	252	...	292	...	342	394
Santos (Brazil)	30	86	103	...	156	...	198	...	262	...	341	...	417	848	428	...
São Goncales (Brazil)	...	...	...	...	8	...	21	...	64	...	430	...	615	...	778	...
São Paolo (Brazil)	240	346	579	880['29]	1,326	...	2,198	...	3,825	...	5,929	...	8,493	12,273	9,626	16,567['91]
Trujillo (Peru)	8['96]	...	20	30['28]	39	...	48	...	100	...	242['72]	...	539	...	521	...
Tucumán (Argentina)	34['95]	94['14]	...	91	149	...	194['47]	...	272	288	361	366	394	499	470	622
Valencia (Venezuela)	...	...	29	37['26]	55	...	89	...	164	...	367	...	616	...	903	1,031
Valparaíso (Chile)	122['95]	162['07]	182	193	210	...	219	...	259	...	293	...	266	...	276	...

A4   Population of Major Cities

NOTES

1. SOURCES: UN and League of Nations, *Statistical Yearbooks*, and the national publications on pp. xii–xv. Official estimates as well as census figures have been used. Where none is available for years ending in 9, 0, or 1, that for the nearest available date has been used, and this has been indicated.
2. With a few exceptions, the cities in this table had a population of 200,000 or more in or about 1970, or the urban agglomeration of which they were the nucleus had a population of at least 500,000. There are a few additions which seem to be of particular historical interest.
3. Statistics to 1930 all relate to the cities proper except as indicated in footnotes. Subsequently two figures are given where available, the first for the cities proper, the second for their urban agglomeration.

FOOTNOTES

[1] The population was said to be 9 thousand in 1731. Including Brooklyn and, from 1850, other places later incorporated in the city.
[2] Including Allegheny, which was consolidated with Pittsburgh between 1900 and 1910, from 1850.
[3] Albany-Schenectady-Troy.
[4] Allentown-Bethlehem-Easton.
[5] Anaheim-Santa Ana-Garden Grove.
[6] Charlotte-Gastonia.
[7] Dallas-Forth Worth (see under Dallas).
[8] Denver-Boulder.
[9] Fort Lauderdale-Hollywood.
[10] Gary-Hammond-East Chicago.
[11] Greensboro-Winston Salem-High Point.
[12] Indianapolis and Marion County were consolidated between 1960 and 1970.
[13] Jacksonville and Duval County were consolidated between 1960 and 1970.
[14] Los Angeles-Long Beach.
[15] Minneapolis-St Paul (see under Minneapolis).
[16] Nashville and Davidson County were consolidated between 1960 and 1970.
[17] Norfolk-Virginia Beach-Portsmouth.
[18] San Francisco-Oakland (see under San Francisco).
[19] Omaha and South Omaha were consolidated between 1910 and 1920. Combined population: 1890–149; 1900–129; 1910–150.
[20] Paterson-Clifton-Passaic.
[21] Providence-Warwick-Pawtucket.
[22] Tampa-St Petersburg (see under Tampa).
[23] Riverside-San Bernardino-Ontario.
[24] Seattle-Everett.
[25] Springfield-Chicopee-Holyoke.
[26] Part of New York metropolitan area.
[27] Youngstown-Warren.
[28] Including suburbs.
[29] Part of Los Angeles metropolitan area.
[30] Part of Miami metropolitan area.
[31] Part of Chicago metropolitan area.
[32] Part of Minneapolis metropolitan area.
[33] Part of San Francisco metropolitan area.

A5   NORTH AMERICA: MID-YEAR POPULATION ESTIMATES (in thousands)

	USA[1]		USA		Canada[2]	Costa Rica	Jamaica	Trinidad	USA
1790	3,929	**1825**	11,252	**1860**	...	...	...	...	31,513
1791	4,050	**1826**	11,580	**1861**	...	...	...	...	
1792	4,194	**1827**	11,909	**1862**	...	...	...	...	33,188
1793	4,332	**1828**	12,237	**1863**	...	...	...	...	34,026
1794	4,469	**1829**	12,565	**1864**	...	...	...	...	34,863
1795	4,607	**1830**	12,901	**1865**	...	...	...	...	35,701
1796	4,745	**1831**	13,321	**1866**	...	...	...	...	36,538
1797	4,883	**1832**	13,742	**1867**	3,463	...	...	...	37,376
1798	5,021	**1833**	14,162	**1868**	3,511	...	...	...	38,213
1799	5,159	**1834**	14,582	**1869**	3,565	...	...	...	39,051
1800	5,297	**1835**	15,003	**1870**	3,625	...	...	...	39,905
1801	5,486	**1836**	15,423	**1871**	3,689	...	...	...	40,938
1802	5,679	**1837**	15,843	**1872**	3,754	...	...	...	41,972
1803	5,872	**1838**	16,264	**1873**	3,826	...	...	...	43,006
1804	6,065	**1839**	16,684	**1874**	3,895	...	...	...	44,040
1805	6,258	**1840**	17,120	**1875**	3,954	...	...	...	45,073
1806	6,451	**1841**	17,733	**1876**	4,009	...	...	...	46,107
1807	6,644	**1842**	18,345	**1877**	4,064	...	...	...	47,141
1808	6,838	**1843**	18,957	**1878**	4,120	...	...	...	48,174
1809	7,031	**1844**	19,569	**1879**	4,185	...	...	...	49,208
1810	7,224	**1845**	20,182	**1880**	4,255	...	558	...	50,262
1811	7,460	**1846**	20,794	**1881**	4,325	...	575	...	51,542
1812	7,700	**1847**	21,406	**1882**	4,375	...	586	...	52,821
1813	7,939	**1848**	22,018	**1883**	4,430	...	590	160	54,100
1814	8,179	**1849**	22,631	**1884**	4,487	...	591	164	55,379
1815	8,419	**1850**	23,261	**1885**	4,537	201	592	169	56,658
1816	8,659	**1851**	24,086	**1886**	4,580	206	597	175	57,938
1817	8,899	**1852**	24,911	**1887**	4,626	211	600	181	59,217
1818	9,139	**1853**	25,736	**1888**	4,678	216	606	187	60,496
1819	9,379	**1854**	26,561	**1889**	4,729	225	617	193	61,775
1820	9,618	**1855**	27,386						
1821	9,939	**1856**	28,212						
1822	10,268	**1857**	29,037						
1823	10,596	**1858**	29,862						
1824	10,924	**1859**	30,687						

A5   NORTH AMERICA: Mid-Year Population Estimates (in thousands)

	Barbados	Canada[2]	Costa Rica	Cuba	Dominican Republic	El Salvador	Guatemala	Haiti
1890	...	4,779	235	...	...	...	...	...
1891	...	4,833	245	...	...	...	...	...
1892	...	4,883	255	...	...	...	...	...
1893	...	4,931	262	...	...	...	...	...
1894	...	4,979	269	...	...	...	...	...
1895	...	5,026	276	...	...	...	...	...
1896	...	5,074	282	...	...	...	...	...
1897	...	5,122	287	...	...	...	...	...
1898	...	5,175	294	...	...	...	...	...
1899	...	5,235	297	1,573	...	...	...	...
1900	...	5,301	307	1,600	600	801	885	1,250
1901	...	5,371c	313	1,679	614	819	910	1,294
1902	...	5,494	318	1,758	628	838	936	1,338
1903	...	5,651	323	1,837	642	856	961	1,381
1904	...	5,827	330	1,879	656	874	987	1,425
1905	...	6,002	336	1,927	670	893	1,013	1,468
1906	...	6,097	341	1,979	684	911	1,029	1,512
1907	...	6,411	347	2,034	698	929	1,046	1,555
1908	...	6,625	353	2,092	712	948	1,062	1,559
1909	...	6,800	358	2,154	726	966	1,079	1,643
1910	172	6,988	364	2,219	740	985	1,096	1,687
1911	173	7,207	370	2,287	753	1,003	1,119	1,730
1912	172	7,389	375	2,358	767	1,021	1,142	1,774
1913	173	7,632	381	2,413	781	1,040	1,165	1,818
1914	173	7,879	387	2,507	795	1,058	1,180	1,862
1915	177	7,981	393	2,585	809	1,076	1,196	1,907
1916	182	8,001	398	2,664	823	1,095	1,211	1,949
1917	185	8,060	404	2,746	837	1,113	1,226	1,993
1918	190	8,148	410	2,828	851	1,131	1,241	2,037
1919	197[7]	8,311	415	2,912	865	1,150	1,257	2,080
1920	...	8,556	421	2,997	879	1,168	1,272	2,124
1921	155	8,788	425	3,083	912	1,193	1,319	2,151
1922	155	8,919	431	3,170	946	1,217	1,367	2,178
1923	155	9,010	439	3,257	981	1,244	1,416	2,206
1924	155	9,143	447	3,345	1,017	1,274	1,471	2,232
1925	156	9,294	456	3,432	1,054	1,301	1,514	2,260
1926	157	9,451	466	3,519	1,092	1,325	1,557	2,292
1927	158	9,637	472	3,606	1,131	1,351	1,602	2,325
1928	159	9,835	479	3,507	1,172	1,385	1,660	2,357
1929	158	10,029	489	3,577	1,213	1,412	1,706	2,390
1930	159	10,208	499	3,647	1,256	1,443	1,755	2,422
1931	159	10,376	508	3,962	1,300	1,456	1,813	2,460
1932	161	10,510	518	3,962	1,345	1,474	1,864	2,498
1933	164	10,633	528	3,962	1,391	1,493	1,909	2,535
1934	166	10,741	540	4,039	1,438	1,512	1,943	2,573
1935	168	10,845	551	4,071	1,484	1,531	1,975	2,611
1936	170	10,950	563	4,109	1,520	1,551	2,023	2,654
1937	173	11,045	576	4,165	1,558	1,571	2,066	2,697
1938	175	11,152	590	4,228	1,595	1,591	2,113	2,741
1939	177	11,267	605	4,253	1,634	1,612	2,150	2,784

A5 NORTH AMERICA: Mid-Year Population Estimates (in thousands)

	Honduras	Jamaica	Martinique	Mexico	Nicaragua	Panama	Puerto Rico	Trinidad & Tobago[3]	USA[4]
1890	...	630	...	...	...	...	...	197	63,056
1891	...	637	...	...	...	...	...	208	64,361
1892	...	648	...,	...	...	...	...	217	65,666
1893	...	661	...	12,257	...	...	...	...[3]	66,970
1894	...	673	...	12,443	...	...	...	224	68,275
1895	...	684	...	12,632	...	...	...	234	69,580
1896	...	695	...	12,822	...	...	...	242	70,885
1897	...	706	...	13,014	...	...	...	249	72,129
1898	...	718	...	13,209	...	...	...	257	73,494
1899	...	731	...	13,406	...	...	...	265	74,799
1900	420	745	...	13,607	420	263	...	273	76,094
1901	436	748	...	13,755	434	270		276	77,584
1902	452	747	...	13,905	448	276		277	79,163
1903	468	781	...	14,056	462	283		290	80,632
1904	484	792	...	14,209	477	290		299	82,166
1905	500	798	...	14,363	491	297		308	83,822
1906	511	805	...	14,519	505	304		315	85,450
1907	521	810	...	14,677	515	311		320	87,008
1908	532	813	...	14,837	524	318		340	88,710
1909	542	820	...	14,998	534	325		342	90,490
1910	553	824	...	15,160	543	332		353	92,407
1911	562	831	...	15,083	553	339		354	93,863
1912	571	839	...	15,007	562	352		342	95,335
1913	579	846	...	14,931	572	364		348	97,225
1914	588	851	...	14,855	581	378		354	99,111
1915	597	861	...	14,780	591	389		361	100,546
1916	606	874	...	14,705	600	401		368	101,961
1917	633	869	...	14,630	610	413		374	103,268[5]
1918	660	864	...	14,556	619	426		379	103,208[5]
1919	688	857	...	14,482	629	437		384	104,514[5]
1920	715	855	...	14,409	638	447	1,312	389	106,461
1921	742	860	244	14,335	643	449	1,336	367	108,538
1922	769	879	...	14,566	647	451	1,359	371	110,049
1923	796	891	...	14,801	652	453	1,383	376	111,947
1924	824	900	...	15,040	656	455	1,407	379	114,109
1925	851	910		15,282	660	457	1,431	382	115,829
1926	878	930	...	15,528	665	459	1,455	385	117,397
1927	893	946	228	15,778	670	462	1,478	388	119,035
1928	911	966	...	16,032	674	464	1,502	392	120,509
1929	928	985	...	16,290	679	466	1,526	398	121,770[4]
1930	948	1,009	...	16,553	683	471	1,552	405	123,188
1931	968	1,039	235	16,840	687	486	1,584	412	124,149
1932	989	1,061	...	17,132	692	501	1,615	417	124,949
1933	1,007	1,082	...	17,429	697	516	1,647	422	125,690
1934	1,023	1,098	...	17,731	711	531	1,679	428	126,485
1935	1,042	1,113	...	18,038	728	546	1,710	435	127,362
1936	1,058	1,130	247	18,350	746	561	1,743	442	128,181
1937	1,076	1,142	...	18,668	765	575	1,777	450	128,961
1938	1,098	1,163	...	18,991	785	590	1,810	458	129,969
1939	1,122	1,191	252	19,320	806	605	1,844	466	131,028

International Historical Statistics: The Americas 1750–1993

A5 NORTH AMERICA: Mid-Year Population Estimates (in thousands)

	Barbados	Canada[6]	Costa Rica	Cuba	Dominican Republic	El Salvador	Guadeloupe	Guatemala	Haiti
1940	179	11,381	619	4,291	1,674	1,633	...	2,201	2,827
1941	179	11,507	633	4,326	1,715	1,654	...	2,252	2,876
1942	180	11,654	647	4,372	1,757	1,675	...	2,300	2,936
1943	182	11,795	661	4,779	1,800	1,697	...	2,339	2,979
1944	183	11,946	677	4,849	1,844	1,719	...	2,384	3,032
1945	187	12,072	695	4,932	1,889	1,742	...	2,438	3,087
1946	193	12,292	709	5,039	1,935	1,764	190	2,498	3,143
1947	199	12,551	726	5,152	1,982	1,788	193	2,567	3,200
1948	202	12,823[6]	746[7]	5,287	1,997	1,811	197	2,642	3,258[7]
		13,167	808						3,233
1949	206	13,475	832	5,399	2,061	1,835	201	2,724	3,293
1950	211	13,737	859	5,516	2,129	1,859	210	2,805	3,097
1951	215	14,050	888	5,638	2,216	1,912	214	2,892	3,149
1952	218	14,496	920	5,759	2,297	1,965	219	2,981	3,200
1953	221	14,886	954	6,129	2,379	2,020	224	3,075	3,251
1954	225	15,330	989	6,254	2,464	2,077	230	3,171	3,302
1955	227	15,736	1,028	6,381	2,554	2,135	237	3,269	3,354
1956	226	16,123	1,069	6,513	2,644	2,195	244	3,371	3,407
1957	226	16,677	1,110	6,641	2,740	2,257	251	3,476	3,460
1958	228	17,120	1,153	6,763	2,839	2,321	258	3,584	3,514
1959	231	17,522	1,200	6,901	2,941	2,386	265	3,695	3,568
1960	233	17,909	1,254	7,027	3,038	2,454	275	3,966	3,623
1961	233	18,271	1,298	7,134	3,126	2,527	281	4,088	3,679
1962	234	18,614	1,343	7,254	3,220	2,627	289	4,214	3,736
1963	237	18,964	1,391	7,415	3,315	2,721	297	4,345[7]	3,793
1964	241	19,325	1,439	7,612	3,412	2,824	308	4,312	3,852
1965	244	19,678	1,490	7,810	3,513	2,928	315	4,437	3,912
1966	247	20,048	1,541	7,985	3,616	3,037	319	4,565	3,972
1967	249	20,412	1,590	8,139	3,723	3,151	320	4,698	4,035
1968	252	20,744	1,634	8,284	3,833	3,266	318	4,837	4,098
1969	253	21,028	1,685	8,421	3,946	3,390	323	4,966	4,163
1970	238	21,324	1,727	8,551	4,062	3,534	327	5,272	4,235
1971	240	21,592	1,798	8,692	4,182	3,647[7]	332[7]	5,425	4,315
1972	241	21,822	1,842	8,862	4,305	3,668	320	5,582	4,368
1973	239	22,072	1,873	9,036	4,476	3,771	325	5,744	4,440
1974	244	22,360	1,922	9,194	4,614	3,887	325	6,050	4,514
1975	246	22,697	1,968	9,299	4,752	4,005	328	6,243	4,584
1976	246	22,993	2,009	9,430	4,890	4,122	329	6,434[7]	4,668
								6,191	
1977	247	23,273	2,066	9,547	5,028	4,255	328	6,364	4,749
1978	248	23,517	2,115	9,644	5,166	4,353	327	6,543	4,833
1979	249	23,747	2,166	9,720	5,305	4,435	327	6,726	4,919
1980	249	24,043	2,245	9,724	5,443	4,508	327	6,917	5,009
1981	250	24,342	2,271	9,724	5,581	4,587	328	7,113	5,100
1982	250	24,583	2,324	9,801	5,744	4,662	328	7,315	5,054
1983	251	24,787	[2,435][8]	9,897	6,123	4,724	336	7,524	5,130
1984	252	24,978	2,417	9,994	6,269	4,780	342	7,740	5,207
1985	253	25,165	2,489[8]	10,098	6,416	4,819	349	7,963	5,285
1986	253	25,353	2,717	10,199	6,565	4,913	356	8,195	5,364
1987	254	25,617	2,781	10,301	6,716	5,009	364	8,434	5,444
1988	254	25,911	2,851	10,412	6,867	5,107	372	8,681	5,526
1989	249	26,240	2,956	10,501	6,964	5,071	381	8,935	6,355
1990	256	26,584	3,035	10,598	7,110	5,172	385	9,197	6,486
1991	260	28,120	3,113	10,692	7,255	5,279	395	9,467	6,619
1992	265	28,436	3,191	10,784	7,399	5,395	408	9,745	6,754
1993	269	28,941	3,269	10,874	7,542	5,517	413	10,030	6,894

A5 NORTH AMERICA: Mid-Year Population Estimates (in thousands)

	Honduras	Jamaica	Martinique	Mexico	Nicaragua	Panama	Puert Rico	Trinidad & Tobago	USA[9]
1940	1,146	1,212	...	19,815	825	620	1,880	476	132,122
1941	1,171	1,230	...	20,332	844	636	1,935	492	133,402
1942	1,195	1,254	...	20,866	863	651	1,987	510	134,860
1943	1,213	1,249	...	21,418	880	669	2,033	525	136,739
1944	1,237	1,259	...	21,988	900	685	2,062	536	138,397
1945	1,261	1,266	...	22,576	923	703[7]	2,099	547	139,928
1946	1,287	1,298	209	23,183	947	727	2,141	561	141,389
1947	1,320	1,327	212	23,811	977	746	2,162	583	144,126
1948	1,353	1,343	215	24,461	1,001	767	2,187	600	146,631
1949	1,389	1,365	218	25,132	1,028	788	2,197	616	149,188
1950	1,445	1,403	222	26,282	1,052	795	2,218	632	151,684
1951	1,485	1,430	226	27,039	1,083	818	2,235	649	154,287
1952	1,528	1,457	230	27,846	1,116	842	2,227	663	156,954
1953	1,572	1,486	234	28,701	1,149	867	2,204	678	159,565
1954	1,617	1,518	239	29,605	1,183	893	2,214	698	162,391
1955	1,665	1,542	247	30,557	1,218	919	2,250	721	165,275
1956	1,715	1,564	253	31,557	1,255	946	2,249	743	168,221
1957	1,768	1,595	258	32,607	1,292	973	2,260	765	171,274
1958	1,823	1,630	271	33,704	1,330	1,002	2,299	789	174,141
1959	1,880	1,598	279	34,851	1,370	1,031	2,321	817	177,073[9]
									177,830
1960	1,943	1,628	285	34,994	1,411	1,062	2,358	841	180,671
1961	2,020	1,646	289	36,158	1,453	1,094	2,402	867	183,691
1962	2,096	1,660	294	37,367	1,496	1,130	2,447	900	186,538
1963	2,169	1,696	294	38,623	1,541	1,162	2,495	924	189,242
1964	2,238	1,740	301	39,928	1,579	1,197	2,550	951	191,889
1965	2,304	1,760	307	41,284	1,619	1,234	2,594	974	194,303
1966	2,384	1,784	314	42,694	1,660	1,272	2,624	995	196,560
1967	2,466	1,802	321	44,161	1,701	1,310	2,645	1,010	198,712
1968	2,552	1,821	326	45,686	1,744	1,351	2,669	1,021	200,706
1969	2,638	1,844	332	47,274[8]	1,788	1,392	2,717	1,028	202,677
1970	2,639	1,869	338	50,695	1,833	1,434	2,718	1,027	205,052
1971	2,720	1,901	341	52,452	1,889	1,478[8]	2,775	1,033	207,661
1972	2,805	1,932	334	54,273	1,954	1,546	2,868	1,045	209,896
1973	2,895	1,972	332	56,161	2,015	1,592	2,870	1,058[8]	211,909
1974	2,991	2,008	330	58,118	2,089	1,634	2,890	1,000	213,854
1975	3,093	2,047	328	60,145[10]	2,162	1,704	2,933	1,009	215,973
1976	3,202	2,083	328	61,979	2,244	1,748	3,024	1,023	218,035
1977	3,318	2,097	327	63,813	2,325	1,792	3,061	1,035	220,239
1978	3,439	2,088	326	65,658	2,410	1,835	3,113	1,049	222,585
1979	3,564	2,112	326	67,517	2,644	1,878	3,149	1,064	225,055
1980	3,691	2,133	326	69,655	2,733	1,956	3,206	1,082	227,757
1981	3,821	2,162	326	71,305	2,860	1,999	3,247	1,094	230,138
1982	3,955	2,200	327	72,968	2,955	2,044	3,263	1,116	232,520
1983	4,092	2,241	331	74,633	3,058	2,089	3,332	1,139	234,799
1984	4,232	2,280	334	76,293	3,163	2,134	3,349	1,170	237,001
1985	4,372	2,311	337	77,938	3,273	2,180	3,378	1,178	239,279
1986	4,514	2,336	341	77,567	3,384	2,227	3,406	1,196	241,625
1987	4,656	2,351	345	81,199	3,502	2,274	3,433	1,212	243,942
1988	4,802	2,356	350	82,721	3,622	2,322	3,461	1,212	246,307
1989	4,734	2,364	356	84,272	3,743	2,351	3,497	1,215	247,342
1990	4,879	2,366	362	86,154	3,871	2,398	3,528	1,236	249,911
1991	5,028	2,133	368	87,836	3,999	2,444	3,549	1,250	252,643
1992	5,180	2,166	373	89,538	4,131	2,491	3,579	1,264	255,407
1993	5,336	2,203	371	91,261	4,265	2,538	3,620	1,278	258,120

A5 SOUTH AMERICA: MID-YEAR POPULATION ESTIMATES
(in thousands)

	Argentina	Brazil	Chile	Guyana	Peru
1850	...	...	1,294	...	...
1851	...	7,344	1,326	...	...
1852	...	7,456	1,358	...	...
1853	...	7,570	1,391	...	...
1854	...	7,686	1,423	...	...
1855	...	7,803	1,454	...	...
1856	...	7,923	1,501	...	...
1857	...	8,044	1,517	...	...
1858	...	8,167	1,551	...	...
1859	...	8,291	1,584	...	...
1860	...	8,418	1,618	...	
1861	...	8,547	1,653	...	...
1862	...	8,678	1,688	...	...
1863	...	8,810	1,725	...	...
1864	...	8,945	1,757	...	...
1865	1,559	9,082	1,795	...	...
1866	1,616	9,221	1,832	...	...
1867	1,675	9,362	1,856	...	...
1868	1,737	9,505	1,880	...	...
1869	1,802	9,650	1,905	...	...
1870	1,859	9,797	1,931	...	...
1871	1,910	9,947	1,956	...	...
1872	1,963	10,099	1,982	...	...
1873	2,017	10,289	2,009	...	...
1874	2,073	10,486	2,035	...	...
1875	2,132	10,687	2,062	...	...
1876	2,192	10,891	2,097	...	...
1877	2,255	11,099	2,138	...	[440][11]
1878	2,320	11,311	2,181	...	...
1879	2,387	11,528	2,224	...	[438][11]
1880	2,457	11,748	2,269	248	...
1881	2,529	11,973	2,314	250	...
1882	2,602	12,202	2,360	255	[505][11]
1883	2,678	12,435	2,408	259	513
1884	2,757	12,673	2,456	262	540
1885	2,839	12,916	2,503	267	571
1886	2,923	13,163	2,536	272	590
1887	3,011	13,414	2,555	276	605
1888	3,108	13,671	2,572	278	631
1889	3,212	13,932	2,591	280	666
1890	3,323	14,199	2,609	280	695
1891	3,434	14,506	2,627	275	707
1892	3,548	14,857	2,646	271	718
1893	3,668	15,216	2,655	275	738
1894	3,793	15,583	2,674	280	762
1895	3,906	15,960	2,698	279	785
1896	4,013	16,346	2,733	277	806
1897	4,152	16,741	2,774	279	830
1898	4,296	17,145	2,816	279	852
1899	4,418	17,560	$2,859_{10}$	282	$\underline{879}_{10}$

A5   SOUTH AMERICA: Mid-Year Population Estimates (in thousands)

	Argentina	Bolivia	Brazil	Chile	Colombia	Ecuador	Guyana	Paraguay	Peru	Uraguay	Venezuela
1900	4,542	1,766	17,984	2,959	3,894	1,300	287	490	3,000	943	2,445
1901	4,674	1,785	18,392	2,994	3,944	1,312	291	506	3,100	965	2,451
1902	4,806	1,803	18,782	3,030	3,994	1,324	298	522	3,200	990	2,458
1903	4,924	1,822	19,180	3,066	4,044	1,336	299	539	3,300	1,019	2,465
1904	5,040	1,840	19,587	3,102	4,094	1,348	295	555	3,400	1,033	2,471
1905	5,197	1,859	20,003	3,139	4,144	1,360	296	571	3,500	1,071	2,492
1906	5,407	1,877	20,427	3,176	4,277	1,372	298	580	3,600	1,103	2,512
1907	5,673	1,896	20,860	3,213	4,409	1,384	299	590	3,700	1,141	2,532
1908	5,988	1,914	21,303	3,253	4,542	1,396	297	600	3,800	1,054	2,554
1909	6,288	1,933	21,754	3,294	4,674	1,408	298	610	3,900	1,095	2,575
1910	6,615	1,951	22,216	3,336	4,807	1,421	301	620	4,000	1,132	2,596
1911	6,934	1,970	22,687	3,378	4,940	1,433	301	630	4,100	1,178	2,612
1912	7,268	1,988	23,168	3,425	5,072	1,445	297	640	4,187	1,226	2,639
1913	7,652	2,007	23,660	3,465	5,193	1,457	302	650	4,267	1,279	2,661
1914	7,917	2,025	24,161	3,509	5,318	1,469	307	657	4,347	1,316	2,633
1915	8,072	2,044	24,674	3,553	5,447	1,481	311	664	4,427	1,346	2,705
1916	8,225	2,062	25,197	3,598	5,579	1,493	314	671	4,508	1,379	2,727
1917	8,374	2,081	25,732	3,644	5,715	1,505	318	678	4,588	1,407	2,750
1918	8,517	2,099	26,277	3,690	5,855	1,517	315	685	4,668	1,439	2,772
1919	8,672	2,118	26,835	3,737	6,029	1,529	309	692	4,748	1,463	2,795
1920	8,861	2,136	27,404	3,785	6,089	1,541	303	679	4,828	1,481	2,818
1921	9,092	2,161	27,969	3,853	6,211	1,570	…	715	4,908	1,499	2,843
1922	9,368	2,186	28,542	3,907	6,336	1,610	298	732	4,989	1,517	2,870
1923	9,706	2,212	29,126	3,961	6,463	1,646	298	749	5,069	1,535	2,898
1924	10,054	2,237	29,723	4,017	6,512	1,685	298	767	5,148	1,553	2,925
1925	10,398	2,263	30,332	4,073	6,724	1,724	300	785	5,229	1,571	2,953
1926	10,692	2,289	30,953	4,130	6,859	1,762	302	803	5,313	1,604	2,981
1927	10,965	2,316	31,587	4,188	6,996	1,800	306	822	5,399	1,636	3,012
1928	11,282	2,343	32,234	4,246	7,136	1,944	307	841	5,482	1,669	3,047
1929	11,592	2,370	32,894	4,305	7,279	1,891	307	860	5,567	1,701	3,082
1930	11,896	2,397	33,568	4,365	7,425	1,944	309	880	5,651	1,734	3,118
1931	12,016	2,425	34,256	4,429	7,574	1,995	312	901	5,748	1,761	3,154
1932	12,402	2,453	34,957	4,495	7,726	2,050	315	922	5,844	1,788	3,191
1933	12,623	2,482	35,673	4,563	7,880	2,095	319	944	5,941	1,815	3,227
1934	12,834	2,511	36,404	4,631	8,068	2,140	322	966	6,037	1,842	3,264
1935	13,044	2,540	37,150	4,700	8,199	2,196	325	988	6,134	1,869	3,300
1936	13,620	2,569	37,911	4,771	8,363	2,249	330	1,012	6,243	1,890	3,382
1937	13,490	2,599	38,687	4,842	8,531	2,298	334	1,036	6,353	1,911	3,464
1938	13,725	2,629	39,480	4,914	8,702	2,355	337	1,061	6,462	1,932	3,546
1939	13,948	2,659	40,289	4,988	8,896	2,412	339[12]	1,086	6,572	1,953	3,628
1940	14,169	2,690	41,114	5,063	9,094	2,466	344	1,111	6,681	1,974	3,710
1941	14,401	2,721	42,069	5,149	9,296	2,521	351	1,137	6,979	1,994	3,803
1942	14,631	2,785	43,069	5,244	9,503	2,575	358	1,164	6,915	2,014	3,914
1943	14,877	2,817	44,093	5,341	9,719	2,641	363	1,191	7,035	2,034	4,028
1944	15,130	1,850	45,141	5,440	9,931	2,712	366	1,219	7,159	2,055	4,146

International Historical Statistics: The Americas 1750–1993

A5 SOUTH AMERICA: Mid-Year Population Estimates (in thousands)

	Argentina	Bolivia	Brazil	Chile	Colombia	Ecuador	Guyana	Paraguay	Peru	Uruguay	Venezuela
1945	15,390	2,850	46,215	5,541	10,152	2,781	370	1,247	7,285	2,076	4,267
1946	15,654	2,883	47,313	5,643	10,378	2,853	377	1,275	7,415	2,098	4,391
1947	15,929	2,916	48,438	5,748	10,609	2,953	390	1,305	7,547	2,121	4,548
1948	16,284	2,950	49,590	5,854	10,845	3,043	400	1,335	7,682	2,144	4,686
1949	16,671	2,984	50,769	5,962	11,087	3,135	412	1,366	7,822	2,169	4,828
1950	17,150	3,019	51,944	6,091	11,334	3,225	423	1,371	7,969	2,195	4,962
1951	17,468	3,065	53,888	6,221	11,615	3,317	434	1,410	8,118	2,224	5,166
1952	17,824	3,125	55,502	6,352	11,986	3,412	446	1,449	8,267	2,255	5,391
1953	18,194	3,189	57,164	6,482	12,369	3,511	459	1,487	8,425	2,288	5,619
1954	18,564	3,256	58,876	6,613	12,765	3,615	472	1,530	8,597	2,319	5,852
1955	18,928	3,322	60,640	6,743	13,172	3,722	486	1,564	8,790	2,348	6,089
1956	19,281	3,392	62,456	6,912	13,593	3,833	500	1,604	9,004	2,375	6,331
1957	19,625	3,464	64,326	7,080	14,028	3,949	515	1,645	9,235	2,400	6,578
1958	19,961	3,539	66,253	7,248	14,476	4,070	532	1,688	9,483	2,429	6,830
1959	20,289	3,729	68,237	7,417	14,938	4,195	550	1,730	9,746	2,459	7,086
1960	20,611	3,825	70,281	7,585	15,416	4,325	568	1,774	10,022	2,491	7,349
1961	20,930	3,920	72,262	7,770	15,908	4,461	585	1,820	10,320	2,523	7,612
1962	21,245	4,019	74,279	7,955	16,417	4,602	601	1,867	10,630	2,555	7,870
1963	21,558	4,121	76,352	8,140	16,941	4,749	618	1,915	10,947	2,586	8,413[8]
1964	21,868	4,226	78,483	8,325	17,484	4,902	631	1,965	11,272	2,617	8,423
1965	22,179	4,334	80,674	8,510	17,996	5,061	645	2,016	11,607	2,647	8,711
1966	22,488	4,445	82,926	8,682	18,468	5,227	661	2,070	11,952	2,677	9,006
1967	22,800	4,561	85,240	8,853	18,956	5,399	677	2,124	12,307	2,709	9,310
1968	23,113	4,680	87,620	9,025	19,462	5,792[8]	690	2,183	12,675	2,740	9,623
1969	23,428	4,774	90,065	9,197	19,984	5,766	699	2,240	13,055	2,771	9,944
1970	23,748	4,931	92,520	9,369	20,527	5,962	709	2,301	13,447	2,802	10,275
1971	24,068	5,063	95,171	9,545	21,088	6,165	724	2,365	13,830	2,833	10,612
1972	24,392	5,195	97,845	9,704	21,668	6,378	741	2,431	14,224	2,865[8]	10,939
1973	24,820	5,331	99,917	9,861	22,343	6,599	758	2,510	14,628	2,840	11,280[8]
1974	25,620	5,470[8]	102,396	10,026	22,981	6,830	769	2,600	14,746	2,840	12,220
1975	26,052	4,894	104,936	10,196	23,644	7,035	781	2,686	15,161	2,829	12,665
1976	26,480	5,027	107,539	10,372	23,968	7,243	794	2,779	15,573	2,847	13,119
1977	26,912	5,163	110,207	10,663	24,434	7,455	806	2,854	15,990	2,862	13,590
1978	27,348	5,304	112,941	10,816	24,906	7,671	820	2,948	16,414	2,877	14,071
1979	27,789	5,449	118,553	10,975	25,376	7,893	848	3,046	16,849	2,896	14,552
1980	28,237	5,600	121,286	11,145	25,892	8,123	865	3,147	17,295	2,914	15,024
1981	28,694	5,755	124,068	11,327	26,426	8,361	883	3,250	17,755	2,932	15,485
1982	29,158	5,919	126,898	11,519	26,965	8,606	901	3,358	18,226	2,951	15,940
1983	29,627	6,082	129,766	11,717	27,502	8,857	918	3,468	18,707	2,970	16,394
1984	30,097	6,253[8]	132,659	11,919	28,056	9,115	936	3,580	19,198	2,989	16,851
1985	30,564	5,895	135,564	12,122	28,624	9,378	...	3,693	19,417	3,008	17,317
1986	31,030	6,025	138,493	12,327	29,188	9,647	972	3,807	19,840	3,026	17,792
1987	31,497	6,157	141,452	12,536	29,729	9,923	989	3,922	20,261	3,043	18,272
1988	31,534	6,293	144,428	12,748	30,241	10,204	1,007	4,039	20,684	3,060	18,757
1989	32,114	6,431	145,803	12,883	31,739	10,490[8]	...	4,190	21,113	3,077	19,025
1990	32,547	6,573	148,477	13,100	32,300	10,264	...	4,317	21,550	3,094	19,502
1991	32,966	6,733	151,152	13,320	32,862	10,502	...	4,444	21,998	3,112	19,972
1992	33,375	6,897	153,824	13,545	33,425	10,741	...	4,572	22,454	3,131	20,441
1993	33,778	7,065	156,941	13,771	33,987	10,981	...	4,701	22,639	3,149	20,910

A5 Mid-Year Population Estimates

NOTES

1. SOURCES:- The national publications listed on pp. xiii–xv; UN, *Demographic Yearbook*; and, for Latin American countries (except Argentina, Brazil, Chile, Costa Rica, and Mexico) from 1900 to about 1950, James W. Wilkie (ed.), *Statistical Abstract of Latin America* vol. 20 (Los Angeles, 1982).
2. Where necessary and possible, and except as indicated in footnotes, statistics for dates other than mid-year have been converted by straight-line interpolation between adjacent estimates.
3. In principle, except as indicated in footnotes, the estimates relate to population actually present.

FOOTNOTES

[1] Earlier estimates are available for the British colonies which later constituted the USA as follows (in thousands):-

1700	251	1730	629	1760	1,594
1710	332	1740	906	1770	2,148
1720	466	1750	1,171	1780	2,780

[2] Estimates to 1901 are at 1 April.
[3] Trinidad only to 1892.
[4] Armed forces overseas are included from 1930. They numbered 111 thousand in that year.
[5] The following figures are available including armed forces overseas for these years (in thousands):-

1917	103,414	1918	104,550	1919	105,063

[6] Newfoundland is included from 1948 (2nd line).
[7] Later revisions were not carried back further than this. In the case of Barbados the figures for 1914–19 are unreliable and are included here only because they provide the basis for the vital rates in table A6.
[8] The reason for this break is not given in the source.
[9] Alaska and Hawaii are included from 1959 (2nd line).
[10] This break occurs on a change of source (see note 1 above).
[11] Estimates at 31 December.
[12] Subsequently including estimates for remote tribes.

International Historical Statistics: The Americas 1750-1993

A6 NORTH AMERICA: VITAL STATISTICS: RATES PER 1,000 POPULATION

Key: B = births; D = deaths; M = marriages

1879-1929

	Barbados			Canada[3]			Costa Rica			El Salvador		
	B	D	M	B	D	M	B	D	M	B	D	M
1879	...	...	...	...	...	...	...	...	...	...	...	...
1880	...	...	...	...	...	...	...	...	...	...	...	...
1881	...	...	...	...	...	...	...	...	...	...	...	...
1882	...	...	...	...	...	...	...	...	...	...	...	...
1883	...	...	...	...	...	...	...	...	...	...	...	...
1884	...	...	...	...	...	...	...	...	...	...	...	...
1885	...	...	...	...	...	...	...	...	...	...	...	...
1886	...	...	...	...	...	...	...	...	...	...	...	...
1887	...	...	...	...	...	...	...	...	...	...	...	...
1888	...	...	...	...	...	...	...	...	...	...	...	...
1889	...	...	...	...	...	...	...	...	...	...	...	...
1890	...	...	...	...	...	...	...	...	...	...	...	...
1891	...	...	...	...	...	...	...	...	...	...	...	...
1892	...	...	...	...	...	...	...	...	...	...	...	...
1893	...	...	...	...	...	...	...	...	...	...	...	...
1894	...	...	...	...	...	...	...	...	...	...	...	...
1895	...	...	...	...	...	...	...	...	...	...	...	...
1896	...	...	...	...	...	...	...	...	...	...	...	...
1897	...	...	...	...	...	...	...	...	...	...	...	...
1898	...	...	...	...	...	...	...	...	...	...	...	...
1899	...	...	...	...	...	...	...	...	...	...	...	...
1900	...	...	...	27.2	16.2	6.9	41.5	23.0	...	...	...	...
1901	...	...	...	31.2	14.1	7.0	36.7	26.3	...	...	...	...
1902	...	...	...	31.3	13.4	6.8	35.2	25.3	...	...	...	...
1903	...	...	...	31.3	13.2	7.3	36.3	22.8	...	...	...	...
1904	...	...	...	31.4	13.5	7.3	38.4	22.6	...	...	...	...
1905	...	...	...	31.0	13.0	7.4	37.8	27.7	...	...	...	...
1906	...	...	...	29.9	13.2	7.5	39.3	24.6	...	...	...	...
1907	...	...	...	29.5	12.8	7.5	42.0	25.2	...	...	...	...
1908	...	...	...	30.3	12.6	7.3	42.3	25.2	...	...	...	...
1909	...	...	...	30.2	12.8	7.7	42.3	24.8	...	...	...	...
1910	37.2	25.5	5.1	30.4	13.1	8.2	41.7	25.6	...	...	...	...
1911	35.2	26.3	4.7	30.1	13.4	8.6	43.3	24.4	...	...	...	...
1912	36.8	41.0	4.1	31.3	13.0	9.4	42.8	23.4	...	...	...	...
1913	31.9	21.3	3.4	31.7	13.1	9.1	43.1	22.8	...	...	...	...
1914	37.4	36.5	3.3	31.9	12.6	8.4	44.3	22.5	...	...	...	...
1915	29.5	19.2	3.1	31.9	12.5	7.9	43.4	21.9	...	...	...	...
1916	32.2	22.7	3.9	30.7	13.0	8.0	41.2	23.0	...	...	...	...
1917	28.8	24.9	3.8	29.1	12.7	7.5	41.7	22.5	...	...	...	...
1918	30.2	20.6	5.4	28.8	15.9	6.8	40.0	30.5	...	...	...	...
1919	34.9	39.3	4.9	27.7	13.7	8.3	36.2	27.6	...	...	...	...
1920	37.5	33.4	5.4	29.2	13.3₃	9.2₃	38.5	28.6	...	36.5	20.9	2.6
1921	32.6	43.3	4.3	29.3	11.6	7.9	38.2	21.0	...	...	...	2.4
1922	34.3	22.4	4.7	28.3	11.6	7.2	38.5	20.9	...	...	...	2.9
1923	37.4	37.1	4.8	26.7₃	11.8₃	7.3₃	38.1	20.1	...	...	...	3.4
1924	32.9	29.5	4.8	26.7	10.9	7.1	38.7	22.3	...	...	...	3.1
1925	34.9	29.5	5.3	26.1	10.7	6.9	38.3₄	24.0₄	...	35.6	20.4	3.4
1926	31.3	29.6	5.8	24.7	11.4	7.0	46.9	23.1	...	36.7	22.7	3.9
1927	31.6	20.2	6.7	24.3	11.0	7.2	47.9	22.6	7.8	36.4	17.9	3.5
1928	33.8	30.1	7.3	24.1	11.2	7.5	48.2	23.6	7.2	38.4	19.3	3.3
1929	32.0	23.7	6.6	23.5	11.4	7.7	46.3	24.2	6.3	35.2	14.2	3.4

A6   NORTH AMERICA: Vital Statistics: Rates per 1,000 Population

	Jamaica[1]			Mexico			Newfoundland			Puerto Rico		
	B	D	M	B	D	M	B	D	M	B	D	M
1879	33.6	23.3	...	...	...	...	...	...	...	...	...	...
1880	38.3	27.0	...	...	...	...	...	...	...	...	...	...
1881	36.7	26.0	3.7	...	...	...	...	...	...	...	...	...
1882	35.3	20.2	4.0	...	...	...	...	...	...	...	...	...
1883	40.7	22.6	4.8	...	...	...	...	...	...	...	...	...
1884	36.3	22.8	5.0	...	...	...	...	...	...	...	...	...
1885	38.1	22.8	5.1	...	...	...	...	...	...	...	...	...
1886	36.4	23.5	4.0	...	...	...	...	...	...	...	...	...
1887	34.9	24.4	4.4	...	...	...	...	...	...	...	...	...
1888	39.5	22.5	5.5	...	...	...	...	...	...	...	...	...
1889	35.6	22.4₁	5.2₁	...	...	...	...	...	...	...	...	...
1890	38.6	25.3	5.6	...	...	...	...	...	...	...	...	...
1891	38.3	22.8	5.3	...	...	...	...	...	...	...	...	...
1892	37.2	20.8	5.1	...	...	...	...	...	...	...	...	...
1893	40.9	22.2	5.6	...	...	...	...	...	...	...	...	...
1894	37.1	21.0	5.3	...	...	...	...	...	...	...	...	...
1895	38.8	22.7	4.7	...	...	...	...	...	...	...	...	...
1896	38.5	22.1	4.3	...	...	...	...	...	...	...	...	...
1897	39.8	23.0	3.7	...	...	...	...	...	...	...	...	...
1898	38.0	21.0	4.6	...	...	...	...	...	...	...	...	...
1899	42.1	22.7	5.1	...	...	...	...	...	...	...	...	...
1900	35.7	21.6	4.3	34.0	32.7	...	...	...	...	...	...	...
1901	42.5	22.8	4.4	34.2	32.3	...	...	...	...	...	...	...
1902	39.3	19.8	4.6	33.7	34.4	...	...	...	...	...	...	...
1903	40.1	24.8	4.5	33.4	32.6	...	...	...	...	...	...	...
1904	36.5	24.9	3.6	34.8	31.4	...	...	...	...	...	...	...
1905	39.4	22.2	3.9	34.1	32.9	...	...	...	...	...	...	...
1906	38.9	26.8	6.8	32.2	33.1	...	...	...	...	...	...	...
1907	36.0	29.2	7.7	32.8	33.0	...	29.5	17.6	7.8	...	...	...
1908	38.7	23.1	4.3	34.3	31.8	...	28.2	17.4	7.4	...	...	...
1909	39.4	22.7	4.3	34.0	32.3	...	30.0	15.4	7.2	...	...	...
1910	38.5	23.1	4.0	32.0	33.3	...	29.7	15.2	7.5	33.6	23.8	...
1911	39.1	22.3	4.3	...	...	...	28.4	16.0	7.3	34.3	23.3	...
1912	39.2	25.4	3.8	...	...	...	31.1	16.7	7.5	35.1	23.4	...
1913	36.0	22.1	3.2	...	...	...	29.9	17.8	7.5	36.5	19.8	...
1914	39.8	21.9	3.2	...	...	...	30.4	15.6	6.3	39.8	18.7	...
1915	35.5₁	22.1₁	3.1₁	...	...	...	30.0	14.0	6.1	37.2	20.7	...
1916	34.2	23.1	3.4	...	...	...	26.5	17.8	6.4	35.1	23.9	...
1917	35.2	27.8	3.4	...	...	...	26.2	17.1	6.9	35.4	30.9	...
1918	35.4	34.2	3.2	...	...	...	28.4	19.6	7.1	40.9	30.9	...
1919	34.9	22.9	3.9	...	...	...	27.0	16.0	8.2	35.9	23.7	...
1920	42.1	26.2	5.0	...	...	...	29.0	15.6	6.9	38.4	22.8	...
1921	34.9	28.3	3.5	...	...	...	27.2	12.8	5.7	38.3	22.5	...
1922	37.4	23.0	3.8	31.4	25.3	3.8	27.8	13.7	5.5	37.4	21.8	...
1923	38.7	23.0	3.8	32.0	24.4	3.8	27.8	13.7	5.2	37.0	19.6	...
1924	37.0	21.9	3.5	30.8	25.6	4.1	25.6	15.9	5.3	38.3	19.4	...
1925	34.9	21.6	4.1	33.1	26.5	4.5	26.0	13.8	6.3	37.1	23.4	...
1926	38.4	20.5	4.3	31.2	24.9	4.9	27.0	13.0	6.4	38.3	22.3	...
1927	34.7	21.1	4.6	30.5	24.0	5.1	26.5	13.7	5.6	39.6	22.8	6.6
1928	35.8	19.7	4.5	32.3	25.3	5.2	24.6	13.8	6.1	35.3	19.8	6.9
1929	34.2	18.4	4.3	39.3	26.8	5.4	24.2	14.4	6.0	34.4	26.8	5.4

A6   NORTH AMERICA: Vital Statistics: Rates per 1,000 Population

1879–1929

| | Trinidad and Tobago[2] | | | USA[5] | | | | |
| | B | D | M | B | | D | | M |
				whites	negroes[6]	whites	negroes[6]	
1879	...	...	...	...	...	...	...	...
1880	...	...	...	...	...	...	...	...
1881	...	...	...	...	...	...	...	...
1882	...	...	...	...	...	...	...	...
1883	37.0	29.2	4.6	...	...	...	...	...
1884	34.7	27.9	4.2	...	...	...	...	...
1885	36.0	28.7	3.4	...	...	...	...	...
1886	36.6	27.9	3.2	...	...	...	...	...
1887	34.1	27.3	3.5	...	...	...	...	...
1888	36.2	31.0	4.1	...	...	...	...	...
1889	35.3	30.1	4.0	...	...	...	...	...
1890	32.0	28.5	5.0[2]	...	...	...	...	...
1891	32.2	27.0	4.9	...	...	...	...	...
1892	33.4[2]	24.8[2]	4.0	...	...	...	...	...
1893	33.8	27.5	4.6	...	...	...	...	...
1894	33.9	24.9	4.3	...	...	...	...	...
1895	34.6	25.3	4.3	...	...	...	...	...
1896	33.8	26.6	4.6	...	...	...	...	...
1897	31.8	28.4	4.1	...	...	...	...	...
1898	31.0	26.3	4.4	...	...	...	...	...
1899	36.5	24.4	5.0	...	...	...	...	...
1900	36.6[2]	25.0[2]	4.4[2]	...	...	17.0	25.0	...
1901	34.7	25.2	4.2	...	...	16.2	24.3	...
1902	35.1	23.5	4.0	...	...	15.3	23.6	...
1903	34.3	24.5	4.1	...	...	15.4	24.5	...
1904	37.1	21.3	4.8	...	...	16.2	26.1	...
1905	36.8	26.3	3.7	...	...	15.7	25.5	...
1906	34.7	25.3	3.5	...	...	15.5	24.2	...
1907	32.8	25.4	4.4	...	...	15.7	24.3	...
1908	33.8	23.1	4.0	...	...	14.5	22.4	...
1909	33.2	21.8	3.9	29.2	...	14.0	21.8	...
1910	32.3	20.8	4.2	29.2	...	14.5	21.7	...
1911	34.3	23.2	4.2	29.1	...	13.7	21.3	...
1912	33.8	29.7	3.7	29.0	...	13.4	20.6	...
1913	33.6	23.1	3.7	28.8	...	13.5	20.3	...
1914	33.0	23.2	3.6	29.3	...	13.0	20.2	...
1915	[31.5][2]	[21.3][2]	[3.7][2]	28.9	...	12.9	20.2	...
1916	32.4	20.4	3.9	28.5	...	13.4	19.1	...
1917	33.6	21.3	3.8	27.9	32.9	13.5	20.4	...
1918	31.0	21.7	3.8	27.6	33.0	17.5	25.6	...
1919	30.1	24.5	3.6	25.3	32.4	12.4	17.9	...
1920	30.1	23.8	3.5	26.9	35.0	12.6	17.7	12.0
1921	30.6	23.2	3.7	27.3	35.8	11.1	15.5	10.7
1922	32.1	22.7	3.9	25.4	33.2	11.3	15.2	10.3
1923	34.7	20.9	3.5	25.2	33.2	11.7	16.5	11.0
1924	33.7	20.0	5.3	25.1	34.6	11.0	17.1	10.4
1925	33.1	20.6	6.3	24.1	34.2	11.1	17.4	10.3
1926	32.0	22.0	6.4	23.1	33.4	11.6	17.8	10.2
1927	30.4	18.7	5.7	22.7	31.1	10.8	16.4	10.1
1928	29.6	19.9	5.5	21.5	28.5	11.4	17.1	9.8
1929	31.7	19.4	5.0	20.5	27.3	11.3	16.9	10.1

A6 NORTH AMERICA: Vital Statistics: Rates per 1,000 Population

1930–1979

	Barbados			Canada[3]			Costa Rica		
	B	D	M	B	D	M	B	D	M
1930	32.7	23.1	6.3	23.9	10.8	7.0	47.4	22.5	6.0
1931	30.4	28.2	6.0	23.2	10.2	6.4	46.9	24.7	5.8
1932	33.5	20.6	6.3	22.5	10.0	5.9	45.7	21.9	6.3
1933	32.5	21.9	6.5	21.0	9.7	6.0	44.6	21.7	5.9
1934	32.4	25.1	6.1	20.7	9.5	6.8	44.2	18.6	6.5
1935	31.6	22.0	4.9	20.5	9.9	7.1	45.2	22.9	6.3
1936	34.8	20.3	5.8	20.3	9.9	7.4	45.2	21.0	6.3
1937	32.8	20.3	5.5	20.1	10.4	7.9	44.5	19.2	7.2
1938	30.5	21.4	5.0	20.7	9.7	7.9	45.5	17.7	6.6
1939	31.1	19.1	6.6	20.6	9.7	9.2	44.7	19.3	6.7
1940	32.4	18.5	6.3	21.6	9.8	10.8	45.3	18.1	6.0
1941	32.3	21.8	5.4	22.4	10.1	10.6	45.5	18.1	6.3
1942	31.0	18.2	6.6	23.5	9.8	10.9	43.7	21.0	6.0
1943	32.3	17.1	8.0	24.2	10.1	9.4	46.1	17.7	5.8
1944	32.4	18.3	7.8	24.0	9.8	8.5	44.2	16.7	6.9
1945	32.3	16.9	7.7	24.3	9.5	9.0	46.8	15.5	6.9
1946	31.9	17.0	7.1	27.2	9.4	10.9	45.0	13.9	6.0
1947	32.7	16.3	5.3	28.9	9.4	10.1	44.7	14.9	7.6
1948	32.5	15.7	4.4	27.3	9.3	9.6	44.5	13.2	4.7
1949	32.0	14.6	4.6	27.3	9.3	9.2	44.2	12.7	7.3
1950	30.5	12.8	4.8	27.1	9.1	9.1	46.5	12.2	7.8
1951	31.6	14.0	5.1	27.2	9.0	9.2	48.5	11.7	8.2
1952	33.5	14.6	4.7	27.9	8.7	8.9	49.8	11.6	7.6
1953	33.0	13.5	4.6	28.1	8.6	8.8	47.9	11.9	7.3
1954	33.6	11.3	5.1	28.5	8.2	8.4	49.4	10.8	7.0
1955	33.4	12.7	4.7	28.2	8.2	48.9	10.7	6.8	
1956	31.3	10.8	4.9	28.0	8.2	8.3	48.5	9.8	6.5
1957	32.4	10.9	5.3	28.2	8.2	8.0	47.9	10.4	6.4
1958	31.2	10.1	4.5	27.5	7.9	7.7	47.2	9.2	6.8
1959	30.8	9.0	4.4	27.4	8.0	7.6	48.3	9.3	6.8
1960	33.6	9.1	4.7	26.7	7.8	7.3	47.5	8.8	7.2
1961	29.0	10.4	4.3	26.0	7.7	7.0	46.9	8.2	6.7
1962	29.4	9.0	4.1	25.2	7.7	7.0	45.4	8.9	5.9
1963	28.5	8.8	4.2	24.6	7.8	6.9	45.3	9.0	5.9
1964	27.0	8.8	3.7	23.4	7.6	7.2	43.0	9.4	5.6
1965	26.1	7.8	3.9	21.3	7.6	7.4	42.3	8.6	5.7
1966	25.6	8.2	…	19.3	7.5	7.8	40.7	7.4	5.6
1967	21.9	8.2	3.9	18.2	7.4	8.1	39.0	7.1	5.6
1968	21.7	8.1	3.8	17.6	7.4	8.3	36.2	6.5	5.8
1969	20.5	7.8	4.0	17.6	7.3	8.7	34.4	6.9	5.8
1970	20.4	8.7	4.6	17.5	7.3	8.8	33.2	6.6	6.3
1971	21.5	8.6	4.5	16.8	7.3	8.9	31.3	5.9	6.4
1972	21.9	8.5	3.9	15.9	7.4	9.2	31.2	5.9	7.0
1973	20.9	9.4	4.0	15.6	7.4	9.0	28.5	5.2	7.0
1974	19.8	8.8	3.8	15.5	7.4	8.9	29.5	4.9	7.4
1975	19.1	8.8	4.1	15.8	7.4	8.7	29.5	4.9	7.5
1976	18.6	9.5	2.9	15.7	7.3	8.4	29.8	4.7	7.3
1977	17.5	8.7	2.8	15.5	7.2	8.1	31.1	4.3	7.5
1978	17.4	8.4	2.8	15.3	7.2	7.9	29.9	4.1	7.8
1979	17.2	8.6	3.8	15.4	7.1	7.9	30.2	4.2	…

A6 NORTH AMERICA: Vital Statistics: Rates per 1,000 Population

1930-1979

	Cuba			El Salvador			Guadeloupe		
	B	D	M	B	D	M	B	D	M
1930	...	...	...	45.9	21.8	3.8	...	...	...
1931	25.2	10.2	3.3	46.0	22.7	3.3	...	...	...
1932	16.7	10.9	3.0	41.2	22.1	3.1	...	...	...
1933	17.0	12.4	2.7	42.3	23.8	3.3	...	...	...
1934	19.2	11.6	4.2	41.6	25.5	3.7	...	...	...
1935	19.5	12.0	4.6	40.2	25.2	3.8	...	...	...
1936	19.5	10.7	4.7	43.5	21.4	3.7	...	...	...
1937	23.1	10.2	5.0	41.8	20.7	4.0	...	...	...
1938	25.3	11.1	4.4	43.5	19.0	3.8	...	...	...
1939	15.5	9.8	3.7	44.2	19.5	3.8	...	...	...
1940	18.1	9.7	...	45.4	19.0	3.7	...	...	...
1941	16.9	9.3	...	43.5	18.3	4.0	...	...	...
1942	...	9.4	...	42.4	22.7	3.9	...	...	...
1943	...	10.4	...	41.9	22.5	3.6	...	...	...
1944	36.0	10.0	...	42.0	19.6	4.0	...	...	...
1945	20.8	10.6	...	42.6	18.1	3.5	...	...	...
1946	23.9	8.0	...	40.6	17.5	4.1	...	16.9	6.9
1947	30.1	7.9	...	46.9	17.1	4.0	...	17.4	7.5
1948	29.9	7.6	...	44.3	16.7	3.6	37.4	16.9	8.0
1949	29.8	7.5	...	45.9	15.3	4.0	39.9	14.3	7.5
1950	29.6	7.1	...	48.5	14.7	5.4	37.3	14.1	5.6
1951	25.4	7.3	...	49.0	15.2	4.5	39.3	13.7	5.2
1952	25.1	6.5	...	49.3	16.5	4.1	38.6	14.7	5.8
1953	29.6	6.3	...	48.7	15.0	4.4	38.8	12.8	5.3
1954	...	5.9	...	49.1	15.3	4.0	39.0	11.6	6.5
1955	...	6.1	4.6	49.2	14.6	3.8	40.3	11.7	5.2
1956	...	5.8	4.7	48.5	12.8	4.0	39.7	10.1	5.2
1957	29.3	6.3	4.8	50.9	14.6	4.2	37.6	11.4	5.4
1958	27.3	6.5	4.5	49.6	14.1	3.8	38.2	9.6	5.0
1959	30.5	6.6	4.6	48.5	12.6	7.2	37.0	8.9	5.4
1960	31.5	6.3	9.2	49.5	11.4	3.8	38.4	9.7	5.8
1961	33.8	6.6	10.4	49.4	11.3	3.5	35.7	8.4	5.5
1962	36.9	7.3	8.4	48.4	11.5	3.6	37.7	8.1	5.1
1963	35.2	6.9	7.6	49.0	10.9	3.7	36.1	8.1	5.5
1964	35.2	6.4	6.2	47.1	10.4	3.9	33.9	7.6	5.4
1965	34.2	6.5	8.9	46.9	10.6	3.5	33.7	8.1	5.3
1966	32.8	6.5	6.1	45.4	10.0	3.3	34.1	7.8	5.1
1967	31.4	6.3	6.4	44.4	9.2	3.3	32.5	8.1	5.6
1968	29.8	6.6	10.3	43.2	9.1	3.3	33.2	8.1	5.6
1969	28.3	6.7	10.2	42.1	9.9	3.3	30.5	7.6	5.5
1970	27.7	6.3	13.4	40.0	9.9	3.3	29.3	7.7	6.0
1971	29.5	6.0	13.0	42.3	7.9	3.7	31.2	7.0	5.3
1972	30.8	5.5	8.9	40.8	8.8	3.8	30.5	7.3	5.3
1973	25.1	5.7	7.0	40.3	8.4	4.0	29.3	7.3	5.2
1974	22.2	5.6	7.3	43.2	7.8	4.2	27.0	7.5	4.6
1975	20.7	5.4	7.0	39.9	7.9	4.2	25.1	7.1	...
1976	19.9	5.6	6.5	40.2	7.5	4.4	21.1	7.2	...
1977	17.7	5.9	6.5	41.7	7.8	4.2	19.3	6.9	4.4
1978	15.4	5.7	6.1	39.7	6.9	4.1	17.2	6.6	4.4
1979	14.8	5.6	6.5	39.3	7.4	4.3	17.8	6.6	4.4

A6 NORTH AMERICA: Vital Statistics: Rates per 1,000 Population

1930–1979

	Guatemala			Honduras[7]			Jamaica		
	B	D	M	B	D	M	B	D	M
1930	56.8	24.7	2.8	37.4	16.1	3.3	37.5	17.3	4.2
1931	54.7	24.3	2.4	38.6	15.4	2.7	35.3	18.9	3.5
1932	50.3	23.6	2.1	...	14.9	...	32.7	17.4	3.7
1933	47.5	27.3	2.1	31.8	14.5	3.9	33.4	19.7	3.3
1934	47.0	30.6	2.2	32.7	13.8	2.3	31.7	17.3	3.9
1935	48.1	27.4	2.3	34.5	13.9	2.9	34.1	18.0	4.2
1936	47.8	24.7	2.0	31.5	16.6	2.6	32.9	17.7	3.9
1937	46.5	24.4	2.2	36.2[7]	18.0[7]	3.0[7]	31.5	15.6	4.6
1938	46.4	26.3	2.5	...	16.3	...	33.3	16.8	4.7
1939	47.4	29.6	2.8	37.5	15.9	2.8	32.3	15.1	4.6
1940	48.2	25.0	2.2	37.1	15.9	3.0	30.8	15.4	3.9
1941	43.8	25.1	2.1	37.3	16.7	2.6	31.4	14.4	4.6
1942	42.6	31.5	2.1	36.7	18.5	2.5	32.7	14.3	4.8
1943	42.2	31.1	2.4	36.3	18.5	2.6	31.5	14.1	4.4
1944	42.2	26.5	2.8	36.3	16.9	3.3	33.2	15.1	5.1
1945	42.9	24.5	2.9	36.5	16.0	3.0	30.0	14.9	5.0
1946	48.2	24.7	3.2	37.9	14.5	3.1	30.8	13.3	5.8
1947	52.2	24.7	2.9	38.8	13.7	3.4	31.9	14.1	4.5
1948	51.9	23.5	3.0	39.5	14.0	3.4	30.7	13.2	4.1
1949	51.6	21.8	3.4	40.0[7]	13.3[7]	3.5[7]	32.3	12.3	4.3
1950	50.9	21.8	3.7	39.9	11.8	3.7	33.5	11.9	4.6
1951	52.3	19.6	3.7	41.0	11.1	4.0	34.6	12.3	4.5
1952	50.9	24.2	3.8	39.7	12.5	4.2	34.3	11.7	4.6
1953	50.9	23.0	3.8	41.7	11.6	32.3	10.6	4.9	
1954	51.3	18.3	4.1	41.7	11.1	4.3	36.4	11.1	5.2
1955	48.6	20.5	3.7	43.0	11.3	3.4	37.5	10.3	5.9
1956	48.4	19.7	4.8	40.7	10.1	4.1	37.2	9.7	6.3
1957	49.0	20.4	4.9	43.2	10.4	3.8	37.9	9.2	6.3
1958	48.2	21.1	4.7	43.1	11.1	3.7	39.0	9.5	5.2
1959	49.2	17.1	5.2	42.0	9.5	9.6	40.0	10.3	5.3
1960	48.9	17.3	4.4	42.3	9.3	3.9	42.0	8.8	6.0
1961	49.3	16.1	4.0	42.5	8.9	3.1	40.2	8.6	5.4
1962	47.3	17.1	3.6	44.0	8.9	3.3	39.1	8.5	5.0
1963	47.2	17.1	3.7	43.2	9.0	3.0	39.0	8.9	4.8
1964	45.5	15.9	3.6	44.9	9.2	3.4	39.3	7.6	4.8
1965	45.3	16.9	3.4	43.3	8.5	3.5	39.6	8.0	4.6
1966	45.2	16.6	3.6	42.1	8.6	3.3	40.0	8.0	4.2
1967	41.8	15.2	3.6	41.6	8.0	3.2	37.3	7.4	4.3
1968	42.6	16.4	3.4	42.1	8.1	3.5	35.7	7.9	4.5
1969	42.2	17.2	3.6	41.1	8.5	3.0	35.1	7.6	4.8
1970	40.4	14.7	3.6	40.6	7.7	3.7	34.4	7.7	4.8
1971	42.0	13.9	3.7	43.2	7.5	3.1	34.9	7.6	4.4
1972	43.6	12.2	3.9	43.6	7.7	3.3	34.3	7.2	4.6
1973	41.8	12.1	4.0	41.9	7.2	3.8	31.4	7.2	4.5
1974	43.1	11.5	4.2	42.2	6.5	3.8	30.6	7.2	4.3
1975	41.4	12.6	3.9	41.9	6.2	3.6	30.0	6.9	5.0
1976	43.1	13.2	4.3	43.2	5.7	4.3	29.6	7.0	4.4
1977	44.7	11.3	4.4	43.9	5.6	4.2	28.6	6.8	4.1
1978	43.8	10.2	4.3	...	...	4.1	27.7	5.9	4.5
1979	44.0	10.7	4.2	...	...	4.0	27.7	6.2	4.2

A6   NORTH AMERICA: Vital Statistics: Rates per 1,000 Population

	Martinique			Mexico			Newfoundland			Panama[8]		
	B	D	M	B	D	M	B	D	M	B	D	M
1930	...	...	...	39.4	26.6	6.1	23.8	14.0	5.9	31.6	13.1	2.9
1931	...	...	...	43.8	25.9	5.9	23.3	13.4	5.6	41.5	16.4	2.3
1932	...	...	...	43.3	26.1	5.6	24.0	12.7	5.5	38.6	15.8	2.2
1933	...	...	...	42.2	25.7	5.8	23.4	12.1	5.6	33.6	15.6	3.1
1934	...	...	...	44.3	23.8	6.7	23.5	12.1	6.5	37.1	15.7	3.4
1935	...	...	...	42.3	22.6	6.6	23.0	13.5	6.6	32.0	11.9	3.6
1936	...	...	...	43.0	23.5	6.5	25.2	13.0	6.7	38.5	12.7	3.7
1937	...	...	...	44.1	24.4	6.9	25.0	13.5	7.1	38.0	13.1	5.0
1938	...	...	...	43.5	22.9	6.9	24.8	12.1	7.3	45.5	14.2	3.6
1939	...	...	...	44.6	23.0	6.9	27.5	11.7	8.4	27.9	11.4	3.5
1940	...	...	...	44.3	23.2	7.9	26.3	11.8	7.7	...	...	...
1941	...	...	...	43.5	22.1	6.2	27.3	12.5	8.8	37.4	13.3	5.6
1942	...	...	...	45.5	22.8	8.5	28.6	12.3	10.6	37.0	12.8	4.5
1943	...	...	...	45.5	22.4	7.5	28.3	11.4	8.7	37.7	13.0	3.5
1944	...	...	...	44.2	20.6	6.8	29.4	12.3	9.5	37.8	12.3	4.0
1945	...	...	...	44.9	19.5	6.7	34.9	10.4	9.8	37.7	11.8	4.6
1946	...	20.5	...	43.7	19.4	5.9	36.5	10.4	9.3	37.0	11.2	4.1
1947	...	21.3	...	46.1	16.6	5.8	37.5	9.9	8.7	37.2[8]	11.7[8]	3.5
1948	35.6	18.9	...	45.2	16.9	6.4	33.8	9.0	7.6	32.8	9.4	3.3
1949	36.9	17.0	...	45.2	17.9	6.6	35.6	8.3	7.1	30.2	9.0	3.3
1950	38.0	13.5	6.0	45.5	16.2	6.9	**incorporated**			31.3	9.0	3.4
1951	38.7	14.8	5.8	44.6	17.3	6.7	**in**			30.5	8.1	3.5
1952	37.9	13.9	5.6	43.8	15.0	6.9	**Canada**			34.5	8.1	3.3
1953	40.2	10.5	7.7	45.0	15.9	6.4				36.2	8.8	3.5
1954	40.0	10.5	5.3	46.4	13.1	7.0				37.3	8.4	3.9
1955	39.6	10.8	5.5	45.1	13.3	6.9				37.6	8.8	3.4
1956	40.1	10.0	5.4	45.2	11.7	7.1				37.6	8.8	3.4
1957	40.7	9.8	5.4	45.5	12.7	6.5				38.8	8.9	3.3
1958	38.7	10.4	4.9	42.9	12.0	6.6				37.7	8.3	5.5
1959	38.2	8.6	5.5	45.6	11.4	6.8				39.1	8.7	14.4
1960	37.4	9.4	5.6	44.6	11.2	6.9				39.1	8.7	3.4
1961	36.6	7.9	5.4	43.8	10.3	6.3				39.5	8.0	3.4
1962	36.2	8.6	5.2	43.9	10.4	6.4				40.0	7.8	3.3
1963	34.7	8.3	5.4	43.8	10.3	6.5				39.5	7.0	3.7
1964	34.4	8.0	5.3	44.6	9.8	6.8				38.9	7.3	3.7
1965	35.0	7.8	5.1	44.1	9.4	6.9				38.4	7.1	3.8
1966	32.1	7.7	5.0	44.1	9.6	7.0				38.8	7.2	3.9
1967	30.9	7.4	5.2	43.2	9.2	6.9				37.3	6.8	4.0
1968	30.6	7.0	5.2	44.3	9.6	7.0				37.4	7.1	4.1
1969	27.4	7.5	5.2	42.6	9.4	7.1				36.5	7.0	4.9
1970	28.5	7.6	5.4	42.1	9.6	7.0				35.8	7.1	5.0
1971	28.2	6.8	5.1	42.5	8.7	7.2				35.9	6.7	5.0
1972	26.4	7.0	4.6	43.2	8.8	7.8				34.9	6.0	4.8
1973	23.4	7.2	4.9	45.8	8.2	8.1				32.2	5.8	4.6
1974	21.3	7.4	4.3	43.4	7.5	8.0				31.8	5.6	4.7
1975	20.5	6.8	4.5	37.5	7.2	7.8				31.6	5.2	4.9
1976	17.9	...	3.9	34.6	7.4	7.7				30.3	5.2	4.7
1977	16.5	6.6	3.8	37.6	7.1	7.3				29.4	4.8	5.0
1978	15.5	6.7	4.0	35.7	6.4	7.0				28.9	3.9	5.0
1979	16.7	6.5	4.0	36.3	6.3	6.8				28.2	...	5.4

A6   NORTH AMERICA: Vital Statistics: Rates per 1,000 Population

	Puerto Rico			Trinidad & Tobago			USA				
	B	D	M	B	D	M	B		D		M
							whites	negroes[6]	whites	negroes[6]	
1930	35.2	20.4	6.4	31.4	19.1	4.5	20.6	27.5	10.8	16.3	9.2
1931	45.3	22.3	6.1	30.0	20.1	4.0	19.5	26.6	10.6	15.5	8.6
1932	41.1	22.0	5.5	29.0	17.1	4.3	18.7	26.9	10.5	14.5	7.9
1933	37.4	22.3	5.8	31.1	19.6	4.6	17.6	25.5	10.3	14.1	8.7
1934	39.1	18.9	7.3	29.8	18.6	4.5	18.1	26.3	10.6	14.8	10.3
1935	39.5	18.0	6.6	33.0	17.5	4.7	17.9	25.8	10.6	14.3	10.4
1936	39.6	20.0	7.9	33.1	16.3	4.7	17.6	25.1	11.1	15.4	10.7
1937	38.2	20.9	7.9	31.6	17.4	5.8	17.9	26.0	10.8	14.9	11.3
1938	38.6	18.7	5.1	33.0	15.9	6.1	18.4	26.3	10.3	14.0	10.3
1939	39.6	17.7	5.8	31.1	16.1	6.5	18.0	26.1	10.3	13.5	10.7
1940	38.6	18.3	10.3	34.7	15.8	6.6	18.6	26.7	10.4	13.8	12.1
1941	39.8	18.3	7.8	33.5	16.1	7.2	19.5	27.3	10.2	13.5	12.7
1942	40.2	16.2	8.1	34.7	17.7	10.0	21.5	27.7	10.1	12.7	13.2
1943	38.7	14.3	7.1	38.5	16.6	8.0	22.1	28.3	10.7	12.8	11.7
1944	40.6	14.4	7.9	39.0	15.0	7.2	20.5	27.4	10.4	12.4	10.9
1945	41.9	13.7	8.3	39.5	14.5	6.2	19.7	26.5	10.4	11.9	12.2
1946	41.6	12.9	9.5	38.8	13.8	5.8	23.6	38.4	9.8	11.1	16.4
1947	42.2	11.8	7.8	38.3	13.4	5.6	26.1	31.2	9.9	11.4	13.9
1948	40.2	12.0	7.0	39.9	12.2	5.8	24.0	32.4	9.7	11.4	12.4
1949	39.0	10.6	7.4	37.2	12.2	6.1	23.6	33.0	9.5	11.2	10.6
1950	38.8	9.9	9.3	37.5	12.1	6.0	23.0	33.3	9.5	11.2	11.1
1951	37.6	10.0	8.1	36.7	12.0	6.5	23.9	33.8	9.5	11.1	10.4
1952	36.1	9.2	8.2	34.6	12.1	6.5	24.1	33.6	9.4	11.0	9.9
1953	35.3	8.2	9.0	37.7	10.7	7.0	24.0	34.1	9.4	10.8	9.8
1954	35.2	7.6	8.8	41.9	9.8	6.7	24.2	34.9	9.1	10.1	9.2
1955	34.6	7.2	8.4	41.9	10.4	6.5	23.8	34.7	9.2	10.0	9.3
1956	34.8	7.4	8.4	37.0	9.6	7.0	24.0	35.4	9.3	10.1	9.5
1957	33.7	7.1	8.5	37.7	9.5	6.1	24.0	35.3	9.5	10.5	8.9
1958	33.2	7.0	8.7	37.6	9.2	7.5	23.3₉	34.3₉	9.4₉	10.3₉	8.4₉
1959	32.4	6.8	8.7	37.4	9.2	6.8	22.9₁₀	32.9₁₀	9.3₁₀	9.9₁₀	8.5₁₀
1960	32.4	6.7	8.6	39.5	7.9	7.1	22.7	32.1	9.5	10.1	8.5
1961	31.4	6.8	8.9	37.9	8.1	6.8	22.2	31.6	9.3	9.6	8.5
1962	31.3	6.7	9.0	37.9	7.2	6.3	21.4	30.5	9.4	9.8	8.5
1963	31.0	6.9	9.2	35.6	7.2	6.0	20.7	29.7	9.5	10.1	8.8
1964	31.0	7.2	9.2	34.6	7.0	6.6	20.0	29.1	9.4	9.7	9.0
1965	30.7	6.8	10.4	32.8	6.9	6.0	18.3	27.6	9.4	9.6	9.3
1966	28.9	6.7	9.7	30.2	7.1	5.6	17.4	26.1	9.5	9.7	9.5
1967	26.9	6.3	10.0	28.2	6.7	5.4	16.8	25.0	9.4	9.4	9.7
1968	25.6	6.5	10.1	27.5	7.0	5.6	16.6	24.2	9.6	9.9	10.4
1969	25.0	6.5	11.0	24.4	6.9	6.1	16.9	24.4	9.5	9.6	10.6
1970	24.9	6.7	10.7	26.2	6.8	6.3	17.4	25.1	9.5	9.4	10.6
1971	25.8	6.5	11.7	26.5	6.8	6.5	16.2	24.7	9.3	9.2	11.0
1972	24.1	6.6	11.7	28.2	7.0	7.0	14.6	22.9	9.5	9.2	10.9
1973	24.0	6.5	11.9	26.6	7.1	6.6	13.9	21.9	9.4	9.1	10.8
1974	24.3	6.4	11.6	26.2	6.3	6.6	14.0	21.4	9.2	8.7	10.5
1975	23.9	6.1	11.2	25.4	6.4	7.0	13.6	20.7	8.9	8.8	10.0
1976	24.3	6.6	11.2	26.5	7.2	7.4	13.8	21.1	9.0	8.2	9.9
1977	24.5	6.5	11.3	26.9	7.1	7.3	14.1	21.4	8.7	8.6	9.9
1978	24.1	6.4	10.7	27.0	6.5	7.4	14.0	21.3	8.8	8.6	10.3
1979	23.4	6.4	10.7	27.9	6.6	8.0	14.5	22.0	8.7	8.4	10.4

A6 NORTH AMERICA: Vital Statistics: Rates per 1,000 Population

	Barbados			Canada			Costa Rica			Cuba		
	B	D	M	B	D	M	B	D	M	B	D	M
1980	16.7	8.1	4.2	15.4	7.1	7.9	29.4	4.1	7.8	14.1	5.7	7.1
1981	17.7	7.5	4.8	15.3	7.0	7.8	29.8	4.0	7.3	14.0	5.9	7.5
1982	18.0	8.0	4.9	15.1	7.1	7.6	30.7	3.9	8.0	16.3	5.8	8.2
1983	17.9	8.2	5.0	15.0	7.0	7.4	30.0	3.9	7.9	16.7	5.9	7.7
1984	16.8	7.8	4.6	15.1	7.0	7.4	31.4	4.1	8.5	16.6	6.0	7.6
1985	16.9	8.4	4.7	14.9	7.2	7.3	33.9	4.2	...	18.0	6.4	8.0
1986	15.9	8.5	5.8	14.7	7.3	6.9	...	3.8	...	16.3	6.2	8.3
1987	15.1	8.7	6.0	14.4	7.2	7.1	28.9	3.8	7.8	17.4	6.3	7.7
1988	14.8	8.8	8.1	14.5	7.3	7.2	28.5	3.8	8.0	18.0	6.5	7.9
1989	15.7	8.9	8.0	14.9	7.3	7.3	28.6	3.9	7.9	17.6	6.4	8.1
1990	16.8	8.7	7.4	15.2	7.2	7.1	29.2	4.1	8.1	17.6	6.8	9.6
1991	16.4	8.8	7.7	14.6	7.0	5.8	28.2	4.1	7.8	16.2	6.7	13.1
1992	15.9	9.1	7.8	14.6	6.9	5.5	27.3	4.2	7.0	14.5	7.0	17.7
1993	14.3	...	...	13.4	7.1	5.4	...	...	7.2	14.0	7.2	

	El Salvador			Guadeloupe			Guatemala			Jamaica		
	B	D	M	B	D	M	B	D	M	B	D	M
1980	37.7	8.6	5.3	19.7	6.5	4.9	43.9	10.3	4.5	26.9	5.8	3.6
1981	35.6	8.2	4.6	19.8	6.5	4.8	43.4	10.6	4.5	26.8	6.1	3.2
1982	33.6	7.1	4.4	20.2	6.4	4.8	42.7	10.4	4.3	26.9	4.9	4.0
1983	30.5	6.9	4.1	20.4	6.7	4.8	40.8	9.9	3.8	27.1	5.5	3.7
1984	29.8	6.0	3.5	20.2	6.8	5.0	40.3	8.5	4.3	25.2	5.9	4.6
1985	...	...	3.8	20.3	6.9	4.8	41.0	8.7	4.8	24.3	6.0	5.1
1986	...	...	3.9	19.2	6.7	5.1	39.0	8.5	...	23.1	5.7	4.6
1987	...	...	...	19.5	7.3	...	38.5	7.9	5.3	22.2	5.3	4.6
1988	...	...	...	...	...	...	39.3	7.5	5.4	22.8	5.2	4.4
1989	...	...	4.0	...	...	...	38.6	7.2	5.1	24.7	6.0	4.7
1990	...	...	4.3	...	...	...	38.3	7.9	5.1	24.7	5.0	5.4
1991	...	...	4.2	19.1	5.4	4.9	37.1	6.8	5.0	25.3	5.6	5.6
1992	...	...	4.2	17.9	5.6	4.7	...	...	...	23.5	5.5	5.4
1993	33.5	7.1	...	...	...	...	...	7.7	...	...	5.8	...

	Martinique			Mexico			Panama			Puerto Rico		
	B	D	M	B	D	M	B	D	M	B	D	M
1980	16.4	6.6	3.6	4.9	6.3	7.2	26.9	...	5.2	22.8	6.4	10.3
1981	16.6	6.3	3.7	35.5	6.0	6.7	26.9	...	5.2	22.0	6.5	9.8
1982	16.5	6.5	4.0	32.8	5.7	7.2	26.7	...	5.5	21.3	6.6	9.3
1983	17.3	6.8	4.1	35.0	5.5	6.8	26.4	...	5.4	20.1	6.6	9.1
1984	17.5	6.3	4.0	32.9	5.4	6.7	26.5	...	5.7	19.4	6.6	9.1
1985	17.3	6.5	4.0	34.1	5.3	7.3	26.6	...	5.7	19.4	7.0	9.2
1986	17.9	6.3	4.6	...	...	7.3	25.9	4.0	5.4	19.4	7.1	...
1987	18.9	6.4	4.6	34.4	5.8	7.4	25.3	4.0	4.9	19.5	7.3	10.1
1988	19.0	6.2	4.6	31.7	...	7.6	24.8	4.0	5.2	19.5	7.6	9.8
1989	18.4	6.1	4.4	31.1	5.0	7.5	24.9	4.0	4.7	19.1	7.4	9.0
1990	17.8	6.1	4.3	33.7	4.9	7.5	25.0	4.1	5.2	18.9	7.4	9.4
1991	17.2	5.9	4.4	32.3	4.7	7.4	24.6	3.9	4.8	18.2	7.4	9.4
1992	16.9	5.8	4.4	32.2	4.6	7.5	23.6	3.5	5.0	18.0	7.7	9.6
1993	...	...	...	27.7	4.6	7.2	22.8	3.5	5.2	18.0	7.9	...

A6 NORTH AMERICA: Vital Statistics: Rates per 1,000 Population

	Trinidad & Tobago			USA				
	B	D	M	B		D		M
				whites	negroes	whites	negroes	
1980	27.6	6.9	8.2	14.9	22.1	8.9	8.8	10.6
1981	28.9	6.6	7.4	14.8	21.6	8.8	8.4	10.6
1982	28.8	6.8	8.4	14.9	21.4	8.7	8.2	10.6
1983	29.2	6.6	7.5	14.6	20.9	8.8	8.3	10.5
1984	27.0	6.7	7.2	14.8	20.1	8.9	8.4	10.5
1985	28.6	6.8	6.7	15.0	20.4	9.0	8.5	10.1
1986	26.6	6.4	7.6	14.8	20.5	9.0	8.6	10.0
1987	24.1	6.6	6.3	14.9	20.8	9.0	8.7	9.9
1988	22.5	6.6	6.0	15.0	21.5	9.1	8.9	9.7
1989	20.7	6.8	5.6	15.4	22.3	8.9	8.9	9.8
1990	18.9	6.7	5.4	15.8	22.4	8.9	8.8	9.4
1991	18.2	6.6	5.7	15.4	21.9	8.9	8.6	9.3
1992	18.6	6.8	5.3	15.0	21.3	8.8	8.5	9.0
1993	16.9	6.5	5.5	14.7	20.5	9.1	8.8	9.1

International Historical Statistics: The Americas 1750–1993

A6 SOUTH AMERICA: VITAL STATISTICS: RATES PER 1,000 POPULATION

1848–1889

	Chile			Uruguay		
	B	D	M	B	D	M
1848	36.8	...	6.9	...	...	...
1849	37.4	...	6.8	...	...	...
1850	41.3	18.8	7.2	...	...	...
1851	38.5	20.5	6.8	...	...	...
1852	40.9	19.5	7.8	...	...	...
1853	44.7	22.9	7.8	...	...	...
1854	43.3	21.7	7.4	...	...	...
1855	44.7	21.1	7.5	...	...	...
1856	45.5	22.7	8.3	...	...	...
1857	44.8	24.5	7.5	...	...	...
1858	41.6	22.3	6.8	...	...	...
1859	41.6	25.0	6.6	...	...	...
1860	47.6	28.9	6.9	...	...	...
1861	39.6	27.0	6.5	...	...	...
1862	40.8	24.4	6.2	...	...	...
1863	40.8	26.8	6.2	...	...	...
1864	42.3	34.6	6.1	...	...	...
1865	36.0	29.4	5.9	...	...	...
1866	38.4	25.5	5.7	...	...	...
1867	39.5	25.7	6.2	...	...	...
1868	41.3	23.4	6.8	...	...	...
1869	42.1	26.1	7.1	...	...	...
1870	42.3	24.7	7.0	...	...	...
1871	41.5	25.4	7.2	...	...	...
1872	44.1	29.2	8.0	...	...	...
1873	44.9	28.2	8.7	...	...	...
1874	44.7	27.6	8.2	...	...	...
1875	42.6	28.3	8.2	...	...	...
1876	40.6	30.2	7.2	...	...	...
1877	38.9	29.4	6.4	...	...	...
1878	36.5	28.0	6.1	...	...	...
1879	40.6	27.7	6.6	...	...	...
1880	38.2	31.2	6.3	...	...	...
1881	44.4	27.4	7.0	...	...	...
1882	40.2	28.0	7.2	43.0	18.1	6.7
1883	40.6	25.7	7.2	42.6	16.3	6.6
1884	41.1	24.2	7.3	38.9	17.3	6.3
1885	25.0	27.0	2.1	40.7	16.7	6.2
1886	29.0	26.7	2.4	41.5	18.3	5.2
1887	29.4	31.6	2.7	42.1	20.2	5.9
1888	32.1	3.3	42.0	18.8	6.4	
1889	38.0	34.7	4.4	41.6	19.1	6.4

A6 SOUTH AMERICA: Vital Statistics: Rates per 1,000 Population

	Argentina			Chile			Colombia		
	B	D	M	B	D	M	B	D	M
1890	...	...	...	37.9	36.7	4.2	...	...	...
1891	...	...	...	30.3	34.1	2.6	...	...	...
1892	...	...	...	39.3	37.6	4.8	...	...	...
1893	...	...	...	39.2	34.3	5.2	...	...	...
1894	...	...	...	41.1	33.7	5.7	...	...	...
1895	...	...	...	39.1	31.4	5.1	...	...	...
1896	...	...	...	37.6	30.5	5.8	...	...	...
1897	...	...	...	39.6	31.2	4.9	...	...	...
1898	...	...	...	37.4	29.1	5.0	...	...	...
1899	...	...	...	37.6	29.5	4.7	...	...	...
1900	...	...	...	38.4	36.0	4.6	...	...	...
1901	...	...	...	39.3	36.7	6.0	...	...	...
1902	...	...	...	38.7	28.8	5.6	...	...	...
1903	...	...	...	38.0	28.4	5.2	...	...	...
1904	...	...	...	37.9	28.1	5.3	...	...	...
1905	...	...	...	38.2	35.2	5.5	...	...	...
1906	...	...	...	36.9	33.0	5.8	...	...	...
1907	...	...	...	38.8	29.7	6.5	...	...	...
1908	...	...	...	39.7	31.9	6.6	...	...	...
1909	...	...	...	39.1	31.7	5.9	...	...	...
1910	38.3	18.9	7.3	38.9	31.7	5.8	...	...	...
1911	37.9	18.2	7.1	39.4	31.9	5.9	...	...	...
1912	38.6	17.0	7.4	39.5	30.4	6.2	...	...	...
1913	38.0	16.2	7.2	40.6	31.0	6.2	...	...	...
1914	36.7	15.4	6.0	39.0	28.6	5.4	...	...	...
1915	35.3	15.8	5.8	38.6	27.3	5.4	28.3	18.6	4.4
1916	35.3	17.1	5.9	40.3	27.9	5.6	...	...	...
1917	33.6	16.1	5.5	41.2	29.6	5.9	...	...	...
1918	32.9	18.2	5.9	36.9	27.5	5.5	...	...	...
1919	32.7	18.4	6.3	35.9	34.1	5.3	...	...	...
1920	32.3	15.5	7.1	39.1	30.7	6.6	...	...	4.8
1921	32.8	15.8	6.9	39.0	32.7	6.6	...	...	4.1
1922	33.1	14.0	7.1	38.4	28.4	6.5	27.5	15.0	4.1
1923	34.0	14.8	7.2	39.2	32.8	6.7	26.6	13.6	4.2
1924	32.8	14.3	7.4	39.7	29.2	8.4	25.5	12.9	4.3
1925	31.8	14.1	...	40.0	27.8	7.3	26.4	13.0	5.0
1926	31.2	13.6	...	40.0	27.2	7.6	27.7	14.4	5.3
1927	30.7	14.1	7.5	41.5	26.3	7.8	27.5	14.5	4.9
1928	30.8	13.2	7.6	52.2	23.7	11.1	29.5	13.7	5.1
1929	30.2	13.8	7.7	41.2	25.8	9.8	30.4	13.1	5.1
1930	29.5	12.7	6.9	39.8	24.7	9.2	28.1	13.3	3.9
1931	28.5	12.7	6.4	34.6	22.0	6.7	27.1	12.1	3.8
1932	28.1	11.1	6.0	34.0	22.8	6.6	22.2	9.8	3.9
1933	26.1	11.8	5.9	33.1	26.8	6.7	28.4	15.5	4.1
1934	25.5	11.7	6.3	33.2	26.8	7.0	29.9	15.6	4.6
1935	25.2	13.1	6.6	33.3	25.0	7.3	30.1	15.3	4.6
1936	24.5	11.9	6.6	33.5	25.3	7.5	29.5	15.5	4.6
1937	24.1	12.0	6.8	32.3	24.0	8.3	30.8	15.4	5.0
1938	24.3	12.4	6.5	32.1	24.5	8.1	32.2	17.3	4.9
1939	24.1	11.3	6.8	33.3	24.6	9.6	31.5	17.6	5.0

A6   SOUTH AMERICA: Vital Statistics: Rates per 1,000 Population

1890–1939

	Guyana			Uruguay			Venezuela		
	B	D	M	B	D	M	B	D	M
1890	...	...	...	40.7	21.2	5.9	...	...	...
1891	26.6	37.4	...	40.6	17.1	4.9	36.6	23.2	2.8
1892	28.0	39.8	...	39.6	17.0	4.7	36.3	23.1	2.8
1893	27.3	35.5	...	37.6	17.2	4.6	35.6	22.7	2.5
1894	24.8	33.4	...	38.1	18.5	4.9	35.5	20.4	1.8
1895	28.9	29.5	...	39.2	15.6	5.8	...	...	...
1896	32.5	26.3	...	37.8	15.6	5.0	...	...	...
1897	33.6	27.9	...	32.1	14.5	3.3	...	...	...
1898	29.7	33.9	...	33.6	14.4	5.0	...	...	...
1899	28.8	29.1	...	34.3	12.8	5.0	...	...	...
1900	36.7	25.1	...	32.6	13.7	4.8	...	...	...
1901	35.9	23.6	...	32.8	12.9	4.6	...	...	...
1902	33.4	28.1	...	31.8	13.6	4.6	...	...	...
1903	29.0	28.9	...	32.0	13.4	4.7	...	...	...
1904	30.3	28.8	...	26.0	11.1	2.6	28.4	19.8	2.6
1905	33.6	27.4	...	31.5	12.7	5.6	27.7	23.4	2.2
1906	32.9	28.8	...	29.5	13.7	5.7	28.1	21.3	2.5
1907	28.3	36.9	...	30.5	14.1	5.7	29.3	20.6	2.4
1908	27.3	30.8	...	33.6	13.6	5.8	27.8	22.3	2.4
1909	29.3	30.0	...	32.5	13.9	6.2	28.1	20.7	2.3
1910	27.5	34.4	...	31.7	14.5	6.1	31.8	21.3	2.4
1911	28.8	31.7	...	31.8	14.0	6.0	32.0	21.2	3.1
1912	33.1	29.2	...	31.9	13.6	6.3	28.7	24.9	3.5
1913	34.6	24.2	...	32.2	12.3	5.8	28.8	19.9	3.7
1914	34.4	27.4	...	29.7	11.8	4.7	28.3	19.3	2.8
1915	31.3	27.7	...	28.6	12.8	4.3	27.7	23.3	2.5
1916	26.5	27.1	...	27.1	14.9	4.3	27.4	24.3	2.5
1917	28.4	30.4	...	26.4	12.5	4.5	28.2	21.0	3.1
1918	25.1	40.6	...	27.4	14.1	4.8	27.4	24.5	4.6
1919	26.0	40.4	...	27.2	13.1	5.2	29.7	22.2	6.1
1920	32.9	26.5	...	26.6	12.9	5.6	26.3	19.4	5.3
1921	34.5	30.9	...	26.2	12.2	5.2	25.2	21.1	2.7
1922	27.8	29.1	3.6	26.0	10.6	4.9	26.6	19.7	2.9
1923	30.4	28.3	3.9	25.4	11.4	5.3	28.3	18.8	3.7
1924	32.4	25.6	3.4	25.8	11.8	5.7	27.9	18.5	3.2
1925	33.5	24.2	3.9	25.1	11.5	5.6	32.4	17.5	3.9
1926	34.7	25.5	3.6	25.4	10.5	5.6	30.7	22.2	5.7
1927	32.6	26.0	3.6	24.6	11.5	5.9	30.1	19.5	4.6
1928	28.3	27.9	3.5	25.0	10.7	6.2	30.2	18.8	4.0
1929	31.7	23.5	3.3	24.2	10.8	6.4	30.2	17.2	3.8
1930	33.8	23.2	3.3	24.4	10.7	6.3	29.7	17.2	3.2
1931	31.6	22.0	3.2	23.3	11.0	5.8	28.1	18.4	2.8
1932	34.3	21.2	3.7	22.5	10.1	5.1	28.4	17.1	3.1
1933	32.8	24.6	4.1	21.0	10.3	4.8	27.9	18.5	2.6
1934	29.0	24.8	3.8	20.6	10.0	5.3	27.0	18.1	3.0
1935	34.7	20.8	4.3	20.4	10.6	5.6	27.8	16.6	2.7
1936	35.7	20.6	4.4	19.8	9.7	5.9	31.9	17.4	3.1
1937	33.8	22.1	4.3	19.9	10.4	6.7	33.7	18.1	4.0
1938	29.9	25.8	4.2	19.8	10.3	7.0	33.7	18.3	4.0
1939	28.3	19.8	4.7	20.1	9.1	7.0	35.9	18.7	4.4

A6 SOUTH AMERICA: Vital Statistics: Rates per 1,000 Population

	Argentina			Chile			Colombia		
	B	D	M	B	D	M	B	D	M
1940	24.0	10.7	6.5	33.4	22.9	9.0	32.2	15.2	4.8
1941	23.7	10.4	6.8	32.6	19.6	8.3	32.7	15.5	5.3
1942	23.3	10.3	7.1	33.1	19.9	8.3	33.1	16.0	5.4
1943	24.2	10.1	7.4	33.1	19.3	8.1	32.1	17.1	5.3
1944	25.2	10.2	7.9	33.2	18.9	8.0	32.2	16.4	5.4
1945	25.2	10.3	8.0	33.3	19.3	7.7	31.7	15.7	5.2
1946	24.7	9.6	8.0	36.2	16.6	7.5	32.8	15.5	5.3
1947	25.0	9.9	8.7	36.0	16.1	7.9	33.8	14.4	5.2
1948	25.3	9.4	8.6	35.3	16.7	7.9	34.9	14.2	5.3
1949	25.1	9.0	8.4	34.7	17.3	7.8	35.1	14.0	5.0
1950	25.5	9.0	8.3	34.0	15.0	7.5	36.5	14.2	5.6
1951	25.2	8.9	8.1	33.9	15.0	7.3	36.1	14.2	5.3
1952	24.7	8.6	7.6	32.6	13.0	8.1	36.4	12.8	5.6
1953	25.0	8.9	7.9	34.5	12.4	8.4	38.1	13.2	5.7
1954	24.7	8.4	7.7	33.4	12.8	8.2	37.2	11.8	6.0
1955	24.4	8.9	7.5	34.9	12.9	8.8	38.8	12.3	5.9
1956	24.6	8.4	7.5	34.3	12.1	8.4	39.6	12.7	5.9
1957	24.4	9.2	7.5	37.1	12.8	7.6	40.1	12.4	5.9
1958	23.7	8.3	7.4	36.3	12.2	7.3	40.5	12.0	5.8
1959	23.5	8.5	7.3	36.1	12.6	7.5	40.7	11.8	5.9
1960	22.9	8.7	7.0	34.4	12.4	7.4	38.8	11.9	6.0
1961	22.8	8.4	6.8	34.7	11.6	7.4	39.4	11.0	6.1
1962	23.1	8.6	6.5	36.3	11.8	6.9	39.6	10.8	5.9
1963	22.8	8.6	6.2	34.0	12.0	7.0	39.3	10.4	5.4
1964	22.7	8.7	6.9	33.1	11.2	7.3	38.6	10.0	...
1965	21.7	8.9	6.9	32.3	10.5	7.6	36.9	9.9	...
1966	21.3	8.6	6.7	30.9	10.2	7.6	35.9	9.5	...
1967	21.1	8.6	6.6	31.6	9.5	7.4	35.3	9.5	...
1968	21.3	9.2	6.7	27.2	9.0	7.2	32.0	8.7	...
1969	24.8	9.5	...	25.7	8.8	7.3	34.6	7.7	...
1970	22.7	9.4	7.7	27.6	8.5	7.6	...	6.6	5.4
1971	22.8	9.3	7.8	28.1	8.8	8.9	37.8	6.9	5.0
1972	22.4	9.0	7.5	27.4	9.0	8.8	34.4	7.5	4.8
1973	22.6	9.1	7.6	26.8	8.2	8.5	33.2	9.1	5.6
1974	23.5	9.0	8.0	25.9	7.8	8.0	32.2	9.0	5.8
1975	23.8	8.8	7.7	24.2	7.3	7.5	31.1	9.0	6.2
1976	23.9	9.1	7.5	23.0	7.4	7.1	30.0	9.0	...
1977	24.7	8.7	6.9	21.4	7.0	7.0	30.4	...	7.0
1978	24.3	8.4	6.6	21.3	6.7	7.2	30.2	...	...
1979	24.8	8.5	6.3	21.4	6.8	7.3	29.9	...	...
1980	24.7	8.5	5.9	22.2	6.7	7.7	29.7	...	...
1981	23.7	8.4	5.6	23.4	6.2	8.0	28.8	...	...
1982	22.8	8.0	...	23.8	6.1	7.0	27.9	...	...
1983	22.5	8.2	6.0	22.2	8.4	7.0	27.7	...	...
1984	22.0	8.5	...	22.2	6.3	7.3	27.6	...	...
1985	22.6	8.0	...	21.6	6.1	7.5	27.4	...	...
1986	22.1	7.9	...	22.1	5.9	7.6	...	...	...
1987	21.3	8.0	...	22.3	5.6	7.6	...	...	...
1988	20.7	8.4	...	23.3	5.8	8.1	...	...	...
1989	20.8	7.9	...	23.4	5.8	8.0	...	...	...
1990	20.9	8.0	5.7	22.4	6.0	7.5	...	...	...
1991	21.1	7.8	...	21.6	5.6	6.9	...	...	...
1992	20.3	7.9	...	21.0	5.4	6.6	...	...	...
1993	19.8	7.9	...	21.7	5.5	6.7	24.0	5.9	...

A6   SOUTH AMERICA: Vital Statistics: Rates per 1,000 Population

1940-1993

	Guyana*			Uruguay			Venezuela		
	B	D	M	B	D	M	B	D	M
1940	35.0	18.6	4.3	19.9	9.6	6.7	36.0	16.6	4.6
1941	35.8	15.7	5.2	20.4	9.4	7.4	35.3	16.4	4.2
1942	38.8	17.4	6.1	19.4	9.4	7.2	35.6	16.2	4.1
1943	33.6	24.8	6.0	19.6	9.4	7.2	36.1	15.9	4.2
1944	28.8	22.0	5.4	20.7	9.0	7.6	35.5	17.0	3.9
1945	36.6	17.9	5.0	[21.6][11]	8.7	8.0	36.2	15.0	4.1
1946	35.6	15.5	4.9	[23.5][11]	8.8	8.1	37.6	14.7	4.5
1947	39.4	14.6	4.6	20.1	9.0	8.2	38.2	13.4	4.4
1948	41.4	14.5	4.4	18.7	8.9	7.8	39.2	12.8	4.6
1949	41.6	13.5	4.9	18.7	8.6	8.2	41.2	11.9	4.9
1950	40.2	14.8	4.7	18.6	8.0	7.9	42.6	10.9	5.0
1951	42.3	13.5	4.5	18.5	8.6	8.2	43.4	11.0	4.9
1952	43.8	13.5	4.4	18.8	8.4	7.5	42.5	10.6	4.9
1953	43.9	13.3	4.1	18.8	8.5	8.8	44.3	9.6	5.2
1954	42.9	12.4	4.1	19.4	8.2	8.9	44.8	9.7	5.3
1955	43.4	11.9	4.3	21.4	8.7	8.7	44.3	9.7	5.0
1956	43.3	11.2	4.2	23.5	8.3	8.5	43.9	9.4	5.7
1957	44.6	11.6	4.1	23.1	8.9	8.6	43.2	9.4	5.3
1958	44.5	10.3	3.7	23.1	8.5	8.5	42.7	8.6	5.1
1959	44.5	10.1	3.7	22.6	9.4	8.3	45.8	8.3	5.6
1960	41.7	9.5	4.0	23.9	8.5	7.8	46.0	7.1	5.3
1961	41.6	9.0	4.0	25.0	8.8	8.4	45.3	7.3	5.1
1962	42.1	8.1	3.8	25.3	8.7	7.8	43.4	7.0	5.2
1963	41.8	8.9	3.3	23.8	8.9	7.6	43.4	7.2	5.2
1964	40.5	8.2	3.7	23.4	9.0	7.5	43.4	7.2	5.6
1965	40.0	8.2	4.1	22.2	9.1	7.7	43.6	7.1	5.7
1966	39.9	8.2	4.2	21.4	9.0	7.6	41.8	6.8	5.8
1967	35.9	7.5	4.0	22.0	9.5	8.0	42.5	6.6	5.7
1968	35.5	7.8	4.0	22.1	9.2	7.9	38.8	6.7	5.8
1969	31.9	7.4	...	20.1	9.7	8.6	38.7	6.8	5.9
1970	33.4	6.8	...	19.5	9.2	8.4	37.0	6.6	5.9
1971	31.7	7.2	...	19.8	10.3	8.4	37.0	6.6	6.2
1972	33.9	8.1	...	19.9	10.6	7.9	35.7	6.7	5.6
1973	31.9	7.4	...	20.0	10.2	8.0	34.4	6.8	6.3
1974	30.0	8.0	...	20.5	10.1	8.9	35.4	6.0	7.1
1975	29.7	7.6	...	20.9	9.7	8.6	35.2	5.9	7.1
1976	30.5	7.9	...	20.8	10.1	8.0	35.2	5.7	7.2
1977	...	7.3	...	20.3	10.1	7.8	34.2	5.5	7.1
1978	...	7.3	...	19.9	9.7	7.9	33.8	5.2	7.1
1979	...	...	...	19.3	9.8	7.9	33.1	5.1	7.0
1980	...	...	...	18.5	10.3	7.7	32.8	5.1	6.2
1981	...	...	...	18.4	9.4	7.7	32.1	5.2	5.9
1982	...	...	...	18.5	9.2	6.8	32.0	4.8	5.7
1983	...	...	...	18.0	9.6	6.5	31.4	4.6	5.7
1984	...	...	...	17.8	10.0	6.8	29.9	4.6	5.5
1985	...	...	...	17.9	9.5	7.4	29.0	4.6	5.4
1986	...	...	...	17.8	9.5	7.2	28.3	4.4	5.6
1987	...	...	...	17.6	9.6	7.2	28.3	4.4	5.7
1988	...	...	...	18.2	9.6	7.0	27.8	4.4	6.0
1989	...	...	...	18.0	9.6	7.4	28.0	4.5	5.9
1990	...	...	...	18.3	9.8	6.5	29.9	4.6	5.5
1991	...	...	...	17.6	9.6	6.6	30.4	4.5	5.4
1992	...	...	...	17.3	...	6.2	27.7	4.5	5.4
1993	25.1	5.5	...	17.9	...	...	...	...	...

A6 Vital Statistics: Rates per 1,000 Population

NOTES

1. SOURCES: The national publications on pp. xiii–xv; UN, *Demographic Yearbook*; and League of Nations, *Statistical Year-Book*. Canadian statistics to 1920 come from O.J. Firestone, Canada's *Economic Development, 1867–1953* (London, Bowes & Bowes, 1958).
2. In principle, birth rates relate to live births and death rates exclude stillbirths.

FOOTNOTES

[1] Data to 1889 are for years ending 30 September. From 1890 to 1915 they are for years ending 31 March in the year following that shown. Birth, death, and marriage rates for the six months from 1 October 1889 to 31 March 1890 were at annual rates of 35.8, 28.2, and 5.9 respectively.

[2] Data to 1892 (1890 for marriage rate) are for Trinidad alone. For the period 1901 to 1914 they relate to years beginning 1 April. The 1915 figures are for the last three quarters of the year.

[3] The figures to 1920 are estimates, the derivation of which is described in the source cited in Note 1 above. Earlier figures for the Province of Quebec are given in the same source and are as follows:

	B		B	D	M		B	D	M
1867	43.5	1879	42.8	...	...	1890	37.8	22.3	6.3
1868	42.8	1880	42.4	...	...	1891	38.9	22.2	6.2
1869	42.3	1881	40.8	...	...	1892	37.1	21.4	6.5
1870	41.6	1882	41.7	...	...	1893	37.5	21.6	6.5
1871	41.6	1883	41.7	...	...	1894	34.9	21.0	6.1
1872	42.7	1884	38.5	19.4	6.6	1895	37.9	20.5	6.6
1873	42.9	1885	37.4	25.2	6.6	1896	38.2	19.9	6.4
1874	44.0	1886	40.2	23.1	6.8	1897	37.1	21.8	6.5
1875	46.0	1887	39.7	20.7	6.9	1898	37.9	20.0	6.8
1876	45.2	1888	39.1	21.6	7.0	1899	35.2	20.4	6.9
1877	44.1	1889	38.5	21.9	6.5	1900	33.0	20.1	6.2
1878	44.4								

M.C. Urquhart and K.A.H. Buckley (eds.), *Historical Statistics of Canada* (Cambridge and Toronto, 1965) give the following decennial estimates for the Roman Catholic population of the Province of Quebec:

	B	D	M		B	D	M		B	D	M
1661–70	59.6	20.3	14.0	1761–70	64.5	11.2	33.5	1861–70	45.0	7.3	21.0
1671–80	55.3	7.5	9.4	1771–80	61.7	9.8	33.0	1871–80	47.0	7.8	24.8
1681–90	42.9	8.1	16.2	1781–90	57.4	9.2	29.9	1881–90	42.6	...	...
1691–1700	49.9	9.8	16.0	1791–1800	57.5	9.6	27.8				
1701–10	57.1	9.0	23.9	1801–10	56.7	9.4	29.1				
1711–20	56.9	10.1	22.1	1811–20	55.1	9.5	27.1				
1721–30	55.5	10.2	24.4	1821–30	56.9	9.4	27.5				
1731–40	56.9	9.5	25.8	1831–40	55.1	9.1	27.9				
1741–50	55.9	10.4	28.7	1841–50	52.1	8.7	23.4				
1751–60	59.6	11.3	38.2	1851–60	45.2	7.3	19.4				

Yukon and Northwest Territories are excluded to 1923, but Newfoundland is included from 1921, though it is also shown separately to 1949.

[4] Subsequent statistics are later revisions which are more complete.

[5] The following estimates of earlier total and white birth rates are given in Henry D. Sheldon, *The Older Population of the United States* (New York, John Wiley & Sons, 1958), and in Warren S. Thompson and P.K. Whelpton, *Population Trends in the United States* (New York, McGraw-Hill, 1933) respectively:

	Total	Whites		Total	Whites		Total	Whites
1800	...	55.0	1840	51.8	48.3	1880	39.8	35.2
1810	...	54.3	1850	...	43.3	1890	...	31.5
1820	55.2	52.8	1860	44.3	41.4	1900	32.3	30.1
1830	...	51.4	1870	...	38.3			

[6] i.e. non-whites.

[7] Data to 1937 are for years ending 31 July. From 1938 to 1949 they are for years ending 30 June.

[8] Excluding the Canal Zone. Revised figures back to 1948 are lower for both birth and death rates than the original series for the first few years after 1948, and it may be presumed that earlier statistics are overstated.

[9] Subsequently including Alaska.

[10] Subsequently including Hawaii.

[11] Late registrations are included.

International Historical Statistics: The Americas 1750–1993

A6a   NORTH AMERICA: COLLVER'S ESTIMATES OF AVERAGE VITAL RATES FOR QUINQUENNIA, 1895–1959

Key: BR = birth rate; DR = death rate; IMR = infant mortality rate

	Cuba			El Salvador			Guatemala		
	BR	DR	IMR	BR	DR	IMR	BR	DR	IMR
1895–99	...	...	...	...	...	...	...	...	...
1900–04	44.6	23.7	136	43.8	29.7	176	45.8	35.4	155
1905–09	47.4	23.3	146	43.5	31.4	188	43.6	34.0	155
1910–14	44.7	21.4	140	44.7	31.1	169	46.6	33.0	142
1915–19	40.7	22.2	136	42.9	41.2	214	43.2	40.8	147
1920–24	36.7	19.3	135	46.6	32.8	185	48.3	33.7	142
1925–29	32.9	15.2	110	47.1	34.1	191	49.2	32.6	123
1930–34	31.3	13.3	76	46.5	32.7	185	46.2	31.7	125
1935–39	30.9	12.7	78	45.4	29.6	164	44.2	30.7	128
1940–44	31.9	10.9	61	45.2	28.5	152	45.2	28.5	127
1945–49	30.0	8.7	52	44.8	22.8	135	49.1	26.5	124
1950–54	...	...	...	47.9	20.0	109	50.9	23.4	116
1955–59	...	...	...	47.9	17.7	107	49.0	20.0	98

	Honduras			Mexico			Panama		
	BR	DR	IMR	BR	DR	IMR	BR	DR	IMR
1895–99	...	...	...	47.3	34.4	226	...	...	...
1900–04	...	...	...	46.5	33.4	220	40.3	21.0	130
1905–09	...	...	...	46.0	32.9	220	40.2	19.7	130
1910–14	43.7	24.5	126	43.2	46.6	228	42.0	19.0	122
1915–19	41.7	27.4	140	40.6	48.3	215	37.3	17.3	121
1920–24	44.3	23.1	111	45.3	28.4	178	40.0	17.3	110
1925–29	44.1	23.1	112	44.3	26.7	153	39.0	16.6	110
1930–34	42.0	21.7	106	44.1	26.7	142	37.4	15.1	101
1935–39	41.9	22.1	118	43.5	23.5	129	37.8	12.6	80
1940–44	43.8	23.9	126	43.8	21.8	120	39.5	12.7	81
1945–49	44.5	19.0	106	44.5	17.8	105	38.3	10.8	70
1950–54	46.0	14.9	74	45.0	15.4	92	38.5	9.1	60
1955–59	46.0	12.5	64	45.8	12.5	78	40.5	9.1	71

A6a   SOUTH AMERICA: COLLVER'S ESTIMATES OF AVERAGE VITAL RATES FOR QUINQUENNIA, 1850–1959

	Argentina			Bolivia		Chile			Colombia		
	BR	DR	IMR	BR	DR	BR	DR	IMR	BR	DR	IMR
1850–54	...	...	...	...	...	44.6	35.0	...	...	...	...
1855–59	...	...	...	...	...	47.5	34.7	...	...	...	...
1860–64	46.8	31.7	188	...	...	46.9	34.3	...	...	...	...
1865–69	46.7	31.4	186	...	...	46.2	34.5	...	...	...	...
1870–74	46.2	30.7	185	...	...	47.5	34.0	...	...	...	...
1875–79	45.6	30.0	181	...	...	44.9	33.7	...	...	...	...
1880–84	45.0	29.1	179	...	...	48.0	33.9	...	...	...	...
1885–89	44.6	27.6	171	...	...	46.6	33.3	...	...	...	...
1890–94	42.9	25.1	162	...	...	45.9	32.7	...	...	...	...
1895–99	42.4	23.8	155	...	...	45.0	30.3	...	...	...	...
1900–04	41.0	21.6	146	...	...	44.7	31.6	261	43.0	26.6	186
1905–09	40.0	20.1	138	...	...	44.6	33.2	269	44.0	26.8	183
1910–14	40.3	17.7	121	...	...	44.4	31.5	261	44.1	26.0	177
1915–19	36.1	16.5	113	...	...	43.3	31.0	248	44.1	25.1	171
1920–24	34.3	14.0	100	...	...	42.2	31.3	250	44.6	23.7	159
1925–29	32.4	13.1	96	...	...	43.8	26.4	223	44.9	22.4	150
1930–34	28.9	11.6	82	...	...	40.2	24.5	212	43.3	22.5	155
1935–39	25.7	11.6	89	...	...	38.4	23.8	207	42.6	21.6	152
1940–44	25.7	10.4	74	45.1	20.5	38.3	20.1	170	42.4	20.3	143
1945–49	25.2	9.6	74	47.0	19.1	37.0	17.5	146	43.4	20.8	143
1950–54	...	...	...	42.4	16.2	37.0	13.7	119	44.0	18.4	125
1955–59	...	...	...	...	...	37.6	12.5	112	45.1	16.0	106

	Ecuador			Peru		Venezuela		
	BR	DR	IMR	BR	DR	BR	DR	IMR
1850–54	...	...	...	...	...	...	...	...
1855–59	...	...	...	...	...	...	...	...
1860–64	...	...	...	...	...	...	...	...
1865–69	...	...	...	...	...	...	...	...
1870–74	...	...	...	...	...	...	...	...
1875–79	...	...	...	...	...	...	...	...
1880–84	...	...	...	...	...	...	...	...
1885–89	...	...	...	...	...	44.4	32.3	176
1890–94	...	...	...	...	...	45.5	28.2	150
1895–99	...	...	...	...	...	43.1	29.4	165
1900–04	...	...	...	...	...	41.8	29.1	169
1905–09	...	...	...	...	...	43.6	29.8	166
1910–14	...	...	...	...	...	44.5	28.3	154
1915–19	46.5	30.2	188	...	...	41.4	29.7	165
1920–24	47.7	28.9	176	...	...	41.2	26.0	153
1925–29	49.1	28.2	167	...	...	43.1	24.6	138
1930–34	48.5	25.7	154	...	...	39.9	21.9	130
1935–39	47.7	25.6	157	...	...	40.2	21.1	130
1940–44	46.0	24.0	149	44.5	28.8	41.5	19.8	120
1945–49	45.9	20.0	134	44.9	24.7	43.6	16.1	102
1950–54	46.4	17.6	120	45.5	22.4	44.2	12.3	88
1955–59	46.5	15.7	112	46.2	18.6	44.3	10.9	76

NOTE

This table has been included because of the generally acknowledged incompleteness of most Latin American vital statistics, at least until recent times. It is compiled from O. Andrew Collver, *Birth Rates in Latin America: New Estimates of Historical Trends and Fluctuations* (Berkeley Institute of International Studies, University of California, 1965).

A7   NORTH AMERICA: INFANT MORTALITY RATES

1879–1889

	Jamaica[1]
1879	163
1880	197
1881	173
1882	141
1883	153
1884	166
1885	159
1886	154
1887	170
1888	162
1889	175[1]
1890	188
1891	175
1892	164
1893	169
1894	168
1895	178
1896	176
1897	177
1898	175
1899	170

	Barbados	Canada[2]	Costa Rica	Cuba	El Salvador
1900	...	187	...	...	...
1901	...	167	...	...	...
1902	...	136	...	...	...
1903	...	134	...	...	...
1904	...	110	...	...	...
1905	...	...	...	...	...
1906	420	130	...	...	...
1907	302	...	...	...	...
1908	319	209	...	...	...
1909	252	139	199	...	...
1910	268	174	197	...	...
1911	263	185	188	...	...
1912	416	161	187	...	...
1913	243	168	200	...	...
1914	403	161	185	...	...
1915	193	153	178	...	...
1916	242	165	184	...	...
1917	289	136	171	...	...
1918	205	138	218	...	...
1919	352	142	196	...	...
1920	270	163[2]	248	...	...
1921	401	102	210	...	...
1922	187	102	225	...	...
1923	368	103[2]	216	...	...
1924	298	94	228	...	...
1925	312	93	257	...	...
1926	314	102	178	...	...
1927	201	95	172	...	129
1928	331	90	169	...	142
1929	239	93	182	...	156
1930	231	91	155	...	130
1931	298	86	179	...	154
1932	198	75	149	113	134
1933	235	74	164	132	141
1934	256	73	136	100	136
1935	220	72	157	127	140
1936	198	68	153	106	120
1937	217	77	142	87	133
1938	221	64	122	83	117
1939	194	61	140	...	116

A7 NORTH AMERICA: Infant Mortality Rates

	Guatemala[6]	Honduras[7]	Jamaica[1]	Mexico	Puerto Rico[3]	Trinidad & Tobago	USA	
							whites	negroes[4]
1900	...	...	174	287	...	...	...	...
1901	...	...	163	266	...	...	...	...
1902	...	...	162	332	...	...	...	...
1903	...	...	187	310	...	...	...	...
1904	...	...	193	267	...	...	...	...
1905	...	...	165	287	...	...	...	...
1906	...	...	198	319	...	...	...	...
1907	...	...	224	311	...	...	...	...
1908	...	...	172	288	...	...	...	...
1909	...	...	175	294	...	...	...	...
1910	...	...	178	323	...	...	...	...
1911	...	...	188	...	168	...	...	...
1912	...	...	194	...	164	...	...	...
1913	...	...	172	...	157	...	...	...
1914	...	...	167	...	125	...	...	...
1915	...	...	176₁	...	141	...	99	181
1916	...	...	[176]	...	152	...	99	185
1917	...	...	185	...	199	...	90	151
1918	...	...	176	...	173	138	97	161
1919	...	...	162	...	142	155	83	130
1920	...	...	173	...	146	175	82	132
1921	...	...	197	...	162	140	72	108
1922	...	...	177	223	152	139	73	110
1923	...	...	171	222	143	130	73	117
1924	...	...	161	232	128	124	67	113
1925	...	...	173	216	148	134	68	111
1926	...	...	168	209	150	143	70	112
1927	...	...	173	193	167	121	61	100
1928	...	...	157	193	146	129	64	106
1929	...	...	160	168	179	128	63	102
1930	84	106	141	132	133	127	60	100
1931	84	95	154	138	133₃	144	57	93
1932	84	...	141	138	132	109	53[8]	86[8]
1933	107	...	150	139	140	131	53[8]	91[8]
1934	108	106	132	130	114	127	54[8]	94[8]
1935	100	87	138	126	115	99	52	83
1936	91	109	131	131	128	97	53	88
1937	99	102	118	131	138	120	50	83
1938	101₆	...₇	129	128	121	98	47	79
1939	128	106	121	123	113	104	44	74

A7 NORTH AMERICA: Infant Mortality Rates

	Barbados	Canada[2]	Costa Rica	Cuba	El Salvador	Guatemala[6]
1940	180	58	132	...	121	109
1941	224	61	123	...	105	108
1942	175	55	157	...	117	144
1943	164	55	117	71	110	120
1944	171	56	125	[58][5]	118	115
1945	149	52	110	[69][5]	108	97
1946	160	48	111	[41][5]	113	114
1947	166	46	108	[42][5]	96	110
1948	154	44	93	[39][5]	100	117
1949	129	43	100	[38][5]	93	102
1950	125	42	90	[35][5]	81	107
1951	136	39	86	[39][5]	77	92
1952	145	38	89	38	85	112
1953	139	36	90	38	83	103
1954	109	32	81	33	82	88
1955	135	31	83	36	77	101
1956	97	32	74	34	70	89
1957	87	31	82	37	87	100
1958	82	30	72	...	89	104
1959	71	28	70	32	78	90
1960	60	27	71	35	76	92
1961	84	27	65	37	70	85
1962	54	28	71	40	71	91
1963	62	26	74	36	68	93
1964	52	25	82	38	65	88
1965	39	24	72	38	71	93
1966	48	23	63	38	62	90
1967	54	22	60	37	63	89
1968	46	21	60	39	59	92
1969	42	19	67	47	63	91
1970	46	19	61	36	67	87
1971	29	18	56	34	52	82
1972	31	17	54	27	58	79
1973	38	16	45	29	59	80
1974	31	15	38	29	53	75
1975	33	14	38	27	58	81
1976	28	13	33	23	55	76
1977	25	12	28	25	59	70
1978	30	12	24	22	51	68
1979	25	11	23	19	53	70
1980	23	10	20	20	42	65
1981	17	10	19	18	44	64
1982	24	9	19	17	42	64
1983	14	8	19	17	44	66
1984	13	8	19	15	35	55
1985	8	8	19	16	...	56
1986	10	8	18	14	...	57
1987	16	7	17	13	...	52
1988	15	7	15	12	...	47
1989	9	7	14	11	...	44
1990	13	7	15	11	...	...
1991	10	7	14	11	...	...
1992	9	6	14	10	...	...
1993	10	6	14	9	45	...

A7 NORTH AMERICA: Infant Mortality Rates

	Honduras[7]	Jamaica	Mexico	Puerto Rico[3]	Trinidad & Tobago	USA	
						whites	negroes[4]
1940	109	112	126	114	106	43	74
1941	106	104	123	116	109	41	75
1942	110	98	118	103	119	37	65
1943	127	93	117	96	93	37	62
1944	109₇	99	114	99	80	37	60
1945	...	102	108	93	84	36	57
1946	90	89	111	84	79	32	49
1947	89	92	96	71	81	30	48
1948	94	87	102	78	75	30	46
1949	93	81	106	68	80	29	47
1950	86	78	96	67	80	27	44
1951	55	81	99	67	78	26	45
1952	64	75	90	66	89	25	47
1953	64	64	95	63	70	25	45
1954	60	67	81	58	60	24	43
1955	55	63	83	56	68	24	43
1956	53	55	71	55	64	23	42
1957	59	55	80	50	56	23	44
1958	65	62	80	53	63	24	46
1959	54	70	74	48	62	23	44
1960	52	51	74	43	45	23	43
1961	50	49	70	41	45	22	41
1962	44	50	70	42	38	22	41
1963	47	50	69	45	41	22	41
1964	45	40	65	52	35	22	41
1965	41	39	61	39	38	21	40
1966	38	35	63	39	42	21	39
1967	35	30	63	37	36	20	36
1968	34	35	64	33	37	19	34
1969	36	33	68	39	40	18	33
1970	33	32	69	34	34	18	31
1971	39	27	63	27	31	17	28
1972	43	31	61	27	25	16	28
1973	40	26	52	24	26	16	26
1974	34	26	47	23	26	15	25
1975	34	23	53	21	26	14	24
1976	31	20	52	20	25	13	23
1977	29	15	49	20	21	12	22
1978	27	...	40	18	20	12	21
1979	...	...	39	20	18	11	20
1980	...	...	39	19	22	11	19
1981	...	...	33	19	16	10	18
1982	...	...	33	17	16	10	17
1983	...	12	30	17	13	10	17
1984	...	13	29	16	14	9	16
1985	...	...	25	15	12	9	16
1986	...	...	...	14	11	9	16
1987	...	...	23	14	11	9	16
1988	...	...	24	13	13	8	16
1989	...	...	26	14	10	8	16
1990	...	...	24	15	13	8	16
1991	...	...	21	13	11	7	15
1992	...	...	19	13	11	7	14
1993	43	...	17	...	11	7	14

A7 SOUTH AMERICA: INFANT MORTALITY RATES (in thousands)

	Argentina	Chile	Colombia	Guyana*	Peru	Uruguay	Venezuela
1901	...	340	...	...	...	...	...
1902	...	270	...	...	...	...	...
1903	...	264	...	205	...	...	...
1904	...	286	...	201	...	...	...
1905	...	249	...	187	...	...	...
1906	...	327	...	201	...	...	...
1907	...	298	...	256	...	...	...
1908	...	318	...	198	...	...	...
1909	...	315	...	209	...	...	...
1910	...	267	...	235	...	...	...
1911	148	333	...	229	...	...	...
1912	143	287	...	190	...	...	...
1913	130	286	...	179	...	...	...
1914	125	255	...	170	...	...	...
1915	124	254	...	184	...	...	...
1916	124	241	...	190	...	...	...
1917	128	269	...	199	...	...	...
1918	138	255	...	223	...	...	...
1919	134	306	...	185	...	...	...
1920	127	263	...	148	...	...	...
1921	116	278	...	195	...	107	...
1922	112	240	...	186	...	94	...
1923	112	283	...	177	...	104	...
1924	116	266	142	165	...	108	...
1925	121	258	122	155	...	115	...
1926	119	251	148	159	...	93	...
1927	126	226	144	158	...	106	...
1928	113	212	129	185	...	100	...
1929	107	224	123	146	...	93	...
1930	100	234	106	146	...	100	150
1931	100	232	125	139	...	110	156
1932	95	235	...	139	...	99	...
1933	87	258	143	154	...	93	162
1934	97	262	117	168	...	96	158
1935	106	251	156	122	...	102	137
1936	97	252	153	120	...	92	134
1937	95	241	150	121	...	96	135
1938	103	236	156	166	...	99	139
1939	90	225	162	120	...	82	132

A7   SOUTH AMERICA: Infant Mortality Rates (in thousands)

	Argentina	Chile	Colombia	Guyana*	Peru	Uruguay	Venezuela
1940	90	217	142	104	128	86	122
1941	85	200	150	84	131	83	121
1942	86	195	154	97	115	93	115
1943	80	194	157	141	126	78	109
1944	81	181	155	136	115	66	117
1945	82	184	151	101	109	...	99
1946	74	160	150	87	113	62	102
1947	78	161	140	85	107	71	100
1948	69	147	136	78	109	61	98
1949	67	155	134	77	105	52	91
1950	68	139	124	86	104	64	81
1951	67	135	120	77	105	55	80
1952	65	129	111	82	100	51	79
1953	63	112	120	81	105	51	74
1954	60	125	103	73	95	49	69
1955	62	120	104	70	95	47	70
1956	57	110	104	68	96	44	67
1957	68	114	100	68	108	53	66
1958	61	121	104	62	103	49	58
1959	59	117	97	57	97	57	61
1960	62	125	100	63	92	47	54
1961	59	111	90	51	89	42	53
1962	59	115	90	49	80	42	47
1963	62	105	90	54	85	44	48
1964	59	108	83	41	54	45	49
1965	57	107	82	52	74	50	48
1966	57	108	80	45	64	43	47
1967	56	100	78	47	72	59	41
1968	55	92	70	42	74	54	43
1969	53	87	61	41	75	49	43
1970	52	79	50	38	65	43	49
1971	50	78	45	42	54	48	50
1972	49	77	53	50	58	50	53
1973	47	66	89	46	...	50	54
1974	46	65	50	...	...9	48	46
1975	44	58	47	...	107	49	44
1976	43	57	47	...	106	46	43
1977	41	50	39	...	105	48	39
1978	38	40	...	...	104	44	35
1979	33	38	...	...	103	40	33
1980	33	33	...	...	101	38	32
1981	34	27	...	...	100	33	
1982	30	24	...	...	99	29	28
1983	30	22	...	...	97	28	26
1984	30	20	...	...	95	30	27
1985	25	19	...	...	93	29	26
1986	26	19	...	...	90	28	25
1987	26	18	...	...	95	24	24
1988	26	19	...	...	95	21	21
1989	26	17	...	...	90	21	23
1990	26	16	...	...	82	20	24
1991	25	15	...	...	89	21	20
1992	24	14	...	...	92	19	...
1993	23	13	...	...	90	20	...

A7   Infant Mortality Rates

NOTES

1. SOURCES: As for table B5.
2. The data relate to deaths of infants under one year old per 1,000 live births.

FOOTNOTES

[1]   Data to 1889 are for years ending 30 September. From 1890 to 1915 they are for years ending 31 March in the year following that shown. The rate for the six months from 1 October 1889 to 31 March 1890 was on an annual basis. The 1916 figure is for the last three quarters of the year.
[2]   Province of Quebec only to 1920. Subsequently the present territory (including Newfoundland), but excluding Yukon and Northwest Territories in 1921–23.
[3]   Data to 1931 are for years ending 30 June.
[4]   i.e. non-whites.
[5]   Excluding infants dying within 24 hours of birth.
[6]   Data to 1938 exclude the live-born who died immediately.
[7]   Data to 1937 are for years ending 31 July, and from 1939 to 1944 they are for years ending 30 June.
[8]   Mexicans are included with negroes.
[9]   Subsequent figures are from national sources. The U.N. *Demographic Yearbooks* give a different series for 1982 onwards, *viz.*

| 1982 | 95 | 1984 | 136 | 1986 | ... | 1988 | 95 | 1990 | 124 | 1992 | 77 |
| 1983 | 141 | 1985 | 91 | 1987 | 122 | 1989 | 129 | 1991 | 79 | 1993 | 75 |

A8 NORTH AMERICA: INTERNATIONAL MIGRATIONS (in thousands)

Key:
a = Immigrants (cabin and other passengers) through Montreal and Quebec
b = Immigrant arrivals
c = East Indian immigrants less those repatriated
d = Immigrants less those repatriated
e = Emigrant departures
f = Arrivals by sea less departures
g = Polynesian and Indian immigrants less those repatriated
h = Total arrivals less departures
i = Total arrivals
j = Total departures

1815–1859

| | Canada | Guadeloupe | | Jamaica[1] | Trinidad & Tobago[3] | USA[4] |
	a	b	c	d	d	b
1815	1.2	…	…	…	…	…
1816	…	…	…	…	…	…
1817	…	…	…	…	…	…
1818	…	…	…	…	…	…
1819	…	…	…	…	…	…
1820	…	…	…	…	…	8.4
1821	…	…	…	…	…	9.1
1822	…	…	…	…	…	6.9
1823	…	…	…	…	…	6.4
1824	…	…	…	…	…	7.9
1825	…	…	…	…	…	10
1826	…	…	…	…	…	11
1827	16	…	…	…	…	19
1828	13	…	…	…	…	27
1829	16	…	…	…	…	23
1830	28	…	…	…	…	23
1831	50	…	…	…	…	23
1832	52	…	…	…	…	[60][4]
1833	22	…	…	…	…	59
1834	31	…	…	- -	…	65
1835	13	…	…	0.9	…	45
1836	28	…	…	1.2	…	76
1837	22	…	…	0.4	…	79
1838	3.3	…	…	–	…	39
1839	7.4	…	…	–	1.0	68
1840	22	…	…	0.1	2.0	84
1841	28	…	…	2.2	2.0	80
1842	44	…	…	1.0	2.9	105
1843	22	…	…	0.4	2.8	[52][4]
1844	20	…	…	0.5	2.5	79
1845	25	…	…	0.6	1.6	114
1846	33	…	…	2.4	2.9	154
1847	74	…	…	2.5	3.1	235
1848	28	…	…	1.9	0.9	227
1849	38	…	…	1.1	1.9	297
1850	32	…	…	0.5	0.8	310[4]
1851	41	…	…	0.8	–0.2	379
1852	39	29	…	- -	1.1	372
1853	37	29	…	–1.1	2.5	369
1854	53	37	0.3	- -	0.7	428
1855	21	25	0.4	0.2	0.1	201
1856	22	23	1.1	–	0.3	200
1857	32	34	1.4	0.4	1.2	251
1858	13	12	1.4	–0.1	1.8	123
1859	8.8	6.3	1.7	–	3.4	121

A8 NORTH AMERICA: International Migrations (in thousands)

1860-1899

	Canada		Guadeloupe	Jamaica[1]	Trinidad & Tobago[3]	USA[4]
	a	b	c	d	d	b
1860	10	6.3	0.8	0.6	2.9	154
1861	20	14	1.9	2.1	2.2	92
1862	22	18	0.9	2.6	2.1	92
1863	19	21	1.5	1.1	1.8	176
1864	19	25	0.6	—	0.9	193
1865	21	19	0.2	—	2.8	248
1866	29	11	1.2	—	2.4	319
1867	31	11	3.1	1.6	3.3	316
1868	34	13	1.0	—	1.4	[139][4]
1869	43	19	0.9	1.4	3.0	353
1870	44	25	0.9	0.9	1.5	387
1871	37	28	0.6	0.4	1.3	321
1872	35	37	0.5	1.1	3.2[3]	405
1873	37	50	1.4	[1.6][2]	2.9	460
1874	24	39	1.3	[1.4][2]	2.1	313
1875	16	27	0.8	[1.2][2]	3.3	227
1876	11	26	1.3	...	1.0	170
1877	7.7	27	0.9	...	1.2	142
1878	10	30	2.2	...	2.6	138
1879	17	40	2.1	...	2.1	178
1880	25	39	2.7	...	2.7	457
1881	...	48	2.8	...	2.2	669
1882	...	112	0.5	...	2.6	789
1883	...	134	1.3	...	1.5	603
1884	...	104	...	...	2.5	519
1885	...	79	...	...	1.1	395
1886	...	69	...	...	1.6	334
1887	...	85	...	...	1.5	490
1888	...	89	...	...	1.4	547
1889	...	92	...	...	2.6	444
1890	...	75	...	...	2.3	455
1891	...	82	...	...	2.9	560
1892	...	31	...	...	2.6	580
1893	...	30	...	...	1.2	440
1894	...	21	...	...	1.8	286
1895	...	19	...	...	1.8	259
1896	...	17	...	...	2.4	343
1897	...	22	...	...	1.1	231
1898	...	32	...	...	0.5	229
1899	...	45	...	...	0.5[3]	312

A8   NORTH AMERICA: International Migrations (in thousands)

	Canada	Cuba	Dominican Rep.	El Salvador	Guatemala	Jamaica[1]	Mexico[8]		Trinidad & Tobago[3]	USA[4]
	b	b	h	h	h	h	b	e	d	b
1900	42	...	...	...	...	...	...	...	−0.1	449
1901	56	23	...	...	...	...	...	...	1.8	488
1902	89	12	...	...	...	0.8	...	...	1.6	649
1903	139	18	...	...	...	–- -	...	...	1.7	857
1904	131	29	...	...	...	−3.1	...	...	0.5	813
1905	141	54			...	−3.9	...	...	2.9	1,026
1906	212	35	...	...	...		...	...	1.7	1,101
1907	272	32	...	...	...	...	...	...	1.1	1,285
1908	143	28	...	...	...	−0.8	...	...	1.7	783
1909	174	31	...	...	...	−3.0	42	...	1.9	752
1910	287	38	...	...	...	−4.9	50	...	2.6	1,042
1911	331	38	...	...	...	0.2	38	36	2.7	879
1912	376	38	...	...	...	−1.8	41	38	1.8	838
1913	401	44	...	...	...	−2.6	27	26	0.4	1,198
1914	150	26	...	...	...	2.9	9.2	7.1	0.4	1,218
1915	37	33	...	...	...	[−2.3][1]	7.2	6.8	[- -][3]	327
1916	56	55	...	...	...	−2.5	13	11	0.5	299
1917	73	57	...	...	...	−8.7[1]	18	9.7	0.7[3]	295
									h	
1918	42	37	...	...	...	−4.1	9.7	8.5	0.8	111
1919	108	80	...	...	...	−14	16	13	3.2	141
1920	139	174	...	...	...	2.2	21	13	2.1	430
1921	92	59	...	...	...	2.6	37	22	3.1	805
1922	64	26	...	...	...	1.9	36	25	2.2	310
1923	134	75	...	...	...	−5.1	41	32	−1.7	523
1924	124	85	...	...	...	−3.5	41	30	−1.6	707
1925	85	56	...	...	0.5	0.2	44	30	−1.5	294
1926	136	32	...	...	0.8	3.6	35	30	−1.5	304
1927	159	31	...	...	0.3	3.9	26	19	−0.3	335
1928	167	27	...	...	0.6	5.4	30[8]	17[8]	1.6	307
1929	165	17	...	...	−0.2	4.1	85	43	1.3	280
1930	105	12	...	...	−0.2	7.6	85	32	4.9	242
1931	28	3	...	...	0.3	12	135	22	1.6	97
1932	21	2	...	...	−0.3	6.8	82	10	—	36
1933	14	3	...	...	−0.8	2.1	37	7.6	1.1	23
1934	12	3	...	0.8	−0.9	−1.0	28	8.1	1.3	29
1935	11	4	...	1.9	−1.0	−0.6	19	9.2	1.2	35
1936	12	4	−0.1	3.2	0.2	−3.2	16	8.0	0.9	36
1937	15	...	−6.2	1.3	–- -	−3.9	12	6.5	1.4	50
1938	17	...	0.1	−1.1	0.3	2.3	13	5.9	1.0	68
1939	17	...	1.2	2.6	...	1.9	2.3	4.7	1.5	83
1940	11	...	1.5	1.0	...	4.7	15	5.4	2.4	71
1941	9	...	−0.7	0.2	1.6	2.5	9.0	7.0	13	52
1942	8	...	−0.6	0.7	0.6	- -	9.8	6.1	7.2	29
1943	9	...	−0.4	−5.7	−0.7	−2.5	6.5	7.3	1.8	24
1944	13	...	−1.3	...	−0.3	14	9.7	6.9	−2.3	29

A8   NORTH AMERICA: International Migrations (in thousands)

	Canada	Cuba	Dominican Republic	El Salvador	Guatemala	Jamaica[1]	Mexico		Trinidad & Tobago[3]	USA[4]
	b	b	h	h	h	h	b	e	d	b
1945	23	…	−1.5	−1.4	0.9	−4.6	9.4	9.2	−1.7	38
1946	72	…	1.2	0.8	2.1	−2.3	10	13	1.5	109
1947	64	…	1.6	−0.6	0.7	−1.8	9.1	11	3.6	147
		h								
1948	125	−4	−0.3	2.3	…	−2.0	8.9	11	−0.5	171
1949	95	−3	0.2	1.1	…	−0.3	11	14	0.4	188
1950	74	3	−1.0	0.8		−11.0	13	13	1.2	249
1951	194	1	−1.1	1.1	−··	−4.5	23	15	−0.8	206
1952	164	1	−1.5	9.5	0.6	−3.9	24	17	−1.6	266
1953	169	…	−1.5	−0.1	−0.3	−4.3	28	13	−·	170
1954	154	…	−0.5	…	1.4	−8.4	29	16	−0.4	208
1955	110	…	4.7	…	2.4	−19.0	27	20	−0.2	238
1956	171	…	−1.9	−2.4	−··	−18.0	29	23	6.1	322
1957	289	…	−2.6	2.2	2.2	−1.4	35	20	0.9	327
1958	132	…	8.6	1.4	−5.0	−11.0	36	20	3.7	253
1959	107	…	…	…	−1.6	−21.0	40	20	4.8	261
1960	104	−38	−1.7	4.2	−8.4	−34.0	43	22	−0.1	265
1961	72	−68	2.5	1.7	−0.1	−39.0	43	22	0.4	271
1962	75	−66	−6.7	−3.4	0.9	−32.0	46	28	2.5	284
1963	93	−12	−0.9	0.3	4.7	−1.5	49	34	3.1	306
1964	113	−12	−11	1.0	−4.4	−14.0	56	36	−0.4	292
1965	147	−17	−2.3	−1.8	6.9	5.1	58	55	−3.0	297
1966	195	…	−9.7	4.5	47.0	−2.9	61	60	−5.1	323
1967	223	…	−13	4.0	−3.9	−16.0	73	60	−9.0	362
1968	184	…	−15	3.1	9.3	…	116	66	−9.1	454
1969	162	…	−16	4.7	−11.0	−29.0	111	65	−16	359
1970	148	…	−9.4	−2.0	12.0	−23	165	65	−17	373
1971	122	…	…	−0.9	18.0	−32	184	61	−7.5	370
1972	122	…	−6.0	−24.1	7.6	−10	220	66	−7.0	385
1973	184	…	−2.5	−10.0	47.0	−10	317	74	−9.6	400
1974	218	…	−15.6	−2.5	94.0	−13	101	79	−6.7	395
1975	188	…	−9.9	−19.4	183	−12	96	79	−7.8	386
1976	149	…	…	−2.5	65	−22	158	74	−2.2	399
1977	115	…	…	−26.6	…	−21	111	66	−2.6	462
1978	86	…	…	−54.2	…	−18	275	80	−10.5	601
1979	112	…	…	−59.6	…	−21	145	76	−9.3	460
1980	143	…	…	−80.6	…	−24.0	213	87	−4.0	531
1981	129	…	…	−23.6	…	−5.9	248	94	−3.2	597
1982	121	…	…	−124.9	…	−9.8	148	75	+2.2	594
1983	189	…	…	−60.7	…	−4.3	…	70	+1.1	560
1984	88	…	…	−40.1	…	−10.0	…	87	−11.8	544
1985	84	…	−113	−27.4	…	−13	…	73	−7.4	570
1986	99	…	−158	…	…	−20	…	…	−15.4	602
1987	152	…	…	…	…	−31	…	…	−10.7	602
1988	162	…	…	…	…	−39	…	…	−45.0	643[9]
1989	192					−10			−19.1	1,091
1990	212					−25			−15.7	1,536
1991	231					−26			−1.1	1,827
1992	242					−20			−2.1	974
1993	265					−21			−7.0	904

A8 SOUTH AMERICA: INTERNATIONAL MIGRATIONS (in thousands)

1815–1834

	Brazil[5]
	b
1815	...
1816	...
1817	...
1818	...
1819	...
1820	1.7
1821	...
1822	...
1823	...
1824	0.1
1825	0.9
1826	0.8
1827	1.1
1828	2.1
1829	2.4
1830	...
1831	...
1832	...
1833	...
1834	...

1835–1884

	Argentina[6]		Brazil[5]	Guyana*[7]	Paraguay	Uruguay	
	b	e	b	d	b	b	e
1835	...	...	...	0.6	...	0.6	
1836	...	...	1.2	1.1	...	3.1	...
1837	...	...	0.6	1.8	...	2.6	
1838	...	...	0.4	1.9	...	5.4	...
1839	...	...	0.4	0.2	...	1.2	...
1840	...	...	0.3	0.9	...	2.5	...
1841	...	...	0.6	8.1	...	7.9	...
1842	...	...	0.6	2.7	...	9.9	...
1843	...	...	0.7	0.6	...	...	...
1844	...	...	...	0.9	...	...	...
1845	...	...	0.1	3.6	...	...	...
1846	...	...	0.4	12.0	...	...	...
1847	...	...	2.4	7.8	...	...	...
1848	...	...	- -	5.5	...	...	...
1849	...	...	- -	0.2	...	...	...
				d			
1850	...	...	2.1	2.0	...	...	...
1851	...	...	4.4	1.3	...	...	...
1852	...	...	2.7	3.6	...	...	...
1853	...	...	11.0	5.3	...	...	...
1854	...	...	9.2	2.3	...	...	...
1855	...	...	12	3.4	...	...	...
1856	...	...	14	2.0	...	...	...
1857	5.0	...	14	2.3	...	...	...
1858	4.7	...	19	2.9	...	...	...
1859	4.7	...	20	4.0	...	...	...
1860	5.7	...	16.0	8.2	...	...	...
1861	6.3	...	13.0	7.2	...	...	...
1862	6.7	...	14.0	8.4	...	...	...
1863	10.0	...	7.6	3.1	...	...	...
1864	12.0	...	9.6	7.9	...	...	...
1865	12	...	6.5	7.0	...	...	...
1866	14	...	7.7	4.2	...	9.3	...
1867	13	...	11.0	4.6	...	17.0	...
1868	26	...	11.0	3.3	...	17.0	...
1869	29	...	12.0	7.9	...	20.0	...
1870	31	...	5.2	5.6	...	21	...
1871	15	11.0	12.0	3.1	...	18	...
1872	26	9.2	19.0	5.5	...	12	...
1873	48	18.0	15.0	11	...	24	...
1874	41	21.0	20.0	7.2	...	14	...
1875	18	26	15	4.1	...	5.3	...
1876	15	13	31	3.0	...	5.6	...
1877	15	18	29	4.5	...	6.2	...
1878	24	15	24	10.0	...	9.5	...
1879	33	24	23	7.4	...	11.0	7.0
1880	27	20.0	30	3.6	...	9.3	6.8
1881	31	22.0	12	2.9[7]	0.1	8.3	6.3
1882	41	8.7	30	3.1	0.2	10.0	6.2
1883	52	9.5	34	1.0	0.2	11.0	6.1
1884	50	14.0	25	3.3	0.3	12.0	6.0

International Historical Statistics: The Americas 1750–1993

A8 SOUTH AMERICA: International Migrations (in thousands)

1885–1929

	Argentina[6]		Brazil[5]	Colombia[7]	Guyana[*7]	Paraguay	Uruguay		Venezuela
	b	e	b	h	d	b	b	e	d
1885	81	15	35	...	5.5	- -	16	6.7	...
1886	66	14	33	...	1.6	0.1	12	6.5	...
1887	95	14	56	...	2.9	0.8	13	6.3	...
1888	129	17	133	...	1.0	1.1	17	7.6	...
1889	219	41	65	...	1.5	1.9	27	11.0	...
1890	78	49	107	...	2.5	0.8	24.0	20	...
1891	28	72	217	...	2.8	0.4	12.0	20	...
1892	40	30	86	...	2.7	0.5	12.0	88	...
1893	52	26	135	...	3.4	0.5	9.5	6.3	...
1894	55	21	61	...	7.2	0.2	12.0	6.0	...
1895	61	20	168	...	0.4	0.3	9.2	6.4	...
1896	103	20	158	...	0.3	0.2	11.0	5.9	...
1897	73	31	146	...	−0.3	0.2	9.1	6.8	...
1898	67	31	78	...	1.2	0.4	9.5	6.4	...
1899	84	38	55	...	3.2	0.3	9.0	5.8	...
1900	85	38	40	...	3.4	0.1	8.9	6.7	...
1901	90	49	85	...	3.1	0.5	9.6	6.7	...
1902	58	45	52	...	0.3	0.6	6.9	6.9	...
1903	75	41	34	...	1.2	0.3	7.3	6.2	...
1904	126	39	46	...	−0.3	0.4	7.0	5.9	...
1905	177	43	70	...	−0.1	0.6	7.9	6.1	...
1906	253	60	74	...	0.3	1.2	8.7	5.8	...
1907	209	90	68	...	- -	...	8.6	6.5	0.9
1908	256	85	95[5]	...	0.4	...	8.9	5.9	3.2
			91	...					
1909	231	95	84		1.1	...	9.3	7.8	2.2
1910	290	98	87	...	0.5	...	11	8.4	1.0
1911	226	121	134	...	0.7	...	14	8.8	3.0
1912	323	120	178	...	1.4	...	18	9.5	1.6
1913	302	157	190	...	0.7[7]	...	17	12.0	0.9
					2.0				
1914	115	179	79	...	2.7	...	10	12	0.9
1915	45	111	30	...	1.3	...	5.6	6.9	1.0
1916	33	73	31	...	1.6	...	4.7	5.0	1.0
1917	18	51	30	...	0.8	...	4.4	4.0	0.7
1918	14	24	20	...	1.8	0.3	5.2	4.3	0.3
1919	41	42	36	...	−0.5	0.4	11.0	6.0	−0.4
1920	87	57	69	...	−0.6	0.3	10.0	7.1	−0.7
1921	98	45	58	...	−0.4	0.6	9.2	5.3	0.9
1922	129	46	65	...	- -	0.2	11.0	6.2	0.8
1923	195	47	85	...	0.7	0.1	17.0	6.6	−0.3
							h		
1924	160	46	96	...	—- -	0.5	15		1.9
1925	125	50	83	...	0.4	0.3	15		1.2
1926	135	56	119	3.0	−0.4	0.3	18		5.1
1927	162	58	98	4.5	−0.4	0.4	19		3.5
1928	129	54	78	2.8	−0.8	0.4	20		0.4
1929	140	58	96	2.4	−0.7	0.3	17		1.9

A8 SOUTH AMERICA: International Migrations (in thousands)

1930–1974

	Argentina		Brazil[5]	Colombia	Guyana[*7]	Paraguay	Uruguay	Venezuela
	b	e	b	h	d	b	h	d
1930	124.0	60.0	63.0	−5.2	−0.4	1.8	27.0	1.6
1931	56.0	53.0	127.0	−2.6	0.3	0.5	15.0	0.6
1932	31.0	43.0	31.0	0.9	0.1	0.9	4.6	−1.2
1933	24.0	35.0[6]	46.0	2.8	0.8	0.4	1.7	−0.6
		50.0						
1934	28.0	42.0	46.0	4.0	0.6	0.6	5.5	−1.0
1935	35.0	37.0	30.0	1.2	0.6	1.1	0.4	0.5
1936	36.0	37.0	13.0	1.1	−0.3	2.5	4.7	3.0
1937	41.0	37.0	35.0	0.9	0.2	4.8	7.6	2.8
1938	38.0	33.0	19.0	3.3	...	4.5	9.3	2.8
1939	15.0	29.0	23.0	1.4	...	2.1	0.4	2.6
1940	6.2	14.0	18.0	0.4	...	0.2	−5.2	0.6
1941	4.7	13.0	9.9	−3.4	...	0.3	−1.8	−2.2
1942	1.8	4.2	2.4	−·-	...	0.1	−4.7	−3.7
1943	0.8	2.9	1.3	0.1	...	...	−6.7	−4.2
1944	0.8	...[6]	1.6	0.7	...	...	−2.0	0.7
1945	1.0	1.3	3.2	2.2	...	- -	...	5.3
1946	4.4	4.6	13.0	3.3	...	- -	...	2.7
1947	39.0	8.9	19.0	1.4	...	2.6	...	9.2
1948	119.0	13.0	22	...	...	...	...	35.0
1949	152.0	17.0	24.0	0.4	...	...	...	24.0
1950	128.0	25.0	35.0	−1.6	−0.5	...	...	27.0
1951	98.0	27.0	63.0	0.5	−0.6	...	...	23.0
1952	64.0	45.0	85.0	−3.1	2.2	...	...	30.0
1953	35.0	32.0	80.0	−·-	...	...	9.8	41.0
1954	44.0	19.0	72.0	−1.3	...	...	...	44.0
1955	30.0	18.0	55.0	...	−1.3	...	18.0	54.0
1956	18.0	18.0	45.0	2.1	−1.7	0.7	25.0	41.0
1957	27.0[6]	24.0	54.0	−1.1	−1.0	2.3	...	44.0
1958	20.0	...	50.0	−1.4	−1.1	1.5	...	10.0
1959	16.0	...	45.0	−3.7	−9.2	...	...	9.8
1960	8.8	...	41.0	−1.9	7.7	1.0	37.0	−10.0
1961	9.1	...	44.0	−2.7	8.6	1.7	21.0	−5.0
1962	9.5	...	31.0	−4.6	−0.9	1.3	−11.0	−8.2
1963	5.7	...	24.0	11.0	−3.0	2.7	...	−7.2
1964	3.7	...	...	10.0	−3.7	1.7	...	12.0
1965	3.9	...	...	15.0	−2.8	1.3	...	7.4
1966	3.2	...	...	−5.2	−0.7	1.7	...	−5.3
1967	3.8	...	11	−5.0	−2.4	1.1	−11.0	−25.0
1968	4.9	...	13.0	−15	−4.8	0.9	...	−59.0
1969	6.3	...	6.6	0.9	−4.6	1.3	...	−36.0
1970	7.4	...	6.9	...	−12.0	1.3	−1.1	−63.0
1971	4.6	...	6.4	...	−2.1	1.5	12.0	39.0
1972	3.5	...	8.8	...	−8.0	2.6	50.0	3.4
1973	...	...	5.9	...	−7.0	4.5	...	9.7
1974	...	...	6.8	7.4	−9.3	6.3	...	71.0

A8 SOUTH AMERICA: International Migrations (in thousands)

					1975–1993
	Brazil b	Colombia h	Guyana d	Paraguay b	Venezuela d
1975	12.0	18.0	−7.7	5.5	28
1976	...	...	...	...	61
1977	...	...	...	...	−12
1978	...	...	...	...	180
1979	6.8	...	...	...	52
1980	...	−4.4	...	5.1	−6
1981	...	−16.0	...	10.0	−95
1982	...	13.0	...	5.9	−21
1983	3.7	32.0	...	...	15
1984	3.5	5.3	...	...	−45
1985	...	1.8	...	...	−26
1986	4.2	2.5	...	...	−19
1987	...	1.0	...	...	31
1988	...	−28.0	...	...	- -
1989	...	...	...	...	9
1990	...	...	...	...	−2
1991	...	...	...	...	−46
1992	...	...	...	...	−12
1993	...	...	...	...	

NOTES

1. SOURCES: The main sources used have been Imre Ferenczi and Walter F. Willcox, *International Migrations*, vol. 1 (New York, 1929); UN, *Sex and Age of International Migrants: Statistics for 1918–1947* (1953); UN, *Economic Characteristics of International Migrants: Statistics for Selected Countries, 1918–1954* (no date); and the annual UN, *Demographic Yearbook*. In addition, the following data came from the national publications on pp. xiii–xv: Canada to 1959; Trinidad and Tobago 1923–47; USA 1869–75; Brazil; British Guiana 1924–38; Venezuela to 1978.
2. Definitions of migrants vary very greatly from time to time and from place to place. So far as possible the changes are indicated in the column headings and in footnotes.
3. Net movements of foreigners 1908–75 are given in Markos J. Mamalakis, *Historical Statistics of Chile*, vol. 2. (Westport, Conn., 1980).

FOOTNOTES

[1] Data for 1873–1917 apply to 'coolies' (i.e. indentured East Indians). For 1902–14 they are for years beginning 1 April. The 1915 figure is for the 9 months ending 31 December.
[2] Exclusive of those repatriated.
[3] Data to 1899 apply to 'coolies', covering only those moving at the public expense from 1873. From 1900 to 1918 only indentured East Indian 'coolies' are covered. From 1900 to 1914 data are for years beginning 1 April. The 1915 figure is for the 9 months ending 31 December.
[4] Alien arrivals at Gulf and Atlantic ports to 1849, with Pacific ports included from 1850 to 1868 (though ports in the control of the Confederacy were excluded during 1861–65. From 1868 data refer, in principle, to aliens arriving with intent to reside, and from 1906 to aliens arriving with intent to settle. Arrivals in Alaska are included irregularly from 1871 to 1903, but regularly thereafter. Arrivals in Hawaii are included from 1901, in Puerto Rico from 1902, and in the US Virgin Islands from 1942. Arrivals at land frontiers were included in a very incomplete fashion in the early years, and not fully until 1908. There were changes in the categories of people included in the statistics at various times. The main ones were the exclusion of immigrants who came as first- or second-class passengers from 1892 to 1903, and the exclusion of aliens in transit from 1904, and of resident aliens returning from visits abroad from 1907. There were changes in the treatment of aliens entering via land frontiers in 1930, 1946 and 1953. Data are for years ending 30 June except for 1820–31 and 1844–50 (which are for years ending 30 September), and 1851–67 (which are for calendar years). The figure for 1832 is for the 15 months ending 31 December, that for 1843 is for the 9 months ending 30 September, and that for 1868 is for the first half-year.
[5] Immigrants were defined as third-class passengers arriving at Brazilian ports to 1907 (1st line). From 1907 (2nd line) to 1964 only aliens were included.
[6] Immigrants and emigrants were defined as alien second- and third-class passengers, except that all classes were counted as emigrants from 1933 (2nd line) to 1943. Only movements by sea are covered to 1957.
[7] Data from 1882 to 1913 (1st line) relate to immigrants from and emigrants to India only.
[8] Aliens only to 1928.
[9] Includes persons who were granted permanent residence under 1986 Immigration Reform & Control Act.

B LABOUR FORCE

The Statistics in this section cover a wide range of topics and come from a variety of sources. The occupation data up to 1966 were largely derived by Professor Bairoch and his colleagues from national censuses of population. The problems of accuracy referred to in the last section appear here also. But a still more significant difficulty is the very considerable variations which have occurred in classification, both between countries and over time. Professor Bairoch's group refer to 'the frequent changes in criteria and methods used in census taking', and say that 'it is practically impossible to come up with statistics that are perfectly comparable in time and space'.[1] The best we can hope for, therefore, is that the figures in table 1 are usable as a guide to structural changes within countries, and for rough international comparisons.

An even greater degree of heterogeneity is to be found in the unemployment statistics, some of which come from trade union records (of varying character and reliability), some from insurance statistics (which can be just as variable), and some from either total registration or sample surveys. In addition to variations in the definition of the unemployed, where percentages are shown there are also likely to be variations in the definition of the total workforce. It will be readily understood, therefore, that comparisons between countries must be made with due regard to changes in the nature of the series, and that comparisons between countries must not be made without taking differences of definition into account. The same applies to the statistics of industrial disputes, shown in table 3, though there is more homogeneity within each country's data. It is noticeable that dictatorships, both of the Right and of the Left, have tended to suppress statistics of both unemployment and industrial disputes, and this accounts for some of the gaps in these series.

Information on wages is often plentiful but of extreme heterogeneity and complexity, and statistics are notoriously intractable. Because of this, it is perhaps best to treat the indices shown in tables 4 and 5 as little more than impressions of the general course of money wages. Apart from the well-known technical problems of index numbers, dealt with in any textbook of statistics, there are problems in each country of availability and selection of data; of weighting different occupations; and of the appropriateness (which often takes the form of assessing obsolescence) of the chosen weights; of the differences between hourly, daily or weekly wage rates, and between rates and actual earnings. Moreover, it must be stressed that these tables are concerned with money wages, not real wages, for which very rough estimates may be made by using the data in section 1. In general, comparisons between countries are extremely difficult, and require a degree of original research which it has not been possible to afford here. In fact, the whole subject, despite its obvious interest to politicians and others with axes to grind, has received very little scholarly attention, though there is a number of studies of individual countries.

---

[1] P. Bairoch *et al*, La Population Active et sa Structure (Brussels, 1968).

B1   NORTH AMERICA: ECONOMICALLY ACTIVE POPULATION BY MAJOR INDUSTRIAL GROUPS (in thousands)[1]

BARBADOS   1946–1993

	Agriculture, Forestry & Fishing	Extractive Industry	Manufacturing Industry[2]	construction	Commerce, Finance, etc	Transport & Communications	Services[3]	Others Occupied
Males								
1946	15	0.4	11	8.0	5	4.0	7	0.3
1960	13	0.4	10	9.0	7	4.0	7	0.1
1970	9	0.3	9	10.0	6[4]	4.0	11[4]	2
1981	6	- -	8	6.0	14	4.0	20	—
1993	3.2	- -	5	6.6	9	3.4	18	4.3
Females								
1946	11	—	7	0.3	7	0.1	15	—
1960	9	0.1	4	0.3	8	0.3	13	—
1970	5	- -	5	0.3	6[4]	0.6	15[4]	1
1981	4	- -	8	0.2	13	1	17	—
1993	2	- -	5	0.3	10	1.2	20	5

CANADA[5]   1891–1991

	Agriculture, Forestry & Fishing	Extractive Industry	Manufacturing Industry[2]	construction	Commerce, Finance, etc	Transport & Communications	Services[3]	Others Occupied
Males								
1891[6]	766	15	176	87	81	60	88	137
1901[6]	751	28	229	89	92	81	101	173
1911	995	63	639		241	211	210	—
1921	1,093	51	748		314	226	250	—
1931	1,199	59	593		323	249	288	551[8]
1941[7]	1,207	93	808	219	414	245	651	41
1951[7]	970	102	1,142	345	578	354	577	55
1961	704	117	1,243	456	750	423	896	117
1971	465	112	1,372	530	1,193	466	1,147	381
1981	487	145	1,696	718	1,799	585	1,431	228
1991	318	283	1,497	798	1,623	735	2,283	—
Females								
1891[6]	12.0	—	62	- -	7	1	116	4
1901[6]	9.0	- -	71	- -	8	1	136	14
1911	16	- -	99		42	7	201	—
1921	18	- -	106		97	21	247	—
1931	25	—	85		63	17	348	129[8]
1941[7]	20	1	183	2	141	19	463	5
1951[7]	38	2	280	6	276	49	501	13
1961	81	5	317	12	404	74	832	42
1971	116	8	416	28	912	97	1,084	92
1981	132	24	441	76	1,832	186	1,779	176
1991	158	42	625	93	1,573	260	3,387	—

COSTA RICA   1950–1993

	Agriculture, Forestry & Fishing	Extractive Industry	Manufacturing Industry[2]	construction	Commerce, Finance, etc	Transport & Communications	Services[3]	Others Occupied
Males								
1950	144	1	25	12	17	9	15	8
1963	191	1	39	23	32	14	27	5
1973	209	1	57	39	61	24	54	9
1984	242	2	83	41	77	19	92	64
1993	236	1.5	131	69	157	47	130	9
Females								
1950	5	—	7	- -	4	1	26	- -
1963	4	—	11	- -	7	1	41	1
1973	5	- -	19	- -	20	1	65	1
1984	8	- -	32	- -	31	2	84	19
1993	20	- -	73	1	92	5	138	4

B1 NORTH AMERICA: Economically Active Population by Major Industrial Groups (in thousands)

CUBA
1919–1981

	Agriculture, Forestry & Fishing	Extractive Industry	Manufacturing Industry[2]	Construction	Commerce, Finance, etc	Transport & Communications	Services[3]	Others Occupied
Males								
1919	454	1	161		145		98	—
1943	620	6	154	26	140	33	103	284
1953	804	9	286	64	212	100	230	10
1970	751	15	416	154	634	150	438	30
1981	678	21	452	279	712[9]	205	[9]	88
Females								
1919	8	—	29		3		50	—
1943	11	—	36	- -	9	1	69	31
1953	15	- -	50	1	20	4	166	1
1970	39	1	101	3	320	11	209	7
1981	113	4	192	34	680[9]	43	[9]	40

DOMINICAN REPUBLIC
1920–1981

	Agriculture, Forestry & Fishing	Extractive Industry	Manufacturing Industry[2]	Construction	Commerce, Finance, etc	Transport & Communications	Services[3]	Others Occupied
Total								
1920	138	23			12	2	15	14
Males								
1950	436	- -	43	20	33	12	32	94
1960	495	2	58	21	43	21	38	54
1970	458	1	83	25	77	39	87	127
1981	378	4	179	78	147	37	157	285
Females								
1950	13	—	16	—	9	- -	36	56
1960	9	—	12	- -	12	- -	54	2
1970	9	- -	20	4	20	4	67	109
1981	42	- -	59	3	68	4	206	131

EL SALVADOR
1950–1991

	Agriculture, Forestry & Fishing	Extractive Industry	Manufacturing Industry[2]	Construction	Commerce, Finance, etc	Transport & Communications	Services[3]	Others Occupied
Males								
1950	399	2	51	19	19	10	30	17
1961	472	1	71	33	27	17	38	6
1971	609	1	78	32	48	24	83	39
1991	79	1	116	50	102	47	116	—
Females								
1950	13	—	25	- -	17	- -	48	5
1961	15	—	34	- -	25	- -	67	2
1971	23	- -	40	- -	46	1	125	17
1991	21	- -	96	2	163	3	134	—

GUATEMALA
1950–1995

	Agriculture, Forestry & Fishing	Extractive Industry	Manufacturing Industry[2]	Construction	Commerce, Finance, etc	Transport & Communications	Services[3]	Others Occupied
Males								
1950	642	1	78	26	36	15	42	4
1964	841	2	114	34	59	28	65	9
1973	866	2	170	62	80	37	86	31[10]
1981	887	2	142	85	113	41	113	65
1995	1,768	3	329	126	155	75	164	48
Females								
1950	18	—	35	- -	17	- -	53	- -
1964	20	- -	37	- -	24	1	84	1
1973	15	- -	47	- -	34	1	108	7[10]
1981	22	- -	43	1	55	2	102	23
1995	30	- -	92	1	71	2	207	13

HAITI
1950–1991

	Agriculture, Forestry & Fishing	Extractive Industry	Manufacturing Industry[2]	Construction	Commerce, Finance, etc	Transport & Communications	Services[3]	Others Occupied
Males								
1950	771	- -	38	10	7	6	26	3
1971	880	1	53	18	21	11	64	178
1982	849	9	67	19	67	14	65	27
1991	1,077	11	83	23	85	17	81	33
Females								
1950	683	- -	48	- -	54	- -	45	2
1971	549	- -	68	- -	176	1	94	213
1982	374	10	56	4	223	2	60	25
1991	458	12	68	4	273	2	73	30

B1   NORTH AMERICA: Economically Active Population by Major Industrial Groups (in thousands)[1]

HONDURAS   1950–1990

	Agriculture, Forestry & Fishing	Extractive Industry	Manufacturing Industry[2]	Construction	Commerce, Finance, etc	Transport & Communications	Services[3]	Others Occupied
Total								
1950	538	3	39	7	8	7	29	17
Males								
1961	376	2	32	11	18	8	27	22
1974	452	2	54	24	40	20	38	7
1990	589	2	68	47	79	25	76	7
Females								
1961	4	—	13	- -	9	1	43	5
1974	9	- -	32	- -	25	1	50	1
1990	17	- -	68	1	108	3	109	- -

JAMAICA   1943–1990

	Agriculture, Forestry & Fishing	Extractive Industry	Manufacturing Industry[2]	Construction	Commerce, Finance, etc	Transport & Communications	Services[3]	Others Occupied
Males								
1943	183	- -	34	31	16	{— 58 —}		
1953	226	8	43	19	19	13	27[11]	27
1960	197	4	49	49	26	17	37	4
1973	{— 174 —}		65	53	32	23	77	5
1982	113	5	47	21	29	16	63	30
1990	181	6.5	102	65	50	35	99	3
Females								
1943	45	- -	25	4	22	{— 87 —}		
1953	74	- -	35	2	33	2	79[11]	8
1960	39	1	44	1	35	2	96	7
1973	{— 47 —}		30	2	68	7	165	3
1982	14	1	14	1	42	5	85	19
1990	63	1	5	2	103	10	201	4

MARTINIQUE   1961–1993

	Agriculture, Forestry & Fishing	Extractive Industry	Manufacturing Industry[2]	Construction	Commerce, Finance, etc	Transport & Communications	Services[3]	Others Occupied
Males								
1961	24	- -	8	8	3	4	8	1
1967	18	- -	8	10	4	5	11	1
1974	12	- -	5	8	7	4	13	5
1982	7	2	3	8	12	4	12	6
1993	7	{— 8 —}		9	12	3	25	—
Females								
1961	11	—	4	- -	6	- -	14	1
1967	8	- -	2	- -	7	- -	14	- -
1974	4	- -	2	- -	7	- -	20	4
1982	3	—	2	- -	16	1	17	2
1993	2	{— 3 —}		- -	10	1	30	—

B1 NORTH AMERICA: Economically Active Population by Major Industrial Groups (in thousands)[1]

MEXICO   1900–1990

	Agriculture, Forestry & Fishing	Extractive Industry	Manufactur- ing Industry[2]	Construction	Commerce, Finance, etc	Transport & Communica- tions	Services[3]	Others Occu- pied
Males								
1900[12]	3,130	97	496		189	58	208[13]	174
1910[12]	3,519	95	422		221	54	316	43
1921	3,459	26	439		222	74	155	439
1930	3,601	51	526	61	234	106	231	170
1940	3,791	105	462	105	456	147	216	144
1960	5,480	132	1,344	394	785	338	760	64
1970	4,837	167	1,771[14]	553	863	351	1,438[14]	509
1980	4,958	354	1,991	1,094	1,464	606	1,177	4,194
1990	5,110	232	3,436	1,551	3,074	1,045	2,891	499
Females								
1900[12]	27	1	262		49	- -	3,799[13]	186
1910[12]	62	1	228		56	- -	566	35
1921	31	2	194		49	1	234	212
1930	26	- -	105	—	40	1	161	372
1940	40	1	72	1	97	3	199	433
1960	664	10	254	14	290	19	767	18
1970	267	14	453	18	334	17	1,127[14]	238
1980	743	159	706	214	698	78	1,274	2,232
1990	189	27	1,057	43	1,591	948	2,192	304
Total								
1950	4,824	97	998[14]	225	684	211	879	355

B1   NORTH AMERICA: Economically Active Population by Major Industrial Groups (in thousands)[1]

NICARAGUA   1940-1991

	Agriculture, Forestry & Fishing	Extractive Industry	Manufactur-ing Industry[2]	Construction	Commerce, Finance,etc	Transport & Communica-tions	Services[3]	Others Occu-pied
Males								
1940	248	5	18[15]	4	...[15]	2	4	17
1950	218	3	28	9	10	6	10	—
1963	269	4	39	16	17	12	22	1
1971	228	3	47	20	30	17	43	7
Females								
1940	10	—	19[15]	—	...[15]	- -	6	22
1950	5	—	11	- -	5	- -	25	—
1963	14	- -	18	—	17	- -	46	1
1971	9	- -	18	- -	24	1	56	2

PANAMA[16]   1940-1990

	Agriculture, Forestry & Fishing	Extractive Industry	Manufactur-ing Industry[2]	Construction	Commerce, Finance,etc	Transport & Communica-tions	Services[3]	Others Occu-pied
Males								
1940	103	- -	9	8	9	4	12	26[17]
1950	124	- -	14	7	15	6	15	15[17]
1960	151	- -	21	14	21	9	27	19[17]
1970	179	1	30	27	44	14	40	19[17]
1980	137	1	48	29	54	24	55	19
1990	189	1	55	33	123	46	86	- -
Females								
1940	6	—	5	- -	2	- -	18	4[17]
1950	7	—	6	- -	5	1	23	4[17]
1960	5	—	7	- -	10	1	41	5[17]
1970	9	- -	13	1	23	2	62	5[17]
1980	6	- -	13	1	31	5	73	5
1990	6	- -	26	1	78	8	141	- -

PUERTO RICO   1940-1992

	Agriculture, Forestry & Fishing	Extractive Industry	Manufactur-ing Industry[2]	Construction	Commerce, Finance,etc	Transport & Communica-tions	Services[3]	Others Occu-pied
Males								
1940	224	1	43	16	45	18	35	3
1950	216	2	56	31	56	26	61	9
1960	134	2	72	51	73	27	78	12
1973	63	1	111	112	140	39	169	4
1980	29	1	109	64	149	43	135	8
1992	40	2	112	84	167	36	266	- -
Females								
1940	6	—	64	- -	6	1	51	1
1950	4	—	54	- -	9	1	64	4
1960	2	—	43	1	19	2	71	7
1973	3	—	87	1	52	5	135	5
1980	1	- -	74	3	56	16	154	7
1992	1	- -	88	2	90	6	241	- -

B1 NORTH AMERICA: Economically Active Population by Major Industrial Groups (in thousands)[1]

TRINIDAD & TOBAGO   1946–1993

	Agriculture, Forestry & Fishing	Extractive Industry	Manufactur- ing Industry[2]	Construction	Commerce, Finance,etc	Transport & Communica- tions	Services[3]	Others Occu- pied
Males								
1946	48	7	48		13	12	26	6
1956	48	15	61		19	19	22	—
1960	44	13	36	29	23	15	33	- -
1971	55		109		29	22	38	—
1980	29	18	34	58	33	23	44	8
1993	42	17	33	65	57	28	68	2
Females								
1946	11	- -	11		6	1	23	1
1956	19	- -	15		12	1	34	—
1960	11	- -	10	1	12	1	34	- -
1971	20		19		18	2	39	—
1980	5	1	12	6	28	4	40	3
1993	8	2	17	15	61	6	75	1

USA   1820–1990

	Agriculture, Forestry & Fishing	Extractive Industry	Manufactur- ing Industry[2]	Construction	Commerce, Finance,etc	Transport & Communica- tions	Services[3]	Others Occu- pied
Total								
1820	2,070[18]	. . .	350		. . .		. . .	460
1830	2,770[18]	. . .	. . .		. . .		. . .	1,160
1840	3,720[18]	15	790		. . .		. . .	895
1850	4,925	90	1,260[20]		420[20]		940	65
1860	6,260	170	1,930[20]		780[20]		1,310	80
1870	6,910[19]	180[19]	2,750[20][19]		1,350[20][19]		1,700[19]	30[19]
	6,490	200	2,250[20]	750	830	640[20]	1,620	140
1880	8,705	310	3,170[20]	830	1,220	860[20]	2,100	195
1890	10,170	480	4,750[20]	1,440	1,990	1,530[20]	3,210	170
1900	10,920	760	6,340[20]	1,660	2,760	2,100[20]	4,160	370
1910	11,590	1,050	8,230[20]	2,300	3,890	3,190[20]	5,880	600
1920	11,400	1,230	10,880[20]	2,170	4,860	4,190[20]	6,500	380
1930	10,750[19]	1,150[19]	10,990[20][19]	3,030[19]	7,450[19]	4,850[20][19]	9,280[19]	1,340[19]
Males								
1940	8,628	1,098	9,652	3,463	6,333	2,540	6,318	1,418
1950	6,568	947	12,192	3,661	8,350	3,186	7,801	1,015
1960	4,069	681	14,557	4,141	9,117	3,031	9,985	1,732
1970	3,040	494	16,750	4,972	11,097	3,262	14,503	—
1980	2,936	870	17,130	6,326	15,135	3,863	15,434	—
1990	2,807	647	15,069	7,758	19,792	4,743	15,762	—
Females								
1940	513	12	2,674	46	2,154	300	6,232	634
1950	612	24	3,915	103	4,497	616	6,240	528
1960	450	33	4,898	162	5,915	684	9,075	1,115
1970	633	38	6,393	251	8,702	1,013	14,251	—
1980	729	133	7,843	527	14,589	1,427	19,027	—
1990	760	119	7,394	712	19,972	2,072	24,814	—

B1   SOUTH AMERICA: ECONOMICALLY ACTIVE POPULATION BY MAJOR INDUSTRIAL GROUPS (in thousands)[1]

ARGENTINA   **1895–1980**

	Agriculture, Forestry & Fishing	Extractive Industry	Manufacturing Industry[2]	Construction	Commerce, Finance,etc	Transport & Communications	Services[3]	Others Occupied
Males								
1895	326		185		133	63	288	524
1914	488	1	487		272	109	229	891
1947[21]	1,534	32	1,053	334	748	375	779	179
1960	1,345	42	1,577	416	734	450	719	601
1970	1,243	43	1,448	699	1,192	541	974	582
1980	1,123	44	1,651	981	1,487	425	1,044	495
Females								
1895	67		181		10	- -	211	664
1914	42	—	353		21	2	241	26
1947[21]	88	1	404	4	107	12	596	22
1960	116	2	424	7	171	28	800	168
1970	88	2	420	12	385	52	1,125	205
1980	78	3	438	22	611	36	1,355	197

BOLIVIA   **1950–1991**

	Agriculture, Forestry & Fishing	Extractive Industry	Manufacturing Industry[2]	Construction	Commerce, Finance,etc	Transport & Communications	Services[3]	Others Occupied
Males								
1950	275	39	96	25	33	21	18	7
1976	604	57	91	82	60	54	166	45
1991	12	18	109	74	108	60	135	31
Females								
1950	397	4	55	1	24	1	52	2
1976	89	3	57	1	60	2	116	9
1991	4	2	49	2	160	4	140	23

BRAZIL   **1872–1990**

	Agriculture, Forestry & Fishing	Extractive Industry	Manufacturing Industry[2]	Construction	Commerce, Finance,etc	Transport & Communications	Services[3]	Others Occupied
Total								
1872	3,261		789		102	22	1,143	—
1900	5,251				323	72	2,478	—
1920	6,452		1,189		498	254	758	—
Males								
1940[22]	8,183	345	1,107		746	460	939	—
1950[16]	9,609		1,842		972	668	1,480	38[23]
1960	10,523	523	1,513[24]	776	1,345	1,044	1,291	1,580[24]
1970	11,833	172	2,813	1,705	2,249	1,183	2,916	551
1980	11,376		5,790	3,096	6,055	1,671	2,317	861
1990	11,235		7,538	3,726	5,060	2,246	10,213	—
Females								
1940[22]	1,270	45	293		55	14	563	—
1950[16]	761		389		102	29	1,218	9[23]
1960	1,175	50	493[24]	8	175	45	1,442	669[24]
1970	1,258	3	618	15	448	62	3,600	162
1980	1,733		1,734	55	5,146	145	2,540	394
1990	2,945		2,733	97	2,916	194	13,198	—

B1 SOUTH AMERICA: Economically Active Population by Major Industrial Groups (in thousands)[1]

CHILE

1920–1994

	Agriculture, Forestry & Fishing	Extractive Industry	Manufacturing Industry[2]	Construction	Commerce, Finance,etc	Transport & Communications	Services[3]	Others Occupied
Males								
1920	442	56	177		96	62	89	71
1930	481	77	205		120	67	91	29
1940	581	94	205	58	124	71	185	2
1952	606	99	277	101	167	90	193	64
1960	639	90	327	135	182	112	232	120
1970	552	79	356	172	245	154	336	186
1982	625	76	408	228	192	423	496	205
1994	720	82	594	350	712	328	542	—
Females								
1920	50	- -	149		23	3	119	6
1930	25	1	91		28	3	109	12
1940	40	2	93	1	39	4	245	2
1952	42	2	133	1	56	6	286	13
1960	24	2	103	1	59	6	312	28
1970	19	2	111	3	102	12	313	55
1982	21	2	105	4	—	—	517	64
1994	88	3	223	10	516	43	725	—

COLOMBIA

1938–1992

	Agriculture, Forestry & Fishing	Extractive Industry	Manufacturing Industry[2]	Construction	Commerce, Finance,etc	Transport & Communications	Services[3]	Others Occupied
Males								
1938[25]	1,758	52	180[27]	84	130	59	133[27]	25
1951[26]	1,930	45	304	131	158	124	236	116
1964	2,311	61	489	217	332	179	374	138
1973	1,493	27	506	195	469	153	352	725
1992	52	15	660	288	895	266	604	8
Females								
1938[25]	52	23	261[27]	2	31	3	178[27]	5
1951[26]	93	16	157	2	45	6	362	19
1964	116	20	180	3	109	12	552	39
1973	53	9	193	5	199	14	486	238
1992	15	4	477	16	682	32	781	6

ECUADOR

1950–1990

	Agriculture, Forestry & Fishing	Extractive Industry	Manufacturing Industry[2]	Construction	Commerce, Finance,etc	Transport & Communications	Services[3]	Others Occupied
Males								
1950	552	5	126	26	50	26	66	37
1962[16]	762	3	149	47	74	42	92	39
1974	857	6	167	84	153	52	192	75
1982	728	7	226	155	215	96	344	29
1990	904	18	248	192	350	123	483	111
Females								
1950	89	- -	108	1	26	1	76	17
1962[16]	40	- -	66	1	23	1	99	5
1974	40	- -	67	2	56	3	138	18
1982	59	- -	74	3	101	5	211	10
1990	131	2	122	5	208	7	354	45

B1　SOUTH AMERICA: Economically Active Population by Major Industrial Groups (in thousands)[1]

GUYANA*　　　　　1946-1980

	Agriculture, Forestry & Fishing	Extractive Industry	Manufacturing Industry[2]	Construction	Commerce, Finance,etc	Transport & Communications	Services[3]	Others Occupied
Males								
1946[16]	51	4	17	7	8	6	11	1
1960	50	6	22	13	13	7	13	- -
1980	44	9	25	6	11	8	36	15
Females								
1946[16]	16	—	6	- -	4	- -	14	- -
1960	10	- -	15	- -	6	- -	16	—
1980	5	1	5	- -	7	1	22	- -

PARAGUAY　　　　　1950-1994

	Agriculture, Forestry & Fishing	Extractive Industry	Manufacturing Industry[2]	Construction	Commerce, Finance,etc	Transport & Communications	Services[3]	Others Occupied
Males								
1950[16]	212	- -	40	13	18	9	34	—[28]
1962[16]	291	- -	50	18	25	15	58	17
1972	347	1	63	27	40	20	59	15
1982	423	1	83	70	66	28	92	65
1994	40	—	132	98	185	50	116	8
Females								
1950[16]	23	—	29	- -	12	- -	34	—[28]
1962[16]	31	—	45	- -	17	1	45	4
1972	21	—	45	- -	25	1	62	3
1982	23	- -	44	- -	38	2	82	15
1994	3	—	55	—	178	6	93	106

PERU　　　　　1940-1991

	Agriculture, Forestry & Fishing	Extractive Industry	Manufacturing Industry[2]	Construction	Commerce, Finance,etc	Transport & Communications	Services[3]	Others Occupied
Males								
1940[16]	1,061	44	166	45	76	49	126	33
1961[16]	1,341	65	307	104	203	89	242	99
1972	1,403	52	361	169	311	158	378	148
1981	1,597	92	436	194	504	196	658	162
1991	1,680	86	313	111	388	141	472	—
Females								
1940[16]	486	1	215	1	36	2	128	8
1961[16]	215	2	116	1	79	5	234	27
1972	133	1	127	2	134	7	286	48
1981	267	5	138	4	250	14	410	110
1991	370	2	140	—	390	12	420	—

URUGUAY　　　　　1963-1992

	Agriculture, Forestry & Fishing	Extractive Industry	Manufacturing Industry[2]	Construction	Commerce, Finance,etc	Transport & Communications	Services[3]	Others Occupied
Males								
1963	177	2	175	55	103	55	134	45
1975	165	2	156	59	121	49	162	61
1985	156	2	157	64	121	51	170	56
1992	50	1.6	159	83	167	59	178	—
Females								
1963	7	- -	70	- -	26	3	135	14
1975	10	- -	66	1	43	5	154	24
1985	14	- -	76	1	61	8	200	24
1992	5	- -	102	2	124	9	268	—

VENEZUELA　　　　　1941-1991

	Agriculture, Forestry & Fishing	Extractive Industry	Manufacturing Industry[2]	Construction	Commerce, Finance,etc	Transport & Communications	Services[3]	Others Occupied
Males								
1941	595	22	69	39	93	42	102	—
1950[16]	669	42	129	90	133	51	171	30
1961[16]	745	44	242	126	265	102	308	110
1971	593	36	353	155	312	115	401	344
1981	515	49	539	378	644	245	578	365
1991	795	65	871	658	1,211	382	951	15
Females								
1941	41	1	98	1	8	- -	130	—
1950[16]	36	3	49	1	17	2	171	7
1961[16]	29	3	79	2	40	4	264	25
1971	18	2	84	4	66	9	376	109
1981	19	6	154	22	283	32	613	107
1991	41	10	335	27	762	39	1,111	6

B1   Economically Active Population by Major Industrial Groups

NOTES

1. SOURCES: The immediate source of most statistics up to 1961 is P. Bairoch *et al*, *The Working Population and its Structure* (Institut de Sociologie, Université Libre de Bruxelles, 1968). The original sources are described in detail there. Later statistics are taken from ILO, *Yearbook of Labour Statistics*. Canadian statistics for 1891 and 1901 are taken from M.C. Urquhart and K.A.H. Buckley (eds.), *Historical Statistics of Canada* (Cambridge and Toronto, 1965); American statistics to 1930 are taken from *Historical Statistics of the United States*; Argentinian statistics for 1895 are taken from Ernesto Tornquist & Co. Ltd, *The Economic Development of the Argentine Republic in the last Fifty Years* (Buenos Aires, 1919).
2. Professor Bairoch and his colleagues 'tried to as great an extent as possible to unify the statistics in different countries during different periods', but were unable to achieve anything like perfect comparability. Comparisons between countries must be made with especially great caution owing to differences in classification, including differences in the definition of 'economically active'
3. Where the original data were for an occupational rather than an industrial classification, this was usually transposed, with, of course, some degree of estimation involved.

FOOTNOTES

[1]   Unless otherwise indicated, all statistics relate to the boundaries of the year concerned.
[2]   Unless otherwise indicated, gas, water, electricity and sanitary service workers are included under this heading.
[3]   Unless otherwise indicated, armed forces are included under this heading.
[4]   Banks, insurance, etc are included with 'Services'.
[5]   In 1881 total numbers engaged in agricultural pursuits were 662 thousand, with 715 thousand in non-agricultural pursuits.
[6]   Labourers and clerical workers are not included in the sector in which they worked but in 'Others Occupied'.
[7]   Excluding Yukon and Northwest Territories.
[8]   Including the armed forces.
[9]   Services are included with Commerce etc.
[10]   Including those seeking employment for the first time.
[11]   Excluding the armed forces.
[12]   A small number of females was probably included with males.
[13]   Including domestics in agriculture and housewives.
[14]   Gas, water, etc, but not electricity, are included in 'Services' rather than in 'Manufacturing Industry'.
[15]   Commerce, finance, etc, are included in 'Manufacturing Industry'.
[16]   Excluding tribal Indians.
[17]   Including those working in the Canal Zone.
[18]   Agriculture only.
[19]   There were changes in classification.
[20]   Public utility employees are included with 'Transport & Communications' rather than 'Manufacturing Industry'.
[21]   Unemployed people are excluded.
[22]   Excluding domestic activities.
[23]   A further 32 thousand were unclassified by either sex or occupation.
[24]   Public utility employees are included with 'Others Occupied' rather than 'Manufacturing Industry'.
[25]   Excluding certain localities and all the indigenous population.
[26]   Excluding the indigenous population of Norte de Santander department.
[27]   Sanitation services are included under 'Services' rather than 'Manufacturing Industry'.
[28]   13 thousand were unclassified either by sex or by occupation.

B2 NORTH AMERICA: UNEMPLOYMENT (numbers in thousands; percentage of appropriate workforce)

	Canada[1]		Mexico[10]	USA[2]	
	No.	%	No.	No.	%
1890	...	...	...	904	4.0
1891	...	...	...	1,265	5.4
1892	...	...	...	728	3.0
1893	...	...	...	2,860	11.7
1894	...	...	...	4,612	18.4
1895	...	...	...	3,510	13.7
1896	...	...	...	3,782	14.4
1897	...	...	...	3,890	14.5
1898	...	...	...	3,351	12.4
1899	...	...	...	1,819	6.5
1900	...	...	...	1,420	5.0
1901	...	...	...	1,205	4.0
1902	...	...	...	1,097	3.7
1903	...	...	...	1,204	3.9
1904	...	...	...	1,691	5.4
1905	...	...	...	1,381	4.3
1906	...	...	...	574	1.7
1907	...	...	...	945	2.8
1908	...	...	...	2,780	8.0
1909	...	...	...	1,824	5.1
1910	...	...	...	2,150	5.9
1911	...	...	...	2,518	6.7
1912	...	...	...	1,759	4.6
1913	...	...	...	1,671	4.3
1914	...	...	...	3,120	7.9
1915	...	...	...	3,377	8.5
1916	...	...	...	2,043	5.1
1917	...	...	...	1,848	4.6
1918	...	...	...	536	1.4
1919	...	...	...	546	1.4
1920	...	...	...	2,132	5.2
1921	192	5.8	...	4,918	11.7
1921	150	4.4	...	2,859	6.7
1923	110	3.2	...	1,049	2.4
1924	158	4.5	...	2,190	5.0
1925	157	4.4	...	1,453	3.2
1926	108	3.0	...	801	1.8
1927	67	1.8	...	1,519	3.3
1928	65	1.7	...	1,982	4.2
1929	116	2.9	...	1,550	3.2
1930	371	9.1	90	4,340	8.7
1931	481	11.6	287	8,020	15.9
1932	741	17.6	339	12,060	23.6
1933	826	19.3	276	12,830	24.9
1934	631	14.5	235	11,340	21.7
1935	625	14.2	191	10,610	20.1
1936	571	12.8	187	9,030	16.9
1937	411	9.1	180	7,700	14.3
1938	522	11.4	209	10,390	19.0
1939	529	11.4	199	9,480	17.2

B2 NORTH AMERICA: Unemployment (numbers in thousands; percentage of appropriate workforce)

	Barbados		Canada[1]		Costa Rica[6]		Guatemala[8]	Honduras	Jamaica	
	No.	%	No.	%	No.	%	No.	No.	No.	%
1940	...	...	423	9.2	...	...	...	...	...	...
1941	...	...	195	4.4	...	...	...	...	...	...
1942	...	...	135	3.0	...	...	...	...	...	...
1943	...	...	76	1.7	...	...	...	...	...	...
1944	...	...	63	1.4	...	...	...	...	...	...
1945	...	...	73	1.6	...	...		...	...	...
1946	...	...	124	2.6	...	...		...	...	...
1947	...	...	92	1.9	...	...		...	...	...
1948	...	...	81	1.6	...	...		...	...	...
1949	...	...	101₄	2.0₄	...	...		...	...	...
1950	...	...	142	2.7	...	...	...	...	...	...
1951	...	...	81	1.5	...	...	...	...	...	...
1952	...	...	105	2.0	...	...	...	...	...	...
1953	...	...	115	2.1	...	...	...	...	...	...
1954	...	...	221	4.0	...	...	...	...	...	...
1955	...	...	214₁	3.8₁	...	...	...	...	...	...
			245	4.4						
1956			197	3.4	...	...	...	...	...	...
1957	...	...	278	4.6	...	...	...	...	...	...
1958	...	...	432	7.0	...	...	...	...	...	...
1959	3.05	...	372	6.0	...	...	0.63	...	...	...
1960	4.56	...	446	7.0	...	...	0.22	...	...	...
1961	4.32	...	466	7.1	...	...	0.15	...	...	...
1962	5.22	...	390	5.9	...	...	0.11	...	...	...
1963	2.06	...	374	5.5	...	...	0.13	...	...	...
1964	1.70	...	324	4.7	...	...	0.10	...	...	...
1965	1.16	...	280	3.9	...	...	0.08	...	...	...
1966	1.61	...	267	3.6	...	...	0.19	...	...	...
1967	1.42	...	315	4.1	...	...	0.33	...	...	...
1968	0.82	...	382	4.8	...	...	0.65	47	[145][9]	[19.9][9]
1969	0.69	...	376	4.7	...	...	0.74	47	132	17.6
1970	0.23	...	487	5.9	...	...	0.66	49	...	...
1971	0.13	...	543	6.4	...	...	0.66	51	...	...
1972	0.21	...	552	6.3	...	...	0.62₈	52	185	23.2
1973	0.42	...	509	5.6	...	...	0.57	53	176	21.9
1974	0.19	...	570₁	5.4₁	...	...	0.44	52	174	21.2
1975	...	...	690	6.9	...	...	0.93	79	175	20.5
1976	0.16	15.6	726	7.1	42	6.3	0.36	81₅	211	22.4
								101		
1977	0.16	15.7	849	8.1	32	4.6	0.22	105	215	24.1
1978	0.14	13.7	908	8.3	33	4.5	0.24	109	223	24.3
1979	[0.12][3]	[11.3][3]	836	7.4	37	4.9	0.22	113	259	27.5
1980	[0.13][3]	[11.4][3]	865₅	7.5₅	46	5.9	0.23	117	262	27.3
1981	0.12	10.8	898	7.5	70	8.7	0.26	113	256	25.9
1982	0.16	13.7	1,308	11.0	79	9.4	0.58	128	278	27.6
1983	0.17	15.0	1,434	11.8	76	9.0	0.31	254	266	26.4
1984	0.19	17.1	1,384	11.2	[44][7]	[5.0][7]	0.40	...	267	25.5
1985	0.21	18.7	1,311	10.5	61	6.8	0.22	...	261	25.0
1986	0.21	17.7	1,215	9.5	57	6.2	0.27	...	250	23.6
1987	0.21	17.4	1,150	8.8	54	5.9	0.22	...	224	21.0
1988	0.21	17.4	1,031	7.8	55	5.5	0.21	...	203	18.4
1989	0.17	13.7	1,065	7.5	38	3.8	1.90	...	177	18.9
1990	0.19	15.0	1,164	8.1	49	4.6	1.70	...	166	16.8
1991	0.21	17.1	1,492	10.4	59	5.5	1.80	...	168	15.7
1992	0.29	23.0	1,640	11.3	44	4.1	1.70	...	171	15.7
1993	0.31	24.5	1,649	11.2	47	4.1	1.60	...	177	15.9

B2 NORTH AMERICA: Unemployment (numbers in thousands; percentage of appropriate workforce)

	Mexico[10]		Panama[11]		Puerto Rico		Trinidad & Tobago		USA[2]	
	No	%	No.	%	No.	%	No.	%	No.	%
1940	185	...	...	...	...	...	...	...	8,120	14.6
1941	181	...	...	...	...	...	...	...	5,560	9.9
1942	158	...	...	...	...	...	...	...	2,660	4.7
1943	...	...	...	...	...	...	...	...	1,070	1.9
1944	...	...	...	...	...	...	...	...	670	1.2
1945	...	...	...	...	...	...	...	...	1,040	1.9
1946	...	...	...	...	[80][12]	[12.0][12]	...	...	2,270	3.9
1947	...	...	...	...	76	11.1	...	...	2,311	3.9
1948	...	...	...	...	71	10.4	...	...	2,276	3.8
1949	...	...	...	...	79	11.2	...	...	3,637	5.9
1950	...	...	...	...	[98][13]	[13.7][13]	...	...	3,288	5.3
1951	...	...	...	...	114	16.2	...	...	2,055	3.3
1952	...	...	...	...	100	15.2	...	...	1,883$_2$	3.0$_2$
1953	...	...	...	...	91	14.4	...	...	1,834	2.9
1954	...	...	...	...	97	15.4	...	...	3,532	5.5
1955	...	...	...	...	92	14.3	...	...	2,852	4.4
1956	...	...	...	...	83	13.0	...	...	2,750	4.1
1957	...	...	...	...	82	13.0	...	...	2,859	4.3
1958	...	...	...	...	89	13.9	...	...	4,602	6.8
1959	...	...	...	...	87	13.8	...	...	3,740	5.5
1960	...	...	...	...	77	12.1	...	...	3,852	5.5
1961	...	...	...	...	85	12.6	...	...	4,714	6.7
1962	...	...	...	...	86	12.6	...	...	3,911	5.5
1963	...	...	21	5.8	83	11.8	...	...	4,070	5.7
1964	...	...	27	7.4	81	11.1	...	...	3,786	5.2
1965	...	...	29	7.6	91	12.0	48	14.0	3,366	4.5
1966	...	...	20	5.1	86	11.8	49	14.0	2,875	3.8
1967	...	...	25	6.2	87	11.7	54	15.0	2,975	3.8
1968	...	...	31	7.0	83	11.1	54	15.0	2,817	3.6
1969	...	...	30	6.6	76	10.0	48	13.5	2,831	3.5
1970	...	...	33	7.1	83	10.8	46	12.5	4,088	4.9
1971	...	...	36	7.6	93	11.6	[46][14]	[12.6][14]	4,993	5.9
1972	...	...	33	6.8	100	11.9	...	...	4,882	5.6
1973	...	...	35	7.0	98	11.6	59	15.4	4,365	4.9
1974	...	...	30[11]	5.8[11]	110	13.2	60	15.3	5,156	5.6
1975	382	7.2	32[11]	6.4[11]	149	18.1	59	15.0	7,929	8.3
1976	375	6.7	34	6.7	167	19.5	...	...	7,406	7.6
1977	472	8.0	45[11]	8.7[11]	174	19.9	57	13.4	6,991	6.9
1978	424	6.9	44	8.1	161	18.1	53	12.0	6,202	6.0
1979	...	5.7 4.5	51	8.8	153	17.0	49$_5$	11.0$_5$	6,137	5.8
1980	...	4.2	...	...	156	17.1	42	10.0	7,637	7.0
1981	...	4.2	...	...	184	19.9	45	10.2	8,273	7.3
1982	...	6.8	51	8.4	208	22.8	44	10.0	10,678	9.5
1983	...	6.0	64	9.7	220	23.4	50	11.0	10,717	9.5
1984	...	4.8	69	10.1	198	20.7	63	13.5	8,539	7.5
1985	...	4.9	88	12.3	211	21.8	73	15.5	8,312	7.2
1986	...	...	76	10.5	188	18.9	81	17.2	8,237	7.0
1987	...	3.9	91	11.8	171	16.8	107	22.3	7,425	6.2
1988	723	3.6	128	16.3	158	15.0	105	22.0	6,701	5.5
1989	...	3.0	133	16.3	163	14.6	103	22.0	6,528	5.3
1990	695	2.8	...	...	160	14.1	94	20.0	6,874	5.5
1991		2.6	136	16.0	186	16.0	91	18.5	8,426	6.7
1992	...	2.8	134	14.7	197	16.6	99	19.6	9,384	7.4
1993	819	3.4	125	13.3	206	17.0	100	19.8	8,734	6.8

B2 SOUTH AMERICA: UNEMPLOYMENT (numbers in thousands; percentages of appropriate workforce)

1931–1959   **1960–1993**

	Chile[15]	Guyana	Surinam[16]		Argentina[17]		Bolivia		Brazil[19]	
	No	No	No		No	%	No	%	No	%
1960				**1960**	...	...	...	...	...	...
1931	29.0			**1961**	...	...	...	...	...	...
1932	107.0	...	...	**1962**	...	...	...	...	...	...
1933	72.0	...	...	**1963**	...	...	...	...	...	...
1934	30.0	...	...	**1964**	[178][18]	[5.7][18]	...	...	...	...
1935	11.0	...	...	**1965**	167	5.3	...	...	...	...
1936	6.5	...	...	**1966**	173	5.6	...	...	...	...
1937	3.2	...	...	**1967**	199	6.4	...	...	...	...
1938	4.6	...	...	**1968**	153	5.0	...	...	710	...
1939	9.4	...	...	**1969**	140	4.3	...	...	698	...
1940	8.6	...	...	**1970**	158	4.8	...	...	725	...
1941	4.1	...	...	**1971**	196	6.0	123	9.0	723	...
1942	2.5	...	...	**1972**	221	6.6	112	8.1	1,034	...
1943	3.6[15]	...	...	**1973**	173	5.6	101	7.1	968	...
	2.8									
1944	3.3	...	...	**1974**	121	3.4	89	6.1	...	...
1945	3.5	...	...	**1975**	97	2.3	77	5.2	...	...
1946	3.4	...	...	**1976**	159	4.5	87	5.5	713	1.8
1947	3.7	...	...	**1977**	103	2.8	89	5.3	953	2.3
1948	3.2	...	...	**1978**	102	2.8	95	5.5	1,003[19]	2.4[19]
1949	3.4	...	...	**1979**	69	2.0	99	5.6	1,210	2.8
1950	2.9	1.6	...	**1980**	82	2.3	106	5.8	...	...
1951	2.6	...	...	**1981**	175	4.5	180	9.7	2,023	4.3
1952	3.3	3.2	...	**1982**	184	4.8	201	10.5	2,533	...
1953	2.8	3.4	...	**1983**	159	4.2	278	14.2	2,474	4.9
1954	3.8	3.5	...	**1984**	152	3.8	303	15.1	2,234	4.3
1955	3.8	3.2	[3.3][13]	**1985**	216	5.3	371	18.0	[1,862][20]	[3.4][20]
1956	6.2	3.9	3.0	**1986**	[178][18]	[4.4][18]	415	20.0	1,380	2.4
1957	7.4	4.3	2.4	**1987**	230	5.3	431	20.5	2,133	3.7
1958	9.4	5.3	3.7	**1988**	251	5.9	388	18.0	2,319	3.9
1959	9.0	4.8	5.2	**1989**	323	7.3	443	20.0	1,891	3.0
				1990	441	9.2	443[30]	19.0[30]	2,367	3.7
				1991	266	5.8	33	5.8	...	...[31]
				1992	321	6.7	59	5.5	4,574	6.5
				1993	520	10.1	70	6.0	4,396	6.2

B2 SOUTH AMERICA: Unemployment (numbers in thousands; percentages of appropriate workforce)

	Chile[15]		Colombia[25]		Guyana[26]	Peru		Surinam[16]	Uruguay[27]		Venezuela[29]	
	No	%	No	%	No	No	%	No	No	%	No	%
1960	12	...	...	...	4.2	...	...	4.0	...	...	...	...
1961	13	...	...	...	4.6	...	...	3.6	...	...	...	...
1962	12	...	...	...	5.5	...	...	3.6	...	...	...	...
1963	11	...	...	...	4.6	...	...	3.9	...	...	...	...
1964	...	...	...	...	5.1	...	...	3.3	...	...	...	...
1965	...[15]	...[15]	...	...	12.3	...	...	3.0	...	...	...	...
1966	[159][21]	[5.7][21]	...	...	12.1	...	...	2.6	...	...	...	...
1967	[132][22]	[4.7][22]	...	...	8.9	...	...	2.5	...	...	217	7.7
1968	137	4.8	...	...	7.6	...	...	2.5	43	8.4	182	6.3
1969	128	4.7	...	...	6.4	243	5.9	2.1	45	8.7	192	6.5
1970	101	3.4	...	...	5.2	201	4.7	2.2	39	7.5	199	6.3
1971	113	3.8	...	...	4.4	196	4.4	1.0	41	7.6	195	6.0
1972	[93][23]	[3.1][23]	...	...	3.4	194	4.2	0.9	[42][14]	[7.7][14]	...	...
1973	...	...	...	...	2.9	191	4.2	2.0	[49][14]	[8.9][14]	...	...
1974	...[15]	...[15]	...	...	2.3	187	4.0	2.2	[38][28]	[3.1][28]	220	...
1975	468	14.7	251	10.5	3.2	237	4.9	2.4	...	...	269	7.6
1976	406	13.0	269	10.4	3.0	258	5.2	1.9	68	12.8	234	6.0
1977	378	11.6	261	9.4	2.5	298	5.8	1.6	64	11.8	193	4.8
1978	495	14.2	244	8.2	2.0	341	6.5	2.7	53	10.2	193	4.6
1979	474	13.6	293	8.9	2.6	388	7.1	2.5	43	8.4	231	5.4
1980	378	10.4	321	9.1	15.6	391	7.0	2.4	40[5]	7.3[5]	272[5]	6.2[5]
1981	417	11.3	266	8.1	20.3	392	6.8	3.8[16]	37	6.6	325	6.4
1982	718	19.6	312	9.1	27.0	417	7.0	7.4	[61][14]	[11.7][14]	374	7.1
1983	552	14.6	407	11.1	7.2	566	9.2	10.7	90	15.4	536	9.8
1984	541[5]	13.9[5]	503	13.1	11.7	667	10.5	12.9	84	13.9	706	13.4
1985	517[24]	12.1[24]	500	14.0	13.3	773	11.8	17.0	78	13.0	767	11.6
1986	374	8.8	483	13.0	10.6	554	8.2	13.4[16]	[64][14]	[11.4][14]	668	9.9
1987	343	7.9	429	11.1	9.2	...	...	2.8	48	9.3	573	7.2
1988	286	6.3	403	10.1	...	...	...[31]	3.0	57	9.1	478	7.3
1989	250	5.3	356	9.9	...	186	7.9	2.4	98	8.0	621	9.2
1990	269	5.6	391	10.3	...	...	...	3.9	106	8.5	741	10.4
1991	254	5.3	502	10.0	...	146	5.8	3.7	111	9.0	701	9.5
1992	217	4.4	487	10.0	...	251	9.4	1.4	113	9.0	579	7.5
1993	234	4.5	408	8.5	...	286	9.9	1.0	105	8.3	498	6.4

B2 Unemployment

NOTES

1. SOURCES: ILO, Yearbook of *Labour Statistics* (1935—), and the national publications on pp. xiii—xv; The US figures to 1928 were derived by *Historical Statistics of the United States* from Stanley Lebergott, *Manpower in Economic Growth* (McGraw-Hill, New York, 1964).
2. Generally speaking, the statistics are averages of monthly or quarterly figures unless otherwise indicated, and relate to persons over the normal age for the end of compulsory schooling.
3. The variety of different indicators of unemployment used is clear from the footnotes. This should serve as a warning against incautious comparisons.

FOOTNOTES

[1]   Persons without a job and seeking work to 1955 (1st line); all unemployed persons aged 14 and over (or 15 and over from 1975) subsequently.
[2]   Unemployed persons aged 14 and over to 1946 or 16 and over subsequently. There are slight breaks in comparability in 1953 and 1962.
[3]   Average of first three quarters only.
[4]   Newfoundland is included from 1950.
[5]   Series subsequently revised.
[6]   In July (except as noted in other footnotes).
[7]   In November.
[8]   Guatemala City only to 1972, with Quezaltenango, Escuintila, and Puerto Barrios added subsequently.
[9]   Average of July and October.
[10] Statistics are for the major metropolitan cities only.
[11] In one month in each year, generally in summer, but in October in 1974 and 1977 and in November in 1975.
[12] Average of March—December.
[13] Average of April—December.
[14] First half-year only.
[15] Applicants for work to 1943 (1st line), registered unemployed subsequently. New series introduced in 1966 and 1975 greatly improved the coverage. From the latter date, statistics relate to the last quarter of each year except as noted in footnote 24. Percentage figures for Greater Santiago covering the gaps in the national statistics are as follows:

1963	5.1	1972	3.3
1964	5.3	1973	4.8
1965	5.4	1974	8.3
1966	5.4	1975	15.0

[16] Paramaribo only to 1981. A new system, requiring frequent re-registration, was instituted in 1987.
[17] Greater Buenos Aires only.
[18] In October.
[19] Data relate to Rio de Janeiro, Guanabara, São Paulo, and other areas ranging according to the survey. The coverage is improved in 1979, and probably again in 1981.
[20] In September.
[21] Average of August and December.
[22] Average of April, August, and December.
[23] In March.
[24] Average of November 1985 to January 1986.
[25] Six main cities only.
[26] Main urban districts only.
[27] Montevideo only, excluding domestic servants.
[28] Average of August 1974 to February 1975.
[29] Most figures relate to only part of the year.
[30] Urban areas only.
[31] Change in compilation methods. Data not strictly transferable.

International Historical Statistics: The Americas 1750–1993

B3 NORTH AMERICA: INDUSTRIAL DISPUTES

Key:- a = number of strikes and lockouts; b = number of workers involved (in thousands); c = number of man-days' work lost (in thousands)

	USA a	USA b		Canada a	Canada b	Canada c	USA a	USA b
1880	...	...	1900	...	...	...	1,839	568
1881	477	130	1901	99	24	738	3,012	564
1882	476	159	1902	125	13	203	3,240	692
1883	506	170	1903	175	38	859	3,648	788
1884	485	165	1904	103	11	193	2,419	574
1885	695	258	1905	96	13	246	2,186	302
1886	1,572	610	1906	150	23	378	...	...
1887	1,503	439	1907	188	34	520	...	...
1888	946	163	1908	76	26	704	...	...
1889	1,111	260	1909	90	18	881	...	...
1890	1,897	373	1910	101	22	731	...	...
1891	1,786	330	1911	100	29	1,821	...	...
1892	1,359	239	1912	181	43	1,136	...	...
1893	1,375	288	1913	152	41	1,036	...	...
1894	1,404	690	1914	63	10	491	1,204	...
1895	1,255	407	1915	63	11	95	1,593	...
1896	1,066	249	1916	120	27	237	3,789	...
1897	1,110	416	1917	160	50	1,124	4,450	...
1898	1,098	263	1918	230	80	648	3,353	...
1899	1,838	432	1919	336	149	3,401	3,630	...

	Canada a	Canada b	Canada c	Mexico[6] a	Mexico[6] b	USA a	USA b	USA c
1920	322	60	800	...	...	3,411	...	...
1921	168	28	1,049	...	...	2,385	...	...
1922	104	44	1,529	...	...	1,112	...	...
1923	86	34	672	...	...	1,553	...	...
1924	70	34	1,295	...	...	1,249	...	...
1925	87	29	1,193	...	...	1,301	...	...
1926	77	24	267	...	...	1,035	...	...
1927	74	22	153	...	...	707	330	26,200
1928	98	18	224	...	...	604	314	12,600
1929	90	13	152	14	3,473	921	289	5,350
1930	67	14	92	15	3,718	637	183	3,320
1931	88	11	204	11	227	810	342	6,890
1932	116	23	255	[56][7]	[3,574][7]	841	324	10,500
1933	125	27	318	[13][7]	[11,084][7]	1,695	1,170	16,900
1934	191	46	575	202	14,685	1,856	1,470	19,600
1935	120	33	289	642	145,212	2,014	1,120	15,500
1936	156	35	277	674	113,885	2,172	789	13,900
1937	278	72	886	576[6]	61,732[6]	4,740	1,861	28,425
1938	147	20	149	319	13,435	2,772	688	9,148
1939	122	41	225	303	14,486	2,613	1,171	17,812

B3 NORTH AMERICA: Industrial Disputes

	Barbados			Canada			Costa Rica			El Salvador		
	a	b	c	a	b	c	a	b	c	a	b	c
1940	...	...	...	168	61	266	...	...	...	...	...	...
1941	...	...	...	231	87	434	...	...	...	...	...	...
1942	...	...	...	354	114	450	...	...	...	...	...	...
1943	...	...	...	402	218	1,041	...	...	...	...	...	...
1944	...	...	...	199	75	490	...	...	...	...	...	...
1945	...	...	...	197	96	1,457	...	...	...	...	...	...
1946	...	...	...	228	139	4,516	...	...	...	...	...	...
1947	...	...	...	236	104	2,397	...	...	...	...	...	...
1948	...	...	...	154	43	886	...	...	...	...	...	...
1949	...	...	...	137	51	1,064	...	...	...	...	...	...
1950	...	...	...	161	192	1,389	...	...	...	...	...	...
1951	...	...	...	259	103	902	...	...	...	...	...	...
1952	...	...	...	222	121	2,880	...	...	...	...	...	...
1953	2	121	...	174	56	1,325	...	...	...	...	...	...
1954	3	331	1.3	174	62	1,475	...	...	...	...	...	...
1955	3	1,257	14.0	159	60	1,875	...	...	...	...	...	...
1956	9	1,467	31.0	229	89	1,246	...	...	...	...	...	...
1957	24	2,207	6.0	249	91	1,635	...	...	...	...	...	...
1958	[1	18,763	169.0][1]	262	112	2,872	...	...	...	...	...	...
1959	4	255	1.0	218	100	2,287	...	...	...	...	...	...
1960	—	—	—	274	49	739	...	...	...	...	...	...
1961	—	—	—	287	98	1,335	...	...	...	...	...	...
1962	10	512	1.3	311	74	1,418	...	...	...	...	...	...
1963	5	289	0.6	332	83	917	...	...	...	...	...	...
1964	4	293	1.0	343	101	1,581	...	...	...	...	...	...
1965	3	366	1.3	501	172	2,350	...	...	...	...	...	...
1966	6	1,969	4.3	617	411	5,178	...	...	...	...	...	...
1967	5	411	2.2	522	252	3,975	...	...	...	...	...	...
1968	—	—	—	582	224	5,083	...	...	...	...	...	...
1969	3	489	2.8	595	307	7,752	...	...	...	...	...	...
1970	—	—	—	542	262	6,540	...	...	...	...	...	...
1971	3[2]	415	54.0	569	240	2,867	...	...	...	12	11.0	197.0
1972	7	1,353	1.5	598	706	7,754	...	...	...	23	3.9	42.0
1973	71	2,549	4.1	724	348	5,776	14	8.3	18.0	6	0.6	7.1
1974	2	550	2.4	1,218	581	9,222	8	15.0	329.0	6	37.0	...
1975	3	823	3.4	1,171	506	10,909	18	11.0	47.0	14	2.9	39.0
1976	2	282	0.1	1,039	1,571	11,610	14	...	...	2	25.0	602.0
1977	—	—	—	803	218	3,308	10	11.0	74.0	19	33.0	155.0
1978	—	—	—	1,058	402	7,393	14	20.0	177.0	29	7.2	73.0
1979	1	45	0.3	1,050	462	7,834	20	26.0	275.0	103	29.0	292.0
1980	7	2,166	14.3	1,028	441	8,975	61	25.0	427.0	[42][3]	[12.0][3]	[44.0][3]
1981	8	2,219	7.0	1,048	339	8,878	6	7.4	167.0	15	5.3	138.0
1982	17	6,084	8.0	677	444	5,795	14	13.0	286.0	4	0.4	5.0
1983	5	1,031	8.9	645	329	4,444	16	8.3	309.0	15	2.7	93.0
1984	3	582	0.9	717	187	3,872	12	13.0	254	36	26.0	233.0
1985	5	886	5.3	829	162	3,125	10	11.0	44.0	54	30.0	351.0
1986	2	85	0.1	748	484	7,151	23	38.0	40.0	54	18.0	2,233.0
1987	7	988	2.3	668[2]	582[2]	3,810[2]	7	5.2	0.9	25	4.0	778.0
				64	533	2,400						
1988	10	862	0.7	548	206	4,901	16	3.0	36.0	36	4.4	15.8
1989	12	2,654	3.9	627	444	3,701	19	7.1	108.1	31	50.9	1,574.2
1990	17	1,083	1.8	579	270	5,079	42	26.0	159.0	20	3.9	153.5
1991	10	604	0.6	463	253	2,516	11	3.7	0.1	26	4.1	815.4
1992	12	4,591	—	404	149	2,108	19	42.3	0.2	47	127.4	1,051.1
1993	5	91	0.5	381	102	1,519	21	8.9	0.1	36	105.0	462.7

B3 NORTH AMERICA: Industrial Disputes

	Guadeloupe			Guatemala			Haiti			Jamaica		
	a	b	c	a	b	c	a	b	c	a	b	c
1940	...	...	...	...	...	...	...	...	...	...	...	...
1941	...	...	...	...	...	...	...	...	...	...	...	...
1942	...	...	...	...	...	...	...	...	...	...	...	...
1943	...	...	...	...	...	...	...	...	...	...	...	...
1944	...	...	...	...	...	...	...	...	...	...	...	...
1945	...	...	...	...	...	...	...	...	...	154	12.0	92.0
1946	...	...	...	...	...	...	...	...	...	110	16.0	239.0
1947	...	...	...	...	...	...	...	...	...	27	13.0	259.0
1948	...	...	...	...	...	...	...	...	...	23	3.2	10.0
1949	...	...	...	...	...	...	...	...	...	7	0.4	2.7
1950	...	...	...	...	...	...	...	...	...	58	13.0	75.0
1951	...	...	...	...	...	...	...	...	...	53	13.0	166.0
1952	...	...	...	...	...	...	...	...	...	42	6.3	79.0
1953	...	...	...	...	...	...	...	...	...	18	4.6	71.0
1954	...	...	...	...	...	...	...	...	...	25	3.2	40.0
1955	...	...	...	...	...	...	...	...	...	28	8.2	132.0
1956	...	...	...	...	...	...	...	...	...	15	5.7	50.0
1957	...	...	...	...	...	...	...	...	...	105	[20.0][5]	[612.0][5]
1958	...	...	...	...	...	...	...	...	...	61	[20.0][5]	[182.0][5]
1959	...	...	...	...	...	...	...	...	...	59	39.0	443.0
1960	2	450	1.4	...	...	...	...	...	...	69	12.0	65.0
1961	2	520	0.9	...	...	...	...	...	...	53	13.0	99.0
1962	3	1,450	5.8	...	...	...	...	...	...	83	16.0	124.0
1963	4	165	0.3	...	...	...	...	...	...	45	11.0	203.0
1964	5	32,000	96.0	...	...	...	...	...	...	41	8.6	68.0
1965	5	310	1.3	...	...	...	...	...	...	37	25.0	290.0
1966	2	89	0.1	...	...	...	...	...	...	69	30.0	181.0
1967	18	4,900	39.0	8	4.0	51.0	...	...	...	95	18.0	174.0
1968	3	3,127	30.0	4	7.5	324.0	...	...	...	94	23.0	225.0
1969	3	236	0.8	2	3.1	16.0	...	...	...	46	8.6	91.0
1970	4	121	0.9	36	27.0	51.0	...	...	...	70	23.0	335.0
1971	6	12,818	[146.0][4]	1	0.1	0.5	...	...	...	77	19.0	76.0
1972	8	1,485	67.0	4	4.9	33.0	...	...	...	55	30.0	266.0
1973	8	4,277	17.0	16	23.0	257.0	...	...	...	90	19.0	237.0
1974	3	249	0.5	53	44.0	563.0	...	...	...	137	21.0	769.0
1975	4	267	1.8	7	8.3	53.0	...	...	...	205	11.0	113.0
1976	4	267	20.0	16	5.8	168.0	...	...	...	142	12.0	140.0
1977	51	5,021	19.0	9	8.7	61.0	2,647	0.8	...	163[8]	13.0	82.0
1978	48	5,847	17.0	229	145.0	1,479.0	1,337	1.6	9.1	678	...	...
1979	35	...	22.0	7	42.0	41.0	751	2.1	20	608	...	...
1980	...	2,746	11.0	51	69.0	817.0	2,946	3.7	22	557	...	...
1981	...	...	...	3	1.3	37.0	2,728	3.7	22	625	...	...
1982	...	...	...	—	—	—	2,642	3.5	24	129	...	...
1983	41	1,976	11.0	—	—	—	2,161	2.8	...	86	...	...
1984	30	1,066	9.7	...	...	...	1,845	2.6	...	62	...	...
1985	31	1,396	27.0	...	...	...	1,653	3.0	2,094	83	...	...
1986	14	858	9.3	33	...	...	1,767	3.8	645	391	...	...
1987	17	515	6.4	12	...	...	...	...	...	370	...	...
1988	27	1,555	15.0	...	...	...	...	...	...	66	18.0	46.0
1989	22	1,455	21.3	9	...	...	...	...	...	64	6.5	28.7
1990	41	3,891	31.6	19	...	...	...	...	...	65	10.2	30.7
1991	31	1,542	23.0	...	...	...	...	...	...	46	22.4	47.7
1992	...	...	...	25	...	...	...	...	...	43	23.3	154.2
1993	...	...	...	35	...	...	...	...	...	58	19.4	83.3

B3 NORTH AMERICA: Industrial Disputes

	Martinique			Mexico[6]			Panama		
	a	b	c	a	b	c	a	b	c
1940	...	...	...	357	19,784	...	...	...	...
1941	...	...	...	142	12,892	...	...	...	...
1942	...	...	...	98	13,643	...	...	...	...
1943	...	...	...	766	81,557	...	...	...	...
1944	...	...	...	887	44,166	...	...	...	...
1945	...	...	...	220	48,055	...	...	...	...
1946	...	...	...	...	...	...	...	...	...
1947	...	...	...	...	...	...	...	...	...
1948	...	...	...	...	...	...	...	...	...
1949	...	...	...	...	...	...	...	...	...
1950	...	...	...	...	...	...	...	...	...
1951	...	...	...	...	...	...	...	...	...
1952	...	...	...	...	...	...	...	...	...
1953	...	...	...	167	38,552	...	...	...	...
1954	...	...	...	93	25,759	...	...	...	...
1955	...	...	...	135	10,710	...	...	...	...
1956	...	...	...	159	7,573	...	...	...	...
1957	...	...	...	193	7,134	...	...	...	...
1958	...	...	...	740	60,611	...	...	...	...
1959	...	...	...	379	62,770	...	...	...	...
1960	2	2,900	29.0	377	63,567	...	...	...	...
1961	3	21,700	505.0	373	33,184	...	...	...	...
1962	—	—	—	725	80,989	...	...	...	...
1963	6	24,800	216.0	504	26,035	...	...	...	...
1964	5	7,440	23.0	568	16,508	...	...	...	...
1965	6	12,530	37.0	67	...	...	...	...	...
1966	7	1,983	8.2	91	...	...	...	...	...
1967	8	5,563	55.0	78	8,457	...	...	...	...
1968	5	3,106	12.0	156	...	...	3	1.1	0.6
1969	4	2,369	18.0	144	...	...	9	1.8	1.0
1970	4	2,332	16.0	206	14,329	...	6	7.5	13.0
1971	9	3,968	32.0	204	9,299	...	280	16.0	...
1972	8	7,710	268.0	207	2,684	...	...	...	...
1973	5	656	10.0	211	8,395	...	11	1.4	...
1974	2	6,150	48.0	742	17,863	...	3	0.2	1.1
1975	5	5,725	131.0	236	9,680	...	8	...	...
1976	15	7,664	25.0	547	23,684	...	15	2.1	19.0
1977	...	...	...	476	13,411	...	4	0.2	0.9
1978	...	...	...	758	14,976	...	3	0.9	3.0
1979	...	...	...	795	17,264	...	10	1.2	44.0
1980	23	1,862	6.4	1,339	...	...	18	2.4	159.0
1981	...	...	...	1,066	...	...	16	7.8	248.0
1982	...	...	...	1,925	...	1,363	7	1.3	546.0
1983	...	...	...	216	...	775	9	6.7	87.0
1984	...	...	...	427	...	238	12	0.8	16.0
1985	...	...	...	159	57.4	334	7	0.8	20.0
1986	...	...	...	312	82.7	1,836	13	8.1	316.0
1987	...	...	...	174	201.7	2,677	7	1.7	450.0
1988	...	...	...	132	117.8	2,097	3	0.5	25.0
1989	...	...	...	118	57.8	1,519	—	—	—
1990	...	...	...	150	49.3	1,598	—	—	—
1991	...	...	...	136	64.8	1,619	—	—	—
1992	...	...	...	156	91.4	1,601	1	0.1	--
1993	...	...	...	155	31.7	1843	—	—	—

B3   NORTH AMERICA: Industrial Disputes*

	Puerto Rico			Trinidad & Tobago			USA		
	a	b	c	a	b	c	a	b	c
1940	...	...	...	...	...	...	2,508	577	6,701
1941	...	...	...	...	...	...	4,288	2,363	23,048
1942	...	...	...	...	...	...	2,968	840	4,183
1943	...	...	...	...	...	...	3,752	1,981	13,501
1944	64	34.0	...	...	...	...	4,956	2,116	8,721
1945	56	145.0	...	...	...	...	4,750	3,467	38,025
1946	81	25.0	...	...	...	...	4,985	4,600	116,000
1947	81	11.0	81	...	...	...	3,693	2,170	34,600
1948	52	6.8	61	...	...	...	3,419	1,960	34,100
1949	60	153.0	1,014	...	...	...	3,606	3,030	50,500
1950	24	4.2	20	...	3.1	16.0	4,843	2,410	38,800
1951	55	20.0	118	13	0.9	6.9	4,737	2,220	22,900
1952	49	27.0	224	5	...	...	5,117	3,540	59,100
1953	43	26.0	94	7	1.2	49.0	5,091	2,400	28,300
1954	49	23.0	64	5	2.7	13.0	3,468	1,530	22,600
1955	33	18.0	347	3	0.4	21.0	4,320	2,650	28,200
1956	26	4.6	48	6	11.0	244.0	3,825	1,900	33,100
1957	39	4.8	50	6	0.8	0.8	3,673	1,390	16,500
1958	39	12.0	94	13	1.8	13.0	3,694	2,060	23,900
1959	39	6.1	94	69	13.0	24.0	3,708	1,880	69,000
1960	47	6.7	105	31	21.0	181.0	3,333	1,320	19,100
1961	52	10.0	125	35	12.0	145.0	3,367	1,450	16,300
1962	50	8.5	65	75	16.0	165.0	3,614	1,230	18,600
1963	47	14.0	85	48	18.0	205.0	3,362	941	16,100
1964	54	7.9	59	44	8.1	96.0	3,655	1,640	22,900
1965	40	9.6	98	4	7.2	88.0	3,963	1,550	23,300
1966	64	13.0	137	—	—	—	4,405	1,960	25,400
1967	52	7.0	48	5	0.6	3.1	4,595	2,870	42,100
1968	49	9.0	55	9	0.7	18.0	5,045	2,649	49,018
1969	73	12.0	114	9	2.8	20.0	5,700	2,481	42,869
1970	93	19.0	191	64	11.0	100.0	5,716	3,305	66,414
1971	77	14.0	232	75	18.0	136.0	5,138	3,280	47,589
1972	107	24.0	223	34	8.7	24.0	5,010	1,714	27,066
1973	76	18.0	141	74	16.0	95.0	5,353	2,251	27,948
1974	95	22.0	289	78	56.0	253.0	6,074	2,778	47,991
1975	65	20.0	165	88	36.0	777.0	5,031[9]	1,746[9]	31,237[9]
							235	965	17,563
1976	37	8.6	332	44	27.0	141.0	231	1,518	23,962
1977	35	15.0	326	16	54.0	104.0	298	1,212	21,258
1978	33	11.0	699	38	11.0	113.0	219	1,006	23,774
1979	27	3.6	49	42	10.0	216.0	235	1,021	20,409
1980	27	5.8	118	27	7.5	118.0	187	795	20,844
1981	31	7.4	82	14	2.6	51.0	145	729	16,908
1982	13	7.9	383	11	2.5	21.0	96	656	9,061
1983	9	1.4	10	38	4.7	55.0	81	909	17,461
1984	12	1.9	37	38	12.0	260.0	62	376	8,499
1985	11	0.7	27	45	6.9	77.0	54	324	7,079
1986	14	2.8	39	16	1.2	81.0	69	533	11,861
1987	7	1.2	4	10	2.7	31.0	46	174	4,469
1988	6	0.5	18	11	1.0	7.1	40	118	4,381
1989	6	0.7	10	24	6.7	91.0	51	452	16,529
1990	3	0.4	0.1	14	3.8	10.4	44	185	5,925
1991	—	—	—	16	2.8	15.7	40	392	4,584
1992	5	5	5	17	5.9	69.7	35	364	3,989
1993	8	0.4	0.4	24	11.7	29.1	35	182	3,981

B3 SOUTH AMERICA: INDUSTRIAL DISPUTES

	Argentina[10]			Chile[11]			Uruguay		
	a	b	c	a	b	c	a	b	c
1924	71	279.0	...	...	...	...	22	0.9	22.0
1925	86	14.0	...	...	...	...	11	0.3	11.0
1926	62	15.0	...	...	...	...	5	0.6	12.0
1927	56	27.0	363	...	...	...	13	4.7	53.0
1928	137	74.0	251	...	...	...	3	0.3	421.0
1929	116	53.0	543	...	...	...	31	2.0	91.0
1930	127	38.0	853	...	...	...	8	1.4	11.0
1931	42	8.4	58	...	...	...	56	1.8	103.0
1932	122	165.0	136	6	0.6	...	6	2.1	...
1933	52	3.3	40	10	0.7	...	2	0.4	87.0
1934	42	26.0	742	13	3.1	...	17	0.9	71.0
1935	69	52.0	2,643	30	5.4	...	2	8.7	3.5
1936	109	85.0	1,344	20	7.8	...	...	...	...
1937	82	50.0	518	21	3.0	...	23	2.0	12.0
1938	44	8.9	229	15	11.0	...	...	4.9	20.0
1939	49	9.7	241	26	11.0	...	20	17.0	539.0
1940	53	13.0	225	45	19.0	...	13	0.8	16.0
1941	54	6.6	248	31	2.9	...	17	1.1	24.0
1942	113	40.0	634	19	2.7	33	17	1.3	6.7
1943	85	6.8	87	127	49.0	40	14	1.2	52.0
1944	27	9.1	41	91	...	...	6	9.5	40.0
1945	47	44.0	509	...	...	...	...	...	...
1946	142	334.0	2,048	196	95.0	...	...	...	...
1947	64	54.0	3,467	176	68.0	1,116	...	...	...
1948	103	278.0	3,159	40	11.0	647	...	...	...
1949	36	29.0	510	50	21.0	739	...	...	...

B3 SOUTH AMERICA: Industrial Disputes*

	Argentina[10]			Bolivia		Brazil	Chile			Colombia		
	a	b	c	a	c	a	a	b	c	a	b	c
1950	30	97.0	2,032.0	...	...	...	218	79.0	2,278	...	...	...
1951	23	16.0	152.0	...	...	...	193	89.0	1,565	...	...	...
1952	14	16.0	313.0	...	...	...	215	152.0	1,767	...	...	...
1953	40	5.5	59.0	...	...	...	208	123.0	1,453	...	...	...
1954	18	120.0	1,449.0	...	...	...	364	99.0	1,795	...	...	...
1955	21	12.0	144.0	...	...	...	274	128.0	1,099	...	...	...
1956	50	854.0	5,167.0	...	...	...	147	105.0	1,657	...	...	...
1957	56	304.0	3,391.0	...	...	...	80	30.0	228	...	...	...
1958	84	277.0	6,245.0	...	...	...	120	48.0	196	...	...	...
1959	45	1,411.0	10,078.0	...	...	...	204	82.0	870	...	...	...
1960	26	130.0	1,662.0	...	...	...	257	89.0	...	...	...	...
1961	43	236.0	1,755.0	...	...	...	262	112.0	...	...	...	...
1962	15	42.0	269.0	...	...	...	401	84.0	...	...	...	...
1963	20	207.0	812.0	...	...	...	416	117.0	...	...	...	...
1964	27	144.0	636.0	...	...	...	564	138.0	...	...	...	...
1965	32	204.0	591.0	...	...	...	723	182.0	...	...	...	...
1966	27	236.0	1,004.0	...	...	...	1,073	195.0	2,015	...	...	...
1967	6	0.5	2.7	...	...	...	1,114	225.0	1,990	...	...	...
1968	7	1.6	16.0	...	...	...	1,124	293.0	3,652	...	...	...
1969	8	6.7	150.0	...	...	...	1,277	362.0	1,179	...	...	...
1970	5	2.9	33.0	...	...	...	1,819	656.0	2,805	...	...	...
1971	16	69.0	159.0	...	...	...	2,696	299.0	1,388	...	...	...
1972	12	61.0	153.0	...	...	...	3,325	394.0	1,678	...	...	...
1973	...[10]	...[10]	...[10]	...	...	...	2,050	711.0	2,503	...	...	...
1974	543	272.0	652.0	...	...	...	...	...	...	...	...	...
1975	1,266	...	...	...	...	...	...	...	...	...	...	...
1976	...	...	...	...	...	...	...	...	...	...	...	...
1977	...	...	...	...	...	...	...	...	...	...	...	...
1978	...	...	...	...	...	...	...	...	...	266	23.0	...
1979	...	...	...	...	...	...	...	...	...	137	30.0	...
1980	...	...	...	...	0.16	81	89	30.0	428	261	31.0	...
1981	...	...	...	31	0.04	79	...	25.0	676	219	23.0	...
1982	...	...	...	301	...	126	...	2.4	52	149	60.0	...
1983	...	...	...	261	0.74	312	41	4.4	58	146	54.0	2.305
1984	...	...	...	500	2.57	534	38	3.6	42	147	31.0	0.925
1985	...	...	...	319	1.62	843	42	8.5	132	87	10.0	0.461
1986	...	...	...	188	0.90	1,493	41	3.9	61	15	3.8	0.728
1987	638	5,464.1	10,561.8	207	1.25	2,369	81	9.9	104	17[13]	6.7[13]	0.432[13]
1988	463	3,256.7	7,876.9	164	0.98	1,954	72	5.6	87	243	25.0	0.185
1989	193	1,737.2	2,331.2	177	0.90	3,164	101	17.9	298	117	19.6	2.106
1990	...	...	...	30	0.12	1,846	176	25.0	245	514	42.4	...
1991	...	...	...	110	...	659	219	45.9	730	234	17.7	...
1992	...	...	...	40	...	347	237	25.3	329	638	23.6	...
1993	...	...	...	35	...	...	224	25.1	312	292	9.9	...

B3   SOUTH AMERICA: Industrial Disputes

	Guyana			Peru			Surinam			Venezuela		
	a	b	c	a	b	c	a	b	c	a	b	c
1950	...	...	...	...	...	...	...	...	...	...	...	...
1951	...	...	...	...	...	...	...	...	...	...	...	...
1952	...	...	...	...	...	...	...	...	...	...	...	...
1953	30	36.0	584.0	...	...	...	...	...	...	...	...	...
1954	26	5.5	69.0	...	...	...	3	131	0.3	...	...	...
1955	21	8.4	33.0	...	...	...	1	107	0.1	...	...	...
1956	56	7.2	23.0	...	...	...	4	1,666	16.0	...	...	...
1957	41	13.0	65.0	161	45	192	2	43	0.1	...	...	...
1958	51	8.1	16.0	213	48	1,263	1	1,218	56.0	15	...	39.0
1959	35	5.2	16.0	233	...	...	...	...	...	15	6.8	105.0
1960	43	6.3	17.0	285	...	...	1	80	0.1	36	9.6	41.0
1961	55	11.0	29.0	341	...	...	5	245	1.6	14	12.0	49.0
1962	53	13.0	55.0	380	...	...	5	1,782	10.0	19	4.8	48.0
1963	56	36.0	459.0	422	...	...	—	—	—	9	2.0	28.0
1964	45	11.0	42.0	398	...	...	—	—	—	27	3.5	13.0
1965	146	48.0	137.0	397	136	803	4	578	1.1	24	4.7	18.0
1966	172	38.0	109.0	394	127	1,461	2	196	0.7	12	3.2	8.0
1967	170	31.0	152.0	414	142	1,047	4	727	3.2	29	3.0	5.6
1968	136	56.0	306.0	364	108	422	4	1,919	25.0	14	6.5	11.0
1969	126	18.0	39.0	372	92	486	26	5,063	62.0	83	21.0	...
1970	159	84.0	454.0	345	111	723	7	420	1.5	64	24.0	234.0
1971	198	41.0	142.0	377	161	1,360	49	6,641	22.0	106	39.0	
1972	175	45.0	135.0	409	131	791	15	2,826	44.0	172[12]	[25.0][7]	[146.0][7]
1973	186	35.0	93.0	788	416	1,961	30	5,073	32.0	250	46.0	145.0
1974	151	62.0	155.0	570	363	1,677	12	3,438	27.0	116	17.0	130.0
1975	129	69.0	551.0	779	617	2,534	8	1,999	17.0	100	26.0	101.0
1976	400	82.0	229.0	440	258	853	24	2,044	9.1	171	34.0	91.0
1977	383	90.0	964.0	234	1,315	1,726	12	2,845	6.5	214	64.0	86.0
1978	300	52.0	76.0	364	1,398	4,518	11	772	3.2	140	25.0	40.0
1979	219	106.0	324.0	653	841	1,676	8	2,186	11.0	145	23.0	50.0
1980	333	41.0	68.0	739	481	2,240	17	3,439	15.0	195	68.0	315.0
1981	621	88.0	126.0	871	857	2,497	13	6,250	7.2	129	30.0	256.0
1982	653	82.0	141.0	809	572	2,844	53	8,421	27.0	102	15.0	330.0
1983	731	104.0	290.0	643	786	2,537	6	2,613	6.5	67	17.0	418.0
1984	493	60.0	152.0	509	697	1,712	51	11,847	120.0	73	12.0	108.0
1985	718	94.0	1.4	566	235	1,528	9	3,772	19.0	99	13.0	96.0
1986	453	48.0	0.8	648	249	2,108	10	2,538	17.0	...	...	...
1987	497	58.0	0.9	726	312	1,147	3	460	9.8	...	...	...
1988	349	39.3	232.6	815	691	4,740	8	663	5.6	...	...	...
1989	138	113.3	686.3	667	208	1,902	8	2,005	7.5	...	...	...
1990	329	61.5	244.5	613	258	1,883	6	1,023	6.2	...	...	...
1991	307	98.4	110.9	315	180	1,110	2	534	2.2	...	...	...
1992	258	69.3	126.8	219	114	299	7	1,558	4.3	...	...	...
1993	475	53.5	129.3	151	41	271	27	3,301	22.6	...	...	...

B3 Industrial Disputes

NOTES

1. SOURCES:ILO, *Yearbook of Labour Statistics*, and the national publications on pp. xiii–xv.
2. Except as indicated in footnotes, the number of workers involved and the days' work lost by them relate to all those clearly affected by a particular dispute, not just to those directly involved.
3. The reporting systems of countries differ considerably, and comparisons should not be made without taking these differences into account.

FOOTNOTES

[1] This relates to a dispute on the sugar estates only.
[2] Subsequent statistics relate only to disputes involving 500 workers or more.
[3] First half-year only.
[4] Excluding agriculture.
[5] These figures relate to a smaller number of disputes than the total.
[6] Excluding lockouts from 1938 and workers indirectly involved throughout.
[7] Incomplete statistics.
[8] Subsequent statistics are from national sources and clearly have a more comprehensive coverage.
[9] Subsequent statistics relate only to disputes involving 1,000 workers or more and lasting at least one full shift.
[10] Buenos Aires City to 1972 and Greater Buenos Aires thereafter. Lockouts, general strikes, and strikes less than one day are excluded, as are workers indirectly involved.
[11] Excluding lockouts and workers indirectly involved.
[12] Including 57 for which no data are available.
[13] Subsequently including "paros" (suspensions of work activities). The numbers of days lost are as given by the I.L.O., although they seems to be improbably small.

B4 NORTH AMERICA: MONEY WAGES IN INDUSTRY

Key:- a = average daily wages of artisans in the Philadelphia area; b = daily wage rates on the Erie Canal; c = average daily wage rates of
5 skilled grades in manufacturing establishments; d = average annual earnings of non-farm employees; e = average hourly earnings
in manufacturing; f = daily wage rates of carpenters, masons, labourers, and painters in the Toronto area for year ending 30 June to
1901 (1st line); average daily wages in non-agricultural occupations from 1901 (2nd line) to 1958 (1st line); and weekly earnings in
manufacturing subsequently; g = weekly earnings in manufacturing; h = average daily earnings in manufacturing; i = average monthly
earnings in manufacturing; j average daily earnings to 1949, and monthly earnings (including salaries) subsequently; k = minimum
hourly rates to 1956; weekly earnings 1956–64; and minimum daily rates from 1974; l = monthly earnings in manufacturing and mining
to 1945 and in manufacturing alone from 1946 to 1956; minimum hourly earnings of unskilled workers in manufacturing subsequently;
m = average daily earnings in non-agricultural sectors in East Central Colombia to 1953; average hourly earnings in manufacturing
from 1955 to 1979, and average monthly earnings subsequently.

	USA			USA			Canada		USA		
	a			a	b		f		b	c	d
	1830 = 100			1830 = 100	1830 = 100				1830 = 100	1865 = 100	1865 = 100
1785	77	1825	101	...		1860	...		140	65	71
1786	58	1826	98	...		1861	...		130	67	72
1787	58	1827	100	...		1862	...		120	71	75
1788	56	1828	101	80		1863	...		160	80	90
1789	58	1829	104	100		1864	...		180	93	99
1790	58	1830	100	100		1865	...		200	100	100
1791	61	1831	...	100		1866	...		240	105	96
1792	58	1832	...	80		1867	...		220	104	94
1793	72	1833	...	100		1868	...		200	103	97
1794	80	1834	...	100		1869	...		240	104	97
1795	96	1835	...	100		1870	...		200	104	96
1796	101	1836	...	100		1871	...		200	103	94
1797	106	1837	...	100		1872	...		200	106	95
1798	91	1838	...	100		1873	...		200	105	91
1799	94	1839	...	120		1874	...		200	99	86
1800	95	1840	...	120		1875	...		200	96	83
1801	90	1841	...	120		1876	...		200	90	79
1802	76	1842	...	120		1877	...		160	87	76
1803	83	1843	...	100		1878	...		160	86	74
1804	92	1844	...	100		1879	...		200	86	73
1805	91	1845	...	80		1880	...		200	90	75
1806	96	1846	...	80		1881	...		200	...	80
1807	97	1847	...	100		1882	...		...	...	84
1808	85	1848	...	110		1883	...		...	...	86
1809	90	1849	...	130		1884	...		...	...	86
1810	99	1850	...	120		1885	...		...	...	87
1811	102	1851	...	120		1886	...		...	...	88
1812	91	1852	...	120		1887	...		...	...	90
1813	88	1853	...	120		1888	...		...	...	91
						1891 = 100					
1814	94	1854	...	140		1889	101		...	...	92
1815	110	1855	...	140							
1816	109	1856	...	140							
1817	99	1857	...	140							
1818	108	1858	...	120							
1819	94	1859	...	120							
1820	90										
1821	79										
1822	95										
1823	85										
1824	90										

B4 NORTH AMERICA: Money Wages in Industry

	Canada	Mexico		USA	
	f	g	d	e	g
	1891 = 100	1955 = 100	1865 = 100	1955 = 100	1955 = 100
1890	99.0	...	93	9.5	...
1891	100.0	...	94	9.6	...
1892	101.0	...	94	9.7	...
1893	101.0	...	89	9.8	...
1894	96.0	...	82	9.6	...
1895	95.0	...	86	9.6	...
1896	97.0	...	86	9.8	...
1897	94.0	...	86	9.7	...
1898	98.0	...	86	9.7	...
1899	93.0	...	92	10.0	...
1900	94.0	...	94	10.3	...
1901	98.0 [1]	...	...	10.5	...
	1955 = 100				
	13.1				
1902	13.8	...	...	10.8	...
1903	14.3	...	...	11.3	...
1904	14.6	...	...	11.3	...
1905	14.9	...	...	11.4	...
1906	15.5	...	...	11.8	...
1907	15.9	...	...	12.3	...
1908	16.4	...	...	11.9	...
1909	16.7	...	...	12.0	12.9
1910	17.2	...	...	12.4	...
1911	16.9	...	...	12.6	...
1912	17.5	...	...	13.1	...
1913	18.0	...	...	13.6	...
1914	18.2	...	...	13.7	14.4
1915	18.3	...	...	13.7	14.8
1916	19.6	...	...	15.3	16.7
1917	22.5	...	...	17.4	19.8
1918	26.4	...	...	21.4	25.3
1919	31.1	...	...	25.3	28.9
1920	36.9	...	...	29.6	34.4
1921	33.7	...	...	27.4	29.0
1922	31.4	...	...	25.8	28.1
1923	32.3	...	...	28.0	31.1
1924	32.7	...	...	29.0	31.3
1925	32.3	...	...	29.0	31.8
1926	32.5	...	...	29.0	32.2
1927	33.2	...	...	29.0	32.3
1928	33.7	...	...	30.1	32.6
1929	34.2	...	...	30.1	32.7
1930	34.4	...	...	29.6	30.4
1931	33.3	...	...	27.4	27.3
1932	30.9	...	...	23.7	22.3
1933	29.4	...	...	23.7	22.0
1934	29.6	...	...	28.5	24.0
1935	30.5	...	...	29.0	26.3
1936	31.1	...	...	29.6	28.5
1937	33.4	...	...	33.3	31.5
		1955 = 100			
1938	34.4	20.9	...	33.3	29.2
1939	34.5	22.1	...	33.9	31.2

B4 NORTH AMERICA: Money Wages in Industry

	Barbados	Canada	Costa Rica	Dominican Republic	El Salvador[6]	Guatemala[7]	Honduras
	g[2]	f	i[5]	j[5]	g[2]	e	h
	1959 = 100	1955 = 100	1973 = 100	1955 = 100	1959 = 100	1955 = 100	1955 = 100
1940	...	35.9	...	...	...	...	...
1941	...	39.0	...	...	...	...	...
1942	...	42.3	...	...	...	...	...
1943	...	46.1	...	...	...	...	...
1944	...	47.6	...	...	...	...	...
1945	...	48.9	...	...	...	...	...
1946	...	53.6	...	...	...	...	...
1947	...	59.9	...	78.5	...	...	...
1948	...	67.5	...	86.3	...	...	...
1949	...	70.6	...	83.5	...	...	...
1950	...	74.5	...	84.9$_1$	...	...	...
1951	...	84.1	...	93.3	...	...	...
1952	...	90.1	...	109.5	...	[85.6][8]	...
1953	...	94.3	...	105.9	...	85.9	78.4
1954	...	97.3	...	100.6	...	96.4	88.6
1955	...	100.0	...	100.0	...	100.0	100.0
1956	...	104.9	...	100.6	...	100.7	99.6
1957	...	110.4	...	100.8	95.3	101.3	87.3
1958	...	114.7$_1$	...	104.2	98.0	106.2	76.6
1959	100.0	120.6	...	108.7	100.0	109.5	83.6
1960	108	123.7	...	101.4$_5$	...$_4$	109.5	100.7
					94.5		
1961	101	127.7	...	104.7	105.8	111.8	...
1962	133	131.6	...	182.9	107.2	115.4	114.5
1963	122	136.4	...	166.6	107.5	118.3	113.5
1964	123	142.3	...	228.5	110.2	116.7	129.5
1965	140	149.0	...	213.9	115.5	121.9	123.1
1966	147	157.2	...	200.4	123.1	126.8	142.0
1967	[139][3]	166.1	...	161.6	127.4	131.0	...
1968	159	178.4	...	180.1	134.5	135.3	...
1969	174	191.6	...	207.8	136.2	141.5	...
1970	206	205.3	...	201.3	140.6	141.5	...
1971	223	223.2	...	204.3	142.6	142.2	...
1972	[231][3]	242.6	...	218.3	142.5	142.5	...
1973	283	261.5	100.0	207.9	151.7	142.5$_7$	...
1974	355	291.6	119.0	238.2	170.4	144.4	...
1975	411	335.2	141.4	335.9	157.2	150.3	...
1976	459	378.9	162.4	380.7	200.7	161.4	...
1977	544	417.9	181.9	371.3	216.0	173.2	...
1978	...	448.7	206.7	407.1	234.9	196.7	...
1979	...	488.8	237.4	414.7	264.5	205.2	...
1980	...	537.5	281.1	434.7	363.3	297.1	...
1981	...	602.8	341.0	465.9	384.2	333.7	...
1982	...	666.5$_4$	519.1	519.1	391.2	350.0	...
1983	...	692.2	836.1	532.8	455.2	382.7	...
1984	...	731.4	[1,077]	597.1	460.8	284.3	...
1985	...	766.8	1,314	705.6	497.0	290.8	...
1986	...	791.7$_4$	1,452	...	...	...	...
1987	...	816.1	2,001	...	...	...	...
1988	...	855.6	2,220	...	...	...	...
1989	...	902.4	2,542	...	...	...	...
1990	...	949.2	2,911	...	...	...	...
1991	...	996.0	3,999	...	...	...	...
1992	...	1,029	4,865	...	...	...	...
1993	...	1,049	5,724	...	...	...	...

B4 NORTH AMERICA: Money Wages in Industry

	Mexico	Nicaragua	Panama	Puerto Rico	Trinidad & Tobago	USA	
	g	e	e	e	k	e	g
	1955 = 100	1959 = 100	1955 = 100	1955 = 100	1955 = 100	1955 = 100	1955 = 100
1940	23.6	...	...	...	...	35.5	33.0
1941	24.1	...	...	...	...	39.2	39.0
1942	30.0	...	...	...	...	45.7	48.5
1943	33.2	...	...	...	...	51.6	56.9
1944	36.5	...	...	...	...	54.3	60.4
1945	41.6	...	...	...	...	54.8	58.4
1946	45.6	...	...	[62.7][11]	...	58.1	57.2
	i						
1947	49.4	...	...	72.7	...	65.6	65.0
1948	54.4	...	...	75.5	...	71.5	70.2
1949	59.0	...	...	75.4	...	74.2	71.2
1950	64.2	...	...	74.8	...	77.4	77.0
1951	71.4	...	...	79.8	75.0	83.9	83.7
1952	74.6	...	...	84.3	80.6	88.7	88.7
1953	79.2	...	...	88.0	92.6	93.5	93.1
1954	87.3	...	...	91.4	95.4	95.7	93.1
1955	100.0	...	100.0	100.0	100.0	100.0	100.0
1956	108.8	...	84.1	112.5	105.6,	104.8	104.1
1957	113.2	...	88.6	133.5	121.7	110.2	107.8
1958	124.5	99.4	93.2	145.4	140.9	113.4	109.3
1959	138.3	100.0	100.0	152.5	137.5	117.7	116.6
1960	151.9	99.4	118.2₄	162.3	141.9	121.5	118.5
1961	158.9	105.6	113.6	173.9	194.8	124.7	122.0
1962	172.5	118.8	122.7	186.6	202.2	128.5	127.6
1963	203.0	125.0	136.4	198.2	202.7	132.3	131.6
1964	221.6	118.8	143.2	208.1	219.4	136.0	136.0
1965	236.9	130.0	147.7	217.4	...	140.3	142.0
1966	247.8	...	152.3	228.0	...	146.2	148.4
1967	262.6	179.4	159.1	245.4	...	152.2	151.8
1968	276.2	190.0	165.9	272.4	...	161.8	161.8
1969	290.0	204.4	168.2	291.2	...	171.5	171.1
1970	204.7	202.5	181.8	309.9	...	180.1	176.7
1971	331.1	204.4	184.1	329.2	...	191.9	188.2
1972	349.9	214.6	186.4	352.1	...	205.4	204.4
1973	393.9	230.1	197.7	375.0	1974 = 100[1]	219.9	217.3
					100		
1974	501.6	267.1	222.7	408.5		237.6	233.6
1975	610.4	297.2	243.2	450.7	126.2	259.7	252.0
1976	763.3	319.7	254.5	489.4	156.4	280.6	276.5
1977	1,001	338.5	270.5	531.7	182.8	305.4	302.4
1978	1,152	356.7	270.5	591.5	216.7	331.7	329.3
1979	1,346	462.4	284.1	649.6	271.4	360.2	355.7
1980	1,636	584.7	...	707.7	340.7	390.9	381.2
1981	2,145	...	340.9	772.9	443.4	429.6	420.1
1982	3,362	...	347.7	816.9	532.0	456.5	436.3
1983	4,983	...	384.1	850.4	621.6	474.7	467.8
1984	7,921	...	411.4	883.8	679.0	494.1	494.1
1985	12,568₄	...	413.6	913.7	715.6	512.9	510.4
1986	20,770	...	...	934.9	742.3	523.1	523.1
1987	45,407	...	...	957.7	727.8	532.8	536.7
1988	92,046	...	...	961.3	729.9	547.3	552.2
1989	111,639	...	...	1019.4	...	563.4	568.4
1990	141,298	...	...	1094.2	...	582.3	584.3
1991	176,617	...	...	1171.7	...	601.1	601.5
1992	215,129	...	...	1260.3	...	616.1	621.3
1993	239,033	...	...	1354.4	...	631.2	642.5

B4 SOUTH AMERICA: MONEY WAGES IN INDUSTRY

	Argentina[9] e	Brazil e	Chile h	Colombia m	Ecuador g	Peru[12] h	Uruguay[13] i	Venezuela i
	1955 = 100	1955 = 100	1955 = 100	1948 = 100	1959 = 100	1955 = 100	1970 = 100	1964 = 100
1937	8.1	...	2.7	...	...	...	...	...
1938	8.1	...	3.1	42.1	...	...	...	...
1939	8.2	...	3.6	44.2	...	...	...	...
1940	8.2	...	4.4	45.4	...	...	...	...
1941	8.5	...	5.4	45.1	...	...	...	...
1942	9.0	...	7.1	46.9	...	...	...	...
1943	9.6	...	7.9	49.9	...	...	...	...
1944	10.4	...	9.4	61.5	...	...	...	...
1945	11.4₁	...	10.6	68.7	...	...	...	...
1946	14.2	24.9	12.3	76.4	...	21.2	...	...
1947	...	29.1	16.6	91.9	...	32.6	...	...
1948	27.4	32.9	20.4	100.0	...	41.8	...	...
1949	37.1	36.9	24.3	123.0	...	54.0	...	...
1950	45.2	40.8	28.2	167.8	...	66.8	...	...
1951	57.2	43.5	31.0	162.7	...	73.5	...	...
1952	70.4	50.3	40.0	149.0	...	81.5	...	...
1953	76.8	51.6	45.3	154.0	...	89.6	...	...
1954	89.4	75.6	58.0	...	...	93.9	...	...
				1955 = 100				
1955	100	100	100	100	...	100	...	...
1956	113.6₁	125.1	158.9	110.6	...	111.8₄	...	...
1957	149.9	151.9	212.0	147.0	[99.7][11]	117.8	...	...
1958	207.3	175.4	453.9	166.7	98.5	130.8	...	...
1959	354.7	238.5₁	554.5	181.8₄	100	153.3	...	...
			i⁵					
1960	464.0	...	638.1	237.9	100.1	172.8	...	...
1961	572.4	...	733.2	274.2	102.4	187.5	...	...
1962	714.9	662.8	867.2	315.2	107.5	203.4	...	...
1963	872.0	1,337.1	1,153.6	437.9	111.7	214.6	...	...
1964	1,128.4	2,480.9	1,754.7	498.5	121.8	253.3	...	100
		1964 = 100						
1965	1,496.8	155.5₄	2,446.0	553.0	125.5	295.2	...	105.0
1966	2,040.5	273.7	3,541.8	628.8	131.3	320.3	...	106.8
1967	2,642.3	358.7	4,514.0	693.9	140.1	...	33.8	111.9
1968	2,745.1	468.7	6,055.0	765.2	153.6	393.1	70.3	121.0
1969	3,018.5	593.5	8,329.1	837.8	186.2	439.8	90.4	117.7
	1969 = 100			1969 = 100				
1970	118.0	741.9	143.1	980.3₄	199.1	471.0	100	127.1
1971	162.4	929.1	206.1	1,100.0	224.9	502.8	128.3	135.2
1972	236.8	1,177.3	328.4	1,198.5	265.7	622.9	191.0	144.8
1973	416.4	1,454.6	985.0	1,363.6	299.0	764.1	363.0	144.6
1974	535.9	1,899.7	6,332.8	1,621.2	370.4	946.1	638.7	170.6
			1974 = 100		e			
1975	1,454.5	2,687.4	451.1	1,993.9	452.6	998.3	1,051.8	195.0
1976	4,458.7	3,943.6	1,789.3	2,474.2	559.0	1,270.3	1,431.7	200.4
1977	9,944.9	...	5,104.6	3,107.6	624.1	1,540.0	1,944.2	218.8
1978	16,959	...	8,759.0	4,021.2	682.4	2,106.7	2,670.3	247.5
1979	43,220	...	13,013	5,397.0₁	867.8	3,072.2₄	4,007.6	441.3
	1979 = 100		1979 = 100	1979 = 100		1979 = 100	1979 = 100	
1980	244.4	...	153.3	132.5	1,227.7	189.2	155.6	553.8
1981	571.2	...	207.3	172.3	1,368.3	314.2	222.6	643.8
1982	1,668.9	...	231.3	222.4	1,478.1	523.5	256.9	...
1983	10,464	...	264.1	281.3	1,899.9	903.2	304.1	...
1984	84,603	...	313.1	348.0	2,469.1	1,597.5	460.9	...
	1984 = 100							
1985	645.2	...	388.4	421.1	...	3,399.5₄	782.6	...
1986	1,369.9	...	477.8	521.3	...	11,529	1,485.1	672.1
1987	2,757.3	...	577.7	639.8	...	20,478	2,638.7	983.5
1988	7,687.1	...	700.6	813.0	...	96,457	4,375.5	...
1989	150,766	...	715.3	...	...	116,374	4,744.6	...
						1989 = 100		
1990	4,396,820	...	739.6	...	...	27	5,527.3	...
1991	44,069,760	...	772.3	...	...	598	7,329.7	...
	1991 = 100							
1992	1,470	...	801.9	...	...	1,007	9,718.4	...
1993	1,560	...	819.8	...	...	1,477	13,229.6	...

B4 Money Wages in Industry

NOTES

1. SOURCES: The main sources used were ILO, *Year Book* (1931–34); ILO, *Yearbook of Labour Statistics* (1935–); and the national publications on pp. xiii–xv. In addition the following were used: Canada to 1958–M.C.'Urquhart and K.A.H. Buckley, *Historical Statistics of Canada* (Cambridge and Toronto, 1965).
2. In principle, the indices relate to annual averages, but it is clear that in practice most are based on a limited number of observations in each year. Where an individual figure is known to deviate from the norm for a series this is indicated.
3. The currency unit applicable to the base-year of each index is employed throughout the currency of that index, irrespective of the date when the unit may have been changed.

FOOTNOTES

[1] See key to this table.
[2] Adult males only.
[3] March and September only.
[4] A new series has been spliced on to the old without, in principle, changing the scope.
[5] Including extractive industries and services to 1960 (1st line).
[6] Department of San Salvador only.
[7] Guatemala City only to 1973
[8] Last quarter-year only.
[9] An earlier index of monthly earnings of workers in Buenos Aires is available as follows (1939 = 100):-

1930	93	1933	87	1936	93
1931	87	1934	83	1937	96
1932	84	1935	90	1938	95

[10] Including salaries.
[11] April–December only.
[12] Lima and Callao only.
[13] Montevideo only.

B5 NORTH AMERICA: WAGES IN AGRICULTURE

	USA[1]
	1909 = 100
1818	44.4
1826	41.5
1830	41.5
1850	50.9
1860	64.1
1870	77.8
1880	54.9
1890	65.4
1899	68.4
1909	100.0

	Canada[2]	Mexico[3]	USA[1]
	1955 = 100	1955 = 100	1909 = 100
1914	17.7	...	...
1915	18.8	...	...
1916	22.2	...	...
1917	39.0	...	...
1918	43.4	...	...
1919	49.2	...	194.9
1920	54.3	...	...
1921	41.9	...	...
1922	36.6	...	...
1923	37.9	...	...
1924	36.6	...	...
1925	36.3	...	...
1926	37.4	...	...
1927	38.5	18.8	...
1928	38.3	19.6	...
1929	37.3	17.7	189.7
1930	33.1	16.0	...
1931	25.2	15.4	...
1932	19.0	13.1	...
1933	17.7	12.5_3	...
1934	18.7	20.7	...
1935	19.9	20.7	...
1936	21.5	23.0	...
1937	23.3	23.0	134
1938	23.9	24.9	130
1939	25.1	24.9	130
1940	30.0_2 / 29.2	24.7	131.7
1941	34.7	24.7	160.0
1942	43.1	25.7	206.0
1943	55.5	25.7	271.0
1944	60.3	31.4	322.0
1945	64.5	31.4	356.0
1946	69.5	39.0	386.0
1947	74.5	39.0	407.0
1948	80.5	45.6	427.2_1
			1955 = 100
			85.9
1949	82.3	45.6	82.8

B5   NORTH AMERICA: Wages in Agriculture

	Barbados[4]	Canada[2]	Costa Rica[6]	Mexico	USA[1]
	1955 = 100	1955 = 100	1955 = 100	1955 = 100	1955 = 100
1950	...	79.0	...	50.6	83.1
1951	...	90.3		50.6	92.6
1952	...	98.4	69.1	86.5	97.9
1953	100.0	101.6	100.0	86.5	99.6
1954	100.0	98.4	100.0	92.0	97.9
1955	100.0	100.0	100.0	100.0	100.0
1956	104.0	106.5	100.0	113.9	104.4
1957	116.0	112.9	106.3	113.9	107.9
1958	130.0	114.5	112.8	130.4	112.1
1959	130.0	116.1	112.8	159.1	118.2
1960	130.0	119.4	112.8	178.3	121.2
1961	144.0	124.2	112.8	178.3	123.6
1962	172.0	124.2	[120.2][7]	207.6	126.8
1963	172.0	129.0	120.2	207.6	130.4
1964	186.0	135.5	120.2	256.1	133.9
1965	186.0[4]	143.5	136.2	256.1	140.9
1966	113.5	154.8	136.2	298.9	152.6
1967	102.3	166.1	136.2	298.9	165.9
1968	118.0	177.4	136.2	348.3	179.3
1969	133.0	193.5	142.6	348.3	197.0
1970	138.6	201.6	142.6	403.0	210.4
1971	164.7	211.3[5]	159.6	446.4	219.3
1972	209.9	229.3	171.3	527.2	234.1
1973	211.5	264.1	171.3	...	256.3
1974	270.2	312.0	242.6	...	284.4[5]
1975	321.9	372.9	268.1	876.4	304.3
1976	403.3	431.4	319.1	1,322.2	328.9
1977	403.6	487.5	360.6	1,454.0	358.2
1978	...	518.6	425.5	1,682.5	376.9
1979	...	555.6	476.6	2,030.6	419.1
1980	...	584.6	560.6	2,550.6	447.2
1981	...	614.9	696.8	3,400.6	...
1982	...	646.8	1,276.6	4,783.8	...
1983	...	675.7	1,959.6[6]	8,004.8	...
1984	...	697.8	[2,508.5][6]	12,360.0	...
1985	...	...	2,915.4	19,703.0	...
1986	...	...	3,324.5	33,633.0	...
1987	...	...	4,277.6	73,289.0	...
1988	...	...	5,088.1	137,224.0	...
1989			7,185.0	...	
1990			8,533.2		
1991			10,273.6		
1992			12,329.4		
1993			15,031.7		

B5 SOUTH AMERICA: WAGES IN AGRICULTURE

	Chile[8]	Peru[9]		Chile[8]	Peru[9]		Chile[8]	Peru[9]		Chile[8]	Peru[9]
1938 = 100	1955 = 100			1938 = 100	1955 = 100		1938 = 100	1955 = 100		1938 = 100	1955 = 100
1929	67.1	...	1934	...[8]	9.8	1939	121.2	7.9	1944	257.9	18.1
1930	69.7	...	1935	74.6	10.1	1940	140.3	8.1	1945	259.6	21.7
1931	73.6	8.7	1936	80.3	11.3	1941	161.3	10.2	1946	406.4	21.7
1932	78.8	7.3	1937	80.3	8.9	1942	182.6	14.5	1947	484.2	...
1933	84.1	9.3	1938	100	8.2	1943	229.7	15.7			

	Argentina[10]	Chile[8]	Colombia[11]	Guyana[12]	Peru[9]	Uruguay[13]
	1969 = 100	1938 = 100	1955 = 100	1955 = 100	1955 = 100	1969 = 100
1948	...	661.2	58.7	...	...	...
1949	...	838.2	61.3	...	...	...
1950	...	1,015.2	72.0	...	...	...
1951	...	1,057.3	77.3	...	...	...
1952	...	1,380.4	77.3	...	73.4	...
1953	...	1,825.9[8]	83.5	94.7	98.8	...
		1955 = 100				
		49.0				
1954	...	62.9	93.3	96.0	99.9	...
1955	...	100.0	100.0	100.0	100.0	...
1956	...	144.9	102.7	102.5	122.1	...
1957	...	190.4	116.8	101.2	142.3	...
1958	...	229.2	126.7	101.6	180.9	...
1959	...	316.9	139.5	103.4	191.0	...
1960	12.2	348.3	155.2	114.3	199.5	...
1961	13.3	398.9	176.0	141.0	224.3	...
1962	18.1	466.3	197.1	142.2	254.8	4.6
1963	20.9	719.1	256.0	160.9	...	4.6
1964	33.2	1,078.7	306.7	171.1	...	6.6
1965	48.4	1,831.5	318.7	173.6	...	6.6
1966	64.1	2,303.3	380.3	180.7	...	15.5
1967	84.2	2,696.6	393.3	184.5	...	32.5
1968	89.7	3,134.8	414.7	183.9[12]	...	84.7
1969	100.0	4,202.2	506.7	212.6	...	100.0
		1969 = 100				
1970	125.4	160.4	514.7	227.7	...	125.0
1971	192.5	267.4	...	235.1	...	159.0
1972	275.0	[401.1][9]	...	249.2	...	229.0
1973	493.8	[846.7][10]	...	246.2	...	408.4
1974	705.0	11,000.0	...	283.7	...	866.4
		1974 = 100				
1975	1,851.1	528.7	...	330.7	...	1,487.4
1976	5,531.2	2,164.6	1,646.7	394.0	...	1,891.7
1977	11,694	5,036.6	2,456.8	387.0	...	3,321.3
1978	20,933	7,347.1	3,176.8	514.7	...	4,779.8
1979	53,858	9,719.6	3,936.8	491.0	...	7,574.0
	1979 = 100	1979 = 100				1979 = 100
1980	243.8	135.4	4,840	620.1	...	143.0
1981	567.7	160.7	...	746.2	...	174.6
1982	1,663.5	259.4	...	...	...	192.1
1983	10,774	265.9	...	...	...	265.7
1984	82,353	272.4	...	...	...	517.2
	1984 = 100				1986 = 100	
1985	550.9	337.6	...	...	...	913.8
1986	1,156.4	389.9	...	...	100.0	1,542.1
1987	2,456.8	...	...	...	239.7	2,438.4
1988	...	...	...	...	1,117.6	4,142.6

B5　Wages in Agriculture

NOTE

All the notes to table B4 also apply to this table.

FOOTNOTES

[1]　Average monthly earnings with board to 1948 (1st line), subsequently average hourly rates. The figures for 1940 and 1948 are based on Lebergott's series reproduced in *Historical Statistics of the United States*, with statistics for 1937–39 and 1941–47 interpolated on the basis of data derived from the ILO.

[2]　The general index of farm wage rates to 1940 (1st line); subsequently day rates of general male farm hands paid wholly in cash.

[3]　Minimum rates for regular day workers. The series from 1934 is completely new and cannot be compared with earlier figures.

[4]　Middle rate per hour to 1965 and average weekly earnings subsequently. The index is for male sugar cane day labour.

[5]　A new series has been spliced on to the old without, in principle, changing the scope.

[6]　Minimum hourly rates of general farm hands on coffee plantations to 1983, and earnings of similar workers in July subsequently (November in 1984).

[7]　Beginning December.

[8]　Minimum daily rates for adult male permanent workers to 1953 (1st line), and for all adult male workers subsequently. The series from 1935 onwards cannot be compared with earlier figures.

[9]　Average daily earnings of males to 1962 and of all workers in 1986–88.

[10]　October 1972 to December 1973.

[11]　Average daily rates of adult males.

[12]　Day rates of sugar cane workers to 1968 and average weekly earnings subsequently.

[13]　Average monthly earnings of workers paid wholly in cash.

C AGRICULTURE

Apart from figures for sugar in Europe's West Indian colonies, there are few agricultural statistics until around 1840, and few on a regular annual basis until the 1890s or later, though they begin for the USA in the 1860s. The main exceptions to this statement are foreign trade data, which are generally available for the countries for which trade in agricultural commodities became of major importance by the time such importance had been attained, if not earlier: by the 1850s, at least, and considerably earlier for sugar, cotton, and tobacco.

There is no reason to suppose that the agricultural statistics proper, once they were collected, are in any way grossly or systematically unreliable. However, in many countries, and for many of the major subsistence crops, 'collection' has not always been an appropriate word to apply to the process by which the statistics have been engendered. All crop statistics are a matter of estimation, whether by local crop reporters or by officials sitting at desks in the Ministry of Agriculture or in the FAO; and some of the estimation, particularly for crops like cassava, or for areas with little or no official presence in rural areas distant from major cities, can only be described as guesswork. Judging by some of the revisions which have been made to previously-published figures, the guesswork has not always been well-informed. The principle employed here in all of the first 14 tables has been to include estimates, from whatever source, provided they seem reasonable in the light of later recorded figures.

Tables 1 to 9 and 11 to 13 present a selection of statistics of crop areas and outputs and of the output of major livestock products. Data, where available, are shown for commodities which are of some significance in each particular country. The same applies to fish landings in table 14 and to the livestock species whose numbers are given in table 10. In interpreting these latter, it should be remembered that changes in the time of year at which a livestock count is taken can have a considerable effect on numbers, and that changes in the average age of flocks and herds have had a major effect, over time, on the productivity of a given stock of animals.

The export statistics, which occupy tables 15 to 19 are a small selection of those available. The intention is to show the major international movements of agricultural and forest products for the period for which they have been significant. With the exception of sugar, tobacco, and cotton, this period began at the earliest when trans-oceanic freight rates became low enough for commodities with relatively high bulk-to-value ratios to be shipped to Western Europe. By their nature these commodities were not much susceptible to illegal trade, and whilst the same cannot be said of tobacco (and, perhaps, sugar), it is the import statistics of Europe which are likely to have been affected, rather than those of the exporters. In any case, such trade was mainly a phenomenon of the colonial period in American history.

C1 NORTH AMERICA: AREA OF MAIN ARABLE CROPS (in thousands of hectares)

Key:- Bwt = buckwheat; P = potatoes; SP = sweet potatoes; SB = sugar beet; SC = sugar cane

	Canada			
	Wheat	Barley	Oats	Rye
1851	489	30	406	37
1861	661	104	661	62
1871	667	…	…	…
1881	948	…	…	…

	Guadeloupe		Jamaica	Trinidad & Tobago[2]
	Sugar Cane		SC	SC
1848	17	1876	19	…
1849	15	1877	19	…
		1878	19	…
		1879	18	…
1850	15	1880	17	…
1851	15	1881	16	…
1852	16	1882	16	…
1853	18	1883	17	…
1854	20	1884	17	…
1855	14	1885	16	…
1856	14	1886	15	…
1857	15	1887	14	24
1858	16	1888	14	24
1859	18	1889	13	24
1860	18	1890	13	24
1861	18	1891	13	24
1862	19	1892	13	24
1863	18	1893	13	24
1864	18	1894	13	24
1865	…	1895	13	24
1866	16	1896	12	24
1867	16	1897	12	23
1874	19	1898	11	23[2]
1879	22	1899	11	22
1884	26	1900	10	21
		1901	11	21
1889	23	1902	11	21
		1903	10	24
1894	24	1904	10	24
1899	23	1905	11	25
		1906	12	26
1902	27	1907	12	24
		1908	11	27
1906	25	1909	12	26

C1 NORTH AMERICA: Area of Main Arable Crops (in thousands of hectares)

	Barbados	Canada[1]						
	SC	Wheat	Barley	Oats	Rye	Mixed Grain	P's	SB
1882	...	[802]	...	...	...	...	[75]	...
1883	...	[719]	[343]	[561]	...	...	[65]	...
1884	...	[795]	[331]	[661]	...	...	[72]	...
1885	...	[766]	[300]	[653]	...	...	[73]	...
1886	...	[822]	[263]	[688]	...	...	[70]	...
1887	...	[740]	[317]	[716]	...	...	[60]	...
1888	...	[734]	[333]	[744]	...	...	[61]	...
1889	...	[693]	[391]	[818]	...	...	[62]	...
1890	...	[746]	[387]	[867]	...	...	[64]	...
1891	...	1,094[942]	351[298]	1,603[935]	...	...	[77]	—
1892	...	[922]	[260]	[869]	...	...	[70]	...
1893	...	[1,009]	[242]	[888]	...	...	[63]	...
1894	...	[920]	[236]	[941]	...	...	[63]	...
1895	...	[817]	[245]	[1,115]	...	...	[73]	...
1896	...	[853]	[256]	[1,156]	...	...	[81]	...
1897	...	[863]	[239]	[1,160]	...	...	[77][1]	...
1898	...	[1,034][1]	[245][1]	[1,174][1]	...	...	[74]	...
1899	...	[1,320]	[251]	[1,288]	...	...	[94]	...
1900	...	[1,404]	[280]	[1,317]	...	...	[92]	—
1901	...	1,209	353	2,172	47	110	[178][1]	...
1902	12	[1,543]	[347]	[1,400]	...	...	[97]	...
1903	...	[1,514]	[418]	[1,501]	...	...	[92]	...
1904	...	[1,707]	[490]	[1,665]	...	...	[91]	...
1905	...	[1,711]	[495]	[1,742]	...	...	[78]	...
1906	...	[1,978]	[529]	[1,853]	...	...	[75]	...
1907	...	[2,440][1]	[551][1]	[2,041][1]	...	...	[80][1]	...
1908	14	[2,449]	[681]	[2,928]	...	...	[202]	...
1909	12	2,657	706	3,201	40	236	...	...

International Historical Statistics: The Americas 1750-1993

C1 NORTH AMERICA: Area of Main Arable Crops (in thousands of hectares)

						USA[3]						
	Wheat	Barley	Oats	Rye	Maize	Bwt	Rice	P	SP	SB	SC
1866	6,235	305	3,211	611	12,147	312	…	496	…	…	…
1867	6,774	428	3,309	667	12,997	328	…	522	…	…	…
1868	7,746	431	3,601	656	14,211	316	…	567	132	…	…
1869	8,577	501	3,867	660	14,501	308	…	599	142	…	…
1870	8,476	539	4,188	631	15,535	299	…	584	142	…	…
1871	8,996	546	4,476	643	16,998	293	…	605	152	…	…
1872	9,292	575	4,771	633	17,638	311	…	631	153	…	…
1873	10,063	596	4,860	628	17,840	304	…	624	159	…	…
1874	11,052	659	5,170	635	19,279	302	…	669	164	…	…
1875	11,486	689	5,510	626	21,224	321	…	724	172	…	…
1876	11,446	798	5,904	716	22,370	330	…	722	186	…	…
1877	11,316	794	5,996	746	23,795	340	…	760	184	…	…
1878	13,508	748	6,406	771	24,143	339	…	760	194	…	…
1879	14,304	779	6,457	739	25,183	341	…	794	183	…	…
1880	15,417	805	6,643	709	25,311	331	…	796	190	…	…
1881	14,890	891	6,846	708	25,506	324	…	824	178	…	…
1882	14,769	985	7,719	842	26,773	324	…	897	190	…	…
1883	14,402	1,001	8,345	859	27,587	325	…	960	190	…	…
1884	15,574	1,090	8,893	850	27,856	316	…	934	193	…	…
1885	14,202	1,158	9,450	768	29,078	334	…	945	192	…	…
1886	14,695	1,225	9,885	788	29,911	325	…	968	195	…	…
1887	14,922	1,319	10,632	803	29,662	323	…	998	200	…	…
1888	14,151	1,329	11,253	883	31,353	329	…	1,054	208	…	…
1889	14,608	1,357	11,613	910	31,426	327	…	1,053	211	…	…
1890	14,846	1,315	11,442	856	30,264	332	…	1,035	215	…	…
1891	16,629	1,453	11,232	882	31,912	335	…	1,066	217	…	…
1892	17,393	1,561	11,399	906	31,126	340	…	1,019	220	…	…
1893	16,507	1,493	11,844	875	32,307	326	…	1,058	221	…	…
1894	16,255	1,473	11,961	877	32,403	326	…	1,161	222	…	…
1895	15,782	1,694	12,507	971	36,616	324	118	1,250	221	…	…
1896	16,523	1,672	12,241	1,052	36,047	346	109	1,201	225	…	…
1897	17,569	1,667	11,667	940	36,408	335	117	1,137	215	…	…
1898	20,439	1,665	11,868	892	35,525	321	127	1,164	221	…	…
1899	21,182	1,810	11,839	833	38,280	325	137	1,189	215	…	…
1900	19,912	1,903	12,565	861	38,385	320	146	1,213	219	…	…
1901	20,577	2,008	12,501	975	38,211	327	171	1,194	226	…	…
1902	18,714	2,215	12,690	989	39,326	328	221	1,245	226	…	…
1903	19,609	2,522	13,026	915	37,860	333	221	1,246	229	…	…
1904	17,464	2,662	13,253	892	38,537	336	232	1,298	231	…	…
1905	18,739	2,694	13,527	930	38,747	334	185	1,320	232	…	…
1906	18,709	2,729	13,633	872	38,698	332	204	1,317	237	…	…
1907	17,862	2,774	13,937	839	38,888	337	228	1,349	241	…	…
1908	18,252	2,998	13,885	862	38,561	341	241	1,383	251	…	…
1909	17,912	3,115	14,189	895	40,550	352	268	1,487	259	170	118

C1 NORTH AMERICA: Area of Main Arable Crops (in thousands of hectares)

	Barbados	Canada[1]							Costa Rica		
	SC	Wheat	Barley	Oats	Rye	Mixed Grain	P's	SB	Maize	Rice	SC
1910	12	3,136	755	3,765	37	236	184	...	27	3	13
1911	12	3,587	519	3,503	47	173	209	8	...	...	...
1912	12	4,490	616	3,902	53	213	208	8	...	...	10
1913	12	4,450	640	4,033	51	201	214	7	...	...	...
1914	13	4,458	653	4,222	48	192	217	5	31	3	12
1915	14	4,166	605	4,072	45	187	224	7	...	...	...
1916	14	6,114	695	4,677	49	189	191	6	...	...	...
1917	14	6,220	730	4,450	60	167	266	6	...	...	...
1918	14	5,972	968	5,388	86	201	298	7	...	...	...
1919	14	7,023	1,276	5,985	225	373	331	10	...	...	...
1920	14	7,740	1,071	6,051	305	365	317	15	...	...	...
1921	14	7,378	1,033	6,414	263	329	284	11	...	...	...
1922	14	9,413	1,132	6,859	745	348	277	6	29	6	17
1923	14	9,074	1,052	5,885	852	316	227	7	26	7	17
1924	14	8,857	1,127	5,823	586	342	227	13	20	7	18
1925	14	8,926	1,379	5,864	361	343	221	14	20	7	16
1926	14	8,413	1,426	5,081	260	348	212	12	24	8	18
1927	14	9,266	1,476	5,156	305	387	232	11	32	7	18
1928	14	9,089	1,419	5,358	301	406	242	14	32	6	15
1929	14	9,761	1,975	5,316	340	448	220	13	34	6	12
1930	14	10,180	2,398	5,050	401	453	231	17	...	...	...
1931	14	10,076	2,250	5,366	586	486	236	17	...	...	...
1932	15	10,666	1,534	5,195	323	484	211	18	...	...	...
1933	15	11,000	1,521	5,321	313	479	214	18	...	...	...
1934	15	10,518	1,480	5,475	236	472	230	15	...	...	...
1935	16	9,706	1,462	5,557	277	469	205	21	29	9	13
1936	16	9,759	1,573	5,704	291	466	203	21	...	...	...
1937	16	10,362	1,796	5,377	253	474	215	19	19	11	11
1938	16	10,348	1,753	5,280	362	456	211	18	...	...	...
1939	16	10,494	1,802	5,265	300	469	210	24	27	...	...
1940	17	10,828	1,759	5,176	446	493	221	33	28	11	12
1941	16	11,625	1,757	4,977	419	494	205	29	29	11	13
1942	15	8,882	2,150	4,969	376	581	205	26	29	13	13
1943	15	8,725	2,784	5,476	529	599	216	21	28	11	13
1944	15	6,772	3,293	5,963	208	507	216	23	30	9	10
1945	15	9,177	2,836	5,428	263	516	205	24	31	12	...
1946	17	9,388	2,810	5,346	199	489	211	27	...	13	...
1947	16	9,865	2,503	4,768	288	471	201[1]	24	...	12	5
1948	16	9,762	2,991	4,343	486	397	206	24	...	10	13
1949	17	9,593	2,590	4,392	952	537	207	34	51	22	15

International Historical Statistics: The Americas 1750–1993

C1 NORTH AMERICA: Area of Main Arable Crops (in thousands of hectares)

	Cuba			Dominican Republic			El Salvador			
	Maize	Rice	SC	Maize	Rice	SC	Maize	Rice	Sorghum	SC
1910	…	…	…	…	…	…	…	…	…	…
1911	…	…	…	…	…	…	…	…	…	…
1912	…	…	542	…	…	…	…	…	…	…
1913	…	…	540	…	…	…	…	…	…	…
1914	…	…	…	…	…	24	…	…	…	…
1915	…	…	…	…	…	25	89	…	…	…
1916	…	…	…	…	…	…	127	…	…	…
1917	…	…	…	…	…	21	…	…	…	9
1918	…	…	…	…	…	36	91	11	…	7
1919	…	…	…	…	…	40	180	6	…	…
1920	…	…	…	…	…	…	252	…	…	…
1921	…	…	…	…	…	…	…	…	…	12
1922	…	…	…	…	…	…	…	…	…	…
1923	…	…	…	…	…	…	…	…	…	…
1924	…	…	…	…	…	…	258	5	…	11
1925	…	…	…	…	…	…	…	…	…	…
1926	…	…	…	…	…	…	…	…	…	…
1927	…	…	…	…	…	…	…	…	…	…
1928	…	…	…	…	…	…	…	…	…	…
1929	…	…	1,192	…	…	…	133	…	…	…
1930	…	…	…	…	…	…	140	8	…	10
1931	…	13	…	…	…	…	140	8	…	9
1932	…	…	582	…	…	…	136	8	…	10
1933	…	18	581	…	…	…	139	10	…	11
1934	25	…	559	…	…	…	133	11	…	8
			574							
1935	…	…	…	36	…	…	159	13	…	10
1936	…	…	…	…	…	…	156	9	…	10
1937	…	7	582	…	…	…	158	12	…	9
1938	21	8	581	…	…	…	84	9	…	8
1939	38	11	637	…	52	97	106	13	…	10
1940	29	11	747	…	…	…	117	13	…	12
1941	…	11	847	…	…	…	158	14	…	14
1942	…	13	646	…	39	…	160	22	…	15
1943	…	11	968	…	33	…	142	19	…	15
1944	…	9	948	…	47	…	154	23	…	16
1945	…[4]	54	1,019	61	45	…	154	23	…	…
1946	244	…	1,151	73	36	…	124	14	…	5
1947	250	60	1,220	82	32	92	157	21	73	5
1948	280	60	1,150	77	47	97	198	29	114	…
1949	270	50	1,193	62	44	97	…	13	…	12

C1   NORTH AMERICA: Area of Main Arable Crops (in thousands of hectares)

	Guadeloupe	Guatemala				Haiti			Honduras	
	SC	Wheat	Maize	Rice	SC	Maize	Rice	SC	Maize	SC
1910	...	...	...	...	...	...	...	...	...	...
1911	28	...	...	...	...	...	...	...	...	...
1912	...	...	...	...	...	...	...	...	...	...
1913	...	...	...	...	...	...	...	...	...	...
1914	...	...	201	8	...	...	...	...	...	...
1915	37	...	230	6	...	...	...	...	...	...
1916	38	...	267	6	...	...	...	...	...	...
1917	40	18	250	12	...	...	...	...	...	...
1918	...	4	263	18	...	...	...	...	...	...
1919	...	9	273	6	...	...	...	...	...	...
1920	...	10	224	3	...	...	...	...	...	...
1921	...	8	125	3	13	...	...	...	...	...
1922	35	11	185	3	23	...	...	...	...	...
1923	35	6	151	3	13	...	...	...	...	...
1924	35	14	172	2	11	...	...	...	...	...
1925	35	9	155	1	13	...	...	...	176	14
1926	35	10	102	1	12	...	...	...	178	17
1927	28	9	117	2	11	...	...	...	177	24
1928	28	8	121	1	12	...	...	18	185	26
1929	28	7	141	2	12	...	...	18	184	20
1930	28	9	169	2	12	...	...	18	192	21
1931	28	6	147	2	13	...	81	16	182	20
1932	28	6	147	2	11	...	91	16	200	18
1933	28	7	135	3	9	...	91	16	206	16
1934	20	7	139	2	8	...	92	16	203	14
1935	21	9	137	5	8	...	92	16	196	14
1936	22	20	280	8	14	...	...	...	214	15
1937	22	17	311	9	16	...	...	...	208	14
1938	...	17	333	...	...	...	...	...	222	15
1939	30	19	385	10	15	...	...	...	228	16
1940	31	21	505	11	19	...	...	...	232	15
1941	37	25	523	12	19	...	...	...	239	15
1942	32	26	584	13	18	...	...	...	242	16
1943	24	22	358	8	18	...	...	...	239	18
1944	24	22	328	5	15	...	...	...	245	18
1945	25	21	221	5	...	...	...	...	256	19
1946	13	21	208	...	...	...	10	...	255	20
1947	15	16	197	3	15	120	10	18	262	21
1948	15	...	...	...	...	120	23	...	274	21
1949	15	31	540	8	18	...	33	...	279	22

C1   NORTH AMERICA: Area of Main Arable Crops (in thousands of hectares)

| | Jamaica | Martinique | Mexico | | | | | | | Nicaragua | | Panama | Puerto Rico | Trinidad & Tobago |
	SC	SC	Wheat	Barley	Oats	Maize	Rice	P	SC	Maize	Rice	Rice	SC	SC
1910	13	...	1,063	555	...	...	84	...	...	...	...	...	74	25
1911	14	...	696	577	...	...	86	...	...	...	...	...	...	21
1912	13	...	...	...	...	2,466	...	...	...	...	...	...	85	18
1913	13	...	600	610	...	...	...	...	...	...	...	...	...	21
1914	13	...	...	...	...	1,922	...	...	...	...	...	...	82	20
1915	14	...	...	...	...	...	...	...	...	...	...	...	82	22
1916	14	...	...	...	...	...	...	...	...	...	...	...	83	21
1917	15	...	...	...	...	...	...	...	...	...	...	...	104	24
1918	17	...	950	1,928	...	1,608	...	...	...	...	...	...	97	30
1919	19	...	...	...	...	...	...	...	...	...	...	...	92	18
1920	23	...	...	...	...	...	...	...	...	...	...	...	97	24
1921	18	...	923	283	...	2,946	20	...	...	...	...	...	98	23
1922	19	...	1,060	282	...	2,856	22	...	...	...	...	...	99	25
1923	19	...	1,236	282	...	3,209	22	...	...	...	...	...	96	24
1924	18	...	568	288	...	3,267	43	...	...	...	...	...	96	14
1925	21	...	455	175	...	2,936	50	...	65	...	...	...	98	13
1926	18	...	518	181	...	3,137	53	...	70	...	...	...	96	13
1927	...	...	528	176	...	3,181	50	...	67	...	...	...	96	13
1928	17	...	516	178	...	3,122	45	...	65	...	...	...	102	18
1929	18	...	521	161	...	2,865	35	...	70	...	...	...	103	18
1930	17	...	490	146	...	3,075	37	...	77	25	...	...	113	...
1931	17	...	604	150	...	3,378	36	...	78	28	...	...	119	24
1932	16	...	445	160	3	3,243	34	...	75	36	...	...	121	25
1933	...	...	472	159	4	3,198	34	...	64	50	...	...	121	25
1934	...	...	493	157	3	2,970	32	...	63	...	...	...	121	27
1935	16	...	460	148	4	2,966	31	...	76	...	...	...	121	29
1936	16	...	508	145	3	2,852	40	...	92	...	...	...	121	33
1937	17	...	484	144	...	3,000	40	...	87	42	...	...	121	33
1938	18	...	501	149	...	3,094	39	...	87	27	...	...	127	33
1939	18	16	563	146	19	3,267	45	...	94	...	...	...	123	33
1940	...	...	601	142	35	3,342	62	18	98	...	...	...	136	33
1941	...	...	583	168	34	3,392	53	23	116	...	...	30	137	33
1942	26	...	600	156	34	3,758	65	27	127	...	...	30	129	33
1943	26	...	510	161	36	3,083	66	27	139	...	...	33	127	33
1944	25	...	527	162	36	3,355	68	27	140	89	16	35	136	33
1945	25	14	468	165	33	3,451	59	27	141	77	15	40	142	24
1946	...	13	415	171	31	3,313	64	27	148	50	9	46	148	26
1947	32	14	499	171	44	3,512	72	28	157	86	10	52	149	26
1948	32	11	577	202	33	3,722	82	28	173	76	15	54	152	33
1949	42	13	535	215	79	3,792	108	29	201	98	15	60	150	34

C1 NORTH AMERICA: Area of Main Arable Crops (in thousands of hectares)

						USA[3]							
	Wheat	Barley	Oats	Rye	Maize	Bwt	Rice	Sorghum	P	SP	SB	SC
1910	18,532	3,054	14,910	915	41,386	340	270	...	1,475	257	161	126
1911	19,823	3,081	15,034	992	41,032	326	257	...	1,429	244	192	128
1912	19,592	3,052	15,072	1,102	41,056	315	260	...	1,418	237	225	83
1913	21,049	3,105	15,073	1,250	40,552	313	292	...	1,407	241	235	103
1914	22,506	3,097	15,060	1,272	39,577	304	261	...	1,383	231	195	88
1915	24,404	2,946	15,703	1,383	40,721	305	299	...	1,389	254	247	74
1916	21,655	3,085	15,822	1,428	40,696	318	341	...	1,325	266	269	92
1917	18,934	3,421	16,837	2,049	44,877	375	386	...	1,538	293	269	100
1918	24,713	3,722	17,185	2,715	41,357	412	446	...	1,456	299	240	95
1919	29,825	2,662	16,026	2,908	39,718	297	438	1,465	1,335	320	280	73
1920	25,235	3,010	17,293	1,960	41,019	295	526	1,630	1,336	310	353	77
1921	26,129	2,863	18,429	1,969	41,745	259	401	1,497	1,456	331	330	93
1922	24,847	2,671	16,319	2,740	40,608	295	426	1,363	1,579	331	214	98
1923	23,035	2,894	16,287	2,002	40,923	279	354	1,701	1,367	273	266	88
1924	21,231	2,848	16,939	1,596	40,639	298	339	1,427	1,257	228	330	66
1925	21,223	3,313	17,903	1,541	41,007	300	345	1,585	1,137	257	262	77
1926	22,912	3,204	17,342	1,387	40,247	275	411	1,704	1,138	261	274	52
1927	24,131	3,830	16,329	1,403	39,804	309	416	1,724	1,288	293	292	30
1928	23,968	5,154	16,239	1,344	40,605	275	393	1,665	1,416	257	261	53
1929	25,654	5,489	15,440	1,270	39,580	255	348	1,426	1,226	262	278	78
1930	25,348	5,111	16,126	1,475	41,061	232	391	1,407	1,270	271	314	76
1931	23,352	4,525	16,266	1,278	43,247	205	391	1,798	1,412	346	289	74
1932	23,411	5,344	16,875	1,356	44,749	184	354	1,781	1,444	429	309	89
1933	20,001	3,902	14,782	973	42,864	186	323	1,762	1,385	367	398	86
1934	17,542	2,662	11,920	777	37,309	192	329	959	1,456	388	312	95
1935	20,762	5,033	16,232	1,645	38,839	204	331	1,860	1,404	382	309	102
1936	19,880	3,371	13,619	1,090	37,698	153	397	1,130	1,198	311	314	99
1937	25,968	4,034	14,383	1,548	38,012	170	445	1,989	1,236	311	305	115
1938	28,003	4,294	14,586	1,654	37,296	181	435	1,902	1,161	321	374	120
1939	21,314	5,155	13,541	1,547	35,725	150	423	1,899	1,138	295	372	103
1940	21,559	5,473	14,338	1,297	34,977	157	433	2,579	1,146	262	369	97
1941	22,636	5,777	15,443	1,446	34,543	136	491	2,434	1,090	296	306	103
1942	20,142	6,863	15,458	1,535	35,356	152	590	2,424	1,081	278	386	117
1943	20,783	6,030	15,748	1,073	37,255	204	596	2,788	1,311	347	223	115
1944	24,180	4,978	16,083	863	38,046	206	599	3,667	1,125	294	225	111
1945	26,372	4,231	16,891	749	35,461	162	607	2,559	1,078	261	289	107
1946	27,156	4,201	17,325	646	35,444	155	640	2,699	1,023	258	325	116
1947	30,157	4,450	15,332	806	33,544	204	691	2,218	810	221	356	119
1948	29,307	4,818	15,896	833	34,308	134	730	2,961	802	184	281	125
1949	30,720	3,995	15,295	629	34,639	109	752	2,560	710	191	278	172

International Historical Statistics: The Americas 1750–1993

C1 NORTH AMERICA: Area of Main Arable Crops (in thousands of hectares)

	Barbados	Canada[1]								Costa Rica		
	SC	Wheat	Barley	Oats	Rye	Maize	Mixed Grain	P's	SB	Maize	Rice	SC
1950	17	11,083	2,397	4,447	488	124	586	204	41	49	34	23
1951	18	11,052	2,635	4,526	461	127	575	115	38	62	36	22
1952	19	10,220	3,173	4,815	456	137	617	124	37	52	29	24
1953	19	10,588	3,431	4,475	500	146	636	134	33	75	37	17
1954	19	10,677	3,605	3,995	609	169	627	125	37	66	33	20
1955	19	10,335	3,174	4,068	318	205	676	129	33	50	36	22
1956	19	9,146	4,001	4,435	302	206	688	130	32	...	37	...
1957	19	9,219	3,395	4,237	221	208	631	130	34	...	37	...
1958	19	8,725	3,806	3,573	220	202	583	126	40	...	45	...
1959	20	8,963	3,758	3,737	208	198	566	119	37	...	58	...
1960	19	9,915	3,192	3,678	216	184	594	119	35	...	53	...
1961	20	10,245	2,237	3,457	227	162	634	125	34	50	54	30
1962	19	10,853	2,139	4,277	258	178	616	118	34	54	54	35
1963	21	11,156	2,500	3,779	284	224	593	116	39	59	51	35
1964	21	12,018	2,224	3,231	282	265	621	113	41	65	50	35
1965	22	11,453	2,477	3,384	323	302	663	121	34	80	54	36
1966	22	12,016	3,019	3,207	294	326	715	130	33	78	56	31
1967	20	12,189	3,284	3,009	277	354	675	124	34	81	38	32
1968	20	11,907	3,576	3,058	275	387	675	125	32	82	40	33
1969	20	10,104	3,859	3,098	375	396	704	126	32	70	38	38
1970	20	5,052	4,064	2,893	411	484	785	129	28	42	47	38
1971	20	7,854	5,658	2,764	387	571	832	110	33	52	36	41
1972	20	8,640	5,062	2,470	257	537	836	100	31	55	32	45
1973	19	9,575	4,839	2,711	256	530	810	106	28	52	65	43
1974	17	8,934	4,775	2,471	341	591	728	115	27	41	80	37
1975	16	9,487	4,468	2,411	320	635	736	106	32	65	87	37
1976	16	11,252	4,353	2,409	250	709	645	107	32	60	80	38
1977	16	10,114	4,751	2,131	250	724	624	113	26	44	71	30
1978	16	10,579	4,259	1,829	318	783	606	111	25	37	76	43
1979	16	10,489	3,724	1,541	330	893	593	113	24	50	80	45
1980	16	11,098	4,634	1,515	310	958	569	107	27	39	60	49
1981	16	12,427	5,476	1,561	445	1,139	545	111	29	47	80	51
1982	16	12,554	5,189	1,633	447	1,107	531	113	29	54	77	44
1983	14	13,697	4,333	1,400	428	1,075	511	113	31	62	88	36
1984	14	13,158	4,566	1,406	370	1,192	462	118	27	61	72	52
1985	14	13,729	4,750	1,263	353	1,123	439	115	12	74	74	49
1986	14	14,239	4,829	1,287	315	994	383	109	23	76	60	50
1987	13	13,486	5,005	1,263	313	999	391	114	22	75	56	48
1988	12	12,987	4,151	1,371	257	981	386	111	21	61	58	48
1989	11	13,627	4,658	1,708	501	1,003	381	113	22	48	68	40
1990	11	14,098	4,529	1,154	341	1,062	390	120	24	39	63	31
1991	10	14,161	4,217	842	181	1,105	244	120	25	32	52	35
1992	9	13,830	3,790	1,238	138	858	290	124	23	24	62	36
1993	9	12,377	4,159	1,341	161	985	...	125	22	19	46	36

C1   NORTH AMERICA: Area of Main Arable Crops (in thousands of hectares)

	Cuba			Dominican Republic			El Salvador			
	Maize[4]	Rice	SC	Maize	Rice	SC	Maize	Rice	Sorghum	SC
1950	166	50	1,257	72	47	102	177	14	82	13
1951	180	69	1,425	71	46	104	...	16	...	11
1952	150	...	1,040	65	51	103	203	16	93	...
1953	...	85	1,070	65	51	108	185	14	102	...
1954	176	93	1,072	...	...	...	177	12	107	6
1955	176	134	...	...	...	...	173	10	122	6
1956	183	162	...	...	49	...	187	12	124	7
1957	175	109	...	...	49	158	171	16	86	8
1958	155	110	1,068	...	...	147	179	13	89	14
1959	185	168	1,156	...	...	183	178	9	84	15
1960	191	160	1,261	...	...	146	178	11	87	12
1961	160	150	1,132	35	58	147	190	9	98	13
1962	153	164	1,074	32	58	130	199	11	93	15
1963	141	85	1,002	30	60	135	172	9	96	15
1964	132	71	1,055	30	65	116	165	15	87	24
1965	120	38	979	25	76	120	193	13	111	24
1966	127	32	1,039	25	76	142	208	20	107	24
1967	121	44	1,013	25	81	120	192	28	104	24
1968	120	88	944	28	88	138	200	27	114	19
1969	120	146	1,460	27	84	146	194	11	114	20
1970	120	195	1,251	26	83	151	206	12	124	20
1971	130	168	1,181	26	74	150	210	15	126	28
1972	130	170	1,073	27	67	150	204	11	130	30
1973	130	225	1,103	26	66	145	202	10	119	33
1974	130	204	1,180	29	67	152	211	11	127	36
1975	...	178	1,224	25	66	154	246	17	132	42
1976	...	163	1,137	33	114	164	234	14	125	42
1977	...	152	1,237	24	113	172	245	12	132	41
1978	...	152	1,313	24	103	174	264	14	137	41
1979	...	147	1,392	19	109	178	276	15	143	37
1980	...	147	1,209	24	111	180	292	17	119	34
1981	...	144	1,327	29	111	185	276	14	115	27
1982	...	151	1,200	21	93	188	239	11	119	32
1983	...	149	1,350	27	119	188	242	13	111	41
1984	...	161	1,348	58	118	188	243	15	116	39
1985	...	159	1,329	38	110	175	253	17	114	40
1986	...	171	1,358	32	112	180	257	12	120	42
1987	...	169	1,297	36	112	180	279	12	125	41
1988	...	172	1,351	34	100	170	282	14	122	34
1989	...	167	1,350	33	105	170	276	16	120	29
1990	...	141	1,350	26	99	206	282	14	129	32
1991	...	143	1,435	30	92	210	307	16	123	43
1992	...	130	1,550	34	102	207	321	17	149	48
1993	...	78	1,150	35	79	215	305	16	143	49

C1   NORTH AMERICA: Area of Main Arable Crops (in thousands of hectares)

	Guadeloupe	Guatemala				Haiti			Honduras	
	SC	Wheat	Maize	Rice	SC	Maize	Rice	SC	Maize	SC
1950	16	...	...	...	...	...	30	10	291	22
1951	16	42	534	9	22	...	...	...	299	23
1952	...	36	478	8	...	...	...	...	307	25
1953	25	38	483	10	...	...	...	...	304	26
1954	18	33	520	8	25	...	...	...	254	28
1955	19	34	551	8	24	...	...	...	291	23
1956	19	35	615	8	25	...	...	...	325	23
1957	20	33	620	9	24	...	...	...	339	23
1958	21	33	624	10	25	335	65	...	360	23
1959	23	34	682	11	26	...	...	...	376	24
1960	27	31	652	10	13	...	...	...	374	25
1961	27	34	625	9	26	300	48	...	252	25
1962	28	39	639	10	28	...	54	...	266	25
1963	28	38	688	13	28	...	55	90	263	26
1964	28	39	698	11	34	...	60	...	294	26
1965	32	27	676	8	38	...	65	...	279	27
1966	30	31	659	8	45	305	70	...	280	28
1967	30	36	697	12	42	320	70	...	280	28
1968	29	30	691	14	45	300	72	...	281	28
1969	32	29	735	14	45	305	75	...	282	31
1970	32	30	695	9	36	310	75	75	283	30
1971	28	31	660	20	40	320	75	...	283	27
1972	27	37	832	16	42	330	50	...	284	27
1973	27	28	844	22	53	238	43	...	287	26
1974	27	43	562	15	58	...	45	...	286	26
1975	27	39	514	19	63	...	48	...	331	26
1976	23	37	514	19	91	239	50	...	381	28
1977	22	45	641	12	82	248	40	...	431	28
1978	21	52	591	11	77	...	52	...	418	27
1979	21	59	622	13	74	234	54	...	352	30
1980	21	50	655	13	79	225	50	80	339	24
1981	19	41	681	11	83	200	...	...	339	35
1982		37	669	8	78	185	...	...	287	52
1983	16	41	800	12	90	171	...	...	308	52
1984	13	30	599	16	89	200	55	...	367	39
1985	12	33	660	15	94	...	35	85	289	45
1986	14	27	675	15	90	175	...	...	345	42
1987	14	28	749	18	84	...	50	...	284	41
1988	14	28	644	27	96	253	50	85	362	41
1989	18	38	600	15	97	230	45	85	404	41
1990	13	38	634	14	112	200	54	86	367	41
1991	13	37	653	19	123	180	50	86	429	42
1992	13	41	707	16	126	285	58	30	433	41
1993	13	32	726	17	129	250	50	59	430	42

C1   NORTH AMERICA: Area of Main Arable Crops (in thousands of hectares)

	Jamaica	Martinique	Mexico							
	SC	SC	Wheat	Barley	Oats	Maize	Rice	Sorghum	P's	SC
1950	46	13	644	230	80	4,328	106	...	30	183
1951	47	13	673	231	82	4,428	104	...	31	198
1952	45	13	593	231	82	4,236	82	...	31	210
1953	62	13	657	222	86	4,857	94	...	31	222
1954	62	...	765	231	87	5,253	90	...	32	247
1955	62	14	800	241	88	5,371	96	...	35	258
1956		14	937	246	89	5,460	115	...	37	199
1957	61	14	958	237	96	5,392	117	...	41	258
1958	68	13	840	239	98	6,372	121	120	45	282
1959	76	13	937	243	96	6,324	127	107	48	315
1960	82	13	840	240	80	5,558	143	116	44	346
1961	77	13	837	233	85	6,288	146	117	46	348
1962	77	12	748	193	86	6,372	134	118	46	362
1963	61	13	819	232	91	6,793	135	198	50	378
1964	60	9	818	212	91	7,461	133	276	48	446
1965	60	9	858	226	92	7,718	138	314	39	461
1966	60	7	731	241	78	8,287	153	576	41	488
1967	60	7	778	237	53	7,611	168	673	38	489
1968	55	8	791	251	42	7,676	139	830	47	505
1969	55	8	841	238	40	7,104	153	883	32	526
1970	58	8	886	250	60	7,440	150	971	38	547
1971	59	8	614	255	40	7,692	154	937	40	481
1972	59	9	687	385	39	7,292	156	1,110	39	465
1973	58	9	640	262	47	7,606	150	1,185	55	505
1974	63	8	774	173	60	6,717	173	1,153	54	491
1975	62	6	778	286	59	6,694	257	1,116	57	479
1976	65	7	894	364	66	6,783	159	1,251	56	496
1977	51	7	709	248	64	7,470	180	1,413	54	488
1978	44	6	760	296	65	7,191	121	1,399	61	537
1979	47	5	599	222	54	5,502	149	1,456	56	538
1980	49	5	739	329	48	6,955	132	1,579	71	546
1981	43	5	861	274	70	8,150	180	1,767	68	522
1982	44	5	1,013	225	69	5,643	175	1,275	68	526
1983	44	4	857	303	70	7,421	133	1,518	74	505
1984	40	4	1,033	283	117	6,972	153	1,622	71	517
1985	47	4	1,224	282	99	7,498	220	1,236	72	540
1986	37	4	1,201	264	...	6,417	158	1,533	...	469
1987	36	3	988	286	...	6,801	155	1,853	...	519
1988	36	4	912	247	...	6,506	126	1,800	70	415
1989	38	4	1,145	263	...	6,470	151	1,621	68	368
1990	40	3	933	263	...	7,341	105	1,818	81	571
1991	42	3	985	284	...	6,947	85	1,381	75	546
1992	41	3	914	290	...	7,217	84	1,417	72	557
1993	41	3	865	265	...	7,833	85	833	73	530

C1 NORTH AMERICA: Area of Main Arable Crops (in thousands of hectares)

	Nicaragua			Panama			Puerto Rico	Trinidad & Tobago
	Maize	Rice	SC	Maize	Rice	SC	SC	SC
1950	112	16	14	69	68	...	154	34
1951	97	13	...	71	66	15	170	34
1952	122	24	...	73	67	20	170	34
1953	136	34	16	86	79	14	162	...
1954	119	14	17	86	83	...	152	34
1955	160	19	...	83	87	14	151	35
1956	179	25	18	83	85	...	142	32
1957	147	24	19	86	89	17	129	32
1958	133	23	20	90	95	14	135	32
1959	130	21	20	86	97	16	135	33
1960	132	21	22	79	89	17	129	33
1961	165	24	28	92	100	22	121	34
1962	173	23	17	82	100	14	144	34
1963	161	22	21	94	103	26	119	23
1964	175	23	21	99	121	18	113	33
1965	195	25	25	105	133	17	107	33
1966	198	26	25	108	132	18	103	36
1967	228	26	27	113	130	17	93	36
1968	215	32	28	100	129	17	71	35
1969	257	40	30	103	126	17	74	35
1970	250	40	34	69	96	18	74	35
1971	266	26	34	63	96	20	60	38
1972	211	26	35	66	105	22	60	37
1973	221	29	35	68	105	25	53	39
1974	263	30	36	76	112	26	49	38
1975	210	30	38	74	115	30	52	32
1976	228	21	39	66	97	30	50	34
1977	212	25	42	76	105	37	47	32
1978	228	28	45	65	99	41	41	34
1979	140	19	42	66	99	44	39	39
1980	197	42	32	66	98	48	34	34
1981	200	42	39	56	100	53	31	28
1982	164	45	44	59	95	50	24	25
1983	183	44	46	71	107	38	24	20
1984	189	41	43	63	93	38	23	27
1985	161	41	46	79	91	35	21	14
1986	156	37	46	84	86	34	21	14
1987	191	40	41	78	86	31	22	18
1988	183	38	36	77	83	31	22	22
1989	221	40	42	75	88	31	21	24
1990	228	46	39	69	98	27	18	23
1991	194	40	41	83	85	30	17	24
1992	192	53	42	92	104	30	14	24
1993	210	57	42	78	93	33	15	24

C1 NORTH AMERICA: Area of Main Arable Crops (in thousands of hectares)

	Wheat	Barley	Oats	Rye	Maize	B'wheat	Rice	Sorghum	P's	SP's	SB	SC
							USA[3]					
1950	24,931	4,514	15,907	709	33,111	102	662	4,187	687	198	374	170
1951	25,039	3,814	14,258	697	32,670	81	808	3,458	546	126	280	164
1952	28,785	3,333	14,978	564	32,755	66	808	2,155	565	130	269	172
1953	27,454	3,513	15,190	579	32,561	72	874	2,547	622	139	301	175
1954	21,997	5,411	16,410	726	32,450	61	1,032	4,575	572	134	355	159
1955	19,138	5,877	15,974	829	32,119	43	739	5,217	569	138	299	151
1956	20,140	5,201	13,489	657	30,451	40	635	3,727	555	112	318	138
1957	17,707	6,018	13,786	695	29,082	40	542	7,965	550	111	355	148
1958	21,467	5,986	12,645	727	29,228	35	573	6,687	578	104	361	137[8]
1959	20,929	6,017	11,233	590	33,145	24	642	5,893	539	104	367	165
1960	20,995	5,607	10,760	683	32,649	19	645	6,314	561	77	387	165
1961	20,870	5,183	9,666	624	26,469	19	643	4,445	599	74	436	179
1962	17,680	4,944	9,056	802	26,092	17	718	4,683	545	82	446	193
1963	18,415	4,547	8,623	643	27,647	18	717	5,393	535	69	500	220
1964	20,138	4,564	7,996	686	26,462	20	723	4,520	515	61	565	265
1965	20,056	3,700	7,478	596	26,129	...	726	5,273	560	68	505	236
1966	20,077	4,130	7,228	516	26,640	...	796	5,185	592	63	470	239
1967	23,614	3,714	6,482	430	28,319	...	797	6,065	590	56	454	241
1968	22,162	3,929	7,095	403	26,144	...	952	5,621	557	55	571	234
1969	19,079	3,857	7,256	522	25,641	...	861	...	572	55	624	217
1970	17,630	3,896[5]	7,543	577	26,799[6]	...	735	5,491	575	52	574	236
		3,936			23,212							
1971	19,293	4,109	6,383	710	25,919	...	736	6,597	563	46	543	262
1972	19,135	3,929	5,473	439	23,237	...	736	5,410	507	46	538	284
1973	21,800	4,231	5,692	418	25,047	...	878	6,415	528	46	493	300
1974	26,552	3,306	5,344	363	26,449	...	1,026	5,615	563	49	491	297
1975	28,081	3,453	5,298	295	27,318	...	1,140	6,214	512	47	614	313
1976	28,640	3,358	4,834	292	28,854	...	1,004	5,958	556	48	598	302
1977	26,895	3,871	5,442	285	28,680	...	910	5,703	550	46	492	307
1978	22,863	3,743	4,503	375	29,109	...	1,202	5,427	556	45	514	301
1979	25,275	3,044	3,917	352	29,300	...	1,161	5,221	514	46	453	297
1980	28,727	2,944	3,501	273	29,555	...	1,340	5,068	467	41	481	297
1981	32,784	3,706	3,810	286	30,230	...	1,535	5,551	501	44	497	306
1982	31,963	3,688	4,297	292	29,554	...	1,320	5,766	515	45	416	307
1983	24,843	3,938	3,671	363	20,834	...	878	4,047	503	41	427	311
1984	27,085	4,545	3,304	397	29,103	...	1,134	6,214	527	42	444	302
1985	26,197	4,696	3,309	290	30,442	...	1,009	6,792	551	43	446	312
1986	24,574	4,859	2,776	274	27,988	...	955	5,609	494	38	482	322
1987	22,646	4,070	2,802	272	23,960	...	944	4,291	578	38	507	333
1988	21,524	3,090	2,239	241	23,593	...	1,174	3,659	510	36	526	342
1989	25,167	3,364	2,785	196	26,184	...	1,087	4,493	519	35	524	345
1990	28,066	3,047	2,406	152	27,094	...	1,142	3,678	555	36	557	321
1991	23,352	3,405	1,945	160	27,861	...	1,123	3,994	556	32	561	363
1992	25,399	2,948	1,820	158	29,169	...	1,268	4,877	532	33	571	374
1993	25,379	2,733	1,539	291	25,464	...	1,147	3,608	533	32	570	384

C1   SOUTH AMERICA: AREA OF MAIN ARABLE
CROPS (in thousands of hectares)

	Argentina			Guyana
	Wheat	Maize	SC	SC
1872	73	130	2.5	...
1882	...	...	...	31
1883	...	...	...	32
1884	243	...	...	32
1885	...	...	...	31
1886	...	...	...	31
1887	...	...	...	31
1888	815	802	23.0	31
1889	...	...	...	31

	Argentina							Chile			
	Wheat	Barley	Oats	Rye	Maize	P	SC	Wheat	Barley	Maize	P
1890	1,202	...	...	...	...	...	...	...	...	...	...
1891	1,320	...	...	...	...	...	...	...	...	...	...
1892	1,600	...	...	...	...	...	...	...	...	...	...
1893	1,840	...	...	...	...	...	...	...	...	...	...
1894	2,050	...	...	...	...	...	...	...	...	...	...
1895	2,260	...	...	...	1,244	21	48	...	...	...	...
1896	2,500	...	...	...	...	...	...	...	...	...	...
1897	2,600	...	22	...	...	...	...	...	...	...	...
1898	3,200	...	22	...	850	...	...	...	...	...	...
1899	3,250	49	23	...	1,009	32	...	...	...	...	...
1900	3,380	52	32	1	1,255	...	50	...	...	...	...
1901	3,296	52	33	2	1,406	35	54	...	...	...	...
1902	3,695	13	56	1	1,802	44	60	350	41	20	47
1903	4,320	31	48	3	2,100	38	60	268	50	22	48
1904	4,903	48	51	4	2,287	39	63	422	76	29	36

	Guyana	Uruguay			
	SC	Wheat	Barley	Oats	Maize
1890	32	...	...	...	...
1891	32	...	...	...	...
1892	32	159	2	- -	...
1893	31	207	4	- -	...
1894	31	204	3	- -	...
1895	28	...	...	...	...
1896	28	...	...	...	...
1897	27	...	...	...	...
1898	26	274	2	- -	...
1899	26	328	1	- -	146
1900	27	277	1	- -	182
1901	29	293	1	- -	178
1902	31	266	1	- -	162
1903	32	...	1	- -	...
1904	30	261	1	- -	177

C1 SOUTH AMERICA: Area of Main Arable Crops (in thousands of hectares)

					Argentina				
	Wheat	Barley	Oats	Rye	Maize	Millet	Rice	P's	SC
1905	5,675	50	72	4	2,717	...	...	40	66
1906	5,692	50	146	5	2,851	...	...	44	71
1907	5,759	94	386	9	2,719	...	...	48	71
1908	6,063	61	633	10	2,974	...	...	48	71
1909	5,837	60	575	11	3,005	...	8	49	79
1910	6,253	60	801	13	3,215	...	8	52	94
1911	6,897	68	1,031	15	3,422	...	3	108	97
1912	6,918	108	1,192	40	3,830	...	4	112	99
1913	6,574	169	1,249	92	4,152	...	4	119	106
1914	6,261	161	1,161	93	4,203	...	3	124	125
1915	6,645	175	1,038	86	4,018	...	7	130	134
1916	6,511	157	1,022	73	3,630	...	5	134	86
1917	7,234	244	1,295	10	3,527	...	7	135	112
1918	6,870	249	1,206	...	3,340	...	7	134	91
1919	7,045	271	931	83	3,312	...	7	150	93
1920	6,076	250	834	88	3,274	...	11	158	95
1921	5,763	251	852	98	2,972	...	11	136	85
1922	6,578	242	1,059	148	3,177	...	6	146	100
1923	6,897	227	864	155	3,435	...	4	163	104
1924	6,465	165	692	65	2,912	...	5	118	109
1925	7,130	291	906	144	3,899	...	5	106	122
1926	7,670	328	898	170	3,667	...	4	113	131
1927	8,173	317	705	216	3,562	...	4	126	122
1928	9,076	369	890	351	3,518	...	3	123	122
1929	6,436	325	874	220	4,220	...	4	133	141
1930	7,902	321	908	202	4,685	...	4	176	142
1931	6,486	409	826	388	3,852	...	6	141	143
1932	7,200	519	894	480	3,764	...	13	140	144
1933	7,301	558	668	290	4,112	...	19	138	145
1934	6,942	633	855	533	5,702	...	15	148	145
1935	4,730	507	553	232	5,135		15	122	147
1936	7,115	538	776	273	4,361	...	16	79	148
1937	6,979	455	716	204	2,957	118	16	113	188
1938	7,897	499	722	433	3,502	105	31	125	189
1939	5,065	621	880	541	5,695	132	31	189	188
1940	6,718	605	570	300	4,932	66	21	183	190
1941	5,933	338	470	214	4,089	69	33	215	187
1942	4,875	320	626	253	1,767	37	34	180	213
1943	5,989	530	1,067	803	3,700	49	52	189	230
1944	4,361	411	1,021	328	2,054	57	39	186	239

C1 SOUTH AMERICA: Area of Main Arable Crops (in thousands of hectares)

	Bolivia					Brazil					
	Wheat	Barley	Maize	Rice	P's	Wheat	Maize	Rice	P's	Cassava	SC
1905	...	...	...	...	...	...	...	...	...	...	...
1906	...	...	...	...	...	...	...	...	...	...	...
1907	...	...	...	...	...	...	...	...	...	...	...
1908	...	...	...	...	...	...	...	...	...	...	...
1909	...	...	...	...	...	...	...	...	...	...	...
1910	...	...	...	...	...	...	...	...	...	...	...
1911	...	...	...	...	...	...	...	...	...	...	...
1912	...	...	...	...	...	...	...	...	...	...	...
1913	...	...	...	...	...	...	...	...	...	...	...
1914	...	...	...	...	...	...	...	...	...	...	...
1915	...	...	...	...	...	...	...	...	...	...	...
1916	...	...	...	...	...	...	3,058	...	...	...	...
1917	...	...	...	...	...	...	...	...	...	...	...
1918	...	...	...	...	...	...	...	...	...	...	...
1919	...	...	...	...	...	...	...	...	...	...	...
1920	...	...	...	...	...	100	2,252	366	...	...	...
1921	...	...	...	...	...	...	2,592	567	50	...	551
1922	...	...	...	...	...	107	3,058	243	32	...	...
1923	90	160	260	21	204	62	3,424	344	30	...	300
1924	93	170	274	19	220	98	2,500	544	45	...	...
1925	98	185	280	22	231	97	2,550	...	50	...	320
1926	102	187	265	24	264	97	2,514	389	50	...	305
1927	...	...	...	...	...	133	2,204	...	31	...	273
1928	15	93	345	12	260	145	4,934	1,100	38	...	485
1929	26	95	350	11	248	...	...	...	...	...	...
1930	43	98	348	10	260	...	...	...	...	...	...
1931	50	98	350	...	300	142	3,170	719	24	...	348
1932	...	...	...	...	...	164	3,722	856	44	...	328
1933	...	...	...	...	...	168	4,352	865	42	...	430
1934	...	...	...	...	...	172	3,988	807	34	...	474
1935	...	...	...	...	...	145	4,076	949	54	...	438
1936	...	...	...	...	...	154	3,872	888	46	...	461
1937	...	...	...	...	...	162	3,877	888	62	388	454
1938	...	...	...	...	...	174	4,254	979	78	473	474
1939	34	37	27	6	26	212	4,379	1,076	80	538	496
1940	...	...	...	...	...	201	3,904	872	66		
1941	...	...	...	...	...	272	4,112	1,001	70		
1942	...	...	...	...	...	277	4,059	1,059	72		
1943	...	...	...	...	...	290	4,290	1,170	102		
1944	...	50	100	12	70		4,101	1,428	84		

C1   SOUTH AMERICA: Area af Main Arable Crops (in thousands of hectares)

	Chile					Colombia					
	Wheat	Barley	Oats	Maize	P's	Wheat	Barley	Maize	Rice	P's	SC
1905	390	102	...	33	...	...	...	...	...	...	...
1906	365	73	...	21	27	...	...	...	...	...	...
1907	460	56	...	26	...	...	...	...	...	...	...
1908	445	52	...	25	...	...	...	...	...	...	...
1909	442	44	25	27	28	...	...	...	...	...	...
1910	392	34	24	19	27	...	...	...	...	...	...
1911	442	42	28	23	27	...	...	...	...	...	...
1912	446	53	38	26	32	...	...	...	...	...	...
1913	412	62	49	24	33	...	...	...	...	...	...
1914	435	57	61	32	32	...	...	...	...	...	...
1915	462	49	65	27	32	57	13	168	6	21	83
1916	515	51	51	20	29	...	...	...	...	...	...
1917	527	40	32	26	33	...	...	...	...	...	...
1918	494	44	20	23	29	...	...	...	...	...	...
1919	484	51	26	25	31	...	...	...	...	...	...
1920	509	58	32	28	34	...	...	...	...	...	...
1921	544	57	28	32	33	...	...	...	...	...	...
1922	596	62	33	28	32	...	...	...	...	...	...
1923	621	63	41	28	29	...	...	...	...	...	...
1924	578	71	54	17	29	...	...	148	17	57	106
1925	585	80	58	22	26	...	...	149	17	57	111
1926	600	63	55	25	31	...	...	156	18	60	117
1927	665	68	68	47	45	...	...	200	17	102	98
1928	694	78	89	47	45	60	...	114	19	67	...
1929	699	62	120	38	43	...	...	...	...	...	...
1930	651	67	78	37	45	...	...	...	...	...	...
1931	614	43	67	54	51	110	...	...	...	...	...
1932	593	63	69	66	56	109	...	596	45	32	...
1933	851	95	107	48	54	109	...	...	...	...	...
1934	858	60	76	46	56	148	...	555	47	27	...
1935	776	66	87	42	43	150	...	...	...	...	...
1936	776	72	113	50	51	206	...	...	...	...	...
1937	765	98	121	43	51	200	...	556	67	68	272
1938	828	82	137	43	54	...	...	...	...	...	...
1939	828	53	107	45	46	...	...	...	...	...	...
1940	780	52	80	52	54	...	...	...	...	...	...
1941	730	49	68	48	52	...	...	...	...	...	...
1942	751	47	88	55	55	...	...	...	...	...	...
1943	797	44	102	53	53	...	...	...	...	...	...
1944	805	53	120	45	49	...	...	...	...	...	...

C1 SOUTH AMERICA: Area of Main Arable Crops (in thousands of hectares)

	Ecuador			Guyana		Peru					
	Maize	Rice	Cassava	Rice	SC	Wheat	Barley	Maize	Rice	P's	SC
1905	...	...	...	...	31	...	...	...	...	...	...
1906	...	...	...	10	32	...	...	...	...	...	...
1907	...	...	...	10	30	...	...	...	...	...	...
1908	...	...	...	12	29	...	...	...	...	...	...
1909	...	...	...	15	30	80	65	52	50	...	...
1910	...	...	...	13	30	75	67	53	56	...	...
1911	...	...	...	15	29	...	...	...	...	...	37
1912	...	...	...	17	29	...	...	...	...	...	40
1913	...	...	...	...	29	...	...	...	...	...	41
1914	...	...	...	...	30	...	...	...	...	...	43
1915	...	...	...	...	31	...	...	...	25	...	11
1916	...	...	...	...	32	...	...	...	25	...	45
1917	...	...	...	...	31	70	40	74	28	36	50
1918	...	...	...	...	30	98	...	...	31	...	
1919	...	...	...	30	29	83	...	...	29	...	40
1920	...	...	...	27	27	83	...	...	27	...	49
1921	...	...	...	23	26	94	...	...	27	...	50
1922	...	...	...	20	25	113	...	...	29	...	51
1923	...	...	...	16	22	123	...	...	36	...	53
1924	...	...	...	16	23	90	...	...	35	...	56
1925	...	...	...	16	23	93	...	...	31	...	53
1926	...	...	...	20	24	88	...	...	27	...	53
1927	...	...	...	20	23	115	...	...	26	...	57[11]
											32
1928	...	...	...	22	23	105	125	280	35	285	29
1929	...	...	...	26	22	142	...	...	30	...	41
1930	...	15	...	26	22	143	...	...	47	...	30
1931	...	12	...	34	22	117	...	...	48	...	36
1932	...	...	...	36	23	118	...	...	54	...	31
1933	...	...	...	35	22	121	...	...	60	...	31
1934	...	...	...	29	24	106	...	...	46	...	33
1935	...	...	...	34	26	97	...	...	47	...	32
1936	...	...	...	25	26	108	...	...	47	...	31
1937	...	...	...	29	25	114	...	...	37	...	31
1938	...	...	...	25	28	122	...	...	42	...	...
1939	130	40	10	29	26	136	...	...	42	...	32
1940	...	...	...	25	26	135	...	...	49	...	30
1941	...	...	...	42	25	120	...	...	62	...	34
1942	...	...	...	39	25	117	...	...	47	...	30
1943	...	...	...	35	25	106	...	...	51	...	29
1944	...	...	...	37	24	102	...	...	58	...	32

C1 SOUTH AMERICA: Area of Main Arable Crops (in thousands of hectares)

| | Surinam | Uruguay | | | | | |
	Rice	Wheat	Barley	Oats	Maize	Sorghum	P's
1905	...	288	2	1	166	...	...
1906	...	252	2	2	212	...	...
1907	...	248	2	2	174	...	...
1908	...	277	2	4	204	...	...
1909	...	...	3	7	216	...	...
1910	...	258	1	12	202	...	...
1911	...	323	3	35	239	...	...
1912	...	330	1	20	255	...	...
1913	...	369	6	39	280	...	...
1914	...	317	2	33	319	...	...
1915	...	384	4	43	282	...	...
1916	...	316	5	57	254	...	...
1917	...	395	2	67	239	...	...
1918	...	340	2	34	224	- -	2.0
1919	...	275	2	33	200	- -	2.0
1920	5	283	2	52	231	- -	4.0
1921	9	329	1	43	194	- -	4.0
1922	...	268	1	35	230	- -	3.0
1923	...	427	2	49	186	- -	5.0
1924	...	344	3	56	164	- -	5.0
1925	...	387	3	60	164	- -	4.0
1926	...	400	2	41	176	- -	3.0
1927	...	466	3	65	231	- -	4.0
1928	...	439	3	54	177	- -	5.0
1929	...	444	6	83	215	- -	4.0
1930	...	388	4	42	195	- -	6.0
1931	11	437	4	60	210	- -	6.0
1932	11	383	4	59	205	- -	7.0
1933	13	481	6	86	230	- -	7.0
1934	11	445	9	78	243	- -	8.0
1935	12	513	14	83	215	- -	8.0
1936	15	399	11	73	218	1	7.0
1937	14	556	16	90	214	1	4.7
1938	16	508	21	99	219	1	7.9
1939	18	471	18	87	209	1	8.9
1940	17	375	23	91	232	1	8.6
1941	17	454	22	62	213	1	9.0
1942	14	399	20	78	186	1	10.0
1943	12	331	25	163	237	- -	13.0
1944	11	351	22	60	186	1	11.0

C1   SOUTH AMERICA: Area of Main Arable Crops (in thousands of hectares)

	Argentina										
	Wheat	Barley	Oats	Rye	Maize	Millet	Rice	Sorghum[7]	P's	SP's	SC
1945	4,044	704	741	570	2,749	145	43	...	180	...	240
1946	5,619	982	805	923	2,615	298	44	...	180	...	218
1947	4,717	660	667	701	2,602	350	41	...	157	34	...
1948	4,343	538	642	567	2,667	167	49	...	170	37	236
1949	4,534	393	516	467	2,036	149	43	...	171	36	210
1950	5,241	580	631	985	942	84	42	...	199	32	250
1951	2,740	351	418	152	1,714	161	47	...	227	31	250
1952	5,579	840	963	1,414	1,431	274	56	73	154	30	256
1953	4,996	653	729	836	2,356	329	61	86	191	33	272
1954	5,462	786	695	1,110	2,414	126	63	84	223	33	284
1955	4,062	828	654	890	1,863	141	55	99	217	29	287
1956	5,392	1,012	956	1,220	2,240	194	54	63	205	31	303
1957	4,394	833	876	893	1,958	166	57	57	203	36	286
1958	5,242	897	796	1,064	2,448	155	60	69	183	32	281
1959	4,378	907	798	1,317	2,361	208	52	91[7] 645	189	29	275
1960	3,599	719	768	733	2,415	207	56	610	215	35	242
1961	4,421	742	597	695	2,744	201	46	787	203	38	223
1962	3,745	361	412	287	2,757	159	53	861	143	36	207
1963	5,676	695	693	655	2,645	145	52	828	166	36	224
1964	6,135	553	570	773	2,971	168	54	984	179	35	231
1965	4,601	384	421	331	3,062	115	68	820	204	36	250
1966	5,214	411	412	420	3,275	163	47	1,123	165	36	242
1967	5,812	496	519	565	3,451	188	62	1,033	163	42	191
1968	5,837	539	443	604	3,378	210	71	1,266	200	41	185
1969	5,191	457	327	528	3,556	197	88	1,456	203	46	195
1970	3,701	356	300	360	4,017	132	102	2,111	190	44	192
1971	4,315	479	357	433	4,066	151	77	2,369	179	42	211
1972	4,965	602	399	747	3,147	116	83	1,564	147	35	243
1973	3,958	502	395	656	3,662	198	77	2,282	117	42	272
1974	4,233	369	282	375	3,486	208	83	2,324	105	33	298
1975	5,271	439	338	300	3,070	194	93	2,010	111	41	293
1976	6,428	476	383	340	2,766	231	87	1,903	108	38	339
1977	3,910	310	430	240	2,532	255	91	2,461	111	36	350
1978	4,685	355	500	260	2,630	244	95	2,254	115	34	343
1979	4,787	246	410	225	2,800	238	102	2,044	110	34	306
1980	5,023	173	350	210	2,490	182	82	1,279	112	34	314
1981	6,400	115	299	162	3,394	187	82	2,135	117	24	320
1982	7,320	119	408	174	3,170	132	114	2,510	102	32	309
1983	6,880	96	414	153	2,970	160	81	2,551	108	28	313
1984	5,900	107	384	157	3,014	114	129	2,392	114	31	319
1985	5,382	76	333	115	3,340	125	105	2,002	...	32	288
1986	4,893	94	312	65	3,231	94	113	1,322	107	32	296
1987	4,789	131	476	96	2,900	62	95	1,005	105	29	290
1988	4,651	134	446	55	2,438	55	92	956	113	30	297
1989	5,422	164	445	75	1,684	45	109	593	112	30	300
1990	5,797	148	324	101	1,672	49	117	689	119	28	280
1991	4,547	230	350	55	1,918	50	86	676	124	28	275
1992	4,134	226	407	48	2,367	40	136	764	117	21	255
1993	4,590	199	287	73	2,505	36	106	724	99	23	226

C1 SOUTH AMERICA: Area of Main Arable Crops (in thousands of hectares)

			Bolivia			
	Wheat	Barley	Maize	Rice	Potatoes	Sugar Cane
1945	18	...	...	...	24	...
1946	...	50	...	...	60	...
1947	19	54	118	11	59	...
1948	35	54	117	12	59	...
1949	37	52	...	...	62	...
1950	...	...	...	...	...	...
1951	...	...	...	...	69	...
1952	...	...	...	...	71	...
1953	...	...	...	...	...	...
1954	84	62	116	17	113	10
1955	...	...	...	18	...	...
1956	...	...	...	19	...	13
1957	...	...	...	17	...	16
1958	22	76	98	7	62	...
1959	20	83	89	13	53	...
1960	...	50	...	16	...	40
1961	70	91	207	24	...	27
1962	80	92	214	27	109	30
1963	106	92	218	29	112	30
1964	109	93	220	31	110	30
1965	63	98	214	33	115	22
1966	74	93	203	34	110	24
1967	45	86	210	31	103	33
1968	75	91	217	34	88	37
1969	76	92	218	49	92	40
1970	78	78	219	53	95	40
1971	81	98	225	48	97	27
1972	63	101	215	46	112	40
1973	69	104	215	41	116	44
1974	74	108	219	53	118	46
1975	77	112	230	74	128	52
1976	81	116	235	72	128	72
1977	73	112	244	65	126	75
1978	87	90	262	66	157	70
1979	98	82	278	51	130	67
1980	100	76	293	66	169	66
1981	96	83	313	63	177	70
1982	104	84	286	54	174	68
1983	71	46	261	44	108	71
1984	89	90	322	115	143	70
1985	100	94	349	113	198	78
1986	106	95	249	92	144	70
1987	95	93	302	93	142	66
1988	82	89	293	96	144	58
1989	87	88	279	105	127	53
1990	84	79	256	109	120	63
1991	104	82	273	130	125	80
1992	120	75	283	100	110	77
1993	133	86	286	121	126	81

C1 SOUTH AMERICA: Area of Main Arable Crops (in thousands of hectares)

	Brazil							Chile				
	Wheat	Maize	Rice	P's	SP's	Cassava	SC	Wheat	Barley	Oats	Maize	P's
1945	316	4,092	1,498	87	108	898	657	728	44	70	46	60
1946	301	4,323	1,681	117	114	908	758	745	53	75	47	57
1947	392	4,323	1,650	128	121	911	773	819	62	90	48	49
1948	536	4,347	1,662	128	121	913	819	867	55	99	47	52
1949	630	4,517	1,758	155	114	941	797	833	45	91	46	53
1950	652	4,678	1,964	148	102	957	828	816	51	99	55	50
1951	725	4,682	1,967	152	101	964	874	762	53	107	50	53
1952	810	4,864	1,873	152	103	1,015	920	779	67	99	48	53
1953	910	5,120	2,072	163	103	1,062	991	761	47	89	52	54
1954	1,081	5,528	2,425	165	107	1,103	1,027	805	61	95	54	57
1955	1,196	5,651	2,511	179	113	1,149	1,073	779	61	98	57	58
1956	886	5,998	2,555	185	116	1,178	1,124	766	60	103	57	65
1957	1,154	6,095	2,525	190	120	1,193	1,172	807	60	106	64	69
1958	1,446	5,790	2,515	192	112	1,227	1,208	886	66	112	76	80
1959	1,186	6,189	2,683	188	126	1,239	1,291	885	65	111	75	83
1960	1,141	6,681	2,966	199	133	1,342	1,340	838	65[9]	108	74[9]	85
1961	1,022	6,886	3,174	191	137	1,381	1,367	849[9]	45	113[9]	83	93
								769		83		
1962	743	7,348	3,350	196	145	1,476	1,467	769	43	83	85	91
1963	793	7,958	3,722	200	152	1,618	1,509	751	39	80	84	89
1964	734	8,106	4,182	209	158	1,716	1,519	748	42	70	88	85
1965	767	8,771	4,619	202	168	1,750	1,705	727	38	70	88	91
1966	717	8,703	4,005	199	175	1,780	1,636	780	39	66	81	76
1967	831	9,274	4,291	217	185	1,914	1,681	719	50	68	92	77
1968	970	9,584	4,459	227	182	1,998	1,687	700	72	109	89	80
1969	1,407	9,654	4,621	221	185	2,029	1,672	743	44	81	58	76
1970	1,895	9,858	4,979	214	181	2,025	1,725	740	47	73	74	72
1971	2,269	10,550	4,764	250	184	2,050	1,692	727	53	75	77	80
1972	2,320	10,539	4,533	202	185	2,100	2,000	712	67	84	84	79
1973	1,839	9,908	4,795	206	159	2,104	1,959	534	64	76	86	67
1974	2,471	10,294	4,164	181	...	2,008	2,159	571	80	97	107	93
1975	2,931	10,473	5,279	193	153	2,098	2,022	686	66	94	92	72
1976	3,539	11,176	6,583	202	138	2,105	2,095	698	58	79	96	68
1977	3,153	11,797	5,992	196	117	2,176	2,270	628	63	75	116	86
1978	2,811	11,125	5,624	211	98	2,149	2,391	580	64	75	94	91
1979	3,831	11,319	5,452	204	92	2,111	2,537	560	60	79	130	81
1980	3,122	11,451	6,243	181	84	2,016	2,608	546	49	92	116	89
1981	1,920	11,502	6,102	171	84	2,067	2,826	432	46	80	126	90
1982	2,829	12,601	6,016	182	82	2,133	3,086	374	57	68	115	77
1983	1,879	10,706	5,108	169	77	2,061	3,479	359	38	85	118	67
1984	1,742	12,018	5,351	173	81	1,816	3,656	471	33	96	138	81
1985	2,677	11,798	4,755	155	80	1,868	3,912	506	35	85	131	63
1986	3,864	12,466	5,585	161	79	2,052	3,952	569	23	64	105	53
1987	3,456	13,503	5,980	177	76	1,936	4,314	677	16	56	87	58
1988	3,468	13,182	5,961	173	68	1,757	4,117	577	24	61	90	62
1989	3,281	12,932	5,250	157	76	1,881	4,076	540	25	69	125	63
1990	2,681	11,394	3,947	158	63	1,938	4,273	583	26	78	101	55
1991	2,049	13,064	4,122	161	69	1,945	4,210	466	32	77	100	59
1992	1,956	13,364	4,867	173	58	1,826	4,203	461	28	64	107	62
1993	1,491	11,833	4,431	162	60	1,807	3,934	395	23	68	106	63

C1   SOUTH AMERICA: Area of Main Arable Crops (in thousands of hectares)

					Colombia			
	Wheat	Barley	Maize	Rice	Sorghum	Potatoes	Cassava	Sugar Cane
1945	...	...	...	...	...	...	...	...
1946	180	32	668	124	—	96	...	180
1947	95	23	460	91	—	126	...	...
1948	177	24	685	149	—	102	...	...
1949	181	45	707	112	—	115	85	168
1950	145	44	652	133	—	39	141	259
1951	174	47	768	145	—	50	160	269
1952	188	51	844	150	—	61	160	269
1953	175	63	700	153	—	58	154	264
1954	195	53	680	175	—	62	148	270
1955	182	43	830	188	—	56	144	273
1956	170	50	828	190	—	55	140	273
1957	178	48	624	190	—	61	140	273
1958	160	43	693	197	—	43	133	279
1959	166	60	721	206	—	62	125	276
1960	160	56	730	227	3	54	120	290
1961	160	48	711	237	3	48	115	294
1962	150	49	697	280	3	75	138	293
1963	113	58	689	254	5	68	142	317
1964	100	58	772	302	24	76	125	325
1965	120	46	869	375	30	66	142	326
1966	110	55	846	350	30	67	142	327
1967	68	61	790	291	40	79	144	361
1968	108	47	788	266	40	81	152	368
1969	58	49	681	280	44	84	155	379
1970	45	51	661	257	54	89	244	247
1971	47	56	666	242	92	88	249	247
1972	61	63	624	258	84	89	251	261
1973	56	52	580	291	135	99	250	273
1974	45	59	570	355	151	92	250	272
1975	30	76	573	372	134	110	257	249
1976	33	68	648	366	174	125	223	254
1977	34	47	581	324	190	130	210	255
1978	30	68	671	406	225	137	217	278
1979	31	74	616	442	221	151	222	286
1980	38	63	614	416	206	142	208	292
1981	44	36	629	421	231	160	207	279
1982	45	35	636	446	291	165	171	270
1983	46	18	582	397	272	161	173	275
1984	43	17	593	364	238	160	153	291
1985	45	31	541	386	192	139	154	346
1986	46	38	592	325	227	160	153	347
1987	41	47	623	345	259	157	159	347
1988	38	53	664	383	266	170	149	337
1989	46	50	759	516	239	173	171	322
1990	57	54	837	521	273	161	207	312
1991	47	50	822	435	257	151	174	313
1992	43	33	696	424	245	147	181	315
1993	51	36	767	388	201	185	173	325

C1 SOUTH AMERICA: Area of Main Arable Crops (in thousands of hectares)

	Ecuador							Guyana	
	Wheat	Barley	Maize	Rice	P's	Cassava	SC	Rice	SC
1945	...	...	...	...	...	...	...	43	24
1946	...	...	...	...	26	...	...	41	26
1947	71	75	...	...	25	...	33	41	28
1948	76	90	99	84	21	...	20	37	27
1949	60	100	70	100	22	...	25	42	28
1950	38	59	73	67	25	...	20	39	29
1951	...	108	...	81	16	...	...	47	33
1952	44	108	109	59	17	...	36	62	32
1953	43	103	110	81	25	...	47	55	32
1954	50	107	115	78	27	...	44	65	31
1955	65	110	...	63	32	16	45	70	31
1956	65	112	146	59	...	...	48	55	34
1957	69	120	151	50	33	19	59	55	35
1958	59	128	191	70	31	19	59	74	...
1959	55	128	203	84	34	22	61	79	40
1960	...	...	209	88	33	27		89	44
1961	79	93	228	95	32	25	63	91	41
1962	85	151	212	112	33	23	65	105	39
1963	67	165	247	113	32	27	72	81	39
1964	71	164	300	109	39	24	93	126	43
1965	69	157	307	103	44	25	97	136	42
1966	65	143	267	101	44	28	113	125	47
1967	80	144	364	114	48	34	108	103	43
1968	79	123	383	107	44	39	86	127	51
1969	99	125	300	109	47	40	108	113	43
1970	76	134	292	71	47	35	95	111	43
1971	67	135	352	92	53	37	100	102	54
1972	56	102	352	80	38	41	100	80	53
1973	47	93	265	85	44	54	89	93	56
1974	56	61	272	103	39	49	101	116	56
1975	70	72	277	132	39	43	115	134	41
1976	76	72	239	130	41	33	85	83	54
1977	41	60	247	107	36	31	109	136	51
1978	27	32	185	77	30	24	104	115	56
1979	30	31	219	111	27	20	103	88	57
1980	32	26	226	127	30	25	108	95	52
1981	31	29	244	131	32	26	104	88	57
1982	33	34	217	132	35	20	92	93	52
1983	26	30	206	93	27	20	80	78	51
1984	24	31	245	139	33	24	89	97	48
1985	18	29	255	136	37	22	87	78	39
1986	41	64	480	228	54	20	97	74	47
1987	39	61	476	276	56	22	97	99	44
1988	39	61	450	288	48	21	108	99	43
1989	38	55	469	278	49	22	100	100	37
1990	38	53	439	269	51	25	85	51	40
1991	37	60	474	284	52	19	89	76	42
1992	41	62	501	310	64	21	97	81	42
1993	32	64	329	205	57	19	110	95	42

C1 SOUTH AMERICA: Area of Main Arable Crops (in thousands of hectares)

	Paraguay				Peru							
	Wheat	Maize	Cassava	SC	Wheat	Barley	Maize	Rice	P's	SP's	Cassava	SC
1945	4	72	…	19	99	…	…	60	129	…	…	29
1946	3	…	…	…	97	…	…	51	150	…	…	31
1947	2	98	…	11	142	179	380	57	207	25	20	30
1948	2	79	51	12	147	165	345	56	176	40	28	32
1949	1	…	85	8	146	186	…	48	199	42	29	32
1950	1	…	…	7	162	185	…	42	228	35	32	32
1951	1	101	…	…	162	182	252	51	242	36	33	29
1952	1	82	…	11	170	185	283	59	242	12	20	36
1953	2	84	62	13	172	191	226	66	238	29	15	36
1954	2	84	…	14	166	194	232	65	246	10	15	36
1955	2	92	61	13	159	185	236	62	235	12	17	38
1956	…	…	68	20	139	169	234	67	224	10	20	39
1957	15	105	…	19	146	170	238	60	219	12	19	…
1958	20	98	66	21	138	190	262	71	218	13	22	41
1959	15	110	67	21	158	202	253	70	221	16	24	47
1960	12	…	68	22	154	198	253	87	238	15	24	47
1961	8	92	70	22	153	183	327	81	258	12	41	52
1962	10	95	71	22	154	180	331	87	253	12	39	55
1963	10	96	71	23	153	180	339	73	254	13	44	54
1964	11	159	103	27	149	179	347	82	262	13	50	51
1965	7	162	108	27	153	176	342	75	251	12	41	64
1966	8	151	102	26	148	178	350	96	255	12	40	59
1967	21	173	97	26	151	185	357	107	272	12	42	61
1968	32	180	101	21	136	173	311	76	262	12	37	54
1969	34	128	103	21	139	182	364	110	304	13	38	57
1970	45	187	127	26	136	186	382	140	289	14	39	57
1971	42	190	121	40	139	183	374	147	286	14	36	56
1972	32	184	97	31	138	182	301	105	263	13	37	56
1973	20	186	80	28	164	185	430	110	277	12	37	51
1974	30	243	80	42	154	187	320	89	280	13	37	54
1975	25	223	107	41	134	163	363	122	251	14	38	57
1976	29	257	106	42	134	163	385	133	253	14	36	63
1977	28	288	116	48	135	180	415	138	250	16	38	56
1978	32	276	120	35	107	160	383	110	255	16	38	54
1979	52	353	126	35	96	153	361	131	242	14	35	54
1980	47	377	136	37	69	165	258	96	194	15	38	49
1981	49	400	178	41	102	170	316	151	202	6	32	39
1982	70	420	180	36	84	168	347	169	217	5	27	46
1983	75	370	145	40	81	81	340	195	156	11	33	45
1984	106	447	184	40	79	91	380	249	172	10	33	53
1985	170	470	186	55	81	95	371	193	188	7	32	53
1986	162	376	200	59	98	98	429	161	192	14	35	50
1987	198	567	205	64	102	107	454	229	212	8	45	47
1988	250	486	230	56	115	119	478	219	236	7	37	46
1989	226	506	234	57	118	114	484	213	192	10	44	47
1990	241	518	241	47	82	78	323	185	146	13	40	48
1991	154	243	240	70	102	112	343	158	183	10	37	53
1992	170	258	179	56	70	82	276	166	135	9	37	46
1993	180	249	184	60	81	101	360	174	178	13	28	48

C1 SOUTH AMERICA: Area of Main Arable Crops (in thousands of hectares)

	Surinam	Uruguay							Venezuela[10]			
	Rice	Wheat	Barley	Oats	Maize	Sorghum	P's		Maize	Rice	Cassava	SC
1945	13	354	24	71	201	2	8		...	...	...	...
1946	17	267	19	43	153	2	8		...	...	...	...
1947	16	505	18	55	158	3	8		230	14	...	...
1948	18	502	30	79	161	2	8		376	8	12	68
1949	18	501	30	99	137	2	9		351	...	54	71
1950	18	496	27	59	160	2	11		342	31	...	...
1951	19	545	22	58	332	2	19		...	...	...	...
1952	20	514	26	58	259	3	15		270	40	53	...
1953	20	737	42	67	301	5	14		277	46	54	...
1954	22	732	44	41	263	3	16		259	63	49	56
1955	22	780	33	50	247	...	19		257	55	40	56
1956	25	561	62	65	308	...	17		474	40	40	53
1957	28	778	28	121	299	...	18		283	30	45	41
1958	31	691	67	90	357	...	...		297	12	...	41
1959	29	293	44	39	310	...	30		280	28	43	47
1960	30	520	67	80	259		31		398	42	61	51
1961	26	436	46	86	284	33	16		389	58	33	55
1962	27	400	40	81	267	33	20		483	69	26	61
1963	28	354	47	85	236	33	23		427	74	25	63
1964	30	527	39	81	167	31	25		443	91	25	64
1965	34	547	32	126	192	32	26		462	105	25	62
1966	29	380	46	92	231	37	26		467	110	26	62
1967	34	222	30	54	226	32	22		616	114	35	57
1968	35	532	40	88	162	38	15		626	115	41	57
1969	36	336	39	75	175	41	22		641	119	39	59
1970	36	337	41	83	183	44	21		588	130	39	59
1971	39	340	52	69	180	54	24		588	113	40	66
1972	37	185	31	65	181	42	23		465	65	41	70
1973	45	283	35	78	226	113	25		439	113	34	70
1974	44	430	22	61	193	100	26		462	117	40	77
1975	48	456	44	84	153	54	26		506	114	37	78
1976	48	508	38	58	172	54	26		489	93	40	75
1977	50	297	43	30	138	95	23		496	166	38	84
1978	55	192	53	34	163	89	19		506	166	41	76
1979	59	313	40	66	94	39	21		519	218	38	77
1980	65	227	36	36	132	50	13		366	226	41	77
1981	66	296	63	25	146	74	21		312	243	43	74
1982	70	234	32	48	95	57	21		305	223	30	77
1983	73	255	52	53	93	56	19		310	164	41	79
1984	75	226	68	50	83	47	19		313	151	41	82
1985	75	212	64	33	89	63	22		467	181	40	87
1986	75	186	51	42	76	40	17		650	124	40	105
1987	71	157	61	58	88	31	15		685	136	40	117
1988	70	177	83	52	74	45	19		640	135	41	117
1989	70	227	91	68	49	38	15		442	93	43	115
1990	52	234	71	51	61	26	18		462	115	38	102
1991	60	116	80	48	66	47	19		460	152	42	105
1992	69	148	124	39	69	47	17		374	142	42	109
1993	69	175	79	47	65	40	18		342	150	42	105

C1 Area of Main Arable Crops

NOTES

1. SOURCES: The national publications on pp. xiii–xv; International Institute of Agriculture, *Yearbook of Agricultural Statistics*; and FAO, *Yearbook of Food and Agricultural Statistics*.
2. Most statistics are of areas sown, or, to be more precise, of areas under crops on a particular date during the summer. Some statistics are of areas harvested and where this is known it is indicated in footnotes.
3. For some countries and crops data may be reported for either of the calendar years in which the crop-year lies, and practice in this respect has not always been consistent. So far as possible, the series shown here *are* consistent, and the year of harvest has been preferred where a choice is available.

FOOTNOTES

[1] Statistics in square brackets relate to Ontario and Manitoba only to 1898 (except that 1883 is for Ontario only, as is the potato figure in 1888). From 1899 to 1907 they relate to Ontario, Manitoba, Alberta, New Brunswick and Saskatchewan, and the potato statistics are for Ontario, Manitoba and New Brunswick. The 1908 figures, and the 1901 figure for potatoes, are exclusive of British Columbia.
[2] Trinidad only to 1898.
[3] Statistics are of area harvested, for grain in the case of small grains and for all purposes in the case of maize.
[4] Subsequent statistics are estimates derived from the F.A.O. A series with much lower figures is available in national sources from 1970, said to cover both state and private sectors, as follows:-

1970	36	1974	31	1978	47	1982	54
1971	50	1975	29	1979	48	1983	62
1972	31	1976	26	1980	51	1984	58
1973	29	1977	53	1981	53	1985	63

[5] All barley from 1970 (2nd line), barley for grain previously.
[6] Maize for grain only from 1970 (2nd line).
[7] The definition of sorghum was widened from 1959 (2nd line).
[8] Subsequently including Hawaii.
[9] Subsequently area harvested rather than area sown.
[10] The following earlier estimates are available for maize and sugar cane in Rafael Cartay, *Historia Economica de Venezuela* 1830–1900 (Valencia, 1988):-

	Maize	Cane		Maize	Cane
1872–3	15	...	1888	...	40
1875	15	35	1924	97	...
1884	27	39	1937	229	59

C2 NORTH AMERICA: OUTPUT OF MAIN ARABLE CROPS (in thousands of metric tons)*

Key: Bwt = buckwheat; P = potatoes; SP = sweet potatoes

	Canada						
	Wheat	Barley	Oats	Rye	Maize	Bwt	P
1827	[80][1]	[8][1]	[38][1]	...	...	[19][1]	[185][1]
1831	[93][1]	...	[49][1]	...	...	[23][1]	[200][1]
1842	[88][2]	[22][2]	[74][2]	[7][2]	[18][2]	[8][2]	[220][2]
1844	[26][1]	[26][1]	[112][1]	[8][1]	[3][1]	[8][1]	[270][1]
1848	[206][2]	[11][2]	[109][2]	[11][2]	[29][2]	[9][2]	[129][2]
1851	429	24	314	16	[56][3]	[45][3]	[386][3]
1861	742	101	598	46	...	...	...
1871	455	250	655	27	[97][4]	81	1,288
1881	880	367	1,087	53	...	107	1,507
1891	1,149	375	1,287	34	...	109	1,456
1900	1,512	484[5]	2,336[5]	...	...	...	1,507[6]
1901	2,404	527	1,864	59	...	99	735
1902	2,642	754	2,421	...	...	...	559
1903	2,229	761	2,515	...	...	...	711
1904	1,955	828	2,467	...	...	...	671

	Guatemala	Mexico			
	Maize	Wheat	Barley	Maize	Rice
1894	159	226	535	1,902	14
1895	...	265	100	1,770	12
1899	297	...	...	...	...
1901	...	327	163	2,305	...
1902	...	230	128	1,927	...
1903	...	286	...	2,402	...
1904	...	256	156	2,174	...

* *For sugar see table C3, p. 188.*

C2 NORTH AMERICA: Output of Main Arable Crops (in thousands of metric tons)

					USA				
	Wheat	Barley	Oats	Rye	Maize[7]	B'wheat	Rice	P	SP
1839	2,313	87	1,785	474	9,602	159	...	...	...
1849	2,722	109	2,134	360	15,037	195	...	1,791	955
1859	4,708	348	2,511	536	21,311[7]	383	...	3,024	1,050
1866	4,627	392	3,367	448	18,568	258	...	3,038	...
1867	5,742	523	3,237	498	20,168	243	...	2,712	...
1868	6,695	501	3,338	437	23,369	229	...	3,274	712
1869	7,892	631	4,122	455	19,864	227	...	3,935	567
1870	6,913	631	3,890	397	28,576	201	...	2,936	771
1871	7,402	610	4,442	431	29,008	202	...	3,667	701
1872	7,375	697	4,746	426	32,488	225	...	3,635	677
1873	8,763	675	4,456	410	25,604	226	...	3,524	830
1874	9,689	784	3,963	440	26,900	218	...	3,568	752
1875	8,546	718	5,298	430	36,831	239	...	4,894	811
1876	8,409	893	4,746	489	37,543	209	...	3,337	953
1877	10,777	849	6,314	555	38,508	258	...	4,727	878
1878	12,220	806	6,430	553	39,753	261	...	3,902	966
1879	12,492	914	6,024	503	44,503	256	...	4,611	844
1880	13,662	980	6,067	490	43,360	240	...	4,495	1,001
1881	11,049	1,067	6,474	487	31,624	189	...	3,472	619
1882	15,023	1,306	7,838	679	44,579	232	...	5,370	1,041
1883	11,947	1,241	8,796	645	41,962	156	...	6,180	776
1884	15,540	1,480	9,304	676	49,481	221	...	5,660	808
1885	10,886	1,393	9,783	552	52,275	252	...	5,365	1,001
1886	13,989	1,611	19,899	606	45,290	235	...	5,309	974
1887	13,363	1,568	10,102	572	40,769	210	...	4,344	961
1888	11,539	1,655	11,220	722	57,178	212	...	6,522	1,119
1889	13,716	1,764	12,062	750	58,270	254	...	5,931	1,117
1890	12,220	1,524	8,840	670	41,912	261	...	4,630	1,122
1891	18,452	2,047	12,149	751	59,337	280	...	7,174	1,142
1892	16,656	2,068	10,480	729	48,186	264	...	5,176	1,157
1893	13,771	1,894	10,262	678	48,262	225	...	5,558	1,138
1894	14,751	1,611	10,886	680	41,023	240	...	5,380	1,239
1895	14,751	2,264	13,426	752	64,392	271	152	8,222	1,120
1896	14,233	2,112	11,249	809	67,846	300	106	7,150	1,048
1897	16,492	2,243	12,047	791	58,117	312	140	5,393	1,037
1898	20,901	2,134	12,222	738	59,718	265	170	6,541	1,266
1899	17,826	2,569	13,601	660	67,211	244	183	7,418	1,054
1900	16,302	2,112	13,717	696	67,617	255	200	7,068	1,140
1901	20,765	2,700	11,612	782	43,588	330	259	5,645	1,201
1902	18,697	3,179	15,633	860	70,462	295	297	8,071	1,222
1903	18,044	3,244	12,846	735	63,884	311	390	7,519	1,319
1904	15,132	3,614	14,689	723	68,252	337	392	9,512	1,385

C2   NORTH AMERICA: Output of Main Arable Crops (in thousands of metric tons)

	Canada								Costa Rica	
	Wheat	Barley	Oats	Rye	Maize	B'wheat	Mixed Grain	P's	Maize	Rice
1905	2,913	895	2,857	...	...	...	...	618	...	...
1906	3,690	1,009	3,109	...	...	...	...	667	...	...
1907	2,535	881₅	2,529₅	...	...	...	...	825	...	...
		967	3,353							
1908	3,060	1,018	3,861	...	...	...	...	857₆	...	...
								2,249		
1909	4,538	1,206	5,451	43	581	156	346	3,020	...	...
1910	4,538	1,206	5,451	44	489	170	352	2,697	...	...
1911	3,595	628	3,784	39	364	157	237	1,509	...	...
1912	6,293	968	5,640	64	487	184	285	1,944	...	...
1913	6,100	1,075	6,040	65	430	229	312	2,310	...	...
1914	6,306	1,052	6,241	58	426	182	287	2,138	...	...
1915	4,389	788	4,828	51	354	188	297	2,332	...	...
1916	10,710	1,176	7,171	63	365	171	318	1,643	...	...
1917	7,152	931	6,326	73	160	130	192	1,723	...	...
1918	6,361	1,199	6,215	98	197	156	293	2,174	...	...
1919	5,146	1,683	6,575	216	361	248	647	2,840	...	...
1920	5,260	1,228	6,082	259	430	230	505	3,418	...	...
1921	7,163	1,378	8,185	287	364	196	588	3,642	...	...
1922	8,188	1,300	6,573	545	379	179	404	2,921	...	...
1923	10,880	1,565	7,576	822	350	211	503	2,529	...	...
1924	12,905	1,676	8,698	590	346	212	540	2,517	6	4
1925	7,133	1,934	6,261	349	305	248	581	2,570	6	4
1926	10,763	1,897	6,204	233	268	230	601	1,824	7	5
1927	11,080	2,177	5,913	309	198	215	615	2,129	8	4
1928	13,054	2,111	6,781	396	108	237	683	2,107	8	2
1929	15,423	2,970	6,973	371	133	237	710	2,277	...	...
1930	8,224	2,228	4,362	334	132	228	649	1,811	...	...
1931	11,449	2,943	6,526	559	148	237	803	2,188	...	...
1932	8,745	1,467	5,063	135	138	151	715	2,373	...	...
1933	12,058	1,759	6,039	215	128	183	708	1,788	...	...
1934	7,672	1,379	4,742	106	128	185	599	1,939	...	...
1935	7,507	1,388	4,952	120	173	188	688	2,182	...	...
1936	7,673	1,828	6,082	244	197	173	717	1,754	...	...
1937	5,966	1,566	4,191	109	155	187	610	1,797	19	10
1938	4,904	1,810	4,140	147	138	169	656	1,930	...	...
1939	9,798	2,226	5,727	279	195	154	711	1,630	24	12
1940	14,169	2,246	5,928	389	206	149	800	1,651	26	12
1941	14,701	2,270	5,868	355	177	146	783	1,919	25	12
1942	8,565	2,404	4,720	283	347	90	828	1,680	25	14
1943	15,133	5,574	9,893	614	373	97	1,117	1,801	25	11
1944	7,685	4,537	7,118	163	203	116	546	1,812	26	9

C2 NORTH AMERICA: Output of Main Arable Crops (in thousands of metric tons)

| | Cuba | | Dominican Republic | | El Salvador | | Guatemala | | | Honduras |
	Maize	Rice	Maize	Rice	Maize	Rice	Wheat	Maize	Rice	Maize
1911	...	...	8	...	...	...	...	...	...	...
1912	...	...	8	...	...	...	...	300	...	...
1913	...	...	8	...	...	...	10	...	2	...
1914	...	...	8	...	...	7	11	461	8	...
1915	...	...	8	...	...	18	17	500	11	...
1916	...	...	8	...	...	...	16	...	6	...
1917	...	...	...	...	...	...	19	512	15	...
1918	...	...	...	...	106	6	3	377	13	...
1919	...	...	9	...	127	10	7	243	4	...
1920	...	...	9	...	271	...	9	200	2	...
1921	...	...	...	...	...	...	10	312	2	...
1922	...	...	...	...	...	...	6	297	3	...
1923	...	...	...	...	250	10	4	249	...	...
1924	...	...	...	...	270	10	6	243	2	...
1925	...	...	...	...	...	...	4	215	1	...
1926	...	...	...	...	...	...	7	176	1	134
1927	...	...	...	...	...	...	6	213	2	123
1928	...	...	...	...	...	...	5	207	1	141
1929	...	28	...	...	228	11	5	280	2	130
1930	...	...	...	...	280	...	5	302	2	145
1931	...	18	...	...	120	5	4	292	2	111
1932	...	...	...	...	107	5	5	316	2	150
1933	...	26	...	...	136	7	5	305	3	157
1934	89	...	...	...	136	9	5	285	2	141
1935	...	...	...	...	188	17	6	307	7	118
1936	...	...	64	38	152	11	16	284	7	171
1937	...	7	51	39	161	14	11	286	...	133
1938	22	10	49	42	345	13	13	323	...	164
1939	45	15	76	46	131	16	15	461	19	175
1940	41	22	71	39	158	17	18	624	19	170
1941	...	30	74	45	217	20	22	687	21	198
1942	...	29	70	42	211	25	23	692	27	195
1943	...	45	61	42	192	16	12	315	12	159
1944	...	36	75	55	157	19	13	264	9	167

C2   NORTH AMERICA: Output of Main Arable Crops (in thousands of metric tons)

| | Mexico | | | | | | Nicaragua | | Panama |
	Wheat	Barley	Oats	Maize	Rice	P	Maize	Rice	Rice
1905	303	140	...	2,135	...	...	...	...	...
1906	350	161	...	2,715	...	...	...	...	...
1907	312	229	- -	1,572	33	17	...	...	...
1908	257	...	...	2,679	...		...	...	...
1909	272	152	...	...	...	...	...	...	...
1910	326	134	...	2,059	28	...	...	...	...
1911	326	142	...	1,720	...	...	...	...	...
1912	326	122	...	2,096	...	...	...	...	...
1913	291	215	- -	3,374	25	15	...	...	...
1914	218	236	...	1,993	25		...	...	...
1915	109	218	...	2,683	...	...	...	...	...
1916	291	215	...	3,374	25	15	...	...	...
1917	...	...	...	...	...	...	...	...	...
1918	...	386	...	1,930	18	12	...	...	...
1919	285	...	...	2,857	...	...	...	...	...
1920	280	...	...	2,349	...	...	...	...	...
1921	139	86	...	1,804	30	...	...	...	...
1922	371	85	...	1,734	33	25	...	...	...
1923	372	85	...	2,574	32	22	...	...	...
1924	282	108	...	2,701	53	40	...	...	...
1925	298	83	...	1,969	86	38	...	...	...
1926	334	94	...	2,135	91	43	...	...	...
1927	385	98	...	2,059	83	53	...	...	...
1928	357	86	...	2,173	83	54	...	...	...
1929	367	55	...	1,469	67	39	...	...	...
1930	370	59	...	1,377	75	46	31	...	...
1931	525	69	...	2,139	72	50	35	1	...
1932	313	66	2	1,974	72	52	45	1	...
1933	392	71	4	1,924	67	52	63	2	...
1934	354	73	2	1,724	69	59	...	...	...
1935	397	82	3	1,656	71	60	...	...	...
1936	439	80	3	1,597	86	76	...	...	...
1937	342	78	...	1,635	75	69	15	2	...
1938	386	75	...	1,693	80	71	19	3	...
1939	429	97	11	1,977	103	71	...	...	...
1940	464	112	19	1,640	108	71	...	...	...
1941	434	114	31	2,124	109	92	...	16	43
1942	489	108	28	2,363	108	118	...	16	44
1943	364	93	25	1,808	115	124	...	15	48
1944	374	101	21	2,316	104	125	...	10	51

C2 NORTH AMERICA: Output of Main Arable Crops (in thousands of metric tons)

	Wheat	Barley	Oats	Rye	Maize	Bwt	Rice	Sorghum	P	SP
					USA					
1905	19,214	3,745	16,025	792	75,035	348	327	...	8,184	1,461
1906	20,166	3,897	14,849	752	77,041	322	363	...	9,293	1,441
1907	17,118	3,288	11,627	718	66,398	310	424	...	9,066	1,430
1908	17,499	3,723	12,033	728	65,204	321	457	...	8,307	1,554
1909	18,615	3,767	14,718	764	66,322	322	481	...	10,619	1,472
1910	17,009	3,092	16,054	739	72,469	316	505	...	9,309	1,505
1911	16,819	3,157	12,860	797	62,867	302	463	...	8,238	1,379
1912	19,867	4,289	19,639	963	74,882	329	484	...	11,055	1,413
1913	20,438	3,462	15,081	1,026	57,736	222	494	...	9,048	1,397
1914	24,412	3,875	15,473	1,070	64,112	281	479	...	10,022	1,351
1915	27,460	4,507	20,829	1,188	71,859	273	533	...	9,165	1,578
1916	17,282	3,462	16,533	1,095	61,597	224	807	...	7,359	1,535
1917	16,873	3,963	20,945	1,534	73,866	296	709	...	10,850	1,815
1918	24,602	4,899	20,742	2,123	62,004	314	816	...	9,420	1,711
1919	25,909	2,852	16,068	2,003	68,049	277	876	1,829	8,092	1,953
1920	22,942	3,723	20,960	1,578	78,006	265	1,054	2,235	10,040	1,921
1921	22,289	2,896	15,168	1,555	74,374	257	802	1,803	8,854	1,839
1922	23,051	3,331	16,663	2,569	68,761	256	850	1,270	11,305	1,955
1923	20,656	3,462	17,810	1,425	73,028	252	678	1,575	9,971	1,593
1924	22,915	3,592	20,553	1,485	56,466	272	666	1,499	10,455	1,120
1925	18,207	4,180	20,394	1,077	71,072	273	674	1,448	8,068	1,251
1926	22,643	3,614	16,721	888	64,696	239	858	1,803	8,753	1,579
1927	23,813	5,204	15,865	1,300	66,449	279	908	2,057	10,060	1,769
1928	24,875	7,141	19,044	967	67,719	220	895	1,956	11,628	1,476
1929	22,425	6,118	16,141	899	63,909	190	807	1,270	9,073	1,622
1930	24,140	6,575	18,492	1,153	52,834	152	917	965	9,357	1,362
1931	25,637	4,354	16,315	833	65,433	194	911	1,829	10,459	1,679
1932	20,493	6,510	18,202	993	74,425	146	850	1,676	10,197	2,160
1933	15,023	3,331	10,683	523	60,912	170	769	1,372	9,340	1,862
1934	14,315	2,547	7,896	414	36,806	196	797	483	11,063	1,938
1935	17,091	6,292	17,563	1,446	58,397	185	805	1,473	10,312	2,027
1936	17,145	3,222	11,510	616	38,254	140	1,017	762	8,817	1,491
1937	23,786	4,833	17,084	1,241	67,135	148	1,090	1,778	10,245	1,700
1938	25,038	5,595	15,807	1,422	64,747	147	1,072	1,702	9,685	1,711
1939	20,166	6,053	13,905	980	65,560	125	1,103	1,321	9,318	1,540
1940	22,180	6,771	18,086	1,009	62,410	141	1,119	2,184	10,258	1,290
1941	25,637	7,903	17,171	1,145	67,363	131	1,048	2,896	9,680	1,560
1942	26,371	9,340	19,494	1,344	77,956	144	1,319	2,794	10,040	1,633
1943	22,969	7,032	16,547	729	75,339	192	1,327	2,794	12,489	1,775
1944	28,848	6,009	16,678	572	78,438	195	1,405	4,521	10,449	1,703

C2 NORTH AMERICA: Output of Main Arable Crops (in thousands of metric tons)

	Canada								Costa Rica	
	Wheat	Barley	Oats	Rye	Maize	Bwt	Mixed Grain	P	Maize	Rice
1945	11,290	4,078	7,311	215	304	103	888	2,004	28	13
1946	8,609	3,240	5,417	149	270	94	733	1,446	...	23
1947	11,202	3,197	5,565	221	280	86	864	1,894	21	14
1948	9,212	3,046	4,167	346	175	91	548	1,724	21	13
1949	10,380	3,315	5,325	699	323	68	974	2,014	22	18
1950	9,961	2,570	4,697	259	355	58	877	1,927	100	33
1951	12,696	3,647	6,196	330	358	64	1,140	1,988	87	33
1952	15,068	5,344	7,617	447	404	66	1,260	1,358	69	41
1953	19,104	6,348	7,266	610	538	62	1,162	1,676	80	48
1954	17,255	5,707	6,384	733	586	78	1,229	1,896	62	34
1955	9,035	3,814	4,725	325	632	54	1,155	1,459	47	34
1956	14,129	5,467	6,160	352	903	53	1,202	1,823	42	50
1957	15,595	5,858	7,210	214	707	69	1,209	1,920	60	34
1958	10,688	4,703	4,887	213	750	48	1,139	1,984	...	57
1959	10,834	5,178	5,332	196	757	44	1,158	1,797	...	55
1960	14,108	4,695	5,308	214	785	31	1,136	1,615	...	56
1961	7,713	2,452	4,379	166	742	26	1,112	2,012	53	57
1962	15,393	3,611	7,597	311	848	24	1,310	2,127	59	60
1963	19,691	4,817	6,876	350	919	26	1,283	2,099	63	65
1964	16,349	3,668	5,352	314	1,342	28	1,291	2,157	70	68
1965	17,674	4,753	6,169	453	1,511	19	1,466	2,087	84	72
1966	22,516	6,558	5,778	437	1,685	25	1,478	2,490	82	77
1967	16,137	5,414	4,691	304	1,882	28	1,560	2,130	85	81
1968	17,686	7,084	5,591	331	2,062	30	1,747	2,409	86	84
1969	18,623	8,238	5,728	419	1,865	37	1,783	2,362	73	104
1970	9,023	9,051	5,673	570	2,564	62	2,012	2,511	47	79
1971	14,412	13,099	5,606	557	2,946	52	2,186	2,066	61	92
1972	14,514	11,285	4,630	344	2,528	37	2,129	1,869	64	89
1973	16,159	10,223	5,041	363	2,803	30	1,980	2,056	87	104
1974	13,304	8,790	3,929	480	2,620	26	1,648	2,511	61	127
1975	17,081	9,510	4,480	523	3,645	20	1,833	2,205	68	196
1976	23,587	10,513	4,831	440	3,771	20	1,569	2,350	92	150
1977	19,858	11,802	4,283	407	4,249	44	1,607	2,525	85	169
1978	21,137	10,397	3,568	605	4,480	73	1,639	2,513	62	196
1979	17,196	8,478	2,879	525	5,276	36	1,559	2,752	73	220
1980	19,292	11,394	2,911	455	5,753	25	1,511	2,478	75	231
1981	24,802	13,724	3,188	927	6,683	53	1,459	2,647	83	222
1982	26,736	13,966	3,637	913	6,522	29	1,484	2,781	82	146
1983	26,465	10,209	2,773	828	5,931	36	1,162	2,556	94	247
1984	21,188	10,279	2,576	664	6,778	23	1,238	2,793	103	223
1985	24,252	12,387	2,736	569	6,970	22	1,265	2,994	119	224
1986	31,378	14,569	3,251	609	5,912	39	1,083	2,761	120	185
1987	25,992	13,957	2,995	493	7,015	44	1,087	3,033	127	163
1988	15,996	10,212	2,993	268	5,369	31	864	2,778	98	205
1989	24,578	11,616	3,546	873	6,379	32	999	2,811	83	238
1990	32,098	13,441	2,692	599	7,066	42	1,051	2,860	72	219
1991	31,946	11,617	1,794	339	7,413	23	614	2,860	52	193
1992	29,871	10,919	2,823	278	4,883	...	606	3,607	40	233
1993	27,232	12,972	3,549	319	6,501	...	...	3,316	34	170

C2 NORTH AMERICA: Output of Main Arable Crops (in thousands of metric tons)

	Cuba		Dominican Republic		El Salvador			Guatemala			Haiti	
	Maize	Rice	Maize	Rice	Maize	Rice	Sorghum	Wheat	Maize	Rice	Maize	Rice
1945	...	64	82	59	157	19	...	14	191	6	...	...
1946	216	81	77	52	118	16	...	13	294	9	...	12
1947	223	70	77	49	171	23	121	8	166	6	60	22
1948	252	70	79	62	255	34	166	...	...	...	95	24
1949	278	60	69	59	...	20	...	16	378	8	102	31
1950	165	75	83	60	203	20	95	...	...	...	...	31
1951	180	117	98	70	...	26	...	26	428	11	...	...
1952	210	164	88	73	181	27	91	22	433	10	...	...
1953	251	192	82	74	181	24	108	20	413	11	...	...
1954	178	181	92	78	175	16	119	18	368	10	...	...
1955	170	215	90	74	158	13	124	15	365	9	...	...
1956	180	279	97	79	186	16	134	20	450	10	...	...
1957	178	261	94	99	178	27	98	18	429	11	...	...
1958	147	253	98	116	142	20	82	22	469	12	230	42
1959	196	326	99	113	151	19	75	22	500	15	...	...
1960	212	323	101	120	178	20	82	21	506	14	...	...
1961	160	213	50	113	176	18	84	25	518	13	228	55
1962	152	230	48	111	214	26	88	32	559	16	229	60
1963	140	140	46	118	207	21	91	36	589	18	230	64
1964	129	123	43	143	192	33	88	36	643	20	232	68
1965	117	55	38	167	203	35	106	27	646	13	234	72
1966	127	68	43	178	266	50	115	30	594	15	234	76
1967	120	93	39	147	209	78	108	32	607	21	246	77
1968	115	100	40	181	258	83	124	33	689	25	220	77
1969	115	205	43	195	279	38	128	33	709	27	242	83
1970	115	366	45	210	363	44	147	31	786	15	240	80
1971	125	355	49	212	377	55	156	33	747	59	252	81
1972	89	316	50	214	238	36	146	38	802	44	257	92
1973	87	322	47	226	406	37	156	47	813	25	204	118
1974	95	437	49	252	353	32	131	51	799	20	204	119
1975	94₈ 20	447	46	219	439	61	175	45	934	28	180	108
1976	...	451	67	312	342	36	156	48	846	24	180	131
1977	...	456	65	308	380	33	151	56	842	25	168	90
1978	...	457	66	351	507	51	162	60	906	26	161	114
1979	17	425	38	377	523	58	160	57	941	37	183	122
1980	23	478	35	398	529	61	140	58	902	42	179	120
1981	23	461	41	400	500	50	136	55	997	33	176	116
1982	22	520	31	447	414	35	124	49	1,100	49	171	113
1983	30	518	42	501	443	43	123	70	1,046	46	186	124
1984	29	555	84	507	527	63	140	61	922	44	186	124
1985	33	524	91	494	495	69	133	54	1,073	38	196	129
1986	35	576	47	468	432	47	148	56	1,196	48	206	135
1987	42	466	47	515	578	42	26	57	1,172	44	205	120
1988	₁₀40	489	56	463	596	57	153	45	1,301	57	202	121
1989	95	536	47	467	589	64	149	51	1,263	63	196	108
1990	95	447	38	405	603	62	161	32	1,293	62	163	130
1991	95	366	43	446	504	61	163	20	1,145	61	190	120
1992	95	275	49	566	632	68	219	24	1,366	72	226	116
1993	90	186	42	449	640	75	207	32	1,295	75	200	90

C2   NORTH AMERICA: Output of Main Arable Crops (in thousands of metric tons)

	Honduras	Mexico							Nicaragua		Panama	
	Maize	Wheat	Barley	Oats	Maize	Rice	Sorghum	P	Maize	Rice	Maize	Rice
1945	187	347	112	22	2,186	121	...	127	26	19	31	52
1946	180	340	119	25	2,383	139	...	124	34	6	...	54
1947	177	422	117	33	2,518	138	...	129	54	10	...	61
1948	207	477	149	18	2,832	163	...	128	48	14	46	75
1949	196	503	160	59	2,871	185	...	130	81	20	...	80
1950	210	587	162	59	3,122	187	...	135	104	23	62	84
1951	223	590	164	50	3,424	180	...	138	91	13	68	83
1952	222	512	165	51	3,202	151	...	139	123	37	72	92
1953	219	671	165	50	3,720	152	...	149	139	50	77	111
1954	184	839	167	61	4,488	170	...	150	96	25	76	99
1955	210	850	192	70	4,490	210	...	l67	142	22	81	98
1956	235	1,243	197	71	4,382	235	...	180	138	30	74	96
1957	246	1,377	174	79	4,500	240	...	197	105	33	78	86
1958	265	1,337	178	84	5,277	252	156	224	108	33	78	114
1959	285	1,266	180	80	5,563	261	179	250	99	32	79	117
1960	293	1,190	180	68	5,420	328	209	294	119	34	63	96
1961	258	1,402	174	68	6,246	333	291	303	140	39	74	109
1962	280	1,455	151	74	6,337	289	296	380	150	37	72	110
1963	284	1,703	186	79	6,870	296	402	414	142	47	76	111
1964	333	2,203	171	80	8,454	274	526	413	158	48	82	128
1965	236	2,150	193	81	8,936	378	747	319	171	54	84	151
1966	335	1,647	220	63	9,721	372	1,411	348	176	63	84	140
1967	336	2,122	200	48	8,603	418	1,605	377	202	68	89	151
1968	337	2,081	251	41	9,062	347	2,128	472	216	87	84	163
1969	338	2,326	201	41	8,411	395	2,453	488	231	110	88	165
1970	339	2,676	213	63	8,879	405	2,565	422	236	81	56	127
1971	340	1,831	306	34	9,786	369	2,335	442	243	82	54	136
1972	341	1,809	294	28	9,223	375	2,441	461	131	74	44	125
1973	343	2,091	392	39	8,609	451	3,270	640	191	78	55	162
1974	344	2,789	250	51	7,848	469	3,499	603	203	80	59	178
1975	358	2,798	440	87	8,449	717	4,126	693	192	89	65	185
1976	389	3,363	549	48	8,017	463	4,027	687	201	57	64	144
1977	439	2,456	418	49	10,138	567	4,325	631	181	76	80	186
1978	455	2,785	505	60	10,930	402	4,193	923	254	85	64	162
1979	354	2,287	368	50	8,458	494	3,917	1,053	173	115	64	170
1980	387	2,785	530	60	12,374	445	4,812	1,065	182	116	55	170
1981	481	3,189	559	77	14,766	644	6,296	861	193	164	57	195
1982	366	4,462	396	71	10,030	521	4,717	941	109	176	66	176
1983	458	3,460	557	251	13,061	441	4,846	835	99	171	74	199
1984	507	4,506	619	180	12,932	484	5,009	1,017	124	162	71	175
1985	424	5,214	544	138	14,103	809	6,550	989	234	156	96	186
1986	484	4,770	515	...	11,721	545	4,833	...	234	144	96	180
1987	443	4,415	617	...	11,607	591	6,298	...	277	149	98	180
1988	440	3,665	350	...	10,600	456	5,895	931	280	111	92	183
1989	510	4,374	433	...	10,953	527	5,002	966	298	104	90	707
1990	558	3,935	492	...	14,640	394	5,978	810	293	121	94	216
1991	567	4,061	580	...	14,253	347	4,250	1,286	199	119	108	186
1992	562	3,621	550	...	17,003	361	5,345	1,213	252	154	111	154
1993	638	3,582	547	...	18,600	325	2,602	1,210	283	178	94	178

C2 NORTH AMERICA: Output of Main Arable Crops (in thousands of metric tons)

					USA					
	Wheat	Barley	Oats	Rye	Maize[7]	Bwt	Rice	Sorghum	P	SP
1945	30,154	5,813	22,121	602	72,875	141	1,391	2,438	11,414	1,528
1946	31,352	5,770	21,453	470	81,715	148	1,474	2,693	13,263	1,517
1947	36,985	6,140	17,070	648	59,819	156	1,597	2,362	10,586	1,238
1948	35,243	6,880	21,047	658	91,571	132	1,736	3,328	12,244	1,075
1949	29,882	5,160	17,708	460	82,248	108	1,849	3,582	10,929	1,125
1950	27,732	6,619	19,871	544	78,108	96	1,761	5,944	11,753	1,237
1951	26,888	5,595	18,550	547	74,323	72	2,091	4,140	8,880	726
1952	35,543	4,964	17,665	410	83,620	70	2,186	2,311	9,575	728
1953	31,923	5,378	16,736	480	81,537	70	2,397	2,947	10,509	862
1954	26,780	8,252	20,466	659	77,676	59	2,912	5,690	9,958	780
1955	25,446	8,774	21,714	739	81,791	40	2,536	6,172	10,328	980
1956	27,351	8,208	16,707	541	87,506	40	2,243	5,207	11,149	788
1957	26,018	9,645	18,724	724	86,363	36	1,947	14,428	11,001	819
1958	39,652	10,385	20,336	843	94,619	33	2,030	14,758	12,106	797
1959	30,426	9,144	15,241	586	106,608	22	2,433	12,904	11,125	856
1960	36,876	9,340	16,736	841	109,580[7]	18	2,476	15,749	11,662	674
1961	33,529	8,540	14,665	694	91,388	19	2,458	12,192	13,298	654
1962	29,718	9,314	14,693	1,034	91,604	18	2,996	12,955	12,018	777
1963	31,212	8,554	14,015	741	102,093	21	3,187	14,860	12,306	652
1964	34,928	8,407	12,371	825	88,504	22	3,319	11,761	10,941	589
1965	35,805	8,559	13,493	846	104,217	...	3,460	17,095	13,211	702
1966	35,514	8,539	11,661	706	105,861	...	3,856	18,162	13,941	620
1967	41,031	8,139	11,523	608	123,458	...	4,054	19,186	13,870	612
1968	42,365	9,279	13,800	583	113,023	...	4,724	18,568	13,405	607
1969	39,264	9,298	14,020	767	119,056	...	4,169	18,541	14,174	652
1970	36,784	9,060	13,285	936	105,471	...	3,801	17,363	14,779	609
1971	44,053	10,069	12,745	1,252	143,421	...	3,890	22,245	14,489	532
1972	42,082	9,193	10,025	741	141,733	...	3,875	20,550	13,447	565
1973	46,561	9,091	9,568	667	144,042	...	4,208	23,623	13,613	569
1974	48,497	6,503	8,719	490	119,420	...	5,098	15,983	15,531	631
1975	57,886	8,255	9,275	405	148,361	...	5,826	19,128	14,605	600
1976	58,481	8,339	7,845	380	159,751	...	5,246	18,284	16,223	610
1977	55,671	9,314	10,927	440	165,235	...	4,501	20,143	16,118	617
1978	48,323	9,901	8,443	611	184,613	...	6,040	18,575	16,616	596
1979	58,081	8,343	7,646	569	201,383	...	5,985	20,546	15,533	606
1980	64,800	7,863	6,659	419	168,647	...	6,629	14,712	13,737	497
1981	75,806	10,309	7,396	478	206,222	...	8,289	22,333	15,358	578
1982	75,251	11,233	8,602	532	209,180	...	6,969	21,372	16,109	648
1983	65,858	11,080	6,923	689	106,041	...	4,523	12,384	15,146	548
1984	70,618	13,046	6,875	825	194,928	...	6,296	22,004	16,448	589
1985	65,999	12,876	7,559	524	225,478	...	6,120	28,456	18,466	674
1986	56,926	13,292	5,608	496	209,555	...	6,049	23,829	16,398	575
1987	57,363	11,529	5,429	495	181,142	...	5,879	18,778	17,484	547
1988	49,303	6,314	3,158	373	125,193	...	7,253	14,648	16,168	497
1989	55,429	8,800	5,423	347	191,156	...	7,007	15,632	16,803	516
1990	74,473	9,192	5,189	259	201,532	...	7,080	14,562	18,239	572
1991	53,917	10,109	3,534	248	189,885	...	7,144	14,856	18,943	508
1992	66,922	9,970	4,271	290	240,719	...	8,149	22,227	19,294	545
1993	65,210	8,665	3,001	263	160,954	...	7,081	13,569	19,445	501

C2   SOUTH AMERICA: OUTPUT OF MAIN ARABLE CROPS (in thousands of metric tons)

	Argentina							
	Wheat	Barley	Oats	Rye	Maize	Millet	Rice	P
1890	845	...	...	...	...	...	...	...
1891	980	...	...	...	...	...	...	...
1892	1,593	...	...	...	...	...	...	...
1893	2,238	...	...	...	...	...	...	...
1894	1,670	...	...	...	...	...	...	...
1895	1,263	...	...	...	2,240	...	...	...
1896	860	...	...	...	...	...	...	...
1897	1,453	...	...	...	...	...	...	...
1898	2,857	...	...	...	1,700	...	...	...
1899	2,767	...	22	...	1,413	...	...	...
1900	2,034	...	25	...	2,511	...	...	...
1901	1,534	...	33	...	2,134	...	...	...
1902	2,824	...	57	...	3,783	...	...	...
1903	3,529	...	48	...	4,450	...	...	...
1904	4,103	...	51	...	3,574	...	...	...
1905	3,672	...	80	...	4,951	...	...	...
1906	4,245	...	180	...	1,823	...	...	...
1907	5,239	36	493	...	3,456	...	...	...
1908	4,250	36	464	...	4,500	...	...	...
1909	3,566	28	530	...	4,450	...	...	303
1910	3,973	20	685	10	7,030	...	...	304
1911	4,523	22	1,004	11	7,515	...	...	660
1912	5,100	25	1,100	36	4,995	...	8	719
1913	2,850	86	618	85	6,684	...	9	725
1914	4,604	84	717	46	8,260	...	8	682
1915	4,600	72	1,093	51	4,093	...	17	861
1916	2,180	13	461	22	1,495	...	12	863
1917	5,973	42	996	...	4,335	...	17	848
1918	4,670	49	490	...	5,696	...	17	862
1919	5,905	56	829	22	6,571	...	16	974
1920	4,249	80	736	21	5,853	...	26	1,018
1921	5,199	130	444	43	4,475	...	26	864
1922	5,330	169	807	90	4,473	...	15	905
1923	6,744	259	1,108	99	7,030	...	9	960
1924	5,202	152	776	37	4,732	...	12	690
1925	5,202	371	1,168	120	8,170	...	10	645
1926	6,262	400	962	132	8,150	...	9	1,045
1927	7,683	317	759	168	7,765	...	7	688
1928	9,500	366	946	228	5,886	...	6	694
1929	4,427	351	991	112	7,128	...	6	879
1930	6,322	305	885	105	10,660	...	5	1,251
1931	5,979	431	1,059	248	7,603	...	10	920
1932	6,556	700	1,010	320	6,802	...	24	786
1933	7,787	735	833	184	6,526	...	34	919
1934	6,550	781	901	397	11,480	...	35	776
1935	3,850	442	521	153	10,051	...	34	516
1936	6,802	442	804	216	8,640	...	38	322
1937	5,650	394	757	131	4,424	55	48	952
1938	10,319	440	732	275	4,864	90	104	849
1939	3,558	726	803	370	10,375	98	97	1,071

C2   SOUTH AMERICA: Output of Main Arable Crops (in thousands of metric tons)

	Bolivia					Brazil					
	Wheat	Barley	Maize	Rice	P	Wheat	Maize	Rice	P	SP	Cassava
1909	...	...	...	...	...	...	...	45	...	...	...
1910	...	...	...	...	...	...	...	...	...	...	...
1911	...	...	...	...	...	...	...	...	...	...	...
1912	...	...	...	...	...	...	...	...	...	...	...
1913	...	...	...	...	...	...	...	...	...	...	...
1914	...	...	...	...	...	...	...	...	...	...	...
1915	...	...	...	...	...	...	...	[224]	...	...	...
1916	...	...	...	...	...	...	5,175	296	180	...	...
1917	...	...	...	...	...	...	2,421	372	...	...	...
1918	...	...	...	...	...	...	...	[309]	141	...	...
1919	...	...	...	...	...	87	5,000	832	146	...	2,899
1920	...	...	...	...	...	136	5,388	693	191	...	...
1921	...	...	...	...	...	139	5,514	767	286	...	...
1922	...	...	...	...	...	80	5,603	918	208	...	...
1923	48	230	280	24	286	118	4,940	666	241	...	...
1924	45	242	291	23	306	106	4,481	709	232	...	...
1925	50	255	298	25	315	154	4,369	779	278	...	...
1926	51	251	270	25	309	135	5,097	910	246	...	...
1927	...	...	...	...	...	126	4,691	1,013	228	...	...
1928	12	76	690	37	338	126	5,271	967	257	...	...
1929	21	80	630	32	372	171	5,027	913	309	...	...
1930	36	90	710	31	364	134	4,750	1,078	361	...	5,210
1931	40	98	660	...	510	164	5,770	1,202	400	...	4,848
1932	...	...	...	...	...	156	5,608	1,186	380	...	4,983
1933	...	...	...	11	...	145	5,292	1,185	315	...	5,293
1934	...	...	...	...	...	146	5,933	1,367	359	...	4,541
1935	...	...	...	...	...	144	5,721	1,214	335	...	4,947
1936	...	...	...	...	...	149	5,776	1,232	323	...	5,013
1937	...	...	...	...	...	161	5,560	1,529	382	...	6,021
1938	...	...	...	...	...	150	5,394	1,485	457	...	7,122
1939	...	...	...	...	...	102	4,876	1,320	444	...	7,332
1940	33	...	...	...	...	232	5,438	1,688	453	...	7,763
1941	54	...	...	...	...	217	5,276	1,881	417	...	7,916
1942	...	...	...	10	...	223	5,210	1,894	518	...	8,936
1943	...	...	...	...	...	...	5,575	2,110	...	...	10,333
1944	14	60	150	15	403	...	4,847	2,147	596	968	11,415

C2 SOUTH AMERICA: Output of Main Arable Crops (in thousands of metric tons)

	Chile					Colombia				
	Wheat	Barley	Oats	Maize	P	Wheat	Barley	Maize	Rice	P
1900	...	...	...	...	...	...	...	...	...	...
1901	...	...	...	...	...	...	...	...	...	...
1902	375	73	...	31	409	...	...	...	...	...
1903	273	76	...	29	282	...	...	...	...	...
1904	489	145	...	38	167	...	...	...	...	...
1905	329	104	...	32	178	...	...	...	...	...
1906	331	81	...	22	85	...	...	...	...	...
1907	...	...	...	...	...	...	...	...	...	...
1908	575	82	20	34	219	...	...	...	...	...
1909	481	86	34	30	174	...	...	...	...	...
1910	536	80	37	35	214	...	...	...	...	...
1911	612	71	49	39	263	...	...	...	...	...
1912	642	100	65	42	238	...	...	...	...	...
1913	446	121	64	38	250	...	...	...	...	...
1914	517	83	103	47	260	...	...	...	...	...
1915	550	95	99	40	316	28	4	166	13	33
1916	612	105	81	34	247	...	...	...	...	...
1917	629	72	46	37	262	...	...	...	...	...
1918	552	80	29	33	242	...	...	...	...	...
1919	542	80	38	37	282	...	...	...	...	...
1920	631	110	46	43	326	...	...	...	...	...
1921	643	99	42	45	315	...	...	...	...	...
1922	706	110	41	43	308	...	...	...	...	...
1923	765	115	58	35	266	...	...	...	...	...
1924	666	108	66	27	283	...	...	...	15	146
1925	726	150	80	36	273	...	...	125	16	154
1926	634	99	71	40	306	...	...	129	16	155
1927	833	126	93	72	430	52	...	200	15	226
1928	808	133	103	71	434	42	...	100	16	238
1929	913	100	151	60	402	...	...	...	...	...
1930	577	84	74	69	447	47	...	...	...	...
1931	577	67	72	75	410	77	...	...	...	...
1932	782	144	103	82	478	68	...	475	59	161
1933	961	146	104	67	611	77	...	...	...	...
1934	820	83	69	69	463	99	...	500	55	225
1935	866	107	99	52	344	102	...	...	107	...
1936	779	97	100	69	445	124	...	...	75	...
1937	824	163	120	56	437	91	...	491	100	236
1938	967	109	153	63	487	...	...	...	100	...
1939	860	73	85	77	417	...	...	...	95	...
1940	783	75	68	65	428	57	...	...	127	...
1941	783	69	67	68	522	64	...	...	111	458
1942	856	73	78	69	512	60	...	...	119	628
1943	994	75	114	71	414	65	...	...	120	131
1944	921	84	101	57	444	51	...	...	121	345

C2 SOUTH AMERICA: Output of Main Arable Crops (in thousands of metric tons)

	Ecuador			Guyana	Paraguay		Peru				
	Wheat	Maize	Rice	Rice	Maize	Cassava	Wheat	Barley	Maize	Rice	P
1909	...	...	...	6	...	...	78	60	80	102	...
1910	...	...	...	6	16	...	...	...	160	84	...
1911	...	...	...	5	13	...	...	...	...	...	...
1912	...	...	...	7	16	...	...	...	...	...	...
1913	...	...	...	4	20	...	...	...	...	...	...
1914	...	...	...	7	21	...	...	...	...	44	...
1915	...	...	...	8	23	...	78	41	121	42	224
1916	...	...	...	12	...	...	71	37	117	60	201
1917	...	...	...	11	20	...	71	37	106	65	175
1918	...	...	...	11	...	...	62	...	...	64	...
1919	...	...	...	10	...	...	72	...	...	55	...
1920	...	...	...	12	52	...	64	...	...	55	...
1921	...	...	...	13	47	...	82	...	...	55	...
1922	...	...	...	17	58	...	82	...	...	66	...
1923	...	...	...	20	34	...	76	...	...	65	...
1924	...	...	...	21	36	...	78	...	...	37	...
1925	...	...	...	26	58	...	87	...	...	44	...
1926	...	...	...	21	39	...	73	...	...	40	...
1927	...	...	...	23	...	...	86	...	...	54	...
1928	...	...	...	19	65	...	84	119	452	59	820
1929	...	...	42	19	63	...	121	...	...	104	...
1930	...	...	15	21	62	...	123	...	...	102	...
1931	...	...	26	25	63	...	95	...	...	136	...
1932	...	...	24	15	...	...	85	...	...	88	...
1933	...	...	30	21	...	...	73	...	...	85	...
1934	...	...	39	19	...	...	48	...	...	77	...
1935	...	...	41	19	45	...	58	...	...	104	...
1936	...	...	39	18	66	...	82	...	...	66	...
1937	...	...	52	17	69	...	90	...	...	91	...
1938	...	...	42	22	77	...	103	...	...	93	...
1939	23	74	65	27	...	...	112	...	...	123	...
1940	28	...	92	52	...	...	102	...	...	151	...
1941	25	...	123	87	119	1,024	100	...	...	100	...
1942	24	...	164	83	115	1,019	101	...	...	117	...
1943	21	...	131	89	...	...	90	...	...	158	...
1944	26	...	99	100	...	...	84	...	...	131	...

C2 SOUTH AMERICA: Output of Main Arable Crops (in thousands of metric tons)

	Surinam	Uruguay						Venezuela		
	Rice	Wheat	Barley	Oats	Maize	P		Maize	Rice	P
1875	...	...	...	...	...	...		102	...	...
1884	...	...	...	...	...	...		252	- -	18
1892	...	91	1	- -	...	...		...	...	...
1893	...	157	3	- -	...	...		...	...	...
1894	...	245	1	- -	...	...		102	4	5
1898	...	195	1	- -	...	...		...	...	...
1899	...	188	4	- -	77			...	...	...
1900	...	100	4	1	142	...		...	...	...
1901	...	207	10	1	129	...		...	...	...
1902	...	143	7	2	134	...		...	...	...
1903	...	...	...	...	...	...		...	...	...
1904	...	206	6	4	112	...		...	...	...
1905	...	125	8	5	82	...		...	...	...
1906	...	187	16	18	136	...		...	...	...
1907	...	202	19	35	102	...		...	...	...
1908	...	233	31	67	169	...		...	...	...
1909	2	...	...	...	166			...	...	...
1910	2	163	1	9	92	...		...	...	...
1911	2	284	2	27	202	...		...	...	...
1912	2	149	1	13	136	...		...	...	...
1913	2	160	4	27	181	...		...	...	...
1914	2	98	1	14	289	...		...	...	...
1915	4	269	3	33	117	...		...	...	...
1916	6	147	2	28	173	...		...	...	...
1917	4	355	2	54	191	...		...	...	...
1918	3	188	2	19	167	4		...	...	...
1919	9	162	2	22	117	4		...	...	...
1920	7	211	2	36	200	4		...	...	...
1921	9	271	1	30	122	8		...	...	...
1922	10	140	1	15	165	5		...	...	...
1923	11	363	2	31	117	9		...	...	...
1924	14	270	2	46	136	13		154	5	5
1925	10	273	2	35	136	9		...	...	...
1926	16	279	2	21	85	9		...	...	...
1927	15	419	3	48	225	11		...	...	...
1928	18	335	2	37	53	15		...	...	...
1929	24	358	6	56	182	9		...	...	...
1930	21	201	3	20	146	15		...	...	...
1931	24	306	3	45	161	24		...	...	...
1932	25	147	1	11	106	30		...	...	...
1933	27	399	5	47	132	30		...	...	...
1934	13	290	7	32	162	28		...	...	...
1935	26	411	13	56	124	22		...	...	...
1936	34	252	7	29	116	30		164	4	11
1937	35	451	15	48	133	18		361	13	6
1938	36	421	17	52	159	38		...	...	...
1939	41	270	14	40	127	38		...	...	...

C2   SOUTH AMERICA: Output of Main Arable Crops (in thousands of metric tons)

					Argentina					
	Wheat	Barley	Oats	Rye	Maize	Millet	Rice	Sorghum	P	SP
1940	8,150	689	540	240	10,238	41	56	...	1,053	...
1941	6,487	370	450	140	9,034	39	108	...	1,442	...
1942	6,400	350	580	151	1,943	39	99	...	1,032	...
1943	6,800	719	925	557	8,730	28	175	...	1,400	...
1944	4,085	573	1,099	189	2,966	43	139	...	1,027	...
1945	3,907	836	797	293	3,574	67	158	...	1,182	355
1946	5,615	1,171	685	552	5,815	...	140	...	814	398
1947	6,664	834	801	521	6,500	...	112	...	1,063	384
1948	5,200	613	733	305	3,450	57	121	57	1,013	358
1949	5,144	395	540	277	836	62	130	62	1,167	344
1950	5,796	762	733	631	2,670	136	141	136	1,559	314
1951	2,100	336	438	81	2,040	208	174	50	960	256
1952	7,634	1,175	1,269	1,335	3,500	290	194	68	1,376	321
1953	6,200	894	991	607	4,450	104	212	62	1,671	358
1954	7,690	1,112	890	844	2,546	123	172	74	1,375	284
1955	5,250	951	723	654	3,870	229	164	53	1,548	303
1956	7,100	1,364	1,140	880	2,698	157	193	46	1,311	375
1957	5,810	1,010	995	630	4,806	163	217	64	1,374	316
1958	6,720	1,050	850	817	4,932	216	162	951	1,398	241
1959	5,837	1,116	983	1,060	4,108	247	190	831	1,860	356
1960	3,960	773	843	505	4,850	261	149	1,477	2,072	388
1961	5,725	800	700	510	5,220	215	182	1,598	1,184	365
1962	5,700	345	487	163	4,360	155	178	1,176	1,453	366
1963	8,940	1,020	906	538	5,350	189	190	1,487	1,492	342
1964	11,260	826	805	652	5,140	110	268	1,059	2,489	341
1965	6,079	404	480	245	7,040	186	165	2,386	1,484	362
1966	6,247	438	540	270	8,510	224	217	1,618	1,797	444
1967	7,320	588	690	352	6,560	229	283	2,033	1,967	379
1968	5,740	556	490	360	6,860	196	345	2,616	2,340	480
1969	7,020	570	425	377	9,360	125	407	4,068	2,336	438
1970	4,920	367	360	181	9,930	183	288	4,784	1,958	454
1971	5,680	553	475	256	5,860	105	294	2,502	1,340	328
1972	7,900	880	566	690	9,700	227	260	5,159	1,535	474
1973	6,560	732	561	613	9,900	229	316	6,074	2,173	295
1974	5,970	430	327	306	7,700	200	351	5,000	1,349	419
1975	8,570	523	433	273	5,855	200	309	4,938	1,528	348
1976	11,000	760	530	330	8,300	294	320	5,167	1,769	348
1977	5,300	353	570	170	9,700	340	310	6,730	1,593	330
1978	8,100	554	676	210	8,700	330	312	7,200	1,694	320
1979	8,100	339	522	202	6,400	310	266	6,200	1,568	322
1980	7,780	217	433	155	12,900	188	286	2,960	2,247	302
1981	8,300	132	339	149	9,600	238	437	7,603	1,817	247
1982	15,000	211	637	148	9,000	154	277	8,060	2,013	368
1983	13,000	166	593	130	9,500	179	480	8,156	2,118	310
1984	13,600	238	610	140	11,900	136	379	6,930	2,244	325
1985	8,700	118	400	105	12,100	158	439	6,256	2,022	377
1986	8,700	133	495	60	9,250	107	371	4,061	1,836	409
1987	9,000	282	718	88	9,200	77	415	3,040	1,915	462
1988	8,540	317	620	41	4,260	91	469	3,200	2,867	460
1989	10,294	358	668	71	4,900	50	428	1,360	2,600	450
1990	11,014	303	434	95	5,047	65	348	2,016	2,500	400
1991	9,867	565	400	45	7,768	75	733	2,252	2,600	400
1992	9,813	379	649	34	10,699	76	593	2,766	1,961	266
1993	9,153	459	600	64	10,987	59	606	2,839	2,090	271

C2   SOUTH AMERICA: Output of Main Arable Crops (in thousands of metric tons)

	Bolivia					Brazil					
	Wheat	Barley	Maize	Rice	P's	Wheat	Maize	Rice	P	SP	Cassava
1945	14	...	...	...	82	233	5,721	2,759	432	924	11,556
1946	...	54	...	...	380	248	5,503	2,596	575	871	12,223
1947	14	36	190	15	400	359	5,607	2,554	585	934	11,845
1948	24	36	188	18	406	405	5,449	2,720	585	934	12,455
1949	28	...	...	...	...	438	6,162	3,218	748	923	12,616
1950	...	...	...	...	...	532	6,024	3,182	707	833	12,532
1951	...	...	...	...	270	424	5,907	2,931	735	823	11,918
1952	...	...	...	...	...	690	5,984	3,072	735	831	12,809
1953	...	...	...	28	...	772	6,789	3,367	815	895	13,441
1954	46	44	138	29	189	871	6,690	3,737	815	958	14,493
1955	...	...	...	32	...	1,101	6,999	3,489	898	1,042	14,863
1956	16	35	94	27	...	885	7,763	4,151	1,003	1,043	15,316
1957	12	55	110	11	155	781	7,370	3,829	999	1,086	15,443
1958	11	60	100	21	160	589	7,787	4,101	1,017	1,053	15,380
1959	40	50	200	23	189	611	8,672	4,795	1,025	1,188	16,575
1960	40	52	205	23	500	713	9,036	5,392	1,113	1,283	17,613
1961	35	60	259	34	617	545	9,587	5,557	1,080	1,356	18,058
1962	40	61	265	39	531	706	10,418	5,740	1,134	1,448	19,843
1963	55	63	271	43	546	392	9,408	6,345	1,168	1,546	22,249
1964	57	62	200	47	561	643	12,112	7,580	1,264	1,598	24,356
1965	55	60	277	51	575	585	11,371	5,802	1,246	1,721	24,993
1966	41	60	269	52	549	615	12,824	6,792	1,329	1,913	24,710
1967	27	56	278	57	520	629	12,814	6,652	1,467	2,226	27,268
1968	45	60	288	66	598	856	12,693	6,394	1,606	2,120	29,203
1969	53	61	289	83	627	1,374	14,216	7,553	1,507	2,175	30,074
1970	62	62	280	73	655	1,844	14,130	6,593	1,583	2,134	29,464
1971	69	66	293	85	698	2,132	14,891	6,761	1,580	2,210	30,258
1972	51	70	269	75	704	983	14,186	7,160	1,589	2,249	31,000
1973	57	72	276	67	730	2,031	16,273	6,764	1,337	1,814	26,559
1974	62	75	277	85	749	2,859	16,335	7,782	1,672	1,673	24,715
1975	62	80	305	127	834	1,788	17,751	9,757	1,655	1,600	25,812
1976	70	92	338	113	824	3,216	19,256	8,994	1,898	1,378	24,839
1977	57	60	305	121	679	2,066	13,569	7,296	1,896	1,074	25,929
1978	57	59	337	91	738	2,691	16,306	7,595	2,014	882	25,459
1979	68	52	378	76	730	2,927	20,372	9,776	2,154	819	24,962
1980	60	49	383	95	787	2,702	21,117	8,228	1,940	726	23,466
1981	67	57	504	101	867	2,210	21,842	9,735	1,912	762	24,516
1982	66	61	450	86	900	1,827	18,731	7,742	2,155	747	24,009
1983	40	30	337	62	316	2,237	21,164	9,027	1,827	682	21,848
1984	75	72	489	166	675	1,983	22,018	9,025	2,171	763	21,466
1985	74	75	554	173	768	4,320	20,531	10,374	1,947	756	23,125
1986	81	78	457	137	697	5,690	26,803	10,419	1,836	769	25,621
1987	77	79	481	164	815	6,035	24,750	11,806	2,331	757	23,464
1988	63	69	446	171	826	5,738	24,748	11,107	2,315	677	21,674
1989	61	57	400	227	659	5,553	26,573	11,044	2,129	750	23,668
1990	54	45	407	211	620	3,094	21,348	7,421	2,234	637	24,332
1991	103	63	510	257	855	2,917	23,624	9,488	2,265	700	24,531
1992	113	51	430	195	649	2,796	30,506	10,006	2,432	603	21,919
1993	146	61	504	223	756	2,201	29,967	10,193	2,360	624	21,719

C2 SOUTH AMERICA: Output of Main Arable Crops (in thousands of metric tons)

	Chile					Colombia						
	Wheat	Barley	Oats	Maize	P	Wheat	Barley	Maize	Rice	Sorghum	P	Cassava
1945	905	69	64	61	635	60	...	615	123	—	418	...
1946	899	92	70	68	569	120	24	620	197	—	460	...
1947	1,071	107	72	74	524	78	26	570	219	—	499	...
1948	1,113	94	85	71	533	118	29	636	303	—	486	...
1949	821	64	64	61	461	128	51	738	319	—	538	841
1950	975	83	82	71	424	102	50	620	241	—	360	768
1951	916	82	88	69	452	127	49	585	318	—	550	870
1952	989	140	91	66	537	140	61	928	330	—	600	870
1953	955	56	97	97	606	140		800	289	—	610	870
1954	1,078	89	108	102	610	146	48	943	278	—	650	871
1955	1,048	101	107	97	646	166	52	940	324	—	580	674
1956	988	98	112	100	636	110	59	741	300	—	623	700
1957	1,214	102	131	132	782	100	60	746	378	—	682	700
1958	1,205	115	119	156	614	155	75	851	410	—	565	700
1959	1,114	117	111	146	668	140	101	701	422	—	785	720
1960	1,123	105	132	145	815	145	106	864	450	6	653	680
1961	1,031	72	101	163	765	142	99	758	474	7	551	650
1962	970	73	82	181	848	162	108	754	585	8	871	780
1963	1,136	70	94	176	808	90	118	782	550	12	572	800
1964	1,159	80	86	242	703	85	114	968	600	60	867	700
1965	1,116	74	82	270	803	110	90	871	672	70	762	800
1966	1,346	88	107	285	717	125	95	850	680	60	760	840
1967	1,204	118	115	362	725	80	95	850	662	90	800	850
1968	1,220	157	163	321	603	105	75	886	786	110	850	886
1969	1,214	80	95	154	684	75	76	920	689	100	900	950
1970	1,307	97	111	239	836	54	87	877	737	118	962	1,956
1971	1,368	114	112	258	733	53	107	819	864	240	869	1,990
1972	1,195	139	111	283	624	69	98	806	1,000	210	823	2,010
1973	747	107	109	294	1,012	72	81	739	1,151	280	1,031	1,998
1974	939	150	150	366	738	59	97	792	1,540	337	1,012	2,026
1975	1,003	121	131	329	539	39	122	723	1,614	335	1,320	2,021
1976	866	89	96	248	928	45	71	884	1,560	428	1,516	1,846
1977	1,219	143	124	355	981	39	81	753	1,307	406	1,609	1,960
1978	893	126	93	257	770	38	119	862	1,715	517	1,996	2,044
1979	995	112	150	489	903	42	137	870	1,830	501	2,066	1,909
1980	966	105	173	405	1,007	46	109	854	1,784	431	1,727	2,150
1981	686	91	131	518	842	62	56	880	1,878	532	2,105	2,150
1982	650	118	118	425	684	71	56	899	2,023	568	2,149	1,552
1983	586	73	146	512	1,036	78	28	864	1,814	595	2,187	1,555
1984	988	74	163	721	909	59	28	864	1,715	590	2,463	1,386
1985	1,165	85	170	772	792	76	60	763	1,742	499	1,910	1,367
1986	1,626	68	124	721	727	82	73	788	1,521	600	2,281	1,335
1987	1,874	48	128	617	928	74	92	860	1,473	704	2,243	1,260
1988	1,734	82	157	661	882	63	97	908	1,777	707	2,520	1,282
1989	1,766	85	165	938	829	61	85	1,044	2,102	695	2,697	1,509
1990	1,718	92	205	823	844	54	100	1,213	2,117	777	2,313	1,939
1991	1,589	107	207	826	1,023	103	102	1,274	1,739	738	2,225	1,645
1992	1,557	109	183	911	926	113	56	1,056	1,735	752	2,281	1,651
1993	1,322	84	202	899	900	146	73	1,064	1,650	631	2,860	1,723

C2 SOUTH AMERICA: Output of Main Arable Crops (in thousands of metric tons)

	Ecuador					Guyana	Paraguay		
	Wheat	Barley	Maize	Rice	P	Rice	Wheat	Maize	Cassava
1945	...	...	...	158	...	108	2	...	...
1946	...	35	...	157	122	109	1	168	810
1947	25	...	...	173	90	95	2	106	739
1948	28	62	69	135	58	109	2	105	1,239
1949	28	69	64	169	59	63	1	84	...
1950	20	42	68	94	82	89	...	...	...
1951	26	...	79	95	47	111	1	100	991
1952	26	77	99	116	82	125	7	95	900
1953	26	83	80	160	127	134	1	107	...
1954	34	93	145	113	...	152	2	116	940
1955	42	83	...	153	268	151	3	100	...
1956	40	85	147	131	...	133	...	...	...
1957	42	82	138	120	281	97	12	120	...
1958	39	92	155	176	246	170	14	130	995
1959	47	92	157	175	260	176	10	125	1,005
1960	58	78	160	186	302	214	9	143	979
1961	78	70	153	163	271	238	7	110	994
1962	67	106	138	187	305	242	7	124	997
1963	53	130	192	191	275	174	9	120	1,000
1964	47	81	129	167	324	264	7	206	1,449
1965	61	93	191	157	396	279	7	210	1,512
1966	64	78	177	185	352	249	9	166	1,437
1967	73	82	231	173	403	198	25	225	1,460
1968	80	62	177	288	367	210	32	180	1,504
1969	94	62	210	233	457	191	31	153	1,549
1970	81	110	256	232	542	210	33	259	1,580
1971	63	102	250	243	681	185	46	230	1,690
1972	51	106	258	189	473	159	17	210	1,197
1973	45	79	246	235	539	169	13	273	1,108
1974	55	56	256	266	503	281	35	282	1,109
1975	65	63	273	364	499	292	18	301	1,428
1976	65	63	275	356	499	173	29	351	1,573
1977	40	41	218	328	417	355	28	401	1,719
1978	29	22	176	225	343	305	38	335	1,838
1979	31	21	218	318	255	240	58	550	1,888
1980	31	24	242	381	323	256	62	585	2,031
1981	41	27	281	434	392	251	84	521	2,012
1982	39	35	324	384	416	276	99	619	2,511
1983	27	30	229	270	314	224	139	730	2,610
1984	25	25	326	437	390	283	140	730	2,775
1985	18	27	371	372	423	236	187	801	2,861
1986	33	44	415	576	389	259	240	469	2,875
1987	31	43	397	781	354	226	318	1,001	3,468
1988	34	50	408	955	338	200	524	961	3,891
1989	26	56	485	867	362	219	432	1,000	3,978
1990	30	42	465	840	369	144	300	1,139	3,550
1991	25	45	519	848	372	250	241	401	2,585
1992	24	45	522	1,030	497	247	272	466	2,591
1993	22	44	487	814	428	247	300	500	2,680

C2 SOUTH AMERICA: Output of Main Arable Crops (in thousands of metric tons)

				Peru			
	Wheat	Barley	Maize	Rice	P	SP	Cassava
1945	87	...	...	153	599	...	...
1946	90	...	544	192	657	...	...
1947	127	208	612	179	1,265	...	200
1948	137	190	621	207	1,077	...	277
1949	129	213		162	1,115	...	300
1950	144	218	...	213	1,364	...	313
1951	157	202	436	207	1,325	...	330
1952	162	217	458	265	1,315	85	218
1953	169	226	418	277	1,385	92	215
1954	163	226	304	251	1,453	73	201
1955	152	208	304	249	1,309	83	228
1956	123	159	265	243	1,013	77	278
1957	138	166	294	246	1,046	86	275
1958	127	202	333	285	1,222	108	298
1959	161	195	339	249	1,217	152	319
1960	154	217	340	358	1,145	129	350
1961	154	198	451	332	1,492	145	407
1962	153	185	460	374	1,416	146	390
1963	153	182	480	270	1,427	159	438
1964	143	183	503	351	1,531	166	497
1965	147	179	557	291	1,568	124	449
1966	135	154	574	374	1,499	133	487
1967	141	172	584	461	1,712	150	507
1968	113	146	526	286	1,592	145	399
1969	127	164	585	444	1,856	156	450
1970	125	170	615	587	1,929	178	498
1971	122	159	615	591	1,968	168	482
1972	120	163	628	482	1,713	154	446
1973	123	155	599	483	1,713	156	460
1974	127	151	606	494	1,722	146	469
1975	126	149	634	537	1,640	162	400
1976	127	150	726	570	1,667	163	402
1977	115	146	734	594	1,616	158	414
1978	104	130	590	468	1,695	153	410
1979	102	131	621	560	1,695	149	403
1980	77	116	453	420	1,380	142	555
1981	119	127	587	712	1,705	155	486
1982	101	127	631	775	1,800	151	513
1983	76	87	585	798	1,200	157	510
1984	84	108	776	1,156	1,463	166	535
1985	92	109	702	878	1,557	100	341
1986	121	116	876	726	1,658	143	344
1987	131	114	909	1,169	1,707	123	466
1988	153	134	908	1,129	2,108	121	392
1989	159	125	1,010	1,091	1,690	142	472
1990	100	74	632	966	1,154	209	413
1991	127	115	669	814	1,480	140	406
1992	73	69	520	829	998	126	386
1993	108	112	785	950	1,493	183	290

C2 SOUTH AMERICA: Output of Main Arable Crops (in thousands of metric tons)

	Surinam*	Uruguay							Venezuela			
	Rice	Wheat	Barley	Oats	Maize	Rice	Sorghum	P	Maize	Rice	P	Cassava
1940	32	192	10	19	119	11	- -	30	...	...	...	...
1941	51	372	14	36	117	20	- -	28	...	6	...	...
1942	41	337	13	39	47	15	- -	35	...	15	...	...
1943	33	301	24	78	232	17	- -	30	...	18	...	...
1944	34	181	15	31	66	21	- -	58	315	26	7.0	...
1945	37	217	16	38	140	31	- -	34	...	19	...	...
1946	51	182	11	20	82	35	- -	30	...	15	...	...
1947	39	424	11	38	115	37	- -	30	300	10	15	...
1948	58	518	26	51	137	45	- -	38	300	10	17	74
1949	50	452	27	59	85	40	- -	31	323	...	27	149
1950	50	435	25	34	89	37	- -	40	361	32	22	...
1951	58	478	18	38	278	47	- -	88	313	36	32	188
1952	54	427	22	38	117	53	- -	51	343	49	24	209
1953	58	819	40	60	208	62	- -	57	355	57	34	253
1954	67	854	41	33	156	68	- -	83	326	98	36	194
1955	65	829	30	41	192	66	...	74	317	75	45	157
1956	71	589	43	56	218	64	...	60	350	50	65	204
1957	55	598	22	52	209	57	...	68	340	22	106	190
1958	85	360	25	33	276	58	...	...	358	19	70	189
1959	79	183	29	21	133	49	...	114	336	39	93	218
1960	81	420	49	62	78	53	...	115	439	72	134	340
1961	72	372	28	64	224	61	15	88	420	81	74	300
1962	79	452	35	57	155	61	15	87	540	103	121	323
1963	75	237	18	56	206	77	16	115	430	131	111	342
1964	88	646	40	86	91	47	17	100	475	166	124	312
1965	101	620	28	97	63	90	16	125	521	200	136	301
1966	112	329	31	72	182	84	15	142	557	195	126	320
1967	120	144	14	33	117	110	28	105	633	223	133	316
1968	116	470	48	73	69	104	30	52	661	245	143	341
1969	113	403	41	60	129	134	51	138	670	244	124	310
1970	145	388	45	78	139	139	35	118	710	226	125	317
1971	145	302	32	60	166	122	72	150	713	153	115	323
1972	123	187	29	59	141	128	57	106	506	165	109	318
1973	164	297	31	55	229	137	225	133	454	302	124	272
1974	162	526	28	47	225	158	193	129	554	297	152	293
1975	175	456	34	61	157	186	77	121	653	363	152	317
1976	173	505	47	48	210	217	118	166	417	206	132	353
1977	203	173	38	17	121	228	162	120	774	496	179	322
1978	224	174	57	23	172	226	184	102	591	502	171	304
1979	236	435	71	59	71	248	54	135	612	614	191	350
1980	258	307	55	32	126	288	84	99	575	619	199	325
1981	281	388	85	21	181	330	192	177	452	681	171	327
1982	301	363	45	27	97	419	123	149	501	609	217	342
1983	268	419	81	50	104	323	107	109	488	449	225	325
1984	302	349	113	48	112	340	119	144	547	408	245	331
1985	299	246	80	20	108	423	152	163	868	472	191	310
1986	300	232	77	28	92	394	105	111	1,173	322	196	322
1987	272	308	124	58	104	335	90	126	1,267	373	216	318
1988	265	414	204	64	118	381	121	143	1,281	383	221	328
1989	261	542	203	68	60	537	79	128	921	313	226	348
1990	196	539	133	43	112	347	59	174	1,002	401	200	302
1991	229	188	138	51	124	522	136	196	964	660	215	381
1992	261	341	307	37	116	600	137	155	800	595	238	382
1993	260	300	140	35	128	700	130	170	700	845	154	382

C2 Output of Main Arable Crops

NOTES

1. SOURCES: As for table C1, with Venezuelan data to 1924 and in 1937 from Rafael Cartay, *Historia Economica de Venezuela 1830–1890* (Valancia, 1988).
2. Where statistics were given in units of volume in the source, they have been converted to units of weight by applying the ratios used by the FAO.
3. For some countries and crops data may be reported for either of the calender years in which the crop-year lies, and practice in this respect has not always been consistent. So far as possible, the series shown there *are* consistent for each country, and the year of harvest has been preferred if a choice is available.

FOOTNOTES

[1]   Lower Canada only. Figures under the buckwheat heading are of all grains not separately specified.
[2]   Upper Canada only.
[3]   Upper & Lower Canada, New Brunswick, and Nova Scotia.
[4]   All grains not separately specified.
[5]   From 1901 to 1907 (1st line) Alberta, Manitoba, New Brunswick, Ontario, and Saskatchewan only.
[6]   From 1901 to 1908 (1st line) Manitoba, New Brunswick, and Ontario only.
[7]   Corn harvested for grain only prior to 1866 and from 1961.
[8]   Later figures are from national sources. No explanation of the discrepancy is available.
[9]   Rio Grande do Sul and São Paulo only.
[10] This increase is probably due to a change in source.

C3 NORTH AMERICA: OUTPUT OF SUGAR (in thousands of metric tons)

Key: SB = Sugar Beet Output

1750-1784

	Barbados[1]	Guade-loupe[1]	Jamaica[1]	Martin-ique[1]
1750	7	...	21	20
1751	4	...	20	...
1752	7	...	19	18
1753	9	...	22	21
1754	6	...	24	...
1755	9	...	22	...
1756	7	...	22	...
1757	7	...	25	...
1758	7	...	24	...
1759	6	...	36	...
1760	8	...	40	...
1761	9	...	29	...
1762	10	...	25	...
1763	9	...	34	...
1764	10	...	33	...
1765	10	...	27	11
1766	9	...	33	9
1767	6	8	36	7
1768	8	...	41	8
1769	8	...	37	9
1770	9	...	37	12
1771	5	...	35	10
1772	7	...	42	10
1773	6	...	52	11
1774	7	...	46	13
1775	4	...	48	12
1776	6	...	37	13
1777	4	...	26	13
1778	2	...	33	...
1779	4	...	41	...
1780	3	...	45	...
1781	...	...	...	4
1782	...	...	...	9
1783	...	...	...	11
1784	...	...	...	11

1785-1829

	Barbados[1]	Cuba[1]	Guade-loupe[1]	Jamaica[1]	Martin-ique[1]	Puerto Rico	Trinidad[1]
1785	...	...	...	...	...	...	...
1786	...	13	...	...	12	...	...
1787	...	12	...	...	12	...	...
1788	...	14	...	60	13	...	...
1789	...	14	...	60	5	...	...
1790	...	16	9	56	...	...	...
1791	...	17	...	61	...	...	...
1792	9	19	...	56	...	...	...
1793	...	18	...	52	...	...	...
1794	...	21	...	65	...	...	...
1795	...	14	...	64	...	...	...
1796	...	24	...	65	...	...	...
1797	...	24	...	52	...	...	...
1798	...	27	...	64	...	...	...
1799	...	34	...	74	...	...	3
1800	6	29	...	71	...	...	3
1801	...	32	...	92	...	...	6
1802	...	42	...	94	...	...	5
1803	...	32	...	77	...	...	5
1804	...	39	...	76	...	...	6
1805	...	35	...	101	...	...	10
1806	...	32	...	99	...	...	10
1807	8	37	...	91	...	...	10
1808	...	26	...	79	...	...	9
1809	6	59	...	77	...	...	8
1810	9	38	...	75	...	...	7
1811	...	...	...	89	...	...	6
1812	...	...	...	63	...	...	7
1813	...	...	...	68	...	...	7
1814	11	...	...	74	...	...	7
1815	10	44	...	81	...	...	8
1816	15	41	5	71	...	...	7
1817	12	44	18	87	...	...	7
1818	13	42	21	84	16	...	7
1819	14	39	19	82	18	...	8
1820	9	44	22	90	21	...	8
1821	11	48	23	85	22	...	8
1822	8	53	23	72	20	...	9
1823	16	61	24	72	21	...	8
1824	12	50	31	74	20	...	8
1825	13	...	24	57	26	...	9
1826	12	...	34	76	28	...	10
1827	10	...	28	67	24	...	12
1828	17	...	36	69	33	9	13
1829	13	74	39	70	29	13	14

C3 NORTH AMERICA: Output of Sugar (in thousands of metric tons)

	Barbados[1]	Cuba[1]	Guadeloupe[1]	Jamaica[1]	Martinique[1]	Puerto Rico	Trinidad[1]
1830	17	...	23	70	28	15	10
1831	16	...	35	71	28	14	17
1832	14	...	33	73	22	16	16
1833	20	....	31	69	20	16	15
1834	20	...	38	64	26	16	17
1835	18	...	32	58	24	20	15
1836	19	168	35	53	22	23	16
1837	23	...	25	46	20	21	15
1838	24	149	35	54	26	31	15
1839	20	132	37	40	29	31	14
1840	11	163	30	27	22	37	12
1841	13	165	29	28	25	38	14
1842	16	...	35	41	28	42	15
1843	18	...	27	34	25	32	16
1844	17	...	35	28	33	37	14
1845	18	...	34	38	30	42	18
1846	15	...	26	29	26	40	18
1847	24	...	38	38	31	47	20
1848	20	...[1]	20	32	18	46	20
1849	25	227	18	32	20	46	22
1850	27	268	13	29	15	51	19
1851	30	256	20	32	23	54	22
1852	38	327	17	26	26	42	25
1853	29	380	17	22	22	50	24
1854	34	398	24	26	25	49	27
1855	30	354	22	23	21	46	21
1856	32	361	23	19	28	53	25
1857	30	391	22	21	26	39	22
1858	38	545	28	27	28	56	28
1859	30[1]	454	28	23	30	40	27
1860	38	473	29	26	38	53	27
1861	44	533	17	27	32	59	27
1862	41	515	31	28	32	58	25
1863	38	584	30	26	30	53	31
1864	32	630	16	24	24	42	34
1865	42	622	...	25	30	55	28
1866	51	607	27	27	35	51	41
1867	47	761	28	25	29	55	43
1868	52	738	...	29	38	56	42
1869	30	738	...	23	37	66	47

C3 NORTH AMERICA: Output of Sugar (in thousands of metric tons)

	Barbados	Canada SB	Costa Rica	Cuba	Dominican Republic	El Salvador	Guadeloupe[1]	Guatemala
1870	35	…	…	556	…	—	40	…
1871	48	…	…	701	…	—	41	…
1872	35	…	…	787	…	—	40	…
1873	33	…	…	692	…	—	38	…
1874	42	…	…	730	…	—	41	…
1875	58	…	…	599	…	—	53	…
1876	33	…	…	528	…	—	43	…
1877	44	…	…	542	…	—	43	…
1878	39	…	…	681	…	—	56	…
1879	51	…	…	539	…	—	54	…
1880	48	…	…	502	…	—	47	…
1881	46	…	…	605	…	—	37	…
1882	49	…	…	468	…	—	58	…
1883	47	…	…	563	…	—	60	…
1884	55	…	…	662	…	—	57	…
1885	54	…	…	743	…	—	45	…
1886	41	…	…	657	…	—	58	…
1887	61	…	…	667	…	—	49	…
1888	65	…	…	569	…	—	…	…
1889	58	…	…	643	…	—	67	…
1890	76	…	…	829	…	—	40	…
1891	45	…	…	993	…	—	30	…
1892	53	…	…	829	…	—	46	…
1893	60	…	…	1,071	…	—	47	…
1894	59	…	…	1,020	…	1	44	…
1895	34	…	…	229	…	1	42	…
1896	46	…	…	215	…	3	51	…
1897	52	…	…	310	…	4	45	…
1898	48	…	…	341	…	4	45	…
1899	47	…	…	305	…	5	47	.
1900	50	…	…	646	…	5	28	…
1901	64	…	…	864	…	6	41	10
1902	59	…	…	1,015	…	7	39	9
1903	65	…	…	1,057	…	6	37	8
1904	58	…	…	1,182	48	6	29	8
1905	53	…	…	1,198	55	6	44	7
1906	57	…	…	1,451	56	6	41	7
1907	39	…	…	977	64	5	37	8
1908	37	…	…	1,538	77	6	26	7
1909	46	99	3	1,833	95	6	43	7

C3 NORTH AMERICA: Output of Sugar (in thousands of metric tons)

	Jamaica[1]	Martinique[1]	Mexico	Nicaragua	Puerto Rico	Trinidad & Tobago[12]	USA[1]	
							SB	Sugar from cane
1870	25	38	...	—	89	42	...	...
1871	30	42	...	—	94	54	...	...
1872	29	30	...	—	81	47	...	...
1873	24	38	...	—	86	61	...	...
1874	23	43	...	—	71	45	...	...
1875	23	51	...	—	74	28	...	...
1876	24	39	...	—	66	43	...	...
1877	22	41	...	—	51	55	...	...
1878	21	44	...	—	76	58	...	...
1879	26[1]	47[1]	...	—	155	54[1]	...	...
1880	28	39	...	—	101	58	...	...
1881	18	42	...	—	57	48	...	...
1882	33	48	...	—	84	59	...	...
1883	31	47	...	—	80	58	...	...
1884	30	49	...	—	99	66	...	...
1885	25	39	...	—	89	67	...	146
1886	17	30	...	—	64	50	...	92
1887	23	40	...	—	81	71	...	180
1888	25	30	...	—	62	63	...	165
1889	16	36	...	—	64	60	...	146
1890	19	34	...	—	58	60	...	246
1891	24	32	...	—	48	54	...	183
1892	22	20	55	—	67	56	...	248
1893	25	33	49	1	43	50	...	303
1894	24	37	54	1	48	53	...	361
1895	23	29	144	1	60	57	...	271
1896	21	34	71	2	56	60	...	321
1897	20	35	66	4	58	56	...	353
1898	25	32	68	4	55	59[2]	...	283
1899	28	32	69	4	36	60	...	162
1900	24	30	75	4	74	47	...	314
1901	25	35	68	4	94	62	...	366
1902	30	29	82	4	91	60	...	375
1903	23	24	100	5	126	49	...	260
1904	19	30	102	4	137	52	...	314
1905	21	42	95	4	195	39	...	383
1906	32	37	93	4	188	64	...	262
1907	29	36	115	4	209	51	...	387
1908	24	38	99	4	252	50	...	404
1909	19	40	125	4	315	54	3,846	326[1]
								307

C3   NORTH AMERICA: Output of Sugar (in thousands of metric tons)

	Barbados	Canada SB	Costa Rica	Cuba	Dominican Republic	El Salvador	Guadeloupe	Guatemala	Haiti	Honduras
1910	32	78	3	1,873	88	7	38	7	...	...
1911	34	171	3	1,926	91	7	39	8	...	...
1912	15	159	3	2,468	84	11	27	11	...	...
1913	35	182	3	2,639	116	5	40	11	...	...
1914	35	134	5	2,650	118	9	34	13	...	...
1915	61	99	6	3,082	137	12	34	16	...	...
1916	58	128	5	3,103	132	12	31	15	...	...
1917	39	64	4	3,528	126	9	27	23	...	...
1918	57	107	5	4,073	168	17	19	13	5	...
1919	43	163	5	3,794	179	14	24	15	5	...
1920	35	218	5	3,996	168	18	27	10	5	...
1921	32	374	5	4,097	187	19	21	25	12	...
1922	58	243	5	3,705	187	20	25	25	10	...
1923	50	172	...	4,177	216	19	28	13	6	...
1924	56	196	...	5,273	316	19	39	26	7	...
1925	55	303	...	5,011	360	19	35	17	11	2
1926	62	416	28	4,581	308	18	36	25	13	10
1927	72	461	32	4,107	353	17	33	39	13	21
1928	72	336	50	5,239	360	16	23	56	13	24
1929	57	379	...	4,746	366	15	27	57	19	18
1930	43	332	...	3,172	358	12	19	41	19	15
1931	84	424	...	2,490	405	...	37	36	21	12
1932	98	396	...	1,935	341	22	46	31	25	8
1933	84	459	...	2,210	362	20	42	30	23	5
1934	47	401	...	2,460	402	19	30	33	33	1
1935	107	375	...	2,477	426	27	40	35	38	—
1936	110	416	...	2,883	458	30	47	33	37	—
1937	91	504	...	2,887	454	32	59	35	41	—
1938	138	383	...	2,888	428	29	58	35	41	—
1939	71	452	28	2,698	431	31	60	35	40	—
1940	76	532	35	2,336	456	41	61	41	32	- -
1941	91	748	32	3,247	400	46	62	44	35	- -
1942	135	646	32	2,760	483	47	70	43	44	1
1943	86	650	17	4,051	428	48	47	44	58	1
1944	101	430	...	3,354	509	46	29	40	46	1
1945	110	513	...	3,728	369	...[3]	28	...	...	1
1946	132	562	8	4,061	463	22	28	58	40	1
1947	123	668	15	5,850	464	27	35	62	45	1
1948	79	550	21	6,057	428	27	28	58	41	1
1949	155	571	25	5,228	477	24	43	64	43	2

C3 NORTH AMERICA: Output of Sugar (in thousands of metric tons)

| | Jamaica | Martinique | Mexico | Nicaragua | Panama | Puerto Rico | Trinidad & Tobago | USA | | |
								SB	Sugar from beet	from cane
1910	29	36	122	3	—	317	53	3,754	...	328
1911	29	40	136	3	—	337	48	4,592	...	334
1912	18	40	146	2	—	361	42	5,124	...	151
1913	13	39	157	4	—	319	43	5,340	...	279
1914	22	39	145	5	—	314	56	5,067	...	229
1915	19	34	104	2	—	439	60	5,907	...	128
1916	32	21	102	3	—	456	65	5,650	...	288
1917	37	21	103	3	—	412	72	5,425	...	228
1918	36	8	108	3	—	368	46	5,397	...	263
1919	39	17	115	4	—	444	49	5,825	...	113
1920	33	27	118	4	—	446	59	7,746	...	163
1921	23	39	111	4	3	370	56	7,060	...	303
1922	40	26	128	4	4	269	48	4,702	...	274
1923	35	33	137	5	6	369	42	6,356	...	152
1924	49	48	165	5	5	600	53	6,811	...	82
1925	57	45	163	5	6	547	71	6,696	...	129
1926	63	40	192	5	4	571	75	6,553	...	44
1927	54	45	184	6	3	682	53	7,033	...	65
1928	59	38	167	6	4	532	83	6,442	1,030	123
1929	68	38	181	6	4	786	91	6,636	988	198
1930	51	40	216	6	4	711	81	8,345	1,173	195
1931	59	43	263	7	4	900	100	7,169	1,122	167
1932	56	51	229	7	4	757	99	8,228	1,317	240
1933	74	51	187	7	4	1,010	123	10,006	1,594	227
1934	78	47	190	7	4	708	107	6,821	1,126	238
1935	93	50	268	8	4	840	120	7,174	1,150	347
1936	108	51	305	8	3	904	157	8,190	1,266	397
1937	120	52	279	8	5	977	157	7,946	1,250	416
1938	120	65	307	8	5	773	136	10,430	1,636	530
1939	101	60	330	8	4	924	131	9,780	1,595	459
1940	159	64	294	9	4	845	94	11,062	1,721	301
1941	158	49	330	11	4	1,041	134	9,382	1,441	377
1942	168	21	420	14	4	943	106	10,600	1,566	415
1943	154	3	412	14	5	656	72	5,939	905	451
1944	155	8	390	17	6	874	76	6,094	958	396
1945	167	35	373	12	5	825	78	7,816	1,159	431
1946	181	16	376	17	7	987	111	9,600	1,382	386
1947	173	25	490	16	9	1,005	112	11,343	1,665	342
1948	196	23	612	18	11	1,158	118	8,549	1,243	433
1949	242	23	645	19	11	1,178	162	9,250	1,424	473

C3   NORTH AMERICA: Output of Sugar (in thousands of metric tons)

	Barbados	Canada SB	Costa Rica	Cuba	Dominican Republic	El Salvador	Guadeloupe	Guatemala	Haiti	Honduras
1950	159	779	21	5,558	474	24	65	71	50	3
1951	191	1,012	21	5,759	533	28	75	52	58	5
1952	171	875	30₄ 60	7,225	577	27₃ 36	96	58	58	6₄ 27
1953	163	928	61	5,159	602	36	87	82	55	30
1954	182	816	64	4,890	655	42	104	88	46	31
1955	174	911	64	4,528	626	59	117	98	53	26
1956	154	890	48	4,740	754	59	130	109	58	27
1957	208	810	65	5,673	806	73	118	135	57	30
1958	155	956	66	5,784	808	70	117	142	46	32
1959	187	1,202	78	5,964	809	74	142	129	49	32
1960	156	1,124	84	5,862	1,112	80	152	141	60	36
1961	162	997	102	6,767	873	71	168	127	73	...
1962	161	1,003	104	4,815	865	82	170	157	70	41
1963	194	1,003	123	3,821	806	88	167	167	69	48
1964	164	1,166	177	4,398	825	88	167	161	61	48
1965	199	1,177	142	6,051	580	135	190	155	65	51
1966	175	1,036	170	4,455	691	142	167	187	59	59
1967	204	1,057	177	6,236	819	148	137	225	61	68
1968	162	992	158	5,315	668	163	141	200	63	86
1969	142	870	161	4,724	864	138	162	222	59	98
1970	157	978	153	8,538	1,015	122	160	171	64	81
1971	137	1,103	157	5,950	1,131	158	151	204	69	92
1972	113	970	176	4,688	1,201	187	82	239	70	71
1973	118	902	198	5,350	1,153	190	121	271	66	97
1974	113	753	219	6,044	1,230	232	96	314	69	155
1975	101	943	196	6,432	1,234	257	87	386	58	85
1976	106	1,172	188	6,279	1,287	262	96	545	54	86
1977	124	1,011	191	6,607	1,258	286	91	519	48	107
1978	101	947	208	7,457	1,199	288	81	410	52	125
1979	114	855	212	8,048	1,200	277	105	377	61	165
1980	132	901	191	6,787	1,039	179	92	397	54	191
1981	94	1,216	195	7,926	1,108	174	59	444	52	198
1982	89	1,018	182	8,279	1,255	194	72	...	66	218
1983	85	1,167	193	7,460	1,219	234	57	532	49	210
1984	100	926	241	8,331	1,156	245	41	464	50	218
1985	100	400	218	8,101	921	270	53	576	57	219
1986	111	945	220	7,467	895	270	66	589	41	230
1987	83	989	217	7,232	866	247	63	629	33	190
1988	80	771	225	8,119	777	202	76	712	30	172
1989	67	828	210	7,579	733	176	78	701	45	190
1990	70	942	138	8,445	590	213	26	839	35	185
1991	67	1,085	160	7,623	584	304	53	918	28	177
1992	54	776	284	7,104	640	346	38	1,062	23	182
1993	49	783	283	4,200	738	368	63	1,049	30	191

C3 NORTH AMERICA: Output of Sugar (in thousands of metric tons)

	Jamaica	Martinique	Mexico	Nicaragua	Panama	Puerto Rico	Trinidad & Tobago	SB	USA sugar from beet	from cane
1950	276	37	740	2	14	1,123	149	12,279	1,823	512
1951	272	50	816	2	16	1,234	143	9,509	1,405	380
1952	270	21	868	31₄ / 54	19₄ / 29	1,061	140	9,225	1,365	549
1953	336	54	894	57	28	1,092	155	10,962	1,647	572
1954	369	71	979	57	29	1,058	176	12,775	1,853	553
1955	403	82	1,021	61	24	1,047	196	11,096	1,578	521
1956	368	86	926	55	25	898	163	11,789	1,784	509
1957	377	70	1,198	67	32	847	170	14,066	1,985	483
1958	351	67	1,303	82	34	986	191	13,744	1,996	525
1959	382	77	1,414	91	33	925	184	15,436	2,123	559
1960	431	79	1,648	84	30	1,007	221	14,897	2,223	572
1961	447	90	1,528	83	32	915	252	16,061	2,181	778
1962	441	84	1,547	108	32	987	206	16,557	2,357	774
1963	492	92	1,943	116	42	898	233	21,163	2,812	1,075
1964	482	62	2,178	125	56	814	233	21,218	3,023	1,041
1965	497	70	2,333	139	55	801	257	18,976	2,625	1,002
1966	508	53	2,361	80	47	742	214	18,454	2,566	1,101
1967	456	47	2,677	119	69	586	204	17,415	2,435	1,322
1968	452	37	2,496	124	75	439	247	23,009	3,145	1,101
1969	389	31	2,744	135	79	417	244	25,162	3,021	973
1970	376	27	2,365	140	75	291	221	23,930	3,014	1,136
1971	385	29	2,562	170	85	268	221	24,581	3,222	1,094
1972	379	22	2,526	166	80	229	235	25,773	3,294	1,466
1973	331	23	2,821	149	81	261	184	22,225	2,917	1,288
1974	372	14	2,834	168	104	271	186	20,070	2,645	1,325
1975	361	16	2,727	199	133	274	167	26,947	3,645	1,560
1976	369	14	2,720	246	143	279	207	26,658	3,533	1,583
1977	295	15	2,728	225	184	239	179	22,686	2,819	1,480
1978	292	17	3,072	219	180	185	148	23,394	2,983	1,366
1979	283	12	3,078	223	226	174	144	19,954	2,611	1,512
1980	232	6	2,765	171	200	158	114	21,321	2,856	1,507
1981	205	3	2,586	196	155	137	94	24,982	3,073	1,809
1982	202	2	2,873	228	162	102	79	18,955	2,482	1,626
1983	198	4	3,108	...	181	90	77	19,044	2,448	1,859
1984	193	5	3,297	249	174	87	70	20,080	2,632	1,604
1985	225	9	3,489	248	158	98	81	20,438	2,721	1,892
1986	206	8	4,031	262	131	87	92	22,826	3,098	1,836
1987	189	6	4,061	198	120	87	85	25,466	3,626	2,205 [7]
1988	222	7	3,806	209	105	93	91	22,507	3,221	
1989	200	7	3,698	205	209	83	97	22,798	3,442	3,176
1990	209	6	3,278	201	97	62	118	24,959	3,809	3,004
1991	234	6	3,365	220	137	67	100	25,585	3,729	3,430
1992	225	6	3,290	224	127	61	110	26,438	4,147	3,416
1993	224	7	4,212	205	149	58	111	23,812	...	...

International Historical Statistics: The Americas 1750–1993

C3 SOUTH AMERICA: OUTPUT OF SUGAR (in thousands of metric tons)

1827–1869

	Guyana		Argentina	Brazil	Ecuador	Guyana	Peru	Venezuela
1827	44	1870	1	...	—	68	...	...
1828	63	1871	...	...	—	76	...	...
1829	57	1872	...	...	—	94	...	...
		1873	...	...	—	78	16	...
1830	60	1874	...	...	—	85	34	...
1831	61							
1832	59	1875	...	...	—	88	50	...
1833	56	1876	3	...	—	84	71	...
1834	55	1877	...	...	—	106	78	...
		1878	...	...	—	99	85[1]	...
1835	48	1879	7	246	—	77	80	...
1836	59							
1837	50	1880	9	161	—	94	50	...
1838	56	1881	9	247	—	97	30	...
1839	49	1882	15	224	—	91	24	...
		1883	20	329	—	123	6	...
1840	34	1884	24	274	—	115	32	...
1841	36							
1842	30	1885	25	112	—	124	35	...
1843	32	1886	25	226	—	95	52	...
1844	33	1887	25	270	—	110	54	...
		1888	35	230	—	133	64	...
1845	35	1889	49	120	—	107	41	...
1846	35							
1847	23	1890	41	175	—	114	41	...
1848	42	1891	46	185	—	104	52	...
1849	41	1892	58	200	—	116	60	...
		1893	62	275	—	115	75	...
1850	30	1894	85	275	—	110	79	...
1851	33							
1852	38	1895	130	229	—	104	76	...
1853	50	1896	163	214	—	103	111	...
1854	39	1897	112	205	—	109	110	...
		1898	76	151	—	102	109	...
1855	49	1899	90	180	6	98	118	2
1856	49							
1857	46	1900	117	307	6	86	120	3
1858	52	1901	158	354	7	96	124	3
1859	52	1902	123	190	6	107	147	3
		1903	143	199	6	122	157	3
1860	49	1904	128	198	7	128	160	3
1861	55							
1862	64	1905	136	279	8	108	161	3
1863	58	1906	117	272	5	127	145	3
1864	69	1907	109	217	5	122	157	3
		1908	161	276	5	101	155	3
1865	65	1909	124	294	6	119	150	3
1866	77							
1867	81							
1868	74							
1869	80							

C3 SOUTH AMERICA: Output of Sugar (in thousands of metric tons)

	Argentina	Brazil	Colombia	Ecuador	Guyana	Peru	Venezuela
1910	146	332	...	6	118	179	3
1911	175	302	...	5	110	188	3
1912	147	[147][5]	...	7	88	179	3
1913	274	[158][5]	...	4	108	223	4
1914	333	312	...	7	119	258	4
1915	148	[190][5]	13	8	121	276	9
1916	84	[244][5]	...	12	116	253	19
1917	87	441	...	11	110	288	11
1918	127	400	...	11	109	295	17
1919	295	...	...	10	88	330	19
1920	207	646	...	12	89	314	23
1921	199	710	...	13	113	269	16
1922	210	761	...	17	92	319	16
1923	258	813	...	20	93	321	18
1924	250	832	38	21	109	317	21
1925	395	883	39	26	100	276	22
1926	477	693	41	21	116	376	21
1927	424	847	35	23	118	375	20
1928	375	967	30	19	119	362	20
1929	341	1,020	...	19	130	428	23
1930	383	1,050	21	21	128	400	20
1931	348	982	26	25	151	390	21
1932	350	1,027	40	15	144	388	24
1933	320	1,085	37	21	134	390	20
1934	346	1,155	36	19	181	399	19
1935	391	1,019	33	19	199	410	23
1936	437	940	31	18	190	389	21
1937	371	956	42	17	200	356	23
1938	466	1,100	41	22	192	368	26
1939	522	1,258	41	27	170	471	18
1940	540	1,281	48	28	191	462	19
1941	408	1,234	62	31	195	468	19
1942	361	1,272	67	28	136	390	30
1943	410	1,255	73	27	141	418	35
1944	459	1,250	81	23	160	423	33
1945	455	1,265	81	31	164	...	27
1946	635	1,460	81	34	160	391	27
1947	606	1,582	76	35	174	420	29
1948	565	1,751	83	44	166	412	27
1949	549	1,646	109	41	188	472	41[4] / 149

C3   SOUTH AMERICA: Output of Sugar (in thousands of metric tons)

	Argentina	Brazil	Colombia	Ecuador	Guyana	Peru	Venezuela
1950	615	1,845	157	46₄ 68	194	451	174
1951	651	1,862	198	76	193	490	168
1952	560	2,114	197	81	247	494	164
1953	710	2,296	190	89	244	626	173
1954	778	2,395	241	85	243	638	179
1955	584	2,383	253	80	254	677	217
1956	728	2,518	261	81	268	718	282
1957	714	3,108	234	105	290	703	275
1958	1,102	3,715	264	107	311	708	233
1959	969	3,533	277	119	289	733	243
1960	850	3,724	329	[109]⁶	340	827	256
1961	694	3,890	363	[125]⁶	330	823	279
1962	798	3,574	402	171	331	805	294
1963	1,055	3,616	368	171	322	852	317
1964	998	4,008	428	183	263	791	358
1965	1,310	5,016	485	221	314	783	410
1966	1,040	4,567	537	249	294	830	410
1967	785	4,646	597	232	349	821	351
1968	936	4,623	683	248	322	768	392
1969	978	4,713	709	277	370	650	424
1970	979	5,762	672	310	316	771	460
1971	996	6,045	744	317	375	882	526
1972	1,303	6,639	824	310	320	899	551
1973	1,638	7,293	810	329	270	897	506
1974	1,530	9,641	895	373	345	992	590
1975	1,353	6,186	970	287	311	964	535
1976	1,559	7,598	935	301	343	930	482
1977	1,666	8,760	854	295	246	900	450
1978	1,397	7,767	963	353	330	856	402
1979	1,411	7,027	1,114	357	303	695	351
1980	1,716	8,547	1,189	370	273	542	374
1981	1,624	8,393	1,148	321	306	478	304
1982	1,623	9,314	1,303	254	288	613	333
1983	1,625	9,576	1,379	220	248	442	385
1984	1,545	9,332	1,178	329	238	603	372
1985	1,174	8,274	1,367	273	265	727	504
1986	1,120	8,649	1,297	286	249	599	542
1987	1,063	8,458	1,390	341	225	560	584
1988	1,132	8,582	1,364	294	169	571	480
1989	1,018	7,793	1,492	317	167	594	524
1990	1,351	7,835	1,589	355	132	601	499
1991	1,570	9,238	1,702	349	163	575	542
1992	1,282	9,986	2,077	349	247	439	539
1993	1,008	10,038	2,151	341	247	401	529

C3 Output of Sugar

NOTES

1. SOURCES:- As for table C1, with output for Barbados to 1859, Cuba to 1841, Guadeloupe, Jamaica, Martinique, and Trinidad to 1879, and Peru to 1878 from Noel Deerr, *The History of Sugar* (London, 1949), where some data are available for years before 1750. There may be some slight break in continuity between these and later figures. Data for U.S.A. to 1909 (1st line) are from *Anuario Azucarero de Cuba*.
2. Data may be reported for either calendar year in which the crop-year lies, and practice in this respect may not always have been consistent, though most statistics appear to relate to the second year.

FOOTNOTES

[1] See note 1 above.
[2] Trinidad only to 1898.
[3] Centrifugal sugar only from 1946 to 1952 (1st line).
[4] Previously centrifugal sugar only.
[5] Data are for 148 factories out of 215.
[6] Centrifugal sugar only.
[7] Output including Hawaii was 3,023 in 1987 and 2,988 in 1988.

C4   AREA OF FLAX, GROUNDNUTS AND SOYA BEANS (in thousands of hectares)[1]

1888-1934

| | NORTH AMERICA | | | | SOUTH AMERICA | | |
| | Canada | USA | | | Argentina | | Uruguay |
	Flax	Flax	Groundnuts	Soya Beans	Flax	Groundnuts	Flax
1888	...	...	...	...	121	...	...
1889	...	544	...	...	...	...	0.1
1890	...	924	...	...	...	...	...
1891	...	826	...	...	...	...	...
1892	...	576	...	...	...	...	0.1
1893	...	521	...	...	...	...	0.1
1894	...	590	...	...	...	...	0.9
1895	...	825	...	...	387	...	...
1896	...	748	...	...	...	...	...
1897	...	552	...	...	...	...	...
1898	...	764	...	...	333	...	1.4
1899	...	851	...	...	355	...	1.3
1900	...	1,118	...	...	607	...	4.0
1901	9	1,284	...	...	783	...	11.0
1902	...	1,569	...	...	1,307	...	34.0
1903	...	847	...	...	1,488	...	...
1904	...		...	...	1,083	...	19.0
1905	...	987	...	...	1,023	...	18.0
1906	...	1,039	...	...	1,191	...	30.0
1907	...	1,092	...	...	1,391	...	26.0
1908	...	951	...	...	1,534	...	18.0
1909	56	842	217	1	1,456	...	...
1910	56	899	188	...	1,504	...	38.0
1911	236	1,065	191	...	1,630	...	58.0
1912	547	1,190	194	...	1,733	...	57.0
1913	818	791	188	...	1,779	...	52.0
1914	628	632	213	...	1,723	...	41.0
1915	439	452	250	...	1,619	...	18.0
1916	187	525	355	...	1,298	...	15.0
1917	266	761	532	...	1,309	...	15.0
1918	372	722	537	...	1,384	...	21.0
1919	432	523	387	46	1,766	...	33.0
1920	442	667	403	...	1,930	...	32.0
1921	578	463	397	...	1,575	...	25.0
1922	216	450	332	...	1,747	...	34.0
1923	229	815	323	...	2,169	33	42.0
1924	255	1,431	439	181	2,177	37	59.0
1925	517	1,223	403	168	2,453	53	75.0
1926	341	1,107	348	180	2,520	60	71.0
1927	299	1,118	439	230	2,741	53	71.0
1928	193	1,057	491	234	2,808	56	78.0
1929	153	1,234	511	287	2,117	53	118.0
1930	155	1,530	434	435	2,731	45	210.0
1931	236	984	583	462	3,344	50	179.0
1932	262	805	607	405	2,588	47	136.0
1933	187	543	493	422	1,974	78	106.0
1934	99	405	613	630	2,875	83	162.0

C4 Area of Flax, Groundnuts and Soya Beans (in thousands of hectares)[1]

1935–1974

	NORTH AMERICA					
	Canada		Mexico	USA		
	Flax	Soya Beans	Soya Beans	Flax	Groundnuts	Soya Beans
1935	92	...	...	860	606	1,180
1936	124	...	...	455	672	955
1937	193	4	...	375	622	1,047
1938	98	4	...	366	685	1,228
1939	85	4	...	879	772	1,746
1940	121	4	...	1,288	830	1,945
1941	155	4	...	1,322	769	2,383
1942	422	18	...	1,784	1,358	4,004
1943	622	14	...	2,303	1,428	4,208
1944	1,208	15	...	1,056	1,242	4,146
1945	493	19	...	1,532	1,279	4,346
1946	353	24	...	984	1,271	4,019
1947	359	25	...	1,671	1,367	4,618
1948	725	38	...	2,013	1,334	4,323
1949	792	42	...	2,043	934	4,242
1950	126	57	...	1,655	915	5,587
1951	236	63	...	1,580	802	5,510
1952	469	70	...	1,337	584	5,842
1953	449	87	...	1,849	613	6,001
1954	387	103	...	2,292	561	6,899
1955	477	87	...	1,989	675	7,535
1956	743	98	...	2,215	560	8,345
1957	1,231	104	...	1,940	599	8,441
1958	1,411	106	...	1,489	614	9,710
1959	1,032	102	...	1,187	581	9,158
1960	830	104	...	1,352	565	9,573
1961	844	86	10	1,017	480	10,928
1962	585	89	11	1,136	567	11,173
1963	681	92	27	1,284	565	11,580
1964	800	93	31	1,143	565	12,461
1965	937	107	27	1,123	582	13,941
1966	716	113	54	1,042	575	14,789
1967	414	117	70	799	568	16,108
1968	617	119	133	847	582	16,750
1969	947	130	163	1,054	589	16,728
1970	1,363	136	112	1,153	594	17,097
1971	715	149	123	625	589	17,280
1972	535	164	229	466	602	18,453
1973	587	190	312	685	605	22,580
1974	587	168	315	677	596	21,192

C4 Area of Flax, Groundnuts and Soya Beans (in thousands of hectares)[1]

	SOUTH AMERICA					
	Argentina			Brazil		Uruguay
	Flax	Groundnuts	Soya Beans	Groundnuts	Soya Beans	Flax
1935	2,268	73	...	...	...	126
1936	3,086	89	...	...	...	144
1937	2,303	103	...	...	...	134
1938	2,342	93	...	...	...	183
1939	2,180	49	...	...	...	236
1940	2,409	77	...	...	...	171
1941	2,322	62	...	...	...	85
1942	2,271	108	...	...	...	137
1943	2,018	109	...	...	...	103
1944	1,254	145	...	41	...	163
1945	1,392	142	...	33	...	240
1946	1,537	154	...	46	...	167
1947	1,351	114	...	49	...	121
1948	869	119	...	142	...	189
1949	960	73	...	136	...	233
1950	847	76	1	137	...	140
1951	448	105	1	141	34	149
1952	869	142	1	137	60	184
1953	552	175	...	139	63	221
1954	633	182	1	166	68	92
1955	444	149	—	163	74	89
1956	1,077	196	1	170	81	105
1957	1,075	222	1	228	97	116
1958	995	240	1	249	107	168
1959	1,117	260	1	255	114	118
1960	957	190	1	291	171	98
1961	1,172	189	1	436	241	118
1962	1,315	280	10	476	314	144
1963	1,217	266	19	423	340	160
1964	1,084	344	12	430	360	132
1965	1,004	378	16	541	432	113
1966	801	333	16	644	491	69
1967	616	328	17	694	612	66
1968	810	287	20	606	722	51
1969	791	244	28	613	906	82
1970	834	211	26	670	1,319	144
1971	440	310	36	662	1,589	92
1972	441	294	68	670	2,274	74
1973	390	379	157	506	3,615	48
1974	501	345	334	362	5,143	42

C4 Area of Flax, Groundnuts and Soya Beans (in thousands of hectares)[1]

	SOUTH AMERICA					
	Argentina			Brazil		Uruguay
	Flax	Groundnuts	Soya Beans	Groundnuts	Soya Beans	Flax
1975	446	357	356	348	5,824	70
1976	833	309	434	375	6,416	98
1977	884	367	660	229	7,070	69
1978	817	428	1,150	254	7,782	79
1979	978	393	1,600	289	8,256	61
1980	726	279	2,030	313	8,774	98
1981	818	197	1,880	245	8,501	37
1982	939	179	1,986	237	8,202	18
1983	804	125	2,281	212	8,137	7
1984	643	146	2,910	151	9,421	13
1985	688	145	3,269	193	10,153	13
1986	745	173	3,316	162	9,182	11
1987	655	238	3,510	144	9,134	8
1988	557	190	4,373	102	10,524	4
1989	416	150	3,931	85	12,211	...
1990	490	168	4,919	84	11,487	...
1991	457	179	4,754	88	9,617	...
1992	343	153	4,941	101	9,441	...
1993	177	110	4,902	85	10,644	...

NOTES

1. SOURCES: As for table C1
2. Note 2 of table C3 also applies to this table.

FOOTNOTE

[1] For areas of cotton see table C6.

C5   NORTH AMERICA: OUTPUT OF MAJOR OIL CROPS (in thousands of metric tons)

Key: C = cottonseed; G = groundnuts; L = linseed; OO = olive oil; SB = soya beans

1865–1899   **1900–1939**

	USA			Canada	Mexico		USA		
	C	L		L	C		C	G	L	SB
1865	...	...	1900	...	...		4,082	...	406	...
1866	784	...	1901	5	...		3,834	...	701	...
1867	945	...	1902	...	...		4,290	...	917	...
1868	884	...	1903	...	...		3,973	...	645	...
1869	1,014	...	1904	...	...		5,413	...	574	...
1870	1,620	...	1905	...	...		4,264	...	729	...
1871	1,109	...	1906	...	...		5,351	...	701	...
1872	1,471	...	1907	...	...		4,473	...	605	...
1873	1,559	...	1908	...	...		5,337	...	523	...
1874	1,422	...	1909	41	...		4,030	161	495	...
1875	1,732	...	1910	60	...		4,677	174	290	...
1876	1,657	...	1911	116	...		6,323	166	470	...
1877	1,809	...	1912	420	...		5,477	164	714	...
1878	1,911	...	1913	711	...		5,703	174	384	...
1879	2,200	183	1914	477	...		6,491	191	328	...
1880	2,560	191	1915	195	...		4,502	218	287	...
1881	2,068	198	1916	166	...		4,613	302	300	...
1882	2,751	218	1917	225	...		4,547	449	213	...
1883	2,223	218	1918	162	...		4,845	429	325	...
1884	2,202	241	1919	165	...		4,599	312	173	30
1885	2,566	236	1920	149	...		5,412	316	277	...
1886	2,542	254	1921	218	...		3,201	308	206	...
1887	2,772	249	1922	112	...		3,928	237	267	...
1888	2,789	254	1923	136	...		4,085	258	422	...
1889	3,010	269	1924	194	...		5,488	323	793	133
1890	3,449	488	1925	264	86		6,486	327	566	133
1891	3,599	424	1926	170	149		7,247	300	470	142
1892	2,682	300	1927	163	75		5,224	383	640	188
1893	2,991	264	1928	133	117		5,733	383	485	215
1894	4,035	267	1929	98	106		5,811	407	404	256
1895	2,879	544	1930	56	74		5,469	316	551	378
1896	3,427	450	1931	138	88		6,632	479	300	471
1897	4,425	335	1932	67	41		5,275	427	292	414
1898	4,645	470	1933	74	106		4,999	372	175	367
1899	3,767	508	1934	17	96		3,861	460	145	631
			1935	25	126		4,204	523	378	1,931
			1936	45	161		4,964	572	135	917
			1937	49	135		7,116	559	180	1,257
			1938	21	118		4,491	585	203	1,685
			1939	34	119		4,417	550	498	2,452

C5 NORTH AMERICA: Output of Major Oil Crops (in thousands of metric tons)

1940–1993

	Canada		El Salvador[1]	Guatemala[1]	Mexico		Nicaragua	USA			
	L	SB	C	C	C	SB	C	C	G	L	SB
1940	56	—	4	2	110	...	3	4,795	801	785	2,123
1941	83	—	4	2	137	...	4	4,130	669	815	2,917
1942	185	6	5	2	170	...	2	4,719	995	1,041	5,103
1943	421	24	6	- -	193	...	2	4,253	987	1,270	5,174
1944	502	16	6	1	174	...	2	4,447	944	551	5,228
1945	242	19	5	- -	161	...	1	3,324	926	879	5,258
1946	169	23	8	2	149	...	- -	3,188	924	574	5,536
1947	184	29	7	2		...	- -	4,247	990	1,031	5,076
1948	376	30	8	2	199	...	1	5,393	1,060	1,392	6,183
1949	502	50	10	2	346	...	9	5,950	846	1,092	6,374
1950	61	71	11	2	443	...	11	3,724	923	1,021	8,143
1951	135	90	17	5	485	...	35	5,703	753	881	7,724
1952	258	105	16	7	447	...	25	5,615	615	767	8,132
1953	317	112	20	10	469	...	46	6,122	714	958	7,326
1954	265	136	33	13	661	...	95	5,179	457	1,049	9,283
1955	299	130	50	15	871	...	70	5,482	702	1,026	10,170
1956	517	163	55	16	681	...	84	4,905	729	1,194	12,228
1957	952	143	63	22	753	...	95	4,181	651	638	13,156
1958	523	176	72	26	917	...	92	4,353	823	950	15,793
1959	608	179	57	24	636	...	53	5,435	691	539	14,503
1960	468	185	81	33	787	...	59	5,340	779	772	15,107
1961	368	180	110	43	767	20	99	5,423	752	564	18,468
1962	407	180	138	86	825	22	126	5,569	780	819	18,212
1963	536	136	121	107	908	56	159	5,617	881	788	19,029
1964	516	190	155	115	932	60	207	5,658	952	620	19,074
1965	741	219	86	131	953	58	189	5,522	1,084	899	23,014
1966	559	245	65	103	858	95	195	3,592	1,096	594	25,270
1967	238	220	59	124	811	131	171	2,912	1,124	509	26,575
1968	500	246	73	124	966	275	158	4,209	1,155	685	30,127
1969	700	209	78	94	637	287	116	3,690	1,150	887	30,839
1970	1,243	283	76	92	550	215	111	3,690	1,351	751	30,675
1971	567	280	91	92	655	232	125	3,846	1,363	462	32,009
1972	447	375	110	134	679	366	163	4,892	1,485	353	34,581
1973	493	397	121	155	572	585	178	4,550	1,576	409	42,118
1974	351	280	124	193	846	491	234	4,091	1,664	344	33,102
1975	445	367	125	193	345	599	197	2,919	1,745	395	42,140
1976	277	250	98	187	349	302	184	3,739	1,696	199	35,043
1977	653	580	119	230	659	516	191	5,009	1,685	384	48,098
1978	572	516	134	249	576	334	201	3,873	1,793	219	50,860
1979	815	657	119	268	605	707	186	5,242	1,800	305	61,526
1980	465	690	109	251	538	322	37	4,056	1,044	201	48,922
1981	467	607	68	189	530	712	120	5,803	1,806	198	54,136
1982	734	857	63	115	289	648	102	4,304	1,560	296	59,611
1983	444	735	60	76	355	686	119	2,791	1,495	175	44,518
1984	694	944	45	92	436	685	126	4,671	1,998	178	50,644
1985	897	1,048	44	91	314	928	98	4,789	1,870	211	57,113
1986	1,026	988	26	66	226	710	77	3,448	1,679	293	54,622
1987	729	1,270	15	42	414	828	93	5,234	1,640	189	52,737
1988	373	1,153	14	65	491	226	48	5,499	1,806	41	42,153
1989	498	1,219	15	59	255	992	34	4,243	1,810	31	52,354
1990	889	1,262	8	60	293	575	37	5,415	1,634	97	52,416
1991	635	1,460	6	59	307	725	40	6,283	2,235	158	54,066
1992	334	1,455	5	32	50	594	36	5,652	1,943	84	59,612
1993	627	1,851	6	21	80	520	2	5,754	1,549	88	50,919

C5 **SOUTH AMERICA: OUTPUT OF MAJOR OIL CROPS** (in thousands of metric tons)

1890–1939

	Argentina			Brazil	Colombia	Peru	Uruguay
	C	G	L	C	C	C	L
1890	...	...	...	...	...	...	...
1891	...	...	...	...	...	...	...
1892	...	...	50	...	...	...	...
1893	...	...	120	...	...	...	...
1894	...	...	270	...	...	...	1
1895	...	...	232	...	...	...	...
1896	...	...	185	...	...	...	...
1897	...	...	160	...	...	...	...
1898	...	...	219	...	...	...	...
1899	...	...	225	...	...	...	1
1900	...	...	390	...	...	...	2
1901	...	...	365	...	...	...	9
1902	...	...	711	...	...	...	21
1903	...	...	938	...	...	...	...
1904	...	...	740	...	...	...	14
1905	...	...	592	...	...	...	11
1906	...	...	826	...	...	...	22
1907	...	...	1,101	...	...	...	18
1908	...	...	1,049	...	...	...	13
1909	...	...	717	...	...	...	...
1910	...	...	595	...	...	...	17
1911	...	...	572	...	...	...	22
1912	...	...	1,130	...	...	...	33
1913	...	...	938	...	...	...	25
1914	...	...	1,143	...	...	...	15
1915	...	...	895	...	...	...	10
1916	...	...	102	...	...	...	3
1917	...	...	498	...	...	...	9
1918	...	...	782	...	...	...	13
1919	...	...	1,267	...	...	...	24
1920	...	...	1,524	233	...	...	25
1921	...	...	916	251	...	68	13
1922	...	...	1,209	245	...	84	18
1923	14	40	1,473	253	...	75	30
1924	31	37	1,145	362	...	78	39
1925	36	48	1,908	332	6	78	52
1926	68	69	1,755	275	8	71	50
1927	31	59	2,100	251	13	87	50
1928	51	65	1,991	240	6	95	52
1929	67	...	1,270	291	5	82	82
1930	79	66	1,990	223	...	104	128
1931	74	66	2,262	263	...	94	123
1932	84	59	1,575	177	5	91	38
1933	78	78	1,590	353	6	91	73
1934	107	104	2,025	664	6	101	86
1935	164	93	1,519	694	5	129	76
1936	200	114	1,978	820	5	146	77
1937	77	72	1,539	945	8	142	95
1938	128	69	1,410	1,019	11	135	112
1939	161	45	1,080	1,000	11	142	135

C5 SOUTH AMERICA: Output of Major Oil Crops (in thousands of metric tons)

1935–1993

	Argentina					Brazil			Colombia	Peru	Uruguay
	C	G	L	OO	SB	C	G	SB	C	C	L
1940	160	84	1,720	...	...	1,094	14	...	7	122	55
1941	93	61	1,600	...	...	1,174	12	...	10	114	47
1942	155	83	1,348	...	...	880	12	...	8	96	46
1943	205	96	1,573	...	...	1,158	25	...	10	114	73
1944	232	199	787	...	...	1,167	29	...	5	118	103
1945	135	158	964	...	...	746	31	...	10	119	131
1946	118	139	1,034	...	...	744	41	...	9	118	
1947	128	107	942	...	...	683	50	12	12	107	72
1948	170	120	433	1	...	629	139	18	13	100	98
1949	190	85	676	2	...	780	139	...	16	113	117
1950	249	61	559	3	...	774	136	35	21	119	75
1951	187	93	313	2	1	620	118	61	19	127	90
1952	239	155	584	2	1	942	151	78	32	147	142
1953	238	204	410	3	...	695	146	88	51	146	109
1954	258	170	405	2	1	742	168	117	80	185	65
1955	221	118	238	7	—	814	186	107	70	174	63
1956	222	216	620	4	1	762	181	115	64	181	50
1957	201	318	630	8	1	744	192	122	58	170	72
1958	330	240	620	4	1	751	228	131	73	192	73
1959	181	241	825	7	1	886	357	152	157	199	72
1960	165	209	562	8	1	1,019	408	206	194	220	50
1961	229	266	818	4	1	1,158	584	271	197	221	67
1962	200	433	839	8	11	1,205	648	342	218	247	96
1963	257	312	771	7	19	1,239	604	323	177	247	84
1964	198	333	815	10	14	1,121	470	305	176	231	62
1965	267	439	570	12	17	1,258	743	523	162	218	71
1966	213	411	577	11	18	1,181	895	595	208	204	38
1967	158	354	385	13	21	1,072	751	716	265	161	40
1968	138	283	510	12	22	1,266	754	654	334	174	27
1969	218	217	640	20	32	1,372	754	1,057	357	158	56
1970	272	235	680	10	27	1,271	928	1,509	376	156	90
1971	167	388	316	21	59	947	945	1,977	322	143	42
1972	173	252	330	9	78	1,277	956	3,666	412	108	43
1973	244	440	297	24	272	1,215	590	5,012	335	148	29
1974	238	290	381	19	496	1,070	453	7,877	420	155	26
1975	314	375	377	17	485	1,138	442	9,893	401	120	39
1976	267	338	750	12	695	806	510	11,227	409	99	62
1977	324	600	810	12	1,400	1,008	321	12,513	480	122	46
1978	414	371	600	15	2,500	975	325	9,541	330	166	40
1979	330	671	743	22	3,700	1,085	455	10,240	282	191	31
1980	272	293	585	12	3,500	1,072	483	15,156	353	172	65
1981	153	289	600	15	3,770	1,107	355	15,007	366	163	21
1982	270	293	795	13	4,150	1,238	317	12,836	154	124	11
1983	202	236	660	16	4,000	995	284	14,582	130	140	5
1984	326	329	550	11	7,000	1,380	249	15,541	243	178	8
1985	293	343	460	11	6,500	1,810	339	18,278	185	...	8
1986	207	379	622	12	7,100	1,466	217	13,335	184	167	7
1987	174	500	535	9	7,000	1,070	196	16,969	241	130	6
1988	467	443	416	10	9,900	1,620	167	18,016	243	180	3
1989	318	243	485	9	6,500	1,131	150	24,071	200	205	2
1990	495	335	458	8	11,315	1,088	138	19,898	182	146	1
1991	538	540	342	9	10,726	1,250	139	14,938	240	110	6
1992	435	364	177	10	11,315	1,170	172	19,215	178	68	6
1993	275	333	112	8	10,673	717	150	22,710	108	60	2

NOTES

1. SOURCES: As for table C1
2. Note 2 of table C3 also applies to this table.

FOOTNOTE

[1] Earlier figures are available but the amounts are negligible.

C6 NORTH AMERICA: AREA AND OUTPUT OF COTTON AND TOBACCO (in thousands of hectares and thousands of metric tons)

| | USA | | | | Mexico | | USA | | | |
| | Cotton | | | | Cotton | Tobacco | Cotton | | Tobacco | |
	Output				Output	Output	Area	Output	Area	Output
1790	0.7	**1825**	121	**1865**	...	...	...	475	...	...
1791	0.9	**1826**	166	**1866**	...	...	3,102	476	159	143
1792	1.4	**1827**	128	**1867**	...	...	3,182	572	150	118
1793	2.3	**1828**	154	**1868**	...	...	2,822	537	149	130
1794	3.9	**1829**	173	**1869**	...	...	3,137	683	160	120
1795	3.9	**1830**	166	**1870**	...	...	3,738	987	172	156
1796	4.8	**1831**	183	**1871**	...	...	3,353	674	170	148
1797	5.2	**1832**	185	**1872**	...	...	3,877	892	199	175
1798	7.0	**1833**	211	**1873**	...	...	4,451	945	208	173
1799	9.5	**1834**	218	**1874**	...	...	4,352	870	153	98
1800	17.0	**1835**	241	**1875**	...	...	4,592	1,050	302	276
1801	23.0	**1836**	256	**1876**	...	...	4,754	1,015	253	211
1802	26.0	**1837**	324	**1877**	...	...	5,101	1,082	319	282
1803	29.0	**1838**	248	**1878**	...	...	5,479	1,151	263	206
1804	31.0	**1839**	375	**1879**	...	...	5,857	1,305	256	214
1805	33.0	**1840**	306	**1880**	...	...	6,443	1,498	263	213
1806	38.0	**1841**	317	**1881**	...	...	6,670	1,237	282	193
1807	38.0	**1842**	462	**1882**	...	...	6,328	1,576	301	263
1808	36.0	**1843**	397	**1883**	...	...	6,594	1,296	304	231
1809	39.0	**1844**	472	**1884**	...	...	6,819	1,289	305	263
1810	40.0	**1845**	410	**1885**	...	...	7,253	1,491	330	277
1811	38.0	**1846**	364	**1886**	...	...	7,434	1,475	343	276
1812	36.0	**1847**	483	**1887**	...	...	7,605	1,598	292	213
1813	36.0	**1848**	593	**1888**	...	4	7,899	1,574	361	300
1814	33.0	**1849**	469	**1889**	...	5	8,171	1,695	307	238
1815	47.0	**1850**	484	**1890**	...	6	8,473	1,962	344	294
1816	59.0	**1851**	635	**1891**	...	7	8,702	2,049	386	339
1817	62.0	**1852**	710	**1892**	16	10	7,636	1,520	420	343
1818	59.0	**1853**	627	**1893**	9	3	8,197	1,699	444	348
1819	79.0	**1854**	614	**1894**	17	9	8,857	2,062	402	348
1820	76.0	**1855**	731	**1895**	37	57	8,029	1,624	407	338
1821	86.0	**1856**	652	**1896**	39	15	9,401	1,935	420	345
1822	100.0	**1857**	683	**1897**	33	9	10,170	2,472	396	319
1823	88.0	**1858**	852	**1898**	46	45	10,002	2,558	452	412
1824	102.0	**1859**	1,022	**1899**	23	10	9,778	2,120	446	395
		1860	871							
		1861	1,019							
		1862	362							
		1863	102							
		1864	68							

C6 NORTH AMERICA: Area and Output of Cotton and Tobacco (in thousands of hectares and thousands of metric tons)

	Canada		Cuba		Dominican Republic		El Salvador	
	Tobacco		Tobacco		Tobacco		Cotton	
	Area	Output[1]	Area	Output	Area	Output	Area	Output
1900	...	...	...	...	...	...	...	...
1901	...	5.1	...	...	...	...	...	...
1902	...	...	...	21	...	...	...	...
1903	...	...	...	26	...	...	...	...
1904	...	...	...	26	...	...	...	...
1905	...	...	...	30	...	10	...	...
1906	...	...	...	24	...	14	...	...
1907	...	...	...	50	...	12	...	...
1908	...	...	...	13	...	15	...	...
1909	...	...	...	47	...	14	...	...
1910	...	...	...	38	...	19	...	...
1911	...	8.0	...	30	...	16	...	...
1912	...	...	...	19	...	8	...	...
1913	4	2.9	...	33	...	11	...	...
1914	4	5.7	...	37	...	4	...	...
1915	4	4.5	...	23	...	9	...	...
1916	2	4.1	...	19	...	9	...	...
1917	3	2.7	...	28	...	...	...	...
1918	5	3.9	...	37	...	...	...	...
1919	13	6.5	...	...	...	14	...	...
1920	21	15.0	...	57	...	23	...	...
1921	5	22.0	...	20	...	7	...	...
1922	10	6.0	...	24	...	7	...	...
1923	10	12.0	...	18	...	16	...	...
1924	9	9.7	...	27	...	16	...	...
1925	11	8.5	...	27	...	20	...	...
1926	14	13.0	...	26	16	8	...	...
1927	18	13.0	...	28	...	18	...	...
1928	17	20.0	61	27	...	14	...	...
1929	15	19.0	...	31	...	20	...	...
1930	17	13.0	...	37	...	11	...	...
1931	22	17.0	69	37	...	...	...	...
1932	22	23.0	38	16	...	6	...	...
1933	19	24.0	45	17	...	6	...	...
1934	17	20.0	42	21	...	10	...	...
1935	19	18.0	47	19	...	7	...	...
1936	22	25.0	44	19	...	9	...	...
1937	28	21.0	49	25	...	9	...	...
1938	34	33.0	45	25	...	14	...	...
1939	37	46.0	41	21	...	11	...	...
1940	27	49.0	44	26	...	6	3	2
1941	29	29.0	36	19	...	6	3	2
1942	32	43.0	40	23	...	6	4	2
1943	29	41.0	32	19	...	12	5	3
1944	36	31.0	51	30	...	5	5	3

C6   NORTH AMERICA: Area and Output of Cotton and Tobacco (in thousands of hectares and thousands of metric tons)

	Mexico				USA			
	Cotton		Tobacco		Cotton		Tobacco	
	Area	Output	Area	Output	Area	Output	Area	Output
1900	...	22	...	9	10,071	2,296	439	386
1901	...	22	...	12	10,947	2,156	444	402
1902	...	23	...	4	11,154	2,411	481	435
1903	...	37	...	13	11,235	2,234	490	443
1904	...	55	...	13	12,172	3,048	415	389
1905	...	148	...	18	11,231	2,399	446	426
1906	...	59	...	16	12,709	3,010	454	441
1907	...	34	...	9	12,436	2,519	422	402
1908	...	25	...	7	12,582	3,003	408	379
1909	...	...	...	...	12,365	2,269	523	478
1910	...	44	...	...	12,751	2,633	566	518
1911	...	35	...	...	14,130	3,559	459	427
1912	...	52	...	...	13,175	3,108	540	507
1913	...	45	...	12	14,247	3,210	524	450
1914	...	...	...	...	14,413	3,654	509	470
1915	...	21	...	...	12,121	2,534	574	525
1916	...	18	...	12	13,383	2,596	600	547
1917	...	14	...	...	13,049	2,559	654	601
1918	...	79	...	13	14,179	2,726	696	655
1919	...	...	...	19	13,317	2,527	793	655
1920	...	...	...	...	13,924	3,046	783	684
1921	...	32	...	7	11,606	1,802	542	456
1922	...	44	5	11	12,691	2,212	654	569
1923	...	38	10	11	14,387	2,300	751	689
1924	...	43	12	13	15,986	3,091	689	565
1925	172	44	16	9	17,962	3,653	709	624
1926	248	78	16	9	18,052	4,077	659	585
1927	132	39	17	10	15,516	2,938	630	549
1928	203	60	18	13	17,172	3,283	754	623
1929	199	53	17	13	17,495	3,362	801	695
1930	158	39	13	11	17,176	3,160	860	748
1931	129	46	14	11	15,663	3,878	805	710
1932	78	22	13	11	14,525	2,949	569	462
1933	172	57	13	10	11,891	2,959	704	622
1934	169	48	14	12	10,872	2,185	515	492
1935	266	68	16	14	11,133	2,413	582	591
1936	343	86	15	13	12,033	2,812	583	528
1937	336	74	22	20	13,607	4,297	709	712
1938	260	66	21	19	9,813	2,709	648	629
1939	262	68	19	21	9,634	2,680	809	853
1940	254	65	21	24	9,656	2,850	571	662
1941	316	81	20	20	8,999	2,437	529	572
1942	362	103	22	19	9,147	2,907	557	639
1943	409	116	17	14	8,745	2,592	590	638
1944	390	106	20	20	7,939	2,774	708	885

C6 NORTH AMERICA: Area and Output of Cotton and Tobacco (in thousands of hectares and thousands of metric tons)

	Canada		Cuba		Dominican Republic		El Salvador		Guatemala	
	Tobacco		Tobacco		Tobacco		Cotton		Cotton	
	Area	Output	Area	Output	Area	Output	Area	Output	Area	Output
1945	38	48	53	32	...	16	10	2	...	...
1946	45	42	57	36	26	32	11	4	3	...
1947	51	64	58	36	15	21	15	4	3	...
1948	45	48	43	26	20	20	13	7	4	1
1949	44	57	60	...	15	26	17	5	3	2
1950	41	63	58	...	20	22	19	7	2	2
1951	48	55	54	36	18	18	30	10	8	2
1952	37	70	56	35	18	17	28	11	9	3
1953	41	63	62	50	19	17	21	13	11	6
1954	53	63	62	50	21	19	30	20	16	8
1955	44	84	62	50	20	18	46	31	21	10
1956	52	61	58	46	20	19	38	32	13	10
1957	55	73	60	52	22	21	40	36	18	14
1958	54	75	60	53	24	21	54	40	28	16
1959	52	89	56	41	20	18	39	31	18	15
1960	55	77	59	52	22	23	43	41	26	21
1961	56	95	55	47	19	26	77	61	46	26
1962	53	92	53	45	22	27	94	72	72	53
1963	46	91	58	48	25	25	88	75	90	66
1964	35	70	55	44	19	28	114	82	98	72
1965	38	77	65	44	19	19	111	52	100	82
1966	53	106	60	51	20	21	82	39	84	59
1967	57	97	54	45	19	19	49	35	90	78
1968	55	99	54	46	18	16	41	43	96	74
1969	54	112	45	36	18	21	51	46	85	56
1970	44	101	60	46	20	23	56	55	74	57
1971	39	102	59	40	21	26	62	55	71	56
1972	42	85	64	44	25	28	73	68	70	81
1973	49	117	66	45	31	44	85	69	89	96
1974	50	116	69	50	31	34	95	75	104	121
1975	42	106	66	42	16	35	88	74	111	107
1976	37	81	69	52	25	45	74	60	84	99
1977	44	104	60	46	28	35	79	70	122	136
1978	49	116	61	40	40	54	99	79	123	149
1979	47	79	57	33	37	45	102	65	122	161
1980	46	108	20	7	27	37	85	62	123	151
1981	47	112	68	54	33	40	58	43	100	114
1982	31	70	65	42	35	34	53	40	66	71
1983	47	112	51	30	30	34	49	41	56	55
1984	41	89	54	45	29	28	37	30	58	59
1985	40	97	63	45	21	27	37	25	63	59
1986	31	67	58	46	27	29	27	14	61	44
1987	30	61	56	39	23	29	13	12	40	28
1988	29	70	57	39	23	30	14	10	40	44
1989	31	76	47	42	27	30	13	9	47	41
1990	29	63	50	44	15	18	10	7	46	40
1991	30	79	50	44	18	24	6	5	39	38
1992	27	66	50	44	22	20	4	9	22	55
1993	31	77	50	44	19	15	4	10	14	36

C6 NORTH AMERICA: Area and Output of Cotton and Tobacco (in thousands of hectares and thousands of metric tons)

	Mexico				Nicaragua		USA			
	Cotton		Tobacco		Cotton		Cotton		Tobacco	
	Area	Output	Area	Output	Area	Output	Area	Output	Area	Output
1945	366	98	19	19	...	...	6,891	2,045	737	903
1946	327	91	37	36	...	...	7,116	1,960	793	596
1947	333	96	35	38	...	...	8,632	2,690	749	956
1948	405	120	36	36	3	4	9,272	3,374	629	898
1949	549	208	35	34	15	1	11,104	3,658	657	893
1950	761	260	35	35	17	4	7,221	2,271	647	921
1951	884	288	35	36	35	9	10,906	3,436	720	1,058
1952	784	265	35	36	30	12	10,490	3,433	717	1,023
1953	753	274	36	37	42	19	9,850	3,734	661	934
1954	922	391	37	38	86	47	7,791	3,106	675	1,018
1955	1,059	508	43	53	87	35	6,851	3,339	605	995
1956	873	426	45	54	70	42	6,319	3,019	552	987
1957	916	478	51	70	61	48	5,487	2,487	454	757
1958	1,028	526	52	71	74	49	4,795	2,611	436	787
1959	751	380	53	72	67	28	6,118	3,302	467	815
1960	899	470	54	72	61	33	6,195	3,238	462	882
1961	794	450	52	67	78	57	6,327	3,247	475	935
1962	787	486	43	53	95	74	6,301	3,228	495	1,050
1963	847	535	52	68	119	94	5,751	3,330	476	1,063
1964	809	565	52	68	135	125	5,688	3,297	436	1,011
1965	813	577	52	69	162	111	5,509	3,255	395	841
1966	695	521	40	57	151	115	3,866	2,080	394	856
1967	662	495	40	61	147	102	3,236	1,621	388	893
1968	705	552	35	47	126	93	4,111	2,379	356	776
1969	513	397	40	72	109	69	4,472	2,175	372	818
1970	411	334	43	80	96	73	4,514	2,219	364	865
1971	458	397	41	65	110	79	4,642	2,281	339	773
1972	523	417	43	82	143	103	5,254	2,984	341	793
1973	421	392	39	61	143	106	4,844	2,825	359	790
1974	567	513	40	72	182	146	5,086	2,513	390	902
1975	227	206	40	68	179	123	3,560	1,807	440	990
1976	235	224	40	67	144	110	4,416	2,304	423	969
1977	420	418	40	55	198	118	5,372	3,133	387	868
1978	350	366	45	70	212	123	5,018	2,364	390	918
1979	405	349	47	72	174	113	5,192	3,185	335	692
1980	372	373	49	94	45	22	5,348	2,422	373	810
1981	355	335	35	56	94	76	5,601	3,406	395	936
1982	200	196	40	67	93	64	3,937	2,605	367	905
1983	232	229	37	53	116	81	2,973	1,692	319	648
1984	316	280	37	41	115	87	4,200	2,827	320	784
1985	193	220	35	48	115	69	4,140	2,924	278	686
1986	157	144	44	64	59	49	3,427	2,119	235	527
1987	222	220	44	53	60	49	4,059	3,214	238	540
1988	298	312	45	69	59	36	4,835	3,355	257	622
1989	189	162	46	67	40	26	3,861	2,655	274	620
1990	205	201	27	34	31	23	4,738	3,375	297	738
1991	249	202	17	29	44	30	5,245	3,835	309	755
1992	46	33	15	21	36	26	4,509	3,531	317	781
1993	31	24	35	32	2	2	5,175	3,512	302	732

C6 SOUTH AMERICA: Area and Output of Cotton and Tobacco (in thousands of hectares and thousands of metric tons)

	Argentina				Brazil			
	Cotton		Tobacco		Cotton		Tobacco	
	Area	Output	Area	Output	Area	Output	Area	Output
1900	...	0.2	13	...	...	34	...	...
1901	...	0.3	11	...	...	55	...	...
1902	...	0.1	10	...	...	51	...	...
1903	...	0.5	10	...	...	48	...	...
1904	...	0.7	18	...	...	59	...	...
1905	...	0.5	17	4	...	80	...	...
1906	...	0.5	14	5	...	76	...	...
1907	...	0.4	10	6	...	50	...	...
1908	...	0.4	10	10	...	58	...	...
1909	2	0.4	10	7	...	59	...	...
1910	2	0.4	10	6	...	78	...	...
1911	2	0.4	10	6	...	91	...	...
1912	3	0.7	10	5	...	103	...	...
1913	2	0.5	15	5	...	101	...	...
1914	3	0.8	15	4	...	73	...	...
1915	4	0.9	8	11	204	74	...	45
1916	3	0.7	10	6	203	87	...	...
1917	12	3.0	11	4	294	118	...	...
1918	13	3.0	6	...	245	97	...	...
1919	13	3.0	8	10	277	108	...	74
1920	24	6.0	13	15	326	100	...	87
1921	16	4.0	14	17	575	108	...	80
1922	23	6.0	7	8	612	105	63	71
1923	63	13.0	9	11	628	108	79	62
1924	105	15.0	8	10	637	155	67	59
1925	110	29.0	9	10	534	142	65	57
1926	72	13.0	5	11	399	118	82	65
1927	85	25.0	9	14	525	108	...	87
1928	104	26.0	11	11	519	103	110	110
1929	122	33.0	13	13	581	125	90	88
1930	127	30.0	13	11		95	...	98
1931	136	37.0	15	13	738	113	...	100
1932	138	33.0	14	15	634	76	...	92
1933	195	43.0	12	10	889	151	9	100
1934	286	64.0	22	24	1,589	284	124	102
1935	309	81.0	16	15	1,765	297	96	91
1936	289	31.0	12	11	1,968	352	102	84
1937	330	51.0	12	8	2,236	405	105	91
1938	340	71.0	19	20	2,350	437	107	93
1939	295	79.0	20	19	2,273	429	96	95
1940	298	50.0	22	18	2,412	469	96	95
1941	308	81.0	17	15	2,493	503	96	93
1942	336	108.0	19	18	1,931	377	102	92
1943	370	120.0	20	19	2,424	496	...	...
1944	359	72.0	22	22	2,808	592	...	...

C6 SOUTH AMERICA: Area and Output of Cotton and Tobacco
(in thousands of hectares and thousands of metric tons)

	Colombia		Paraguay		Peru	
	Tobacco		Tobacco		Cotton	
	Area	Output	Area	Output	Area	Output
1900	...	...	...	...	...	7
1901	...	...	...	...	...	8
1902	...	...	...	...	...	7
1903	...	...	...	...	...	8
1904	...	...	...	...	...	8
1905	...	...	...	...	...	9
1906	...	...	...	...	...	10
1907	...	...	...	...	...	12
1908	...	...	...	...	...	16
1909	...	...	...	...	...	21
1910	...	...	8	9	...	14
1911	...	...	6	7	...	16
1912	...	...	7	8	...	19
1913	...	...	7	8	...	24
1914	...	...	9	10	56	23
1915	7	6	8	10	56	21
1916	...	...	...	...	65	28
1917	...	...	14	14	64	27
1918	...	...	...	...	90	31
1919	...	...	...	...	90	34
1920	...	...	10	12	109	38
1921	...	...	9	10	108	40
1922	...	...	13	11	114	43
1923	...	...	11	10	114	46
1924	16	12	12	12	118	47
1925	16	13	...	12	120	46
1926	17	13	9	9	128	53
1927	13	10	...	9	128	53
1928	7	9	8	13	115	49
1929	...	...	8	13	127	66
1930	...	...	9	14	134	59
1931	...	...	9	14	127	51
1932	...	8	...	...	123	53
1933	...	8	...	1	130	60
1934	...	11	...	5	149	74
1935	...	10	18	16	162	85
1936	...	11	6	6	166	84
1937	7	15	4	4	157	82
1938	6	...	9	8	191	86
1939	9	...	...	...	177	82
1940	8	19	7	4	180	83
1941		...	5	4	170	71
1942		...	6	4	156	70
1943	15	...	6	6	125	57
1944		...	6	...	132	67

C6   SOUTH AMERICA: Area and Output of Cotton and Tobacco (in thousands of hectares and thousands of metric tons)

	Argentina				Brazil			
	Cotton		Tobacco		Cotton		Tobacco	
	Area	Output	Area	Output	Area	Output	Area	Output
1945	332	62	28	27	2,722	378	114	109
1946	361	69	30	29	2,480	378	136	119
1947	420	78	26	27	2,470	347	134	111
1948	465		17	22	2,308	320	144	118
1949	517	130	24	26	2,497	396	145	115
1950	458	99	24	27	2,689	393	142	108
1951	461	142	36	26	2,487	349	160	106
1952	561	125	37	39	3,035	515	154	118
1953	533	123	38	36	2,587	375	168	132
1954	551	137	33	33	2,487	395	184	147
1955	550	114	31	32	2,617	428	196	148
1956	533	122	35	41	2,663	400	180	144
1957	545	105	40	45	2,771	397	179	140
1958	641	171	28	25	2,707	381	181	144
1959	496	100	30	28	2,746	466	191	151
1960	461	89	36	41	2,930	536	213	161
1961	499	124	46	48	3,234	609	228	168
1962	537	108	38	47	3,458$_2$	634	232	187
					2,226			
1963	519	133	42	55	2,226	652	250	207
1964	520	99	44	49	2,327	590	251	210
1965	534	138	48	53	2,327	662	274	248
1966	441	116	48	45	2,226	622	265	228
1967	330	87	59	63	2,023	564	261	243
1968	282	72	59	62	2,266	666	276	258
1969	406	112	54	54	2,631	697	258	250
1970	452	145	69	66	2,873	673	245	244
1971	367	84	65	62	2,428	499	255	254
1972	398	85	68	74	2,631	672	260	263
1973	457	125	74	71	2,428	640	234	234
1974	474	127	83	98	2,307	646	226	296
1975	505	172	88	98	2,226	577	239	286
1976	414	140	79	95	1,902	417	286	299
1977	518	160	75	90	2,145	627	311	357
1978	607	220	62	63	2,023	518	328	405
1979	669	174	75	70	2,023	540	326	422
1980	568	145	58	62	3,699	553	316	405
1981	282	84	47	52	3,511	571	298	366
1982	399	152	55	69	3,644	639	319	420
1983	343	112	60	74	2,926	540	312	393
1984	470	180	61	75	3,114	723	282	414
1985	447	171	58	60	3,590	926	269	411
1986	339	120	49	66	3,160	735	279	387
1987	273	100	51	70	1,968	552	298	397
1988	492	282	55	72	2,558	837	283	430
1989	502	195	52	80	2,126	625	287	444
1990	529	302	50	68	1,904	660	274	445
1991	634	324	65	94	1,831	675	286	413
1992	520	253	60	109	1,061	651	345	576
1993	213	151	69	112	465	405	372	657

C6   SOUTH AMERICA: Area and Output of Cotton and Tobacco (in thousands of hectares and thousands of metric tons)

	Colombia				Paraguay		Peru	
	Cotton		Tobacco		Tobacco		Cotton	
	Area	Output	Area	Output	Area	Output	Area	Output
1945	…	…	16	16	7	6	150	71
1946	…	…	16	19	9	11	125	70
1947	63	5	18	18	11	13	130	67
1948	87	6	20	20	7	9	150	67
1949	36	6	18	20	4	5	134	74
1950	37	8	19	20	5	5	160	84
1951	40	7	20	22	7	7	190	96
1952	55	11	20	22	7	7	190	96
1953	67	17	20	26	7	7	205	97
1954	82	28	26	26	10	10	209	114
1955	84	25	22	39	6	6	217	109
1956	69	22	21	36	5	6	227	114
1957	63	21	22	37	5	5	231	104
1958	77	26	23	38	7	7	238	116
1959	131	66	23	39	10	10	236	120
1960	150	67	15	25	8	9	252	133
1961	150	76	14	28	12	15	244	134
1962	169	62	19	39	20	25	253	149
1963	141	73	22	42	10	12	257	149
1964	150	66	22	41	14	18	246	139
1965	148	65	26	40	7	9	238	131
1966	164	88	27	44	11	14	204	121
1967	175	97	23	43	18	22	181	97
1968	199	120	23	43	20	24	166	105
1969	236	125	24	45	13	18	169	95
1970	267	128	23	42	14	18	144	92
1971	219	112	23	39	16	18	136	86
1972	242	145	24	36	17	23	129	68
1973	251	116	26	40	20	27	152	89
1974	258	146	25	41	24	33	142	81
1975	281	139	34	58	28	39	97	63
1976	286	142	30	39	30	41	98	65
1977	377	162	33	58	22	27	118	72
1978	328	111	18	47	21	26	123	87
1979	186	97	19	60	15	20	135	100
1980	217	122	18	47	8	11	149	102
1981	221	129	30	50	10	19	157	94
1982	99	57	31	49	12	22	134	36
1983	119	77	29	48	15	20	84	76
1984	223	92	21	35	16	25	99	99
1985	196	118	18	27	14	17	150	99
1986	190	119	18	29	9	15	162	89
1987	229	134	21	35	9	14	120	67
1988	187	97	21	36	6	14	133	93
1989	200	105	21	34	4	7	171	103
1990	250	119	20	33	3	5	138	78
1991	248	158	23	34	4	8	118	59
1992	210	117	15	28	4	8	86	35
1993	114	72	13	24	5	8	64	31

NOTES

1. SOURCES: As for table C1.
2. Note 2 of table C3 also applies to this table.

FOOTNOTES

[1]   Earlier figures are available as follows: 1871 0.7, 1891 1.9.
[2]   Figures from 1962 (2nd line) are derived from the International Cotton Advisory Committee, which the FAO has preferred to the earlier official series.

C7 NORTH AMERICA: OUTPUT OF COCOA, COFFEE AND TEA (in thousands of metric tons)

1875–1919

	Costa Rica	Cuba	Dominican Republic		El Salvador	Guatemala	Mexico		Puerto Rico	Trinidad & Tobago
	Coffee	Coffee	Cocoa	Coffee	Coffee	Coffee	Cocoa	Coffee	Coffee	Cocoa
1875	...	...	...	...	...	...	...	...	...	...
1876	...	...	...	...	...	...	...	...	...	...
1877	...	...	...	...	...	...	...	8	...	...
1878	...	...	...	...	...	...	...	...	...	...
1879	...	...	...	...	...	...	...	...	...	...
1880	...	...	...	...	...	...	...	...	...	...
1881	...	...	...	...	...	...	...	...	...	...
1882	...	...	...	...	...	...	...	...	...	...
1883	...	...	...	...	...	...	...	...	...	...
1884	19	...	...	...	...	23	...	...	...	...
1885	...	...	...	...	...	24	...	...	...	...
1886	...	...	...	...	...	...	...	...	...	...
1887	...	...	...	...	...	...	...	...	...	...
1888	14	...	...	...	...	27	...	...	...	...
1889	16	...	...	...	...	...	...	...	...	...
1890	15	...	...	...	...	...	...	...	...	...
1891	17	...	...	...	...	27	...	...	...	...
1892	17	...	...	...	...	34	...	11	...	...
1893	15	...	...	...	...	35	...	3	...	...
1894	...	...	...	...	...	36	...	17	...	9.8
1895	...	...	...	...	...	36	...	19	...	12.0
1896	...	...	...	...	...	38	...	13	...	11.0
1897	...	...	...	...	...	30	...	26	23	11.0
1898	...	...	...	...	...	44	...	16	...	11.0
1899	16	...	...	...	...	45	...	38	...	13.0
1900	17	...	...	...	...	36	...	21	...	14.0
1901	14	...	7	...	...	42	1	27	...	12.0
1902	17	...	9	...	...	47	1	10	...	17.0
1903	13	...	8	...	...	36	1	29	...	15.0
1904	18	...	13	...	...	...	1	34	...	22.0
1905	14	...	12	...	...	...	1	40	...	22.0
1906	17	3	14	...	...	...	1	39	...	13.0
1907	9	...	10	...	...	...	1	50	...	18.0
1908	12	...	19	...	...	...	1	40	...	21.0
1909	13	...	15	...	...	...	1	...	...	23.0
1910	13	...	16	...	...	...	2	32	...	26.0
1911	12	...	19	...	...	...	2	...	...	22.0
1912	13	...	20	...	...	54	2	32	...	19.0
1913	17	...	19	...	...	42	2	37	...	21.0
1914	12	...	20	...	...	47	2	...	...	28.0
1915	17	...	20	...	...	49	2	37	...	24.0
1916	12	...	21	...	...	45	2	9	...	24.0
1917	12	...	23	...	...	24	2	37	...	31.0
1918	14	...	19	...	...	49	2	48	...	26.0
1919	14	...	22	...	...	45	2	58	24	27.0

C7   NORTH AMERICA: Output of Cocoa, Coffee and Tea (in thousands of metric tons)

	Costa Rica	Cuba	Dominican Republic		El Salvador	Guatemala	Haiti
	Coffee	Coffee	Cocoa	Coffee	Coffee	Coffee	Coffee
1920	13	...	23	...	...	24	...
1921	19	...	26	...	...	48	...
1922	11	...	19	...	48	48	...
1923	18	...	19	...	54	33	...
1924	15	...	23	...	43	38	...
1925	18	20	23	...	46	44	...
1926	16	16	20	...	30	61	...
1927	19	21	26	...	68	62	...
1928	20	20	19	...	61	41	...
1929	23	21	21	...	65	44	...
1930	23	24	20	...	75	41	...
1931	19	27	26	16	48	54	...
1932	28	27	21	22	64	50	...
1933	19	26	19	20	58	36[2]	...
1934	24	28	21	19	59	52	...
1935	21	37	26	24	57	56	...
1936	26	31	22	29	72	58	...
1937	24	32	21	19	64	57	37
1938	22	31	29	19	68	54	37
1939	18	32	30	21	67	52	41
1940	22	30	24	20	58	50	28
1941	24	31	20	22	65	50	35
1942	24	36	21	20	67	52	26
1943	19	35	25	18	62	59	23
1944	22	26	25	19	58	60	30
1945	27	21	24	20	50	53	42
1946	16	35	25	17	62	56	36
1947	18	35	31	21	68	51	35
1948	18	28	28	22	90	57	35
1949	22	40	26	28	78	56	40
1950	24	33	33	25	72	54	33
1951	21	29	31	31	59	63	29
1952	33	27	32	34	78	58	27
1953	23	36	31	32	60	61	36
1954	35	39	33	33	77	65	24
1955	25	56	36	33	73	69	41
1956	34	37	28	32	91	74[1]	27
1957	46	44	35	36	84	86	45
1958	51	30	36	32	93	84	27
1959	50	48	33	35	103	105	39
1960	54	42	40	35	99	99	26
1961	62	37	35	36	123	101	44
1962	58	58	33	34	98	108	35
1963	64	35	38	41	123	105	35
1964	50	32	41	41	123	108	33
1965	61	24	25	47	109	126	37
1966	73	33	28	45	123	106	31
1967	76	34	26	42	145	109	32
1968	69	30	27	45	124	108	30
1969	85	30	26	44	144	114	27

C7 NORTH AMERICA: Output of Cocoa, Coffee and Tea (in thousands of metric tons)

	Honduras	Mexico		Nicaragua	Puerto Rico	Trinidad & Tobago
	Coffee	Cocoa	Coffee	Coffee	Coffee	Cocoa
1920	...	2	45	...	23	28
1921	...	2	34	...	20	35
1922	...	2	40	...	20	23
1923	...	2	41	...	10	30
1924	...	2	28	...	12	25
1925	4	2	48	...	11	22
1926	5	1	50	...	13	22
1927	5	1	52	...	11	23
1928	6	1	53	...	7	26
1929	5	1	52	...	2	28
1930	5	1	49	...	6	24
1931	5	1	47	...	5	27
1932	6	1	41	...	5	18
1933	6	1	55	...	4	22
1934	6	1	46	...	4	13
1935	6	1	52	...	9	16
1936	6	1	63	...	9	16
1937	6	1	60	...	8	12
1938	6	1	57	...	9	16
1939	6	2	55	...	11	7
1940	6	1	52	...	7	11
1941	6	1	52	...	13	8
1942	8	2	52	...	8	5
1943	8	2	52	...	10	4
1944	9	2	60	...	14	5
1945	10	2	55	...	7	4
1946	10	3	57	14	13	4
1947	9	7	55	15	11	4
1948	11	7	53	14	10	8
1949	13	7	59	20	11	6
1950	14	9	66	24	8	
1951	14	9	68	20	14	7
1952	15	9	71	22	8	10
1953	18	8	88	20	14	7
1954	18	13	85	24	9	8
1955	18	14	93	20	16	9
1956	18	14	88	23	7	8
1957	20	15	97	22	16	8
1958	22	15	122	22	11	8
1959	22	13	98	24	16	7
1960	23	17	124	24	12	6
1961	21	27	127	23	16	6
1962	28	30	140	28	18	6
1963	29	17	137	30	14	5
1964	29	21	156	31	17	5
1965	32	24	162	40	14	5
1966	30	25	183	32	13	4
1967	40	24	225	37	15	6
1968	31	26	213	30	12	5
1969	40	20	173	34	9	5

International Historical Statistics: The Americas 1750–1993

C7 NORTH AMERICA: Output of Cocoa, Coffee and Tea (in thousands of metric tons)

	Costa Rica	Cuba	Dominican Republic		El Salvador	Guatemala	Haiti
	Coffee	Coffee	Cocoa	Coffee	Coffee	Coffee	Coffee
1970	73	29	38	43	130	127	33
1971	89	28	33	45	145	128	32
1972	79	29	36	45	148	143	32
1973	96	30	36	59	127	149	33
1974	84	29	38	54	159	157	31
1975	80	20	31	52	165	139	39
1976	82	27	33	57	148	158	32
1977	87	17	34	60	147	168	31
1978	98	15	37	43	158	170	27
1979	99	23	36	60	186	161	40
1980	106	19	28	60	184	163	28
1981	113	22	33	52	156	177	33
1982	115	29	43	63	146	194	32
1983	124	18	45	68	155	171	36
1984	137	22	35	72	164	143	36
1985	124	24	41	52	134	169	37
1986	128	25	44	62	143	158	38
1987	138	26	39	67	148	182	30
1988	145	29	41	68	120	180	32
1989	147	29	42	65	117	220	33
1990	151	27	43	59	156	202	37
1991	158	23	44	55	149	208	37
1992	168	19	47	41	162	205	27
1993	148	18	53	41	165	215	34

	Honduras	Mexico		Nicaragua	Puerto Rico	Trinidad & Tobago
	Coffee	Cocoa	Coffee	Coffee	Coffee	Cocoa
1970	36	29	185	39	15	6
1971	42	26	187	42	11	4
1972	47	38	203	35	12	5
1973	42	33	222	37	14	3
1974	45	35	221	41	10	4
1975	47	34	228	49	11	5
1976	48	31	212	57	11	3
1977	50	25	182	55	9	3
1978	60	42	242	65	12	3
1979	72	38	220	56	9	3
1980	64	38	220	59	12	2
1981	75	30	244	61	14	3
1982	72	41	313	71	13	2
1983	79	33	313	44	16	2
1984	72	36	240	51	12	2
1985	75	49	270	50	14	1
1986	76	47	375	43	11	1
1987	80	41	318	37	16	2
1988	91	57	283	43	13	2
1989	90	50	326	44	15	1
1990	120	44	440	28	13	2
1991	102	44	334	47	13	2
1992	112	44	360	45	13	1
1993	110	54	336	42	13	2

C7 SOUTH AMERICA: OUTPUT OF COCOA, COFFEE AND TEA (in thousands of metric tons)

1840–1879

	Ecuador[4] Cocoa
1840	6
1841	5
1842	3
1843	7
1844	4
1845	4
1846	5
1847	5
1848	10
1849	6
1850	5
1851	4
1852	6
1853	6
1854	5
1855	7
1856	6
1857	7
1858	9
1859	6
1860	8
1861	8
1862	7
1863	7
1864	5
1865	6
1866	10
1867	9
1868	5
1869	8
1870	11
1871	8
1872	8
1873	11
1874	11
1875	8
1876	10
1877	9
1878	5
1879	14

1880–1924

	Brazil Cocoa	Brazil Coffee	Colombia Cocoa	Ecuador[4] Cocoa	Venezuela[6] Cocoa
1880	...	...	...	15	...
1881	...	...	...	10	...
1882	...	...	...	9	...
1883	...	...	...	9	...
1884	...	...	...	8	...
1885	...	...	...	10[5]	...
				12	
1886	...	...	...	19	...
1887	...	...	...	16	...
1888	...	...	...	13	...
1889				27	
1890	...	...	...	18	...
1891	...	...	...	10	...
1892	...	...	...	16	...
1893	...	...	...	20	...
1894	...	...	...	19	...
1895	...	...	...	18	...
1896	...	...	...	17	...
1897	...	...	...	16	...
1898	...	...	...	21	...
1899	...	...	...	27	...
1900	...	690	...	19	...
1901	18	975	3	23	9
1902	20	778	3	24	8
1903	21	699	3	23	8
1904	23	635	3	28	14
1905	21	662	3	21	12
1906	25	1,224	3	22	14
1907	24	680	3	19	12
1908	32	782	3	31	16
1909	33	927	3	31	16
1910	29	660	3	36	16
1911	35	794	3	39	18
1912	30[2]	727	3	36	14
1913	29	868	3	42	18
1914	41	810	3	44	17
1915	44	958	4	35	18
1916	43	766	3	49	15
1917	55	951	3	46	20
1918	41	584	3	37	19
1919	62	789	4	37	19
1920	67	788	4	39	17
1921	35	1,027	4	40	22
1922	59	857	4	40	21
1923	57	857	4	29	22
1924	68	952	5	30	17

International Historical Statistics: The Americas 1750–1993

C7 SOUTH AMERICA: Output of Cocoa, Coffee and Tea (in thousands of metric tons)

1925–1969

	Argentina	Brazil		Colombia		Ecuador		Venezuela	
	Tea	Cocoa	Coffee	Cocoa	Coffee	Cocoa	Coffee	Cocoa	Coffee
1925	...	60	888	5	...	30	...	23	...
1926	...	72	960	5	...	18	...	15	...
1927	...	71	1,102	5	...	20	...	17	...
1928	...	73	1,671	6	...	20	...	20	...
1929	...	64	1,577	5	...	15	...	21	...
1930	...	69	1,634	5	195	17	...	16	67
1931	...	77	1,302	6	204	14	...	16	58
1932	...	104	1,536	11	203	15	...	16	49
1933	...	100	1,777	9	217	10	...	17	48
1934	...	108	1,653	11	230	19	...	14	57
1935	...	127	1,136	10	210	20	...	15	64
1936	...	127	1,577	9	252	19	...	17	72
1937	...	119	1,462	11	262	21	17	18	60
1938	...	142	1,404	11	268	19	17	20	39
1939	...	135	1,157	12	265	15	17	15	65
1940	...	128	1,002	14	267	11	15	15	48
1941	...	132	962	12	286	14	18	17	39
1942	...	109	830	12	329	14	15	17	33
1943	...	178	922	9	317	18	...	18	33
1944	...	117	...	8	332	14	25	16	45
1945	...	120	835	10	329	17	14	15	45
1946	...	122	917	11	346	17	17	17	44
1947	...	119	948	8	365	16	18	20	47
1948	...	129	1,037	11	368	16	20	17	47
1949	...	162	1,068	14	368	20	13	23	51
1950	1	136	1,071	15	338	21	23	17	34
1951	1	105	1,080	15	302	32	22	18	43
1952	1	97	1,125	15	403	24	24	16	54
1953	1	123	1,111	15	384	29	[23][5]	18	45
1954	2	172	1,037	15	403	26	[35][5]	17	53
1955	2	158	1,370	14	377	34	[23][5]	19	53
1956	3	168	979	12	335	31	40	16	46
1957	2	147	1,409	12	365	27	51	15	57
1958	10	164	1,696	12	469	33	46	18	60
1959	3	178	2,629	13	462	41	39	19	61
1960	5	163	1,797	14	480	44	33	17	59
1961	7	156	2,110[3] 2,229	17	450	44	54	19	57
1962	8	140	2,190	17	482	45	56	21	54
1963	10	144	1,651	16	450	36	43	21	61
1964	13	154	1,042	18	468	48	50	20	56
1965	11	161	2,294	17	492	50	66	20	54
1966	19	170	1,203	18	456	43	74	20	61
1967	15	195	1,508	17	477	60	66	21	62
1968	15	149	1,058	18	480	85	63	19	46
1969	20	211	1,284	19	480	48	56	18	61

C7 SOUTH AMERICA: Output of Coffee, Cocoa and Tea (in thousands of metric tons)[1]

	Argentina	Brazil		Colombia		Ecuador		Venezuala	
	Tea	Cocoa	Coffee	Cocoa	Coffee	Cocoa	Coffee	Cocoa	Coffee
1970	17	201	755	19	501	54	72	19	61
1971	21	182	1,550	21	485	71	62	19	58
1972	29	164	1,475	22	480	68	71	17	40
1973	29	159	873	23	468	63	75	20	66
1974	25	242	1,615	25	540	91	70	18	46
1975	28	265	1,272	26	480	75	76	20	65
1976	35	251	376	29	558	65	87	15	40
1977	22	226	975	27	648	72	83	16	58
1978	26	279	1,268	31	720	72	75	15	59
1979	29	309	1,333	32	762	77	90	15	54
1980	36	296	1,061	34	756	91	69	13	58
1981	23	336	2,032	38	808	80	86	15	60
1982	33	364	958	43	728	85	84	14	58
1983	41	380	1,672	37	824	45	81	14	59
1984	41	330	1,420	39	694	49	97	12	62
1985	47	431	1,911	43	678	131	121	11	64
1986	41	459	1,041	47	713	90	118	12	66
1987	45	329	2,203	54	652	58	112	13	70
1988	32	375	1,369	54	709	85	144	14	71
1989	35	392	1,352	55	664	83	129	14	73
1990	45	356	1,465	56	845	97	135	16	76
1991	49	320	1,525	58	971	100	139	14	73
1992	38	329	1,294	55	1,146	94	138	17	69
1993	38	340	1,278	57	1,080	83	137	16	66

NOTES

1. SOURCES: As for table C1, with cocoa statistics for the Dominican Republic and Colombia to 1949, Ecuador and Venezuela to 1954 and Brazil to 1919, taken from *Cocoa Statistics*, published annually by Gill & Duffus.
2. Statistics are not always for calendar years, but so far as possible they have been shown against the year in which the bulk of the production was harvested. (Most cocoa statistics, for example, are for years ended 30 September.)

FOOTNOTES

[1] Registered production only to 1956, estimated to be about 90% of the total.
[2] Subsequent figures are revised and not strictly comparable with earlier ones.
[3] Data to 1961 (1st line) are derived from the Brazil Coffee Institute. Official data are preferred subsequently.
[4] Data to 1885 (1st line) are of cocoa received for shipment at Guyaquil.
[5] Exportable crop only.
[6] Rafael Cartay, *Historia Economica de Venezuela 1830–1900* gives the following earlier figures:-

	Cocoa	Coffee
1875	5	40
1884	8	55
1894	11	106

C8 NORTH AMERICA: OUTPUT OF FRUIT (in thousands of metric tons)

1880-1929

	Canada	Costa Rica[1]	Guatemala[2]	Honduras[4]	Jamaica	Mexico	Nicaragua[6]	USA	
	Apples	Bananas	Bananas	Bananas	Bananas[5]	Oranges	Bananas	Apples	Citrus Fruit[8]
1883	...	2.8	...	...	...	...	...	...	...
1884	...	11.0	...	...	...	...	...	...	...
1885	...	10.0	...	...	...	...	...	...	...
1886	...	15.0	...	...	...	...	...	...	...
1887	...	23.0	...	...	21	...	...	...	...
1888	...	22.0	...	...	45	...	...	...	...
1889	...	25.0	...	...	42₅	...	...	2,921	...
1890	...	26.0	...	...	...	...	...	...	...
1891	...	29.0 ·	...	...	70	...	...	...	...
1892	...	30.0	...	...	44	...	...	...	...
1893	...	32.0	...	...	60	...	...	...	...
1894	...	35.0	...	...	75	...	...	...	...
1895	...	40.0	...	...	68	...	...	...	...
1896	...	43.0	...	...	61	...	...	...	...
1897	...	50.0	...	...	70	...	...	...	...
1898	...	59.0	...	...	101	...	...	...	...
1899	...	75.0	...	...	116	...	...	3,580	250
1900	...	87.0	...	...	119	...	...	...	...
1901	...	98.0	...	...	159	...	...	...	...
1902	...	106.0	...	...	205	...	...	...	...
1903	...	131.0	...	...	113	...	...	...	...
1904	...	154.0	...	...	129	...	...	...	...
1905	...	185.0	...	...	217	...	...	...	...
1906	...	275.0	...	...	232	...	...	...	...
1907	...	258.0	...	...	202	38	...	...	...
1908	...	256.0	...	...	211₅	...	...	...	...
1909	...	238.0	...	...	242	...	...	2,968	827
1910	...	231.0	...	...	204	...	...	...	...
1911	...	236.0	...	...	239	...	...	...	...
1912	...	270.0	...	...	194	...	...	...	...
1913	...	284.0	...	...	168	...	...	...	...
1914	...	258.0	...	...	234	...	...	...	...[8]
1915	...	242.0	...	...	118	...	...	...	786
1916	...	256.0	...	...	50	...	... ·	1,376	905
1917	...	200.0	...	...	35	...	...		393
1918	...	...	...	...	46	...	...		897
1919	...	185.0	69	...	140	...	17	2,787₇	840
1920	...	220.0	100	...	131	...	25	4,566	1,104
1921	...	211.0	121	...	144	...	40	2,021	754
1922	236	182.0	138	...	184	...	55	4,137	1,123
1923	235	189.0	153	...	180	...	71	4,140	1,372
1924	207	205.0	199	...	173	...	59	3,505[1]	1,100
1925	178	212.0	132	632	217	...	63	3,519	1,234
1926	181	217.0	122	670	265	...	46	5,032	1,440
1927	172	200.0	120	784	306	100	50	2,520	1,156
1928	198	186.0	127	954	247	101	65	3,815	1,990
1929	237	155.0	146	946	319	101	86	2,721	1,230₈
									1,829

C8 NORTH AMERICA: Output of Fruit (in thousands of metric tons)

1930–1969

	Canada	Costa Rica[1]	Dominican Republic	Guadeloupe	Guatemala[2]	Honduras[4]	Jamaica	
	Apples	Bananas	Bananas	Bananas	Bananas	Bananas	Bananas[5]	Citrus Fruit
1930	...	148	...	...	...	1,003	356	...
1931	232	129	...	...	138	1,159	323	...
1932	171	110	...	...	123	1,027	295	...
1933	335	109	...	...	130	893	153	...
1934	267	82	...	...	121	843	231	...
1935	276	74	...	...	129	690	295	...
1936	252	99	...	...	173	675	272	...
1937	310	140	...	...	198	589	390	...
1938	320	140	...	...	218	618	345	...
1939	335	...	...	...	236	656	272	...
1940	263	80	...	...	169	746	100	...
1941	219	123	...	...	141	699	81	...
1942	265	58	...	...	102	509	19	...
1943	262	61	...	...	52	499	4	...
1944	364	48	...	...	100	650	16	...
1945	156	56	...	...	174	742	26	...
1946	394	112	342	48	222	787	84	...
1947	319	140	366	...	290	867	80	78
1948	274	190	250	72	273	847	88[5] / 147	78
1949	370	223	380	72	120	789	155	78
1950	330	222	389	75	...	845	122	99
1951	278	217[1] / 413	375	90	120	872	80	72
1952	246	531	376	105	87	850	103	71
1953	239	...	...	108	174	863	240	94
1954	296	429	393	115	144[2] / 154	747	264	102
1955	391	456	277	110	134	700	266	103
1956	254	342	326	125	125	899	279	79
1957	319	...	343	125	130	869[4] / 705	254	74
1958	347	...	364	140	152	735	245	73
1959	317	...	457	165	178	900	254	90
1960	304	...	488	170	244	832	254	86
1961	337	410	424	165	197[3]	881	263	111
1962	410	521	400	163	139	840	272	119
1963	469	466	290	168	185	801	281	102
1964	409	486	252	162	138	831	290	108
1965	455	567	270	162	52	1,090	327	110
1966	430	399	238	180	96	1,002[4] / 1,151	320	116
1967	446	512	238	180	76	1,011	275	105
1968	410	703	343	140	76	1,002	210	93
1969	444	967	267	145	80[3]	994	155	116

C8   NORTH AMERICA: Output of Fruit (in thousands of metric tons)

1930–1969

	Martinique	Mexico		Nicaragua[6]	Panama[1]	USA	
	Bananas	Bananas	Oranges	Bananas	Bananas	Apples	Citrus Fruit[8]
1930	...	...	111	82	...	3,197	2,920
1931	...	...	125	63	...	4,193	2,621
1932	...	...	113	71	...	2,997	2,624
1933	...	...	92	78	...	3,034	2,466
1934	...	...	113	57	...	2,167	3,390
1935	...	...	113	63	...	2,870	2,758
1936	...	...	146	40	...	2,003	3,314
1937	...	...	147	53	...	3,129	4,065
1938	...	...	167	38	152	2,161	4,723[8]
1939	...	...	183	...	...	2,845	4,093
1940	...	...	208	23	119	2,277	5,134
1941	...	...	229	15	115	2,505	5,004
1942	...	...	240	2	48	2,618	5,711
1943	...	...	264	—	19	1,818	6,432
1944	...	...	284	—	23	2,546	7,463
1945	...	...	295	2	52	1,363	6,673
1946	8	302	342	6[6]	159	2,437	7,135
1947	25	298	345	7	106	2,307	7,069
1948	45	300	400	14	130	1,945	6,020
1949	55	308	411	15	218	2,917	5,866
1950	85	257	555	13	189	2,710	6,832
1951	95	187	502	9	136[1] / 356	2,425	6,682
1952	82	204	534	8	298	2,056	6,635
1953	...	203	557	9	335	2,076	7,458
1954	62	205	598	12	345	2,436	7,316
1955	65	207	595	9	430	2,314	7,466
1956	98	246	625	4	390	2,206	7,567
1957	115	270	656	2	465	2,596	6,441
1958	115	274	662	2	445	2,776	7,357
1959	155	276	674	2	486	2,762	7,202
1960	146	317	766	4	439	2,363	6,847
1961	185	341	772	1	452	2,756	7,802
1962	170	367	883	7	417	2,739	5,946
1963	130	940	855	19	422	2,609	5,656
1964	120	949	845	27	485	2,866	6,930
1965	220	960	1,401	8	579	2,781	7,874
1966	260	978	1,537	14	586	2,612	10,375
1967	240	986	1,805	42	592	2,447	7,555
1968	245	1,040	1,721	42	949	2,468	10,175
1969	220	1,025	1,626	22	1,019	3,063	10,313

C8 NORTH AMERICA: Output of Fruit (in thousands of metric tons)

Key: CF = Citrus fruit

	Canada	Costa Rica	Dominican Republic	Guadeloupe	Guatemala	Honduras	Jamaica	
	Apples	Bananas	Bananas	Bananas	Bananas	Bananas	Bananas	CF
1970	406	1,146	275	126	487	985	185	130
1971	398	1,250	286	148	495	977	194	150
1972	393	1,250	290	174	510	969	199	149
1973	375	1,198	310	175	520	961	160	77
1974	406	1,151	302	162	500	871	132	95
1975	460	1,121	318	165	520	907	127	95
1976	409	1,187	318	148	550	944	144	95
1977	411	1,125	314	142	...	982	148	93
1978	452	1,183	315	170	...	1,022	160	101
1979	435	1,154	275	116	556	1,068	130	...
1980	553	1,107	301	83	527	1,058	165	102
1981	422	1,141	320	150	536	1,022	174	84
1982	478	1,153	320	...	601	948	188	89
1983	485	1,155	320	142	...	939	160	89
1984	434	1,169	...	163	483	...	181	82
1985	479	1,008	314	127	538	1,263	190	89
1986	388	1,096	422	144	551	1,167	191	100
1987	506	1,139	373	148	525	1,392	208	121
1988	501	1,162	391	150	406	1,408	146[12]	147[12]
1989	537	1,400	384	94	420	1,092	42	23
1990	540	1,740	395	102	454	999	61	43
1991	511	1,700	389	95	460	973	75	25
1992	564	1,657	420	147	478	1,023	77	48
1993	620	1,827	460	150	479	1,013	77	28

	Martinique	Mexico		Nicaragua	Panama	USA	
	Bananas	Bananas	Oranges	Bananas	Bananas	Apples	CF
1970	158	1,136	1,555	217	947	2,838	10,307
1971	165	1,116	1,999	219	1,013	2,758	10,837
1972	240	1,149	1,318	230	988	2,663	11,044
1973	170	1,070	1,466	260	964	2,824	12,604
1974	220	1,070	1,778	305	977	2,941	12,168
1975	180	1,194	2,322	234	989	3,416	13,237
1976	275	1,199	1,787	236	999	2,939	13,415
1977	290	1,276	1,857	237	1,028	3,026	13,828
1978	305	1,384	1,902	240	1,056	3,446	12,932
1979	184	1,553	1,717	240	1,000	3,694	12,092
1980	94	1,501	1,950	231	1,050	4,004	14,955
1981	187	1,591	1,789	239	1,045	3,517	13,703
1982	...	1,572	1,995	237	1,057	3,681	10,934
1983	178	1,640	2,069	212	1,045	3,798	12,344
1984	181	2,093	1,720	200	1,056	3,779	9,793
1985	181	1,151	1,745	212	1,067	3,594	9,559
1986	212	1,473	1,909	186	907	3,598	10,026
1987	212	1,770	1,934	204	1,251	4,875	10,874
1988	209	1,566	2,099	229	1,081	4,118	11,565
1989	241	1,185	1,166	90	1,254	4,498	11,961
1990	255	1,986	2,220	104	1,166	4,398	9,912
1991	226	1,889	2,369	133	1,106	4,458	10,362
1992	231	2,095	2,541	135	1,093	4,798	11,296
1993	214	2,344	2,852	85	819	4,861	13,849

C8 SOUTH AMERICA: OUTPUT OF FRUIT (in thousands of metric tons)

1933–1969

	Argentina			Brazil		Ecuador		Paraguay		Peru	Venezuala	
	Apples	Bananas	CF	Bananas	CF[9]	Bananas[10]	CF[11]	Bananas	CF	CF	Bananas	CF
1933	...	...	...	...	1,037	...	...	...	...	...	...	...
1934	...	...	...	...	1,152	...	...	...	...	...	...	...
1935	...	...	...	...	1,146	...	...	...	...	...	...	...
1936	...	...	...	...	1,221	...	...	...	...	...	...	...
1937	...	...	...	...	1,136	...	...	...	...	...	...	...
1938	...	...	...	...	1,242	55	...	...	...	...	...	...
1939	...	...	...	1,755	1,189	...	...	...	...	...	...	...
1940	...	...	487	1,503	1,273	47	48	...	...	...	...	...
1941	...	...	482	1,620	1,263	34	58	...	...	...	...	...
1942	...	...	639	1,600	1,240	22	26	...	...	...	...	...
1943	...	...	401	1,698	1,246	15	61[11]	...	...	...	...	...
1944	...	...	392	1,854	973	14	...	...	...	...	...	...
1945	...	...	320	2,146	1,001	17	...	...	...	...	...	...
1946	...	...	391	2,344	1,048	36	...	...	...	...	...	...
1947	...	...	382	2,549	1,035	69	10	...	206	113	...	...
1948	173	...	407	2,726	1,062	174	7	...	207	302	59	...
1949	229	...	448	2,854	1,226	199	6	...	244	356	42	...
1950	196	...	407	3,257	1,246	...	5	...	180	363	60	...
1951	284	...	437	3,393	1,203	246	4[11]	...	130	399	...	...
1952	224	...	419	3,703	1,236[9]	430	...	...	...	415	...	...
		...			1,262							
1953	268	...	442	3,257	1,364	406	176	...	203	...	49	...
1954	242		475	3,964	1,409	492	...	...	...	...	52	...
1955	361	...	516	4,086	1,436	613	184	...	...	...	...	...
1956	256	11	536	4,481	1,516	579	...	...	148	...	700	...
1957	442	5	719	4,665	1,598	669[10]	156	...	143	...	1,074	...
						1,160						
1958	283	3	755	4,595	1,648	1,340	155	...	135	...	924	37
1959	464	3	791	4,885	1,759	2,024	166	161	135	...	...	37
1960	431	9	732	5,127	1,853	2,304	161	141	134	...	1,332	40
1961	415	12	844	3,529	1,951	2,204	171	145	150	170	1,004	...
1962	397	47	813	3,909	2,053	2,109	182	141	202	180	874	...
1963	474	36	821	4,070	2,321	2,098	173	196	209	191	1,456	127
1964	371	66	854	4,397	2,263	3,300	170	195	215	205	742	138
1965	544	37	663	4,531	2,529	3,304	217	232	229	213	825	151
1966	...	104	962	4,626	2,588	2,956	230	251	235	248	840	142
1967	...	130	823	5,236	2,748	3,163	230	259	243	270	859	146
1968	...	53	1,079	5,484	2,983	2,693	232	250	240	297	949	158
1969	...	141	1,344	6,023	3,179	2,800	231	250	259	357	948	170

C8 SOUTH AMERICA: Output of Fruit (in thousands of metric tons)

	Argentina			Brazil		Ecuador		Paraguay		Peru	Venezuela	
	Apples	Bananas	CF	Bananas	CF	Bananas	CF	Bananas	CF	CF	Bananas	CF
1970	445	223	1,425	6,408	3,537	2,700	221	249	259	357	968	184
1971	424	225	1,598	6,806	3,500	3,512	219	250	263	334	989	194
1972	512	311	1,302	7,000	4,228	3,296	201	250	250	337	997	206
1973	233	352	1,444	7,128	5,276	3,203	208	255	182	284	902	217
1974	786	399	1,546	6,974	6,625	3,397	377	258	250	312	937	231
1975	608	374	1,483	5,311	6,743	2,544	401	259	192	322	860	245
1976	577	278	1,399	5,761	7,871	2,571	393	254	199	275	900	250
1977	820	220	1,480	6,415	7,592	2,451	586	252	298	245	875	320
1978	810	129	1,450	6,240	6,810	2,152	613	254	293	273	900	314
1979	972	144	1,365	6,133	7,370	2,032	618	306	336	258	961	369
1980	958	146	1,478	6,721	9,363	2,269	648	300	343	238	890	351
1981	908	77	1,465	6,710	10,008	2,010	636	305	345	217	915	368
1982	804	89	1,394	6,821	10,181	1,999	618	314	347	237	921	372
1983	817	126	1,394	6,566	10,179	1,642	307	315	360	233	934	434
1984	922	161	1,371	7,062	14,035	1,678	370	325	360	237	965	362
1985	982	163	1,431	4,815	15,049	1,970	337	311	492	246	989	370
1986	594	190	1,525	5,052	14,422	2,316	283	325	478	277	1,007	384
1987	1,074	243	1,776	5,131	15,830	2,387	308	423	524	276	1,038	388
1988	940	250	1,562	5,156	16,168	2,576	199	449	552	340	1,100	424
1989	891	240	1,445	5,502	18,856	3,055	203	425	521	313	1,134	483
1990	980	260	1,620	5,506	18,556	3,525	185	310	513	318	1,167	491
1991	950	270	1,590	5,526	19,547	3,995	183	144	515	319	1,215	490
1992	1,043	146	1,985	5,624	20,846	4,422	147	152	483	441	1,239	535
1993	709	135	1,839	5,587	19,911	4,715	163	153	484	401	1,116	503

NOTES

1. SOURCES: The national publications on pp. xiii–xv; International Institute of Agriculture, Year-book of Agricultural Statistics; and FAO, Yearbook of Food and Agricultural Statistics.
2. Statistics refer to commercial production.
3. Note 2 of table C3 also applies to this table.

FOOTNOTES

[1] Exports to 1951 (1st line).
[2] Exports to 1954 (1st line).
[3] The FAO Yearbooks do not indicate any breaks, but the markedly lower figures between 1962 and 1969 are FAO estimates, whereas the others are from official national sources, and it seems probable that the latter covered plantains as well as bananas.
[4] Except from 1957 (2nd line) to 1966 (1st line), data relate to plantains as well as bananas.
[5] Exports to 1948 (1st line). Data are for years ending 30 September to 1889 and years beginning 1 April from 1891 to 1908.
[6] Exports to 1946.
[7] Statistics to 1919 (except for citrus fruit in 1915-19) are derived from censuses. In 1924 the census figure for apples was 3,122.
[8] Data to 1929 (1st line) relate to orange output in California and Florida only. From 1929 (2nd line) to 1938 they are for the citrus fruit output of the seven main producing states. The census figure for total citrus fruit output in 1919 was 1,400 thousand tons.
[9] Oranges only to 1952 (1st line)
[10] Exports to 1957 (1st line).
[11] Oranges only to 1943. Exports from 1947 to 1951.
[12] National sources used from this point.

C9 SOUTH AMERICA: AREA OF VINEYARDS AND OUTPUT OF WINE (in thousands of hectares and thousands of hectolitres)

	Argentina		Brazil		Chile		Uruguay	
	Area[1]	Output	Area	Output	Area	Output	Area[2]	Output
1896	28	574	...	...	...	...	...	...
1897	...	...	...	...	...	...	...	...
1898	...	...	...	...	...	...	4	34
1899	...	...	...	...	...	...	...	...
1900	...	1,151	...	...	...	...	...	...
1901	...	1,844	...	...	30	1,062	...	...
1902	48	1,360	...	...	30		4	70
1903	50	1,892	...	...	30	597	...	...
1904	54	1,741	...	...	38	756	4	105
1905	54	1,838	...	...	38	728	4	116
1906	61	2,426	...	...	32	553	5	95
1907	74	2,621	...	...	...	...	5	115
1908	122	2,843	...	...	59	1,900	5	186
1909	122	2,338	...	...	66	2,300	6	162
1910	122	3,396	...	...	66	2,227	6	170
1911	105	3,781	...	...	52	1,332	6	147
1912	100	4,260	...	...	57	1,964	6	106
1913	102	4,989	...	...	61	2,263	6	194
1914	106	5,151	...	...	66	2,952	6	165
1915	132	3,940	...	...	71	3,081	6	114
1916	124	4,406	...	...	57	1,614	6	206
1917	115	5,133	...	...	64	2,243	6	192
1918	116	4,529	...	...	89	2,066	7	256
1919	113	4,575	...	...	67	1,658	7	194
1920	113	5,134	...	480	66	1,789	7	194
1921	120	6,155	...	473	67	1,861	7	361
1922	121	5,155	...	750	67	2,137	7	230
1923	126	5,435	...	442	68	2,353	8	320
1924	146	5,463	...	707	68	2,124	8	343
1925	137	6,635	...	717	69	1,590	9	362
1926	123	5,282	...	819	71	1,966	10	293
1927	128	4,649	...	861	71	3,085	10	399
1928	133	7,656	...	841	81	3,451	11	359
1929	...	8,368	...	753	82	3,278	12	409
1930	141	5,734	...	1,367	85	3,202	12	495
1931	143	5,585	...	1,248	86	2,425	13	379
1932	157	2,187	...	933	84	2,315	14	533
1933	157	7,347	...	686	84	3,078	14	473
1934	169	7,548	...	526	86	2,925	15	583
1935	169	4,365	...	762	89	2,220	15	357
1936	169	5,812	...	858	101	3,438	15	561
1937	...	7,948	...	772	102	3,547	16	725
1938	...	9,262	24	828	104	3,595	16	684
1939	143	6,631	24	802	102	2,818	16	599
1940	138	6,707	32	750	102	2,656	17	446
1941	139	7,615	34	629	101	2,784	...	616
1942	139	6,916	35	626	100	2,710	...	689
1943	120	10,662	34	709	99	2,849	...	773
1944	135	8,489	31	...	99	3,808	...	718

C9   SOUTH AMERICA: Area of Vineyards and Output of Wine (in thousands of hectares and thousands of hectolitres)

	Argentina		Brazil		Chile		Uruguay	
	Area	Output	Area	Output	Area	Output	Area	Output
1945	117	7,101	32	782	...	2,881	...	531
1946	159	8,940	32	850	87	2,627	...	...
1947	159	10,344	33	970	87	2,615	18	658
1948	157	11,624	37	900	89	2,366	18	720
1949	157	10,397	35	621	91	3,140	18	807
1950	157₁ 170	12,509	36	977	90	3,603	17	731
1951	170	11,503	37	821	88	3,395	17	961
1952	177	10,794	41	852	98	2,200	...	719
1953	198	13,001	42	1,020	...	3,646	18	971
1954	207	10,686	45	743	...	3,526	20	901
1955	213	17,672	48	743	108	3,045	19	769
1956	216	13,422	50	1,376	108	3,654	...	874
1957	224	8,616	54	1,698	...	3,579	...	...
1958	229	14,098	56	1,670	108	3,720	...	680
1959	230	17,767	59	1,560	108	3,638	...	967
1960	234	15,826	61	1,500	100	3,688	...	810
1961	239	16,750	65	1,580	101	4,853	20	800
1962	245	19,172	70	1,390	108	5,529	20	703
1963	253	20,744	71	1,180	108	4,563	20	842
1964	261	19,533	68	999	108	4,837	20	782
1965	267	18,271	69	1,928	103	3,648	20	867
1966	271	21,917	67	1,830	113	4,736	19	1,061
1967	276	28,171	65	1,750	109	4,885	20	934
1968	291	19,513	73	1,988	114	5,360	20	837
1969	298	17,916	60	1,580	112	4,024	20	760
1970	295	18,360	66	1,900	125	4,006	20	910
1971	322	21,783	67	1,900	130	5,251	20	910
1972	319	19,986	60	2,300	125	6,400	22	900
1973	313	22,567	56	2,362	...	5,690	...	900
1974	325	27,183	53	2,036	...	4,665	...	900
1975	331	22,103	58	2,036	...	4,649	...	900
1976	339	28,197	62	2,195	...	5,143	...	820
1977	341	23,319	60	2,641	...	5,786	...	470
1978	346	29,267	58	2,850	101	5,612	...	470
1979	366	25,975	60	2,850	106	5,925	16	550
1980	312	23,302	57	2,000	108	5,860	12	571
1981	320	21,633	58	2,900	110	5,943	12	971
1982	318	24,984	58	2,750	112	6,100	18	836
1983	319	24,719	58	2,750	121	5,200	18	751
1984	317	18,808	57	2,730	112	4,000	17	666
1985	265	16,800	58	2,800	112	4,500	...	710
1986	262	18,559	59	2,800	...	4,500	...	710
1987	282	18,383	59	2,820	115	3,000	...	740
1988	274	17,861	58	3,760	118	3,800	19	740
1989	260	17,229	58	2,740	118	3,900	19	850
1990	210	17,131	59	3,110	120	3,980	20	900
1991	209	17,111	57	3,110	121	3,900	20	800
1992	208	16,193	60	3,580	121	3,170	12	800
1993	203	14,558	60	3,600	112	3,810	12	1,070

C9　Area of Vineyards and Output of Wine

NOTES

1. SOURCES: As for table C1, with Argentinian output for 1900–39 taken from *Anuario Geografico Argentino* (Buenos Aires, 1941).
2. It is only recently that data on wine output in the U.S.A. have been published. Statistics since 1970 are as follows:-

1970	9,688	1975	14,535	1980	18,400	1985	18,100
1971	13,699	1976	14,366	1981	16,300	1986	17,700
1972	12,040	1977	14,179	1982	19,500	1987	17,000
1973	15,813	1978	16,160	1983	14,760	1988	18,450
1974	14,241	1979	16,050	1984	16,656	1989	18,500
						1990	17,955
						1991	—
						1992	18,318
						1993	15,572

FOOTNOTES

[1]　Data to 1950 (1st line) are of vines in bearing only.
[2]　In 1892–94 the area was given as 3 thousand hectares.

C10 NORTH AMERICA: NUMBERS OF LIVESTOCK (in thousands, poultry in millions)

	Canada[1]				
	Horses	Cattle	Pigs	Sheep	Poultry[3]
1851	[401][2]	[1,707][2]	[828][2]	[2,066][2]	...
1861	722	2,316	1,228	2,506	...
1871	837	2,624	1,366	3,156	...
1881	1,059	3,515	1,208	3,049	...
1891	1,471	4,121	1,734	2,564	...
1901	1,578	5,576	2,354	2,510	16.7
1906	1,963	7,202	3,379	2,543	...
1907	2,106	7,153	3,701	2,350	...
1908	2,248	6,995	3,546	2,380	...
1909	2,327	6,651	3,287	2,327	...
1910	2,478	6,515	3,304	2,246	...
1911	2,599	6,526	3,635	2,174	29.8
1912	2,694	6,686	3,684	2,172	...
1913	2,827	6,855	3,683	2,333	...
1914	2,992	6,911	3,640	2,310	...
1915	3,115	7,221	3,464	2,359	...
1916	3,167	7,499	3,562	2,334	34.1
1917	3,210	7,789	3,292	2,422	34.9
1918	3,346	8,251	3,677	2,636	35.8
1919	3,445	8,485	3,623	2,949	37.6
1920	3,404	8,153	3,152	3,179	35.6
1921	3,452	8,370	3,324	3,200	41.1
1922	3,401	8,267	3,493	3,045	45.5
1923	3,341	7,975	3,986	2,601	47.1
1924	3,384	8,135	4,594	2,499	48.3
1925	3,348	7,976	4,009	2,628	48.7
1926	3,361	7,818	4,037	2,830	49.7
1927	3,297	7,604	4,302	2,968	50.9
1928	3,265	7,458	4,217	3,128	54.2
1929	3,264	7,518	4,048	3,350	59.8
1930	3,191	7,686	3,735	3,438	60.5
1931	3,114	7,973	4,700	3,627	61.3
1932	3,084	8,548	4,670	3,604	59.7
1933	2,973	8,954	3,854	3,307	54.7
1934	2,918	9,070	3,736	3,291	55.0
1935	2,911	8,973	3,651	3,224	52.5
1936	2,878	8,829	4,136	3,159	54.4
1937	2,845	8,915	4,016	3,071	52.2
1938	2,770	8,491	3,527	3,047	51.7
1939	2,761	8,374	4,364	2,911	55.7
1940	2,780	8,380	6,002	2,887	57.0
1941	2,789	8,517	6,081	2,840	59.0
1942	2,759	8,712	6,808	2,972	66.3
1943	2,667	9,122	7,413	3,107	68.8
1944	2,568	9,544	6,790	3,213	77.2

	Costa Rica			
	Horses	Cattle	Pigs	Poultry[4]
1910	60	333	70	...
1914	52	336	64	...
1915	65	347	76	...
1922	95	477	114	...
1923	105	426	92	...
1924	116	404	76	...
1925	104	433	71	...
1926	127	423	76	...
1927	126	478	129	...
1928	102	443	104	...
1929	85	399	83	1.0

For Cuba see next page

	Dominican Republic					
	Horses	Mules	Asses	Cattle	Pigs	Goats
1920	156	49	...	609	557	656
1921	163	65	...	647	674	706
1922	115	34	76	577	843	360
1923	126	37	85	635	927	381
1924	139	41	93	701	1,020	419
1930	150	45	105	900	1,100	650
1935	266	45	93	913	880	373
1939	245	48	68	819	783	447

C10   NORTH AMERICA: Numbers of Livestock (in thousands, poultry in millions)

	Horses	Mules	Cattle	Pigs	Sheep	Goats
			Cuba			
1846	240[5]		1,027	929	83	
1862	330[5]		1,241	723	79	
1881	205[5]		916	325	60	
1892	647		2,585	535	95	
1894	585		2,486	570	78	
1899	108		377	359	29	
1902	168	31	1,000	...	...	...
1903	208	33	1,304	...	...	...
1904	269	44	1,700	...	...	...
1905	343	46	2,176	...	...	...
1906	402	51	2,579	...	...	...
1907	453	55	2,754	...	...	...
1908	500	57	2,969	...	...	...
1909	555	59	3,076	...	...	...
1910	613	61	3,212	...	...	...
1911	457	31	2,329	...	...	...
1912	561	41	2,830	...	...	...
1913	625	46	3,141	...	...	...
1914	673	50	3,395	...	...	...
1915	720	54	3,704	...	...	...
1916	750	58	3,962	...	...	...
1917	...	...	...	...	...	...
1918	779	65	3,966	...	...	...
1919	...	...	...	...	...	...
1920	841	71	4,593	...	...	...
1921	859	72	4,771	...	...	...
1922	889	78	4,877	...	...	...
1923	844	77	5,085	...	...	...
1924	785	71	4,600	...	...	...
1925	685	72	4,512	...	...	...
1926	747	72	4,704	...	...	...
1927	759	73	4,786	...	...	...
1928	634	68	4,421	...	...	...
1929	758	92	4,865	591	102	33
1930	635	85	4,991	650	112	37
1931	623	73	4,349	715	...	41
1932	599	80	4,462	787	135	45
1933	552	62	4,123	865	149	49
1934	569	64	4,515	952	164	54
1935	599	80	4,651	952	164	54
1936	...	...	...	...	...	...
1937	588	84	5,074	...	...	...
1938	636	86	5,559	...	...	...
1939	572	77	4,900	...	...	...
1940	391	33	5,334	857	141	...

C10   NORTH AMERICA: Numbers of Livestock (in thousands, poultry in millions)

El Salvador

	Horses[6]	Cattle	Pigs	Poultry[3]
1905	74	284	423	…
1929	66	338	335	…
1930	83	374	360	…
1931	103	438	367	…
1932	123	454	230	…
1933	150	523	336	…
1934	165	577	396	…
1935	181	609	425	…
1936	187	609	425	…
1937	201	670	543	…
1938	221	680	577	…
1939	114	451	598	1.2
1940	143	542	328	1.5
1941	192	716	481	2.4
1942	207	743	518	2.4
1943	183	673	417	1.9
1944	222	779	503	2.2

Guatemala

	Horses	Mules	Cattle	Pigs	Sheep	Goats	Poultry
1913	64	…	557	188	514	11	…
1914	114		655	177	402	59	…
1915	116		620	103	383	…	…
1920	63	…	297	41	105	…	…
1921	86	…	319	96	185	17	…
1922	55	…	246	33	113	9	…
1923	69	…	233	57	248	10	…
1924	72	…	245	53	114	18	…
1925	94	…	564	93	148	24	…
1926	55	…	260	51	98	16	…
1927	75	…	310	70	216	20	…
1928	53	…	298	89	241	24	…
1929	59	…	396	72	189	19	…
1930	63[7]	…	416[7]	79[7]	184[7]	21[7]	…
1931	57	…	387	87	147	16	…
1932	65	…	369	89	166	18	…
1933	79	…	451	103	179	22	…
1934	77	…	469	112	181	15	…
1935	81	…	445	120	196	17	…
1936	85	…	489	125	234	20	0.8[8]
1937	96	…	548	163	246	20	…
1938	127	…	523	155	241	22	…
1939	168	…	605	…	378	51	…
1940	117	…	612	276	383	44	…
1941	106	…	630	290	435	42	…
1942	107	…	729	290	438	44	…
1943	96	…	657	240	368	38	…

Haiti

	Horses	Asses	Cattle	Pigs	Sheep	Goats
1926	110	270	57	170	2	189
1927	115	310	67	185	5	216
1928	250	340	75	200	5	220
1929	280	340	80	220	8	240
1930	310	380	90	240	10	260
1931	350	400	92	260	12	280
1932	400	600	100	250	15	300
1933	400	650	105	350	15	310
1934	400	…	110	360	16	320
1935	400	…	125	375	16	330

Honduras

	Horses	Cattle	Pigs	Goats	Poultry
1910	64	466	…	[24][9]	…
1914	68	489	150	[23][9]	…
1930	167	517	298	9	2.0

For Jamaica see next page

Mexico

	Horses	Mules	Asses	Cattle
1900	859	334	288	5,142
1920	[929][10]	[354][10]	[288][10]	[2,163][10]
1926	1,036	686	850	5,585
1930	1,887	751	2,160	10,082
1940	1,757	933	2,342	11,622

	Pigs	Sheep	Goats	Poultry
1900	616	3,424	…	…
1920	[1,654][10]	[1,090][10]	[1,988][10]	…
1926	2,903	2,698	5,244	…
1930	3,698	3,674	6,544	20.7
1940	5,068	4,401	6,850	36.4

C10   NORTH AMERICA: Numbers of Livestock (in thousands, poultry in millions)

| | Jamaica | | | |
	Horses & Mules	Cattle	Pigs	Sheep
1869	74	122	...	...
1881	43	82	...	...
1882	48	85	...	...
1883	46	84	...	...
1884	62	133	...	...
1885	63	131	...	...
1886	66	118	...	...
1887	66	116	...	...
1888	68	114	...	...
1889	68	113	...	...
1890	68	113	...	14
1891	70	108	...	14
1892	69	98	...	16
1893	71	101	...	17
1894	69	104	...	15
1895	46	100	...	13
1896	47	120	...	14
1897	49	121	...	15
1898	49	122	...	15
1899	50	122	17	15
1900	55	119	18	16
1901	58	120	20	17
1902	58	120	20	17
1903	52	119	25	18
1904	74	108	27	20
1905	73	112	28	17
1906	68	110	29	16
1907	50	105	29	15
1908	52	102	30	14
1909	53	110	31	13
1910	52	111	32	12
1911	59	108	31	12
1912	54	116	31	12
1913	53	116	31	10
1914	55	115	31	11

| | Jamaica | | | | |
	Horses & Mules	Asses	Cattle	Pigs	Sheep
1915	51	...	114	31	9
1916	47	...	114	32	12
1917	50	...	167	...	12
1918	...	...	...	...	...
1919	...	17	170	...	...
1920	29	17	158	...	8
1921	...	17	141	...	8
1922	...	17	141	...	8
1923	...	16	112	...	5
1924	...	15	133	...	4
1925	...	15	133	...	5
1926	...	15	114	...	8
1927	...	14	116	...	5
1928	...	14	114	...	7
1929	...	13	106	...	7
1930	...	11	109	...	7
1931	...	10	110	...	8
1932	...	10	123	...	8
1933	...	8	124	...	8
1934	...	9	126	...	8
1935	...	9	122	...	8
1936	...	8	102	...	10
1937	...	10	126	...	9
1938	...	10	124	...	11
1943	38	51	226	218	13[12]

| | Nicaragua | | | |
	Horses	Cattle	Pigs	Poultry
1908	28	...	12	...
1930	150	800	400	1.5

| | Panama | | | |
	Horses	Cattle	Pigs	Poultry[3]
1916	15	200	30	...
1928	...	...	60	...
1929	...	...	67	...
1930	...	...	90	...
1931	...	...	105	...
1934	...	370	...	...
1935	...	...	...	0.3
1942	...	334	138	1.1
1943	...	382	150	1.2
1944	...	445	165	1.3

C10 NORTH AMERICA: Numbers of Livestock (in thousands, poultry in millions)

	Puerto Rico				
	Horses	Cattle	Pigs	Goats	Poultry[10]
1910	58	316	106	49	...
1920	57	279	137	58	...
1930	50	311	104	56	...
1935	43	285	113	57	...
1940	...	343	...	111	0.9

	USA											
	Horses	Mules	Cattle	Pigs	Sheep		Horses	Mules	Cattle	Pigs	Sheep	Poultry[11]
1867	6,820	1,000	28,636	34,389	44,997	**1905**	18,491	3,586	66,111	53,176	40,410	...
1868	7,051	1,057	29,238	33,304	43,808	**1906**	18,806	3,680	65,009	53,633	41,965	...
1869	7,304	1,130	30,060	32,570	39,802	**1907**	19,090	3,814	63,754	56,543	43,460	...
						1908	19,444	3,949	61,989	58,388	45,095	...
1870	7,633	1,245	31,082	33,781	36,449	**1909**	19,731	4,085	60,774	52,508	47,098	340
1871	8,054	1,305	32,107	36,688	34,063							
1872	8,441	1,360	33,078	39,296	34,312	**1910**	19,972	4,239	58,993	48,072	46,939	356
1873	8,767	1,419	33,830	39,794	35,782	**1911**	20,418	4,429	57,225	55,366	46,055	382
1874	9,055	1,485	34,821	38,377	36,234	**1912**	20,726	4,551	55,675	55,394	42,972	367
						1913	21,008	4,683	56,592	53,747	40,544	365
1875	9,333	1,548	35,361	35,834	37,237	**1914**	21,308	4,870	59,461	52,853	38,059	367
1876	9,606	1,608	36,140	35,715	37,477							
1877	9,910	1,674	37,333	39,333	38,147	**1915**	21,431	5,062	63,849	56,600	36,263	379
1878	10,230	1,746	39,396	43,375	38,942	**1916**	21,334	5,200	67,438	60,596	36,260	369
1879	10,574	1,816	41,420	43,767	41,678	**1917**	21,306	5,353	70,979	57,578	35,246	359
						1918	21,238	5,485	73,040	62,931	36,704	363
1880	10,903	1,878	43,347	44,327	44,867	**1919**	20,922	5,568	72,094	64,326	38,360	391
1881	11,187	1,912	44,501	43,076	47,371							
1882	11,444	1,928	45,738	42,566	48,883	**1920**	20,091	5,651	70,400	60,159	37,328	381
1883	11,794	1,975	47,387	43,440	50,935	**1921**	19,369	5,768	68,714	58,942	35,426	370
1884	12,215	2,047	49,804	45,961	51,101	**1922**	18,764	5,824	68,795	59,849	33,565	395
						1923	18,125	5,893	67,546	69,304	32,597	415
1885	12,700	2,102	52,463	47,330	49,620	**1924**	17,378	5,907	65,996	66,576	32,859	435
1886	13,276	2,162	54,868	45,457	46,654							
1887	13,821	2,213	56,602	42,563	44,217	**1925**	16,651	5,918	63,373	55,770	34,469	435
1888	14,490	2,260	58,599	42,134	43,011	**1926**	16,083	5,903	60,576	52,105	35,719	438
1889	15,064	2,295	59,178	44,508	42,365	**1927**	15,388	5,804	58,178	55,496	38,067	461
						1928	14,792	5,656	57,322	61,873	40,689	475
1890	15,732	2,322	60,014	48,130	42,693	**1929**	14,234	5,510	58,877	59,042	43,481	449
1891	16,329	2,377	59,968	47,435	43,882							
1892	16,846	2,459	58,126	45,165	44,628	**1930**	13,742	5,382	61,003	55,770	45,577	468
1893	17,289	2,550	55,119	43,652	44,567	**1931**	13,195	5,273	63,030	54,835	47,720	450
1894	17,709	2,632	51,713	46,522	43,414	**1932**	12,664	5,148	65,801	59,301	47,682	437
						1933	12,291	5,046	70,280	62,127	47,303	445
1895	17,849	2,708	49,510	47,628	41,827	**1934**	12,052	4,945	74,369	58,621	48,244	434
1896	17,876	2,782	49,205	49,154	39,609							
1897	17,803	2,836	50,447	51,232	38,891	**1935**	11,861	4,822	68,846	39,066	46,139	390
1898	17,698	2,918	52,868	53,282	40,097	**1936**	11,598	4,628	67,847	42,975	44,435	403
1899	17,728	3,012	55,927	51,558	42,688	**1937**	11,342	4,460	66,098	43,083	45,251	424
						1938	10,995	4,250	65,249	44,525	44,972	390
1900	17,856	3,139	59,739	51,055	45,065	**1939**	10,629	4,163	66,029	50,012	45,463	419
1901	17,955	3,190	62,576	50,681	46,126							
1902	17,968	3,264	64,418	47,858	46,196	**1940**	10,444	4,034	68,309	61,165	46,266	438
1903	18,121	3,353	66,004	48,100	44,436	**1941**	10,193	3,911	71,755	54,353	47,441	423
1904	18,331	3,465	66,442	51,623	41,908	**1942**	9,873	3,782	76,025	60,607	49,346	477
						1943	9,605	3,626	81,204	73,881	48,196	542
						1944	9,192	3,421	85,334	83,741	44,270	582

C10   NORTH AMERICA: Numbers of Livestock (in thousands, poultry in millions)

	Canada					Costa Rica			
	Horses	Cattle	Pigs	Sheep	Poultry[3]	Horses	Cattle	Pigs	Poultry[4]
1945	2,374	9,632	4,964	3,032	74.5	...	...	...	...
1946	2,136	9,174	4,277	2,792	73.2	...	...	...	...
1947	1,937	9,085	4,957	2,465	78.1	...	506	...	...
1948	1,789	8,984	3,946	2,050	62.6	...	515	...	...
1949	1,642	8,641	4,452	1,773	63.6	77	641	112	1.28
1950	1,496	8,343	4,372	1,579	55.8	80	685	112	1.32
1951	1,304	8,363	4,914	1,461	64.5	71	657	120	...
1952	1,179	9,153	5,428	1,534	59.0	80	696	103	1.39
1953	1,055	9,806	3,970	1,592	64.9	90	762	115	...
1954	917	10,170	4,440	1,636	69.4	80	705	115	...
1955	832	10,603	4,800	1,634	65.0	...	954	95	1.28
1956	782	11,011	4,731	1,620	67.5	...	...	...	...
1957	722	11,265	4,758	1,628	71.6	...	...	...	...
1958	661	10,990	5,931	1,630	72.3	...	1,002	...	...
1959	601	11,058	6,519	1,608	71.6	...	1,057	...	...
1960	555	11,337[12]	5,070[12]	1,607[12]	67.3[12]	94	1,097	130	1.60
		10,704	5,003	1,069	68.8				
1961	514	10,940	5,138	984	69.4	96	1,126	135	1.75
1962	480	11,214	4,995	904	64.9	100	1,122	135	1.81
1963	457	11,560	5,350	878	66.5	100	1,051	145	2.05
1964	427	11,908	5,577	852	68.6	101	1,117	171	2.20
1965	401	11,651	5,108	783	67.4	101	1,106	196	2.40
1966	389	11,757	5,785	700	71.7	103	1,294	221	2.78[4]
									3.25
1967	373	11,783	6,060	671	80.1	105	1,288	165	3.46
1968	363	11,409	5,697	620	76.9	107	1,350	170	3.68
1969	344	11,634	6,460	616	83.3	108	1,414	175	3.92
1970	328	11,992	7,735	670	92.5	109	1,496	198	3.98
1971	357	12,275	7,402	617	90.2	111	1,574	210	4.33
1972	353	12,615	6,960	597	91.0	113	1,655	225	4.45
1973	345	13,218	6,455	580	96.2	101	1,766	216	4.60
1974	345	14,016	5,913	559	87.0	110	1,741	220	4.80
1975	345	14,055	5,708	467	83.3	112	1,790	225	5.0
1976	350	13,710	6,170	418	70.6	107	1,841	215	5.0
1977	350	12,870	6,653	389	76.4	109	1,920	215	5.0
1978	350	12,328	8,074	430	78.5	111	2,002	215	5.0
1979	350	12,403	9,688	481	78.5	112	2,093	207	6.0
1980	370	12,166	10,190	530	80.4	113	2,181	223	5.0
1981	370	12,088	10,035	564	82.5	113	2,275	240	5.0
1982	370	12,638	10,286	809	77.0	113	2,276	243	5.0
1983	380	12,284	10,795	791	94.0	113	2,365	236	6.0
1984	380	12,160	10,154	748	93.0	113	2,429	223	6.0
1985	385	11,788	9,885	694	96.0	113	2,509	220	6.0
1986	340	11,750	10,476	701	98.0	114	2,415	222	5.0
1987	340	12,060	10,890	697	108.0	114	2,360	238	5.0
1988	340	12,195	10,763	728	107.0	114	1,753	223	4.0
1989	415	12,249	10,532	759	108.0	114	1,735	223	4.0
1990	415	12,843	10,172	780	110.0	114	1,762	224	4.0[13]
1991	415	11,713	10,498	654	98.0	114	2,175	225	14.0
1992	420	11,786	10,841	662	96.0	114	2,132	245	14.0
1993	420	12,306	11,200	691	96.0	114	2,122	244	14.0

C10   NORTH AMERICA: Numbers of Livestock (in thousands, poultry in millions)

			Cuba				
	Horses	**Mules**	**Cattle**	**Pigs**	**Sheep**	**Goats**	**Poultry[3]**
1945	311	25	3,884	669	114	85	...
1946	409	34	4,115	1,338	154	139	7.2
1947	...	...	4,100	...	...	...	...
1948	...	...	4,000	...	...	...	...
1949	...	...	4,100	...	...	...	...
1950	...	...	...	1,344	...	...	...
1951	...	...	4,116	1,286	...	...	6.9
1952	412	31	4,042	1,285	193	161	7.4
1953	...	...	...	1,340	...	...	...
1954	...	...	4,150	1,365	...	...	...
1955	400	32	4,500	1,395	210	180	7.7
1956	...	...	...	1,440	...	...	...
1957	...	...	...	1,500	...	...	...
1958	...	...	5,840	...	...	...	...
1959	...	...	5,760	...	...	...	...
1960	470	30	5,025	1,700	222	190	...
1961	480	30	5,776	1,750	215	170	...
1962	490	30	6,200	1,750	219	180	...
1963	500	30	6,378	1,540	148	190[13]	...
						65	
1964	500	24	6,611	1,746	170	71	...
1965	536	27	6,700	1,810	240	80	...
1966	550	31	6,774	1,670	245	81	...
1967	711	37	7,172	1,531	260	82	...
1968	695	37	7,250	1,500	270	82	...[14]
1969	696	38[13]	7,100[13]	1,490	280	84	12.4
		32	6,100				
1970	747	29	5,738	1,460	290	83	13.6
1971	765	27	5,487	1,450	300	83	13.3
1972	783	27	5,354	1,450	310	86	16.4
1973	799	26	5,486	1,450	320	88	15.9
1974	804	29	5,450	1,450	330	90	18.3
1975	811	27	5,622	1,460	340	92	18.1
1976	815	27	5,644	1,506	346[14]	94[14]	19.9
					112	23	
1977	819	27	...	...	123	22	19.7
1978	807	23	5,274	...[14]	134	20	22.4
1979	814	24	...	691	163	20	24.9
1980	812	25	5,057	765	209	21	24.6
1981	810	26	...	840	259	22	24.0
1982	790	26	...	853	318	25	23.1
1983	781	28	...	911	352	24	25.7
1984	759	29	5,115	1,009	441	30	26.7
1985	740	30	5,020	1,038	495	30	25.9
1986	740	30	5,007	1,101	...	...	25.0
1987	718	31	4,984	1,093	...	...	26.0
1988	703	32	4,927	1,169[33]	382	...	27.0
1989	630	31	4,920	1,850	385	...	28.0
1990	629	31	4,920	1,850	385	...	28.0
1991	629	32	4,700	1,900	385	...	28.0
1992	625	32	4,500	1,703	350	...	28.0
1993	580	32	4,500	1,603	310	...	25.0

C10 NORTH AMERICA: Numbers of Livestock (in thousands, poultry in millions)

	Dominican Republic							El Salvador				
	Horses	Mules	Asses	Cattle	Pigs	Goats	Poultry[3]	Horses[5]	Mules	Cattle	Pigs	Poultry[3]
1945	143	43	83	...	...	346	2.07	156	...	650	342	1.77
1946	136	42	77	597	547	304	1.99	157	...	686	284	1.76
1947	139	45	79	602	537	333	1.82	183[5]	...	765	348	1.89
1948	139	46	79	...	546	331	2.04	...	...	...	...	...
1949	142[13]	47	80	885	533	334[13]	2.17	...	...	...	...	...
1950	243	43	81	694	1,158	596	2.16	122	37	825	419	2.76
1951	...	45	79	769	641	...	1.53	...	...	...	...	...
1952	...	46[13]	75	857	833	...	1.73	...	...	615	265	...
1953	250	71	78[13]	933	888	...	2.69	87	29	827	261	1.77
1954	242	70	135	917	947	503	1.35	90	34	968	339	2.08
1955	242	70	136	923	1,408	700	1.05	90	37	1,304	291	1.83
1956	242	79	137	930	1,414	724	3.63	90	37	1,371	301	2.01
1957	242	81	139	936	1,523	749	3.50	91	37	917	267	1.77
1958	242	83	140	943	1,584	774	3.75	75	27	...	...	1.46
1959	241	84	142	949	1,648	801	4.79	...	...	827	221	...
1960	253	85	145	1,005	1,713	828	...	...	...	916	324	...
1961	255	85	145	1,005	1,171	852	4.9	74	27	...	323	1.85
1962	255	85	145	972	1,036	878	5.0	74	27	918	323	1.88
1963	255	85	145	981	900	902	5.2	74	27	919	323	1.90
1964	255	85	145	990	1,000	928	5.25	74	27	920	322	1.92
1965	203	89	149	1,000	1,175	954	5.3	74	27	925	322	1.98
1966	200	90	150	1,050	1,200	790	5.3[13] 6.3	70	27	1,340	408	2.00
1967	200	90	153	1,082	1,250	780	6.5	69	25	1,371	416	2.05
1968	190	91	154	1,090	1,275	780	6.7	68	24	1,410	417	2.10
1969	180	92	158[13] 129	1,100	1,300	775	7.0	67	23	1,241	421	2.14
1970	183	93	126	1,399	1,050	760	7.2	79	23	993	408	...
1971	180	94	125	1,423	1,100	750	7.3	81	22	1,000	415	...
1972	178	94	123	1,500	760	328	7.4	81	22	1,008	465	...
1973	200	94	121	1,837	750	335	7.1	81	22	1,038	480	...
1974	201	94	119	1,900	700	340	7.2	81	22	1,031	420	2.60
1975	202	95	119	1,950	705	350	7.3	81	21	1,109	425	2.76
1976	202	95	119	2,000	753	355	7.4	86	21	1,283	430	3.36
1977	203	96	119	2,050	718	360	7.6	87	21	1,350	515	4.41
1978	203	97	119	2,150	600	370	7.8	88	21	1,387	503	5.14
1979	204	97	119	2,153	250	380	8.0	89	22	1,440	560	5.30
1980	204	98	120	1,810	...	385	8.2	88	22	1,211	421	5.06
1981	204	99	120	1,949	...	385	8.3	88	22	1,106	386	5.0
1982	204	99	120	2,154	375	463	8.0	89	23	954	400	6.0
1983	204	99	120	2,020	...	465	9.0	90	23	937	400	4.0
1984	300	130	120	1,922	...	465	14.0	90	23	980	375	5.0
1985	300	130	140	2,055	368	480	17.0	92	23	1,050	397	5.0
1986	300	130	140	2,092	389	521	17.0	92	23	1,088	411	5.0
1987	310	132	142	2,129	409	534	19.0	93	23	1,144	418	5.0
1988	310	132	142	2,245	429	543	22.0	93	23	1,176	442	5.0
1989	310	132	142	2,240	431	550	25.0	93	23	1,220	450	5.0
1990	310	133	143	2,365	769	550	26.0	94	23	1,243	317	5.0
1991	315	133	143	2,356	750	560	30.0	95	23	1,257	308	4.0
1992	320	133	143	2,371	780	574	33.0	95	23	1,197	315	4.0
1993	320	135	145	2,450	900	587	33.0	96	24	1,256	325	4.0

C10   NORTH AMERICA: Numbers of Livestock (in thousands, poultry in millions)

	Horses	Mules	Cattle	Pigs	Sheep	Goats	Poultry[15]
				Guatemala			
1945	...	...	...	...	...	...	...
1946	...	...	...	...	...	...	...
1947	155	56	911	374	618	64	...
1948	157	60	893	415	718	79	...
1949	183	58	903	415	712	79	...
1950	...	...	...	...	...	...	4.5
1951	...	...	1,194	415	889	77	...
1952	...	62	1,270	462	813	134	...
1953	189	59	1,218	435	865	91	...
1954	171	57	993	390	739	86	...
1955	169	59	1,033	362	756	78	...
1956	177	57	1,049	401	826	84	...
1957	171	57	1,113	403	840	88	...
1958	174	55	1,142	406	792	89	...
1959	161	54	1,062	431	841	93	...
1960	166	54	1,134	409	677	89	...[15]
1961	156	53	1,122	388	792	86	4.8
1962	164	55	1,263	381	702	89	4.5
1963	156	53	1,324	438	748	89	5.4
1964	155	53	1,384	495	794	89	5.5
1965	154	53	1,328	543	818	90	5.7
1966	153	52	1,242	594	632	91	5.9
1967	152	51	1,371	662	565	92	6.1
1968	151	50	1,395	728	550	92	6.3
1969	150	50	1,443	806	631	66	6.6[15] / 9.3
1970	145	48	1,585	896	521	82	9.6
1971	140	45	1,740	881	528	80	9.7
1972	130	45	1,808	881	572	77	9.9
1973	130	40	1,562	646	414	76	10.1
1974	125	40	1,713	659	540	76	11.0
1975	102	43	2,270	522	470	76	12.2
1976	100	43	1,431	667	612	76	9.2
1977	100	43	1,500	704	600	76	11.2
1978	100	43	1,575	747	685	76	13.5
1979	100	43	1,653	792	679	76	13.8
1980	100	43	1,730	835	734	76	14.0
1981	100	43	2,280	...	...	76	14.2
1982	100	37	2,185	806	613	73	15.0
1983	100	37	2,224	806	657	76	15.0
1984	100	37	2,254	834	680	76	15.0
1985	100	38	2,160	862	660	75	15.0
1986	110	38	2,004	850	666	76	14.0
1987	112	38	2,010	820	667	76	15.0
1988	112	38	2,023	800	660	76	10.0
1989	112	38	2,032	1,100	670	77	10.0
1990	113	38	2,077	1,100	675	77	10.0
1991	114	38	2,097	650	430	78	15.0
1992	114	38	2,236	715	440	78	16.0
1993	116	38	2,210	720	440	78	16.0

C10 NORTH AMERICA: Numbers of Livestock (in thousands, poultry in millions)

	Haiti							
	Horses	**Mules**	**Asses**	**Cattle**	**Pigs**	**Sheep**	**Goats**	**Poultry**
1950	...	...	...	...	...	...	...	3.9
1951	...	...	...	...	...	...	...	...
1952	...	...	...	...	...	...	...	...
1953	...	...	...	...	...	...	...	4.7
1954	...	...	...	...	...	...	...	4.3
1955	...	...	...	...	...	...	...	4.1
1956	...	...	...	...	...	...	...	4.3
1957	...	...	...	...	...	...	...	4.7
1958	255	56	163	669	1,136	52	891	4.7
1959	...	...	...	...	...	...	...	4.8
1960	255	56	163	672	1,138	53	890	4.8
1961	255	60	163	675	1,235	54	967	4.4
1962	283	62	163	685	1,268	58	993	4.6[13]
								3.3
1963	290	64	163	690	1,301	59	1,019	3.3
1964	297	65	163	694	1,334	61	1,045	3.2
1965	303	67	150	699	1,367	62	1,070	3.0
1966	334	74	145	769	1,504	69	1,177	3.3
1967	367	81	141	845	1,654	76	1,295	3.6
1968	319	83	140[13]	900	1,700	78	1,300	3.6
1969	327	73	209	713	1,480	73	1,189	3.6
1970	335	74	214	718	1,520	74[13]	1,221	3.6[13]
						69		3.2
1971	344	76	219	722	1,560	71	1,245	3.2
1972	352	78	225	727	1,602	73	1,287	3.3
1973	361	80	230	732	1,645	75	1,321	3.4
1974	370	81	235	737	1,690	77	1,356	3.4
1975	379	83	240	742	1,735	79	1,380	3.5
1976	385	84	242	850	1,800	81	1,100	3.9
1977	392	85	245	900	1,900	83	945	4.0
1978	400	79	202	900	2,000	85	997	4.6
1979	407	80	204	1,000	1,500	87	995	4.7
1980	410	80	206	1,000	1,500	89	1,000	4.8
1981	415	81	208	1,100	1,100	90	1,000	4.9
1982	420	82	210	1,200	600	91	1,000	5.0
1983	425	83	212	1,300	500	92	1,100	7.0
1984	425	83	212	1,350	500	92	1,100	8.0
1985	425	83	212	1,350	500	92	1,100	8.0
1986	425	84	215	1,400	700	92	1,100	10.0
1987	430	84	216	1,474	750	93	1,150	12.0
1988	430	85	216	1,545	800	94	1,200	13.0
1989	432	86	217	1,550	800	95	1,250	14.0
1990	435	86	218	1,450	950	93	1,250	15.0
1991	435	86	218	1,400[13]	930[13]	92	1,200	15.0
1992	400	81	210	800	200	86	910	16.0
1993	400	80	210	800	200	83	910	16.0

C10 NORTH AMERICA: Numbers of Livestock (in thousands, poultry in millions)

	Horses	Mules	Asses	Cattle	Pigs	Goats	Poultry
				Honduras			
1945	147	66	20	849	318	24	...
1946	156	67	21	918	323	22	...
1947	155	75	21	945	399	24	...
1948	209	72	20	823	376	21	...
1949	198	69	22	856	407	33	...
1950	140	81	23	889	523	36	...
1951	188	77	28	907	521	39	2.0
1952	...	90	23	1,168	530	53	3.5
1953	...	93	23	1,124	...	...	6.6
1954	...	85	21	1,120	592	46	5.6
1955	192	86	22	1,121	615	46	5.6
1956	...	...	...	...	...	...	...
1957	...	...	...	...	...	...	...
1958	...	...	...	...	...	...	...
1959	...	...	...	...	...	...	...
1960	238	95	32	1,387	695	41	5.7
1961	252	99	35	1,454	711	43	5.2
1962	266	103	39	1,587	727	46	5.0
1963	274	106	40	1,635	749	47	4.6
1964	281	110	40	1,700	785	48	5.2
1965	282	110	40	1,720	901	50	5.8
1966	285	110	41	1,510	775	52	5.9
1967	288	115	42	1,540	787	53	6.1
1968	290	117	43	1,559	795	54	6.5
1969	285	118	44	1,578	803	55	6.8
1970	280	118	46	1,598	811	56	7.0
1971	275	118	48	1,618	824	57	7.3
1972	277	118	49	1,641	837	58	7.6
1973	280	118	50	1,795	511	59	7.7
1974	278	117	48	1,817	511	57	7.6
1975	280	118	49	1,839	520	58	7.6
1976	280[13]	118[13]	49[13]	1,862	525	16	7.8[13]
1977	152	68	22	1,900	530	15	4.2
1978	150	68	22	2,234	531	22	4.3
1979	149	68	21	2,262	534	22	4.4
1980	150	68	21	2,358	406	22	4.8
1981	151	68	21	2,499	409	22	4.9
1982	152	68	21	2,086	410	24	5.0
1983	167	68	22	2,695	491	26	5.0
1984	168	68	22	2,770	558	27	5.0
1985	169	68	22	2,803	563	28	5.0
1986	170	68	22	2,859	567	29	7.0
1987	170	69	22	2,824	600	25	8.0
1988	170	69	22	2,759	600	25	8.0
1989	170	69	22	2,424	728	27	7.0
1990	171	69	22	2,424	734	26	8.0
1991	172	69	22	2,388	740	27	11.0
1992	172	69	22	2,351	591	28	10.0
1993	172	69	22	2,077	596	27	14.0

C10 NORTH AMERICA: Numbers of Livestock (in thousands, poultry in millions)

	Jamaica						
	Horses & Mules	Asses	Cattle	Pigs	Sheep	Goats	Poultry
1945	...	...	...	...	...	...	...
1946	...	...	...	...	...	...	...
1947	...	...	...	...	...	...	...
1948	...	...	...	...	...	...	...
1949	...	...	...	...	...	...	...
1950	38	51	248	142	17	350	...
1951	38	51	248	142	17	350	...
1952	38	51	248	142	17	350	...
1953	38	51	248	142	17	350	...
1954	38	51	248	151	17	350	...
1955	38	51	248	152	17	350	...
1956	38	51	248	...	...	...	...
1957	24	64	276	212	12	224	1.3
1958	23	66	300	196	13	269	1.3
1959	22	66	300	196	13	269	1.4
1960	24	66	295	196	13	269	...
1961	17	39	240	128	10	270	1.6
1962	17	39	240	128	10	269	1.9
1963	17	39	240	128	10	270	2.0
1964	17	39	240	128	10	267	2.1
1965	17	39	240	150	10	312	2.1
1966	17	38	240	150	10	321	2.1
1967	17	37	240	160	11	330	2.2
1968	17	36	248	170	12	340	2.2
1969	17	34	270	180	13	358	2.2[13]
1970	16	32	270	190	7	360	2.2 / 3.1
1971	15	30	270	200	5	360	4.2
1972	15	30	272	210	5	300	3.5
1973	15	30	274	222	5	300	3.6
1974	15	30	276	230	5	320	3.6
1975	15	28	280	235	5	330	3.7
1976	15	27	282	240	6	340	3.8
1977	14	26	285	245	6	350	3.9
1978	14	26	290	250	6	370	4.0
1979	14	25	300	255	6	380	4.1
1980	13	25	305	260	6	390	4.2
1981	13	24	310	265	6	400	4.3
1982	14	24	310	230	3	410	4.0
1983	14	24	290	240	3	420	5.0
1984	14	23	280	245	3	430	5.0
1985	14	23	290	245	3	430	5.0
1986	14	23	290	246	3	440	5.0
1987	14	23	290	250	3	440	6.0
1988	[13]14	23	290	220	3	440	5.0
1989	4	23	290	240	3	440	6.0
1990	4	23	310	250	2	440	8.0
1991	4	23	320	250	2	440	8.0
1992	4	23	320	180	2	440	8.0
1993	4	23	330	180	2	440	8.0

C10 NORTH AMERICA: Numbers of Livestock (in thousands, poultry in millions)

	Horses	Mules	Asses	Cattle	Pigs	Sheep	Goats	Poultry[16]
				Mexico				
1945	2,641	1,001	2,471	12,783	...	4,742	6,885	...
1946	...	...	...	...	...	...	...	...
1947	2,685	1,120	2,505	12,743	5,622	4,897	6,894	38.0
1948	2,722	1,225	2,636	13,217	5,704	4,965	6,946	39.5
1949	...	...	...	...	...	...	...	...
1950	3,581	1,539	2,768	15,713	6,896	5,086	8,522	34.3
1951	...	...	...	...	...	...	...	...
1952	...	...	...	...	...	...	...	...
1953	4,235	1,975	2,990	18,078	7,919	5,385	9,394	81.4
1954	4,417	2,102	3,049	18,725	8,199	5,463	9,626	88.9
1955	4,607	2,237	3,109	19,397	8,489	5,542	9,865	97.2
1956	4,806	2,381	3,170	20,093	8,789	5,623	10,110	106.3
1957	5,013	2,535	3,233	20,814	9,101	5,705	10,362	116.2
1958	5,228	2,698	3,297	21,561	9,423	5,788	10,620	127.1
1959	...:13	...:13	...:13	...:13	...	...	...	...:16
1960	4,047	1,579	2,861	31,385	10,689	5,853	8,928	100.0
1961	4,169	2,141	2,946	30,800	11,231	5,994	9,197	96.0
1962	4,377	1,660	2,849	30,184	12,079	5,724	10,446	80.0
1963	4,600	1,731	3,087	28,914	12,507	5,783	11,367	63.4
1964	4,800	1,817	3,241	31,516	13,132	6,073	11,936	85.1
1965	4,750	1,908	3,403	22,395	13,751₁₃ 9,650	6,376	12,582₁₃ 9,300	89.3
1966	4,890	2,003	3,573	22,800	9,730	6,695	9,350	94.0
1967	5,038	2,775	3,353	23,294	9,756	6,639	9,392	99.0
1968	5,048	2,745	3,330	23,628	9,979	6,706	9,416	104.4
1969	5,743	3,173	3,519	24,876	10,298	6,113	9,127	132.6
1970	5,026	2,603	3,199	25,124	9,970	5,320	8,488	140.3
1971	4,423	2,655	3,039	25,827	10,983	5,480	8,063	142.6
1972	6,066	3,259	3,392	27,042	10,753	5,644	8,996	144.9
1973	6,127	2,719	3,289	27,585	10,860	5,380	9,871	147.2
1974	6,376	3,295	2,891	27,863	11,466	5,280	8,556	...
1975	6,490	3,302	3,318	28,376	11,694	5,300	8,627	133.6
1976	6,551	3,270	3,282	28,935	11,986	7,860	8,343	143.6
1977	6,479	3,239	3,245	29,333	12,321	7,856	8,193	150.2
1978	6,447	3,207	3,233	29,920	12,578	7,850	8,103	161.5
1979	6,300	3,109	3,233	34,590	13,222	7,318	7,185	169.8
1980	5,625	3,283	2,807	35,689	17,562	6,567	10,004	187.8
1981	5,635	3,447	2,812	36,839	18,373	6,657	10,320	204.8
1982	6,134	3,130	3,182	37,522	19,364	6,270	9,809	201.3
1983	6,134	3,130	3,182	30,374	19,393	6,120	9,553	203.7
1984	6,135	3,130	3,183	31,489	18,579	6,373	9,981	213.6
1985	6,140	3,130	3,183	31,123	18,397	5,699	10,079	219.0
1986	6,150	3,150	3,184	31,156	18,662	5,926	10,442	246.0
1987	6,160	3,160	3,185	31,200	15,884	5,761	10,086	224.0
1988	6,170	3,170	3,186	34,999	16,157	5,863	10,241	234.0
1989	6,170	3,170	3,186	30,900	17,300	5,846	9,086	238.0
1990	6,175	3,180	3,187	32,054	15,786	6,003	10,532	234.0
1991	6,180	3,186	3,188	29,847	16,502	5,300	11,008	248.0
1992	6,185	3,200	3,189	30,157	16,832	5,876	11,066	282.0
1993	6,191	3,210	3,190	30,649	18,000	5,905	10,450	285.0

C10   NORTH AMERICA: **Numbers of Livestock** (in thousands, poultry in millions)

	Nicaragua					Panama			
	Horses	Mules	Cattle	Pigs	Poultry	Horses	Cattle	Pigs	Poultry[3]
1945	...	...	...	...	...	...	534	184	1.4
1946	...	...	939	...	...	...	...	...	...
1947	185	57	978	664	...	119	576	209	1.5
1948	...	...	1,018	...	...	...	...	...	...
1949	...	...	1,060	...	...	...	...	...	...
1950	...	...	1,103	...	...	158	570	182	1.6
1951	114	...	1,182	234	1.2	...	...	...	...
1952	...	...	...	...	...	...	568	241	...
1953	...	...	...	...	...	171	579	226	1.7
1954	...	...	...	...	...	...	578[17]	215[17]	2.1[17]
1955	...	...	...	...	...	...	587	182	1.9
1956	...	...	...	...	...	...	614	182	1.9
1957	...	...	1,331	...	...	...	638	218	1.8
1958	...	...	...	...	...	...	661	246	2.1
1959	...	...	1,425	...	...	...	666	248	2.2
1960	164	40	1,496	388	1.8	160	773	...	2.4
1961	169	42	1,374	405	2.0	160	761	222	2.5
1962	175	44	1,651	423	2.2	160	835	204	2.4
1963	175	44	1,734	423	2.2	160	842	213	2.4
1964	175	44	1,821	424	2.3	160	891	189	2.2
1965	174	44	1,540	450	2.4	162	969	176	2.5
1966	173	44	2,020	524	2.7	161	1,011	167	2.7
1967	172	44	2,155	552	2.8	160	1,037	169	2.6
1968	171	44	2,293	583	2.8	159	1,119	174	2.6
1969	210	43	2,431	615	3.0	158	1,157	196	2.9
1970	...	42	...	624	3.1	163	1,188	195	2.9
1971	...	41	...	630	3.2	164	1,260	152	3.8
1972	230	41	2,295	590	3.3	164	1,289	159	3.7
1973	240	40	2,462	600	3.4	164	1,312	188	3.7
1974	250	44	2,558	650	3.9	164	1,333	175	3.8
1975	260	44	2,660	670	4.1	164	1,348	166	3.7
1976	270	44	2,768	690	4.3	164	1,361	179	4.3
1977	275	44	2,782	710	4.5	164	1,374	202	4.4
1978	280	44	2,737	725	4.1	164	1,395	204	4.9
1979	275	45	2,401	500	4.7	165	1,437	190	4.9
1980	270	45	2,324	510	4.8	165	1,405	195	4.8
1981	275	45	2,379	520	5.0	166	1,426	209	5.1
1982	270	45	2,116	540	5.0	166	1,456	206	5.0
1983	270	45	2,344	744	5.0	167	1,459	197	6.0
1984	270	45	2,369	745	5.0	168	1,452	195	6.0
1985	270	45	2,100	750	5.0	169	1,447	208	6.0
1986	255	45	1,850	749	7.0	170	1,430	250	7.0
1987	250	45	1,700	700	7.0	170	1,410	229	7.0
1988	250	45	1,650	680	7.0	171	1,423	211	6.0
1989	250	45	1,680	690	7.0	171	1,417	202	7.0
1990	250	45	1,600	695	7.0	151	1,388	226	7.0
1991	250	45	1,640	550	5.0	156	1,399	256	5.0
1992	155	45	1,645	530	6.0	155	1,427	292	6.0
1993	156	45	1,650	535	6.0	156	1,437	290	6.0

C10 NORTH AMERICA: Numbers of Livestock (in thousands, poultry in millions)

	Puerto Rico					USA[19]					
	Horses	Cattle	Pigs	Goats	Poultry[18]	Horses	Mules	Cattle	Pigs	Sheep	Poultry[11]
1945	...	...	...	...	...	8,715	3,235	85,573	59,373	39,609	516
1946	...	...	...	...	...	8,081	3,027	82,235	61,306	35,525	523
1947	50	384	220	103	...	7,340	2,789	80,554	56,810	31,805	467
1948	39	388	...	...	...	6,704	2,575	77,171	54,590	29,486	500
1949	36	400	...	...	...	6,096	2,402	76,830	56,257	26,940	431
1950	33	422[13]	227[13]	106[13]	...	5,548	2,233	77,963	58,937	26,182	457
1951	39	375	96	32	...	7,036		82,083	62,269	27,251	431
1952	31	386	91	31	0.8	6,150		88,072	62,117	27,944	427
1953	36	405	86	27	1.0	5,403		94,241	51,755	27,593	398
1954	40	408	97	24	0.8	4,791		95,679	45,114	27,079	397
1955	...	404	75	23	0.8	4,309		96,592	50,474	27,137	391
1956	...	408	97	24	0.7	3,958		95,900	55,354	26,890	384
1957	30	403	97	31	0.8	3,632		92,860	51,897	26,348	391
1958	31	412	102	26	1.1	3,415		91,176	51,517	27,167	374
1959	31	433	104	26	1.1	3,189		93,322	58,045	28,108	387
1960	31	473	163	26	1.2	3,089		96,236[19]	59,026[19]	28,849[19]	369[19]
1961	28	476	164	25	1.3[18] / 3.2	...		97,700	55,560	28,320	366
1962	23	495	163	25	3.5	...		100,369	56,619	26,719	377
1963	22	515	154	25	3.8	...		104,488	57,993	25,122	376
1964	21	498	162	25	3.6	...		107,903	56,757	23,455	382
1965	21	495	176	24	3.4	...		109,000	50,792	21,843	394
1966	19	490	180	24	3.6	...		108,862	47,414	21,456	393
1967	20	497	184	24	3.5	...		108,645	53,249	20,661	429
1968	19	507	194	23	3.6	...		109,152[20]	58,777	19,105	425
1969	18	518	191	21	3.9	...		109,885	60,632	18,332	424
1970	17	530	198	20	4.0	...		112,303	57,046	17,411	433
1971	18	538	210	20	4.4	...		114,578	67,433	16,898	406
1972	18	548	224	20	4.6	...		117,862	62,507	15,767[21] / 18,710	404
1973	19	541	233	20	4.5	...		121,534	59,180	17,724	409
1974	19	546	244	21	4.8	...		127,670	61,106	16,394	384
1975	19	561	269	21	5.0	...		132,028	54,693	14,515	380[11] / 2,950
1976	20	571	332	21	5.5	...		127,976	49,267	13,376	3,273
1977	20	562	279	21	5.5	...		122,810	54,934	12,766	3,394
1978	20	524	232	21	5.8	...		116,375	56,539	12,421	3,614
1979	20	479	212	21	6.8	...		110,864	60,356	12,365	3,951
1980	20	489	230	21	7.1	...		111,192	67,353	12,687	3,963
1981	20	536	216	21	7.5	...		114,321	64,512	12,936	4,148
1982	21	576	205	...	6.0	...		115,604	58,688	12,966	4,149
1983	21	593	203	...	6.0	...		115,001	54,534	12,140	4,184
1984	21	580	210	...	6.0	...		113,700	56,694	11,487	4,282
1985	21	600	206	15	7.0	...		109,749	54,073	10,443	4,479
1986	22	580	199	14	8.0	...		105,468	52,313	9,983	4,646
1987	22	579	195	14	9.0	...		102,118	50,920	10,334	5,003
1988	22	592	195	14	11.0	...		99,622	54,620	10,572	5,238
1989	22	601	199	15	10.0	...		98,065	55,469	10,858	5,517
1990	22	599	203	17	11.0	...		98,162	53,821	11,364	5,864
1991	23	429	209	22	12.0	...		98,896	54,427	11,200	6,137
1992	23	429	197	21	10.0	...		97,856	57,649	8,965	6,402
1993	23	429	194	20	11.0	...		99,176	58,202	8,305	6,694

C10   SOUTH AMERICA: NUMBERS OF LIVESTOCK (in thousands, poultry in millions)

				Argentina				
	Horses	**Mules**	**Asses**	**Cattle**	**Pigs**	**Sheep**	**Goats**	**Poultry**
1875	3,916	124	267	13,338	257	57,501	2,863	...
1888	4,263	...	...	21,964	403	66,701	...	...
1895	4,467	483	...	21,702	653	74,380	2,749	...
1908	7,531	465	...	29,117	1,404	67,212	...	18.1
1909	...	...	...	...	...	...	...	...
1910	8,435	...	...	28,828	...	73,013	...	...
1911	8,894	535	319	28,786	2,900	80,402	4,302	...
1912	9,239	556	328	29,123	3,045	83,546	4,431	...
1913	9,366[22]	584[22]	345[22]	30,796[22]	3,197[22]	81,485[22]	4,564[22]	...[22]
1914	8,324	565	260	25,867	2,901	43,225	4,325	28.9
1915	...	...	...	26,388	...	43,677	...	...
1916	...	...	...	...	...	...	...	...
1917	8,823	595	276	27,053	3,260	44,855	4,583	...
1918	...	...	...	...	...	...	...	...
1919	9,293	611	284	27,721	3,199	45,767	4,763	...
1920	9,367	618	287	27,943	3,237	45,996	4,796	...
1921	...	...	...	28,138	3,221	46,134	4,820	...
1922	9,432	623	289	37,065	1,437	36,209	4,820	...
1930	9,858	660	377	32,212	3,769	44,413	5,647	47.1
1934	...	...	...	38,868	...	39,330	...	...
1937	8,319	517	264	33,207	3,966	43,883	4,649	52.9
1938	8,262	...	...	34,318	3,382	45,917	4,761	...
1942	6,757	509	...	31,460	5,707	50,904	2,838	...

				Bolivia				
	Horses	**Mules**	**Asses**	**Cattle**	**Pigs**	**Sheep**	**Goats**	**Poultry**
1910	97	45	173	734	114	1,449	468	...
1925	198	155	189	2,145	362	3,436	348	...
1926	204	175	190	2,320	498	4,220	442	...
1927	320	...	...	1,404	268	4,151	416	...
1928	373	246	140	1,855	336	5,552	748	...
1929	384	256	156	1,960	384	4,786	978	...
1930	386	260	158	2,050	390	5,020	979	...
1931	390	264	160	2,064	398	5,232	987	5.1
1938	...	...	...	1,842	523	2,608	...	...

C10   SOUTH AMERICA: Numbers of Livestock (in thousands, poultry in millions)

			Brazil				
	Horses	**Mules & Asses**	**Cattle**	**Pigs**	**Sheep**	**Goats**	**Poultry**[28]
1912	7,290	3,208	30,705	18,401	10,550	10,049	...
1916	6,065	3,222	28,962	17,329	7,205	6,920	...
1920	5,254	1,865	34,271	16,169	7,933	5,087	...
1931	6,836	2,813	47,530	22,147	10,709	5,273	...
1935	6,052	3,233	40,514	23,183	12,645	5,871	...
1937	6,202	3,387	40,860	25,398	13,560	6,019	...
1938	6,713	4,119	41,883	23,543	14,167	5,906	...
1939	6,583	3,948	40,745	21,763	10,745	6,006	...
1940	6,462	3,712	41,546	21,687	10,855	6,221	59.3

		Chile				
	Horses	**Cattle**	**Pigs**	**Sheep**	**Goats**	**Poultry**[23]
1900	...	830	...	1,335	...	...
1902	...	969	...	1,009	...	...
1906	...	2,675	339	4,528	...	...
1907	...	...	...	...	...	...
1908	517	2,304	216	4,224	...	...
1909	...	...	...	...	...	...
1910	347	1,635	178	1,636	205	...
1911	352	1,640	160	3,538	210	...
1912	421	1,760	166	4,169	273	...
1913	489	2,084	184	4,567	288	...
1914	458	1,969	221	4,602	299	...
1915	458	1,944	229	4,545	394	...
1916	443	1,869	260	4,568	386	...
1917	403	2,030	301	4,183	376	...
1918	411	2,225	326	4,434	451	...
1919	392	2,163	292	4,500	460	...
1922	329	1,996	263	4,569	525	...
1925	324	1,918	247	4,094	357	...
1930	441	2,388	331	6,263	789	...
1935	...	2,463	...	...	...	...
1936	528	2,573	572	5,749	810	...
1937	...	2,460	...	...	...	...
1938	...	2,635	...	...	...	...
1939	...	2,356	...	...	...	1.1
1940	...	2,421	...	...	...	0.9
1941	...	2,418	...	...	...	1.2
1942	...	2,346	...	...	...	1.2
1943	...	2,391	...	...	...	1.3
1944	...	2,311	...	...	...	1.6

C10 SOUTH AMERICA: Numbers of Livestock (in thousands, poultry in millions)

		Colombia					
	Horses	Mules	Asses	Cattle	Pigs	Sheep	Goats
1915	526	340		3,005	711	...	164
1924	964	354	160	6,500	1,338	771	405
1925	978	354	138	6,476	1,366	780	407
1926	980	360	140	6,500	1,400	800	410
1927	978	346	157	6,727	1,366	771	407
1928	...	...	...	...	...	...	...
1929	929	329	149	7,343	1,434	810	427
1932	926	453	288	7,592	1,545	831	518
1934	972	476	303	7,972	1,622	872	544
1935	...	...	...	8,337	...	...	...
1938	...	...	...	9,018	...	...	...

	Ecuador		
	Horses	Pigs	Goats
1934	85	...	300
1935	80	...	350
1938	103	...	...
1939	104	350	...
1941	117	820	...
1943	117	836	...

				Falkland Islands					
	Sheep		Sheep		Sheep		Sheep		Sheep
1850	0.6	1870	65	1980	667	1910	725	1930	607
1851	0.5	1871	78	1891	643	1911	706	1931	609
1852	1.0	1872	125	1892	771	1912	711	1932	616
1853	2.0	1873	149	1893	763	1913	698	1933	615
1854	2.5	1874	179	1894	791	1914	701	1934	607
1855	3.0	1875	185	1895	762	1915	891	1935	616
1856	3.0	1876	271	1896	732	1916	690	1936	609
1857	4.5	1877	283	1897	786	1917	697	1937	604
1858	7.7	1878	351	1898	780	1918	670	1938	602
1859	7.9	1879	411	1899	762	1919	670	1939	601
1860	11	1880	...	1900	778	1920	646	1940	605
1861	12	1881	...	1901	762	1921	668	1941	624
1862	15	1882	429	1902	714	1922	667	1942	634
1863	19	1883	473	1903	681	1923	647	1943	633
1864	26	1884	517	1904	702	1924	635	1944	628
1865	27	1885	486	1905	701	1925	631		
1866	31	1886	563	1906	703	1926	606		
1867	35	1887	582	1907	696	1927	607		
1868	58	1888	590	1908	689	1928	631		
1869	60	1889	676	1809	716	1929	613		

C10 SOUTH AMERICA: Numbers of Livestock (in thousands, poultry in millions)

	Guyana				Guyana		
	Cattle	Pigs	Sheep		Cattle	Pigs	Sheep
1903	70	12	12				
1904	86	12	17				
1905	77	13	18	**1925**	135	16	24
1906	85	16	24	**1926**	138	16	29
1907	72	13	17	**1927**	141	18	24
1908	70	13	18	**1928**	154	24	26
1909	72	13	17	**1929**	154	23	27
1910	72	17	18	**1930**	155	24	29
1911	81	17	19	**1931**	181	21	22
1912	72	17	18	**1932**	186	18	33
1913	81	14	19	**1933**	160	19	35
1914	90	11	20	**1934**	150	14	18
1915	98	14	22	**1935**	128	23	28
1916	93	12	23	**1936**	131	23	26
1917	99	12	22	**1937**	130	27	33
1918	77	13	21	**1938**	135	26	33
1919	79	15	19	**1939**	133	27	32
1920	112	17	21	**1940**	135	24	33
1921	123	12	20	**1941**	141	23	34
1922	112	13	17	**1942**	158	25	48
1923	102	12	15	**1943**	160	42	36
1924	113	13	16	**1944**	171	46	37

	Paraguay				
	Horses	Cattle	Pigs	Sheep[30]	Goats
1915	478	5,249	61	600	87
1918	490	5,500	87	600	93
1926	210	2,973	45	195	…
1932	372	3,984	52	229	…
1933	296	3,244	49	203	…
1934	237	2,920	29	142	…
1935	186	3,052	33	136	…
1936	198	3,219	35	146	…
1940	…	…	…		
1941	…	…	…	220	
1942	214	4,030	50	…	
1943	…	…	…	250	
1944	135	3,187	59	255	

	Peru						
	Horses	Mules	Asses	Cattle	Pigs	Sheep & Goats	Poultry
1917	…	…	…	1,000	400	6,900	…
1921	…	…	…	1,302	…	11,056	…
1922	…	…	…	1,293	429	11,334	…
1924	193	…	…	…	…	…	…
1929	432	130	265	1,806	689	11,209	3.2

C10   SOUTH AMERICA: Numbers of Livestock (in thousands, poultry in millions)

	Horses[24]	Mules & Asses[24]	Cattle	Pigs[24]	Sheep[24]	Poultry[3]
			Uruguay			
1860	518	813	3,632	6	1,990	...
1897	357	...	4,963	30	14,452	...
1898	364	...	4,927	35	15,538	...
1899	395	...	5,219	34	15,122	...
1900	561	...	6,827	94	18,609[24]	...
1901	575	...	6,327	48	17,625	...
1902	660	...	7,029	52	17,927	...
1903	578	...	6,948	49	18,559	...
1904	479	...	7,305	41	14,416	...
1905	450[24]	...	6,029	36[24]	13,916[24]	...
1908	556	...	8,193	180	26,286	...
1916	555	...	7,802	304	11,473	...
1924	513	...	8,432	251	14,443	...
1927	...	...	...	...	22,500	...
1930	623	...	7,128	308	20,558	...
1932	...	...	7,372	...	15,406	...
1937	644	...	8,297	346	17,931	4.8

	Horses	Mules	Asses	Cattle	Pigs	Sheep	Goats
				Venezuela			
1804	180	90	...	1,200	...	...	...
1839	78	39	141	2,086	363	1,910 (sheep & goats)	
1873	94	47	281	1,390	363	1,128 (sheep & goats)	
1876	385 (horses & mules)		520	2,158	660	2,309 (sheep & goats)	
1883	292	248	659	2,927	976	3,491 (sheep & goats)	
1886	622 (horses & mules)		770	5,275	1,439	4,646 (sheep & goats)	
1887	365	289	813	6,687	1,666	5,158 (sheep & goats)	
1888	388	301	859	8,476	1,930	5,728 (sheep & goats)	
1894	209	89	383	2,352	1,618	134	1,561
1899	191	—	—	2,004	...	1,844 (sheep & goats)	
1910	111	28	141	1,750	195	1,026 (sheep & goats)	
1918	157	53	195	1,516	501	113	2,155
1920	...	...	...	2,078	...	...	...
1921	168	55	200	2,600	512	...	...
1922	...	...	...	2,278	...	...	...
1924	115	49	121	2,327	295	1,079 (sheep & goats)	
1929	...	...	...	2,750	500	125	2,250
1936	194	43	191	3,091	...	...	...
1937	209	47	248	4,300	296	108	1,365

C10   SOUTH AMERICA: Numbers of Livestock (in thousands, poultry in millions)

	Argentina							
	Horses	Mules	Asses	Cattle	Pigs	Sheep	Goats	Poultry
1945	7,473	...	...	...	8,010	56,182	...	...
1946	...	...	...	...	...	...	...	...
1947	7,238	330	170	41,268	2,981	50,857	4,934	...
1948	...	...	...	...	3,500	...	...	...
1949	...	...	...	...	...	...	...	...
1950	...	...	...	...	...	...	...	...
1951	7,265	...	...	...	...	...	...	...
1952	...	...	...	...	...	...	...	...
1953	7,181	402	...	45,750	4,020	56,216	...	43.8
1954	...	...	...	43,596	3,512	46,772	...	...
1955	...	...	...	...	...	43,785	...	44.5
1956	5,872	...	...	46,940	4,011	45,166	1,476	...
1957	5,428	...	...	43,980	3,489	45,931	...	...
1958	4,846	...	...	40,736	3,142	47,010	...	...
1959	4,701	...	...	41,206	3,501	48,847	...	...
1960	4,800	...	...	44,550	3,800	50,200	...	45.0
1961	4,184	300	100	43,165	3,787	50,150	5,000	47.5
1962	3,930	300	100	43,300	3,075	47,305	4,970	41.8
1963	3,761	300	100	40,009	3,417	46,158	4,980	41.0
1964	3,763	300	100	42,300	3,400	47,500	4,998	31.5
1965	3,760	300	100	46,709	3,700	49,000	5,098	35.0
1966	3,780	300	100	48,800	3,100	48,500	5,200	34.0
1967	3,800	280	98	51,227	3,000	48,000	5,280	38.5
1968	3,700	270	97	51,465	3,400	47,800	5,300	42.1
1969	3,650	270	95	48,298	4,098	44,320	5,330	44.7
1970	3,620	260[13] 200	94	48,440	4,400	43,000	5,380	50 8
1971	3,600	...	94	49,786	4,900	41,000	5,300	34.5
1972	3,540	...	90	52,300	4,500	40,000	5,250	35.2
1973	3,500	170	85	54,771	5,000	40,000	5,500	34.0
1974	3,500	167	88	55,355	4,127	34,691	5,400	36.0
1975	3,400	165	90	58,700	4,200	34,000	4,000	34.7
1976	3,500	165	90	58,174	4,127	34,485	4,000	32.4
1977	3,073	165	90	61,054	3,332	35,220	3,500	31.3
1978	3,050	165	90	57,791	3,600	34,200	3,200	32.0
1979	3,000	165	90	56,864	3,552	35,220	3,000	35.4
1980	3,000	165	90	55,760	3,800	32,000	3,000	38.8
1981	3,073	165	90	54,235	3,900	31,418	3,000	40.0
1982	3,000	165	90	52,717	3,900	30,401	3,000	42.0
1983	3,050	165	90	53,937	3,800	30,000	2,900	43.0
1984	2,970	165	90	54,594	3,800	33,800	3,098	42.0
1985	3,000	165	90	54,000	4,000	29,441	3,100	42.0
1986	3,000	165	90	53,480	4,100	29,243	3,100	47.0
1987	3,000	165	90	51,683	4,100	28,750	3,100	42.0
1988	2,900	168	90	50,782	4,100	29,167	3,200	45.0
1989	2,900	170	90	50,582	4,200	29,345	3,200	43.0
1990	3,400	172	90	50,080	4,400	31,473	3,300	43.0
1991	3,400	172	90	50,020	4,600	28,571	3,320	40.0
1992	3,300	173	90	50,856	2,100	25,706	3,350	54.0
1993	3,300	174	90	50,000	2,200	18,468	3,370	58.0

C10   SOUTH AMERICA: Numbers of Livestock (in thousands, poultry in millions)

	Bolivia							
	Horses	Mules	Asses	Cattle	Pigs	Sheep	Goats	Poultry[3]
1947	256	102	301	3,041	1,020	4,289	1,089	...
1948	442	109	519	3,499	1,465	4,195	1,910	...
1949	...	...	...	...	1,200	...	...	
1950	...	...	...	3,849	...	...	...	1.6
1951	...	...	...	2,227	...	...	...	...
1952	...	...	...	...	...	...	...	...
1953	...	...	207	...	...	...	...	...
1954	...	...	...	2,260	...	6,464	...	...
1955	...	...	...	...	...	...	...	...
1956	...	...	...	...	...	...	...	...
1957	...	...	...	...	...	...	...	...
1958	...	...	...	...	...	...	...	...
1959	189	49	399	2,449	596	5,549	1,176	2.0
1960	...	...	...	...	...	...	...	...
1961	191	56	445	...	619	5,965	1,700	...
1962	193	59	468	2,490	631	6,174	1,764	2.1
1963	194	62	490	2,739	642	6,300	1,940	2.2
1964	195	66	513	2,672	654	6,097	1,250	2.2
1965	214	72	550	2,693	704	6,144	1,259	2.2
1966	223	73	560	2,700	710	6,150	2,000	2.9
1967	244	75	590	2,132	719	6,378	2,100	3.0
1968	264	81	620	2,184	777	6,460	2,150	3.0
1969	284	85	640	2,238	837	6,723	2,300	3.1
1970	290	86	650	2,291	900	6,787	2,400	3.1
1971	300	88	670	2,132	953	6,965	2,300	3.2
1972	300	90	660	2,200	1,000	7,144	2,543	3.3[13]
								4.8
1973	310	90	660	2,277	1,050	7,323	2,645	5.0
1974	320	92	683	2,366[13]	1,103	7,506	2,748	5.0
				2,755				
1975	340	92	701	2,877	1,158	7,694	2,793	5.2
1976	360	94	720	3,398	1,232	7,988	2,893	7.1
1977	370	96	740	3,578	1,292	8,229	2,914	8.0
1978	380	98	760	3,772	1,351	8,462	2,946	8.2
1979	390	100	770	3,990	1,412	8,722	2,978	8.3
1980	400	102[25]	770[25]	4,699[13]	1,601	9,057	2,007	8.5
1981	410	104	780	4,488	1,647	9,308	2,013	8.8
1982	410[13]	105[13]	790[13]	4,602	1,706	9,677	2,045	9
1983	300	82	600	4,878	1,910	10,632	1,757	10
1984	293	80	600	4,149	...	5,152	1,296	6
1985	311	80	600	4,333	1,725	5,553	1,298	7
1986	310	80	600	4,584	1,650	5,995	1,383	9
1987	315	80	610	4,898	1,902	6,478	1,507	11
1988	315	80	620	5,402	2,019	7,005	...	12
1989	320	80	630	5,476	2,127	...	...	14
1990	320	80	630	5,543	2,176	...	...	18
1991	320	80	630	5,607	2,177	7,342	1,448	30
1992	322	81	631	5,779	2,226	7,472	1,441	32
1993	322	81	631	5,794	2,273	7,512	1,450	33

C10   SOUTH AMERICA: Numbers of Livestock (in thousands, poultry in millions)

				Brazil				
	Horses	Mules	Asses	Cattle	Pigs	Sheep	Goats	Poultry[28]
1946	6,522	2,717	1,344	44,613	24,344	13,283	6,768	...
1947	6,768	2,952	1,374	46,358	23,815	15,542	7,363	...
1948	6,907	2,908	1,464	47,927	22,503	14,640	7,869	...
1949	6,928	3,097	1,536	50,178	23,881	13,804	8,309	57.3
1950	...	...	...	...	...	...	...	59.1
1951	6,937	3,101	1,572	52,655	26,059	14,251	8,526	61.0
1952	6,994	3,181	1,593	53,513	27,801	15,891	8,840	65.8[28]
								116.3
1953	7,111	3,215	1,611	55,854	30,916	16,264	8,822	127.3
1954	7,059	3,133	1,612	57,626	32,721	16,800	8,915	...
1955	7,286	3,241	1,674	61,442	35,555	17,503	9,481	146.7
1956	7,564	3,390	1,774	63,608	38,606	18,484	9,879	146.7
1957	7,935	3,576	1,876	66,695	41,416	18,867	10,339	157.8
1958	8,128	3,760	1,967	69,548	44,190	20,164	10,640	161.0
1959	8,185	3,917	1,946	71,420	45,262	19,921	10,194	166.9
1960	8,333	4,047	2,031	72,829	46,823	18,995	10,644	175.4
1961	8,273	4,081	2,175	73,962	47,944	18,162	11,195	185.8
1962	8,374	4,205	2,256	76,176	50,051	19,162	11,560	197.5
1963	8,692	4,421	2,393	79,076	52,941	19,718	12,397	208.2
1964	8,903	4,586	2,552	79,855	55,990	21,033	13,210	238.2
1965	9,222	4,749	2,727	84,167	58,705	21,906	13,826	254.4
1966	9,344	4,856	2,851	90,505	62,534	22,312	14,253	255.6
1967	9,155	4,745	2,858	89,969	62,080	22,170	13,927	263.0
1968	9,238	4,804	2,971	89,896	63,406	23,065	14,332	270.6
1969	9,146	4,830	2,996	92,739[13]	64,924	24,606	14,815	275.9
				72,966				
1970	9,100	4,796	2,958	75,447	65,867[13]	24,449	14,637	281.1
					30,846			
1971	9,114	4,793	2,952	78,452	31,541	24,270	14,609	224.1
1972	8,992	4,710	2,800	81,000	32,100	25,000	14,440	235.3
1973	9,350[13]	4,700[13]	2,800[13]	85,000	33,000	25,500[13]	16,000[13]	255.0
1974	6,889	1,702	1,984	90,437	37,587	18,356	6,394	271.7
1975	5,217	1,755	1,568	92,495	34,192	18,877	7,171	274.3
1976	5,507	1,822	1,691	102,532	37,640	17,828	7,101	311.9
1977	5,157	1,631	1,464	107,349	38,742	18,002	7,485	339.0
1978	4,934	1,514	1,423	107,297	34,532	18,009	7,424	331.6
1979	4,853	1,488	1,363	106,943	33,699	17,418	7,665	345.7
1980	4,928	1,586	1,340	109,177	35,695	17,806	8,070	387.7
1981	5,055	1,605	1,330	118,971	34,183	18,381	8,326	441.3
1982	5,227	1,750	1,331	121,785	32,429	19,054	8,865	450.0
1983	5,260	1,829	1,316	123,488	33,176	18,588	9,037	469.9
1984	5,289	1,836	1,237	124,186	31,678	18,121	8,936	450.8
1985	5,442	1,946	1,246	127,655	32,327	18,447	9,675	462.8
1986	5,550	1,943	1,274	128,423	32,248	18,473	10,020	470.1
1987	5,735	1,921	1,286	128,918	32,121	19,660	10,595	495.6
1988	5,855	1,952	1,295	131,503	32,480	20,085	10,792	514.5
1989	6,098	2,009	1,322	144,154	33,015	20,041	11,669	531.2
1990	6,121	2,032	1,343	147,102	33,623	20,014	11,994	546.2
1991	6,237	2,035	1,364	152,135	34,290	20,128	12,172	594.4
1992	6,329	2,046	1,381	154,441	34,532	19,955	12,160	640.1
1993	6,314	1,993	1,302	155,134	34,184	18,008	10,618	654.2

C10 SOUTH AMERICA: Numbers of Livestock (in thousands, poultry in millions)

	Chile					
	Horses	**Cattle**	**Pigs**	**Sheep**	**Goats**	**Poultry**[23]
1945	...	2,348	...	5,900	...	1.7
1946	...	2,397	...	5,700	...	2.2
1947	523	2,338	585	6,432	636	2.2
1948	523	2,324	585	6,435	636	2.2[23]
1949	...	2,344	600	6,435	636	...
1950	...	2,331	660	...	...	...
1951	...	2,186	875	5,794	...	...
1952	500	2,592	894	5,797	...	...
1953	451	2,594	913	5,800	...	...
1954	605	2,595	978	5,933	1,099	...
1955	500	2,856	741	6,540	1,300	...
1956	571	2,560	1,032	5,947	1,300	...
1957	573	2,900	986	6,067	...	...
1958	555	2,912	931	6,136	...	...
1959	554	2,809	964	6,298	...	...
1960	558	2,913	958	6,343	1,380	...
1961	555	2,990	950	6,436	1,400	9.6
1962	547	3,046	950	6,422	1,421	10.3
1963	494	3,017	959	6,552	1,030	11.0
1964	478	2,845	1,022	6,690	980	11.7
1965	475	2,870	1,007	6,596	933	12.0
1966	470	2,900	1,022	6,502	930	13.0
1967	465	3,097	1,085	6,675	925	14.0
1968	460	2,876	1,090	6,600	920	15.5
1969	480	2,911	1,120	6,500	910	16.5
1970	478	2,999	1,140	6,400	900	17.0
1971	475	2,860	1,040	5,907	870	18.0
1972	480	3,188	966	5,529	850	19.0
1973	470	3,165	968	5,353	830	19.5
1974	450	3,457	866	5,544	830	18.0
1975	450	3,606	701	5,644	800	18.5
1976	443	3,389	895	5,674	584	19.5
1977	450	3,427	924	5,699	600	20
1978	450	3,487	979	5,692	600	22
1979	450	3,575	1,036	5,928	600	24
1980	450	3,664	1,068	6,064	600	25
1981	450	3,750	1,100	6,185	600	26
1982	430	3,800	1,150	6,000	600	21
1983	450	3,865	1,100	6,200	600	20
1984	480	3,650	1,070	6,000	600	18
1985	490	3,400	1,100	5,800	600	19
1986	490	3,217	1,150	5,980	600	19
1987	490	3,371	1,300	6,470	600	23
1988	490	3,468	1,360	6,429	600	26
1989	500	3,336	1,400	6,600	600	27
1990	520	3,336	1,500	6,650	600	29
1991	530	3,404	1,300	6,400	600	35
1992	530	3,461	1,226	4,689	600	42
1993	500	3,557	1,288	4,629	600	43

C10 SOUTH AMERICA: Numbers of Livestock (in thousands, poultry in millions)

	Colombia							
	Horses	**Mules**	**Asses**	**Cattle**	**Pigs**	**Sheep**	**Goats**	**Poultry**
1945	...	...	...	12,570	...	...	...	...
1946	1,077	476	252	13,169	1,679	1,168	653	...
1947	1,183	528	260	14,542	2,162	1,022	470	...
1948	...	...	...	...	2,470	1,062	531	...
1949	...	...	...	...	...	1,198	...	18.6
1950	1,298	542	461	15,512	2,782	1,339	638	21.1
1951	...	...	...	...	...	1,350	...	...
1952	...	...	...	...	...	1,341	...	...
1953	...	...	...	...	...	...	...	...
1954	[1,159][26][27]	[410][26][27]	[282][26][27]	[10,994][26][27]	[1,824][26][27]	[1,114][26][27]	[294][26][27]	[14.4][26]
1955	[1,285][26]	[459][26]	[325][26]	[12,500][26]	[1,727][26]	[1,128][26]	[342][26]	[15.0][26]
1956	1,331	492	353	[13,390][26]	[1,455][26]	[1,126][26]	[215][26]	[14.0][26]
1957	...	...	...	...	...	...	...	...
1958	...	...	...	14,840	...	...	...	...
1959	...	...	...	15,100	...	...	...	...
1960	1,155	440	359	15,400	1,994	1,260	[350][26]	18.0
1961	1,100	420	361	15,627	2,000	1,100	[357][26]	19.7
1962	937	360	297	15,861	2,700	1,400	[360][26]	22.0
1963	960	370	298	16,099	2,400	1,500	[370][26]	25.0
1964	983	380	298	14,116	2,326	1,630	[374][26]	25.5
1965	951	356	368	15,020	2,400	1,702	688	21.5
1966	975	375	400	18,082	2,300	1,720	765	25.3
1967	1,086	400	436	18,883	2,058	1,966	865	30.3
1968	1,098	400[13]	438[13]	19,576	3,708	1,500	886	32.7
		350	330					
1969	778	353	315	20,200	1,420	1,818	630	35.4
1970	839	367	327	20,800	1,470	1,962	654	32.0
1971	866	381	340	21,400	1,520	2,025	660	33.2
1972	859	385	356	22,100	1,540	2,036	660	33.5
1973	860[13]	420	450	23,032	1,729	1,619	637	35.0
	1,331							
1974	1,379	484	526	22,501	1,805	1,888	675	40.0
1975	1,435	499	543	23,222	1,877	1,921	626	42.7
1976	1,485	515	560	23,859	1,876	2,026	623	47.1[13]
1977	1,535	531	578	24,335	1,876	2,138	626	28.9
1978	1,588	548	597	24,342	1,884	2,255	632	30.8
1979	1,644	552	616	24,132	1,916	2,357	639	27.1
1980	1,696	587	640	23,945	2,078	2,413	645	30
1981	1,710	590	645	24,251	2,094	2,427	652	31
1982	1,744	595	650	24,499	2,179	2,749	657	33
1983	1,779	600	650	24,000	2,244	2,660	729	34
1984	1,815	600	650	22,441	2,312	2,689	797	35
1985	1,906	600	650	23,271	2,381	2,500	879	35
1986	1,950	600	650	23,593	2,440	2,568	905	35
1987	1,950	600	650	23,971	2,511	2,652	932	36
1988	1,950	612	693	24,245	2,580	2,614	970	39
1989	1,974	618	703	24,598	2,600	2,650	930	40
1990	1,975	618	703	24,550	2,640	2,690	990	42
1991	1,980	620	705	24,350	2,642	2,550	964	43
1992	2,000	620	705	24,772	2,644	2,553	968	55
1993	2,000	620	710	25,324	2,635	2,540	960	62

C10 SOUTH AMERICA: Numbers of Livestock (in thousands, poultry in millions)

	Ecuador								Falkland Islands
	Horses	Mules	Asses	Cattle	Pigs	Sheep	Goats	Poultry[3]	Sheep
1945	...	...	...	...	...	...	...	...	619
1946	117	31	65	1,185	819	1,447	...	...	612
1947	111	54	100	1,520	...	1,802	1,382	...	604
1948	111	54	100	1,600	547	1,800	...	...	619
1949	...	...	...	...	...	...	...	...	619
1950	...	...	...	...	...	...	...	...	611
1951	98	30	41	1,200	259	1,559	349	...	597
1952	...	...	...	...	...	...	...	...	584
1953	...	...	...	...	...	...	...	...	594
1954	...	...	...	1,169	...	...	...	...	600
1955	...	...	...	1,274	994	1,242	137	3.7	611
1956	...	...	...	1,363	...	...	...	...	598
1957	...	...	...	1,363	1,081	1,502	137	3.8	600
1958	...	...	...	...	...	...	...	...	611
1959	...	...	...	1,530	...	...	...	...	621
1960	186	86	150	1,550	1,340	1,667	...	...	610
1961	199	92	150	1,720	1,410	1,703	152	4.2	617
1962	212	98	150	1,909	1,117	1,749	158	4.4	619
1963	225	104	166	2,000	1,182	1,644	164	4.7	637
1964	226	105	167	2,100	1,246	1,681	164	5.0	627
1965	227	106	167	2,200	1,260	1,718	165	5.3	627
1966	227	106	170	2,300	1,270	1,749	171	5.3	621
1967	230	108	172	2,393	1,294	1,780	178	5.4	628
1968	233	110	173	2,400	1,300	1,811	184	5.4	621
1969	237	112	175	2,434	1,330[10]	1,830	185	5.4	623
1970	240	113[10] / 92	180	2,500	1,920	1,895	187	5.4	629
1971	250	...	183	2,518	1,980	1,900	189	5.4[13] / 7.1	637
1972	255	...	185	2,580	2,047	1,980	192	7.7	634
1973	270	89	187	2,700	2,200	2,020	194	9.8	613
1974	285	90	190	2,800	2,366	2,060	196	10.0	628
1975	285	90	192	2,800	2,543	2,105	201	12.9	644
1976	289	92	194	2,793	2,734	2,147	230	15.1	645
1977	291	90	190	2,860	2,935	2,174	240	21.1	638
1978	297	92	196	2,767	3,150	2,198	246	23.3	648
1979	309	97	204	2,846	3,385	2,318	251	23.0	659
1980	314	98	207	2,916	3,549	2,318	257	22.5[13]	663
1981	318	99	210	3,135	3,318	2,335	263	38	650
1982	322	101	212	3,200	3,520	2,341	269	39	...
1983	327	102	215	3,270	3,735	2,303	275	42	669
1984	331	104	218	3,456	3,792	2,311	280	43	679
1985	337	112	189	3,578	4,049	2,086	287	41	692
1986	372	105	162	3,765	4,181	1,959	228	50	699
1987	404	113	215	3,847	4,160	1,293	262	49	705
1988	438	116	279	4,007	4,160	1,296	301	48	745
1989	460	124	242	4,176	4,160	1,329	298	49	705
1990	492	131	253	4,361	2,220	1,350	300	51	729
1991	516	141	259	2,327	2,327	1,501	309	56	713
1992	512	151	262	2,425	2,425	1,565	330	56	721
1993	510	152	263	2,540	2,540	1,602	335	57	727

C10   SOUTH AMERICA: Numbers of Livestock (in thousands; poultry in millions)

	Guyana				Paraguay					
	Cattle	Pigs	Sheep	Poultry[3,29]	Horses	Cattle	Pigs	Sheep[30]	Goats[30]	Poultry[31]
1945	185	43	44	0.5	...	...	...		306	...
1946	189	35	48	0.5	333	3,453	65		337	...
1947	193	30	51	0.4	404	3,365	...		222	2.8
1948	186	28	44	0.4	354	...	...		195	4.0
1949	166	28	37	0.4	294	3,865	...		206	...
1950	166	28	37	...	...	3,857	...		210	...
1951	174	25	43	0.4	361	4,132	250		217	...
1952	170	22	41	0.4	354	4,163	...		223	2.9
1953	167	22	39	0.5	337	4,336	...		218	3.8
1954	172	37	36	0.6[29]	354	4,008	...		222[30]	3.8
1955	172	...	...	...	517[20]	4,426	439	351	57	...
1956	172	37	37	...	329	3,929	456	370	60	...
1957	172	37	36	...	307	3,703	461	386	62	...
1958	175	...	40	...	292	3,666	476	402	64	...
1959	175	...	...	...	321	4,004	523	442	71	...
1960	180	37	40	1.1	342	4,695	575	486	78	5.3
1961	220	40	52	1.2	563	5,300	512	361	59	5.4
1962	225	45	45	1.3	570	5,353	525	360	59	5.5
1963	270	50	54	1.4	629	5,407	752	420	50	5.7
1964	332	66	87	2.6	673	5,461	810	438	48	6.3
1965	350	65	87	3.0	691	5,461	861	442	48	6.1
1966	315	68	83	3.5	710	5,516	786	441	47	6.4
1967	306	83	100	4.6	720	5,485	710	402	50	6.4
1968	250	79	98	5.9	730	5,529	636	363	54	6.4
1969	257	81	99	6.4	694	4,340	589	325	59	6.2
1970	258	82	99	7.0	326	4,459	579	333	59	6.3
1971	260	90	100	8.0	316	4,548	617	340	87	6.4
1972	265	100	102	8.8	331	4,756	725	335	100	6.6[31] 8.2
1973	270	110	104	9.0	326	4,845	841	354	...	8.3
1974	275	120	106	9.5	325	5,043	975	366	108	9.0
1975	280	125	108	10.0	325	5,568	1,102	370	108	9.3
1976	260	130	110	10.8	326	5,800	1,174	374	113	10.1
1977	270	130	112	11.5	328	5,810	1,201	403	120	11.4
1978	290	134	113	12.0	329	5,203	1,273	423	126	12.5
1979	295	135	114	...	330	5,300	1,300	430	130	13
1980	300	137	115	13	330	5,400	1,310	430	135	13
1981	305	140	116	14	330	5,500[13]	1,330	435	140	14
1982	170	142	117	14	330	6,400	1,350	440	145	14
1983	180	170	118	15	313	6,795	1,109	372	113	13
1984	199	160	118	15	314	6,956	1,278	378	118	13
1985	200	180	120	15	317	7,151	1,508	388	123	15
1986	210	185	120	15	323	7,374	1,809	398	125	15
1987	210	185	120	15	328	7,780	2,108	387	138	16
1988	210	185	120	15	330	8,074	2,305	430	146	17
1989	210	185	120	15	334	8,524	2,444	449	148	17
1990	220	60	120	15	335	7,627	2,580	357	102	11
1991	230	58	130	11	350	7,800	2,700	365	115	12
1992	190	36	130	11	327	7,886	2,950	378	117	12
1993	190	50	130	11	339	8,000	3,300	386	122	13

International Historical Statistics: The Americas 1750-1993

C10 SOUTH AMERICA: Numbers of Livestock (in thousands, poultry in millions)

								Peru
	Horses	**Mules**	**Asses**	**Cattle**	**Pigs**	**Sheep**	**Goats**	**Poultry[32]**
1945	453	120	349	2,662	770	15,000	950	...
1946	453	123	350	...	775	16,000	962	8.0
1947	453	123	349	2,662	777	17,288	962	9.5
1948	518	150	433	2,639	864	17,748	924	...
1949	550	159	432	2,883	960	18,518	1,093	9.1
1950	432	156	415	2,824	995	17,752	2,207	...
1951	529	178	404	3,140	1,203	16,268	1,917	...
1952	533	181	407	3,188	1,270	15,905	2,038	10.8
1953	533	181	407	3,413	1,346	16,190	2,285	12.1
1954	533	181	407	3,477	1,352	16,822	2,456	11.2
1955	529	177	397	3,439	1,341	16,505	2,254	11.3
1956	518	173	388	3,380	1,281	15,204	3,464	11.0
1957	512	171	384	3,224	1,364	14,130	3,555	11.8
1958	560	183	420	3,372	1,432	14,760	5,196	12.4
1959	567	189	426	3,590	1,464	15,136	5,075	12.4
1960	580	193	435	3,820	1,625	16,009	3,769	15.5
1961	589	197	442	3,824	1,540	15,937	3,831	17.6
1962	616	197	442	3,927[13]	1,620[13]	16,340[13]	3,950	21.6[13]
				3,326	1,807	14,087		23.2
1963	615	200	445	3,466	1,897	14,115	4,099	24.6
1964	494	165	370	3,625	1,997	14,548	3,950	26.4
1965	532	177	399	3,644	1,843	15,218	3,959	13.9
1966	595	199	447	3,686	1,782	15,233	3,916	15.9
1967	600	200	450	3,711	1,829	16,041	1,866	18.0
1968	620	210	460	3,810	1,813	16,220	1,821	20.0
1969	640	220	485	4,060	1,939	16,811	1,855	21.0
1970	667	230	505	4,127	1,930	17,063	1,860	21.5[32]
								19.3
1971	700	228	530	4,310	2,071	16,918	1,946	24.4
1972	685	211	514[13]	4,145	2,075	15,033	1,950	24.7
1973	634	212	476	4,103	2,083	15,105	1,950	26.1
1974	636	212	478	4,144	2,132	15,400	2,012	29.4
1975	637	211	479	4,150	2,136	15,280	2,050	34.8
1976	...	...	...	4,189	2,141	15,294	2,060	37.7
1977	643	214	483	4,184	2,052	15,150	2,070	39.6
1978	645	215	485	4,229	2,043	15,000	2,000	37.5
1979	648	216	486	4,310	2,071	14,800	2,000	36.2
1980	650	217	488	4,207	2,058	14,700	2,000	42.0
1981	653	218	489	4,265	2,116	14,099	1,950	45.2
1982	653	218	489	4,318	2,211	14,277	1,900	47.9
1983	653	218	489	4,050	2,145	12,928	1,786	45.1
1984	655	220	490	4,051	2,214	12,701	1,700	42.7
1985	655	220	490	4,000	2,046	12,929	1,700	41
1986	655	220	490	3,980	2,170	13,060	1,720	48
1987	655	220	490	3,820	2,240	13,118	1,740	50
1988	655	220	490	3,850	2,271	12,922	1,751	58
1989	660	220	490	4,009	2,289	12,970	1,682	54
1990	660	220	490	4,003	2,351	12,257	1,709	59
1991	660	220	490	4,053	2,417	12,429	1,747	67
1992	665	224	520	4,042	2,396	11,911	1,776	63
1993	665	224	520	3,972	2,400	11,915	1,780	60

C10   SOUTH AMERICA: Numbers of Livestock (in thousands, poultry in millions)

	Uruguay					Venezuela							
	Horses	Cattle	Pigs	Sheep	Poultry[3]	Horses	Mules	Asses	Cattle	Pigs	Sheep	Goats	Poultry[3]
1945	...	...	...	19,559	...	...	...	...	...	...	...	...	...
1946	575	6,821	274	19,800	...	...	...	...	...	...	...	...	...
1947	...	...	...	22,000	...	...	...	...	...	...	...	...	...
1948	546	...	...	...	...	...	...	...	...	...	...	...	...
1949	...	...	...	22,646	...	...	...	...	...	...	...	...	...
1950	...	...	259	23,409	...	335	62	387	5,674	1,451	101	1,273	9.3
1951	667	8,154	259	24,543	5.1	...	...	...	...	...	...	...	...
1952	...	...	275	25,677	...	...	...	...	...	...	...	...	...
1953	...	8,013	260	25,699	...	...	...	...	...	...	...	...	...
1954	...	7,819	235	24,492	...	...	...	...	6,230	...	...	...	...
1955	...	7,433	381	23,303	5.7	...	...	...	6,380	...	...	...	...
1956	...	...	...	...	...	533	130	427	7,162	2,362	176	921	11.7
1957	557	...	...	...	...	...	...	...	...	...	...	...	...
1958	...	...	...	...	...	...	...	...	...	...	...	...	...
1959	...	6,902	...	21,293	...	...	...	...	...	...	...	...	...
1960	...	7,505	...	...	...	388	65	402	6,441	1,781	83	1,251	12.5
1961	498	8,792	383	21,738	6.5	390	65	410	6,459	1,820	85	1,250	12.7
1962	480	8,835	400	22,300	6.8	397	67	420	6,502	1,814	99	1,250	17.7
1963	475	8,866	413	21,829	7.0	397	68	435	6,572	1,847	99	1,249	13.4
1964	463	9,145	431	21,905	7.3	401	70	453	6,650	1,882	98	1,247	13.6
1965	451	8,142	438	21,84	7.5	406	71	471	7,380	1,977	89	1,626	13.9
1966	450	8,188	383	21,800	7.5	410	73	475	7,612	1,552	93	1,495	14.2
1967	450	8,300	375	21,900	7.8[13] / 4.7	414	74	480	7,852	1,548	94	1,556	14.4[13] / 16.0
1968	440	8,600	380	22,100	4.7	419	75	485	8,102	1,480	99	1,598	16.6
1969	440	8,900	380	22,606	4.6	423	76	495	8,289	1,601	101	1,424	17.3
1970	421	8,564	419	19,893	5.3	428	77	500	8,485	1,609	96	1,383	18.7
1971	420	8,727	400	17,220	6.3	432	78	510	8,549	1,761	99	1,397	20.5
1972	410	9,273	420	15,452	6.5	445	79	522	8,730	1,767	99	1,413	19.8
1973	430	9,860	430	15,902	7.0	450	80	533	8,843	1,570	100	1,419	22.8
1974	450	10,790	415	15,373	7.2	454	81	545	9,089	1,795	101	1,427	24.6
1975	470	11,536	418	15,062	7.3	458	77	480	9,404	1,880	103	1,285	29.4
1976	509	10,385	445	15,546	7.5	463	76	470	9,546	1,916	275	1,286	35.7
1977	491	10,128	461	16,030	7.6	470	75	460	9,919	2,040	298	1,339	32.4
1978	520	10,007	398	16,161	7.6	474	75	455	10,249	2,046	320	1,354	37.0
1979	525	10,301	412	17,234	7.7	478	74	450	10,625	2,141	344	1,338	40.9
1980	530	11,173	450	20,034	8	482	74	450	11,052	2,280	336	1,381	44
1981	506	11,421	450	20,391	6	481	74	448	11,500	2,303	382	1,312	41
1982	495	11,237	430	20,307	6	412	73	445	11,575	2,459	356	1,322	42
1983	453	9,704	440	20,447	6	491	72	445	12,286	2,699	365	1,335	48
1984	469	9,062	235	20,738	6	495	72	440	11,844	2,935	422	1,340	51
1985	464	9,629	200	21,195	6	495	72	440	12,083	3,091	...	...	54
1986	469	9,300	195	23,858	7	495	72	440	12,331	3,351	425	1,400	56
1987	437	9,945	220	25,560	7	495	72	440	12,641	3,349	425	1,450	59
1988	466	10,331	215	24,689	8	495	72	440	12,856	3,053	508	1,511	61
1989	470	9,447	215	24,872	7	495	72	440	13,076	2,326	523	1,530	57
1990	465	8,723	215	25,220	8	495	72	440	13,272	2,455	525	1,530	70
1991	470	8,889	215	25,986	9	495	72	440	13,368	2,300	525	1,620	80
1992	475	9,508	220	25,941	9	495	72	440	14,192	2,100	525	1,620	88
1993	477	10,093	223	25,702	9	495	72	440	14,660	2,250	525	1,620	90

C10   Numbers of Livestock

NOTES

1. SOURCES: As for table C1 with most Venezuelan statistics to 1937 from Rafael Cartay, *Historia Economica de Venezuela 1830–1900* (Valencia, 1988). Valencia
2. Statistics in this table relate to a count taking place at some point during the year shown, or, in the case of FAO estimates, to a 12-month period ending in September. The exact date is not always given in the sources, and in some cases there were changes which affected the comparability of the figures. Where this is known it has been indicated in footnotes, but a number of unexplained discrepancies probably arise from this.
3. Where estimates are continued unchanged over several years, it is probably wise to regard them with some caution. Where a later count has rendered estimates previously made for the years preceding such a count unbelievable, they have been ignored here, and 'not available' symbols substituted.

FOOTNOTES

[1]   Statistics for some part of Canada are available for various dates before 1851. The following are those for the 18th and 19th centuries (in thousands):

Lower Canada	Horses	Cattle	Pigs	Sheep
1706	2	14	...	2
1719	4	18	14	8
1720	5	25	18	12
1721	6	23	16	14
1734	5	33	24	20
1765	13	50	29	28
1784	30	99	70	85
1827	142	389	242	829
1831	117	470	295	543
1844	147	592	198	603
New Brunswick				
1840	18	90	72	141
Nova Scotia				
1827	13	111	71	174

Upper Canada	Horses	Cattle	Pigs	Sheep
1826	24	112	...	...
1827	25	124	...	...
1828	26	134	...	...
1829	28	143	...	...
1830	31	147	...	...
1831	33	156	...	...
1832	37	167	...	...
1833	40	173	...	...
1834	43	179	...	...
1835	48	196	...	...
1836	55	215	...	...
1837	57	218	...	...
1837	57	218	...	...
1838	57	218	...	...
1839	66	221	...	...
1840	73	247	...	...
1841	75	264	...	...
1842	114	505	394	576
1848	151	566	484	835

[2]   Excluding Prince Edward Island.
[3]   Chickens only.
[4]   Chickens only to 1966 (1st line).
[5]   Including asses.
[6]   Most, and perhaps all statistics up to 1947 include mules and asses. These numbered 28 thousand in 1939.
[7]   The count was in April instead of the usual June.
[8]   Excluding geese.
[9]   Including sheep.
[10]   Incomplete figures.
[11]   Chickens only (but excluding broilers) to 1975 (1st line). All chickens and turkeys subsequently.
[12]   Earlier statistics are for 1 June, later for 1 December.
[13]   The reason for this break is not given in the source.
[14]   Later figures relate to animals on state-operated farms only.
[15]   Chickens only from 1961 to 1969 (1st line).
[16]   Chickens only from 1960.
[17]   Earlier statistics are for June, later for September.
[18]   Chickens on agricultural holdings only to 1961 (1st line).
[19]   Alaska and Hawaii are included from 1961.
[20]   Subsequently at 1 December in the year before that indicated.
[21]   Stock sheep only to 1972 (1st line), lambs included subsequently. Earlier figures which include lambs are available in the FAO, *Yearbook of Agricultural Statistics*.
[22]   The date of the count was changed from summer to winter.
[23]   Chickens only to 1948.

C10 Numbers of Livestock

[24] Excluding Montevideo is 1905, except for sheep in 1900.
[25] National sources give a figure of 2,318 for mules and asses together in this year.
[26] These statistics exclude the *Intendencias and Comisarias.*
[27] Earlier statistics are for May or June, later for October.
[28] Chickens only to 1952 (1st line).
[29] Excluding chickens on sugar plantations to 1954.
[30] Statistics to 1954 are incomplete. For 1940–54 they are said, in official sources, to cover sheep and goats. It is probable that the earlier figures of sheep, from 1926 on, given by the FAO also include goats.
[31] Chickens only to 1972 (1st line)
[32] Chickens only from 1970 (2nd line).
[33] Change of source is probably responsible for jump in figures.

C11   NORTH AMERICA: OUTPUT OF COW'S MILK (in thousands of metric tons)

	Canada	Costa Rica	Guatemala	Honduras	USA
1889	...	...	...	...	20,324
1899	...	...	...	...	28,343
1909	...	...	...	...	29,126
1919	...	...	...	...	30,447
1920	4,979	...	...	...	...
1921	5,397	...	...	...	...
1922	5,492	...	...	...	...
1923	5,809	...	...	...	...
1924	5,980	...	...	...	40,479
1925	6,088	...	...	...	41,140
1926	6,112	...	...	57	42,332
1927	5,858	...	...	58	43,169
1928	5,764	...	...	58	43,474
1929	5,629	...	...	61	44,900
1930	6,088	...	121	62	45,431
1931	6,504	...	92	63	46,733
1932	6,349	...	186	65	47,087
1933	6,388	...	193	67	47,519
1934	6,555	...	142	68	46,095
1935	6,610	...	143	70	45,906
1936	6,859	...	182	71	46,452
1937	6,861	...	608	73	46,225
1938	7,176	...	468	75	47,993
1939	7,158	...	415	77	48,440
1940	7,007	363	418	78	49,628
1941	7,288	356	435	80	52,203
1942	7,592	345	497	83	53,766
1943	7,590	337	...	84	53,078
1944	7,642	...	...	86	53,081

	Canada	Costa Rica	Cuba	Dominican Republic
1945	7,640	...	...	55
1946	7,317	...	...	53
1947	7,413	...	499	52
1948	7,158	...	499	54
1949	7,220	...	421	55
1950	6,950	...	...	57
1951	6,944	179	...	60
1952	6,944	124₁ / 108	...	61
1953	7,274	119	624	...
1954	7,497	144	750	...
1955	7,687	95	735	...
1956	7,696	123	760	...
1957	7,727	76	806	...
1958	8,016	...	828	...
1959	7,998	...	979	...
1960	8,057	...	1,130₁ / 767	...
1961	8,325	...₁	700 / 350	...
1962	8,346	127	370	181
1963	8,369	149	390	182
1964	8,402	163	420	186
1965	8,336	160	440	200
1966	8,345	150	462	210
1967	8,267	157	566	231
1968	8,337	178	530	240
1969	8,495	186	520	260
1970	8,314	194	500₁ / 690	283
1971	7,932	202	675	304
1972	8,026	219	758	315
1973	7,667	210	781	330
1974	7,633	248	799	340
1975	7,751	259	860	320
1976	7,693	261	1,000	340
1977	7,742	279	1,066	325
1978	7,615	294	1,150	340
1979	7,095	316	1,180	409
1980	7,855	318	1,080	431
1981	8,025	308	1,180	440
1982	8,258	302	1,091	450
1983	8,019	325	1,109	460
1984	8,096	347	...	495
1985	7,891	376	1,100	379
1986	7,925	414	1,111	337
1987	7,986	410	1,128	289
1988	8,229	415	1,122	290
1989	7,980	418	1,131	294
1990	7,900	429	1,100	326
1991	7,455	450	1,070	374
1992	7,633	430	856	364
1993	7,501	470	700	382

C11 NORTH AMERICA: Output of Cow's Milk (in thousands of metric tons)

	El Salvador	Guatemala	Honduras	Jamaica	Mexico[2]	Nicaragua	Panama	Puerto Rico[3]	USA[4]
1945	...	...	88	...	...	...	...	...	54,353
1946	...	...	91	...	...	...	...	105	53,386
1947	102	...	94	...	...	147	...	...	52,986
1948	107	...	96	...	...	153	...	134	51,107
1949	...	...	99	30	...	183	...	...	52,663
1950	...	206	102	38	1,539	190	...	160	52,890
1951	...	...	105	38	...	...	...	147	52,018
1952	138	175	108	40	...	169	33	148	52,014
1953	164	175	113	40	1,730	...	51	153	54,531
1954	193	89	116	40	1,895	...	37	182	55,381
1955	...	92	105	...	1,985	...	36	194	55,767
1956	...	92	105	...		...	44	220	56,636
1957	...	93	108	37	2,750	...	54	262	56,530
1958	...	128	111	37		...	51	269	55,892
1959	...	127	115	35	2,489	...	51	301	55,333[4]
1960	...	144	119	35	2,370	...	45	324	55,841
1961	...	126	125	33[1] 40	2,327	190	48	339	57,020
1962	...	183	123	38	2,284	192	53	313	57,266
1963	...	209	128	39	2,237	175	56	325	56,791
1964	...	199	131	40	2,304	181	60	333	57,591
1965	...	213	135	40	2,373	182	63	350	56,324
1966	...	208	137	41[1] 30	2,444	183	71	354	54,382
1967	...	231	156	33	2,591	185	73	356	53,856
1968	159	234	167	39	2,671	176	72	367	53,172
1969	167	253	167	43	3,023	191	79	371	52,665
1970	169	262	162	46	3,053[1] 3,919	201	73	370	53,073
1971	170	270	169	47	4,068	210	76	374	53,780
1972	172	280	176	49	4,190	218[1]	72	383	54,442
1973	187	290	182	48	4,227	385	66	384	52,386
1974	200	300	175	47	4,523	415	64	374	52,429
1975	235	310	180	46	4,980	446	73	380	52,343
1976	294	320	190	47	5,344	462	75	407	54,512
1977	244	314	192	48	5,731	462	86	436	55,635
1978	253	310	202	48	6,426	465	98	440	55,093
1979	264	315	202	48	6,848	386	95	438	55,978
1980	291	320	277	48	6,951	165	94	407	58,244
1981	293	325	209	51	6,885	124	98	416	60,161
1982	268	319	279	48	7,138	124	93	399	61,599
1983	249	320	281	48	7,171	125	88	384	63,354
1984	213	360	244	49	7,101	125	96	351	61,439
1985	234	370	247	...	7,173	167	98	363	65,166
1986	232	364	269	48	6,373	191	111	340	65,036
1987	240	366	283	49	7,499	181	119	353	64,731
1988	295	...	299	49	6,350	197	112	346	65,840
1989	294	...	300	49	5,750	163	122	398	65,426
1990	326	...	305	49	6,332	158	137	402	67,260
1991	273	382	373	53	6,925	165	144	388	67,348
1992	275	385	396	53	7,204	171	141	375	68,440
1993	278	355	380	53	7,657	182	157	364	68,303

C11   SOUTH AMERICA: OUTPUT OF COW'S MILK (in thousands of metric tons)

	Argentina[4]	Brazil[5]	Chile	Colombia	Ecuador	Paraguay	Peru	Uruguay	Venezuela
1925	1,158	1,856	170	...	...	...	...	...	...
1926	1,212	1,901	187	...	...	...	...	...	...
1927	1,056	1,957	202	...	...	...	...	...	...
1928	1,067	2,016	283[2]	...	...	...	...	...	...
1929	973	2,076	...	...	...	...	191	...	...
1930	1,159	2,138	...	...	...	...	...	...	...
1931	1,343	2,321	...	...	...	...	...	...	...
1932	1,345	2,371	...	...	...	...	...	...	...
1933	1,218	2,459	...	...	...	...	...	...	...
1934	1,155	2,514	...	...	...	...	...	...	...
1935	1,143	2,521[5]	230	...	...	...	...	...	...
1936	1,283	3,828	235	...	...	...	...	...	...
1937	1,288	3,862	...	...	...	...	191	368	...
1938	1,399	3,934	...	...	...	...	...	...	...
1939	1,568	4,305[5]	...	...	...	...	...	...	...
1940	1,687	...	...	...	...	...	...	...	...
1941	2,006	...	...	...	...	...	...	...	...
1942	1,903	...	...	...	...	...	...	...	...
1943	2,178	...	436	...	...	...	...	406	...
1944	2,245	...	524	...	...	...	...	...	...
1945	2,083	...	516	...	...	...	263	356	...
1946	2,403[4]	...	588	...	...	...	273	...	...
1947	4,169	...	598	...	...	...	300	...	...
1948	4,214	...	575	1,740	...	...	318	361	...
1949	4,002	2,377	663	...	168	...	332	395	361
1950	4,032	2,495	698	2,007	...	...	315	446	...
1951	4,061	2,562	704	1,949	...	...	321	498	...
1952	4,478	2,833	634	...	169	124	345	546	...
1953	4,891	3,215	701	1,801	...	126	387	566	...
1954	4,801	3,441	771	1,780	270	126	389	586	289
1955	4,999	3,673	825	2,095	...	...	390	600	327
1956	5,126	4,238	...	2,085	330	129	392	630	374
1957	4,662	4,407	...	2,085	360	130	390	702	377
1958	4,481	4,603	764	...	375	132[1] 75	372	627	...
1959	4,478	4,792	754	1,965	386	75	397	619	387
1960	4,511	5,052	784	1,905[1] 1,753	414	76	419	773	434
1961	4,486[1] 4,151	5,227	799	1,753	405	78	437	746	458
1962	4,143	5,460	762	1,785	397	79	453	765	496
1963	4,367	5,550	821	1,833	386	80	475	781	538
1964	4,534	6,340	856	1,860	400	82	499	763	604
1965	4,276	6,775	835	1,973	400	84	714	736	645
1966	4,732	6,889	856	2,020	440[1] 500	86	725	742	683
1967	4,366	6,905	873	2,080	600	87	726	619	717
1968	4,683	7,235	939	2,070	677	86	730	680	771
1969	4,556	7,253	1,012	2,160	685	87	762	762	889
1970	4,190	7,353	1,104	2,250	705	88	825	763	952
1971	4,825	7,346	969	2,340	717	89	897	706	1,000
1972	5,385	7,323	907	2,450	730	92	816	727	1,081
1973	5,221	7,763	882	2,300	763	95	804	675	1,055
1974	5,292	9,022	933	2,027	766	110	813	711	1,134

C11 SOUTH AMERICA: Output of Cow's Milk (in thousands of metric tons)

	Argentina	Brazil	Chile	Colombia	Ecuador	Paraguay	Peru	Uruguay	Venezuela
1975	5,650	9,971	986	2,096	784	121	813	745	1,224
1976	5,799	10,667	1,054	2,276	809	128	821	765	1,198
1977	5,309	9,862	1,035	2,303	849	136	820	730	1,244
1978	5,213	10,500	1,008	2,360	866	149	822	753	1,270
1979	5,349	10,503	983	2,395	754	162	824	784	1,302
1980	5,307	11,956	1,080	2,165	924	163	780	820	1,311
1981	5,155	...	1,163	2,623	916	168	785	830	1,352
1982	5,781	11,817	1,056	2,570	967	124	805	843	1,472
1983	5,300	11,818	900	2,647	981	160	752	896	1,511
1984	5,200	12,303	880	2,858	1,020	175	780	851	1,570
1985	5,742	12,452	1,012	2,816	988	182	809	922	1,532
1986	6,118	12,879	1,092	3,017	1,260	188	819	959	1,580
1987	6,444	13,399	1,128	3,142	1,270	194	830	988	1,598
1988	6,168	13,941	1,149	3,155	1,406	200	850	990	1,715
1989	6,725	14,518	1,268	3,557	1,443	206	802	1,005	1,549
1990	6,400	15,003	1,423	3,500	1,539	226	777	1,311	1,497
1991	6,400	15,547	1,450	4,131	1,606	240	786	1,101	1,505
1992	6,795	15,784	1,540	4,214	1,510	240	768	1,111	1,576
1993	7,716	15,671	1,650	4,425	1,673	250	803	1,163	1,451

NOTES

1. SOURCES: As for table C1.
2. The basis on which the statistics have been collected has varied from country to country and over time, so that comparisons must be made with caution.
3. Where necessary, conversions from liquid measures have been made on the assumption that the specific gravity of milk is 1.031.

FOOTNOTES

[1] This break is not explained in the source.
[2] One earlier figure is available, *viz.* 1940-1,368.
[3] One earlier figure is available, *viz.* 1939-63.
[4] Including Alaska and Hawaii from 1960.
[5] Statistics to 1946 are of deliveries to dairies.
[6] Statistics to 1935 exclude milk for butter and cheese manufacture. Those for 1936-39 include goat's milk.

C12 NORTH AMERICA: OUTPUT OF BUTTER (in thousands of metric tons)

	Canada	USA		Canada	USA		Canada	Mexico	USA
1849	...	142	1910	91[1]	774	1950	131	...	748
1850	15	...		[26]		1951	129	...	655
			1911	...	799	1952	138	...	636
1859	...	209	1912	...	722	1953	146	...	729
1960	23	...	1913	...	729	1954	150	...	738
			1914	...	764				
1869	...	233				1955	151	...	701
			1915	[38]	794	1956	144	...	704
1870	34	187	1916	[37]	813	1957	143	...	696
1871	...	213	1917	[40]	746	1958	158	...	674
1872	...	197	1918	[42]	682	1959	153	...	640
1873	...	257	1919	[47]	747				
1874	...	265				1960	150	...	651[3]
			1920	[51][1]	714				670
1875	...	252		98		1961	165	...	697
1876	...	307	1921	107	793	1962	169	...	716
1877	...	316	1922	118	848	1963	164	...	659
1878	...	329	1923	124	904	1964	164	13	666
1879	...	366	1924	130	937				
						1965	157	14	611
1880	47	370	1925	125	944	1966	155	14	512
1881	...	264	1926	127	967	1967	153	15	562
1882	...	337	1927	126	992	1968	156	16	533
1883	...	383	1928	121	962	1969	162	17	511
1884	...	394	1929	122	991				
						1970	153	18	518
1885	...	423	1930	128	975	1971	134	19	520
1886	...	449	1931	146	1,016	1972	136	20	500
1887	...	444	1932	142	1,016	1973	118	21	417
1888	...	444	1933	144	1,077	1974	109	22	436
1889	...	586	1934	151	1,037				
						1975	133	23	446
1890	51	531	1935	153	1,003	1976	118	23	444
1891	...	495	1936	157	983	1977	117	24	493
1892	...	480	1937	155	968	1978	105	25	451
1893	...	475	1938	163	1,021	1979	101	24	447
1894	...	482	1939	161	1,002				
						1980	107	21	519
1895	...	588	1940	156	1,016	1981	117	21	557
1896	...	728	1941	163	1,029	1982	126	23	570
1897	...	695	1942	157	966	1983	108	24	589
1898	...	668	1943	158	914	1984	112	25	500
1899	...	677	1944	151	825				
						1985	100	25	566
1900	64	699	1945	150	771	1986	103	21	545
1901	...	714	1946	138	681	1987	98	26	508
1902	...	635	1947	147	744	1988	109	32	548
1903	...	674	1948	145	682	1989	102	29	598
1904	...	699	1949	141	766				
						1990	104	31	608
1905	...	756				1991	101	31	621
1906	...	701				1992	85	28	648
1907	[21][1]	697				1993	82	22	625
1908	...	800							
1909	...	736							

C12   SOUTH AMERICA: OUTPUT OF BUTTER (in thousands of metric tons)

	Argentina	Brazil[2]		Argentina	Brazil[2]		Argentina	Brazil[2]
1904	8.8	...						
1905	8.8	...	**1935**	28	21	**1965**	42	25
1906	8.0	...	**1936**	32	21	**1966**	46	25
1907	6.7	...	**1937**	32	21	**1967**	41	36
1908	7.2	...	**1938**	29	27	**1968**	39	32
1909	7.2	...	**1939**	34	34	**1969**	35	43
1910	7.5	...	**1940**	37	35	**1970**	28	45
1911	7.9	...	**1941**	44	...	**1971**	36	50
1912	9.5	...	**1942**	41	...	**1972**	49	52
1913	10	...	**1943**	47	14	**1973**	37	60
1914	9.3	...	**1944**	47	15	**1974**	35	60
1915	10	...	**1945**	43	18	**1975**	40	63
1916	11	...	**1946**	51	21	**1976**	40	66
1917	15	6.4	**1947**	51	20	**1977**	30	69
1918	25	6.6	**1948**	42	20	**1978**	29	90
1919	26	6.6	**1949**	39	22	**1979**	33	92
1920	29	8.6	**1950**	45	25	**1980**	29	94
1921	33	6.9	**1951**	43	20	**1981**	32	95
1922	33	8.9	**1952**	46	26	**1982**	37	70
1923	41	9.2	**1953**	58	25	**1983**	34	70
1924	39	9	**1954**	61	24	**1984**	28	73
1925	33	9.6	**1955**	57	28	**1985**	33	74
1926	35	10	**1956**	66	28	**1986**	32	72
1927	29	12	**1957**	56	27	**1987**	34	77
1928	31	13	**1958**	52	30	**1988**	34	79
1929	28	13	**1959**	61	29	**1989**	45	80
1930	34	12	**1960**	60	25	**1990**	40	75
1931	36	12	**1961**	55	26	**1991**	38	70
1932	27	19	**1962**	49	30	**1992**	37	65
1933	33	20	**1963**	51	22	**1993**	48	68
1934	29	24	**1964**	51	25			

NOTE

SOURCES: As for table C1.

FOOTNOTES

[1]   Creamery butter only in 1907 and from 1910 (2nd line) to 1920 (1st line).
[2]   Government-inspected butter only.
[3]   Subsequently including Alaska and Hawaii.

C13   NORTH AMERICA: OUTPUT OF MEAT (in thousands of metric tons)

	Canada	Cuba	Dominican Republic	El Salvador	Guatemala	Honduras	Mexico	USA
1899	...	...	...	...	...	...	...	5,763
1900	...	...	...	...	...	...	...	5,827
1901	...	...	...	...	...	...	...	5,961
1902	...	...	...	...	...	...	...	5,727
1903	...	...	...	...	...	...	...	6,061
1904	...	...	...	...	...	...	...	6,165
1905	...	...	...	...	...	...	...	6,450
1906	...	...	...	...	...	...	...	6,564
1907	...	...	...	...	...	...	...	6,705
1908	...	...	...	...	...	...	...	6,982
1909	...	...	...	...	...	...	...	6,686
1910	...	...	...	...	...	...	...	6,349
1911	...	...	...	...	...	...	...	6,744
1912	...	...	...	...	...	...	...	6,556
1913	...	...	...	...	...	...	...	6,566
1914	...	...	...	...	...	...	...	6,397
1915	...	...	...	...	...	...	...	6,752
1916	...	...	...	...	...	...	...	7,215
1917	...	...	...	...	...	...	...	7,031
1918	...	...	...	...	...	...	...	7,866
1919	...	...	...	...	...	...	...	7,412
1920	488	...	...	...	...	...	...	6,955
1921	458	...	...	...	...	...	...	6,885
1922	522	...	...	...	...	...	...	7,320
1923	534	...	...	...	...	...	...	8,032
1924	566	...	...	...	...	...	...	7,981
1925	570	...	...	...	...	...	...	7,529
1926	582	...	...	...	...	8	...	7,552
1927	591	...	...	...	...	8	...	7,448
1928	579	63	...	...	...	8	...	7,370
1929	576	84	...	...	...	8	...	7,324
1930	532	87	...	...	...	8	...	7,265
1931	548	79	...	...	...	9	169	7,464
1932	567	65	...	...	...	9	167	7,447
1933	583	60	...	...	...	10	180	7,900
1934	624	70	...	...	26	10	199	8,544
1935	603	65	...	...	38	11	204	6,544
1936	655	68	17	...	28	11	214	7,603
1937	677	86	17	...	26	11	220	7,125
1938	636	77	15	24	26	11	217	7,475
1939	643	81	14	24	27	11	219	7,958
1940	763	87	14	26	34	11	222	8,653
1941	913	97	15	26	...	12	228	8,876
1942	991	109	15	28	...	12	169	9,939
1943	1,079	...	19	28[2]	...	13	161	11,105
1944	1,187	...	...	...	...	13	155	11,421

C13   NORTH AMERICA: Output of Meat (in thousands of metric tons)

	Canada	Cuba	Dominican Republic	El Salvador[2]	Guatemala	Honduras	Jamaica	Mexico	Nicaragua	Panama	Puerto Rico	USA
1945	1,127	...	...	...	...	13	...	181	...	...	...	10,746
1946	975	...	...	...	...	13	...	...	...	...	...	10,396
1947	949	...	23	...	...	13	10	203	...	...	...	10,586
1948	887	77	22	...	...	14	11	203	15	...	...	9,662
1949	853	84	21	...	...	15	12	201	18	...	...	9,826
1950	827	...	...	...	36	14	13	221	...	...	...	10,013
1951	815	84	...	...	35	14	13	213	...	...	...	9,933
1952	923	63	...	21	35	15	13	219	...	16	...	10,430
1953	882	...	...	20	35	15	16	...	...	...	...	11,198
1954	924	...	...	19	39	...	17	317	...	...	...	11,437
1955	979	...	20	20	41	...	16	324	...	19	17	12,199
1956	1,017	...	22	20	35	...	...	...	...	20	18	12,716
1957	1,052	...	22	...	36	...	15	396	...	22	19	12,183
1958	1,069	...	25	...	38	15	15	415	...	23	20	11,638
1959	1,161	...	31	...	38	16	16	411	...	24	21	12,392
1960	1,114	...	29	...	41	...	15	423	...	23	20	12,795
1961	1,101	...	29	...	40	18	17	430	22	27	25	12,981
1962	1,102	...	21	22	40	18	16	462	22	31	19	13,135
1963	1,155	229	26	24	43	21	16	485	22	32	26	13,861
1964	1,273	236	25	23	40	19	17	505	43	32	30	14,820
1965	1,335	242	26	23	42[1] / 52	21[1] / 28	17	532	39	32	32	14,288
1966	1,331	217	27	23	52	30	17	538	44	35	32	14,779
1967	1,401	217	34	38	62	32	17	583[6] / 788	48	34	32	15,510
1968	1,435	224	40	25	63	35	17	798	55	35	32	15,984
1969	1,363	225	42	26	70	39	19	816	62	37	32	16,009
1970	1,476	212	43	30	72	40	19	839	72	39	31	16,448
1971	1,578	200	45	...	78	48	15	904	75	42	33	17,144
1972	1,558	191	53	36	79	50	17	879	74	45	35	16,810
1973	1,547	169	56	39	76	52	21	825	77	44	37	15,830
1974	1,595	152	57	45	70	44	21	920	64	46	37	17,188
1975	1,638	157	57	40	75	48	21	923	82	50	36	16,675
1976	1,706	169	63	45	91	51	20	944	92	54	40	17,965
1977	1,685	190	63	42	83	50	21	1,028	100	54	45	18,013
1978	1,682	204	69	47	86	63	21	1,058	100	47	51	17,497
1979	1,689	208	70	45	83	69	19	1,870[8]	98	45	51	17,066
1980	1,832	206	62	44	72	73	21	2,044	66	48	38	17,680
1981	1,861	213	53	35	79	72	22	2,199	56	54	36	17,707
1982	1,866	214	55	35	72	57	21	2,284	68	60	37	17,045
1983	1,893	220	59	35	75	44	23	2,485	59	61	38	17,815
1984	1,865	229	61	36	74	46	24	2,432	59	64	39	17,819
1985	1,939	233	72	35	74	45	23	2,279	57	71	42	17,872
1986	1,953	243	74	36	57	38	23	2,269	59	73	50	17,824
1987	1,922	237	79	34	66	56	22	2,139	55	71	52	17,717
1988	...	237	82	34	74	57	22	2,256	46	61	44	18,115
1989	...	231	93	42	74	60	23	3,004	60	60	46	18,251
1990	...	234	92	44	80	59	24	2,685	53	68	49	17,852
1991	...	233	90	45	74	59	23	2,506	53	71	51	18,217
1992	...	187	129	30	78	59	22	2,218	59	68	68	18,854
1993	...	168	141	32	80	59	23	2,230	59	75	75	18,741

C13   SOUTH AMERICA: Output of Meat (in thousands of metric tons)

	Argentina[3]	Brazil	Chile[5]	Colombia	Uruguay[3]	Venezuela
1910	...	...	...	...	...	...
1911	...	...	...	...	...	...
1912	...	...	...	...	...	...
1913	...	...	...	...	...	...
1914	1,118	...	...	...	...	...
1915	1,104	...	...	...	...	...
1916	1,226	...	...	...	...	...
1917	1,291	...	...	...	...	...
1918	1,519	...	...	...	...	...
1919	1,233	...	...	...	...	...
1920	1,113	...	...	...	...	...
1921	1,186	...	...	...	...	...
1922	1,571	...	...	...	...	...
1923	1,884	...	...	...	...	...
1924	2,117	...	...	...	...	...
1925	2,034	724	...	...	...	...
1926	1,868	634	...	...	...	...
1927	1,944	740	...	...	...	...
1928	1,775	712	...	...	...	...
1929	1,747	677	...	...	...	...
1930	1,788	757	...	...	...	...
1931	1,638	745	135	...	252	...
1932	1,653	674	135	...	198	...
1933	1,741	864	135	...	218	...
1934	1,812	934	130	232	236	...
1935	1,839	1,076	128	232	262	...
1936	1,909	1,072	147	230	222	...
1937	2,068	1,123	137	226	242	...
1938	2,022	1,081	135	227	233	...
1939	2,135	1,085	145	222	248	53
1940	2,011	979	157	221	230	64
1941	2,247	1,016	167	224	252	61
1942	2,234	1,019	167	248	252	63
1943	2,248	947	169[5] / 202	...	285	60
1944	2,371	903	202	...	...	64
1945	2,113	901	216	...	303	70
1946	2,207	1,011	219	...	...	77
1947	2,459	1,053	194	...	293	73
1948	2,345	1,165	196	...	313	74
1949	2,387	1,218	155	328	376	81

C13 SOUTH AMERICA: Output of Meat (in thousands of metric tons)

	Argentina[3]	Bolivia[4]	Brazil	Chile[5]	Colombia	Ecuador	Paraguay	Peru	Uruguay[3]	Venezuela
1950	2,372	...	1,226[1] / 1,461	152	335	...	...	...	381	88
1951	2,171	...	1,577	141	...	...	...	...	386	86
1952	2,117	...	1,494	153	...	...	70	...	382	88
1953	2,113	...	1,555	160	...	...	...	...	409	96
1954	2,176	...	1,611	188	...	...	...	...	349	98
1955	2,501	...	1,576	153	...	...	...	...	342	101
1956	2,856	...	1,752	...	...	...	...	...	355	105
1957	2,827	...	1,843	182	...	...	...	...	...	113
1958	2,893	29	2,011	198	...	...	...	...	298	120
1959	2,281	18	1,964	202	...	58	...	148	297	135
1960	2,250	27	1,872	183	...	59	...	151	324	142
1961	2,509	28	1,945	199	427	61	...	151	...	164
1962	2,704	20	1,989	217	429	61	...	148	341	167
1963	2,913	35	1,983	237	418	71	127	153	392	177
1964	2,308	37	2,065	208	468	72	141	164	442	190
1965	2,371	42	2,148	210	448	73	138	153	403	196
1966	2,742	42	2,173	225	480	70	151	170	334	212
1967	2,953	42[4] / 74	2,226	223	483	83	153	174	323	223
1968	2,963	79	2,469	247	485	84	141	173	428	228
1969	3,292	82	2,619	242	500	86	136	186	451	259
1970	3,021	90	2,669	249	489	89	162	190	466	253
1971	2,448	91	2,657	228	531	92	164	191	356	267
1972	2,550	99	2,925	181	495	97	166	192	362	275
1973	2,545	106	2,961	161	499	98	164	189	368	309
1974	2,524	109	2,902	251	515	108	167	190	408	297
1975	2,825	113	2,981	269	577	114	156	188	412	357
1976	3,204	120	3,035	244	654	119	162	189	466	371
1977	3,192	128	3,337	223	650	128	186	189	405	363
1978	3,265	133	3,218	219	685	145	184	190	377	400
1979	3,415	142	3,066	232	703	154	190	187	318	421
1980	3,210	143	3,115	232	698	146	195	185	388	455
1981	3,313	150	3,119	261	747	139	204	195	454	434
1982	2,898	158	3,292	305	709	145	206	197	462	430
1983	2,708	172	3,302	319	689	150	210	216	493	442
1984	2,888	181	2,905	308	725	155	219	201	360	426
1985	3,077	194	3,061	259	740	157	225	195	393	454
1986	3,085	187	2,835	270	736	166	228	191	392	462
1987	3,041	198	3,311	282	720	168	212	216	381	425
1988	2,990	222	2,868	316	733	172	253	236	379	470
1989	3,014	241	3,883	364	946	194	253	269	462	478
1990	3,011	255	4,011	397	924	200	270	271	415	490
1991	3,041	266	4,049	413	955	212	305	267	436	480
1992	2,797	218	4,484	364	826	235	399	265	455	492
1993	2,836	215	4,360	395	729	237	423	261	407	496

C13   Output of Meat

NOTES

1. SOURCES: As for table C1.
2. Except as indicated in footnotes, the statistics in this table generally relate to the carcass weight of beef and veal, lamb and mutton, and pork (excluding offal and edible fat) from indigenous animals. In some cases where it was a significant amount, goat meat is also included.

FOOTNOTES

[1]   The reason for this break is not given in the source.
[2]   Including meat from imported animals.
[3]   Excluding production on farms.
[4]   Commercial production only to 1967 (1st line).
[5]   Excluding cold storage production and production on farms to 1943 (1st line).
[6]   This break probably occurs through the inclusion of slaughterings on farms and in most small towns, which were previously excluded.
[7]   Beef and pork only.
[8]   There was a large unexplained increase in pork production in this year.

C14 NORTH AMERICA: LANDINGS OF FISH (in thousands of metric tons)

Year	Newfound-land[2]	Year	Canada[1]	Newfound-land[2]	USA[3]	Year	Canada[1]	Cuba	Mexico	Newfound-land[2]	USA[3]
1805	...	1850	...	55	...	1895	133	...	...	67[2]	...
1806	39	1851	...	52	...	1896	132	...	...	58	...
1807	34	1852	...	49	...	1897	131[1]	...	...	58	...
1808	29	1853	...	47	...	1898	123	...	...	62	...
1809	41	1854	...	39	...	1899	155	...	...	66	...
1810	45	1855	...	56	...	1900	144	...	...	63	...
1811	47	1856	...	64	...	1901	163	...	...	65	...
1812	36	1857	...	71	...	1902	156	...	...	73	...
1813	45	1858	...	53	...	1903	131	...	...	69	...
1814	48	1859	...	62	...	1904	129	...	...	61	...
1815	55	1860	...	68	...	1905	127	...	...	75	908
1816	53	1861	...	63	...	1906	114	...	...	72	928
1817	52	1862	...	65	...	1907	...	...	...	77	875
1818	51	1863	...	51	...	1908	121	...	...	88	931
1819	47	1864	...	52	...	1909	140[1]	...	...	76	...
1820	46	1865	...	49	...	1910	162[1] / 350	...	...	60	...
1821	46	1866	...	45	...	1911	338	...	...	71	...
1822	45	1867	...	51	...	1912	322	...	...	72	...
1823	44	1868	...	45	...	1913	326	...	...	63	...
1824	44	1869	70	56	...	1914	316	...	...	56	...
1825	49	1870	79	59	...	1915	325	...	...	72	...
1826	49	1871	92	59	...	1916	300	...	...	80	...
1827	46	1872	112	57	...	1917	302	...	...	93	1,214
1828	46	1873	120	67	...	1918	313	...	...	85	...
1829	47	1874	109	81	...	1919	322[1] / 335	...	...	91	...
1830	48	1875	102	58	...	1920	306	...	...	69	...
1831	38	1876	113	54	...	1921	264	...	...	81	1,023
1832	31	1877	111	53	...	1922	325	...	4	75	1,188
1833	35	1878	123	53	...	1923	289	...	10	64	1,236
1834	41	1879	145	71	...	1924	334	...	7	59[2]	1,116
1835	36	1880	149	70	774	1925	358	...	13	63	1,311
1836	43	1881	146	78	...	1926	400	...	12	73[2]	1,302
1837	40	1882	123	71	...	1927	349	...	16	80	1,273
1838	37	1883	146	78	...	1928	390	...	15	66	1,388
1839	44	1884	139	74	...	1929	346	...	12	64[2]	1,583
1840	47	1885	147	65	...	1930	347	...	11	59	1,462
1841	51	1886	147	68	...	1931	294	...	8	52	1,193
1842	51	1887	147	55	...	1932	266	...	8	53	1,185
1843	48	1888	143	60	...	1933	286	...	6	57	1,359
1844	43	1889	123[1] / 146	55	764	1934	315	...	12	52	1,862
1845	51	1890	141[1]	53	797	1935	311	7	11	53	1,876
1846	45	1891	143	63	775	1936	371	7	11	56	2,189
1847	43	1892	153	53	749	1937	353	8	12	47	1,974
1848	47	1893	146	54	...	1938	339	8	19	53	1,930
1849	60	1894	153	56	...	1939	374	7	57	46	2,016

C14   NORTH AMERICA: Landings of Fish (in thousands of metric tons)

	Canada[1]	Cuba	Mexico	Newfoundland[2]	Panama	USA[3]
1940	431	7	63	58	...	1,842
1941	385	6	52	35	...	2,223
1942	399	4	54	39	...	1,758
1943	386	4	61	39	...	1,888
1944	390	5	...	39	...	2,056
1945	474	5	...	51	...	2,086
1946	492	5	...	52$_2$	...	2,026
				377		
1947	454	9	54	363	...	1,973
1948	545	8	68	335	...	2,047
1949	489$_1$	8	68	...	...	2,179
	1,000					
1950	1,048	8	74	...	...	2,223
1951	1,013	6	75	...	...	2,011
1952	940	9	58	...	...	2,010
1953	924	10	67	...	1	2,035
1954	1,027	12	91	...	...	2,155
1955	965	13	106	...	...	2,181
1956	1,106	16	145	...	...	2,390
1957	997	22	118	...	...	2,172
1958	1,008	22	164	...	...	2,153$_3$
1959	1,054	28	192	...	15	2,323
1960	935	31	198	...	11	2,242
1961	1,020	31	225	...	11	2,353
1962	1,124	35	219	...	14	2,429
1963	1,198	37	243	...	13	2,199
1964	1,211	37	249	...	26	2,060
1965	1,262	41	256	...	39	2,167
1966	1,346	44	287	...	72	1,980
1967	1,296	66	350	...	72	1,839
1968	1,499	66	364	...	72	1,887
1969	1,405	80	353	...	32	1,967
1970	1,389	106	387	...	52	2,230
1971	1,290	126	425	...	72	2,276
1972	1,132	140	426	...	63	2,760
1973	1,121	150	448	...	92	2,796
1974	974	165	402	...	69	2,847
1975	993	143	467	...	117	2,842
1976	1,102	194	479	...	184	3,050
1977	1,235	185	517	...	239	2,980
1978	1,367	213	782	...	139	3,416
1979	1,415	153	955	...	165	3,528
1980	1,347	186	1,222	...	216	3,654
1981	1,417	165	1,536	...	149	3,794
1982	1,403	195	1,321	...	117	4,033
1983	1,349	198	1,064	...	169	4,319
1984	1,284	200	1,104	...	142	4,991
1985	1,453	220	1,226	...	291	4,949
1986	1,512	245	1,305	...	132	5,167
1987	1,567	215	1,419	...	156	5,989
1988	1,612	231	1,373	...	125	5,952
1989	1,575	192	1,470	...	190	5,775
1990	1,626	188	1,401	...	144	5,868
1991	1,544	165	1,453	...	150	5,486
1992	1,276	109	1,248	...	149	5,588
1993	1,172	93	1,201	...	158	5,939

C14 SOUTH AMERICA: LANDINGS OF FISH (in thousands of metric tons)

	Argentina	Brazil[3]	Chile	Colombia	Ecuador	Peru	Venezuela
1930	44	...	...	...	...	...	...
1931	34	...	17	...	...	...	...
1932	33	...	23	...	...	...	...
1933	29	...	27	...	...	...	...
1934	34	...	26	...	...	...	...
1935	45	...	29	...	...	...	...
1936	47	...	35	...	...	...	...
1937	50	...	37	...	...	...	...
1938	55	...	32	...	2	5	...
1939	55	103	37	...	2	5	22
1940	55	111	38	...	...	6	33
1941	60	116	37	...	...	12	43
1942	58	120	32	...	...	21	37
1943	62	123	41	...	...	27	59
1944	57	115	40	...	...	30	65
1945	54	122	47	...	...	32	68
1946	57	122	61	...	...	28	77
1947	65	140	61	...	3	37	76
1948	71	144	65	15	3	48	92
1949	65	153	77	...	5	45	75
1950	58	153	88	...	15	74	78
1951	78	158	94	16	10	127	75
1952	79	175	119	16	9	137	63
1953	77	161	107	16	9	148	63
1954	78	172	144	16	13	176	52
1955	79	190	214	18	15	213	70
1956	75	208	188	21	22	322	61
1957	83	212	213	30	26	511	84
1958	84	212[3]	226	25	31	961	78
1959	90	239	273	21	36	2,187	83
1960	105	251	340	30	44	3,569	85
1961	102	275	430	43	39	5,291	85
1962	101	379	643	48	43	7,164	95
1963	131	346	762	45	50	7,091	97
1964	169	369	1,161	50	46	9,322	111
1965	205	389	709	54	54	7,632	117
1966	251	393	1,383	59	48	8,845	114
1967	241	420	1,053	93	58	10,199	109
1968	224	495	1,393	...	69	10,556	126
1969	181	492	1,095	58	87	9,244	134
1970	216	526	1,181	55	91	12,535	126
1971	218	582	1,487	38	107	10,529	139
1972	278	602	792	111	108	4,724	152
1973	276	699	664	105	154	2,329	162
1974	214	726	1,128	62	174	4,145	145

C14　SOUTH AMERICA: Landings of Fish (in thousands of metric tons)

	Argentina	Brazil	Chile	Colombia	Ecuador	Peru	Venezuela
1975	214	753	899	67	224	3,446	153
1976	266	653	1,379	75	298	4,343	146
1977	380	748	1,319	64	433	2,549	146
1978	519	752	1,959	80	617	3,443	166
1979	568	779	2,630	63	605	3,652	169
1980	385	735	2,817	76	639	2,709	185
1981	361	755	3,394	95	539	2,717	185
1982	475	733	3,673	71	607	3,513	221
1983	416	754	3,978	58	372	1,569	231
1984	315	835	4,499	79	883	3,317	259
1985	406	838	4,804	72	1,087	4,136	265
1986	420	794	5,572	83	1,003	5,616	284
1987	559	733	4,815	86	680	4,587	298
1988	493	750[4]	5,210	89	876	6,641	286
1989	487	850	6,454	98	740	6,854	329
1990	556	803	5,195	128	391	6,875	332
1991	641	800	6,003	109	384	6,949	352
1992	705	790	6,502	159	347	6,843	321
1993	931	780	6,038	146	331	8,451	390

NOTES

1. SOURCES: The national publications on pp. xiii–xv; League of Nations and UN, *Statistical Yearbooks*; and FAO, *Yearbook of Fisheries Statistics*.
2. The definitions of fish landings vary from country to country, but except as indicated in footnotes they are generally consistent for each country.
3. In general the statistics relate to fresh round weight.

FOOTNOTES

[1]　Statistics to 1909 relate to cod, with haddock included from 1889 (1st line). The cod statistics are derived from O.E. Sette, *Statistics of the Catch of Cod off the East Coast of North America to 1926* (Ottawa, 1927), who converted marketings to fresh round weight. The haddock statistics are derived from A.W.H. Needler, *Statistics of the Haddock Fishery in North American Waters* (Ottawa, 1929), who converted marketings to fresh gutted weight. Haddock landings data are available for 1880–88 also, but were regarded as of doubtful accuracy by Needler. For what they are worth they are as follows:

1880	20	1883	31	1886	39
1881	21	1884	39	1887	39
1882	32	1885	34	1888	43

Statistics from 1910 (2nd line) onwards relate to the main species landed on both the Atlantic and Pacific Coasts, with inland fisheries included from 1919 (2nd line). The statistics are based on the records of the Dominion Bureau of Statistics, except that figures of West Coast halibut landings derived from Bell, Dunlop and Fremen, *Pacific Coast Halibut Landings 1888 to 1950 and Catch according to Area of Origin* have been preferred for the period 1915–50. (See *Historical Statistics of Canada*, pp. 389 and 392 for the reasons for this choice.) Data for 1909–16 are for years beginning 1 April. There is an adjustment to the recorded figure for 1897. Newfoundland is included from 1949.

[2]　Data to 1946 (1st line) relate to exports of dried cod only. From 1896 to 1924 and from 1927 to 1929 the statistics are for years beginning 1 July. Newfoundland is included in Canada from 1949.

[3]　Including whales to 1958.

[4]　Change of source from this point onwards.

C15 EXPORTS OF WHEAT BY MAIN TRADING COUNTRIES (in thousands of metric tons)

	NORTH AMERICA		SOUTH AMERICA		NORTH AMERICA		SOUTH AMERICA
	Canada[1]	USA[2]	Argentina		Canada[1]	USA[2]	Argentina
1852	...	73	...	1900	265	2,775	1,930
1853	...	92	...	1901	711	3,594	904
1854	...	219	...	1902	898	4,215	645
				1903	457	3,108	1,681
1855	...	22	...	1904	400	1,204	2,305
1856	...	222	...				
1857	...	397	...	1905	1,099	120	2868
1858	...	243	...	1906	1,073[1]	962	2,248
1859	...	82	...	1907	1,188	2,084	2,681
				1908	1,337	2,732	1,636
1860	...	113	...	1909	1,354	1,821	2,514
1861	...	850	...				
1862	...	1,015	...	1910	1,247	1,270	1,884
1863	...	984	...	1911	1,755	646[2]	2,286
1864	...	645	...	1912	2,536	1,760	2,629
				1913	3,277	2,708	2,812
1865	...	270	...	1914	1,957	4,732	981
1866	...	152	...				
1867	...	167	...	1915	4,293	5,605	2,512
1868	76	434	...	1916	5,161	4,193	2,295
1869	97	478	...	1917	4,093	2,890	936
				1918	1,138	3,026	2,996
1870	48	996	—	1919	2,122	4,030	3,286
1871	81	934	- -				
1872	119	719	- -	1920	3,517	5,941	5,008
1873	179	1,067	- -	1921	3,715	7,622	1,704
1874	119	1,933	0.4	1922	5,853	4,482	3,802
				1923	6,991	2,682	3,706
1875	165	1,444	—	1924	5,219	4,526	4,384
1876	65	1,499	- -				
1877	120	1,097	0.2	1925	6,795	2,355	2,993
1878	180	1,971	2.5	1926	6,763	3,764	2,035
1879	139	3,330	26	1927	7,264	4,580	4,226
				1928	10,082	2,621	5,296
1880	69	4,170	1.2	1929	4,817	2,452	6,613
1881	105	1,376	1.7				
1882	160	2,593	1.7	1930	5,912	2,390	2,213
1883	20	2,895	61	1931	5,207[1]	2,185	3,639
1884	64	1,915	108	1932	6,211	1,494	3,442
				1933	5,234	242	3,929
1885	93	2,304	78	1934	4,570	463	4,794
1886	153	1,572	38				
1887	59	2,775	238	1935	4,509	6	3,860
1888	13	1,790	179	1936	6,614	51	1,610
1889	11	1,263	23	1937	2,613	948	3,887
				1938	3,108	2,365	1,940
1890	57	1,480	328	1939	4,434	1,720	4,746
1891	237	1,500	396				
1892	252	4,280	470	1940	3,788	391	3,640
1893	252	3,188	1,008	1941	5,352	357	2,390
1894	240	2,406	1,608	1942	5,892	180	2,176
				1943	5,967	322	1,955
1895	270	2,071	1,010	1944	7,938	273	2,326
1896	214	1,651	532				
1897	516	2,165	102				
1898	280	4,034	645				
1899	458	3,783	1,713				

C15 Exports of Wheat by Main Trading Countries (in thousands of metric tons)

| | NORTH AMERICA | | SOUTH AMERICA | | | NORTH AMERICA | | SOUTH AMERICA |
	Canada[1]	USA[2]	Argentina			Canada	USA	Argentina
1945	8,973	3,504	2,358		1970	10,746	17,443	2,302
1946	4,288	5,093	1,387		1971	12,869	16,221	811
1947	4,366	4,552	2,284		1972	13,832	21,317	1,640
1948	3,692	8,913	2,174		1973	12,305	37,444	2,971
1949	5,726	9,261	1,847		1974	10,122	25,733	1,726
1950	4,436	5,605	2,767		1975	11,039	30,966	1,758
1951	6,452	11,497	2,455		1976	10,553	26,527	3,155
1952	9,140	10,056	63		1977	14,272	23,826	5,635
1953	7,890	6,408	2,527		1978	14,423	32,395	1,608
1954	5,667	5,226	2,943		1979	11,696	31,719	4,279
1955	5,167	6,025	3,617		1980	16,760	33,972	4,495
1956	8,227	11,131	2,526		1981	15,472	41,717	3,766
1957	6,323	11,276	2,660		1982	19,205	38,745	3,801
1958	7,393	8,994	2,113		1983	21,808	36,570	10,181
1959	7,173	9,731	2,399		1984	21,091	40,135	7,245
1960	6,606	13,745	2,486		1985	16,983	23,571	9,583
1961	9,964	17,158	1,066		1986	15,957	23,280	4,021
1962	8,047	14,139	2,832		1987	22,140	29,100	4,192
1963	10,731	17,473	1,831		1988	20,087	38,490	3,643
1964	13,615	20,575	3,710		1989	11,274	36,568	4,322
1965	11,882	17,700	6,661		1990	17,954	27,557	5,837
1966	14,577	22,483	5,055		1991	23,260	31,088	5,544
1967	9,535	17,474	2,060		1992	23,644	33,877	6,071
1968	9,246	16,118	2,423		1993	18,210	35,665	5,777
1969	6,686	12,086	2,345					
1970	10,746	17,443	2,302					
1971	12,869	16,221	811					
1972	13,832	21,317	1,640					
1973	12,305	37,444	2,971					
1974	10,122	25,733	1,726					

NOTES

1. SOURCES: The national publications on pp. xiii–xv, and F.A.O. *Yearbook of Food and Agricultural Statistics.*
2. Earlier figures are available for the USA, and for some individual Canadian colonies, but the amounts involved are small.

FOOTNOTES

[1] Data to 1906 are for years beginning 1 July, and from 1907 to 1931 they are for years beginning 1 April.
[2] Years ending 30 June to 1911.

C16 NORTH AMERICA: EXPORTS OF SUGAR BY MAIN TRADING COUNTRIES (in thousands of metric tons)

	Barbados[1]	Guadeloupe	Jamaica	Martinique	Puerto Rico[2]	Trinidad & Tobago
1816	...	5.3	...	...	...	...
1817	...	18	...	...	...	...
1818	...	21	...	...	...	...
1819	...	19	...	16	...	...
1820	...	22	...	21	...	...
1821	...	23	...	22	...	...
1822	...	23	...	20	...	...
1823	...	24	...	21	...	...
1824	...	31	...	20	...	...
1825	...	24	...	26	...	...
1826	...	34	...	28	...	...
1827	...	28	...	25	...	...
1828	...	36	...	33	...	...
1829	...	39	...	29	...	...
1830	...	23	...	28	...	...
1831	...	35	73	28	...	...
1832	...	33	73	22	...	...
1833	19	31	62	20	...	17
1834	20	38	71	26	...	19
1835	18	32	69	24	...	16
1836	19	35	61	22	...	18
1837	23	25	55	20	...	14
1838	23	35	64	26	...	15
1839	20	37	43	29	...	15
1840	10	30	29	22	...	13
1841	13	29	30	25	...	14
1842	14	35	45	28	...	15
1843	18	27	35	25	...	17
1844	16	35	31	33	...	16
1845	19	34	42	30	...	18
1846	15	26	31	26	...	18
1847	25	38	45	31	...	21
1848	20	20	34	18	...	19
1849	25	18	35	20	...	21
1850	32	13	30	15	...	17
1851	35	20	25	23	...	20
1852	44	17	27	26	...	17
1853	33	17	21	22	114	22
1854	40	24	28	25	71	23
1855	36	22	26	21	...	20
1856	39	23	23	28	...	25
1857	34	22	28	26	...	26
1858	47	28	32	28	...	31
1859	39	29	28	30	...	26

C16 NORTH AMERICA: Exports of Sugar by Main Trading Countries (in thousands of metric tons)

	Barbados[1]	Cuba[4]	Dominican Republic[3]	Guadeloupe	Jamaica[5]	Martinique	Puerto Rico[2]	Trinidad & Tobago[6]
1860	42	…	…	29	30	33	…	27
1861	48	…	…	17	33	32	…	28
1862	43	…	…	31	31	32	…	37
1863	41	…	…	30	28	30	…	34
1864	36	…	…	16	27	24	…	36
1865	45	…	…	24	25	30	…	28
1866	54	…	…	34	31	35	…	41
1867	52	…	…	23	26	29	…	42
1868	55	…	…	31	32	38	…	42
1869	31	…	…	29	25	37	…	47
1870	38	…	…	34	30	38	107	42
1871	52	…	…	38	36	42	…	54
1872	38	…	…	32	34	40	…	47
1873	36	…	…	36	27	38	…	61
1874	46	…	…	35	27	43	…	45
1875	63	…	…	48	27	51	…	59
1876	37	…	…	35	28	39	…	52
1877	46	…	…	43	29	41	…	47
1878	42	…	…	48	25	44	…	53
1879	55	…	…	48	28	47	…	68
1880	52	…	4.5	41	31	39	…	54
1881	50	…	4.2	42	20	42	…	44
1882	52	…	8.5	58	37	48	…	56
1883	48	…	8.4	52	30	47	…	55
1884	56	…	16	55	30	49	…	62
1885	41	…	19	41	25	39	90	65
1886	42	…	10	37	17	30	66	49
1887	63	…	9.4	55	23	40	81	68
1888	67	…	…	48	25	30	62	56
1889	60	…	…	45	16[5]	36	62	51
1890	78	472	…	47	19	34	58	53
1891	46	649	…	30	22	32	51	47
1892	54	900	…	46	19	20	42	51
1893	61	836	…	41	21	33	43	47
1894	60	965	…	44	20	37	48	48
1895	33	837	…	30	20	29	60	56
1896	45	496	…	43	16	34	56	56
1897	54	261	49	40	14	35	58	50
1898	49	200	51	37	18	32	56	52
1899	42	301	56	40	20	32	36	53
1900	46	320[4]	54	28	15	34	74	41[6]
1901	59	499	46	39	16	40	94	46
1902	48	808	46	41	21	40	83	48
1903	35	974	49	39	14	29	103	41
1904	57	1,131	48[3]	36	10	24	118	48

C16 NORTH AMERICA: Exports of Sugar by Main Trading Countries (in thousands of metric tons)

	Barbados[1]	Cuba[4]	Dominican Republic[3]	Guadeloupe	Jamaica[5]	Martinique	Puerto Rico[2]	Trinidad & Tobago[6]
1905	42	1,103	48	27	12	30	123	37
1906	52	1,205	55	43	14	42	186	46
1907	35	1,326	49	39	11	37	185	47
1908	36	905	63	36	[6.3][5]	36	213	40[6]
1909	31	1,425	71	25	10	38	222	46
1910	46	1,778	93	43	20	40	258	47
1911	45	1,442	...	37	20	35	293	39
1912	48	1,950	...	38	10	40	330	34
1913	32	2,485	79	27	5	32	347	33
1914	55	2,529	101	40	16	39	291	49
1915	41	2,600	103	34	15	39	267	51
1916	75	2,978	123	34	29	34	385	59
1917	71	2,922	132	31	33	21	443	64
1918	58	2,309	120	27	27	21	364	36
1919	71	4,081	162	19	38	22	330	38
1920	49	3,169	159	24	37	20	401	49
1921	37	2,908	184	25	27	24	447	47
1922	52	5,064	172	20	52	19	364	53
1923	64	3,513	170	23	26	23	325	36
1924	55	4,029	221	27	24	31	382	44
1925	67	5,060	301	38	38	46	564	62
1926	65	4,809	338	34	49	43	521	67
1927	74	4,273	296	25	51	36	534	43
1928	83	4,038	348	31	50	38	614	75
1929	86	5,029	323	1	38	35	463	83
1930	76	3,311	351	25	60	37	736	70
1931	57	2,763	321	17	45	20	687	87
1932	98	2,659	440	45	39	48	813	87
1933	104	2,321	294	41	46	48	692	110
1934	118	2,341	334	29	55	45	753	95
1935	71	2,466	498	38	70	50	744	107
1936	122	2,640	435	43	79	51	785	145
1937	127	2,710	430	61	97	46	826	145
1938	103	2,641	406	45	107	51	775	122
1939	154	2,784	409	59	105	66	833	116
1940	87	2,099	418	60	83	58	763	79
1941	91	3,230	389	32	140	29	823	110
1942	66	1,799	193	17	130	16	814	86
1943	130	3,752	395	0.4	143	9.7	819	55
1944	119	3,935	755	43	134	34	649	56

C16   NORTH AMERICA: Exports of Sugar by Main Trading Countries (in thousands of metric tons)

	Barbados[1]	Cuba[4]	Dominican Republic[3]	Guadeloupe	Jamaica[5]	Martinique	Puerto Rico[2]	Trinidad & Tobago
1945	123	3,752	330	113	120	48	806	60
1946	118	3,710	416	36	151	17	778	88
1947	106	5,486	469	29	130	14	841	91
1948	70	5,820	384	30	153	14	886	97
1949	142	4,883	442	42	196	18	1,042	141
1950	152	5,079	438	54	226	33	854	128
1951	175	5,389	482	72	216	46	945	119
1952	163	4,968	548	93	203	33	1,022	116
1953	154	5,391	555	84	279	50	1,025	132
1954	167	4,149	508	103	327	66	896	152
1955	159	4,613	575	126	294	78	972	172
1956	143	5,331	694	123	379	72	1,022	140
1957	196	5,366	766	113	308	59	820	144
1958	147[1] 132	5,451	669	114	283	61	740	161
1959	159	4,876	668	136	317	69	861	154
1960	132	5,513	1,099	148	358	71	...	191
1961	143	6,500	769	159	386	74	...	219
1962	138	5,100	813	173	385	79	...	171
1963	174	3,477	652	165	401	84	...	196
1964	143	4,051	650	162	424	53	...	196
1965	162	5,167	521	168	431	74	...	216
1966	157	4,315	548	158	414	33	...	173
1967	178	5,476	647	123	358	38	...	163
1968	161	5,410	605	162	390	28	...	205
1969	121	5,535	618	120	299	24	...	204
1970	132	7,498	764	...	298	16	...	177
1971	118	5,511	994	...	202	17	...	174
1972	94	4,140	1,099	77	280	9.5	...	191
1973	111	4,797	1,065	114	265	17	...	148
1974	90	5,491	1,040	71	274	2.6	...	176
1975	73	5,744	939	71	258	4.4	...	110
1976	84	5,764	963	86	233	2.9	...	158
1977	101	6,238	1,101	82	217	1.7	...	140
1978	79	7,197	901	66	199	2.3	...	103
1979	83	7,199	986	93	191	0.2	...	88
1980	109	6,170	794	86	132	—	...	64
1981	54	7,055	855	56	121	0.1	...	67
1982	59	7,727	827	54	135	- -	...	50
1983	48	7,011	916	41	137	- -	...	63
1984	80	7,007	828	45	157	—	...	64
1985	55	7,206	655	30	152	—	...	66
1986	81	6,697	449	64	143	—	...	57
1987	74	6,479	553	5.8	136	—	...	47
1988	56	6,967	514	90	153	—	...	54
1989	48	6,819	496	55	132	—	...	57
1990	53	7,171	358	55	146	—	...	62
1991	55	6,767	320	53	157	—	...	57
1992	52	6,104	321	39	139	—	...	59
1993	38	3,662	320	56	150	—	...	52

C16   SOUTH AMERICA: EXPORTS OF SUGAR BY MAIN TRADING COUNTRIES
(in thousands of metric tons)

1821–1859				1860–1899		
	Brazil[7]	Guyana*[3]			Brazil[7]	Guyana*[8]	Peru
1821	35	...		1860	90	60	...
1822	37	...		1861	65	69	...
1823	54	...		1862	155	62	...
1824	45	...		1863	145	74	...
				1864	95	71	...
1825	35	...					
1826	35	44		1865	108	83	...
1827	50	63		1866	131	88	...
1828	68	57		1867	87	80	...
1829	55	60		1868	124	87	...
				1869	65	73	...
1830	65	61					
1831	63	59		1870	138	92	...
1832	76	56		1871	116	101	...
1833	[45][7]	55₃		1872	173	86	...
		46		1873	196	92	...
1834	56	40		1874	155	95	...
1835	72	53		1875	207	90	...
1836	83	57		1876	122	115	...
1837	73	49		1877	183	108	...
1838	90	43		1878	171	84	...
1839	68	30		1879	147	103	...
1840	81	32		1880	216	107	58
1841	98	27		1881	161	101	44
1842	72	29		1882	247	134	45
1843	77	29		1883	179	125	35
1844	83	31		1884	329	134	34
1845	110	28		1885	274	103	46
1846	104	20		1886	112	120	44
1847	104	35		1887	226₇	145	36
1848	114	34		1888	158	110	41
1849	125	30		1889	106	117	53
1850	116	36		1890	134	107	39
1851	132	42		1891	185	119₈	38
1852	111	53		1892	162	115	48
1853	158	52		1893	104	110	44
1854	119	55		1894	152	104	34
1855	120	53		1895	164	103	59
1856	109	50		1896	173	119	72
1857	113	56		1897	128	103	105
1858	107	57		1898	126	98	106
1859	156	54		1899	50	86	104

C16   SOUTH AMERICA: Exports of Sugar by Main Trading Countries (in thousands of metric tons)

1900–1944	Brazil	Guyana[*8]	Peru	1945–1993	Brazil	Guyana[*]	Peru
1900	92	96	112	1945	27	135	322
1901	187	107	115	1946	22	150	260
1902	137	122	117	1947	17	188	276
1903	22	128	128	1948	342	139	352
1904	7.9	108	132	1949	57	177	285
1905	38	118	134	1950	24	176	291
1906	85	117	137	1951	18	183	264
1907	13	102[8]	111	1952	43	238	285
1908	32	117	125	1953	256	215	408
1909	68	110	125	1954	162	248	423
1910	58	103	123	1955	573	246	483
1911	36	101	124	1956	19	250	428
1912	4.8	79	148	1957	424	260	496
1913	5.4	89	143	1958	759	305	411
1914	32	109	176	1959	617	259	480
1915	59	120	220	1960	771	314	...
1916	54	104	239	1961	783	318	557
1917	138	116	...	1962	445	315	479
1918	116	96	...	1963	524	278	496
1919	69	85	272	1964	253	238	425
1920	109	85	250	1965	760	317	366
1921	172	110	239	1966	1,005	283	430
1922	252	92	274	1967	1,001	298	475
1923	153	85	293	1968	1,026	298	467
1924	35	87	266	1969	1,099	332	270
1925	3.2	99	208	1970	1,126	283	435
1926	17	86	330	1971	1,261	342	432
1927	49	113	300	1972	2,535	305	430
1928	30	117	306	1973	2,798	229	452
1929	15	102	363	1974	2,254	307	429
1930	85	116	339	1975	1,515	289	420
1931	11	121	330	1976	807	300	299
1932	41	139	325	1977	1,830	230	434
1933	25	129	369	1978	1,347	285	249
1934	24	132	418	1979	1,394	268	283
1935	85	177	326	1980	1,961	252	54
1936	90	182	326	1981	1,785	269	—
1937	0.3	185	313	1982	1,550	255	140
1938	8.1	185	250	1983	1,721	211	17
1939	50	182	272	1984	1,848	215	40
1940	67	145	302	1985	1,356	230	60
1941	25	157	378	1986	1,234	219	52
1942	46	137	309	1987	1,101	195	30
1943	12	133	181	1988	984	143	36
1944	70	181	223	1989	549	170	43
				1990	926	129	77
				1991	977	150	59
				1992	1,346	230	56
				1993	2,133	237	50

C16 Exports of Sugar by Main Trading Countries

NOTES

1. SOURCES: The main sources have been the national publications on pp. xiii–xv; League of Nations, *International Trade Statistics*; UN, *Yearbook of International Trade Statistics*; and FAO, *The World Sugar Economy in Figures, 1880–1959* (Rome, 1961). The Peru statistics to 1910 are from Rosemary Thorp and Geoffrey Bertram, *Peru, 1890–1977* (London, 1978). Dominican Republic statistics to 1904 are from Noel Deerr, *The History of Sugar* (London, 1949), who has a somewhat different series for the years that follow. His data apparently apply to crop-years beginning in the year shown, and they are probably incomplete prior to 1897. Deerr is also the source of British Guiana figures to 1832 (1st line), and this series is also different for later years than that shown here, which comes from the Sessional Papers of the UK Parliament. He gives earlier figures for British Guiana as follows (in thousands of metric tons):

1745	0.7	1755	...	1765	2.3	1775	...	1785	3.0
1746	0.8	1756	1.2	1766	2.5	1776	2.4		
1747	0.3	1757	1.0	1767	2.5	1777	1.9	1804	1.4
1748	1.3	1758	0.5	1768	1.8	1778	4.2		
1749	2.2	1759	...	1769	2.1	1779	3.6		
1750	1.5	1760	0.5	1770	3.5	1780	2.4		
1751	0.9	1761	0.7	1771	1.9	1781	1.0		
1752	1.6	1762	1.8	1772	2.0	1782	...		
1753	0.3	1763	1.8	1773	2.3	1783	...		
1754	0.2	1764	1.8	1774	3.2	1784	2.4		

2. Most statistics are of raw and refined sugar aggregates, but it is possible that in some the refined sugar component has been converted to raw equivalent.

FOOTNOTES

[1] Including the sugar equivalent of fancy molasses to 1958 (1st line).
[2] Years ending 30 June. Small amounts of exports other than to the USA may be excluded in 1910–19.
[3] See Note 1 above.
[4] Exports to the USA only to 1900.
[5] Years beginning 1 April from 1890 to 1907. The 1908 figure is for the last three quarters of the year.
[6] Years beginning 1 April from 1901 to 1908.
[7] Years ending 30 June from 1834 to 1887. The 1833 figure is for the first half-year. Exports in the second half of 1887 were 95 thousand tons.

C17 EXPORTS OF PRINCIPAL LIVESTOCK PRODUCTS BY MAIN TRADING COUNTRIES (in thousands of metric tons)

| | NORTH AMERICA | | | SOUTH AMERICA | | | |
| | Canada[1] | | USA[2] | Argentina | | Uruguay | |
	Butter	Cheese	Meat	Meat[3]	Wool[4]	Meat[5]	Wool
1850	...	...	...	...	7.7	...	...
1851	...	...	...	...	...	...	...
1852	...	...	2.6	...	...	...	...
1853	...	...	8.3	...	7.4	...	...
1854	...	...	21	...	8.1	...	...
1855	...	...	17	...	9.4	...	...
1856	...	...	19	...	12	...	...
1857	...	...	20	...	14	...	...
1858	...	...	9.5	...	14	...	...
1859	...	...	5.4	...	18	...	...
1860	...	...	12	...	18	...	...
1861	...	...	23	...	22	...	...
1862	...	...	64	...	24	...	...
1863	...	...	99	...	32	...	...
1864	...	...	50	...	35	...	...
1865	...	...	21	...	47	...	...
1866	...	...	17₂ 39	...	55	...	...
1867	...	...	30	...	56	...	...
1868	4.8	2.8	43	...	65	...	...
1869	4.9	2.0	46	...	58	32	19
1870	5.6	2.6	41	...	58	26	13
1871	7.0	3.8	70	...	57	26	16
1872	8.6	7.4	150	...	67	34	16
1873	6.9	8.8	223	...	72	37	16
1874	5.5	11	206	...	69	36	17
1875	4.2	15	161	...	66	23	10
1876	5.6	16	190	...	79	...	...
1877	6.7	16	281	...	84	23	17
1878	5.9	17	344	...	91₄	33	17
1879	6.5	21	412	...	92	23	18
1880	8.4	18	448	...	98	37	19
1881	8.0	18	456	...	104	26	15
1882	6.9	23	302	...	111	26	21
1883	3.7	26	239	...	118	37	31
1884	3.7	32	279	...	114	49	27
1885	3.3	36	290	...	128	36	29
1886	2.1	35	302	...	132	47	32
1887	2.5	33	284 303	12	109	29	26
1888	2.0	38	280	18	132	39	38
1889	0.8	40	321	17	142	39	45
1890	0.9	43	473	20	118	39	22
1891	1.7	48	487	23	139	...	26
1892	2.6	54	473	25	155	40	28
1893	3.2	61	395	25	123	44	29
1894	2.5	70	400	36₃	162	56	39

C17 Exports of Principal Livestock Products by Main Trading Countries
(in thousands of metric tons)

1895–1934

| | NORTH AMERICA | | | SOUTH AMERICA | | | |
| | Canada[1] | | USA[2] | Argentina | | Uruguay | |
	Butter	Cheese	Meat	Meat[3]	Wool[4]	Meat[5]	Wool
1895	1.7	66	424	43	206	56	51
1896	2.7	75	446	48	192	56	43
1897	5.2	74	519	55	211	57	52
1898	5.1	89	587	66	228	52	41
1899	9.1	86	602	66$_3$	244	60	39
1900	11	84	564	82	106	58	27
1901	7.4	89	577	109	235	47	46
1902	13	91	519	152	203	44	43
1903	15	104	411	164	200	58	45
1904	11	106	441	189	176	63	45
1905	14	98	428	233	199	50	33
1906	15$_1$	98$_1$	506	222	157	53	41
1907	[8.2]	[81]	448$_2$ / 620	210	162	56	45
1908	2.2	86	385	263	183	59	53
1909	2.9	75	289	282	185	63	58
1910	2.1	82	187	340	159	67	47
1911	1.4	83	242	414	141	69	61
1912	4	74	220	431	174	63	81
1913	0.4	70	230	425	131	81	68
1914	0.6	66	215	441	125	88	45
1915	1.2	62	594	430	137	122	38
1916	1.6	77	591	524	141	100	31
1917	3.6	82	600	536	161	122	40
1918	2.2	77	1,113	737	125	130	34
1919	6.2	69	1,004	581	167	155	66
1920	8	57	496	487	106	118	33
1921	4.4	61	361	471	170	96	57
1922	3.8	61	337	524	200	124	48
1923	10	52	456	703	153	157	44
1924	6.2	53	352	897	128	159	45
1925	11	58	269	828$_3$ / 886	144	179$_5$ / 155	41
1926	...	69	211	837	146	150	54
1927	...	48	160	902	158	132	69
1928	...	51	163	707	127	88	53
1929	0.6	42	185	688	130	99	51
1930	0.5	36	181	639	136	140	75
1931	4.8	38	128	629	141	100	66
1932	1.6	39	94	574	131	72	43
1933	2	34	109	561	159	68	52
1934	0.2	28	120	560	111	59	24

C17 Exports of Principal Livestock Products by Main Trading Countries
(in thousands of metric tons)

1935–1974

| | NORTH AMERICA | | | SOUTH AMERICA | | | |
| | Canada[1] | | USA[2] | Argentina | | Uruguay | |
	Butter	Cheese	Meat	Meat[3]	Wool	Meat[4]	Wool
1935	3.5	25	85	560	137	59	50
1936	2.3	37	78	586	140	48	46
1937	1.9	40	76	648	116	71	41
1938	1.8	37	94	639	152	75	54
1939	5.6	41	112	661	149	67	49
1940	0.6	48	100	537	136	62	55
1941	0.7	42	78	637	169	95	44
1942	0.7	64	47	697	100	70	19
1943	4.3	59	32	658	89	75	56
1944	2.1	60	44	789	90	...	60
1945	2.5	61	34	514	159	36	73
1946	2.0	48	53	548	206	41	57
1947	1.4	25	142	687	172	13	68
1948	0.4	18	63	509	182	40	56
1949	0.5	24	62	497	96	72	48
1950	0.7	29	61	346	142	76	90
1951	0.2	14	71	294	60	67	34
1952	0.4	1.0	84	236	106	54	46
1953	0.1	7.5	89	269	155	49	80
1954	0.1	2.3	78	284	98	52	54
1955	3.3	6.2	86	392	109	4.1	50
1956	1.0	5.5	115	574	109	35	64
1957	- -	3.8	122	601	88	38	28
1958	- -	7.1	77	655	105	21	59
1959	4.8	9.1	90	538	141	24	35
1960	1.4	8.6	89	438	140	52	35
1961	- -	8.9	88	436	140	43	72
1962	- -	12	84	570	159	55	46
1963	2.5	12	119	670	147	66	41
1964	17	14	143	544	102	125	22
1965	1.3	15	105	469	130	80	56
1966	0.1	16	106	560	151	65	41
1967	- -	13	112	546	122	65	45
1968	- -	20	131	407	139	110	52
1969	- -	16	149	578	109	126	38
1970	- -	18	131	513	102	160	45
1971	2.0	16	142	346	92	104	47
1972	- -	9.9	161	517	85	122	27
1973	...	5.5	193	425	81	106	21
1974	...	5.1		182	46	109	29

C17 Exports of Principal Livestock Products by Main Trading Countries (in thousands of metric tons)

| | NORTH AMERICA | | SOUTH AMERICA | | | |
| | Canada | USA | Argentina | | Uruguay | |
	Cheese	Meat	Meat	Wool	Meat	Wool
1975	3.6	197	166	84	92	36
1976	2.4	263	364	92	155	24
1977	1.9	257	389	110	116	29
1978	2.2	284	435	107	103	32
1979	3.2	296	449	86	69	16
1980	3.1	282	293	91	111	41
1981	4.8	314	317	113	167	47
1982	5.1	299	345	84	141	45
1983	4.8	300	266	81	172	37
1984	5.4	307	163	74	106	28
1985	11.0	284	155	66	103	26
1986	12.0	352	158	69	150	40
1987	11.0	399	147	63	63	30
1988	10.0	474	170	61	92	34
1989	10.7	677	235	43	132	26
1990	8.6	597	268	61	162	37
1991	12.1	…	170	43	85	26
1992	11.0	793	125	37	82	14
1993	9.3	771	136	50	76	17

NOTES

1. SOURCES: The national publications on pp. xiii–xv; League of Nations, *International Trade Statistics*; and UN, *Yearbook of International Trade Statistics*.
2. The definition of meat is very variable, but it is believed that all changes have been noted in footnotes. Lard, tallow, etc, are probably not included in any case.

FOOTNOTES

[1] Data to 1906 are for years ending 30 June, and those for 1908 to 1931 are for years beginning 1 April. The 1907 figures are for the nine months from 1 July 1907 to 31 March 1908.
[2] Data to 1866 (1st line) are of bacon and hams only. From 1866 (2nd line) salt and fresh beef and pickled and fresh pork are also included. Mutton is included from 1877, but the effect of this on the continuity of the series is negligible, as is the exclusion of fresh pork and pickled beef from 1883. Canned beef is included from 1887 (2nd line). From 1907 (2nd line) the statistics relate to all meat and meat products except lard and tallow.
[3] Frozen mutton to 1894, frozen and chilled beef and mutton from 1895 to 1899, with preserved meat included from 1900. In both cases the break is negligible. From 1925 (2nd line) all kinds of meat are included.
[4] Exports from Buenos Aires for years ending 31 October to 1878.
[5] All kinds of meat to 1925 (1st line). Fresh, frozen, and chilled beef, mutton, and pork subsequently.

C18   NORTH AMERICA: EXPORTS OF VARIOUS AGRICULTURAL COMMODITIES BY MAIN TRADING COUNTRIES
(in thousands of metric tons, except as otherwise indicated)

1790–1834   1835–1874

| | Trinidad[1] | USA[2] | | | Costa Rica | Guatemala | Trinidad[1] | USA[2] | |
	Cocoa	Cotton[3]	Tobacco		Coffee	Coffee	Cocoa	Cotton[3]	Tobacco
			(million hogsheads)						(million hogsheads)
1790	...	...	118	1835	...	...	1.6	176	94
1791	...	- -	101	1836	...	...	1.4	192	109
1792	...	- -	112	1837	...	...	1.0	201	100
1793	...	- -	60	1838	...	...	1.2	270	111
1794	...	1	77	1839	...	...	1.2	188	79
1795	...	3	61	1840	...	...	1.0	337	119
1796	...	3	69	1841	...	...	1.1	240	148
1797	...	2	58	1842	...	...	1.3	265	159
1798	...	4	69	1843	...	...	0.9	[359][2]	[94][2]
1799	...	5	96	1844	...	...	1.0	301	163
1800	...	8	79	1845	...	...	1.4	396	147
1801	...	10	104	1846	...	...	1.1	249	150
1802	...	13	78	1847	...	...	1.6	239	136
1803	...	19	86	1848	...	...	1.0	369	131
1804	...	17	83	1849	...	...	2.1	464	102
1805	...	17	71	1850	...	...	1.6	288	146
1806	...	16	83	1851	...	...	2.5	421	96
1807	...	29	62	1852	...	...	3.1	496	137
1808	...	5	10	1853	...	...	2.2	504	160
1809	...	23	54	1854	...	...	1.5	448	126
1810	...	42	84	1885	...	...	2.1	457	150
1811	...	28	36	1856	7.6	...	2.1	613	117
1812	...	13	26	1857	11	...	2.2	475	157
1813	...	9	5	1858	6.1	...	2.5	507	128
1814	...	8	3	1859	11	...	2.7	629	199
1815	...	38	85	1860	9.1	...	1.9	802	167
1816	...	37	69	1861	5.1	...	3.0	139	161
1817	...	39	62	1862	4.9	...	1.7	[2.3][5]	107
1818	...	43	84	1863	3.9	...	3.4	[5.2][5]	112
1819	...	40	69	1864	5.1	...	2.3	[5.4][5]	110
									(thousand metric tons)
1820	...	58	84	1865	5.1	...	3.1	[3.9][5]	68
1821	...	57	67	1866	6.1	...	2.7	295	87
1822	...	66	83	1867	8.2	...	3.6	300	84
1823	...	79	99	1868	9.1	...	3.5	356	93
1824	...	64	78	1869	7.9	...	2.9	292	83
1825	...	80	76	1870	9.4	...	3.4	435	84
1826	...	93	64	1871	11	6.0	3.1	664	98
1827	...	133	100	1872	7.0	6.4	3.3	423	107
1828	...	96	96	1873	11	6.9	4.2	544	97
1829	...	120	77	1874	9.1	7.4	5.1	616	144
1830	...	135	84						
1831	...	126	87						
1832	...	146	107						
1833	1.3	147	83						
1834	1.3	175	88						

C18   NORTH AMERICA: Exports of Various Agricultural Commodities by Main Trading Countries (in thousands of metric tons, except as otherwise indicated)

1875–1924

	Costa Rica	Cuba	Dominican Republic		El Salvador		Guatemala
	Coffee	Tobacco	Cocoa	Tobacco	Coffee	Cotton	Coffee
1875	11	...	...	...	...	—	7.5
1876	4.8	...	...	...	...	—	9.5
1877	11	...	...	...	...	—	9.6
1878	8.2	...	...	...	...	—	9.5
1879	11	...	...	...	...	—	11
1880	11	...	...	...	...	—	13
1881	7.8	...	...	...	...	—	12
1882	4	...	...	...	...	—	14
1883	9.2	...	...	...	10	—	18
1884	17	...	...	...	10	—	17
1885	9.2	...	...	...	...	—	24
1886	9.1	...	...	...	...	—	24
1887	13	...	...	...	...	—	22
1888	10	...	...	...	...	—	17
1889	13	...	...	...	...	—	25
1890	15	...	...	...	...	—	23
1891	14	...	...	...	...	—	24
1892	11	...	...	...	...	—	22
1893	11	...	...	...	...	—	27
1894	11	...	...	...	...	—	28
1895	11	14	...	...	15	—	32
1896	12	7.6	...	...	...	—	32
1897	14	...	...	...	...	—	35
1898	20	...	...	...	...	—	38
1899	15	...	...	...	...	—	39
1900	16	...	...	...	...	—	34
1901	17	5.7	...	...	20	—	31
1902	14	7.5	...	...	19	—	36
1903	17	19	7.8	...	27	—	27
1904	13	13	14	...	35	—	30
1905	18	15	13	...	28	—	37
1906	14	13	15	...	29	—	32
1907	17	8.7	10	...	26	—	51
1908	9.0	18	19	...	25	—	26
1909	12	22	15	...	29	—	41
1910	12	16	17	10	28	—	31
1911	13	14	20	14	30	—	36
1912	12	19	21	5.8	27	—	33
1913	13	14	15	10	29	—	40
1914	18	16	21	3.7	35	—	38
1915	12	17	20	...	30	—	36
1916	17	18	22	...	36	—	40
1917	12	13	23	...	36	—	42
1918	11	12	19	...	36	—	36
1919	14	16	22	...	33	—	41
1920	14	13	23	16	38	—	43
1921	13	12	27	9	28	—	43
1922	19	16	19	8	43	—	43
1923	11	13	20	16	42	- -	44
1924	18	14	23	16	49	0.4	41

C18 NORTH AMERICA: Exports of Various Agricultural Commodities by Main Trading Countries (in thousands of metric tons, except as otherwise indicated)

1875–1924

	Haiti[5]	Mexico		Nicaragua	Trinidad	USA[2]	
	Coffee	Coffee	Cotton	Coffee	Cocoa	Cotton[3]	Tobacco
1875	...	...	...	...	3.5	572	102
1876	...	...	...	...	4.9	676	99
1877	...	...	...	...	5.0	656	128
1878	...	4.4	- -	...	4.9	729	129
1879	...	7.1	- -	...	6.1	739	146
1880	...	6.8	...	...	5.3	826	98
1881	...	8.7	...	...	5.2	994	103
1882	...	10	...	...	5.6	789	102
1883	...	8.6	—	...	5.8	1,038	107
1884	...	6.9	- -	...	6.7	845	94
1885	...	5.8	- -	...	6.8	858	99
1886	...	8.4	...	...	9.0	934	128
1887	...	8.3	- -	...	6.2	984	133
1888	...	6.5	- -	...	11	1,027	113
1889	...	9.2	—	...	7	1,082	96
1890	...	10	—	...	11	1,121	111
1891	...	15	—	...	8.4	1,319	108
1892	...	11	—	...	13	1,331	109
1893	...	15	- -	...	9.9	1,003	112
1894	...	19	- -	...	11,[1] / 9.8	1,217	122
1895	...	17	- -	9.0	12	1,595	...
1896	...	11	- -	...	11	1,059	...
1897	...	15	- -	...	11	1,408	...
1898	...	20	- -	...	11	1,746	114
					Trinidad & Tobago		
1899	...	18	- -	...	13	1,712	123
1900	...	23	0.3	...	14,[1]	1,406	152
1901	...	15	0.1	...	14	1,511	139
1902	29	22	0.2	8.9	17	1,588	132
1903	22	19	- -	8.4	16	1,607	162
1904	22	18	- -	9.8	18	1,389	138
1905	28	19	- -	8.3	22	1,953	149
1906	29	19	- -	8.8	13	1,648	137
1907	27	14	8.0	9.1	23	2,049	151
1908	29	21	3.5	9.3	22,[1]	1,731	147
1909	19	27	0.2	8.4	23	2,018	128
1910	36	19	0.3	12	26	1,455	160
1911	24	19	0.2	7.6	23	1,830	160
1912	36	21	0.4	6.2	19	2,511	170
1913	26	...	...	12	22	2,069	188
1914	...	...	...	10	29	2,160	203
1915	16	...	...	9.1	25	1,998	158
1916	20	...	...	10	24	1,653	216
1917	24	...	...	8.4	32	1,123	114
1918	20	...	...	12	27	961	183
1919	49	...	...	15	28	1,528	347
1920	31	11	24	7.0	22	1,442	212
1921	21	15	36	14	34	1,515	234
1922	27	25	16	8.9	23	1,430	195
1923	36	18	2.9	14	31	1,244	215
1924	29	18	16	18	26	1,580	248

C18 NORTH AMERICA: Exports of Various Agricultural Commodities by Main Trading Countries (in thousands of metric tons, except as otherwise indicated)

1925-1969

	Costa Rica	Cuba	Dominican Republic		El Salvador		Guatemala	
	Coffee	Tobacco	Cocoa	Tobacco	Coffee	Cotton	Coffee	Cotton
1925	15	15	23	22	32	2.2	45	—
1926	18	18	20	10	51	0.3	43	—
1927	16	18	27	20	36	- -	53	—
1928	19	21	19	14	53	- -	44	—
1929	20	21	21	17	47	- -	44	—
1930	24	26	21	13	59	0.1	57	
1931	23	18	26	6.8	55	- -	36	—
1932	19	16	17	4.4	40	- -	46	—
1933	28	13	20	5.7	56	- -	35	—
1934	19	12	22	9.7	50	- -	49	—
1935	24	14	28	6.9	50	—	40	—
1936	21	10	18	4.8	49	—	50	—
1937	23	12	20	3.2	67	- -	47	—
1938	22	13	28	7.4	53	—	49	—
1939	18	13	28	8.6	55	—	44	—
1940	18	12	23	3.6	56	- -	42	—
1941	21	13	19	...	41	0.6	43	—
1942	20	12	18	3.4	52	0.9	56	—
1943	24	15	28	7.5	56	1	50	—
1944	19	15	26	0.9	63	0.9	51	—
1945	22	14	19	9.1	57	0.6	51	—
1946	16	21	25	29	48	1.0	50	—
1947	18	12	30	15	63	0.9	56	—
1948	24	13	26	14	60	3.3	49	—
1949	17	12	20	21	75	1.7	55	—
1950	17	62	26	14	69	3.0	55	—
1951	19	17	23	16	66	3.4	50	—
1952	21	18	22	15	67	6.5	61	—
1953	28	16	25	9.5	66	9.5	57	—
1954	23	19	21	12	62	9.1	52	5.2
1955	28	22	23	13	72	14	58	6.6
1956	23	21	18	13	65	30	63	8.2
1957	29	25	24	12	83	27	62	7.2
1958	46	26	21	12	81	33	71	10
1959	43	26	22	12	83	47	83	11
1960	47	26	27	15	90	30	80	13
1961	52	...	15	22	87	40	79	22
1962	57	...	21	18	105	60	84	32
1963	55	13	26	17	101	64	98	46
1964	51	17	28	25	109	65	76	64
1965	48	18	23	15	100	68	95	64
1966	55	11	26	13	97	44	109	82
1967	66	11	24	20	121	29	81	57
1968	69	16	25	16	118	22	94	65
1969	68	15	25	18	113	34	101	73

C18 NORTH AMERICA: Exports of Various Agricultural Commodities by Main Trading Countries (thousands of metric tons)

1925–1969

	Haiti[5]	Mexico		Nicaragua		Trinidad & Tobago	USA[2]	
	Coffee	Coffee	Cotton	Coffee	Cotton	Cocoa	Cotton[3]	Tobacco
1925	31	24	12	11	—	22	1,989	212
1926	36	21	28	18	—	23	2,128	217
1927	29	26	26	10	—	24	2,221	230
1928	41	32	23	18	—	26	2,028	261
1929	29	30	21	13	—	28	1,806	252
1930	34	31	3.0	15	—	24	1,584	254
1931	26	27	11	16	—	26	1,663	229
1932	23	20	5.5	8.1	—	19	2,180	176
1933	42	41	1.4	14	—	23	2,052	191
1934	34	38	3.5	15	—	12	1,428	190
1935	19	32	27	19	—	20	1,467	173
1936	36	43	52	13	—	13	1,349	185
1937	25	35	9.4	16	—	12	1,462	190
1938	25	35	22	14	—	19	1,108	215
1939	29	35	7.7	17	—	7.6	1,162	148
1940	16	26	5.4	15	—	11	928	98
1941	23	28	13	13	—	8.5	283	119
1942	18	22	0.5	13	—	4.6	244	108
1943	26	34	5.4	12	—	3.6	382	178
1944	23	36	29	13	—	4.8	241	127
1945	30	36	29	12	—	3.5	582	213
1946	24	33	46	12	0.1	3.0	907	291
1947	25	33	85	10	0.1	4.1	626	224
1948	23	31	49	15	0.1	8.3	669	188
1949	33	49	123	6.8	0.4	5.8	1,228	224
1950	23	46	163	21	0.3	7.4	1,344	214
1951	25	52	178	16	4.4	8.8	1,188	235
1952	31	52	230	19	9.5	6.4	971	177
1953	23	74	235	19	13	9.9	679[3] 642	233
1954	32	70	259	17	23	8.0	944	204
1955	20	84	352	23	44	7.5	564	243
1956	31	74	422	17	36	9.9	1,033	230
1957	18	89	284	22	36	7.3	1,574	223
1958	35	79	341	23	43	8.3	1,044	173
1959	22	74	407	16	62	7.3	834	208
1960	24	83	316	22	27	7.2	1,708	224
1961	20	93	305	21	33	5.7	1,450	227
1962	31	95	425	21	56	5.9	873	213
1963	23	68	370	24	73	6.6	989	229
1964	23	104	322	23	93	4.6	1,189	232
1965	23	81	409	28	125	4.9	807	212
1966	24	95	429	23	111	4.8	816	250
1967	17	78	271	26	110	4.7	901	259
1968	19	99	316	28	105	5.9	878	272
1969	19	97	370	27	91	3.9	544	262

C18 NORTH AMERICA: Exports of Various Agricultural Commodities by Main Trading Countries (in thousands of metric tons)

	Costa Rica	Cuba	Dominican Republic		El Salvador		Guatemala	
	Coffee	Tobacco	Cocoa	Tobacco	Coffee	Cotton	Coffee	Cotton
1970	69	14	34	20	112	42	96	50
1971	64	11	29	26	99	49	101	48
1972	86	12	33	33	104	59	115	75
1973	73	15	26	31	120	63	115	85
1974	90	16	28	42	145	44	122	107
1975	77	14	23	37	144	79	136	98
1976	64	15	25	33	154	52	119	93
1977	67	19	26	20	135	51	133	124
1978	86	14	28	27	65	77	132	128
1979	97	13	26	42	186	56	144	147
1980	72	2.7	24	21	147	53	129	137
1981	96	7.9	28	40	132	30	103	77
1982	94	18	40	12	141	32	141	67
1983	108	14	35	14	159	37	143	39
1984	113	9.8	32	16	161	5.5	127	52
1985	124	18	31	14	148	24	173	51
1986	94	15	36	18	123	5.9	155	37
1987	139	19	39	13	146	2.6	146	16
1988	120	19	47	17	125	3.5	141	32
1989	130	15	41	9	95	0.9	430	26
1990	140	18	46	16	144	1.2	201	26
1991	145	14	41	12	123	1.0	174	16
1992	110	14	44	9	125	0.7	195	12
1993	144	10	45	12	171	0.1	221	3

	Haiti	Mexico		Nicaragua		Trinidad & Tobago	USA	
	Coffee	Coffee	Cotton	Coffee	Cotton	Cocoa	Cotton	Tobacco
1970	16	85	214	30	68	6.1	677	234
1971	22	97	166	33	78	3.6	936	217
1972	19	101	204	33	102	5.0	701	278
1973	19	137	179	38	100	3.5	1,246	284
1974	19	120	166	32	132	3.8	1,173	301
1975	18	143	157	41	133	4.8	871	265
1976	27	168	143	53	113	3.0	779	266
1977	16	103	131	50	116	3.2	1,013	291
1978	19	107	191	55	129	3.2	1,333	321
1979	14	115	212	56	114	2.7	1,508	260
1980	25	175	172	47	20	2.2	1,809	274
1981	14	122	183	53	75	3.0	1,269	267
1982	15	160	126	48	60	2.4	1,393	261
1983	24	220	70	56	79	1.7	1,204	240
1984	19	174	122	42	82	1.5	1,500	249
1985	18	227	77	40	67	1.3	1,095	251
1986	17	208	56	39	49	1.3	657	218
1987	13	223	52	38	47	1.5	1,195	199
1988	14	170	89	33	35	1.7	1,173	220
1989	13	272	58	27	22	1.4	1,533	230
1990	9	209	58	37	24	1.6	1,697	230
1991	7	221	25	28	23	1.1	1,532	229
1992	8	195	7	37	23	1.4	1,413	263
1993	9	196	27	30	0.2	1.3	1,141	212

C18   SOUTH AMERICA: EXPORTS OF VARIOUS AGRICULTURAL COMMODITIES BY MAIN TRADING COUNTRIES (in thousands of metric tons)

	Brazil[4]				Colombia	Ecuador
	Cocoa	Coffee	Cotton	Rubber	Coffee	Cocoa
1821	1.0	7.7	11	...	...	...
1822	0.7	11	13	...	...	...
1823	0.7	14	13	...	...	...
1824	1.3	16	12	...	...	...
1825	1.5	13	15	...	...	...
1826	1.6	19	5.1	...	...	...
1827	2.0	26	10	- -	...	...
1828	0.7	27	14	0.1	...	...
1829	1.2	28	14	0.1	...	...
1830	0.7	29	16	0.2	...	...
1831	0.9	33	16	0.1	...	...
1832	1.8	43	10	0.2	...	...
1833	[0.8][4]	[34][4]	[7.3][4]	[0.1][4]	...	...
1834	1.2	67	12	0.2	...	...
1835	0.8	58	11	0.2	...	...
1836	1.3	63	13	0.2	...	...
1837	1.2	55	13	0.3	...	...
1838	2.8	69	11	0.2	...	...
1839	3.0	80	9.4	0.4	...	...
1840	3.0	83	10	0.4	...	...
1841	2.9	74	10	0.4	...	...
1842	2.7	82	9.4	0.2	0.7	...
1843	2.2	87	10	0.2	1.1	...
1844	2.8	92	12	0.2	1.2	...
1845	2.0	92	12	0.4	1.4	...
1846	2.9	103	9.5	0.4	...	...
1847	3.0	143	8.9	0.6	...	...
1848	2.4	140	9.4	0.7	...	...
1849	3.7	126	13	0.8	...	...
1850	4.1	87	17	0.9	...	...
1851	3.9	149	13	1.4	...	...
1852	4.3	140	13	1.6	...	...
1853	3.4	146	15	1.6	...	...
1854	4.6	128	13	2.3	...	...
1855	2.2	191	13	2.9	2.1	...
1856	2.4	171	15	2.1	2.1	...
1857	3.5	191	16	1.6	2.5	...
1858	3.6	143	15	1.6	2.9	...
1859	4.1	164	17	1.7	3.3	6.8
1860	3.2	151	11	2.5	3.9	7.7
1861	3.5	214	9.0	2.5	...	10.0
1862	3.0	145	13	2.3	...	7.2
1863	3.9	128	16	3.1	...	7.1
1864	3.4	120	20	3.4	...	5.9

C18 SOUTH AMERICA: Exports of Various Agricultural Commodities by Main Trading Countries (in thousands of metric tons)

	Argentina		Brazil[4]				Colombia	Ecuador		Peru
	Linseed	Maize	Cocoa	Coffee	Cotton	Rubber	Coffee	Cocoa	Coffee	Cotton
1865	—	...	3.2	159	25	3.3	0.4	5.2	...	...
1866	—	...	2.6	146	43	3.5	4.7	10	...	...
1867	—	...	2.9	189	39	4.7	4.1	9.2	...	...
1868	—	...	3.9	214	42	5.0	6.2	9.8	...	...
1869	—	...	2.8	228	39	4.7	3.8	8.0	0.1	...
1870	—	...	4.6	187	43	4.8	4.0	11	0.1	...
1871	—	0.1	4.5	230	45	5.0	6.4	8.5	0.2	...
1872	—	0.1	5.5	244	79	5.7	8.0	8.4	0.3	...
1873	—	1.5	4.3	210	46	5.1	7.4	12	0.3	...
1874	—	3.5	4.6	166	56	6.7	10	11	0.5	...
1875	—	0.2	5.3	231	44	5.8	4.6	8.1	0.5	...
1876	—	8.1	5.2	204	28	5.7	3.4	10	0.4	...
1877	—	9.8	5.8	213	31	6.2	2.2	9.3	0.5	...
1878	0.1	17	4.6	231	18	6.6	4.6	4.6	...	...
1879	0.2	30	5.1	294	25	6.5	4.7	14	0.3	...
1880	1	15	5.0	157	11	6.9	6.5	17	0.8	2.3
1881	6.4	25	6.8	220	13	6.7	...	10	0.6	2.0
1882	23	107	7.5	245	22	6.8	...	9.3	0.6	2.2
1883	23	19	6.8	401	34	7.5	...	7.7	0.8	2.1
1884	34	114	7	319	33	9.2	...	8.5	0.6	1.6
1885	69	198	6.2	374	24	7.9	...	11	0.9	2.2
1886	38	232	4.2	326	15	8.2	...	17	1.4	3.6
1887	81	362	6.9[4]	365[4]	23[4]	8.6[4]	6.7	16	1.1	2.5
1888	40	162	10	207	22	17	...	11	1.4	3.7
1889	28	433	9.0	335	14	16	...	12	1	3.4
1890	31	707	6.2	307	13	15	...	16	1.2	4.2
1891	12	66	10	322	20	17	...	9.7	1.3	4.8
1892	43	446	6.5	427	12	18	...	15	1.7	9.8
1893	72	85	10	318	39	19	...	19	1.9	8.0
1894	104	55	8.5	335	27	20	28	18	2.7	4.5
1895	276	772	11	403	9.5	28	29	17	2.6	5
1896	230	1,571	9.0	405	7.2	24	38	16	1.6	4.7
1897	162	375	10	568	12	22	34	15	1.2	5.6
1898	158	717	11	556	8.1	21	38	20	1.7	6.7
1899	218	1,116	13	586	3.7	21	23	24	1.2	5.9
1900	223	713	15	549	21	24	...	18	1.5	7.2
1901	338	1,112	16	886	12	30	...	22	1.3	8.0
1902	341	1,193	21	789	32	29	...	22	2.2	6.7
1903	594	2,104	21	776	28	32	...	23	1.8	7.7
1904	881	2,470	23	602	13	32	...	29	3.5	7.5
1905	655	2,222	21	649	24	35	31	21	2.2	8.6
1906	538	2,694	25	838	32	35	38	23	2.7	10
1907	764	1,277	24	941	28	36	34	20	1.1	12
1908	1,056	1,712	33	759	3.6	38	36	32	3.7	16
1909	887	2,273	34	1,013	10	39	42	32	3.3	21

C18 SOUTH AMERICA: Exports of Various Agricultural Commodities by Main Trading Countries (in thousands of metric tons)

	Argentina		Brazil				Colombia	Ecuador		Peru
	Linseed[6]	Maize	Cocoa	Coffee	Cotton	Rubber	Coffee	Cocoa	Coffee	Cotton
1910	605	2,660	29	583	11	39	34	36	3.9	14
1911	416	125	35	675	15	37	38	39	4.6	16
1912	515	4,835	30	725	17	42	56	38	2.8	19
1913	1,017	4,807	30	796	37	36	61	39	3.7	24
1914	842	3,542	41	576	30	33	62	45	3	23
1915	981	4,331	45	1,024	5.2	35	68	35	2.3	21
1916	640	2,874	44	782	1.1	31	73	44	3.2	24
1917	141	894	56	636	5.9	34	63	42	2.7	17
1918	391	665	42	446	2.6	23	69	37	1.6	22
1919	855	2,485	63	778	12	33	101	42	1.7	38
1920	1,063	4,475	55	691	25	24	87	43	1.6	34
1921	1,357	2,830	43	742	20	17	141	41	6.1	36
1922	938	2,833	46	760	34	20	106	44	4.1	40
1923	1,036	2,839	65	868	19	18	124	31	5.6	43
1924	1,358	4,527	69	854	6.5	22	133	33	5.8	40
1925	961	2,936	64	809	31	24	117	33	4.1	42
1926	1,673	4,907	63	825	17	23	147	22	6.1	50
1927	1,895	8,344	75	907	...	26	141	24	5.9	57
1928	1,944	6,372	72	833	10	19	160	23	9.2	47
1929	1,617	5,048	66	857	4.8	20	170	18	7.3	46
1930	1,170	4,670	67	917	30	14	190	20	9.5	55
1931	1,880	9,767	76	1,071	21	13	182	15	8.3	47
1932	2,028	7,055	98	716	0.5	6.2	191	15	8.0	46
1933	1,392	5,019	99	928	12	9.5	200	11	7.0	55
1934	1,374	5,471	102	849	127	11	185	19	14	68
1935	1,778	7,052	112	920	139	12	226	20	13	78
1936	1,488	8,382	122	851	200	13	236	20	14	81
1937	1,802	9,087	105	727	236	15	248	21	15	81
1938	1,265	2,642	128	1,027	269	12	254	18	14	69
1939	1,183	3,196	132	890	324	12	222	14	13	77
1940	752	1,875	107	723	224	12	267	11	15	51
1941	665	553	133	663	288	11	175	14	12	83
1942	315	220	72	437	154	12	259	14	6.1	34
1943	646	190	115	607	78	15	315	18	12	36
1944	275[6]	550	102	813	108	21	294	14	14	26
1945	46	572	83	850	164	19	309	17	11	60
1946	148	2,200	130	930	353	18	340	17	7.6	120
1947	214	2,366	99	890	285	14	320	20	10	56
1948	46	2,534	72	1,050	259	5.4	335	17	20	52
1949	69	1,063	132	1,162	140	3.2	325	20	10	42
1950	206	794	132	890	129	4.5	269	26	20	66
1951	258	298	96	982	143	5.4	288	24	17	62
1952	28	652	58	949	28	3.2	302	24	20	83
1953	113	1,083	109	933	140	3.7	398	22	18	90
1954	245	2,185	121	655	309	4.3	345	31	21	84

C18 SOUTH AMERICA: Exports of Various Agricultural Commodities by Main Trading Countries (in thousands of metric tons)

	Argentina		Brazil				Colombia	Ecuador		Peru
	Linseed[6]	Maize	Cocoa	Coffee	Cotton	Rubber	Coffee	Cocoa	Coffee	Cotton
1955	156	362	122	822	176	3.4	352	25	23	85
1956	61	1,065	126	1,008	143	2.6	304	30	26	109
1957	141	789	110	859	66	3.0	289	27	29	82
1958	162	1,679	103	773	40	2.4	326	22	30	108
1959	218	2,686	80	1,046	78	3.0	385	29	24	115
1960	169	2,570	125	1,009	95	3.5	356	36	32	100
1961	204	1,730	120	1,018	206	8.1	339	33	23	114
1962	264	2,931	73	983	216	5.8	394	32	33	140
1963	213	2,447	83	1,171	222	2.7	368	35	30	125
1964	205	3,339	86	987	217	4.2	385	27	25	116
1965	239	2,804	110	810	196	7.9	338	39	48	116
1966	121	3,752	135	1,114	236	4.7	334	32	43	115
1967	211	4,318	136	1,116	189	5.7	366	45	58	70
1968	79	2,893	96	1,119	248	4.6	395	70	49	68[7]
										67
1969	147	4,024	137	1,140	439	4.8	...	35	38	88
1970	—	5,232	141	983	396	5.3	394	40	52	69
1971	183	6,128	163	1,058	261	5.0	390	...	...	52
1972	106	3,005	157	1,084	305	4.1	391	54	61	50
1973	97	4,033	134	1,111	283	4.0	405	39	76	48
1974	80	5,525	186	721	83	1.8	412	80	60	46
1975	84	3,887	223	813	107	1.7	490	53	61	37
1976	113	3,080	177	849	6	1.0	373	50	87	39
1977	199	5,431	146	544	35	1.0	310	60	54	21
1978	240	5,895	226	665	45	0.9	536	71	99	18
1979	184	5,960	270	615	0.3	0.3	659	75	84	16
1980	223	3,481	245	826	9	0.1	663	72	56	30
1981	175	9,164	254	874	30	0.1	544	66	59	31
1982	176	5,226	240	938	56	- -	532	61	79	53
1983	203	6,525	271	986	180	- -	553	13	80	20
1984	212	5,518	248	1,032	32	0.1	599	54[8]	72	8
								47		
1985	142	7,069	323	1,034	87	- -	585	69	75	25
1986	126	7,411	272	478	37	- -	667	38	109	21
1987	183	3,987	275	988	174	—	662	44	102	9
1988	152	4,217	278	904	35	- -	568	45	76	10
1989	130	1,907	263	1,009	9	- -	629	68	102	37
1990	160	3,038	274	913	9	- -	811	92	101	14
1991	117	3,898	235	1,173	14	- -	740	64	75	34
1992	126	6,093	234	1,083	15	- -	968	43	57	8
1993	35	4,871	237	1,032	12	- -	788	81	75	20

C18   Exports of Various Agricultural Commodities by Main Trading Countries

NOTE

SOURCES: The national publications on pp. xiii–xv; League of Nations, *International Trade Statistics*; and UN, *Yearbook of International Trade Statistics*. Colombian statistics to 1887 are taken from Robert C. Beyer, *The Colombian Coffee Industry: Origins and Major Trends, 1740–1940* (PhD thesis, University of Minnesota, 1947).

FOOTNOTES

[1]   Data to 1894 (1st line) include re-exports. Data for 1901 to 1908 are for years beginning 1 April.
[2]   Data to 1842 are for years ending 30 September. From 1844 to 1915 they are for years ending 30 June. The 1843 figures are for the nine months from 1 October 1842 to 30 June 1843.
[3]   Data to 1953 (1st line) are of unmanufactured cotton. Subsequently they are of raw cotton excluding linters.
[4]   Data from 1834 to 1887 are for years ending 30 June. The 1833 figures are for the first half-year only. Figures for the second half of 1887 are as follows: cocoa—2.9; coffee—102; cotton–16; rubber—6.7.
[5]   Years ending 30 September.
[6]   Linseed to 1944, linseed oil subsequently. Linseed exports in 1945 and 1946 were 135 and 38 thousand tons respectively, and were negligible subsequently. Linseed oil exports prior to 1945 were as follows: 1939–2; 1940–6; 1941–10; 1942–34; 1943–35; 1944–25.
[7]   Subsequently excluding linters.
[8]   Subsequently only beans.

C19 EXPORTS OF TIMBER PRODUCTS BY MAIN TRADING COUNTRIES

1900–1939   1940–1993

	Canada[1]			USA			Canada[1]			USA
	Lumber (thousand million feet)	Newsprint (thousand tons)	Woodpulp (thousand tons)	Lumber (thousand million feet)		Lumber (thousand million feet)	Newsprint (thousand tons)	Woodpulp (thousand tons)	Lumber (thousand million feet)
1900	...	...	...	1.7	1945	2.0	2,775	1,302	0.4
1901	...	...	...	1.5	1946	2.1	3,500	1,287	0.6
1902	...	...	...	1.4	1947	2.7	3,829	1,541	1.4
1903	...	...	...	1.9	1948	2.5[1]	3,926[1]	1,631[1]	0.6
1904	...	...	...	2.0	1949	2.2	4,345	1,412	0.7
1905	...	...	...	1.8	1950	3.6	4,480	1,675	0.5
1906	...	...	...	2.1	1951	3.4	4,638	2,035	1.0
1907	...	...	...	2.3	1952	3.3	4,833	1,761	0.7
1908	...	...	218	1.8	1953	3.4	4,876	1,769	0.6
1909	...	...	255	2.0	1954	4.0	5,009	1,978	0.7
1910	...	...	298	2.3	1955	4.6	5,228	2,146	0.8
1911	...	...	236	2.7	1956	4.0	5,413	2,154	0.8
1912	...	...	316	2.9	1957	3.6	5,435	2,071	0.8
1913	...	...	270	3.0	1958	3.9	5,156	2,013	0.7
1914	...	...	386	2.1	1959	4.2	5,369	2,238	0.8
						(million cubic metres[2])			
1915	...	...	330	1.3	1960	12	5,621	2,423	0.9
1916	...	477	507	1.3	1961	13	5,673	2,660	0.8
1917	...	541	464	1.1	1962	13	5,578	2,840	0.8
1918	...	577	530	1.1	1963	14	5,635	3,122	0.9
1919	...	642	643	1.5	1964	16	6,183	3,402	1.0
1920	1.9	691	744	1.7	1965	17	6,522	3,606	0.9
1921	1.0	643	478	1.3	1966	16	7,095	3,850	1.0
1922	2.0	870	742	2.0	1967	17	6,771	3,978	1.1
1923	2.4	1,032	794	2.5	1968	18	6,785	4,619	1.2
1924	2.1	1,098	709	2.7	1969	17	7,471	5,360	1.1
1925	2.2	1,272	872	2.6	1970	19	7,339	5,153	1.3
1926	2.2	1,571	913	2.8	1971	21	7,075	5,270	1.1
1927	2.2	1,707	797	3.1	1972	24	7,350	5,663	1.4
1928	1.9	2,002	784	3.2	1973	24	7,617	6,017	2.0
1929	2.0	2,282	754	3.2	1974	21	7,892	6,534	1.7
1930	1.6	2,116	689	2.4	1975	16	6,350	5,043	1.6
1931	1.1	1,822	565	1.7	1976	26	6,997	6,269	1.8
1932	0.8	1,612	410	1.2	1977	33	7,266	6,243	1.7
1933	1.1	1,667	552	1.3	1978	35	7,868	6,751	1.7
1934	1.5	2,190	550	1.3	1979	35	7,778	7,196	2.1
1935	1.4	2,336	601	1.3	1980	34	7,707	7,354	2.3
1936	1.9	2,715	684	1.3	1981	32	7,987	6,869	2.3
1937	2.0	3,134	790	1.4	1982	31	7,078	6,342	2.0
1938	1.8	2,200	503	1.0	1983	39	7,475	11,550	2.2
1939	2.2	2,412	640	1.1	1984	43	8,127	7,193	2.1
1940	2.5	2,942	970	1.0	1985	44	8,285	7,263	1.9
1941	2.3	2,959	1,281	0.7	1986	43	8,563	7,856	2.4
1942	2.2	2,726	1,371	0.5	1987	48	8,772	8,504	3.2
1943	1.7	2,549	1,412	0.3	1988	49	8,554	8,643	4.5
1944	1.9	2,546	1,277	0.4	1989	48	8,165	8,241	4.2
					1990	29	8,722	7,884	3.8
					1991	27	8,561	8,776	4.0
					1992	36	8,696	8,922	3.6
					1993	27	9,000	9,379	3.4

NOTE

SOURCES: The national publications on pp. xiii–xv, except for Canadian lumber exports 1960–75, which come from FAO, *Yearbook of Forestry Statistics.*

FOOTNOTES

[1] Newfoundland became part of Canada from 1 April 1949.
[2] The figure for 1959 in million cubic metres is 11.

D INDUSTRY

Apart from table 1, which gives indices of industrial production, and table 13, showing the number of cotton spindles, all the tables in this section consist of physical output and external trade volume statistics for major commodities which possess an adequate degree of homogeneity to allow aggregation and meaningful comparisons between countries. Inevitably, these are mostly basic commodities rather than finished goods; yarn and cloth rather than clothing, metals rather than machinery. The picture they give of industrial development is necessarily biased and partial. However, until very recent times there is little that could be added to them in the way of continuous statistical series for industries making finished products.

Probably enough has been written about the problems of constructing indices of industrial production for most users to be aware of their pitfalls. Even given all the desired basic information, an index which accurately reflects the composition of industrial output in any one year will not, in a changing world, have precisely the right weighting of activities for another year. Where the components of an index are expressed in terms of values rather than volume, changes in relative prices will be an added source of possible misrepresentation. Changing the weights and linking indices is one solution to this problem and often the best one; but it takes away exact precision of comparability. Such precision, however, can easily become unreal and meaningless where new commodities and activities are added to, and sometimes displace, old ones. All worthwhile indices of industrial production, then, are compromises between relevance and exact comparability over time. The skill of the constructor is in picking the base-years and linking points which produce least distortion and appear to represent best the reality of industrial activity and change. Judgement on these matters inevitably contains subjective elements, and it is safe to say that there is no objectively perfect index.

Technical problems have been compounded in many cases by lack of sufficient basic information.

As was mentioned above, statistics on the more complex products of industry have not been collected until quite recently, with rare exceptions in the most industrialized countries. Moreover, some of the statistics have been concerned with taxation in one form or another, and clearly such data are not unbiased. On the whole, it seems wise to treat nineteenth-century indices of production, and all of those for less-developed countries, with a measure of caution.

The remaining tables in this section are reasonably straightforward, though not always so much so as they seem at first glance. Most of the commodities covered are fairly homogeneous, though hardly one is perfectly so. The main reasons for such variations as are not obvious are referred to in the notes following each table and in the footnotes.

D1 NORTH AMERICA: INDICES OF INDUSTRIAL PRODUCTION

Key: MF = manufacturing

1860–1899   1900–1944

1860–1899 (USA)

Year	Mf (1899 = 100)	Mining (1899 = 100)
1860	16	...
1861	16	...
1862	15	...
1863	17	...
1864	18	...
1865	17	...
1866	21	...
1867	22	...
1868	23	...
1869	25	...
1870	25	...
1871	26	...
1872	31	...
1873	30	...
1874	29	...
1875	28	...
1876	28	...
1877	30	...
1878	32	...
1879	36	...
1880	42	35
1881	46	39
1882	49	44
1883	50	46
1884	47	47
1885	47	48
1886	57	54
1887	60	59
1888	62	62
1889	67	67
1890	72	72
1891	73	74
1892	79	78
1893	70	74
1894	68	71
1895	81	79
1896	74	82
1897	80	85
1898	91	90
1899	100	100

1900–1944

Base years: Canada 1938 = 100 (Mf from 1923, Mining from 1924). Mexico 1900 = 100 (1900–1914), then 1938 = 100 (Mf from 1876 figure/1915 onward; Mining 1938 = 100 from 1929). USA 1899 = 100 (1900–1914), then 1938 = 100 (from 1876/1915 onward).

Year	Canada Mf	Canada Mining	Mexico Mf	Mexico Mining	USA Mf	USA Mining
1900	...	...	100	...	101	105
1901	...	...	102	...	112	111
1902	...	...	106	...	129	114
1903	...	...	113	...	129	130
1904	...	...	120	...	124	131
1905	...	...	127	...	142	148
1906	...	...	130	...	151	154
1907	...	...	135	...	153	189
1908	...	...	139	...	123	157
1909	...	...	145	...	158	177
1910	...	...	147	...	164	188
1911	...	...	139	...	155	186
1912	...	...	113	...	187	200
1913	...	...	130	...	196	212
1914	...	...	98	...	186	197
(1938 = 100)			30		63	61
1915	...	...	36	...	74	66
1916	...	...	33	...	88	74
1917	...	...	30	...	87	78
1918	...	...	29	...	86	79
1919	...	...	37	...	75	69
1920	...	...	35	...	82	80
1921	...	...	35	...	66	67
1922	...	...	47	...	84	71
1923	66	*(1938 = 100)*	54	...	95	97
1924	65	61	56	...	91	92
1925	71	67	58	...	101	95
1926	81	72	66	...	107	103
1927	86	73	58	...	108	105
1928	94	82	62	...	111	104
1929	100	85	66	118 *(1938 = 100)*	124	114
1930	90	71	69	...	106	101
1931	79	61	83	...	89	85
1932	66	54	60	...	67	69
1933	67	55	55	...	78	75
1934	78	66	83	...	85	82
1935	86	73	81	88	102	87
1936	95	81	93	92	120	104
1937	109	95	97	104	128	116
1938	100	100	100	100	100	100
1939	108	108	98	96	127	111
1940	133	115	104	94	147	123
1941	174	120	111	96	195	135
1942	212	119	121	105	244	142
1943	230	105	127	106	294	145
1944	234	95	138	97	287	150

International Historical Statistics: The Americas 1750–1993

D1   NORTH AMERICA: Indices of Industrial Production 1958 = 100

	Canada		Dominican Republic[1]	El Salvador[1]	Guatemala[1]	Mexico		Nicaragua[1]	Panama[1]	USA	
	Mf	Mining				Mf	Mining			Mf	Mining
1944	75	34	...	...	...	43	89	...	...	91	83
1945	66	33	...	...	...	46	90	...	...	77	80
1946	60	31	...	...	60	47	70	...	...	63	79
1947	66	35	...	...	63	48	88	...	...	69	89
1948	69	40	...	...	65	50	81	...	...	72	92
1949	71	45	...	...	66	52	82	...	...	68	80
1950	75	49	...	...	69	56	90	...	...	79	89
1951	82	55	...	...	68	60	87	...	...	86	97
1952	84	58	...	...	72	59	93	...	...	89	95
1953	90	62	...	...	71	60	89	63	...	96	97
1954	87	71	...	82	72	71	86	72	...	91	93
1955	96	82	...	81	76	80	93	82	...	102	103
1956	103	94	...	88	82	88	99	82	...	107	108
1957	102	100	...	102	92	95	97	89	...	107	108
1958	100	100	100	100	100	100	100	100	100	100	100
1959	107	113	96	95	106	104	109	...	109	112	105
1960	109	114	112	106	106	119	107	133	133	114	108
1961	113	117	101	108	113	123	108	145	149	116	109
1962	123	125	123	120	111	131	110	152	193	125	112
1963	131	132	127	141	126	143	115	159	237	133	117
1964	143	149	135	183	133	163	121	178	237	142	122
1965	158	155	109	224	147	179	117	202	271	156	127
1966	168	158	132	228	154	196	122	213	300	172	134
1967	172	167	141	263	159	209	125	235	321	175	136
1968	184	179	136	252	158	227	132	260	358	186	142
1969	195	182	161	263	176	248	138	283	387	195	150
1970	193	206	183	289	183	264	142	317	417	186	153
1971	205	215	204	301	196	272	137	362	471	189	150
1972	213	229	235	310	207	297	144	400	492	209	153
1973	238	256	244	344	225	325	153	438	517	228	156
1974	245	256	262	321	236	347	169	416	512	226	156
1975	234	235	273	370	234	362	160	463	504	203	154
1976	248	240	295	411	257	372	170	486	494	227	155
1977	256	249	326	427	290	385	171	486	530	241	160
1978	267	222	335	449	307	420	175	467	556	257	169
1979	284	244	363	438	328	458	183	332	620	270	171
1980	275	249	390	378	349	494	223	386	620	241	180
1981	278	234	374	344	335	531	258	397	664	268	189
1982	242	229	406	317	321	510	285	394	682	249	175
1983	259	247	406	325	314	472	273	...	676	263	165
1984	297	281	437	328	318	495	277	...	651	292	178
1985	314	289	452	344	318	528	280	...	664	299	175
1986	322	291	...	...	...	503	268	...	682	302	160
1987	333	311	...	...	...	522	278	...	707	324	162
1988	346	333	...	...	...	536	279	...	...	331	165
1989	350	321	...	...	...	569	279	...	...	335	163
1990	339	319	...	...	...	596	289	...	...	335	167
1991	319	323	...	...	...	622	291	...	...	330	163
1992	323	331	...	...	...	636	295	...	...	339	161
1993	334	339	...	...	...	631	295	...	...	348	159

D1 SOUTH AMERICA: INDICES OF INDUSTRIAL PRODUCTION

1938 = 100

	Brazil			Brazil	Chile			Brazil	Chile	
	MF			MF	MF	Mining		MF	MF	Mining
1914	8		1925	36	...	...	1935	70	89	81
1915	10		1926	40	...	...	1936	80	91	83
1916	13		1927	46	58	82	1937	94	98	114
1917	20		1928	60	64	123	1938	100	100	100
1918	20		1929	56	77	132	1939	120	100	99
1919	25									
1920	25		1930	49	78	94	1940	151	111	107
1921	25		1931	48	58	64	1941	166	123	123
1922	32		1932	46	66	35	1942	171	121	119
1923	49		1933	50	72	43	1943	183	123	118
1924	37		1934	57	79	70	1944	204	117	118

1958 = 100

	Argentina		Brazil		Chile		Colombia		Ecuador[1]	Peru[1]	Uruguay[1]	Venezuela	
	MF	Mining	MF	Mining	MF	Mining	MF	Mining				MF	Mining
1935	38	28	12	...	39	68	...	...	...	...	...	...	...
1936	40	33	13	...	40	70	...	...	...	...	...	...	...
1937	42	39	16	...	43	96	...	...	...	...	...	...	...
1938	45	44	17	42	44	85	...	...	...	...	...	...	...
1939	47	50	20	...	44	84	...	...	...	...	...	...	...
1940	46	56	25	...	49	90	...	...	...	...	...	...	...
1941	48	58	28	...	54	104	...	...	...	...	...	...	...
1942	54	61	29	...	54	101	...	...	...	...	...	...	...
1943	56	59	31	...	54	100	...	...	...	...	...	...	...
1944	62	61	34	51	52	100	...	...	...	...	...	...	...
1945	59	58	37	52	58	98	...	...	...	48	...	...	...
1946	64	53	37	49	62	87	...	...	...	47	...	...	...
1947	74	56	43	51	63	98	...	...	...	49	...	...	...
1948	72	56	41	56	66	104	48	...	...	50	...	25	44
1949	67	58	46	59	69	90	...	...	...	57	...	29	43
1950	68	58	52	59	66	89	56	70	...	58	...	34	49
1951	70	67	57	67	79	94	58	78	...	65	...	39	57
1952	68	72	60	68	87	94	63	78	...	68	...	47	61
1953	68	77	63	70	94	83	70	82	71	76	94	55	60
1954	73	81	68	69	98	88	78	84	...	82	86	65	67
1955	81	84	76	74	94	97	84	86	81	87	84	75	79
1956	85	88	81	82	100	100	92	94	86	92	89	81	91
1957	91	92	86	85	97	101	96	98	94	101	96	92	106
1958	100	100	100	100	100	100	100	100	100	100	100	100	100
1959	92	114	108	125	114	115	108	116	109	109	96	117	107

D1   SOUTH AMERICA: Indices of Industrial Production

1958 = 100

	Argentina		Brazil		Chile		Colombia		Ecuador[1]	Peru[1]	Uruguay[1]	Venezuela	
	Mf	Mining	Mf	Mining	Mf	Mining	Mf	Mining				Mf	Mining
1960	101	156	124	142	112	112	115	120	125	125	99	121	112
1961	111	203	138	168	120	120	122	113	139	132	97	125	108
1962	106	228	149	166	131	131	130	113	144	146	97	137	116
1963	101	228	149	197	139	135	137	127	152	157	96	147	116
1964	116	236	155	201	147	143	145	137	188	172	104	162	126
1965	136	245	149	268	154	140	152	147	208	188	103	174	129
1966	137	259	166	288	164	152	162	142	227	202	105	178	126
1967	139	291	171	300	163	144	167	144	255	216	100	185	130
1968	148	326	198	334	163	147	178	138	279	227	105	194	133
1969	164	360	220	355	169	153	190	163	307	232	110	200	137
1970	174	383	244	345	169	152	207	160	345	270	115	213	143
1971	186	399	271	359	195	156	225	162	379	297	113	228	137
1972	196	406	310	359	200	150	244	151	414	322	113	238	124
1973	203	395	361	359	192	152	267	159	452	346	113	260	131
1974	213	403	390	379	185	180	281	149	514	386	116	268	119
1975	202	383	405	376	133	168	283	141	559	405	124	272	94
1976	200	391	458	380	139	192	303	138	615	425	126	321	…
1977	211	433	469	381	153	194	316	134	690	405	134	380	…
1978	188	443	491	401	165	190	345	140	751	392	141	408	…
1979	218	473	525	452	178	198	360	138	821	405	150	465	…
1980	213	497	570	508	189	207	368	148	873	426	155	567	…
1981	179	502	513	498	191	223	357	159	891	414	147	606	…
1982	177	502	513	528	160	247	345	171	917	345	122	663	…
1983	193	502	485	615	168	246	345	193	882	362	109	674	…
1984	197	502	519	798	184	259	379	239	935	375	118	861	…
1985	179	487	565	889	185	268	390	…	987	398	122	997	…
1986	200	487	627	925	199	270	415	…	1,022	469	130	1,235	…
1987	198	468	633	915	209	272	437	…	1,048	535	144	1,762	…
1988	185	518	609	925	225	286	446	…	1,100	464	141	…	…
1989	171	…	627	995	250	308	454	…	1,143	375	138	…	…
1990	175	…	567	1,055	247	312	476	…	1,221	366	152	…	…
1991	196	…	555	1,075	267	346	476	…	1,377	393	140	…	…
1992	…	…	534	1,085	307	366	501	…	1,481	384	140	…	…
1993	…	…	576	1,095	315	380	512	…	1,507	402	131	…	…

NOTES

1. SOURCES: Based on the national publications listed on pp. xiii–xv, the League of Nations and UN, *Statistical Yearbooks* and *Yearbook of Industrial Statistics* (under various names). The US manufacturing production series is based on the index in Edwin Frickey, *Production in the United States, 1860–1914* (Cambridge, Mass., 1947) to 1888, on the index in John W. Kendrick, *Productivity Trends in the United States* (Princeton, 1961) from 1889 to 1950, and on the Federal Reserve Board index subsequently. The US mining production series is based on the Bureau of Mines index.
2. All indices have been converted, where necessary, to a base year in 1899, 1938, or 1958, and different indices have been crudely spliced together.
3. Except as indicated in the footnote or headings, indices relate to manufacturing production alone, excluding mining, construction, and usually utilities also.

FOOTNOTE

[1]   This is a general index of industrial production, not just manufacturing.

D2 NORTH AMERICA: OUTPUT OF COAL (in thousands of metric tons)

1800–1849   1850–1899

	USA			Canada[1]	Mexico		USA	
	Bituminous	**Anthracite**					**Bituminous**	**Anthracite**
1800	98	- -	1850	...	...		3,655	3,925
1801	103	- -	1851	...	...		4,164	5,274
1802	11	- -	1852	...	...		4,453	5,817
1803	115	- -	1853	...	...		5,534	6,036
1804	128	- -	1854	...	...		6,676	6,956
1805	132	- -	1855	...	...		6,843	7,808
1806	138	- -	1856	...	...		7,250	8,128
1807	144	- -	1857	...	...		7,961	7,818
1808	150	1	1858	228	...		8,025	7,990
1809	154	1	1859	266	...		8,280	9,155
1810	160	2	1860	314	...		8,216	9,965
1811	171	2	1861	328₁ 332	...		7,943	9,294
1812	184	2	1862	404	...		8,513	9,241
1813	198	2	1863	436	...		9,507	11,128
1814	213	2	1864	[401]²	...		10,356	11,818
1815	230	2	1865	785₁	...		11,203	10,956
1816	252	2	1866	...	...		11,807	14,319
1817	275	2	1867	572	...		12,553	14,576
1818	299	3	1868	565	...		14,736	16,064
1819	290	3	1869	624	...		18,056	16,639
1820	299	4	1870	683	...		18,571	18,106
1821	317	4	1871	} 2,751 {	...		20,736	17,658
1822	327	5	1872		...		24,776	22,438
1823	336	9	1873		...		28,668	23,248
1824	376	14	1874	965	...		27,881	22,015
1825	396		1875	934	...		29,626	20,975
1826	447	55	1876	903	...		28,868	20,677
1827	483	73	1877	941	...		31,194	23,278
1828	516	93	1878	989	...		33,038	19,677
1829	551	135	1879	1,021	...		36,673	27,404
1830	586	213	1880	1,345	...		46,046	25,991
1831	630	234	1881	1,394	...		47,124	28,957
1832	699	455	1882	1,676	...		53,449	31,861
1833	747	601	1883	1,650	...		58,840	34,888
1834	827	464	1884	1,801	...		65,079	33,708
1835	961	689	1885	1,743	...		65,111	34,778
1836	968	839	1886	1,921	...		67,717	35,412
1837	971	1,056	1887	2,204	...		80,342	38,182
1838	1,035	887	1888	2,361	...		92,569	42,293
1839	1,135	1,024	1889	2,411	...		86,804	41,320
1840	1,220	1,024	1890	2,799	...		100,972	42,156
1841	1,229	1,145	1891	3,246	200		106,958	45,963
1842	1,336	1,307	1892	2,983	350		115,083	47,603
1843	1,465	1,502	1893	3,432	260		116,469	48,959
1844	1,627	1,930	1894	3,490	300		107,792	47,102
1845	1,902	32,382	1895	3,155	270		122,577	52,616
1846	2,112	2,751	1896	3,398	253		124,865	49,302
1847	2,387	3,380	1897	3,435	359		133,917	47,729
1848	2,794	3,630	1898	3,786	367		151,132	48,428
1849	3,191	3,785	1899	4,468	409		175,380	54,810

D2   NORTH AMERICA: Output of Coal (in thousands of metric tons)

	Canada[1]		Mexico	USA		
	Hard Coal	Brown Coal		Bituminous[4]		Anthracite
1900	5,241		388	192,610		52,043
1901	5,884		670	204,868		61,210
1902	6,774		710	236,065		37,534
1903	7,221		780	256,506		67,682
1904	7,489		832	252,796		66,367
1905	7,863		920	285,820		70,452
1906	8,857		768	311,051		64,666
1907	9,535		1,025	358,119		77,659
1908	9,876		866	301,706		75,540
1909	9,526		1,300	344,498		73,545
1910	11,711		1,304	378,397		76,644
1911	10,272		1,400	368,233		82,068
1912	13,166		982	408,329		76,532
1913	13,619		600	434,029		83,030
1914	12,372		780	383,471		82,392
1915	12,036		450	401,542		80,735
1916	13,139		300	455,879		79,449
1917	12,743		431	500,577		90,367
1918	13,588[1]		782	525,610		89,653
1919	12,627		728	422,621		79,916
1920	12,021	3,353	716	515,886		80,282
1921	10,684	2,976	735	377,318		82,076
1922	10,588	3,163	933	383,075		49,608
1923	12,164	3,250	1,262	512,165		84,676
1924	9,139	3,233	1,227	438,794		79,766
1925	8,628	3,288	1,444	471,784		56,079
1926	11,637	3,262	1,309	520,150		76,600
1927	12,341	3,469	1,031	469,707		72,662
1928	12,440[2]	3,495[2]	1,022	454,268		68,355
	15,504	428				
1929	15,345	526	1,054	485,334		66,976
1930	12,973	526	1,294	424,133		62,945
1931	10,504	603	922	346,625		54,110
1932	9,843	806	691	280,964		45,228
1933	9,954	845	647	302,665		44,943
1934	11,700	829	782	326,013		51,862
				Hard Coal	Brown Coal	
1935	11,760	839	1,255	335,316	2,495	47,318
1936	12,886	930	1,308	395,513	2,821	49,514
1937	13,411	955	1,242	401,259	2,920	47,043
1938	12,039	929	1,093	313,475	2,720	41,820
1939	13,364	872	877	355,446	2,760	46,708
1940	14,939	997	816	415,339	2,666	46,706
1941	15,333	1,201	856	463,910	2,518	51,136
1942	15,933	1,182	914	525,951	2,659	54,729
1943	14,689	1,512	1,053	532,906	2,494	55,015
1944	14,201	1,245	904	559,953	2,317	57,789

D2   NORTH AMERICA: Output of Coal (in thousands of metric tons except as indicated)

	Canada[1]		Mexico	USA		
				Bituminous[4]		Anthracite
	Hard Coal	Brown Coal		Hard Coal	Brown Coal	
1945	13,584	1,391	915	521,584	2,421	49,835
1946	14,776	1,382	978	481,946	2,420	54,891
1947	12,971	1,425	1,040	569,486	2,607	51,882
1948	15,296	1,442	1,057	541,075	2,799	51,837
1949	15,649	1,697	1,075	394,422	2,805	38,739
1950	15,364	1,999	912	465,332	3,057	39,986
1951	14,845	2,017	1,119	481,147	2,986	38,710
1952	14,058	1,890	1,317	420,774	2,737	36,816
1953	12,591	1,834	1,432	412,261	2,586	28,076
1954	11,609	1,921	1,314	352,771	2,579	26,384
1955	11,362	2,081	1,342	418,636	2,872	23,773
1956	11,407	2,125	1,548	451,774	2,611	26,218
1957	9,925	2,041	1,548	444,609	2,365	22,986
1958	8,558	2,044	1,476[3]	370,148	2,202	19,206
1959	7,874	1,767	961	371,402	2,384	18,732
1960	8,020	1,969	1,074	374,455	2,491	17,071
1961	7,429	2,004	1,063	362,833	2,738	15,827
1962	7,283	2,047	1,106	380,196	2,771	15,326
1963	7,894	1,700	1,225	413,879	2,454	16,572
1964	8,460	1,809	1,277	439,121	2,676	15,589
1965	8,641	1,872	943	461,797	2,761	13,466
1966	8,449	1,885	1,261	480,808	3,521	11,740
1967	8,296	1,812	1,424	497,261	4,073	11,118
1968	7,928	2,041	1,558	490,268	4,370	10,397
1969	7,849	1,832	2,458	503,935	4,547	9,501
1970	11,598	3,465	2,959	541,562	5,409	8,826
1971	13,728	2,994	3,513	495,132	5,808[4]	7,917
1972	15,810	2,978	3,614	530,147	9,978	6,447
1973	16,618		4,263	523,966	12,848	6,196
1974	17,784		5,166	531,160	14,041	6,003

(million metric tons)

1975	15,751	9,507	5,193	570.3	18.0	5.6
1976	14,389	11,086	5,650	592.4	23.1	5.6
1977	15,317	13,203	6,610	601.6	26.5	5.3
1978	17,141	13,343	6,756	571.1	32.3	4.6
1979	18,610	14,587	7,357	666.2	38.0	4.4
1980	20,173	16,514	7,010	704.9	42.3	5.5
1981	21,739	18,349	8,086	695.9	46.5	4.9
1982	22,379	20,528	7,634	708.2	47.9	4.2
1983	22,563	22,224	8,996	652.9	52.9	3.7
1984	32,063	25,339	9,522	751.7	57.3	3.8
1985	34,310	26,544	9,790	731.6	65.7	4.3
1986	30,542	26,506	10,157	747.0	66.8	3.9
1987	32,651	28,556	11,137	759.6	70.7	3.3
1988	38,585	32,059	10,586	780.7	78.1	3.8
1989	38,794	31,733	11,500	811.3	78.0	2.9
1990	37,672	30,659	11,940	853.6	79.9	3.4
1991	39,911	31,224	10,981	825.0	78.5	2.4
1992	32,315	33,047	9,852	823.2	81.7	2.8
1993	35,310	33,706	11,060	776.4	81.2	...

D2 SOUTH AMERICA: OUTPUT OF COAL (in thousands of metric tons)

	Argentina	Brazil	Chile	Colombia	Peru	Venezuela[6]
1895	...	...	200	...	...	...
1896	...	...	205	...	...	...
1897	...	...	244	...	...	...
1898	...	...	283	...	10	...
1899	...	...	242	...	...	...
1900	...	...	325	...	48	...
1901	...	...	600	...	45	...
1902	...	...	750	...	...	...
1903	...	...	827	...	...	...
1904	...	...	752	...	60	...
1905	...	...	794	...	75	...
1906	...	...	932	...	77	...
1907	...	...	833	...	186	...
1908	...	...	940	...	311	...
1909	...	...	899	...	311	...
1910	...	...	1,074	...	307	
1911	...	...	1,188	...	324	...
1912	...	...	1,334	...	268	...
1913	...	26	1,283	...	274	7
1914	...	...	1,807	...	284	9
1915	...	...	1,172	...	291	13
1916	...	...	1,418	...	319	18
1917	...	...	1,539	...	354	20
1918	...	...	1,516	...	346	...
1919	...	...	1,485	...	344	30
1920	...	302	1,063	...	378	...
1921	...	260	1,275	...	357	28
1922	...	400	1,053	...	303	29
1923	...	324	1,164	...	253	26
1924	...	298	1,539	...	155	25
1925	...	378	1,453	...	102	25
1926	...	361	1,491	...	170	16
1927	...	347	1,482	...	162	16
1928	...	330	1,376	...	178	16[6]
						18
1929	...	373	1,508		221	19
1930	...	385	1,442	...	201	9
1931	...	...	1,100	...	141	1
1932	...	541	1,080	...	26	1
1933	...	641	1,538	90	30	5
1934	...	719	1,808	251	35	6
1935	...	826	1,900	378	85	1
1936	...	649	1,875	392	90	6
1937	...	763	1,988	341	99	7
1938	...	907	2,044	331	75	6
1939	1	1,047	1,850	349	108	3
1940	1	1,336	1,938	521	113	5
1941	1	1,408	2,060	403	117	6
1942	4	1,775	2,151	578	149	9
1943	9	2,078	2,265	483	187	11
1944	5	1,908	2,279	499	173	9

D2 SOUTH AMERICA: Output of Coal (in thousands of metric tons)

	Argentina	Brazil	Chile		Colombia	Peru	Venezuela[6]
			Hard Coal	Brown Coal			
1945	3	2,073	2,079		534	201	7
1946	3	1,897	1,966		551	230	4
1947	14	1,999	2,067		506	215	3
1948	17	2,025	1,994		514	189	3
1949	18	2,129	2,141		521[5]	170	2
1950	26	1,959	2,217		1,011	196	1[6]
1951	40	1,962	1,956	257	1,115	186	28
1952	112	1,960	2,174	273	966	225	25
1953	37	2,025	2,038	267	1,230	210	29
1954	33	2,055	1,879	238	1,500	206	32
1955	75	2,268[7] / 1,676	1,889	229	1,850	136	31
1956	97	1,550	1,887	210	2,000	145	31
1957	123	1,466	1,748[8]	173[8]	2,000	141	35
1958	136	1,312	1,670	75	2,440	223	36
1959	184	1,284	1,655	79	2,480	173	34
1960	175	1,277	1,297	68	2,600	162	35
1961	236	1,256	1,531	91	2,800	167	31
1962	211	1,583	1,638	84	3,000	162	27
1963	207	1,542	1,515	89	3,200	131	42
1964	335	1,782	1,592	85	3,000	147	36
1965	374	2,186	1,544	85	3,072	129	31
1966	357	2,144	1,462	80	2,500	150	34
1967	411	2,295	1,357	40	3,100	167	34
1968	472	2,364	1,417	57	3,100	161	31
1969	522	2,437	1,491	68	3,300	162	32
1970	616	2,361	1,351	63	2,268	156	40
1971	632	2,498	1,492	65	2,540	103	43
1972	675	2,497	1,310	63	2,631	104	40
1973	451	2,427	1,374	61	3,048	10	50
1974	626	3,181	1,444	41	3,266	–	57
1975	502	2,817	1,461	46	3,447	23	60
1976	615	3,391	1,261	28	3,629	20	87
1977	533	4,009	1,306	30	3,814	25	121
1978	434	4,582	1,129	30	4,019	26	81
1979	727	5,028	926	35	4,618	28	55
1980	390	5,241	968	40	4,112	44	44
1981	498	5,689	1,099	36	4,325	94	46
1982	515	6,346	985	40	4,422	73	47
1983	486	6,737	990	40	5,192	92	39
1984	509	7,519	1,184	40	6,637	105	51
1985	400	7,712	1,291	35	8,974	125	41
1986	365	7,391	1,633	35	10,800	155	57
1987	373	6,884	1,567	36	14,594	105	238
1988	511	7,331	1,926	37	15,101	187	1,072
1989	375	6,671	1,949	38	18,902	189	2,129
1990	270	4,595	2,183	40	12,809	81	2,178
1991	280	5,184	2,208	40	11,862	70	2,362
1992	370	4,728	1,626	60	12,758	85	2,379
1993	335	4,560	1,355	42	12,795	83	3,753

D2　Output of Coal

NOTES

1. SOURCES: The national publications listed on pp. xiii–xv; League of Nations and UN, *Statistical Yearbooks*; and UN, *Yearbook of Industrial Statistics* (under various names). US figures to 1885 were derived by *Historical Statistics of the United States*, from H. N. Eavenson, *The First Century and a Quarter of American Coal Industry* (Pittsburgh, 1942).
2. Lignite is normally included with brown coal. Where there is no indication, output was usually of hard coal only, except where hard and brown coal are later distinguished separately.

FOOTNOTES

[1]　Nova Scotia only to 1865, the figures to 1861 (1st line) being of shipments from mines. Dominion statistics to 1918 are of sales plus colliery consumption.
[2]　Lignite is included with hard coal from 1928 (2nd line).
[3]　Waste coal is excluded subsequently. In the year of the change it was calculated as 38% of production.
[4]　Texas lignite is not included until 1972.
[5]　Coal shipped by rail to 1949.
[6]　Excluding state mines to 1928 (1st line) and mines outside Guárico State until 1951.
[7]　The reason for this break is not given in the source. A revised figure for 1948, comparable with the later statistics was given, viz. 1,424.
[8]　A small amount of production was transferred between categories.
[9]　Sub-bituminous coal is counted as brown coal from 1975.

D3 NORTH AMERICA: OUTPUT OF CRUDE PETROLEUM (in thousands of metric tons)

1859–1942

	Canada[1]	USA		Canada[1]	Mexico[3]	Trinidad & Tobago[4]	USA
1859	...	- -					
1860	...	67	1900	93	—	—	8,483
1861	...	282	1901	81	1	—	9,252
1862	...	408	1902	69	6	—	11,836
1863	...	348	1903	64	11	—	13,395
1864	...	282	1904	66	19	—	15,611
1865	...	333	1905	83	38	—	17,962
1866	...	480	1906	74	75	—	16,866
1867	25	446	1907	102	151	—	22,146
1868	26	486	1908	69	589	—	23,804
1869	29	562	1909	55	407	...	24,423
1870	33	701	1910	41	545	17	27,941
1871	35	694	1911	38	1,881	40	29,393
1872	40	839	1912	32	2,481	70	29,725
1873	48	1,319	1913	30	3,851	90	33,126
1874	22	1,457	1914	28	3,931	146	35,435
1875	29	1,172	1915	28	4,901	[93][7]	37,481
1876	41	1,218	1916	26	6,079	129	40,102
1877	41	1,780	1917	28	8,290	223	44,709
1878	41	2,053	1918	40	9,569	308	47,457
1879	75	2,655	1919	31	13,054	256	52,099
1880	46	3,505	1920	26	23,549	290	62,122
1881	48	3,688	1921	26	27,707	342	64,718
1882	51	4,047	1922	25	26,114	340	76,415
1883	62	3,127	1923	23	21,431	424	100,371
1884	75	3,229	1924	22	20,011	564	98,024
1885	77	2,915	1925	43	16,549	610	104,622
1886	76	3,742	1926	47	12,954	737	106,474
1887	93	3,771	1927	61	9,186	797	123,486
1888	91	3,682	1928	80	7,184	1,139	123,592
1889	92	4,689	1929	144	6,401	1,217	138,104
1890	104	6,110	1930	196	5,662	1,315	123,117
1891	99	7,239	1931	198	4,733	1,371	116,683
1892	102	6,735	1932	134	4,699	1,425	107,645
1893	104	6,457	1933	142	4,870	1,345	122,536
1894	108	6,579	1934	135	5,462	1,576	122,715
1895	95	7,052	1935	128	5,758	1,688	134,679
1896	95	8,128	1936	122	5,871	1,915	148,611
1897	93	8,063	1937	309	6,711	2,243	172,865
1898	99	7,382	1938	873	5,510	2,566	164,107
1899	106	7,609	1939	1,017	6,138	2,865	170,946
			1940	1,128	6,301	3,226	182,873
			1941	1,330	6,160	2,976	189,496
			1942	1,360	4,982	3,204	187,390

D3 NORTH AMERICA: Output of Crude Petroleum (in thousands of metric tons)

	Canada[1]	Cuba	Mexico	Trinidad & Tobago	USA
1943	1,295	- -	5,031	3,104	203,468
1944	1,304	2	5,467	3,141	226,751
1945	1,091	10	6,231	3,061	231,582
1946	966	11	7,045	2,936	234,323
1947	982	17	8,053	2,988	250,952
1948	1,660	13	8,372	2,846	273,007
1949	2,815	9	7,818	3,011	248,919
1950	3,925	2	10,363	3,015	266,708
1951	6,435	2	11,062	3,026	303,754
1952	8,276	1	11,059	3,086	309,447
1953	10,941	1	10,362	3,162	318,535
1954	12,984	3	11,967	3,343	312,846
1955	17,492	48	12,786	3,523	335,744
1956	23,260	71	12,970	4,093	353,698
1957	24,594	52	12,627	4,820	353,646
1958	22,383	45	13,380	5,286	330,955
1959	24,832	25	13,969	5,790	347,929
1960	25,630	14	14,171	5,994	347,975
1961	29,863	10	15,278	6,476	354,303
1962	33,020	12	16,000	6,916	361,658
1963	34,845	31	16,483	6,888	372,001
1964	37,147	37	16,535	7,036	376,609
1965	39,457	57	16,874	6,913	384,946
1966	43,248	69	17,317	7,727	409,170
1967	47,333	116	18,702	9,197	434,573
1968	50,433	198	20,015	9,467	449,885
1969	53,767	206	21,058	8,126	455,602
1970	62,000	159	21,508	7,223	475,289
1971	66,193	120	21,416	6,671	466,704
1972	75,421	112	22,166	7,246	466,956
1973	88,028	138	23,257	8,804	654,190
1974	82,529	168	29,593	9,641	432,794
1975	70,166	226	36,889	11,216	413,090
1976	64,523	234	41,336	10,990	401,252
1977	64,668	256	49,303	11,832	405,712
1978	64,333	288	62,346	11,854	428,490
1979	73,279	288	75,461	11,072	420,818
1980	70,405	274	99,938	10,983	424,196
1981	62,928	259	120,203	9,780	421,804
1982	62,163	541	142,783	9,144	425,591
1983	66,408	742	139,758	8,255	427,515
1984	70,668	770	139,946	8,758	438,127
1985	72,004	868	135,755	9,097	441,479
1986	72,302	938	126,211	8,722	428,154
1987	75,411	895	132,086	8,061	419,442
1988	79,324	717	130,675	7,858	410,637
1989	76,539	718	130,665	7,714	382,677
1990	76,226	726	132,469	7,863	371,032
1991	75,939	748	139,115	7,442	373,918
1992	78,858	936	139,073	7,009	362,661
1993	82,185	975	139,001	6,396	345,323

D3 SOUTH AMERICA: OUTPUT OF CRUDE PETROLEUM (in thousands of metric tons)

	Argentina	Bolivia	Brazil	Chile	Colombia	Ecuador	Peru	Venezuela
1915	76	—	—	—	—	—	344	5
1916	130	—	—	—	—	—	346	10
1917	180	—	—	—	—	—	347	18
1918	199	—	—	—	—	—	335	48
1919	172	—	—	—	—	—	349	63
1920	243	—	—	—	—	—	373	70
1921	323	—	—	—	—	—	489	218
1922	439	—	—	—	46	—	701	335
1923	497	—	—	—	61	—	752	639
1924	677	—	—	—	64	—	1,046	1,335
1925	924	—	—	—	144	23	1,220	2,864
1926	1,143	—	—	—	920	30	1,427	5,207
1927	1,263	—	—	—	2,144	76	1,341	8,969
1928	1,318	1	—	—	2,841	154	1,592	15,349
1929	1,362	3	—	—	2,911	196	1,777	19,891
1930	1,305	4	—	—	2,782	221	1,656	20,109
1931	1,652	2	—	—	2,484	250	1,340	17,221
1932	1,875	5	—	—	2,237	227	1,313	17,120
1933	1,951	14	—	—	1,792	230	1,762	17,334
1934	1,998	20	—	—	2,399	232	2,162	19,935
1935	2,037	21	—	—	2,434	245	2,253	21,723
1936	2,212	13	—	—	2,594	272	2,324	22,619
1937	2,340	16	—	—	2,807	285	2,300	27,204
1938	2,444	18	—	—	2,984	297	2,097	27,485
1939	2,663	28	—	—	3,300	305	1,794	29,967
1940	2,948	38	- -	—	3,535	310	1,609	26,896
1941	3,150	31	- -	—	3,408	205	1,583	33,184
1942	3,392	40	4	—	1,465	301	1,810	21,650
1943	3,553	43	6	—	1,853	305	1,948	26,238
1944	3,467	41	8	—	3,133	382	1,914	37,597
1945	3,274	50	10	—	3,157	345	1,827	47,304
1946	2,976	47	9	—	3,102	307	1,639	56,822
1947	3,126	49	13	—	3,455	311	1,699	63,611
1948	3,323	60	19	—	3,284	338	1,879	70,215
1949	3,232	88	14	7	4,111	338	1,968	
1950	3,357	80	38	8	4,711	347	2,007	. . .
1951	3,501	68	90	99	5,311	357	2,151	. . .
1952	3,552	67	98	119	6,351	375	2,191	. . .
1953	4,078	78	120	164	5,454	391	2,137	92,140
1954	4,231	221	130	226	5,530	415	2,292	98,998
1955	4,365	351	265	336	5,493	466	2,303	113,041
1956	4,437	417	530	462	6,104	451	2,455	129,178
1957	4,858	466	1,321	565	6,327[3]	421	2,567	145,830
1958	5,102	448	2,473	726	6,342	410	2,502	135,636
1959	6,206	413	3,083	838	7,261	364	2,368	144,850

D3 SOUTH AMERICA: Output of Crude Petroleum (in thousands of metric tons)

	Argentina	Bolivia	Brazil	Chile	Colombia	Ecuador	Peru[5]	Venezuela[6]
1960	8,898	466	3,870	943	7,584	360	2,572	149,372
1961	11,752	390	4,549	1,208	7,238	386	2,587	152,616
1962	13,661	364	4,367	1,524	7,059	340	2,822	167,147
1963	13,514	443	4,669	1,722	8,228	325	2,867	169,671
1964	13,961	428	4,353	1,784	8,597	369	3,181	178,230
1965	13,672	438	4,488	1,656	10,123	376	3,081	182,409
1966	14,559	779	5,548	1,620	9,938	342	3,075	176,418
1967	15,953	1,838	7,079	1,620	9,603	290	3,453	185,489
1968	17,525	1,897	7,823	1,785	9,010	233	3,613	189,231
1969	18,166	1,876	8,360	1,711	10,934	209	3,519	187,916
1970	20,026	1,122	7,980	1,468	11,327	193	3,550	194,306
1971	21,578	1,710	8,303	1,402	11,127	179	3,053	185,280
1972	22,130	2,031	8,138	1,417	10,142	4,016	3,204	168,342
1973	21,476	2,196	8,276	1,276	9,493	10,615	3,482	175,774
1974	21,139	2,112	8,617	1,110	8,686	8,989	3,815	156,167
1975	20,773	1,874	8,352	994	8,102	8,155	3,553	122,400
1976	20,810	1,890	8,344	938	7,553	9,488	3,779	120,170
1977	22,167	1,612	8,025	928	7,106	9,283	4,571	117,189
1978	23,236	1,506	8,002	780	6,755	10,223	7,528	113,628
1979	24,279	1,294	8,262	1,010	6,410	10,874	9,413	124,106
1980	25,281	1,107	9,083	1,604	6,501	10,417	9,664	114,788
1981	25,534	1,029	10,675	1,950	6,912	10,745	9,538	111,688
1982	25,196	1,134	12,984	2,003	7,320	10,746	9,729	100,391
1983	25,200	1,030	16,595	1,919	7,851	12,088	8,589	94,470
1984	24,637	969	23,216	1,879	8,653	13,088	9,358	94,850
1985	23,607	917	27,493	1,591	8,887	14,243	9,296	88,186
1986	22,283	816	28,784	1,485	15,289	14,551	9,027	93,933
1987	21,999	876	28,463	1,319	19,415	8,856	8,754	95,449
1988	23,119	893	27,853	1,057	18,939	15,806	7,579	101,120
1989	23,641	925	29,845	946	20,382	14,556	6,975	100,090
1990	24,784	971	31,614	842	22,155	14,936	6,895	112,009
1991	25,329	1,029	31,229	755	21,450	15,639	6,142	124,605
1992	28,617	1,029	31,569	619	22,170	16,756	6,199	127,785
1993	30,331	969	32,162	584	23,063	17,966	6,252	130,106

D3   Output of Crude Petroleum

NOTES

1. SOURCES: As for table D2
2. Output from oil shale is not included in this table.
3. Data for many countries is given originally in measures of capacity (i.e. the barrel of 42 US gallons). The conversion ratios used by UN and League of Nations statisticians have been followed generally here, when they are available. For periods prior to 1921, the ratios used in the early 1920s have been employed.

FOOTNOTES

[1] The conversion ratio used to 1920 is 7.66 barrels = 1 ton. Crude petroleum from tar sands is not included. Since the beginning of extraction in 1967 production has been as follows (in thousands of tons):

1967	61	1970	1,625	1973	2,481
1968	774	1971	2,020	1974	2,270
1969	1,357	1972	2,531	1975	2,120

[2] The conversion ratio used to 1917 is 7.50 barrels = 1 ton.
[3] The conversion ratio used to 1927 is 6.98 barrels = 1 ton.
[4] The conversion ratio used to 1920 is 7.18 barrels = 1 ton. Data to 1914 are for years beginning 1 April, the 1915 figure being for the period April—December.
[5] Production began in 1907 and statistics to 1914 are available as follows: 1908 2; 1909 2; 1910 3; 1911 2; 1912 9; 1913 18; 1914 41.
[6] Earlier statistics are available as follows:

1884	1	1890	4	1895	13	1900	38	1905	50	1910	168
1885	1	1891	15	1896	13	1901	39	1906	71	1911	195
1886	1	1892	22	1897	13	1902	32	1907	100	1912	234
1887	2	1893	15	1898	20	1903	37	1908	126	1913	273
1888	2	1894	13	1899	27	1904	39	1909	188	1914	245
1889	2										

The conversion ratio used to 1920 is 7.57 barrels = 1 ton.
[7] Production in 1914 was 2 thousand tons. The conversion ratio used to 1920 is 6.70 barrels = 1 ton.

D4   NORTH AMERICA: OUTPUT OF NATURAL GAS (in millions of cubic metres to 1966, and Petajoules subsequently)

	Canada	Mexico	Trinidad & Tobago	USA[3]		Canada	Mexico	Trinidad & Tobago	USA[3]
1900	...	...	...	3,625	1945	1,371	976	393	114,457
1901	...	...	...	5,097	1946	1,356	974	402	117,600
1902	...	...	...	5,833	1947	1,491	1,189	407	129,748
1903	...	...	...	6,768	1948	1,659	1,248	465	145,775
1904	...	...	...	7,277	1949	1,712	1,293	489	153,477
1905	...	...	...	9,061	1950	1,921[1]	1,793[1,2]	475	177,886
1906	...	...	...	11,015		1,870	920		
1907	...	...	...	11,525	1951	2,130	1,310	471	211,159
1908	...	...	...	11,383	1952	2,450	1,440	478	226,903
1909	...	...	...	13,620	1953	2,785	1,440	501	237,777
					1954	3,330	1,440	515	247,574
1910	...	...	...	14,413					
1911	330	...	...	14,527	1955	4,130	1,850	498	266,320
1912	433	...	...	15,914	1956	4,630	1,800	547	285,490
1913	580	...	...	16,480	1957	6,025	2,380	600	302,424
1914	614	...	...	16,764	1958	9,320	3,810	663	312,335
					1959	11,390	4,730	714	341,105
1915	570	...	...	17,811					
1916	721	...	...	21,323	1960	14,270	4,900	766	361,634
1917	776	...	...	22,512	1961	17,730	5,260	832	373,273
1918	570	...	...	20,416	1962	25,270	5,410	850	390,800
1919	565	...	...	21,124	1963	25,705	6,100	832	415,323
					1964	34,575	7,000	1,089	437,835
1920	477	...	...	22,993					
1921	399	...	...	19,086	1965	37,389	7,440	1,174	454,202
1922	416	...	...	21,974	1966	34,119	7,580	1,379	487,268
1923	452	...	...	29,025		1,290	387	54	17,932
1924	421	...	...	32,904	1967	1,406	443	59	18,932
					1968	1,600	442	62	20,156
1925	479	...	...	34,263	1969	1,863	436	62	21,571
1926	544	...	...	37,831					
1927	605	...	...	41,654	1970	2,113	451	73	22,860
1928	639	...	...	45,194	1971	2,314	420	71	23,517
1929	804	...	...	55,274	1972	2,612	461	73	23,524
					1973	2,794	502	71	23,410
1930	832	...	...	56,039	1974	2,735	522	65	22,080
1931	733	...	...	48,762					
1932	663	257	...	45,137	1975	2,795	523	59	20,724
1933	655	313	...	45,222	1976	2,820	520	77	20,552
1934	656	347	...	51,423	1977	2,962	573	92	18,921
					1978	2,856	701	114	18,846
1935	705	...	...	55,756	1979	3,041	832	128	19,415
1936	796	...	...	63,005					
1937	917	118	...	70,028	1980	2,790	1,036	146	19,256
1938	947	...	...	66,771	1981	2,748	1,033	134	19,057
1939	996	1,165	325	71,868	1982	2,825	1,638	148	17,655
					1983	2,740	1,452	157	15,986
1940	1,168	1,163	391	77,418	1984	2,972	1,112	158	17,341
1941	1,232	1,126	391	81,949					
1942	1,294	1,055	419	89,085	1985	3,189	1,068	192	16,365
1943	1,254	879	393	99,562	1986	2,988	1,005	151	17,495
1944	1,276	934	358	108,029	1987	3,254	1,011	158	18,079
					1988	3,763	968	146	18,604
					1989	3,983	902	193	18,830
					1990	4,114	955	202	19,373
					1991	4,344	948	234	19,225
					1992	4,767	935	232	19,379
					1993	5,263	977	202	20,008

D4 SOUTH AMERICA: OUTPUT OF NATURAL GAS (in millions of cubic metres to 1966, and Petajoules subsequently)

	Argentina	Bolivia	Brazil	Chile	Colombia	Ecuador	Peru	Venezuela
1929	260	...	—	...	...	...	...	...
1930	265	...	—	...	...	...	...	...
1931	330	...	—	...	...	...	...	...
1932	450	...	—	...	...	6	...	534
1933	605	...	—	...	...	9	...	532
1934	732	...	—	...	...	10	...	584
1935	618	...	—	...	493	10	...	617
1936	534	...	—	...	508	19	...	642
1937	505	...	—	...	512	46	...	668
1938	491	...	—	...	512	55	...	810
1939	519	...	—	...	496	58	...	...
1940	536	...	—	...	599	59	...	
1941	593	...	—	...	678	42	...	518
1942	676	...	1	...	553	54	...	424
1943	677	...	6	...	533	49	...	346
1944	662	...	4	...	682	64	...	568
1945	609	...	1	...	678	70	...	654
1946	566	...	9	...	620	66	...	803
1947	583	...	1	...	563	87	...	1,128
1948	606	...	3	...	349	106	...	1,177
1949	664	...	2	...	494	109	...	1,089
1950	755	...	5	...	510	132	405	1,117
1951	830	...	8	...	489	152	410	1,440
1952	898	...	7	59	204	...	410	1,752
1953	698	...	27	70	484	...	410	2,172
1954	707	...	63	90	545	...	410	2,448
1955	719	6	62	112	539	...	410	2,748
1956	764	7	84	150	621	...	415	2,994
1957	852	8	158	250	633	...	500	3,624
1958	866	6	300	450	794	...	425	3,929
1959	861	7	429	600	908₂ / 388	...	420	4,192
1960	1,383	6	535	823	404	...	415	4,606
1961	2,357	50	527	1,201	417	...	420	4,891
1962	2,978	57	511	1,570	592	...	430	5,189
1963	3,406	59	503	1,532	702	...	440	5,610
1964	3,751	85	532	1,300	762	...	448	6,103
1965	4,222	80	684	1,284	906	...	437	6,538
1966	4,577	93	789	1,134	1,099	...	457	6,856
	159	3	5	41	...		13	291
1967	167	3	5	43	...	...	12	319
1968	186	3	5	44	...	1	14	329
1969	185	4	5	43	49	1	14	339

D4 SOUTH AMERICA: Output of Natural Gas (in Petajoules)

	Argentina	Bolivia	Brazil	Chile	Colombia	Ecuador	Peru	Venezuela
1970	209	1	3	48	55	1	16	382
1971	224	1	5	51	61	1	15	398
1972	219	37	9	52	72	1	16	402
1973	234	57	10	46	75	1	15	480
1974	252	60	21	46	73	1	16	494
1975	265	59	25	46	73	2	24	480
1976	268	61	20	46	75	2	21	453
1977	270	64	40	54	85	2	19	510
1978	255	68	32	59	113	2	20	528
1979	303	74	35	41	121	2	19	611
1980	327	84	41	27	140	2	21	643
1981	340	90	37	33	150	3	25	647
1982	393	93	43	34	157	4	26	682
1983	457	90	63	37	172	4	19	668
1984	478	86	77	37	173	4	24	741
1985	509	85	97	38	172	4	24	727
1986	553	92	110	34	169	4	25	805
1987	657	91	114	34	171	2	25	799
1988	775	101	139	45	159	4	24	826
1989	784	104	149	66	149	4	22	839
1990	793	106	150	69	153	5	23	956
1991	886	107	147	61	159	5	20	997
1992	899	108	159	70	149	5	18	957
1993	925	107	173	67	149	5	18	1,031

NOTES

1. SOURCES: As for table D2.
2. The statistics normally relate to natural gas from gasfields only (exclusive of waste), and exclude methane from coalfields.

FOOTNOTES

[1] Subsequent figures exclude shrinkage.
[2] Subsequent figures exclude repressured and wasted gas.
[3] Marketed production.

D5 NORTH AMERICA: OUTPUT OF IRON ORE (in thousands of metric tons)

Key: A = crude weight, B = weight of Fe content

	Canada	Cuba[1]	Mexico	Newfoundland	USA
	A	A	B	A	A
1860	...	...	...	...	2,919
1870	...	...	...	...	3,893
1875	...	...	...	...	4,082
1880	...	...	...	...	7,234
1881	...	...	...	...	7,234
1882	...	...	...	...	9,144
1883	...	...	...	...	8,534
1884	...	...	...	...	8,332
1885	...	...	...	...	7,722
1886	58	...	...	...	10,160
1887	69	...	...	...	11,481
1888	72	...	...	...	12,257
1889	76	...	...	...	14,751
1890	70	370	...	...	16,293
1891	63	268	...	19	14,825
1892	93	348	...	...	16,559
1893	114	357	...	38	11,774
1894	100	160	...	41	12,071
1895	93	388	...	...	16,214
1896	83	420	...	67	16,262
1897	46	461	...	93	17,799
1898	53	171	...	136	19,746
1899	68	383	...	338	24,994
1900	111	454	3	323	27,738
1901	285	561	3	758	29,058
1902	367	711	2	767	35,866
1903	239	634	10	641	35,358
1904	199	393	23	660	27,941
1905	264	554	20	753	43,080
1906	226	664	31	928	48,516
1907	284	658[1]	23	898	52,551
1908	216	833	24	950	36,560
1909	243	945	49	1,020	52,117
1910	235	1,441	55	1,127	57,930
1911	190	1,183	64	1,191	44,581
1912	196	1,422	58	1,272	56,035
1913	279	1,608	13	1,456	62,975
1914	222	834	—	575	42,105
1915	361	841	2	788	56,417
1916	249	724	20	918	76,374
1917	195	562	19	801	76,497
1918	192	654	26	770	70,776
1919	179	203	31	453	61,943
1920	117	84	26	600	68,689
1921	54	132	34	348	29,964
1922	16	452	42	1,018	47,885
1923	28	374	51	733	70,464
1924	—	481	52	993	55,138

D5 NORTH AMERICA: Output of Iron Ore (in thousands of metric tons)

	Canada		Cuba		Mexico	Newfoundland[2]		USA	
	A	B	A	B	B	A	B	A	B
1925	—	—	567	...	76	1,150	598	62,902	
1926	—	—	587	...	49	877	456	68,708	
1927	—	—	422	...	41	1,229	639	62,732	
1928	—	—	401	225	48	1,509	785	63,195	31,649
1929	—	—	682	383	76	1,518	789	74,200	37,226
1930	—	—	249	109	62	1,473	766	59,346	29,681
1931	—	—	227	104	39	546	283	31,632	15,876
1932	—	—	188	87	16	323	168	10,005	5,028
1933	—	—	229	129	50	326	170	17,835	8,918
1934	—	—	80	45	68	514	267	24,983	12,504
1935	—	—	182	102	67	673	350	31,030	15,608
1936	—	—	362	203	79	908	471	49,572	25,078
1937	—	—	400	224	90	1,635	850	73,251	36,991
1938	—	—	125[1]	70[1]	99	1,707	887	28,903	14,322
			145	81					
1939	112	60	46	26	111	1,680	874	52,562	26,423
1940	376	201	96	54	70	1,533	798	74,879	37,918
1941	468	250	57	32	72	983	508	93,893	47,819
1942	494	264	100	56	103	1,212	630	107,219	54,767
1943	582	293	51	29	138	551	284	102,873	52,127
1944	502	276	13	8	187	472	244	95,628	48,653
1945	1,030	567	—	—	175	983	511	89,794	45,822
1946	1,406	773	—	—	171	1,237	648	71,980	36,154
1947	1,741	958	39	22	226	1,467	763	94,586	47,709
1948	1,213	667	23	13	227	1,492	789	102,624	50,891
1949	3,334[2]	1,834[2]	7	4	247	...	...	86,300	43,288
1950	3,270	1,799	7	4	286	...	...	99,618	49,306
1951	4,247	2,335	10	6	313	...	...	118,375	60,123
1952	4,783	2,630	52	30	340	...	...	99,489	50,013
1953	5,906	3,248	164	92	331	...	...	119,888	60,376
1954	6,679	3,673	16	9	314	...	...	79,383	39,952
1955	14,772	8,125	141	79	429	...	...	104,656	53,635
1956	20,274	11,151	...	4	489	...	...	99,448	51,185
1957	20,205	11,113	...	8	569	...	...	107,851	55,424
1958	14,266	7,847	...	6	581	...	...	68,796	36,701
1959	22,215	12,218[3]	...	5	535	...	...	61,243	32,129
		12,663							
1960	19,551	11,140	...	1	521	...	...	90,209	47,867
1961	18,470	10,528	...	1	687	...	...	72,474	39,103
1962	24,820	14,148	...	1	1,354	...	...	72,982	39,671
1963	27,346	16,150	...	1	1,397	...	...	74,780	41,542
1964	34,769	20,766	...	1	1,392	...	...	86,197	47,681
1965	34,208	21,822	...	1	1,593	...	...	88,842	50,175
1966	36,914	22,702	...	...	1,481	...	...	91,594	51,750
1967	38,390	23,610	...	...	1,617	...	...	85,530	49,152
1968	43,040	26,469	...	...	1,921	...	...	87,243	50,172
1969	36,336	22,347	...	...	2,097	...	...	89,745	52,512
1970	47,458	29,187	...	...	2,612	...	...	91,200	53,308
1971	42,957	26,418	...	...	2,819	...	...	82,058	49,235
1972	38,735	23,822	...	...	3,053	...	...	76,644	46,754
1973	47,498	29,211	...	...	3,113	...	...	89,076	54,336
1974	46,785	28,772	...	...	3,338	...	...	85,709	52,283

D5 OUTPUT OF IRON ORE (in thousands of metric tons)

NORTH AMERICA

	Canada		Mexico	USA	
	A	B	B	A	B
1975	44,893	27,609	3,369	80,132	49,041
1976	55,416	34,081	3,644	81,277	50,154
1977	53,621	32,977	3,587	56,645	35,043
1978	42,931	26,403	3,556	82,892	51,579
1979	59,617	36,664	4,041	87,091	54,500
1980	49,068	30,177	5,087	70,730	44,592
1981	49,551	30,654	5,749	74,348	47,286
1982	33,198	20,501	5,382	36,002	23,005
1983	32,959	20,105	5,306	38,165	24,554
1984	39,930	24,357	5,489	52,092	33,640
1985	39,502	24,096	5,161	49,533	31,797
1986	36,167	22,062	4,817	39,486	25,293
1987	37,702	23,060	4,965	47,648	30,525
1988	39,934	24,302	5,564	57,515	36,468
1989	40,509	24,592	5,373	59,032	37,413
1990	34,855	22,178	5,327	56,408	35,695
1991	36,383	22,152	4,976	56,761	35,801
1992	32,697	19,604	5,154	55,593	35,251
1993	30,568	19,349	5,597	55,661	34,617

SOUTH AMERICA

	Chile			Argentina	Brazil		Chile	
	A			A	A[4]	B	A	B
1911	29		**1925**	...	...	...	1,234	814
1912	7		**1926**	...	...	...	1,396	921
1913	14		**1927**	...	...	...	1,508	995
1914	64		**1928**	...	...	...	1,525	1,006
			1929	...	...	...	1,812	1,196
1915	147		**1930**	...	...	...	1,689	1,118
1916	56		**1931**	...	...	...	742	440
1917	5		**1932**	...	...	...	172	167
1918	—		**1933**	...	...	...	565	350
1919	1		**1934**	...	...	...	973	584
1920	3		**1935**	...	...	...	862	517
1921	8		**1936**	...	110	75	1,462	815
1922	290		**1937**	3	242	164	1,558	916
1923	673		**1938**	2	486	330	1,615	950
1924	1,050		**1939**	4	363	246	1,691	995
			1940	3	404	274	1,804	1,061
			1941	4	828	561	1,697	1,011
			1942	1	704	477	409	245
			1943	- -	811	550	5	3
			1944	2	770	522	18	11

International Historical Statistics: The Americas 1750–1993

D5 SOUTH AMERICA: OUTPUT OF IRON ORE (in thousands of metric tons)

	Argentina		Brazil		Chile		Colombia		Peru		Venezuela	
	A	B	A	B	A	B	A	B	A	B	A	B
1945	1	- -	650	442	277	173	—	—	—	—	—	—
1946	52	27	583	396	1,177	738	—	—	—	—	—	—
1947	...	...	611	415	1,738	1,084	—	—	—	—	—	—
1948	33	17	1,572	1,069	2,711	1,681	—	—	—	—	—	—
1949	38	19	1,888	1,284	2,743	1,662	—	—	—	—	—	—
1950	40	20	1,987	1,351	2,950	1,770	—	—	—	—	199	127
1951	55	27	2,407	1,637	3,160	1,960	—	—	—	—	1,270	813
1952	67	34	3,162	2,150	2,362	1,426	—	—	—	—	1,970	1,261
1953	77	36	3,617	2,460	2,939	1,747	—	—	...	577	2,296	1,470
1954	77	30	3,071	2,088	2,285	1,310	...	35	...	1,157	5,389	3,469
1955	76	38	3,382	2,300	1,720	940	...	149	...	1,059	8,439	5,401
1956	65	33	4,075	2,771	3,002	1,563	...	168	...	1,614	11,105	7,107
1957	67	32	4,977	3,384	3,081	1,706	...	253	...	2,148	15,296	9,024
1958	66	29	5,185	3,526	3,759	2,296	...	238	...	2,017	15,485	9,136
1959	105	48	8,841	6,057	4,649	2,936	...	172	...	2,145	17,201	10,149
1960	135	58	9,345	6,355	6,041	3,804	655	178	5,232	3,947	19,490	12,474
1961	139	60	10,221	6,950	6,990	4,426	673	...	5,376	4,723	14,565	9,322
1962	123	54	10,778	7,301	8,092	5,160	643	...	5,917	3,445	13,266	8,490
1963	100	46	11,218	7,629	8,510	5,481	690	...	6,624	4,975	11,747	7,518
1964	65	45	16,960	11,452	9,910	6,361	731	...	6,528	4,187	15,645	10,013
1965	116	54	18,159	13,725	12,721	7,756	706	...	9,000	4,459	17,650	11,296
1966	156	69	24,818	15,763	12,212	7,788	660	...	11,683	4,554	17,841	11,418
1967	226	100	22,661	14,772	10,789	6,853	856	...	11,484	5,314	17,124	10,959
1968	277	121	24,776	16,682	11,916	7,428	578	...	11,931	5,421	12,665	9,922
1969	299	133	27,959	18,748	11,534	7,161	352	...	11,960	5,853	19,745	12,410
1970	239	107	36,381	24,739	11,265	6,940	453	...	12,585	6,249	22,070	14,080
1971	282	125	37,486	25,490	11,228	6,854	442	170	11,603	5,617	20,240	12,522
1972	259	115	46,471	31,600	8,640	5,303	416	180	9,414	6,086	17,327	11,267
1973	237	105	55,019	37,413	9,416	5,797	480	202	8,964	5,852	22,155	14,096
1974	415	212	91,488	62,212	10,297	6,299	510	209	9,525	6,220	25,983	16,384
1975	286	139	108,162	73,550	11,007	6,772	595	247	7,753	5,067	24,772	15,359
1976	506	273	107,395	73,027	10,055	6,186	542	229	4,776	2,199	18,685	11,958
1977	1,030	544	100,817	68,556	8,021	4,941	505	212	6,185	4,107	13,683	8,757
1978	909	483	103,896	70,649	7,813	4,769	497	209	4,923	3,275	13,515	8,650
1979	611	396	117,502	79,901	8,225	4,978	397	174	5,444	3,629	15,261	9,766
1980	437	275	139,697	94,993	8,835	5,344	506	226	5,704	3,844	16,102	10,304
1981	398	249	122,709	83,442	8,514	5,190	433	189	6,069	4,073	15,722	9,935
1982	587	389	119,939	81,559	6,470	3,874	470	205	5,774	3,904	11,680	6,605
1983	609	390	114,190	77,649	5,974	3,602	456	210	4,287	2,949	9,297	5,949
1984	571	346	143,842	97,813	7,116	4,250	441	203	3,979	2,784	13,055	8,355
1985	639	389	168,120	113,718	6,510	3,945	455	209	4,881	3,476	14,753	9,442
1986	810	514	175,725	119,493	7,009	4,311	523	209	5,026	3,343	16,753	10,722
1987	567	360	182,745	134,106	6,690	4,078	611	283	5,100	3,358	17,111	11,380
1988	1,119	379	200,617	146,002	7,866	4,801	614	287	4,189	2,839	18,321	12,116
1989	1,017	539	222,024	157,973	9,030	5,313	573	261	4,507	2,954	18,053	11,769
1990	992	681	213,079	152,242	7,903	5,035	628	289	3,307	2,181	20,119	13,034
1991	259	171	211,057	151,764	8,692	5,164	607	274	3,593	1,450	21,196	13,187
1992	4	2	205,346	146,447	8,270	4,450	674	310	2,848	1,109	18,070	12,088
1993	10	5	...	...	8,500	4,517	715	316	3,344	2,038	16,851	10,798

D5 Output of Iron Ore

NOTES

1. SOURCES: The national publications listed on pp. xiii–xv League of Nations and UN, *Statistical Yearbooks*, and British Iron and Steel Federation, *Statistical Year Books*.

FOOTNOTES

[1] Data to 1907 are of exports, and from 1908 to 1938 (1st line) they are of total output
[2] Newfoundland production is included in Canada from April 1949.
[3] The reason for this break is not given in the source.
[4] Production for several years prior to 1936 was estimated at 30,000 tons.

D6 OUTPUT OF MAIN NON FERROUS METAL ORES

ANTIMONY (Sb content) (in metric tons)

	NORTH AMERICA			SOUTH AMERICA				NORTH AMERICA				SOUTH AMERICA	
	Canada	Mexico	USA[1]	Boliva[2]	Peru[3]			Canada	Guatemala	Mexico	USA	Bolivia	Peru
1893	...	- -	...	...	...		1945	707	...	8,754	1,751	5,535	2,301
1894	...	80	...	...	...		1946	291	...	6,572	2,272	6,964	1,213
							1947	522	...	6,926	4,823	10,857	1,292
1895	...	600	...	...	...		1948	141	...	7,380	5,887	12,260	1,636
1896	...	3,200	...	...	...		1949	72	...	5,753	1,484	10,275	739
1897	...	5,900	...	...	...								
1898	...	10,000	...	...	...		1950	292	...	5,878	2,265	8,781	2,274
1899	...	3,010	...	...	...		1951	3,040	...	6,825	3,150	11,816	1,115
							1952	1,057	...	5,532	1,960	9,806	715
1900	...	2,313	...	...	...		1953	675	...	3,687	337	5,784	963
1901	...	5,103	...	...	...		1954	591	...	4,182	695	5,218	846
1902	...	1,218	...	...	...								
1903	...	2,304	...	...	...		1955	917	...	3,818	574	5,359	871
1904	...	1,694	...	...	...		1956	971	...	4,556	535	5,112	969
							1957	617	...	5,202	643	6,374	835
1905	...	1,978	...	...	...		1958	389	...	2,747	640	5,278	874
1906	...	2,418	...	...	...		1959	752	...	3,286	615	5,502	719
1907	...	4,615	...	...	...								
1908	...	4,046	...	...	...		1960	749	...	4,231	576	5,327	817
1909	...	3,730	...	...	...		1961	604	...	3,609	625	6,740	789
							1962	876	...	4,769	572	6,651	522
1910	...	3,730	2,022	298	...		1963	726	...	4,826	585	7,563	611
1911	...	4,131	2,045	175	...		1964	722	...	4,788	573	9,640	682
1912	...	1,698	1,768	51	...								
1913	...	937	—	35	—		1965	590	...	4,467	767	8,760	647
1914	...	1,047	—	104	—		1966	638	14	4,478	841[2]	10,667	848
											8,076		
1915	...	739	4,535	10,037	522		1967	575	50	3,738	809	8,387	742
1916	...	829	4,082	12,739	1,876		1968	526	9	3,464	777	8,283	786
1917	...	2,647	961	10,288	901		1969	372	100	3,225	851	9,025	613
1918	...	3,269	173	3,010	323								
1919	...	471	—	105	60		1970	329	1,297	4,468	1,025	11,766	1,050
							1971	147	885	3,361	930	11,878	796
1920	...	623	—	484	10		1972	213	900	2,976	444	13,338	791
1921	...	45	—	282	9		1973	2,400	873	2,388	494	14,933	417
			— [1]				1974	2,500	435	2,407	600	13,060	851
1922	...	464	4	185	...								
1923	...	490	9	312	...		1975	2,654	856	3,137	804	16,089	277
1924	...	775	29	621	...		1976	3,324	1,120	2,546	257	17,015	603
							1977	3,165	916	2,698	553	16,341	819
1925	...	1,398	30	1,384	28		1978	3,005	230	2,457	724	13,336	745
					— [3]		1979	2,954	660	2,872	655	14,420	546
					17								
1926	...	2,614	39	3,440	99		1980	2,361	556	2,176	311	15,465	394
1927	...	1,924	—	4,005	—		1981	1,670	510	1,800	586	15,296	433
1928	...	3,342	78	3,543	140		1982	455	—	1,565	456	13,978	394
1929	...	2,925	—	3,779	108		1983	385	—	2,518	760	9,950	323
							1984	554	74	3,064	505	9,281	372
1930	...	3,032	—	1,160	59								
1931	...	5,443	—	1,348	30		1985	1,075	1,638	4,266	...[4]	8,925	377
1932	...	1,735	380	1,470	31		1986	3,805	1,530	3,337	...[4]	10,243	356
1933	...	1,950	533	1,896	40		1987	3,531	1,575	2,839	...[4]	10,635	318
1934	...	2,668	367	2,024	168		1988	3,387	1,335	2,185	...[4]	10,632	246
							1989	2,818	1,191	1,906	...	9,211	304
1935	...	4,570	507	3,402	343								
1936	—	7,303	685	6,524	1,244		1990	565	868	1,800	...	8,454	307
1937	22	10,639	1,148	7,128	1,419		1991	429	590	2,900	...	7,287	600
1938	11	8,069	590	9,437	1,688		1992	796	275	1,064	...	6,022	339
1939	556	7,873	357	10,060	1,549		1993	741	90	1,294	...	4,155	400
1940	1,177	12,267	448	11,753	881								
1941	1,445	11,138	1,101	14,872	1,564								
1942	1,379	11,695	2,671	17,643	1,584								
1943	505	13,682	5,040	17,973	2,681								
1944	879	10,930	4,296	7,448	1,258								

D6 Output of Main Non-ferrous Metal Ores

BAUXITE (in thousands of metric tons)

	NORTH AMERICA	SOUTH AMERICA	
	USA[7]	Guyana[8]	Surinam
1885	—	...	—
1886	—	...	—
1887	—	...	—
1888	—	...	—
1889	1	...	—
1890	2	...	—
1891	4	...	—
1892	11	...	—
1893	9	...	—
1894	11	...	—
1895	17	...	—
1896	18	...	—
1897	21	...	—
1898	25	...	—
1899	34	...	—
1900	23	...	—
1901	20	...	—
1902	27	...	—
1903	46	...	—
1904	52	...	—
1905	58	...	—
1906	72	...	—
1907	96	...	—
1908	51	...	—
1909	134	...	—
1910	153	...	—
1911	160	...	—
1912	164	...	—
1913	214	...	—
1914	222	...	—
1915	305	...	—
1916	432	...	—
1917	578	2.1	—
1918	616	4.3	—
1919	383	2.0	—
1920	529	32.0	—
1921	142	20.0	—
1922	315	...	13
1923	531	136.0	13
1924	353	188.0	60
1925	322	197.0	87
1926	398	222.0	46
1927	326	193.0	176
1928	381	201.0	214
1929	372	220.0	210
1930	336	149.0	265
1931	199	160.0	173
1932	98	85.0	126
1933	157	42.0	104
1934	160	66.0	103
1935	238[7] / 249	140.0	113
1936	386	213.0	235
1937	432	367.0	392
1938	316	455.0	377
1939	381	478.0	512

	NORTH AMERICA				SOUTH AMERICA		
	Dominican Republic[4]	Haiti[5]	Jamaica[6]	USA[7]	Brazil	Guyana[8]	Surinam
1940	—	—	—	446	6	614	614
1941	—	—	—	952	13	1,112	1,116
1942	—	—	—	2,644	30	1,178	1,250
1943	—	—	—	6,333	69	1,973	1,694
1944	—	—	—	2,869	15	928	762
1945	—	—	—	997	20	680	747
1946	—	—	—	1,122	4	1,134	1,020
1947	—	—	—	1,221	7	1,381	1,742
1948	—	—	—	1,480	15	1,996	1,983
1949	—	—	—	1,167	16	1,827	2,162
1950	—	—	—	1,356	19	1,679	2,045
1951	—	—	—	1,878	19	2,107	2,700
1952	—	—	420	1,694	14	2,426	3,168
1953	—	—	1,240	1,605	19	2,311 / 3,359	3,273
1954	—	—	2,098	2,027	28	3,373	3,362
1955	—	—	2,709	1,817	45	3,523	3,123
1956	—	—	3,256	1,772	70	3,369	3,485
1957	—	318	4,708	1,439	64	2,989	3,377
1958	—	329	5,874	1,332	70	2,185	2,988
1959	771	298	5,304	1,727	97	2,325	3,430
1960	689	346	5,841	2,030	121	3,422	3,455
1961	749	306	6,566	1,248	111	3,253	3,453
1962	675	506	7,705	1,391	191	3,592	3,297
1963	723	442	7,078	1,549	170	2,861	3,508
1964	820	411	7,828	1,627	188	3,483	3,993
1965	893	428	8,722[6]	1,681	169	4,302	4,360
1966	818	412	9,226	1,825	268	3,348	5,563
1967	1,091	370	9,396	1,681	261	3,475	5,466
1968	1,008	430	8,415	1,692	285	3,545	5,660
1969	1,103	748	10,624	1,873	351	4,306	6,236
1970	1,086	673	12,106	2,562	510	4,418	6,011
1971	1,032	715	12,543	2,458	566	4,234	6,717
1972	1,087	725	12,989	2,235	765	3,727	6,777
1973	1,086	779	13,489	2,324	849	3,622	6,718
1974	1,196	793	15,086	2,408	858	3,606	6,863
1975	785	522	11,157	2,199	969	3,830	4,751
1976	621	733	10,473	2,420	998	3,203	4,587
1977	576	685	11,417	2,436	1,352	3,344	4,856
1978	558	639	11,732	2,066	1,401	3,014	5,025
1979	524	518	11,502	2,186	2,884	1,994	4,769
1980	510	477	12,049	1,869	6,688	1,629	4,893
1981	406	488	11,683	1,847	6,969	1,511	4,125
1982	152	431	8,158	896	6,290	1,172	3,060
1983	—	—	7,725	679	7,199	1,088	2,793
1984	—	—	8,605	856	10,355	1,349	3,375
1985	—	—	6,219	674	9,963	1,601	3,738
1986	—	—	6,953	510	6,463	1,467	3,731
1987	211	—	7,702	576	8,750	1,362	2,522
1988	185	—	7,315	588	8,083	1,339	3,434
1989	164	—	9,487	670	8,665	1,340	3,457
1990	85	—	10,965	495	9,876	1,424	3,267
1991	7	—	11,610	50	10,414	1,346	3,136
1992	—	—	11,367	45	9,366	913	3,252
1993	—	—	11,184	40	9,410	897	3,220

D6 Output of Main Non-ferrous Metal Ores

CHROMIUM (Cr_2O_3 content) (in thousands of metric tons)

	NORTH AMERICA		SOUTH AMERICA		NORTH AMERICA		SOUTH AMERICA
	Cuba	USA[10]	Brazil		Cuba	USA[10]	Brazil
1915	...	2	...	1950	15	- -	2
1916	...	25	...	1951	...	3	2
1917	...	24	...	1952	6	9	1
1918	...	45	...	1953	22	22	2
1919	...	28	...	1954	25	57	1
1920	1	1	4	1955	27	54	2
1921	1	- -	...	1956	19	78	2
1922	- -	- -	...	1957	42	59	4
1923	11	- -	...	1958	27	52	3
1924	8	- -	...	1959	17	[37][10]	4
1925	12	- -	...	1960	10	[37][10]	4
1926	36	- -	2	1961	9	[29][10]	10
1927	16	- -	2	1962	10	—	16
1928	15	- -	- -	1963	19	—	17
1929	23	- -	—	1964	11	—	8
1930	18	- -	—	1965	14	—	3
1931	7	- -	—	1966	13	—	10
1932	- -	- -	—	1967	15	—	9
1933	8	- -	—	1968	17	—	12
1934	16	- -	—	1969	16	—	15
1935	16	- -	—	1970	8	—	28
1936	23	- -	2	1971	5	—	83
1937	31	1	- -	1972	13	—	146
1938	12	- -	- -	1973	13	—	124
1939	17	2	2	1974	9	—	110
1940	16	1	2	1975	9	—	183
1941	74	5	2	1976	5	—	231
1942	86	40	3	1977	5	—	178
1943	100	60	4	1978	7	—	249
1944	68	18	2	1979	7	—	232
1945	62	6	1	1980	7	—	217
1946	53	2	—	1981	5	—	241
1947	44	- -	—	1982	7	—	159
1948	17	2	1	1983	8	—	111
1949	11	- -	2	1984	9	—	129
				1985	9	—	131
				1986	12	—	90
				1987	13	—	94
				1988	13	—	101
				1989	12	—	129
				1990	11	—	124
				1991	15	—	100
				1992	15	—	140
				1993	15	—	130

D6 Output of Main Non-ferrous Metal Ores

COPPER (Cu content) (in thousands of metric tons)

	NORTH AMERICA	SOUTH AMERICA
	USA	Chile
1844	...	8
1845	- -	8
1846	- -	10
1847	- -	9
1848	1	9
1849	1	10
1850	1	12
1851	1	8
1852	1	15
1853	2	13
1854	2	15
1855	3	19
1856	4	21
1857	5	24
1858	6	25
1859	6	23
1860	7	34
1861	8	33
1862	10	37
1863	9	32
1864	8	42
1865	9	41
1866	9	33
1867	10	43
1868	12	41
1869	13	51
1870	13	44
1871	13	39
1872	13	49
1873	16	42
1874	18	48
1875	18	48
1876	19	52
1877	21	44
1878	22	48
1879	23	46

	NORTH AMERICA				SOUTH AMERICA		
	Canada[11]	Cuba	Mexico	USA[12]	Bolivia[2]	Chile	Peru
1880	...	...	...	27	...	40	...
1881	...	...	...	33	3	40	1
1882	...	...	- -	41	3	45	- -
1883	...	...	- -	52	2	32	- -
1884	...	...	1.0	66	2	45	- -
1885	...	...	- -	75	2	40	- -
1886	2	...	- -	72	1	38	- -
1887	2	...	2.0	82	1	30	- -
1888	3	...	3.0	103	2	34	- -
1889	3	...	4.0	103	1	25	- -
1890	3	...	4.0	117	2	27	- -
1891	4	...	5.7	129	2	21	- -
1892	3	...	7.9	156	...	21	- -
1893	4	...	9.6	149	2	23	- -
1894	3	...	12.0	161	2	23	- -
1895	4	...	12.0	173	2	22	1
1896	4	...	11.0	209	2	24	1
1897	6	...	12.0	224	2	21	1
1898	8	...	16.0	239	2	26	3
1899	7	...	19.0	259	2	26	5
1900	9	...	22.0	275	2	28	8
1901	17	...	34.0	273	2	30	10
1902	16	...	36.0	299	2	27	9
1903	19	...	46.0	317	2	30	10
1904	19	1	52.0	369	2	31	10
1905	22	1	65.0	409	2	29	12
1906	25	- -	62.0	416[12] 417	2	26	13
1907	26	- -	57.0	384	2	29	21
1908	29	3	38.0	434	3	42	20
1909	24	3	57.0	511	3	43	20
1910	25	4	48.0	494	3	38	27
1911	25	4	56.0	506	2	36	28
1912	35	4	57.0	567	2	42	27
1913	35	3	53.0	560	4	42	28
1914	34	6	27.0	521	3	45	27
1915	46	9	- -	675	8	52	35
1916	53	10	28.0	910	8	71	43
1917	50	11	51.0	860	10	102	45
1918	54	13	70.0	866	8	107	44
1919	34	8	52.0	550	7	80	39
1920	37	8	49.0	555	10	100	33
1921	22	8	15.0	211	10	59	33
1922	19	11	27.0	438	11	130	36
1923	39	11	53.0	670	11	182	44
1924	47	12	49.0	729	7	190	38

D5 Output of Main Non-ferrous Metal Ores

COPPER (Cu content) (in thousands of metric tons)

	NORTH AMERICA							SOUTH AMERICA		
	Canada[11]	Cuba	Haiti	Mexico	Newfound-land	Nicaragua	USA	Bolivia	Chile	Peru
1925	51	12	—	51	...	—	761	7	192	38
1926	—[13] 60	12	—	54	...	—	783	8	203	41
1927	64	14	—	59	—	—	748	9	243	48
1928	92	17	—	65	- -	—	821	9	287	53
1929	112	14	—	81	1	—	905	7	321	54
1930	138	16	—	73	1	—	640	4	220	48
1931	133	13	—	54	2	—	480	2	223	46
1932	112	5	—	35	2	—	216	2	103	22
1933	136	7	—	40	3	—	173	2	163	25
1934	165	6	—	44	4	—	215	2	257	28
1935	190	6	—	39	3	—	345	2	267	30
1936	191	12	—	30	5	—	557	3	256	33
1937	240	13	—	46	9	—	764	4	413	36
1938	259	14	—	42	8	—	506	3	351	38
1939	276	11	—	44	10	—	661	4	341	36
1940	297	10	—	38	9	—	797	7	365	44
1941	292	10	—	49	7	—	869	7	469	37
1942	274	10	—	51	6	—	980	6	484	35
1943	261	7	—	50	6	—	990	6	497	33
1944	248	7	—	41	5	—	882	6	498	32
1945	216	9	—	62	5	—	701	6	470	32
1946	167	12	—	61	5	—	552	6	361	25
1947	205	13	—	64	4	—	769	6	427	23
1948	218[11]	16	—	59	4	—	757	7	445	18
1949	239	17	—	57	...	—	683	5	371	28
1950	240	21	—	62	...	—	825	5	363	30
1951	245	20	—	67	...	—	842	5	381	32
1952	234	18	—	59	...	—	839	5	409	30
1953	230	15	—	60	...	—	840	5	361	34
1954	275	15	—	55	...	—	758	4	364	38
1955	296	18	—	55	...	—	906	4	434	43
1956	322	15	—	55	...	—	1,002	4	490	48
1957	326	14	—	61	...	—	986	4	486	54
1958	313	13	—	65	...	—	888	3	467	56
1959	359	9	—	57	...	1	748	2	546	54

D6 Output of Main Non-ferrous Metal Ores

COPPER (Cu content) (in thousands of metric tons)

	NORTH AMERICA						SOUTH AMERICA		
	Canada	Cuba	Haiti	Mexico	Nicaragua	USA	Bolivia[2]	Chile	Peru
1960	399	12	1	60	5	980	2	536	209
1961	398	5	3	49	6	1,057	2	553	223
1962	415	6	4	47	7	1,114	2	592	176
1963	411	6	6	56	7	1,101	3	602	180
1964	442	6	6	53	9	1,131	5	634	176
1965	461	6	10	69	10	1,226	5	590	199
1966	459	5	8	74	10	1,297	6 5	661	200
1967	556	5	4	56	9	866	6	664	193
1968	575	5	6	61	12	1,093	6	667	213
1969	520	4	6	66	4	1,401	8	699	210
1970	610	- -	5	61	3	1,560	8	711	218
1971	655	—	7	63	4	1,381	7	717	213
1972	720	2	—	79	2	1,510	8	726	226
1973	824	2	—	81	2	1,559	8	743	215
1974	821	3	—	83	2	1,449	7	905	222
1975	734	3	—	78	2	1,282	6	831	166
1976	731	3	—	89	2	1,457	5	1,013	228
1977	759	3	—	90	2	1,364	3	1,053	327
1978	659	3	—	87	2	1,358	3	1,029	376
1979	636	3	—	107	2	1,447	2	1,068	397
1980	716	3	—	175	2	1,181	2	1,063	336
1981	718	3	—	230	2	1,538	3	1,105	323
1982	612	3	—	239	2	1,147	2	1,255	354
1983	653	3	—	206	1	1,038	2	1,255	319
1984	722	3	—	189	1	1,103	2	1,307	354
1985	739	3	—	168	1	1,105	2	1,360	401
1986	699	3	—	175	1	1,144	- -	1,399	397
1987	802	3	—	231	1	1,244	—	1,413	406
1988	777	3	—	268	1	1,417	- -	1,472	298
1989	723	3	—	242	—	1,498	—	1,628	364
1990	794	2	—	291	—	1,588	—	1,616	317
1991	811	3	—	296	—	1,631	—	1,855	375
1992	769	2	—	277	—	1,765	—	1,969	369
1993	734	2	—	301	—	1,787	—	2,079	374

D6   Output of Main Non-ferrous Metal Ores

GOLD (in metric tons)

	NORTH AMERICA				NORTH AMERICA			SOUTH AMERICA		
	Mexico[14]	USA[15]		Canada[16]	Mexico[14]	USA[15]		Brazil	Chile	Colombia
1835	...	1.2	1880	...	1.4	54		...	...	...
1836	...	0.8	1881	...	1.4	52		...	...	...
1837	...	0.5	1882	...	1.6	49		...	...	...
1838	...	0.7	1883	...	1.4	45		...	0.1	...
1839	...	0.7	1884	1.4	1.0	46		...	0.1	5.8
1840	...	0.7	1885	1.7	1.0	48		...	0.1	3.8
1841	...	0.9	1886	2.2	1.0	52		...	0.2	3.8
1842	...	1.3	1887	1.8	1.0	50		...	0.5	4.5
1843	...	1.8	1888	1.6	1.0	50		...	0.9	4.5
1844	...	1.7	1889	2	1.4	50		...	0.4	5.2
1845	...	1.5	1890	1.7	1.6	49		...	0.7	5.4
1846	...	1.7	1891	1.4	1.9	50		...	0.6	5.2
1847	...	1.3	1892	1.4	1.8	50		...	1.0	5.2
1848	...	15	1893	1.5	7.0	54		...	0.8	4.4
1849	...	60	1894	1.7	9.0	59		3.2	1.5	4.4
1850	...	75	1895	3.1	10	70		3.3	2.1	4.4
1851	...	83	1896	4.1	11	80		1.5	1.1	3.3
1852	...	90	1897	9.1	14	86		1.8	0.5	3.4
1853	...	98	1898	21	12	97		2.4	1.3	3.2
1854	...	90	1899	32	14	107		3.2	2.0	2.8
1855	...	83	1900	42	15[14]	119		4.2	2.4	1.8
1856	...	83	1901	36	14	118		4.2	1.6	4.2
1857	...	83	1902	32	15	120		3.1	1.0	3.8
1858	...	75	1903	28	16	111		3.4	1.0	4.1
1859	...	75	1904	25	19	121[15] 122		3.0	1.0	2.9
1860	...	69	1905	21	24	133		3.0	1.4	3.9
1861	...	65	1906	17	27	146		3.6	1.4	3.3
1862	...	59	1907	13	29	131		3.0	1.9	4.9
1863	...	60	1908	15	32	138		3.3	0.5	5.1
1864	...	69	1909	14	34	149		3.4	0.7	4.8
1865	...	80	1910	15	41	143		2.9	0.7	5.0
1866	...	80	1911	15	37	146		5.7	0.5	4.8
1867	...	78	1912	19	32	139		5.4	2.6	4.4
1868	...	72	1913	25	26	134		3.4	0.2	4.4
1869	...	74	1914	24	8.6	137		3.2	0.3	7.0
1870	3.4	75	1915	29	7.4	148		3.6	1.2	8.2
1871	1.5	65	1916	29	12	137		4.3	1.9	9.3
1872	2.0	54	1917	23	24	121		4.5	1.9	7.5
1873	1.6	54	1918	22	25	100		4.2	1.9	7.3
1874	1.6	50	1919	24	24	86		3.0	2.0	9.0
1875	1.5	50	1920	24	23	74		3.9	1.7	8.7
1876	1.1	60	1921	29	21	73		4.2	1.4	9.0
1877	1.3	71	1922	39	23	71		4.6	2.5	7.5
1878	1.4	77	1923	38	24	75		4.5	2.0	5.9
1879	1.5	59	1924	47	25	76		4.5	2.1	8.9

D6 Output of Main Non-ferrous Metal Ores

GOLD (in metric tons)

	NORTH AMERICA			SOUTH AMERICA		
	Canada[16]	Mexico	USA	Brazil	Chile	Colombia
1925	54	25	72	3.4	1.9	7.9
1926	55	24	69	3.2	1.8	5.6
1927	58	22	66	3.2	1.9	5.1
1928	59	22	67	3.3	1.1	4.5
1929	60	20	64	3.7	1.0	4.2
1930	65	21	67	4.2	0.6	4.9
1931	84	19	69	3.9	0.7	6.0
1932	95	18	71	3.7	1.2	7.7
1933	92	20	71	3.7	4.6	9.3
1934	92	21	86	3.5	7.4	11
1935	102	21	101	3.7	8.3	10
1936	117	23	118	3.9	7.7	12
1937	127	26	128	4.5	8.5	14
1938	147	29	133	4.4	9.1	16
1939	158	26	145	4.6	10.2	18
1940	165	27	151	4.7	10.4	20
1941	166	25	148	4.6	8.2	20
1942	151	25	108	4.9	5.8	19
1943	114	20	42	5.0	5.4	18
1944	91	16	31	5.2	6.3	17
1945	84	16	30	5.1	5.6	16
1946	88	13	49	4.4	7.2	14
1947	95	14	66	4.2	5.3	12
1948	110[16]	11	63	4.1	5.1	10
1949	128	13	62	3.7	5.6	11
1950	138	13	74	4.0	5.8	12
1951	137	12	62	4.1	5.4	13
1952	139	14	59	4.4	5.2	13
1953	126	15	61	3.6	4.1	14
1954	136	12	57	3.7	3.9	12
1955	141	12	56	3.4	3.8	12
1956	136	11	57	3.8	2.9	14
1957	137	11	56	3.8	3.2	10
1958	142	10	54	3.6	3.5	12
1959	139	9.8	50	3.5	2.4	12
1960	144	9.1	52	3.7	3.4	13
1961	139	8.4	48	3.8	1.5	12
1962	130	7.4	48	4.0	1.8	12
1963	125	7.4	45	4.1	2.4	10
1964	119	6.5	45	4.4	2.0	11

D6   Output of Main Non-ferrous Metal Ores

GOLD (in metric tons)

	NORTH AMERICA			SOUTH AMERICA		
	Canada	Mexico	USA	Brazil	Chile	Colombia
1965	112	6.7	53	5.6	1.6	9.9
1966	102	6.6	56	6.1	1.6	8.7
1967	92	5.7	49	6.1	1.8	8.0
1968	85	4.6	46	6.1	1.8	7.5
1969	79	5.6	54	6.1	1.8	6.8
1970	75	6.2	54	5.8	1.6	6.3
1971	70	4.7	47	5.1	2.0	5.9
1972	65	4.5	50	7.2	2.9	5.9
1973	61	4.1	37	6.9	3.2	6.7
1974	53	4.2	35	5.9	3.7	8.2
1975	51	4.5	33	5.4	4.0	9.6
1976	53	5.1	33	4.9	4.0	9.5
1977	54	6.6	34	5.4	3.6	8.0
1978	54	6.3	31	9.4	3.2	7.6
1979	51	5.9	30	4.5	3.5	8.4
1980	51	6.1	30	14	6.8	16
1981	49	6.3	43	17	12	16
1982	65	6.1	46	26	17	15
1983	74	6.9	62	54	18	14
1984	83	7.1	65	37	17	25
1985	88	7.5	75	30	17	36
1986	103	7.8	116	23	18	40
1987	116	8.0	154	36	17	27
1988	135	9.1	201	56	21	29
1989	159	8.6	266	103	22	30
1990	167	8.3	294	85	27	29
1991	176	8.4	296	80	29	30
1992	157	8.9	329	86	34	30
1993	151	9.7	331	85	33	27

D6 Output of Main Non-ferrous Metal Ores

LEAD (Pb content) (in thousands of metric tons)

	NORTH AMERICA		
	Canada[11]	Mexico[14]	USA[17]
1883	—	15	...
1884	—	15	...
1885	—	18	...
1886	—	16	...
1887	0.1	18	...
1888	0.3	30	...
1889	0.1	28	...
1890	- -	22	...
1891	- -	30	...
1892	0.4	48	...
1893	1.0	64	...
1894	2.6	57	...
1895	7.5	68	...
1896	11	63	...
1897	18	70	...
1898	14	71	...
1899	10	85	...
1900	29	64[14]	...
1901	24	94	...
1902	10	107	...
1903	8.2	101	...
1904	17	95	...
1905	25	101	...
1906	25	74	...
1907	22	76	331
1908	20	127	300
1909	21	118	349
1910	15	124	347
1911	11	117	387
1912	16	105	401
1913	17	68	438
1914	16	21	458
1915	21	57	492
1916	19	20	546
1917	15	64	570
1918	23	99	510
1919	20	71	390

	NORTH AMERICA				SOUTH AMERICA			
	Canada[11]	Mexico	New-foundland	USA[17]	Argentina	Bolivia[2]	Brazil	Peru
1920	16	83	...	451	...	1.0	...	0.6
1921	30	61	...	376	...	2.9	...	0.5
1922	42	110	...	433	...	4.1	...	0.7
1923	50	156	...	496	...	5.5	...	0.7
1924	80	165	- -	541	1.2	20.0	...	0.8
1925	115	172	—	621	2.6	22.0	...	3.5
1926	129	211	—	620	5.4	18.0	...	10
1927	141	244	—	604	4.0	15.0	...	5.2
1928	153	235	—	569	1.9	13.0	...	17
1929	148	247	11	588	3.1	15.0	...	21
1930	151	233	18	506	3.0	12.0	...	20
1931	121	227	25	367	3.9	6.7	...	2.6
1932	116	137	36	266	2.8	5.5	...	4.6
1933	121	119	35	247	4.3	7.8	...	2
1934	157	166	38	261	2.8	11	...	9.1
1935	154	184	36	300	2.5	10	...	28
1936	174	216	31	338	6.8	14	...	30
1937	187	218	29	422	15.0	18	...	42
1938	190	282	32	335	22.0	13	...	58
1939	176	220	27	376	28.0	14	...	46
1940	214	196	30	415	29.0	12	...	50
1941	209	155	30	419	23.0	16	...	50
1942	232	198	25	450	26.0	12	...	45
1943	201	218	33	411	18.0	11	...	48
1944	138	185	30	378	19.0	9	...	52
1945	157	205	25	354	16.0	9.5	...	54
1946	161	140	25	304	20.0	8.4	...	44
1947	147	223	21	348	19.0	11	...	55
1948	152	193	20	354	18.0	26	...	48
1949	145	221	...	372	15.0	26	...	65
1950	150	238	...	391	17.0	31	...	65
1951	143	225	...	352	20.0	31	...	82
1952	153	246	...	354	17.0	30	...	96
1953	176	221	...	311	18.0	24	2.9	115
1954	198	217	...	295	19.0	18	2.7	110
1955	184	211	...	307	22.0	19	3.7	119[13]
1956	171	200	...	320	28.0	22	3.5	132
1957	165	215	...	307	30.0	26	3.5	151
1958	169	202	...	243	29.0	23	5.8	137
1959	169	191	...	232	30.0	22	5.5	150

D6　Output of Main Non-ferrous Metal Ores

LEAD (Pb content) (in thousands of metric tons)

	NORTH AMERICA			SOUTH AMERICA			
	Canada[11]	Mexico	USA[17]	Argentina	Bolivia[2]	Brazil[18]	Peru
1960	187[11] 192	191	224	27	21	10	166
1961	166	181	238	28	20	4.9	176
1962	192	193	215	30	19	14	167
1963	180	190	230	26	20	10	149
1964	187	175	259	26	18	13[18] 22	151
1965	275	170	273	32	17	24	154
1966	293	182	297	29	21[2] 20	23	161
1967	308	164	287	32	21	24	160
1968	328	174	326	27	21	27	154
1969	300	171	462	39	22	28	162
1970	358	177	519	36	22	28	164
1971	368	157	525	40	21	28	172
1972	335	161	562	38	22	30	190
1973	342	167	547	35	21	26	198
1974	294	193	602	38	18	26	179
1975	349	163	564	30	18	22	154
1976	256	165	553	33	19	23	175
1977	281	163	537	34	19	24	176
1978	320	170	530	30	18	31	183
1979	311	173	526	32	16	22	184
1980	252	145	550	33	17	22	174
1981	273	157	445	33	17	22	205
1982	272	146	512	33	12	19	198
1983	272	167	449	32	12	19	207
1984	264	183	323	28	7	19	194
1985	268	207	414	29	6	17	224
1986	334	183	340	27	3	14	190
1987	373	177	311	26	9	15	190
1988	351	171	385	28	12	13	148
1989	269	163	411	27	16	14	179
1990	233	174	484	23	20	9	187
1991	248	158	466	23	25	7	203
1992	337	173	398	18	19	8	194
1993	182	181	357	12	21	8	218

D6   Output of Main Non-ferrous Metal Ores

MERCURY (Hg content) (in metric tons)

1850–1879

| | NORTH AMERICA | | NORTH AMERICA | | NORTH AMERICA |
	USA		USA		USA
1850	268	1860	347	1870	1,044
1851	964	1861	1,246	1871	1,099
1852	694	1862	1,459	1872	1,097
1853	773	1863	1,408	1873	959
1854	1,041	1864	1,648	1874	963
1855	1,145	1865	1,839	1875	1,744
1856	1,145	1866	1,615	1876	2,523
1857	979	1867	1,631	1877	2,755
1858	1,076	1868	1,656	1878	2,216
1859	451	1869	1,173	1879	2,556

MANGANESE (Mn content) (in thousands of metric tons)   **MERCURY** (Hg content) (in metric tons)

| | NORTH AMERICA | | SOUTH AMERICA | | NORTH AMERICA | |
	Cuba	USA[20]	Brazil[21]	Chile	Mexico	USA
1880	...	5.8	...	...	...	2,040
1881	...	4.9	...	...	...	2,072
1882	...	4.6	...	...	...	1,780
1883	...	6.2	...	...	...	1,590
1884	...	10	...	...	...	1,087
1885	...	23	...	...	...	1,092
1886	...	31	...	...	...	1,021
1887	...	35	...	...	...	1,152
1888	...	30	...	...	...	1,132
1889	...	25	...	...	...	902
1890	22	20	...	49	...	780
1891	22	23	...	35	250	780
1892	15	14	...	50	240	954
1893	14	8	...	50	286	1,027
1894	15	6	...	48	300	1,036
1895	16	10	5	24	213	1,230
1896	12	10	14	26	218	1,047
1897	—	11	16	24	294	907
1898	—	16	26	21	253	1,058
1899	—	10	65	41	324	1,037

D6 Output of Main Non-ferrous Metal Ores

	MANGANESE (Mn content) (in thousands of metric tons)					MERCURY (Hg content) (in metric tons) 1900–1939	
	NORTH AMERICA			SOUTH AMERICA		NORTH AMERICA	
	Cuba[19]	Mexico	USA[20]	Brazil[21]	Chile	Mexico	USA
1900	22	—	12	108	26.0	124	964
1901	25	—	12	100	19.0	128	1,012
1902	40	—	8	157	13.0	191	1,168
1903	21	—	3	162	17.0	188	1,213
1904	18	—	3	208	2.3	190	1,177
1905	8	—	4	224	1.3	190	1,036
1906	14	—	7	121	—	200	893
1907	35	—	6	237	—	200	734
1908	1	—	6	166	—	200	672
1909	3	—	2[20]	240	—	200	717
1910	6	—	2	254	—	251	701
1911	10	—	2	174	—	165	723
1912	11	—	2	155	—	165	853
1913	12[19]	—	4	122	—	166	688
1914	2	—	3	184	—	162	563
1915	60	—	10	289	—	94	716
1916	37	—	32	502	—	52	1,019
1917	43	0.1	131	533	—	33	1,223
1918	76	2.9	311	395	—	164	1,118
1919	32	2.8	56	206	—	119	728
1920	23	1.1	96	459	—	76	456
1921	0.6	0.6	14	276	—	46	216
1922	9.2	0.7	14	341	0.4	42	217
1923	20	2.2	32	236	2.1	45	270
1924	29	1.8	57	159	2.0	37	342
1925	24	3.3	100	312	5.3	39	312
1926	25	3.3	47	320	5.3	45	260
1927	130	1.0	45	242	3.7	81	384
1928	87	0.7	48[20] 20	362[21] 174	4.4	87	616
1929	84	0.7	27	141	1.5	83	816
1930	2.1	0.7	30	92	2.9	166	743
1931	1.2	0.3	16	46	0.2	251	860
1932	3.5	0.3	8	10	0.2	253	435
1933	15	0.6	8	12	10.0	154	333
1934	32	0.9	12	1	1.9	158	532
1935	23	1.4	13	22	2.0	216	604
1936	18	1.3	17	56[21]	2.3	183	571
1937	57	1.5	23	126	5.7	170	569
1938	63[19] 148	0.8	12	147	4.4	294	620
1939	145	0.5	13	124	5.3	254	642

D6 Output of Main Non-ferrous Metal Ores

| | MANGANESE (Mn content) (in thousands of metric tons) | | | | | MERCURY (Hg content) (in metric tons) | | | 1940–1993 |
| | NORTH AMERICA | | | SOUTH AMERICA | | NORTH AMERICA | | | SOUTH AMERICA |
	Cuba	Mexico	USA[20]	Brazil	Chile	Canada	Mexico	USA	Peru
1940	161	0.3	18	150	9.7	140	402	1,302	...
1941	318	1.0	40	217	9.9	243	797	1,549	...
1942	231	11	92	170	15	470	1,118	1,753	...
1943	123	23	99	123	24	767	976	1,790	11[9]
1944	184	29	119	114	9.6	334	795	1,299	5.3[9]
1945	242	19	94	119	3.5	—	567	1,060	7.2[9]
1946	227	11	76	83	4.2	—	402	874	0.2[9]
1947	2.1	14	70	81	4.4	—	334	801	—
1948	4.7	24	69	72	11	—	165	496	—
1949	6.0	24	64	102	14	—	181	342	—
1950	12	14	69	86	17	—	130	156	—
1951	42	28	48	90	19	—	278	251	—
1952	116	41	57	110	24	—	301	433	—
1953	163	76	75	102	25	—	401	494	—
			108						
1954	123	83	100	71	17	—	509	639	2
1955	111	36	151	93	20	—	1,030	653	5
1956	105	62	165	137	22	—	673	833	12
1957	60	80	181	404	25	—	726	1,194	14
1958	29	79	145	388	17	—	777	1,312	68
1959	25	77	109	454	18	—	566	1,077	87
1960	18	72	47	438	20	—	693	1,145	105
1961	19	69	33	447	15	—	624	1,091	103
1962	33	63	34	515	19	—	650	906	120
1963	15	54	48	552	21	—	562	658	107
1964	28	64	35	649	9.2	252	433	488	113
1965	34	59	47	659	7.8	69	662	675	107
1966	35	31	45	634	8.4	...	761	759	142
1967	29	31	42	572	6.6	172	497	820	104
1968	28	27	35	842	11	196	593	995	104
1969	11	60	57	1,045	11	731	777	1,022	124
1970	11	99	47	1,202	11	827	1,043	941	110
1971	10	96	24	1,264	10	638	1,220	616	119
1972	7	106	17	1,057	7	505	776	253	125
1973	6	131	23	1,142	6	475	700	75	123
1974	11	145	32	1,232	11	532	894	75	112
1975	8	154	17	1,245	8	456	490	254	53
1976	...	163	28	1,268	7	—	518	797	—
1977	...	175	25	1,204	7	—	333	974	—
1978	...	188	35	1,207	8	—	76	833	—
1979	...	177	28	1,236	9	—	68	1,018	—
1980	...	161	21	1,339	9	—	145	1,057	—
1981	...	208	22	1,393	9	—	240	962	—
1982	...	183	4	2,225	5	—	295	888	—
1983	...	133	3	1,141	8	—	221	864	—
1984	...	181	8	1,537	8	—	384	657	—
1985	...	151	4	1,105	12	—	264	570	—
1986	...	174	2	1,134	11	—	345	483	—
1987	...	146	...	979	11	—	344	34	—
1988	...	169	...	994	14	—	345	379	—
1989	...	150	...	1,143	14	—	345	414	—
1990	...	139	...	950	13	—	345	562	—
1991	...	78	...	826	13	—	...	...	—
1992	...	138	...	647	15	—	...	...	—
1993	...	116	...	722	19	—	...	...	—

D6   Output of Main Non-ferrous Metal Ores

MOLYBDENUM (Mo content) (in metric tons)

1910–1993

	NORTH AMERICA			SOUTH AMERICA				NORTH AMERICA			SOUTH AMERICA	
	Canada	Mexico	USA	Chile	Peru			Canada	Mexico	USA	Chile	Peru
1910	...	...	—	—	...		1950	28	—	20,205	992	1
1911	...	...	—	—	...		1951	104	—	17,217	1,725	3
1912	...	...	—	—	...		1952	138	—	19,376	1,644	3
1913	...	...	—	—	...		1953	88	—	24,414	1,364	5
1914	...	...	1	—	...		1954	205	71	29,039	1,204	1
1915	...	...	83	—	...		1955	378	25	29,352	1,273	—
1916	...	...	93	—	...		1956	382	14	25,912	1,408	—
1917	...	...	159	—	...		1957	355	13	25,920	1,338	—
1918	...	...	391	—	...		1958	403	26	19,200	1,285	1
1919	...	...	135	—	...		1959	340	26	23,487	2,299	—
1920	...	...	15	—	...		1960	348	60	31,725	1,852	—
1921	...	...	...	—	...		1961	350	2	30,279	1,831	—
1922	...	...	...	—	...		1962	371	58	22,909	2,440	5
1923	...	...	10	—	...		1963	378	41	29,865	2,906	538
1924	...	...	135	—	...		1964	556	53	29,528	3,852	639
1925	6	1	523	—	...		1965	4,335	49	35,067	3,752	680
1926	6	—	650	—	...		1966	9,342	90	41,581	4,668	672
1927	—	—	1,037	—	...		1967	9,696	38	37,011	4,740	924
1928	—	—	1,510	—	...		1968	10,190	48	42,296	3,853	810
1929	4	—	1,771	—	...		1969	13,450	202	46,725	4,841	224
1930	—	—	1,706	—	—		1970	15,319	141	50,068 / 50,508	5,701	1,012
1931	—	4	1,413	—	1		1971	10,279	79	49,710	6,321	1,337
1932	—	3	1,076	—	4		1972	12,925	78	50,865	5,885	1,278
1933	—	40	2,613	—	5		1973	13,786	41	52,553	4,940	1,056
1934	—	466	4,253	—	9		1974	13,942	43	50,808	9,757	1,085
1935	—	686	4,941	—	8		1975	13,026	17	48,072	9,091	739
1936	—	534	8,147	—	10		1976	14,618	16	51,362	10,899	850
1937	4	629	13,663	—	58		1977	16,568	1	55,524	10,938	456
1938	3	483	11,670	—	111		1978	13,943	11	59,803	13,196	730
1939	1	523	14,704	30	205		1979	11,175	48	65,303	13,560	1,196
1940	5	309	11,489	267	166		1980	11,889	74	68,351	13,668	2,688
1941	47	522	17,407	229	146		1981	14,134	451	63,458	15,360	2,488
1942	43	855	30,135	580	153		1982	16,460	5,190	38,274	20,048	2,893
1943	178	1,137	24,474	680	85		1983	10,194	5,866	15,237	15,264	2,628
1944	509	716	17,882	1,051	62		1984	11,557	4,054	47,021	16,861	3,085
1945	228	468	15,279	841	29		1985	7,852	3,761	49,173	18,389	3,833
1946	184	818	7,315	560	4		1986	11,251	3,350	42,627	16,581	3,491
1947	207	136	10,065	402	2		1987	14,771	4,400	34,072	16,941	3,352
1948	83	—	13,457	532	2		1988	13,535	4,456	43,063	15,527	2,370
1949	—	—	10,560	558	2		1989	13,543	4,189	63,105	16,550	3,177
							1990	12,188	3,200	61,611	13,830	2,510
							1991	11,437	2,550	53,607	14,434	3,031
							1992	9,602	2,300	45,098	14,840	3,220
							1993	9,836	2,400	32,671	14,899	2,860

D6 Output of Main Non-ferrous Metal Ores

NICKEL (Ni content) (in metric tons)

1885-1993

	NORTH AMERICA Canada[11]		NORTH AMERICA Canada[11]	Cuba	USA		NORTH AMERICA Canada[11]	Cuba	USA
1885	...	1920	28.0			1955	159	14	4.0
1886	...	1921	8.8			1956	162	15	6.7
1887	...	1922	8.0			1957	171	20	12
1888	...	1923	28			1958	127	18	12
1889	0.4	1924	31			1959	169	18	12
1890	0.6	1925	33			1960	195	13	13
1891	1.8	1926	30			1961	211	15	12
1892	1.1	1927	30			1962	211	17	12
1893	1.8	1928	44			1963	197	20	12
1894	2.2	1929	50			1964	207	23	14
1895	1.8	1930	47	—	...	1965	235	28	15
1896	1.5	1931	30	—	...	1966	203	28	14
1897	1.8	1932	14	—	...	1967	226	33	14
1898	2.5	1933	38	—	...	1968	240	38	16
1899	2.6	1934	58	—	...	1969	194	35	15
1900	3.2	1935	63	—	...	1970	277	37	14
1901	4.2	1936	77	—	...	1971	267	36	15
1902	4.9	1937	102	—	...	1972	235	37	15
1903	5.7	1938	96	—	...	1973	249	35	17
1904	4.8	1939	103	—	...	1974	269	34	15
1905	8.6	1940	111	—	...	1975	242	37	15
1906	9.7	1941	128	—	...	1976	241	37	15
1907	9.6	1942	129	—	...	1977	233	37	13
1908	8.7	1943	131	2.4	...	1978	128	35	12
1909	12	1944	125	4.7	...	1979	126	32	14
1910	17	1945	111	11	...	1980	185	38	13
1911	15	1946	87	11	...	1981	155	40	11
1912	20	1947	108	2.0	...	1982	89	38	3
1913	23	1948	120	—	...	1983	125	39	—
1914	20	1949	117	—	...	1984	174	33	13
1915	31	1950	112	—	...	1985	170	36	6
1916	38	1951	125	—	...	1986	164	35	1
1917	38	1952	128	8.1	...	1987	189	37	—
1918	42	1953	130	13	...	1988	199	44	—
1919	20	1954	151	13	1.8	1989	195	47	—
						1990	195	38	—
						1991	188	35	5
						1992	185	32	6
						1993	188	29	5

D6 Output of Main Non-ferrous Metal Ores

SILVER (metal content) (in metric tons)

	NORTH AMERICA	SOUTH AMERICA			NORTH AMERICA			SOUTH AMERICA				
	USA	Chile			Canada	Mexico[14]	USA[15]	Argentina	Bolivia[23]	Chile	Colombia	Peru
1865					...	...	271	...	...	22	...	...
1834	0.2	...		1866	...	...	241	...	...	38	...	...
				1867	...	...	325	...	...	65	...	...
1835	0.6	...		1868	...	...	289	...	...	70	...	...
1836	0.6	...		1869	...	...	289	...	...	83	...	...
1837	0.6	...										
1838	0.6	...		1870	...	967	385	...	...	46	...	...
1839	0.6	...		1871	...	516	553	...	...	54	...	...
				1872	...	489	692	...	...	37	...	...
1840	0.6	...		1873	...	514	860	...	...	65	...	...
1841	0.6	...		1874	...	523	898	...	...	75	...	...
1842	0.6	...										
1843	0.6	...		1875	...	570	763	...	...	74	...	...
1844	0.6	28		1876	5.6	607	933		82	35	...	58
				1877	3.7	614	997	...	67	43	...	58
1845	1.2	36		1878	5.5	673	1,089	...	88	41	...	58
1846	1.2	41		1879	1.6	715	982	10	265	60	...	58
1847	1.2	41										
1848	1.2	50		1880	1.6	715	943	...	265	84	...	58
1849	1.2	71		1881	1.6	723	1,034	...	265	38	...	47
				1882	1.6	775	1,126	...	265	97	18	46
1850	1.2	92		1883	5.0	812	1,111	...	385	77	...	46
1851	1.2	80		1884	5.0	836	1,174	10	241	67	18	46
1852	1.2	86										
1853	1.2	57		1885	5.0	917	1,241	12	241	156	9.6	48
1854	1.2	69		1886	5.0	962	1,235	1.4	241	155	9.6	96
				1887	11	1,011	1,298	0.7	199	194	24	75
1855	1.2	62		1888	14	957	1,424	10	230	183	24	75
1856	1.2	57		1889	12	1,023	1,558	15	263	124	15	69
1857	1.2	35										
1858	1.2	27		1890	12	1,151	1,696	15	301	74	20	66
1859	2.4	16		1891	13	1,350	1,814	15	373	34	41	70
				1892	10	1,423	1,975	15	393	101	41	59
1860	3.6	34		1893	13	1,423	1,866	22	424	97	53	59
1861	48	28		1894	26	1,491	1,540	37	684	145	53	108
1862	108	48										
1863	204	49		1895	49	1,557	1,733	10	684	137	53	98
1864	265	36		1896	100	1,715	1,830	10	198	150	106	120
				1897	173	1,772	1,675	12	255	141	157	102
				1898	138	1,716	1,693	12	342	132	171	165
				1899	106	1,817	1,703	12	337	129	110	203
				1900	139	1,773[14]	1,793	1.2	341	73	58	227
				1901	172	1,795	1,717	1.4	404	68	59	111
				1902	133	1,898	1,726	1.2	279	51	55	133
				1903	100	2,019	1,689	2.9	189	51	35	171
				1904	111	1,973	1,794[15] 1,742	2.0	117	27	29	145
				1905	187	1,891	1,750	4.7	96	26	21	191
				1906	264	1,803	1,784	0.4	110	26	24	230
				1907	398	1,954	1,633	0.7	149	28	33	208
				1908	688	2,221	1,582	3.9	157	30	43	199
				1909	856	2,213	1,783	8.2	157	44	13	208

D6 Output of Main Non-ferrous Metal Ores

SILVER (metal content) (in metric tons)

	NORTH AMERICA					SOUTH AMERICA				
	Canada[22]	Honduras	Mexico	Newfound-land	USA	Argentina	Bolivia[23]	Chile	Colombia	Peru
1910	1,022	...	2,417	—	1,791	8.1	144	42	27.0	253
1911	1,013	...	2,518	—	1,901	6.3	128	35	25.0	289
1912	994	...	2,527	—	2,054	2.5	124	40	18.0	324
1913	991	...	2,199	—	2,214	1.1	124	40	18.0	299
1914	885	...	857	—	2,166	...	71	37	11.0	287
1915	828	...	1,231	—	2,250	...	77	40	11.0	293
1916	792	...	926	—	2,453	0.7	78	47	10.0	335
1917	691	...	1,307	—	2,198	0.9	76	53	10.0	338
1918	665	...	1,945	—	2,117	0.8	76	47	...	304
1919	498	...	2,050	—	1,614	0.8	76	41	15.0	305
1920	415	...	2,069	—	1,758	0.9	68[24] 192	81	15.0	286
1921	421	...	2,005	—	1,436	0.8	187	80	16.0	307
1922	579	...	2,522	—	1,904	0.8	167	84	0.1	410
1923	579	...	2,825	—	2,188	0.9	162	104	0.1	580
1924	614	...	2,844	—	1,993	0.6	151	94	0.1	582
1925	629	...	2,889	—	2,075	0.6	135	101	0.1	645
1926	696	...	3,044	—	1,944	0.5	181	101	0.1	701
1927	707	...	3,248	—	1,855	0.5	168	47	4.1	572
1928	682	...	3,374	—	1,800	0.5	175	45	1.5	679
1929	720	...	3,386	17	1,893	0.5	150	49	1.7	660
1930	823	...	3,272	17	1,484	0.5	221	24	2.1	479
1931	640	...	2,677	30	929	...	179	9.0	2.7	273
1932	571	...	2,156	42	708	1.6	128	3.1	2.8	211
1933	472	122	2,118	38	719	1.6	170	8.0	3.4	232
1934	511	96	2,306	34	1,020	1.9	166	33	4.0	322
1935	517	83	2,351	35	1,509	1.6	193	40	4.1	548
1936	570	99	2,409	39	1,902	16	318	47	4.7	619
1937	715	106	2,634	45	2,221	66	294	58	5.2	543
1938	691	112	2,520	51	1,919	82	198	43	6.0	639
1939	720	139	2,360	44	2,002	148	225	37	7.5	585
1940	741	133	2,570	47	2,191	116	175	47	8.1	602
1941	677	118	2,437	62	2,085	91	229	39	8.4	470
1942	644	120	2,640	34	1,682	89	253	28	7.7	499
1943	539	111	2,686	39	1,290	72	227	31	6.5	456
1944	424	112	2,286	36	1,072	53	211	31	6.2	492
1945	403	110	1,900	34	903	90	208	25	5.2	404
1946	390	102	1,346	35	713	96	190	17	4.7	384
1947	389	94	1,830	30	1,114	76[13]	194	23	3.4	335
1948	501[22]	97	1,789	27	1,185	212	235	27	3.4	289
1949	549	127	1,538	...	1,079	240	206	24	3.3	330
1950	722	136	1,528	...	1,321	235	204	29	3.6	416
1951	719	125	1,362	...	1,237	240	223	37	4.0	541
1952	784	[111][5]	1,566	...	1,227	340	220	44	3.8	597
1953	880	[173][5]	1,463	...	1,169	223	190	47	3.7	611
1954	968	[107][5]	1,241	...	1,149	155	157	46	3.5	635

D6   Output of Main Non-ferrous Metal Ores

SILVER (metal content) (in metric tons)

	NORTH AMERICA				SOUTH AMERICA				
	Canada	Honduras	Mexico	USA	Argentina	Bolivia[23]	Chile	Colombia	Peru
1955	870	56	1,492	1,157	100	184	53	3.5	714
1956	884	63	1,340	1,204	50	235	57	3.4	746
1957	896	70	1,466	1,187	69	167	48	3.3	773
1958	969	86	1,462	1,061	48	188	47	3.3	806
1959	993	98	1,371	970	67	139	55	3.2	847
1960	1,058	92	1,385	957	70	152	45	4.2	953[13]
									1,016
1961	976	110	1,255	1,082	64	121	68	4.0	1,055
1962	947	99	1,282	1,145	65	117	58	4.1	1,031
1963	931	98	1,330	1,096	60	151	79	3.3	1,095
1964	930	100	1,298	1,130	60	150	87	4.1	1,070
1965	1,004	114	1,254	1,238	71	128	86	3.6	1,134
1966	1,039	120	1,306	1,358	69	103	100	3.4	1,149
1967	1,130	120	1,190	1,006	53	110	98	3.4	999
1968	1,400	168	1,245	1,018	77	113	116	3.1	1,127
1969	1,354	116	1,334	1,303	97	150	96	2.4	1,175
1970	1,423	117	1,332	1,400	88	148	76	2.4	1,217
1971	1,431	76	1,140	1,293	99	145	85	2	1,264
1972	1,393	108	1,166	1,158	102	143	146	2	1,269
1973	1,477	104	1,206	1,166	76	165	157	2	1,287
1974	1,332	118	1,168	1,050	96	179	208	2	1,215
1975	1,234	89	1,183	1,087	72	204	194	3	1,201
1976	1,281	114	1,326	1,068	70	177	228	3	1,202
1977	1,314	88	1,463	1,187	76	209[23]	263	3	1,132
						181			
1978	1,267	87	1,579	1,225	64	196	255	3	1,337
1979	1,147	76	1,537	1,179	69	179	272	3	1,364
1980	1,070	54	1,473	1,006	73	190	299	5	1,337
1981	1,203	56	1,655	1,265	78	205	361	4	1,470
1982	1,291	53	1,550	1,252	84	170	382	4	1,663
1983	1,197	83	1,911	1,351	78	187	468	3	1,739
1984	1,327	89	1,987	1,387	62	142	490	4	1,651
1985	1,197	83	2,153	1,227	68	111	517	5	1,899
1986	1,088	84	2,303	1,074	66	100	500	5	1,853
1987	1,375	23	2,415	1,241	60	140	500	5	1,905
1988	1,443	58	2,359	1,661	79	232	507	7	1,568
1989	1,312	50	2,306	2,008	83	267	545	7	1,748
1990	1,381	36	2,346	2,121	83	310	655	7	1,725
1991	1,261	43	2,290	1,855	70	337	676	8	1,769
1992	1,147	43	2,317	1,804	45	282	1,025	8	1,570
1993	888	40	2,128	1,645	43	300	970	8	1,573

D6 Output of Main Non-ferrous Metal Ores

TIN (Sn content) (in metric tons)

	SOUTH AMERICA Bolivia
1870	102
1871	...
1872	...
1873	...
1874	...
1875	305
1876	315
1877	315
1878	325
1879	335
1880	366
1881	305
1882	356
1883	501
1884	207
1885	228
1886	360
1887	998
1888	1,385
1889	1,411
1890	1,691
1891	1,584
1892	2,864
1893	2,956
1894	3,538
1895	4,166
1896	4,104
1897	5,594
1898	4,536
1899	5,588
1900	9,198
1901	13,124
1902	10,604
1903	12,533
1904	12,902
1905	16,582
1906	17,624
1907	16,607
1908	17,692
1909	21,340

	NORTH AMERICA Canada	SOUTH AMERICA Argentina	Bolivia
1910	—	...	23,129
1911	—	...	22,434
1912	—	...	23,027
1913	—	...	26,355
1914	—	...	22,355
1915	—	...	21,794
1916	—	...	21,145
1917	—	...	27,858
1918	—	...	29,280
1919	—	...	27,389
1920	—	...	29,542
1921	—	...	28,957
1922	—	...	28,129
1923	—	...	31,128
1924	—	...	32,059
1925	—	...	32,741
1926	—	...	30,543
1927	—	...	36,383
1928	—	22	42,074
1929	—	2	47,081
1930	—	—	38,756
1931	—	—	31,234
1932	—	6	20,919
1933	—	51	14,961
1934	—	234	23,224
1935	—	640	25,408
1936	—	904	24,438
1937	—	1,356	25,531
1938	—	1,747	25,894
1939	—	1,729	27,916
1940	—	1,480	38,531
1941	29	1,189	42,740
1942	562	872	38,907
1943	353	785	40,960
1944	235	1,002	39,341

	NORTH AMERICA Canada	SOUTH AMERICA Argentina	Bolivia	Brazil
1945	385	1,101	43,168	...
1946	396	795	38,222	...
1947	324	558	33,800	...
1948	314	284	37,935	187
1949	280	224	34,662	...
1950	362	261	31,714	183
1951	157	241	33,664	200
1952	97	265	32,472	233
1953	[292][25]	156	35,384	212
1954	[151][25]	97	29,287	170
1955	[224][25]	86	28,369	148
1956	[343][25]	86	27,273	178
1957	[322][25]	185[13]	28,242	298
1958	[361][25]	90	18,013	416
1959	339	107	24,193	468[13]
1960	282	140	20,543	1,581
1961	508	261	20,996	590
1962	296	235	22,150	743
1963	421	229	22,603	1,172
1964	160	348	24,587	802
1965	171	505	23,407	1,842
1966	322	465	25,932	1,624
1967	198	815	27,721	1,761
1968	162	712	29,568	1,865
1969	131	869	30,045[13]	2,033
1970	120	1,172	30,100	3,610
1971	145	711	20,290	2,098
1972	159	559	32,405	2,813
1973	132	432	28,568	3,742
1974	324	556	29,151	4,400
1975	319	538	31,952	4,512
1976	275	358	30,315	5,482
1977	328	537	33,740	5,761
1978	360	362	30,881	6,320
1979	337	386	27,791	6,645
1980	243	351	27,271	6,930
1981	248	413	29,801	8,297
1982	135	342	24,343	8,218
1983	140	291	25,278	13,275
1984	209	274	19,911	19,957
1985	119	451	16,136	26,514
1986	2,356	379	10,479	26,405
1987	3,388	186	8,128	28,523
1988	3,787	446	10,713	44,102
1989	3,479	405	15,849	50,151
1990	3,844	123	17,248	39,096
1991	4,392	—	16,829	29,300
1992	58	—	16,516	21,700
1993	—	—	17,800	24,096

D6 Output of Main Non-ferrous Metal Ores

TUNGSTEN (WO3 content) (in metric tons)

	NORTH AMERICA			SOUTH AMERICA			
	Canada[11]	Mexico	USA	Argentina	Bolivia[26]	Brazil	Peru[27]
1900	—	...	20	—	...	—	...
1901	—	...	77	—	...	—	...
1902	—	...	80	—	...	—	...
1903	—	...	126	—	...	—	...
1904	—	...	319	—	...	—	...
1905	—	...	347	—	...	—	...
1906	—	...	401	—	...	—	...
1907	—	...	708	—	...	—	...
1908	—	...	289	—	...	—	...
1909	—	...	699	—	...	—	...
1910	—	...	786	—	...	—	...
1911	—	...	492	—	...	—	...
1912	13	...	574	—	...	—	...
1913	—	...	664	—	282	—	...
1914	—	...	427	—	276	—	...
1915	—	...	1,007	—	793	—	...
1916	—	...	2,556	—	3,035	—	...
1917	- -	...	2,653	—	3,888	—	...
1918	12	...	2,185	—	3,417	—	...
1919	—	...	142	—	1,995	—	...
1920	—	...	93	—	708	—	...
1921	—	...	...	—	161	—	...
1922	—	...	...	—	7	—	...
1923	—	...	103	—	—	—	...
1924	—	...	244	—	- -	—	...
1925		...	513	—	73[26]	—	4
					50		
1926	—	...	597	—	65	—	—
1927	—	...	503	5	52	—	—
1928	—	—	522	15	17	—	—
1929	—	6	358	38	977	—	1
1930	—	17	303	59	532	—	—
1931	—	—	606	12	246	—	—
1932	—	—	171	4	411	—	—
1933	—	—	386	—	143	—	
1934	—	74	885	238	530	—	11
1935	—	50	1,034	351	817	—	54
1936	—	52	1,128	426	1,044	—	55
1937	—	31	1,511	453	1,081	5	18
1938	—	70	1,315	685	1,518	2	102
1939	4	109	1,851	518	2,002	6	160
1940	5	103	2,296	812	2,510	8	183
1941	38	91	2,835	660	2,613	24	202
1942	236	92	4,029	913	3,363		222
1943	684	245	5,156	926	4,141	875	433
1944	402	160	4,439	1,245	4,761	1,492	381

D6   Output of Main Non-ferrous Metal Ores

TUNGSTEN (WO3 content) (in metric tons)

	NORTH AMERICA			SOUTH AMERICA			
	Canada[11]	Mexico	USA	Argentina	Bolivia[26]	Brazil[27]	Peru[28]
1945	- -	64	2,389	628	2,311	1,529	314
1946	—	45	2,242	44	1,273	1,107	305
1947	225	46	1,335	54	1,581	920	347
1948	474	80	1,741	101	1,491	792	212
1949	114	39	1,194	103	1,526	352	272
1950	129	40	2,081	14	1,476	434	309
1951	1	195	2,709	79	1,631	952	281
1952	677	267	3,286	331	2,224	788	350
1953	1,109	409	4,140	417	2,295	940	545
1954	985	327	5,910	599	2,667	791	462
1955	881	341	7,085	595	3,231	583	486
1956	1,030	342	6,363	663	2,860	783	676
1957	872	160	2,383	739	2,618	614	661
1958	313	4	1,636	601	1,337	1,276	540
1959	—	75	1,576	473	1,454	1,044	295
1960	—	110	3,162	487	1,290	847	293
1961	—	105	3,560	486	1,694	617	233
1962	2	47	3,639	351	1,523	620	237[28]
1963	555	20	2,442	100	1,368	278	175
1964	485	5	3,991	37	1,244	212	587
1965	1,734	110	3,432	87	1,112[26] 1,038	252	430
1966	1,934	86	3,250	87	1,344	349	514
1967	122	188	2,980	135	1,740	378	495
1968	1,626	266	3,568	233	1,770	460	677
1969	1,843	289	3,177	184	1,848	526	869
1970	1,690	288	4,224	181	1,990	597	1,014
1971	2,097	408	. . .	173	2,238	866	958
1972	2,018	362	. . .	199	2,537	905	1,203
1973	2,105	348	3,202	105	2,376	1,001	1,077
1974	1,280	309	3,554	94	1,776	985[27] 1,641	703
1975	1,280	277	2,490	58	2,311	1,644	625
1976	1,172	235	2,662	62	3,132	1,685	838
1977	1,719	191	2,732	70	3,063	2,026	526
1978	1,811	234	3,130	97	3,073	1,937	582
1979	2,289	252	3,014	59	3,114[13] 2,384	1,934	564
1980	2,580	266	2,738	35	2,661	1,897	331
1981	3,178	199	3,545	11	2,778	2,550	334
1982	2,052	99	1,575	17	2,534	2,602	682
1983	2,938	90	980	41	2,490	1,842	762
1984	328	274	1,203	38	1,893	1,892	699
1985	3,715	282	996	17	1,643	2,050	645
1986	3,005	294	780	20	1,160	1,502	440
1987	1,273	213	34	15	804	634	53
1988	—	206	230	14	1,126	585	825
1989	—	170	400	20	1,375	538	1,228
1990	—	183	450	30	1,278	422	1,410
1991	—	194	100	15	1,343	500	1,237
1992	—	162	100	10	1,073	250	543
1993	—	160	. . .	—	330	245	388

D6 Output of Main Non-ferrous Metal Ores

VANADIUM (V content) (in metric tons)

	NORTH AMERICA				SOUTH AMERICA		
	USA		USA		Peru[29]		Peru
1905	...	1950	2,085	1905	—	1950	432
1906	...	1951	2,758	1906	—	1951	655
1907	...	1952	3,255	1907	25	1952	437
1908	...	1953	4,212	1908	252	1953	331
1909	...	1954	4,472	1909	392	1954	190
1910	...	1955	4,521	1910	802	1955	71
1911	249	1956	5,113	1911	504	1956-1988	—
1912	272	1957	6,617	1912	683		
1913	392	1958	6,592	1913	...		
1914	410	1959	6,706	1914	14		
1915	569	1960	7,300	1915	803		
1916	417	1961	5,769	1916	773		
1917	439	1962	6,937	1917	819		
1918	250	1963	5,486	1918	375		
1919	258	1964	4,703	1919	502		
1920	478	1965	5,117	1920	1,111		
1921	183	1966	5,157	1921	199		
1922	24	1967	4,616	1922	...		
1923	58	1968	6,446	1923	354		
1924	...	1969	5,205[13]	1924	614		
			5,059				
1925	196	1970	4,825	1925	246		
1926	300	1971	4,765	1926	857		
1927	...	1972	4,433	1927	717		
1928	...	1973	3,971	1928	73		
1929	...	1974	4,418	1929	902[29]		
					510		
1930	...	1975	4,303	1930	268		
1931	...	1976	6,691	1931	—		
1932	245	1977	5,900	1932	—		
1933	2	1978	3,875	1933	—		
1934	6	1979	5,008	1934	74		
1935	23	1980	4,360	1935	67		
1936	64	1981	4,650	1936	161		
1937	493	1982	3,718	1937	583		
1938	732	1983	1,969	1938	826		
1939	900	1984	1,467	1939	569		
1940	981	1985	...	1940	1,150		
1941	1,140	1986	...	1941	991		
1942	2,014	1987	...	1942	1,015		
1943	2,534	1988	...	1943	881		
1944	1,600			1944	518		
1945	1,344			1945	688		
1946	577			1946	322		
1947	961			1947	435		
1948	811			1948	511		
1949	1,434			1949	456		

D6 Output of Main Non-ferrous Metal Ores

ZINC (Zn content) (in thousands of metric tons)

	NORTH AMERICA				SOUTH AMERICA
	Canada	Mexico	Newfoundland	USA[17]	Peru
1893	...	0.4	—	...	—
1894	...	0.3	—	...	—
1895	...	0.5	—	...	—
1896	...	0.5	—	...	—
1897	...	0.6	—	...	—
1898	0.4	1.2	—	...	—
1899	0.4	0.7	—	...	—
1900	0.1	1.1	—	...	—
1901	—	0.9	—	...	—
1902	0.1	0.7	—	...	—
1903	0.4	1	—	...	—
1904	0.2	0.8	—	...	—
1905	8.1	2.0	—	...	—
1906	0.9	23	—	...	—
1907	1.8	23	—	230	—
1908	—	16	—	212	—
1909	16	3.0	—	274	—
1910	4.5	1.8	—	294	—
1911	2.7	1.6	—	301	—
1912	5.4	1.3	—	350	—
1913	7.2	1	—	375	—
1914	9.9	0.8	—	377	—
1915	14	5.8	—	533	—
1916	11	37	—	638	—
1917	13	45	—	647	—
1918	16	21	—	577	—
1919	15	12	—	498	—
1920	18	16	—	533	—
1921	24	1.3	—	233	—
1922	26	6.1	—	428	—
1923	27	18	—	554	—
1924	45	25	—	579	0.1
1925	50	46	—	645	1.9
1926	68	105	—	703	15
1927	75	138	—	652	11
1928	84	162	—	631	5.5
1929	89	174	23	657	12
1930	121	124	30	540	11
1931	108	120	44	372	—
1932	78	57	66	259	0.2
1933	90	89	75	349	0.2
1934	135	125	88	398	5.6
1935	145	136	72	470	4.7
1936	151	150	64	522	11
1937	168	155	64	568	29
1938	173	172	67	469	25
1939	179	134	60	530	36

D6 Output of Main Non-ferrous Metal Ores

ZINC (Zn content) (in thousands of metric tons)

	NORTH AMERICA				SOUTH AMERICA
	Canada[11]	Mexico	Newfoundland	USA[17]	Peru
1940	192	115	65	603	18
1941	232	155	63	680	23
1942	263	189	51	697	24
1943	277	197	60	675	33
1944	250	219	64	652	49
1945	235	210	51	557	61
1946	214	139	49	521	53
1947	189	196	40	578	58
1948	212[11]	179	39	571	59
1949	261	178	...	538	72
1950	284	223	...	565	88
1951	309	180	...	618	101
1952	337	227	...	604	128
1953	364	226	...	497	139
1954	341	224	...	430	159
1955	393	269	...	467	166
1956	383	249	...	492	178
1957	375	243	...	482	178
1958	386	224	...	374	160[15]
					123
1959	359	264	...	386	133
1960	390	262	...	395	157
1961	402	269	...	421	171
1962	455	251	...	459	184
1963	451	240	...	480	195
1964	662	236	...	521	237
1965	826	225	...	554	254
1966	950	219	...	519	258
1967	1,135	241	...	498	305
1968	1,155	240	...	480	291
1969	1,194	253	...	502	313
1970	1,239	266	...	485	361
1971	1,134	265	...	456	386
1972	1,129	272	...	434	448
1973	1,227	271	...	434	459
1974	1,127	263	...	454	440
1975	1,055	229	...	426	365
1976	982	259	...	439	456
1977	1,070	265	...	408	403
1978	1,067	245	...	303	457
1979	1,100	245	...	267	491
1980	884	238	...	317	419
1981	995	212	...	312	410
1982	966	232	...	300	460
1983	988	257	...	275	492
1984	1,063	290	...	253	466
1985	1,049	275	...	226	608
1986	988	271	...	203	598
1987	1,158	271	...	216	612
1988	1,347	262	...	244	485
1989	1,216	281	...	276	597
1990	1,203	299	...	515	584
1991	1,148	301	...	518	638
1992	1,325	341	...	524	602
1993	1,007	334	...	488	639

D6 Output of Main Non-ferrous Metal Ores

NOTES

1. SOURCES: The national publications listed on pp. xiii–xv; League of Nations and UN, *Statistical Yearbooks*; Imperial Institute, *Statistical Summary of the Mineral Industry of the British Empire and Foreign Countries*; and R.P. Rothwell, *The Mineral Industry: its Statistics, Technology and Trade in the United States and other Countries* (New York, 1892–).
2. So far as possible, and except as indicated in footnotes, the data in this table relate to the recoverable metallic content of ores (including concentrates).

FOOTNOTES

[1]   Excluding antimony recovered as a by-product by primary lead refineries. Data to 1921 relate to the weight of ore.
[2]   Statistics to 1966 (1st line) are of exports.
[3]   Statistics to 1925 (1st line) are of the gross weight of output.
[4]   Dried equivalent of crude ore.
[5]   Exports
[6]   Dried equivalent of crude ore from 1966.
[7]   Statistics are of production for 1919–28 and 1940–75, production or shipments (the terms were used interchangeably) for 1929–34, and of shipments for all other years. From 1935 (2nd line) they are of dried bauxite equivalent.
[8]   Dried equivalent of crude ore to 1953 (1st line).
[9]   Output in 1939 was 9 thousand tons. Earlier figures of exports are 1936 7, 1937 9, and 1938 13.
[10] Statistics are of shipments (for government only in 1959–61). Content up to 1927 has been estimated on the assumption that it was 54% of gross weight. Small amounts were produced from 1880 onwards, but the amounts involved are insignificant.
[11] Statistics are of shipments from mines. Newfoundland is included from 1949. There is no break in the case of nickel or tungsten.
[12] Statistics to 1906 (1st line) are of smelter production from domestic ores. Subsequently they are of estimated recoverable content of domestically-mined ores.
[13] There was a change in the method of calculating output.
[14] Years beginning 1 July to 1900.
[15] Production at refinery stage to 1904 (1st line), content of mined ores subsequently. Total gold production for the period 1792 to 1834 was 21 tons.
[16] Including Newfoundland from 1949, its output in 1948 being 0.3 tons.
[17] Estimated recoverable content of domestically-mined ores.
[18] Primary production only to 1964 (1st line).
[19] Statistics from 1914 to 1938 (1st line) are of exports.
[20] Shipments from mines of ores of 40% or more Mn content to 1910, of 35% or more Mn content from then to 1953 (1st line), and of 10% or more Mn content subsequently. Gross weight to 1928 (1st line).
[21] Statistics to 1936 are of exports. Gross weight to 1928 (1st line).
[22] Including Newfoundland from 1949.
[23] Statistics to 1977 (1st line) are of exports.
[24] This break occurs on a change of source.
[25] Tin content of exports and of tin-lead alloys.
[26] Gross weight of exports to 1925 (1st line), and content of exports from then to 1965 (1st line).
[27] Concentrated tungsten from 1974 (2nd line)
[28] Exports to 1962.
[29] Gross weight to 1929 (1st line).

D7 OUTPUT OF MAIN NON-METALLIC MINERALS (in thousands of metric tons)

1880–1924

	ASBESTOS		PHOSPHATE ROCK	POTASH (K₂O content)	NATIVE SULPHUR (unrefined)	
	NORTH AMERICA		NORTH AMERICA	NORTH AMERICA	NORTH AMERICA	SOUTH AMERICA
	Canada[1]	USA	USA	USA	USA[2]	Chile
1880	...	...	214	...	1	...
1881	...	...	271	...	1	...
1882	...	...	337	...	1	...
1883	...	...	384	...	1	...
1884	...	...	439	...	- -	...
1885	...	...	684	...	1	...
1886	2.7	...	438	...	2	...
1887	4.5	...	489	...	3	...
1888	3.6	...	459	...	—	...
1889	5.4	...	555	...	- -	...
1890	9.1	...	518	...	—	...
1891	8.2	...	597	...	1	...
1892	5.4	...	693	...	2	...
1893	5.4	...	956	...	1	...
1894	7.3	...	1,013	...	- -	1
1895	8.2	...	1,056	...	2	1
1896	11.0	...	946	...	5	1
1897	27.0	...	1,056	...	2	1
1898	22.0	...	1,330	...	1	1
1899	24.0	...	1,540	...	4	1
1900	26.0	...	1,515	...	3	3
1901	36.0	...	1,508	...	7	3
1902	36.0	...	1,514	...	7	3
1903	38.0	...	1,607	...	7	...
1904	44.0	...	1,904	...	86	4
1905	62.0	...	1,978	...	224	4
1906	74.0	...	2,114	...	300	5
1907	82.0	...	2,301	...	192	3
1908	83.0	...	2,424	...	370	3
1909	79.0	...	2,376	...	278	5
1910	93.0	...	2,698	...	251	4
1911	115.0	...	3,102	...	208	5
1912	123.0	...	3,021	...	801	4
1913	146.0	...	3,161	...	499	7
1914	107.0	...	2,778	...	425	10
1915	124.0	...	1,865	1	529	10
1916	140.0	...	2,014	9	660	15
1917	140.0	...	2,625	30	1,152	19
1918	143.0	...	2,531	35	1,376	20
1919	144.0	...	2,308	42	1,210	19
1920	181.0	...	4,170	37	1,275	13
1921	84.0	...	2,098	4	1,909	10
1922	149.0	0.1	2,457	10	1,860	12
1923	210.0	0.2	3,055	17	2,069	11
1924	205.0	0.3	2,914	20	1,240	10

D7 Output of Main Non-metallic Minerals (in thousands of metric tons)

	ASBESTOS			PHOSPHATE ROCK	POTASH (K$_2$O content)		NATIVE SULPHUR (unrefined)			
	NORTH AMERICA			NORTH AMERICA	NORTH AMERICA		NORTH AMERICA		SOUTH AMERICA	
	Canada[1]	USA		USA	Canada	USA[3]	Mexico	USA[2]		Chile
1925	249	1.1		3,538	...	24	...	1,432		9
1926	253	1.2		3,262	...	23	...	1,920		10
1927	249	2.7		3,222	...	45	...	2,146		12
1928	248	2.0		3,557	...	54	...	2,014		16
1929	278	2.9		3,821	...	53	...	2,400		16
1930	220	3.8		3,989	...	52	...	2,600		13
1931	149	2.9		2,576	...	58	...	2,163		11
1932	112	3.2		1,734	...	51	...	904		9
1933	143	4.3		2,530	...	126	...	1,429		13
1934	142	4.6		2,880	...	103	...	1,444		21
1935	191	8.1		3,091	...	204	...	1,659		20
1936	273	10		3,406	...	202	...	2,049		26
1937	372	11		4,019	...	242	...	2,786		23
1938	263	9		3,799	...	259	...	2,432		28
1939	330	14		3,817	...	332	...	2,125		32
1940	315	18		4,067	...	357	...	2,776		35
1941	433	22		4,765	...	482	...	3,190		25
1942	399	14		4,719	...	618	...	3,516		24
1943	432	5		5,208	...	664	...	2,580		26
1944	380	6		5,463	...	742	...	3,270		26
1945	424	11		5,900	...	789	10	3,813		21
1946	506	13		6,971	...	842	6	3,922		9
1947	600	22		9,172	...	955	3	4,512		12
1948	650	34		8,808	...	1,037	3	4,947		13
1949	521	39		9,131	...	1,017	5	4,821		8
1950	794	38		11,292	...	1,158₂ 1,168	11	5,276	...	15
1951	883	47	...	10,948	...	1,288	10	5,363	...	30
1952	843	49	...	12,259	...	1,511	12	5,378	...	49
1953	827	49	...	12,704	...	1,734	12	5,238	...	33
1954	838	43	...	14,043	...	1,768	63	5,669	...	44
1955	965	40	...	12,462	...	1,875	492	5,893	...	57
1956	920	37	...	16,000	...	1,970	771	6,588	...	38
1957	949	40	...	14,200	...	2,056	1,040	5,668	...	19
1958	839	40	...	15,118	...	1,948	1,243	4,720	...	24
1959	953	41	...	16,124	...	2,162	1,314	4,714	...	21
1960	1,015	41	...	17,797	...	2,394	1,302	5,118	...	31
1961	1,065	48	...	18,857	...	2,479	1,191	5,565	...	39
1962	1,103	48	...	19,693	135	2,225	1,395	5,106	...	54
1963	1,157	60	...	20,174	569	2,598	1,553	4,960	...	42
1964	1,288	92	...	23,328	779	2,628	1,734	5,312	...	44

D7 Output of Main Non-metallic Minerals (in thousands of metric tons)

1965–1993

| | ASBESTOS | | | PHOSPHATE ROCK | POTASH (K$_2$O content) | | NATIVE SULPHUR (unrefined) | | | |
| | NORTH AMERICA | | SOUTH AMERICA | NORTH AMERICA | NORTH AMERICA | | NORTH AMERICA | | SOUTH AMERICA | |
	Canada	USA	Brazil[4]	USA	Canada	USA[2]	Mexico	USA	Brazil	Chile
1965	1,259	107	...	26,704	1,353	2,849	1,581	6,214	...	46
1966	1,351	114	...	35,420	1,806	3,012	1,701	7,114	...	53
1967	1,318	112	2	36,079	2,163	2,993	1,891	7,127	...	56
1968	1,448	109	5	37,422	2,647	2,469	1,685	7,580	...	62
1969	1,462	114	10	34,224	3,168	2,544	1,716	7,261	...	99
1970	1,508	114	18	35,143	3,103	2,476	1,381	7,196	...	109
1971	1,483	119	20	35,277	3,629	2,347	1,178	7,138	...	106
1972	1,530	119	33	37,041	3,494	2,412	944	7,407	...	78
1973	1,690	136	45	38,226	4,453	2,361	1,608	7,727	1	31
1974	1,644	99	62	41,446	5,776	2,315	2,322	8,028	9	32
1975	1,056	89	74	44,276	4,676	2,269	2,164	7,327	20	21
1976	1,536	105	93	44,662	5,215	2,177	2,150	6,365	30	
1977	1,517	92	93	47,256	5,764	2,229	1,856	5,915	44	32
1978	1,422	93	123	50,037	6,344	2,253	1,818	5,648	57	32
1979	1,493	93	138	51,611	7,074	2,225	2,025	6,357	92	77
1980	1,323	80	170	54,415	7,201	2,239	2,102	6,391	131	87
1981	1,133	76	138	53,624	6,549	2,156	2,077	6,348	102	115
1982	837	64	146	37,414	5,295	1,784	1,815	4,210	146	105
1983	829	70	159	42,573	6,294	1,429	1,602	3,202	193	99
1984	837	58	135	49,197	7,527	1,564	1,826	4,193	216	54
1985	750	58	165	50,835	6,661	1,296	2,020	5,011	229	79
1986	662	51	204	40,320	6,753	1,202	2,051	4,043	271	57
1987	665	51	213	40,954	7,668	1,661	2,304	3,202	313	37
1988	705	18	228	45,389	8,190	1,853	2,138	3,174	322	38
1989	701	17	206	49,817	7,014	1,972	1,528	3,888	302	16
1990	686	—	210	46,343	7,372	2,053	1,450	3,726	318	29
1991	687	20	210	48,096	7,406	1,750	1,100	2,869	334	17
1992	587	16	...	46,965	7,040	1,710	710	2,320	304	24
1993	509	—	...	35,500	6,834	1,510	102	1,900	329	1

NOTE

SOURCES: The national publications listed on pp. xiii–xv; League of Nations and U.N., *Statistical Yearbooks*.

FOOTNOTES

[1] Shipments from mines.
[2] Production of Frasch-process mines. Sulphur from coal, gases, pyrites, etc.
[3] Sales by producers to 1950 (1st line).
[4] Asbestos fibres only.

D8 OUTPUT OF PIG IRON (in thousands of metric tons)

	NORTH AMERICA		NORTH AMERICA				NORTH AMERICA			SOUTH AMERICA
	USA		Canada[1]	Mexico[2]	USA		Canada[1]	Mexico[2]	USA	Brazil
1810	54	1855	—	...	711	1900	90	...	14,011	...
1811	...	1856	—	...	801	1901	249	...	16,133	...
1812	...	1857	—	...	724	1902	325	...	18,107	...
1813	...	1858	—	...	640	1903	270	...	18,298	...
1814	...	1859	—	...	763	1904	275	...	16,762	...
1815	...	1860	—	...	835	1905	477	...	23,361	...
1816	...	1861	—	...	664	1906	543	25	25,713	...
1817	...	1862	—	...	715	1907	591	16	26,195	...
1818	...	1863	—	...	860	1908	572	17	16,192	...
1819	...	1864	—	...	1,031	1909	687	59	26,209	...
1820	20	1865	—	...	845	1910	726	45	27,742	...
1821	...	1866	—	...	1,225	1911	832	...	24,029	...
1822	...	1867	—	...	1,326	1912	920	...	30,204	...
1823	...	1868	—	...	1,454	1913	1,024	...	31,463	...
1824	...	1869	—	...	1,739	1914	710	...	23,707	...
1825	...	1870	—	...	1,692	1915	829	...	30,396	...
1826	...	1871	—	...	1,735	1916	1,061	...	40,068	...
1827	...	1872	—	...	2,590	1917	1,062₁ / 1,103	...	39,241	...
1828	132	1873	—	...	2,602	1918	1,124	...	39,681	...
1829	144	1874	—	...	2,439	1919	877	...	31,513	...
1830	168	1875	—	...	2,057	1920	1,015	...	37,519	...
1831	194	1876	—	...	1,899	1921	627	42	16,956	...
1832	203	1877	—	...	2,100	1922	411	24	27,657	...
1833	...	1878	—	...	2,338	1923	937	44	41,009	25
1834	...	1879	—	...	2,786	1924	638	19	31,910	25
1835	...	1880	—	...	3,896	1925	606	49	37,289	30
1836	...	1881	—	...	4,211	1926	827	62	40,045	21
1837	...	1882	—	...	4,697	1927	778	41	37,152	15
1838	...	1883	—	...	4,669	1928	1,100	49	38,769	26
1839	...	1884	—	...	4,164	1929	1,188	60	43,298	36
1840	291	1885	—	...	4,110	1930	825	58	32,261	35
1841	...	1886	—	...	5,774	1931	474	53	18,715	28
1842	219	1887	23	...	6,520	1932	163	20	8,921	29
1843	...	1888	20	...	6,594	1933	262	54	13,590	47
1844	...	1889	24	...	7,726	1934	444	65	16,398	59
1845	...	1890	20	...	9,350	1935	667	63	21,715	64
1846	777	1891	22	...	8,412	1936	767	86	31,571	78
1847	813	1892	39	...	9,304	1937	997	58	37,758	98
1848	813	1893	51	...	7,238	1938	774	98	19,474	122
1849	660	1894	45	...	6,764	1939	845	99	32,321	160
1850	572	1895	39	...	9,598					
1851	...	1896	61	...	8,762					
1852	508	1897	53	...	9,808					
1853	...	1898	70	...	11,963					
1854	668	1899	93	...	13,839					

D8   Output of Pig Iron (in thousands of metric tons)

	NORTH AMERICA			SOUTH AMERICA					
	Canada[1]	Mexico[2]	USA	Argentina[3]	Brazil[4]	Chile[3]	Colombia	Peru[3]	Venezuela
1940	1,323	92	43,027	...	186	7	—	...	—
1941	1,572	95	51,456	- -	209	17	—		—
1942	1,981	122	55,317	—	214	13	—	...	—
1943	1,774	160	56,969	1	248	18	—	...	—
1944	1,836	159	57,060	3	292	13	—	...	—
1945	1,769	210	49,855	3	260	14	—	...	—
1946	1,402	240	42,024	12	371	14	—	...	—
1947	1,987	236	54,559	16	481	11	—	...	—
1948	2,140	176	56,166	17	552	14	—	...	—
1949	2,146	206	49,820	19	512	19	—	...	—
1950	2,266	227	60,211	18	729	110	—	...	—
1951	2,557	254	65,746	19	776	240	—	...	—
1952	2,643	305	57,507	32	812[4]	270	—	...	—
1953	2,872	242	70,035	36	894	286	—	...	—
1954	2,111	237	54,206	40	1,109	305	88	...	—
1955	3,089	312	71,906	35	1,087	256	99	...	—
1956	3,455	409	70,461	29	1,188	368	128	...	—
1957	3,559	414	73,409	34	1,289	382	142	...	—
1958	2,878	478	53,402	29	1,407	304	149	18	—
1959	3,917	556	56,367	32	1,588	290	145	40	—
1960	4,025	683	62,250	181	1,783	266	280	39	—
1961	4,594	867	60,524	399	1,976	285	327	51	5
1962	4,912	912	61,358	396	2,009	383	294	39	123
1963	5,519	832[2]	66,873	424	2,415	418	204	29	302
		858							
1964	6,090	959	78,772	589	2,488	437	198	27	323
1965	6,582	985	82,480	663	2,590	309	199	20	334
1966	6,696	1,464	85,279	520	2,950	433	167	12	351
1967	6,450	1,699	81,168	601	3,016	498	203	31	422
1968	7,747	2,040	82,883	574	3,173	442	198	111	539
1969	6,954	2,222	88,536	589	3,792	485	201	167	520
1970	8,424	2,353	85,141	815	4,296	481	229	77	510
1971	8,010	2,428	75,722	861	4,812	500	243	136	515
1972	8,722	2,778	82,861	849	5,511	487	288	163	536
1973	9,737	2,885	94,102	804	5,781	458	271	253	534
1974	9,670	3,307	89,423	1,066	7,704	516	269	303	562
1975	9,309	3,082	74,253	1,088	7,393	439	294	308	538
1976	10,026	3,548	80,541	1,321	8,477	445	287	231	425
1977	9,854	4,206	75,371	1,143	9,746	475	224	245	508
1978	10,578	5,058	81,053	1,470	10,447	587	298	246	429
1979	11,081	5,026	80,629	1,183	12,073	663	241	258	534
1980	11,182	5,330	63,748	1,080	13,116	708	280	263	559
1981	10,025	5,555	68,121	952	11,151	618	234	187	474
1982	8,218	5,223	40,033	1,057	11,175	459	208	161	255
1983	8,806	5,161	44,898[5]	962	13,286	552	243	140	226
1984	9,864	5,588	48,232	894	17,628	607	253	66	383
1985	9,887	5,331	46,789	1,351	19,420	587	235	207	528
1986	9,486	5,312	41,022	1,668	20,881	603	318	273	575
1987	9,968	5,377	44,669	1,798	21,867	628	327	252	551
1988	9,739	5,564	50,676	1,640	24,172	794	352	253	588
1989	10,139	5,394	50,687	2,062	24,363	679	297	199	489
1990	7,346	6,170	49,668	1,883	21,141	675	323	93	314
1991	8,268	5,501	44,123	1,366	22,695	703	305	207	...
1992	8,621	5,798	47,377	971	23,152	750	308	147	...
1993	8,633	6,159	48,155	980	23,900	702	238	147	...

D8   Output of Pig Iron

NOTES

1. SOURCES: The national publications listed on pp. xiii–xv UN, *Statistical Yearbook*; and British Iron and Steel Federation, *Statistics of the Iron and Steel Industries*.
2. Output of ferro-alloys is normally included in these statistics.

FOOTNOTES

[1]   Excluding ferro-alloys to 1917 (2nd line).
[2]   Excluding ferro-alloys to 1963 (2nd line).
[3]   Excluding ferro-alloys.
[4]   Excluding ferro-alloys to 1953.
[5]   Subsequently including silico-manganese.

D9   NORTH AMERICA: OUTPUT OF CRUDE STEEL (in thousands of metric tons)

	Canada	Mexico[3]	USA[1]		Canada	Mexico	USA[1]		Canada	Cuba[2]	Mexico[3]	USA[1]
1867	...	...	20	**1910**	746	68	26,514	**1950**	3,070	...	390	87,848
1868	...	...	27	**1911**	800	...	24,056	**1951**	3,237	...	467	95,435
1869	...	...	32	**1912**	869	...	31,753	**1952**	3,359	...	537	84,520
				1913	1,061	...	31,803	**1953**	3,734	...	462	101,250
1870	...	...	70	**1914**	752	...	23,890	**1954**	2,898	...	454	80,115
1871	...	...	74									
1872	...	...	145	**1915**	926	...	32,667	**1955**	4,114	...	510	106,173
1873	...	...	202	**1916**	1,296	...	43,460	**1956**	4,809	...	591	104,522
1874	...	...	219	**1917**	1,584	...	45,784	**1957**	4,598	...	687	102,253
				1918	1,700	...	45,176	**1958**	3,955	...	988[3]	77,342
1875	...	...	396	**1919**	935	...	35,228	**1959**	5,354	...	1,213	84,773
1876	...	...	542									
1877	...	...	579	**1920**	1,118	32	42,809	**1960**	5,270	...	1,500	90,067
1878	...	...	744	**1921**	678	43	20,101	**1961**	5,886	...	1,725	88,917
1879	...	...	950	**1922**	494	53	36,173	**1962**	6,507	...	1,851	89,202
				1923	899	60	45,665	**1963**	7,436	63	1,974	99,120
1880	...	...	1,267	**1924**	661	38	38,540	**1964**	8,282	52	2,284	115,281
1881	...	...	1,614									
1882	...	...	1,765	**1925**	765	76	46,122	**1965**	9,132	36	2,394	119,260
1883	...	...	1,700	**1926**	789	79	49,069	**1966**	9,093	67	2,780	121,655
1884	...	...	1,576	**1927**	922	66	45,656	**1967**	8,797	120	3,059	115,406
				1928	1,255	81	52,371	**1968**	10,161	120	3,270	119,262
1885	...	...	1,739	**1929**	1,400	102	57,339	**1969**	9,350	119	3,470	128,152
1886	...	...	2,604									
1887	...	...	3,393	**1930**	1,026	103	41,352	**1970**	11,198	140	3,846	119,309
1888	...	...	2,946	**1931**	683	76	26,363	**1971**	11,040	111	3,784	109,265
1889	...	...	3,440	**1932**	345	58	13,901	**1972**	11,859	187	4,396	120,875
				1933	417	76	23,605	**1973**	13,386	221	4,652	136,804
1890	...	...	4,346	**1934**	770	103	26,474	**1974**	13,623	250	5,046	132,196
1891	...	...	3,967									
1892	...	...	5,007	**1935**	957	111	34,640	**1975**	13,025	298	5,196	105,897
1893	...	...	4,085	**1936**	1,134	113	48,534	**1976**	13,290	250	5,243	116,121
1894	26	...	4,483	**1937**	1,425	106	51,380	**1977**	13,581	330	5,529	113,701
				1938	1,174	142	28,805	**1978**	14,898	324	6,712	124,314
1895	17	...	6,213	**1939**	1,407	142	47,898	**1979**	16,078	313	7,023	123,688
1896	16	...	5,366									
1897	19	...	7,272	**1940**	2,045	147	60,765	**1980**	15,901	292	7,003	101,456
1898	22	...	9,076	**1941**	2,460	142	75,150	**1981**	14,811	317	7,448	109,614
1899	22	...	10,811	**1942**	2,821	174	78,047	**1982**	11,871	290	6,926	67,656
				1943	2,725	167	80,592	**1983**	12,832	352	6,747	76,762
1900	24	...	10,352	**1944**	2,736	175	81,322	**1984**	14,699	325	7,293	83,940
1901	27	...	13,690									
1902	185	...	15,187	**1945**	2,611	230	72,304	**1985**	13,459	401	7,174	80,067
1903	184	...	14,768	**1946**	2,111	258	60,421	**1986**	14,081	412	6,960	74,032
1904	151	...	14,082	**1947**	2,672	290	77,015	**1987**	14,737	402	7,210	80,876
				1948	2,903	292	80,413	**1988**	15,193	321	7,311	90,631
1905	410	...	20,345	**1949**	2,892	373	70,740	**1989**	15,458	314	7,329	87,722
1906	580	33	23,774									
1907	641	32	23,737					**1990**	12,281	270	8,221	89,726
1908	534	29	14,248					**1991**	12,987	270	7,462	79,738
1909	685	60	24,339					**1992**	13,924	200	7,848	84,322
								1993	14,387	100	8,188	88,793

D9 SOUTH AMERICA: OUTPUT OF CRUDE STEEL (in thousands of metric tons)

	Argentina[6]	Brazil[4]	Chile[5]	Colombia[5]	Peru	Uruguay	Venezuela
1940	24	141	...	—	—	...	
1941	45	155	...	—	—	...	...
1942	53	160	...	—	—	...	...
1943	73	186	...	—	—	...	...
1944	150	221	...	—	—	...	...
1945	...	206	...	—	—	...	...
1946	133	343	21	—	—	...	...
1947	125	387	31	—	—	...	...
1948	122	483	30	—	—	...	...
1949	125	615	32	—	—	...	...
1950	130	789	56	—	—	...	...
1951	132	843	178	—	—	...	...
1952	126	893	243	—	—	...	...
1953	174	1,016	313	—	—	...	...
1954	186	1,148	321	—	—	...	...
1955	218	1,162	290	77	—	...	...
1956	202	1,375	381	90	—	...	...
1957	221	1,299	388	114	7	...	...
1958	244	1,362	348	121	20	...	...
1959	214	1,608	415	109	51	...	50
1960	277	2,260	422	157	60	10	47
1961	442	2,443	363	181	76	9	75
1962	644	2,396	495	194	71	9	225
1963	913	2,737	489	200	76	7	364
1964	1,267	2,938	544	200	82	14	441
1965	1,371	2,983	441	204	94	13	625
1966	1,286	3,782	540	174	80	10	537
1967	1,348	3,734	596	207	80	14	690
1968	1,579	4,453	526	199	106	8	860
1969	1,720	4,925	601	206	194	14	840
1970	1,859	5,390	547	239	94	16	927
1971	1,743	6,011	610	248	179	15	924
1972	1,929	6,518	581	275	181	13	964
1973	1,995	7,149	508	263	356	12	907
1974	2,196	7,507	596	244	450	14	895
1975	2,043	8,308	458	266	432	16	919
1976	2,244	9,169	448	252	349	14	937
1977	2,671	11,164	509	209	379	18	855
1978	2,651	12,107	574	265	374	7	860
1979	3,090	13,891	657	234[5] 400	436	16	1,473
1980	2,556	15,337	704	420	447	18	1,784
1981	2,389	13,226	644	420	364	14	1,818
1982	2,752	12,995	492	422	273	28	2,215
1983	2,828	14,671	618	482	299	46	2,320
1984	2,508	18,386	692	507	337	41	2,770
1985	2,775	20,456	689	525	414	39	3,061
1986	3,116	21,233	706	632	486	31	3,402
1987	3,463	22,227	726	691	503	30	3,721
1988	3,527	24,657	899	777	496	29	3,650
1989	3,909	25,005	800	711	364	37	3,404
1990	3,636	20,567	772	733	284	34	3,140
1991	2,972	22,617	805	700	404	44	2,933
1992	2,902	23,898	1,013	657	343	53	2,446
1993	2,950	25,155	1,063	715	417	53	2,568

D9 Output of Crude Steel

NOTES

1. SOURCES: As for table D8.
2. Except as indicated in footnotes, the statistics in this table relate to ingots and castings produced by the Bessemer, Siemens-Martin, and later-invented processes.

FOOTNOTES

[1] Excluding steel for castings made in foundries by companies not producing ingots.
[2] Crude steel for casting only.
[3] Ingots only to 1958.
[4] Excluding alloy steels. Earlier figures are available as follows:

1925	8	1930	21	1935	64
1926	10	1931	23	1936	74
1927	8	1932	34	1937	76
1928	21	1933	54	1938	98
1929	27	1934	62	1939	114

[5] Ingots only (to 1979 (1st line) in the case of Colombia).
[6] Production began in 1939, when output was 18 thousand tons.

D10 OUTPUT OF ALUMINIUM (in thousands of metric tons)

	NORTH AMERICA				NORTH AMERICA				SOUTH AMERICA	
	Canada	USA			Canada	Mexico	USA		Brazil[1]	Venezuela
		primary	secondary				primary	secondary		
1895	—	- -	...	1940		—	187	73	—	—
1896	—	1	...	1941		—	280	97	—	—
1897	—	1	...	1942		—	473	178	—	—
1898	—	1	...	1943		—	835	285	—	—
1899	—	2	...	1944		—	695	295	—	—
1900	—	3	...	1945		—	449	271	—	—
1901	0.1	3	...	1946		—	372	252	—	—
1902	0.9	3	...	1947		—	519	313	—	—
1903	0.8	3	...	1948		—	566	260	—	—
1904	1.0	4	...	1949		—	547	164	—	—
1905	1.2	5	...	1950	360	—	652	221	—	—
1906	2.1	6	...	1951	406	—	759	265	—	—
1907	2.7	6	...	1952	453	—	850	276	—	—
1908	0.4	7	...	1953	497	—	1,136	334	1.2	—
1909	2.8	5	...	1954	506	—	1,325	265	1.5	—
1910	4.4	14	...	1955	556	—	1,420	305	1.7	—
1911	4.4	16	...	1956	563	—	1,523	308	6.3	—
1912	5.5	17	...	1957	505	—	1,495	328	8.9	—
1913	6.4	22	5	1958	575	—	1,420	263	12	—
1914	6.6	26	5	1959	538	—	1,773	326	18	—
1915	8.3	41	7	1960	691	—	1,827	299	18	—
1916	9.6	53	17	1961	602	—	1,727	309	20	—
1917	10	59	15	1962	626	—	1,921	419	20	—
1918	11	56	14	1963	653	4.8	2,098	459	18	—
1919	9.8	58	17	1964	764	15	2,316	500	27	—
1920	10	63	15	1965	753	19	2,499	581	30	—
1921	2.9	24	8	1966	807	20	2,693	629	33	—
1922	5.8	34	15	1967	874	21	2,966	633	37	3
1923	11	58	19	1968	888	22	2,953	741	51	10
1924	12	68	24	1969	979	32	3,441	817	56	14
1925	14	64	40	1970	962	34	3,607	709	48	23
1926	18	67	40	1971	1,002	40	3,561	741	49	22
1927	38	74	42	1972	907	40	3,740	948	61	23
1928	38	95	44	1973	930	39	4,109	1,040	97	24
1929	29	103	44	1974	1,007	41	4,448	1,079	98	43
1930	35	104	35	1975	878	40	3,519	1,049	118	49
1931	31	80	38	1976	631	42	3,857	1,244	139	45
1932	18	48	22	1977	973	43	4,117	1,355	167	43
1933	16	39	30	1978	1,048	43	4,358	1,410	186	66
1934	16	34	42	1979	860	43	4,557	1,500	238	193
1935	21	54	47	1980	1,068	43	4,654	1,469	291	328
1936	27	102	47	1981	1,116	43	4,489	1,667	256	313
1937	43	133	57	1982	1,065	42	3,274	1,549	299	274
1938	65	130	35	1983	1,091	40	3,353	1,648	401	335
1939	75	149	49	1984	1,222	44	4,099	1,606	455	385
				1985	1,282	43	3,500	1,762	549	403
				1986	1,355	46	3,037	1,773	757	421
				1987	1,540	79	3,343	1,986	843	430
				1988	1,535	75	3,944	2,122	874	443
				1989	1,555	68	4,030	2,054	888	566
				1990	1,567	57	4,048	2,393	931	599
				1991	1,822	43	4,121	2,286	1,139	610
				1992	1,972	17	4,042	2,757	1,193	508
				1993	2,309	26	3,695	2,944	1,172	568

NOTES

SOURCES: The national publications listed on pp. xiii–xv, League of Nations and UN, *Statistical Yearbooks.*

FOOTNOTE

[1] Output of main establishments only

D11 NORTH AMERICA: OUTPUT OF REFINED COPPER, LEAD, TIN, AND ZINC (in thousands of metric tons)

	USA				Canada		USA	
	Lead[1,2]	Zinc[3]			Copper	Lead	Lead[2]	Zinc[3]
1821	1.7	...		1860	...	...	14	0.7
1822	1.7	...		1861	...	...	13	1.4
1823	1.9	...		1862	...	...	13	1.4
1824	1.8	...		1863	...	...	13	1.5
				1864	...	...	14	1.6
1825	2.0	...						
1826	2.2	...		1865	...	...	13	1.9
1827	4.1	...		1866	...	...	15	1.8
1828	6.8	...		1867	...	...	14	2.9
1829	7.8	...		1868	...	...	15	3.4
				1869	...	...	16	3.9
1830	7.3	...						
1831	6.8	...		1870	...	...	16	4.9
1832	9.1	...		1871	...	...	18	6.3
1833	10	...		1872	...	...	23	7.1
1834	11	...		1873	...	...	38	8.7
				1874	...	...	46	12
1835	12	...						
1836	14	...		1875	...	...	53	15
1837	12	...		1876	...	...	57	15
1838	14	...		1877	...	...	73	14
1839	16	...		1878	...	...	81	18
				1879	...	...	82	19
1840	15	...						
1841	19	...		1880	...	...	87	23
1842	22	...		1881	...	...	104	27
1843	23	...		1882	...	...	118	31
1844	24	...		1883	...	...	127	33
				1884	...	...	124	35
1845	27	...						
1846	25	...		1885	...	...	114[2]	37
1847	25	...		1886	...	...	120	39
1848	23	...		1887	...	...	142	46
1849	21	...		1888	...	...	142	51
				1889	...	...	162	53
1850	20	...						
1851	17	...		1890	...	...	143[2]	58
1852	14	...		1891	...	...	180	73
1853	15	...		1892	...	...	189	79
1854	15	...		1893	...	...	203	72
				1894	...	...	194	68
1855	14	...						
1856	15	...		1895	...	...	214	81
1857	14	...		1896	...	...	234	74
1858	14	- -		1897	0.1	...	256	91
1859	15	- -		1898	0.6	...	274	105
				1899	0.9	...	270	117
				1900	0.5	...	334	112
				1901	0.4	...	337	128
				1902	0.3	...	334	142
				1903	7.2	...	335	144[3]
				1904	8.0	3.4	357	169

D11 NORTH AMERICA: Output of Refined Copper, Lead, Tin, and Zinc (in thousands of metric tons)

	Canada			Mexico		
	Copper[4]	Lead[13]	Zinc	Copper[5]	Lead	Zinc
1905	11	7.2	—	...	...	—
1906	14	9.3	—	...	...	—
1907	14	12	—	...	...	—
1908	14	17	—	...	...	—
1909	13	19	—	...	...	—
1910	13	15	—	...	...	—
1911	9.7	11	0.9	...	...	—
1912	16	16	1.9	...	...	—
1913	15	17	2.5	44	55	—
1914	14	17	3.3	...	...	—
1915	...	20	4.5	...	...	—
1916	...	15	11	...	...	—
1917	...	15	14	...	...	—
1918	...	14	16	...	...	—
1919	...	16	15	...	79	—
1920	...	13	18	33	82	—
1921	15	28	24	7.5	60	—
1922	13	37	25	21	114	—
1923	14	46	27	38	150	—
1924	16	59	25	32	134	—
1925	24	97	35	33	143	1.3
1926	31	117	56	38	174	5.9
1927	33	134	66	40	214	6.4
1928	57	137	74	46	215	11
1929	73	138	78	58	230	15
1930	102	138	110	53	231	29
1931	111	126	108	43	208	36
1932	96	115	78	34	137	30
1933	118	115	83	40	117	27
1934	152	143	122	47	162	29
1935	176	149	136	41	174	32
1936	173	165	137	33	203	31
1937	210	181	144	46	201	34
1938	216	182	156	37	231	37
1939	229	173	159	39	214	36
1940	256	200	168	31	192	34
1941	255	207	194	41	151	32
1942	244	221	196	45	193	52
1943	233	203	187	43	212	54
1944	224	129	153	33	178	49
1945	198	148	165	53	201	49
1946	151[4] 152	150	168	52	138	42
1947	184	147	162	58	218	57
1948	201	145	178	49	187	48
1949	205	133	187	49	212	54

D11   NORTH AMERICA: Output of Refined Copper, Lead, Tin, and Zinc (in thousands of metric tons)

	USA							
	Copper		Lead		Tin		Zinc	
	Primary	Secondary	Primary	Secondary[7]	Primary	Secondary	Primary	Secondary[7]
1905	...	...	352	...	—	—	185	...
1906	489	...	367	...	—	—	204	...
1907	468	...	375	23	—	—	227	23
1908	516	...	360	17	—	—	191	21
1909	631	...	405	38	—	—	232	44
1910	645	59	427	50	—	—	244	63
1911	650	69	442	49	—	—	260	68
1912	711	97	436	61	—	—	307	85
1913	733	83	420	66	—	—	314	81
1914	696	80	492	55	—	11	320	77
1915	741	110	499	72	—	12	444	99
1916	1,025	159	518	87	2.1	17	606	117
1917	[1,099][6]	177	554	85	5.5	18	607	120
1918	1,086	160	581	88	9.3	22	470	124
1919	803	138	437	111	11	22	423	118
1920	692	153	480	113	16	21	420	128
1921	431	120	407	94	11	15	182	84
1922	569	184	483	145	8.3	18	321	146
1923	898	246	561	176	6.8	27	463	149
1924	1,025	241	626	186	0.4	28	469	142
1925	1,000	264	696	206	—	28	520	142
1926	1,053	306	725	252	0.3	30	561	152
1927	1,055	308	723	250	...	34	537	153
1928	1,128	332	709	280	0.1	33	547	165
1929	1,243	421	703	282	0.1	31	567	160
1930	978	310	583	232	0.3	24	452	116
1931	681	237	402	213	- -	18	265	93
1932	309	164	256	180	- -	13	188	64
1933	336	236	239	204	- -	20	279	109
1934	404	282	282	189	- -	23	330	86
1935	534	328	294	245	0.2	25	382	117
1936	746	347	362	238	0.2	25	446	146
1937	968	371	424	250	0.2	27	505	151
1938	719	242	348	204	...	...	405	108
1939	916	260	439	219	...	...	460	172
1940	1,192	303	484	236	1.4	30	613	201
1941	1,266	374	518	361	1.8	38	746	258
1942	1,283	387	514	293	16	34	809	300
1943	1,251	388	426	310	22	34	855	334
1944	1,108	414	422	301	31	30	789	313
1945	1,006	451	402	329	41	32	694	327
1946	797	369	307	356	44	25	661	273
1947	1,052	457	400	464	34	27	728	282
1948	1,005	459	369	454	37	27	715	295
1949	842	348	433	374	36	23	739	216

D11 NORTH AMERICA: Output of Refined Copper, Lead, Tin, and Zinc (in thousands of metric tons)

	Canada				Mexico		
	Copper		Lead[13]	Zinc	Copper[5]	Lead	Zinc
	Primary	Secondary					
1950	216	...	155	185	48	231	54
1951	223	...	147	188	59	214	60
1952	178	...	166	202	51	237	50
1953	215	...	150	228	52	214	53
1954	230	...	151	194	43[5] 32	209	55
1955	262	...	135	233	35	202	56
1956	298	...	134	232	32	191	56
1957	293	...	130	224	28	207	57
1958	299	...	121	229	28	197	58
1959	331	...	123	232	29	186	56
1960	378	...	144	237	28	185	53
1961	369	...	156	243	27	175	52
1962	347	...	138	254	31	189	57
1963	344	...	141	258	31	185	57
1964	370	...	137	306	35	171	59
1965	394[4]	...	169	325	46	165	59
1966	379	23	168	347	48	179	59
1967	421	33	177	367	48	161	71
1968	447	29	183	387	52	147	80
1969	380	28	170	423	57	144	80
1970	460	33	186	413	54	151	81
1971	449	29	168	373	53	151	78
1972	470	26	187	476	60	154	84
1973	469	29	187	533	57	142	71
1974	533	26	126	438	68	158	137
1975	501	28	171	427	63	138	154
1976	485	25	176	472	75	128	175
1977	476	32	187[13] 241	495	73	137	174
1978	418	28	246	495	75	150	173
1979	365	32	252	580	82	158	162
1980	475	30	235	592	86	131	144
1981	477	29	238	619	61	138	126
1982	338	24	242	512	61	129	127
1983	464	35	242	617	81	153	174
1984	504	32	252	683	61	154	166
1985	500	25	240	692	65	185	175
1986	493	24	258	571	59	173	174
1987	491	24	226	610	120	175	188
1988	529	38	268	703	126	175	108
1989	515	38	243	670	134	172	103
1990	516	47	184	592	126	169	108
1991	538	27	212	661	121	169	91
1992	539	37	255	672	121	194	115
1993	562	40	232	610	106	178	115

D11   NORTH AMERICA: Output of Refined Copper, Lead, Tin, and Zinc (in thousands of metric tons)

	USA							
	Copper		Lead		Tin		Zinc	
	Primary	Secondary	Primary	Secondary	Primary	Secondary	Primary	Secondary[7]
1950	1,125	440	461	438	33	32	765	296
1951	1,095	416	379	470	31	31	800	285
1952	1,068	376	429	428	23	29	820	282
1953	1,173	390	424	442	38	28	831	267
1954	1,099	369	442	430	27	27	728	247
1955	1,218	467	435	455	23	29	874	276
1956	1,309	425	492	460	18	30	892	255
1957	1,319	403	484	444	1.6	25	894[8]	240
1958	1,227	373	427	364	5.4	23	709	209
1959	996	427	309	409	11	24	724	251
1960	1,378	390	347	426	14	22	725	241
1961	1,406	373	408	411	8.7	23	768	216
1962	1,462	377	341	403	5.6	22	798[8]	238
1963	1,448	383	358	448	1.5	23	810	243
1964	1,503	430	408	491	4.0	24	865	271
1965	1,553	466	379	522	3.1	25	902	321
1966	1,552	485	400	520	3.9	26	930	327
1967	1,028	438	345	502	3.1	23	852	290
1968	1,304	472	424	500	3.6	23	926	322
1969	1,581	522	579	548	0.4	23	944	341
1970	1,601	457	605	542	4.5	20	796	308
1971	1,444	404	590	542	4.1	20	695	326
1972	1,699	415	617	560	4.4	21	574	352
1973	1,695	422	612	593	4.9	21	629	348
1974	1,501	451	611	634	6.1	19[11] / 2.0	504	307[7] / 71
1975	1,309	312	577	597	6.5	1.9	397	52
1976	1,396	340	592	659	5.7	1.5	453	62
1977	1,357	350	549	758	6.7	1.7	408	46
1978	1,449	420	566	769	5.9	1.6	407	35
1979	1,517	498	578	743	4.6	1.8	472	53
1980	1,215	515	550	675	3.0	1.7	340	29
1981	1,544	494	495	658	2.0	1.6	347	50
1982	1,227	467	517	581	3.5	1.1	228	74
1983	1,182	402	519	515	2.5	1.2	236	69
1984	1,174	306	389	591	4.0	1.1	253	78
1985	1,057	372	494	573	3.0	1.3	261	73
1986	1,074	406	370	581	3.2	1.1	253	63
1987	1,127	415	374	668	3.9	1.4	261	83
1988	1,406	446	392	698	1.5	0.6	241	88
1989	1,477	480	397	891	1.0	0.6	263	98
1990	1,577	441	404	922	...	0.6	263	96
1991	1,577	418	346	885	...	0.2	255	126
1992	1,711	433	305	916	...	0.2	272	128
1993	1,792	461	335	904	...	0.2	240	142

D11 SOUTH AMERICA: OUTPUT OF REFINED COPPER, LEAD, TIN, AND ZINC
(in thousands of metric tons)

| | Chile | | | Argentina | Chile | Peru | |
	Copper[9]			Lead	Copper[9]	Copper	Lead
1847	9.8		1895	...	23	—	...
1848	10		1896	...	24	—	...
1849	11		1897	...	21	—	...
			1898	...	26	—	...
1850	12		1899	...	26	—	...
1851	8.4						
1852	17		1900	...	28	—	...
1853	15		1901	...	30	—	...
1854	17		1902	...	27	—	...
			1903	...	30	—	...
1855	22		1904	...	31	—	...
1856	24						
1857	25		1905	...	29[9]	—	...
1858	25				23		
1859	23		1906	...	19	1.5	...
			1907	...	17	8.8	...
1860	34		1908	...	20	13	...
1861	34		1909	...	19	16	...
1862	37						
1863	32		1910	...	18	19	...
1864	43		1911	...	16	21	...
			1912	...	17	20	...
1865	41		1913	1.0	20	20	...
1866	33		1914	...	25	25	...
1867	43						
1868	42		1915	...	35	33	...
1869	52		1916	...	57	40	...
			1917	...	85	43	...
1870	34		1918	...	102	44	...
1871	39		1919	...	73	38	...
1872	49						
1873	42		1920	3.5	93	32	...
1874	48		1921	2.5	47	31	...
			1922	3.6	113	36	...
1875	48		1923	3.6	162	43	...
1876	52		1924	4.5	174	34	...
1877	44						
1878	49		1925	7.7	175	37	...
1879	46		1926	8.5	190	38	...
			1927	7.8	226	46	...
1880	40		1928	8.4	274	52	...
1881	40		1929	9.0	302	53	...
1882	45						
1883	40		1930	9.0	208	47	...
1884	45		1931	7.6	215	44	...
			1932	7.1	97	21	...
1885	40		1933	9.6	157	25	...
1886	38		1934	5.0	247	27	1.2
1887	30						
1888	34		1935	4.1	259	29	6.4
1889	25		1936	11	245	33	8.9
			1937	9.1	396	34	19
1890	27		1938	11	337	36	26
1891	21		1939	15	326	34	24
1892	21						
1893	23						
1894	23						

D11　SOUTH AMERICA: Output of Refined Copper, Lead, Tin, and Zinc (in thousands of metric tons)

	Argentina		Bolivia	Brazil			Chile	Peru		
	Lead[12]	Zinc	Tin	Lead[12]	Tin[10]	Zinc	Copper[9]	Copper[9]	Lead	Zinc
1940	13	—	—	—	—	—	347	34	31	0.2
1941	20	—	—	—	—	—	456	28	33	0.7
1942	24	0.4	—	—	—	—	477	29	38	0.9
1943	29	0.7	—	—	0.1	—	488	28	43	1.5
1944	22	1.0	—	—	0.2	—	490	26	39	1.5
1945	21	1.0	—	0.1	0.2	—	462	25	42	1.6
1946	22	1.8	—	0.4	0.2	—	359	19	38	0.9
1947	21	2.6	- -	0.4	0.2	—	408	18	33	1
1948	24	1.6	0.1	…	0.2	—	425	13	35	0.7
1949	18	2.7	—	1.1	0.2	—	351	21	37	0.6
1950	19	3.7	0.4	4.2	0.1	—	345	20	32	1.3
1951	24	8.6	- -	3.0	0.1	—	360	23	44	0.9
1952	20	12	0.3	1.3	0.1	—	383	20	50	5
1953	13	13	2	2.9	0.6	—	336[9] 216	24[9] 23	59	8.9
1954	26	11	0.2	2.7	1.9	—	191	25	58	15
1955	18	14	0.1	3.7	1.2	—	241	28	61	17
1956	24	14	0.5	3.5	1.6	—	240	18	60	9.5
1957	26	14	0.3	3.5	1.4	—	222	28	69	30
1958	33	15	0.7	5.8	0.6	—	186	28	64	29
1959	31	13	0.9	5.5	1.2	—	260	28	57	27
1960	26	17	1.0	10	1.3	—	225	30	74	32
1961	28	15	2.0	4.9	1.5	—	226	34	78	32
1962	24	18	2.1	14	2.4	—	263	34	68	32
1963	24	18	2.5	16	2.1	—	259	37	81	54
1964	23	21	3.7	13	1.2	—	278	38	90	60
1965	32	23	3.5	9.2	1.4	0.4	289	40	87	61
1966	22	22	1.1	14	1.8	0.5	357	37	89	63
1967	22	22	1.1	14	1.9	1.9	386	36	82	62
1968	25	22	0.1	19	1.7	5.0	399	38	86	66
1969	22	25	0.1	21	2.7	4.2	453	35	78	65
1970	38	29	0.3	20	3.3	13	461	36	73	71
1971	44	30	6.8	26	4.4	16	399	33	68	59
1972	40	40	6.5	25	4.6	16	461	39	86	70
1973	32	37	7.0	38	4.5	23	415	39	83	70
1974	37	35	6.1	42[12] 63	6.6	10	538	39	81	71
1975	36	37	7.6	63	6.8	31	535	54	71	66
1976	40[12] 50	31	9.8	69	6.7	43	632	132	74	67
1977	45	29	13	77	7.7	47	676	188	84	67
1978	30	24	16	80	9.3	56	749	185	80	63
1979	50	35	16	99	10	63	782	230	91	68
1980	42	28	18	90	8.8	78	811	231	87	64
1981	35	29	20	71	7.8	92	775	200	84	126
1982	31	31	17	53	9.3	96	729	224	82	160
1983	31	32	14	63	13	100	693	195	65	154
1984	28	30	16	64	19	107	753	219	71	148
1985	29	33	14	70	25	116	725	227	83	163
1986	31	31	10	72	25	131	784	226	67	156
1987	32	34	8.1	74	29	139	795	225	71	147
1988	35	35	11	85	42	140	853	175	57	123
1989	26	34	9.5	86	44	156	1,071	224	74	127
1990	27	33	12	75	35	150	991	182	69	121
1991	25	36	15	64	29	157	1,013	244	76	155
1992	30	37	14	67	21	160	1,242	251	83	126
1993	20	34	17	67	23	160	1,255	261	86	159

D11 Output of Refined Copper, Lead, Tin, and Zinc

NOTES

1. SOURCES: As for table D10.
2. Secondary production (i.e. remelted from scrap) is shown separately if it is significant, where possible, but is generally included with primary production in earlier years. Secondary production normally does not include production from 'new' scrap (i.e. the recycled waste of primary production).

FOOTNOTES

[1] Average annual production for 1801-10 was 1 thousand short tons, and for 1811-20 it was 1,500 short tons (= 0.9 and 1.4 thousand metric tons respectively).
[2] Including lead from imported ores from 1886 and from imported base bullion from 1891.
[3] Production from domestic ores only to 1903.
[4] Smelter production to 1946 (1st line). Secondary production is included with primary to 1965.
[5] Smelter production to 1954 (1st line).
[6] Includes some refined copper imports.
[7] Including production from 'new' scrap and zinc recovered in alloys to 1974 (1st line).
[8] Including zinc in concentrates used directly in alloying operations in 1958-62.
[9] Smelter production to 1953 (1st line) (from 1905 (2nd line) in the case of Chile), refined copper output subsequently. Earlier data for Chile are of the metal content of ore.
[10] Smelter production.
[11] This break probably arises from the exclusion of tin recovered in alloys.
[12] Primary soft lead only to 1977 (1st line) for Canada, 1976 (1st line) for Argentina, and 1974 (1st line) for Brazil.

D12 RAW COTTON CONSUMPTION (in thousands of metric tons)

	NORTH AMERICA			NORTH AMERICA			SOUTH AMERICA	
	Canada[1]	USA		Canada[1]	Mexico	USA	Brazil	Peru
1860	...	184	1900	27	...	803	...	...
1861	...	183	1901	25	43	785	...	...
1862	...	80	1902	___[1]	28	888	...	...
1863	...	62	1903	27	29	912	...	...
1864	...	48	1904	25	31	867	...	...
1865	...	75	1905	28	36	985	...	...
1866	...	134	1906	31	37	1,062	...	...
1867	...	156	1907	29	36	1,083	...	...
1868	...	184	1908	27	35	978	...	...
1869	...	187	1909	34	35	1,141	...	...
1870	...	174	1910	30	35	1,045	...	...
1871	...	224	1911	34	...	1,024	...	...
1872	...	250	1912	36	...	1,169	...	...
1873	...	243	1913	36	...	1,260	...	...
1874	...	264	1914	33	...	1,281	...	...
1875	...	239	1915	44	...	1,308	...	...
1876	...	273	1916	44	...	1,585	...	3.2
1877	...	286	1917	39	...	1,667	...	3.4
1878	...	318	1918	49	...	1,673	...	3.6
1879	...	317	1919	39	...	1,355	...	3.4
1880	...	327	1920	52	...	1,472	84	3.1
1881	5.3	406	1921	40	36	1,178	76	2.9
1882	8.8	403	1922	50	35	1,426	86	2.9
1883	13	444	1923	51	32	1,592	83	3.1
1884	9.4	395	1924	42	31	1,354	88	3.2
1885	11	367	1925	57	41	1,492	106	3.3
1886	14	456	1926	61	42	1,581	97	3.6
1887	15	446	1927	62	41	1,741	92	3.9
1888	15	480	1928	61	39	1,658	102	3.9
1889	18	503	1929	62	39	1,735	79	3.7
1890	17	548	1930	46	41	1,505	68	4.1
1891	18	567	1931	42	35	1,301	73	3.8
1892	21	620	1932	44	34	1,198	90	4.3
1893	19	526	1933	55	41	1,502	94	5.1
1894	16	501	1934	65	50	1,408	...	6.2
1895	26	650	1935	55	50	1,324	...	6.7
1896	18	544	1936	68	54	1,543	...	6.7
1897	19	619	1937	72	56	1,909	...	6.5
1898	29	756	1938	84	51	1,407	...	6.8
1899	25	799	1939	...	49	1,678	139	7.4
			1940	115	52	1,926	...	7.8
			1941	109	57	2,413	...	10
			1942	112	65	2,756	...	12
			1943	92	68	2,700	...	11
			1944	83	69	2,462	...	...
			1945	82	69	2,406	...	...
			1946	82	...	2,225	...	...
			1947	82	...	2,397	...	...

D12 Raw Cotton Consumption (in thousands of metric tons)

	NORTH AMERICA				SOUTH AMERICA						
	Canada[1]	Cuba	Mexico	USA	Argentina[3]	Brazil	Chile[3]	Colombia[3]	Peru	Uruguay[3]	Venezuela[3]
1948	80	...	75	2,288[2] 2,077	81	182	11	22	13	6.1	5.4
1949	83	...	68	1,735	81	179	15	25	14	4.1	4.8
1950	91	5.9	67	1,957	85	179	18	24	13	4.6	2.8
1951	104	6.7	73	2,313	100	182	14	24	13	5.6	3.3
1952	74	5.6	68	2,014	108	179	14	23	12	5.2	3.5
1953	77	4.3	72	2,074	81	174	20	27	12	4.8	4.6
1954	63	6.7	72	1,884	92	195	20	29	15	6.9	4.1
1955	73	6.1	84	1,936	107	217	20	33	16	8.7	5.2
1956	79	6.5	97	2,020	114	228	21	35	15	6.5	6.3
1957	77	8	102	1,894	118	223	20	37	15	7.8	8
1958	71	8.2	104	1,756	113	228	17	40	14	8.7	7.4
1959	72	6.9	104	1,906	119	249	13	42	15	7.2	8
1960	69	9.1	105	1,971	105	257	18	47	17	9.8	9.3
1961	73	12	108	1,802	108	271	23	51	17	7.6	9.1
1962	84	14	111	1,945	105	282	24	53	18	5.6	11
1963	81	16	111	1,833	76	282	25	56	18	5	12
1964	91	17	121	1,877	101	271	26	58	18	6.9	15
1965	93	18	130	2,002	112	266	28	63	20	7.6	17
1966	91	20	141	2,059	113	260	28	63	20	8.7	18
1967	92	18	145	2,057	107	271	28	65	18	6.3	18
1968	85	20	154	1,947	94	271	28	65	17	7.4	17
1969	85	20	149	1,787	103	288	28	67	17	5.9	21
1970	78	20	149	1,733	103	293	29	71	20	5.6	21
1971	76	20	146	1,749	107	299	28	75	26	6.7	22
1972	79	20	163	1,743	108	325	29	78	30	5.2	25
1973	74	20	174	1,691	101	369	24	84	31	4.8	27
1974	71	19	146	1,749	113	299	29	75	26	6.7	22
1975	51	23	178	1,276	112	412	29	65	30	6.1	28
1976	56	26	181	1,583	117	444	27	61	32	4.1	34
1977	48	28	165	1,453	117	455	23	79	41	4.8	30
1978	52	30	160	1,417	104	488	22	88	55	6	26
1979	56	33	165	1,383	109	531	24	70	55	6	24
1980	59	35	165	1,416	102	564	16	82	52	6	20
1981	48	37	159	1,232	76	570	12	59	50	5	16
1982	49	39	144	1,128	85	569	11	47	42	5	17
1983	55	42	124	1,274	96	560	11	47	41	5	21
1984	51	44	119	1,232	110	581	11	58	49	5	33
1985	52	44	131	1,276	118	654	11	67	63	5	39
1986	48	47	127	1,477	132	731	12	77	76	4	34
1987	45	46	133	1,706	133	735	15	86	82	2	30
1988	45	45	151	1,567	124	811	16	93	69	2	44
1989	41	46	169	1,694	133	822	15	89	68	2	46
1990	41	44	164	1,872	98	775	15	96	80	2	25
1991	40	44	167	1,742	120	775	14	105	78	2	35
1992	38	44	170	1,785	114	827	12	110	77	2	37

NOTES

1. SOURCES: The national publications listed on pp. xiii–xv for Canada, USA to 1948 (1st line), and all other countries to 1947 (except 1939). Other data are from the publications of the International Federation of Cotton and Allied Textile Industries (under various names).
2. Data from the last-mentioned source are for years ending 31 July.

FOOTNOTES

[1] Imports of raw cotton and waste for years ending 30 June to 1902. Subsequently, to 1937, imports of raw cotton.
[2] Note the change of year indicated in Note 2 above.
[3] Figures for the year ended 31 July 1939 are available as follows: Argentina 33, Chile 4.3, Colombia 12, Uruguay 0.4, Venezuela 2.4.

D13 COTTON SPINDLES (in thousands)

	NORTH AMERICA				
	Canada	Cuba	El Salvador	Mexico	USA
1900	774	...	...	491	20,318
1914	860	...	...	750	31,520
1920	1,200	...	...	720	35,834
1930	1,277	...	...	767	34,031
1939	1,159	...	14	884	25,911
1950	1,121	...	32	986	23,007
1960	817	...	73	1,350	19,916
1970	755	237	127	2,704	19,559

	SOUTH AMERICA							
	Argentina	Brazil	Chile	Colombia	Ecuador	Peru		Venezuela
1853	...	4	...	...	...	...	...	...
1866	...	14	...	...	...	...	...	...
1885	...	66	...	...	...	...	...	...
1900	...	288	...	...	...	...	...	...
1914	...	1,400	...	...	...	...	...	...
1920	...	1,600	...	...	...	...	...	...
1930	...	2,775	...	...	...	...	...	...
1939	329	2,765	33	105	42	118	...	42
1950	531	3,291	175	358	49	148	...	60
1960	1,038	3,840	219	485	88	210	135	132
1970	1,070	3,588	403	649	116	265	180	287

NOTES

1. SOURCES: The main source used has been the publications of the International Federation of Cotton and Allied Textile Industries (IFCATI) (under various names). Data for Brazil 1853–85, 1905, 1910, and 1915, are from Stanley J. Stein, *The Brazilian Cotton Manufacture* (Cambridge, Mass., 1957).
2. In principle, the statistics in this table relate to spinning spindles in place. Rayon spinning spindles are included.
3. IFCATI data refer to 1 March to 1912, 31 July from then to 1958, and 31 December subsequently.
4. Annual figures, where available, are given in earlier editions of this work, up to 1974.

D14 OUTPUT OF COTTON YARN (in thousands of metric tons)

	NORTH AMERICA			SOUTH AMERICA			
	Canada[1]	Mexico[2]	USA	Argentina	Brazil[5]	Chile[6]	Paraguay
1928	...	3.8	...	...	...	...	
1929	...	4.1	...	...	...	...	
1930	...	3.8	...	...	...	...	
1931	...	3.5	...	...	...	...	
1932	...	3.9	...	...	...	...	
1933	...	4.7	...	...	...	...	
1934	...	7.0	...	...	...	...	
1935	...	7.1	...	16	...	...	
1936	59	7.6	...	21	...	...	
1937	62	7.3	1,410	26	...	2.3	
1938	54	7.7	...	24	...	3.5	
1939	65	7.8	1,424	29	...	3.6	
1940	89	8.5	...	33	...	3.4	
1941	96	9.3	...	38	...	3.4	
1942	97	12	...	50	...	3.9	
1943	85	12	...	55	125	6.2[6]	
1944	76	11	...	63	149	2.1	
1945	74	8.0	...	64	159	2.0	
1946	74	7.6	...	65	168	1.5	
1947	76	4.9	1,715	66	...	2.8	
1948	82	5.9	...	70	196	3.3	
1949	81	5.2	...	70	210	4.1	
1950	93	6.5	...	77	...	4.4	
1951	90	4.9	...	91	76	1.6	
1952	71	5.2	...	82	74	2.9	
1953	67	4.5	...	76	71	3.9	
1954	62	4.9	1,695	85	87	11	
1955	67	5.7[2]	...	95	91	16	
1956	71	44	...	101	96	13	
1957	68	49	...	99	91	...	
1958	60	50	1,645	99	95	...	
1959	68	51	1,839	86	101	...	
1960	65	50	1,655	95	106	...	
1961	70	51	1,763	95	112	...	
1962	77	50[3]	1,805	77	114	21	11
1963	79	104	1,761	73	111	23	13
1964	87	117	1,871	89	110	25	11
1965	89	120	1,958	98	100	26	14
1966	77	136	2,006	94	109	26	9
1967	81	139	1,877	84	98	26	9
1968	79[1]	106	1,694	85	111	26	10
1969	85	145	1,594	89	118	26	13
1970	77	132	1,525	90	118[5]	27	12
1971	78	130	1,567	94	...	27	5
1972	86	131	1,517	89	275	29	13
1973	77	163	1,388	85	322	23	22
1974	78	179	1,261	89	335	...	24

D14   Output of Cotton Yarn (in thousands of metric tons)

| | NORTH AMERICA | | | SOUTH AMERICA | | | |
	Canada	Mexico	USA	Argentina	Brazil	Chile	Paraguay
1975	62	157	1,101	89	360	...	32
1976	63	153	1,221	98	380	...	34
1977	61	143	1,141	105	390	...	73
1978	66₈	146	1,096	86	460	...	91
1979	26	154	1,112	90	500	3.8	73
1980	24	...	1,114	75	510	4.8	75
1981	41	...	987	79	483	4.0	106
1982	45	...	932	80	493	4.6	91
1983	45	126	1,055	93	473	3.6	77
1984	45	92	956	105	674	7.5	105
1985	43	117	977	91	963	8.3	160
1986	40	107	1,127	114	793	9.4	100
1987	37	118	1,288	100	633	9.9	84
1988	36	137	1,225	100	680	4.3	188
1989	34	143	1,358	90	661	4.1	209
1990	34	142	1,342	89	645	3.6	219
1991	33	145	1,534	93	670	4.0	209
1992	...	...	1,678	...	...	3.1	144
1993	...	...	1,765	...	...	3.4	132

NOTES

1. SOURCES: The national publications listed on pp. xiii–xv, UN, *Statistical Yearbooks*, and *Cotton-World Statistics*.
2. Except as indicated in footnotes, tyre cord yarns are excluded and yarns made from waste and from mixed fibres of more than 50% cotton are included.

FOOTNOTES

[1] Excluding yarn made in carpet mills to 1968. Including tyre cord yarn.
[2] Production for sale only to 1955. The reason for the break between 1962 and 1963 is not given in the source. Mixed yarns are not included.
[3] Including tyre cord yarns.
[4] Mixed yarns are not included.
[5] São Paulo state only to 1970.
[6] Yarns for sale only from 1944.
[7] Yarns for sale only from 1951 (2nd line), including tyre cord yarns from 1962. Data relate to years ended 30 June.
[8] Shipments from factories subsequently.

D15 OUTPUT OF COTTON TISSUES

	NORTH AMERICA			SOUTH AMERICA					
	Canada	Mexico	USA (million square metres)	Argentina	Brazil	Chile	Colombia	Peru	Venezuela
	millions metres	(thousand tons)		(thousand tons)	(million metres)	(million metres)	(million metres)	(millions metres)	(million metres)
1853	...	...	...	...	1.2	...	...	...	...
1866	...		...	...	3.6	...	...	...	...
1882	...		...	...	22	...	...	...	...
1885	...		...	...	21	...	...	...	...
1899	...		3,312	...	...	...	...	...	...
1904	...		3,657	...	242	...	...	...	...
1909	...		4,757	...	...	...	...	...	...
1911	...		...	...	379	...	...	...	...
1912	...		...	...	400	...	...	...	...
1913	...		...	...	385	...	...	...	...
1914	...	...	5,059	...	314	...	...	...	...
1915	...	...	...	...	471	...	...	...	...
1916	...	...	...	...	474	...	...	...	...
1917	...	...	...	...	548	...	...	...	...
1918	...	...	...	...	494	...	...	...	...
1919	...	...	5,673	...	584	...	...	...	...
1920	...	...	...	...	587	...	...	...	...
1921	...	...	5,135	...	552	...	...	...	...
1922	...	...	...	...	627	...	...	...	...
1923	...	...	6,228	...	940	...	...	...	...
1924	...	...	...	...	580	...	...	...	...
1925	121	...	5,782	...	536	...	...	...	...
1926	98	...	...	...	539	...	...	...	...
1927	144	...	6,844	...	594	...	...	...	...
1928	103₁ 208	...	...	...	582	...	...	...	...
1929	196	...	6,432₃ 6,805	...	478	...	...	...	...
1930	176	...	...	...	476	...	...	...	...
1931	173	...	5,840	...	634	...	...	...	...
1932	177	...	...	...	631	...	...	...	...
1933	208	...	6,455	...	639	...	...	...	...
1934	214	...	...	...	716	...	...	...	...
1935	204	...	5,843	...	753	...	...	...	...
1936	218	...	...	...	915	...	...	...	...
1937	236	38	7,728 (million metres) 7,921	...	964	13	...	...	...
1938	195	38	...	...	846	13	...	...	3.0
1939	241	36	7,578	...	894	13	...	...	4.2
1940	283	38	...	...	840	15	73	...	5.1
1941	321	44	9,539	...	990	17	65	...	6.8
1942	306	46	10,157	...	1,069	17	111	...	20
1943	254	47	9,668	...	1,414	20	...	...	24
1944	241	48	8,730	...	1,383	23	...	...	22
1945	224	48	7,974	...	1,085	24	142	...	21
1946	217	47	8,361	...	1,142	23₆ 47	...	...	22
1947	233	46	8,977	...	1,063	45	157	67	23
1948	229	47	8,815	66	1,120	45	166	71	21
1949	205	42	7,686	...	1,137	52	164	...	14

D15 Output of Cotton Tissues

	Canada[1]	Cuba	Mexico	USA	Argentina	Brazil	Chile[6]	Colombia	Peru[7]	Venezuela[7]
	(million metres)	(million sq. metres)	(thousand tons)	(million metres)	(thousand tons)	(million metres)	(million metres)	(million metres)	(million metres)	(million metres)
1950	297	...	44	9,156[4]	...	1,189	70	160	...	9.2
1951	277	...	37	9,268	...	1,112	73	157	...	11
1952	238[1]	...	35	8,701	78	997	75	180	...	13
1953	229	...	37	9,330	72	...	81	181	...	14
1954	242	...	29	9,044	74	...	86	173	...	14
1955	287	...	36	9,304	80	1,240	86	166	...	16
1956	286	...	43	9,434	86	1,252	88	211	...	16
1957	276	...	46	8,718	84	1,106	...[5]	203	...	21
1958	259	...	44	8,206	84	1,273	68	219	...	23
1959	250	...	49	8,781	73	...	72	249	85	32
1960	240	...	49	8,564	82	...	83	277	91	36
1961	278	...	46	8,383	81	...	84	281	87	40
1962	281	94	47[2]	8,456	65	...	77	307	91	50
1963	290	90	99	8,009	63	...	89	299	85	59
1964	302	105	113	8,199	77	...	89	309	94	69
1965	271	96	115	8,447	83	1,262	92	298	83	72
	(million square metres)									
	292									
1966	259	108	115	8,083	73	1,343	95	295	93	72
1967	270	112	125	7,569	71	1,230	99	...	76	71
1968	250	105	95	6,837	73	1,409	102	298	84	72
1969	227	91	128	6,369	77	1,426[5]	101	300	...	81
1970	181	76	119	5,711	76	784	97	...	...	80
1971	175	87	116	5,613	78	774	94	...	...	78
1972	202	98	115	5,174	75	777	82	...	...	94
1973	169	117	138	4,650	74	846	82	...	95	...
1974	269	127	150	4,242	72	818	86	...	112	...
									(million tons)	
1975	...	138	123	3,744	70	864[5]	53	...	34	...
1976	...	134	73	4,314	93	1,075	50	...	25	...
1977	...	145	69	3,983	98	1,011	59	...	30	...
1978	...	147	67	3,664	87	1,123	68	...	...	...
1979	...	143	68	3,225	101	1,207	67	...	...	...
				(million square metres)			(million tons)			
				4,069						
1980	...	148	67	3,726	85	1,252	53	...	...	...
1981	...	149	71	3,272	74	1,018	36	38	...	...
1982	...	138	66	3,173	75	...[2]	27	30	...	...
1983	...	156	66	3,505	88	1,643	28	27	...	...
1984	...	156	64	3,346	98	1,490	41	29	21	...
1985	...	177	71	3,278	81	1,816	45	34	22	...
1986	...	183	71	3,648	106	1,968	52	27	33	...
1987	...	202	87	3,990	87	1,974	51	29	31	...
1988	...	203	83	3,873	88	1,805	32	36	25	...
1989	...	184	87	3,837	80	1,823	32	37	28	...
1990	...	...	86	3,732	79	1,591	26	41	29	...
1991	...	...	87	3,682	83	1,405	26	43	29	...
1992	...	...	...	3,846	...	1,353	21	...	...	...
1993	...	...	...	...	...	1,312	15	...	...	...

D15 Output of Cotton Tissues

NOTES

1. SOURCES: The national publications listed on pp. xiii–xv, UN, *Statistical Yearbooks*, and *Cotton-Worl d Statistics*.
2. Fabrics of mixed fibres with cotton predominating are included in this table.

FOOTNOTES

[1] Broad-woven fabrics only to 1928 (1st line). Data from 1953 are of factory shipments.
[2] Subsequently including finished fabrics.
[3] A more inclusive classification was employed subsequently.
[4] The reason for this break is not given in the source.
[5] Production by main establishments only in 1970–75.
[6] Incomplete data to 1946 (1st line).
[7] Including finished fabrics.

D16 WOOL INDUSTRY INDICATORS

	NORTH AMERICA					SOUTH AMERICA	
	Canada			**USA**		**Argentina**[6]	**Uruguay**[6]
	Yarn[1] **Output**	**Tissues**[3] **Output**	**Wool Consumption**	**Yarn Output**	**Tissues Output** (million square metres)	**Wool Consumption**	**Wool Consumption**
	(thousand tons)	(million metres)	(thousand tons)	(thousand tons)		(thousand tons)	(thousand tons)
1899	...	...	...	[27]	357	...	...
1904	...	...	...	50	423	...	...
1909	...	...	...	59	477	...	...
1914	...	...	...	56	472	...	...
1918	...	...	181	...	...	...	...
1919	...	...	149	53	428	...	...
1920	...	...	143	...	...	...	...
1921	...	...	156	55	413	...	...
1922	...	...	184	...	...	...	...
1923	...	...	192	78	525	...	...
1924	...	...	155	...	...	...	...
1925	...	...	159	66	485	...	...
1926	...	...	155	...	...	...	...
1927	...	...	161	61	467	...	...
1928	...	8.5	151	...	...	...	...
1929	...	8.5	167	67	430$_5$	...	...
					348		
1930	...	6.3	119	...	...	...	...
1931	...	8.4	141	57	271	...	...
1932	...	10	104	...	...	...	...
1933	4.0	13	144	55	304	...	...
1934	4.0	13	104	...$_4$	...	...	...
1935	4.7	15	189	44	400	...	...
1936	5.2	16	184	...	393	...	...
1937	5.2	17	173	34$_4$	394	...	...
				262			
1938	4.1$_1$	13	129	...	301$_5$	...	...
	11				(million metres)		
1939	18	16	180	270	340	...	...
1940	31	25	185	...	...	...	...
1941	31	25	294	...	...	...	...
1942	32	27	274	...	483	...	...
1943	30	26	289	...	491	...	...
1944	28	24	282	388	483	...	...
1945	29	25	293	375$_2$	451	...	...
1946	31	27	335	417	552	...	...
1947	32	27	317	350	458	23	3.6
1948	31	26	314	362	455	27	3.6
1949	27	25	227	312	379$_5$	32	3.5
1950	28	23	288	367$_2$	383	34	6
1951	28	24	220	358	343	32	7.5
1952	25	24	212	341	321	30	13
1953	22	22$_3$	224	343	307	25	19
1954	19	15	173	279	260	28	16

D16 Wool Industry Indicators

	NORTH AMERICA					SOUTH AMERICA	
	Canada		USA			Argentina[6]	Uruguay[6]
	Yarn[1] Output (thousand tons)	Tissues Output (million metres)	Wool Consumption (thousand tons)	Yarn Output (thousand tons)	Tissues Output[6] (million metres)	Wool Consumption (thousand tons)	Wool Consumption (thousand tons)
1955	21	21	188	317	290	31	18
1956	24	21	200	346	297	27	21
1957	21	18	167	308	269	32	12
1958	18	15	150	294	248	28	15
1959	19	17	197	250	284	26	20
1960	16	14₃ / 25	186	238	262	20	17
1961	13	27	187	230	262	25	20
1962	18	28	195	238	284	16	19
1963	16	30	187	244	260	16	21
1964	19	32	162	217	233	24	22
1965	19	30	176	248	244	24	18
1966	17	32	139	226	241	21	22
1967	14	28	143	281	218	21	22
1968	14_1	30	150	286	222	22	23
	(million square metres)						
	15	31					
1969		31	142	173	203	25	21
1970	15	28	109	141	163	27	22
1971	16	23	87	116	104	34	20
1972	16	27	99	116	93	36	19
1973	17	31	67	89	97	31	18
1974	12	29	41	64	73	32	12
1975	2.7	31	48	59	72	32	18
1976	3.2	29	53	61	89	32	23
1977	3.8	28	47	64	93	37	21
1978	4.0	28	50	63	107	35	23
1979	4.2	...	54₇ / 65	64	106	26₇ / 26	21
1980	3.5	...	62	57	105	22	26
1981	...	...	70	62	96	13	30
1982	...	...	58	54	59	20	27
1983	...	...	72	59	61	25	29
1984	...	...	77	57	86	27	32
					(m. square metres)		
					133		
1985	...	...	61	50	116	26	33
1986	...	...	70	62	167	28	...
1987	...	...	68	61	141	28	...
1988	...	...	60	55	160	...	...
1989	...	...	...	54	148	...	...
1990	...	...	...	50	118	...	...
1991	...	...	...	61	142	...	...
1992	...	...	...	61	147	...	...
1993	...	...	...	57	184	...	...

D16 Wool Industry Indicators

NOTE

1. SOURCES: The national publications listed on pp. xiii-xv and League of Nations and UN, Statistical Yearbooks.
2. In principle, the output of mixed yarn and tissues in which wool predominates is included in this table.

FOOTNOTES

[1] Worsted yarn only to 1938 (1st line). Excluding yarn made in carpet mills to 1968.
[2] A proportion of worsted yarn is excluded from 1946 to 1950.
[3] Factory shipments form 1954 and deliveries from 1960 (2nd line).
[4] Yarns for sale only to 1937 (1st line). The reason for the break between 1933 and 1935 is not given in the source.
[5] Apparel fabrics only from 1929 (2nd line) to 1938, but excluding upholstery to 1921. The reason for the break between 1949 and 1950 is not given in the source, but it is not of major significance.
[6] Years ended 30 September.
[7] Consumption at the spinning stage subsequently.

D17 OUTPUT OF ARTIFICIAL AND SYNTHETIC FIBRES (in thousands of metric tons)

Key: a = rayon and acetate filaments; b = non-cellulosic filaments

| | NORTH AMERICA | | | | | SOUTH AMERICA | | |
| | Canada | | Mexico | USA | | Argentina | Brazil | Colombia |
	a	b	a^2	a^3	b	a	a	a
1910	—	—	—	...	—	—	—	...
1911	—	—	—	1.0	—	—	—	...
1912	—	—	—	1.3	—	—	—	...
1913	—	—	—	1.8	—	—	—	...
1914	—	—	—	2.3	—	—	—	...
1915	—	—	—	3.0	—	—	—	...
1916	—	—	—	3.0	—	—	—	...
1917	—	—	—	3.1	—	—	—	...
1918	—	—	—	2.7	—	—	—	...
1919	—	—	—	4.2	—	—	—	...
1920	—	—	—	3.9	—	—	—	...
1921	—	—	—	9.0^3	—	—	—	...
1922	—	—	—	11	—	—	—	...
1923	—	—	—	17	—	—	—	...
1924	—	—	—	17	—	—	—	...
1925	0.2	—	—	24	—	—	—	...
1926	0.9	—	—	28	—	—	0.1	...
1927	1.1	—	—	34	—	—	0.3	...
1928	1.5	—	—	44	—	—	0.3	...
1929	1.7	—	—	55	—	—	0.2	...
1930	2.1	—	—	58	—	—	0.3	...
1931	2.7	—	—	69	—	—	0.5	...
1932	3.3	—	—	62	—	—	0.7	...
1933	3.8	—	—	98	—	—	0.9	...
1934	4.8	—	—	96	—	—	1.2	...
1935	6.0	—	—	119	—	—	1.6	...
1936	6.2	—	—	131	—	0.2	2.2	...
1937	7.5	—	—	155	—	0.8	3.3	...
1938	6.2	—	—	130	—	1.2	5.5	...
1939	6.4	—	—	172	—	2.4	7.2	0.1
1940	8.9	—	—	214	1.2	2.7	7.8	0.3
1941	9.5	—	—	260	3.4	3.5	8.5	0.5
1942	8.6	—	- -	287	5.5	3.8	8.7	0.6
1943	8.0	—	0.2	301	8.0	3.5	7.7	0.6
1944	9.4	—	0.2	328	11	3.8	9.8	0.7
1945	10	—	0.2	359	13	4.4	10	1.0
1946	9.8	—	0.2	387	...	5.1	11	1.4
1947	13	—	1.3	442	...	4.8	13	...
1948	15	1.2	4.6	510	30	4.7	12	1.5
1949	17	—	9.8	452	...	7.1	16	1.4

D17 Output of Artificial and Synthetic Fibres (in thousands of metric tons)

	NORTH AMERICA						SOUTH AMERICA					
	Canada		Mexico		USA		Argentina		Brazil		Colombia	
	a	b	a[2]	b	a	b	a	b	a	b	a	b
1950	24	2.3	9.1	—	571	56	7.4	0.1	20	—	1.7	—
1951	26	2.9	11	—	587	77	7.4	0.2	25	—	1.8	—
1952	28	3.7	11	—	515	96	7.4	0.2	26	—	3.7	—
1953	29	4.5	11	—	543	112	8.6	0.1	27	—	5.4	—
1954	32	5.5	14	0.1	493	129	9.9	0.2	30	—	5.2	—
1955	36	5.6	17	0.1	572	172	11	0.3	32	0.2	6.8	—
1956	35	6.3	19	0.1	521	182	12	0.3	34	0.4	6.3	—
1957	34	9.3	16	0.2	517	234	13	0.4	35	1.3	8.1	—
1958	30	11	18	0.3	469	222	14	0.4	34	1.9	7.8	—
1959	39	13	20	0.4	529	293	11	0.6	36	2.9	7.8	- -
1960	34	17	21	0.7	467	307	11	1.1	41	4.5	7.7	- -
1961	34	19	21	1.3	497	341	16	1.8	42	5.7	6.9	0.1
1962	40	23	23[2]	2.9	577	405	12	2.2	42	8.7	11	0.9
1963	44	26	22	4.6	612	524	10	4.6	40	10	13	0.9
1964	49	30	25	6.0	650	638	18	9.7	41	13	13	0.9
1965	52	38	26	8.8	693	807	20	13	42	15	10	3.0
1966	46	45	27	12	689	945	16	15	46	19	8.7	3.2
1967	44	51	29	15	620	1,067	13	17	46	18	9.0	5.3
1968	46	69	30	22	723	1,465	11	18	53	27	9.7	8.0
1969	43	76	33	26	715	1,600	11	23	48	30	9.0	11
1970	35	73	34	39	623	1,627	9.8	25	48	44	8.8	13
1971	38	86[1]	35	62	631	1,946	14	33	53	52	11	15
1972	41	80	34	85	632	2,430	16	39	55	73	9	20
1973	43	94	37	99	616	2,862	18	46	59	103	7.4	24
1974	41	92	34	126	544	2,823	18	47	54	116	7.0	23
1975	28	96	33	148	340	2,670	14	47	49	126	5.6	27
1976	27	98	34	133	381	3,007	10	41	54	157	3.4	34
1977	37	115	25	158	403	3,324	11	43	50	160	3.3	39
1978	39	123	25	171	410	3,522	8	39	46	180	3.4	41
1979	45	122	24	183	422	3,828	10	52	50	214	3.4	37
1980	44	122	26	194	366	3,242	3.6	35	51	231	2.4	39
1981	42	110	26	213	349	3,275	1.1	25	46	202	1.8	44
1982	37	97	28	201	265	2,603	1.6	31	44	198	1.8	40
1983	40	112	20	219	299	3,008	1.7	43	40	185	1.8	40
1984	44	129	18	222	285	2,937	3.6	52	47	216	1.8	47
1985	35	133	19	235	253	2,864	2.9	37	47	217	1.8	48
1986	38	140	19	221	281	2,919	8.5	58	50	237	1.8	47
1987	37	130	20	237	275	3,094	5.8	57	49	248	2.3	49
1988	42	134	20	…	279	3,147	3.5	51	51	240	1.5	50
1989	47	125	22	…	263	3,119	3.4	45	55	246	1.0	52
1990	40	123	23	…	229	2,886	2.3	48	55	208	2.0	56
1991	41	127	25	…	221	2,903	3.3	54	53	219	1.9	73
1992	36	119	24	…	225	2,981	3.2	52	54	230	2.0	75
1993	16	107	23	…	229	2,976	9.5	47	57	234	1.8	81

NOTE

SOURCES: The national publications listed on pp. xiii–xv and League of Nations and UN, *Statistical Yearbooks*.

FOOTNOTES

[1] Subsequently excluding olefin.
[2] Excluding high tenacity yarn to 1962.
[3] Statistics to 1921 may contain a very small amount of imports.

D18 OUTPUT OF SULPHURIC ACID, HYDROCHLORIC ACID, NITRIC ACID, AND CAUSTIC SODA (in thousands of metric tons)

Key: CS = caustic soda; HA = hydrochloric acid; NA = nitric acid; SA = sulphuric acid

| | NORTH AMERICA | | | | | SOUTH AMERICA | | | |
| | Canada | USA | | | | Argentina | | Chile | Peru |
	SA	SA[1]	HA	NA[1]	CS	SA	CS	SA	SA
1899	...	1,068	...	...	151[3]	...	...	...	...
1904	...	1,289	...	...	79[3]	...	...	...	...
1909	...	2,045	...	...	120[3]	...	...	...	...
1914	...	2,809	...	...	265[3]	...	...	...	...
1919	41	3,830	...	...	284	...	...	...	...
1920	62	...	...	...	...	...	...	...	...
1921	40	3,015	...	...	217	...	...	...	...
1922	52	...	...	...	...	...	...	...	...
1923	74	4,521	...	...	396	...	...	...	...
1924	61	...	...	...	...	...	...	...	...
1925	70	4,831	...	...	451	...	...	...	...
1926	91	...	...	...	...	...	...	...	...
1927	83	5,059	...	...	520	...	...	...	...
1928	81	...	...	...	...	...	...	...	...
1929	94	5,857	74	130	691	...	...	...	...
1930	91	...	...	...	...	...	...	...	...
1931	101	4,198	50	106	598	...	...	...	...
1932	116	...	...	...	...	...	...	...	...
1933	125	...	57	87	623	...	...	...	...
1934	174	...	...	...	...	...	...	...	...
1935	190	4,436	79	87	689	...	...	...	...
1936	204	...	...	...	...	...	...	...	...
1937	239	5,469	110	160	879	...	...	...	...
1938	227	3,799	...	...	...	...	...	...	...
1939	216	4,350	112	152	948	41	15	3	...
1940	273	5,208[1]	...	...	...[8]	...	...	2	...
1941	304	6,142	207	315	1,297	53	20	5	...
1942	421	7,034	269	388	1,428	57	23	4	1.7
1943	474	7,658	311	438	1,614	61	22	4	5.9
1944	580	8,384	346	428	1,698	71	23	4	5.9

D18　NORTH AMERICA: Output of Sulphuric Acid, Hydrochloric Acid, Nitric Acid, and Caustic Soda (in thousands of metric tons)

	Canada				Cuba	Mexico		USA			
	SA	HA	NA	CS	SA	SA	CS	SA[1]	HA	NA[1]	CS
1945	603	...	...	...	...	...	...	8,638	370	406	1,691
1946	538	...	...	...	...	...	...	8,349	310	521	1,699
1947	607	...	...	...	...	...	...	9,779	402	1,079	1,908
1948	616	...	...	...	...	...	...	10,393	416	1,028	2,156
1949	642	...	...	101	...	...	...	10,371	448	1,025	2,017
1950	686	...	...	138	25	43	...	11,820	561	1,212	2,278
1951	745	...	...	150	27	57	...	12,131	631	1,372	2,818
1952	741	...	...	172	24	92	9.1	12,075	620	1,487	2,750
1953	746	...	...	174	26	103	13	12,703[1]	702	1,602[1]	2,960
1954	838	6.1	211	181	28	110	18	13,042	693	2,077	3,093
1955	862	6.2	215	205	28	125	23	14,746	760	2,352	3,552
1956	954	7.3	209	232	32	157	26	14,964	822	2,352	3,835
1957	1,170	7.8	182	239	32	186	34	14,932	860	2,580	3,934
1958	1,439	16	208	285	...	200	40	14,470	749	2,453	3,623
1959	1,578	19	255	309	...	243	52	15,974	867	2,789	4,308
1960	1,518	19	243	338	44	269	66	16,223	880	3,007	4,510
1961	1,464	17	248	376	58	276	65	16,191	826	3,066	4,458
1962	1,559	22	289	392	136	339	73	17,873	954	3,329	4,976
1963	1,625	24	310	440	135	387	88	18,993	956	3,849	5,275
1964	1,761	26	353	498	189	433	80	20,796	1,122	4,293	5,796
1965	1,964	31	344	583	192	508	102	22,540	1,243	4,444	6,197
1966	2,268	41	392	650	226	579	110	25,750	1,380	5,002	6,891
1967	2,495	42	384	731	265	640	118	26,141	1,479	5,863	7,618
1968	2,587	47	358	766	316	780	140	25,895	1,585	5,772[2] / 6,343	8,045
1969	2,175	60	475	856	319	1,067	154	26,795	1,733	6,553	8,997
1970	2,475	64	503	860	315	1,235	166	26,784	1,827	6,897	9,200
1971	2,661	70	543	869	361	1,433	171	26,340	1,905	6,929	8,769
1972	2,749	75	610	921	392	1,518	174	28,290	2,089	7,241	9,269
1973	2,980	81	715	1,029	377	1,966	188	28,613	2,282	7,658	9,694
1974	2,821	91	436	1,030	376	2,091	222	29,982	2,181	7,425	10,341
1975	2,723	88	365	845	410	2,047	209	28,290	1,790	6,418	8,410
1976	2,842	109	...	1,000	392	2,178	228	30,460	2,203	6,813	9,202
1977	3,140	136	...	1,014	375	2,295	263	34,771	2,420	7,244	9,977
1978	3,261	155	...	1,036	347	2,372	247	37,472	2,533	7,196	10,258
1979	3,666	154	...	1,138	296	2,041	231	39,186	2,803	8,087	11,572
1980	4,295	177	713	1,459	401	2,359	224	40,050	2,619	8,373	10,544
1981	4,117	186	861	1,458	413	2,619	296	36,953	2,335	8,247	9,633
1982	3,085	143	977	1,367	332	2,732	365	30,143	2,222	6,703	8,512
1983	3,679	170	855	1,528	356	2,996	363	33,975	2,238	6,320	9,106
1984	4,043	161	1,101	1,575	336	3,196	350	37,914	2,442	7,073	9,899
1985	3,890	158	1,128	1,589	373	2,222	363	35,964	2,546	6,924	9,805
1986	3,536	153	1,024	1,697	395	2,149	382	32,650	2,170	6,110	9,643
1987	3,437	164	1,000	1,770	370	...	331	35,612	2,718	6,554	10,480
1988	3,805	179	907	1,720	391	...	320	38,628	2,928	7,249	9,556
1989	3,719	180	1,027	1,679	377	...	349	39,282	2,965	7,574	10,599
1990	3,830	...	...	...	...	...	380	40,222	2,848	7,194	11,116
1991	3,676	193	912	1,498	...	...	293	39,432	3,067	7,189	11,114
1992	3,776	168	919	1,428	...	...	348	40,697	3,235	7,296	11,292
1993	3,713	134	917	1,225	...	...	333	35,693	3,168	7,487	11,308

D18 SOUTH AMERICA: OUTPUT OF SULPHURIC ACID, HYDROCHLORIC ACID, NITRIC ACID, AND CAUSTIC SODA
(in thousands of metric tons)

	Argentina		Brazil		Chile[7]	Colombia	Peru		Venezuela
	SA[4]	CS	SA[6]	CS[5]	SA	SA	SA[9]	NA	SA
1945	71	23	...	...	5	...	5.9	...	...
1946	68	23	...	...	5	...	2.6	...	...
1947	81	28	...	...	5	...	2.8	...	...
1948	75	30	...	...	5	...	6.1	...	...
1949	77	26	...	...	4	...	3.6	...	...
1950	77	28	122	...	9	...	8.4	...	...
1951	64	31	108	...	12	...	10	...	...
1952	60	31	150	...	16	...	10	...	...
1953	56	30	97	20	13	8	10	...	...
1954	57	35	...	15	19	...	12	...	...
1955	68	37	88	31	18	...	12	...	...
1956	78	37	134	50	45	2	10	...	...
1957	72	40	122	50	45	12	13	...	...
1958	64	51	175	60₅	45	9	16	...	...
1959	63	54	202	63	60	15	18	...	7
1960	60₄ 132	47	215	68	84	19	30	14	7
1961	127	54	231	77	117	23	29	23	12
1962	118	55	259	84	129	25	29	28	15
1963	109	58	288	85	136	18	33	28	36
1964	151	61	300	89	178	16	37	35	51
1965	162	76	252	89	193	24	38	36	58
1966	149	75	300	99	180	34	39	32	52
1967	154	69	365	112	220	18	37	35	49
1968	163	79	367	138	249	47	46	36	99
1969	184	88	421	115	327	41	56	40	80
1970	180	95	...	137	373	41	60	32	68
1971	188	113	...	136	425	...	19	...	30
1972	242	123	...	197	530₂	48	61	...	79
1973	233	120	835	210	195	52	67	...	68
1974	243	117	925₂	214	155	51	54	...	93
1975	225	113	...	241	110	47	54	...	117
1976	234	110	1,439	259	130	49	57	...	82
1977	251	121	1,556	317	132	42	63	...	42
1978	244	101	1,596	577	127	45	58	...	92
1979	279	110	1,910	645	100	54	68	...	128
1980	250	104	2,408	691	...	59	62	...	114
1981	232	105	2,516	759	...	49	184	...	79
1982	250	115	2,681	760	...	40	227	...	113
1983	262	128	2,983	746	...	53	210	...	139
1984	254	125	3,484	857	...	...	205	...	158
1985	235	121	3,660	886	...	62	213	...	156
1986	251	129	3,820	988	...	68	209	72	164
1987	253	119	4,004	954	...	68	212	73	197
1988	258	117	4,049	1,007	...	75	174	71	172
1989	214	242	3,809	1,126	...	95	193	61	163
1990	209	230	3,451	1,105	347	76	172	62	210
1991	243	210	3,634	1,211	804	...	207	...	277
1992	219	160	3,257	1,238	887	...	143	56	253
1993	206	156	3,724	1,271	920	...	229	56	...

D18 Output of Sulphuric Acid, Hydrochloric Acid, Nitric Acid and Caustic Soda

NOTES

1. SOURCES: The national publications listed on pp. xiii–xv, and League of Nations and UN, *Statistic Yearbooks*.
2. So far as possible, output is given in terms of 100% H_2SO_4, HCl, HNO_3, and NaOH.

FOOTNOTES

[1] Government plants are excluded to 1954. Coverage of sulphuric acid is not complete to 1939.
[2] The reason for this break is not given in the source.
[3] Amount for sale.
[4] Data to 1960 (1st line) are based on sample surveys.
[5] Data to 1958 are in terms of less than 100% NaOH.
[6] Statistics represent about 90% of total output.
[7] Strength not reported.
[8] Production in the soap, paper, and pulp industries is excluded to 1939.
[9] Excluding weak acid.

D19   NORTH AMERICA: TIMBER INDUSTRY INDICATORS (output in units shown)

Key: a = million board feet; b = thousand metric tons; c = million cubic metres; d = thousand cubic metres

	Canada[1]			USA			
	Lumber	Wood Pulp	Paper[2]	Industrial Roundwood	Lumber	Wood Pulp	Paper[2]
	a	b	b	c	a	b	b
1799	...	...	...	...		...	...
1809	...	...	...	...		...	3
1819	...	...	...	...		...	11
1829	...	...	...	...		...	...
1839	...	...	...	...		...	34
1849	...	...	...	...		...	71
1859	...	...	...	...		...	115
1869	...	...	...	...	12,756	1	350
1879	...	...	...	...	18,125	21	410
1889	...	...	...	...	27,039	278	848
1899	...	...	...	...	35,078	1,070	1,967
1900	...	...	...	206	...	...	...
1901	...	...	...	215	...	...	...
1902	...	...	...	223	...	...	...
1903	...	...	...	233	...	...	...
1904	...	...	...	240	34,127	1,744	2,819
1905	...	...	...	244	30,503	...	...
1906	...	...	...	261	37,551	...	...
1907	...	...	...	271	40,256	2,312	...
1908	3,348	329	...	247	33,224	1,922	...
1909	3,815	404	...	263	44,510	2,264	3,739
1910	4,452	431	...	263	40,018	2,299	...
1911	4,918	451	...	255	37,003	2,437	...
1912	4,390	620	...	264	39,158	...	...
1913	3,817	776	...	260	38,387	...	...
1914	3,946	848	...	243	37,348	2,624	4,675
1915	3,843	975	...	227	31,242	...	...
1916	3,491	1,176	...	242	34,791	3,116	...
1917	4,152	1,328	777	225	33,193	3,184	5,265
1918	3,887	1,412	878	207	29,362	3,006	5,387
1919	3,820	1,557	989	219	34,552	3,191	5,412

D19   NORTH AMERICA: Timber Industry Indicators (output in units shown)

	Canada[1]			Mexico	Newfoundland	USA			
	Lumber	Wood pulp	Paper[2]	Sawn wood	Wood pulp	Industrial Roundwood	Lumber	Wood pulp	Paper[2]
	a	b	b	e	b	c	a	b	b
1920	4,299	1,778	1,102	...	...	220	29,878	3,467	6,518
1921	2,869	1,405	924	...	...	186	26,961	2,609	4,838
1922	3,139	1,950	1,240	...	...	215	31,569	3,195	6,237
1923	3,728	2,246	1,442	...	125	242	37,166	3,437	7,140
1924	3,879	2,236	1,559	...	138	234	35,931	3,377	7,194
1925	3,889	2,516	1,710	...	145	236	38,339	3,594	8,166
1926	4,185	2,930	2,056	...	188	233	36,936	3,987	8,885
1927	4,098	2,975	2,240	...	214	220	34,532	3,913	9,074
1928	4,337	3,273	2,585	...	210	217	34,142	4,092	9,437
1929	4,742	3,648	2,900	...	210	228	36,886	4,412	10,106
1930	3,989	3,283	2,655	...	261	179	26,051	4,200	9,225
1931	2,498	2,874	2,369	...	255	130	16,523	4,000	8,511
1932	1,810	2,416	2,078	...	239	96	10,151	3,411	7,256
1933	1,958	2,703	2,194	...	241	114	13,961	3,879	8,337
1934	2,578	3,299	2,785	...	278	123	15,494	4,024	8,334
1935	2,973	3,509	2,976	...	296	144	19,539	4,469	9,506
1936	3,412	4,069	3,454	...	287	170	24,355	5,166	10,864
1937	4,006	4,665	3,942	...	320	180	25,997	5,963	11,646
1938	3,768	3,328	2,947	...	242	158	21,646	5,383	10,325
1939	3,977	3,779	3,267	...	...	180	25,148	6,344	12,256
1940	4,629	4,800	3,918	...	357	198	28,934	8,128	13,140
1941	4,941	5,190	4,105	...	374	228	33,613	9,412	16,113
1942	4,935	5,086	3,839	...	348	229	36,332	9,782	15,498
1943	4,364	4,784	3,598	...	288	214	34,289	8,782	15,455
1944	4,512	4,782	3,669	...	325	211	32,938	9,170	15,588
1945	4,514	5,081	3,955	...	356	187	28,122	9,223	15,759
1946	5,083	6,001	4,851	...	366	218	34,112	9,623	17,489
1947	5,878	6,581	5,239	...	399	229	35,404	10,837	19,143
1948	5,909₁	6,963₁	5,501₁	...	424	237	37,000	11,677	19,865
1949	5,915	7,124	5,933	...	...	208	32,178	11,074	18,429
1950	6,554	7,687	6,180	...	...	241	38,007	13,471	22,113
1951	6,949	8,450	6,554	...	...	247	37,204	14,990	23,629
1952	6,808	8,136	6,534	926	...	248	37,462	14,944	22,152
1953	7,306	8,235	6,692	887	...	249	36,742	15,909	24,136
1954	7,244	8,775	6,940	890	...	248	36,356	16,603	24,381
1955	7,920	9,209	7,257	923	...	261	37,380	18,812	27,377
1956	7,740	9,738	7,681	936	...	272	38,199	20,008	28,523
1957	7,100	9,458	7,530	815	...	244	32,901	19,777	27,870
1958	7,179	9,197	7,331	...	...	242	33,385	19,773	27,962
1959	7,591₄ 18	9,827	7,756₂ 7,554	896	...	266	37,166	22,120	30,858

D19   NORTH AMERICA: Timber Industry Indicators (output in units shown)

	Canada[1]			Mexico	USA			
	Sawn wood[6]	Wood pulp	Paper[2]	Sawn wood	Industrial Roundwood	Lumber	Wood pulp	Paper[2]
	c	b	b	d	c	a	b	b
1960	19	10,398	7,934	926	253	32,926[7]	22,966	31,247
1961	20	10,574	7,975	801	248	32,019	24,061	32,431
1962	21	11,007	8,055	879	256	33,178	25,318	34,057
1963	23	11,316	8,218	1,043	271	34,706	27,325	35,589
1964	23	12,467	8,961	1,268	288	36,559	29,406	37,832
1965	26	12,861	9,758	1,259	298	36,762	30,838	39,989
1966	25	14,517	10,563	1,384	301	36,584	33,206	42,740
1967	25	14,435	10,316	1,466	295	34,741	33,273	42,571
1968	27	15,261	10,398	1,479	312	36,475	37,097	46,489
1969	27	16,864	11,354	1,422	311	35,824	38,839	49,158
1970	27	16,609	11,251	1,572	315	34,668	39,504	48,549
1971	31	16,508	11,161	1,534	320	36,988	39,855	49,986
1972	33	17,455	12,038	1,803	324	37,745	42,427	53,796
1973	36	18,561	12,578	1,938	333	38,595	41,221	55,973
1974	32	19,656	13,218	2,055	320	34,608	41,379	54,340
1975	27	14,831	10,067	1,986	291	32,619	36,808	47,537
1976	37	17,688	11,791	2,147	325	36,967	40,307	51,757
1977	42	17,773	12,152	2,259	352	39,362	41,618	53,347
1978	45	19,216	13,286	2,299	394	40,498	43,145	55,154
1979	45	19,516	13,486	2,109	422	40,569	45,318	57,410
1980	44	19,945	13,390	1,991	418	35,354	46,187	56,839
1981	40	19,578	13,835	1,928	419	31,672	47,200	57,667
1982	37	17,007	12,408	1,669	397	30,010	44,786	54,899
1983	42	19,221	13,353	1,827	438	34,572	47,660	58,804
1984	50	20,451	14,222	1,975	475	37,065	50,398	62,366
1985	55	20,222	14,448	2,205	476	36,445	49,061	60,959
1986	55	21,512	15,259	2,143	511	41,999	51,927	64,444
1987	62	22,804	16,044	2,410	530	44,886	54,058	67,532
1988	61	23,298	16,639	2,528	533	44,730	55,530	69,587
1989	59	23,834	16,555	2,447	532	43,576	56,225	69,514
1990	55	23,020	16,466	2,366	542	43,466	57,217	71,965
1991	52	23,441	16,559	2,696	505	40,031	58,896	72,774
1992	56	23,169	16,585	2,696	539	...	59,280	75,161
1993	60	23,658	17,557	2,696	537	...	58,310	77,250

D19   SOUTH AMERICA: TIMBER INDUSTRY INDICATORS (output in units shown)

	Brazil	Chile	Colombia			Brazil	Chile	Colombia
	Sawn wood	Sawn wood	Sawn wood			Sawn wood	Sawn wood	Sawn wood
1937	3,500	467	...		1970	8,035	1,075	1,100
					1971	8,100	1,093	1,180
1946	...	853	...		1972	7,550	1,134	1,258
1947	4,011	755	...		1973	7,109	1,059	1,261
1948	3,907	669	...		1974	7,642	1,478	934
1949	4,225	536	...					
1950	2,970	425	...		1975	10,128	1,320	954
1951	4,227	520	...		1976	11,243	1,223	...
1952	4,021	537	...		1977	12,643	1,267	...
1953	4,025	509	730		1978	13,337	1,478	...
1954	4,076	698	...		1979	14,070	2,199	983
1955	4,426	584	...		1980	14,881	2,186	970
1956	4,387[3]	741	...		1981	15,852	1,735	1,006
	7,254				1982	16,470	1,176	721
1957	6,226	786	...		1983	17,199	1,610	...
1958	6,534	...	...		1984	17,781	2,001	...
1959	6,092	721	...					
					1985	17,781	2,194	...
1960	5,700	876	...		1986	18,063	2,026	813
1961	6,100	746	990		1987	...	2,677	...
1962	6,300	1,031	...		1988	18,179	2,710	...
1963	5,363	785	...		1989	18,179	2,684	...
1964	5,531	1,015	910					
					1990	17,179	3,327	...
1965	5,661	1,019	910		1991	18,628	3,218	...
1966	6,072	1,063	920		1992	18,628	3,020	...
1967	6,618	851	930		1993	18,628	3,113	...
1968	6,965	1,055	950					
1969	7,467	1,013	1,052					

NOTES

1. SOURCES: The national publications listed on pp. xiii–xv and League of Nations and UN, *Statistical Yearbooks*.
2. The board foot is a measure of lumber 1 foot long × 1 foot deep × 1 inch wide

FOOTNOTES

[1]   Including Newfoundland from 1949.
[2]   All paper and products. Data for Canada from 1959 (2nd line) are of paper and paperboard.
[3]   A wider definition was employed subsequently.
[4]   Sawn wood and sleepers subsequently.
[5]   Subsequently excluding some paper products.
[6]   Including sleepers.
[7]   Including Alaska and Hawaii subsequently.

D20 NORTH AMERICA: OUTPUT AND ASSEMBLY OF MOTOR VEHICLES (in thousands)

Key: PC = passenger cars; CV = commercial vehicles

	Canada		USA[1]	
	PC	CV	PC	CV
1900	…	…	4.1	…
1901	…	…	7.0	…
1902	…	…	9.0	…
1903	…	…	11	…
1904	…	…	22	0.7
1905	…	…	24	0.7
1906	…	…	33	0.8
1907	…	…	43	1.0
1908	…	…	64	1.5
1909	…	…	124	3.3
1910	…	…	181	6.0
1911	…	…	199	11
1912	…	…	356	22
1913	…	…	461	24
1914	…	…	548	25
1915	…	…	896	74
1916	…	…	1,526	92
1917	…	…	1,746	128
1918	70	7.3	943	227
1919	68	7.9	1,652	225
1920	79	10	1,906	322
1921	57	5.1	1,468	148
1922	79	8.2	2,274	270
1923	106	19	3,625	409
1924	98	18	3,186	417
1925	120	26	3,735	531
1926	154	30	3,692	609
1927	137	30	2,937	465
1928	176	18	3,775	583
1929	189	50	4,455	882
1930	116	17	2,787	575
1931	65	17	1,948	432
1932	48	10	1,104	228
1933	48	12	1,561	329
1934	80	24	2,161	576
1935	112	37	3,274	697
1936	108	34	3,679	782
1937	133	54	3,929	891
1938	105	42	2,020	489
1939	90	47	2,889	700
1940	103	113	3,717	755
1941	91	174	3,780	1,061
1942	12	216	223	819
1943	—	178	0.1	700
1944	—	158	0.6	737
1945	1.9	131	70	656
1946	92	80	2,149	941
1947	167	91	3,558	1,239
1948	167	97	3,909	1,376
1949	194	99	5,119	1,134

D20 NORTH AMERICA: Output and Assembly of Motor Vehicles (in thousands)

	Canada		Mexico		USA[1]	
	PC	CV	PC	CV	PC	CV
1950	284	106	...	...	6,666	1,337
1951	283	133	...	...	5,338	1,427
1952	283	150	21	27	4,321	1,218
1953	360	121	14	22	6,117	1,206
1954	287	70	13	20	5,559	1,042
1955	375	79	12	20	7,920	1,249
1956	374	94	13	26	5,816	1,104
1957	340	73	18	23	6,113	1,107
1958	297	59	20	19	4,258	877
1959	301	67	27	21	5,591	1,137
1960	326	72	25	20	6,675	1,194
1961	324	63	33	20	5,543	1,134
1962	425	80	41	22	6,933	1,240
1963	532	99	50	26	7,638	1,463
1964	560	111	66	33	7,752	1,540
1965	707	140	67	28	9,306	1,752
1966	684	188	85	33	8,598	1,731
1967	712	211	86	39	7,437	1,539
1968	886	261	103	44	8,822	1,896
1969	1,033	300	114	51	8,224	1,919
1970	923	236	137	53	6,547	1,692
1971	1,097	280	160	54	8,585	2,053
1972	1,155	320	170	63	8,824	2,447
1973	1,228	347	208	74	9,658	2,980
1974	1,166	359	260	90	7,331	2,727
1975	1,045	379	262	98	6,713	2,272
1976	1,137	503	229	92	8,498	2,979
1977	1,163	583	196	84	9,201	3,441
1978	1,140	634	249	131	9,165	3,706
1979	961	626	290	148	8,419	3,037
1980	847	528	316	169	6,400	1,667
1981	803	520	369	218	6,255	1,701
1982	808	468	324	152	5,049	1,906
1983	971	554	214	70	6,739	2,414
1984	1,022	808	247	100	7,621	3,075
1985	1,075	856	285	139	8,002	3,357
1986	1,061	785	198	120	7,516	3,393
1987	810	825	278	113	7,085	3,821
1988	1,008	1,018	345	148	7,105	4,121
1989	984	949	448	185	6,825	4,051
1990	940	790	611	199	6,078	3,706
1991	890	790	730	239	5,439	3,372
1992	901	901	798	269	5,664	4,065
1993	838	838	810	217	5,981	4,917

D20 SOUTH AMERICA: OUTPUT AND ASSEMBLY OF MOTOR VEHICLES (in thousands)

	Argentina[2]		Brazil		Chile[3]		Colombia[3]		Peru[3]		Venezuela	
	PC	CV	PC	CV	PC	CV	PC	CV	PC	CV	PC	CV
1949	—	—	—	—	—	—	—	—	—	—	—	1.2
1950	—	—	—	—	—	—	—	—	—	—	0.1	2.9
1951	—	—	—	—	—	—	—	—	—	—	1.9	4.6
1952	—	2.9	—	—	—	—	—	—	—	—	3.9	4.7
1953	—	4.4	—	—	—	—	—	—	—	—	5.9	4.5
1954	1.5	5.1	—	—	—	—	—	—	—	—	7.9	6.3
1955	1.6	7.5	—	—	—	—	—	—	—	—	12	6.1
1956	2.3	5.5	—	6.1	—	—	—	—	—	—	9.2	4.6
1957	9.8	21	9.3	21	—	—	—	—	—	—	8.9	5.9
1958	21	11	17	45	—	—	—	—	—	—	7.5	5.9
1959	21	9.6	30	66	—	—	—	—	—	—	8.7	6.2
1960	50	39	57	76	—	—	—	—	—	0.2	6.5	3.9
1961	85	50	73	73	—	—	0.6	—	—	0.1	8.8	2.9
1962	94	35	97	94	5.2	1.3	2.0	0.5	—	0.6	8.8	2.9
1963	80	26	100	74	6.6	1.3	0.7	0.8	—	0.6	17	5.7
1964	119	47	111	73	6.6	1.2	0.9	1.0	—	1.0	30	11
1965	141	56	113	72	6.7	1.9	0.4	1.1	1.7	1.1	41	15
1966	137	42	135	90	5.1	2.0	0.7	0.6	7.7	5.3	45	13
1967	134	41[6] / 23	141	85	10	3.2	1.5	1.1	12	5.7	42	11
1968	132	3	169	109	14	4.4	1.2	1.5	7.7	2.4	43	15
1969	156	38	243	109	19	3.6	4.2	3.9	13	4.3	56	15
1970	169	30	255	161	21	3.9	7.7	9.8	10	4.2	48	13
1971	196	34	363	152	21	2.2	14	10	11	5.6	56	...
1972	202	36	437	177	23	2.9	18	7.6	16	7.7	64	25
1973	220	37	492	251	16	3	21	5.2	20	12	66	31
1974	214	54	562	337	9	4.9	30	6.6	19	11	79	39
1975	185	42	525	374	5	2.5	21	8.6	21	13	92	52
1976	141	38	527	453	5	2.0	25	11	22	12	97	66
1977	168	51	482	424	9	2.9	28	8.9	18	7.7	99	64
1978	135	33	559	495	17	3.5	32	13	7	4.2	104	79
1979	190	46	568	543[6] / 219	18	2.6	33	16	6	4.9	92	66
1980	218	44	652	232	25	4.1	32	11	11	8.0	94	61
1981	138	23	605	195	22	5.3	25	11	13	8.9	82	72
1982	110	19	686	187	8	2.3	27	9.1	16	5.8	94	61
1983	132	25	746	148	3	1.5	21	6.8	8	1.7	72	40
1984	143	23	673	185	4	2.6	34	11	6	2.7	70	40
1985	118	17	754	208	5	3.5	33	5.9	6	3.2	72	44
1986	143	20	815	241	2	3.0	36	8.1	7	5.6	85	52
1987	166	19	683	237	3	4.5	43	8.9	5	8.4	74	41
1988	142	13	782	263	4	6.2	47	14	2	4.6	68	46
1989	112	16	731	282	7	8.4	40	14	1	2.8	16	6
1990	87	19	663	251	3	8.0	37	13	1	2.8	24	12
1991	114	25	705	255	3	9.4	35	13	0.5	1.9	35	24
1992	221	41	816	257	4	14.4	40	9	—	0.6	42	30
1993	287	55	392	291	3	16.6	63	10	—	1.2	...	...

NOTES

1. SOURCES: The national publications listed on pp. xiii–xv and League of Nations and UN, *Statistical Yearbooks*.
2. Except as indicated in footnotes, the statistics relate to the production and assembly of complete vehicles, other than motor cycles.

FOOTNOTES

[1] Factory sales.
[2] Production and assembly.
[3] Assembly only.
[4] Years ended 30 June.
[5] Subsequently including part-finished vehicles.
[6] The reason for this break is not given in the source. It may result from the exclusion of agricultural tractors.

D21 NORTH AMERICA: OUTPUT OF BEER (in thousands of hectolitres)

	Canada[1]	USA[2]		Canada[1]	Costa Rica[3]	Cuba	Dominican Republic	El Salvador
1870	...	7,744	1915	...	...	...	...	...
1871	...	9,035	1916	...	...	...	...	...
1872	...	10,208	1917	...	...	...	...	...
1873	...	11,264	1918	1,183	...	...	...	...
1874	...	11,264	1919	1,676	...	...	...	...
1875	...	11,147	1920	1,614	...	...	...	...
1876	...	11,616	1921	1,746	...	313	...	...
1877	...	11,499	1922	1,672	...	286	...	...
1878	...	11,968	1923	2,004	...	407	...	...
1879	...	13,024	1924	2,198	...	473	...	...
1880	...	15,606	1925	2,384	...	452	...	...
1881	...	16,779	1926	2,353	...	468	...	...
1882	...	19,947	1927	2,655	...	516	...	...
1883	...	20,886	1928	2,993	...	422	...	...
1884	...	22,294	1929	2,884	...	431	...	...
1885	...	22,528	1930	2,686	...	362	...	...
1886	...	24,288	1931	2,377	...	221	...	...
1887	...	27,104	1932	1,849	...	161	...	7.1
1888	744	28,982	1933	1,860	...	186	...	20
1889	782	29,451	1934	2,368	...	229	...	21
1890	821	32,384	1935	2,598	...	303	...	17
1891	770	35,787	1936	2,742	...	357	10	16
1892	781	37,430	1937	3,062	...	437	9.3	15
1893	832	40,598	1938	2,879	...	406	8.0	14
1894	801	39,190	1939	3,023	...	385	10	19
1895	819	39,424	1940	3,592	...	403	11	8.9
1896	813	42,123	1941	4,595	...	454	12	11
1897	903	40,481	1942	4,954	...	433	17	14
1898	959	44,001	1943	4,731	...	436	12	16
1899	1,059	43,062	1944	5,570	...	597	20	22
1900	1,141	46,347	1945	6,316	...	780	35	24
1901	1,256	47,638	1946	7,083	...	814	35	32
1902	1,171	52,331	1947	7,874	...	844	51	38
1903	1,242	54,795	1948	8,218	...	998	50	42
1904	1,379	56,673	1949	8,204	...	965	67	...
1905	1,511	58,081	1950	8,094	...	1,043	66	94
1906	...	64,182	1951	8,665	25	1,255	71	141
1907	1,764	68,758	1952	9,455	27	1,437	92	194
1908	1,696	68,993	1953	9,672	29	1,188	85	217
1909	1,753	66,059	1954	9,606	38	1,202	76	183
1910	...	69,814	1955	10,098	54	1,179	71	158
1911	2,190	74,273	1956	10,293	60	1,205	83	158
1912	2,360	72,982	1957	10,894	67	1,292	105	200
1913	...	76,620	1958	10,649	74	1,232	132	169
1914	...	77,676	1959	11,202	79	1,557	125	131
			1960	11,489	89	...	94	145
			1961	11,688	91	1,394	87	139
			1962	12,276	86	927	225	142
			1963	12,732	86	891	286	139
			1964	13,056	89	1,036	302	128

D21 NORTH AMERICA: Output of Beer (in thousands of hectolitres)

	Guatemala	Honduras	Jamaica[4]	Mexico	Nicaragua	Panama	Puerto Rico[5]	USA[2]
1915	...	...	...	...				70,166
1916	...	...	...	...				68,758
1917	...	...	...	...				71,340
1918	...	...	...	...				59,019
1919	...	...	...	...				32,502
1920	...	...	...	...				10,795
1921	...	...	...	...				10,795
1922	...	...	...	...				7,392
1923	...	...	...	...				6,219
1924	...	...	...	...				5,749
1925	...	...	...	540				5,884
1926	...	...	...	680				5,749
1927	...	...	...	720				5,163
1928	...	...	...	679				4,928
1929	...	...	...	720				4,576
1930	...	...	...	720	...	...	...	4,319
1931	16	...	...	547	...	...	...	3,681
1932	11	...	...	425	...	...	...	3,245
1933	12	...	...	530	...	73	...	11,496[2]
1934	8.3	...	...	674	...	68	...	44,209
1935	8.2	...	...	825	...	75	...	53,069
1936	11	...	...	989	...	84	...	60,794
1937	22	...	11	1,208	...	90	...	68,932
1938	25	...	12	1,298	4.9	102	...	66,107
1939	26	...	11	1,605	7.9	105	...	63,210
1940	27	...	7.7	1,792	12	129	...	64,408
1941	...	...	13	1,836	13	170		64,785
1942	...	...	12	2,198	15	232	...	74,762
1943	44	...	12₄	2,593	17	275	[104][6]	83,225
1944	59	...	20	3,161	15	246	131	95,762
1945	79	...	25	3,687	18	262	159	101,458
1946	82	...	34	4,205	18	233	158	99,551
1947	104	...	41	3,222	16	218	175	102,912
1948	102	...	54	3,360	18	172	120	106,996
1949	97	...	32	4,045	17	145	98	105,292
1950	96	...	37	4,949	17	131	110	104,202
1951	95	...	49	6,015	19	147	132	104,400
1952	96	...	63	5,721	26	169	363	105,133
1953	113	94	71	5,657	30	164	515	106,111
1954	112	101	82	6,559	34	154	548	108,606
1955	111	131	91	6,589	43	149	552	105,356
1956	130	161	100	7,292	47	153	501	106,420
1957	155	178	106	7,525	40	182	536	105,463
1958	187	161	120	7,308	47	184	581	104,441
1959	202	147	138	7,908	42	189	642	106,744
1960	166	139	153	8,525	41	209	688	110,938
1961	161	139	178	8,403	45	233	732	109,704
1962	154	150	204	8,500	57	246	793	113,132
1963	179	144	183	8,550	76	272	802	114,943
1964	203	175	225	10,280	97	276	870	120,876

D21   NORTH AMERICA: Output of Beer (in thousands of hectolitres)

	Canada[1]	Costa Rica[3]	Cuba	Dominican Republic	El Salvador
1965	13,584	92	993	200	133
1966	14,344	95	1,089	201	131
1967	14,786	99	1,360	176	129
1968	15,057	102	784	252	135
1969	15,921	105	659	314	153
1970	16,864	109	1,002	374	184
1971	18,404	112	1,309	427	204
1972	19,224	140	1,666	488	229
1973	20,347	200	1,851	484	237
1974	20,902	220	1,808	486	329
1975	21,500	270	2,111	445	386
1976	21,712	139	2,169	475	484
1977	21,898	168	2,199	648	578
1978	22,032	170	2,338	804	581
1979	24,106	...	2,307	991	414
1980	22,655	...	2,365	1,173	351
1981	23,085	...	2,243	1,101	427
1982	22,658	...	2,421	1,119	420
1983	23,332	...	2,582	999	344
1984	23,558	...	2,607	945	...
1985	23,237	...	2,736	1,038	...
1986	23,547	...	2,931	1,099	...
1987		...	3,288	1,269	...
1988		...	3,324	...	...
1989			3,333	...	
1990				1,376	
1991				1,459	
1992				1,956	
1993				1,992	

	Guatemala	Honduras	Jamaica	Mexico	Nicaragua	Panama	Puerto Rico[5]	USA
1965	226	190	266	11,080	111	292	894	126,739
1966	241	186	294	11,660	125	307	942	128,759
1967	244	185	311	12,254	140	321	759	136,770
1968	247	201	335	12,519	180	308	824	137,897
1969	272	226	401	13,649	128	353	934	143,920
1970	299	258	432	14,321	137	366	937	157,996
1971	328	283	430	12,656	144	378	593	157,354
1972	356	287	506	15,137	...	284	708	164,671
1973	421	323	567	17,325	...	349	814	167,789
1974	480	298	578	19,732	...	393	454	179,523
1975	526	302	663	19,684	150	423	493	185,389
1976	572	233	606	19,358	160	433	601	179,523[2]
1977	598	309	558	21,642	160	355	463	167,789
1978	700	374	612	22,568	165	433	509	195,434
1979	700	380	515	25,461	357	559	736	216,155
1980	789	433	636	26,876	477	670	721	227,772
1981	718	471	563	28,635	480	694	692	227,303
1982	645	397	581	28,028	470	713	546	228,007
1983	672	469	604	24,139	503	708	377	228,945
1984	715	511	517	25,616	522	734	347	228,955
1985	613	500	568	27,215	...	797	260	228,960
1986	795	548	632	27,353	...	925	261	230,588
1987	869	580	700	31,482	...	1,014	266	229,321
1988	...	656	809	33,261	...	871	360	231,985
1989	...	...	852	37,335	...	1,042	525	232,510
1990	...	...	887	38,734	...	1,162	628	236,670
1991	...	...	715	41,092	...	1,219	644	...
1992	...	...	828	42,262	...	1,163	545	237,092
1993	...	...	786	43,780	...	1,204	397	237,345

D21   SOUTH AMERICA: OUTPUT OF BEER (in thousands of hectolitres)

	Argentina	Bolivia	Brazil[7]	Chile	Colombia	Ecuador	Paraguay	Peru[9]	Uruguay[10]	Venezuela
1891	...	...	...	...	...	...	...	...	[7.5][10]	...
1892	...	...	...	...	...	...	...	...	22	...
1893	...	...	...	...	...	...	...	...	16	...
1894	...	...	...	...	...	...	...	...	19	...
1895	156	...	...	...	...	...	...	...	15	...
1896	...	...	...	...	...	...	...	...	13	...
1897	...	...	...	...	...	...	...	...	12	...
1898	...	...	...	...	...	...	...	...	11	...
1899	...	...	...	...	...	...	...	...	1	...
1900	...	...	...	...	...	...	...	...	15	...
1901	...	...	...	...	...	...	...	...	16	...
1902	...	...	...	...	...	...	...	...	17	...
1903	...	...	...	...	...	...	...	...	19	...
1904	...	...	...	...	...	...	...	...	18	...
1905	...	...	...	...	...	...	...	...	22	...
1906	648	...	...	...	...	...	...	...	30	...
1907	701	...	...	...	...	...	...	...	31	...
1908	816	...	...	...	...	...	...	...	35	...
1909	863	...	...	...	...	...	...	...	39	...
1910	981	...	...	...	...	...	...	...	44	...
1911	1,003	...	681	...	...	...	...	...	52	...
1912	1,094	...	863	...	...	...	...	...	66	...
1913	1,255	...	976	...	...	...	...	...	79	...
1914	751	...	879	...	...	...	...	...	68	...
1915	733	...	765	...	...	...	...	...	47	...
1916	772	...	726	...	...	...	...	...	50	...
1917	788	...	586	430	...	...	...	...	53	...
1918	962	...	600	430	...	...	...	...	60	...
1919	...	...	799	...	...	...	...	...	68	...
1920	...	...	819	450	...	...	...	...	89	...
1921	...	...	898	394	...	...	...	...	87	...
1922	...	...	1,108	355	...	...	...	...	91	...
1923	...	...	1,243	531	...	...	...	...	97	...
1924	...	...	1,277	613	...	...	...	...	95	...
1925	2,002	...	1,423	515	...	...	...	...	109	...
1926	2,030	...	1,426	...	...	...	...	...	117	...
1927	2,127	...	1,580	412	...	...	...	20	143	...
1928	1,981	...	1,742	418	...	...	...	17	135	...
1929	2,132	...	1,766	508	...	...	...	18	159	...
1930	1,828	...	1,456	552	...	...	17	112	152	...
1931	1,347	...	1,063	371	...	...	...	88	147	...
1932	1,158	...	1,076	367	...	...	4.6	71	121[10]	...
1933	983	...	1,141	392	...	...	4.6	70	102	...
1934	1,344	...	1,181	444	...	...	7.1	88	116	...
1935	1,330	...	1,792	578	...	...	13	104	112	...
1936	1,237	...	1,905	623	648	...	11	122	123	...
1937	1,436	129	1,953	699	581	...	7.7	142	142	115
1938	1,412	155	1,857	619	...	125	7.2	149	149	141
1939	1,539	155	2,077	675	...	118	7.7	186	156	192

D21 SOUTH AMERICA: Output of Beer (in thousands of hectolitres)

	Argentina	Bolivia	Brazil[7]	Chile	Colombia	Ecuador	Paraguay	Peru[9]	Uruguay	Venezuela
1940	1,478	149	2,061	781	783	127	7.8	194	178	219
1941	1,476	175	2,013	726	881	147	7.8	209	166	216
1942	1,848	193	1,982	635	914	209	10	239	187	217
1943	2,161	224	2,257	664	913	262	16	262	189	241
1944	2,298	215	3,139	642	...	274	23	311	193	316
1945	2,575	214	...	684	1,226	257	31	345	210	401
1946	2,467	215	...	790	...	257	35	368	239	437
1947	3,151	221	...	852	1,842	269	28	351	276	502
1948	3,446	267	...	880	2,334	234	39	316	213	578
1949	3,738	278	...	920	2,514	222	40	334	368	683
1950	3,894	274	...	915	3,327	262	32	444	411	806
1951	4,009	305	...	914	3,380	356	41	556	459	1,007
1952	3,881	299	...	1,072	3,856	437	53	663	561	1,187
1953	3,447	290	...	1,240	4,423	492	57	811	...	1,244
1954	3,732	285	...	1,203	4,657	582	55	923	...	1,280
1955	3,689	219	7,131	1,332	4,512	570	52	963[9]	...	1,348
1956	3,522	220	6,553	1,421	4,727	553[8] 332	45	984	...	1,395
1957	3,568	194	6,242	1,416	5,182	370	52	1,219	621	1,539
1958	3,875	196	7,502	1,199	5,990	399	53	1,171	626	1,891
1959	2,323	168	...	1,118	5,923[8] 6,155	402	55	1,203	629	2,162
1960	2,430	176	...	1,307	6,425	406	51	1,461	525	2,411
1961	2,436	199	...	1,199	6,471	390	64	1,429	1,038	2,407
1962	1,987	216	7,360	1,309	6,514	378	62	1,541	638	2,477
1963	1,239	235	7,167	1,253	6,529	345	82	1,637	956	2,488
1964	1,722	257	6,605	1,093	6,632	417	86	1,646	689	2,626
1965	2,492	249	7,576	1,649	6,854	441	85	1,726	646	2,779
1966	2,256	287	8,441	1,774	6,837	446	97	2,098	517	2,971
1967	2,496	302	7,845	1,761	5,847	442	103	2,121	494	3,324
1968	3,012	306	7,969	1,727	5,671	502	114	2,188	660	3,559
1969	3,172	341	9,087	1,563	6,395	516	157	2,320	...	4,844
1970	3,565	381	9,132	1,776	7,058	647	175	2,344	810	4,954
1971	2,970	412	10,450	2,192	...	643	164	2,940	860	4,367
1972	2,970	426	9,723	2,293	7,720	740	181	3,000	865	4,504
1973	3,033	442	11,298	2,058	7,649	822	208	3,426	745	4,600
1974	4,456	563	12,157	1,054	8,194	889	253	3,826	620	4,580
1975	3,955	752	12,518[7]	1,833	8,406	1,060	301	4,296	670	4,261
1976	2,839	957	40,825	1,083	9,577	1,370	332	5,096	600	4,400
1977	2,710	1,058	21,519	1,361	10,578	1,677	451	4,691	650	4,600
1978	2,048	1,113	31,897	1,404	11,317	1,957	514	3,964	660	4,750
1979	2,148	814	[30,089][7]	1,591	11,467	2,010	591	4,600	670	4,900
1980	2,280	1,162	27,824	1,808	12,871	632	621	5,325	...	...
1981	2,102	1,141	28,928	1,904	13,536	728	632	5,141	...	...
1982	2,225	901	...	1,797	13,383	769	696	5,556	...	...
1983	3,157	717	25,861	1,760	14,494	626	717	5,230	...	...
1984	4,079	701	25,980	1,781	...	...	753	5,388	...	...
1985	3,827	606	27,092	1,892	15,509	...	768	5,724	468	...
1986	5,548	803	34,002	2,050	16,915	...	887	7,477	678	...
1987	5,861	...	33,893	2,548	15,355	...	918	8,559	709	...
1988	5,232	1,179	36,445	2,650	11,973	...	903	7,018	603	...
1989	5,110	965	42,343	2,765	14,027	...	1,055	5,548	...	...
1990	6,173	1,031	43,849	2,657	15,098	...	1,076	5,732	...	...
1991	7,991	1,278	54,545	2,788	...	...	1,126	6,774	...	...
1992	9,518	1,333	43,509	3,349	...	1,826	1,163	6,764	...	...
1993	10,305	1,047	45,336	3,631	...	...	1,710	7,060	817	...

D21 Output of Beer

NOTES

1. SOURCES: The national publications listed on pp.xiii–xv and League of Nations and UN, *Statistical Yearbooks*.
2. All types of beer have been aggregated in this table, including virtually non-alcoholic malt liquor, though home-brewed beer is not covered.

FOOTNOTES

[1] Years beginning 1 April.
[2] Years ending 30 June to 1976 and years ending 30 September thereafter. Alaska and Hawaii are included throughout except for the period 7 April to 30 June 1933.
[3] Years ending 30 September.
[4] Years beginning 1 April to 1943.
[5] Years ending 30 June.
[6] 11 months.
[7] Production by main establishments only to 1975 and In 1979.
[8] The reason for this break is not given in the source.
[9] Consumption of domestically produced beer to 1955.
[10] Years ending 30 June from 1892 to 1932. The 1891 figure is for the first half-year only.

D22 NORTH AMERICA: OUTPUT OF ELECTRIC ENERGY (in gigaWatt hours)

	Bahamas[1]	Barbados[2]	Canada[3]	Cuba[4]	Dominican Republic[5]	Guatemala[6]	Jamaica[7]
1919	...	...	5,497	...	...	...	...
1920	...	...	5,895	...	...	...	...
1921	...	...	5,614	...	...	...	...
1922	...	...	6,741	...	...	...	...
1923	...	...	8,099	...	...	...	...
1924	...	...	9,315	...	...	...	...
1925	...	...	10,110	...	...	...	...
1926	...	...	12,093	...	...	...	...
1927	...	...	14,549[3]	...	...	...	...
			15,377				
1928	...	...	17,509	236	...	...	...
1929	2.9	...	19,306	263	...	...	...
1930	...	...	19,468	265	...	...	...
1931	...	...	17,620	235	...	...	...
1932	...	...	17,453	213	...	...	...
1933	...	...	18,697	208	...	...	...
1934	...	...	22,749	235	...	...	...
1935	...	...	24,927	252	...	...	...
1936	...	...	27,099	274	13	...	...
1937	4.9	...	30,225	307	15	25	16
1938	5.3	3.1	28,603	324	24	27	18
1939	...	...	30,979	343	23	28	20
1940	...	...	33,062	356	28	29	27
1941	...	...	36,479	370	28	30	30
1942	...	...	41,007	379	28	32	31
1943	...	...	43,950	397	25	35	29
1944	...	...	43,571	430	29	32	35

D22   NORTH AMERICA: Output of Electric Energy (in gigaWatt hours)

	Martinique	Mexico[5]	Panama[8]	Puerto Rico	Trinidad & Tobago[10]	USA[5]
1902	...	...	...	...	...	5,969
1907	...	...	...	...	...	14,121
1912	...	...	...	...	...	24,752
1917	...	...	...	...	...	43,429
1920	...	...	...	...	...	56,559
1921	...	...	...	...	...	53,125
1922	...	...	...	...	...	61,204
1923	...	...	...	...	...	71,399
1924	...	...	...	...	...	75,892
1925	...	...	...	...	...	84,666
1926	...	1,262	...	...	...	94,222
1927	...	1,381	...	...	...	101,390
1928	...	...	...	...	...	108,069
1929	...	...	...	...	...	116,747
1930	...	1,464	...	...	...	114,637
1931	...	1,490	...	...	...	109,373
1932	...	1,425	...	...	...	99,359
1933	...	1,529	...	...	3.5	102,655
1934	...	1,834	...	...	3.7	110,404
1935	2.0	2,064	...	...	4.1	118,935
1936	2.7	2,245	...	...	4.3	136,006
1937	2.7	2,480	27	120	4.7	146,476
1938	3.3	2,512	29	134	5.4	141,955
1939	3.8	2,462	31	155	7.4	161,308
1940	4.8	2,529	37	173	8.5	179,907
1941	6.0	2,524	44	214	14.0	208,306
1942	6.1	2,625	45	235	18.0	233,146
1943	4.9	2,739	50	265	23.0	267,540
1944	5.4	2,750	54	283	25.0	279,525

D22   NORTH AMERICA: Output of Electric Energy (in gigaWatt hours)

	Bahamas[1]	Barbados[2]	Belize	Bermuda	Canada[3]	Costa Rica	Cuba[4]	Dominician Republic[5]
1945	...	...	...	...	42,720	...	488	34
1946	...	...	...	...	44,663	...	532	40
1947	...	...	...	...	47,174	...	571	49
1948	13	10	...	...	47,262	...	639	58
1949	15	...	...	...	50,890[3]	...	690	72
1950	16	11	...	38	55,382	180	758	79
1951	19	11	...	41	61,776	190	836	96
1952	22	12	...	44	66,497	200	918	112
1953	24	17	...	48	70,301	219	1,006	167
1954	28	18	...	51	74,540	241	1,088	185
1955	32	20	...	57	82,221	271	1,200[4] 1,842	195
1956	37	22	...	60	88,455	328	2,063	232
1957	45	25	...	69	91,115	347	2,358	258
1958	51	28	4.4	76	97,526	365	2,589	284
1959	65	33	5.2	80	104,671	387	2,806	316
1960	76	38	5.8	92	114,457	438	2,981	349
1961	89	43	6.2	103	113,713	461	3,030	372
1962	101	47	6.8	118	117,469	491	2,998	439
1963	113	53[2]	9.2	124	122,325	518	3,057	452
1964	123	66	11.0	133	143,987	573	3,250	532
1965	137[1]	75	12.0	146	144,274	660	3,423	500
1966	250	78	14.0	163	158,135	697	4,074	623
1967	300	95	15.0	174	165,625	757	4,486	697
1968	370	110	18.0	190	176,378	833	4,700	761
1969	422	131	22.0	208	191,102	901	4,266	864
1970	489	146	23.0	226	204,723	1,028	4,888	1,003
1971	543	160	26.0	251	216,472	1,148	5,021	1,068
1972	631	188	28.0	278	240,213	1,266	5,265	1,687
1973	645	212	32.0	300	263,335	1,346	5,703	2,254
1974	662	203	35.0	299	280,256	1,467	6,018	2,406
1975	684	214	39.0	299	273,392	1,531	6,583	2,556
1976	649	228	43.0	311	294,043	1,701	7,191	2,580
1977	687	264	45.0	327	326,184	1,828	7,706	2,243
1978	743	287	48.0	333	345,165	1,998	8,481	2,395
1979	829	315	53.0	333	363,176	2,000	9,403	3,268
1980	853	332	54.0	332	337,518	2,202	9,990	3,317
1981	762	349	55.0	342	390,937	2,349	10,576	3,582
1982	814	355	57.0	353	387,460	2,457	11,071	3,206
1983	871	375	58.0	368	408,443	2,918	11,551	3,400
1984	866	383	67.0	382	437,990	3,069	12,292	4,009
1985	900	390	71.0	390	459,045	2,826	12,199	4,229
1986	905	390	74.0	390	468,593	2,949	13,176	4,614
1987	907	425	80.0	426	496,335	3,133	13,594	5,296
1988	910	449	90.0	450	505,966	3,193	14,543	5,244
1989	925	441	95.0	441	499,536	3,350	15,240	5,300
1990	950	468	105	468	482,025	3,544	14,678	5,325
1991	965	527	105	527	507,913	3,808	12,741	5,330
1992	975	537	110	537	520,857	4,144	11,127	5,330
1993	980	548	110	548	527,316	4,386	11,054	6,182

D22 NORTH AMERICA: Output of Electric Energy (in gigaWatt hours)

	El Salvador	Guadeloupe	Guatemala[6]	Haiti	Honduras	Jamaica[7]	Martinique	Mexico[5]
1945	...	...	35	...	...	37	5.9	3,069
1946	...	...	39	...	...	46	7.4	3,317
1947	...	...	41	...	...	52	8.8	3,599
1948	...	2.4	45[6] / 55	...	...	56	9.8	3,969
1949	...	3.0	62	...	...	67	11	4,328
1950	65	4.0	70[6] / 80	[9.6][13]	46	76[6] / 166	12	4,423
1951	70	6.0	95	18.0	55	188	12	4,908
1952	93	...	105	16.0	60	209	13	5,337
1953	125	7.1	115	19	62	228	14	5,703
1954	133	7.3	125	21	54	257	15	6,282
1955	144	8.5	140	23	59	285	16	7,002
1956	165	9.4	171	27	66	328	17	8,173
1957	185	11	193	34	75	373	18	8,463
1958	213	14	219	47	80	390	20	9,057
1959	235	17	243	53	86	453	21	9,693
1960	256	21	281	60	97	508	23	10,813
1961	273	24	291	65[14] / 90	102	580	25	11,754
1962	300	29	324	95	108	610	28	12,608
1963	340	34	364	95	115	649	32	13,645
1964	379	40	434	95	128	712	37	15,736
1965	418	46	449	96	175	798	45	17,245
1966	477	52	492	100	204	867	54	18,843
1967	524	62	531	105	232	977	63	20,658
1968	569	75	589	110	268[14]	1,069	74	22,781
1969	617	88	720	115	282	1,275	87	25,554
1970	671	99	759	118	315	1,541	103	28,707
1971	743	110	847	120	347	1,676	128	31,313
1972	836	123	936	133	389	2,022	143	34,457
1973	912	140	1,020	141	436	2,187	161	37,084
1974	986	155	1,104	145	490	2,283	171	40,766
1975	1,059	167	1,167	158	545	2,331	179	43,329
1976	1,161	190	1,245	209	606	2,378	194	48,387
1977	1,303	220	1,443	215	682	2,375	220	52,704
1978	1,451	255	1,554	246	756	2,279	242	57,257
1979	1,578	265	1,618	280	847	2,218	253	62,860
1980	1,543	310	1,671	315	928	2,195	275	66,954
1981	1,474	345	1,668	325	1,014	2,213	298	73,559
1982	1,489	395	1,623	360	1,090	2,252	340	80,589
1983	1,600	410	1,617	373	1,150	2,399	392	82,243
1984	1,684	461	1,587	385	1,060	2,288	409	86,971
1985	1,800	491	1,651	411	1,065	2,286	442	93,405
1986	1,762	546	1,823	438	1,075	2,452	477	97,117
1987	1,976	622	1,966	445	1,085	2,606	536	104,791
1988	2,043	681	2,160	470	1,090	2,585[22]	585	109,861
1989	2,098	637	2,313	470	2,033	1,886	639	118,102
1990	2,296	747	2,330	475	2,287	2,008	682	122,448
1991	2,364	824	2,493	470	2,319	2,053	738	126,807
1992	2,457	901	2,822	430	2,313	2,140	789	130,108
1993	2,858	960	3,084	394	2,464	2,216	792	134,925

D22 NORTH AMERICA: Output of Electric Energy (in gigaWatt hours)

	Netherlands Antilles	Nicaragua	Panama[8]	Panama Canal Zone[9]	Puerto Rico[9]	Trinidad & Tobago[10]	USA[5,11]	US Virgin Islands[5]
1945	...	...	53	...	306	30	271,255	...
1946	...	...	61	...	344	32	269,361	...
1947	...	...	69	...	419	35	307,310	...
1948	...	77	70	266	476	40	336,808	...
1949	...	79	74	270	517	45	345,066	...
1950	660	80	85[8] / 103	252	580	48[10] / 168	388,674	4.9
1951	660	84	108	235	660	192	433,358	6.8
1952	660	90	116	254	735	211	463,055	7.7
1953	660	96	124	267	837	236	514,169	10
1954	665	105	132	254	895	260	544,645	12
1955	670	110	142	253	1,050	279	629,010	16
1956	686	119	157	258	1,225	311	684,804	19
1957	719	128	175	255	1,494	330	716,356	22
1958	784	143	197	250	1,641	383	724,752[11]	25
1959	813	166	217	246	1,875	449	797,567	29
1960	825	183	230	269	2,151	470	844,188	34
1961	824	195	263	301	2,438	504	881,496	44
1962	859	212	325	330	2,742	570	946,526	52
1963	869	251	348	368	3,164	626	1,011,418	69
1964	1,022	281	420	418	3,638	817	1,083,741	76
1965	1,080	311	510	444	4,100	908	1,157,583	97
1966	1,168	366	524	489	4,730	1,007	1,249,444	125
1967	1,144	411	582	585	5,409	1,035	1,317,301	172
1968	1,178	484	670	614	6,182	1,119	1,436,028	258
1969	1,267	551	859	638	7,110[9]	1,213	1,552,757	388
1970	1,289	627	956	570	7,308	1,202	1,639,771	578
1971	1,419	657	1,037	634	8,818	1,226	1,717,521	621
1972	1,500	754	1,151	713	10,299	1,307	1,853,390	670
1973	1,550	714	1,359	678	11,642	1,210	1,964,830	705
1974	1,600	874	1,434	735	11,781	1,314	1,967,289	720
1975	1,690	932	1,447	708	10,974	1,207	2,003,002	720
1976	1,660	1,038	1,546	674	12,839	1,412	2,123,406	720
1977	1,650	1,142	1,630	543	13,554	1,576	2,211,031	740
1978	1,834	1,136	1,564	634	13,850	1,675	2,285,880	760
1979	2,060[14] / 1,675	951	1,893	552	13,340	1,818	2,318,783	790
1980	1,090	1,068	1,813		13,206	2,056	2,354,384	800
1981	1,100	1,106	1,905		12,866	2,301	2,359,258	845
1982	1,250	1,054	2,092		11,863	2,683	2,302,287	855
1983	1,275	941	2,262		12,066	2,905	2,367,634	875
1984	1,175	973	2,272		12,557	2,998	2,479,297	880
1985	1,125	1,059	2,450		12,316	3,018	2,567,276	900
1986	...	1,063	2,689		12,870	3,297	2,597,518	920
1987	...	1,063	2,902		13,757	3,479	2,716,004	963
1988	...	1,068	2,638		14,403	3,470	2,853,740	970
1989	...	1,361	2,664		14,310	3,436	2,971,356	950
1990	...	1,398	2,771		15,328	3,578	2,835,241	980
1991	...	1,468	2,910		15,730	3,754	3,073,448	1,000
1992	...	1,586	3,016		16,434	3,945	3,114,856	1,020
1993	...	1,683	3,286		16,540	3,817	3,201,843	1,040

D22 SOUTH AMERICA: OUTPUT OF ELECTRIC ENERGY (in gigaWatt hours)

	Argentina[14]	Bolivia[14]	Brazil[15]	Chile[16]	Colombia[17]	Paraguay[18]	Peru[19]	Uruguay[20]	Venezuela[21]
1909	...	...	...	...	...	...	...	7	...
1910	...	...	...	...	...	...	...	10	...
1911	...	...	...	...	...	...	...	14	...
1912	...	...	...	...	...	...	...	20	...
1913	...	...	...	...	...	...	...	23	...
1914	...	...	...	...	...	...	...	23	...
1915	...	...	...	...	...	...	...	24	...
1916	...	...	...	...	...	...	...	30	...
1917	...	...	...	...	...	...	...	34	...
1918	...	...	...	...	...	...	...	37	...
1919	...	...	...	...	...	...	...	45	...
1920	...	...	...	...	...	...	...	51	...
1921	...	...	...	...	...	...	...	54	...
1922	...	...	...	...	...	...	...	56	...
1923	...	...	...	113	...	...	...	61	...
1924	...	...	...	165	...	...	...	65[20]	...
								76	
1925	...	...	...	214	...	...	...	84	...
1926	...	...	...	239	...	...	...	87	...
1927	1,045	...	...	255	...	...	...	97	...
1928	1,130	...	520	257	...	...	...	109	...
1929	1,292	...	540	285	...	...	...	125	...
1930	1,433	...	535	312	...	...	...	142	...
1931	1,474	...	541	312	...	...	41	158	...
1932	1,550	...	555	293	...	...	36	151	...
1933	1,615	...	610	320	92	...	38	148	...
1934	1,735	...	687	365	110	...	45	162	...
1935	1,861	...	768	391	131	...	53	166	...
1936	2,051	...	849	422	165	...	60	201	...
1937	2,199	48	1,025	477	186	...	69	203	...
1938	2,328	67	1,122	502	213	...	76	229	106
1939	2,461	71	1,210	509	251	...	87	245	112
1940	2,550	85	1,276	570	254	...	98	282	137
1941	2,644	93	1,391	614	270	13	110	...	160
1942	2,773	98	1,498	640	280	14	122	...	170
1943	2,927	118	1,621	697	302	15	129	...	175
1944	3,064	118	1,778	730	340	17	138	...	189

D22   SOUTH AMERICA: Output of Electric Energy (in giga Watt hours)

	Argentina[4]	Bolivia[4]	Brazil[15]	Chile[16]	Colombia[17]	Ecuador
1945	2,976	131	1,899	893	396	...
1946	3,263	138	2,032	987	463	...
1947	3,576	145	2,204	1,083	517	...
1948	4,034	171	2,452[15]	1,166[16]	545	105
			6,797	2,906		
1949	4,121	172	7,610	2,844	625	125
1950	4,430[4]	174[4]	8,208	2,943	705[17]	118
	5,155	226			1,147	
1951	5,468	225	8,758	3,224	1,254	141
1952	5,551	230	10,029	3,361	1,440	153
1953	5,963	370	10,341	3,337	1,663	167
1954	6,466	390	11,871	3,590	1,950	188
1955	7,035	387	13,655	3,866	2,250	259
1956	7,665	400	15,447	4,046	2,403	281
1957	8,191	421	16,963	4,190	2,850	299
1958	9,418	444	19,766	4,146	3,034	324
1959	9,544	433	21,108	4,605	3,413	349
1960	10,459	447	22,865	4,592	3,750	387
1961	11,547	463	24,405	4,880	3,776	411
1962	11,887	495	27,158	5,286	4,280	451
1963	12,449	531	27,869	5,623	5,268	495
1964	13,928	534	29,094	5,932	5,916	551
1965	15,383	566	30,128	6,131	5,824	572
1966	15,927	619	32,654	6,662	6,319	609
1967	16,687	640	34,238	6,892	7,055	672
1968	17,952	702	38,181	6,918	7,197	749
1969	20,014	739	41,648	7,214	8,157	850
1970	21,727	787	45,460	7,550	8,750	949
1971	23,624	832	50,988	8,524	9,500	1,050
1972	25,306	872	56,995	8,934	10,999	1,117
1973	26,660	918	64,727	8,766	11,881	1,256
1974	27,951	993	71,698	9,297	12,613	1,430
1975	29,468	1,057	78,936	8,732	13,345	1,650
1976	30,216	1,132	89,979	9,276	14,757	1,885
1977	32,413	1,260	100,822	9,776	15,369	2,260
1978	33,434	1,354	112,575	10,360	17,358	2,565
1979	37,640	1,432	124,673	11,133	19,139	2,954
1980	39,676	1,564	139,485	11,751	20,624	3,352
1981	38,838	1,677	142,198	11,979	20,704	3,730
1982	39,804	1,677	151,999	11,872	26,183	4,118
1983	42,998	1,668	161,969	12,624	27,334	4,289
1984	44,914	1,511	178,532	13,498	29,888	4,207
1985	45,265	1,510	192,731	14,040	30,268	4,806
1986	48,984	1,515	201,353	14,820	33,564	5,301
1987	52,165	1,520	202,349	15,636	31,103	5,353
1988	53,062[22]	1,883	214,951	16,914	33,201	5,603
1989	46,010	2,009	221,731	17,810	34,602	5,736
1990	47,412	2,133	222,821	18,372	35,396	6,327
1991	50,619	2,275	234,366	19,961	36,661	6,952
1992	54,521	2,412	241,731	22,362	35,993	7,165
1993	59,353	2,445	251,484	24,004	40,298	7,447

D22 SOUTH AMERICA: Output of Electric Energy (in gigaWatt hours)

	French Guiana	Guyana	Paraguay[18]	Peru[19]	Surinam	Uruguay[20]	Venezuela
1945	...	...	19	150	...	...	212
1946	...	...	21	164	...	350	239
1947	...	...	21	182	...	...	282
1948	...	...	28[18]	204	...	532	344
			37				
1949	0.2	...	40	232	...	574	409
1950	0.4	...	44	237[19]	35	616	520[21]
				322			1,220
1951	0.7	38	48	344	35	682	1,460
1952	1.0	43	52	461[19]	38	753	1,670
				1,051			
1953	...	44	55	1,219	40	845	1,988
1954	1.7	50	60	1,384	42	927	2,190
1955	2.3	55	64	1,524	43	1,024	2,385
1956	2.6	59	65	1,594	55	1,065	2,650
1957	2.9	67	75	1,792	66	1,155	3,103
1958	3.2	70	82	1,990	66	1,237	3,791
1959	3.8	72	87	2,219	72	1,176	4,497
1960	4.4	92	96	2,656	79	1,244	4,651
1961	4.7	124	107	2,945	87	1,327	5,217
1962	5.8	147	107	3,067	112	1,559	5,922
1963	7.4	143	125	3,419	119	1,578[20]	6,771
						1,639	
1964	8.7	212	129	3,689	128	1,819	7,597
1965	11	220	135	3,839	244	1,744	8,197
1966	13	240	151	4,336	681	1,918	8,593
1967	20	260	165	4,770	843	1,944	9,277
1968	29	287	179	5,008	1,076	1,940	10,646
1969	42	312	203	5,288	1,242	2,090	11,494
1970	55	323	218	5,529	1,322	2,200	12,708
1971	60	329	246	5,949	1,362	2,360	13,386
1972	62	340	273	6,289	1,465	2,405	14,829
1973	67	361	379	6,655	1,528	2,520	16,077
1974	63	370	504	7,275	1,588	2,358	18,222
1975	66	383	599	7,486	1,201	2,444	19,591
1976	65	392	604	7,911	1,335	2,665	20,539
1977	71	431	532	8,627	1,421	2,876	23,452
1978	89	409	516	8,765	1,511	3,046	25,955
1979	102	407	644	9,265	1,530	2,960	32,033
1980	113	414	725	10,039	1,577	3,355	35,932
1981	124	429	747	10,757	1,367	3,603	37,542
1982	138	354	681	11,350	1,332	3,593	39,964
1983	164	400	818	10,675	1,107	7,343	43,493
1984	181	400	920	11,717	1,250	7,244	44,330
1985	207	390	1,260	12,115	1,300	6,602	47,997
1986	223	390	1,643	12,941	1,325	7,429	51,093
1987	249	385	2,290	13,785	1,729	7,578	54,706
1988	282	385	2,900	13,544	1,918	6,998	57,773
1989	313	...	...	13,358	1,370	5,749	57,620
1990	353	...	3,334	13,817	1,504	7,443	59,507
1991	405	...	3,608	14,492	1,400	7,017	60,237
1992	445	...	3,331	13,145	1,386	8,898	69,460
1993	446	...	3,858	14,326	1,392	7,989	71,388

D22 Output of Electric Energy

NOTES

1. SOURCES: The national publications listed on pp. xiii–xv; League of Nations and UN, *Statistical Yearbooks*; UN, *World Energy Supplies*.
2. Except as indicated in footnotes, the statistics are of gross output (i.e. inclusive of electricity consumed in the power stations and of transmission losses).

FOOTNOTES

[1] Excluding Out islands to 1965.
[2] Years ended 30 June to 1963.
[3] Net output, excluding output of industrial and railway establishments to 1927 (1st line). Newfoundland is included from 1950. Its output in 1930 was 795.
[4] Public supply only to 1955 (1st line).
[5] Net output.
[6] Consumption in Guatemala City and neighbourhood to 1948 (1st line). Public supply only in 1949 and 1950 (1st line).
[7] Public supply only to 1950 (1st line).
[8] Public supply of Panama City and Colón only to 1950 (1st line).
[9] Years ended 30 June, beginning 1970 in the case of Puerto Rico.
[10] Public supply only, excluding San Fernando to 1950 (1st line).
[11] Including Alaska and Hawaii from 1959.
[12] Belize town only to 1962.
[13] January–September.
[14] The reason for this break is not given in the source.
[15] Rio de Janeiro and São Paulo cities only to 1948 (1st line). Total production to 1939 was 2,987.
[16] Public supply only to 1948 (1st line). Total supply in 1938 was 1,634.
[17] Three main enterprises only to 1950 (1st line).
[18] Ascension only to 1948 (1st line).
[19] Lima and Callao only to 1950 (1st line). Public supply only in 1949 and 1950 (1st line).
[20] Public supply only to 1963 (1st line). Data to 1924 (1st line) are for Montevideo only and are for years beginning 1 July.
[21] Public supply in the state of Miranda plus 24 enterprises in the rest of the country to 1950 (1st line). Total public supply in 1950 was 552.
[22] This break can be explained by a change to national sources.

D23 IMPORTS AND EXPORTS OF COAL BY MAIN TRADING COUNTRIES
(in thousands of metric tons)

| | NORTH AMERICA | | | | SOUTH AMERICA |
| | Canada[1] | | USA | | Argentina[2] |
	Imports	Exports	Imports	Exports	Imports
1867	...	...	518	289	...
1868	...	240	400	283	...
1869	...	399	445	...	...
1870	...	260	423	232	...
1871	...	288	438	272	...
1872	...	269	493	407	...
1873	...	367	469	594	...
1874	...	379	501	776	...
1875	...	261	444	528	...
1976	...	252	409	577	...
1877	...	227	504	752	...
1878	...	308	582	671	...
1879	...	287	495	673	...
1880	886	313	479	625	...
1881	1,051	381	664	664	...
1882	1,157	382	808	882	...
1883	1,520	403	657	1,038	...
1884	1,813	410	763	1,316	...
1885	1,762	435₁	787	1,292	...
1886	1,781	473	826	1,231	...
1887	2,069	527	847	1,557	409
1888	3,084	534	1,128	1,860	336
1889	2,341	603	1,039	1,822	661
1890	2,417	657	965	1,961	516
1891	2,774	881	1,110	2,374	354
1892	2,881	748	1,420	2,594	522
1893	2,915	871	1,174	3,156	586
1894	2,729	1,002	1,258	3,678	751
1895	2,750	917	1,423	3,907	854
1896	3,015	1,004	1,367	3,654	869
1897	2,927	894	1,334	3,742	784
1898	3,061	1,043	1,297	4,098	885
1899	3,804	1,173	1,279	5,272	1,101

D23 Imports and Exports of Coal by Main Trading Countries (in thousands of metric tons)

| | NORTH AMERICA | | | | SOUTH AMERICA | |
| | Canada[1] | | USA | | Argentina[2] | Brazil |
	Imports	Exports	Imports	Exports	Imports	Imports
1900	4,013	1,622	1,735	7,179	780	...
1901	4,413	1,428	2,009	7,882	939	793
1902	4,707	1,898	2,145	6,410	1,060	944
1903	5,007	1,774	3,847	7,335	1,079	920
1904	6,293	1,412	2,051	8,802	1,431	988
1905	6,741	1,483	1,581	9,082	1,501	1,055
1906	6,753[1]	1,665	1,882	9,523	2,358	1,208
1907	9,662	1,718	1,727	11,695	2,357	1,301
1908	9,341	1,569	2,029	12,840	2,869	1,355
1909	8,957	1,441	1,251	12,052	2,234	1,348
1910	9,614	2,156	1,659	13,650	3,354	1,582
1911	13,208	1,362	1,793	15,640	3,746	1,736
1912	13,241	1,930	1,323	18,693	3,739[2] 3,532	2,099
1913	16,513	1,417	1,605	20,562	3,801	2,262
1914	13,355	1,291	1,396	19,849	3,221	1,540
1915	11,309	1,603	1,547	20,631	2,525	1,164
1916	15,949	1,937	1,560	23,515	1,728	1,024
1917	18,921	1,572	1,325	27,077	627	818
1918	19,667	1,648	952	24,783	712	637
1919	15,688	1,878	993	22,762	1,170	927
1920	17,095	2,321	1,158	39,844	1,909[2] 2,046	1,121
1921	16,603	1,803	1,149	25,227	1,721	843
1922	11,815	1,650	4,803	13,664	2,220	1,176
1923	19,042	1,500	1,979	24,080	2,579	1,470
1924	15,173	701	485	19,158	3,299	1,620
1925	14,832	713	894	18,725	3,148	1,703
1926	15,040	933	1,179	35,654	2,808	1,772
1927	16,408	1,010	607	19,358	3,489	2,008
1928	15,609	784	845	17,690	3,122	1,950
1929	16,514	765	891	18,901	3,136	2,067
1930	17,031	567	831	16,719	3,061	1,746
1931	11,903	327	766	12,613	2,619	1,134
1932	10,849	259	720	9,178	2,387	1,099
1933	10,164	235	592	9,137	2,246	1,207
1934	11,771	278	597	11,038	2,480	1,080
1935	10,958	379	701	10,297	2,388	1,315
1936	11,905	374	805	11,188	2,633	1,290
1937	13,309	322	578	13,661	3,075	1,516
1938	11,804	320	548	11,248	2,787	1,382
1939	13,507	341	608	12,864	2,925	1,201
1940	15,810	458	460	17,358	2,023	1,150
1941	18,496	482	422	21,881	1,012	1,013
1942	22,622	740	579	24,841	519	593
1943	25,500	1,007	726	27,193	576	538
1944	26,058[1]	916	435	27,413	617	468

D23 Imports and Exports of Coal by Main Trading Countries (in thousands of metric tons)

| | NORTH AMERICA | | | | SOUTH AMERICA | |
| | Canada[1] | | USA | | Argentina[2] | Brazil |
	Imports	Exports	Imports	Exports	Imports	Imports
1945	22,736	763	424	28,710	768	698
1946	23,684	782	404	43,267	1,144	1,038
1947	26,210	649	272	70,014	1,215	1,531
1948	28,008	1,155	265	47,723	2,177	1,060
1949	[20,135][1]	392	286	29,742	1,341	767
1950	24,453	358	331	26,635	1,447	1,083
1951	24,313	395	289	56,861	2,168	1,005
1952	22,619	353	264	47,387	1,740	885
1953	21,102	231	234	33,098	1,184	742
1954	16,852	199	186	30,746	1,506	408
1955	17,907	538	306	49,377	1,177	564
1956	20,510	539	323	66,948	1,352	446
1957	17,669	359	334	73,281	1,156	894
1958	13,144	307	344	47,693	1,354	567
1959	12,912	430	343	35,417	1,321	634
1960	12,303	774	237	34,456	1,402	1,035
1961	11,164	852	150	33,026	1,216	858
1962	11,443	811	218	36,482	620	892
1963	12,130	957	247	45,754	769	866
1964	13,597	1,258	266	44,946	691	1,352
1965	15,054	1,398	167	46,295	657	1,048
1966	14,910	1,449	161	45,421	698	1,744
1967	14,618	1,522	206	45,455	806	1,537
1968	15,429	1,699	203	46,408	520	1,408
1969	15,678	1,771	99	51,584	431	1,921
1970	17,033	4,512	33	65,096	746	1,989
1971	16,462	7,626	101	51,986	717	1,717
1972	17,484	8,264	43	51,474	428	1,856
1973	14,951	11,645	115	48,627	781	1,696
1974	12,389	11,407	1,887	55,043	821	1,596
1975	15,258	12,060	853	60,172	1,027	2,761
1976	14,553	12,241	1,092	54,466	802	3,174
1977	15,266	12,573	1,495	49,285	1,246	3,563
1978	13,226	14,188	2,680	36,946	952	3,640
1979	17,541	14,440	1,868	59,929	405	4,479
1980	15,618	14,701	1,033	83,250	788	4,526
1981	14,620	16,612	946	102,124	878	4,353
1982	15,432	15,885	673	96,440	739	4,236
1983	14,451	17,376	1,153	70,574	492	6,295
1984	18,767	24,816	1,167	73,940	537	8,104
1985	14,727	28,019	1,771	84,102	764	8,260
1986	13,311	25,904	2,007	77,543	1,157	8,442
1987	14,345	26,740	1,585	72,186	1,254	9,660
1988	17,477	31,732	1,936	86,203	1,383	9,282
1989	14,522	32,817	2,587	91,457	1,500	9,710
1990	14,806	32,606	2,163	95,912	862	10,146
1991	11,706	33,051	2,760	98,809	659	10,758
1992	13,749	26,695	3,091	92,955	993	10,399
1993	8,718	29,081	6,631	67,603	967	11,200

D23   Imports and Exports of Coal by Main Trading Countries

NOTES

1. SOURCES: The national publications listed on pp. xiii–xv; League of Nations, *International Trade Statistics*; and UN, *Yearbook of International Trade Statistics*.
2. All kinds of coal are aggregated, but, except as indicated, coke is not included.
3. Coal used for ships' bunkers is not normally included.

FOOTNOTES

[1]   Data to 1885 for exports and to 1906 for imports are for years ending 30 June. Newfoundland is included as part of Canada from 1 April 1949. Briquettes are included to 1944.
[2]   Data to 1912 (1st line) include coke. From 1912 (2nd line) to 1920 (1st line) they are of net imports.

D24 NORTH AMERICA: IMPORTS AND EXPORTS OF PETROLEUM BY MAIN TRADING COUNTRIES (in thousands of metric tons, except as otherwise indicated)

Key: CP = crude petroleum, PP = petroleum products

	Canada[1]		Mexico	Trinidad & Tobago	USA[3]	
	CP		CP & PP	CP & PP	CP	
	Imports[2]	Exports	Exports	Exports	Imports	Exports[4]
	(thousand barrels)			(million gallons)	(thousand barrels)	
1870	...	—	—	—	...	248
1871	...	—	—	—	...	269
1872	...	—	—	—	...	390
1873	...	—	—	—	...	468
1874	...	—	—	—	...	344
1875	...	—	—	—	...	394
1876	...	—	—	—	...	603
1877	...	—	—	—	...	685
1878	...	—	—	—	...	573
1879	...	—	—	—	...	681
1880	20	—	—	—	...	875
1881	41	—	—	—	...	963
1882	86	—	—	—	...	1,072
1883	88	31	—	—	...	1,405
1884	90	10	—	—	...	1,897
1885	108	7	—	—	...	1,939
1886	109	14	—	—	...	1,818
1887	123	6	—	—	...	1,920
1888	129	7	—	—	...	1,846
1889	133	12	—	—	...	2,028
1890	145	13	—	—	...	2,299
1891	145	9	—	—	...	2,303
1892	161	3	—	—	...	2,486[3]
1893	171	2	—	—	...	2,660
1894	188	1	—	—	...	2,903
1895	217	—	—	—	...	2,650
1896	229	—	—	—	...	2,641[3]
1897	240	—	—	—	...	2,893
1898	259[2]	—	—	—	...	2,736
1899	8	—	—	—	...	2,802
1900	10	—	—	—	...	3,290
1901	10	—	—	—	...	3,024
1902	17	—	—	—	...	3,458
1903	61	—	—	—	...	3,012
1904	123	—	—	—	...	2,647
1905	643	—	—	—	...	3,004
1906	[379][1]	—	—	—	...	3,525
1907	712	—	—	—	...	3,007
1908	903	—	—	—	...	3,552
1909	...	—	—	- -	...	4,056
1910	1,532	—	—	—	...	4,288
1911	2,047	—	100	8	...	4,806
1912	3,431	1	1,220	4	...	4,493
1913	4,630	—	3,250	14	17,809	4,633
1914	5,577	—	3,560	12	17,247	2,970

D24   NORTH AMERICA: Imports and Exports of Petroleum by Main Trading Countries (in thousands of metric tons, except as otherwise indicated)

	Canada		Mexico	Trinidad & Tobago			USA			
	CP		CP & PP	CP		PP	CP		PP	
	Imports[2]	Exports	Exports	Imports	Exports	Exports	Imports	Exports	Imports	Exports
	(thousand barrels)			(million gallons)			(thousand barrels)		(million barrels)	
1915	5,503	1	3,760	—	14		18,140	3,768	...	...
1916	7,231	4	4,060	—	34		30,570	4,096	...	...
1917	9,328	—	7,000	—	15	23	30,127	4,098	...	...
1918	10,789	8	7,820	—	13	33	37,736	4,901	...	...
1919	11,585	17	11,380	—	14	35	52,822	6,019	...	...
							(million barrels)			
1920	8,312	77	21,687	—	5	32	106	9.3 / 8.8	2.6	70
1921	10,158	154	25,656	—	4	39	125	9.6	3.4	62
1922	12,014	201	26,951	—	9	47	127	11	8.7	64
1923	11,219	68	20,564	—	12	74	82	18	18	84
1924	13,317	522	19,371	—	12	90	78	18	17	99
1925	12,584	211	14,443	—	11	100	62	13	16	100
1926	16,298	601	10,261	—	13	113	60	15	21	117
1927	19,562	537	6,324	—	16	108	58	16	13	126
1928	24,404	615	4,327	5	26	143	80	19	12	136
1929	30,291	805	3,909	—	32	179	79	26	30	137
1930	28,931	550	4,047	6	37	154	62	24	43	133
1931	29,070	465	3,367	2	93	115	47	26	39	99
1932	25,432	208	3,394	2	92	132	45	27	30	74
1933	27,270	305	3,302	14	41	136	32	37	14	68
1934	30,643	—	3,792	24	17	200	36	41	15	72
1935	33,052	—	3,535	15	10	255	32	51	20	74
1936	35,833	—	3,701	18	15	308	32	50	25	79
1937	38,915	—	3,605	14	22	333	27	67	30	102
1938	34,245	—	1,223	18	23	418	26	77	28	116
1939	37,095	—	1,977	12	8	351	33	72	26	117
1940	42,623	—	1,744	14	6	192	43	51	41	79
1941	46,791	—	2,097	8	6	42	51	33	47	76
1942	44,120	1	828	3	—	14	12	34	24	83
1943	49,754	—	779	—	—	12	14	41	50	109
1944	57,048	—	664	38	—	13	45	34	48	173
1945	56,806	—	1,105	74	—	118	74	33	39	150
1946	63,407	—	1,255	101	3	421	86	42	52	111
1947	68,447	—	1,892	206	31	498	98	46	62	118
1948	75,559	1	1,784	310	73	652	129	40	59	95
1949	73,947	—	1,921	395	89	732	154	33	82	86

D24 NORTH AMERICA: Imports and Exports of Petroleum by Main Trading Countries (in thousands of metric tons, except as otherwise indicated)

1950–1993

| | Canada | | Mexico | | Trinidad & Tobago | | | USA | | | |
| | CP | | CP | PP | CP | | PP | CP | | PP | |
	Imports[2]	Exports	Exports	Exports	Imports	Exports	Exports	Imports	Exports	Imports	Exports
1950	11,351	—	1,836		1,587	310	2,594	24,880	4,705	18,598	6,121
1951	12,018	46	1,138		2,302	278	2,909	25,070	3,865	18,449	11,711
1952	11,717	192	2,184		2,425	267	2,932	29,340	3,610	20,203	12,537
1953	11,469	337	2,354		2,447	289	3,034	33,105	2,695	21,340	12,245
1954	11,367	315	3,514		2,361	430	3,185	34,111	1,838	20,242	10,659
1955	12,500	1,995	4,190		2,522	406	3,721	39,942	1,564	24,225	11,040
1956	15,370	5,771	3,791		2,803	550	4,573	47,922	3,868	26,780	11,536
1957	16,087	7,488	2,326		2,616	488	5,045	52,632	6,790	29,181	15,392
1958	15,133	4,261	1,736		3,660	407	5,944	48,906	587	34,093	7,656
1959	16,210	4,487	1,913		4,465	465	7,057	49,279	341	39,420	7,211
1960	17,749	5,681	1,202		5,733	698	7,761	51,874	418	39,874	6,106
1961	18,664	8,772	2,119		8,749	803	10,136	53,098	436	42,225	4,481
1962	18,850	12,318	2,735		8,966	967	11,019	57,094	242	45,603	4,240
1963	20,645	12,223	2,706		9,728	1,052	13,774	57,361	230	47,604	5,712
1964	20,216	13,619	2,560		11,805	1,501	15,153	60,829	184	50,873	4,828
1965	20,192	14,527	2,603		13,082	1,559	15,546	62,404	136	59,556	4,149
1966	20,271	16,636	2,071		13,048	1,473	16,370	61,573	201	65,841	3,960
1967	23,909	20,221	2,003		11,382	1,962	16,073	56,676	3,586	69,159	5,552
1968	25,042	22,527	2,124		12,948	2,178	17,592	64,915	244	77,083	4,740
1969	25,107	26,542	2,600		14,561	2,469	18,322	70,497	194	86,488	4,336
1970	29,293	32,096	—	2,629	15,713	2,849	17,556	66,239	674	103,087	4,428
1971	34,221	34,848	—	1,872	14,634	2,594	16,488	83,837	68	108,210	3,597
1972	40,519	42,615	—	755	14,841	2,042	16,492	111,114	26	120,400	3,185
1973	43,359	50	—	816	14,096	3,329	15,315	161,269	94	141,883	2,996
1974	41,723	40,111	818	825	12,999	4,506	15,188	172,573	145	122,567	1,894
1975	41,424	30,833	4,848	354	7,895	6,835	9,646	203,124	290	93,079	1,845
1976	36,585	19,960	4,861	152	11,532	6,284	13,138	261,670	397	98,405	1,722
1977	33,613	14,074	10,147	206	8,922	6,993	11,311	325,976	2,461	106,353	1,144
1978	31,158	12,265	18,760	80	7,946	7,161	9,026	313,076	7,783	100,047	1,613
1979	30,928	13,517	26,586	426	7,225	6,267	8,097	321,695	11,555	91,896	1,152
1980	28,095	9,591	34,669	2,189	7,346	6,251	9,344	261,440	14,148	77,404	4,021
1981	25,779	8,041	56,518	3,454	6,928	5,817	6,148	218,244	11,213	70,115	9,350
1982	17,206	10,291	77,573	2,158	3,669	4,375	5,595	174,626	11,632	66,457	19,480
1983	12,564	14,016	79,907	4,039	—	4,841	710	166,934	8,082	66,921	17,314
1984	12,451	17,560	80,206	5,273	—	4,378	3,538	171,943	8,930	76,952	16,262
1985	14,249	23,942	74,340	6,148	189	4,806	3,466	160,861	10,046	65,396	18,168
1986	17,799	28,762	66,746	4,943	217	4,498	3,520	209,471	7,595	78,337	17,680
1987	20,053	30,512	70,048	4,440	249	3,882	3,795	233,923	7,550	74,155	18,361
1988	22,152	34,968	68,140	5,458	648	3,638	3,953	256,123	7,807	86,469	19,405
1989	23,943	31,803	66,442	3,684	600	3,300	3,467	291,923	7,103	83,237	22,171
1990	27,388	30,014	63,804	4,515	720	4,394	3,910	299,851	5,460	85,237	23,140
1991	26,508	37,044	67,822	3,943	1,570	3,884	5,152	289,609	5,845	74,505	30,324
1992	25,270	40,039	68,844	5,255	1,026	3,002	5,552	313,665	4,487	72,240	29,787
1993	28,343	45,022	55,849	6,001	2,345	2,760	4,772	347,433	4,950	77,975	29,468

D24 SOUTH AMERICA: IMPORTS AND EXPORTS OF PETROLEUM BY MAIN TRADING COUNTRIES (in thousands of metric tons)

1900–1944

	Brazil		Colombia	Netherlands Antilles			Peru	Venezuela	
	CP	PP	CP	CP		PP	CP & PP	CP	PP
	Imports	Imports	Exports	Imports	Exports	Exports	Exports	Exports	Exports
1900	...	...	...	...	...	...	—	...	—
1901	...	...	...	...	...	...	—	...	—
1902	...	68	...	...	...	...	1.6	...	—
1903	...	65	...	...	...	...	14	...	—
1904	...	68	...	...	...	...	11	...	—
1905	...	77	...	...	...	...	7.9	...	—
1906	...	77	...	...	...	...	17	...	—
1907	...	85	...	...	...	...	32	...	—
1908	...	86	...	...	...	...	49	...	—
1909	...	92	...	...	...	...	100	...	—
1910	...	113	...	...	...	...	74	...	—
1911	...	103	...	...	...	...	100	...	—
1912	...	141	...	...	...	...	161	...	—
1913	...	162	...	...	...	...	180	...	—
1914	...	143	...	...	...	...	137	...	—
1915	...	193	...	...	...	...	220	...	—
1916	...	241	...	...	...	...	280	...	—
1917	...	172	...	...	...	...	217	9	—
1918	...	80	...	...	...	...	182	22	—
1919	...	327	...	...	...	...	256	2	—
1920	...	339	...	...	...	...	178	41	—
1921	...	401	...	...	...	...	321	184	—
1922	...	298	...	...	...	...	529	286	—
1923	...	332	...	...	...	...	572	546	—
1924	...	452	- -	...	...	...	786	1,253	—
1925	...	542	—	...	...	...	951	2,720	—
1926	...	500	644	3,982	333	2,743	1,199	4,893	- -
1927	...	706	1,875	4,264	670	4,022	1,171	8,420	8
1928	...	735	2,488	9,867	449	10,603	1,271	14,715	43
1929	...	793	2,577	12,331	516	11,032	1,542	19,220	40
1930	...	769	2,656	16,047	1,589	13,033	1,448	20,458	53
1931	...	728	2,376	13,329	1,014	14,122	1,200	17,280	...
1932	...	615	2,211	13,040	1,086	11,640	1,126	16,192	713
1933	...	787	1,695	13,954	1,203	12,456	1,588	16,718	837
1934	...	832	2,351	15,431	1,223	13,552	1,976	18,780	902
1935	2.4	843	2,279	17,289	885	15,310	2,026	20,446	1,033
1936	13	978	2,356	18,790	1,272	17,110	2,063	22,343	973
1937	38	1,068	2,546	21,941	762	19,907	2,058	25,112	853
1938	48	1,132	2,648	23,789	1,083	22,290	1,708	26,611	930
1939	42	1,233	2,441	22,200	828	19,486	1,447	28,269	985
1940	49	1,209	3,050	17,940	247	16,700	1,157	23,438	1,318
1941	46	1,061	3,015	21,863	—	21,903	1,240	28,796	3,287
1942	11	736	1,002	12,739	—	13,098	1,461	18,082	3,375
1943	37	748	1,444	20,575	—	18,751	1,543	22,853	1,968
1944	18	736	2,524	25,796	—	24,812	1,311	32,461	1,907

D24 SOUTH AMERICA: Imports and Exports of Petroleum by Main Trading Countries (in thousands of metric tons)

	Brazil		Colombia	Netherlands Antilles				Peru		Venezuela
	CP	PP	CP	CP		PP	CP	PP	CP	PP
	Imports	Imports	Exports	Imports	Exports	Exports	Exports	Exports	Exports	Exports
1945	10	936	2,650	29,973	47	28,545	1,223		41,653	3,473
1946	37	1,594	2,422	33,600	703	30,585	1,056		30,150	3,962
1947	8.7	2,471	2,665	38,079	1,869	32,987	926		56,391	4,091
1948	—	3,149	2,561	38,998	2,102	38,238	1,033		62,682	4,775
1949	—	3,516	3,287	...	...	46,276	1,079		60,020	5,388
1950	11	4,339	3,910	42,180	1,237	39,687	848		64,460	8,741
1951	20	5,008	3,932	45,473	757	42,713	869		72,010	10,883
1952	18	5,941	3,752	43,995	949	43,587	854		76,115	12,044
1953	30	6,315	3,559	40,549	1,139	39,704	649		69,920	15,184
1954	142	7,427	4,339	43,741	2,069	34,470	698		75,650	16,630
1955	3,513	5,003	3,510	45,117	2,946	35,740	841		84,820	19,630
1956	4,889	4,386	4,056	45,071	2,336	37,443	982		97,010	22,814
1957	4,846	3,592	3,729	41,281	926	34,512	1,007		109,080	23,468
1958	5,652	4,137	3,298	36,699	1,243	33,030	668		100,619	26,600
1959	5,742	3,528	3,981	39,107	1,563	31,734	641		103,200	29,759
1960	5,684	4,097	4,353	38,833	945	31,539	762		104,628	34,629
1961	7,549	2,973	3,861	40,846	1,436	32,367	648		106,280	36,362
1962	9,961	1,069	3,402	41,342	1,430	34,106	586		115,583	39,150
1963	10,375	1,093	4,364	40,210	940	34,751	493		115,720	41,817
1964	10,803	818	4,248	40,834	486	35,575	431		122,385	44,165
1965	10,247	803	5,610	40,811	375	34,674	435		121,390	46,684
1966	11,322	858	4,920	39,761	344	33,333	330		117,920	46,171
1967	10,559	959	4,308	41,436	597	34,487	431		126,462	46,888
1968	12,525	1,744	2,551	40,325	318	34,228	587		129,050	45,338
1969	14,910	716	4,002	42,469	356	36,352	290		129,451	46,879
1970	15,797	558	4,203	47,413	660	39,449	235	—	127,591	51,502
1971	18,731	1,114	3,512	39,967	305	32,042	150	33	120,798	48,161
1972	25,257	640	2,016	39,054	566	31,745	145	142	111,478	46,248
1973	34,879	800	1,340	45,293	1,855	40,192	160	200	110,907	51,565
1974	34,831	809	68	41,334	784	36,893	—	402	92,450	47,829
1975	35,730	198	—	25,522	549	24,802	195	317	76,718	28,948
1976	40,996	1,109	—	35,060	908	23,366	364	295	71,565	38,001
1977	40,592	964	—	28,979	1,874	21,119	85	496	69,069	31,225
1978	44,750	372	—	28,548	1,023	22,396	1,445	506	65,216	35,049
1979	50,158	552	—	26,500	998	22,100	2,568	821	74,455	33,928
1980	43,333	1,902	—	31,177	1,001	22,765	2,390	806	68,369	28,008
1981	42,211	1,165	—	25,700	500	21,153	2,000	875	66,923	23,402
1982	39,810	2,907	—	24,500	600	18,516	1,500	1,222	56,115	23,323
1983	36,438	1,173	—	24,000	653	18,925	1,132	1,901	51,235	22,954
1984	32,425	439	—	20,000	200	16,694	1,000	2,503	52,546	22,667
1985	26,980	1,257	—	8,450	100	6,414	1,190	2,567	43,327	23,715
1986	29,871	1,779	4,425	8,150	100	5,950	656	2,361	49,766	25,100
1987	30,643	2,113	7,336	9,867	552	7,649	166	2,565	53,866	19,539
1988	31,739	3,456	7,314	10,200	300	7,549	271	2,205	52,156	24,405
1989	29,666	3,127	8,176	10,500	—	7,504	53	2,209	...	29,076
1990	28,246	2,504	10,306	11,195	1,796	7,757	159	2,168	...	28,331
1991	25,293	3,423	9,110	11,800	—	8,098	55	2,399	...	34,405
1992	26,268	4,078	9,505	13,000	1,116	7,936	42	2,395	...	30,167
1993	22,551	10,689	9,692	14,150	956	8,662	45	2,387	...	30,407

D24 Imports and Exports of Petroleum by Main Trading Countries

NOTES

1. SOURCES: Data to 1949 are from the national publications listed on pp. xiii–xv supplemented by League of Nations and UN, *International Trade Statistics*. Data from 1950 are from UN, *World Energy Supplies*.
2. Definitions of both crude petroleum and petroleum products have varied from time to time in most countries. So far as possible changes are indicated in footnotes.
3. Data on products from 1950 relate only to energy products.

FOOTNOTES

[1] Data to 1885 for exports and 1905 for imports are for years beginning 1 July. The 1906 import figures are for the nine months from 1 July 1906 to 31 March 1907; the 1907 and 1908 figures are for years beginning 1 April.
[2] Including refined products to 1898.
[3] Data for 1893–96 are for years ending 30 June.
[4] All crude mineral oils to 1916 and including re-exports to 1928. Shipments to Puerto Rico are included to 1920 (1st line).

D25 IMPORTS AND EXPORTS OF IRON ORE BY MAIN TRADING COUNTRIES (in thousands of metric tons)

1870–1914

	NORTH AMERICA				SOUTH AMERICA
	Canada[2]		USA		Chile
	Imports	Exports	Imports	Exports	Exports
1870	...	...	...	...	...
1871	...	...	24	...	...
1872	...	...	24	...	...
1873	...	...	47	...	...
1874	...	...	59	...	...
1875	...	...	58	...	...
1876	...	...	17	...	...
1877	...	...	31	...	...
1878	...	...	28	...	...
1879	...	...	289	...	...
1880	...	...	501	...	...
1881	...	...	796	...	...
1882	...	...	599	...	...
1883	...	...	499	...	...
1884	...	...	496	...	...
1885	...	...	397	...	...
1886	...	...	1,056	...	...
1887	...	...	1,213	...	...
1888	...	...	596	...	...
1889	...	...	868	...	...
1890	...	...	1,267	...	—
1891	...	...	928	...	1.7
1892	...	...	820	...	—
1893	...	...	535	...	—
1894	...	...	170	...	—
1895	...	...	532	...	0.3
1896	...	...	694	...	—
1897	...	...	498	...	—
1898	...	...	190	...	—
1899	...	...	685	42	—
1900	...	5	912	52	—
1901	...	—	983	66	—
1902	...	—	1,184	89	..
1903	...	—	996	82	—
1904	...	—	496	217	—
1905	...	—	860	211	..
1906	...	68	1,077	269	—
1907	...	24	1,249	283	—
1908	...	4	789	314	—
1909	...	20	1,722	463	—
1910	...	103	2,633	761	—
1911	...	34	1,841	780	29
1912	[1,858][1]	107	2,139	1,215	6.5
1913	1,762	114	2,637	1,059	14
1914	1,041	122	1,373	561	64

D25 Imports and Exports of Iron Ore by Main Trading Countries (in thousands of metric tons)

1915–1959

	NORTH AMERICA				SOUTH AMERICA			
	Canada[2]		USA		Brazil	Chile	Peru	Venezuela
	Imports	Exports	Imports	Exports	Exports	Exports	Exports	Exports
1915	1,364	73	1,363	719	...	147	...	—
1916	2,123	146	1,347	1,203	...	—	...	—
1917	2,042	149	988	1,150	...	—	...	—
1918	1,997	118	800	1,276	...	—	...	—
1919	1,527	13	484	1,013	...	—	...	—
1920	1,800	18	1,293	1,163	...	—	...	—
1921	600	4	321	447	...	8.0	...	—
1922	805	2	1,153	612	...	290	...	—
1923	1,762	7	2,812	1,135	...	673	...	—
1924	828	5	2,080	605	...	1,050	...	—
1925	941	4	2,226	641	...	1,234	...	—
1926	1,330	1	2,596	883	...	1,396	...	—
1927	1,349	2	2,663	913	...	1,508	...	—
1928	2,017	3	2,492	1,303	...	1,525	...	—
1929	2,221	4	3,189	1,325	...	1,816	...	—
1930	1,348	1	2,820	764	...	1,558	...	—
1931	733	2	1,490	443	...	712	...	—
1932	62	1	591	84	...	199	...	—
1933	187	2	875	157	...	510	...	—
1934	886	3	1,451	619	...	953	...	—
1935	1,370	3	1,516	672	...	845	...	—
1936	1,195	3	2,268	655	...	1,350	...	—
1937	1,928	5	2,481	1,284	186	1,473	...	—
1938	1,182	—	2,156	601	369	1,571	...	—
1939	1,601	10	2,452	1,074	397	1,592	...	—
1940	2,194	228	2,519	1,408	256	1,713	...	—
1941	2,953	256	2,382	1,939	421	1,622	...	—
1942	2,451	269	743	2,555	316	418	...	—
1943	3,544	340	405	2,464	323	—	...	—
1944	2,836	280	471	2,193	206	—	...	—
1945	3,393	700	1,217	2,096	300	218	...	—
1946	200	1,039	2,798	1,530	64	1,814	...	—
1947	3,578	1,588	4,975	2,856	197	1,747	...	—
1948	3,901	971	6,190	3,130	599	2,625	...	—
1949	[2,225][2]	[2,315][2]	7,510	2,464	676	2,675	...	—
1950	2,786	2,021	8,414	2,592	890	2,596	...	—
1951	3,475	2,264	10,303	4,398	1,320	2,687	...	—
1952	3,872	3,490	9,918	5,205	1,561	1,828	...	—
1953	3,781	4,373	11,252	4,320	1,547	2,442	890	1,973
1954	2,753	4,909	16,045	3,196	1,678	1,720	1,927	5,449
1955	4,118	13,217	23,849	4,589	2,565	1,237	1,697	7,791
1956	4,599	18,384	30,899	5,596	2,745	2,071	2,674	10,905
1957	4,118	18,261	34,191	5,082	3,550	3,074	3,677	15,587
1958	3,096	12,590	27,986	3,630	2,831	3,638	2,510	16,068
1959	2,541	18,850	36,189	3,015	3,988	4,261	3,320	17,379

D25 Imports and Exports of Iron Ore by Main Trading Countries (in thousands of metric tons)

| | NORTH AMERICA | | | | SOUTH AMERICA | | | | |
| | Canada[2] | | USA | | Argentina | Brazil | Chile | Peru | Venezuela |
	Imports	Exports	Imports	Exports	Imports	Exports	Exports	Exports	Exports
1960	4,587	16,837	35,133	5,358	—	5,240	5,191	5,171	19,320
1961	4,199	15,107	26,219	5,038	317	6,282	6,197	5,573	14,565
1962	4,679	21,993	33,945	5,993	515	7,650	7,246	5,149	13,285
1963	5,411	24,238	33,797	6,921	757	8,268	7,092	5,749	12,319
1964	5,317	30,963	43,089	7,075	1,019	9,730	9,114	5,824	14,893
1965	4,840	31,294	45,827	7,199	1,033	12,731	10,729	7,246	17,006
1966	4,393	31,186	47,001	7,904	707	12,910	11,095	7,680	17,037
1967	2,439	31,911	45,386	6,001	880	14,279	9,894	8,497	16,487
1968	2,794	40,332	44,646	5,978	616	15,050	10,497	8,710	15,053
1969	2,297	31,256	36,975	5,243	467	21,478	9,655	9,503	18,992
1970	2,160	39,348	45,612	5,580	1,448	28,061	9,908	9,644	21,089
1971	1,384	34,164	40,768	3,110	1,592	31,020	10,304	9,468	19,162
1972	1,753	29,275	36,335	2,129	1,029	30,512	5,454	8,941	16,509
1973	2,689	37,668	43,991	2,791	1,235	44,963	8,122	9,002	21,659
1974	2,333	37,448	48,800	2,360	1,003	59,439	9,390	8,398	26,277
1975	4,842	36,034	47,493	2,578	1,520	72,522	9,066	5,620	19,405
1976	3,020	44,685	45,102	2,960	1,745	67,086	8,965	4,515	15,671
1977	2,505	45,060	38,513	2,177	2,377	56,762	6,705	6,433	11,835
1978	4,686	31,929	34,156	4,282	2,395	66,370	3,129	4,869	12,828
1979	5,913	48,849	34,312	5,348	2,919	75,588	6,980	5,529	12,976
1980	5,875	38,994	25,460	5,780	2,391	78,958	7,600	5,500	11,752
1981	5,792	41,452	28,789	5,635	2,559	85,798	6,640	5,156	12,423
1982	3,357	27,281	14,951	3,229	2,106	80,927	5,767	5,596	6,616
1983	4,013	25,528	13,542	3,842	1,904	74,200	4,594	4,194	6,245
1984	4,947	30,737	17,435	5,073	2,213	90,294	5,230	4,089	8,456
1985	5,800	32,259	16,221	5,114	2,455	94,218	4,824	5,224	9,032
1986	5,367	31,030	17,018	4,553	3,183	91,135	4,650	4,209	10,027
1987	5,213	29,679	16,849	5,094	3,342	95,332	5,384	4,429	11,700
1988	4,856	30,523	20,183	5,289	3,260	112,839	6,682	4,520	12,128
1989	...	30,222	19,596	5,365	4,000	118,431	6,863	4,000	...
1990	...	27,098	18,054	3,199	3,140	113,469	6,528	3,700	...
1991	...	29,651	13,335	4,045	2,410	113,301	6,306	2,600	...
1992	...	25,132	12,504	5,055	3,574	108,183	6,537	3,000	...
1993	...	26,140	14,097	5,061	3,204	115,131	5,757	4,700	...

NOTES

1. SOURCES: The national publications listed on pp. xiii–xv League of Nations, *International Trade Statistics*; and UN, *Yearbook of International Trade Statistics*.
2. Statistics refer to crude weight of ore.

FOOTNOTES

[1] Nine months ending 31 December.
[2] Including Newfoundland and Labrador as part of Canada from April 1949.

E. EXTERNAL TRADE

Because it has long been an important source of revenue to governments, external trade provides more statistical material at an earlier date for most countries than does any other economic activity. It was always one of the first things to be recorded by colonial administrations, though the Spanish and Portuguese were less diligent in this respect than other colonizers. However, as independent regimes established their authority they began to follow West European practice in this field. Unfortunately, it was standard practice in most Latin American countries until around the middle of the nineteenth century, or later, to record the values of imports and exports in terms of officially fixed 'prices' for each commodity. Since these were not normally kept up-to-date, the recorded values, both for individual goods and in the aggregate, tended to become increasingly misleading as a representation of the actual values of imports and exports. The size of the gap which could develop is well illustrated by the Uruguayan figures in table 1 for 1913, when the system was changed.

Most Latin American countries have followed the practice of continental Europe in recording their external trade in two forms—'general' and 'special' trade. The former includes all commodities entering or leaving a country; the latter relates only to commodities intended for internal use or to commodities which have been, in some sense, produced within the country. It is the latter, the 'special' trade, or its equivalent in Anglo-Saxon countries, which has been shown in this section wherever possible. It must be noted, however, that the exact definition of 'special' trade has not been rigidly fixed, though the scope for major variations is obviously lacking. Moreover, statements of origin or intention to sell can be both honestly and dishonestly mistaken. However, these sources of unreliability or lack of comparability in the figures are not likely to be of very great significance. Nor, for the period and countries covered here, is smuggling, since most of the goods exported were of relatively low bulk-to-value ratios and tariffs on both imports and exports were not usually very high except where the means of enforcement were reasonably well developed. For practical purposes, therefore, it seems possible to take most of the statistics in this section as reasonably, though not perfectly, accurate. The main exceptions are probably some of the small countries of Central America, where the bureaucracies were incapable of policing and recording foreign trade effectively until well into the twentieth century.[1]

It is clear that one major influence on the course of these statistics has been the changes which have taken place in price levels, above all since 1914. It has not been found practicable to include a list showing variations in exchange rates, though these obviously have a bearing on any analysis of external trade. Information on these for the period since World War II is to be found in the UN, *Yearbook of International Trade*; and an idea of changing price levels in those countries and periods for which data are available can be got from section I below. Alterations in the internal value of currency units are listed on p. xii above.

Table 2, showing the trade of each country with others which have at various times been its chief trading partners, presents its own peculiar problems. The main one of these is that the records of no two countries tell precisely the same story about their trade with each other. The main cause of this is confusion between countries of shipment, of consignment, and of origin. Different systems have been used at various times in most countries, and even when allowance is made for this, it is clear that the system supposedly in use has not always been followed with precise accuracy in every case. This table does not cover all the countries for which data are available, though it is only smaller ones, and colonial and ex-colonial territories where trade has been overwhelmingly with the colonizing country, which have been omitted.

It would be extremely useful to have statistics showing a breakdown of the trade of the various countries by major commodity groups. Unfortunately, changes in definition occur in the published statistics of every country

---

[1] The British Department of Overseas Trade, *Report on the Financial and Commercial Conditions in the Republic of Honduras* (London, 1921), said that 'there exists a large clandestine export of goods which fails to appear in the records of the Custom Houses.' It seems unlikely that this was true of only one country in the area.

with very great frequency, and to produce reasonably consistent and comparable series for even one country is a considerable enterprise. Reluctantly, therefore, such commodity group statistics have been omitted. However, it has been possible to include, in table 3, series showing the value of the major individual commodities exported by a number of countries, since most of these commodities have been either fairly homogeneous basic ones, or else the exports of industrial countries with unusually well-presented national data.

E1 NORTH AMERICA: EXTERNAL TRADE AGGREGATES IN CURRENT VALUES

1790–1839

	Barbados[1]		Cuba		Guadeloupe[2]		Jamaica[1,3]		Martinique[2]	
	Imports	Exports	Imports	Exports	Imports	Exports	Imports	Exports	Imports	Exports
	(thousand pounds)		(million pesos fuertes)		(million francs)		(thousand pounds)		(million francs)	
1790	...	...	5.9	11	...	...	...	...	...	...
1791	...	...	12	13	...	...	...	...	...	...
1792	...	...	11	7.3	...	...	...	...	...	...
1793	...	...	6.9	12	...	...	...	...	...	...
1794	...	...	5.5	18	...	...	...	...	...	...
1795	...	...	19	17	...	...	...	...	...	...
1796	...	...	...	...	...	...	...	...	...	...
1797	...	...	...	...	...	...	...	...	...	...
1798	...	...	...	...	...	...	...	...	...	...
1799	...	...	...	...	...	...	...	...	...	...
1800	...	...	...	...	...	...	...	...	...	...
1801	...	...	...	...	...	...	...	...	...	...
1802	...	...	...	...	...	...	...	...	...	...
1803	...	...	12	8.1	...	...	...	...	...	...
1804	...	...	10	8.2	...	...	...	...	...	...
1805	...	...	12	5.8	...	...	...	...	...	...
1806	...	...	11	6.4	...	...	...	...	...	...
1807	...	...	7.8	5.5	...	...	...	...	...	...
1808	...	...	9.1	3.8	...	...	...	...	...	...
1809	...	...	13	9.2	...	...	...	...	...	...
1810	...	...	16	7.9	...	...	...	...	...	...
1811	...	...	12	7.3	...	...	...	...	...	...
1812	...	...	5.9	4.0	...	...	...	...	...	...
1813	...	...	9.3	6.1	...	...	...	...	...	...
1814	...	...	11	11	...	...	...	...	...	...
1815	...	...	...	...	...	...	...	...	...	...
1816	...	...	13	84	...	...	...	...	...	...
1817	...	...	...	...	...	...	...	...	...	...
1818	...	...	...	...	...	...	...	...	...	...
1819	...	...	...	...	...	...	...	...	...	...
1820	...	...	...	...	...	...	...	...	...	...
1821	...	...	...	...	11	16	...	...	16	16
1822	...	...	...	...	10	20	...	...	14	19
1823	...	...	...	...	13	14	...	...	16	14
1824	...	...	...	...	18	25	...	...	16	16
1825	...	...	...	...	15	17	...	...	20	17
1826	...	...	15	14	20	20	...	...	27	21
1827	...	...	17	14	19	18	...	...	23	18
1828	...	...	20	13	20	22	...	...	21	19
1829	...	...	19	4	22	23	...	...	21	18
1830	...	...	16	16	11	18	...	...	12	17
1831	...	...	16	13	13	24	...	...	14	17
1832	461	286	15	14	22	24	1,593	2,814	19	17
1833	439	418	19	14	12	19	1,519	2,490	12	13
1834	454	625	19	14	14	18	1,590	3,149	14	13
1835	505	579	21	14	16	19	2,019	3,095	17	14
1836	616	637	23	15	20	19	2,109	3,316	15	13
1837	627	787	23	20	16	18	1,957	2,828	17	13
1838	718	848	25	20	15_2	17_2	1,877	3,299	15_2	12_2
					19	24			19	20
1839	784	687	25	21	19	29	2,244	2,485	21	22

International Historical Statistics: The Americas 1750-1993

E1 NORTH AMERICA: External Trade Aggregates in Current Values

1790-1839

	Mexico[4]		Newfoundland[1,5]		Trinidad[1]		USA[1,6]	
	Imports	Exports	Imports	Exports	Imports	Exports	Imports	Exports
	(thousand pounds)		(thousand pounds)		(thousand pounds)		(million US dollars)	
1790	...	...	...	...	...	...	23	20
1791	...	...	...	...	...	...	29	19
1792	...	...	...	...	...	...	32	21
1793	...	...	...	...	...	...	31	26
1794	...	...	...	...	...	...	35	33
1795	...	...	...	...	...	...	70	48
1796	7,969	8,308	...	...	...	...	81	59
1797	2,234	1,423	...	...	...	...	75	51
1798	3,247	3,371	...	...	...	...	69	61
1799	6,722	8,716	...	...	...	...	79	79
1800	4,709	6,058	...	...	...	...	91	71
1801	3,487	1,971	...	...	...	...	111	93
1802	21,999	38,447	...	...	...	...	76	72
1803	19,867	14,483	...	...	...	...	65	56
1804	16,526	21,458	...	...	...	...	85	78
1805	3,914	341	...	...	...	...	121	96
1806	7,138	5,479	...	...	...	...	129	102
1807	16,737	22,507	...	...	...	...	139	108
1808	10,413	13,599	...	...	...	...	57	22
1809	20,431	28,278	...	...	...	...	59	52
1810	20,431	15,917	...	...	...	...	85	67
1811	11,347	9,867	...	...	...	...	53	61
1812	5,241	5,118	...	...	...	...	77	39
1813	7,932	12,100	...	...	...	...	22	28
1814	9,670	10,393	...	...	...	...	13	7
1815	10,986	9,181	...	...	...	...	113	53
1816	10,006	6,675	...	...	...	...	147	82
1817	8,686	8,520	...	...	...	...	99	88
1818	5,765	4,731	...	...	...	...	122	93
1819	10,999	8,675	...	...	...	...	87	70
1820	3,552	10,894	...	...	...	...	74	70
1821	...	...	...	...	...	...	63	65
1822	...	...	...	...	...	...	83	72
1823	3,919	2,346	...	...	...	...	77	74
1824	12,082	4,099	...	...	...	...	80	76
1825	19,094	5,503	...	...	...	...	96[6]	100[6]
							96	99
1826	15,451	9,006	...	...	...	...	84	77
1827	15,882	18,672	...	...	...	...	78	80
1828	10,508	14,489	...	...	...	...	88	71
1829	...	...	...	...	...	...	74	70
1830	...	...	...	...	...	...	70	73
1831	...	...	...	...	...	...	102	78
1832	...	...	574	594	230	236	100	86
1833	...	...	596	715	287	268	107	90
1834	...	...	556	663	253	381	123	103
1835	...	...	577	737	316	370	148	120
1836	...	...	580	787	469	488	183	128
1837	...	...	711	864	444	469	138	114
1838	...	...	580	728	409	494	102	107
1839	...	...	624	818	466	359	160	116

E1 NORTH AMERICA: External Trade Aggregates in Current Values

1840–1884

	Barbados[1]		Canada[7]		Costa Rica[8]		Cuba		Dominican Republic	
	Imports	Exports	Imports	Exports	Imports	Exports	Imports	Exports	Imports	Exports
	(thousand pounds)		(million Canadian dollars)		(million pesos)		(million pesos fuertes)		(million pesos)	
1840	599	344	...	...	...	...	25	26	...	...
1841	578	410	...	...	...	...	25	27	...	...
1842	578	557	...	...	...	...	25	27	...	...
1843	617	547	...	...	...	...	23	25	...	...
1844	594	562	...	...	...	...	25	25	...	...
1845	654	562	...	...	...	...	28	19	...	...
1846	679	513	...	...	...	...	23	22	...	...
1847	546	738	...	...	...	...	32	28	...	...
1848	426	560	...	...	...	...	25	26	...	...
1849	572	659	...	...	...	...	26	22	...	...
1850	734	832	...	...	...	...	29	26	...	...
1851	788	888	...	...	...	...	32	31	...	...
1852	768	952	...	...	...	...	30	27	...	...
1853	571	775	...	...	...	...	28	31	...	...
1854	597	946	...	...	1.0	0.8	31	33	...	...
1855	645	790	...	...	0.7	0.8	31	35	...	...
1856	841	971	...	...	0.9	0.8	32	32	...	...
1857	976	1,345	...	...	- -	1.3	35	33	...	...
1858	1,335	1,468	...	...	1.0	1.0	39	34	...	...
1859	1,049	1,226	...	...	0.9	1.4	43	57	...	...
1860	942	984	...	...	1.1	1.3	34	42	...	...
1861	924	1,075	...	...	0.8	1.8	...	...	...	...
1862	913	1,068	...	...	0.9	1.7	41	55	...	...
1863	878	981	...	...	1.1	1.4	...	...	...	...
1864	910	926	...	...	1.6	1.6	...	...	...	...
1865	953	1,161	...	...	1.5	1.6	...	...	...	...
1866	988	1,247	...	...	1.4	1.8	...	...	...	...
1867	990	1,245	67	53	1.3	2.2	...	...	...	...
1868	1,134	1,270	63	56	0.9	2.2	...	...	1.1	...
1869	1,026	935	67	66	1.2	2.4	...	...	1.4	...
1870	1,070	973	84	67	1.4	2.7	...	...	1.3	...
1871	1,192	1,299	105	79	1.7	3.6	...	...	1.3	...
1872	1,125	1,021	125	86	2.8	2.8	...	...	1.1	1.2
1873	1,194	1,024	123	87	3.8	6.0	...	...	...	...
1874	1,031	1,141	117	77	2.9	4.6	...	...	...	...
1875	1,187	1,475	93	80	2.9	4.6	...	...	...	...
1876	1,028	964	94	75	3.3	2.3	...	...	...	...
1877	1,144	1,098	90	79	...	5.0	59	67	...	...
1878	1,103	1,078	79	71	2.5	3.4	...	...	...	...
1879	1,023	1,259	70	86	3.4	4.2	...	...	...	...
1880	1,171	1,166	90	97	2.4	3.5	...	...	1.7	1.3
1881	1,119	1,140	111	102	2.2	2.4	...	...	1.6	1.5
1882	1,163	1,193	122	97	...[8]	3.7[8]	...	...	2.0	1.9
					(million colones)					
1883	1,155	1,141	106	89	5	4	...	...	3.1	2.1
1884	1,156	1,319	100	87	8	8	...	...	2.5	2.6

E1   NORTH AMERICA: External Trade Aggregates in Current Values

	El Salvador		Guadeloupe[2]		Guatemala[10]		Jamaica[1,3]		Martinique[2]	
	Imports (thousand gold pesos)	Exports (thousand silver pesos)	Imports	Exports (million francs)	Imports (thousand gold pesos)	Exports (thousand silver pesos)	Imports	Exports (thousand pounds)	Imports	Exports million francs
1840	...	...	22	23	...	...	2,184	2,209	26	19
1841	...	...	22	23	...	...	1,335	1,910	24	20
1842	...	...	20	23	...	...	1,877	2,231	21	21
1843	...	...	27	19	...	...	1,696	1,847	29	20
1844	...	...	32	22	...	...	1,476	1,609	26	22
1845	...	...	29	26	...	...	1,559	1,851	26	24
1846	...	...	27₂	19	...	...	1,420	1,479	29₀	19₂
1847	...	...	27	27	...	...	1,322	1,938	28	24
1848	...	...	12	14	...	...	1,023	1,341	14	15
1849	...	...	17	13	...	...	1,118	1,068	26	14
1850	...	...	18	9.2	...	...	1,218	1,217	22	12
1851	...	...	26	12	1,404	1,404	1,129	980	36	15
1852	...	...	25	12	1,581	869	838	927	30	19
1853	...	...	21	10	971	599	864	837	27	16
1854	...	...	23	16	874	2,033	985	660	29	19
1855	...	787	24	16	826	1,283	900	1,003	26	16
1856	...	765	24	16	1,206	1,707	962	935	32	21
1857	...	1,285	28	14	1,066	1,605	765	1,235	29	19
1858	...	1,304	28	20	1,136	2,025	1,040	1,170	33	21
1859	1,336	1,761	25	19	1,224	1,767	853	961	28	22
1860	950	1,391	30	20	1,520	1,871	1,203	1,226	28	23
1861	1,349	2,291	27	18	1,495	1,107	1,089	1,215	31	22
1862	1,304	2,686	25	23	1,093	1,368	1,142	1,113	30	22
1863	...	1,673	23	21	745	1,498	1,088	1,008	26	25
1864	1,234	1,665	19	14	1,415	1,563	1,143	947	27	19
1865	1,689	2,848	19	18	1,650	1,833	1,051₃	912	29	20
1866	1,664	2,135	21	21	1,699	1,680	1,031	1,153	30	22
1867	1,876	2,896	19	16	1,575	1,920	859	1,045	30	21
1868	1,949	3,448	19	22	1,665	2,188	1,025	1,139	30	29
1869	3,729	3,769	21	25	1,753	2,291	1,224	1,163	31	32
1870	4,199	3,894	19	27	1,375	2,045	1,300	1,283	27	30
1871	2,580	3,810	24	29	2,403	2,658	1,331	1,249	33	35
1872	2,951	3,881	28	26	2,269	2,704	1,560	1,418	35	32
1873	2,103	3,477	28	25	1,192	2,364	1,733	1,226	32	28
1874	2,835	3,841	25	22	3,054	2,301	1,763	1,442	28	33
1875	2,690	3,180	25	31	2,586	3,217	1,760	1,410	30	36
1876	2,102	3,605	22	23	2,717	3,767	1,700	1,517	26	28
1877	2,586	3,961	27	35	3,134	3,773	1,552	1,459	29	34
1878	2,501	3,626	25	35	3,238	3,919	1,493	1,211	30	30
1879	2,549	4,128	29	28	2,929	4,606	1,347	1,358	30	34
1880	2,295	4,073	27	31	3,036	4,425	1,475	1,513	32	34
1881	2,705	4,902	26	32	3,665	4,084	1,393₃	1,179	27	32
1882	3,170	5,227	27	42	2,652	3,719	1,318	1,549	28	39
1883	2,401	5,861	28	32	2,031	5,718	1,625	1,469	33	36
1884	2,647	6,066	25	27	3,830	4,938	1,569	1,484	28	26

E1 NORTH AMERICA: External Trade Aggregates in Current Values

1840–1884

	Mexico[4]		Newfoundland[1.5]		Nicaragua[11]		Trinidad[1]		USA[1.6]	
	Imports	Exports	Imports	Exports	Imports	Exports	Imports	Exports	Imports	Exports
	(thousand pounds)		(thousand pounds)		(thousand gold pesos or cordobas)		(thousand pounds)		(million US dollars)	
1840	...	...	671	896	...	...	537	362	104	129
1841	...	...	666	908	...	...	533	474	127	118
1842	...	...	650	787	...	...	386	458	99	103
1843	...	...	667	913	...	...	430	407	[47][6]	[84][6]
1844	...	...	709	853	...	...	437	404	107	110
1845	...	...	655	875	...	...	450	430	116	112
1846	...	...	727	689	...	...	494	497	121	112
1847	...	...	760	807	...	...	394	512	125	158
1848	...	...	634	860	...	...	284	268	152	143
1849	...	...	725[5]	891[5]	...	...	416	388	144	143
1850	...	...	867	976	...	...	477	319	177	147
1851	...	...	943	960	...	...	548	390	213	196
1852	...	...	796	966	...	...	493	459	209	170
1853	...	...	912	1,171	...	...	504	446	266	205
1854	...	...	965	1,020	...	...	559	381	302	238
1855	...	...	1,153	1,142	...	...	555	388	261	220
1856	...	...	1,272	1,339	...	...	666	575	313	282
1857	...	44,000	1,413	1,651	...	...	801	1,074	354	298
1858	...	...	1,173	1,319	...	...	826	786	271	275
1859	...	...	1,324	1,357	...	...	735	821	336	296
1860	...	...	1,254	1,272	...	...	829	715	360	342
1861			1,153	1,093	...	...	857	645	293	222
1862			1,1007	1,172	...	...	734	740	192	192
1863			1,077	1,233	...	...	711	796	247	206
1864	25,842	1,165	1,067	1,111	...	...	884	1,102	318	164[6]
1865			1,104	1,144	...	...	810	820	242	175
1866			1,205	1,186	...	...	930	1,032	438	364
1867			1,156	1,056	...	...	859	1,087	401	317
1868	...	...	897	888	...	...	928	1,116	362	303
1869	...	...	1,095	1,270	...	...	1,027	1,381	424	307
1870	...	...	1,387	1,298	...	...	1,043	1,278	450	418
1871	...	...	1,258	1,311	...	...	1,218	1,497	534	475
	(million pesos)									
1872	20	32	1,399	1,189	...	...	1,234	1,440	632	474
1873	23	28	1,410	1,361	...	...	1,324	1,734	655	562
1874	22	27	1,532	1,528	...	...	1,343	1,412	576	619
1875	...	...	1,533	1,340	...	...	1,508	1,625	540	538
1876	...	...	1,501	1,367	...	...	1,666	1,637	469	565
1877	28	28	1,534	1,425	...	...	1,708	2,094	466	632
1878	...	30	1,431	1,173	...	...	1,901	1,839	453	720
1879	...	33	1,513	1,233	...	...	2,223	2,265	461	730
1880	...	30	1,451	1,174	...	...	2,382	2,186	680	850
1881	...	29	1,430	1,629	1,284	1,433	2,226	2,099	654	919
1882	...	42	1,740	1,459	1,182	1,517	2,400	2,452	733	768
1883	34	47	1,902	1,471	...	...	2,663	2,687	734	841
1884	36	47	1,682	1,368	...	...	3,084	2,770	683	767

E1 NORTH AMERICA: External Trade Aggregates in Current Values

1885–1929

	Barbados[1]		Canada[7]		Costa Rica[8]		Cuba[9]		Dominican Republic		El Salvador	
	Imports	Exports	Imports	Exports	Imports	Exports	Imports	Exports	Imports	Exports	Imports	Exports
			(million Canadian								(thousand gold pesos)	(thousand silver pesos)
	(thousand pounds)		dollars)		(million colones)		(million pesos fuertes)		(million pesos)			
1885	891	1,004	96	85	8	5	...	...	2.1	2.5	2,134	5,716
1886	863	740	105	90	8	5	...	...	...	...	4,428	4,755
1887	983	1,063	101	90	12	10	...	...	2.1	2.7	3,275	5,230
1888	1,058	1,075	109	87	11	9	...	...	...	...	4,082	6,758
1889	1,211	1,030	112	94	14	10	...	...	2.4	2.9	2,886	5,674
1890	1,194	1,204	112	97	14	14	...	...	2.4	3.9	2,401	7,579
1891	1,068	814	115	112	18	13	...	...	2.7	2.9	3,200	7,073
1892	1,082	927	115	114	12	10	56	90	2.4	3.6	5,758	6,838
1893	1,373	1,243	109	116	13	9	...	...	2.8	5.7	1,854	7,492
1894	1,279	985	101	109	9	11	...	...	2.9	5.4	2,171	6,611
1895	957	587	105	116	8	11	...	...	...	...	...	...
1896	1,049	758	107	134	10	12	...	...	3.4	4.4	...	...
1897	1,009	736	126	160	12	12	...	...	3.4	9.3	...	...
1898	1,059	769	149	155	9	12	...	...	3.4	11.6	...	...
1899	998	846	173	183	10	11	...	...	...	...	...	...
							(million US dollars)					
1900	1,045	919	178	195	14	14	71	45	...	...	...	...
											(million colones)	
1901	1,022	950	197	210	9	12	65	63	...	...	6.5	11
1902	873	592	225	225	10	12	65	51	...	...	6.9	10
1903	822	553	244	211	12	16	59	78	...	...	7.7	14
1904	1,069	861	252	201	13	15	70	93	...	...	9.0	17
1905	1,043	936	284	247	11	17	84	99	2.7	6.9	11	14
1906	1,192	875	[250][7]	[192][7]	16	19	104	105	4.0	6.6	10	16
1907	1,272	847	352	263	17	20	96	111	4.9	7.9	8.6	15
1908	1,226	880	289	260	12	17	97	97	4.9	9.6	11	15
1909	1,119	822	370	299	13	18	84	116	4.4	8.6	11	17
1910	1,345	1,004	453	290	17	18	98	144	6.3	10.8	11	18
							(million pesos)					
							103	150				
1911	1,540	931	522	308	19	19	113	123	6.9	11.0	13	22
1912	1,465	996	671	377	22	21	123	172	8.2	12.4	16	22
1913	1,353	761	619	455	19	22	140	164	9.3	10.5	15	23
1914	1,300	846	456	461	16	23	118	173	6.7	10.6	14	27
1915	1,270	1,053	508	779	10	21	140	235	9.1	15.2	11	26
1916	1,851	2,002	846	1,179	14	24	215	321	10.7	21.5	17	29
1917	2,285	1,939	964	1,586	12	24	256	356	17.4	22.4	18	27
1918	2,986	2,223	920[7]	1,269[7]	8	21	293	407	19.7	22.4	15	25
1919	3,876	2,754	941	1,290	16	38	355	573	22.0	39.6	21	34
1920	5,135	4,371	1,337	1,298	48	27	556	794	46.5	58.7	26	36
1921	2,642	1,425	799	814	20	26	353	278	24.6	20.6	18	18
1922	2,484	1,245	762	894	18	31	178	325	14.3	15.2	15	33
1923	2,522	2,130	903	1,016	21	28	267	421	18.2	26.0	18	35
1924	2,556	1,820	808	1,042	48	66	288	435	21.6	30.3	28	49
1925	2,296	1,375	890	1,252	55	66	296	354	25.3	26.8	39	34
1926	2,155	1,205	1,008	1,277	55	76	259	302	23.8	24.9	52	49
1927	2,300	1,537	1,087	1,231	65	72	258	324	27.8	31.2	30	28
1928	2,349	1,470	1,222	1,364	72	79	213	278	26.8	28.8	38	49
1929	2,040	1,247	1,299	1,178	81	73	216	272	22.7	23.7	36	37

E1   NORTH AMERICA: External Trade Aggregates in Current Values

1885–1929

	Guadeloupe		Guatemala[10]		Haiti[1,13]		Honduras[14]		Jamaica[3]		Martinique	
	Imports	Exports	Imports (thousand gold pesos)	Exports (thousand silver pesos)	Imports	Exports	Imports	Exports	Imports	Exports	Imports	Exports
	(million francs)				(million gourdes)		(thousand gold pesos)		(thousand pounds)		(million francs)	
1885	20	18	3,103	6,070	...	...	...	...	1,488	1,409	22	21
1886	17	16	3,236	6,720	...	...	...	...	1,326	1,280	24	20
1887	20	22	3,743	9,039	...	...	...	...	1,322	1,509	23	21
1888	24	26	5,344	7,087	...	...	...	...	1,696	1,829	23	23
1889	24	26	7,587	13,248	...	...	...	...	1,598₃	1,615₃	23	23
1890	23	21	7,640	14,402	...	...	...	...	2,189	1,903	30	23
1891	20	15	7,807	14,175	...	...	...	...	1,760	1,722	34	23
1892	21	22	6,010	14,869	...	...	...	...	1,941	1,760	33	18
1893	20	23	6,383	14,087	...	...	...	...	2,158	2,076	26	24
1894	23	21	6,180	20,325	...	...	...	...	2,192	1,921	29	23
				(thousand gold pesos)								
1895	16	12	8,689	...	6.2	14	...	...	2,289	1,873	21	20
1896	20	18	11,429	9,973	6.1	9.4	1,325	3,131	1,856	1,470	23	21
1897	18	15	8,585	7,910	6.4	13	3,263	2,649	1,661	1,441	21	19
1898	18	17	4,851	4,882	5.5	13	...	...	1,815	1,663	24	22
1899	18	18	4,118	8,371	3.9	13	1,410	2,657	1,844	1,868	25	26
1900	20	15	3,127	7,393	7.2	14	1,074	2,636	1,722	1,797	25	27
1901	20	17	4,259	7,519	5.5	13	1,737	2,576	1,756	1,939	26	23
1902	16	17	4,017	9,032	...	...	1,294	1,763	2,029	2,292	19	16
1903	16	18	2,972	6,719	...	...	1,434	1,715	2,014	1,543	20	15
1904	13	13	5,041	7,552	...	...	2,223	2,173	1,682	1,437	15	13
1905	13	16	6,844	8,238	...	...	2,363	2,419	1,942	1,843	15	18
1906	13	15	7,221	7,136	...	...	2,512	2,880	2,261	1,992	15	19
1907	13	16	7,317	10,174	...	...	2,332	2,080	2,914	2,376	16	19
1908	15	17	5,812	6,756	...	...	2,830	1,834	2,420₃	2,268₃	15	21
1909	14	12	5,251	10,079	5.9	...	2,592	1,991	2,562	2,628	16	22
1910	17	24	6,514	10,982	7.7	...	2,696	2,296	2,615	2,568	20	28
1911	19	20	8,167	11,006	7.9	...	3,561	2,908	2,866	2,948	20	23
1912	20	26	9,822	13,157	9.9	17	4,238	2,049	3,050	2,709	22	31
1913	20	18	10,062	14,450	8.7	...	5,133	3,048	2,837	2,430₃ 2,249	22	29
1914	18	26	9,331	12,742	7.6	...	6,625	3,397	2,553	2,831	22	30
1915	20	27	5,072	11,551	4.3	...	5,875	3,458	2,327	2,227	23	43
1916	25	42	8,539	10,634	1.9	1.8	4,452	4,191	3,032	2,803	34	61
1917	40	51	8,700	7,828	1.7	1.7	6,293	5,353	3,298	2,479	57	81
1918	40	51	8,412	11,312	...	...	4,784	4,587	3,376	2,686	55	51
1919	64	104	14,216	22,408	17	21	6,931	5,998	4,872	5,626	75	173
			(million quetzales)									
1920	118	146	18	18	27	19	12,861	5,867	10,309	6,830	132	129
1921	79	75	13	12	12₁₃	5₁₃	16,723	5,429	5,460	3,053	85	89
1922	72	85	10	12	62	54	12,467	4,650	4,834	4,170	67	95
1923	86	105	13	15	71	73	14,342	8,681	5,556	4,278	95	118
1924	108	185	17	24	74	71	9,618	6,985	5,085	3,134	142	180
1925	133	155	23	29	101	97	12,003	10,030	5,631	3,934	162	179
1926	145	168	27	29	94	101	9,475	11,635	5,633	4,248	223	222
1927	158	183	26	34	79	76	10,330	16,118	5,997	4,857	213	229
1928	153	178	31	28	101	113	12,567	21,870	6,374	4,181	228	252
1929	231	135	30	25	86	84	14,861	23,075	7,023	4,656	266	310

International Historical Statistics: The Americas 1750-1993

E1 NORTH AMERICA: External Trade Aggregates in Current Values

1885-1929

	Mexico[4]		Newfoundland[1,5]		Nicaragua[11]		Panama[15]		Trinidad[1,12]		USA[1,6]	
	Imports	Exports	Imports	Exports	Imports	Exports	Imports	Exports	Imports	Exports	Imports	Exports
					(thousand gold pesos							
	(million pesos)		(thousand pounds)		or cordobas)		(million balboas)		(thousand pounds)		(million US dollars)	
1885	39	44	1,396	985	...	...	...	...	2,241	2,247	595	776
1886	41	49	1,254	1,013	...	...	...	...	2,504	2,509	653	710
1887	43	49	1,124	1,078	...	...	...	...	1,919	1,871	709	742
1888	40	60	1,546	1,371	...	...	...	...	1,944[12]	2,133[12]	739	724
1889	52	62	1,376	1,276	...	...	...	...	2,127	2,348	763	779
1890	...	63	1,326	1,271			...	...	2,272	2,199	810	893
1891	...	75	1,431	1,549	...	...	...	...	2,121	2,083	863	907
1892	43	88	...	...	...	...	...	...	2,105	2,272	847	1,063
1893	30	79	1,578	1,309	...	...	...	...	2,289	2,336	889	889
1894	34	91	1,493	1,211	...	...	...	...	2,168	2,017	668	942
1895	42	105	1,233[5]	1,278[5]	4,235	5,138	...	...	2,291	2,076	752	855
1896	42	111	1,230	1,364	...	...	...	...	2,477	2,177	809	944
1897	44	129	1,220	1,012	2,642	3,058	...	...	2,173	2,000	796	1,113
1898	51	138	1,066	1,074	2,866	3,184	...	...	2,294	2,332	647	1,286
1899	61[4] 120	150	1,297	1,425	...	...	...	...	2,536	2,573	728	1,283
1900	133	158	1,541	1,773	3,517	3,961	...	...	2,500	2,585	885	1,451
1901	151	172	1,536	1,718	2,302	3,478	...	...	2,652	2,446	859	1,552
1902	191	207	1,611	1,964	1,273	3,047	...	...	2,672	2,472	931	1,432
1903	178	210	1,743	2,051	2,461	3,652	...	...	2,526	2,275	1,050	1,464
1904	178	209	1,942	2,134	3,202	3,926	...	...	2,629	2,479	1,019	1,510
1905	220	271	2,113	2,193	3,407	3,542	...	...	3,304	3,169	1,145	1,568
1906	232	248	2,141	2,484	3,409	4,231	7.4	1.1	3,121	2,872	1,271	1,810
1907	222	243	2,143	2,487	3,224	3,364	9.6	2.0	3,375	2,500	1,458	1,938
1908	157	231	2,367	2,429	2,959	3,648	7.8	1.8	2,683[12]	3,908[12]	1,228	1,919
1909	195	260	2,349	2,230	2,583	3,989	8.8	1.5	3,289	3,218	1,326	1,719
1910	206	294	2,631	2,431	2,856	4,545	10.0	1.8	3,343	3,468	1,592	1,800
1911	183	298	2,751	2,462	5,724	6,579	9.9	2.9	5,019	4,769	1,573	2,114
1912	192	300	3,029	2,852	4,967	2,932	9.9	2.1	4,682	4,473	1,700	2,269
1913	171	319	3,291	3,016	5,770	6,609	11.2	5.4	4,968	5,206	1,854	2,538
1914	[86][4]	[160][4]	3,123	3,111	4,134	3,968	9.9	3.8	4,183	4,201	1,924	2,420
1915	[53][4]	251	2,539	2,700	3,159	3,572	9.0	3.4	4,430[12] 3,013	5,379[12] 4,027	1,703[6]	2,820[6]
1916	[85][4]	487	3,377	3,899	4,778	4,243	9.2	5.7	3,565	4,188	2,424	5,554
1917	190[4]	307	4,382	4,601	6,393	4,808	9.2	5.6	4,157	4,702	3,005	6,318
1918	276	376	5,528	6,198	5,930	6,016	7.8	2.9	4,476	4,516	3,102	6,402
1919	237	394	6,844	7,561	7,912	10,153	11.4	3.8	5,159	6,187	3,993	8,159
1920	397	855	8,332	7,167	13,864	8,910	17.6	3.6	8,487	8,025	5,366	8,342
1921	493	757	5,943	4,613	5,310	6,629	11.4	2.5	6,846	4,402	2,572	4,537
1922	309	644	3,743	4,004	5,123	6,345	10.3	2.5	4,576	3,990	3,184	3,895
1923	315	568	3,972	4,308	7,268	9,604	12.7	2.4	4,285	4,612	3,866	4,239
1924	321	615	5,687	4,712	8,807	12,001	13.8	3.0	4,273	4,700	3,684	4,701
					(million gold cordobas)							
1925	391	682	7,480	5,051	10.4	11.7	16.1	3.7	4,346	4,895	4,292	5,009
1926	381	692	5,661	5,665	10.3	12.2	15.7	3.5	4,349	5,285	4,501	4,901
1927	346	634	5,305	6,339	10.2	8.4	14.7	3.9	5,072	5,573	4,240	4,941
1928	358	592	5,678	6,916	13.4	11.3	16.2	4.1	5,252	6,139	4,159	5,215
1929	382	591	6,008	7,564	11.8	10.4	19.3	4.1	5,932	6,392	4,463	5,324

E1 NORTH AMERICA: External Trade Aggregates in Current Values

1930–1974

	Barbados[1]		Canada[7]		Costa Rica		Cuba		Dominican Republic		El Salvador	
	Imports	Exports	Imports	Exports	Imports	Exports	Imports	Exports	Imports	Exports	Imports	Exports
	(thousand pounds)		(million Canadian dollars)		(million colones)		(million pesos)		(million pesos)		(million colones)	
1930	1,732	1,038	1,008	883	43	65	163	167	15.2	18.6	24	27
1931	1,492	1,043	628	600	35	57	80	119	10.2	13.1	15	23
1932	1,657	1,369	453	498	24	38	51	81	7.8	11.0	13	14
1933	1,740	1,370	401	535	29	49	42	84	9.3	9.4	16	20
1934	1,915	1,470	513	656	37	37	73	107	10.6	12.6	21	24
1935	1,841	1,123	550	738	47	49	96	128	9.8	15.2	22	26
1936	2,004	1,483	635	951	58	54	103	155	9.9	14.8	21	24
1937	2,220	1,632	809	1,012	67	65	130	186	11.7	17.9	26	37
1938	2,086	1,340	677	849	71	57	106	142	11.3	14.7	23	26
					(million US dollars)							
					12.6	9.3						
1939	2,378	2,028	751	936	16.9	8.6	106	148	11.6	18.4	22	30
	(million local dollars)											
1940	11.1	8.1	1,082	1,193	16.8	7.0	104	127	10.5	18.0	20	26
1941	11.1	9.1	1,449	1,640	17.8	9.8	134	211	11.7	16.6	21	25
1942	9.7	6.5	1,644	2,385	12.3	10.2	147	182	11.5	19.8	21	43
1943	14.1	11.2	1,735	3,001	20.4	12.2	177	351	14.4	36	29	54
1944	16.4	12.1	1,759	3,483	21.5	10.4	208	433	18.5	60	31	55
1945	16.7	13.8	1,556	3,267	26.9	11.5	238	410	18.1	43	34	52
1946	24.0	15.1	1,865	2,339	33.0	14.3	299	476	28	65	52	63
1947	34.2	17.8	2,574	2,812	48.1	31.0	520	747	53	83	92	99
1948	30.5	14.6	2,637[7]	3,110[7]	42.3	45.9	527	710	65	83	104	112
1949	33.9	22.5	2,761[7]	3,022[7]	43.4	48.2	451	578	46	74	101	135
1950	38.7	27.6	3,174	3,157	46.0	55.6	515	642	44	87	121	171
1951	51.9	35.5	4,085	3,963	55.7	63.4	640	766	59	119	157	212
1952	54.2	40.0	4,030	4,356	67.9	73.3	618	675	97	115	173	218
1953	45.5	41.0	4,383	4,173	73.7	80.1	490	640	86	105	181	222
1954	48.8	40.4	4,093	3,947	80.0	84.7	488	539	83	120	217	263
1955	55.2	38.8	4,712	4,351	87.5	80.9	575	594	98	115	230	267
1956	61.3	36.2	5,705	4,863	91.2	67.4	649	666	108	121	262	282
1957	68.3	49.0	5,623	4,920	103	83.4	773	808	116	147	288	346
1958	73.4	40.1	5,192	4,926	99	91.9	777	733	129	128	270	290
1959	74.9	46.7	5,654[16]	5,179[16]	103	76.7	673	637	117	130	249	283
			5,509	5,140								
1960	83.3	40.9	5,483	5,387	110	85.8	580	618	87	174	306	292
1961	80.3	43.3	5,781	5,902	107	84.1	639[9]	625	69	143	272	298
1962	89.1	50.3	6,294	6,357	113	93.0	759	521	129	172	312	341
1963	98.9	69.8	6,578	6,990	124	95.0	867	544	160	174	379	385
1964	109	60.3	7,488	8,303	139	114	1,019	714	192	179	478	445
1965	116	64.3	8,633	8,767	178	112	866	691	87	125	501	472
1966	131	70.0	10,072	10,325	178	136	925	598	161	137	550	472
1967	134	71.6	10,872	11,420	191	144	999	705	175	156	560	518
1968	168	80.2	12,358	13,624	214	171	1,102	651	197	163	534	530
1969	195	74.3	14,130	14,890	245	190	1,222	671	217	183	523	505
1970	235	79.1	13,952	16,820	317	231	1,311	1,050	278	214	534	571
1971	244	80.3	15,617	17,820	350	225	1,387	861	310	241	619	608
1972	270	84.5	18,669	20,150	343	279	1,190	771	338	348	695	754
1973	329	104	23,324	25,420	455	345	1,467	1,153	422	442	934	896
1974	418	172	31,692	32,441	720	440	2,226	2,236	673	637	1,409	1,156

International Historical Statistics: The Americas 1750–1993

E1 NORTH AMERICA: External Trade Aggregates in Current Values

1930–1974

	Guadeloupe		Guatemala[10]		Haiti[1]		Honduras[14]		Jamaica		Martinique	
	Imports	Exports	Imports	Exports	Imports	Exports	Imports	Exports	Imports	Exports	Imports	Exports
	(million francs)		(million quetzales)		(million gourdes)		(thousand gold pesos)		(thousand pounds)		(million francs)	
1930	229	193	16	23	64	71	15,946	25,096	6,099	4,080	237	282
1931	189	137	13	15	48	45	10,193	18,558	4,943	3,334	220	180
1932	167	190	7.4	11	37	36	7,497	14,839	4,751	3,240	191	201
1933	153	191	7.5	9.2	38	47	6,114	12,313	4,365	2,499	192	200
1934	150	152	9.9	15	46	52	8,330	10,477	4,765	3,174	187	184
1935	112	160	12	12	41	36	9,465	8,621	5,009	3,813	140	166
1936	125	171	14	17	38	47	8,213	6,993	5,072	3,803	156	191
1937	195	294	21	18	46	45	9,887	7,476	6,135	4,962	214	231
1938	251	296	21	18	38	35	9,468	5,443	6,423	5,028	235	310
							(million lempiras)					
							[18.8][14]	[31.8][14]				
1939	241	278	19	19	41	36	19.4	45	6,501	4,753	234	319
1940	184	282	16	12	40	27	20	44	6,152	3,204	225	330
1941	201	137	16[10]	14	37	33	20	42	6,442	3,959	215	183
1942	168	82	14	20	42	43	22	41	5,460	4,050	207	90
1943	158	30	18	20	49	53	19	18	7,209	4,236	136	81
1944	385	286	21	24	80	81	24	39	8,968	4,478	526	248
1945	451	986	23	30	66	86	26	55	9,586	4,959	602	580
1946	1,116	1,495	36	37[17] 53	80	114	37	60	12,450	8,750	1,583	1,563
1947	2,803	3,589	57	66	136	157	56	85	18,941	10,168	3,667	4,117
1948	5,415	3,835	68	67	161	154	71	98	19,678	11,387	6,406	4,696
1949	6,987	6,842	68	63	157	155	67	114	19,225	12,134	8,638	5,185
							(million local dollars)					
1950	7,422	6,008	71	79	181	192	67	131	45	32	7,432	5,306
1951	9,147	8,102	81	84	223	248	79[14]	128[14]	61	36	10,912	7,498
1952	12,440	9,966	76	95	253	265	115	124	73	37	13,405	6,932
1953	11,744	8,785	80	100	226	189	108	135	71	52	12,198	6,883
1954	12,684	11,709	86	105	238	278	103	112	75	63	12,637	8,857
1955	13,056	11,881	104[10]	107[10]	196	174	108	98	91	69	13,754	8,972
1956	12,695	10,181	138	123	232	233	117	146	117	80	13,079	9,893
1957	16,842	12,380	147	116	191	165	137	130	133	103	17,455	12,915
	(million new francs)										(million new francs)	
1958	201	142	150	107	227	211	131	139	129	96	174	122
1959	207	172	134	108	169	130	124[14]	137	137	96	211	155
1960	238	171	138	117	202	191	143	126	155	113	233	159
1961	259	178	134	113	164	152	144	146	151	127	251	166
1962	284	174	136	118	186	204	160	163	159	130	281	166
1963	342	188	171	154	180	216	190	167	161	144	364	176
1964	392	172	202	164	180	190	203	188	207	154	389	145
1965	421	187	228	188	186	189	244	253	206	153	449	186
1966	448	183	208	229	180	192	298	291	234	163	457	221
1967	492	160	247	202	182	168	329	316	253	163	520	212
1968	504	180	249	227	188	178	369	358	320	183	537	197
1969	546	176	250	255	194	186	368	342	363	212	651	182
1970	709	209	284	290	275	202	441	363	438	289	810	167
1971	692	231	303	283	302	237	387	388	460	283	860	189
1972	747	201	324	328	345	220	386	419	489	300	872	228
1973	896	285	431	436	416	264	524	523	615	355	1,083	244
1974	1,104	278	701	572	626	358	760	588	851	549	1,405	347

E1 NORTH AMERICA: External Trade Aggregates in Current Values

1930–1974

	Mexico		Newfoundland[1,5]		Nicaragua[11]		Panama[15]		Trinidad & Tobago		USA	
	Imports	Exports	Imports	Exports	Imports	Exports	Imports	Exports	Imports	Exports	Imports	Exports
	(million pesos)		(thousand pounds)		(million gold cordobas)		(million balboas)		(thousand pounds)		(million US dollars)	
1930	350	459	6,549	8,232	8.2	7.9	18.3	3.3	5,334	5,150	3,104	3,897
1931	217	400	5,190	6,895	6.0	6.2	13.5	2.6	3,911	4,045	2,119	2,451
1932	181	305	3,727	6,612	3.5	4.2	8.9	2.0	3,692	3,937	1,342	1,625
1933	244	365	3,117	6,044	3.8	4.5	9.3	2.3	4,002	3,777	1,510	1,694
1934	334	644	3,350	5,355	4.6	4.6	13.6	2.7	4,486	4,350	1,758	2,149
1935	406	750	3,954	5,567	5.1	5.1	15.6	3.6	4,372	4,336	2,402	2,302
1936	464	775	4,251	5,794	5.6	3.8	19.0	3.7	5,664	5,607	2,605	2,468
1937	614	892	4,846	5,684	5.6	6.2	21.8	8.4	7,466	6,176	3,176	3,361
1938	494	838	5,593	7,001	5.1	4.3	17.7	7.5	7,395	6,483	2,191	3,102
1939	630	914	5,134	6,714	6.4	4.8	20	6.7	7,242	5,836	2,403	3,192
1940	669	960	6,341	7,450	7.1	3.7	23	6.9	9,394	5,180	2,684	4,025
1941	915	730	7,974	8,388	10.4	4.6	33	6.2	11,976	3,393	3,392	5,153
1942	753	990	14,513	8,854	6.8	5.9	38	3.8	11,478	2,477	2,797	8,081
1943	910	1,130	11,770	6,950	14	7.7	40	3.7	12,456	2,353	3,409	12,996
1944	1,895	1,047	14,042	9,988	10	7.8	38	3.9	14,373	2,614	3,952	14,386
									(million local dollars)			
1945	1,604	1,272	14,792	10,946	12	6.9	46	6	65	58	4,186	9,897
1946	2,637	1,975	…	…	15	11	56	7.9[17] 13	75	61	5,000	9,775
1947	3,230	2,162	…	…	21	13	76	15[15]	118	86	5,824	15,369
1948	2,950	2,595	…	…	24	19	64	24	131	132	7,195	12,665
1949	3,524	3,389	…	…	21	16	60	24	154	138	6,696	12,074
1950	4,402	4,339	included with Canada		25	27	61	23	168	176	8,962	10,282
1951	7,112	5,447			30	37	66	25	219	214	11,070	15,041
1952	6,984	5,126			40	42	73	23	244	230	10,820	15,206
1953	6,985	4,836			44	46	71	26	236	256	11,010	15,782
1954	8,926	6,936			58[11]	55	72	31	249	262	10,372	15,114
1955	11,046	9,484			70	72	75	36	294	285	11,568	15,556
1956	13,396	10,671			69	58	83	31	301	330	12,906	19,102
1957	14,440	8,729			81	64	99	35	356	393	13,418	20,873
1958	14,108	8,846			78	64	94	33	412	425	13,351	17,920
1959	12,583	9,007			67	65	93	35	448	449	15,692	17,655
1960	14,831	9,247			72	63	109	21	504	491	15,075	20,612
1961	14,233	9,997			74	68	124	24	584	593	14,761	21,036
1962	14,287	11,029			98	90	145	40	606	592	16,457	21,715
1963	15,496	11,504			111	107	181	60	646	641	17,211	23,389
1964	18,657	12,492			136	125	181	70	731	699	18,750	26,652
1965	19,496	13,610			160	144	208	79	817	690	21,431	27,532
1966	20,064	14,535			182	142	235	89	778	735	25,620	30,434
1967	21,824	13,798			202	152	251	94	724	763	26,892	31,627
1968	24,527	14,759			183	162	266	99	854	943	33,226	34,636
1969	25,974	17,312			176	159	294	113	966	948	36,043	38,006
1970	28,994	16,025			198	179	357	110	1,085	961	39,756	42,590
1971	28,130	17,070			210	187	396	117	1,327	1,039	45,516	43,498
1972	33,981	20,926			218	249	440	123	1,468	1,068	55,282	48,959
1973	47,668	25,881			326	278	502	138	1,553	1,372	68,658	70,246
					(million paper cordobas)							
1974	75,709	37,021			3,939	2,671	822	211	3,778	4,166	107,112	97,144

E1 NORTH AMERICA: External Trade Aggregates in Current Values

	Barbados[1]		Canada		Costa Rica		Cuba		Dominican Republic		El Salvador	
	Imports	Exports	Imports	Exports	Imports	Exports	Imports	Exports	Imports	Exports	Imports	Exports
	(million local dollars)		(million local dollars)		(million US dollars)		(million pesos)		(million pesos)		(million colones)	
1975	437	217	34,691	32,246	694	493	3,113	2,952	773	894	1,495	1,329
1976	475	173	37,444	38,397	770	593	3,180	2,692	764	716	1,837	1,858
1977	549	191	42,332	44,554	1,021	828	3,462	2,918	848	780	2,323	2,431
1978	629	261	50,102	53,183	1,166	865	3,574	3,440	861	675	2,568	2,002
1979	848	304	62,871	65,641	1,397	934	3,687	3,499	1,080	869	2,598	2,828
1980	1,055	455	69,274	76,159	1,540	1,002	4,627	3,967	1,498	962	2,404	2,684
1981	1,148	393	79,482	83,812	1,208	1,008	5,114	4,224	1,450	1,188	2,461	1,992
1982	1,107	518	67,856	84,530	889	870	5,531	4,933	1,256	768	2,142	1,749
1983	1,238	646	75,608	90,612	988	873	6,222	5,535	1,279	785	2,229	1,838
1984	1,321	784	95,460	112,384	1,094	1,006	7,227	5,476	1,257	868	2,444	1,813
1985	1,222	708	104,355	119,475	1,098	976	8,035	5,991	3,875	2,347	2,403	1,697
1986	1,181	553	112,678	120,490	1,147	1,120	7,569	5,325	4,165	2,086	4,284	3,563
1987	1,036	311	116,076	125,087	1,383	1,158	7,611	5,401	6,885	2,710	4,970	2,955
1988	1,170	349	131,554	137,695	1,410	1,246	7,579	5,518	11,362	5,518	5,034	3,043
1989	1,354	374	141,866	144,248	1,717	1,414	8,124	5,392	...	...	5,806	2,482
1990	1,408	430	143,837	148,912	1,990	1,448	6,745	4,910	...	...	8,816	3,891
1991	1,398	414	142,913	145,658	1,876	1,598	3,690	3,585	...	...	11,360	4,731
1992	1,048	380	156,246	162,596	2,440	1,829	...	...	...	...	14,210	4,984
1993	1,154	374	179,425	187,346	2,885	2,049	...	...	...	...	16,630	6,365

	Guadeloupe		Guatemala		Haiti		Honduras		Jamaica		Martinique	
	Imports	Exports	Imports	Exports	Imports	Exports	Imports	Exports	Imports	Exports	Imports	Exports
	(million francs)		(million quetzales)		(million gourdes)		(million lempiras)		(million local dollars)		(million Francs)	
1975	1,315	353	724	623	745	399	809	606	1,021	690	1,453	408
1976	1,515	429	839	760	1,034	622	906	794	830	573	1,965	594
1977	1,844	387	1,052	1,160	1,063	743	1,159	1,037	782	699	2,099	630
1978	1,910	499	1,286	1,090	1,166	777	1,398	1,225	1,260	1,142	2,241	567
1979	2,540	648	1,504	1,241	1,360	927	1,652	1,467	1,755	1,446	2,870	567
1980	3,074	446	1,598	1,520	1,771	1,131	2,017	1,659	2,087	1,715	3,564	492
1981	3,334	509	1,673	1,226	2,240	757	1,891	1,458	2,623	1,735	4,188	895
1982	4,117	548	1,388	1,120	1,936	813	1,384	1,336	2,460	1,367	4,835	764
1983	5,039	627	1,126	1,159	2,203	769	1,605	1,344	2,841	1,392	5,578	867
1984	5,231	751	1,278	1,128	2,361	893	1,787	1,451	4,509	2,897	5,648	924
1985	5,745	669	1,175	1,057	2,208	871	1,776	1,529	6,147	3,128	6,050	1,300
1986	5,457	748	960	1,044	1,774	922	1,750	1,708	5,322	3,226	6,065	1,445
1987	6,229	564	1,479	981	1,872	1,068	1,797	1,616	6,790	3,874	6,708	1,163
1988	7,169	909	1,557	1,021	1,721	896	1,866	1,737	7,983	4,830	7,692	1,172
1989	7,888	707	1,654	1,108	1,455	720	1,937	1,717	10,668	5,747	8,387	1,277
1990	8,937	649	1,641	1,163	1,661	801	1,870	1,662	13,923	8,305	9,681	1,512
1991	9,217	830	1,851	1,202	2,414	1,005	5,080	4,215	20,830	13,079	9,520	1,208
1992	8,021	690	2,531	1,295	2,728	719	5,696	4,395	38,267	24,099	9,267	1,312
1993	7,903	726	2,599	1,340	4,556	1,029	7,386	5,291	52,847	26,361	8,812	1,078

E1   NORTH AMERICA: External Trade Aggregates in Current Values

	Mexico		Nicaragua		Panama		Trinidad & Tobago		USA	
	Imports	Exports	Imports	Exports	Imports	Exports	Imports	Exports	Imports	Exports
	(million pesos)		(million cordobas)		(million galboas)		(million local dollars)		(million US dollars)	
1975	82,131	37,405	3,632	2,636	816	286	3,239	3,875	105,880	108,113
1976	90,900	53,675	3,739	3,808	780	238	4,904	5,392	132,498	115,413
1977	126,352	96,779	5,353	4,474	778	251	4,365	5,231	160,411	121,293
1978	177,278	134,313	4,173	4,539	845	256	4,721	4,895	186,044	143,766
1979	287,135	201,109	3,334	5,244	1,063	303	5,051	6,265	222,228	182,025
	(thousand million pesos)									
1980	446	351	8,916	4,526	1,289	358	7,626	9,785	256,984	220,786
1981	614	476	10,044	5,023	1,393	328	7,499	9,026	273,352	233,666
1982	743	1,230	7,794	4,078	1,407	375	8,873	7,372	254,885	212,277
1983	1,096	2,692	8,109	4,309	1,412	321	6,197	5,646	269,878	200,537
1984	2,006	4,054	8,303	3,873	1,423	276	4,606	5,216	341,177	223,999
1985	3,536	5,588	25,558	7,991	1,392	333	3,739	5,247	361,626	218,828
1986	7,187	9,299	57,915	16,187	1,229	341	4,860	4,989	382,295	227,158
1987	19,343	27,505	64,581	20,993	1,306	336	4,387	5,265	424,442	254,122
1988	47,507	46,949	...	...	815	292	4,310	5,424	459,542	322,427
1989	65,427	55,251	...	...	965	297	5,190	6,707	492,922	363,812
1990	92,524	74,824	...	...	1,489	340	4,712	8,331	516,987	393,592
1991	120,584	80,286	...	...	1,695	358	5,994	7,542	508,363	421,730
1992	155,633	84,533	...	...	2,024	501	4,964	7,188	553,923	448,163
1993	159,653	93,080	...	...	2,188	553	7,495	8,801	603,438	464,773

E1   SOUTH AMERICA: EXTERNAL TRADE AGGREGATES IN CURRENT VALUES

1821–1854

	Brazil[19]		Colombia		Guyana[1,21]		Peru[27]		Surinam		Venezuela[23]	
	Imports	Exports	Imports	Exports	Imports	Exports	Imports	Exports	Imports	Exports	Imports	Exports
	(million paper milreis)		(million gold pesos)		(thousand pounds)		(million pesos)		(million guilders)		(million bolivares)	
1821	21	20	...	...	...	...	4.6	5.9	...	...	...	...
1822	22	20	...	...	...	...	3.3	3.2	...	...	...	...
1823	19	21	...	...	...	...	...	...	...	...	...	...
1824	24	19	...	...	...	...	...	...	...	...	...	...
1825	23	21	...	...	...	...	...	...	...	...	...	...
1826	19	17	...	...	...	...	4.5	4.0	...	...	...	...
1827	27	25	...	...	...	...	...	...	...	...	...	...
1828	32	32	...	...	...	...	...	...	...	...	...	...
1829	36	33	...	...	...	...	...	...	...	...	...	...
1830	42	35	...	...	...	...	...	...	...	...	8.2	8.7
1831	33	32	...	...	...	...	8.0	5.0	...	...	13	11
1832	32[19]	32[19]	...	...	573	1,719	5.5	5.1	...	...	13	12
1833	36	33	...	...	558	1,837	...	...	...	...	13	14
1834	37	33	...	...	653	1,529	...	...	...	...	17	17
1835	41	41	3.8	1.7	711	1,771	...	...	...	...	15	20
1836	45	34	4.8	2.8	912	2,094	...	...	...	...	23	25
1837	41	34	3.1	3.1	957	1,698	...	...	...	...	15	21
1838	49	42	3.7	1.5	1,059	1,680	...	...	...	...	22	27
1839	52	43	3.7	3.8	1,209	1,348	4.6	5.3	...	...	31	30
1840	58	42	4.0	...	988	1,888	...	...	...	...	37	31
1841	56	39	1.6	0.7	886	1,166	...	...	...	...	32	38
1842	51	41	2.7	1.3	672	1,136	...	...	...	...	26	34
1843	55	44	5.0	...	715	991	...	...	...	...	22	30
1844	55	47	4.8	2.9	664	1,119	...	...	...	...	25	28
1845	52	54	3.5	2.6	831	992	5.1	4.8	...	...	27	36
1846	56	52	2.0	2.0	884	776	4.3	5.1	...	...	25	32
1847	47	58	1.4	2.0	771	1,109	4.9	6.2	...	...	19	28
1848	52	56	2.3	1.4	601	887	5.8	7.7	...	...	14	28
1849	59	55	3.3	1.0	570	673	...	...	...	...	21	25
1850	77	68	5.0	3.9	785	815	...	...	2.1	3.9	28	32
1851	93	67	8.0	4.6	855	865	6.1	7.5	...	...	30	33
1852	87	74	7.0	5.0	965	978	...	...	1.9	2.8	23	30
1853	86	77	5.4	3.7	847	1,015	7.2	8.6	2.0	3.0	29	36
1854	85	91	4.0	5.5	916	1,405	7.6	8.9	2.2	3.1	31	34

E1 SOUTH AMERICA: External Trade Aggregates in Current Values

1855–1894

	Argentina[18]		Brazil[19]		Chile[20]		Colombia		Ecuador[25]		Guyana[1,21]	
	Imports	Exports	Imports	Exports	Imports	Exports	Imports	Exports	Imports	Exports	Imports	Exports
	(million gold pesos)		(million paper milreis)		(million gold pesos)		(million gold pesos)		(million sucres)		(thousand pounds)	
1855	...	...	93	94	...	...	5.9	5.1	...	...	886	1,331
1856	...	...	125	115	...	...	9.4	5.6	...	...	...	...
1857	...	...	130	96	51	50	8.0	7.1	...	...	...	...
1858	...	...	127	107	46	46	7.2	9.1	...	...	...	...
1859	...	...	113	113	47	50	8.3	9.2	...	...	1,180	1,229
1860	...	...	124	123	54	62	10.2	10.8	...	...	1,146	1,513
1861	...	...	111	121	41	50	9.9	10.9	...	...	1,340	1,584
1862	...	...	99	122	43	56	10.2	10.5	...	...	1,107	1,365
1863	...	...	126	131	50	49	17.9	9.5	...	...	1,122	1,679
1864	23	22	132	141	46	67	25.5	22.6	...	...	1,509	1,845
1865	30	26	138	157	54	65	23.6	16.9	...	...	1,359	2,090
1866	37	27	143	156	49	69	27.8	15.1	...	...	1,531	2,171
1867	39	33	141	185	65	80	23.2	12.0	...	...	1,499	2,366
1868	42	30	167	203	66	76	24.6	14.7	...	...	1,618	2,232
1869	41	32	168	197	70	71	24.1	17.6	...	...	1,572	2,164
1870	49	30	162	168	72	68	23.8	15.4	...	...	1,897	2,383
1871	46	27	150	191	68	82	24.8	15.8	...	...	1,897	2,749
1872	62	47	159	215	89	96	30.0	19.8	...	...	2,014	2,463
1873	73	47	153	190	94	95	39.0	15.3	...	...	1,765	2,217
1874	58	45	168	208	97	93	33.6	20.4	...	...	1,873	2,762
1875	58	52	172	184	95	87	17.8	28.9	...	...	1,837	2,337
1876	36	48	157	196	88	85	21.9	14.5	...	...	1,983	3,031
1877	40	45	164	186	73	69	19.9	12.7	...	...	2,230	3,049
1878	44	37	164	204	63	70	22.5	16.2	...	...	2,151	2,508
1879	46	49	174	222	57	78	26.0	18.3	...	...	2,065	2,716
1880	46	58	180	231	64	88	23.5	19.4	...	...	2,003	2,618
1881	56	58	182	210	84	104	26.5	20.7	...	...	1,784	2,597
1882	61	60	190	197	108	140	26.9	17.8	...	5.5	2,100	3,209
1883	80	60	203	217	115	149	27.0	14.6	...	4.9	2,225	3,172
1884	94	68	178	226	112	122	25.3	10.6	7.6	10	1,999	2,322
1885	92	84	198	195	85	108	16.1	7.3	...	4.9	1,467	1,801
1886	95	70	207	264	93	108	20.9	8.9	...	6.6	1,436	1,843
1887	117	84	[104][19]	[125][19]	103	127	25.8	11.7	...	10	1,603	2,191
1888	128	100	216	237	129	154	26.1	10.2	...	9.1	1,586	2,025
1889	165	123	218	256	137	139	21.7	9.2	9.7	7.9	1,804	2,471
1890	142	101	295	326	144	144	25.1	12.2	10	9.7	1,887	2,162
1891	67	103	512	574	135	139	24.1	18.2	7.2	7.4	1,708[21]	2,533[21]
1892	91	113	590	784	165	135	19.8	9.7	8.4	12	1,780	2,433
1893	96	94	652	706	144	152	20.6	11.0	11	15	1,921	2,359
1894	93	102	782	767	114	152	16.3	10.3	...	...	1,669	2,040

E1 SOUTH AMERICA: External Trade Aggregates in Current Values

1855–1894

	Netherlands Antilles[28]		Paraguay[26]		Peru[27]		Surinam		Uruguay[22]		Venezuela[23]	
	Imports	Exports	Imports	Exports	Imports	Exports	Imports	Exports	Imports	Exports	Imports	Exports
	(million guilders)		(thousand gold pesos)		(million pesos)		(million guilders)		(million pesos fuertes)		(million bolivares)	
1855	…	…	…	…	…	…	2.4	3.4	…	…	28	36
1856	…	…	…	…	…	…	2.6	4.3	…	…	37	39
1857	…	…	…	…	…	…	3.0	5.6	…	…	37	29
1858	…	…	…	…	15	16	3.5	3.4	…	…	40	44
1859	…	…	…	…	15	17	2.9	3.3	…	…	34	43
1860	…	…	…	…	15	35	3.1	4.5	…	…	24	30
1861	…	…	…	…	15	37	3.3	3.5	…	…	22	38
1862	…	…	…	…	…	…	2.9	3.6	8.2	8.8	17	31
					(million soles)							
1863	…	…	…	…	15	35	3.7	3.1	…	…	14	25
1864	…	…	…	…	…	…	4.8	3.1	8.4	6.3	48	42
1865	…	…	…	…	…	…	4.5	2.2	…	…	41	46
1866	…	…	…	…	15	22	…	…	14.6	10.7	31	38
1867	…	…	…	…	11	23	…	…	17.7	12.1	22	17
1868	…	…	…	…	12	20	4.0	3.1	16.1	12.1	32	27
1869	…	…	…	…	11	20	3.6	2.6	16.8	13.9	15	35
1870	…	…	…	…	12	21	4.0	2.7	15.0	12.8	23	55
1871	…	…	…	…	12	21	4.0	2.9	14.9	13.3	40	60
1872	…	…	…	…	13	19	3.7	3.2	18.8	15.5	46	70
1873	…	…	…	…	15	21	3.6	2.6	21.1	16.3	27	74
1874	…	…	…	…	14	20	4.0	3.2	17.2	15.2	53	87
1875	…	…	…	…	16	19	3.1	2.4	12.4	12.7	75	81
1876	…	…	…	…	20	21	3.2	2.8	12.8	13.7	73	71
1877	…	…	…	…	24	32	3.5	3.8	15.0	15.9	65	75
1878	…	…	…	…	23	25	3.6	2.0	15.9	17.5	42	58
1879	…	…	956	1,582	…	…	3.6	3.1	15.9	16.6	49	52
1880	…	…	1,030	1,613	…	…	3.9	3.6	19.5	19.8	45	69
1881	…	…	1,293	1,929	…	…	4.8	3.9	17.9	20.2	58	70
1882	…	…	1,417	1,651	…	…	4.3	3.7	18.2	22.1	86	99
1883	…	…	1,040	1,766	5.3	2.0	5.2	3.7	20.3	25.2	70	74
1884	…	…	1,448	1,573	8.2	2.0	5.3	4.1	24.6	24.8	59	77
1885	…	…	1,477	1,601	8.2	2.4	4.8	3.1	25.3	25.3	62	82
1886	…	…	1,918	2,103	9.9	2.4	4.6	3.0	20.2	23.8	73	91
1887	3.2	0.5	…	…	11	10	5.1	3.5	24.6	18.7	79	90
1888	2.8	0.6	3,320	2,589	9.6	11	4.3	3.3	29.5	28.0	81	97
1889	3.4	0.7	3,222	2,301	10	11	4.9	3.5	36.8	26.0	84	101
1890	3.7	0.8	2,726	3,504	12	12	5.3	4.3	32.4	29.1	67	120
1891	4.1	0.5	1,845	3,166	15	12	5.9	4.0	19.0	27.0	71	105
1892	3.4	0.3	2,190	1,687	15	18	5.2	3.9	18.4	26.0	53	89
1893	4.1	0.3	2,533	1,302	11	17	5.7	5.5	19.7	27.7	73	108
1894	3.2	0.3	2,222	1,808	12	12	6.2	5.1	23.8	33.5	62	99

E1 SOUTH AMERICA: External Trade Aggregates in Current Values

1895–1934

	Argentina[18]		Bolivia		Brazil[19]		Chile[20]		Colombia	
	Imports	Exports	Imports	Exports	Imports	Exports	Imports	Exports	Imports	Exports
	(million gold pesos)		(million bolivianos)		(million paper milreis or cruzeiros)		(million gold pesos)		(million gold pesos)	
1895	95	120	...	...	844	883	146	154	17.8	10.5
1896	112	117	...	...	864	864	156	156	22.9	13.0
1897	98	101	...	...	846	1,011	139	137	22.3	12.0
1898	107	134	...	...	933	1,011	102	168	16.2	13.1
1899	117	185	13	27	865	955	106	163	13.7	12.8
1900	113	155	13	36	645	850	129	168	9.0	9.1
1901	114	168	17	37	448	861	139	174	15.7	9.3
1902	103	179	14	28	471	736	133	187	12.5	8.1
1903	131	221	16	25	486	743	142	196	18.3	10.5
1904	187	264	21	31	513	770	157	218	22.4	16.6
1905	205	323	28	42	455	685	189	273	15.0	12.9
1906	270	292	35	56	499	800	238	287	16.7	13.7
1907	286	296	38	50	645	861	294	280	17.8	13.2
1908	273	366	41	47	567	706	267	319	17.4	12.0
1909	303	397	37	64	593	1,017	262	298	16.9	14.4
1910	352[18]	373[18]	49	75	714	939	297	371	17.4	14.4
	(million paper pesos)									
	862	884								
1911	920	778	58	83	794	1,004	349	383	18.1	18.5
1912	1,016	1,140	50	90	951	1,120	334	397	24.0	25.6
1913	1,128	1,180	55	94	1,007	982	326	442	28.5	29.9
1914	733	916	40	66	562	756	270	309	21.0	26.4
1915	694	1,323	23	95	583	1,042	152	335	17.8	25.6
1916	832	1,302	31	101	811	1,137	222	523	29.7	30.6
1917	864	1,250	50	158	838	1,192	339	723	24.8	31.9
1918	1,138	1,822	70	183	989	1,137	395	811	21.8	34.9
1919	1,490	2,343	62	144	1,334	2,179	387	331	47.5	78.1
1920	2,125	2,373	65	156	2,091	1,752	441	804	113.6	64.4
1921	1,703	1,525	71	67	1,690	1,710	368	456	37.0	53.2
1922	1,567	1,536	50	95	1,653	2,332	237	350	47.0	46.8
1923	1,974	1,753	63	108	2,267	3,297	329	562	67.2	56.0
1924	1,883	2,299	63	115	2,780	3,864	363	636	62.3	84.2
1925	1,993	1,973	68	111	3,377	4,022	403	635	97.2	83.2
1926	1,869	1,800	70	114	2,706	3,191	430	496	124.0	110.2
1927	1,947	2,294	66	121	3,273	3,644	358	559	139.2	107.6
1928	1,902	2,396	64	109	3,695	3,970	399	655	162.4	132.5
1929	1,959	2,168	71	123	3,528	3,860	539	775	141.5	121.7
1930	1,680	1,396	58	88	2,344[19]	2,888[19]	467	449	70	104
1931	1,174	1,456	30	57	1,881	3,358	235	280	46	80
1932	836	1,288	22	46	1,519	2,501	71	94	34	67
1933	897	1,121	41	67	2,165	2,780	61	112	56	68
1934	1,110	1,438	67	116	2,503	3,459	71	154	98	124

E1   SOUTH AMERICA: External Trade Aggregates in Current Values

	Ecuador[25]		Guyana[1,21]		Netherlands Antilles[28]		Paraguay[26]	
	Imports	Exports	Imports	Exports	Imports	Exports	Imports	Exports
	(million sucres)		(thousand pounds)		(million guilders)		(thousand gold pesos)	
1895	...	...	1,444	1,769	2.6	0.3	2,460	2,121
1896	...	22	1,342	1,899	3.0	0.4	2,786	2,049
1897	18	31	1,283	1,784	2.7	0.3	2,211[26]	2,555[26]
1898	9.9	14	1,371	1,776	2.0	0.3	2,608	2,463
1899	...	17	1,319	1,928[21]	1.9	0.3	2,511	2,291
1900	13	15	1,307	1,982	2.7	0.3	2,556	2,652
1901	15	16	1,297	1,716	2.2	0.3	3,023	2,565
1902	14	18	1,371	1,757	2.4	0.3	2,426	3,073
1903	11	19	1,600	1,754	3.0	0.3	3,506	4,047
1904	15	23	1,479	1,932	2.7	0.5[28]	3,566	3,196
1905	16	19	1,584	1,916	3.2	1.0	4,679	2,833
1906	17	22	1,634	1,786	3.2	1.0	6,324	2,695
1907	20	23	1,698	1,644	3.8	1.3	7,513	3,236
1908	21	27	1,778	2,044	2.8	0.9	4,073	3,867
1909	19	25	1,710	1,921	3.2	0.9	3,788	5,137
							(million gold pesos)	
1910	16	28	1,652	1,722	3.2	1.7	6.4	4.9
1911	...	26	1,665[21]	2,084[21]	4.2[28]	2.0	6.7	4.7
1912	21	25	1,632	1,727	...	...	5.4	4.2
1913	18	32	1,611	2,110	4.8	2.3	8.1	5.6
1914	17	26	1,597	2,454	4.7	2.2	5.1	5.6
1915	15	25	1,833	3,201	4.7	2.3	3.1	8.9
1916	19	35	2,190	3,476	6.2	2.4	7.0	8.9
1917	21	32	2,906	3,951	6.9	2.8	9.2	11.7
1918	17	27	3,394	3,083	7.3	2.7	11.1	11.4
1919	25	43	3,275	3,925	8.7	2.8	15.8	19.0
1920	44	50	4,723	5,686	7.3	11	13.1	15.0
1921	24	34	3,273	3,424	19	13	8.4	9.3
1922	34	46	2,293	2,925	20	14	5.7	9.9
1923	37	38	2,669	3,758	30	19	8.6	12.5
1924	52	61	2,744	3,394	51	32	15.7	12.4
1925	55	73	2,908	3,131	71	60	17.7	15.7
1926	47	64	2,599	2,733	107	95	12.2	15.5
1927	57	82	2,471	3,339	142	135	12.0	14.3
1928	81	93	2,471	3,110	268	260	14.3	15.9
1929	84	86	2,216	2,557	361	309	13.8	13.5
1930	64	81	1,971	2,222	407	417	15.1	14.2
1931	44	57	1,595	2,011	248	343	10.1	12.9
1932	25	49	1,690	2,205	140	182	6.4	12.9
1933	32	44	1,801	2,075	150	195	7.2	9.5
1934	62	102	1,749	1,892	155	161	11.3	12.4

E1 SOUTH AMERICA: External Trade Aggregates in Current Values

1895–1934

	Peru[27]		Surinam		Uruguay[22]		Venezuela[23]	
	Imports	Exports	Imports	Exports	Imports	Exports	Imports	Exports
	(million soles)		(million guilders)		(million pesos fuertes)		(millio bolivares)	
1895	11	15	5.2	5.5	25.4	32.5	61	111
1896	18	25	5.3	4.4	25.5	30.4	69	93
1897	16	28	5.3	5.2	19.5	29.3	44	74
1898	19	30	5.7	5.2	24.8	30.3	72	93
1899	21	33	6.1	5.5	25.7	36.6	54	78
1900	23	45	6.2	5.5	24.0	29.4	$\cdots_{23}$	$\cdots_{23}$
1901	27	43	7.1	5.4	23.7	27.7	56	80
1902	34	37	6.2	4.1	23.5	33.6	64	76
1903	38	39	6.3	4.3	25.1	37.3	28	40
1904	44	41	7.4	3.7	21.2	38.5	59	81
1905	44	58	6.6	4.4	30.8	30.8	48	73
1906	50	58	6.3	4.8	34.5	33.4	45	81
1907	55	57	6.9	5.9	37.5	34.9	52	81
1908	53	55	7.0	6.0	37.5	40.3	54	78
1909	43	65	7.2	6.6	36.9	45.1	49	83
1910	50_{27} 45	71	7.4	8.3	40.8	40.9	64	91
1911	52	74	8.3	9.2	44.8	42.5	95	114
1912	50	93	7.5	8.4	49.8	48.8	107_{23}	124
1913	60	91	7.1	9.5	50.4	45.1_{22} 68.5	85	151
1914	46	87	6.4	6.5	37.2_{22}	58.2	68	108
1915	30	115	5.4	6.9	40.6	73.3	69	114
1916	75	165	5.9	8.1	52.9	73.9	101	108
1917	107	186	7.6	8.9	66.6	103	101	115
1918	96	200	6.2	7.1	101	116	73	100
1919	119	269	9.0	9.0	113	147	140	256
1920	177	351	14	7.5	133	81	306	168
1921	167	165	13	6.6	94	70	96	127
1922	106	186	11	5.7	82	77	100	133
1923	139	238	7.9	8.4	$[102]^{22}$	101	153	153
1924	178	247	7.5	7.4	82	107	193	212
1925	182	214	9.5	9.9	95	99	274	327
1926	194	237	10.0	7.7	…	94	402	391
1927	194	310	9.3	11.8	…	96	359	440
1928	176	314	9.2	11.5	…	101	384	604
1929	190	334	8.6	7.8	…	93	443	774
1930	137	224	9.1	8.2	94	101	359	735_{29}
				(million US dollars)				960
					137	149		
1931	102	175	6.6	5.8	109	76	207	639
1932	76	169	5.6	4.2	44	46	153	666
1933	107	245	4.9	3.3	51	53	143	326
1934	171	300	5.3	3.8	50	56	131	414

E1 SOUTH AMERICA: External Trade Aggregates in Current Values

1935-1974

	Argentina		Bolivia		Brazil[19]		Chile[20]		Colombia	
	Imports	Exports	Imports	Exports	Imports	Exports	Imports	Exports	Imports	Exports
	(million paper pesos)		(million bolivianos)		(million paper cruzeiros)		(million gold pesos)		(million gold pesos)	
1935	1,175	1,569	71	149	3,856	4,104	98	155	120	124
			(million US dollars)							
1936	1,117	1,656	15	29	4,268	4,895	116	183	134	137
1937	1,558	2,311	16	35	5,314	5,092	143	311	170	152
1938	1,461	1,400	19	27	5,195	5,097	166	225	159	144
1939	1,338	1,573	17	34	4,994	5,610	137	220	183	136
1940	1,499	1,428	20	49	4,960	4,961	169	226	148	125
1941	1,277	1,465	28	60	5,503	6,726	175	256	170	134
1942	1,274	1,789	33	65	4,678	7,500	208	288	105	171
1943	942	2,192	39	81	6,220	8,729	212	287	147	219
1944	1,007	2,360	38	77	8,121	10,727	233	315	175	227
1945	1,154	2,498	40	80	8,743	12,198	252	330	281	246
1946	2,332	3,973	51	74	13,028	18,230	318	350	403	352
1947	5,349	5,505	60	81	22,789	21,179	429	451	639	446
1948	6,190	5,542	69	113	20,984	21,697	435	532	589	505
	(million US dollars)				(million US dollars)				(million US dollars)	
	1,562	1,629			1,121	1,180			324	277
1949	1,180	1,044	78	101	1,103	1,096	492	479	265	321
1950	964	1,178	56	94	1,085	1,355	400	458	365	396
1951	1,480	1,169	86	151	1,987	1,769	532	601	419	463
1952	1,179	688	93	141	1,986	1,418	599	736	415	473
1953	795	1,125	68	113	1,318	1,539	542	663	547	596
1954	979	1,027	66[24]	92	1,629	1,562	555	652	672	657
1955	1,173	929	81	100	1,306	1,423	609	768	669	580
1956	1,128	944	84	107	1,234	1,482	572	881	657	599
1957	1,310	975	90	95	1,488	1,392	714	741	483	511
1958	1,233	994	80	63	1,353	1,243	671	629	400	461
1959	993	1,009	65	76	1,374	1,282	668	804	416	473
1960	1,249	1,079	72	66	1,462	1,269	808	793	519	465
1961	1,460	964	78	73	1,460	1,403	956	822	557	434
1962	1,357	1,216	97	75	1,475	1,214	828	861	540	463
1963	981	1,365	103	81	1,487	1,406	1,031	877	506	447
1964	1,077	1,410	103	112	1,263	1,430	983	1,013	586	548
1965	1,199	1,493	134	129	1,096	1,595	977	1,113	453	539
1966	1,124	1,593	138	127	1,496	1,741	1,225	1,425	674	508
1967	1,096	1,465	151	150	1,667	1,654	1,176	1,477	497	510
							(million US dollars)			
							722	908		
1968	1,169	1,368	153	152	2,129	1,881	744	936	643	558
1969	1,576	1,612	165	172	2,265	2,311	908	1,068	685	607
1970	1,694	1,773	159	190	2,849	2,739	930	1,234	843	727
1971	1,868	1,740	170	181	3,701	2,904	980	961	929	689
1972	1,905	1,941	185	201	4,783	3,990	941	855	859	969
1973	2,230	3,266	230	260	6,999	6,199	1,098	1,231	1,062	1,177
1974	3,635	3,931	366	556	14,168	7,951	1,681	1,247	1,597	1,417

E1   SOUTH AMERICA: External Trade Aggregates in Current Values

1935–1974

	Ecuador[25]		Guyana[1,21]		Netherlands Antilles[28]		Paraguay	
	Imports	Exports	Imports	Exports	Imports	Exports	Imports	Exports
	(million sucres)		(thousand pounds)		(million guilders)		(million gold pesos)	
1935	97[25]	103	1,834	2,269	174	167	11.6	11.4
1936	118	108	2,003	2,490	197	202	9.8	9.4
1937	132	145	2,443	2,830	296	270	12.4	12.1
1938	148	133	2,252	2,772	389	341	13.1	12.0
1939	147	126	2,290	3,065	322	344	12.6	13.2
1940	171	137	2,991	3,166	256	251	14.9	11.4
1941	149	170	3,632	4,075	300	345	12.2	15.2
1942	198	267	3,825	4,016	262	214	17.2	16.5
1943	218	366	5,200	4,905	345	298	22.0	20.2
1944	331	440	4,708	5,097	385	397	22.9	24.2
							(million guaranies)	
1945	323	362	4,426[21]	4,496[21]	473	443	55	69
			(million local dollars)					
1946	414	512	26	27	504	512	66	83
1947	604	594	42	34	633	566	68	66
1948	671	623	48	37	869	767	75	87
1949	622	438	51	46	975	814	88	102
	(million US dollars)						(million US dollars)	
1950	41.2	74.0	56	51	1,130	1,037	18.8	33.1
1951	52.5	70.5	67	58	1,449	1,325	25.4	37.7
1952	58.0	102	83[21]	81[21]	1,523	1,377	30.7	31.3
1953	62.8	92.3	72	83	1,389	1,349	24.3	30.7
1954	100	125	80	85	1,544	1,458	32.9	34.0
1955	95.0	114	95	90	1,567	1,516	29.0	35.1
1956	89.9	116	100	95	1,657	1,588	24.6	36.7
1957	97.8	133	119	108	1,813	1,645	27.4	32.9
1958	104	133	116	97	1,694	1,525	32.6	34.1
1959	97.3	141	111	103	1,465	1,342	26.2	31.2
1960	115	145	147	125	1,286	1,241	32.4	27.0
1961	106	127	147	147	1,353	1,337	34.7	30.7
1962	97.1	143	126	161	1,360	1,297	34.7	33.5
1963	128	148	118	173	1,313	1,242	32.6	40.2
1964	152	159	150	167	1,225	1,188	33.8	49.8
1965	169	170	179	166	1,164	1,136	47.4	57.3
1966	172	184	202	183	1,165	1,116	50.2	49.4
1967	214	190	225	192	1,261	1,146	60.7	48.3
1968	255	226	219	229	1,267	1,130	61.5	47.6
1969	242	153	236	234	1,307	1,178	70.3	51.0
1970	274	190	268	266	1,504	1,275	63.8	64.1
1971	340	199	268	288	1,660	1,366	70.3	65.2
1972	319	326	298	300	1,565	1,364	69.9	86.2
1973	537	487	373	288	2,868	2,465	105	127
1974	962	926	567	602	6,536	5,815	171	170

E1 SOUTH AMERICA: External Trade Aggregates in Current Values

	Peru[27]		Surinam		Uruguay		Venezuela[23]	
	Imports	Exports	Imports	Exports	Imports	Exports	Imports	Exports
	(million soles)		(million guilders)		(million US dollars)		(million bolivares)	
1935	181	309	5.4	3.4	48	77	[165][23]	447
1936	200	332	5.7	4.5	53	72	[212][23]	582
1937	235	365	6.8	5.2	65	78	[304][23]	599
1938	260	336	6.8	5.8	62	62	311	559
1939	256	377	7.8	7.3	52	63	328	510
1940	319	398	8.5	7.3	55	66	311	487
1941	358	484	9.4	11	63	71	288	718
1942	333	489	15	13	64	58	216	501
1943	449	459	22	14	64	100	222	620
1944	514	547	16	6.9	72	98	372	867
1945	550	673	12	7.4	94	122	602	1,112
1946	802	974	16	12	147	153	983	1,614
1947	1,092	957	31	25	215	162	1,857	2,324
1948	1,091	1,021	36	26	200	179	2,431	3,360
1949	2,692	2,031	38	34	182	192	2,376	3,483
1950	2,704	2,887	39	31	201	254	1,991	3,889
1951	3,972	3,744	46	40	309	236	2,271	4,533
1952	5,453	4,423	56	46	237	209	2,528	4,858
	(million US dollars)							
	287	234						
1953	293	219	54	50	193	270	2,733	4,841
1954	250	245	52	55	274	249	3,063	5,661
1955	299	271	52	50	228	184	3,155	6,275
1956	384	311	62	59	213	211	3,438	7,090
1957	448	330	73	65	255	128	5,587	7,921
1958	334	291	71	62	151	139	4,783	7,720
1959	317	314	85	77	160	98	4,717	7,937
1960	373	434	102	82	244	129	3,553	8,147
1961	468	496	101	78	206	175	3,522	8,092
1962	539	543	103	80	230	153	3,871	8,689
1963	553	540	110	87	177	165	3,655	8,807
1964	571	666	152	90	198	179	4,886	9,241
1965	719	666	179	110	150	191	5,590	12,076
1966	816	763	169	171	164	186	5,120	11,941
1967	820	755	193	198	171	159	5,632	11,238
1968	630	866	188	217	157	179	6,532	11,175
1969	600	865	208	246	197	200	6,748	11,104
1970	622	1,044	217	255	231	233	7,382	11,691
1971	750	893	237	295	229	206	8,252	13,996
1972	796	944	259	306	212	214	9,471	12,993
1973	1,024	1,049	281	316	285	32	10,856	20,431
1974	1,595	1,517	411	481	487	382	16,249	47,435

E1   SOUTH AMERICA: External Trade Aggregates in Current Values

	Argentina		Bolivia		Brazil		Chile		Colombia	
	Imports	Exports	Imports	Exports	Imports	Exports	Imports	Exports	Imports	Exports
	(million US dollars)		(million US dollars)		(million US dollars)		(million US dollars)		(million US dollars)	
1975	3,947	2,961	575	444	12,210	8,670	1,338	1,552	1,495	1,465
1976	3,033	3,916	594	568	13,532	10,128	1,684	2,083	1,708	1,745
1977	4,162	5,652	591	632	13,069	12,120	2,414	2,190	2,028	2,443
1978	3,834	6,400	769	629	14,538	12,659	3,002	2,478	2,836	3,003
1979	6,700	7,810	980	760	19,372	15,244	4,218	3,894	3,233	3,300
1980	10,541	8,021	678	942	24,961	20,132	5,124	4,671	4,663	3,945
1981	9,430	9,143	975	912	24,079	23,293	6,364	3,906	5,199	2,956
1982	5,337	7,625	577	828	21,069	20,175	3,831	3,709	5,478	3,095
1983	4,504	7,836	589	755	16,801	21,899	2,969	3,835	4,968	3,081
1984	4,585	8,107	492	724	13,916	27,005	3,480	3,657	4,497	3,462
1985	3,814	8,396	552	623	13,153	25,639	3,007	3,823	4,141	3,552
1986	4,724	6,852	716	564	15,557	22,349	3,157	4,191	3,861	5,102
1987	5,818	6,360	776	566	16,581	26,225	4,023	5,224	4,322	4,642
1988	5,322	9,135	591	601	16,055	33,494	4,924	7,052	5,002	5,037
1989	4,203	9,579	611	828	19,875	34,383	6,734	8,080	5,010	5,717
1990	4,076	12,353	687	926	22,524	31,414	7,272	8,373	5,589	6,766
1991	8,275	11,978	970	849	22,950	31,620	7,424	8,942	4,906	7,232
1992	14,872	12,235	1,090	710	23,068	35,793	10,129	10,007	6,516	6,917
1993	16,784	13,117	1,206	728	27,740	38,597	11,125	9,199	9,832	7,116

	Ecuador[25]		Guyana		Netherlands Antilles[28]		Paraguay	
	Imports	Exports	Imports	Exports	Imports	Exports	Imports	Exports
	(million US dollars)		(million local dollars)		(million guilders)		(million US dollars)	
1975	943	897	811	858	5,088	4,315	179	176
1976	959	1,258	927	711	6,601	4,544	180	181
1977	1,189	1,436	804	662	5,631	4,764	255	279
1978	1,627	1,494	711	750	5,682	4,754	318	257
1979	1,986	2,067	810	746	7,911	7,138	438	305
1980	2,253	2,481	1,010	992	10,216	9,292	517	310
1981	2,246	2,542	1,236	974	10,551	9,750	506	295
1982	2,189	2,341	841	724	9,157	8,803	561	330
1983	1,465	2,203	691	567	8,148	7,937	506	284
1984	1,716	2,581	945	808	7,258	6,719	563	386
1985	1,674	2,780	1,082	875	4,061[28]	3,023[28]	719	403
1986	1,867	2,171	1,036	991	2,002	1,664	733	275
1987	2,052	1,927	2,590	2,684	2,703	2,354	590	379
1988	1,714	2,192	2,156	2,353	2,527	2,040	671	657
1989	1,855	2,354	7,009	6,232	2,888	2,608	694	1,163
1990	1,862	2,714	12,290	10,599	3,833	3,204	...	...
1991	2,399	2,851	34,275	29,831	3,828	2,862	...	...
1992	2,500	3,008	...	36,126	3,344	2,790	...	...
1993	2,562	2,904	...	...	3,485	2,297	...	...

International Historical Statistics: The Americas 1750–1993

E1 SOUTH AMERICA: External Trade Aggregates in Current Values

	Peru		Surinam		Uruguay		Venezuela	
	Imports	Exports	Imports	Exports	Imports	Exports	Imports	Exports
	(million US dollars)		(million guilders)		(million US dollars)		(thousand million bolivares)	
1975	2,380	1,315	450	495	556	384	22.8	39.9
1976	1,798	1,296	525	492	587	547	25.8	41.1
1977	1,598	1,647	710	553	730	607	42.0	43.5
1978	1,356	1,805	724	734	774	686	45.6	42.0
1979	1,475	3,380	734	793	1,206	788	41.3	64.0
1980	2,573	3,265	900	918	1,680	1,059	45.8	85.5
1981	3,803	3,249	1,014	846	1,641	1,215	50.7	86.4
1982	3,080	3,227	913	765	1,110	1,023	50.1	70.6
1983	2,147	3,027	808	655	787	1,045	33.7	64.5
1984	1,869	3,130	617	635	777	934	47.6	99.9
1985	1,806	2,978	533	587	708	909	55.6	116
1986	2,909	2,531	435	597	870	1,088	67.4	78.6
1987	3,562	2,661	525	546	1,142	1,182	115	122
1988	3,348	2,701	626	731	1,178	1,404	213	155
1989	2,749	3,488	791	966	1,203	1,599	240	448
1990	3,470	3,231	842	844	1,343	1,693	348	833
1991	4,195	3,329	909	648	1,637	1,605	638	863
1992	4,861	3,484	1,142	645	2,045	1,702	962	975
1993	4,859	3,514	1,798	2,318	2,326	1,645	1,107	1,272

E1 APPENDIX: Trade of Canadian Colonies before Confederation (in thousand pounds)

1830–1867

	Ontario & Quebec[30]		New Brunswick		Nova Scotia		Prince Edward Island		British Columbia	
	Imports	Exports	Imports	Exports	Imports[32]	Exports	Imports[37]	Exports	Imports	Exports
1830	...	...	...	...	...	...	...	...	—	—
1831	...	...	...	...	...	...	...	...	—	—
1832	1,568	952	532	472	766	392	...	8	—	—
1833	1,665	965	549	469	769	460	...	4	—	—
1834	1,064	1,019	568	491	713	427	...	11	—	—
1835	1,496	897	622	577	625	487	...	9	—	—
1836	1,941	1,035	864	548	745	481	...	12	—	—
1837	1,602	909	731	588	800	520	...	7	—	—
1838	1,413	969	720	656	933	558	...	12	—	—
1839	2,137	1,099	1,012	690	1,223	686	...	14	—	—
1840	1,903	1,626	846	637	1,290	782	...	15	—	—
1841	1,936	1,884	843	667	1,426	917	...	12	—	—
1842	1,923	1,327	329	368	1,009	669	...	9	—	—
1843	1,127	1,381	428	482	816	442	...	11	—	—
1844	2,384	1,758	672	546	912	422	...	15	—	—
1845	2,600	2,185	893	721	876_{32}	447	...	26	—	—
1846	2,363	1,953	861	796	837	476	51	29	—	—
1847	2,162	2,079	926	618	1,045	597	75	30	—	—
1848	1,426	1,329	517	562	768	459	36	15	—	—
1849	$1,570_{31}$	$1,333_{31}$	596_{31}	547_{31}	796_{31}	473_{31}	61_{31}	21_{31}	—	—
1850	3,489	2,660	816	658	1,056	671	123	60	—	—
1851	4,404	2,838	980	772	1,125	494	134	69	—	—
1852	4,168	3,146	1,111	796	1,062	785	172	106	—	—
1853	6,572	4,891	1,716	1,072	1,417	1,079	211	127	—	—
1854	8,327	4,730	2,069	1,104	1,791	1,248	274	151	—	—
1855	7,415	5,792	1,431	826	1,883	1,472	268	147	—	—
1856	8,956	6,585	1,521	1,073	1,870	1,373	238	112	—	—
1857	8,102	5,549	1,419	918	1,936	1,394	259	134	—	—
1858	5,975	4,823	1,163	811	1,615	1,264	186	135	—	—
1859	6,895	5,089	1,416	1,073	1,620	1,378	235	179	—	—
1860	7,078	7,116	1,447	916	1,702	1,324	230	201	257	611
1861	8,847	7,523	1,238	947	1,523	1,155	210	163	699	13
1862	9,986	6,903	1,292	803	1,689	1,129	211	151	1,305	12
1863	$9,445_{30}$	$8,596_{30}$	1,596	1,029	2,040	1,309	293	209	1,232	58
1864	10,365	9,108	1,864	1,053	2,521	1,435	338	203	1,242	1,856
1865	9,296	8,850	1,476	1,153	2,876	1,766	381	292	1,092	1,159
1866	11,209	11,342	2,083	1,328	2,876	1,609	445	247	...	...
1867	12,302	9,752	...	...	...	...	294	260	332	777

E1 External Trade Aggregates in Current Values

NOTES

1. SOURCES: The national publications listed on pp. xiii–xv; League of Nations, *International Trade Statistics*; UN, *Yearbook of International Trade Statistics*. Colombian data for 1835–44 are from Jorge E. Rodriguez and William P. McGreavey in Miguel Urrutia and Mario Arrubla (eds.), *Compendio de Estadisticas Historicas de Colombia* (Bogotà, 1970), and those for 1845–1929 are from William P. McGreavey, *An Economic History of Colombia, 1845–1930* (Cambridge, 1971). Peruvian data to 1896 are based on Laura Randall, *A Comparative Economic History of Latin America 1500–1914, vol 4 Peru* (New York, 1977).
2. Except as indicated in footnotes, statistics are, in principle, of merchandise trade only, and are of 'special' rather than 'general trade—i.e. imports for domestic consumption and exports of domestic origin plus re-exports of commodities originally entered for domestic consumption. In some cases, however, it is impossible to discover the exact composition of the statistics.
3. Imports are normally valued c.i.f. and exports f.o.b.

FOOTNOTES

[1] 'General' trade including bullion and specie until or unless otherwise indicated.
[2] Trade with France only to 1838 (1st line). These statistics are at official (i.e. fixed) values, as is the French component of the subsequent statistics to 1846.
[3] Years ending 30 September to 1889 and years beginning 1 April from 1890 to 1908. Bullion and specie are included to 1913 (1st line), there being no break in that year in the import series. Import data for 1866–81 are of 'special' rather than 'general' trade.
[4] 'General' trade. Data are for years beginning 1 July from 1861 to 1913. The 1914 figures are for the second half-year only. Total exports from 1519 to 1776 were valued at 155,161 million pesos and from 1779 to 1791 at 244,052 million pesos. Up to 1899 (1st line) the gold peso was used to value imports. The import figures for 1915 and 1916 are not strictly comparable with those for other years, since they were calculated in paper money at the compulsory rates enforced. The 1917 import figure is an official estimate.
[5] Excluding trade with British North America to 1849. Data from 1896 are for years ending 30 June.
[6] Excluding movements of gold from 1825 (2nd line) and domestic exports of silver from 1825 (2nd line) to 1864. Data to 1842 are for years ending 30 September, and for 1844 to 1915 they are for years ending 30 June. The 1843 figures are for the period 1 October 1842 to 30 June 1843.
[7] Data to 1905 are for years beginning 1 July, and for 1907–18 they are for years beginning 1 April. The 1906 figures are for the period 1 July 1906 to 31 March 1907. Imports are on a 'general' trade basis to 1916 and exports to 1919. Gold is included to 1939. Newfoundland became part of Canada on 1 April 1949. Earlier statistics for the separate provinces are shown in the Appendix to this table on p. 442.
[8] Data to 1882 are believed to be for years ending 30 April. The import figures are known to be defective for that period.
[9] Statistics of trade with Spain and the USA are available for 1891–96 and with the USA for 1877–90 (see table F2). The 1877 and 1892 figures are for years ending 30 June. Imports are valued f.o.b. to 1961.
[10] 'General' trade to 1955, with imports valued free alongside ship to 1941.
[11] Excluding trade on government account. Imports are valued f.o.b. to 1954.
[12] Tobago is included from 1889. From that year to 1908 statistics are for years beginning 1 April. Bullion movements and transit trade are included to 1915 (1st line).
[13] Statistics to 1921 are known to be very defective. Bullion and specie are not included after that date.
[14] Years ending 31 July to 1937 and 30 June from 1939 to 1951. The 1938 figures are for the period 1 August 1937 to 30 June 1938. Imports are valued f.o.b to 1959.
[15] Part of Colombia to 1905. Imports are valued f.o.b. to 1963. Exports from the free zone of Colon are excluded from 1946.
[16] A new basis of valuation was adopted which excluded armed forces' stores, settlers' effects and gifts from the export statistics, and similar items from those of imports.
[17] Banana exports were undervalued previously.
[18] Data to 1910 (1st line) are in official (i.e. fixed) values. The 1910 figures in current values but in million gold pesos are imports 379 and exports 389.
[19] Years beginning 1 July from 1833 to 1886. The figures for 1887 are for the second half-year only. Figures for the first half-year of 1833 are imports 18, exports 21 million milreis. Statistics of imports are on a 'general' trade basis to 1957 and those of exports are on a 'general' trade basis to 1930. Bullion is included to 1930.
[20] Statistics are given here in terms of the gold peso of 18 pence (up to 1967), though trade was actually recorded in pesos of different values at different times.
[21] Years beginning 1 April from 1892 to 1911. Trans-shipments are included in exports to 1899. Bullion and specie are included to 1945 (1st line). Statistics are of 'special' trade from 1953.
[22] Official (i.e. fixed) values to 1913 (1st line) for exports, and to 1914 for imports. The official and the 'effective' values for imports in 1913 coincide but the latter was considerably higher in 1915 and later years. No calculation of 'effective' value was made for 1914. The 1923 import figure is an official estimate of 'effective' value.
[23] Imports are valued f.o.b., except in 1935–37, and include bullion and specie to 1912. Data to 1900 are for fiscal years beginning 1 July.
[24] Valued f.o.b. to September 1954.
[25] 'General' trade exclusive of bullion and specie. Imports are valued f.o.b. to 1935.
[26] Official (i.e. fixed) values to 1897.
[27] Excluding trade on government account. Bullion and specie are included to 1910 (1st line). There is no break in the export series in that year.
[28] Data for imports are for Curaçao only to 1911, and those for exports are for the other islands only (i.e. exclusive of Curaçao) to 1904. From 1955 data relate to Curaçao, Aruba, and Bonaire only, and from 1969 to the first two of these only, but there is no break at the level of rounding used here. Aruba is excluded from 1986.
[29] Petroleum exports were undervalued previously.
[30] Years ending 30 June from 1864.
[31] Excluding the intercolonial trade of British North America to 1849. Bullion and specie are included.
[32] Imports to Prince Edward Island are included with Nova Scotia to 1845.

E2 NORTH AMERICA: EXTERNAL TRADE (IN CURRENT VALUES) WITH MAIN TRADING PARTNERS

CANADA (million Canadian dollars)[1]

	Germany		Japan		UK		USA	
	Imports	Exports	Imports	Exports	Imports	Exports	Imports	Exports
1872	1.0	...	...	...	64	...	36	...
1873	1.1	0.1	...	...	69	39	48	43
1874	1.0	0.1	...	...	64	46	55	37
1875	0.8	0.1	...	...	61	41	51	30
1876	0.5	0.1	...	...	41	41	47	32
1877	0.4	- -	...	...	40	42	52	26
1878	0.4	0.1	...	...	36	47	49	26
1879	0.4	0.1	...	...	31	37	44	28
1880	0.5	0.1	...	...	35	46	30	34
1881	0.9	0.1	...	...	44	54	37	37
1882	1.5	0.2	...	...	51	46	49	49
1883	1.8	0.1	...	...	53	48	57	42
1884	2.0	0.2	...	...	44	44	51	39
1885	2.1	0.3	...	...	42	42	48	40
1886	2.2	0.3	1.5	- -	41	42	45	37
1887	3.2	0.4	1.6	- -	45	45	45	38
1888	3.4	0.2	1.2	0.1	39	40	48	43
1889	3.7	- -	1.2	- -	42	38	51	44
1890	3.8	0.5	1.3	- -	43	48	52	41
1891	3.8	0.5	1.3	- -	42	49	54	41
1892	5.6	0.9	1.9	- -	41	65	53	39
1893	3.8	0.8	1.5	- -	43	64	58	44
1894	5.8	2.0	1.4	- -	39	69	53	36
1895	4.8	0.6	1.6	- -	31	62	55	41
1896	5.9	0.8	1.6	- -	33	67	59	44
1897	6.5	1.0	1.3	0.1	29	77	62	49
1898	5.6	1.8	1.4	0.1	32	105	79	46
1899	7.4	2.2	2.0	0.1	37	99	93	45
1900	8.4	1.7	1.8	0.1	45	108	110	69
1901	7.0	2.1	1.6	0.2	43	105	110	72
1902	11	2.7	1.5	0.3	49	117	121	71
1903	12	2.1	1.4	0.3	59	131	138	72
1904	8.2	1.8	1.9	0.3	62	118	151	73
1905	6.7	1.1	1.9	0.5	60	102	163	77
1906	7.0[1]	1.9[1]	1.7[1]	0.5[1]	69[1]	133[1]	176[1]	98[1]
1907	8.2	2.3	2.2	0.7	95	126	211	91
1908	6.1	1.5	2.0	0.8	71	126	180	85
1909	7.9	2.5	2.2	0.7	95	139	228	104
1910	10	2.7	2.4	0.6	110	132	285	105
1911	11	3.8	2.5	0.5	117	147	357	102
1912	14	3.0	3.5	1.1	139	170	441	140
1913	15	4.0	2.6	1.6	132	215	411	164
1914	5.1	2.2	2.8	1.0	90	187	429	174
1915	0.1	—	4.0	1.0	80	452	399	201
1916	- -[1]	—	8.1[1]	1.3	122[1]	742	678[1]	281
1917	- -	—	12	5.0	81	845	804	418
1918	- -	—	14	12	73	541	750	455
1919	- -	0.6[1]	14	7.7[1]	126	489[1]	801	464[1]

E2   NORTH AMERICA: External Trade (in Current Values) with Main Trading Partners

CANADA (million Canadian dollars)[1]

	Germany		Japan		UK		USA	
	Imports	Exports	Imports	Exports	Imports	Exports	Imports	Exports
1920	1.5	8.2	11	6.4	214	313	856	542
1921	2.0	4.5	8.2	15	117	299	516	293
1922	2.6	10	7.2	15	141	379	541	369
1923	5.4	16	6.3	27	154	360	601	431
1924	6.8	24	7.0	22	151	396	510	417
1925	10	31	9.6	35	164	508	610	475
1926	15	34	11	30	164	447	687	466
1927	17	42	13	33	186	411	719	478
1928	21	47	13	42	194	430	868	500
1929	22	25	13	31	189	282	847	515
1930	16	13	9.3	19	150	210	584	350
1931	12[1]	10[1]	6.0[1]	17[1]	98[1]	174[1]	352[1]	235[1]
1932	9.8	7.8	4.6	12	94	179	264	165
1933	9.3	9.9	3.1	13	98	211	217	173
1934	10	6.2	4.4	17	113	271	294	224
1935	9.8	3.6	3.6	15	117	304	312	273
1936	11	6.8	4.3	20	123	396	369	345
1937	12	12	5.9	26	147	403	491	372
1938	9.9	18	4.6	21	119	341	425	279
1939	8.9	7.8	4.9	28	114	324	497	390
1940	0.4	—	6.1	12	161	512	744	452
1941	- -	—	2.4	1.6	219	661	1,004	610
1942	- -	—	1.0	—	161	748	1,305	897
1943	—	—	- -	—	135	1,037	1,424	1,167
1944	—	—	—	—	111	1,238	1,447	1,335
1945	- -	2.7	—	—	122[3]	971	1,202	1,227
1946	- -	6.9	- -	1.0	141[3]	599	1,405	909
1947	0.5	6.7	0.4	0.6	189	754	1,975	1,057
1948	1.7	13	3.1	8.0	300	687	1,806	1,522
1949	7.1[1]	23[1]	5.5[1]	5.9[1]	307[1]	709[1]	1,952[1]	1,524[1]
1950	11	8.9	12	21	404	473	2,130	2,050
1951	31	37	13	73	421	636	2,813	2,334
1952	23[2]	95[2]	13	103	360	751	2,977	2,349
	23	95						
1953	36	84	14	119	453	669	3,221	2,463
1954	44	87	19	96	392	658	2,961	2,367
1955	52	91	37	91	401	774	3,452	2,612
1956	84	134	61	128	485	818	4,162	2,879
1957	93	152	61	139	522	728	3,999	2,942
1958	103	201	70	105	527	779	3,572	2,915
1959	124	129	103	140	597	797[1]	3,829[1]	3,207[1]
						786	3,836	3,094
1960	127	166	110	179	589	915	3,689	2,943
1961	136	189	117	232	618	909	3,866	3,120
1962	141	178	125	214	563	909	4,302	3,621
1963	144	171	130	296	527	1,007	4,447	3,781
1964	170	217	174	332	574	1,207	5,168	4,452
1965	209	193	230	317	619	1,185	6,048	5,051
1966	235	180	253	395	645	1,132	7,140	6,254
1967	257	181	305	574	673	1,178	8,028	7,350
1968	299	232	360	608	696	1,225	9,051	9,218
1969	355	281	496	626	791	1,113	10,318	10,593

E2 NORTH AMERICA: External Trade (in Current Values) with Main Trading Partners

CANADA (million Canadian dollars)

	West Germany		Japan		UK		USA	
	Imports	Exports	Imports	Exports	Imports	Exports	Imports	Exports
1970	383	388	601	796	762	1,500	10,233	11,039
1971	429	319	802	792	832	1,361	10,957	12,197
1972	512	316	1,105	962	949	1,328	12,927	13,974
1973	607	444	1,018	1,800	1,005	1,589	16,511	17,115
1974	767	542	1,427	2,224	1,127	1,895	21,268	21,316
1975	786	593	1,205	2,120	1,222	1,784	23,511	21,598
1976	818	705	1,526	2,382	1,153	1,845	25,704	25,658
1977	963	772	1,802	2,496	1,281	1,882	29,559	30,469
1978	1,195	751	2,181	2,935	1,533	1,895	33,560	35,411
1979	1,550	1,234	2,157	4,046	1,926	2,579	43,908	43,907
1980	1,441	1,433	2,792	4,355	1,967	2,932	47,299	46,571
1981	1,599	1,297	4,039	4,476	2,230	3,020	53,447	53,885
1982	1,376	1,268	3,527	4,535	1,894	2,595	47,372	56,048
1983	1,564	1,122	4,413	4,453	1,787	2,381	53,146	64,282
1984	2,168	1,116	5,711	5,230	2,298	2,337	67,392	82,624
1985	2,705	1,126	6,114	5,363	3,274	2,235	72,625	91,046
1986	3,450	1,236	7,632	5,557	3,735	2,498	75,454	90,231
1987	3,532	1,545	7,550	6,410	4,339	2,799	78,282	93,284
1988	3,841	1,773	9,259	8,725	4,622	3,560	86,166	101,195
1989	3,703	1,857	9,555	8,798	4,567	3,459	87,709	100,139
1990	3,828	2,117	9,517	7,997	4,839	3,367	87,202	110,552
1991	3,733	2,403	10,249	7,109	4,181	3,024	92,080	108,069
1992	3,534	2,266	10,767	7,433	4,106	3,056	95,894	124,352
1993	3,504	2,4609	10,691	8,456	4,429	2,746	112,587	148,530

COSTA RICA (thousand gold pesos TO 1896, million colones subsequently)

	Germany		UK		USA	
	Imports	Exports	Imports	Exports	Imports	Exports
1882	...	...	...	...	...	...
1883	989	263	953	1,165	741	661
1884	105	441	2,025	1,698	944	1,310
1885	605	375	1,688	1,362	857	1,059
1886	582	335	1,379	1,440	1,010	1,023
1887	816	251	1,771	3,126	1,441	2,479
1888	834	294	1,649	2,884	1,794	2,078
1889	1,229	201	1,862	3,647	4,852	3,035
1890	1,262	...	1,449	...	2,255	...
1891	1,697	268	2,119	3,222	2,369	2,514
1892	948	198	1,784	2,521	1,296	1,868
1893	1,124	164	1,724	2,264	1,400	1,831
1894	566	593	907	1,297	941	2,770
1895	737	934	855	2,230	1,198	1,582
1896	844	940	1,221	2,772	1,478	1,579
			(million colones)			
1897	2.5	...	3.2	...	4.0	...
1898	1.4	...	1.8	...	4.0	...
1899	1.5	...	2.0	...	5.4	...
1900	1.9	...	3.8	...	6.5	...
1901	...	...	...	...	...	...
1902	1.2	...	2.2	...	5.0	...
1903	1.2	0.7	2.3	7.7	5.3	6.6
1904	1.6	0.6	2.5	7.1	5.4	6.8

E2   NORTH AMERICA: External Trade (in Current Values) with Main Trading Partners

COSTA RICA (million colones)

	Germany		UK		USA	
	Imports	Exports	Imports	Exports	Imports	Exports
1905	1.3	0.6	2.0	8.2	4.7	8.2
1906	1.6	1.1	3.2	8.5	7.1	9.0
1907	1.7	1.1	3.7	8.6	7.1	9.4
1908	1.8	0.5	2.6	7.2	5.4	8.8
1909	1.8	0.4	2.3	6.3	6.7	10.0
1910	2.0	0.6	2.7	6.4	7.8	11
1911	3.6	0.6	3.3	7.6	8.8	11
1912	3.2	1.2	3.0	8.9	9.4	11
1913	2.9	1.1	2.8	9.3	9.6	11
1914	2.3	1.0	2.3	11	8.7	11
1915	0.1	- -	1.2	9.5	6.5	10
1916	- -	—	1.7	7.9	10	15
1917	- -	—	1.5	5.4	8.4	17
1918	—	—	0.6	0.4	4.7	19
1919	- -	- -	1.2	14	13	21
1920	6.5	0.1	6.8	6.7	25	23
1921	0.4	0.1	3.3	6.4	11	17
1922	0.8	0.3	2.5	11	11	17
1923	1.4	0.2	3.3	11	12	15
1924	3.8	1.3	7.9	29	27	32
1925	5.8	4.0	8.6	30	30	28
1926	6.8	6.6	8.0	35	31	31
1927	10	5.9	9.7	40	33	24
1928	11	7.5	10	42	36	24
1929	14	7.9	10	41	39	20
1930	5.3	6.5	5.3	39	22	17
1931	3.6	6.3	3.9	34	18	13
1932	2.8	2.8	2.6	17	13	15
1933	3.6	7.6	3.9	21	14	17
1934	4.5	6.8	4.9	17	17	10
1935	2.5	1.7	0.7	2.4	2.7	3
1936	2.0	1.4	0.6	2.2	3.7	3.7
1937	2.7	2.2	0.9	2.3	5	5.2
1938	2.5	1.9	0.9	2.5	6.2	4.6
1939	3.0	2.3	0.7	1.5	9.9	4.1
1940	0.6	—	0.8	1.9	13	4.4
1941	0.1	—	0.7	- -	14	8.3
1942	- -	—	0.4	- -	9.0	7.5
1943	—	—	0.5	- -	12	9.2
1944	—	—	0.4	- -	14	7.8
1945	—	—	0.4	- -	19	9.8
1946	—	—	0.6	0.1	25	11
1947	- -	—	1.0	0.4	39	18
1948	- -	- -	1.7	0.5	33	25
1949	0.4	- -	1.7	0.1	32	24

E2 NORTH AMERICA: External Trade (in Current Values) with Main Trading Partners

COSTA RICA (million US dollars)

	Germany		Japan		UK		USA	
	Imports	Exports	Imports	Exports	Imports	Exports	Imports	Exports
1950	1.9	0.2	...	...	2.3	- -	31	25
1951	4.1	0.5	0.6	- -	2.7	0.2	37	49
1952	4.7	1.2	0.8	- -	3.6	0.2	43	53
1953	5.6	7.4	1.7	- -	5.6	0.1	44	53
1954	8.0	15	1.4	0.1	5.8	0.3	47	50
1955	8.0	21	2.2	—	5.9	0.7	52	44
1956	8.5₂	20₂	1.9	- -	5.6	0.4	50	34
1957	9.5	20	3.5	- -	5.0	0.4	57	43
1958	11	25	5.1	0.3	5.7	1.0	51	46
1959	10	19	5.9	0.5	6.3	0.9	50	38
1960	13	20	8.0	0.4	6.4	0.7	52	45
1961	12	18	7.4	0.5	5.8	0.6	50	49
1962	13	20	7.5	0.6	5.8	0.8	53	54
1963	15	17	8.6	0.6	6.5	0.7	59	55
1964	14	20	10	0.4	7.1	0.5	64	61
1965	17	13	17	0.6	8.3	0.5	71	56
1966	18	16	16	1.3	8.5	0.7	70	60
1967	15	11	16	1.5	12	0.5	74	69
1968	16	11	15	2.0	8.9	0.4	81	80
1969	20	13	22	1.9	15	0.6	86	90
1970	26	19	29	11	16	0.8	110	98
1971	27	21	39	7.0	17	0.6	114	92
1972	27	32	40	5.3	20	0.7	123	113
1973	31	44	41	1.7	15	1.7	160	115
1974	44	56	71	7.1	18	0.9	248	142
1975	39	56	61	8.2	23	0.7	239	207
1976	44	63	89	7.2	22	1.5	290	237
1977	59	107	137	7.3	24	2.1	373	262
1978	62	125	158	6.9	28	2.7	413	342
1979	73	110	174	10	27	3.5	460	347
1980	74	117	173	8.5	26	2.7	550	360
1981	57	124	121	5.4	19	11	459	329
1982	37	125	38	6.2	18	21	387	295
1983	...	111	...	4.8	...	22	...	297
1984	55	130	82	4.7	14	27	394	358
1985	58	119	105	5.2	20	27	380	378
1986	64	161	121	10	22	42	408	467
1987	78	168	118	12	23	25	511	513
1988	60	173	94	10	24	27	549	494
1989	72	177	122	9	25	32	934	652
1990	94	173	164	15	31	29	1,074	657
1991	64	175	119	20	23	30	1,146	775
1992	87	173	168	13	29	24	1,382	879
1993	101	188	218	12	30	38	1,295	872

E2 NORTH AMERICA: External Trade (in Current Values) with Main Trading Partners

CUBA (million pesos)[4]

	Germany		Spain		UK		USA	
	Imports	Exports	Imports	Exports	Imports	Exports	Imports	Exports
1848	1.5	3.9	7.1	3.9	5	7.1	6.9	8.3
1854	1.4	1.8	9.1	3.6	6.6	11	7.9[4]	12[4]
1876	...	...	...	...	...	...	13	56
1877	...	...	...	...	...	...	13	66
1878	...	...	...	...	...	...	12	57
1879	...	...	...	...	...	...	13	64
1880	...	...	...	...	...	...	11	65
1881	...	...	...	...	...	...	11	63
1882	...	...	...	...	...	...	12	70
1883	...	...	...	...	...	...	15	66
1884	...	...	...	...	...	...	11	57
1885	...	...	...	...	...	...	9	42
1886	...	...	...	...	...	...	10	51
1887	...	...	...	...	...	...	11	50
1888	...	...	...	...	...	...	10	49
1889	...	...	...	...	...	...	12	52
1890	...	...	...	...	...	...	13	54
1891	...	...	22	7.1	...	...	12	62
1892	...	...	28	9.6	...	...	18	78
1893	...	...	25	5.7	...	...	24	79
1894	...	...	26	7.3	...	...	20	76
1895	...	...	27	7.2	...	...	13	53
1896	...	...	26	4.3	...	...	9.6	42
1897	...	...	...	...	...	...	...	...
1898	...	...	...	...	...	...	...	...
1899	...	...	...	...	...	...	...	...
1900	2.6	2.9	11	1	12	4.4	34	37
1901	3.4	6.7	10	0.6	9.3	5.9	29	46
1902	3.5	3.9	9.7	1.3	9.6	6	29	38
1903	3.7	3.8	10	1.7	9.2	6.4	26	63
1904	4.6	5.1	11	1.2	12	5.9	30	78
1905	5.1	3.8	10	1.1	12	6.2	38	86
1906	6.6	4.3	11	1.6	15	5.9	49	90
1907	6.4	3.1	8.3	0.7	14	4.4	48	102
1908	7.8	3.7	9.3	1	15	5.1	47	94
1909	6.4	4.5	7.4	1.5	11	5	43	101
1910	6.9	4.3	8.9	0.5	14	11	50	122
1911	7.2	3.7	8.5	0.7	14	5.1	57	113
1912	8.4[4]	6.2[4]	10[4]	0.5[4]	16[4]	11[4]	63[4]	123[4]
1913	9.7	4.7	10	0.7	16	18	75	132
1914	5	2.4	9.9	1.6	12	16	69	146

E2 NORTH AMERICA: External Trade (in Current Values) with Main Trading Partners

CUBA (million pesos)[4]

	Germany		Spain		USSR		UK		USA	
	Imports	Exports	Imports	Exports	Imports	Exports	Imports	Exports	Imports	Exports
1915	0.8	—	11	0.9	...	...	15	33	90	195
1916	- -	—	14	3.0	...	...	19	53	153	243
1917	- -	—	16	5.4	...	...	15	74	190	255
1918	—	—	10	6.4	...	...	9.2	95	219	289
1919	0.2	- -	16	8.2	...	...	8.8	83	272	441
1920	2.9	0.1	28	7.2	...	...	18	98	404	627
1921	5.4	0.5	14	2.5	...	...	17	27	264	223
1922	3.5	0.6	8.4	3.1	...	...	9.1	38	120	262
1923	7.9	0.6	13	1.6	...	...	13	32	182	368
1924	9.8	1.7	15	1.4	...	...	12	49	192	363
1925	9.4	2.2	13	1.9	...	...	12	56	187	265
1926	7.7	1.7	12	1.3	...	...	13	22	160	244
1927	7.8	2.3	11	1.5	...	...	12	33	160	257
1928	6.6	2.8	9.4	4.3	...	...	10	45	129	203
1929	7.5	2.3	8.9	3.3	...	...	12	34	127	209
1930	6.1	2.2	7.6	2.5	...	...	8.9	25	92	116
1931	3.0	1.5	4.2	1.8	...	...	4.0	17	46	89
1932	2.1	0.7	3.0	1.5	...	...	3.0	12	28	57
1933	1.9	0.8	2.6	2.2	...	...	2.4	16	23	57
1934	2.9	0.8	4.1	2.4	...	...	3.9	15	41	81
1935	4.4	2.3	4.8	1.8	...	...	4.1	14	56	102
1936	4.8	2.4	3.5	1.1	...	...	5.1	20	66	122
1937	5.8	3.1	1.8	0.6	...	...	6.3	20	89	150
1938	4.7	2.8	1.6	1.4	...	...	4.5	20	75	108
1939	3.4	1.5	1.3	2.2	...	...	3.1	18	78	111
1940	0.2	0.1	1.7	3.0	...	...	3.5	10	80	105
1941	- -	—	1.2	2.2	...	...	3.4	17	115	181
1942	—	—	0.5	0.6	...	...	2.8	5.6	120	164
1943	—	—	1.2	2.2	...	...	4.3	35	135	297
1944	—	—	1.4	4.9	...	...	2.5	23	161	386
1945	- -	—	3.5	8.4	...	...	2.8	35	188	323
1946	- -	—	5.2	6.7	...	...	4.3	64	299	320
1947	- -	6.9	7.4	8.4	—	—	6.9	133	437	498
1948	0.1	62	6.8	11	—	—	8.4	95	421	367
1949	0.7	27	6.9	2.9	—	—	6.5	70	376	367
1950	4.8	14	6.5	3.8	—	—	8.6	96	407	381
1951	11	19	13	9.0	—	—	19	105	493	416
1952	9.6	15	9.6	9.2	—	—	16	57	463	409
1953	9.2₂	17₂	9.6	5.0	—	—	10	75	371	393
1954	12	8.5	9.8	11	—	0.8	13	22	367	369
1955	15	15	12	12	—	36	12	7.0	423	401
1956	18	19	9.8	11	—	14	18	29	488	431
1957	21	37	12	14	—	42	21	44	578	468
1958	24	7.5	13	18	—	14	22	37	543	491
1959	22	14	8.4	5.1	- -	13	27	9.1	459	445

E2 NORTH AMERICA: External Trade (in Current Values) with Main Trading Partners

CUBA (million pesos)[4]

	Germany				Spain		USSR		UK		USA	
	Exports		Imports		Imports	Exports	Imports	Exports	Imports	Exports	Imports	Exports
	East	West	East	West								
1960	4.4	22	0.5	13	…	7.3	88	104	23	8.5	310	329
1961	18	25	7.7	13	…	5.1	289	301	17	13	26	30
1962	27	14	25	0.4	1.6	8.6	411	220	12	12	0.6	4.2
1963	36	12	40	0.3	14	23	461	164	11	23	35	—
1964	39	19	16	0.8	39	68	410	275	38	26	—	—
1965	25	…	28	0.7	47	33	428	322	50	12	—	—
1966	36	…	31	…	75	33	521	274	25	11	—	—
1967	50	12	36	0.7	29	33	582	367	29	13	—	—
1968	39	11	36	2.1	21	41	672	290	31	14	—	—
1969	43	30	38	1.4	48	41	658	233	66	14	—	—
1970	50	34	49	0.9	36	41	691	529	59	20	—	—
1971	63	17	49	2.7	33	36	731	304	61	17	—	—
1972	36	23	38	3.2	155	40	714	224	43	12	—	—
1973	40	39	46	2.8	40	52	811	477	54	30	—	—
1974	52	107	103	5.7	62	176	1,025	810	84	45	—	—
1975	76	140	70	4.6	152	226	1,251	1,662	128	13	—	—
1976	99	80	79	10	186	101	1,490	1,638	154	53	—	—
1977	153	65	96	8.1	154	112	1,858	2,066	48	16	—	—
1978	139	75	98	17	75	60	2,328	2,495	57	10	—	—
1979	136	73	116	27	105	79	2,513	2,370	61	19	—	—
1980	165	83	122	17	139	46	2,904	2,253	77	15	—	—
1981	171	99	176	14	163	64	3,234	2,357	63	16	—	—
1982	206	54	164	44	95	88	3,744	3,290	50	24	—	—
1983	251	65	200	68	107	94	4,245	3,882	93	31	—	—
1984	268	91	217	14	108	64	4,782	3,952	92	15	—	—
1985	280	82	234	16	177	103	5,373	4,479	105	27	—	—
1986	305	85	258	12	106	88	5,314	3,934	79	17	—	—
1987	339	53	282	28	163	85	5,496	3,867	70	13	—	—
1988	341	57	311	73	146	82	5,364	3,688	60	42	—	—
1989	358	77	286	71	184	86	5,522	3,231	82	114	—	—

E2 NORTH AMERICA: External Trade (in Current Values) with Main Trading Partners

EL SALVADOR (imports: thousand gold pesos to 1919, million quetzales subsequently)

	Germany		Guatemala		Honduras		Japan		UK[8]		USA	
	Imports	Exports	Imports	Exports	Imports	Exports	Imports	Exports	Imports	Exports	Imports	Exports
1901	447	1,294	...	...	8	39	...	...	984	2,448	733	2,087
1902	361	1,363	...	...	6	23	...	...	976	1,939	863	1,624
1903	558	1,679	...	...	31	105	6	...	1,109	3,579	839	2,355
1904	404	2,396	...	...	28	55	31	...	1,303	3,706	1,002	2,758
1905	473	2,469	...	...	85	72	11	...	1,314	2,214	1,355	3,063
1906	437	2,235	...	...	41	100	25	...	1,412	1,115	1,290	5,726
1907	366	2,529	...	...	90	175	25	...	1,018	822	1,197	5,046
1908	443	2,646	...	...	103	109	46	...	1,539	1,177	1,287	5,116
1909	482	2,830	...	...	36	26	69	...	1,442	1,126	1,344	5,012
1910	407	3,962	...	...	13	83	62	...	1,170	1,217	1,347	5,699
1911	533	3,928	...	...	29	92	80	...	1,550	1,310	1,815	7,271
1912	665	5,156	...	...	13	32	56	...	1,908[8]	1,015[8]	2,628	6,642
1913	661	4,028	2.0	7.9	0.2	54	88	...	1,660	1,672	2,407	6,692
1914	488	6,536	1.4	17	2.5	18	97	...	1,284	1,489	2,023	6,655
1915	40	...	...	...	...	...	56	...	967	...	2,474	...
1916	1.7	96	3.9	13	3.4	68	114	...	1,339	168	3,587	10,256
1917	0.1	...	...	30	...	30	...	...	1,680	...	4,260	...
1918	- -	—	0.6	147	0.6	19	204	...	1,560	202	3,455	21,094
1919	...	24	...	...	...	...	...	...	1,610	160	9,064	8,340
1920	370	139	43	16	29	31	633	...	1,939	753	7,783	11,623
1921	215	408	5.8	7.7	6.4	13	166	12	1,239	164	5,901	3,297
1922	190	1,374	9.3	13	0.8	8.7	294	19	1,307	205	5,973	3,748
1923	606	824	8.3	11	- -	24	328	...	1,603	115	6,771	6,518
1924	1,350	4,492	13	52	26	51	...	...	1,815	196	8,497	6,333

————————— (thousand colones) —————————

	Germany		Guatemala		Honduras		Japan		UK[8]		USA	
	Imports	Exports	Imports	Exports	Imports	Exports	Imports	Exports	Imports	Exports	Imports	Exports
1925	2,736	9,879	15	13	76	29	708	15	4,190	1,471	26,180	5,613
1926	2,291	...	...	...	...	...	...	...	2,619	...	21,407	9,123
1927	2,378	9,462	13	23	...	221	762	4	4,795	295	14,980	3,130
1928	3,895	14,214	21	2.8	221	274	1,315	4	4,967	230	20,161	7,435
1929	3,067	11,705	133	20	199	337	793	3	5,175	429	18,438	7,922
1930	2,200	8,021	332	118	74	191	816	3	3,133	149	11,726	6,396
1931	1,267	6,471	227	197	58	83	360	1	1,790	97	7,444	3,435
1932	1,292	4,634	83	138	67	157	353	—	1,407	35	6,412	2,414
1933	2,028	5,265	97	91	87	317	574	—	2,235	24	7,383	4,245
1934	1,888	7,342	186	106	369	208	2,284	3	2,769	27	9,594	6,464
1935	5,569	3,529	377	176	463	235	20	9	3,116	897	8,710	13,086
1936	6,769	3,601	306	194	260	291	18	5.8	2,242	237	7,757	14,502
1937	7,772	4,329	264	231	416	567	35	8.2	2,835	430	10,085	23,532
1938	4,815	2,698	217	269	672	1,007	7.2	9.2	2,083	378	10,687	16,897
1939	3,871	2,853	194	1,040	629	1,318	9.9	10	1,520	58	11,720	19,068
1940	266	—	177	429	679	1,295	26	4.7	1,536	70	13,671	22,991
1941	55	—	402	1,001	608	1,383	13	—	974	82	16,182	22,138
1942	5.6	—	2,053	1,982	910	1,910	1.3	—	996	83	14,340	37,749
1943	18	—	1,439	2,185	1,008	2,735	—	—	1,408	328	20,170	45,280
1944	—	—	400	1,206	1,800	2,812	0.7	—	773	77	20,975	41,976
1945	—	—	474	1,267	2,093	1,799	0.3	—	786	228	22,897	45,128
1946	- -	—	717	2,847	2,671	5,062	0.1	—	1,462	176	37,375	46,701
1947	0.2	—	653	2,936	3,234	4,449	—	—	2,304	93	72,264	77,610
1948	31	16	353	5,242	5,142	4,398	14	—	3,795	47	76,218	88,161
1949	649	103	469	4,442	4,020	4,103	146	—	2,977	339	73,350	114,898

E2 NORTH AMERICA: External Trade (in Current Values) with Main Trading Partners

EL SALVADOR (million colones)

	Germany		Guatemala		Honduras		Japan		UK		USA	
	Imports	Exports	Imports	Exports	Imports	Exports	Imports	Exports	Imports	Exports	Imports	Exports
1950	3.5	0.1	0.7	3.5	5.3	2.6	1.0	- -	4.2	3.2	82	150
1951	6.7	0.2	1.0	1.2	7.9	4.4	2.5	1.8	6.1	3.2	100	184
1952	7.2	7.3	2.4	1.2	6.8	3.0	2.3	0.1	7.9	1.8	106	185
1953	9.0	13	3.9	2.3	10	3.2	2.9	1.4	6.2	2.8	112	182
1954	13	28	3.4	2.9	10	4.7	3.9	4.7	7.4	8.5	128	189
1955	18	45	4.5	3.0	10	4.7	6.3	12	7.9	4.9	131	172
1956	21	83	4.7	6.1	14	3.6	13	31	11	7.3	138	125
1957	23	105	6.2	5.9	12	5.9	17	17	13	4.6	148	158
1958	25	94	7.6	7.4	16	8.6	13	32	12	3.0	131	115
1959	22	79	11	10	16	10	12	42	10	4.5	110	101
1960	31	97	13	15	16	9.9	23	34	12	1.6	131	102
1961	27	91	17	19	16	12	19	47	11	0.3	107	101
1962	30	88	21	19	26	15	22	65	12	0.7	114	115
1963	34	88	32	41	27	21	25	96	15	0.2	128	95
1964	38₂	116₂	41	48	33	26	32	85	18	0.7	166	114
1965	42	110	46	51	39	35	45	77	21	1.6	156	117
1966	44	117	68	59	33	42	36	54	20	0.5	180	119
1967	40	116	75	82	31	50	42	40	34	0.8	174	138
1968	33	103	86	77	37	59	40	37	14	0.8	155	103
1969	37	112	95	90	18	32	45	50	14	0.5	153	108
1970	42	141	102	99	—	—	55	63	16	0.8	158	122
1971	51	113	105	111	—	—	73	73	18	1.1	175	130
1972	55	161	119	137	—	—	77	97	22	5.0	191	111
1973	71	118	149	159	—	—	91	89	24	1.6	273	299
1974	98	157	176	204	—	—	111	76	27	4.0	434	303
1975	89	161	211	199	—	—	103	150	40	29	470	348
1976	105	258	265	249	—	—	174	142	44	3.6	513	588
1977	136	449	320	305	—	—	261	156	72	9.9	692	795
1978	134	203	375	361	—	—	305	137	59	8.3	793	311
1979	122	519	452	438	—	—	205	157	51	12	737	745
1980	72	121	634	434	—	—	107	86	33	9.3	614	534
1981	92	230	619	352	0.9	3.5	84	84	23	4.5	625	255
1982	100	170	525	329	20	9.6	67	54	13	2.0	583	269
1983	91	350	431	308	38	18	78	92	23	0.7	724	715
1984	109	325	467	292	42	17	102	83	26	4.4	786	517
1985	108	321	469	293	42	20	105	81	28	3.3	813	542
1986	212	860	544	239	46	38	166	134	50	5.7	1,525	1,759
1987	249	509	640	364	51	47	312	128	53	14	1,835	1,331
1988	207	632	625	461	68	63	244	132	80	23	1,850	1,122
1989	210	477	631	521	60	75	235	75	51	16	2,143	889
1990	242	686	746	488	80	84	196	28	43	5	2,387	933
1991	308	332	826	545	94	108	344	78	104	8	2,940	1,031
1992	573	359	...	...	239	264	664	30	152	14	5,141	1,554
1993	566	655	1,790	1,372	302	410	849	122	155	14	6,870	1,850

E2   NORTH AMERICA: External Trade (in Current Values) with Main Trading Partners

GUATEMALA (thousand gold pesos to 1919, million quetzales subsequently)

	El Salvador		Germany		Japan		UK		USA	
	Imports	Exports	Imports	Exports	Imports	Exports	Imports	Exports	Imports	Exports
1911	- -	...	1,593	...	...	...	1,314	...	2,696	...
1912	...	...	2,251	6,975	...	...	1,276	1,710	4,532	3,864
1913	...	...	2,043	7,654	...	...	1,650	1,857	5,053	3,924
1914	...	...	...	...	...	...	...	...	...	...
	...	...						...		
1915	...	...	146	50	...	...	577	1,322	3,752	6,889
1916	...	...	5.2	92	...	...	1,062	86	5,228	8,669
1917	...	...	—	—	...	...	1,462	1,229	6,386	5,359
1918	...	...	—	—	...	...	1,438	1,137	5,813	4,582
1919	...	...	—	—	...	...	3,672	1,534	9,088	19,187
					(million quetzales)					
1920	...	...	0.8	0.1	0.3	—	3.9	0.5	12	15
1921	...	...	1.4	1.8	0.1	—	2.4	0.1	8.2	8.1
1922	...	...	1.2	1.9	0.2	- -	1.6	0.3	6.6	7.9
1923	...	...	1.6	2.1	0.4	- -	2.1	0.4	8.1	11
1924	...	...	1.5	8.3	0.3	—	1.9	0.8	9.1	12
1925	...	...	2.0	9.3	0.5	—	2.3	0.5	11	15
1926	...	...	3.5	9.2	0.4	—	3.5	0.5	15	16
1927	...	...	3.5	13	0.7	—	2.8	0.3	14	14
1928	...	...	4.2	9.4	0.5	—	3.2	0.2	17	15
1929	...	...	3.4	9.9	0.3	- -	1.3	0.2	14	11
1930	...	...	1.6	8.3	0.3	- -	2.1	0.7	7.6	9.2
1931	...	...	1.3	5.0	0.2	—	0.9	0.3	5.5	5.4
1932	...	...	0.7	3.0	0.1	—	0.6	0.5	3.0	4.0
1933	...	...	0.7	3.2	0.2	- -	0.8	0.2	3.0	3.2
1934	...	...	0.9	5.5	0.5	- -	0.7	0.4	4.1	4.5
1935	...	...	2.2	2.8	0.5	- -	1.1	- -	4.0	6.5
1936	...	...	3.6	2.8	0.1	- -	1.1	0.3	4.9	9.0
1937	...	...	5.4	2.8	0.1	- -	1.4	0.1	7.6	10
1938	...	...	5.9	2.3	- -	- -	1.0	0.1	7.5	11
1939	- -	0.1	4.1	1.9	- -	- -	0.6	0.1	8.3	12
1940	0.1	0.1	0.4	- -	0.1	- -	0.2	0.2	9.4	11
1941	...	...	- -	- -	...	...	0.5	...	13	13
1942	...	...	...	...	...	...	...	...	...	...
1943	...	...	...	...	...	...	...	...	...	...
1944	...	...	...	...	...	...	...	...	...	...
1945	...	...	...	...	...	...	...	...	...	...
1946	0.9	0.2	...	...	...	...	0.5	...	25	32
1947	0.9	0.3	...	...	...	...	0.8	0.7	43	45
1948	1.6	0.1	- -	- -	...	...	1.5	0.2	52	45
1949	1.6	0.1	0.7_2	0.2_2	0.1	...	1.2	...	50	48

E2 NORTH AMERICA: External Trade (in Current Values) with Main Trading Partners

GUATEMALA (million quetzales)

	El Salvador		West Germany		Japan		UK		USA	
	Imports	Exports	Imports	Exports	Imports	Exports	Imports	Exports	Imports	Exports
1950	1.6	0.1	2.0	0.2	0.2	...	1.7	...	49	60
1951	0.2	0.3	3.8	0.8	...	...	3.2	- -	54	67
1952	0.2	0.9	3.9	2.0	...	...	4.1	1.5	48	73
1953	0.5	1.5	4.3	7.6	...	...	2.7	- -	51	68
1954	0.8	1.5	6.5	7.9	0.3	0.2	3.4	0.7	56	68
1955	0.8	1.7	7.4	3.1	0.6	0.9	4.0	0.6	70	73
1956	0.8	1.4	8.5	10	0.8	0.8	5.0	0.7	93	83
1957	1.0	2.4	12	14	0.9	0.6	6.8	0.7	89	73
1958	1.3	2.9	15	16	1.3	2.6	7.8	0.7	89	66
1959	2.2	4.0	14	18	3.0	2.3	6.3	0.9	74	63
1960	5.9	4.4	17	23	6.1	5.5	5.6	0.8	68	63
1961	6.8	6.2	15	19	6.5	8.5	5.9	1.2	64	59
1962	4.7	6.2	14	21	7.1	11	6.9	1.2	65	56
1963	16	11	17	24	9.0	16	7.3	3.0	80	67
1964	19	17	22	26	12	17	7.6	3.7	90	54
1965	22	20	22	25	15	21	11	1.6	97	68
1966	24	28	18	30	15	19	9.9	1.6	87	70
1967	29	29	25	24	22	17	9.5	1.2	101	62
1968	28	32	26	20	23	24	12	2.2	102	62
1969	33	35	26	26	26	21	10	1.9	86	73
1970	39	39	27	33	29	20	10	1.8	100	82
1971	43	41	31	31	32	19	14	2.6	98	88
1972	46	45	30	34	28	27	14	3.2	105	96
1973	57	56	41	41	43	25	15	8.8	136	146
1974	73	65	57	63	63	29	19	8.6	223	188
1975	60	75	55	62	65	32	24	51	252	144
1976	59	84	59	81	93	63	26	3.3	306	267
1977	45	106	79	159	121	90	31	4.1	367	384
1978	114	120	107	138	130	73	30	10	381	339
1979	105	148	106	103	125	94	33	15	473	309
1980	61	182	89	119	129	49	35	69	525	426
1981	97	179	104	82	113	50	26	13	551	294
1982	117	180	72	76	76	55	17	18	466	296
1983	102	158	66	59	60	42	13	13	401	407
1984	95	174	75	59	68	49	19	12	424	419
1985	49	121	81	65	56	36	20	3.5	404	359
1986	71	149	108	126	84	66	20	11	646	713
1987	184	335	232	179	237	46	71	23	1,413	1,015
1988	212	334	265	247	258	65	83	32	1,543	761
				US Dollars (thousand)						
1989	828	918	965	540	896	188	408	43	5,770	2,671
1990	800	1,442	919	634	984	346	307	113	6,645	4,632
1991	974	1,547	863	454	1,219	340	308	97	7,888	4,545
1992	1,409	1,825	1,133	443	1,466	219	339	101	11,167	4,590
1993	1,388	1,912	1,021	593	1,380	232	372	158	13,132	5,106

E2 NORTH AMERICA: External Trade (in Current Values) with Main Trading Partners

HONDURAS (thousand pesos to 1938, thousand lempiras subsequently)[5]

	El Salvador		Germany		Guatemala		Japan		UK		USA	
	Imports	Exports	Imports	Exports	Imports	Exports	Imports	Exports	Imports	Exports	Imports	Exports
1913	...	106	1,116	352	122	220	...	...	1,426	26	6,914	5,530
1914	...	...	522	165	54	181	34	—	460	53	5,262	2,974
1915	...	...	96	0.7	89	45	...	...	327	14	5,177	3,041
1916	...	...	...	...	...	...	...	...	...	...	...	...
1917	...	...	...	...	...	...	...	...	...	...	...	...
1918	...	...	...	...	...	...	...	...	...	...	...	...
1919	...	...	...	...	...	...	...	...	...	...	...	...
1920	...	—	36	—	...	40	...	...	1,600	8	22,494	13,332
1921	...	...	636	...	...	...	...	...	2,792	...	28,058	...
1922	...	...	1,098	80	54	22	352	—	1,110	132	21,714	9,392
1923	...	...	1,634	...	...	...	...	—	1,252	...	24,032	17,940
1924	...	...	398	20	...	...	18	—	802	...	19,568	14,372
1925	26	2	616	56	126	14	76	—	1,592	408	20,528	22,144
1926	32	—	772	1,104	138	14	56	—	1,286	2,956	16,236	20,614
1927	226	...	912	864	92	110	64	—	1,504	4,270	16,890	26,972
1928	282	2	1,002	3,400	132	116	100	—	1,500	5,234	20,058	35,294
1929	278	864	1,246	5,894	122	166	142	—	1,676	3,958	23,126	36,546
1930	322	904	1,460	7,018	144	282	184	—	1,862	3,906	23,772	38,704
1931	126	678	1,208	6,432	48	76	80	—	965	2,404	14,736	29,000
1932	70	394	608	3,408	46	56	84	—	668	4,032	12,752	23,762
1933	36	250	568	3,716	44	12	136	—	642	2,904	9,288	19,342
1934	118	542	552	2,578	22	22	536	—	900	1,888	11,764	17,782
1935	204	704	650	458	46	16	2,028	—	1,210	254	12,378	17,416
1936	234	394	1,090	384	42	38	1,334	—	620	1,050	11,592	15,038
1937	504	304	1,980	260	36	52	3,032	4	684	116	12,058	17,126
1938	[640][5]	[442][5]	[2,096][5]	[414][5]	[18][5]	[96][5]	[1,752][5]	[46][5]	[572][5]	[284][5]	[11,742][5]	[12,724][5]

――――――――――――――――――――――――― (thousand lempiras) ―――――――――――――――――――――――――

	El Salvador		Germany		Guatemala		Japan		UK		USA	
	Imports	Exports	Imports	Exports	Imports	Exports	Imports	Exports	Imports	Exports	Imports	Exports
1939	...	...	...	...	...	...	...	...	...	...	...	...
1940	...	...	...	...	...	...	...	...	...	...	...	...
1941	...	...	...	...	...	...	...	...	...	...	...	...
1942	1,608	678	13	—	125	44	97	—	272	—	18,265	18,121
1943	1,791	1,027	—	—	233	126	—	—	349	—	14,842	6,989
1944	3,107	1,739	—	—	267	237	0.6	—	391	—	17,791	16,161
1945	1,974	2,192	—	—	420	276	0.1	—	284	- -	21,516	20,190
1946	3,107	2,855	—	—	81	199	—	—	410	—	28,778	21,160
1947	3,539	3,257	8.8	9.1	86	436	—	—	608	117	45,583	22,304
1948	3,632	4,436	- -	—	73	300	2.5	—	756	—	56,031	28,450
1949	4,176	5,695	5.2	29	127	588	13	—	973	378	53,885	29,361

E2　NORTH AMERICA: External Trade (in Current Values) with Main Trading Partners

HONDURAS (million lempiras)[5]

	El Salvador		Germany		Guatemala		Japan		UK		USA	
	Imports	Exports	Imports	Exports	Imports	Exports	Imports	Exports	Imports	Exports	Imports	Exports
1950	3.5	6.1	0.2	- -	0.2	0.3	0.2	—	1.3	0.9	54	30
1951	3.6$_5$	7.1$_5$	1.4$_5$	0.1$_5$	0.3$_5$	0.4$_5$	1.5$_5$	- -$_5$	2$_5$	- -$_5$	58$_5$	34$_5$
1952	2.8	7.4	2.3	1.5	0.9	0.2	1.3	- -	3.8	0.1	85	94
1953	2.9	7.9	4.5	0.6	0.6	0.4	2.5	- -	2.9	0.1	77	106
1954	3	7.3	6.4	0.8	- -	0.3	4.1	- -	3	0.4	71	86
1955	3.5	8	6.8	6.5	- -	1.1	5.3	- -	2.8	0.6	72	66
1956	2.6	12	7.5	8.5	0.1	0.7	6.2	- -	2.9	1.5	79	96
1957	4.5	10	9.2$_2$	8.6$_2$	0.2	1.6	8.6	- -	3.4	1	88	83
1958	7.2	11	9.2	7.3	0.5	2	8	3.8	3.4	1.2	78	86
1959	7.5	13	9.2	12	0.6	2.6	10	5	3.9	1.4	66	73
1960	8.2	13	11	9	2.2	3.2	8.8	1.5	5.4	2.1	80	72
1961	9.3	12	8.9	7.9	3.1	4.1	11	0.8	4.2	1.7	75	96
1962	11	18	9.7	11	6	6.1	9.6	0.6	4.8	1.5	83	93
1963	16	18	10	16	9.2	6.1	17	2.6	5.6	1.4	91	98
1964	18	22	13	20	12	7.8	11	6.9	6.4	1.1	99	99
1965	25	26	14	28	16	10	13	9.8	7.6	1.1	115	148
1966	34	21	16	45	20	9.4	11	7.3	8.9	0.9	148	164
1967	40	23	18	69	24	13	15	8.8	9.1	1.1	159	143
1968	46	28	17	67	28	14	20	14	9.2	1.4	170	162
1969	25	14	24	42	36	12	24	19	9.5	1.8	161	164
1970	—	—	24	37	57	14	36	4.9	12	1.3	183	185
1971	—	—	21	45	16	4.7	44	1.6	13	1.5	183	238
1972	—	—	20	53	19	3.2	30	11	14	1.4	170	218
1973	—	—	22	58	32	5.1	53	21	13	1.9	214	276
1974	—	—	37	55	42	14	53	19	17	1.2	308	243
1975	—	—	28	66	47	23	53	24	24	1.2	342	304
1976	—	—	42	93	53	32	80	25	19	0.7	396	444
1977	—	—	41	196	66	43	127	56	29	2.0	497	502
1978	—	—	49	152	88	51	124	29	38	12	586	692
1979	—	—	47	143	102	63	128	60	41	19	716	842
1980	—	—	57	204	115	75	199	68	43	44	952	863
1981	3	4.5	69	114	122	61	126	91	35	13	784	784
1982	7.5	20	45	117	92	50	90	77	28	11	547	692
1983	16	28	56	70	117	56	73	79	30	18	592	727
1984	18	27	74	74	82	23	88	116	30	32	648	756
1985	21	16	70	117	88	7.9	103	103	31	40	636	739
1986	27	15	62	182	74	16	152	158	28	29	665	807
1987	25	21	60	169	55	21	177	79	34	25	705	900
1988	27	19	64	183	68	20	173	123	32	28	721	894
1989	29	22	66	118	96	29	161	96	25	41	858	556
1990	32	19	76	110	70	21	132	56	22	23	816	570
1991	108	87	147	230	228	47	307	188	48	60	2,498	1,761
1992	160	127	122	535	254	65	276	102	47	80	2,942	2,138
1993	288	118	244	605	501	89	460	125	68	69	4,354	2,465

E2 NORTH AMERICA: External Trade (in Current Values) with Main Trading Partners

JAMAICA (thousand pounds)[6]

	UK		USA			UK		USA	
	Imports	Exports	Imports	Exports		Imports	Exports	Imports	Exports
1850	...	910	...	70	1900	815	339	717	1,146
1851	...	732	...	87	1901	858	410	733	1,273
1852	...	733	...	66	1902	1,029	437	811	1,560
1853	...	627	...	93	1903	948	282	857	908
1854	...	769	...	90	1904	788	271	719	768
1855	550	788	191	130	1905	950	357	756	1,058
1856	565	678	224	154	1906	1,126	430	864	1,139
1857	448	965	221	155	1907	1,382	510	1,268	1,401
1858	700	1,016	231	82	1908	$1,003_6$	489_6	$1,132_6$	$1,312_6$
1859	494	800	220	95	1909	1,126	557	1,164	1,617
1860	701	991	299	158	1910	1,113	530	1,182	1,391
1861	606	1,045	285	92	1911	1,292	434	1,200	1,826
1862	603	926	330	97	1912	1,333	359	1,273	1,619
1863	581	845	344	52	1913	1,088	424	1,327	1,396
1864	628	814	322	65	1914	986	530	1,221	1,769
1865	643	723	271	74	1915	772	849	1,258	1,043
1866	684	971	206	101	1916	1,009	1,226	1,783	921
1867	534	841	192	92	1917	624	1,112	2,329	695
1868	624	938	205	103	1918	548	1,348	2,281	628
1869	775	849	267	142	1919	1,013	3,567	3,365	1,343
1870	760	898	267	61	1920	3,062	2,963	6,041	1,794
1871	777	1,030	312	104	1921	1,601	953	2,991	1,425
1872	933	1,153	366	150	1922	1,302	1,065	2,092	2,066
1873	1,045	999	427	103	1923	1,524	$1,241_6$	2,337	$2,109_6$
							1,219		2,102
1874	1,017	1,141	453	153	1924	1,437	770	1,956	1,355
1875	966	1,154	540	163	1925	1,631	1,022	2,143	1,586
1876	968	1,228	468	152	1926	1,377	892	2,100	1,860
1877	833	1,159	453	221	1927	1,656	874	1,939	2,002
1878	757	955	471	171	1928	1,853	817	1,922	1,608
1879	686	995	423	203	1929	1,771	830	2,089	1,568
1880	778	1,018	474	304	1930	1,732	1,089	1,934	1,357
1881	646	783	550	224	1931	1,405	1,063	1,430	1,030
1882	726	968	403	276	1932	1,887	1,571	817	553
1883	942	800	423	260	1933	1,695	1,342	688	224
1884	899	644	422	462	1934	1,798	1,680	847	281
1885	790	533	470	595	1935	1,954	2,070	880	328
1886	662	509	460	563	1936	1,875	2,000	834	265
1887	724	583	445	663	1937	2,006	2,679	1,083	231
1888	1,049	734	479	790	1938	2,050	2,914	1,359	180
1889	884_6	603_6	545_6	810_6	1939	1,842	2,925	1,471	260
1890	1,232	615	738	1,051	1940	1,883	1,869	962	258
1891	862	563	654	877	1941	1,712	1,469	869	747
1892	1,001	512	677	955	1942	1,562	1,168	981	807
1893	1,191	554	719	1,190	1943	2,466	715	1,381	846
1894	1,106	513	803	1,128	1944	1,325	917	2,843	916
1895	1,106	518	953	1,067	1945	1,321	2,210	2,882	522
1896	927	403	731	832	1946	2,671	5,467	3,193	438
1897	777	318	720	897	1947	3,796	$7,873_6$	6,376	275_6
1898	819	343	808	982			7,902		310
1899	873	358	801	1,182	1948	7,758	8,388	3,825	389
					1949	8,669	7,505	3,174	450

E2 NORTH AMERICA: External Trade (in Current Values) with Main Trading Partners

JAMAICA (million local dollars)[6]

	UK		USA				UK		USA	
	Imports	Exports	Imports	Exports			Imports	Exports	Imports	Exports
1950	19	17	6.4	1.6		1970	84	46	192	149
1951	25	20	12	1.8		1971	90	58	182	124
1952	30	24	15	2.8		1972	94	65	184	128
1953	30	29	12	6.8		1973	101	80	233	143
1954	32	33	12	8.8		1974	105	102	300	308
1955	37	34	19	10		1975	134	172	382	274
1956	44	39	29	12		1976	90	99	308	236
1957	51	38	30	22		1977	76	139	281	308
1958	50	34	27	30		1978	131	264	464	392
1959	48	31	29	26		1979	172	277	555	647
1960	53	35	38	29		1980	140	333	659	641
1961	50	32	37	44		1981	168	321	952	687
1962	47	34	44	47		1982	192	251	869	459
1963	42	42	49	45		1983				
1964	51	44	63	53		1984	245	378	2,036	1,392
1965	51	41	65	57		1985	327	526	2,546	1,040
1966	52	42	86	61		1986	361	620	2,689	1,109
1967	50	42	99	64		1987	465	682	3,345	1,448
1968	65	43	123	70		1988	543	865	3,799	660
1969	78	40	150	78		1989	664	875	5,460	1,507
						1990	734	1,248	6,818	2,444
						1991	1,163	1,418	10,247	2,432
						1992	1,926	2,754	20,373	8,983

MEXICO (million Mexican dollars or pesos)[7]

	France		Germany		UK[8]		USA	
	Imports	Exports	Imports	Exports	Imports	Exports	Imports	Exports
1873	...	4.6	...	0.8	...	13.0	...	11
1874	...	4.1	...	0.2	...	9.8	...	12
1875	...	5.7	...	0.4	...	9.2	...	10
1876	...	...	...	...	...	...	...	...
1877	...	...	...	...	...	...	...	...
1878	...	5.4	...	0.5	...	10	...	12
1879	...	5.2	...	0.6	...	10	...	12
1880	...	5.2	...	1.5	...	11	...	13
1881	...	3.1	...	1.4	...	10	...	14
1882	...	2.2	...	1.3	...	10	...	14
1883	...	4.2	...	1.1	...	17	...	16
1884	...	2.9	...	1.2	...	19	...	22
1885	...	2.2	...	1.4	...	15	...	26
1886	...	3.9	...	1.6	...	12	...	25
1887	...	5.1	...	2.2	...	13	...	28
1888	...	4.5	...	2.2	...	11	...	31
1889	5.0	3.5	2.8	2.1	6.3	13	23	41
1890	6.2	3.2	3.7	1.7	8.5	14	29	43
1891	...	3.7	...	2.8	...	11	...	45
1892	...	4.6	...	4.3	...	15	...	50
1893	4.8	3.7	2.9	3.3	5.7	15	26	64
1894	4.4	5.3	2.7	7.0	5.8	15	14	95

E2 NORTH AMERICA: External Trade (in Current Values) with Main Trading Partners

MEXICO (million Mexican dollars or pesos)[7]

	France		Germany		Japan		UK[8]		USA	
	Imports	Exports	Imports	Exports	Imports	Exports	Imports	Exports	Imports	Exports
1895	5.6	2.4	3.4	2.8	...	5.9	6.7	12	15	61
1896	6.1	2.1	4.4	3.1	...	3	7.9	15	20	67
1897	5.0	2.1	4.0	3.0	...	1.7	6.9	16	23	80
1898	5.4	1.9	4.8	4.4	...	2.1	8.1	14	22	87
1899	5.9	6.3	5.7	4.0	...	...	9.2	14	24	104
1900	6.8	6.6	6.7	5.0	...	...	10	12	31	116
1901	6.6	2.8	7.1	5.0	...	...	9.9	12	35	117
1902	6.3	2.2	6.5	4.8	...	...	8.3	11	39	130
1903	6.5	3.7	9.6	9.5	...	...	10	27	41	140
1904	7.5	6.3	9.6	11	...	0.3	10	25	43	142
1905	8.6[7]	5.9[7]	9.8[7]	16[7]	...	10[7]	17[7]	17[7]	48[7]	140[7]
1906	16	8.0	21	21	...	...	20	42	146	186
1907	17	8.1	24	20	...	...	23	32	146	176
1908	20	12	28	22	...	...	33	26	118	170
1909	12	11	17	13	...	...	20	24	91	173
1910	17	12	20	8.4	...	...	22	29	113	197
1911	19	9.3	26	8.7	...	15	24	36	113	224
1912	16	8.3	24	10	...	...	22	40	98	224
1913	18[7]	7.2[7]	25[7]	16[7]	...	...[7]	26[7]	31[7]	97[7]	232[7]
1914	...	...	...	...	...	...	...	...	...	...
1915	...	...	...	...	...	...	...	...	...	...
1916	...	...	...	...	...	...	...	...	...	...
1917	...	...	...	...	...	...	...	...	...	...
1918	...	...	...	...	...	...	...	...	...	...
1919	...	...	...	...	...	...	...	...	...	...
1920	22	4.8	7.0	1.3	...	...	33	15	267	359
1921	47	8.2	24	2.7	...	...	45	49	339	596
1922	20	16	[38][10]	3.0	...	...	24	50	198	518
1923	14	8.2	20	3.6	...	...	22	35	235	472
1924	16	8.4	23	18	...	...	23	35	233	493
1925	21	12	30	33	1.5	- -	31	45	275	518
1926	18	16	28	32	1.2	- -	28	49	269	491
1927	17	19	30	64	1.3	- -	23	49	233	417
1928	18	23	33	40	1.5	1.0	26	46	242	404
1929	19	23	31	45	1.4	1.4	26	61	264	359
1930	20	20	33	33	1.1	0.8	21	55	239	268
1931	12	17	20	31	1.0	1.2	16	48	145	244
1932	10	5.6	21	20	0.7	0.8	14	12	115	199
1933	17	16	29	27	1.5	1.4	22	80	147	175
1934	17	20	35	41	3.0	7.4	36	132	203	334
1935	16	17	49	53	4.9	12	23	76	265	471
1936	17	16	71	82	7.3	19	24	68	275	471
1937	20	21	99	84	11	10	29	99	382	502
1938	20	19	93	65	8.8	3.6	20	79	285	565
1939	23	14	80	51	7.3	9.4	17	53	416	679
1940	13	8.6	8.4	0.3	18	24	22	9.6	527	859
1941	0.1	0.1	2.1	- -	25	21	31	0.8	771	665
1942	- -	0.1	- -	—	1.1	—	28	0.1	655	905
1943	- -	- -	- -	- -	- -	—	18	0.1	805	992
1944	- -	- -	- -	- -	—	—	17	0.1	1,699	890

E2   NORTH AMERICA: External Trade (in Current Values) with Main Trading Partners

MEXICO (million pesos to 1974, million US dollars subsequently)

	France		Germany		Japan		UK[8]		USA	
	Imports	Exports	Imports	Exports	Imports	Exports	Imports	Exports	Imports	Exports
1945	0.4	0.3	- -	—	—	—	24	1.0	1,322	1,062
1946	9.3	7.2	- -	—	- -	—	51	9.8	2,204	1,366
1947	26	17	- -[2]	0.2[2]	- -	- -	65	39	2,856	1,655
1948	13	54	1.6	7.6	0.2	14	86	78	2,561	2,006
1949	22	55	14	16	2.5	0.1	79	71	3,068	2,854
1950	52	26	62	21	9.8	32	101[8]	36[8]	3,717	3,750
1951	135	24	139	158	23	50	142	190	5,515	3,840
1952	92	52	152	138	21	144	166	99	5,240	4,031
1953	102	19	232	58	20	370	167	166	5,173	3,175
1954	157	19	305	147	38	461	171	477	7,185	5,162
1955	113	31	429	345	67	576	256	386	8,762	7,167
1956	124	121	607	505	72	652	313	357	10,491	7,448
1957	151	138	795	245	81	386	403	198	11,122	6,838
1958	301	81	711	235	100	392	457	169	10,862	6,864
1959	220	64	834	263	154	834	481	195	9,174	6,579
1960	290	75	913	226	214	555	722	152	10,706	5,691
1961	289	75	999	165	247	663	649	142	9,976	6,275
1962	404	133	1,160	225	246	855	541	97	9,782	6,917
1963	415	122	1,027	236	322	746	544	119	10,628	7,406
1964	474	153	1,206	219	351	800	625	114	12,791	7,522
1965	606	170	1,526	436	489	834	670	97	12,815	7,913
1966	977	256	1,553	549	571	1,033	652	144	12,823	8,146
1967	915	585	1,646	480	942	858	846	190	13,745	7,812
1968	795	165	2,076	531	957	896	933	480	15,471	9,090
1969	1,077	108	1,968	577	1,178	1,200	812	305	16,222	10,147
1970	1,307	110	2,313	348	1,075	861	895	133	19,594	10,585
1971	946	95	2,565	423	1,124	817	844	103	18,489	11,474
1972	1,045	121	3,295	491	1,443	1,477	1,161	177	22,180	16,212
1973	1,252	261	3,481	747	2,224	2,223	1,133	396	32,617	22,636
1974	1,649	501	5,955	1,369	2,795	2,205	1,700	574	47,240	21,729
					(million US dollars)					
1975	161	39	480	87	306	144	192	36	4,129	1,845
1976	183	43	420	89	320	180	181	44	3,779	2,158
1977	172	39	323	96	311	130	137	63	3,528	2,879
1978	312	32	568	175	586	175	211	71	4,867	4,510
1979	516	72	822	213	735	256	283	45	7,999	6,237
1980	520	567	972	256	989	671	405	44	11,979	10,072
1981	588	901	1,189	212	1,205	1,157	429	242	15,470	10,702
1982	349	931	914	240	855	1,450	278	913	9,006	11,129
1983	389	845	396	298	426	1,535	186	918	7,502	15,488
1984	312	940	565	291	656	1,905	234	1,028	10,013	16,572
1985	307	824	584	297	843	1,723	302	679	11,244	15,858
1986	195	335	599	333	550	834	173	155	6,137	8,294
1987	240	567	643	298	449	1,261	176	156	6,222	12,497
1988	454	561	1,224	436	1,171	1,228	370	193	13,036	13,453
1989	474	480	919	358	818	1,311	284	179	15,552	16,092
1990	716	546	1,646	321	1,283	1,442	590	182	19,846	18,491
1991	980	606	2,328	557	2,061	1,229	496	224	24,652	18,729
1992	1,304	547	2,476	482	3,040	883	617	246	30,129	37,263
1993	1,012	444	2,652	424	3,056	705	541	220	48,295	42,912

E2 NORTH AMERICA: External Trade (in Current Values) with Main Trading Partners

NICARAGUA (thousand gold cordobas)

	Germany		Japan		UK		USA	
	Imports	Exports	Imports	Exports	Imports	Exports	Imports	Exports
1910	369	849	...	...	684	676	1,629	1,600
1911	643	1,075	...	...	1,412	523	2,755	1,703
1912	604	702	...	...	939	515	2,549	1,767
1913	619	1,888	...	...	1,151	999	3,244	2,722
1914	391	560	...	...	718	367	2,566	2,428
1915	37	—	...	...	302	439	2,593	3,080
1916	0.3	—	...	...	611	38	3,886	3,731
1917	- -	—	...	...	655	1.9	4,103	4,074
1918	—	—	...	...	597	16	4,630	6,413
1919	—	—	...	...	690	438	6,688	7,664
1920	145	2	...	...	1,635	306	11,248	9,295
1921	101	54	...	...	654	109	3,857	6,265
1922	74	26	7.7	—	485	225	4,127	5,618
1923	231	19	33	—	873	241	5,509	7,896
1924	396	409	33	—	1,043	431	6,425	7,442
1925	607	482	49	—	1,230	517	7,272	7,971
1926	727	694	75	—	1,128	255	7,117	6,904
1927	688	782	68	—	1,170	628	6,778	5,016
1928	1,179	884	134	—	1,494	346	8,384	6,025
1929	1,086	1,293	166	—	1,276	399	7,390	5,754
1930	736	972	94	- -	799	290	5,024	4,150
1931	565	943	44	—	544	461	3,684	3,506
1932	299	425	30	—	357	295	2,181	2,964
1933	270	686	45	0.2	493	354	2,394	2,437
1934	378	709	208	0.2	549	365	2,712	2,598
1935	855	700	324	7.0	593	119	2,538	3,151
1936	1,337	743	143	136	697	84	2,580	2,505
1937	857	1,504	243	335	477	53	3,045	3,897
1938	513	867	80	120	422	136	3,058	3,961
1939	777	906	55	40	333	104	4,352	6,432
1940	56	- -	162	192	210	37	5,921	8,941
1941	4.2	—	217	147	153	- -	9,142	11,457
1942	7.3	—	27	—	143	2.0	5,185	13,542
1943	1.9	—	—	—	272	1.4	8,257	13,560
1944	—	—	—	—	179	40	7,601	14,061
1945	—	—	—	—	137	131	8,926	12,572
1946	—	0.3	—	—	200	520	11,397	14,137
1947	2.9	0.5	—	- -	370	351	17,904	16,234
1948	0.2	43	—	365	448	169	20,180	19,940
1949	759	16	- -	- -	351	384	16,790	15,057

E2   NORTH AMERICA: External Trade (in Current Values) with Main Trading Partners

NICARAGUA (million gold cordobas).

	Germany		Japan		UK		USA	
	Imports	Exports	Imports	Exports	Imports	Exports	Imports	Exports
1950	0.2	0.4	0.2	0.2	0.8	3.7	20	24
1951	1.5	0.4	0.1	2.3	1.2	7.9	22	25
1952	1.6	2.4	0.4	1.3	1.5	6.7	28	27
1953	3.2	5.3	1.2	3.4	1.6	7.2	28	25
1954	5.2	8.5	1.2	6.8	1.9	2.3	38	26
1955	4.4	13	1.4	11	2.3	2.1	45	25
1956	5	15	1.3	6.0	2.8	2.1	43	20
1957	8.5	12	2.2	3.3	3.0	4.3	47	23
1958	6.1	12	3.0	7.5	3.2	3.0	43	21
1959	5.0	10	3.4	16	2.9	2.6	35	15
1960	5.6	8.6	4.7	8.7	3.0	2.6	38	23
1961	6.1	8.2	4.5	13	3.3	2.0	36	27
1962	7.1	13_2	5.7	18	4.1	3.4	49	32
1963	8.1	12	6.5	23	6.0	3.1	54	39
1964	11	24	8.3	28	5.2	3.9	64	32
1965	10	21	11	48	5.9	3.3	76	35
1966	13	21	9.9	42	6.3	2.5	83	30
1967	14	20	13	46	5.2	1.9	87	41
1968	11	18	14	42	5.5	3.3	70	45
1969	12	17	13	28	6.8	2.1	67	51
1970	11	21	13	25	6.9	1.7	72	58
1971	15	14	17	33	6.5	1.1	70	65
1972	16	19	18	45	7.3	0.8	69	82
1973	25	25	23	34	7.3	0.7	113	94
1974	27	30	29	25	9.7	0.5	125	51
1975	21	24	27	34	8.8	8.4	118	73
1976	24	37	30	49	9.4	1.1	116	117
1977	36	60	54	49	11	1.3	154	105
1978	30	83	38	51	10	1.9	172	143
1979	15	57	15	32	4.8	2.0	97	195
1980	28	56	29	13	7.3	1.8	243	161
1981	60	51	28	56	11	2.2	263	136
1982	29	38	19	45	4.3	2.8	148	98
1983	19	51	20	66	5.1	3.2	158	79
1984	22	54	24	96	6.9	4.4	135	49
1985	50	110	81	161	28	2.7	189	74
1986	…	…	…	…	…	…	…	…
1987	…	…	…	…	…	…	…	…
1988	…	…	…	…	…	…	…	…

E2 NORTH AMERICA: External Trade (in Current Values) with Main Trading Partners

TRINIDAD & TOBAGO (thousand pounds)[9]

	UK		USA			UK		USA	
	Imports	Exports	Imports	Exports		Imports	Exports	Imports	Exports
1850	264	282	89	1	1900	882	983	605	792
1851	308	375	98	1	1901	921	706	674	817
1852	255	408	107	4	1902	983	626	702	822
1853	255	434	91	1	1903	945	604	676	945
1854	278	359	109	4	1904	939	817	677	695
1855	272	360	114	10	1905	958	828	651	851
1856	306	431	158	92	1906	922	702	677	975
1857	388	787	173	138	1907	1,051	821	817	1,016
1858	373	673	195	24	1908	944_9	444_9	717_9	924_9
1859	353	657	169	73	1909	968	647	805	1,016
1860	357	526	178	63	1910	980	746	969	1,030
1861	372	429	199	10	1911	$1,419_9$	$1,129_9$	$1,034_9$	$1,271_9$
1862	289	604	202	8	1912	945	508	819	750
1863	295	622	185	26	1913	893	477	814	954
1864	426	912	179	42	1914	999_9	548	853_9	915
1865	431	638	135	14	1915	969	1,507	914	1,427
1866	501	825	187	39	1916	999	1,358	1,296	1,202
1867	403	887	131	38	1917	905	1,886	1,589	1,163
1868	423	890	138	27	1918	681	1,736	1,607	1,252
1869	369	1,170	169	55	1919	871	2,338	2,041	1,446
1870	448	1,033	151	21	1920	2,219	3,598	3,474	1,931
1871	535	1,217	214	94	1921	1,727	1,865	2,458	1,080
1872	640	1,125	205	73	1922	$1,367_7$	$1,544_7$	$1,249_7$	937_7
1873	562	1,380	192	53		1,363	1,544	1,247	937
1874	489	981	269	70	1923	1,259	2,144	1,052	890
					1924	1,402	2,229	932	926
1875	532	1,220	279	108	1925	1,324	2,409	930	947
1876	572	1,248	303	122	1926	1,225	1,582	1,143	1,500
1877	493	1,417	362	253	1927	1,574	1,541	1,376	1,580
1878	644	1,247	343	252	1928	1,795	1,951	1,103	1,642
1879	774	1,461	368	104	1929	1,859	1,851	1,492	2,077
1880	831	1,164	408	262	1930	1,889	1,283	1,279	1,571
1881	828	996	398	194	1931	1,375	729	718	944
1882	808	1,076	403	342	1932	1,583	1,090	469	630
1883	878	814	438	717	1933	1,780	1,736	513	285
1884	887	863	426	608	1934	1,746	1,809	619	256
1885	655	1,186	394	564	1935	1,892	1,785	684	352
1886	666	950	352	634	1936	2,207	2,446	923	403
1887	752	749	361	723	1937	2,685	2,947	1,746	459
1888	794_9	862_9	350_9	669_9	1938	2,690	3,198	1,721	283
1889	764	972	383	763	1939	2,592	3,092	1,846	268
1890	822	857	429	725	1940	2,990	2,512	2,623	359
1891	778	729	422	736	1941	2,474	1,077	2,979	376
1892	760	793	457	811	1942	2,144	1,071	3,725	291
1893	874	864	466	754	1943	1,751	798	4,083	352
1894	835	832	446	559	1944	1,606	932	4,005	389
1895	989	907	443	564	1945	1,930	1,282	3,636	370
1896	979	944	458	670	1946	4,462	5,505	2,424	378
1897	858	714	451	628	1947	5,681	6,763	5,634	797
1898	796	713	496	863	1948	8,927	9,442	4,484	1,229
1899	950	890	628	886	1949	11,978	8,851	5,092	1,542

E2 NORTH AMERICA: External Trade (in Current Values) with Main Trading Partners

TRINIDAD & TOBAGO (million local dollars)[9]

	UK		USA			UK		USA	
	Imports	Exports	Imports	Exports		Imports	Exports	Imports	Exports
1950	68	46	14	13	1970	144	93	176	447
1951	78	59	18	12	1971	176	93	233	422
1952	86	68	22	7.8	1972	188	87	274	452
1953	89	103	19	12	1973	176	64	255	723
1954	95	103	21	13	1974	207	93	402	2,531
1955	112	112	28	8.4	1975	286	148	702	2,575
1956	105	116	36	19	1976	366	249	953	3,548
1957	129	129	50	29	1977	458	103	921	3,674
1958	135	102	57	79	1978	589	137	969	3,234
1959	146	143	59	68	1979	553	231	1,310	3,478
1960	150	153	70	97	1980	774	153	2,021	5,466
1961	137	143	67	146	1981	669	165	1,935	4,795
1962	136	137	77	149	1982	724	156	3,119	3,425
1963	134	145	104	179	1983	715	177	2,614	3,172
1964	130	152	103	204	1984	452	469	1,745	2,961
1965	136	114	139	233	1985	358	204	1,460	3,196
1966	127	102	110	271	1986	474	241	2,065	3,043
1967	105	97	118	321	1987	405	163	1,800	2,972
1968	126	102	126	249	1988	426	148	1,602	2,933
1969	134	97	142	295	1989	396	165	2,601	3,756
					1990	400	250	2,173	5,027
					1991	522	188	2,808	4,215
					1992	477	136	2,571	3,860
					1993	602	178	2,964	4,195

E2 NORTH AMERICA: External Trade (in Current Values) with Main Trading Partners

USA (million dollars)[10]

	British North America		France		Germany		Mexico		UK	
	Imports	Exports	Imports	Exports	Imports	Exports	Imports	Exports	Imports	Exports
1790	...	...	...	1	...	- -	...	...	...	7
1791	...	...	...	1	...	- -	...	...	...	6
1792	...	...	...	2	...	1	...	...	...	5
1793	...	...	...	2	...	2	...	...	...	6
1794	...	...	...	1	...	5	...	...	...	6
1795	...	...	...	8	...	10	...	...	...	6
1796	...	...	...	3	...	10	...	...	...	17
1797	...	...	...	4	...	10	...	...	...	6
1798	...	...	...	1	...	15	...	...	...	12
1799	...	...	...	...	...	18	...	...	...	19
1800	...	...	...	- -	...	8	...	...	...	19
1801	...	...	...	4	...	11	...	...	...	31
1802	...	...	...	8	...	6	...	...	...	16
1803	...	...	...	4	...	4	...	...	...	18
1804	...	...	...	9	...	6	...	...	...	13
1805	...	...	...	13	...	4	...	...	...	15
1806	...	...	...	11	...	6	...	...	...	16
1807	...	...	...	13	...	3	...	...	...	23
1808	...	...	...	3	...	- -	...	...	...	3
1809	...	...	...	...	...	2	...	...	...	6
1810	...	...	...	- -	...	2	...	...	...	12
1811	...	...	...	2	...	- -	...	...	...	14
1812	...	...	...	3	...	...	...	...	...	6
1813	...	...	...	4	...	- -	...	...	...	...
1814	...	...	...	- -	...	...	...	...	...	...
1815	...	...	...	7	...	2	...	...	18	18
1816	...	...	...	10	...	4	...	...	30	30
1817	...	...	...	9	...	3	...	...	33	33
1818	...	...	...	12	...	3	...	...	38	38
1819	...	...	...	9	...	4	...	...	24	24
1820	...	...	...	8	...	3	...	...	24	24
1821	- -	2	4	6	1	2	...	...	24	19
1822	- -	2	6	6	2	3	...	...	35	24
1823	- -	2	6	9	2	3	...	...	28	22
1824	- -	2	7	10	2	2	...	...	28	21
1825	- -	3	11	10	3	3	1	6	37	37
1826	- -	2	8	11	3	2	1	6	26	21
1827	- -	2	8	11	2	3	1	4	30	26
1828	- -	2	9	9	3	3	1	3	33	20
1829	- -	2	9	10	2	3	1	2	25	24
1830	- -	3	8	11	2	2	1	5	24	26
1831	1	3	14	6	4	3	1	6	44	31
1832	1	3	12	12	3	4	1	3	37	29
1833	1	4	13	14	2	3	1	5	38	32
1834	1	3	15	15	3	5	1	5	41	44
1835	1	3	22	19	4	4	1	9	60	52
1836	2	3	32	21	5	4	1	6	76	58
1837	2	3	21	19	6	4	1	4	45	52
1838	1	2	16	15	3	3	1	2	36	52
1839	2	4	32	18	5	3	1	3	65	57

E2 NORTH AMERICA: External Trade (in Current Values) with Main Trading Partners

USA (million dollars)[10]

	Canada[11]		France		Germany		Japan		Mexico		UK	
	Imports	Exports	Imports	Exports	Imports	Exports	Imports	Exports	Imports	Exports	Imports	Exports
1840	1	6	16	20	3	4	...	...	1	3	33	55
1841	1	6	24	18	2	5	...	...	1	2	46	47
1842	1	6	17	17	2	5	...	...	1	2	34	40
1843	[- -][10]	[3][10]	[5][10]	[12][10]	[1][10]	[4][10]	...	...	[1][10]	[1][10]	[12][10]	[41][10]
1844	1	6	17	13	2	4	...	...	1	2	41	49
1845	1	6	21	12	3	6	...	...	1	1	45	45
1846	1	7	24	14	3	5	...	...	1	2	45	46
1847	1	7	24	19	4	5	...	...	- -	1	48	87
1848	3	8	28	15	6	4	...	...	1	4	60	67
1849	2	8	24	13	8	3	...	...	1	2	58	78
1850	5	10	27	18	9	5	...	...	1	2	75	71
1851	5	12	31	21	10	6	...	...	1	2	93	101
1852	5	10	25	19	8	6	...	...	1	2	89	81
1853	7	12	33	22	14	7	...	...	1	4	130	103
1854	9	24	36	25	17	9	...	...	1	3	146	117
1855	15	28	32	29	13	9	- -	- -	1	3	106	92
1856	21	29	49	35	15	13	- -	...	1	4	122	128
1857	22	24	46	32	15	15	- -	- -	1	4	127	135
1858	16	24	33	28	14	12	- -	- -	1	3	89	129
1859	19	28	41	30	18	15	- -	- -	1	3	126	133
1860	24	23	43	39	19	15	- -	- -	2	5	138	169
1861	23	23	32	15	15	11	- -	- -	1	2	105	108
1862	19	21	8	20	14	10	- -	- -	1	2	75	86
1863	17	28	11	14	13	14	- -	- -	3	9	113	128
1864	30	27	11	13	14	13	- -	- -	6	9	142	97
1865	33	29	7	11	10	20	- -	- -	6	16	85	103
1866	49	24	23	51	26	22	2	1	2	5	202	288
1867	25	21	29	34	27	22	3	1	1	5	172	225
1868	26	24	25	26	22	31	2	1	2	6	132	198
1869	29	23	30	33	25	38	3	1	2	5	159	185
1870	36	25	43	46	27	42	3	1	3	6	152	248
1871	33	32	28	27	25	35	5	1	3	8	221	273
1872	36	29	43	31	46	41	7	1	4	6	249	265
1873	38[11]	35[11]	34	34	61	62	8	1	4	6	237	317
	37	33										
1874	34	42	52	43	44	63	6	1	4	6	180	345
1875	28	35	60	34	40	50	8	2	5	6	155	317
1876	29	33	51	40	35	51	15	1	5	6	123	336
1877	24	37	48	45	33	58	14	1	5	6	114	346
1878	25	37	43	55	35	55	7	2	5	7	107	387
1879	26	30	51	90	36	57	10	3	5	7	109	349
1880	33	29	69	100	52	57	15	3	7	8	211	454
1881	38	38	70	94	53	70	14	1	8	11	174	481
1882	51	37	89	50	56	54	14	3	8	15	196	408
1883	44	44	98	59	57	66	15	3	8	17	189	425
1884	38	44	71	51	65	61	11	3	9	13	163	386
1885	37	38	57	47	63	62	12	3	9	8	137	398
1886	37	33	63	42	69	62	15	3	11	8	154	348
1887	38	35	68	57	81	59	17	3	15	8	165	366
1888	43	36	71	39	78	56	19	4	17	10	178	362
1889	43	41	70	46	82	68	17	5	21	11	178	383

E2 NORTH AMERICA: External Trade (in Current Values) with Main Trading Partners

USA (million dollars)[10]

	Canada[11]		France		Germany		Japan		Mexico		UK	
	Imports	Exports	Imports	Exports	Imports	Exports	Imports	Exports	Imports	Exports	Imports	Exports
1890	39	40	78	50	99	86	21	5	23	13	186	448
1891	39	38	77	61	97	93	19	5	27	15	195	445
1892	35	43	69	99	83	106	24	3	28	14	156	499
1893	38	47	76	47	96	84	27	3	34	20	183	421
1894	31	57	48	55	69	92	19	4	29	13	107	431
1895	37	53	62	45	81	92	24	5	16	15	159	387
1896	41	60	66	47	94	98	26	8	17	19	170	406
1897	40	65	68	58	111	125	24	13	19	23	168	483
1898	32	84	53	95	70	155	25	20	19	21	109	541
1899	31	88	62	61	84	156	27	17	23	25	118	512
1900	39	95	73	83	97	187	33	29	29	35	160	534
1901	42	106	75	79	100	192	29	19	29	36	143	631
1902	48	110	83	72	102	173	38	21	40	40	166	549
1903	55	123	90	77	120	194	44	21	41	42	190	524
1904	52	131	81	84	109	215	47	25	44	46	166	537
1905	62	141	90	76	118	194	52	52	46	46	176	523
1906	68	157	108	98	135	235	53	38	51	58	210	583
1907	73	183	128	114	162	257	69	39	57	66	246	608
1908	75	167	102	116	143	277	68	41	47	56	190	581
1909	79	163	108	109	144	235	70	27	48	50	209	515
1910	95	216	132	118	169	250	66	22	59	58	271	506
1911	101	270	115	135	163	287	79	37	57	61	261	577
1912	109	329	125	135	171	307	81	53	66	53	273	564
1913	121	415	137	146	189	332	92	58	78	54	296	597
1914	161	345	141	160	190	345	107	51	93	39	294	594
1915	160[10]	301[10]	77[10]	369[10]	91[10]	29[10]	99[10]	41[10]	78[10]	34[10]	256[10]	912[10]
1916	237	605	109	861	6	2	182	109	105	54	305	1,887
1917	414	829	99	941	—	—	254	186	130	111	280	2,009
1918	452	887	60	931	—	—	302	274	159	98	149	2,061
1919	495	734	124	893	11	93	410	366	149	131	309	2,279
1920	612	972	166	676	89	311	415	378	179	208	514	1,825
1921	335	594	142	225	80	372	251	238	119	222	239	942
1922	364	577	143	267	117	316	354	222	132	110	357	856
1923	416	652	150	272	161	317	347	267	140	120	404	882
1924	399	624	148	282	139	440	340	253	167	135	366	983
1925	454	649	157	280	164	470	384	230	179	145	414[11]	1,041
											413	1,034
1926	476	739	152	264	198	364	401	261	169	135	383	973
1927	475	837	168	229	201	482	402	258	138	109	358	840
1928	489	915	159	241	222	467	384	288	125	116	349	847
1929	503	948	171	266	255	410	432	259	118	134	330	848
1930	402	659	114	224	177	278	279	165	80	116	210	678
1931	266	396	79	122	127	166	206	156	48	52	135	456
1932	174	241	45	112	74	134	134	135	37	32	75	288
1933	185	211	50	122	78	140	128	143	31	38	111	312
1934	232	302	61	116	69	109	119	210	36	55	115	383
1935	286	323	58	117	78	92	153	203	42	66	155	433
1936	376[10]	384	65[10]	129	80[10]	102	172[10]	204	49[10]	76	200[10]	440
1937	398	509	76	165	92	126	204	289	60	109	203	536
1938	260	468	54	134	65	107	127	240	49	62	118	521
1939	340	489	62	182	52	46	161	232	56	83	149	505

E2   NORTH AMERICA: External Trade (in Current Values) with Main Trading Partners

USA (million dollars)[10]

	Canada[11]		France		Germany		Japan		Mexico		UK	
	Imports	Exports	Imports	Exports	Imports	Exports	Imports	Exports	Imports	Exports	Imports	Exports
1940	424	713	37	252	5	—	158	227	76	97	155	1,011
1941	554	994	5	2	3	—	78	60	98	159	136	1,637
1942	717	1,334	1	1	—	—	—	—	124	148	134	2,529
1943	1,024	1,444	—	—	—	—	—	2	192	187	105	4,505
1944	1,260	1,441	—	18	—	—	—	—	204	264	84	5,243
1945	1,125	1,178	13	472	1	2	—	1	231	307	90	2,193
1946	883[11]	1,442[11]	63	709	3	83	81	102	232	505	158	855
1947	1,127	2,114	47	817	6	128	35	60	247	630	205	1,103
1948	1,593	1,944	73	591	32	863	63	325	246	522	290	644
1949	1,551	1,959	61	497	45	822	82	468	243	468	228	700
1950	1,960	2,039	132	475	104	441	182	418	315	526	335	548
1951	2,275	2,693	263	843	233[2]	523[2]	205	601	326	730	466	1,000
1952	2,386	3,003	167	1,013	212	405	229	633	410	683	485	787
1953	2,462	3,197	186	1,236	277	363	262	686	355	663	546	826
1954	2,377	2,966	157	783	278	505	279	693	328	649	501	808
1955	2,653	3,404	202	536	366	607	432	683	397	719	616	1,006
1956	2,894	4,149	236	829	494	943	558	998	401	860	726	982
1957	2,907	4,041	256	708	607	1,330	601	1,319	430	917	766	1,162
1958	2,674	3,539	308	570	629	887	666	987	454	904	864	905
1959	3,042	3,825	462	483	920	878	1,029	1,079	435	755	1,137	1,097
1960	2,901	3,810	396	699	897	1,272	1,149	1,447	443	831	993	1,487
1961	3,270	3,826	435	704	856	1,343	1,055	1,837	538	828	898	1,206
1962	3,660	4,045	428	735	962	1,581	1,358	1,574	578	821	1,005	1,128
1963	3,829	4,251	431	813	1,003	1,582	1,498	1,844	594	873	1,079	1,213
1964	4,239	4,915	495	990	1,171	1,606	1,768	2,009	643	1,107	1,143	1,532
1965	4,833	5,642	615	971	1,341	1,649	2,414	2,080	638	1,104	1,405	1,615
1966	6,125	6,661	698	1,007	1,796	1,674	2,963	2,364	750	1,180	1,786	1,737
1967	7,107	7,165	690	1,025	1,955	1,706	2,999	2,695	749	1,222	1,710	1,960
1968	9,005	8,072	842	1,095	2,721	1,709	4,054	2,954	910	1,378	2,058	2,289
1969	10,384	9,137	842	1,195	2,603	2,142	4,888	3,490	1,029	1,450	2,120	2,335
1970	11,092	9,079	942	1,483	3,127	2,741	5,875	4,652	1,219	1,704	2,194	2,536
1971	12,691	10,365	1,088	1,373	3,650	2,831	7,259	4,055	1,262	1,620	2,499	2,369
1972	14,907	12,415	1,369	1,609	4,250	2,808	9,068	4,980	1,632	1,982	2,987	2,658
1973	17,715	15,104	1,732	2,263	5,345	3,757	9,676	8,313	2,306	2,937	3,656	3,564
1974	22,285	19,936	2,305	2,941	6,429	4,985	12,456	10,679	3,386	4,855	4,023	4,573
1975	22,151	21,744	2,164	3,031	5,410	5,194	11,425	9,563	3,066	5,141	3,773	4,527
1976	26,237	24,106	2,509	3,446	5,592	5,731	15,504	10,145	3,598	4,990	4,254	4,801
1977	29,599	25,788	3,032	3,503	7,238	5,989	18,550	10,529	4,694	4,822	5,141	5,951
1978	33,525	28,374	4,051	4,166	9,962	6,957	24,458	12,885	6,094	6,680	6,514	7,116
1979	38,046	33,096	4,768	5,587	10,955	8,478	26,248	17,581	8,800	9,847	8,028	10,635
1980	41,459	35,395	5,265	7,485	11,693	10,960	30,714	20,790	12,580	15,145	9,842	12,694
1981	46,414	39,564	5,851	7,341	11,379	10,277	37,612	21,823	13,265	17,789	12,835	12,439
1982	46,477	33,720	5,545	7,110	11,975	9,291	37,744	20,966	15,566	11,817	13,095	10,645
1983	52,130	38,244	6,025	5,961	12,695	8,737	41,183	21,894	16,776	9,082	12,470	10,621
1984	66,478	46,524	8,113	6,037	16,996	9,084	57,135	23,575	18,020	11,992	14,492	12,210
1985	69,006	47,251	9,482	6,096	20,239	9,050	68,783	22,631	19,132	13,635	14,937	11,273
1986	68,253	45,333	10,129	7,216	25,124	10,561	81,911	26,882	17,302	12,392	15,396	11,418
1987	71,085	59,814	10,730	7,943	27,069	11,748	84,575	28,249	20,271	14,582	17,341	14,114
1988	80,746	69,651	13,068	10,133	27,414	14,000	93,165	37,346	23,518	20,621	18,698	18,097
1989	97,107	77,894	13,501	11,358	25,667	16,824	97,107	44,484	27,442	24,843	18,815	20,462
1990	93,875	82,435	13,602	13,009	28,977	18,581	93,875	48,560	30,766	28,245	20,906	22,794
1991	95,712	84,708	13,767	13,510	26,882	21,221	95,711	48,026	31,767	33,144	18,915	21,435
1992	100,216	89,666	15,260	13,739	29,592	21,243	100,216	47,604	35,856	40,329	20,664	21,807
1993	111,986	99,365	15,689	12,978	29,458	18,756	110,415	47,874	40,708	41,486	22,354	22,468

E2 SOUTH AMERICA: EXTERNAL TRADE (IN CURRENT VALUES) WITH MAIN TRADING PARTNERS

ARGENTINA (million pesos)[12]

	Brazil		Germany		UK		USA	
	Imports	Exports	Imports	Exports	Imports	Exports	Imports	Exports
1870	3.4	0.6	1.6	0.2	13	2.5	2.9	3.8
1871	2.6	0.6	1.2	0.1	12	6.1	2.1	3.7
1872	3.3	1.0	1.8	0.6	16	13	3.2	4.3
1873	3.0	0.8	3.2	0.4	19	14	5.2	3.0
1874	2.7	0.6	2.3	0.8	16	15	3.9	3.7
1875	...	...	...	...	...	...	...	...
1876	2.2	1.2	1.8	1.5	9.0	7.4	1.9	2.5
1877	2.5	1.9	2.1	1.2	9.8	5.5	2.3	2.5
1878	2.2	1.8	2.2	1.0	12	3.6	2.9	2.6
1879	2.3	3.4	2.3	1.6	12	3.9	3.9	3.9
1880	2.4	2.0	2.4	2.5	13	5.3	3.2	5.1
1881	2.7	1.8	3.5	4.0	16	3.9	4.3	4.1
1882	2.2	2.2	4.8	4.8	20	7.6	5.1	3.0
1883	2.2	1.7	7.0	4.8	31	6.0	4.9	3.5
1884	2.3	1.5	8.9	6.8	31	7.2	7.5	4.1
1885	2.2	2.2	7.3	8.5	35	13	7.0	5.6
1886	2.3	1.9	8.0	7.0	33	10	7.7	3.6
1887	2.5	1.8	12	9.8	35	17	11	5.9
1888	2.4	2.5	13	13	44	17	9.9	6.7
1889	2.6	3.7	15	17	57	15	17	6.7
1890	3.6	4.1	12	12	58	19	9.3	6.1
1891	1.5	5.2	6.2	12	28	17	3.4	4.2
1892	2.1	5.1	11	17	36	20	7.4	4.8
1893	2.1	5.2	11	10	33	19	9.6	3.4
1894	2.0	6.8	11	12	33	20	10	5.3
1895	4.1	8.1	11	13	40	15	6.7	8.9
1896	5.2	9.8	14	13	45	14	11	6.4
1897	4.8	8.7	11	14	36	13	10	8.3
1898	5.0	7.9	13	20	39	19	11	5.9
1899	4.8	7.0	13	29	44	22	15	7.7
1900	3.9	6.2	17	20	39	24	13	6.9
1901	4.4	9.7	17	21	36	30	16	9.3
1902	4.6	8.4	13	23	37	35	13	10
1903	5.4	8.5	17	27	45	36	17	8.1
1904	6.0	10	25	30	65	36	24	10
1905	5.3	13	29	37	68	45	29	16
1906	6.6	12	38	39	95	43	39	13
1907	7.8	14	46	36	98	54	39	11
1908	7.3	15	38	35	93	78	36	13
1909	8.2	17	45	41	99	81	43	26
1910	9.1[12]	18[12]	61[12]	45[12]	109[12]	81[12]	48[12]	25[12]
1911	8.5	18	66	43	109	92	52	24
1912	9.5[12]	23[12]	64[12]	54[12]	119[12]	121[12]	59[12]	32[12]
	11	24	74	56	138	127	69	34
1913	11	26	84	62	154	129	73	25

E2 SOUTH AMERICA: External Trade (in Current Values) with Main Trading Partners

ARGENTINA (million pesos)

	Brazil		Germany		UK		USA	
	Imports	Exports	Imports	Exports	Imports	Exports	Imports	Exports
1913	25	59	191	141	350	294	166	56
1914	25	41	108	81	249	268	99	112
1915	32	52	17	—	207	391	172	213
1916	46	59	1	—	235	383	243	272
1917	86	52	1	—	189	366	314	367
1918	112	76	1	—	284	695	385	375
1919	108	85	3	21	351	669	529	430
1920	115	51	101	54	497	636	705	350
1921	102	65	162	115	395	466	457	135
1922	111	61	211	120	367	341	347	181
1923	105	57	269	145	470	429	412	204
1924	85	73	236	230	440	532	415	163
1925	83	76	229	202	436	472	469	163
1926	96	68	212	186	361	452	461	164
1927	99	85	220	377	378	649	495	190
1928	73	92	222	329	373	687	441	198
1929	74	85	225	217	345	697	516	212
1930	69	65	198	123	333	510	371	135
1931	72	44	136	120	247	567	185	88
1932	53	21	77	112	180	465	113	44
1933	58	49	90	86	210	411	107	87
1934	63	61	97	120	292	553	146	79
1935	69	76	100	108	291	538	160	189
1936	61	104	103	96	263	582	161	202
1937	79	132	166	157	323	672	251	295
1938	75	98	151	164	293	459	255	119
1939	93	67	123	90	297	565	220	189
1940	113	76	10	—	325	545	450	253
1941	140	87	6	3	269	477	450	543
1942	226	106	7	—	231	601	397	511
1943	202	143	—	—	195	780	179	533
1944	344	220	—	—	80	942	152	536
1945	334	238	—	—	116	649	159	554
1946	338	150	—	2	308	877	665	596
1947	439	249	2	30	446	1,651	2,431	547
1948	521	260	13	133	775	1,535	2,287	537
1949	357	405	11	152	722	849	689	399
1950	460	430	106	264	569	973	787	1,109
1951	956	704	571₂	459₂	788	1,148	2,199	1,183
1952	881	326	687	227	509	619	1,537	1,115
1953	643	1,116	821	262	355	1,404	965	1,363

E2 SOUTH AMERICA: External Trade (in Current Values) with Main Trading Partners

ARGENTINA (million US dollars)

	Brazil		West Germany		Japan		UK		USA	
	Imports	Exports	Imports	Exports	Imports	Exports	Imports	Exports	Imports	Exports
1954	120	93	81	112	43	47	76	205	141	122
1955	110	129	70	54	75	19	76	201	154	118
1956	85	65	107	115	71	36	53	212	231	118
1957	123	75	90	99	7.6	10	101	237	307	112
1958	128	76	115	95	18	25	102	237	203	128
1959	58	89	112	92	18	26	90	235	191	108
1960	63	83	151	87	28	40	113	221	327	92
1961	78	27	211	76	33	52	140	174	383	86
1962	63	69	186	121	64	27	121	205	399	89
1963	58	78	106	94	47	39	78	200	242	154
1964	101	97	107	110	23	40	81	154	256	94
1965	163	107	110	99	44	32	73	153	273	96
1966	132	99	108	88	32	37	66	154	257	127
1967	124	101	112	79	41	34	69	139	243	123
1968	139	129	128	67	42	29	79	105	270	162
1969	174	130	174	74	65	72	93	155	346	144
1970	186	139	186	105	86	109	92	123	420	159
1971	197	107	219	115	157	89	113	120	416	162
1972	175	187	246	226	143	58	129	170	388	192
1973	205	309	239	265	256	143	104	214	480	268
1974	297	341	393	156	392	179	111	190	617	334
1975	359	213	424	127	494	136	137	79	644	197
1976	371	422	341	205	250	209	129	121	544	282
1977	372	465	427	297	364	308	169	146	781	389
1978	340	577	453	410	267	381	170	198	712	547
1979	654	886	618	435	356	395	222	235	1,414	581
1980	1,072	765	985	407	977	211	343	203	2,379	718
1981	893	595	905	355	965	166	322	218	2,094	863
1982	688	568	479	336	430	283	68	74	1,177	1,024
1983	667	358	475	249	307	377	3.5	- -	987	773
1984	831	478	443	298	376	271	0.4	- -	847	877
1985	612	496	404	290	266	361	1.8	0.2	694	1,028
1986	691	698	523	353	337	391	6.0	19	833	706
1987	819	539	766	383	441	224	7.4	72	952	931
1988	966	608	556	485	387	333	4.2	85	886	1,217
1989	722	1,124	394	413	180	270	1.5	116	892	1,185
1990	715	1,423	376	637	181	395	48.1	186	820	1,699
1991	1,532	1,488	653	732	602	454	109	197	1,498	1,245
1992	3,388	1,671	1,083	731	697	375	197	169	3,226	1,349
1993	3,568	2,814	1,023	625	668	467	258	162	3,859	1,277

E2 SOUTH AMERICA: External Trade (in Current Values) with Main Trading Partners

BOLIVIA (million gold bolivianos)

	Germany		Japan		UK		USA	
	Imports	**Exports**	**Imports**	**Exports**	**Imports**	**Exports**	**Imports**	**Exports**
1900	3.1	...	...	...	2.3	...	0.8	...
1901	3.2	...	...	...	2.3	...	1.7	...
1902	2.5	...	...	...	2.4	...	1.1	...
1903	3.0	2.6	2.8	...	2.8	6.3	1.1	- -
1904	3.9	0.7	3.8	...	3.8	3.2	1.3	- -
1905	3.6	1.0	3.3	2.7	3.3	2.7	1.7	- -
1906	...	...	...	...	...	...	...	...
1907	9.1	...	...	...	6.1	...	7.8	...
1908	10	...	...	...	6.6	...	8.1	...
1909	5.3	...	...	...	8.4	...	11	...
1910	8.5	15	...	...	16	46	5.5	0.2
1911	10	11	...	...	12	60	9.9	0.6
1912	17	11	...	...	9.1	67	4.6	0.4
1913	20	8.0	...	...	11	76	4.0	0.6
1914	11	3.7	- -	—	7.8	52	4.6	2.5
1915	1.6	0.1	- -	—	3.6	67	4.8	25
1916	- -	—	- -	—	4.1	66	9.4	29
1917	- -	—	- -	—	4.1	90	11	57
1918	0.1	—	0.1	- -	4.1	91	11	76
1919	- -	—	0.2	—	4.0	71	15	60
1920	2.1	0.1	0.3	—	14	70	20	72
1921	3.9	0.2	0.3	—	17	36	20	26
1922	2.8	0.4	0.3	- -	11	49	12	38
1923	6.7	- -	0.5	—	14	64	15	38
1924	7.0	0.8	0.4	—	13	82	18	26
1925	7.9	2.5	0.3	—	14	96	18	9.8
1926	8.1	4.4	0.6	—	15	96	20	12
1927	7.1	6.0	0.3	—	13	101	19	11
1928	7.5	3.4	0.3	—	11	97	19	7.1
1929	9.7	1.9	0.3	—	12	108	24	19
1930	7.9	2.4	0.3	—	9.7	78	16	13
1931	5.1	0.6	0.3	- -	4.9	50	7.5	3.0
1932	2.7	0.3	0.1	- -	4.1	40	5.4	1.8
1933	2.4	0.5	0.2	- -	9.1	63	12	3.5
1934	9.0	1.2	1.6	- -	8.4	128	25	3.5
1935	16	1.5	2.3	- -	6.8	133	18	6.0
1936	7.0	1.5	3.5	- -	6	75	16	7.8
1937	7.9	1.3	2.9	- -	4.7	75	16	9.1
1938	13	1.1	4.9	0.3	4.9	59	18	4.4
1939	...	...	...	...	3.7	76	15	4.0
1940	1.3	0.5	...	...	5.5	118	49	47
1941	0.3	- -	8.4	4.4	5.8	75	43	127
1942	- -	—	0.1	- -	7.4	73	50	149
1943	—	—	—	—	8.0	104	47	172
1944	—	—	—	—	5.0	98	47	165
1945	—	—	—	—	4.6	102	43	174
1946	—	—	—	—	6.1	95	63	154
1947	—	—	—	- -	7.6	103	98	170
1948	- -	- -	- -	...	14	146	112	239
1949	0.7	0.2	0.1	- -	14	116	136	225

E2 SOUTH AMERICA: External Trade (in Current Values) with Main Trading Partners

BOLIVIA (million US dollars)

	Argentina		Germany		Japan		UK		USA	
	Imports	Exports	Imports	Exports	Imports	Exports	Imports	Exports	Imports	Exports
1950	9.9	2.2	- -	- -	- -	—	3.9	28	24	63
1951	12	1.3	2.1	0.1	0.2	—	7.0	48	36	100
1952	13	1.1	5.1	0.2	0.5	- -	7.7	44	38	93
1953	9.7	1.0	3.3₂	- ₂	0.2	- -	4.6	52	22	69
1954	7.7	1.3	4.0	0.1	0.3	- -	4.4	42	25	65
1955	8.4	2.4	7.9	1	0.9	—	6.1	33	31	61
1956	12	2.7	7.8	1.4	0.6	- -	4.9	40	39	57
1957	6.0	4.6	11	3.2	1.8	—	6.0	52	43	33
1958	6.5	6.0	9.8	1.8	2.3	0.2	4.8	33	37	21
1959	8.1	4.6	7.6	3.5	1.5	2.9	3.1	35	29	27
1960	4.2	3.9	9.1	3.3	4.2	2.5	3.7	37	31	16
1961	6.6	2.6	9.5	4.6	5.8	2.0	3.8	39	33	21
1962	7.9	1.9	11	4.6	8.5	1.7	6.0	41	39	23
1963	4.1	2.1	14	4.7	7.7	1.5	5.8	41	50	28
1964	3.2	1.0	11	5.3	9.7	2.8	5	55	53	41
1965	7.3	0.9	15	6.7	18	2.7	7	59	59	56
1966	8.7	3.3	17	7.9	16	2.7	6.4	68	57	59
1967	9.0	5.3	18	8.2	18	4.0	6.9	67	62	72
1968	11	8.2	18	5.7	17	5.3	7.2	77	66	60
1969	17	11	20	5.2	27	12	8.3	91	51	61
1970	16	11	20	6.1	26	22	8.0	87	49	74
1971	18	12	21	5.6	28	13	8.6	97	53	59
1972	31	33	18	9.9	20	13	6.8	62	44	66
1973	34	6.8	20	12	23	19	7.9	67	50	77
1974	58	114	31	33	55	32	10	76	103	200
1975	74	137	50	17	87	18	15	53	154	165
1976	86	136	51	24	79	17	16	52	135	222
1977	79	130	58	28	77	17	14	79	141	269
1978	80	126	95	33	102	14	34	93	208	214
1979	93	136	81	44	82	21	25	84	242	241
1980	70	245	61	41	60	9.4	39	73	167	301
1981	90	342	73	27	106	9.3	44	36	206	272
1982	71	400	35	34	53	16	19	30	142	258
1983	75	362	29	23	39	16	21	21	149	192
1984	70	382	30	26	28	8.4	8.7	41	83	146
1985	117	376	52	31	66	2.9	30	63	141	95
1986	76	341	46	38	65	2.6	31	51	151	94
1987	107	260	53	33	76	2.9	6.8	61	161	96
1988	89	227	32	34	70	4.5	9.0	72	128	123
1989	68	228	47	51	62	2.1	8.1	110	151	157
1990	73	236	49	40	69	3.1	9.4	114	154	185
1991	111	263	83	28	122	1.7	8.9	104	231	197
1992	103	153	85	32	135	1.6	27	128	249	153
1993	115	127	66	12	129	2.3	67	114	248	214

E2 SOUTH AMERICA: External Trade (in Current Values) with Main Trading Partners

BRAZIL (million milreis or cruzeiros)

	Argentina		Germany		UK		USA	
	Imports	Exports	Imports	Exports	Imports	Exports	Imports	Exports
1901	56	19	39	127	130	111	52	371
1902	42	21	54	116	133	128	58	272
1903	44	16	60	110	138	143	55	307
1904	53	22	65	108	142	126	57	390
1905	54	20	61	103	121	126	47	285
1906	53	29	73	141	140	128	57	281
1907	58	28	99	147	193	138	82	277
1908	57	30	84	111	163	104	69	283
1909	60	34	92	159	159	164	73	408
1910	61	35	114	110	203	233	92	340
1911	60	39	133	146	231	151	106	358
1912	71	44	164	160	240	133	148	438
1913	75	47	176	137	247	129	158	317
1914	54	36	87	70	135	108	102	312
1915	93	52	8.7	- -	128	125	188	428
1916	114	68	0.4	—	165	131	318	520
1917	109	107	0.9	—	151	149	395	533
1918	188	173	—	—	202	115	356	394
1919	204	96	3.2	11	216	158	640	902
1920	157	120	105	112	452	140	880	725
1921	200	113	137	165	345	118	527	628
1922	226	159	147	141	427	230	379	905
1923	278	177	236	187	601	229	506	1,364
1924	339	208	342	253	667	130	675	1,656
1925	396	215	466	272	751	201	838	1,814
1926	266	202	342	266	512	111	794	1,526
1927	390	219	348	379	695	127	930	1,684
1928	426	235	461	445	795	137	982	1,804
1929	386	245	448	338	678	251	1,063	1,630
1930	312	199	267	265	453	237	566	1,179
1931	277	203	195	314	327	240	472	1,488
1932	113	150	136	224	292	176	457	1,173
1933	278	151	262	229	420	213	455	1,310
1934	311	164	351	454	430	419	591	1,347
1935	500	202	800	680	478	378	898	1,617
1936	702	199	1,003	646	480	585	946	1,902
1937	737	242	1,270	872	642	549	1,229	1,851
1938	615	230	1,299	972	539	447	1,258	1,749
1939	420	310	958	672	462	540	1,672	2,031
1940	535	358	92	112	469	860	2,575	2,096
1941	620	617	101	81	313	821	3,325	3,832
1942	787	993	9.2	—	270	1,233	2,540	3,422
1943	1,146	801	—	—	437	1,231	3,310	4,420
1944	1,698	1,473	—	—	234	1,356	4,895	5,693

E2   SOUTH AMERICA: External Trade (in Current Values) with Main Trading Partners

BRAZIL (million cruzeiros to 1952, million US dollars subsequently)

	Argentina		Germany		Japan		UK		USA	
	Imports	Exports	Imports	Exports	Imports	Exports	Imports	Exports	Imports	Exports
1945	1,863	1,457	—	—	...	...	341	1,484	4,749	6,020
1946	1,020	1,363	—	—	...	...	1,035	1,596	7,583	7,693
1947	1,461	2,004	- -	10	...	...	1,548	1,652	13,975	8,214
1948	1,496	2,055	20	230	0.5	16	2,116	2,048	10,876	9,388
1949	2,174	1,550	111	314	...	...	2,665	1,713	8,770	10,121
1950	2,031	1,402	353	336	24	199	2,506	2,078	7,005	13,587
1951	2,313	2,163	2,073	1,557	394	302	3,158	3,196	15,563	15,936
1952	702	2,055	3,449	1,469	296	349	3,179	709	15,483	13,439
					(million US dollars)					
1953	185	77	108	147	11	41	49	71	366	745
1954	105	100	157	188	79	68	17	74	537	579
1955	152	100	88	104	45	56	18	60	308	602
1956	77	65	80₂	94₂	50	37	43	53	354	735
1957	90	103	127	83	23	37	51	66	547	660
1958	88	107	141	79	33	25	44	54	483	534
1959	105	43	141	86	27	31	37	73	461	592
1960	95	56	136	90	38	31	51	65	443	564
1961	30	67	141	114	79	43	47	62	514	563
1962	86	48	152	110	60	29	46	54	457	485
1963	88	46	134	112	62	32	53	55	457	531
1964	116	91	103	134	34	28	37	63	436	474
1965	132	141	96	142	37	30	30	62	325	520
1966	117	113	135	134	44	41	44	74	590	581
1967	123	98	168	135	50	56	56	61	572	548
1968	153	119	236	148	73	59	95	73	684	627
1969	156	171	286	220	106	105	90	99	682	610
1970	171	185	359	236	178	145	158	130	918	676
1971	132	201	474	256	260	158	213	127	1,064	760
1972	218	154	652	337	366	180	215	180	1,339	931
1973	344	198	884	555	549	425	268	312	2,004	1,122
1974	382	302	1,762	570	1,250	557	354	374	3,434	1,737
1975	252	383	1,460	702	1,256	672	359	340	3,380	1,337
1976	473	331	1,190	919	970	639	347	387	3,103	1,843
1977	504	373	1,127	1,066	936	685	292	421	2,623	2,149
1978	594	349	1,207	1,062	1,336	650	385	513	3,178	2,869
1979	990	718	1,461	1,115	1,179	887	500	708	3,619	2,941
1980	841	1,092	1,735	1,337	1,191	1,232	483	550	4,626	3,496
1981	634	880	1,177	1,317	1,379	1,220	367	735	3,931	4,111
1982	594	650	932	1,179	973	1,304	270	672	3,160	4,140
1983	373	655	754	1,131	617	1,433	253	719	2,615	5,063
1984	539	853	681	1,256	609	1,515	304	708	2,525	7,709
1985	493	548	932	1,309	613	1,398	273	632	2,825	6,951
1986	776	678	1,390	1,099	979	1,514	375	646	3,488	6,306
1987	612	832	1,545	1,229	939	1,676	408	756	3,428	7,325
1988	739	754	1,515	1,459	1,136	2,274	447	1,034	3,229	8,388
1989	1,294	569	1,594	1,540	1,516	2,410	461	1,014	4,030	7,744
1990	1,514	645	1,830	1,774	1,611	2,348	460	945	4,505	7,733
1991	1,747	148	2,030	2,146	1,349	2,557	489	1,057	5,396	6,387
1992	1,808	307	2,019	2,063	1,257	2,324	444	1,294	5,352	7,138
1993	2,816	366	2,422	1,809	1,664	2,313	565	1,140	6,260	8,024

E2 SOUTH AMERICA: External Trade (in Current Values) with Main Trading Partners

CHILE (million gold pesos)[13]

	Argentina		Germany		UK		USA	
	Imports	Exports	Imports	Exports	Imports	Exports	Imports	Exports
1873	1.4	0.1	4.2	0.5	18	19	2.1	1.9
1874	1.4	0.3	3.7	0.7	17	22	2.2	0.6
1875	2.7	0.2	4.2	0.9	16	21	2.1	0.4
1876	3.1	0.5	3.7	1.1	13	21	2.6	1.1
1877	3.1	0.4	3.4	1.3	9.4	15	1.9	0.9
1878	2.6	0.3	2.9	1.5	7.9	17	1.5	0.5
1879	1.6	0.2	2.8	1.6	8.9	33	1.4	0.7
1880	1.5	1.1	4.8	2.1	13	40	1.7	2.5
1881	2.0	0.1	7.4	2.9	18	43	1.7	3.2
1882	2.2	0.3	9.0	3.8	23	53	2.6	2.6
1883	3.6	0.3	10	4.8	22	59	3.6	1.7
1884	3.4	– –	10	3.9	21	42	4.2	1.3
1885	3.2	– –	7.1	3.2	16	40	2.7	1.6
1886	4.1	– –	8.3	3.2	17	38	2.6	2.7
1887	2.2	– –	12	5.1	20	45	3.2	2.6
1888	4.3	– –	14	4.8	26	57	3.1	2.1
1889	5.2	– –	15	5.4	28	48	3.8	3.8
1890	4.4	– –	16	6.4	29	46	5.2	8.5
1891	5.2	– –	12	7.6	28	43	4.1	6.6
1892	5.8	0.2	21	7.1	34	47	4.6	3.1
1893	5.4	0.2	17	6.2	31	55	4.5	2.9
1894	4.2	0.1	12	9.7	25	53	3.8	1.7
1895	5.1	0.1	17	8.0	32	54	4.6	2.2
1896	4.1	0.2	20	10	30	54	6.8	2.2
1897	3.3	0.3	16	11	29	42	4.5	3.3
1898	3.7	0.4	26	25	38	111	9.4	7.6
1899	2.2	0.3	30	21	44	111	8.2	7.4
1900	2.5	0.4	34	20	42	123	12	6.4
1901	3.4	0.2	34	58	50	39	17	15
1902	3.2	0.4	36	55	52	63	14	27
1903	4.3	0.4	39	43	54	62	12	33
1904	6.0	0.9	42	63	57	71	14	31
1905	6.3	1.6	48	73	71	101	19	43
1906	7.6	2.2	58	54	88	132	25	48
1907	10	3.6	74	56	114	141	31	25
1908	11	3.4	76	68	84	151	24	44
1909	18	2.2	62	66	87	129	26	54
1910	15	2.9	72	63	94	131	37	68
1911	21	3.3	90	72	112	146	43	54
1912	11	3.1[13]	91	77[13]	106	151[13]	46	67
		4.5		78		152		
1913	8.9	4.3	81	84	99	153	55	83
1914	5.9	6.3	71	50	61	110	55	86

E2 SOUTH AMERICA: External Trade (in Current Values) with Main Trading Partners

CHILE (million gold pesos)[13]

	Argentina		Germany		UK		USA	
	Imports	Exports	Imports	Exports	Imports	Exports	Imports	Exports
1915	6.7	11	9.8	—	36	112	51	138
1916	6.9	14	1.2	—	55	133	94	252
1917	21	23	0.2	—	65	152	174	425
1918	31	26	- -	—	81	182	203	489
1919	11	14	0.7	0.1	78	71	192	131
1920	17	14	21	7.3	116	164	140	344
1921	7.5	6.8	33	15	103	68	105	74
1922	8.5	7.1	33	22	57	39	64	120
1923	14	7.9	44	25	79	155	88	247
1924	7.3	9.4	51	37	76	189	85	251
1925	12	9.5	45	41	85	215	113	244
1926	23	6.8	52	33	74	143	141	266
1927	17	11	45	61	66	201	106	175
1928	17	12	56	61	71	225	123	222
1929	25	13	83	66	95	102	174	194
1930	19	10	79	35	71	65	156	113
1931	3.6	4.5	39	25	38	45	81	92
1932	2.5	2.7	11	13	9.2	30	17	26
1933	6.4	3.6	6.9	7.4	7.4	28	14	23
1934	2.0	2.8	8.2	8.2	19	38	23	35
1935	3.1	2.1	20	11	19	28	28	40
1936	3.2	3.4	33	18	15	31	29	40
1937	6.1	3.7	37	30	16	62	42	71
1938	7.2	3.3	43	23	18	50	46	36
1939	6.0	4.3	31	29	11	28	43	68
1940	11	6.3	5.7	- -	18	13	81	135
1941	13	11	1.3	1.9	16	11	99	167
1942	25	17	0.4	—	11	7.0	94	201
1943	36	13	- -	—	15	6.7	79	198
1944	41	26	—	—	15	3.7	103	207
1945	52	31	—	—	12	6.0	106	189
1946	46	28	- -	0.1	18	46	128	136
1947	46	35	0.2	1.8	23	48	190	201
1948	42	22	2.5	1.7	29	42	185	282
1949	22	18	1.4	10	39	40	267	241
1950	22	27	8.3	15	46	24	191	248
1951	42	41	27	26	38	36	293	318
1952	50	63	35	39	52	41	309	426
1953	50	72	36	36	34	23	286	427
1954	86	59	42	46	28	89	226	303

E2 SOUTH AMERICA: External Trade (in Current Values) with Main Trading Partners

CHILE (million gold pesos to 1969, million US dollars subsequently)[13]

	Argentina		Germany		Japan		UK		USA	
	Imports	Exports	Imports	Exports	Imports	Exports	Imports	Exports	Imports	Exports
1955	64	72	68	78	11	2.9	33	129	262	326
1956	40	49	65[12]	99[12]	49	15	28	150	261	394
1957	26	30	88	96	31	30	40	111	370	307
1958	30	38	77	104	57	7.7	45	88	345	254
1959	43	39	69	129	23	35	44	121	354	313
1960	64	29	94	123	56	44	57	140	387	295
1961	89	37	133	101	101	127	66	124	385	301
1962	69	24	104	98	71	165	53	120	315	314
1963	85	23	125	99	60	192	73	120	362	299
1964	99	33	109	124	58	271	67	128	354	349
1965	83	43	103	147	45	359	62	125	384	345
1966	104	45	161	136	83	427	67	214	482	355
1967	125	64	148	115	43	510	79	201	417	273
1968	129	78	136	122	63	597	69	230	462	341
1969	150	107	151	162	87	694	78	250	566	302

(million US dollars)

	Argentina		Germany		Japan		UK		USA	
1970	93	78	115	135	28	150	58	154	344	177
1971	111	60	103	123	44	183	64	110	268	77
1972	144	51	88	177	33	148	54	94	165	82
1973	166	75	113	175	35	221	64	126	184	107
1974	323	169	151	337	49	407	70	217	416	286
1975	324	166	127	239	78	187	90	137	587	146
1976	222	133	109	300	59	231	49	137	523	223
1977	206	164	149	258	195	258	59	112	455	269
1978	188	165	211	312	242	319	70	144	682	339
1979	161	287	270	799	319	518	123	244	954	414
1980	234	277	288	419	417	508	117	266	1,302	458
1981	181	186	344	309	734	409	156	154	1,530	541
1982	144	150	174	388	196	429	96	202	792	692
1983	200	118	173	444	157	325	74	225	689	944
1984	161	117	216	360	313	407	80	197	748	873
1985	106	84	209	364	189	389	84	247	655	797
1986	123	161	250	443	296	426	89	217	641	835
1987	159	175	335	483	387	561	152	318	773	1,141
1988	279	168	365	778	392	877	150	397	1,002	1,242
1989	399	110	483	897	737	1,110	152	436	1,348	1,364
1990	503	113	522	902	568	1,369	159	494	1,372	1,341
1991	554	256	499	638	646	1,663	148	367	1,582	1,267
1992	634	456	631	571	965	1,708	188	531	1,984	1,458
1993	580	588	620	438	883	1,543	215	481	2,477	1,433

E2 SOUTH AMERICA: External Trade (in Current Values) with Main Trading Partners

COLOMBIA (thousand gold pesos to 1909, millions subsequently)[14]

	Germany		UK		USA			Germany		UK		USA	
	Imports	Exports	Imports	Exports	Imports	Exports		Imports	Exports	Imports	Exports	Imports	Exports
1839	—	...	2,181	...	197	...	1910	...	...	...	...	...	7.8
							1911	3.2	1.9	5.8	4.6	5.4	12
1840	—	...	2,244	...	228	...	1912	4.2	1.9	7.8	4.4	7.6	16
1841	—	...	63	...	2	...	1913	4.0	3.2	5.8	5.6	7.6	19
1842	—	...	1,669	...	131	...	1914	2.6	1.8	6.3	5.9	6.5	22
1843	...	...	...	...	...	...							
1844	...	...	2,461	...	186	...	1915	—	—	5.4	3.7	8.7	27
							1916	—	−9	8.0	0.7	16	30
1855	68	382	1,402	1,493	344	712	1917	—	−9	7.0	0.7	15	31
1856	100	338	1,480	2,930	684	754	1918	—	—	5.8	0.3	12	31
1857	34	1,341	1,749	3,467	302	494	1919	- -	0.2	7.0	2.7	29	57
1858	55	1,641	792	1,275	263	391							
1859	321	1,293	1,069	562	406	452	1920	...	...	...	...	...	...
							1921	...	...	...	...	...	...
1867	...	...	3,220	958	...	...	1922	2.6	0.4	9.5	4.0	21	41
1868	...	...	...	...	...	...	1923	5.2	0.4	15	2.7	28	51
1869	378	...	3,975	...	414	...	1924	5.1	0.9	11	3.2	27	69
1870	—	2,680	2,892	1,939	407	645	1925	8.8	1.3	19	3.2	44	70
1871	306	1,543	3,304	3,877	484	1,116	1926	14	1.4	18	4.3	53	96
1872	...	1,875	...	2,752	...	1,263	1927	18	2.8	19	5.6	57	91
1873	772	2,526	5,778	5,483	557	1,179	1928	23	2.9	19	8.4	66	104
1874	676	2,636	4,976	3,844	807	1,557	1929	18	2.7	18	6.0	58	95
1875	603	3,133	2,965	3,352	767	1,470	1930	8.1	3.7	7.8	3.3	29	83
1880	...	...	3,857	4,012	...	...	1931	5.1	2.7	6.6	2.1	17	65
1881	...	...	4,732	6,849	...	...	1932	4.7	2.9	6.1	0.8	13	51
1882	...	...	4,352	7,449	...	...	1933	8.8	3.4	11	2.1	18	49
1883	...	...	5,057	6,871	...	...	1934	13	6.9	15	2.9	38	81
1884	...	...	3,803	4,710	...	...	1935	20[14]	15[14]	18[14]	2.0[14]	44[14]	75[14]
							1936	27	23	23	2.4	50	74
1885	...	...	...	...	...	...	1937	23	19	32	0.7	82	86
1886	553	894	2,906	3,151	829	3,490	1938	28	21	18	0.7	79	76
1887	844	1,311	3,612	3,455	937	3,021	1939	23	13	17	2.5	99	78
1888	1,169	1,532	4,617	4,202	1,004	6,878							
1889	1,508	1,396	4,796	4,634	1,928	5,290	1940	1.1	0.1	11	3.2	106	76
							1941	1.0	—	8.6	0.8	125	92
1890	1,636	2,475	4,990	4,835	1,218	4,636	1942	- -	—	6.9	0.5	60	155
1891	1,685	1,309	5,413	4,532	1,644	4,123	1943	- -	—	8.2	0.6	89	185
1892	1,315	1,451	4,290	5,967	1,816	4,855	1944	- -	—	3.8	- -	113	179
1898	1,539	2,000	2,874	4,041	1,788	4,705	1945	- -	—	8.2	1.8	185	193
							1946	- -	- -	18	1.4	274	288
1903	5,741	3,626	5,878	...	...	7,211	1947	0.2	- -	25	3.0	455	377
1904	...	...	5,677	...	...	...	1948	0.8	0.7	33	2.6	405	420
							1949	4.6	12	28	0.7	366	503
1905	...	...	...	...	...	...							
1906	...	716	...	124	...	4,708	1950	33	32	33	1.0	498	635
1907	...	631	...	821	...	4,809	1951	78	62	46	3.9	644	880
1908	...	1,456	...	2,553	...	8,621	1952	54	54	52	5.6	697	952
1909	...	1,549	...	3,051	...	8,588	1953	86	73	61	1.1	845	1,193

E2 SOUTH AMERICA: External Trade (in Current Values) with Main Trading Partners

COLOMBIA (million US dollars)[14]

	Germany		Japan		UK		USA	
	Imports	Exports	Imports	Exports	Imports	Exports	Imports	Exports
1954	54	36	8.3	0.5	30	1.3	421	518
1955	64	44	7.9	0.8	29	4.6	421	432
1956	77₂	35₂	8.5	1.0	22	3.5	406	383
1957	45	37	5.4	0.5	22	7.6	289	359
1958	46	44	3.7	1.2	17	7.8	238	319
1959	41	45	9.8	1.8	19	25	249	324
1960	53	55	13	4.5	30	20	296	298
1961	59	58	19	3.3	33	22	293	262
1962	54	57	17	2.9	32	16	273	267
1963	52	55	19	4.1	28	7.9	257	234
1964	58	66	26	3.2	35	10	274	283
1965	52	63	16	3.6	23	21	212	252
1966	73	69	28	6.4	37	21	312	222
1967	49	68	22	5.8	35	20	224	222
1968	58	74	26	8.9	34	21	321	234
1969	64	82	44	13	31	14	300	238
1970	72	104	59	21	36	15	390	268
1971	97	104	69	18	43	9.7	386	260
1972	85	121	72	34	49	19	330	295
1973	101	147	90	49	44	20	420	445
1974	145	170	140	21	73	22	632	531
1975	138	218	138	27	57	41	614	468
1976	177	283	160	62	63	34	679	542
1977	160	490	212	83	74	45	713	699
1978	199	648	280	71	95	44	999	904
1979	201	584	295	92	105	25	1,279	983
1980	334	741	434	148	112	42	1,840	1,069
1981	328	583	498	126	146	49	1,787	692
1982	316	560	608	127	116	46	1,891	714
1983	241	567	552	137	107	54	1,769	872
1984	245	578	431	154	93	86	1,535	1,097
1985	266	574	429	150	99	106	1,457	1,165
1986	256	1,051	350	249	103	133	1,389	1,530
1987	322	592	465	204	112	100	1,457	1,997
1988	341	525	540	262	122	88	1,813	1,974
1989	347	496	470	250	140	101	1,805	2,478
1990	477	571	496	259	143	193	1,979	3,005
1991	271	547	505	232	146	190	1,737	2,824
1992	417	592	584	197	131	186	2,394	2,722
1993	578	563	1,096	238	175	146	3,278	3,015

E2 SOUTH AMERICA: External Trade (in Current Values) with Main Trading Partners

ECUADOR (million sucres to 1948, million US dollars subsequently

	Germany		UK		USA	
	Imports	Exports	Imports	Exports	Imports	Exports
1900	2.6	...	4.0	...	3.4	...
1901	2.7	...	3.6	...	4.0	...
1902	2.1	...	5.8	...	3.0	...
1903	2.0	...	3.2	...	2.9	...
1904	3.0	...	4.0	...	4.9	...
1905	3.1	...	4.6	...	4.5	...
1906	3.1	3.6	5.6	1.3	4.7	6.8
1907	3.6	3.0	7.2	2.3	5.0	6.0
1908	4.3	2.0	7.2	3.5	4.1	7.7
1909	3.3	3.2	6.3	2.5	4.8	6.8
1910	3.2	4.6	5.1	2.3	4.6	8.4
1911	...	...	...	...	...	...
1912	4.3	3.1	6.3	4.2	5.5	8.1
1913	3.2	5.4	5.4	3.3	5.8	7.9
1914	...	1.5	...	2.3	...	7.0
1915	0.1	...	6.9	...	6.6	...
1916	- -	—	4.9	7.3	11	18
1917	—	—	5.0	0.2	12	26
1918	—	—	3.9	2.0	9.5	21
1919	- -	—	3.3	7.3	17	21
1920	1.1	1.8	10	8.7	25	28
1921	1.9	10	6.9	1.1	8.9	11
1922	2.5	5.7	9.5	3.0	15	18
1923	5.4	2.6	9.0	2.9	15	17
1924	6.2	7.9	13	5.0	21	19
1925	5.7	7.7	12	4.1	25	30
1926	5.1	4.1	11	3.4	20	25
1927	6.7	8.1	9.8	12	28	32
1928	10	8.1	13	2.5	37	37
1929	11	5.1	16	2.3	35	39
1930	8.3	5.8	12	2.5	26	38
1931	5.9	3.0	8.0	2.0	17	26
1932	3.2	2.5	4.3	3.1	20[15]	22
1933	4.5	1.9	5.3	1.0	10	22
1934	7.1	7.0	8.0	4.4	21	49
1935	14	11	12	8.5	28	53
1936	25	21	11	4.9	34	67
1937	32	36	13	4.4	52	54
1938	36	30	11	7.9	51	63
1939	27	11	8.1	6.2	72	83
1940	3.4	0.1	13	3.5	103	100
1941	1.2	—	10	1.2	110	146
1942	0.1	—	8.1	5.5	139	169
1943	—	—			104	139
1944	—	—	16	3.0	182	186
1945	—	—	12	0.7	190	175
1946	...	...	20	1.8	272	150
1947	...	...	41	6.8	430	217
1948	- -	1.2	36	1.5	413	????

	Germany		Japan		UK		USA	
	Imports	Exports	Imports	Exports	Imports	Exports	Imports	Exports
	(million US dollars)							
1949	0.3	0.1			2.3	0.1	31	16
1950	2.1	2.5			2.5	0.5	28	36
1951	4.1	2.7	0.6	0.1	3.3	0.4	36	31
1952	3.4	2.5	0.7	5.2	3.4	0.5	37	41
1953	5.8	4.8	1.0	5.3	3.6	0.3	42	45
1954	9.1	7.3	1.1	0.1	5.1	0.7	46	64
1955	10	7.8	1.2	0.1	5.6	0.5	47	54
1956	9.4[12]	11[12]	0.8	0.1	4.8	2.2	42	56
1957	11	11	0.9	0.2	5.0	1.2	48	56
1958	11	11	1.0	1.8	4.3	0.9	43	54
1959	11	11	1.2	1.4	5.4	0.5	47	57
1960	13	11	2.6	1.8	5.8	0.8	49	65
1961	12	13	2.9	0.9	6.0	0.3	48	58
1962	10	14	2.9	3.3	6.0	0.4	43	74
1963	12	14	4.6	14	6.2	0.4	52	73
1964	17	21	6.2	9.0	7.8	1.8	69	66
1965	20	19	10	2.6	8.6	0.4	69	79
1966	27	21	12	4.9	12	0.5	66	75
1967	31	21	9.0	19	9.0	0.6	79	81
1968	31	19	17	24	13	0.5	86	73
1969	29	19	21	19	11	0.4	95	60
1970	...	18	24	34	...	0.3	108	81
1971	40	27	45	45	15	0.5	135	101
1972	35	28	39	50	19	0.6	121	113
1973	47	25	55	22	22	1.1	134	181
1974	73	48	89	18	30	1.3	243	460
1975	91	31	149	10	37	1.9	379	420
1976	84	37	160	14	36	1.4	378	476
1977	94	56	219	20	45	2.1	451	626
1978	137	61	242	23	53	2.9	576	673
1979	139	62	181	27	48	4.2	621	712
1980	164	30	307	304	59	5.5	862	806
1981	106	21	232	288	38	4.5	689	768
1982	150	24	239	17	42	2.4	656	988
1983	122	9.5	140	28	37	3.2	545	1,295
1984	127	31	242	17	32	8.1	528	1,655
1985	141	54	189	59	36	6.1	619	1,658
1986	177	78	250	57	41	5.4	547	1,332
1987	172	68	282	47	49	6.6	548	1,056
1988	107	91	238	54	35	9.0	568	1,006
1989	125	79	153	59	46	11.0	671	1,425
1990	142	78	171	51	31	11.9	587	1,438
1991	143	137	233	63	40	11.4	742	1,402
1992	134	108	327	62	26	15.2	814	1,415
1993	131	71	345	51	38	15.4	810	1,374

E2   SOUTH AMERICA: External Trade (in Current Values) with Main Trading Partners

GUYANA (thousand pounds)[16]

	Canada[17]		UK		USA			Canada[17]		UK		USA	
	Imports	Exports	Imports	Exports	Imports	Exports		Imports	Exports	Imports	Exports	Imports	Exports
1850	...	...	501	757	150	2	1900	78	38	673	949	396	909
1851	...	...	486	814	145	2	1901	84	80	703	752	405	808
1852	...	...	626	918	177	3	1902	83	123	729	766	453	784
1853	...	...	457	959	200	7	1903	107	607	869	674	476	410
1854	...	...	511	1,302	214	8	1904	101	538	787	761	443	547
1855		...	465	1,249	195	19	1905	117	651	860	862	471	327
1856	...	...	...	...	...	...	1906	114	475	922	802	479	414
1857	...		...	...	...	...	1907	136	865	925	615	508	38
1858	...	...	...		...	...	1908	126[17]	765[17]	977	907	524	225
1859	...	...	638	1,139	254	54	1909	138	657	831	893	481	197
1860	...	...	620	1,348	226	91	1910	144	576	834	728	427	257
1861	...	...	732	1,434	258	44	1911	116	875[16]	834[16]	713[16]	441[16]	362[16]
1862	...	...	569	1,196	272	55	1912	144	724	898	726	424	141
1863	...	...	562	1,421	246	95	1913	112	797[16]	907	1,015[16]	377	80[16]
1864	...	...	888	1,589	317	113			796		955		75
							1914	197	668	832	1,480	379	54
1865	...	...	741	1,729	286	228	1915	277	1,141	883	1,328	459	79
1866	...	...	823	1,743	344	283	1916	320	1,406	952	1,089	650	329
1867	...	...	750	1,824	361	362	1917	440	1,568	950	1,682	1,231	134
1868	...	...	817	1,334	391	693	1918	544	1,166	873	1,365	1,511	106
1869	...	...	760	1,138	399	779	1919	720	1,635	1,103	1,287	1,235	114
1870	...	...	998	1,388	371	741	1920	828	2,331	1,950	1,817	1,570	644
1871	...	...	1,025	1,266	429	1,204	1921	610	1,011	1,528	1,953	814	67
1872	...	...	1,031	1,289	400	896	1922	495	1,048[16]	1,022	1,192[16]	463	116[16]
1873	...	...	935	1,535	350	375			1,048		1,162		109
1874	...	...	952	1,940	389	543	1923	555	1,241	1,385	1,666	417	154
1875	...	...	927	1,745	365	290	1924	556	1,403	1,482	1,241	394	174
1876	...	...	1,068	2,332	386	453	1925	599	844	1,539	1,312	446	186
1877	...	...	1,080	1,955	495	734	1926	617	901	1,231	952	396	197
1878	...	...	1,092	1,870	521	199	1927	538	1,210	1,264	1,051	346	196
1879	...	...	1,072	2,169	419	225	1928	549	1,130	1,360	924	299	187
							1929	416	928	1,258	798	274	180
1880	94	64	1,005	1,685	407	601							
1881	89	74	834	1,771	398	514	1930	311	850	1,130	622	225	138
1882	108	79	1,214	1,962	388	913	1931	229	747	935	573	177	177
1883	177	97	1,266	1,590	422	1,213	1932	207	576	1,078	979	117	131
1884	112	37	1,100	1,777	323	282	1933	225	378	1,115	1,079	114	64
							1934	229	479	983	877	129	70
1885	91	20	725	1,294	345	308							
1886	101	33	787	1,071	296	563	1935	271	940	1,010	727	167	117
1887	95	42	916	1,148	317	814	1936	274	967	1,088	817	172	142
1888	85	30	918	1,003	322	774	1937	345	1,225	1,285	814	235	163
1889	35	42	1,051	1,317	401	883	1938	327	1,430	1,115	715	252	96
							1939	406	1,540	1,009	922	322	89
1890	62	42	1,129	959	379	951							
1891	72[16]	45[16]	927[16]	1,221[16]	375[16]	1,109[16]	1940	682	1,682	1,112	883	557	88
1892	91	64	949	1,271	437	981	1941	1,381	1,834	826	1,525	776	234
1893	90	99	1,047	1,234	481	898	1942	1,350	1,469	642	1,375	1,208	322
1894	97	26	882	1,274	436	597	1943	1,909	1,877	840	598	1,385	518
							1944	1,736	1,531	716	1,382	1,221	128
1895	69	42	790	968	382	658							
1896	87	20	784	964	300	779	1945	1,822	1,507	858	1,539	1,056	160
1897	63	17	741	949	342	705	1946	1,992	2,333	1,735	2,086	978	254
1898	58	7	762	818	381	849	1947	2,812	2,664	2,266	3,224	2,174	354
1899	66	18	747	964	376	838	1948	3,582	2,976	7,234	7,179	2,022	260
							1949	4,971	3,433	8,047	9,009	1,523	663

E2 SOUTH AMERICA: External Trade (in Current Values) with Main Trading Partners

GUYANA (million local dollars)[16]

	Canada		UK		USA			Canada		UK		USA	
	Imports	Exports	Imports	Exports	Imports	Exports		Imports	Exports	Imports	Exports	Imports	Exports
1950[18]	8.8	5.0	14	16	2.4	0.7	1970	24	48	84	50	64	72
1951	9.4	29	29	19	8.9	3.2	1971	15	30	83	72	65	76
1952	13[16]	37[16]	34[16]	28[16]	13[16]	5.1[16]	1972	15	20	89	87	72	74
1953	10	30	35	32	8.3	6.3	1973	20	14	95	85	91	60
1954	8.2	33	38	31	11	6.5	1974	28	31	116	122	146	164
1955	5.9	32	45	32	12	8.0	1975	35	26	174	240	239	187
1956	8.6	38	45	30	13	10	1976	39	17	213	180	264	134
1957	.10	40	52	43	21	7.9	1977	47	35	150	207	216	119
1958	8.6	31	54	47	19	5.9	1978	29	54	135	195	162	149
1959	9.0	28	50	43	15	9.0	1979	27	69	150	210	207	136
1960	16	32	58	47	29	21	1980	31	72	187	249	208	238
1961	10	38	56	36	29	31	1981	48	46	197	252	296	202
1962	9.4	44	45	38	29	35	1982						
1963	9.7	59	40	41	25	25	1983						
1964	14	49	50	33	34	26	1984						
1965	14	38	55	41	43	31	1985						
1966	18	40	66	41	46	41	1986						
1967	25	36	58	48	62	46	1987						
1968	20	43	64	46	52	56	1988						
1969	20	43	64	57	50	60							

PARAGUAY (thousand gold pesos)

	Argentina		USA			Argentina		USA	
	Imports	Exports[19]	Imports	Exports[21]		Imports	Exports[19]	Imports	Exports
1908	767	2,000	223	—	1925	6,115	[12,285][20]	2,601	[91][20]
1909	589	2,547	210	—	1926	4,099	11,957	1,938	1,152
					1927	4,009	12,080	2,224	99
1910	697	2,858	319	—	1928	5,515	14,010	2,291	60
1911	775	2,722	390	—	1929	4,852	11,454[19]	2,593	6
1912	703	2,446	316	—			7,397		
1913	1,090	3,516	488	—	1930	4,360	7,369	2,410	26
1914	930	2,294	429	13	1931	2,957	6,399	1,628	62
					1932	2,487	6,633	823	68
1915	1,026	5,578	282	480	1933	4,391	4,161	377	159
1916	2,403	6,509	873	426	1934	6,696	4,757	396	138
1917	3,347	8,957	1,562	370					
1918	2,479	4,102	816	752	1935	5,868	3,624	889	72
1919	6,760	11,059	2,704	1,008	1936	4,082	3,174	558	94
					1937	4,926	2,313	943	942
1920	5,022	8,685	3,130	1,325	1938	4,962	2,567	1,243	1,475
1921	3,216	6,540	1,444	1,095	1939	4,745	2,933	1,262	2,666
1922	1,842	7,338	1,221	1,613					
1923	[2,268][20]	[6,032][20]	[1,036][20]	[992][20]	1940	6,716	2,623	3,177	2,384
1924	[3,471][20]	[6,142][20]	[1,306][20]	[945][20]	1941	6,150	2,042	2,385	2,879
					1942	7,691	2,249	3,342	2,430
					1943	17,601	5,242	6,445	2,627
					1944	17,831	10,614	6,041	6,985

E2 SOUTH AMERICA: External Trade (in Current Values) with Main Trading Partners

PARAGUAY (million US dollars)

	Argentina		Brazil		USA			Argentina		Brazil		USA	
	Imports	Exports	Imports	Exports	Imports	Exports[21]		Imports	Exports	Imports	Exports	Imports	Exports
1945	9.1	6.1	...	...	2.4	2.8	1970	12	19	2.0	0.9	15	8.9
1946	9.9	7.1	...	...	4.5	1.1	1971	10	18	5.1	0.8	18	11
1947	7.8	8.8	...	...	6.5	0.5	1972	11	16	10	0.7	14	15
1948	8.2	9.2	...	...	6.6	0.3	1973	30	16	...	...	20	17
1949	6.3	12	...	...	8.5	0.4	1974	53	39	27	6.1	18	20
1950	7.5	12	...	...	5.0	1.0	1975	36	50	37	5.7	25	14
1951	6.7	12	...	...	4.9	4.7[21]	1976	41	18	34	10	22	22
1952	3.3	4.6	...	...	10	10	1977	48	36	59	16	37	40
1953	...	...	...	...	...	...	1978	54	24	68	20	41	23
1954	9.2	15	...	...	6.5	6.3	1979	82	51	106	29	58	18
1955	13	16	...	...	4.0	6.4	1980	121	74	154	40	59	17
1956	7.1	13	...	...	3.3	6.6	1981	114	69	142	54	58	17
1957	11	11	...	- -	6.5	8.3	1982	131	59	166	83	61	9.1
1958	7.2	13	0.7	- -	8.9	8.3	1983	103	32	147	52	40	23
1959	7.4	6.4	0.1	- -	5.3	10	1984	98	41	182	53	50	18
1960	7.5	7.7	0.3	0.1	7.6	7.2	1985	86	16	174	60	40	3.8
1961	8.3	8.7	0.2	0.1	5.3	7.4	1986	83	35	174	92	78	9.4
1962	5.0	9.6	0.2	0.1	11	7.0	1987	53	54	186	62	62	15
1963	7.6	8.6	0.5	0.4	9.6	9.1	1988	69	34	166	117	58	19
1964	9.4	12	0.3	0.1	7.2	12	1989	81	49	193	328	107	42
1965	9.8	15	1.5	0.1	10	14	1990	17	55	222	312	170	41
1966	10	16	1.6	0.2	10	12	1991	18	45	251	203	219	35
1967	13	14	1.6	0.2	12	11	1992	23	64	283	171	199	53
1968	13	13	2.4	0.2	17	12	1993	24	65	370	215	238	57
1969	13	19	1.6	0.3	16	9.0							

PERU (million soles)

	Germany		Japan		UK		USA	
	Imports	Exports	Imports	Exports	Imports	Exports	Imports	Exports
1890	...	...	...	...	...	...	...	...
1891	4.1	1.6	...	...	8.9	8.2	1.9	0.4
1892	3.3	1.5	...	...	7.4	13	1.4	1.3
1893	2.0	1.0	...	...	4.4	9.4	0.8	0.9
1894	1.8	0.8	...	...	4.1	6.7	0.8	1.0
1895	...	...	...	...	...	...	...	...
1896	...	...	...	...	...	...	...	...
1897	2.7	2.1	...	...	6.1	14	1.5	1.3
1898	3.4	2.7	...	...	8.6	17	2.1	2.9
1899	3.5	3.4	...	...	7.6	15	2.2	5.2
1900	3.6	5.2	...	...	11	21	3.0	9.6
1901	4.6	4.2	...	...	10	23	4.5	5.8
1902	6.2	3.0	...	...	11	16	5.9	7.1
1903	4.5	3.3	...	...	15	15	5.8	4.9
1904	7.0	3.4	...	...	16	20	7.6	3.8

E2 SOUTH AMERICA: External Trade (in Current Values) with Main Trading Partners

PERU (million soles)

	Germany		Japan		UK		USA	
	Imports	**Exports**	**Imports**	**Exports**	**Imports**	**Exports**	**Imports**	**Exports**
1905	6.8	4.0	...	...	15	30	7.3	5.3
1906	7.8	5.2	...	...	15	24	10	6.4
1907	8.9	3.7	...	...	16	24	12	14
1908	8.6	4.0	...	...	15	23	14	13
1909	6.9	3.5	...	...	16	27	8.5	15
1910	7.9	3.6	...	...	18	25	9.2	20
1911	9.5	5.7	...	...	17	25	12	21
1912	9.3	6.6	- -	—	14	32	12	36
1913	11	6.1	- -	- -	16	34	18	30
1914	6.5	3.3	0.1	- -	13	33	16	30
1915	1.0	—	0.2	0.1	6.7	36	15	64
1916	0.1	—	0.9	0.1	15	30	51	104
1917	0.4	—	1.3	0.2	19	38	88	109
1918	0.4	—	2.7	0.7	16	63	53	93
1919	—	0.5	3.2	0.9	16	84	76	125
1920	3.1	0.2	3.4	1.0	27	127	102	163
1921	7.4	0.9	2.8	1.2	23	58	82	65
1922	11	3.9	1.9	0.4	20	66	42	66
1923	15	7.3	1.6	0.2	29	80	57	95
1924	19	5.7	2.0	0.6	34	95	70	84
1925	20	3.7	1.9	0.6	34	74	71	76
1926	19	3.9	2.4	0.2	31	68	91	84
1927	20	16	2.0	0.2	31	88	81	86
1928	18	25	2.1	1.5	28	75	72	90
1929	19	20	2.4	0.1	28	61	79	112
1930	17	18	2.4	—	23	45	52	95
1931	9.6	17	1.7	- -	14	42	41	72
1932	8.2	13	1.3	- -	13	64	22	31
1933	11	19	5.3	1.0	19	93	29	40
1934	15	34	10	5.1	30	103	46	43
1935	27	35	9.4	8.9	25	66	60	64
1936	39	41	7.9	14	27	76	64	65
1937	46	47	8.1	3.9	24	83	83	81
1938	53	36	8.7	2.0	26	68	89	92
1939	38	23	8.0	9.1	22	75	105	116
1940	4.5	0.2	19	32	29	49	169	174
1941	4.3	—	16	82	18	12	224	214
1942	- -	—	7.6	—	19	28	189	199
1943	- -	—	- -	—	27	43	254	196
1944	- -	—	- -	—	14	19	277	200
1945	—	—	- -	—	18	42	310	299
1946	- -	—	- -	—	52	83	451	250
1947	0.2	0.1	- -	- -	72	86	636	293
1948	0.6	3.5	- -	20	75	171	591	260
1949	21	29	2.1	0.2	250	318	1,697	608

E2 SOUTH AMERICA: External Trade (in Current Values) with Main Trading Partners

PERU (million soles to 1967, million US dollars subsequently)

	Germany		Japan		UK		USA	
	Imports	Exports	Imports	Exports	Imports	Exports	Imports	Exports
1950	77	60	5.8	31	476	496	1,517	757
1951	226	108	21	118	473	912	2,378	889
1952	256	86	32	118	407	304	2,511	1,031
1953	307	163	69	199	424	350	2,697	1,431
1954	393	220	77	307	439	678	2,550	1,706
1955	512[2]	355[2]	100	193	511	524	2,883	1,854
1956	673	304	118	282	620	675	3,441	2,182
1957	748	371	185	457	639	634	3,646	2,193
1958	829	421	145	193	621	620	3,674	2,590
1959	[933][22]	740	[216][22]	438	[585][22]	842	[3,662][22]	2,707
1960	1,169	1,187	338	729	707	919	4,487	4,270
1961	1,467	1,222	517	1,005	885	1,174	5,551	4,779
1962	1,780	1,590	781	935	924	1,407	5,694	5,044
1963	1,893	1,554	944	1,126	1,082	1,325	5,567	5,117
1964	1,921	2,174	867	1,634	1,005	1,343	6,329	5,577
1965	2,287	2,246	1,398	1,644	1,017	1,038	7,783	6,055
1966	2,898	2,262	1,592	2,039	1,005	586	8,586	8,721
1967	2,991	2,560	1,911	3,141	1,095	519	8,981	9,829
				(million US dollars)				
	102	85	65	104	37	17	306	327
1968	64	82	35	115	27	18	190	305
1969	68	105	43	140	26	27	186	301
1970	75	157	49	142	27	26	199	348
1971	91	137	72	111	40	26	220	257
1972	95	106	61	131	34	25	239	313
1973	124	80	113	179	36	31	308	369
1974	159	119	184	204	38	41	478	547
1975	270	86	192	151	109	43	854	318
1976	182	92	123	177	63	74	527	335
1977	118	71	118	200	68	61	463	492
1978	140	84	107	234	39	50	517	677
1979	138	165	112	363	46	130	564	1,220
1980	215	181	268	287	98	115	945	1,060
1981	326	95	232	375	8.3	58	1,477	702
1982	206	75	368	417	68	130	1,082	987
1983	152	63	227	266	46	87	850	857
1984	133	79	167	234	37	98	639	1,093
1985	...	...	180	233	48	120	508	1,009
1986	199	...	215	196	64	30	644	632
1987	259	92	240	219	79	73	675	644
1988	211	138	121	270	62	244	691	599
1989	119	207	87	301	55	125	621	730
1990	173	253	90	420	50	149	744	764
1991	167	189	173	311	52	113	723	589
1992	171	111	268	277	58	132	978	661
1993	174	198	331	299	52	146	1,251	708

E2 SOUTH AMERICA: External Trade (in Current Values) with Main Trading Partners

URUGUAY (million gold pesos)

	Argentina		Brazil		Germany		UK		USA	
	Imports	Exports	Imports	Exports	Imports	Exports	Imports	Exports	Imports	Exports
1874	0.6	0.7	2.0	2.1	0.8	- -	3.9	4.9	1.1	1.3
1875	0.4	0.5	1.7	1.5	0.5	- -	2.5	4.6	0.8	1.0
1876	...	...	...	...	...	...	...	...	...	...
1877	0.4	0.9	1.9	3.7	0.8	0.1	4.2	3.7	1.0	1.1
1878	0.3	0.6	2.0	4.2	0.8	0.1	4.9	4.4	1.0	1.1
1879	0.4	0.5	2.0	3.5	0.9	- -	4.9	3.5	1.1	2.0
1880	0.5	0.9	2.4	3.9	1.1	0.1	5.8	4.3	1.3	2.8
1881	0.5	1.0	2.2	3.5	1.2	0.1	5.4	3.2	1.3	3.9
1882	0.6	1.0	2.2	2.8	1.4	0.3	4.5	5.4	1.4	2.3
1883	0.7	2.1	2.2	3.4	2.0	0.7	5.5	4.8	1.2	2.2
1884	0.6	1.9	2.4	3.9	2.3	0.8	6.8	5.2	1.6	1.8
1885	0.7	1.4	2.2	3.3	2.3	0.4	7.4	4.9	2.0	4.4
1886	0.5	1.2	1.5	4.5	2.1	0.4	5.6	5.0	1.2	2.7
1887	0.4	1.1	1.8	2.6	2.8	0.3	6.7	4.1	1.7	1.5
1888	0.8	2.1	2.6	5.4	3.0	1.2	9.5	5.1	1.6	2.3
1889	1.5	2.3	2.5	3.3	3.4	1.3	10.0	3.6	3.4	1.4
1890	2.6	2.6	2.5	3.3	2.8	1.0	8.8	3.9	2.4	2.0
1891	1.6	2.5	1.7	4.7	1.8	1.5	5.5	5.0	0.9	1.8
1892	1.1	3.0	1.3	4.5	2.1	2.0	5.6	4.5	1.1	2.2
1893	1.2	4.8	1.6	5.5	2.1	1.6	6.4	3.3	1.1	1.4
1894	1.4	6.0	1.9	8.0	2.7	1.5	8.0	4.0	1.7	1.9
1895	2.2	4.1	2.2	6.9	3.0	1.7	7.9	4.9	1.8	3.1
1896	3.5	4.9	1.4	7.2	2.8	2.5	7.3	2.0	1.8	1.7
1897	3.0	4.0	1.6	5.9	1.8	3.1	4.8	1.8	1.5	2.9
1898	3.3	5.3	1.9	5.9	2.3	2.8	6.8	2.9	1.9	1.0
1899	3.9	7.0	1.5	7.0	2.6	4.4	6.9	2.4	2.2	1.6
1900	2.7	2.8	1.3	7.6	3.5	2.8	6.3	2.0	2.2	1.7
1901	3.1	4.3	1.5	4.5	2.9	3.2	6.2	2.4	2.1	1.9
1902	2.8	6.5	1.5	4.6	3.3	3.8	6.1	3.3	2.1	3.2
1903	3.1	6.4	1.5	5.3	3.5	4.8	6.6	3.3	2.1	1.7
1904	3.4	6.5	1.5	4.9	2.6	5.1	5.4	2.5	2.1	2.1
1905	4.6	5.8	1.6	3.2	4.2	3.3	7.9	1.8	3.0	2.0
1906	3.2	6.1	1.8	3.3	5.4	4.3	9.8	1.8	3.4	2.0
1907	2.6	7.3	1.7	2.8	6.1	4.6	12	3.0	3.4	1.6
1908	2.5	8.1	1.8	3.5	6.2	5.5	12	3.0	3.3	2.3
1909	2.7	8.2	2.0	4.0	5.8	6.7	11	2.7	3.7	3.8

E2 SOUTH AMERICA: External Trade (in Current Values) with Main Trading Partners

URUGUAY (million gold pesos)[23]

	Argentina		Brazil		Germany		UK		USA	
	Imports	Exports	Imports	Exports	Imports	Exports	Imports	Exports	Imports	Exports
1910	2.8	5.8	2.0	4.1	6.8	4.0	12	3.4	4.3	2.7
1911	4.0	4.9	2.0	3.2	7.6	6.7	12	3.9	5.5	1.5
1912	4.4	7.1	2.6	3.7	8.1	7.6	13	6.3	6.2	2.6
1913	5.8	10.0[23]	3.4	4.9[23]	7.8	13.0[23]	12	7.7[23]	6.4	2.8[23]
1914	4.7	8.2	2.9	1.9	3.2	5.5	8.9	11	6.6	9.7
1915	7.4	8.9	4.9	1.1	0.7	—	6.9	13	7.3	12
1916	7.3	11	4.1	1.4	0.2	—	7.1	14	8.9	17
1917	8.0[23]	13	5.4[23]	1.3	0.1[23]	—	6.8[23]	23	11.0[23]	30
1918	25	9.9	22	4.3	0.1	—	17	26	23	23
1919	22	6.9	15	2.0	0.1	1.4	20	27	40	43
1920	28	3.6	13	2.5	3.3	5.9	26	18	38	20
1921	12	2.9	14	2.0	5.7	11	16	17	24	19
1922	11	6.0	9.1	2.4	8.3	10	15	25	17	16
1923	...	7.1	...	2.1	...	15	...	28	...	16
1924	8.2	11	7.4	6.0	8.9	18	15	24	20	17
1925	8.2	8.0	5.4	5.2	11	15	16	24	27	7.1
1926	7.2	8.6	3.8	4.4	8.1	14	11	24	21	12
1927	9.1	13	4.4	4.5	8.8	18	12	19	25	11
1928	8.0	17	4.7	4.7	12	15	15	23	28	7.4
1929	8.4	12	6.6	2.8	9.0	13	15	21	28	11
1930	9.0	13	7.1	3.2	8.9	12	16	34	23	11
1931	11	10	8.4	0.7	9.7	11	17	28	17	7.6
1932	9.7	5.2	5.7	0.7	5.3	9.1	10	16	5.3	3.5
1933	10	4.0	7.3	1.2	5.5	9.8	12	22	5.5	2.4
1934	6.1	5.1	4.0	4.6	5.4	11	12	18	9.0	5.6
1935	4.3	6.9	4.7	4.7	5.2	13	10	24	10	7.3
1936	3.1	10	4.6	2.8	6.5	10	12	23	9.0	11
1937	5.8	9.4	5.0	2.7	8.4	13	13	24	11	14
1938	3.4	9.2	5.7	3.5	12	23	15	25	9.0	3.8
1939	4.5	2.2	5.5	6.1	11	12	12	19	3.5	14
1940	10	2.2	6.3	6.1	1.0	2.2	14	23	12	29
1941	8.4	3.1	7.4	5.6	0.3	—	8.5	31	15	58
1942	10	2.7	8.3	2.8	- -	—	5.4	28	12	41
1943	13	3.1	9.5	2.9	- -	—	4.5	51	10	86

E2   SOUTH AMERICA: External Trade (in Current Values) with Main Trading Partners

URUGUAY (million US dollars)

	Argentina		Brazil		Germany		UK		USA	
	Imports	Exports	Imports	Exports	Imports	Exports	Imports	Exports	Imports	Exports
1944	9.3	2.7	17	3.4	—	—	9.4	34	19	47
1945	12	1.9	19	2.9	...	...	12	31	48	58
1946	12	1.9	17	3.1	...	...	20	38	67	48
1947	25	3.2	18	2.0	...	...	27	25	98	47
1948	17	4.1	20	10	0.5	4.1	25	33	67	52
1949	2.2	7.6	20	14	1.2	21	43	42	40	51
1950	3.1	1.3	17	2.4	...12	...12	49	36	39	130
1951	1.4	2.4	20	7.0	25	9.2	40	41	140	103
1952	0.5	0.6	19	25	19	21	29	33	61	51
1953	1.1	—	22	9.3	23	20	25	84	35	51
1954	1.0	- -	34	34	23	16	42	46	45	33
1955	1.2	- -	38	26	18	7.1	25	25	44	16
1956	4.1	0.3	25	24	15	18	15	21	33	25
1957	5.3	0.4	24	8.8	23	8.9	24	21	56	12
1958	2.7	1.3	25	9.0	5.9	8.9	8.0	21	16	11
1959	2.7	0.4	23	1.4	12	9.1	6.8	9.1	32	11
1960	9.8	2.4	15	0.3	18	12	19	31	65	20
1961	12	1.8	17	1.8	26	15	21	42	47	25
1962	8.6	1.6	21	3.0	32	15	24	25	44	24
1963	9.6	0.9	14	9.7	18	12	21	39	27	19
1964	18	4.1	19	1.9	21	17	15	30	31	15
1965	8.8	3.1	13	5.4	18	16	15	31	20	32
1966	12	5.2	22	11	19	15	8.7	26	20	23
1967	11	3.3	21	5.2	17	8.8	14	34	24	12
1968	15	2.9	15	7.4	15	12	7.4	38	36	22
1969	21	4.9	26	11	22	20	12	27	27	14
1970	28	6.4	35	12	26	31	16	20	30	20
1971	32	5.9	36	24	22	35	18	15	23	9.8
1972	27	4.1	36	11	16	28	12	16	19	7.4
1973	62	8.0	48	16	22	44	14	20	25	11
1974	72	31	74	92	31	33	17	16	36	14
1975	47	28	67	65	41	45	26	18	54	26
1976	66	25	90	68	41	67	21	21	49	59
1977	83	32	94	95	51	71	34	27	71	87
1978	86	38	85	127	53	81	31	30	62	120
1979	197	97	181	182	95	128	46	28	111	84
1980	174	142	286	191	111	137	69	37	161	83
1981	129	115	322	169	106	123	48	53	158	95
1982	86	109	141	146	77	92	27	37	135	76
1983	82	90	107	112	55	79	18	41	59	99
1984	87	88	127	115	46	79	16	38	66	126
1985	86	63	126	143	49	66	17	36	54	130
1986	124	90	212	284	66	97	24	58	74	130
1987	157	113	279	206	93	122	35	54	91	177
1988	179	162	307	236	75	120	36	58	93	162
1989	191	177	329	441	77	122	37	64	150	177
1990	219	161	330	506	92	131	42	71	140	161
1991	272	163	373	384	75	137	37	60	153	158
1992	346	250	475	284	90	132	39	66	187	173
1993	432	279	608	366	79	104	37	61	211	147

E2 SOUTH AMERICA: External Trade (in Current Values) with Main Trading Partners

VENEZUELA (million bolivares)[24]

	Canada		France[25]		Germany		Netherlands Antilles[26]		UK[25]		USA	
	Imports	Exports	Imports	Exports	Imports	Exports	Imports	Exports	Imports	Exports	Imports	Exports
1904	...	...	5.8	28	12	4.0	...	...	19	5.9	15	21
1905	...	...	4.3	14	12	3.5	...	...	12	8.1	14	25
1906	...	...	2.7	21	8.9	4.3	...	...	13	6.6	14	25
1907	...	...	0.4	20	10	5.0	...	...	20	7.0	13	30
1908	...	...	0.8	27	9.7	4.5	...	...	19	7.2	15	28
1909	...	...	1.5	25	12	4.5	...	...	15	7.6	14	37
1910	...	...	3.8	29	11	8.3	...	...	15	9.7	18	31
1911	...	...	9.6	27	14	16	...	...	23	11	21	32
1912	...	...	14	39	16	23	...	...	27	11	32	43
1913	...	...	14	36	17	20	...	...	23	8.5	35	51
1914	...	...	5.5	44	12	22	...	...	21	9.6	29	45
1915	...	...	2.3	12	1.5	1.1	...	...	11	8.4	34	63
1916	...	...	5.0	21	...	...	...	...	20	7.8	55	67
1917	...	...	5.4	10	...	...	...	...	25	11	89.69	
1918	...	...	3.9	8.2	...	...	...	...	19	13	53	50
1919	...	...	2.7[24,25]	56[24,25]	...[24]	...[24]	...	...	28[24,25]	15[24,25]	92[24]	110[24]
1920	...	...	21	14	14	0.9	1.3	22	71	14	152	80
1921	...	...	7.2	12	4.1	5.3	1.2	25	17	5.8	55	49
1922	...	...	5.9	18	5.6	6.3	0.3	34	22	3.9	53	43
1923	...	...	8.9	14	14	7.6	1.4	52	36	8.1	72	42
1924	...	...	11	16	15	12	2.5	98	40	7.8	119	33
1925	...	...	15	17	25	20	3.9	144	57	10	163	54
1926	- -	—	26	12	38	21	4.4[26] / 5.0	166[26] / 212	54	6.5	229	98
1927	- -	0.1	25	19	33	32	3.6	233	45	5.8	190	104
1928	0.1	—	23	12	34	23	4.7	360	47	6.4	239	162
1929	0.2	0.6	20	22	42	36	2.6	434	58	9.0	249	216
1930	0.1	13	20	13	42	23	3.0	494	40	14	186	175
1931	0.1	1.7	14	15	25	20	2.7	436	25	14	101	135
1932	0.2	2.4	10	17	19	13	1.6	431	22	5.8	70	131
1933	0.1	6.1	9.1	11	16	9.1	1.2	466	22	11	70	91
1934	0.1	4.9	6.1	11	11	8.8	1.1	498	43	14	72	108
1935	0.1	7.8	13	8.5	19	11	2.2	530	60	19	100	114
1936	0.2	5.9	11	15	32	16	1.6	543	21	29	100	135
1937	0.1	15[24]	8.5	14[24]	41	21[24]	1.7	630[24]	28	47[24]	161	119[24]
1938	0.2	8.0	9.2	11	37	28	2.2	675	22	29	175	118
1939	2.9	14	9.7	17	31	17	1.7	685	20	42	200	151
1940	5.8	14	6.3	9.4	1.1	—	1.1	574	24	19	229	194
1941	4.6	22	0.1	- -	1.8	—	1.3	789	17	9.4	224	227
1942	2.0	28	0.2	- -	- -	—	2.3	437	16	4.9	156	110
1943	2.1	3.4	0.1	- -	- -	—	1.9	18	15	0.7	145	64
1944	4.3	1.0	0.1	- -	- -	—	1.6	12	8.8	0.3	280	46
1945	8.7	12	1.2	1.6	- -	—	1.2	242	15	6.5	442	234
1946	31	24	6.4	23	- -	—	2.2	824	54	36	694	425
1947	35	41	24	54	- -[2]	- -[2]	4.5	1,279	107	41	1,372	548
1948	55	74	28	75	7.3	3.0	15	2,033	181	26	2,195	930
1949	61	69	48	68	28	15	11	1,875	177	62	1,654	960

E2 SOUTH AMERICA: External Trade (in Current Values) with Main Trading Partners

VENEZUELA (million bolivares)

	Canada		France		West Germany		Japan		Netherlands Antilles		UK		USA	
	Imports	Exports	Imports	Exports	Imports	Exports	Imports	Exports	Imports	Exports	Imports	Exports	Imports	Exports
1950	69	99	35	60	53	21	9.8	0.7	8.3	2,012	133	126	1,233	1,164
1951	86	94	57	59	91	30	14	0.7	12	2,224	143	121	1,452	1,375
1952	112	...	62	0.4	79	2.9	25	...	12	22	180	2.2	1,657	205
1953	104	101	64	64	128	42	27	1.6	15	1,880	194	85	1,853	1,802
1954	109	110	98	57	188	33	34	2.4	12	2,209	208	133	1,733	2,096
1955	117	116	109	36	265	47	56	0.6	15	2,362	231	[250][27]	1,742	2,443
1956	115	155	119	62	295	60	55	2.4	10	2,146	271	424	2,033	2,782
1957	135	157	152	154	460	101	89	...	14	1,863	357	654	4,106	3,195
1958	149	162	117	111	404	182	82	...	11	1,817	352	482	2,745	3,268
1959	157	227	114	118	443	128	123	3.0	5.0	1,916	338	556	2,513	3,310
1960	131	259	81	142	316	89	127	2.6	1.9	1,966	215	641	1,847	3,732
1961	148	312	117	137	308	114	133	4.9	1.2	2,049	192	650	1,934	3,151
1962	176	742	116	131	340	188	161	58	3.2	2,073	237	687	2,050	2,998
1963	183	787	94	154	292	179	162	91	9.6	1,989	223	704	1,999	2,946
1964	280	782	140	160	393	210	281	153	17	1,945	261	710	2,634	3,132
1965	360	1,153	181	231	485	201	297	123	31	2,874	333	962	2,885	4,515
1966	278	1,034	165	145	509	190	273	139	26	2,665	286	911	2,644	4,744
1967	313	1,238	214	201	527	205	345	193	38	2,898	306	881	2,879	4,632
1968	306	1,558	179	159	570	180	365	113	67	2,651	436	863	3,359	4,427
1969	292	1,653	217	178	650	227	451	102	11	2,739	356	716	3,374	4,685
1970	293	1,617	227	223	663	250	591	107	13	2,891	382	692	3,607	5,088
1971	388	1,590	380	212	859	206	740	57	9.3	2,597	428	812	3,692	5,530
1972	316	1,674	393	231	1,004	158	853	88	12	2,494	502	530	4,234	5,156
1973	372	2,430	345	242	1,388	196	883	86	12	3,759	387	540	4,470	9,374
1974	613	5,669	481	480	1,442	500	1,526	194	43	9,362	503	1,298	7,619	21,235
1975	834	4,780	708	313	2,071	537	2,012	115	106	8,032	912	1,481	12,091	15,222
1976	726	5,349	633	331	2,497	559	2,240	148	143	9,148	826	868	12,106	16,450
1977	1,210	5,085	889	348	5,060	341	4,499	190	111	8,136	1,182	529	16,203	17,725
1978	1,461	4,262	1,609	359	4,172	265	4,355	149	155	8,727	1,674	540	18,810	15,879
1979	1,710	6,194	1,054	574	2,885	584	3,398	623	302	11,902	1,210	1,451	18,984	22,823
1980	2,126	7,983	1,372	1,404	2,900	920	3,654	2,990	326	18,214	1,289	876	22,049	22,644
1981	2,721	8,311	1,440	2,119	2,710	856	4,123	3,710	166	18,643	1,186	896	24,511	9,934
1982	2,261	...	1,934	...	2,958	...	5,872	...	162	...	1,284	...	26,308	...
1983	1,360	2,208	1,107	875	1,431	2,345	1,490	1,727	523	1,177	584	1,082	12,245	20,327
1984	1,814	4,922	1,698	1,234	2,481	3,752	2,454	2,614	905	18,496	1,484	2,381	22,027	47,466
1985	1,869	5,458	2,032	1,129	3,242	4,336	3,204	5,451	807	1,289	1,874	2,359	25,739	54,233
1986	1,533	105	2,652	51	4,375	207	4,117	1,636	—	—	2,455	62	27,602	4,036
1987	3,066	112	4,091	82	9,918	61	7,004	3,538	847	446	3,913	163	51,463	9,294
1988	7,148	259	9,134	145	25,805	271	16,015	6,766	664	326	8,093	258	114,647	7,679
1989	5,272	17,806	7,262	3,275	18,894	21,040	9,856	17,338	1,984	28,637	7,464	5,567	106,227	249,597
1990	8,984	22,565	10,796	7,872	30,820	31,294	12,016	23,909	1,156	2,698	9,307	8,027	145,698	440,807
1991	15,773	33,347	12,795	7,109	39,593	36,736	28,281	23,542	1,483	52,338	15,207	10,309	271,559	446,023
1992	19,204	10,190	16,401	6,992	55,724	23,465	64,201	24,557	2,714	91,375	20,002	6,341	401,310	524,306
1993	33,040	11,142	29,636	5,345	56,473	30,911	77,684	20,186	3,346	122,605	25,888	6,972	469,396	764,562

E2 External Trade (in Current Values) with Main Trading Partners

NOTES

1. SOURCES: The main sources used have been the same as for table E1. Colombian data to 1909 are from Miguel Urrutia and Mario Arrubla (eds.), *op.cit.* in Note 1 to table E1.
2. In principle, and except as indicated in footnotes, statistics are of merchandise trade, and are on a 'special' rather than a 'general' basis.
3. Except as indicated in footnotes, statistics are believed to relate to countries of first or last consignment.

FOOTNOTES

[1] Years ending 30 June to 1906 and years beginning 1 April from 1907 to 1931. Re-exports are included with exports to 1906. Imports are on a 'general' basis to 1916 and exports to 1919. Gold is included to 1939. Newfoundland became part of Canada on 1 April 1949. A new basis of reckoning was adopted in 1959 which affected the comparability of some series.

[2] West Germany only subsequently.

[3] Adjusted for Canadian-owned military equipment returned to Canada.

[4] 'General' trade. Years ending 30 June from 1876 to 1912.

[5] Years ending 31 July to 1937 and 30 June from 1939 to 1951. The 1938 figures are for the period 1 August 1937 to 30 June 1938.

[6] 'General' trade. Years beginning 1 April from 1890 to 1908. Exports include re-exports to 1923 (1st line) and from 1947 (2nd line).

[7] In gold dollars to 1905 and in new standard dollars (or pesos) subsequently. Data to 1913 are for years ending 30 June.

[8] Including Malta and Gibraltar to 1950.

[9] 'General' trade, though only imports for consumption to 1914. Tobago is included from 1889. Data are for years beginning 1 April from 1889 to 1908. Up to 1911 they relate to countries of shipment, subsequently to those of origin or destination.

[10] 'General' trade. Years ending 30 September to 1842 and 30 June for 1844 to 1915. The 1843 figures are for the period 1 October 1842 to 30 June 1843. Imports relate to countries of origin rather than last consignment from 1937.

[11] British North America to 1873 (1st line). Newfoundland is included from 1947.

[12] Official (i.e. fixed) values to 1910. Imports for domestic consumption and exports of domestic produce to 1912 (1st line).

[13] Statistics are given here in terms of the gold peso of 18 pence to 1969 though trade was actually recorded in pesos of different value at different times. Exports to 1912 (1st line) are of domestic produce only. There is no break in the series of exports to the USA.

[14] 'General' trade. Countries of purchase and sale from 1936.

[15] Including 9.5 million sucres of gold coins.

[16] 'General' trade to 1952. Years beginning 1 April from 1892 to 1911. Re-exports are included to 1913 (1st line) and bullion and specie to 1922 (1st line)

[17] British North America to 1908.

[18] The 1950 figures in thousand pounds are as follows:-

	Canada	UK	USA
imports	5,368	8,850	1,442
exports	3,055	9,837	444

[19] Including transit trade to 1929 (1st line).

[20] Official (i.e. fixed) values.

[21] Direct shipments only to 1951.

[22] Excluding imports of the Southern Peru Copper Corporation through Ilo.

[23] Official (i.e. fixed) values to 1917 for imports and 1914 for exports.

[24] 'General' trade, including bullion and specie in exports to 1937 (1st line). Data to 1919 are for years ending 30 June.

[25] The French Empire or the British Empire to 1919.

[26] Curaçao only to 1926 (1st line).

[27] Including Gibraltar.

E3   NORTH AMERICA: MAJOR COMMODITY EXPORTS BY MAIN EXPORTING COUNTRIES (in currency units)

	USA[1] (million dollars)			Barbados (thousand pounds)	Jamaica[2] (thousand pounds)	Trinidad[3] (thousand pounds)	USA[1] (million dollars)		
	Raw Cotton	Leaf Tobacco		Sugar	Sugar	Sugar	Raw Cotton	Leaf Tobacco	Wheat
1802	5	6	1830	...	...	...	30	6	- -
1803	8	6	1831	...	...	...	25	5	- -
1804	8	6	1832	262	1,396	204	32	6	- -
			1833	377	1,212	209	36	6	- -
1805	9	6	1834	562	1,540	308	49	7	- -
1806	8	7							
1807	14	5	1835	517	1,484	296	65	8	- -
1808	2	1	1836	581	1,767	407	71	10	- -
1809	9	4	1837	733	1,559	347	63	6	- -
			1838	758	1,777	382	62	7	- -
1810	15	5	1839	629	1,177	297	61	10	- -
1811	10	2							
1812	3	2	1840	300	959	296	64	10	2
1813	2	- -	1841	371	1,015	389	54	13	1
1814	3	- -	1842	374	1,167	386	48	10	1
			1843	501	880	339	[49][1]	[5][1]	[- -][1]
1815	18	8	1844	486	732	317	54	8	1
1816	24	13							
1817	23	9	1845	502	998	343	52	7	- -
1818	31	10	1846	433	738	413	43	8	2
1819	21	8	1847	657	1,032	398	53	7	6
			1848	515	670	207	62	8	3
1820	22	8	1849	601	593	297	66	6	2
1821	20	6							
1822	24	6	1850	597	585	242	72	10	1
1823	20	6	1851	654	428	294	112	9	1
1824	22	5	1852	740	442	357	88	10	3
			1853	555	412	350	109	11	4
1825	37	6	1854	729	431	289	94	10	12
1826	25	5							
1827	29	7							
1828	22	5							
1829	27	5							

E3   NORTH AMERICA: Major Commodity Exports by Main Exporting Countries (in currency units stated)

	Barbados (thousand pounds)	Canada[5] (million Canadian dollars)					Costa Rica[6] (thousand gold pesos)	
	Sugar	Lumber[5]	Machinery	Non-ferrous Metals	Wheat & Flour	Wood Pulp	Bananas	Coffee
1855	545	...	...	...	...	...	...	...
1856	662	...	...	...	...	...	...	751
1857	881	...	...	...	...	...	...	1,181
1858	1,052	...	...	...	...	...	...	692
1859	807	...	...	...	...	...	...	1,282
1860	658	...	...	...	...	...	...	1,122
1861	751	...	...	...	...	...	...	...
1862	677	...	...	...	...	...	...	1,403
1863	634	...	...	...	...	...	...	1,340
1864	554	...	...	...	...	...	...	1,576
1865	708	...	...	...	...	...	...	1,483
1866	837	...	...	...	...	...	...	1,949
1867	806	...	...	...	...	...	...	2,442
1868	857	...	...	...	...	...	...	...
1869	481	17	...	0.7	...	...	...	...
1870	595	19	...	0.4	...	—	...	...
1871	809	20	...	0.9	...	—	...	...
1872	590	21	...	2.5	6.7	—	...	...
1873	563	25	...	2.6	9.0	—	...	...
1874	710	24	...	1.6	12	—	...	4,464
1875	977	22	...	2.2	6.6	—	...	3,984
1876	570	18	...	2.4	13	—	...	2,103
1877	711	21	...	1.6	5.7	—	...	4,859
1878	653	18	...	1.3	15	—	...	3,252
1879	860	12	...	1.6	13	—	...	4,030
1880	814	15	...	1.4	17	—	...	3,436
1881	784	23	...	1.0	12	—	...	2,242
1882	806	21	...	1.1	11	—	...	3,512[6]
1883	753	23	...	1.1	15	—	47	1,695
1884	871	23	...	1.2	4.9	—	282	3,038
1885	632	19	...	1.3	5.8	—	233	1,913
1886	437	20	...	1.6	7.1	—	333	1,580'
1887	660[4] 703	19	...	1.3	10	—	504	3,934
1888	752	19	...	1.1	8.0	—	375	3,340
1889	668	21	...	1.0	2.5	—	374	4,070
1890	870	24	...	1.2	3.1	0.2	410	6,050
1891	518	23	...	1.6	5.6	0.3	431	2,562
1892	606	21	...	1.4	14	0.4	363	5,376
1893	856	25	...	1.2	12	0.5	350	4,115
1894	626	24	...	1.8	11	0.5	443	3,713
1895	282	20	0.9	2.5	8.4	0.6	628	4,198
1896	436	22	0.9	3.9	8.9	0.7	670	4,318
1897	447	27	1.0	7.1	11	0.7	778	4,102
1898	435	23	1.8	10	27	1.2	923	4,210
1899	474	24	2.3	8.8	17	1.3	1,173	2,943
1900	510	26	2.4	19	19	1.8	1,354	3,800
1901	565	25	2.4	33	18	1.9	1,742	2,823
1902	302	28	2.4	27	30	2.0	1,878	3,180
							(thousand colones)	
1903	260	31	2.9	23	34	3.2	4,972	8,971
1904	440	29	3.2	28	24	2.4	6,520	6,536

E3 NORTH AMERICA: Major Commodity Exports by Main Exporting Countries (in currency units stated)

| | Cuba | | El Salvador (million colones) | Guatemala (million pesos)[7] | Honduras[12] | | Jamaica[2] | |
| | (million pesos) | | | | (million gold pesos) | | (thousand pounds) | |
	Sugar	Tobacco	Coffee	Coffee	Bananas	Coffee	Bananas	Sugar
1855	...	...	...	...	...	...	...	365
1856	...	...	...	...	...	...	...	425
1857	...	...	...	...	...	...	...	599
1858	...	...	...	...	...	...	...	631
1859	...	...	...	...	...	...	...	497
1860	...	...	...	- -	...	...	...	646
1861	...	...	...	0.1	...	...	...	595
1862	...	...	...	0.1	...	...	...	563
1863	...	...	...	...	...	...	...	480
1864	...	...	...	0.2	...	...	...	503
1865	...	...	...	...	...	...	...	430
1866	...	...	...	0.4	...	...	...	557
1867	...	...	...	0.4	...	...	...	447
1868	...	...	...	0.8	...	...	...	551
1869	...	...	...	...	...	...	...	443
1870	...	...	...	...	...	...	...	492
1871	...	...	...	1.3	...	...	...	592
1872	...	...	...	1.7	...	...	...	578
1873	...	...	...	4.1	...	...	3	483
1874	...	...	...	3.7	...	...	6	483
1875	...	...	...	4.8	...	...	6	454
1876	...	...	...	3.3	...	...	13	413
1877	...	...	...	3.4	...	...	16	530
1878	...	...	...	3.9	...	...	31	379
1879	...	...	...	4.0	...	...	33	415
1880	...	...	...	4.1	...	...	39	498
1881	...	...	...	3.6	...	...	23	337
1882	...	...	...	3.1	...	...	89	614
1883	...	...	...	4.8	...	...	94	552
1884	...	...	...	4.4	...	...	192	428
1885	...	...	...	5.2	...	...	130	308
1886	...	...	...	5.8	...	...	166	203
1887	...	...	...	8.1	...	...	146	265
1888	...	...	...	6.6	...	...	271	288
1889	...	...	...	13[7] / 9.6	...	...	252[2]	244[2]
1890	...	...	...	11	...	...	444	233
1891	...	...	...	11	...	...	263	255
1892	...	...	...	10	...	...	340	242
1893	...	...	...	15	...	...	473	282
1894	77	20	...	9.7	...	...	429	239
1895	...	...	...	...	...	...	317	195
1896	...	...	...	3.5	0.2	0.1	302	149
1897	...	...	...	7.6	...	...	446	121
1898	...	...	...	5.0	0.4	0.1	469	150
1899	19	...	...	7.4	0.4	0.1	603	195
1900	...	...	...	6.5	0.7	- -	619	166
1901	...	10	8.3	6.8	0.8	- -	825	137
1902	31	15	7.7	6.5	0.8	- -	1,135	168
1903	42	26	10	5.8	0.6	- -	585	122
1904	56	25	13	6.5	0.9	- -	514	116

E3   NORTH AMERICA: Major Commodity Exports by Main Exporting Countries (in currency units stated)

| | Mexico[8] | | | | | | Nicaragua | | Trinidad[3] |
| | (million pesos) | | | | | | (thousand gold pesos or cordobas) | | (thousand pounds) |
	Coffee	Copper[9]	Cotton	Lead	Silver	Zinc[9]	Bananas	Coffee	Sugar
1855	...	...	...	...	...	...	...	...	285
1856	...	...	...	...	...	...	...	...	450
1857	...	...	...	...	...	...	...	...	781
1858	...	...	...	...	...	...	...	...	558
1859	...	...	...	...	...	...	...	...	599
1860	...	...	...	...	...	...	...	...	503
1861	...	...	...	...	...	...	...	...	377
1862	...	...	...	...	...	...	...	...	517
1863	...	...	...	...	...	...	...	...	468
1864	...	...	...	...	...	...	...	...	742
1865	...	...	...	...	...	...	...	...	470
1866	...	...	...	...	...	...	...	...	592
1867	...	...	...	...	...	...	...	...	629
1868	...	...	...	...	...	...	...	...	622
1869	...	...	...	...	...	...	...	...	912
1870	...	...	...	...	...	...	...	...	719
1871	...	...	...	...	...	...	...	...	938
1872	...	...	...	...	24	...	...	...	817
1873	...	...	...	...	18	...	...	...	974
1874	...	...	...	...	17	...	...	...	669
1875	...	...	...	...	20	...	...	...	812
1876	...	...	...	...	20	...	...	...	659
1877	1.2	- -	- -	0.1	25	...	...	...	924
1878	2.2	- -	- -	- -	25	...	...	...	730
1879	2.0	- -	—	- -	28	...	...	...	833
1880	2.2	0.1	—	- -	29	...	...	...	858
1881	2.4	- -	—	0.1	29	...	...	310	688
1882	1.7	- -	- -	- -	30	...	...	484	875
1883	1.6	- -	- -	0.2	32	...	...	...	886
1884	1.2	- -	- -	0.3	33	...	...	...	642
1885	1.7	- -	—	0.5	34	...	...	...	685
1886	2.6	- -	- -	0.3	38	...	...	...	546
1887	2.4	0.6	- -	0.4	39	...	...	...	801
1888	3.9	0.8	—	0.5	41	...	...	...	724[3]
1889	4.8	0.7	—	0.6	39	...	...	...	875
1890	6.2	0.9	—	1.1	42	...	...	...	631
1891	5.5	0.9	—	2.4	47	...	...	...	663
1892	8.7	2.3	- -	0.3	55	...	...	...	675
1893	12	2.0	- -	- -	58	...	...	...	758
1894	13	2.1	- -	1.8	58	...	...	...	598
1895	8.1	3.9	- -	2.5	61	...	...	...	596
1896	9.9	3.9	- -	2.8	64	...	...	...	700
1897	11	2.3	—	2.9	70	...	...	...	537
1898	7.9	4.1	- -	3.8	72	...	...	...	602
1899	11	9.9	- -	3.5	70	...	...	...	715
1900	7.0	11	- -	5.1	74	- -	...	...	550
1901	10	14	- -	5.7	73	- -	...	...	452
1902	9	19	- -	5.6	83	—	...	...	410
1903	8.7	19	- -	4.8	82	- -	...	...	436
1904	9.3	24	- -	5.5	78	0.1	286	1,044	722

E3 NORTH AMERICA: Major Commodity Exports by Main Exporting Countries (in currency units stated)

	Coal[10]	Cotton	Iron & Steel	Machinery	Meat[12]	Motor Vehicles	Petroleum & Products	Leaf Tobacco	Wheat[13]
					USA[1] (million US dollars)				
1855	...	88	...	...	16	...	...	15	1
1856	...	128	...	...	16	...	...	12	15
1857	...	132	...	...	14	...	...	20	22
1858	...	131	...	...	12	...	...	17	9
1859	...	161	...	...	11	...	...	21	3
1860	...	192	...	...	14	...	...	16	4
1861	...	34	...	...	17	...	...	14	38
1862	...	[1][11]	...	...	30	...	...	12	43
1863	...	[7][11]	...	...	48	...	...	20	47
1864	...	[10][11]	...	...	66	...	...	23	31
1865	...	[7][11]	...	...	35	...	...	42	19
1866	...	281	...	...	22	...	...	29	8
1867	...	201	...	...	34	...	...	20	8
1868	...	153	...	...	24	...	...	23	30
1869	...	163	...	...	45	...	...	21	24
1870	...	227	...	...	21	...	...	21	47[13] / 68
1871	...	218	...	...	30	...	...	20	69
1872	...	181	...	...	55	...	...	24	57
1873	...	227	...	...	71	...	...	23	71
1874	...	211	...	...	71	...	...	30	131
1875	...	191	...	...	68	...	...	25	83
1876	...	193	...	...	79	...	...	23	93
1877	...	171	...	...	101	...	...	29	69
1878	...	180	...	...	107	...	...	25	122
1879	...	162	...	...	102	...	...	25	160
1880	...	212	...	...	114	...	...	16	226
1881	...	248	...	...	134[12]	...	...	19	213
1882	4	200	1	14	69	...	52	19	149
1883	4	247	1	17	61	...	46	19	175
1884	5	197	2	16	64	...	48	18	126
1885	5	202	1	11	63	...	52	22	125
1886	4	205	1	10	54	...	52	27	89
1887	5	206	1	11	53	...	49	26	143
1888	6	223	2	12	52	...	49	22	111
1889	7	238	2	16	59	...	52	19	87
1890	7	251	3	20	78	...	54	21	102
1891	8	291	3	21	81	...	56	21	106
1892	9	258	3	21	83	...	49	20	237
1893	10	189	3	22	79	...	47	22	169
1894	12	211	3	22	80	...	45	23	129
1895	11	205	3	24	81	...	50	...	95
1896	11	190	5	29	81	...	67	...	92
1897	12	231	11	38	88	...	68	...	116
1898	12	230	19	44	104	...	62	22	215
1899	14	210	29	61	109	...	63	25	177
1900	21	242	39	78	114	...	84	29	141
1901	24	314	40	73	121	...	78	27	166
1902	22	291	26	68	121	1	81	27	179
1903	23	316	21	76	104	1	77	25	162
1904	30	371	31	84	101	2	88	29	105

E3 NORTH AMERICA: Major Commodity Exports by Main Exporting Countries (in currency units stated)

	Barbados (thousand pounds)	Canada[5]							
		(million Canadian dollars)							
	Sugar	Lumber[14]	Machinery	Motor Vehicles	Non-Ferrous Metals	Paper etc.	Petroleum & Products	Wheat & Flour	Wood Pulp
1905	451	29	3.2	...	26	...	...	18	3.4
1906	351	36	3.4	...	29	2.0	...	40	3.5
1907	260	[31][5]	[3.2][5]	...	[28][5]	[1.7][5]	...	[26][5]	[3.0][5]
1908	288	41[14]	4.4[4]	0.2	34	3.5	...[4]	53	4
		44	4.0					48	
1909	153	39	4.3	0.2	31	3.5	...	63	4.3
1910	396	47	5.2	0.4	33	3.2	...	66	5.2
1911	289	45	6.9	0.6	34	3.9	...	62	5.7
1912	313	41	6.7	1.5	35	3.9	...	83	5.1
1913	91	43	7.4	2.4	50	11	...	109	5.5
1914	253	43	8.7	3.8	54	13	...	142	6.4
1915	503	43	4.3	3.1	51	15	...	110	9.3
1916	1,101	51	4.9	9.4	67	20	...	220	10
1917	1,056	56	5.9	5.6	76	26	...	340	20
1918	687	52	8.4	5.4	72[4]	38	...	466	26
					90				
1919	1,232	70	15	8.9	79	48	...	191	35
1920	2,203	105	18	15	55	63	...	252	41
1921	515	116	18	18	46	92	...	377	72
1922	503	71	7.9	9.2	28	70	...	233	36
1923	1,226	103	8.5	29	44	80	...	312	43
1924	998	127[4]	13	37	66	97	...	331	46
		129							
1925	686	111	16	31	90	100	...	322	42
1926	594	118	19	43	97[4]	110	...	434	50
					75				
1927	816	110	22	36	79	123	...	422	50
1928	875	101	22	27	93	135	...	412	47
1929	722	94	23	46	118	148	...	494	45
1930	473	92	26	38	93	152	...	261	45
1931	361	62	13	17	56	132	...	210	35
1932	733	41	6.2	4.4	44	107	...	136	28
1933	788	25	5.3	7.8	67	77	...	148	18
1934	775	40	4.7	13	90	77	...	139	25
1935	319	47	8.9	22	116	88	...	151	26
1936	772	56[5]	12[5]	27[5]	134	97[5]	...	168[5]	28[5]
		67	13	23		111		248	31
1937	911	84	20	27	195	136	...	148	42
1938	683	70	18	25	180	113	...	107	28
1939	1,278	86	18	26	183	124	...	125	31
1940	649	113	27	65	195	160	...	146	61
1941	841	121	33	149	244	157	...	207	86
1942	846	133	54	257	309	149	...	168	95
1943	1,498	125	63	455	333	150	...	301	100
1944	1,317	156	112	386	340	165	...	474	102
1945	1,589	169	104	300	353	188	11	574	120
1946	1,790	161	65	78	248	287	4.6	377	114
1947	1,879	322	83	92	304	373	6.9	462	175
1948	1,202	314	114	55	396	417	9.3	368	209
1949	3,274	244[5]	124[5]	39[5]	427[5]	453[5]	2.6[5]	533[5]	167[5]

E3 NORTH AMERICA: Major Commodity Exports by Main Exporting Countries (in currency units stated)

	Costa Rica (thousand colones)		Cuba (million pesos)		Dominican Republic (thousand US dollars)			El Salvador (million colones)
	Bananas	Coffee	Sugar	Tobacco	Cocoa	Coffee	Sugar	Coffee
1905	7,829	7,995	73	28	2,212	157	3,292	10
1906	9,538	7,217	59	34	2,263	220	2,392	12
1907	10,167	7,148	66	28	2,988	252	2,100	11
1908	10,075	4,399	53	32	4,269	325	3,092	10
1909	9,366	5,617	81	32	2,759	128	3,305	12
1910	9,097	5,916	111	28	2,932	333	5,752	13
1911	9,309	6,109	79	32	3,902	319	4,160	16
1912	10,648	7,624	124	35	4,249	566	5,841	17
1913	11,171	7,753	118	32	4,120	257	3,651	19
1914	10,163	10,028	133	28	3,896	346	4,943	23
	(million colones)							
1915	9.5	8.0	193	24	4,864	458	7,458	21
1916	10	9.1	267	26	5,959	468	12,028	23
1917	8.7	8.1	295	30	4,856	228	13,386	21
1918	7.1	8.0	339	37	3,917	537	22,372	19
1919	7.3	25	502	48	8,011	947	20,702	10
1920	8.7	15	725	49	6,168	266	45,535	12
1921	12	8.2	232	33	3,083	241	14,338	6.8
1922	11	15	276	35	3,054	609	9,200	14
1923	11	10	368	36	2,917	428	18,734	15
1924	24	34	375	39	2,794	864	21,686	45
1925	25	34	281	41	3,875	1,295	15,452	30
1926	26	42	242	37	3,831	1,890	14,700	47
1927	24	42	264	37	7,477	1,750	16,668	25
1928	22	50	215	39	4,250	2,136	17,710	45
1929	18	49	205	37	3,870	2,444	12,292	34
1930	18	42	105	33	2,710	1,483	10,167	24
1931	13	40	79	22	1,789	1,182	7,601	22
1932	11	25	54	13	1,027	1,255	6,869	13
1933	9.0	36	58	13	1,274	1,832	4,401	19
1934	6.8	26	74	14	1,739	1,676	6,756	23
	(million US dollars)							
1935	1.5	5.0	90	16	2,095	1,269	9,486	24
1936	2.1	4.6	113	13	1,585	2,020	8,569	23
1937	3.1	6.1	127	15	2,524	1,765	10,740	35
1938	2.8	4.9	100	14	1,915	1,039	8,654	24
1939	1.9	4.6	117	14	2,014	1,731	11,881	37
1940	1.9	4.0	96	12	1,617	772	13,001	30
1941	3.5	5.0	138	14	2,250	1,475	7,965	29
1942	1.9	6.0	108	16	2,482	1,454	10,653	51
1943	2.1	8.0	226	28	4,039	2,648	22,685	59
1944	1.8	6.3	237	52	4,000	3,135	44,027	69
					(million US dollars)			
1945	2.2	7.5	259	51	3.1	4.9	22	75
1946	4.4	6.5	315	56	4.5	5.4	35	95
1947	5.6	11	610	35	13	5.1	51	143
1948	27	14	586	33	17	6.6	42	90
1949	28	11	495	30	7.5	11	39	119

E3 NORTH AMERICA: Major Commodity Exports by Main Exporting Countries (in currency units stated)

| | Guadeloupe | | Guatemala (million gold pesos or quetzales) | Haiti (million gourdes) | Honduras[15] | | Jamaica[2] | |
| | (million francs) | | | | (million gold pesos) | | (thousand pounds) | |
	Bananas	Sugar	Coffee	Coffee	Bananas	Coffee	Bananas	Sugar
1905	...	...	7.3	...	0.9	- -	843	122
1906	...	...	6.2	...	1.0	- -	881	119
1907	...	...	9.0	...	1.0	- -	1,039	110
1908	...	...	5.7	...	0.8	0.1	1,045₂	77₂
1909	...	...	8.8	...	0.9	0.1	1,404	119
1910	...	...	6.6	...	...	...	1,142	261
1911	...	...	7.3	...	...	...	1,457	247
1912	...	...	9.1	...	1.3	0.1	1,241	133
1913	...	...	12	...	1.1	- -	988	52
1914	...	...	10	...	1.7	0.1	1,491	196
1915	...	...	8.9	...	...	...	600	256
1916	...	...	8.1	...	...	...	222	503
1917	...	...	5.4	30	...	...	227	704
1918	...	...	8.6	22	...	...	298	614
1919	...	...	20	97	...	...	1,141	1,318
					(million lempiras)			
1920	...	...	14	65	5.8	0.4	1,320	2,994
1921	...	...	9.2	21	...	...	1,303	510
1922	...	...	9.2	37	...	0.1	1,788	912
1923	...	...	10	54	...	...	2,265	675
1924	...	...	19	52	12	...	1,225	498
1925	...	...	24	77	15	0.6	1,511	545
1926	...	...	23	82	20	0.9	2,072	655
1927	...	...	28	57	27	1.0	2,365	792
1928	...	...	22	90	37	1.7	1,774	710
1929	...	...	19	64	42	1.1	2,510	483
1930	...	...	19	52	46	0.8	2,310	592
1931	...	...	11	33	35	0.5	1,983	379
1932	...	...	7.2	26	28	0.6	1,869	343
1933	...	...	5.7	36	23	0.6	1,018	424
1934	...	...	11	36	19	0.7	1,665	448
1935	...	...	8.8	19	16	0.3	2,174	558
1936	...	...	11	29	12	0.6	1,912	632
1937	...	...	11	23	12	0.8	2,657	865
1938	86	125	10	17	[8.5][15]	[0.3][15]	2,917	860
1939	...	...	9.6	19	12	0.5	2,439	990
1940	...	...	4.1	10	13	0.4	1,045	848
1941	...	...	6.6	23	13	0.3	901	1,585
1942	...	...	14	17	12	1.0	273	1,621
1943	...	...	14	28	3.9	0.9	47	1,832
1944	...	...	15	26	9.2	0.8	198	1,859
1945	...	...	18	36	13	0.9	359	1,938
1946	...	...	20	38	12	1.8	1,631	2,762
1947	...	...	32	61	16	1.1	2,049	2,082
1948	1,261	539	31	54	15₁₅ 82	2.5	2,321	3,561
1949	1,201	3,219	37	92	80	2.8	2,271	4,624

E3 NORTH AMERICA: Major Commodity Exports by Main Exporting Countries
(in currency units stated)

	Mexico[8] (million pesos)						
	Coffee	Copper[9]	Cotton	Lead	Petroleum & Products	Silver	Zinc[9]
1905	9.3	23	- -	4.4	...	76	0.3
1906	7.2	22	3.7	3.7	...	77	2.0
1907	11	18	1.7	5.3	...	85	0.9
1908	13	15	0.1	6.4	...	77	1.0
1909	8.0	18	0.2	6.8	...	76	1.2
1910	8.6	20	- -	6.5	...	81	0.9
1911	13	27	- -	6	...	82	...
1912	$\underline{11}_8$	$\underline{31}_8$	$\underline{0.1}_8$	$\underline{4.9}_8$	...	$\underline{91}_8$	$\underline{0.5}_8$
1913	[5.6]	[16]	...	[2.9]	...	...	...
1914	1.7	...	...	...	...	...	...
1915	30	2.5	...	0.1	...	...	...
1916	86	6.3	...	1.3	...	...	...
1917	...	...	...	...	...	...	...
1918	6.7	46	...	36	...	96	...
1919	14	29	...	16	...	103	...
1920	9.3	38	11	29	569	121	5.3
1921	10	9.1	6.0	13	...	77	...
1922	15	17	5.2	27	412	49	...
1923	14	37	1.8	53	270	105	6.2
1924	15	29	17	58	289	111	5.7
1925	24	33	8.9	68	292	126	16
1926	24	42	22	86	228	123	38
1927	29	42	16	28	129	84	56
1928	35	46	17	20	86	87	55
1929	32	73	14	46	77	93	61
1930	28	52	2.1	46	75	74	34
1931	19	22	5.1	46	51	58	25
1932	14	14	1.8	19	72	35	10
1933	27	21	0.5	19	76	42	27
1934	27	30	3.3	55	145	76	42
1935	23	26	19	71	133	164	46
1936	20	24	46	79	136	115	61
1937	28	45	8.4	108	145	128	86
1938	26	33	18	89	73	171	80
1939	34	42	6.5	87	79	137	213
1940	22	45	5.3	95	85	121	92
1941	29	41	14	4.1	68	106	37
1942	33	74	0.8	66	31	106	57
1943	52	53	5.3	102	36	38	88
1944	58	37	29	76	31	23	91
1945	59	43	40	84	40	35	93
1946	63	74	74	136	53	148	91
1947	92	122	217	289	45	159	221
1948	104	100	155	456	249	147	142
1949	229	192	482	446	132	240	182

E3 NORTH AMERICA: Major Commodity Exports by Main Exporting Countries (in currency units stated)

	Netherlands Antilles (million guilders)	Nicaragua (thousand gold cordobas)			Panama (thousand balboas)	Trinidad & Tobago[3] (thousand pounds)	
	Petroleum & Products	Bananas	Coffee	Cotton	Bananas	Sugar	Petroleum & Products
1905	...	296	1,541	...	...	452	...
1906	...	700	1,376	...	...	430	...
1907	...	83	1,318	...	...	521	...
1908	...	268	1,526	...	1,160	462₃	...
1909	...	164	1,557	...	853	565	- -
1910	...	107	2,795	...	92 l	724	—
1911	...	339	4,291	...	2,146	530	33
1912	...	423	1,773	...	1,157	539	18
1913	...	430	5,004	...	2,940	418	75
1914	...	504	2,295	...	2,639	591	67
1915	...	372	1,983	...	2,128	1,070	79
1916	...	494	2,171	...	2,371	1,297	205
1917	...	...	1,762	...	2,467	1,460	413
1918	...	...	2,249	...	2,111	810	572
1919	...	559	6,268	...	2,298	975	844
1920	...	817	2,874	...	2,006	2,576	649
1921	...	1,405	2,352	...	1,851	1,456	726
1922	...	1,970	2,301	...	1,596	1,145	762
1923	...	2,052	3,938	...	1,590	1,022	1,233
1924	...	1,707	7,322	...	1,891	1,234	1,246
1925	...	1,736	5,627	...	2,420	1,092	1,399
1926	...	1,226	8,100	...	2,459	1,003	1,723
1927	...	1,442	4,082	...	2,818	762	1,982
1928	...	1,923	6,792	...	2,910	1,201	2,056
1929	305	1,985	5,903	...	2,942	1,050	2,439
1930	404	2,239	3,792	...	2,008	776	2,206
1931	346	1,981	3,319	...	1,743	903	1,493
1932	181	2,238	1,479	...	1,728	846	1,861
1933	193	1,849	2,214	...	...	1,116	1,492
1934	160	1,546	2,374	...	1,910	916	2,068
1935	166	1,201	3,118	55	2,452	942	2,148
1936	200	770	2,115	134	2,537	1,277	2,751
1937	267	985	3,078	553	2,578	1,274	3,169
1938	336	777	2,031	262	2,755	1,033	4,108
1939	...	654	2,640	253	2,430	1,060	3,699
1940	...	446	2,094	203	3,084	898	2,722
1941	...	280	2,575	125	3,654	1,396	631
1942	...	28	3,588	312	1,813	1,103	267
1943	...	—	3,437	302	755	742	207
1944	366	3.9	3,734	32	922	848	213
1945	434	81	3,668	—	2,048	915	1,601
1946	496	193	4,316	145	4,154	1,369	6,336
1947	479	336	5,333	198	4,277	1,685	9,358
					(million balboas)		
1948	745	659	8,457	—	15	2,553	15,114
1949	...	828	4,362	212	41	3,695	16,117

E3 NORTH AMERICA: Major Commodity Exports by Main Exporting Countries (in currency units stated)

	USA[1] (million US dollars)								
	Coal[10]	Cotton	Iron & Steel	Machinery	Meat	Motor Vehicles	Petroleum & Products	Leaf Tobacco	Wheat[13]
1905	31	380	45	89	99	2	88	30	44
1906	31	401	51	108	115	3	93	29	88
1907	38	481	55	125	108	6	94	33	122
1908	42	438	58	121	102	5	113	34	164
1909	40	417	47	99	82	6	112	31	119
1910	44	450	60	117	62	11	107	38	95
1911	48	585	79	151	66	16	105	39	71
1912	56	566	102	161	72	26	123	43	79
1913	68	547	124	195	68	33	150	49	142
1914	63	610	91	168	68	35	162	54	142
1915	58[1]	376[1]	85[1]	120[1]	132[1]	70[1]	148[1]	44[1]	428[1]
1916	73	545	376	278	198	123	221	63	313
1917	119	575	645	356	274	124	275	46	384
1918	120	674	632	270	668	101	371	123	505
1919	126	1,137	450	362	698	156	377	260	650
1920	360	1,136	498	588	279	303	593	245	821
1921	171	534	236	408	157	84	401	205	551
1922	96	673	136	234	140	103	346	146	292
1923	166	807	167	281	154	171	367	152	205
1924	116	951	150	310	121	210	444	163	328
1925	107	1,060	144	366	127	318	474	153	234
1926	204	814	174	398	107	320	555	137	285
1927	110	826	161	433	71	389	487	139	325
1928	100	920	180	491	68	502	527	154	194
1929	106	771	200	604	79	541	562	146	192
1930	90	497	139	513	66	279	495	145	157
1931	65	326	63	316	36	148	271	110	84
1932	45	345	29	131	19	76	209	65	51
1933	40	398	46	132	26	91	201	82	19
1934	57	373	89	218	35	190	228	125	27
1935	52	391	88	265	28	227	251	134	15
1936	57	361	112	335	25	240	265	137	19
1937	67	369	300	479	25	347	378	134	64
1938	56	229	184	486	28	270	390	155	101
1939	67	243	236	502	32	254	385	77	61
1940	87	213	516	671	22	254	310	44	33
1941	119	83	501	740	99	339	285	65	35
1942	152	99	592	763	358	433	350	68	28
1943	172	184	615	1,194	617	279	517	170	56
1944	182	115	551	1,478	535	643	960	146	76
1945	198[10]	279	457	1,191	290	588	753	239	330
1946	316	536	447	1,369	341	549	436	350	610
1947	632	423	824	2,352	129	1,149	641	270	868
1948	492	511	649	2,259	57	930	657	214	1,393
1949	308	874	732	2,355	51	753	562	252	1,002

International Historical Statistics: The Americas 1750–1993

E3 NORTH AMERICA: Major Commodity Exports by Main Exporting Countries (in currency units stated)

	Barbados (thousand pounds)	Canada[2]								
		(million Canadian dollars)								
	Sugar	Lumber[14]	Iron Ore	Machinery	Motor Vehicles	Non-ferrous Metals	Paper, etc	Petroleum & Products	Wheat & Flour	Wood Pulp
1950	3,868	392[4]	13	113[4]	43	457[4]	515[4]	2.4	419	204[4]
		370		142		414	500			212
1951	4,836	421	19	189	86	487	565	3.9	555	371
1952	5,430	413	22	220	119	595	618	10	737	295
1953	5,628	349	31	182	82	570	636	7.8	670	251
1954	5,871	387	40	184	34	610	653	9.9	463	273
1955	5,526	449	100	183	48	718	691	42	413	300
1956	4,971	392	144	190	49	788	739	116	585	307
1957	7,635	346	152	228	50	989	749	157	442	295
1958	5,528	341	108	255	46	1,035	722	78	516	288
1959	...	367	158	298	50	1,129	759	82	507	315
	(million local dollars)									
1960	27	393	155	317	67	1,245	796	104	473	328
1961	28	406	143	354	43	907	800	162	723	350
1962	27	448	220	423	53	953	798	244	659	374
1963	42	505	271	479	78	986	813	244	849	411
1964	31	530	356	597	158	1,155	898	275	1,124	467
1965	33	551	361	754	336	1,293	939	291	907	500
1966	33	543	369	1,026	891	1,418	1,056	334	1,144	529
1967	37	578	383	1,179	1,612	1,623	1,052	414	804	550
1968	36	725	443	1,403	2,435	1,878	1,091	471	742	634
1969	29	763	333	1,623	3,270	1,808	1,257	556	526	760
1970	31	751	476	1,817	3,294	2,397	1,275	696	747	791
1971	28	900	413	1,900	3,905	2,151	1,254	855	886	805
1972	26	1,229	353	2,110	4,228	2,200	1,375	1,153	964	826
1973	32	1,659	462	2,518	4,814	2,895	1,567	1,719	1,265	1,062
1974	54	1,368	543	2,934	5,216	3,524	2,137	3,890	2,094	1,876
1975	105	1,045	686	3,522	5,818	3,023	2,044	3,423	2,097	1,825
1976	56	1,735	920	3,844	7,502	3,203	2,362	2,647	1,830	2,195
1977	56	2,508	1,064	4,469	9,381	3,540	2,839	2,005	1,942	2,177
1978	54	3,240	754	5,203	10,974	3,728	3,375	1,949	1,987	2,116
1979	67	4,081	1,354	6,651	11,261	4,485	4,056	3,860	2,321	3,098
1980	116	3,591	1,240	7,129	10,705	6,321	4,697	4,643	3,906	3,895
1981	59	3,251	1,465	8,892	13,046	5,501	5,300	4,316	3,910	3,847
1982	68	3,195	1,034	8,690	16,114	4,560	5,091	4,240	4,361	3,270
1983	46	4,385	972	9,490	20,316	5,170	5,133	5,299	4,728	3,089
1984	65	4,767	1,112	12,432	27,936	5,783	6,182	6,502	4,825	3,949
1985	57	5,043	1,174	12,822	31,808	5,634	6,853	8,324	3,863	3,464
1986	57	5,496	1,108	13,033	32,647	5,822	7,424	5,193	2,905	4,142
1987	62	6,590	968	14,083	30,882	6,520	8,231	6,387	3,278	5,554
1988	63	6,187	968	16,767	33,267	8,277	8,907	5,880	4,494	6,550
1989	48	5,565	942	15,661	31,775	6,258	8,340	6,251	2,578	7,032
1990	64	5,414	842	17,176	31,578	6,350	9,057	8,317	3,340	6,170
1991	57	5,185	891	18,073	30,562	6,077	9,118	8,736	3,797	4,981
1992	62	6,575	806	18,727	35,944	6,828	9,410	9,028	4,696	5,098
1993	48	9,587	802	20,848	44,971	6,949	10,131	6,908	2,833	4,652

E3 NORTH AMERICA: Major Commodity Exports by Main Exporting Countries (in currency units stated)

	Costa Rica		Cuba		Dominican Republic			El Salvador
	(million US dollars)		(million pesos)		(million US dollars)			(million colones)
	Bananas	Coffee	Sugar	Tobacco	Cocoa	Coffee	Sugar	Coffee
1950	32	18	551	31	15	13	42	154
1951	34	22	632	39	16	18	61	190
1952	38	24	538	40	15	27	53	194
1953	32	34	502	42	15	25	42	192
1954	36	35	402	41	23	31	37	230
1955	33	37	438	44	17	28	42	229
1956	26	34	392	44	9.0	33	53	218
1957	32	41	629	48	14	25	89	275
1958	27	51	557	52	21	24	57	210
1959	19	40	473	54	15	18	47	178
1960	20	45	468	63	15	23	83	192
1961	21	45	...	40	8.5	14	62	175
1962	27	49	432	25	9.7	20	90	189
1963	26	45	472	22	14	18	89	186
1964	28	48	627	29	12	30	87	233
1965	28	47	593	33	7.1	21	58	240
1966	30	53	504	26	11	21	70	224
1967	31	55	601	29	12	17	82	247
1968	44	55	495	38	14	18	83	234
1969	53	56	488	42	20	21	88	223
1970	68	73	785	33	19	29	104	302
1971	65	59	634	32	13	24	132	269
1972	83	78	549	37	18	30	159	329
1973	91	94	841	51	23	46	187	398
1974	99	125	1,886	59	46	45	324	487
1975	145	99	2,631	53	27	35	552	477
1976	150	165	2,321	61	47	83	247	1,011
1977	152	341	2,411	67	95	186	218	1,514
1978	172	314	2,956	69	86	97	172	964
1979	194	315	2,963	60	75	157	191	1,688
1980	215	248	3,279	37	54	77	287	1,538
1981	229	240	3,301	57	48	76	517	1,145
1982	218	242	3,772	104	57	97	261	1,016
1983	286	175	4,078	103	58	76	262	1,019
1984	253	267	4,090	57	74	95	272	1,131
1985	216	316	4,433	93	63	91	158	1,131
1986	278	277	4,069	77	59	113	134	2,452
1987	438	368	3,987	91	66	63	127	1,769
1988	290	316	4,086	78	64	66	127	1,804
1989	526	286	3,914	85	43	63	157	1,148
1990	644	246	...	...	41	47	143	1,244
1991	742	264	...	...	31	44	132	1,064
1992	804	203	...	...	40	32	109	1,135
1993	...	204	...	...	37	26	126	1,941

International Historical Statistics: The Americas 1750–1993

E3 NORTH AMERICA: Major Commodity Exports by main Exporting Countries (in currency units stated)

	Guadeloupe		Guatemala (million quetzales)	Haiti (million gourdes)	Honduras		Jamaica		
	(million francs)				(million lempiras)		(million pounds)		
	Bananas	Sugar	Coffee	Coffee	Bananas	Coffee	Bananas	Bauxite[16]	Sugar
1950	1,352	3,305	53	103	81	6.4	2.1	...	5.8
1951	2,417	3,831	58	130	87	12	1.3	- -	6.3
1952	2,394	5,685	72	170	82	18	1.8	0.4	7.0
1953	2,954	4,175	68	125	82	24	5.3	2.7	11
1954	4,810	5,407	74	216	69	28	5.4	6.0	11
1955	4,742	5,833	75	120	...	17	5.0	8.7	11
1956	2,423	6,250	92	148	88	27	5.3	10	13
1957	5,045	5,827	82	105	67	24	6.8	21	13
1958	5,587	6,829	78	146	75	22	5.0	22	11
1959	6,424	8,802	78	76	65	23	4.9	20	12
	(million new francs)								
1960	60	95	83	86	57	24	4.8	28	14
1961	65	94	71	67	79	18	4.9	30	15
1962	59	96	69	104	76	23	4.5	30	16
1963	57	104	78	80	66	28	4.8	30	22
1964	36	113	72	97	67	34	6.0	34	21
1965	56	108	92	99	106	44	6.1	35	16
1966	56	102	101	88	145	40	6.3	54	18
1967	56	81	70	72	158	35	6.6	57	16
1968	66	98	75	67	168	42	6.9	56	19
1969	59	97	83	72	152	37	6.2		15
							(million local dollars)		
1970	57	126	103	74	144	52	12	182	29
1971	73	130	98	99	187	46	12	185	32
1972	82	89	107	84	167	54	12	190	35
1973	102	129	146	105	164	95	16	229	35
1974	130	84	175	119	105	85	11	449	79
1975	130	144	166	106	123	114	15	484	140
1976	181	150	244	233	213	201	12	389	56
1977	138	138	355	337	260	336	17	489	68
1978	279	130	476	269	284	422	27	783	93
1979	185	162	433	329	400	394	32	934	100
1980	116	185	465	334	456	408	19	1,310	97
1981	183	147	296	151	427	345	7.6	1,353	83
1982	277	96	359	225	437	302	14	863	85
1983	325	92	351	277	406	302	13	871	112
1984	428	97	365	237	464	338	6.3	1,864	172
1985	289	70	451	226	547	370	23	1,628	253
1986	365	153	502	279	513	644	50	1,689	239
1987	283	19	355	124	644	400	104	1,723	338
1988	626	40	388	183	710	370	86	1,913	430
			US dollars (thousand)						
1989	224	187	238	170	365	416	111	639	389
1990	196	191	323	77	359	290	269	738	614
1991	278	162	286	97	1,029	810	529	1,367	1,059
1992	280	122	249	89	1,606	745	910	2,041	1,898
1993	229	192	268	...	1,416	838	889	2,101	2,432

E3 NORTH AMERICA: Major Commodity Exports by Main Exporting Countries (in currency units stated)

	Martinique (million new francs)		Mexico (million pesos)				Petroleum		
	Bananas	Sugar	Coffee	Copper[9]	Cotton	Lead	& Products	Silver	Zinc[9]
1950	...	...	334	216	780	524	276	266	216
1951	...	...	403	274	1,112	571	301	221	345
1952	...	...	408	357	1,187	636	280	120	413
1953	...	...	575	349	1,119	452	231	218	182
1954	...	...	793	418	1,646	612	444	402	211
1955	...	...	1,301	889	3,153	740	642	373	354
1956	...	...	1,314	1,019	3,288	664	669	319	542
1957	...	...	1,360	516	2,129	648	523	346	523
1958	...	...	990	437	2,378	442	300	328	249
1959	...	...	783	373	2,494	425	286	363	307
1960	66	49	899	323	1,974	420	172	306	369
1961	74	51	938	238	1,999	464	330	265	334
1962	75	52	915	319	2,729	326	403	356	353
1963	61	55	630	298	2,445	343	400	600	373
1964	59	37	1,221	197	2,127	289	378	382	533
1965	87	51	942	142	2,652	325	390	387	536
1966	144	23	1,076	162	2,774	346	388	442	566
1967	101	29	787	111	1,795	318	382	510	560
1968	122	22	863	151	2,129	280	323	914	593
1969	99	21	846	253	2,450	290	399	552	633
						(million US dollars)			
			68	20	142	24	32	44	31
1970	83	14	74	10	83	28	31	29	36
1971	93	15	73	15	63	20	27	30	32
1972	137	9.0	95	40	149	21	20	20	38
1973	117	18	169	48	166	23	105	19	29
1974	153	3.1	161	30	182	63	424	112	141
1975	195	7.8	194	30	174	46	460	131	93
1976	337	5.2	337	19	283	32	544	115	115
1977	353	3.0	458	43	195	46	1,028	103	92
1978	327	5.0	387	21	309	54	1,818	128	102
1979	246	0.4	544	65	346	80	3,915	0.3	102
1980	138	- -	446	189	315	55	9,843	837	107
1981	347	0.6	396	375	356	30	16,325	475	85
1982	416	2.1	328	231	175	22	16,262	302	76
1983	514	1.4	511	256	117	39	15,101	411	117
1984	508	...	522	205	212	52	16,117	346	164
1985	607	...	538	167	96	41	14,502	262	143
1986	709	...	868	176	69	41	5,499	304	91
1987	557	...	541	248	72	49	8,485	364	100
1988	715	...	481	282	114	32	4,927	251	93
1989	...	...	584	331	116	61	7,613	346	157
1990	606	...	373	256	93	99	9,545	277	146
1991	470	...	408	288	80	52	7,822	228	97
1992	575	...	282	246	32	58	7,939	201	56
1993	376	...	285	312	10	47	7,100	179	121

E3   NORTH AMERICA: Major Commodity Exports by Main Exporting Countries (in currency units stated)

	Netherlands Antilles[17] (million guilders)	Nicaragua (million US dollars[18])			Panama (thousand balboas)	Trinidad & Tobago (million local dollars)	
	Petroleum & Products	Bananas[19]	Coffee	Cotton	Bananas	Sugar	Petroleum & Products
1950	1,001	0.6	17	1.8	16	18	126
1951	1,310	0.5	18	5.5	16	19	162
1952	1,358	0.4	22	6.8	13	20	175
1953	1,333	0.3	21	8.4	16	26	194
1954	1,428	0.4[19]	25	17	22	28	193
1955	1,491	0.4	28	31	26	31	213
1956	1,568	0.2	23	24	22	26	262
1957	1,627	0.1	29	22	24	31	314
1958	1,506	0.1	24	25	22	32	362
1959	1,321	0.1	14	29	24	32	387
1960	1,221	0.1	19	15	18	37	410
1961	1,319	0.1	17	18	20	45	516
1962	1,274	0.8	15	31	20	36	510
1963	1,223	1.4	18	40	25	50	539
1964	1,158	2.2	21	52	29	48	81
1965	1,094	0.8	26	67	40	42	568
1966	1,062	0.9	22	57	45	34	585
1967	1,101	3.3	21	57	50	38	593
1968	1,082	3.2	23	61	58	48	721
1969	1,099	2.2	21	47	63	52	731
1970	1,195	0.3	33	35	61	49	743
1971	1,298	- -	30	42	63	48	802
1972	1,290	3.4	33	65	65	57	829
1973	2,454	5.6	45	65	64	44	1,115
1974	5,601	5.3	46	139	50	107	3,562
1975	4,162	4.9	49	99	60	166	3,368
1976	4,344	4.6	119	133	62	117	4,870
1977	4,595	4.5	200	153	66	83	4,479
1978	5,188	6.3	261	189	72	54	4,348
1979	7,031	7.2	180	157	66	84	5,642
1980	9,136	8.4	170	31	62	67	9,039
1981	9,514	21	142	124	69	65	8,041
1982	8,673	9.8	128	89	66	52	6,426
1983	7,802	15	159	112	75	61	4,672
1984	6,600	12	127	137	75	61	4,146
1985	2,894[17]	17	91	93	78	51	4,157
1986	1,573	24	134	36	70	84	3,511
1987	2,241	54	117	57	86	76	3,728
1988	1,940	14	87	35	77	91	3,264
1989	2,461	16	65	26	82	127	4,076
1990	3,095	27	76	38	90	129	5,905
1991	2,699	27	36	45	79	132	5,424
1992	2,524	14	46	26	82	140	4,920
1993	...	5	34	—	78	144	4,876

E3 NORTH AMERICA: Major Commodity Exports by Main Exporting Countries (in currency units stated)

	USA[1] (million US dollars)								
	Coal[10]	Cotton	Iron & Steel	Machinery	Meat	Motor Vehicles	Petroleum & Products	Leaf Tobacco	Wheat[13]
1950	278	1,024	472	2,035	43	723	499	250	489
1951	605	1,146	611[20]	2,615	60	1,191	783	325	997
1952	510	874	621	2,868	52	987	793	245	942
1953	346	521	495	3,013	60	963	692	339	590
1954	312	788	516	2,875	61	1,036	658	303	427
1955	495	477	818	3,057	70	1,238	646	355	483
1956	745	729	1,075[20]	3,813	99	1,357	766	333	798
1957	846	1,059	1,377	4,178	113	1,309	994	359	848
1958	534	661	563	3,682	83	1,087	462	279	686
1959	388	452	372	3,706	106	1,258	480	346	719
1960	362[4]	988[4]	610[4]	4,121[4]	125[4]	1,298[4]	479[4]	370[14]	971[4]
	354	980	635	4,476	115	1,270	468	379	1,029
1961	340	875	454	4,968	133	1,188	432	390	1,300
1962	376	528	455	5,447	138	1,365	430	372	1,136
1963	474	577	505	5,702	144	1,518	479	401	1,331
1964	463	682	664	6,525	177	1,749	461	409	1,532
1965	477	486	607	6,935	162	1,744	418	378	1,184
1966	468	432	537	7,678	159	2,154	434	472	1,536
1967	483	464	539	8,280	151	2,503	539	487	1,207
1968	503	459	583	8,844	162	3,123	454	511	1,101
1969	594	280	941	10,137	199	3,514	433	529	831
1970	962	372	1,188	11,685	175	3,245	488	481	1,112
1971	902	583	798	11,660	195	4,180	481	466	1,005
1972	984	504	800	13,562	252	4,473	444	639	1,452
1973	1,014	929	1,258	17,588	444	5,573	518	681	4,154
1974	2,437	1,335	2,500	24,318	371	7,248	792	832	4,589
1975	3,259	991	2,382	29,215	528	9,290	908	852	5,293
1976	2,910	1,049	1,833	32,113	798	10,132	998	922	4,040
1977	2,655	1,530	1,608	32,630	797	10,887	1,280	1,094	2,883
1978	2,046	1,740	1,646	38,105	958	12,150	1,564	1,358	4,532
1979	3,328	2,198	2,227	45,914	1,127	13,904	1,914	1,184	5,491
1980	4,621	2,864	2,998	57,263	1,293	13,117	2,833	1,334	6,586
1981	5,909	2,260	2,801	64,426	1,482	14,733	3,696	1,457	8,073
1982	5,987	1,955	2,101	59,821	1,285	12,751	5,947	1,547	6,869
1983	4,051	1,817	1,415	54,695	1,191	13,492	4,557	1,462	6,509
1984	4,132	2,441	1,248	61,464	1,208	17,651	4,470	1,511	6,698
1985	4,464	1,633	1,152	60,573	1,153	19,445	4,707	1,521	3,780
1986	3,928	733	1,020	60,809	1,424	17,695	3,639	1,209	3,217
1987	3,366	1,631	1,223	70,080	1,768	19,952	3,922	1,090	3,248
1988	4,009	1,975	2,017	88,531	2,430	23,972	3,679	1,252	5,080
1989	4,396	2,297	3,643	88,242	2,844	26,412	5,009	1,365	5,913
1990	4,610	2,838	3,708	101,036	2,989	30,524	6,868	1,470	3,887
1991	4,781	2,554	4,777	107,630	3,383	33,133	6,945	1,440	3,350
1992	4,243	2,054	4,130	114,546	3,920	37,946	6,261	1,659	4,498
1993	3,093	1,581	3,908	125,226	4,001	41,178	6,149	1,322	4,668

E3 SOUTH AMERICA: MAJOR COMMODITY EXPORTS BY MAIN EXPORTING COUNTRIES (in currency units stated)

| | Brazil[21] | | | | | Chile (million gold pesos of 18 pence) | Colombia (thousand gold pesos) | | Guyana[22] (thousand pounds) | Venezuela (million bolivares) |
| | (million paper milreis) | | | | | | | | | |
	Cocoa	Coffee	Cotton	Rubber	Sugar	Copper[20]	Coffee	Tobacco	Sugar	Coffee
1820	...	...	...	...	...	...	...	...	...	...
1821	0.1	3.3	4.3	...	5.1	...	...	...	...	...
1822	0.1	3.9	4.9	...	3.6	...	...	...	...	...
1823	0.1	4.2	4.5	...	5.3	...	...	...	...	...
1824	0.1	3.5	6.6	...	4.5	...	...	...	...	...
1825	0.2	2.9	1.8	...	4.9	...	...	...	...	...
1826	0.2	3.5	4.0	...	4.9	...	...	...	...	...
1827	0.2	5.3	5.3	- -	9.3	...	...	...	...	...
1828	- -	5.1	5.6	- -	15	...	...	...	...	...
1829	0.1	6.8	7.2	0.1	12	...	...	...	...	...
1830	- -	7.0	7.4	0.1	13	...	...	...	...	3.4
1831	- -	9.3	3.8	0.1	8.2	...	...	...	...	4.3
1832	0.1[21]	12[21]	3.1[21]	0.1[21]	9.4[21]	...	...	...	1,262	4.8
1833	0.1	18	2.9	0.1	6.7	...	...	...	1,258	5.2
1834	0.1	15	3.3	0.1	6.8	...	...	...	1,155	3.6
1835	0.1	16	3.0	0.1	12	...	18	18	1,343	7.3
1836	0.2	14	2.5	0.1	7.4	...	—	191	1,529	8.3
1837	0.5	18	3.1	0.1	8.6	...	36	159	1,258	7.3
1838	0.5	21	4.0	0.3	8.8	...	34	40	1,201	11.3
1839	0.4	20	3.9	0.3	11	...	55	26	948	9.7
1840	0.4	18	3.2	0.2	12	...	...	...	1,195	12
1841	0.5	18	3.5	0.1	8.4	...	67	—	810	17
1842	0.4	17	3.7	0.1	10	...	...	19	845	13
1843	0.4	18	3.3	0.1	10	...	...	...	715	11
1844	0.4	18	2.9	0.2	14	...	87	214	793	12
1845	0.5	21	3.2	0.2	16	...	106	122	694	16
1846	0.5	22	3.6	0.3	15	...	...	...	533	12
1847	0.5	25	3.5	0.2	14	8.6	...	...	809	10
1848	0.6	22	5.8	0.3	16	8.9	...	...	647	18
1849	0.7	23	5.7	0.4	15	9.4	...	...	503	12
1850	0.6	33	4.3	1.0	16	11	...	...	602	13
1851	0.6	33	5.1	0.9	14	7.3	...	...	648	13
1852	0.5	34	4.9	1.4	18	14	...	...	717	13
1853	0.8	35	4.9	3.6	16	13	...	...	703	15
1854	0.4	48	4.7	2.8	17	15	...	...	763	16
1855	0.6	48	5.6	2.3	19	19	288	934	826	15
1856	1.5	54	7.0	1.6	26	21	326	1,460	...	...
1857	1.7	44	6.7	1.2	23	22	434	3,092	...	...
1858	1.3	50	5.5	1.9	28	22	430	1,567	...	...
1859	1.3	60	6.4	3.4	16	21	469	1,580	934	19

E3 SOUTH AMERICA: Major Commodity Exports by Main Exporting Countries (in currency units stated)

| | Argentina | | | | | | Bolivia |
| | (million gold pesos) | | | | | | (million gold bolivianas) |
	Hides & Skins	Linseed	Maize	Meat	Wheat	Wool	Tin[9]
1860	...	...	...	...	...	...	...
1861	...	...	...	...	...	...	...
1862	...	...	...	...	...	...	...
1863	...	...	...	...	...	...	
1864	6.0	...	...	1.2	...	9.5	...
1865	6.1	...	...	1.1	...	12	...
1866	6.6	...	...	1.3	...	12	...
1867	...	...	...	...	...	...	
1868	...	...	...	...	...	...	
1869	...	...	...	...	...	...	
1870	...	...	...	...	...	...	
1871	...	...	...	...	...	...	
1872	...	...	...	...	...	...	
1873	...	...	...	...	...	...	
1874	...	...	...	...	...	...	
1875	19	...	- -	...	- -	21	
1876	14	...	0.1	...	- -	20	
1877	13	...	0.2	...	0.1	19	...
1878	12	- -	0.3	...	1.3	15	...
1879	14	- -	0.5	...	- -	22	
1880	19	0.1	0.3	2.8	- -	27	...
1881	15	0.6	0.5	3.8	0.1	30	...
1882	14	1.6	2.1	2.7	2.4	29	...
1883	16	1.2	0.4	2.7	4.3	30	...
1884	18	1.7	2.3	2.0	4.3	32	...
1885	21	3.5	4.0	4.3	3.1	36	...
1886	18	1.8	4.7	3.7	1.5	37	...
1887	19	4.1	7.2	3.4	9.5	33	...
1888	20	2.1	5.4	4.9	8.2	45	...
1889	25	1.6	13	7.5	1.6	57	...
1890	18	1.2	14	5.5	9.8	36	...
1891	16	0.6	1.5	5.4	16	39	...
1892	20	2.5	8.6	6.1	15	44	...
1893	13	2.9	1.6	6.1	23	25	...
1894	16	3.6	1.0	6.4	27	29	...
1895	19	8.3	10	5.9	19	31	...
1896	15	6.9	16	5.0	13	34	...
1897	17	4.9	5.5	4.7	3.5	37	...
1898	18	5.4	9.3	4.7	22	46	...
1899	23	7.4	13	4.7	38	71	...
1900	21	11	12	9.0	49	28	8.6
1901	21	17	19	12	26	45	9.4
1902	24	18	23	16	19	46	8.8
1903	23	21	33	16	41	50	12
1904	22	28	44	18	67	48	...

E3 SOUTH AMERICA: Major Commodity Exports by Main Exporting Countries (in currency units stated)

| | Brazil[21] | | | | | Chile (million gold pesos of 18 pence) | | Colombia (thousand gold pesos) | |
| | (million paper milreis) | | | | | | | | |
	Cocoa	Coffee	Cotton	Rubber	Sugar	Copper[9]	Nitrate of Soda	Coffee	Tobacco
1860	1.5	80	4.7	2.9	11	30	—	...	...
1861	1.3	59	7.8	2.4	23	30	—	...	...
1862	1.4	57	17	3.3	19	33	—	...	...
1863	1.1	54	30	3.7	20	28	—	...	...
1864	1.2	64	32	3.6	16	38	—	...	...
1865	1.2	61	47	4.6	19	36	—	99	2,458
1866	1.4	70	33	5.8	13	29	—	796	3,003
1867	1.6	84	32	7.6	22	38	—	610	2,810
1868	1.4	91	35	7.8	13	37	—	694	2,696
1869	2.1	77	44	7.1	29	46	—	608	3,008
1870	1.6	85	24	10	18	39	—	1,164	2,360
1871	1.9	72	46	10	28	35	—	974	1,486
1872	1.5	115	27	10	28	43	—	1,264	1,516
1873	1.4	110	24	11	18	37	—	1,931	2,037
1874	2.4	126	20	10	23	42	—	956	2,361
1875	2.7	118	11	10	14	42	—	732	2,728
1876	3.4	112	12	11	30	46	—	1,168	2,130
1877	2.8	110	6.9	12	21	38	—	753	1,375
1878	3.1	134	9.9	11	22	43	—	1,504	564
1879	3.2	126	5.2	12	31	41	—	...	908
1880	3.7	126	5.1	12	26	35	27	...	...
1881	4.2	105	9.7	12	36	35	43	...	...
1882	4.4	123	12	14	23	40	59	...	...
1883	4.0	130	13	9.5	39	35	70	...	...
1884	4.5	152	11	11	23	39	67	...	...
1885	3.1	125	6.5	11	14	35	39	...	...
1886	4.1	187	15	13	16	33	41	...	...
1887	[1.4][21]	[74][21]	[6.7][21]	[12][21]	[11][21]	26	65	...	...
1888	3.8	103	9.3	38	20	30	71	...	...
1889	3.5	172	7.0	25	14	22	73	...	...
1890	2.6	190	6.8	27	17	23	81	...	...
1891	5.9	284	18	43	43	18	70	...	...
1892	5.5	441	11	60	49	19	63	...	...
1893	9.8	452	40	71	41	20	82	...	...
1894	8.1	500	29	85	49	20	94	...	...
1895	7.8	543	12	123	45	20	101	...	...
1896	7.0	524	9.5	101	45	21	92	...	...
1897	11	526	19	135	39	19	82	...	...
1898	19	466	11	179	49	23	87	...	...
1899	19	471	4.8	200	21	23	95	...	...
1900	19	484	29	167	...	24	108	...	...
1901	18	510	9.3	183	32	27	109	...	...
1902	21	410	24	148	19	24	125	...	...
1903	20	384	26	196	4.0	21	140	...	...
1904	22	392	16	221	1.8	23	162	...	...

E2   SOUTH AMERICA: Major Commodity Exports by Main Exporting Countries (in currency units stated)

	Ecuador (million sucres)		Guyana[22] (thousand pounds)	Peru (thousand pounds sterling)							Venezuela (million bolivares)
	Cocoa	Coffee	Sugar	Copper[9]	Cotton	Rubber	Petroleum & Products	Silver	Sugar	Wool	Coffee
1860	...	...	1,088	...	...	...	...	...	...	...	...
1861	...	...	1,124	...	...	...	...	...	...	...	...
1862	...	...	975	...	...	...	...	...	...	...	...
1863	...	...	1,230	...	...	...	...	...	...	...	17
1864	...	...	1,330	...	...	...	...	...	...	...	17
1865	...	...	1,595	...	...	...	...	...	...	...	
1866	...	...	1,698	...	...	...	...	...	...	...	19
1867	...	...	1,781	...	...	...	...	...	...	...	...
1868	...	...	1,649	...	...	...	...	...	...	...	17
1869	...	...	1,549	...	...	...	...	...	...	...	20
1870	...	...	1,811	...	...	...	...	...	...	...	...
1871	...	...	2,191	...	...	...	...	...	...	...	
1872	...	...	1,958	...	...	...	...	...	...	...	43
1873	...	...	1,627	...	...	...	...	...	...	...	47
1874	...	...	1,980	...	...	...	...	...	...	...	59
1875	...	...	1,668	...	...	...	...	...	...	...	57
1876	...	...	2,408	...	...	...	...	...	...	...	37
1877	...	...	2,412	...	...	...	...	...	...	...	55
1878	...	...	1,786	...	...	...	...	...	...	...	38
1879	...	...	2,137	...	...	...	...	...	...	...	...
1880	...	...	2,126	...	104	21	...	481	1,160	165	30
1881	...	...	2,049	...	84	24	...	397	928	217	39
1882	...	...	2,605	...	92	41	...	397	883	266	50
1883	...	...	2,606	...	78	50	...	456	644	178	41
1884	...	...	1,823	...	62	137	...	479	446	661	38
1885	...	...	1,388	...	79	177	...	481	613	304	36
1886	...	...	1,460	...	119	226	...	515	505	265	49
1887	...	...	1,803	...	89	180	...	521	418	328	60
1888	...	...	1,612	...	133	406	...	486	518	276	70
1889	...	...	1,921	...	131	202	...	524	827	345	71
1890	...	...	1,442	10	161	232	...	584	499	267	90
1891	...	...	1,668[22]	17	143	380	...	521	510	313	...
1892	...	...	1,576	16	265	365	...	517	636	279	67
1893	...	...	1,571	24	238	224	...	507	621	332	85
1894	...	...	1,250	21	109	262	...	421	381	304	68
1895	...	...	1,046	23	123	231	...	431	577	242	86
1896	...	...	1,098	41	131	273	...	537	758	269	66
1897	...	...	1,030	58	141	581	...	415	958	288	62
1898	...	...	1,060	186	143	583	...	642	986	230	64
1899	...	...	1,103	448	134	549	...	792	1,069	273	31
1900	11	0.8	1,154	713	256	497	0.2	859	1,240	290	...
1901	12	0.6	1,060	751	244	402	0.2	780	1,041	304	...
1902	13	0.9	1,071	470	209	380	3.3	648	836	294	...
1903	12	0.7	1,155	542	296	528	21	679	1,066	367	...
1904	15	1.0	1,324	551	319	687	18	737	1,329	330	...

E3 SOUTH AMERICA: Major Commodity Exports by Main Exporting Countries (in currency units stated)

	Uruguay[30] (million gold pesos)			Venezuela (million bolivares)		Uruguay[30] (million gold pesos)			Venezuela (million bolivars)	
	Hides & Skins	Meat	Wool	Coffee[33]		Hides & Skins	Meat	Wool	Coffee[33]	Petroleum & Products
1860	...	...	...	19	1905	8.0	4.8	11	31	...
1861	...	...	...	...	1906	8.4	5.2	13	37	0.6
1862	...	...	...	...	1907	7.8	5.1	14	38	1.0
1863	...	...	...	...	1908	9.5	5.0	17	35[33]	0.4
1864	...	...	...	17	1909	11	5.4	19	40	0.7
1865	...	...	...	17	1910	11	5.8	15	42	0.9
1866	...	...	...	...	1911	9.4	5.3	19	42	1.4
1867	...	...	...	19	1912	8.6	4.6[4] 6.7	26	79	1.6
1868	...	...	...	...	1913	7.4[30] 13	7.2[30] 15	20[30] 31	84	3.0
1869	...	...	...	17	1914	9.4	15	20	64	1.5
1870	...	...	...	20	1915	17	31	20	61	1.7
1871	...	...	...	...	1916	18	27	23	55	1.4
1872	...	...	...	...	1917	23	35	38	43	2.1
1873	...	...	...	43	1918	27	43	35	39	2.7
1874	...	...	...	47	1919	26	47	65	151	2.6
1875	...	...	...	59	1920	15	26	32	66	2.0
1876	...	...	...	57	1921	11	22	32	64	9.6
1877	...	...	...	37	1922	17	32	21	70	14
1878	...	...	...	55	1923	19	45	28	69	27
1879	5.7	2.8	3.6	38	1924	15	37	37	100	63
1880	6.9	4.6	4.1	...	1925	15	39[10] 41	29	126	136
1881	7.9	4.0	4.0	30	1926	11	41	28	99	245
1882	6.9	5.0	5.2	39	1927	12	27	33	104	279
1883	7.2	4.6	8.0	50	1928	14	28	31	84	465
1884	7.4	5.7	6.7	41	1929	12	31	29	133	593
1885	7.7	3.6	7.3	38	1930	11	41	26	68	634
1886	7.4	5.9	5.7	36	1931	10	30	20	65	547
1887	5.6	3.8	5.0	49	1932	7.2	19	19	58	532
1888	7.5	6.1	7.6	60	1933	8.4	19	25	34	553
1889	7.1	4.9	9.1	70	1934	8.4	22	18	33	608
1890	9.2	5.5	7.9	71	1935	11	23	38	31	649
1891	12	...	8.2	90	1936	9.2	16	42	40	684
1892	7.9	5.9	7.4	67	1937	12	19	45	38	770
1893	8.5	6.5	7.7	...	1938	10	22	42	26	828
						(million US dollars)				
1894	8.0	8.0	9.1	85	1939	11	15	40	21	895
1895	7.3	7.0	10	68	1940	10	14	54	19	809
1896	6.7	7.7	10	86	1941	14	15	48	24	1,001
1897	6.6	5.5	12	66	1942	15	15	32	37	636
1898	6.3	7.0	11	62	1943	18	13	70	34	786
1899	7.7	8.8	14	64	1944	10	30	41	24	1,057
1900	7.9	7.7	8.0	34	1945	10	31	57	35	1,025
1901	8.2	6.4	8.7	31	1946	22	40	52	64	1,325
1902	10	6.1	10	30	1947	20	25	71	57	2,355
1903	10	7.8	12	21	1948	22	45	66	71	3,597
1904	10	7.7	13	37	1949	28	40	67	52	3,434

E3 SOUTH AMERICA: Major Commodity Exports by Main Exporting Countries (in currency units stated)

	Argentina						Bolivia
	(million gold pesos)						(million gold bolivianos)
	Hides & Skins	Linseed	Maize	Meat	Wheat	Wool	Tin[9]
1905	29	26	46	25	86	64	...
1906	28	26	53	21	67	58	...
1907	25	36	30	21	83	59	30
1908	22	49	42	25	129	47	30
1909	38	44	58	28	106	60	31
1910	39	45	60	48	72	59	37
1911	42	34	2.8	60	81	50	53
1912	50	34	109	64	98	58	60
1913	44	50	112	75	103	45	68
1914	35	43	78	88	37	47	42
1915	50	46	94	96	133	56	45
1916	63	38	74	127	97	64	43
1917	65	13	39	133	61	101	85
1918	52	37	17	249	168	101	130
1919	81	111	77	...	202	130	100
1920	42	116	166	130	342	69	112
1921	34	108	112	118	129	50	43
1922	58	81	99	75	198	46	68
1923	64	90	105	120	181	59	81
1924	85	121	178	159	210	70	84
1925	75	87	116	168	192	69	80
1926	66	112	127	143	118	69	83
1927	84	119	226	137	200	76	98
1928	77	131	228	134	251	75	90
1929	47	120	168	134	278	64	103
1930	42	88	107	131	92	41	75
1931	34	90	169	119	92	34	48
	(million current paper pesos)						
1932	61	187	321	193	226	66	37
1933	81	143	197	192	216	82	56
1934	82	171	302	201	295	105	100
1935	98	216	322	250	274	91	116
1936	116	211	445	268	170	125	66
1937	153	275	599	312	476	136	82
1938	101	181	181	318	183	123	65
1939	114	170	203	332	275	163	84
1940	114	119	85	307	284	195	132
1941	148	67	22	387	157	239	160
1942	170	56	9.4	557	159	187	164
1943	181	157	15	594	163	167	205
1944	194	70	43	732	251	147	198
1945	173	30	59	480	331	271	200
1946	341	8.2	389	593	303	357	200
1947	358	—	674	767	1,039	326	214
1948	420	100	829	662	1,377	413	298
1949	482	98	247	749	839	349	268

E3 SOUTH AMERICA: Major Commodity Exports by Main Exporting Countries (in currency units stated)

| | Brazil[21] | | | | | | Chile (million gold pesos of 18 pence) | | Colombia (million pesos) | | |
	(million paper milreis/cruzeiros)										
								Nitrate of			
	Cocoa	Coffee	Cotton	Iron Ore	Rubber	Sugar	Copper[9]	Soda	Coffee	Tobacco	Petroleum
1905	16	325	17	- -	226	6.4	23	182	4.8	0.4	—
1906	21	418	25	—	210	9.2	27	212	6.1	0.7	—
1907	32	454	28	—	218	2.1	28	207	5.3	0.5	—
1908	32	368	3.3	- -	188	4.9	27	224	5.5	0.4	—
1909	26	534	9.4	- -	302	11	26	212	6.3	0.4	—
1910	21	385	13	- -	377	11	24	232	5.5	0.4	—
1911	25	607	15	—	226	6.1	21	262	9.5	0.3	—
1912	23	698	16	- -	241	0.8	34	287	17	0.5	—
							(million gold pesos of 6 pence)				
1913	24	612	35	- -	156	1.0	93	945	18	0.9	—
1914	31	440	28	—	114	6.8	96	637	16	0.4	—
1915	56	620	5.5	- -	136	14	136	698	16	0.3	—
1916	50	589	2.4	—	152	26	261	1,016	16	0.4	—
1917	48	440	15	—	144	73	369	1,465	13	0.6	—
1918	40	353	9.7	—	74	101	326	1,597	21	1.0	—
1919	93	1,226	37	- -	106	58	148	351	54	2.8	—
1920	64	861	81	- -	58	106	296	1,582	36	...	—
1921	48	1,019	46	—	36	94	128	823	42	...	—
1922	68	1,504	104	—	49	115	288	514	36	0.2	—
1923	93	2,124	119	- -	81	142	408	930	45	0.2	—
1924	98	2,929	39	—	79	30	422	967	69	0.4	—
1925	100	2,900	124	—	192	2.3	403	1,032	67	...	—
1926	104	2,348	41	—	115	8.7	402	710	86	...	9.4
1927	187	2,576	42	—	115	26	459	860	71	...	22
1928	149	2,840	36	—	59	21	621	935	88	...	26
1929	105	2,740	154	—	61	9.0	953	966	77	...	27
1930	92[21]	1,828[21]	85[21]	- -[21]	34[21]	25[21]	460	593	62	...	26
1931	98	2,347	54	- -	26	4.6	308	359	55	...	16
1932	114	1,824	1.8	0.1	11	19	121	44	43	...	16
1933	106	2,053	33	0.4	22	13	127	85	49	...	9.9
1934	130	2,115	456	0.6	34	14	157	151	82	...	28
1935	163	2,157	648	1.4	36	46	179	147	79	...	29
1936	258	2,231	930	4.6	68	44	214	144	92	...	28
1937	229	2,159	944	7.9	76	0.3	506	168	99	...	35
1938	213	2,296	930	20	47	2.9	329	142	89	...	37
1939	225	2,234	1,159	19	57	23	332	127	87	...	32
1940	192	1,589	838	16	77	39	382	141	74	...	40
1941	315	2,017	1,010	30	91	9.7	488	124	83	...	41
1942	217	1,966	644	23	148	47	575	120	145	...	14
1943	342	2,803	414	25	189	17	525	127	176	...	20
1944	308	3,879	668	19	366	114	528	129	165	...	37
1945	229	4,260	1,049	27	346	54	524	187	182	...	39
1946	651	6,441	2,938	5.8	268	72	537	232	270	...	42
1947	1,048	7,755	3,076	14	204	221	842	168	342	...	65
1948	1,066	9,019	3,385	61	47	692	953	260	394	...	79
1949	964	11,611	2,007	103	28	78	754	311	472	...	113

E3 SOUTH AMERICA: Major Commodity Exports by Main Exporting Countries (in currency units stated)

	Ecuador				Guyana[22]		Paraguay				
	(million sucres)				(thousand pounds)		(thousand gold pesos)				
	Bananas[23]	Cocoa	Coffee	Petroleum & Products	Bauxite[16]	Sugar	Cotton	Hides & Skins	Meat	Quebracho Extract	Wood
1905	...	11	0.8	—	...	1,255	...	...	...	...	...
1906	...	12	0.9	—	...	1,097	...	...	...	...	...
1907	...	13	0.4	—	...	1,004[22]	...	...	...	...	...
1908	...	18	1.0	—	...	1,258	...	...	...	...	...
1909	...	15	1.0	—	...	1,205	...	1,167	...	652	998
1910	...	16	1.5	—	...	1,040	...	1,170	8	692	1,028
1911	...	16	2.3	—	...	1,381[22]	...	1,012	10	487	1,022
1912	...	16	1.6	—	...	1,019	...	1,114	4	438	773
1913	...	21	1.7	—	...	1,103	...	1,196	48	703	764
1914	...	21	1.2	—	...	1,575	...	1,034	119	763	496
1915	...	20	1.0	—	...	2,059	...	1,118	124	1,098	...
1916	...	26	1.3	—	...	2,100	...	719	- -	1,268	...
1917	...	22	1.3	—	...	2,500	...	1,639	6	3,737	...
1918	...	17	1.7	—	...	2,067	...	...	...	...	...
1919	...	29	1.3	—	...	2,476	...	2,935	[2,580][24]	4,946	...
1920	...	36	0.9	—	28	4,193	...	1,348	[529][24]	3,609	1,342
1921	...	20	3.2	—	12	2,104	...	660	170	2,495	1,720
1922	...	13	3.6	- -	—	1,453	...	1,257	...	3,024	1,394
1923	...	19	5.4	—	110	2,133	...	2,072	390	2,328	2,304
1924	...	30	9.3	—	163	1,767	[452][25]	[1,327]	[401][25]	[1,901][25]	[814][25]
1925	0.7	34	7.6	0.4	185	1,414	[418][25]	[1,554][25]	[3,015][25]	[3,880][25]	[1,349][25]
1926	1.1	26	12	2.3	192	1,260	437	1,578	2,791	4,144	2,003
1927	1.5	37	9.6	5.3	168	1,831	532	1,521	2,747	3,675	1,832
1928	1.7	30	17	12	175	1,693	645	1,812	3,645	3,817	1,621
1929	1.3	21	12	15	190	1,238	747	1,082	2,499	2,765	1,643
1930	1.2	23	7.6	16	125	1,229	934	1,281	3,533	3,223	1,300
1931	0.7	12	5.9	16	130	1,110	721	1,264	2,912	2,735	1,188
1932	0.4	11	8.0	14	104	1,342	754	1,026	3,037	3,325	586
1933	0.5	8.7	5.6	11	55	1,197	711	1,228	1,626	2,894	368
1934	2.5	27	21	13	66	1,160	2,686	1,862	1,732	2,405	438
1935	3.6	24	15	15	138	1,443	3,229	1,402	730	2,477	451
1936	6.7	31	20	13	215	1,428	2,277	1,202	1,001	2,181	371
1937	5.7[23]	50	25	22	358	1,585	4,435	1,122	1,016	2,305	428
1938	7.6	39	17	26	421	1,578	3,193	1,424	1,487	2,210	317
1939	7	37	15	25	602	1,695	901	1,653	4,215	3,321	469
1940	6.4	29	16	25	838	1,485	...	1,208	1,633	2,511	1,122
1941	4.7	34	24	13	1,456	1,720	1,583	2,049	4,065	2,907	800
1942	3.1	40	17	25	1,503	1,518	1,939	2,561	3,795	3,205	904
	——— (million US dollars) ———										
1943	0.2	3.7	2.4	24	2,271	1,566	4,224	4,322	10,677	6,371	2,566
1944	0.1	3	2.5	30	1,127	2,284	5,190	5,787	11,799	5,474	5,158
								——— (million guaranies) ———			
1945	0.2	3.9	2.5	28	763	2,018	11	7.3	17	11	11
1946	0.6	5.6	2.6	18	1,263	2,571	13	9.2	3.6	12	11
1947	1.7	15	3.8	16	1,402	3,974	10	11	9.4	8.6	8.6
1948	9.1	13	7.1	26	1,982	3,428	13	13	14	16	17
1949	14[23]	8.8	5.4	17	2,502	4,386	15	21	9.1	21	24

International Historical Statistics: The Americas 1750–1993

E3 SOUTH AMERICA: Major Commodity Exports by Main Exporting Countries (in currency units stated)

	Peru								
	(thousand pounds sterling)								
	Copper[9]	Cotton	Lead	Rubber	Petroleum & Products	Silver	Sugar[26]	Wool[27]	Zinc[9]
1905	835	312	...	853	12	242	1,450	441	...
1906	1,157	399	...	910	27	523	1,142	488	...
1907	1,769	519	...	1,050	49	502	1,004	412	...
1908	1,170	588	...	670	90	510	1,196	299	...
1909	1,160	865	...	885	152	447	1,262	379	...
1910	1,537	724	...	1,200	117	925	1,327	506	...
	(million soles)								
1911	16	10	...	6.1	4.0	0.7	15	4.1	...
1912	23	10	...	13	7.6	2.2	14	3.9	...
1913	20	14	0.2	8.2	9.1	1.0	14	5.2	...
1914	17	14	0.1	4.4	8.9	1.6	26	5.1	...
1915	34	13	- -	6.0	11	3.0	30	6.0	...
1916	59	17	0.6	7.0	14	0.3	40	9.4	...
1917	63	29	0.4	6.0	12	0.6	41	17	...
1918	59	38	—	3.2	14	0.7	42	27	...
1919	48	69	—	4.7	23	1.0	83	16	...
1920	35	112	0.2	2.0	14	1.2	156	6.8	...
1921	36	36	0.2	0.1	29	0.2	47	3.0	...
1922	35	44	0.1	1.1	45	0.1	42	5.3	...
1923	43	61	0.2	1.6	47	0.2	63	6.5	...
1924	36	66	0.2	1.6	60	1.8	50	10	...
1925	42	63	0.1	2.2	56	1.2	22	7.4	0.2
1926	42	46	0.2	2.8	74	0.9	36	5.2	2.5
1927	49	68	0.2	1.8	102	- -	46	8.4	4.0
1928	55	59	11	1.4	113	- -	36	11	4.4
1929	66	52	15	1.2	129	- -	34	11	4.7
1930	45	42	11	0.7	70	- -	26	7.1	4.7
1931	39	31	0.3	0.7	53	—	28	6.2	—
1932	14	34	0.6	0.2	77	—	26	5.1	—
1933	23	61	0.8	0.3	95	0.8	34	10	—
1934	28	82	1.2	0.4	121	1.8	26	8.7	—
1935	45	81	7.4	0.4	117	1.2	26	7.6	1.0
1936	43	92	11	0.3	119	0.1	25	13	2.3
1937	51	89	17	0.5	121	0.1	32	16	3.5
1938	58	61	17	0.4	116	- -	25	11	1.2
1939	71	75	12	0.3	111	5.4	41	14	1.2
1940	82	71	11	0.3	101	8.4	44	20	1.3
1941	75	125	16	2.4	112	9.8	60	21	2.1
1942	81	53	11	1.2	115	6.4	113	11	2.4
1943	72	69	17	2.8	104	0.9	75	15	11
1944	62	60	45	4.1	92	0.7	168	18	12
1945	60	141	34	9.2	84	5.0	216	18	15
1946	78	328	34	9.4	91	3.8	291	19	21
1947	64	225	63	8.8	117	39	302	11	35
1948	46	276	103	1.7	188	24	228	13	42
1949	133[4]	631	198	0.9	230	86	341	50	98

E3   SOUTH AMERICA: Major Commodity Exports by Main Exporting Countries (in currency units stated)

	Argentina (million current paper pesos)						Bolivia (million US dollars)	
	Hides & Skins	Linseed	Maize	Meat	Wheat	Wool	Natural Gas	Tin[9]
1950	690 662	316	159	593 618	760	876	—	64
1951	526	482	144	1,009	1,003	916	—	93
1952	413	61	338	884	30	720	—	85
1953	387	125	376	1,288	1,218	1,143	—	73
1954	449	207	587	1,357	1,027	761	—	60
			(million US dollars)					
1955	55	29	23	208	246	124	—	57
1956	66	19	63	244	155	125	—	59
1957	60	33	45	256	159	118	—	57
1958	59	39	81	268	126	100	—	36
1959	70	42	124	245	135	122	—	53
1960	70	41	124	220	143	146	—	43
1961	79	50	83	218	66	144	—	51
1962	92	59	121	230	173	147	—	54
1963	78	42	126	332	116	168	—	57
1964	58	41	168	324	242	135	—	81
1965	50	47	154	325	373	117	—	93
1966	83	21	201	393	280	133	—	93
1967	78	35	223	378	122	108	—	91
1968	72	15	140	333	139	111	—	92
1969	97	30	195	435	138	99	—	102
1970	97	—	265	441	126	89	—	108
1971	69	34	348	416	49	73	—	106
1972	120	18	175	691	110	90	10	114
1973	120	24	365	790	273	188	18	131
1974	98	58	659	440	305	107	29	230
1975	71	53	518	288	301	110	42	171
1976	151	55	363	523	431	133	55	216
1977	207	92	518	640	541	228	67	329
1978	270	76	588	795	174	238	78	374
1979	454	88	606	1,226	606	232	105	396
1980	355	127	513	966	816	283	221	378
1981	369	111	1,308	930	763	333	337	343
1982	298	87	585	805	677	230	382	278
1983	264	75	804	603	1,474	186	378	208
1984	305	103	748	404	966	176	376	248
1985	289	82	766	386	1,133	147	373	187
1986	341	53	654	465	395	135	329	104
1987	354	45	299	599	351	141	249	68
1988	368	49	381	607	355	184	215	77
1989	...	76	236	716	658	124	214	84
1990	...	96	329	873	871	159	227	84
1991	...	48	410	892	479	98	234	80
1992	...	45	637	767	716	90	125	204
1993	...	19	525	748	735	99	90	87

E3   SOUTH AMERICA: Major Commodity Exports by Main Exporting Countries (in currency units stated)

	Brazil (million US dollars)						Chile (million gold pesos of 6 pence)		Colombia (million pesos)	
	Cocoa	Coffee	Cotton	Iron Ore	Soybeans	Sugar	Copper[28]	Nitrate of Soda[29]	Coffee	Petroleum
1950	118	866	142	7	...	7	687	343	600	126
1951	95	1,059	255	13	...	30	815[28] 954	329	849	174
1952	56	1,045	43	23	...	15	1,357	280	950	179
1953	91	1,088	108	22	3	22	1,170	265	1,231	192
1954	147	948	227	22	3	12	1,167	328	1,375	191
									(million US dollars)	
1955	103	844	136	30	6	47	1,599	273	487	65
1956	78	1,030	90	35	4	2	1,926	235	474	73
1957	91	845	47	48	2	46	1,446	214	389	81
1958	105	687	26	57	4	57	1,163	203	355	77
1959	85	733	37	43	5	43	1,623	188	361	82
1960	94	713	48	53	—	58	1,644	126	332	88
1961	61	710	113	60	7	66	1,603	176	308	74
1962	41	643	115	68	8	39	1,677	147	332	68
1963	51	748	118	70	7	72	1,695	146	303	82
1964	46	760	111	81	3	33	1,947	134	394	83
1965	41	707	98	103	15	57	2,278	146	344	96
1966	72	764	113	100	28	81	640	24	328	81
1967	84	705	93	103	39	84	707	22	322	75
1968	72	775	134	104	25	106	727	21[29] 16	351	51
1969	136	813	200	147	53	122	831	17	344	77
1970	106	939	159	209	72	134	977	14	467	73
1971	92	773	141	237	108	162	688	19	395	70
1972	99	989	191	232	295	417	631	15	430	64
1973	143	1,244	221	363	949	592	1,007	18	598	61
1974	323	864	94	571	891	1,383	1,898	32	624	114
1975	294	855	100	921	1,304	1,148	980	27	674	103
1976	312	2,173	9.1	994	1,780	349	1,365	31	975	68
1977	605	2,299	43	907	2,143	510	1,052	29	1,527	87
1978	828	1,947	54	1,028	1,515	387	1,246	36	1,991	121
1979	945	1,918	4.2	1,288	1,650	421	2,305	42	2,023	120
1980	697	2,486	17	1,564	2,277	1,374	2,249	37	2,372	102
1981	597	1,517	45	1,748	3,191	1,133	1,737	34	1,462	36
1982	429	1,858	65	1,847	2,122	562	1,489	75	1,580	215
1983	557	2,096	196	1,513	2,563	553	1,382	30	1,541	435
1984	661	2,564	50	1,605	2,566	617	1,324	28	1,802	480
1985	779	2,369	82	1,658	2,540	401	1,529	33	1,792	451
1986	630	2,006	20	1,615	1,640	433	1,544	36	3,061	464
1987	584	1,959	166	1,615	2,325	366	1,904	34	1,702	1,369
1988	412	1,998	100	1,892	3,046	425	2,835	54	1,641	987
1989	333	1,792	162	2,232	1,153	147	3,095	34	1,524	1,045
1990	341	1,282	131	2,406	909	326	3,504	40	1,414	1,540
1991	272	1,507	151	2,599	448	256	2,901	37	1,336	1,138
1992	257	1,135	124	2,381	809	330	3,032	50	1,262	1,149
1993	265	1,306	57	2,257	945	550	2,646	52	1,152	1,058

E3   SOUTH AMERICA: Major Commodity Exports by Main Exporting Countries (in currency units stated)

	Ecuador (million US dollars)				Guyana (million local dollars)		Paraguay (million guaranies)					
	Bananas	Cocoa	Coffee	Petroleum & Products	Bauxite[16]	Sugar	Cotton	Hides & Skins	Meat	Quebracho Extract	Soybeans	Wood
1950	17	18	19	...	14	24	33	18	19	28	...	45
1951	25	18	16	1.5	16	27	37	15	15	18	...	60
1952	44	18	20	1.0	22	42	91	25	8.4	52	...	46
1953	42	15	19	1.6	24	38	196	30	22	80	...	98
									(million US dollars)			
1954	51	35	27	1.5	23	41	6.9	1.7	2.1	4.0	...	11
1955	62	19	23	1.6	25	40	5.5	1.4	2.3	5.6	...	13
1956	61	18	30	1.1	29	42	5.6	2.0	4.6	6.5	...	12
1957	69	18	30	1.4	30	54	4.5	1.6	3.7	4.5	...	9.4
1958	73	21	26	0.7	21	55	3.7	2.0	8.2	3.5	...	9.7
1959	90	22	18	0.3	25	46	2.1	3.6	9.6	3.6	...	4.0
1960	89	22	22	—	29	58	0.3	2.2	7.1	3.0	...	5.0
1961	81	16	14	—	41	57	1.6	2.0	8.6	2.7	...	6.5
1962	88	16	21	0.2	54	59	2.5	1.7	7.5	2.5	...	6.7
1963	63	20	18	0.3	51	74	3.2	1.7	11	2.8	...	4.7
1964	84	15	22	0.7	57	54	4.2	1.5	15	4.0	...	7.1
1965	84	19	38	0.6	68	44	4.7	1.8	19	3.5	...	9.8
1966	89	17	32	1.4	78	49	2.0	3.1	14	3.1	...	11
1967	105	25	40	1.1	77	55	2.3	2.0	17	2.0	...	7.7
1968	105	41	35	1.1	91	59	1.4	1.8	14	2.1	...	8.0
1969	106	26	26	0.6	102	82	3.2	2.0	12	1.9	- -	11
1970	123	25	50	0.9	139	73	3.7	1.7	16	1.9	—	12
1971	124	29	36	1.0	137	92	0.8	1.7	20	2.2	1.0	8.7
1972	128	30	43	60	131	101	3.3	3.8	25	2.3	3.8	6.8
1973	125	35	67	283	137	76	12	2.3	40	2.4	10	8.4
1974	125	126	67	697	200	285	16	3.8	34	0.9	14	20
1975	157	71	64	588	197	418	20	2.3	31	0.6	17	23
1976	146	95	205	739	229	223	34	0.9	20	3.7	32	7.3
1977	168	245	157	713	253	186	80	1.8	21	5.3	56	13
1978	181	259	281	718	250	216	99	1.8	22	5.2	39	12
1979	197	273	205	1,178	330	236	98	0.4	5.5	3.2	79	29
1980	244	210	130	1,565	486	342	104	...	1.1	4.4	42	44
1981	208	135	106	1,342	430	340	127	...	- -	5.6	48	24
1982	213	88	139	1,472	282	212	121	...	2.1	5.0	101	30
1983	153	19	149	1,644	172	185	82	...	5.3	5.4	111	17
1984	133	116	175	1,797	282	272	131	...	4.6	5.6	109	20
1985	220	151	191	1,825	344	242	141	...	1.4	4.0	105	8.3
1986	263	83	297	912	334	327	80	...	34	3.8	43	16
1987	267	139	192	646	713	777	101	...	21	5.3	123	23
1988	298	132	152	875	910	875	87	...	21	4.4	169	13
1989	300	104	149	1,147	1,993	2,311	305	...	96	5.9	382	25
1990	373	125	119	1,408	3,201	3,749	330	...	133	7.4	267	29
1991	471	107	98	1,152	8,865	10,375	315	...	55	6.5	157	36
1992	719	69	54	1,335	...	...	201	...	47	4.7	137	40
1993	676	78	80	1,250	...	...	157	...	46	3.9	224	42

E3 SOUTH AMERICA: Major Commodity Exports by Main Exporting Countries (in currency units stated)

	Peru (million soles)									
	Copper[9]	Cotton	Fish Meal	Lead	Rubber	Petroleum & Products	Silver	Sugar[26]	Wool[27]	Zinc[9]
1950	161	1,015	4	229	2.2	346	82	443	118	157
1951	244	1,291	7	417	7.4	330	89	520[26]	208	236
1952	261	1,224	13	438	8.0	262	114	506	117	244
1953	292	1,101	16	463	8.2	239	110	585	...	133
1954	390[4] 401	1,254	23	575	15	322	156	633	165	181
1955	579	1,294	38	616	13	407	187	700	112	284
1956	693	1,683	67	732	13	446	146	623	152	296
1957	524	1,293	135	683	19	503	162	942	186	304
1958	584	1,765	271	759	22	382	213	793	141	285
1959	691	1,911	860	830	21	436	267	997	248	412
1960	2,683	1,997	1,056	869	19	484	301	1,294	192	491
1961	2,911	2,140	1,329	856	31	384	392	1,713	199	539
1962	2,557	2,605	2,678	744	80	348	524	1,443	238	413
1963	2,424	2,452	2,802	791	9.8	257	532	1,693	313	450
1964	2,843	2,450	3,846	1,223	—	258	777	1,702	310	1,103
1965	3,323	2,345	4,170	1,311	...	242	639	1,000	244	1,022
1966	5,095	2,292	4,870	1,292	...	193	619	1,243	222	959
1967	6,315	1,696	5,322	1,355	...	260	832	1,625	252	1,101
1968	9,467	2,159	7,906	1,999	...	385	1,395	2,412	365	1,167
1969	10,386	2,522	7,753	2,297	...	240	1,032	1,522	330	1,530
					(million US dollars)					
1970	269	53	294	63	...	7.4	29	66	3.3	47
1971	170	45	277	49	...	5.4	22	71	2.4	47
1972	186	47	233	58	...	7.7	32	79	6.1	69
1973	284	62	136	80	...	13	38	88	12	93
1974	345	94	196	123	...	18	60	156	7.1	160
1975	168	60	156	94	...	44	82	296	11	151
1976	234	76	177	112	...	53	90	94	26	191
1977	398	47	179	133	...	52	116	85	18	163
1978	412	38	192	175	...	180	118	46	28	133
1979	674	44	256	293	...	652	234	63	40	171
1980	752	63	192	383	...	777	312	15	30	210
1981	529	60	141	219	...	692	310	0.3	9.5	272
1982	461	75	202	216	...	719	205	18	7.1	255
1983	443	31	79	293	...	544	391	7.1	8.4	307
1984	442	15	137	233	...	618	227	19	5.1	341
1985	464	31	117	202	...	645	139	43	29	269
1986	450	41	206	172	...	232	107	24	24	246
1987	559	19	224	257	...	273	92	15	19	250
1988	607	23	364	203	...	166	60	22	36	261
1989	344	69	373	38	...	196	95	21	12	176
1990	684	44	365	48	...	325	59	41	13	130
1991	697	55	445	33	...	170	79	33	10	150
1992	689	18	319	37	...	200	75	18	13	145
1993	650	5	560	30	...	199	73	14	16	130

E3 SOUTH AMERICA: Major Commodity Exports by Main Exporting Countries
(in currency units stated)

	Uruguay (million US dollars)			Venezuela (million bolívars)	
	Hide & Skins	Meat	Wool[32]	Coffee	Petroleum & Products
1950	29	43	153[32] 160	55	3,356
1951	26	44	117	65	3,798
1952	23	41	90	115	4,208
1953	24	44	165	158	4,398
1954	19	45	124	111	4,797
1955	15	7.2	105	124	5,491
1956	16	22	126	103	6,349
1957	11	27	64	115	7,865
1958	9.0	15	80	211	7,099
1959	10	19	54	82	6,654
1960	16	31	67	73	6,642
1961	17	27	110	76	6,809
1962	17	31	82	63	7,221
1963	18	33	85	78	7,218
1964	17	74	67	68	10,138
1965	16	61	90	62	10,144
1966	18	45	84	63	9,746
1967	14	40	83	31	10,267
1968	16	60	78	64	10,370
1969	24	58	67	64	10,141
1970	24	82	73	57	10,550
1971	21	65	65	66	12,814
1972	23	99	54	67	12,571
1973	26	121	97	57	18,632
1974	24	137	87	71	45,200
1975	17	83	87	82	35,668
1976	32	117	101	118	37,593
1977	28	110	121	121	39,106
1978	30	96	132	181	37,517
1979	47	105	101	106	58,519
1980	40	182	212	34	78,328
1981	51	255	236	14	81,723
1982	73	201	205	15	67,068
1983	69	247	169	14	59,473
1984	92	146	163	152	85,226
1985	61	118	164	578	77,639
1986	75	199	198	451	53,781
1987	84	129	241	326	100,909
1988	105	152	349	515	118,345
1989	179	241	300	1,022	344,003
1990	103	296	317	1,235	681,112
1991	58	212	256	781	689,551
1992	73	225	70	791	767,683
1993	85	199	61	3,170	1,063,610

E3 Major Commodity Exports by Main Exporting Countries

NOTES

1. SOURCES: The main sources used have been the same as for table E1. The Canadian non-ferrous metals series to 1915 is from K.W. Taylor, *Statistical Contributions to Canadian Economic History* (Toronto, 1931). The Colombian statistics to 1924 are from Miguel Urrutia and Mario Arrubla (eds.), *op. cit.* in Note 1 to table E1. The Peruvian statistics to 1910 are from Rosemary Thorp and Geoffrey Bertram, *Peru, 1890–1977* (London, 1978).
2. Statistics refer to domestic exports and are recorded f.o.b. (except as noted in footnote 19)

FOOTNOTES

[1] Years ending 30 September to 1842 and 30 June from 1844 to 1915. The 1843 figures are for the period 1 October 1842 to 30 June 1843.
[2] Years ending 30 September to 1889, and years beginning 1 April from 1890 to 1908.
[3] Tobago is included from 1889. Data are for years beginning 1 April from that year to 1908.
[4] This break is caused by a change in classification.
[5] Years ending 30 June to 1906 and 31 March from 1908 to 1936 (1st line), except for the non-ferrous metals series, which is for calendar years from 1927. The 1907 figures are for the period 1 July 1906 to 31 March 1907. Newfoundland became part of Canada on 1 April 1949.
[6] Data to 1882 are believed to be for years ending 30 April.
[7] Silver pesos to 1889 (1st line), gold pesos (later called quetzales and equal to the US dollar) subsequently.
[8] Years beginning 1 July to 1912. The 1913 figures are for the second half-year only.
[9] Including ores.
[10] Including coke to 1946.
[11] Excluding exports from ports in the control of the Confederacy.
[12] Meat products are included to 1881. Prior to 1855, there is a series available in the *Reports on Commerce* of meat, fats, hides, and live animals in the aggregate.
[13] Including flour from 1870 (2nd line).
[14] Including manufactured wood other than wood pulp from 1908 (2nd line).
[15] Years ending 31 July to 1937 and 30 June from 1939 to 1951. The 1938 figures are for the period 1 August 1937 to 30 June 1938. Bananas are known to be undervalued to 1948 (1st line).
[16] Including alumina
[17] Excluding Aruba from 1986.
[18] The old gold cordoba was equal to the US dollar.
[19] Bananas are valued c.i.f. from 1955.
[20] Including a small amount of non-ferrous metal articles in 1952–56.
[21] 'General' trade to 1930. Data are for years beginning 1 July from 1833 to 1886. The 1887 figures are for the second half-year only. The figures for the first half-year of 1833 are as follows (in million milreis): cocoa-0.1, coffee-8.9, cotton-5.2, rubber-0.1, sugar-5.3.
[22] All fruit to 1937, bananas being by far the most important. Values are known to be understated to 1949.
[23] Years beginning 1 April from 1892 to 1911. Trans-shipments are included to 1907.
[24] Canned meat only.
[25] Official (i.e. fixed) values.
[26] Including preparations of sugar to 1951.
[27] Including other animal hair.
[28] Copper wire and sheets are included from 1951 (2nd line).
[29] Natural sodium nitrate from 1968 (2nd line).
[30] Official (i.e. fixed) values to 1913 (1st line).
[31] Subsequently excluding wild animal skins.
[32] Including other animal hair from 1950 (2nd line).
[33] Fiscal years to 1908.

F. TRANSPORT AND COMMUNICATIONS

Government has generally been involved more intimately in the provision of means of transport and communication than in agriculture or industry, at any rate until very recently. As a consequence, there is usually more statistical material available from the past than on most other economic activities. Shipping was a matter of close concern to all major maritime powers, though there were few of those in the Americas until quite recently. The railways were frequently of military as well as economic importance, and they necessitated the investment of large lumps of capital, on which the social return seems generally to have exceeded by a considerable margin that which could be captured by investors. Outside the United States, it was fairly unusual for private promoters to attract this capital without some assistance from governments. Some form of reporting to governments, therefore, was required of most railways. Postal services were long recognized as a government function, and telegraphs fell naturally into the same niche in most countries other than the USA, where they were not simply an adjunct of the railways, and telephones generally followed. And outside North America and certain Central American countries influenced by the United States, the potential influence of radio led to its direct control by governments and to some form of licensing system, which produced a statistical by-product. Taxation of motor vehicles had a similar effect.

Table 1, showing the length of railway line open in each country, is fairly straightforward, though there is a variety of different figures for some countries purporting to cover the same thing. The diversity usually arises from different treatment of industrial lines, some of which did, at times, take public traffic and convey paying passengers. For other countries there is a paucity of published figures, and in these cases an effort has been made to build up a series from such benchmark statistics as are available coupled with information about the opening of particular stretches of line culled from a variety of sources—mainly national statistical annuals, but also British and American Consular Reports, and the reports and accounts of individual railway companies.

The principal problems in using the merchant marine statistics of table 4 arise from changes in the size of ships covered and from changes in the method measuring capacity. In most countries, there has been a lower limit of size below which vessels are not included in the register; but this has changed from time to time, and differed between countries. So far as aggregate capacity, especially of mechanically-propelled vessels, is concerned, this limit, and the changes in it, have made little impact, though the numbers, especially of sailing ships, have sometimes changed violently. These are usually apparent in the series, and it is hoped that all are indicated in footnotes. Changes in methods of measuring capacity are a more difficult problem, though the two basic methods—gross and net, representing the inclusion and exclusion respectively of space which cannot be used for carrying cargo—are readily distinguished. Where possible, the tonnage data are given in gross register tons, which is the measure most commonly used since World War II. However, some earlier statistics are only available in net tons and there are unavoidable breaks in continuity in this table.

Tables 5, 6 and 7 are reasonably straightforward and call for little elaboration. The main problem has been the lack of availability for many countries of statistics of the vehicle park during the years of World War II. In many cases these statistics probably were collected, but national statistical abstracts tended not to publish them at that period, and international sources have tended to ignore the war years.

Apart from some early statistics on civil air traffic from national sources, the main reliance in table F7 has been on the publications of the International Civil Aviation Organization, which makes for a large measure of consistency. If should be noted that these data apply to airlines based in each of the countries concerned, not to the actual traffic at the countries' airports.

Postal statistics (and even those of telegrams), which one might expect to be reasonably uniform and homogeneous, are amongst the most intractable, as well as being unavailable for the majority of Latin American countries for long periods. The main problems with them lie in the great variety of definitions of various categories of postal material, and in the penchant of most authorities for making changes in those which they use. There are also variations in the amount of double-counting which occurs, and in the treatment of mail and telegrams in transit. Comparisons both between countries and over time have to be made with caution, therefore. The telephone statistics in table 9, on the other hand, are reasonably easy to use, though, like the motor vehicle statistics, and for the same reason, there are many gaps over the years of World War II.

F1 NORTH AMERICA: LENGTH OF RAILWAY LINE OPEN (in kilometres)

1830–1874

	Canada[1]	Costa Rica	Cuba	Jamaica[2]	Mexico[3]	Panama[4]	USA[5]
1830	...	...	—	—	—	—	37
1831	...	...	—	—	—	—	153
1832	...	...	—	—	—	—	369
1833	...	...	—	—	—	—	612
1834	...	...	—	—	—	—	1,019
1835	...	...	—	—	—	—	1,767
1836	25	...	—	—	—	—	2,049
1837	25	...	26	—	—	—	2,410
1838	25	...	82	—	—	—	3,079
1839	25	...	82	—	—	—	3,705
1840	25	...	82	—	—	—	4,535
1841	25	...	82	—	—	—	5,689
1842	25	...	82	—	—	—	6,479
1843	25	...	82	—	—	—	6,735
1844	25	...	82	—	—	—	7,044
1845	25	...	82	23	—	—	7,456
1846	25	...	198	23	—	—	7,934
1847	86	...	198	23	—	—	9,009
1848	86	...	198	23	—	—	9,650
1849	86	...	...	23	—	—	11,853
1850	106	...	440	23	13	—	14,518
1851	255	...	...	23	16	—	17,674
1852	329	...	...	23	16	—	20,773
1853	814	...	...	23	16	—	24,720
1854	1,229	...	...	23	16	—	26,908
1855	1,411	...	...	23	...	76	29,570
1856	2,275	...	...	23	...	76	35,528
1857	2,323	...	...	23	...	76	39,434
1858	2,998	...	...	23	...	76	43,401
1859	3,209	...	...	23	32	76	46,331
1860	3,323	...	682	23	32	76	49,288
1861	3,453	...	...	23	32	76	50,350
1862	3,522	...	...	23	32	76	51,692
1863	3,522	...	...	23	32	76	53,382
1864	3,522	...	...	23	32	76	54,570
1865	3,604	...	...	23	142	76	56,464
1866	3,666	...	...	23	142	76	59,225
1867	3,666	...	...	23	142	76	62,845
1868	3,666	...	...	23	...	76	67,961
1869	4,061	...	...	37	349	76	75,388
1870	4,211	...	...	37	349	76	85,170
1871	4,337	...	...	37	...	76	97,045
1872	4,665	...	...	37	...	76	106,492
1873	5,814	68	...	37	572	76	113,085
1874	6,167	82	...	42	587	76	116,492

F1 NORTH AMERICA: Length of Railway Line Open (in kilometres)

1875–1924

	Alaska	Barbados	Belize[6]	Canada[1]	Costa Rica	Cuba	Dominican Republic	El Salvador	Guatemala	Haiti
1875	...	—	—	6,970	82	...	...	—	—	—
1876	...	—	—	7,731	82	...	...	—	—	—
1877	...	—	—	8,397	82	...	...	—	—	—
1878	...	—	—	9,305	82	...	...	—	—	—
1879	...	—	—	10,019	82	...	...	—	—	—
1880	...	—	—	11,036	117	1,382	...	—	21	—
1881	...	—	—	11,577	154	...	...	—	21	—
1882	...	21	—	11,798	172	...	...	20	48	—
1883	...	37	—	13,996	172	...	...	20	116	—
1884	...	39	—	15,412	172	...	...	46	186	—
1885	...	39	—	16,532	172	1,600	80	46	186	—
1886	...	39	—	17,337	172	...	...	61	186	—
1887	...	39	—	18,978	172	...	...	61	186	—
1888	...	39	—	19,608	178	...	115	61	186	—
1889	...	39	—	20,253	190	...	115	87	186	—
1890	...	39	—	21,164	241	1,731	115	87	186	—
1891	...	39	—	22,270	241	1,778	115	87	186	—
1892	...	39	—	23,438	241	1,778	115	87	186	—
1893	...	39	—	24,148	241	1,778	150	98	186	—
1894	...	39	—	25,149	241	1,778	150	98	186	—
1895	...	39	—	25,712	249	1,778	150	98	282	—
1896	...	39	—	26,184	254	1,778	150	116	457	—
1897	...	39	—	26,634	254	1,778	150	116	480	—
1898	...	39	—	27,149	291	1,825	...	116	480	—
1899	...	39	—	27,761	388	1,825	...	116	480	16
1900	35	39	—	28,475	388	1,960	182	116	640	37
1901	...	45	—	29,193	379	...	182	156	640	45
1902	...	45	—	30,117	408	...	182	156	640	45
1903	...	45	—	30,558	432	2,548	182	156	640	45
1904	...	45	—	31,271	432	2,548	182	156	640	70
1905	98	45	—	32,970	432	2,604	182	156	640	70
1906	129	45	—	34,364	473	2,857	182	156	654	...
1907	235	45	—	36,123	473	2,857	182	156	654	...
1908	298	45	—	36,961	473	...	182	156	700	103
1909	488	45	31	38,791	619	3,150	182	156	700	103
1910	627	45	40	39,799	619	3,229	241	156	724	103
1911	740	45	40	40,877	619	3,527	241	209	781	103
1912	743	45	40	43,194	619	3,609	241	320	808	103
1913	742	45	40	47,160	619	3,803	241	320	987	180
1914	742	45	40	49,559	619	3,846	241	328	987	180
1915	603	45	40	56,137	619	...	241	328	987	180
1916	611	45	47	59,521	619	...	247	328	987	180
1917	613	45	47	61,748	619	...	247	328	987	180
1918	556	45	47	61,560[1]	647	...	247	355	987	180
1919	371	39	47	61,951	647	...	247	375	987	180
1920	397	39	47	62,450	647	4,366	247	375	987	169
1921	400	39	47	63,071	647	4,396	247	375	1,096	177
1922	1,286	39	40	63,340	647	4,488	247	407	1,096	177
1923	1,284	39	40	63,816	647	4,651	247	409	1,096	177
1924	1,284	39	40	64,468	647	4,821	247	409	1,096	168

F1 NORTH AMERICA: Length of Railway Line Open (in kilometres)

	Honduras[7]	Jamaica[2]	Mexico[3]	Newfoundland[8]	Nicaragua	Panama[4]	Puerto Rico	Trinidad	USA[5]
1875	—	42	663	—	—	76	—	…	119,246
1876	—	42	666	—	—	76	—	26	123,610
1877	—	42	672	—	—	76	—	26	127,270
1878	—	42	737	—	—	76	—	26	131,559
1879	—	42	886	—	—	76	—	26	139,298
1880	60	42	1,080	—	—	76	—	55	150,091
1881	60	42	1,771	—	—	76	—	61	165,936
1882	96	42	3,709	—	35	76	—	71	184,555
1883	96	42	5,437	72	53	76	—	71	195,410
1884	96	42	5,891	72	94	76	—	71	201,723
1885	96	103	6,010	145	143	76	18	87	206,511
1886	96	103	6,089	145	143	76	18	87	219,415
1887	96	103	6,609	145	143	76	18	87	240,137
1888	96	103	7,826	180	143	76	18	87	251,241
1889	96	103₂	8,455	180	143	76	18	87	259,549
1890	96	124	9,718	180	143	76	18	87	268,282₅ 263,284
1891	96	142	10,029	180	143	76	18	87	271,018
1892	96	153	10,477	180	143	76	18	87	276,105
1893	96	188	10,642	475	143	76	18	87	283,986
1894	96	209	10,763	641	143	76	18	87	287,604
1895	96	298	10,776	752	146	76	18	87	290,739
1896	96	298	11,087	911	146	76	223	92	294,151
1897	96	298	11,763	953	146	76	223	98	296,808
1898	96	298	12,680	1,027	146	76	223	130	299,975
1899	96	298	12,901	1,027	225	76	223	130	304,641
1900	96	298	13,585	1,056	225	76	223	130	311,160
1901	96	298	14,523	1,056	225	76	223	130	317,422
1902	96	298	15,135	1,061	225	76	223	130	325,847
1903	96	298	16,114	1,059	257	76	250	130	334,707
1904	96	298	16,523	1,072	257	76	250	130	344,245
1905	96	298	16,934	1,072	275	76	322	130	351,000
1906	111	298	17,510	1,059	275	76	322	130	361,077
1907	138	298	18,068	1,056	275	76	322	130	370,070
1908	138	298	18,968	1,056	275	76	322	130	375,730
1909	138	298	19,438	1,091	275	76	354	130	391,147
1910	170	298	19,748	1,098	275	76	354	130	386,714
1911	170	314	19,831	1,239	322	76	354	130	392,646
1912	170	318	20,447	1,239	322	76	354	130	397,149
1913	241	318	…	1,353	322	76	547	158	401,977
1914	241	318	…	1,408	322	76	547	177	405,724
1915	386	318	…	1,429	322	76	547	177	408,434
1916	515	318	…	1,502	322	76	547	177	409,177₅ 408,171
1917	575	318	…	1,502	322	76	547	177	408,171
1918	575	318	…	1,502	322	76	547	177	408,015
1919	575	318	…	1,502	322	76	547	177	407,409
1920	763	318₂	…	…	322	158	547	177	406,915
1921	895	322	…	…	322	158	547	177	404,229
1922	900	322	…	…	322	158	547	177	403,001
1923	1,306	322	20,894	…	322	158	547	177	402,693
1924	1,236	322	20,872	…	322	158	547	187	402,587

International Historical Statistics: The Americas 1750–1993

F1 NORTH AMERICA: Length of Railway Line Open (in kilometres)

1925–1974

	Alaska	Barbados	Belize[6]	Canada[1]	Costa Rica	Cuba	Dominican Republic	El Salvador	Guatemala	Haiti
1925	1,289	39	40	64,937	665	4,893	247	409	1,096	168
1926	1,271	39	40	64,937	665	4,871	247	530	1,102	176
1927	1,276	39	40	65,291	665	4,861	247	550	1,102	176
1928	1,276	39	40	66,018	665	4,903	240	596	1,155	180
1929	1,271	39	40	66,594	665	4,946	240	596	1,159	217
1930	1,271	39	40	66,668	665	4,891	240	604	1,159	217
1931	1,207	39	40	68,043	665	4,891	240	604	1,159	254
1932	1,207	39	40	68,250	665	4,897	240	604	1,159	254
1933	1,178	39	40	68,133	665	4,887	240	608	1,159	254
1934	1,178	39	40	68,026	665	4,876	240	608	1,159	254
1935	1,178	39	40	69,066	665	4,876	240	608	1,159	254
1936	1,178	39	40	68,480	665	4,945	240	608	1,159	254
1937	1,178	—	40	68,762	665	4,961	240	608	1,159	254
1938	1,178	—	31	68,786	665	4,957	240	608	1,159	254
1939	1,178	—	14	68,617	665	4,965	240	608	1,159	254
1940	863	—	14	68,501	665	4,945	270	608	1,159	254
1941	863	—	14	68,302	665	4,972	270	608	1,159	254
1942	863	—	—	68,136	665	4,952	270	618	1,159	254
1943	882	—	—	68,149	665	4,925	270	618	1,159	254
1944	882	—	—	68,133	665	4,940	270	618	1,159	254
1945	882	—	—	68,158	665	4,922	270	618	1,159	254
1946	875	—	—	68,131	665	4,871	270	618	1,159	254
1947	914	—	—	68,110	665	4,866	270	618	1,159	254
1948	912	—	—	67,991₁	665	4,857	270	618	1,159	254
1949	912	—	—	69,166	665	4,854	270	618	1,159	254
1950	912	—	—	69,167	665	4,860	270	618	1,159	254
1951	912	—	—	69,130	665	4,825	270	618	1,159	254
1952	914	—	—	69,126	665	4,825	270	618	1,159	254
1953	914	—	—	69,464	665	4,825	270	618	1,159	254
1954	914	—	—	69,414	665	5,099	270	618	1,159	254
1955	863	—	—	69,916	665	5,099	270	618	1,159	254
1956	909	—	—	70,251	665	5,099	270	618	1,159	254
1957	922	—	—	70,634	665	5,099	270	618	1,159	254
1958	922	—	—	71,012	665	...	270	618	1,159	254
1959	921	—	—	71,147	665	...	270	618	1,159	254
1960	921	—	—	70,858	665	...	270	618	1,159	254
1961	...	—	—	70,311	564	...	270	618	1,159	254
1962	...	—	—	70,254	596	5,099	270	618	1,159	254
1963	...	—	—	70,204	596	5,099	270	618	1,159	254
1964	...	—	—	69,773	596	5,099	270	618	1,159	254
1965	...	—	—	69,454	596	5,099	270	618	1,159	254
1966	...	—	—	69,512	596	5,099	270	618	1,159	121
1967	...	—	—	69,472	596	5,099	270	618	1,159	121
1968	...	—	—	69,472	596	5,227	270	618	1,159	121
1969	...	—	—	70,188	617	5,227	270	618	819	121
1970	...	—	—	70,784	622	5,227	270	618	819	121
1971	...	—	—	71,057	622	5,227	270	618	819	—
1972	...	—	—	70,851	622	5,227	270	618	819	—
1973	...	—	—	71,185	623	5,227	270	618	819	—
1974	...	—	—	71,239	623	5,086	142	618	819	—

F1 NORTH AMERICA: Length of Railway Line Open (in kilometres)

1925-1974

	Honduras[7]	Jamaica[2]	Mexico[3]	Newfoundland[8]	Nicaragua	Panama[4]	Puerto Rico	Trinidad	USA[5]
1925	1,432	338	20,972	1,460	322	158	547	187	401,367
1926	1,459	338	23,237	1,460	322	158	547	187	400,949
1927	1,459	338	23,575[3]	1,460	322	158	547	187	400,937
			23,055						
1928	1,459	338	23,096	1,460	327	158	547	187	401,224
1929	1,459	338	23,238	1,460	327	158	547	187	401,424
1930	1,459	338	23,345	1,460	327	158	547	190	400,810
1931	1,437	338	23,387	1,460	327	158	547	190	400,451
1932	1,437	338	23,344	1,207	327	158	547	190	398,466
1933	1,437	338	23,041	1,207	327	158	547	190	395,421
1934	1,437	338	23,030	1,207	327	158	547	190	392,450
1935	1,437	338	22,947	1,207	327	158	547	190	389,175
1936	1,437	338	22,937	1,207	354	158	547	190	386,410
1937	1,437	338	22,784	1,207	367	158	547	190	383,891
1938	1,313	338	23,331	1,207	367	158	547	190	381,160
1939	1,313	338	23,473	1,207	367	158	620	190	378,299
1940	...	338	22,979	1,207	367	158	620	190	376,055
1941	...	346	23,145	1,207	367	158	620	190	373,321
1942	...	346	23,135	1,207	367	158	620	190	368,820
1943	...	341	22,914	1,207	367	158	620	190	366,929
1944	1,046	341	22,980	1,207	379	158	620	190	365,860
1945	1,046	341	22,954	1,207	379	158	620	190	364,832
1946	1,046	341	22,954	1,207	379	158	620	190	364,417
1947	1,160	338	22,918	1,207	379	158	620	190	363,400
1948	1,160	333	23,314	1,207	379	158	620	190	362,342
1949	1,281	333	23,259	...	431	158	620	190	361,315
1950	1,297	333	23,332	...	431	158	620	190	360,137
1951	1,318	325	23,329	...	431	158	620	190	359,571
1952	1,313	333	23,397	...	431	158	620	190	358,092
1953	1,316	333	23,301	...	431	158	760	175	356,885
1954	1,312	335	23,282	...	431	158	760	175	355,823
1955	1,293	335	23,370	...	431	158	760	175	355,134
1956	1,272	335	23,425	...	431	158	760	175	354,411
1957	1,263	335	23,383	...	405	158	760	175	352,554
1958	1,251	335	23,457	...	403	158	—	175	351,479
1959	1,240	335	23,292	...	403	158	—	175	350,137[5]
1960	1,230	330	23,369	...	403	158	—	175	350,116
1961	1,219	330	23,487	...	403	158	—	175	348,334
1962	1,200	330	23,501	...	403	158	—	175	346,154
1963	1,148	330	23,793	...	403	158	—	175	345,022
1964	1,078	330	23,619	...	403	158	—	175	341,276
1965	1,029	330	23,672	...	403	158	—	26	340,190
1966	1,027	330	23,826	...	403	158	—	13	338,884
1967	1,036	330	23,977	...	403	158	—	13	336,823
1968	1,017	330	24,129	...	403	158	—	—	334,922
1969	1,016	330	24,119	...	403	158	—	—	333,142
1970	1,028	330	24,468	...	403	158	—	—	331,174
1971	1,045	330	24,501	...	403	158	—	—	329,426
1972	1,059	330	24,700	...	403	158	—	—	326,335
1973	996	330	24,670	...	403	158	—	—	323,586
1974	989	330	24,864	...	403	158	—	—	322,498

F1 NORTH AMERICA: Length of Railway Line Open (in kilometres)

	Canada	Costa Rica	Cuba	Dominican Republic	El Salvador	Guatemala
1975	70,716	648	5,209	142	618	819
1976	70,471	...	5,130	142	602	819
1977	69,967	...	...	142	602	819
1978	67,890	...	5,210	142	602	819
1979	67,725	...	5,215	142	602	819
1980	67,066	...	5,197	142	602	819
1981	66,371	...	5,027	142	602	819
1982	65,899[13] 98,927	760	5,158	142	602	819
1983	99,444	760	4,922	142	602	819
1984	97,389	760	4,909	142	674	819
1985	95,670	700	4,889	142	674	819
1986	93,544	700	4,881	142	674	819
1987	94,184	696	4,807	142	602	953
1988	91,365	556	4,820	142	602	953
1989	89,100	356	4,843	142	602	1,139
1990	86,880	556	4,843	142	602	1,139
1991	86,880	333	4,843	142	602	1,139
1992	85,191	581	4,843	142	602	1,139
1993	83,351	442	4,843	142	564	1,139

	Honduras	Jamaica	Mexico	Nicaragua	Panama	USA (thousands)
1975	977	330	24,912	373	158	320
1976	977	293	24,952	320	...	283
1977	977	293	25,047	345	...	306
1978	977	293	25,101	345	...	307
1979	...	...	25,314	345	...	298
1980	1,004	...	25,510	345	118	288
1981	1,004	257	25,498	345	118	270
1982	1,004	257	25,476	331	118	265
1983	1,004	182	25,799	331	...	259
1984	1,004	208	25,840	331	109	253
1985	1,004	208	25,908	331	109	249
1986	996	208	26,241	331	485	248
1987	996	208	26,287	289	485	245
1988	996	208[14]	26,399	289	485	241
1989	996	128	26,391	245	485	250
1990	996	128	26,360	245	485	244
1991	996	128	26,434	245	485	241
1992	996	128[15]	26,435	218	485	234
1993	996		26,445	218	485	231

F1 SOUTH AMERICA: LENGTH OF RAILWAY LINE OPEN (in kilometres)

1845-1889

	Argentina	Brazil	Chile	Colombia[4]	Ecuador	Guyana	Paraguay	Peru[10]	Uruguay	Venezuela
1845	—	—	...	—	—	—	—	—	—	...
1846	—	—	...	—	—	—	—	—	—	...
1847	—	—	...	—	—	—	—	—	—	...
1848	—	—	...	—	—	10	—	—	—	...
1849	—	—	...	—	—	16	—	—	—	...
1850	—	—	...	—	—	26	—	—	—	...
1851	—	—	...	—	—	26	—	24	—	...
1852	—	—	...	—	—	26	—	24	—	...
1853	—	—	...	—	—	26	—	24	—	...
1854	—	14	...	—	—	29	—	24	—	...
1855	—	14	...	—	—	29	—	24	—	...
1856	—	16	...	—	—	29	—	87	—	...
1857	10	16	...	—	—	29	—	103	—	...
1858	18	109	...	—	—	29	—	103	—	...
1859	23	109	...	—	—	29	—	103	—	...
1860	39	223	195	—	—	29	—	103	—	...
1861	39	251	...	—	—	29	14	103	—	...
1862	47	359	543	—	—	29	...	103	—	...
1863	61	428	...	—	—	29	91	103	—	...
1864	94	474	...	—	—	32	91	103	—	...
1865	213	498	440	—	—	32	91	103	—	...
1866	514	513	...	—	—	32	91	103	—	...
1867	572	598	...	—	—	32	91	103	—	...
1868	572	718	...	—	—	32	91	138	—	...
1869	604	737	459	—	—	32	91	255	20	...
1870	732	745	732	—	—	32	91	669	20	13
1871	852	869	...	27	—	32	91	975	26	13
1872	865	932	...	27	—	32	91	1,272	63	13
1873	1,104	1,129	998	27	—	32	91	1,371	63	13
1874	1,249	1,284	1,180	27	—	32	91	1,398	280	13
1875	1,384	1,801	1,276	27	—	34	91	1,792	304	13
1876	1,665	2,122	1,537	27	41	34	91	2,021	431	13
1877	2,262	2,388	1,624	27	41	34	91	2,030	431	113
1878	2,262	2,709	1,624	45	64	34	91	...	431	113
1879	2,262	2,911	1,624	45	64	34	91	...	431	113
1880	2,313	3,398	1,777	45	64	34	91	...	431	113
1881	2,442	3,946	1,777	45	64	34	91	...	431	113
1882	2,666	4,464	1,856	100	64	34	91	...[9]	431	113
1883	3,123	5,354	2,204	148	64	34	91	1,509	431	113
1884	3,728	6,302	2,204	176	64	34	91	1,580	431	164
1885	4,541	6,930	2,204	203	64	34	91	1,580	478	164
1886	5,964	7,586	2,204	203	64	34	91	1,580	543	164
1887	6,868	8,400	2,204	219	64	34	91	1,580	556	295
1888	7,644	9,321	2,626	238	64	34	91	1,580	642	295
1889	8,113	9,583	2,709	282	64	34	140	1,591	869	295

F1   SOUTH AMERICA: Length of Railway Line Open (in kilometres)

1890–1939

	Argentina	Bolivia	Brazil	Chile	Colombia[4]	Ecuador
1890	9,254	209	9,973	2,747	282	92
1891	11,700	315	10,590	2,868	282	92
1892	12,920	972	11,316	2,871	282	92
1893	13,961	972	11,485	2,871	...	92
1894	14,029	972	12,260	2,871	...	92
1895	14,222	972	12,967	3,497	445	92
1896	14,489	972	13,568	3,961	481	92
1897	14,997	972	14,015	4,215	513	92
1898	15,314	972	14,664	4,215	513	92
1899	16,399	972	14,916	4,215	550	92
1900	16,767	972	15,316	4,354	568	92
1901	17,200	972	15,506	4,354	568	105
1902	17,591	972	15,680	4,464	568	145
1903	18,603	1,129	16,010	4,630	568	201
1904	19,430	1,129	16,306	4,714	568	201
1905	19,682	1,129	16,781	4,778	661	300
1906	20,653	1,129	17,242	4,826	723	375
1907	22,045	1,129	17,613	5,182	723	459
1908	23,654	1,129	18,633	5,557	759	523
1909	25,457	1,149	19,241	5,682	901	543
1910	27,713	1,207	21,326	5,944	988	587
1911	30,462	1,226	22,287	6,028	1,050	587
1912	32,212	1,252	23,491	7,260	1,061	587
1913	33,478[11]	1,284	24,614	8,070	1,061	587
	30,281					
1914	31,186	1,440	26,062	8,147	1,166	587
1915	31,408	1,561	26,647	8,216	1,191	587
1916	32,755	...	27,015	8,420	1,191	587
1917	32,774	2,179	27,453	8,484	1,203	587
1918	32,774	2,179	27,706	8,512	1,231	587
1919	32,817	2,179[11]	28,127	8,196	1,312	626
		1,543				
1920	35,282	1,543	28,535	8,211	1,347	665
1921	35,112	1,666	28,828	8,253	1,424	665
1922	35,333	1,666	29,341	8,127	1,475	665
1923	35,496	1,794	29,295	8,661	1,500	665
1924	36,008	1,822	30,306	8,756	1,585	665
1925	36,117	1,923	30,731	8,641	1,856	752
1926	36,257	1,980	31,333	8,620	2,048	805
1927	36,333	2,015	31,549	9,009	2,387	805
1928	36,571	2,112	31,851	8,779	2,514	1,017
1929	37,478	2,112	31,967	8,465	2,586	1,030
1930	37,978	2,253	32,478	8,937	2,609	1,031
1931	39,383	2,253	32,764	8,875	2,940	1,031
1932	39,841	2,253	32,973	8,673	3,144	1,031
1933	39,962	2,253	33,073	8,718	3,173	1,031
1934	39,992	2,253	33,106	8,715	3,178	1,031
1935	40,171	2,253	33,331	8,718	3,192	1,031
1936	40,266	2,253	33,521	8,745	3,187	1,031
1937	40,355	2,270	34,095	8,762	3,197	1,031
1938	40,973	2,270	34,207	8,770	3,282	1,031
1939	40,973	2,270	34,204	8,663	3,247	1,031

F1   SOUTH AMERICA: Length of Railway Line Open (in kilometres)

1890–1939

	Guyana	Paraguay	Peru[10]	Surinam	Uruguay	Venezuela
1890	34	140	1,599	—	983	454
1891	34	240	1,599	—	1,567	454
1892	34	240	1,621	—	1,568	454
1893	34	240	1,728	—	1,602	502
1894	34	240	1,728	—	1,604	620
1895	34	240	1,734	—	1,604	653
1896	64	240	1,734	—	1,624	760
1897	64	240	1,744	—	1,624	760
1898	64	240	1,756	—	1,625	851
1899	89	240	1,773	—	1,730	851
1900	151	240	1,800	—	1,730	858
1901	153	240	1,806	—	1,944	858
1902	153	240	1,826	—	1,944	858
1903	153	240	1,849	—	1,944	858
1904	153	240	2,043	—	1,947	858
1905	153	240	2,079	60	1,948	858
1906	153	240	2,401	60	1,960	858
1907	153	240	2,555	60	1,960	858
1908	153	240	2,852	...	2,208	858
1909	153	240	2,983	133	2,328	858
1910	153	...	2,995	...	2,488	858
1911	153	373	3,208	...	2,512	858
1912	153	373	3,256	173	2,522	858
1913	153	373	3,276	173	2,576	858
1914	158	373	3,317	173	2,592	858
1915	158	373	3,345	173	2,638	858
1916	158	373	3,407	173	2,672	858
1917	158	373	3,433	173	2,672	858
1918	158	373	3,488	173	2,672	861
1919	158	410	3,489[10] 2,116	173	2,672	861
1920	158	410	2,116	173	2,672	861
1921	158	425	2,159	173	2,672	935
1922	158	457	2,183	173	2,672	935
1923	158	457	2,188	173	2,672	945
1924	158	468	2,459	173	2,672	945
1925	158	468	2,555	173	2,672	945
1926	158	468	2,654	173	2,692	982
1927	158	468	2,582	173	2,720	982
1928	158	468	2,709	173	2,724	982
1929	127	468	2,861	173	2,724	993
1930	127	468	...	173	2,731	993
1931	127	468	2,899	173	2,731	993
1932	127	468	2,972	173	2,731	993
1933	127	468	2,954	...	2,848	993
1934	127	468	2,977	...	2,848	993
1935	127	468	3,038	...	2,848	993
1936	127	481	3,038	...	2,848	993
1937	127	499	3,039	...	2,971	993
1938	127	499	2,938	...	2,971	993
1939	127	499	2,918	...	3,009	993

F1   SOUTH AMERICA: Length of Railway Line Open (in kilometres)

1940–1988

	Argentina	Bolivia	Brazil	Chile	Colombia	Ecuador
1940	41,283	2,270	34,252	8,610	3,335	1,060
1941	41,371	2,270	34,283	8,702	3,343	1,055
1942	41,407	2,270	34,438	8,577	3,415	1,055
1943	...	2,270	34,769	8,502	3,445	1,055
1944	...	2,270	35,163	8,737	3,448	1,055
1945	...	2,270	35,280	...	3,455	1,048
1946	41,600	2,340	35,336	8,672	3,510	1,048
1947	42,757	2,343	35,451	8,255	3,554	1,048
1948	42,757	2,343	35,622	8,516	3,486	1,048
1949	42,838	2,343	35,972	8,506	3,505	1,048
1950	42,864	2,343	36,681	8,503	3,526	1,124
1951	...	2,343	36,845	8,509	3,526	1,124
1952	...	2,343	37,019	8,503	3,349[12]	1,124
					2,977	
1953	...	2,721	37,032	8,493	2,946	1,121
1954	...	2,721	37,190	8,493	2,944	1,121
1955	43,930	2,721	37,092	8,405	3,062	1,121
1956	43,930	2,721	37,049	8,408	3,029	1,121
1957	43,930	2,721	37,422	8,408	3,161	1,152
1958	43,930	3,268	37,967	8,415	3,161	1,152
1959	43,930	3,268	37,710	8,415	3,161	1,152
1960	43,905	3,470	38,287	8,415	3,161	1,152
1961	42,813	...	37,548	8,251	3,436	1,152
1962	39,985	3,745	36,572	8,085	3,436	1,152
1963	43,751	...	35,349	7,965	3,436	1,154
1964	...	3,580	34,262	7,957	3,436	1,154
1965	41,907	3,560	33,864	7,946	3,436	1,154
1966	41,434	3,560	32,463	7,946	3,436	1,154
1967	40,165	3,560	32,182	8,265	3,436	1,154
1968	40,641	3,560	32,054	8,274	3,436	1,154
1969	40,235	3,524	32,939	8,274	3,436	990
1970	39,905	3,524	31,847	8,281	3,436	990
1971	39,822	3,524[11]	31,518	8,281[12]	3,431	990
		3,284		6,432		
1972	39,816	3,284	30,934	6,396	3,431	990
1973	39,805	3,284	30,429	6,393	3,431	990
1974	39,782	3,284	30,439	6,361	3,431	990
1975	39,787	3,269	30,809	6,606	3,431	965
1976	39,779	3,269	30,422	6,378	3,403	965
1977	36,996	3,373	29,778	6,372	3,403	965
1978	34,393	3,473	29,951	6,366	3,403	965
1979	34,350	3,473	30,021	6,365	3,403	965
1980	34,077	3,628	29,659	6,302	3,403	965
1981	34,172	3,628	29,237	6,300	3,403	965
1982	34,098	3,628	29,164	6,236	2,710	966
1983	34,127	3,628	29,207	6,236	3,400	966
1984	34,345	3,628	28,942	6,858	3,255	966
1985	34,447	3,628	29,777	6,740	3,255	966
1986	34,428	3,628	29,814	6,850	3,257	966
1987	34,183	3,701	29,833	6,848	3,239	966
1988	34,192	3,701	29,635	6,850	3,239	966
1989	34,059	3,701	30,402	6,880	2,113	966
1990	34,059	3,701	30,322	6,852	2,113	966
1991	35,753	3,701	30,314	6,869	2,113	956
1992	35,753	3,698	30,302	6,837	2,113	956
1993	35,753	3,694	30,381	6,560	2,113	956

F1 SOUTH AMERICA: Length of Railway Line Open (in kilometers)

	Guyana	Paraguay	Peru[10]	Surinam	Uruguay	Venezuela
1940	127	499	2,898	...	3,009	1,049
1941	127	499	2,886	...	3,009	997
1942	127	499	2,801	...	3,009	997
1943	127	499	2,802	...	3,009	997
1944	127	499	2,936	...	3,009	997
1945	127	499	2,875	136	3,009	997
1946	127	499	2,890	136	3,009	997
1947	127	499	3,062	136	3,009	997
1948	127	499	3,029	136	3,004	997
1949	127	499	3,097	136	3,004	997
1950	127	499	3,097	136	3,004	997
1951	127	499	3,010	136	3,004	997
1952	127	499	3,067	136	3,004	997
1953	127	499	2,789	136	3,004	997
1954	127	441	2,789	136	3,004	997
1955	127	441	2,726	136	3,004	...
1956	127	441	2,726	136	3,004	506
1957	127	441	2,726	136	3,004	506
1958	127	441	2,673	136	3,004	506
1959	127	441	2,578	136	3,004	474
1960	127	441	2,559	136	3,004	474
1961	127	441	2,458	136	3,004	474
1962	127	441	2,558	136	3,004	474
1963	127	441	2,460	102	3,004	474
1964	127	441	2,327	86	3,004	474
1965	127	441	2,244	86	3,004	474
1966	127	441	2,340	86	3,004	474
1967	127	441	2,295	86	3,004	474
1968	127	441	2,209	86	3,004	474
1969	127	441	2,235	86	3,004	226
1970	127	441	2,242	86	2,975	226
1971	127	441	2,282	86	2,975	226
1972	65	441	...	86	2,975	226
1973	30	441	1,892	86	2,975	233
1974	30	441	1,892	86	2,975	226
1975	—	441	1,875		2,975	226
1976	—	441	1,875		2,975	264
1977	—	441	1,875		2,988	284
1978	—	441	1,875		2,998	264
1979	—	441	1,882		3,005	268
1980	—	441	2,099		3,005	268
1981	—	441	2,159		3,005	268
1982	—	441	2,159		3,010	268
1983	—	441	2,159		3,001	...
1984	—	441	2,159		3,001	280
1985	—	441	2,159		2,991	280
1986	—	441	2,159		2,991	445
1987	—	441	2,157	—	2,991	445
1988	—	441	2,397	—	3,006	538
1989	—	441	2,434	—	3,005	538
1990	—	441	2,196	—	3,002	538
1991	—	441	2,196	—	3,002	627
1992	—	441	2,121	—	3,004	627
1993	—	441	2,121	—	3,004	627

F1 Length of Railway Line Open

NOTES

1. SOURCES: The basic sources have been the national publications listed on pp. xiii–xv, but a variety of others has been used to fill in gaps. These include *Jane's World Railways, International Railway Progress*, the publications of the Institut International de Statistique, and British Consular Reports.
2. Except where otherwise indicated, the statistics are for the route length of line open at the end of each year. Narrow gauge line are included but not, in general, mountain railways.
3. In principle, purely industrial lines, which were not open to public traffic, are not included. In practice, this distinction cannot always be made, especially in central American countries. The main endeavour has been to maintain consistency in the series.

FOOTNOTES

[1] Statistics to 1918 are at 30 June. Newfoundland is included from 1949.
[2] Statistics from 1890 to 1920 are at 31 March in the year following the year shown.
[3] Including tramways to 1927 (1st line). The first proper railway was opened in 1865.
[4] Data for Panama are shown separately from Colombia even for the period when the former was part of the latter.
[5] Statistics to 1890 (1st line) are of railway operated, subsequently they are of railway owned. The former series contains some double counting where different companies operated over the same line. Data for 1890 (2nd line) to 1916 are at 30 June. Alaska and Hawaii are included from 1960.
[6] At 31 March following the year shown.
[7] Some industrial lines carried public traffic at some times but not at others and it is not clear how inconsistently this is treated in the data. It also seems likely that the data relate to track rather than route length.
[8] At 30 June.
[9] 450 km were ceded to Chile as a result of the war of 1879–84.
[10] Statistics are of railways in existence to 1919 (1st line) and of railways exploited subsequently.
[11] Subsequently excluding private lines.
[12] The reason for this break is not clear in the sources, but it is probably the subsequent exclusion of some, or all, private lines.
[13] Track kilometres of class I railroads subsequently.
[14] Figures from this point supplied by National Statistical Office.
[15] Service suspended.

F2   NORTH AMERICA: FREIGHT TRAFFIC ON RAILWAYS

Key: a = thousand metric tons; b = million metric ton-kilometres; c = million metric tons;
       d = thousand million metric ton-kilometres

1860–1904

	Canada[1]	Mexico	USA[2]	
	a	a	c	b[3]
1860	...	...	...	...
1861	...	...	50	...
1862	...	...	...	...
1863	...	...	...	...
1864	...	...	...	...
1865	...	...	...	3,150
1866	...	...	...	3,830
1867	...	...	...	4,420
1868	...	...	...	5,020
1869	...	...	...	6,160
1870	...	...	65.8	7,180
1871	...	...	...	8,130
1872	...	...	...	9,370
1873	...	150	...	10,920
1874	...	122	...	11,290
1875	5,145	137	...	11,450
1876	5,744	133	...	12,750
1877	6,223	159	...	12,770
1878	7,151	172	...	15,590
1879	7,574	190	...	19,080
1880	9,017	250	...	21,140
1881	10,945	364	...	23,450
1882	12,316	748	327	23,695[3]
				57,380
1883	12,035	866	363	64,334
1884	12,439	1,026	362	65,297
1885	13,298	1,179	396	71,761
1886	14,216	1,180	437	77,089
1887	14,838	1,478	501	89,877
1888	15,579	1,821	535	95,516
1889	16,265	2,127	562	100,267
				(thousand million ton-kilometres)
1890	18,858	2,734	627[2]	116[2]
				111
1891	19,734	3,233	...	118
1892	20,130	3,191	...	129
1893	19,962	3,796	...	137
1894	18,798	4,121	...	117
1895	19,526	4,073	...	124
1896	22,015	3,988	...	139
1897	22,952	4,878	...	139
1898	26,114	6,078	...	167
1899	28,315	5,425	455	181
1900	32,610	7,553	529	207
1901	33,565	6,759	530	215
1902	38,444	8,488	597	230
1903	42,976	9,911	649	253
1904	43,634	11,141	648	255

F2 NORTH AMERICA: Freight Traffic on Railways

1905–1939

	Canada[1]		Costa Rica	Cuba[4]		El Salvador	Guatemala	Mexico		Nicaragua		USA[2]	
	c	b	a	a	b	a	a	a	b	a	b	c	d
1905	46	...	...	...	...	...	...	14,578	...	...	...	712	272
1906	52	...	...	...	...	...	...	...	...	...	...	813	315
1907	58.0	17,064	...	...	...	...	...	...	...	...	...	886	345
1908	57.2	18,923	...	...	...	...	...	12,310	...	...	...	789	319
1909	60.6	19,214	...	...	...	...	...	14,440	...	...	...	799	319
1910	67.6	22,939	...	...	...	...	...	...	...	...	...	931	372
1911	72.5	23,430	...	...	...	...	...	...	...	...	...	910	371
1912	81.1	28,554	...	...	...	...	...	...	...	...	...	935	386
1913	97.1	33,628	...	15,000	582	91	...	...	...	...	...	1,073	441
1914	92.0	32,212	...	...	...	...	...	...	...	...	...	1,025	421
1915	79.1	25,785	...	...	...	...	...	...	...	...	...	929	405
1916	99.5	41,165	...	...	...	...	...	...	...	...	...	1,146[2]	501[2]
												1,195	535
1917	110.6	45,532	...	...	...	...	...	...	...	...	...	1,254	581
1918	115.7	45,302	...	...	...	...	...	...	...	...	...	1,249	597
1919	105.9[1]	40,477[1]	...	...	...	...	...	...	...	...	...	1,080	536
	101.2	39,347											
1920	115.6	46,565	...	...	...	...	...	...	...	...	...	1,236	604
1921	93.5	38,867	...	...	...	...	...	8,300	2,262	...	...	924	452
1922	98.4	44,336	...	22,800	903	168	...	9,614	2,398	...	...	1,009	500
1923	107.3	49,738	...	23,900	1,072	195	...	11,158	2,886	...	...	1,259	608
1924	96.5	44,549	...	26,100	1,145	203	...	11,146	2,901	...	...	1,168	572
1925	99.7	46,668	...	33,100	1,710	253	...	12,239	3,219	...	...	1,226	609
1926	111.1	49,863	...	30,100	1,237	...	...	12,878	3,608	...	...	1,306	653
1927	114.3	50,956	635	28,000	...	251	...	13,298	3,803	...	...	1,246	631
1928	128.1	60,750	615	27,000	...	310	...	13,393	4,006	...	...	1,244	637
1929	125.1	51,137	592	32,000	...	345	...	13,878	4,035	...	...	1,287	657
1930	104.5	43,222	561	18,549	...	255	...	13,015	4,041	...	12	1,107	563
1931	78.0	37,532	432	...	...	261	...	10,799	3,378	...	11	857	454
1932	61.4	33,779	375	...	...	220	...	9,105	2,884	...	8.0	616	344
1933	57.7	30,795	387	...	...	254	...	9,993	3,245	...	7.1	665	366
1934	68.7	34,047	328	...	...	303	...	12,577	4,154	...	7.1	728	395
1935	69.9	35,514	320	...	...	330	...	13,555	4,596	89	9.1	755	429
1936	76.8	38,564	369	...	...	302	...	14,275	4,927	93	9.0	918	498
1937	83.9	39,311	462	18,320	719	373	642	14,405	5,381	142	13	975	530
1938	76.8	39,178	499	15,287	651	364	690	14,668	5,535	144	12	744	426
1939	85.8	45,938	434	14,619	617	432	714	15,367	5,728	134	12	866	490

F2 NORTH AMERICA: Freight Traffic on Railways

1940-1993

	Canada[1]		Costa Rica		Cuba[4]		El Salvador		Guatemala[8]	
	c	d	a[6]	b[7]	a	b	a	b	a	b
1940	100	55	363[6]	...	17,255	726	380	...	630	...
1941	122	73	377	...	17,289	750	331	...	661	...
1942	141	82	386	...	19,345	926	392	...	693	...
1943	161	93	448	...	16,910	1,580	523	...	743	...
1944	161	96	412	...	23,080	1,734	520	...	874	...
1945	152	92	456	...	17,980	1,405	536	...	951[8]	...
									455	
1946	146	81	433[6]	...	19,600[4]	1,343[4]	537	...	512	...
1947	159	88	447	38	24,450	1,385	631	...	623	...
1948	160	86	442	30	24,310	1,261	525	...	639	...
1949	147[1]	82[1]	443	41	20,560	1,056	487	...	589	...
1950	149	81	465	44	20,250	1,100	513	...	623	239
1951	167	94	468	45	21,600	1,134	560	...	594	209
1952	168	100	485	49	24,900	1,192	618	...	550	193
1953	160	95	538	56	19,660	1,008	564	...	652	256
1954	147	84	556	57	19,010	979	586	...	568	245
1955	171	97	640	63[7]	17,910	952	683	...	661	273
1956	194	115	622	35	17,580	1,008	712	...	692	285
1957	179	104	620	33	...	1,101	686	...	676	259
1958	158	97	679	41	...	...	687	...	590	234
1959	169	99	710	50	...	...	693	...	612	246
1960	162[1]	96	832	59	...	...	680	...	672	270
	144									
1961	139	96	841	59	...	...	580	...	579	255
1962	146	99	907	66	9,298	1,109	633	...	557	192
1963	156	111	935	[77][7]	7,618	1,064	635	...	583	207
1964	172	124	935	33	8,279	1,025	613	...	495	177
1965	178	127	922	31	10,032	1,326	589	...	406	129
1966	186	141	1,299	47	9,102	1,487	529	...	434	133
1967	191	137	1,369	13	10,765	1,705	496	...	414	120
1968	196	139	1,545	18	9,976	1,672	423	...	323	75
1969	188	141	1,795	11	10,259	1,485	396	...	412	106
1970	212	161	2,140	18	11,735	1,625	495	...	415	106
1971	214	173	2,113	13	10,655	1,598	503	...	357	...
1972	216	181[5]	2,191	15	9,569	1,504	525	63	353	93
1973	241	191	1,921	20	10,017	1,617	509	61	463	137
1974	246	202	...	14	10,867	1,654	491	49	525	143
1975	226	197	2,108	...	10,867	1,766	402	46	524	127
1976	239	202	...	16	11,320	1,848	476	46	704	117
1977	247	212	...	...	13,600	2,021	518	52	...	139
1978	239	215	...	...	13,530	1,904	606	76	...	139
1979	258	234	...	...	14,897	1,899	606	78	...	91
1980	254	235	...	...	15,702	2,165	414	55	...	91
1981	247	234	...	...	18,218	2,676	285	31	...	...
1982	213	224	...	...	18,248	2,550	302	31	...	...
1983	223	232	...	...	17,697	2,617	364	31	681	...
1984	255	258	...	...	18,435	2,674	315	24	...	...
1985	251	245	...	...	18,368	2,797	324	25	...	...
1986	250	247	...	...	...	2,155	322	24	650	...
1987	291	268	...	...	...	2,105	353	39	...	...
1988	300	271	...	...	...	2,087	...	36	...	...
1989	281	249	...	...	...	2,416	...	22	...	...
1990	268	248	...	...	...	2,376	...	38	...	...
1991	274	261	...	...	...	1,759	...	36	...	...
1992	265	251	...	...	...	1,411	...	38	...	...
1993	...	257	...	...	...	989	...	35	...	...

F2 NORTH AMERICA: Freight Traffic on Railways

1940–1993

	Honduras	Mexico		Nicaragua		Panama	USA[2]	
	a	a	b	a	b	a	c	d
1940	...	15,023	5,810	129	12	23	970	548
1941	...	15,681	6,076	145	13	26	1,176	697
1942	...	16,898	7,019	183	16	34	1,359	936
1943	...	21,343	8,092	199	17	36	1,412	1,066
1944	...	20,222	8,194	217	16	38	1,420	1,081
1945	...	20,702	8,024	197	15	42	1,354	999
1946	...	21,046	8,185	205	15	44	1,299	869
1947	...	21,138	8,341	188	17	28	1,463	960
1948	...	21,181	8,521	...	19	28	1,433	936
1949	...	21,598	8,701	...	19	23	1,165	772
1950	804	22,907	9,391	244	21	19	1,289	864
1951	943	22,827	9,460	306	23	18	1,403	949
1952	935	23,696[5]	10,087	314	21	20	1,313	902
		26,332						
1953	1,079	25,461	9,593	353	21	24	1,314	889
1954	1,110	26,136	10,304	375	35	35	1,160	806
1955	1,018	27,685	10,961	361	32	35	1,324	915
1956	1,083	29,615	12,015	294	26	36	1,380	951
1957	990	31,536	12,983	330	29	34	1,315	908
1958	915	30,543	12,810	394	36	36	1,131	810
1959	947	30,482	12,231	413	32	34	1,173[2]	845[2]
1960	890	34,359	14,004	286	23	35	1,180	840
1961	848	32,614	13,524	253	23	24	1,137	827
1962	740	32,603	13,521	254	25	32	1,174	870
1963	580	36,336	14,960	203	19	18	1,222	913
1964	682	39,582	16,330	187	16	18	1,288	967
1965	542	42,947	18,332	162	13	17	1,342	1,030
1966	431	42,303	18,407	144	13	10	1,401	1,090
1967	512	45,184	19,690	153	14	12	1,359	1,062
1968	2,076	44,213	20,304	146	13	15	1,374	1,096
1969	1,603	46,890	21,577	136	13	15	1,413	1,130
1970	510	46,784	22,863	126	16	14	1,426	1,126
1971	2,357	48,399	22,374	124	15	22	1,335	1,079
1972	1,827	49,946	24,140	107	14	22	1,389	1,136
1973	...	55,227	26,139	100	12	30	1,466	1,253
1974	...	63,824	30,858	83	11	18	1,469	1,244
1975	341	65,357	33,195	62	8	17	1,334	1,102
1976	...	65,000	34,821	...	12	...	1,343	1,123
1977	...	70,864	36,232	...	11	...	1,378	1,206
1978	...	71,363	36,422	66	10	...	1,298	1,253
1979	...	69,718	36,766	...	6	...	1,400	1,334
1980	...	71,978	41,323	...	12	...	1,393[15]	1,342
							1,353	
1981	...	75,568	43,513	...	14	...	1,318	1,360
1982	...	69,667	38,800	...	7	...	1,151	1,192
1983	...	71,904	42,377	...	2	...	1,173	1,237
1984	...	73,428	44,592	...	5	...	1,296	1,345
1985	...	73,091	45,306	...	4	...	1,197	1,280
1986	...	66,384	40,608	36	...	...	986	1,284
1987	...	66,843	40,475	...	...	...	1,244	1,388
1988	...	57,373	41,177	...	...	...	1,429	1,604
1989	...	55,279	38,750	...	...	...	1,403	1,632
1990	...	51,591	36,408	...	...	...	1,425	1,665
1991	...	46,863	32,986	...	...	...	1,383	1,673
1992	...	48,959	34,229	...	...	...	1,399	1,557
1993	...	50,785	35,901	...	...	...	1,397	1,619

F2 SOUTH AMERICA: FREIGHT TRAFFIC ON RAILWAYS

1855-1894

	Argentina[9]	Chile[10]	Peru	Uruguay[11]	Venezuela
	a	a	a	a	a
1855	...	...	...	...	...
1856	...	...	...	...	...
1857	2.3	...	...	...	...
1858	6.7	...	...	...	...
1859	13	...	...	...	...
1860	...	...	...	...	...
1861	...	...	...	...	...
1862	19	...	...	...	...
1863	24	...	...	...	...
1864	71	...	...	...	...
1865	72	...	...	...	...
1866	83	...	...	...	...
1867	129	...	...	...	...
1868	152	...	...	...	...
1869	206	...	...	...	...
1870	275	...	...	...	...
1871	286	...	...	...	...
1872	343	...	...	...	...
1873	443	...	...	...	...
1874	504	...	...	...	...
1875	661	...	...	...	...
1876	734	603	...	...	...
1877	721	556	...	...	...
1878	734	592	...	...	...
1879	812	659	...	...	...
1880	773	821	...	...	...
1881	957	865	...	...	...
1882	1,308	982	...	...	...
1883	1,918	999	...	...	7.6
1884	2,421	1,069	...	...	49
1885	3,050	1,086	...	...	59
1886	2,949	1,306	...	...	46
1887	3,844	1,340	...	...	55
1888	4,411	1,412	...	...	75
1889	6,642	1,588	...	...	109
1890	5,421	1,667	442	...	113
1891	4,621	1,527	406	...	144
1892	6,038	1,849	488	366	112
1893	7,169	1,960	413	406	143
1894	8,143	1,971	419	521	126

F2 SOUTH AMERICA: Freight Traffic on Railways

1895–1939

	Argentina[9]		Bolivia		Brazil		Chile[10]		Colombia	
	a	b	a	b	a	b	a	b	a	b
1895	9,650	...	...	...	...	...	2,143	...	...	...
1896	10,914	...	...	...	...	...	2,110	...	...	...
1897	8,981	...	...	...	...	...	1,977	...	...	...
1898	9,429	...	...	...	...	...	2,026	...	...	...
1899	11,819	...	...	...	...	...	2,132	...	...	...
1900	12,660	...	...	...	...	...	2,229	...	...	...
1901	13,988	...	...	...	...	...	2,681[12]	...	...	...
							5,764			
1902	14,252	...	...	...	...	...	5,772	...	...	...
1903	17,302	...	...	...	...	...	5,580	...	...	...
1904	20,288	...	...	...	...	...	5,393	...	...	...
1905	22,770	...	...	...	...	...	7,924	...	...	...
1906	26,969	...	...	...	...	...	7,817	...	...	...
1907	27,934	...	...	...	...	...	6,512	...	...	...
1908	32,194	...	...	...	...	...	...	...	...	...
1909	31,200	...	...	...	...	...	8,253	...	...	...
1910	32,562	...	...	...	...	...	12,179	...	...	...
1911	34,961	...	...	...	...	...	9,807	...	568	...
1912	41,312	...	...	...	...	...	9,842	...	...	...
1913	42,917	...	...	...	...	...	10,793	...	...	...
1914	34,296	...	...	...	...	...	8,343	...	...	...
1915	31,939	...	...	...	...	...	8,164	...	797	...
1916	32,005	...	...	...	13,015	1,691	10,587	...	858	...
1917	32,681	...	...	...	15,049	3,003	10,991	...	930	...
1918	30,570	...	...	...	15,382	2,294	15,498	...	825	...
1919	37,342	...	...	...	15,564	2,129	8,209	...	1,055	...
1920	44,783	...	...	...	16,555	2,231	9,293	...	1,331	...
1921	37,533	...	...	...	15,933	2,105	8,131	...	1,504	...
1922	34,457[9]	...	...	...	16,232	2,226	7,072	...	1,129	...
1923	38,804	...	...	...	19,049	2,721	10,170	...	1,582	...
1924	43,181	...	...	...	20,337	2,838	18,161	...	1,820	...
1925	44,281	...	...	...	22,737	3,443	19,796	...	2,101	...
1926	45,134	...	...	...	22,713	3,444	17,684	...	2,650	...
1927	50,880	...	...	...	24,391	3,894	29,529	1,432	3,068	...
1928	52,782	13,779	...	...	24,995	4,231	34,232	1,552	3,315	...
1929	52,596[9]	14,090[9]	...	...	25,764	3,178	38,472	1,711	3,134	...
1930	44,532	11,445	...	108	18,949	3,679	26,835	1,430	2,197	...
1931	44,728	12,063	...	82	20,725	3,570	21,291	1,057	[1,192][12]	[121][12]
1932	44,043	10,720	...	69	20,411	3,404	9,843	874	[1,246][12]	[95][12]
1933	38,825	10,078	...	71	22,245	3,554	13,081	1,096	[1,535][12]	[121][12]
1934	40,162	11,086	...	88	23,283	3,697	23,900[10]	1,410	2,523	179
							7,675			
1935	43,189	11,702	...	123	26,231	4,318	8,019	1,478	2,582	212
1936	42,372	12,276	...	140	22,636	4,851	8,586	1,480	2,820	252
1937	51,027	13,507	...	164	31,169	5,404	9,752	1,686	2,829	276
1938	42,255	11,730	1,224	175	33,479	5,995	10,036	1,768	2,903	294
1939	45,213	12,340	1,323	178	34,829	6,126	9,925	1,842	2,836	296

F2 SOUTH AMERICA: Freight Traffic on Railways

1895–1934

	Ecuador[13]		Paraguay	Peru		Uruguay[11]		Venezuela
	a	b	a	a	b	a	b	a
1895	...	...	...	432	...	617	...	154
1896	...	...	...	475	...	607	...	173
1897	...	...	...	506	...	509	...	158
1898	...	...	...	544	...	513	...	145
1899	...	...	...	596	...	567	...	117
1900	...	...	...	676	...	614	...	137
1901	...	...	...	760	...	701	...	137
1902	...	...	...	678	...	743	...	112
1903	...	...	...	804	...	715	...	156
1904	...	...	...	862	...	746	...	165
1905	...	...	...	922	...	836	...	152
1906	...	...	...	1,020	...	945	...	179
1907	...	...	...	978	...	1,175	...	188
1908	...	...	...	1,450	...	1,211	...	184
1909	...	...	...	1,441	...	1,140	...	164
1910	45	...	...	1,094	...	1,250	...	209
1911	...	...	...	828	...	1,306	...	229
1912	...	...	...	1,680	...	1,378	...	279
1913	...	...	...	1,701	...	1,569	...	283
1914	...	...	156	1,661	...	1,296	...	269
1915	...	...	...	1,813	...	1,324	...	273
1916	...	...	...	2,106	...	1,494	...	306
1917	...	...	...	2,357	...	1,534	...	365
1918	...	...	...	2,677	...	1,673	...	334
1919	...	...	...	2,444	180	1,799	...	362
1920	96	...	...	2,632	173	1,526	...	366
1921	...	...	...	2,292	158	...	...	320
1922	...	...	83	2,342	158	...	...	338
1923	...	...	149	2,390	169	1,375	...	400
1924	132	...	164	2,597	169	1,579	...	440
1925	112	...	186	1,927	126	1,487	...	529
1926	147	...	175	2,733	175	1,692	...	529
1927	157	...	166	2,628	130	...	...	401
1928	164	...	176	2,793	197	2,037	357	493
1929	165	...	165	3,151	206	1,844	355	457
1930	160	...	149	3,072	...	1,993	354	467
1931	136	...	123	2,342	160	2,104	384	411
1932	116	...	...	1,814	119	1,614	297	274
1933	144	...	170	1,620	102	1,387[11]	283[11]	289
1934	187	...	...	1,838	121	1,539	...	285
1935	221	...	147	2,354	213	1,714	354	321
1936	236	58	132	2,986	287	1,896	361	348
1937	243	64	136	2,911	287	1,866	361	341
1938	274[13] 321	67	120	3,000	292	1,963	370	352
1939	279	41	129	3,024	304	2,025	395	454

F2 SOUTH AMERICA: Freight Traffic on Railways

1940–1993

	Argentina[9]		Bolivia		Brazil		Chile[10]		Colombia	
	a	b	a	b	a	b	a	b	a	b
1940	43,178	12,880	1,445	219	35,066	6,075	9,794	2,031	2,768	309
1941	40,540	13,128	1,679	244	34,973	6,490	10,032	1,999	2,854	313
1942	46,163	15,026	1,691	267	36,558	6,592	10,153	2,070	3,246	369
1943	51,286	16,784	1,786	237	38,882	6,992	10,656	2,190	3,999	450
1944	52,925	17,744	1,662	236	41,261	7,385	10,740	2,222	4,041	459
1945	52,697	17,404	1,498	253	39,672	7,218	11,263	2,357	4,423	526
1946	52,914	16,776	1,506	229	40,563	7,417	10,901	2,318	4,543	572
1947	50,139	16,002	1,654		39,378	7,512	11,389	2,317	4,329	546
1948	48,827[0]	17,416[9]	1,829	291	37,800	7,758	12,737	2,295	4,481	577
1949	37,261	16,325	1,734	270	39,378	8,101	15,939	2,175	4,817	608
1950	38,648	17,309	1,683	249	38,040	8,066	14,660	2,102	4,626	558
1951	39,186[9]	17,681[9]	1,966	310	42,655	8,733	13,845	2,368	4,605	546
	34,253	16,429								
1952	32,447	15,255	1,955	319	40,747	9,155	14,012	2,493	4,579	551
1953	33,322	15,016	1,799	294	40,316	10,155	12,863	2,440	4,709	618
1954	34,038	15,197	1,796	296	41,431	9,252	12,731	2,488	4,744	618
1955	32,154	15,392	1,814	…	41,369	9,069	12,589	2,563	4,676	581
1956	31,179	14,873	1,924	…	39,934	9,709	12,452	2,489	4,809	592
1957	30,093	14,367	1,591	300	40,300	10,220	11,421	2,225	5,158	655
1958	30,197	15,043	1,254	228	42,494	10,471	12,861	2,146	5,979	654
1959	33,954[9]	15,526	1,049	…	43,660	12,034	12,655	2,220	5,872	804
	26,799									
1960	26,166	15,188	1,062	186	43,727	12,079	13,032	1,953	5,441	768
1961	21,965	14,014	1,220	203	43,885	11,340	12,839	1,899	5,169	769
1962	18,653	11,655	…	219	47,353	14,921	14,823	2,033	4,487	918
1963	16,914	10,631	1,040	246	53,446	17,914	15,325	2,326	3,655	891
1964	21,340	13,065	1,040	221	52,041	16,387	16,764	2,349	3,317	952
1965	23,407	14,027	945	301	53,747	18,259	19,517	2,621	3,062	934
1966	22,036	13,459	985	288	53,818	18,861	23,024	2,760	3,312	1,114
1967	16,820	11,355	955	321	54,301	19,487	20,085	2,505	3,169	996
1968	19,836	12,914	1,036	316	59,471	21,528	21,413	2,637	3,240	1,125
1969	20,987	13,318	1,189	382	48,073	16,150	19,281	2,652	3,050	1,159
1970	22,123	13,640	1,076	456	49,747	17,267	19,069	2,533	2,781	1,173
1971	21,553	13,654	1,122	351	47,404	17,178	19,490	2,718	2,653	1,150
1972	18,313	12,489	971	361	77,789	33,308	16,580	2,549	2,731	1,198
1973	19,091	12,508	955	365	94,531	42,508	18,039	2,709	2,760	1,331
1974	19,122	12,357	1,122	388	115,190	54,664	17,564	2,539	2,899	1,329
					c	d				
1975	16,272	10,659	1,141	470	124	59	17,366	2,416	2,439	1,139
1976	17,800	11,047	1,080	523	130	63	16,877	2,163	2,411	1,157
1977	20,169	11,578	1,178	583	126	61	15,514	2,150	2,519	1,215
1978	17,158	9,871	1,185	593	133	64	15,261	1,965	2,682	1,232
1979	19,128	10,947	1,196	601	155	74	15,351	1,849	2,394	1,105
1980	16,274	9,468	1,302	646	181	86	16,962	1,943	1,935	862
1981	16,664	9,238	1,047	620	167	79	15,373	1,765	1,347	641
1982	19,098	11,472	994	484	168	78	13,135	1,773	1,097	562
1983	22,509	13,364	1,159	577	164	75	14,182	2,248	1,246	665
1984	19,502	11,208	971	548	196	92	15,148	2,315	1,267	733
1985	17,234	9,501	…	494	208	100	20,023	2,566	1,278	777
1986	15,018	8,761	923	464	213	104	21,343	2,510	1,186	691
1987	13,577	7,952	982	505	215	109	15,667	2,612	1,055	563
1988	14,880	8,983	872	424	231	120	19,418	2,809	934	464
1989	14,220	8,237	1,055	512	246	125	20,561	2,946	…	361
1990	14,223	7,578	1,283	541	235	120	19,134	2,787	…	391
1991	9,731	5,460	1,436	683	235	121	19,499	2,717	…	298
1992	8,666	4,388	…	710	229	117	19,012	2,715	293	243
1993	9,275	4,477	…	692	242	125	17,092	2,464	541	459

F2 SOUTH AMERICA: Freight Traffic on Railways

	Ecuador		Paraguay		Peru		Uruguay		Venezuela	
	a	b	a	b	a	b[14]	a	b	a	b
1940	408	73	129	...	3,017	299	1,983	395	426	...
1941	411	74	126	...	3,062	329	2,165	431	409	...
1942	454	80	160	...	3,195	355	2,160	409	455	...
1943	517	...	201	...	3,271	357	2,580	457	529	...
1944	525	101	192	...	3,472	383	2,399	413	536	...
1945	530	102	194	...	3,564	403	1,911	404	531	...
1946	551	114	170	...	3,668	412	1,841	385	506	...
1947	528	111	153	...	3,378	385	1,519	324	426	...
1948	507	105	...	25	3,331	381	1,456	365	391	...
1949	478	101	...	31	3,534	404	1,545	434	374	...
1950	484	101	...	35	3,630	403	1,186	470	306	17
1951	506	109	...	31	3,874	465	1,187	...	162	10
1952	605	114	...	34	4,078	509	1,128	...	183	11
1953	501	101	...	29	4,309	513	1,159	...	197	13
1954	518	127	137	26	4,216	510	1,530	...	162	25
1955	554	118	126	25	4,382	513	1,888	426	87	6
1956	426	106	138	24	4,799	560[14] 531	1,908	...	87	8
1957	...	...	132	25	4,760	554	1,870	...	87	9
1958	504	...	106	21	3,986	481	1,700	...	62	8
1959	...	...	202	18	3,577	420	1,662	...	98	13
1960	537	121	83	16	4,214	506	1,737	399	172	20
1961	535	110	100	17	4,166	518	1,451	...	118	14
1962	512	96	91	16	3,931	509	1,396	...	195	24
1963	498	97	95	18	4,040	536	1,295	...	174	21
1964	523	104	112	20	4,390	622	1,641	255	221	26
1965	...	84	95	19	4,456	646	1,660	332	249	32
1966	377	72	78	16	4,388	658	1,665	...	207	26
1967	323	63	74	17	3,987	625	1,301	370	136	17
1968	314	59	95	22	3,469	591	1,359	320	113	12
1969	295	61	114	27	3,222	591	1,109	261	92	10
1970	278	56	127	30	...	610	...	250	108	13
1971	275	55	121	30	...	610	...	222	130	12
1972	232	43	161	35	...	547	...	134	236	17
1973	274	57	132	30	...	613	...	196	117	13
1974	214	52	143	32	...	630	...	239	98	10
1975	...	46	97	20	...	605	1,424	281	118	14
1976	...	26	...	16	...	635	...	372	116	14
1977	...	25	...	17	...	612	...	307	167	20
1978	...	34	94	23	...	1,035	...	303	163	20
1979	...	29	163	30	...	1,127	...	269	174	18
1980	...	14	187	32	5,752	1,133	1,400	234	192	21
1981	...	15	215	23	4,166	1,039	1,200	218	122	14
1982	...	14	244	34	4,252	974	...	186	247	29
1983	...	8	138	30	4,013	897	977	220	205	22
1984	...	6	141	16	4,571	1,044	...	273	103	11
1985	...	9	156	13	4,640	1,036	...	185	127	14
1986	...	7	...	17	4,334	1,022	...	210	114	12
1987	...	8	...	17	4,550	1,148	...	210	147	18
1988	...	8	...	18	3,700	971	...	213	291	40
1989	...	6	163	14	3,800	929	...	243	253	39
1990		5	288	4	3,400	848	...	204	267	35
1991		2	239	3	5,300	825	...	203	317	40
1992		3	251	3	5,700	817	...	215	331	36
1993		3	155	3	6,100	844	...	178	...	26

F2   Freight Traffic on Railways

NOTES

1. SOURCES: The national publications listed on pp. xiii–xv with gaps filled from the League of Nations and UN, *Statistical Yearbooks*.
2. It is not always clear whether traffic for the servicing of the railways is included or not, though there appears to be an indicator whenever a change in this respect occurs.
3. Livestock and passengers, baggage are not normally included with freight.

FOOTNOTES

[1]   Years ending 30 June to 1919 (1st line). Newfoundland is included from 1950. Double-counting is eliminated from 1960 (2nd line).
[2]   Freight carried to 1890 (1st line), freight originated subsequently. Freight carried free of charge is not included. Data for 1890 (2nd line) to 1916 (1st line) are for years ending 30 June. Alaska and Hawaii are included from 1960.
[3]   Statistics to 1882 (1st line) relate to 13 companies, seven east and six west of Chicago.
[4]   Years ending 30 June to 1946.
[5]   Including service traffic subsequently.
[6]   For the period 1941–46 the data for the Ferrocarril del Norte are for years beginning 1 July.
[7]   Ferrocarril del Norte only from 1956 (except 1963.)
[8]   Public railways only from 1945 (2nd line).
[9]   Years ending 30 June to 1948. Service traffic is included to 1951 (1st line). The Ferrocarril Central de Chubut is not included in 1923–29. The reason for the break in the tonnage series in 1959 is not clear in the sources, but it may result from the exclusion of suburban railways.
[10] State railways only to 1901 (1st line). The reason for the break in 1934 is not clear from the sources but may be the later exclusion of mineral traffic on private lines, which was never included in the TKm series. More or less complete figures including private lines are available for certain years in the 1950s and 1960s as follows (excluding the Romeral-Guyacan line to 1960 for a and 1963 for b):-

	a	b		a	b
1956	61,087	5,411	1961	92,075	43,927
1957	46,679	4,416	1962	27,718	2,959
1959	19,967	2,674	1963	49,517	4,326
1960	25,057	2,835	1964	53,434	4,469
			1967	39,364	3,774

[11] Years ending 30 June to 1933.
[12] Excluding the Ferrocarril del Nordeste.
[13] Ferrocarril del Sur only to 1938 (1st line).
[14] Excluding service traffic from 1956 (2nd line).
[15] Subsequently Class I railways only.

F3   NORTH AMERICA: PASSENGER TRAFFIC ON RAILWAYS

Key: a = million passenger journeys; b = million passenger kilometres

1870–1909

	Canada[1]	Mexico	USA[2]	
	a	a	a	b
1870	...	...	...	...
1871	...	...	...	...
1872	...	...	...	...
1873	...	0.7	...	...
1874	...	1.0	...	...
1875	5.2	0.8	...	...
1876	5.5	0.7	...	...
1877	6.1	0.9	...	...
1878	6.4	0.8	...	...
1879	6.5	0.8	...	...
1880	6.5	1.0	...	...
1881	6.9	2.0	...	...
1882	9.4	2.4	289	12,373
1883	9.6	3.0	312	13,745
1884	10	3.4	334	14,128
1885	9.7	3.3	351	14,700
1886	9.9	3.5	382	15,546
1887	11	3.6	428	17,011
1888	11	3.9	451	18,010
1889	12	4.3	494	19,256
1890	13	5.4	520[2]	20,152[2]
			492	
1891	13	6.6	531	20,670
1892	14	5.2	561	21,506
1893	14	7.1	594	22,899
1894	14	4.2	541	22,996
1895	14	5.7	507	19,615
1896	15	4.9	512	21,000
1897	16	6.4	489	19,726
1898	18	9.4	501	21,533
1899	19	9.0	523	23,482
1900	22	11	577	25,811
1901	18	11	607	27,929
1902	21	12	650	31,688
1903	22	14	695	33,661
1904	24	15	715	35,282
1905	25	16	739	38,302
1906	28	16	798	40,502
1907	32	...	874	44,609
1908	34	17	890	46,805
1909	33	18	891	46,846

F3   NORTH AMERICA: Passenger Traffic on Railways

1910–1949

	Canada[1]		Costa Rica[4]		Cuba[3]		El Salvador	Guatemala
	a	b	a	b[5]	a	b	a	a
1910	36	3,970	...	...	...	...	...	...
1911	37	4,194	...	...	...	...	...	...
1912	41	4,683	...	...	...	...	...	...
1913	46	5,256	...	...	10	323	0.6	...
1914	47	4,971	...	...	...	...	...	...
1915	46	3,925	...	...	...	...	...	...
1916	49	4,389	...	...	...	...	...	...
1917	48	5,069	...	...	...	...	...	...
1918	45	5,087	...	...	...	...	...	...
1919	44[1]	4,949[1]	...	...	...	...	...	...
	48	5,889						
1920	51	5,670	...	...	...	...	...	...
1921	47	4,765	...	...	...	...	...	...
1922	44	4,529	...	...	23	504	1.1	...
1923	45	4,950	...	...	25	546	1.3	...
1924	43	4,622	...	...	26	653	1.4	...
1925	42	4,685	...	...	28	684	1.5	...
1926	43	4,826	...	...	26	613	...	...
1927	42	4,912	1.3	...	32	...	1.8	...
1928	41	5,055	1.4	...	24	...	1.7	...
1929	39	4,662	1.3	...	23[3]	...[3]	...	...
1930	35	3,899	1.3	...	...	...	1.3	...
1931	26	2,813	0.9	...	...	...	0.7	...
1932	21	2,311	0.5	...	...	...	0.8	...
1933	19	2,242	0.5	...	...	...	1.1	...
1934	21	2,464	0.5	...	...	...	1.1	...
1935	20	2,551	0.6	...	...	...	1.1	...
1936	21	2,778	0.7	...	...	...	1.0	...
1937	22	3,104	0.8	...	7.1	204	1.0	1.8
1938	21	2,869	0.9	...	9.7	221	0.9	1.6
1939	21	2,820	0.9	...	9.5	212	0.9	1.7
1940	22	3,504	0.7[4]	...	5.8	248	0.9	1.5
1941	30	5,160	0.8	...	6.7	270	0.8	1.5
1942	48	8,029	1.0	...	7.7	379	1.4	1.8
1943	57	10,501	1.3	...	11	522	2.1	2.5
1944	60	11,061	1.2	...	14	617	2.7	3.2
1945	53	10,268	1.2[4]	...	16	739	3.2	3.9
1946	43	7,482	1.2	...	16[3]	737[3]	3.2	4.2
1947	41	6,008	1.2	57	15	667	3.3	4.1
1948	38	5,596	1.3	49	14	562	3.5	3.9
1949	35[1]	5,139[1]	1.4	56	13	515	3.3	3.8

F3 NORTH AMERICA: Passenger Traffic on Railways

1910-1949

	Mexico		Nicaragua		Panama	USA[2]	
	a	b	a	b	a	a	b
1910	...	...	...	...	...	972	52,043
1911	...	...	...	...	...	997	53,433
1912	...	...	...	...	...	1,004	53,321
1913	...	...	...	...	...	1,044	55,801
1914	...	...	...	...	...	1,063	56,902
1915	...	...	...	...	...	986	52,263
1916	...	...	...	...	...	1,015[2]	55,215[2]
						1,049	56,681
1917	...	...	...	...	...	1,110	64,535
1918	...	...	...	...	...	1,123	69,543
1919	...	...	...	...	...	1,211	75,378
1920	...	...	...	...	...	1,270	76,235
1921	25	2,134	...	...	...	1,061	60,682
1922	22	1,610	...	...	...	990	57,632
1923	22	1,604	...	...	...	1,009	61,628
1924	21	1,687	...	...	...	950	58,529
1925	24	1,687	...	...	...	902	58,205
1926	24	1,484	...	...	...	875	57,410
1927	23	1,515	...	...	...	840	54,393
1928	22	1,502	...	...	...	798	51,045
1929	21	1,629	...	...	...	786	50,155
1930	21	1,448	...	29	...	708	43,253
1931	17	1,123	...	25	...	599	35,298
1932	15	929	...	20	...	481	27,354
1933	17	1,005	...	17	...	435	26,342
1934	21	1,160	...	17	0.2	452	29,079
1935	24	1,382	0.9	33	...	448	29,787
1936	26	1,571	1.2	46	...	492	36,146
1937	27	1,719	1.5	55	...	500	39,743
1938	29	1,789	1.3	46	...	455	34,854
1939	30	1,841	1.4	49	0.3	454	36,553
1940	28	1,844	1.6	55	0.3	456	38,239
1941	28	1,976	1.7	57	0.3	489	47,324
1942	32	2,284	1.8	64	0.4	672	86,497
1943	36	3,022	2.1	75	0.5	888	141,502
1944	38	3,598	2.4	84	0.5	916	153,955
1945	35	3,405	2.6	98	0.6	897	147,780
1946	33	3,009	2.8	98	0.6	795	104,211
1947	32	2,885	2.8	97	0.6	707	73,985
1948	30	2,664	...	97	0.7	646	66,344
1949	31	2,787	...	95	0.6	557	56,541

F3   NORTH AMERICA: Passenger Traffic on Railways

	Canada[1]		Costa Rica[4]		Cuba[3]		El Salvador		Guatemala
	a	b	a	b[5]	a	b	a	b	a
1950	31	4,532	1.4	52	15	567	3.7	...	3.8
1951	31	5,005	1.5	50	14	563	4.1	...	3.9
1952	30	5,071	1.6	50	12	462	4.0	...	4.0
1953	29	4,806	1.4	51	9.3	357	3.8	...	4.2
1954	28	4,608	1.4	63	8.5	322	3.6	...	4.2
1955	27	4,654	1.3	63	7	295	3.7	...	4.2
1956	26	4,680	1.4	64$_5$	6.3$_3$	278$_3$	3.6	...	3.9
1957	23	4,707	1.4	31	...	...	3.5	...	3.5
1958	21	4,001	1.5	34	...	...	3.3	...	3.0
1959	21	3,936	1.6	36	...	...	3.1	...	2.5
1960	19	3,644	1.6	37	...	...	2.8	...	2.0
1961	19	3,155	1.6	38	...	...	2.7	...	1.8
1962	19	3,249	1.6	36	14	899	2.8	...	1.7
1963	21	3,331	1.5	21	13	918	2.7	...	1.8
1964	23	4,315	1.5	...	11	725	2.5	...	1.8
1965	25	4,287	...	...	12	822	2.2	...	1.6
1966	23	4,166	1.7	[72]^5	15	922	1.8	...	1.6
1967	27	5,103	1.9	60	18	1,168	1.7	...	1.4
1968	25	4,230	2.1	71	20	1,302	1.5	...	1.1
1969	24	3,890	2.3	69	20	1,434	1.5	...	1.1
1970	24	3,657	2.3	55	13	1,130	1.6	33	1.3
1971	24	3,518	2.4	57	12	990	1.6	...	1.3
1972	23	3,288$_6$	2.6	53	10	946	1.7	...	1.5
1973	20	2,573	2.8	85	10	609	1.7	...	1.1
1974	24	3,023	2.9	81$_5$	10	636	1.9	...	1.7
1975	24	2,658	2.6	128	11	668	1.5	23	1.6
1976	...	2,942	...	99	13	767	1.7	26	...
1977	...	2,966	...	...	15	1,076	2.0	30	...
1978	...	3,200	...	...	18	1,571	2.0	31	...
1979	...	3,175	...	...	18	1,636	2.0	30	...
1980	...	3,280	...	...	20	1,802	1.7	27	...
1981	24	3,276	...	...	20	1,916	0.9	14	...
1982	21	2,640	2.4	152	23	2,073	0.4	5.9	...
1983	...	2,932	2.5	...	23	2,144	0.2	3.8	...
1984	22	2,915	2.0	79	25	2,360	0.3	4.7	...
1985	23	3,040	...	...	23	2,257	0.3	4.7	...
1986	23	2,831	...	...	...	2,200	0.3	5.0	...
1987	...	1,920	...	57	...	2,189	0.4	5.6	...
1988	27	2,709	1.3	...	...	2,627	...	6.0	...
1989	...	2,989		44		2,891		5.3	
1990	...	3,178		43		2,865		5.9	
1991	...	2,004				3,026		7.8	
1992	...	1,426				2,594		6.3	
1993	...	1,439				2,512		6.0	

F3   NORTH AMERICA: Passenger Traffic on Railways

	Honduras	Mexico		Nicaragua		Panama	USA[2]	
	a	a	b	a	b	a	a	b
1950	1.4	32	3,025	3.0	100	0.7	488	51,161
1951	1.6	33	3,363	3.1	95	0.8	485	55,748
1952	1.7	31	3,328	3.3	113	0.8	471	54,771
1953	1.6	28	2,987	3.5	118	0.7	458	50,982
1954	1.5	31	3,259	3.6	124	0.7	441	47,170
1955	1.0	34	3,764	3.6	128	0.9	433	45,944
1956	1.0	35	3,861	3.4	118	1.0	430	45,409
1957	0.9	33	3,837	3.1	115	1.0	413	41,705
1958	0.8	29	3,491	2.7	109	0.9	382	37,490
1959	0.7	31	3,725	2.0	77	0.9	354[2]	35,526[2]
1960	0.7	33	4,128	1.5	60	0.8	327	34,253
1961	0.7	34	4,288	1.5	56	0.8	318	32,683
1962	0.7	35	3,770	1.5	59	0.7	313	32,068
1963	0.7	36	3,889	1.4	55	0.6	311	29,803
1964	0.7	37	4,097	1.4	54	0.5	314	29,404
1965	0.6	37	3,882	1.3	51	0.5	306	28,089
1966	0.3	38	4,062	1.2	43	0.4	308	27,620
1967	0.3	39	4,442	1.1	43	0.4	304	24,565
1968	1.6	39	4,344	0.9	35	0.4	301	21,185
1969	1.5	39	4,633	0.8	30	0.4	302	19,657
1970	0.1	37	4,534	0.8	30	0.5	289	17,358
1971	1.3	34	4,362	0.8	31	0.5	276	14,264
1972	0.8	34	4,467	0.7	28	0.5	262	13,795
1973	0.1	29	4,057	0.5	23	0.4	255	14,980
1974	0.1	25	4,614	0.6	22	0.5	275	16,655
1975	...	25	4,123	0.4	18	...	270	15,715
1976	...	24	4,058	...	20	...	272	15,688
1977	...	29	5,040	...	19	...	276	16,565
1978	...	29	5,326	0.4	17	...	262	16,452
1979	...	25	5,253	...	15	...	274	18,025
1980	...	24	5,296	...	19	...	281	17,695
1981	...	23	5,287	0.6	20	...	...[12]	18,371
1982	...	22	5,351	...	25	...	19	16,966
1983	...	23	5,630	...	45	...	19	17,606
1984	...	24	5,951	...	60	...	20	16,564
								17,649[12]
1985	...	23	6,015	2.4	66		21	8,008
1986	...	22	5,874	3.5	...	0.1	20	8,069
1987	...	22	5,828	...	...	- -	21	8,639
1988	...	18	5,619	...	...	- -	21	9,154
1989		16	5,383				21	9,402
1990		17	5,336				22	9,726
1991		15	4,725				22	10,101
1992		10	4,794				22	9,800
1993		11	3,219				22	9,974

International Historical Statistics: The Americas 1750-1993

F3 SOUTH AMERICA: Passenger Traffic on Railways

	1855-1894						1895-1939			
	Argentina[7]	Chile[8]	Peru[9]	Uruguay[10]	Venezuela		Argentina[7]		Bolivia[11]	
	a	a	a	a	a		a	b	a	b
1855	...	...	...	...	...	1895	15	...	...	...
1856	...	...	...	...	...	1896	17	...	...	...
1857	0.1	...	...	...	...	1897	16	...	...	...
1858	0.2	...	...	...	...	1898	16	...	...	...
1859	0.3	...	...	...	...	1899	18	...	...	...
1860	...	...	...	...	...	1900	18	...	...	...
1861	...	...	...	...	...	1901	20	...	...	...
1862	0.4	...	...	...	...	1902	20	...	...	...
1863	0.4	...	...	...	...	1903	21	...	...	...
1864	0.6	...	...	...	...	1904	23	...	...	...
1865	0.7	...	...	...	...	1905	27	...	...	...
1866	1.2	...	...	...	...	1906	34	...	...	...
1867	1.6	...	...	...	...	1907	42	...	...	...
1868	1.7	...	...	...	...	1908	47	...	...	...
1869	1.9	...	...	...	...	1909	51	...	...	...
1870	1.9	...	...	...	...	1910	60	...	...	...
1871	2.5	...	...	...	...	1911	68	...	...	...
1872	2.2	...	...	...	...	1912	69	...	...	...
1873	2.7	...	...	...	...	1913	79	...	...	...
1874	2.6	...	...	...	...	1914	81	...	...	...
1875	2.6	...	...	...	...	1915	68	...	...	...
1876	2.3	1.4	...	...	...	1916	66	...	...	...
1877	2.4	1.3	...	...	...	1917	62	...	...	...
1878	2.5	1.2	...	...	...	1918	54	...	...	...
1879	2.6	1.3	...	...	...	1919	64	...	...	...
1880	2.8	1.4	...	...	...	1920	78	...	...	...
1881	3.3	1.8	...	...	...	1921	87	...	...	...
1882	3.6	2.1	...	...	...	1922	91[7]	...	...	...
1883	4.1	2.3	...	...	- -	1923	115	...	...	...
1884	4.8	2.5	...	...	- -	1924	128	...	...	...
1885	5.8	2.7	...	...	0.1	1925	137	...	...	...
1886	4.7	...	...	...	- -	1926	143	...	...	...
1887	8.2	2.5	...	...	0.1	1927	149	...	...	...
1888	10	3.0	...	...	0.2	1928	154	4,187	...	...
1889	11	3.4	...	...	0.2	1929	162[7]	4,358	...	...
1890	10	3.6	2.6	...	0.2	1930	171	4,344	...	54
1891	11	2.8	2.6	...	0.2	1931	166	4,038	...	38
1892	12	4.2	2.6	0.6	0.2	1932	150	3,719	...	44
1893	13	4.7	2.8	0.5	0.2	1933	144	3,525	...	79
1894	14	5.3	2.6	0.6	0.4	1934	138	3,634	...	89
						1935	139	3,649	...	122
						1936	135	3,865	...	138
						1937	147	4,065	...	176
						1938	159	4,278	1.2	100
						1939	164	4,338	1.3	103

F3 SOUTH AMERICA: Passenger Traffic on Railways

1895–1939

	Brazil		Chile[8]		Colombia		Paraguay	Peru[9]		Uruguay[10]		Venezuela
	a	b	a	b	a	b	a	a	b	a	b	a
1895	...	...	5.3	...	...	...	...	2.6	...	0.7	...	0.4
1896	...	...	5.6	...	...	...	...	3.1	...	0.8	...	0.5
1897	...	...	5.7	...	...	...	...	3.3	...	0.7	...	0.5
1898	...	...	5.9	...	...	...	...	3.2	...	0.7	...	0.5
1899	...	...	6.3	...	...	...	...	3.5	...	0.8	...	0.4
1900	...	...	6.6	...	...	...	...	3.8	...	0.8	...	0.3
1901	...	...	$\underline{7.4}_8$ 8.4	...	...	...	...	4.1	...	0.9	...	0.3
1902	...	...	8.5	...	...	...	...	3.8	...	0.9	...	0.3
1903	...	...	8.9	...	...	...	...	5.5	...	0.9	...	0.3
1904	...	...	9.2	...	...	...	...	6.1	...	1.0	...	0.4
1905	...	...	10	...	...	...	...	8.7	...	1.0	...	0.4
1906	...	...	12	...	...	...	...	9.4	...	1.2	...	0.4
1907	...	...	15	...	...	...	...	$\underline{11.0}_9$	...	1.4	...	0.4
1908	...	...	...	...	...	...	...	2.9	...	1.2	...	0.4
1909	...	...	12	...	...	...	...	2.9	...	1.2	...	0.4
1910	...	...	13	...	...	...	...	3.1	...	1.2	...	0.5
1911	...	...	13	...	1.5	...	...	3.4	...	1.5	...	0.6
1912	...	...	17	...	2.0	...	...	4.2	...	1.7	...	0.6
1913	...	...	28	...	3.4	...	...	4.3	...	2.0	...	0.6
1914	...	...	25	...	3.6	...	0.6	4.1	...	1.9	...	0.6
1915	...	...	19	...	4.0	...	...	3.9	...	1.9	...	0.8
1916	54	1,413	23	...	4.4	...	...	4.1	...	2.1	...	0.9
1917	57	1,529	25	...	5.0	...	...	4.7	...	2.0	...	1.0
1918	59	1,586	$\underline{27}_8$	...	5.0	...	...	1.3	...	2.0	...	1.0
1919	67	1,850	17	...	6.0	...	...	5.8	221	2.4	...	1.2
1920	76	2,194	19	...	7.1	...	...	6.3	233	2.6	...	1.9
1921	78	2,309	17	...	6.7	...	...	7.0	262	...	...	1.9
1922	90	2,673	15	...	7.0	...	0.2	6.3	241	...	...	2.1
1923	104	3,218	16	...	7.5	...	0.3	6.3	246	3.1	134	3.0
1924	116	3,702	18	...	8.2	...	0.5	6.3	231	3.2	135	2.4
1925	124	4,082	17	...	8.7	...	0.5	5.7	...	4.3	...	2.8
1926	126	3,569	16	...	10.0	...	0.5	5.4	212	4.5	153	2.4
1927	131	4,237	18	896	11.0	...	0.5	4.9	210	...	...	2.7
1928	157	4,298	18	950	12.0	...	0.5	4.7	168	4.3	161	2
1929	163	4,846	17	923	12.0	...	0.5	4.8	158	4.0	159	2.1
1930	148	4,397	18	925	9.1	...	0.6	4.4	126	4.0	166	2.7
1931	145	4,734	14	708	7.2	261	0.5	4.2	126	4.4	174	2.9
1932	135	3,734	14	693	7.3	270	...	3.8	136	4.1	157	1.9
1933	146	4,097	18	937	8.2	310	1.1	3.5	132	$\underline{3.9}_{10}$	146_{10}	0.8
1934	156	4,122	20	1,030	11	432	...	3.4	123	4.2	153	0.9
1935	167	4,561	17	1,031	12	451	2.6	4.4	126	4.8	192	1.2
1936	165	4,730	19	1,204	12	468	2.0	4.2	126	5.1	210	1.1
1937	168	5,100	20	1,198	12	484	1.6	3.8	136	5.4	235	0.4
1938	174	5,532	20	1,227	12	482	1.1	3.5	132	5.7	260	0.8
1939	195	7,118	19	1,257	13	487	1.0	3.4	123	6.3	271	1.0

F3 SOUTH AMERICA: Passenger Traffic on Railways

1940-1993

	Argentina[7]		Bolivia[11]		Brazil		Chile[8]		Colombia	
	a	b	a	b	a	b	a	b	a	b
1940	164	4,380	1.6	125	194	6,428	21	1,457	12	457
1941	165	4,631	1.2	122	214	7,130	21	1,337	12	462
1942	173	4,833	2.1	163	224	6,708	23	1,733	13	565
1943	188	5,169	2.1	132	257	7,846	27	2,113	15	651
1944	209	5,818	2.1	128	277	8,771	28	1,779	16	727
1945	246	6,944	1.8	130	287	9,023	29	1,663	17	782
1946	282	7,699	1.9	132	304	9,704	27	1,665	18	851
1947	314	8,973	1.8	...	318	10,139	26	1,682	18	814
1948	351[7]	10,329[7]	1.5	136	350	10,706	24	1,511	18	816
1949	470	13,678	1.6	147	338	10,394	23	1,419	17	838
1950	491	13,229	1.8	158	340	10,267	24	1,588	15	743
1951	525	13,976	2.2	195	339	10,015	27	1,808	15	731
1952	531	13,451	2.5	240	327	10,417	26	1,778	14	694
1953	541	13,654	2.6	251	313	11,593	27	1,789	13	668
1954	572	14,735	3.4	331	353	12,008	31	1,739	12	674
1955	579	14,762	3.4	...	364	12,686	32	1,887	11	586
1956	605	15,384	3.3	...	358	12,607	33	1,821	11	562
1957	619	15,456	2.1	236	375	12,546	29	1,627	11	592
1958	618	15,653	2.2	208	382	13,432	29	1,529	11	652
1959	623	16,586	2.2	...	420	14,639	30	2,407	11	651
1960	604	15,684	2.1	226	421	15,395	26	1,906	9.8	598
1961	580	15,158	2.2[11]	205[11]	457	16,853	24	1,788	9.6	617
1962	453	12,616	1.9	156	478	17,926	25	1,931	9.0	623
1963	450	12,074	1.8	142	459	17,315	25	1,991	8.6	627
1964	480	12,962	1.8	155	440	16,991	24	2,048	7.4	546
1965	482	12,829	1.5	220	406	16,884	28	2,411	6.5	513
1966	480	14,080	1.4	257	352	13,945	23	2,097	5.8	491
1967	449	13,590	1.4	252	345	13,517	23	2,043	4.8	418
1968	491	14,852	1.4	249	367	13,803	21	2,085	3.7	351
1969	492	14,772	1.2	258	356	13,338	22	2,217	2.7	273
1970	440	12,684	1.2	271	333	12,351	21	2,338	2.1	249
1971	435	12,814	1.1	270	309	11,276	21[8]	2,481[8]	2.3	282
1972	406	12,573	1.1	...	314	10,783	25	3,037	3.1	398
1973	391	12,837	1.1	270	308	10,603	28	3,475	4.2	427
1974	423	14,103	...	248	306	10,647	27	2,882	4.6	483
1975	447	14,863	1.1	310	292	10,621	21	2,103	4.2	508
1976	445	14,598	1.2	368	333	11,638	23	2,464	4.0	511
1977	410	12,897	1.3	397	344	11,699	19	2,382	3.0	391
1978	380	11,561	1.2	398	368	11,923	14	2,126	2.6	342
1979	377	12,028	1.2	363	389	11,404	11	1,732	2.5	322
1980	394	12,706	1.7	529	435	12,376	9.4	1,431	2.2	315
1981	343	11,258	1.6	482	451	13,133	11	1,582	1.8	230
1982	302	10,147	1.7	556	461	13,266	10	1,506	1.2	158
1983	290	10,387	2.3	772	499	13,797	9.2	1,575	1.3	175
1984	291	10,469	2.1	684	587	15,578	8.7	1,424	1.5	189
1985	300	10,743		748	650	16,362	8.9	1,522	2.4	228
1986	359	12,451	1.9	657	631	15,782	6.2	1,274	1.4	178
1987	352	12,475	1.4	500	653	15,273	7.2	1,177	1.4	171
1988	296	10,271	1.0	369	623	13,891	6.8	1,013	1.2	148
1989	280	10,533	1.1	386	613	18,813	8.1	1,058	...	177
1990	286	10,512	1.3	388	568	18,209	8.8	1,077	...	141
1991	216	8,045	1.3	350	601	18,859	9.8	1,125	...	79
1992	214	6,749	...	334	498	15,668	9.5	1,010	1.3	16
1993	215	5,836	...	318	475	14,040	9.6	938	...	...

F3   SOUTH AMERICA: Passenger Traffic on Railways

1940-1993

	Ecuador[13]		Paraguay		Peru[9]		Uruguay[10]		Venezuela	
	a	b	a	b	a	b	a	b	a	b
1940	1.3	81	1.2	...	3.3	124	6.0	272	0.8	...
1941	1.3	81	1.2	...	3.0	126	5.7	268	0.7	...
1942	1.8	115	1.6	...	3.7	155	5.4	261	1.2	...
1943	2.4	...	1.8	...	5.1	213	4.7	235	1.5	...
1944	2.7	181	1.9	...	5.5	236	5.4	275	2.0	...
1945	2.6	177	2.0	...	5.8	251	6.0	303	1.8	...
1946	2.2	153	2.2	...	5.8	261	6.5	314	1.4	...
1947	2.1	147	2.0	...	5.6	249	6.6	327	0.9	...
1948	2.0	138	...	45	5.7	248	7.3	356	0.6	...
1949	1.9	129	...	58	5.8	260	8.2	394	0.6	...
1950	1.9	121	...	62	5.4	241	9.2	470	0.6	16
1951	2.0	129	...	58	5.5	246	11	515	0.3	12
1952	2.3	129	...	67	5.5	268	12	548	0.4	18
1953	2.1	106	...	60	5.4	282	13	488	0.4	21
1954	2.0	105	1.9	57	5.8	308	13	556	0.3	14
1955	2.7	118	1.5	48	6.3	335	13	...	0.1	9
1956	1.8	113	1.2	39	6.2	332	13	485	0.1	7
1957	...	...	1.1	39	6.2	342	12	435	0.1	6
1958	1.6	...	0.9	34	5.8	292	12	511	0.1	5
1959	...	...	1.0	31	5.2	260	14	577	0.2	21
1960	1.3	65	0.8	31	5.1	282	10	527	0.3	25
1961	1.3	58	0.6	36	4.7	275	8.6	494	0.4	28
1962	1.8	62	0.5	36	4.4	275	9.8	608	0.4	28
1963	2.4	54	0.5	38	3.8	257	10	630	0.3	29
1964	3.3	64	0.5	39	3.5	252	9.8	603	0.5	37
1965	3.4	52	0.3	35	3.0	236	9.1	552	0.6	44
1966	3.9	53	0.2	20	2.8	224	11	708	0.5	45
1967	4.1	72	0.1	14	2.4	211	...	717	0.4	39
1968	4.9	80	0.2	28	2.5	219	...	...	0.4	34
1969	5.1	86	0.2	28	2.6	254	8.6	500	0.3	29
1970	4.9	85	0.2	24	...	248	...	529	0.4	36
1971	2.2	62	0.2	24	...	270	...	437	0.4	43
1972	2.4	63	0.2	26	...	286	...	336	0.4	44
1973	4.0	70	0.2	26	...	305	...	351	0.4	45
1974	2.9	69	0.2	27	...	393	5.8	353	0.4	43
1975	...	65	0.1	24	...	455	6.1	362	0.4	40
1976	...	59	0.1	16	...	528	...	372	0.4	42
1977	...	72	0.1	18	...	651	...	307	0.4	39
1978	...	65	0.1	17	...	473	...	303	0.4	40
1979	...	69	0.2	21	...	534	...	269	0.2	25
1980	...	70	0.3	22	4.2	586	5.4	234	0.2	28
1981	...	58	0.3	22	3.5	494	3.3	218	0.1	10
1982	...	50	0.3	20	3.4	458	...	274	0.1	19
1983	...	43	0.3	20	3.4	454	...	312	0.2	22
1984	...	49	0.2	22	3.6	483	5.0	334	0.1	12
1985	...	52	...	26	3.6	475	...	241	0.1	8
1986	...	55	0.3	26	3.5	490	...	196	0.1	17
1987	...	63	...	23	3.9	594	...	140[14]	0.2	22
1988	...	77	...	22	4.0	596	...		0.2	29
1989		83	0.7	22	4.4	659			0.3	38
1990		82	0.6	13	3.1	469			0.6	64
1991		53	0.4	10	2.3	320			0.5	55
1992		53	...	10	1.7	226			0.4	47
1993		39	0.2	5	1.5	165			0.4	44

F3 Passenger Traffic on Railways

NOTES

1. SOURCES: As for table F2.
2. It is not always clear whether passengers carried free are included or not, though there appears to be an indication whenever a change in this respect occurs.

FOOTNOTES

[1] Years ending 30 June to 1919 (1st line). Newfoundland is included from 1950.
[2] Paying passengers carried by each line to 1890 (1st line), paying passengers originated subsequently. Data for 1890 (2nd line) to 1916 (1st line) are for years ending 30 June. Alaska and Hawaii are included from 1960.
[3] Statistics to 1929 are for passengers carried by each line. From 1936 to 1956 they relate to class I railways only. Data to 1946 are for years ending 30 June.
[4] For the period 1941–45 the data for the Ferrocarril del Norte component are for years beginning 1 July.
[5] Ferrocarril del Norte only from 1957 to 1974, except 1966.
[6] Including non-paying passengers subsequently.
[7] Years ending 30 June to 1948. The Ferrocarril Central de Chubut is not included in 1923–29.
[8] State railways only to 1901 (1st line). Tramways are included to 1918. The Transandean Railway is excluded from 1972.
[9] Tramways are included to 1907.
[10] Years ending 30 June to 1933.
[11] Coverage is said to be variable prior to 1962.
[12] Subsequent statistics relate to AMTRAK only.
[13] Earlier figures are available as follows:

	a	b
1936	...	31
1937	...	34
1938	1.0	52
1939	0.9	...

[14] Passenger traffic suspended.

F4 NORTH AMERICA: MERCHANT SHIPS REGISTERED

key: a = number of ships; b = thousand gross registered tons; c = thousand net registered tons

	USA			USA		
	b			a	b	
	Sail[1]	Steam		All Ships[1]	Sail[1]	Steam
1789	202	—	1835	...	1,702	123
1790	478	—	1836	...	1,737	146
1791	502	—	1837	...	1,742	155
1792	564	—	1838	...	1,802	193
1794	629	—	1839	...	1,901	195
1795	748	—	1840	...	1,978	202
1796	832	—	1841	...	1,956	175
1797	877	—	1842	...	1,863	230
1798	898	—	1843	...	1,922	237
1799	939	—	1844	...	2,008	272
1800	972	—	1845	...	2,091	326
1801	948	—	1846	...	2,214	348
1802	892	—	1847	...	2,434	405
1803	949	—	1848	...	2,726	428
1804	1,042	—	1849	...	2,872	462
1805	1,140	—	1850	...	3,010	526
1806	1,209	—	1851	...	3,189	584
1807	1,268	- -	1852	...	3,495	643
1808	1,242	- -	1853	...	3,802	605
1809	1,350	1	1854	...	4,126	677
1810	1,424	1	1855	...	4,442	770
1811	1,231	1	1856	...	4,199	673
1812	1,268	2	1857	...	4,235	706
1813	1,164	3	1858	...	4,320	729
1814	1,156	3	1859	...	4,376	768
1815	1,365	3	1860	...	4,486	868
1816	1,366	6	1861	...	4,663	877
1817	1,391	9	1862	...	4,402	710
1818	1,213	13	1863	...	4,580	576
1819	1,243	17	1864	...	4,080	978
1820	1,258	22	1865	...	4,030[2]	1,067[2]
1821	1,276	23	1866	...	3,227	1,084
1822	1,304	23	1867	...	3,113	1,192
1823	1,312	25	1868	28,167	3,153[1]	1,199[2]
1824	1,368	22			2,509[2]	
1825	1,400	23	1869	27,487	2,400	1,104
1826	1,500	34	1870	28,998	2,363	1,075
1827	1,580	40	1871	29,651	2,286	1,088
1828	1,702	39	1872	31,114	2,325	1,112
1829	1,207	54	1873	32,672	2,383	1,156
1830	1,127	64	1874	32,486	2,474	1,186
1831	1,198	69	1875	32,285	2,585	1,169
1832	1,349	91	1876	25,934	2,609	1,172
1833	1,504	102	1877	25,386	2,580	1,168
1834	1,636	123	1878	25,264	2,521	1,168
			1879	25,211	2,423	1,176

F4 NORTH AMERICA: Merchant Ships Registered

	Canada				Cuba		Honduras		Mexico	
	Sail		Steam		Steam		Steam & Motor		Steam[3]	
	a	c	a	c	a	b	a	b	a	b
1867	5,338	722	355	46	...	...	...	...	...	...
1873	6,223	1,005	560	69	...	...	...	...	...	...
1883	6,336	964	1,008	304	...	...	...	...	...	...
1888	...	...	...	...	...	...	...	...	10	4.9
1889	...	...	...	...	...	...	...	...	10	5.0
1890	...	...	...	...	...	...	...	...	12	5.9
1891	...	...	...	...	...	...	...	...	12	5.0
1892	6,004	819	1,000	145	...	...	...	...	11	4.7
1893	...	...	...	...	...	...	...	...	9	4.0
1894	...	...	...	...	...	...	...	...	11	3.9
1895	5,532	671	1,718	154	...	...	...	...	11	4.2
1896	...	...	...	...	...	...	...	...	12	4.7
1897	...	...	...	...	...	...	...	...	18	9.1
1898	4,732	529	1,889	161	...	...	...	...	15	6.6
1899	4,729	...	1,969	...	...	...	...	...	14	6.2
1900	4,634	479	2,101	181	30	4.2	...	...	16	6.5
1901	4,615	483	2,177	183	34	31	...	...	23	13
1902	4,547	469	2,289	184	38	38	...	...	24	12
1903	4,610	477	2,410	206	39	39	...	...	27	17
1904	4,609	459	2,543	214	43	42	...	...	30	18
1905	4,671	456	2,654	214	40	45	1	2.2	31	21
1906	4,702	428	2,810	226	44	54	7	16	24	33
1907	4,521	406	3,007	293	43	58	4	8.7	34	27
1908	4,518	406	3,084	296	41	56	1	1.5	35	29
1909	4,539	406	3,229	313	40	56	1	1.5	33	26
1910	4,572	413	3,332	337	36	50	1	1.5	30	26
1911	4,644	412	3,444	359	38	54	3	4.9	30	31
1912	4,713	447	3,667	389	40	56	2	3.4	30	35
1913	4,698	467	3,847	430	41	56	4	6.3	30	36
1914	4,718	479	4,054	453	38	51	5	9.2	33	42
1915	4,625	470	4,132	459	29	33	5	8.7	29	37
1916	4,458	451	4,202	491	27	28	3	6.3	24	32
1917	4,295	450	4,264	522	35	30	6	9.8	32	33
1918	4,202	461	4,366	556	37	31	7	11	39	29
1919	4,131	487	4,442	605	38	39	7	11	35	32
1920	3,623	476	4,281	677	41	44	7	11	33	31
1921		445		779	44	50	11	21	37	36
1922	3,253	447	4,388	794	49	55	14	31	43	43
									—[3]	—[3]
1923	3,231	445	4,463	786	48	43	14	27	75	54
1924	3,198	453	4,499	768	53	52	24	49	58	57

F4 NORTH AMERICA: Merchant Ships Registered

	Newfoundland[4]				Panama		USA[2]		
	Sail		Steam		Steam & Motor		All Ships[1]	b	
	a	c	a	c	a	b	a	Sail[1]	Steam
1879	1,691	76	27	6.3	...	...	see page 571		
1880	1,803	80	27	6.3	...	...	24,712	2,366	1,212
1881	1,866[4]	83[4]	29	6.8	...	...	24,065	2,350	1,265
1882	1,938	90	...	...	...	...	24,368	2,361	1,356
1883	1,988	...	...	...	...	...	24,217	2,387	1,413
1884	2,033	...	...	...	...	...	24,082	2,414	1,466
1885	1,977	...	...	...	...	...	23,963	2,374	1,495
1886	2,044	...	...	...	...	...	23,534	2,210	1,523
1887	2,053	...	...	...	...	...	23,063	2,170	1,543
1888	2,106	94	...	...	...	...	23,281	2,124	1,648
1889	2,172	94	...	...	...	...	23,623	2,099	1,766
1890	2,207	99	...	...	...	...	23,467	2,109	1,859
1891	2,222	95	...	...	...	...	23,899	2,172	2,016
1892	2,202	92	...	...	...	...	24,383	2,178	2,074
1893	...	...	...	...	...	...	24,512	2,118	2,183
1894	2,339	108	...	...	...	...	23,586	2,023	2,189
1895	2,341	104	...	...	...	...	23,240	1,965	2,213
1896	2,368	106	...	...	...	...	22,908	1,928	2,307
1897	...	...	...	...	...	...	22,633	1,904	2,359
1898	2,429[4]	107[4]	...	...	...	...	22,705	1,836	2,372
1899	2,441	99	37	8.4	...	...	22,728	1,825	2,476
1900	2,546	102	45	10	...	...	23,333	1,885	2,658
1901	2,637	105	47	9.4	...	...	24,057	1,933	2,921
1902	2,751	109	48	9.7	...	...	24,273	1,942	3,177
1903	2,802	111	54	11	...	...	24,425	1,966	3,408
1904	2,880	114	65	12	...	...	24,558	1,945	3,595
1905	2,982	118	66	12	...	...	24,681	1,962	3,741
1906	3,131	125	68	11	...	...	25,006	1,899	3,975
1907	3,241	130	67	12	...	...	24,911	1,814	4,279
1908	3,289	132	66	15	...	...	25,425	1,761	4,711
1909	3,315	132	72	17	...	...	25,868	1,711	4,749
1910	3,318	133	68	14	...	...	25,740	1,655	4,900
1911	3,307	132	71	15	...	...	25,991	1,598	5,074
1912	3,315	132	80	17	...	...	26,528	1,539	5,180
1913	3,327	132	88	21	...	...	27,070	1,508	5,333
1914	3,310	130	92	21	...	...	26,943	1,433	5,428
1915	3,330	134	98	20	...	...	26,701	1,384	5,944
1916	...	138	...	22	...	...	26,444	1,311	6,070
1917	...	140	...	20	...	...	26,397	1,278	6,433
1918	...	152	...	20	...	...	26,711	1,210	7,471
1919	...	149	...	22	...	...	27,513	1,200	10,416
1920	...	152	...	22	...	...	28,183	1,272	13,823
1921	...	151	...	23	1	1.1	28,012	1,294	15,745
1922	...	148	...	21	2	7.5	27,358	1,288	15,982
1923	...	143	...	18	9	38	27,017	1,254	15,821
1924	...	136	...	19	14	84	26,575	1,185	15,315

F4 NORTH AMERICA: Merchant Ships Registered

	Canada[5]				Cuba		Hondurasl		Mexico	
	Sail		Steam & Motor		Steam & Motor		Steam & Motor		Steam & Motor[3]	
	a	c	a	c	a	b	a	b	a	b
1925	3,279	492	4,634	793	53	54	24	53	51	56
1926	3,351	504	4,842	847	55	54	26	58	49	50
1927	3,358	502	5,096	866	51	45	30	72	44	45
1928	3,337	501	5,308	865	52	45	28	69	43	47
1929	...	503	...	891	48	38	33	87	42	47
1930	...	515	...	917	...	...	35	98	41	46
1931	...	515	...	969	42	36	34	97	28	39
1932	...	505	...	970	44	37	31	80	...	...
1933	...	490	...	941	43	33	29	77	...	...
1934	...	476	...	921	44	34	29	75	...	...
1935	...	475	...	914	42	31	28	72	...	...
1936	...	463	...	904	39	29	27	69	28	32
1937	...	...	...	...	36	30	28	70	30	34
1938	2,193	428	6,008	849	35	30	28	71	29	29
1939	2,159[5]	437[5]	6,260	850	33	27	32	84	30	30

	All Ships									
	a	c								
1940	8,396	1,293								
1941	8,667	1,272			...	...	...	...	...	...
1942	8,852	1,210			...	...	...	...	...	...
1943	9,074	1,348			...	...	...	...	...	...
1944	9,369	1,645			...	...	...	...	...	...
1945	9,421	1,673			...	...	...	...	...	...
1946	10,070	1,601			...	...	...	...	...	...
1947	10,931	1,710			27	19	78	278	50	108

	Steam & Motor									
	a	b								
	904	1,870								
1948	984[6]	2,007[6]			34	35	93	324	53	114
1949	1,178	2,097			34	36	123	409	55	120
1950	1,156	1,931			...	...	142	523	59	144
1951	1,126	1,647			...	...	152	508	61	168
1952	1,151	1,692			...	...	145	468	64	160
1953	1,142	1,652			...	...	146	471	64	157
1954	1,122	1,610			...	...	130	439	65	163
1955	1,095	1,521			...	...	117	432	67	172
1956	1,081	1,504			...	...	106	386	64	165
1957	1,105	1,521			...[7]	...[7]	94	368	63	159
1958	1,096	1,516			14	38	89	338	70	162
1959	1,079	1,501			18	49	78	202	76	181
1960	1,043	1,578			19	52	59	154	74	179
1961	1,080	1,669			20	62	58	120	77	177
1962	1,063	1,704			21	71	54	113	79	201
1963	1,087	1,796			24	98	49	103	85	250
1964	1,132	1,823			29[7]	118[7]	46	90	86	265
					53	135				

F4 NORTH AMERICA: Merchant Ships Registered

| | Newfoundland | | | | Panama | | USA | | |
| | Sail | | Steam & Motor | | Steam & Motor | | All Ships[1] | | b |
	a	c	a	c	a	b	a	Sail	Steam & Motor
1925	...	131	...	30	18	98	26,367	1,125	14,976
1926	...	127	...	34	20	101	26,343	1,092	14,848
1927	...	119	...	34	21	47	25,778	989	14,507
1928	...	115	...	39	29	71	25,385	915	14,344
1929	...	111	...	39	27	62	25,326	825	14,162
1930	2,501	102	255	42	28	75	25,214	757	13,757
1931	...	94	...	41	41	131	25,471	673	13,528
1932	...	87	...	39	43	138	25,156	625	13,568
1933	2,001	80	290	42	83	287	24,868	563	12,862
1934	1,970	76	302	43	71	271	24,904	500	12,687
1935	2,065	83	319	42	42	137	24,919	441	12,535
1936	1,987	80	385	44	81	429	25,392	379	12,267
1937	1,907	77	421	44	103	512	26,588	312	12,170
1938	1,849	74	375	46	134	611	27,155	261	12,007
1939	1,696	65	646	52	159	718	27,470	221	11,952
1940	...	...	...	...	...	...	27,212	200	11,353
1941	...	...	...	...	...	...	27,075	182	11,047
1942	...	...	...	...	...	...	27,325	166	11,072
1943	1,578	65	808	52	...	...	27,612	142	14,052
1944	...	...	...	...	...	...	28,690	129	23,217
1945	1,461	55	898	53	...	...	29,797	115	30,247
1946	1,438	54	1,045	52	174	834	31,386	98	35,928
1947	1,379	52	1,011	58	369	1,702	32,760	95	35,149
1948	1,330	49	1,054	62	515	2,716	33,843	87	30,469
1949	...	...	...	...	535	3,016	35,264	87	29,323
1950					573	3,361	36,083	82	28,327
1951					607	3,609	36,745	71	27,424
1952			included with Canada		606	3,740	37,389	66	27,459
1953					593	3,907	38,072	55	27,507
1954					595	4,091	39,008	46	27,631
1955					555	3,923	39,242	40	26,792
1956					556	3,926	39,499	34	26,251
1957					580	4,129	40,191	24	25,785
1958					602	4,358	41,276	23	24,599
1959					639	4,583	42,409	23	24,333
1960					607	4,236	43,088	23	23,553
1961					601	4,049	43,367	18	21,175
1962					592	3,851	43,566	18	20,076
1963					619	3,894	44,077	18	20,079
1964					691	4,269	44,669[1] 3,537	17	20,018

F4 NORTH AMERICA: Merchant Ships Registered

| | Bahamas | | Bermuda | | Canada[5,6] | | Cuba[7] | |
| | Steam & Motor | | Steam & Motor | | Steam & Motor | | Steam & Motor | |
	a	b	a	b	a	c	a	b
1965	89	254	29	200	1,154	1,830	68	161
1966	95	256	31	222	1,188	2,125	99	238
1967	106	282	27	346	1,236	2,305	101	235
1968	113	303	30	380	1,296	2,403	104	238
1969	136	376	29	355	1,278	2,451	200	277
1970	144	276	48	684	1,266	2,400	236	333
1971	145	358	47	814	1,228	2,366	264	385
1972	144	206	48	814	1,235	2,381	267	398
1973	143	179	52	861	1,235	2,423	271	416
1974	129	153	54	1,153	1,231	2,460	259	409
1975	119	190	59	1,450	1,257	2,566	272	477
1976	119	148	69	1,562	1,269	2,639	294	604
1977	109	106	88	1,752	1,283	2,823	315	668
1978	93	84	99	1,814	1,289	2,954	331	779
1979	91	121	112	1,727	1,290	3,016	341	853
1980	91	87	114	1,724	1,324	3,180	405	881
1981	106	197	75	499	1,300	3,159	408	920
1982	96	433	68	474	1,299	3,213	414	949
1983	122	861	67	819	1,300	3,385	418	961
1984	163	3,192	76	822	1,310	3,449	418	959
1985	195	3,907	79	981	1,286	3,344	423	965
1986	302	5,985	97	1,208	1,249	3,160	422	959
1987	469	9,105	105	1,925	1,238	2,971	422	966
1988	572	8,963	116	3,774	1,225	2,902	412	912
1989	724	11,579	107	4,076	1,227	2,825	407	900
1990	807	13,626	105	4,258	1,224	2,744	410	836
1991	973	17,541	100	3,057	1,204	2,685	401	770

F4 NORTH AMERICA: Merchant Ships Registered

	Honduras		Mexico		Panama		USA		
	Steam & Motor		Steam & Motor		Steam & Motor		Steam & Motor		b
									Steam & Motor
	a	b	a	b	a	b	a	Sail	
1965	47	81	90	269	692	4,465	3,416	8	19,730
1966	43	70	95	306	702	4,543	3,332	...	...
1967	45	75	99	330	757	4,756	3,303	...	...
1968	45	69	114	404	798	5,097	3,232	6	19,396
1969	51	66	118	424	823	5,374	3,146	6	19,433
									19,550
1970	52	60	132	381	886	5,646	2,983	6	18,463
1971	54	70	185	401	1,031	6,262	3,327	...	16,266
1972	58	74	216	417	1,337	7,794	3,687	...	15,024
1973	57	67	248	453	1,692	9,569	4,063	...	14,912
1974	56	70	261	515	1,962	11,003	4,086	...	14,429
1975	60	68	274	575	2,418	13,667	4,346	...	14,587
1976	57	71	290	594	2,680	15,631	4,614	...	14,908
1977	63	105	311	674	3,267	19,458	4,740	...	15,300
1978	70	131	336	727	3,640	20,749	4,746	...	16,188
1979	99	193	349	915	3,803	22,324	5,088	...	17,542
1980	124	213	361	1,006	4,090	24,191	5,579	...	18,464
1981	143	201	456	1,135	4,461	27,657	5,869	...	18,908
1982	172	234	545	1,252	5,032	32,600	6,133	...	19,111
1983	191	222	619	1,475	5,316	34,666	6,437	...	19,358
1984	238	277	624	1,489	5,499	37,244	6,441	...	19,292
1985	291	357	638	1,467	5,512	40,674	6,447	...	19,518
1986	424	555	642	1,520	5,252	41,305	6,496	...	19,900
1987	503	506	651	1,532	5,136	43,255	6,427	...	20,178
1988	587	582	659	1,448	5,022	44,604	6,442	...	20,832
1989	677	691	642	1,388	5,121	47,365	6,375	...	20,588
1990	754	712	640	1,320	4,748	39,298	6,348	...	21,328
1991	846	816	649	1,196	4,953	44,949	6,222	...	20,291

F4   SOUTH AMERICA: MERCHANT SHIPS REGISTERED

	Chile					Chile					Chile			
	Sail		Steam			Sail		Steam			Sail		Steam	
	a	c	a	c		a	c	a	c		a	c	a	c
1848	105	13	—	—	1860	259	59	7	1.4	1875	52	13	28	9.9
1849	119	20	—	—	1861	260	59	7	1.4	1876	62	13	28	9.9
1850	157	28	—	—	1862	259	58	10	1.7	1877	89	21	25	11
1851	182	35	—	—	1863	250	55	9	1.6	1878	...	...	...	...
1852	215	43	—	—	1864	263	62	9	1.6	1879	...	...	...	...
1853	214	47	3	0.8										
1854	217	49	5	0.9	1865	248	66	9	1.3	1880	31	5.2	18	5.4
					1866	247	66	11	2.2	1881	56	17	18	4.8
1855	257	59	—	—	1867	...[9]	...[9]	...[9]	...[9]	1882	90	35	24	9.7
1856	257	60	8	2.0	1868	19	2.8	2	0.6	1883	104	41	27	13
1857	267	63	—	—	1869	33	5.5	7	0.6	1884	128	51	30	15
1858	260	62	—	—									Steam & Motor	
1859	261	58	7	1.2	1870	56	11	12	2.4	1885	131	55	35	17
					1871	61	13	14	2.5	1886	136	59	37	19
					1872	57	13	18	3.6	1887	141	59	38	19
					1873	57	12	18	4.2					
					1874	51	11	26	8.0					

	Argentina				Brazil				Chile			
	Sail[10]		Steam & Motor[11]		Sail[10]		Steam & Motor[11]		Sail		Steam	
	a	b	a	b	a	b	a	b	a	c	a	c
1888	86	20	48	23	265	57	121	67	140	63	37	19
1889	101	28	50	24	271	58	125	70	150	69	39	20
1890	106	29	54	25	268	56	129	76	150	72	39	24
1891	105	28	57	29	270	58	147	93	150	69	43	25
1892	113	31	53	25	276	61	180	121	146	66	48	28
1893	115	29	60	36	282	65	176	120	116	57	54	28
1894	124	28	56	33	285	66	172	115	117	57	50	24

	Peru				Uruguay				Venezuela	
	Sail[10]		Steam & Motor[11]		Sail[10]		Steam & Motor[11]		Steam & Motor	
	a	b	a	b	a	b	a	b	a	b
1888	38	24	7	8.4	37	11	10	4.2	5	1.9
1889	36	21	7	8.5	37	10	15	7.8	5	2.5
1890	36	21	5	5.3	40	12	18	8.2	6	2.8
1891	37	22	5	5.3	42	12	19	8.7	6	2.1
1892	36	20	4	4.6	44	12	17	7.6	5	2.0
1893	35	19	3	2.6	46	13	24	7.6	5	2.0
1894	37	17	3	2.6	45	13	17	8.4	5	1.9

F4   SOUTH AMERICA: Merchant Ships Registered

	Argentina				Brazil				Chile			
	Sail[10]		Steam & Motor[11]		Sail[10]		Steam & Motor[11]		Sail		Steam & Motor	
	a	b	a	b	a	b	a	b	a	c	a	c
1895	140	36	54	34	303	71	190	127	111	52	54	28
1896	154	38	61	43	320	74	214	139	113	53	48	26
1897	152	36	61	46	322	72	218	144	...	...	...	...
1898	157	40	64	48	343	68	211	144	112	52	50	25
1899	155	29	68	58	364	80	211	140	...	...	...	...
1900	155	40	76	62	358	80	214	139	82	37	54	31
1901	151	38	75	60	343	77	208	142	83	38	53	30
1902	159	42	81	66	340	77	204	134	84	36	52	29
1903	163	41	93	73	347	76	186	124	76	35	56	37
1904	156	42	120	79	345	76	202	136	...	...	...	...
1905	161	41	101	85	340	74	192	146	64	33	63	35
1906	161	44	132	116	305	66	207	151	63	39	83	56
1907	175	53	128	111	297	64	215	180	68	44	100	54
1908	177	52	126	111	298	63	208	196	63	41	96	53
1909	181	56	123	113	293	61	208	194	63	41	95	54
1910	183	57	130	129	290	61	218	210	48	39	67	57
1911	182	54	141	146	286	62	229	237	57	38	102	58
1912	192	64	143	150	289	61	244	264	45	30	103	53
1913	175[10]	52[10]	147	157	303[10]	68[10]	257	284	35	22	98	43
1914	52	20	150	164	87	17	252	276	35	25	92	44
1915	48	19	144	162	86	15	248	268	28	25	101	51
1916	49	17	135	147	79	13	240	259	28	21	98	45
1917	56	23	160	143	82	16	312	457	39	29	92	43
1918	50	20	140	139	86	19	312	492	35	23	95	47
1919	55	21	142	163	83	20	299	493	26	17	103	45
1920	48	20	140	149	85	22	298	475	25	20	114	52
1921	46[11]	21[11]	148[11]	160[11]	82[11]	22[11]	299[11]	473[11]	24[12]	22[12]	115[12]	56[12]
									23	b	101	b
									14			100
1922	43	20	173	162	50	23	349	469	19	10	107	121
1923	32	18	167	161	45	19	337	459	18	8.3	119	164
1924	33	20	182	179	45	20	330	445	22	20	125	161
1925	34	20	192	203	44	18	330	448	21	20	123	166
1926	33	19	209	216	43	18	338	465	18	16	120	164
1927	39	25	228	238	44	18	332	508	14	11	114	152
1928	40	23	252	265	44	17	344	542	14	11	116	160
1929	38	22	273	275	41	15	350	546	11	10	108	144
1930	43	25	292	298	42	15	346	544	11	8	120	185
1931	41	25	299	303	14	5	297	494	3	4	113	180
1932	41	24	304	312	13	5	296	492	3	4	108	174
1933	41	24	305	318	15	5	295	489	3	4	99	152
1934	40	24	304	316	15	5	293	495	3	4	98	153
1935	42	26	298	317	15	5	293	486	3	4	90	142
1936	42	27	286	305	13	3	283	475	3	4	90	139
1937	43	25	290	293	13	3	286	473	3	4	90	138
1938	42	22	293	281	11	3	286	483	5	5	94	158
1939	42	22	295	291	11	3	293	485	5	5	101	172

F4   SOUTH AMERICA: Merchant Ships Registered

	Peru				Uruguay				Venezuela	
	Sail[10]		Steam & Motor[11]		Sail[10]		Steam & Motor[11]		Steam & Motor	
	a	b	a	b	a	b	a	b	a	b
1895	46	20	5	5.5	51	13	18	8.1	7	4.0
1896	54	22	6	6.4	51	12	19	9.4	5	2.0
1897	58	25	5	6.0	55	14	22	14	7	3.7
1898	63	27	4	5.1	56	14	21	11	6	3.2
1899	60	24	3	5.0	58	15	19	10	4	2.5
1900	57	24	5	6.4	58	16	21	12	7	3.9
1901	55	23	5	6.4	62	20	23	13	6	3.1
1902	55	23	5	6.4	67	26	26	22	7	5.3
1903	56	25	3	4.7	70	30	26	25	6	3.4
1904	56	25	3	4.7	76	32	32	27	8	3.7
1905	55	25	4	8.1	72	31	21	21	6	3.4
1906	53	22	5	8.5	65	26	25	25	6	3.4
1907	58	27	7	9.9	67	31	23	26	6	3.4
1908	60	29	7	11	62	28	28	40	6	3.4
1909	65	31	7	16	64	29	34	58	6	3.4
1910	60	31	9	21	62	27	36	50	6	3.4
1911	57	30	9	26	57	24	29	40	7	4.5
1912	57	29	11	31	53	23	31	45	7	4.5
1913	58[10]	31[10]	12	32	56[10]	25[10]	30	42	7	4.5
1914	40	21	13	39	45	17	19	17	5	3.9
1915	41	21	13	32	45	16	17	14	6	4.2
1916	40	20	11	26	48	23	19	19	7	4.6
1917	40	21	14	27	49	26	26	21	10	4.8
1918	41	23	17	53	45	19	21	37	11	5.2
1919	40	22	14	45	43	18	22	24	9	4.9
1920	40	22	15	33	43	18	27	52	9	4.9
1921	42[11]	30[11]	16[11]	34[11]	44[11]	21[11]	29[11]	62[11]	9	4.9
1922	44	33	30	68	12	11	41	65	9	4.6
1923	22	23	25	59	...	13	...	73	12	5.6
1924	18	20	20	51	...	10	...	70	14	11
1925	17	17	22	59	15	9	50	68	15	11
1926	18	19	28	61	14	8	49	67	...	...
1927	15	19	28	57	10	7	45	24	...	...
1928	16	17	26	52	...	...	...	...	32	45
1929	15	18	23	44	...	...	...	...	36	56
1930	15	20	24	45	...	...	...	...	38	58
1931	15	20	24	45	...	...	...	...	38	59
1932	15	20	24	45	...	...	...	...	36	58
1933	14	17	24	43	...	...	...	...	37	60
1934	13	17	22	33	...	...	...	...	38	63
1935	13	17	21	27	...	...	...	...	41	65
1936	13	17	24	29	...	...	...	...	40	72
1937	4	6	26	31	...	...	...	...	38	71
1938	4	6	29	35	...	...	...	...	43	76
1939	4	6	28	34	...	...	...	...	47	75

F4   SOUTH AMERICA: Merchant Ships Registered

	Argentina		Brazil		Chile		Colombia	
	Steam & Motor		Steam & Motor		Steam & Motor		Steam & Motor	
	a	b	a	b	a	c	a	b
1945	...	...	...	...	84	160	...	...
1946	113	354	166	511	98	191	...	...
1947	312	571	307	603	92	188	...	...
1948	330	683	331	706	91	175	...	...
1949	357	814	331	722			...	...
1950	369	914	328	698	88	169	...	...
1951	363	979	335	688	85	168	...	...
1952	365	1,034	374	794	92	188	...	...
1953	370	1,057	384	854	94	199	...	...
1954	368	1,057	399	895	96	209	...	...
1955	364	1,043	396	893	101	230	...	...
1956	364	1,050	386	862	109	249	...	...
1957	360	1,039	398	891	111	246	...	...
1958	356	1,029	409	911	102	231	...	...
1959	358	1,039	415	952	105	232	...	...
1960	355	1,042	423	1,055	110	246	...	...
1961	374	1,195	455	1,201	113	258	36	114
1962	332	1,262	430	1,204	103	258	37	116
1963	346	1,308	428	1,227	104	286	37	114
1964	318	1,284	421	1,271	111	284	37	132
1965	323	1,289	397	1,253	126	296	38	160
1966	322	1,279	392	1,279	136	290	41	187
1967	315	1,240	394	1,305	134	279	42	196
1968	315	1,197	398	1,294	130	269	47	209
1969	319	1,218	414	1,381	133	288	47	206
1970	327	1,266	422	1,722	134	308	49	235
1971	335	1,312	420	1,731	135	388	50	209
1972	343	1,401	444	1,885	134	382	54	232
1973	351	1,453	469	2,103	138	384	54	224
1974	366	1,408	471	2,429	135	364	54	211
1975	374	1,447	482	2,691	138	386	53	209
1976	379	1,470	520	3,096	142	410	53	212
1977	401	1,677	538	3,330	143	406	52	247
1978	432	2,001	565	3,702	146	466	61	272
1979	495	2,344	585	4,007	154	537	65	292
1980	537	2,546	607	4,534	172	614	69	283
1981	521	2,307	627	5,133	182	564	72	297
1982	523	2,256	666	5,678	192	495	74	314
1983	532	2,470	698	5,808	200	488	82	359
1984	530	2,422	706	5,722	219	473	82	374
1985	549	2,457	702	6,057	234	454	80	366
1986	454	2,117	697	6,212	282	567	90	380
1987	434	1,901	718	6,324	264	547	93	424
1988	451	1,877	719	6,123	287	604	97	412
1989	465	1,833	716	6,078	304	590	100	379
1990	479	1,890	691	6,016	365	616	103	372
1991	490	1,709	669	5,882	387	618	100	313

F4   SOUTH AMERICA: Merchant Ships Registered

	Ecuador		Peru		Uruguay		Venezuela	
	Steam & Motor		Steam & Motor		Steam & Motor		Steam & Motor	
	a	b	a	b	a	b	a	b
1945	...	...	...	...	...	...	...	...
1946	...	...	...	...	...	...	...	...
1947	...	...	41	74	...	...	60	90
1948	...	...	40	87	43	63	64	96
1949	...	...	43	88	47	85	79	137
1950	...	...	41	87	47	85	93	157
1951	...	...	44	91	44	70	97	167
1952	...	...	48	96	43	63	96	173
1953	...	...	49	97	43	63	97	187
1954	...	...	49	97	44	68	97	210
1955	...	...	47	98	41	66	94	216
1956	...	...	48	98	42	73	90	217
1957	...	...	50	102	38	70	92	225
1958	...	...	54	108	38	72	99	233
1959	...	...	55	121	40	77	104	251
1960	...	...	57	120	...	...	100	349
1961	...	...	61	136	...	...	90	324
1962	...	...	56	131	...	...	85	328
1963	...	...	...	...	...	...	81	319
1964	...	...	60	158	37	104	81	330
1965	...	...	78	163	39	113	79	313
1966	...	...	119	169	39	113	83	315
1967	...	...	231	251	40	126	88	350
1968	14	43	275	288	42	131	89	351
1969	16	44	366	338	41	112	90	369
1970	18	45	494	378	41	141	96	393
1971	18	45	601	421	42	163	109	412
1972	21	57	655	446	39	143	113	411
1973	23	76	663	448	38	143	137	479
1974	38	128	675	514	37	130	143	480
1975	44	142	677	518	38	131	152	516
1976	46	181	681	525	43	151	165	543
1977	55	197	681	555	45	193	179	639
1978	59	201	686	575	48	174	201	824
1979	69	234	694	646	53	198	220	882
1980	86	275	698	741	72	198	225	848
1981	100	299	694	826	76	200	227	742
1982	110	354	696	836	81	202	236	911
1983	130	388	679	781	88	217	244	973
1984	135	412	670	788	89	190	250	1,003
1985	152	444	650	818	96	173	269	985
1986	155	438	632	754	89	150	279	998
1987	156	421	635	788	90	144	283	999
1988	154	428	621	675	87	170	286	982
1989	159	402	616	638	86	101	288	1,092
1990	158	385	617	617	91	104	273	935
1991	158	384	618	605	91	105	278	970

F4 Merchant Ships Registered

NOTES

1. SOURCES: The national publications listed on pp. xiii–xv; *Lloyd's Register of Shipping Statistical Tables*; and League of Nations and UN, *Statistical Yearbooks*, with data for Cuba, Honduras, Mexico, and all South American countries to 1921 from the *Shipping World Year Book*.
2. Tonnage figures are normally given in gross capacity.
3. The minimum size of vessel on the register has varied from time to time and from country to country. Where possible changes are indicated. Since 1948 the usual minimum has been 100 GRT.
4. Data since 1947 apply to 31 December. Prior to that, most were for 30 June.
5. The removal of vessels lost, abandoned, sold abroad, etc. was not always done annually, so that the cumulative error sometimes resulted in the inflation of the statistics. When general correction of these errors occurred, the effect was concentrate in a single year and can give a misleading impression.
6. For the period 1953–60 the figures for Costa Rica are large enough to be shown separately. They are as follows:

	a	b		a	b		a	b
1953	50	146	1956	152	508	1959	91	288
1954	70	201	1957	152	519	1960	44	92
1955	114	341	1958	144	510			

FOOTNOTES

[1] Including canal boats and barges to 1868 (1st line) for Sail tonnage series and to 1964 (1st line) for numbers, whereafter the latter relate to steam and motor ships only.
[2] There was a change in the method of measurement between 1865 and 1868, during which period the tonnage figures are 'mixed'. It is noted in *Historical Statistics of the United States* (p. 743) that 'neither the magnitude nor the direction of the change can be stated'.
[3] Excluding motor-assisted sailing ships to 1922.
[4] From 1882 to 1898 all ships are included under Sail.
[5] From 1940 to 1947 (1st line) all ships are included under Sail.
[6] Newfoundland is included in Canada from 1949.
[7] International fleet only from 1958 to 1964 (1st line).
[8] Subsequently from *Lloyd's Register of Shipping Statistical Tables*.
[9] No explanation of this break is given in the source.
[10] Including motor-assisted sailing ships to 1913.
[11] Excluding motor-assisted sailing ships to 1921, when there were also changes in classification affecting sailing vessels.
[12] This break occurs on a change from national sources to *Lloyd's Register of Shipping Statistical Tables*.
[13] Registered tonnage was insignificant in previous years, except 1964, when figures were as follows:

	Bahamas		Bermuda	
	a	b	a	b
1964	86	218	24	168

F5 NORTH AMERICAN INLAND WATERWAY TRAFFIC

Key: a = thousand metric; b = million metric tons; c = thousand million ton — kilometres

	Canada[1]	USA			Canada[1]	USA	
		New York Canals				New York Canals	
			Origin on Erie				Origin on Erie
	Total traffic	Total traffic	Canal		Total traffic	Total traffic	Canal
	a	a	a		a	a	a
1835	...	...	...	**1870**	1,190	5,601	2,797
1836	...	...	...	**1871**	1,341₁	5,868	3,249
1837	...	1,063	605	**1872**	1,209	6,054	3,232
1838	...	1,209	676	**1873**	1,366	5,774	3,268
1839	...	1,302	767	**1874**	1,260	5,266	2,810
1840	...	1,285	753	**1875**	942	4,409	2,529
1841	...	1,380	822	**1876**	998	3,785	2,194
1842	...	1,122	646	**1877**	1,066	4,496	2,952
1843	...	1,373	743	**1878**	879	4,691	3,274
1844	...	1,648	858	**1879**	786	4,865	3,465
1845	...	1,794	942	**1880**	744	5,858	4,181
1846	...	2,058	1,147	**1881**	623	4,698	3,265
1847	...	2,603	1,507	**1882**	718	4,960	3,351
1848	...	2,537	1,451	**1883**	912	5,138	3,254
1849	...	2,535	1,472	**1884**	760	4,545	3,075
1850	...	2,791	1,483	**1885**	712	4,293	2,910
1851	...	3,250	1,774	**1886**	889₁	4,803	3,455
					2,693		
1852	...	3,505	1,932	**1887**	2,559	5,038	3,484
1853	...	3,854	1,992	**1888**	2,506	4,484	3,013
1854	...	3,779	2,018	**1889**	2,872	4,872	3,333
1855	...	3,649	1,998	**1890**	2,643	4,759	2,997
1856	...	3,734	1,912	**1891**	2,634	4,140	2,810
1857	...	3,034	1,421	**1892**	2,751	3,885	2,702
1858	...	3,325	1,603	**1893**	3,218	3,930	2,955
1859	...	3,431	1,591	**1894**	2,670	3,522	2,852
1860	...	4,219	2,044	**1895**	3,026	3,175	2,137
1861	...	4,089	2,269	**1896**	7,249	3,370	2,488
1862	...	5,079	2,907	**1897**	7,712	3,282	2,345
1863	...	5,042	2,681	**1898**	6,004	3,048	2,121
1864	...	4,403	2,300	**1899**	5,648	3,686	2,195
1865	...	4,291	2,289	**1900**	4,549	3,035	1,947
1866	...	5,239	2,627	**1901**	5,139	3,103	2,048
1867	846	5,160	2,650	**1902**	6,816	2,971	1,910
1868	1,054	5,844	3,036	**1903**	8,359	3,280	2,190
1869	1,118	5,315	2,581	**1904**	7,490	2,847	1,765

F5　North American Inland Waterway Traffic

	Canada[1]			Panama Canal[3]	USA		Mississippi Great Lakes[5]	
					New York Canals			
	Total traffic	Origin in Canada	Origin in other countries[2]	Ocean traffic	Total traffic	Origin on Erie Canal	Total traffic	
	a	a	a	a	a	a	b[6]	c
1905	8,502	...	...	—	2,927	1,814	...	...
1906	9,546	...	...	—	3,212	2,164	...	...
1907	18,637	...	...	—	3,092	2,191	...	...
1908	15,878	4,547	11,332	—	2,769	1,975	...	...
1909	30,591	6,693	23,898	—	2,827	1,843	...	...
1910	39,001	7,152	31,849	—	2,788	1,835	...	...
1911	34,500	7,070	27,431	—	2,810	1,843	...	...
1912	43,170	8,507	34,664	—	2,364	1,628	...	...
1913	47,223	10,098	37,125	—	2,361	1,622	...	...
1914	33,587	8,511	25,075	—	1,888	1,235	...	...
1915	13,788	6,159	7,629	4,966	1,686	1,048	...	...
1916	21,394	6,792	14,603	3,143[4]	1,474	833	...	...
1917	20,175	5,356	14,764	7,168	1,177	612	...	...
1918	17,131	3,056	14,074	7,647	1,052	605	...	...
1919	9,067	4,414	4,653	7,021	1,124	764	...	...
1920	7,924	3,714	4,210	9,522	1,290	809	...	...
1921	8,534	4,139	4,395	11,782	1,152	901	...	...
1922	9,095	5,691	3,405	11,058	1,700	1,347	...	...
1923	10,160	6,928	3,231	19,880	1,820	1,475	...	...
1924	11,675	8,035	3,640	27,426	1,844	1,535	186	...
1925	12,819	8,682	4,137	24,341	2,126	1,765	203	...
1926	12,227	8,760	3,466	26,448	2,149	1,756	224	...
1927	15,956	10,763	5,102	28,179	2,342	1,858	218	...
1928	16,982	12,594	4,389	30,091	2,803	2,300	220	...
1929	12,428	8,791	3,638	31,140	2,609	2,197	242	...
1930	13,429	9,938	3,491	30,500	3,271	2,762	226	...
1931	14,686	10,373	4,314	25,467	3,377	2,974	198	...
1932	16,294	12,014	4,280	20,117	3,305	2,890	169	...
1933	17,037	11,544	5,494	18,452	3,696	3,243	180	...
1934	16,392	9,810	6,582	25,100	3,758	3,307	196	...
1935	16,516	10,149	6,368	25,716	4,073	3,537	238	...
1936	19,476	12,215	7,260	26,931	4,549	3,829	283	...
1937	21,184	10,805	10,378	28,559	4,545	3,786	316	...
1938	22,349	11,783	10,567	27,826	4,272	3,038	316	...
1939	21,220	12,837	8,383	28,314	4,254	3,306	356	...
1940	20,748	11,119	9,628	27,737	4,326	3,254	387	...
1941	21,276	9,375	11,901	25,351	4,087	3,187	436	...
1942	18,960	7,044	11,916	13,825	3,211	2,504	437	...
1943	19,483	7,111	12,372	10,770	2,562	1,965	415	...
1944	18,703	7,260	11,442	7,115	2,274	1,569	428	...
1945	20,248	9,517	10,731	8,742	2,693	1,511	408	204
1946	16,924	8,078	8,845	15,218	2,559	1,529	412[6] 157	176
1947	19,517	9,333	10,183	22,019	3,438	2,281	238	209
1948	21,372	10,133	11,240	24,505	4,095	2,832	257	227
1949	22,112	13,427	8,684	25,711	3,610	2,436	243	194

F5　North American Inland Waterway Traffic

	Canada[1]			Panama Canal[3]	USA		Mississippi & Great Lakes[5]	
					New York Canals			
	Total traffic	Origin in Canada	Origin in other countries[2]	Ocean traffic	Total traffic	Origin on Erie Canal	Total traffic	
	a	a	a	b	a	a	b	c
1950	24,892	13,733	11,159	29.3	4,187	3,284	271	225
1951	26,603	14,519	12,085	30.6	4,728	3,332	296	243
1952	28,444	15,644	12,799	34.1	4,071	2,824	292	223
1953	30,275	16,750	13,525	36.7	4,080	2,914	298	264[7]
								248
1954	27,280	15,638	11,642	39.7	3,501	2,173	291	192
1955	31,637	18,146	13,492	41.3	4,188	2,522	331	250
1956	36,303	22,406	13,897	45.8	4,407	2,770	350	244
1957	33,774	19,468	14,307	50.5	4,054	2,427	353	260
1958	31,839	19,807	12,033	48.9	3,629	1,866	335	203
1959	46,335	27,969	18,367	52.0	3,375	1,793	354	213
1960	48,033	26,205	21,828	60.2	3,098	1,608	359	246
1961	51,911	28,565	23,346	64.7	2,924	1,436	353	232
1962	57,868	30,819	26,849	68.6	2,976	1,461	380	247
1963	67,663	38,081	29,582	63.2	2,926	1,398	392	259
1964	84,621	51,074	33,547	71.7	2,898	1,362	416	285
1965	91,077	50,810	40,267	77.8	2,967	1,369	430	301
1966	100,428	60,309	40,119	83.0	2,855	1,192	445	325
1967	89,606	53,459	36,147	87.6	2,921	1,209	455	323
1968	98,226	54,455	43,771	98.1	2,947	1,279	474	339
1969	88,321	43,251	45,070	103	2,947	1,354	499	351
1970	106,139[1]	59,605[1]	46,534[1]	116	2,481	893	503	369
	64,513	...	...	121				
1971	64,213	...	...	111	...	...	508	361
1972	65,874	...	...	128	...	...	542	390
1973	68,192	...	...	150	...	...	541	411
1974	54,555	...	...	142	...	...	547	417
1975	60,686	...	...	143	...	...	531	394
1976	65,176	...	...	119	...	...	554	431
1977	...	...	...	125	...	...	558	420
1978	...	...	...	145	...	...	570	479
1979	...	...	...	157	...	...	573	497
1980	...	...	...	170	...	...	574	474
1981	...	...	...	174	...	...	560	485
1982	...	...	...	188	...	...	521	411
1983	...	...	...	148	...	...	511	425
1984	...	...	...	143	...	...	569	463
1985	...	...	...	141	...	...	...	439
1986	...	...	...	142	...	...	...	449
1987	...	...	...	149	...	...	...	473
1988	...	...	...	156	...	...	...	498
1989				152				519
1990				157				...
1991				163				...
1992				159				...
1993				158				...

F5 North America Inland Waterway Traffic

NOTE

SOURCES: The national publications listed on pp. xiii–xv.

FOOTNOTES

[1] Welland Canal only to 1886 (1st line), and St Lawrence Seaway and Welland Canal (excluding duplication) from 1970 (2nd line). Statistics for the intervening period contain duplication when two or more canals were used. Statistics available since 1976 do not constitute a consistent series.
[2] Mostly, and sometimes entirely, the USA until the 1960s.
[3] Data are for commercial traffic only (i.e. excluding US government traffic), and are for years ending 30 June. The canal was opened on 15 August 1914.
[4] The canal was closed for about seven months during the year.
[5] Covers the whole Mississippi Basin and Great Lakes systems, and canals as indicated in footnotes 6 and 7.
[6] Figures to 1946 (1st line) include traffic on canals and connecting channels, and contain a small element of double-counting.
[7] Figures to 1953 (1st line) include traffic on canals.

F6 NORTH AMERICA: MOTOR VEHICLES IN USE (in thousands)

Key: PC = passenger cars, CV = commercial vehicles

	Canada[1]		Mexico		Puerto Rico[2]		USA[3]	
	PC	CV	PC	CV	PC	CV	PC	CV
1900	...	...	...	...	...		8.0	...
1901	...	...	...	...	...		15	...
1902	...	...	...	...	...		23	...
1903	...	...	...	...	...		33	...
1904	0.5	...	...	...	...		55	0.7
1905	0.6	...	...	...	...		77	1.4
1906	1	...	...	...	...		106	2.2
1907	1.5	...	...	...	...		140	2.9
1908	2.2	...	...	...		0.2	194	4.0
1909	3.2	...	...	...		0.3	306	6.0
1910	5.9	...	...	...		0.3	458	10
1911	14	...	...	...		0.6	619	21
1912	20	...	...	...		1.0	902	42
1913	29	...	...	...		1.2	1,190	68
1914	46	0.4	...	...		1.3	1,664	99
1915	61	0.5	...	...		1.8	2,332	158
1916	78	3.5	...	...		2.6	3,368	250
1917	116	6.1	...	...		3.5	4,727	391
1918	157	9.6	...	...		4.7	5,555	605
1919	196	14	...	...		5.0	6,679	898
1920	252	22	...	...		5.9	8,132	1,108
1921	334	29	...	...		7.0	9,212	1,282
1922	369	38	...	...		7.4	10,704	1,570
1923	513	55	...	...		8.3	13,253	1,849
1924	573	64	33	10		10	15,436	2,177

F6 NORTH AMERICA: Motor Vehicles in Use (in thousands)

1925–1969

	Bahamas		Barbados		Canada[1]		Costa Rica		Cuba	
	PC	CV	PC	CV	PC	CV	PC	CV	PC	CV
1925	...	...	...	...	641	75	...	...	...	...
1926	...	...	1.2	0.2	737	88	...	...	...	...
1927	...	...	1.3	0.2	83	12	...	...	...	...
1928	0.8	0.3	1.3	0.3	931	131	1.1	0.5	26	13
1929	0.9	0.4	1.5	0.3	131	148	1.6	0.6	33	17
1930	...	...	1.4	0.3	162	162	1.4	0.5	27	15
1931	0.8	0.2	1.5	0.4	128	163	...	...	...	...
1932	0.7	0.2	1.6	0.4	948	156	...	...	27	12
1933	0.7	0.2	1.7	0.5	92	153	...	...	...	...
1934	0.8	0.2	1.9	0.5	955	164	...	...	22	11
1935	0.9	0.2	2.0	0.6	992	174	...	...	22	1
1936	1.2	0.2	2.0	0.6	1,420	188	...	...	22	1
1937	1.2	0.2	2.2	0.6	1,150	24	1.9	0.8	26	16
1938	...	...	...	...	1,162	221	2.1	0.8	27	16
1939	...	...	...	...	1,192	235	2.3	0.9	28	16
1940	...	...	...	...	1,237	251	2.4	1.2	29	17
1941	...	...	...	...	1,281	277	...	...	3	18
1942	...	...	...	...	1,219	29	...	...	27	16
1943	...	...	...	...	1,195	3	...	...	23	15
1944	...	...	...	...	1,179	39	...	...	22	16
1945	...	...	...	...	1,161	322	...	...	23	17
1946	...	...	...	...	1,235	37	2.8	1.9	27	21
1947	...	...	2.5	1.1	1,372	438	3.0	2.1	37	26
1948	1.6	0.6	3.2	1.3	1,498₁	53₁	...	...	48	3
1949	...	...	3.4	1.4	1,673	577	4.4	2.9	57	31
1950	2.1	0.7	3.7	1.4	1,913	643	4.6	3.1	7	35
1951	2.3	0.7	4.0	1.5	2,160	723	5.1	3.6	84	39
1952	2.7	0.8	4.5	1.7	2,360	87	5.6	4.3	98	42
1953	2.9	0.9	4.9	1.9	2,528	863	6.7	4.6	13	42
1954	3.0	1.0	4.9	1.8	2,760	91	14		112	44
1955	3.7	1.1	5.2	1.8	2,961	952	17		126	47
1956	4.3	1.2	5.0	1.8	3,223	170	19		139	51
1957	4.9	1.3	6.0	2.1	3,428	134	14[4]	7.7[4]	158	55
1958	6.4	1.3	6.3	2.2	3,631	159	15	8.7	159	51
1959	6.9	1.6	6.8	2.4	3,886	197	19₄ / 14	1.0₄ / 9.0	174	47
1960	7.8	1.7	8.0	2.4	4,140	1,117	16	9.7	18	65
1961	9.0	1.8	8.7	2.5	4,326	1,157	17	9.3	91	41
1962	12.0	2.8	8.8	2.6	4,531	1,210	18	9.2	...	...
1963	12.0	3.1	1.0	2.8	4,789	1,246	19	9.7	...	...
1964	16.0	3.6	11.0	3.5	5,380	1,297	2	11	...	...
1965	2.0	3.5	13.0	3.6	5,279	1,345	23	12	162	14
1966	22.0	4.6	12.0	2.8	5,481	1,447	27	14	...	...
1967	26.0	5.1	15.0	3.0	5,866	1,493	3	16	7	3
1968	32.0	6.2	17.0	3.3	6,160	1,587	32	17	7	31
1969	44.0	7.4	17.0	3.9	6,433	1,683	35	2	71	31

F6 NORTH AMERICA: Motor Vehicles in Use (in thousands)

1925–1969

	Dominican Republic		El Salvador		Guadeloupe		Guatemala		Haiti	
	PC	CV	PC	CV	PC	CV	PC	CV	PC	CV
1925	...	...	...	...	...	...	...	...	...	...
1926	...	...	...	...	...	...	...	...	...	...
1927	...	...	...	...	...	...	...	...	...	...
1928	3.4	1.0	1.5	0.3	1.0	0.2	2.1	1.0	2.0	0.7
1929	3.2	1.1	1.8	0.4	1.2	0.3	2.2	0.8	3.1	0.8
1930	3.2	1.1	1.8	0.4	1.2	0.3	2.0	0.8	2.4	0.6
1931	...	...	...	...	...	...	2.2	1.1	...	...
1932	...	...	...	...	...	...	1.8	1.3	...	...
1933	...	...	...	...	...	...	1.8	1.2	...	...
1934	...	...	1.6	0.5	...	...	1.8	1.1	...	...
1935	...	...	...	...			1.9	1.5	...	...
1936	1.4	0.7	...	...			2.0	1.6	...	...
1937	1.4	0.7	2.4	0.8			2.5	1.6	...	...
1938	1.4	0.7	2.5	0.7			2.5	1.6	1.8	0.6
1939	1.5	0.8	2.5	0.9			2.5	1.7	1.8	0.6
1940	1.5	0.8	2.5	0.9	...	...	2.4	2.2	...	...
1941	...	...	3.5		...	...	...	2.4	2.3	...
1942	1.2	0.9	3.4		...	...	2.4	2.1	...	...
1943	1.2	0.8	2.2	1.1	...	...	2.6	2.1	...	...
1944	1.2	0.8	2.2	1.1	...	...	2.5	2.5	...	...
1945	1.2	0.8	2.1	1.0	...	...	2.6	2.1	...	...
1946	1.8	15	2.6	1.0	1.0	0.6	2.9	2.3	...	...
1947	2.5	2.5	3.3	1.1	1.4	1.1	...	...	2.8	0.8
1948	3.1	2.9	3.7	2.1	1.9	1.6	5.2	4.0	...	...
1949	3.6	3.0	4.0	2.0	2.6	2.1	4.6	4.8	...	...
1950	4.3	3.4	6.7	2.6	3	2.5	7.8	5.0	2.3	1.5
1951	4.6	3.9	7.1	3.6	3.3	2.8	7.6	6.9	2.6	1.7
1952	5.4	4.5	6.7	2.7	3.6	3.2	9.1	6.2	3.9	3.2
1953	5.7	4.4	9.6	4.5	4.6	2.4	9.8	6.9	4.5	2.9
1954	6.4	4.9	9.0	4.8	5.1	3.1	11	7.8	4.9	3.3
1955	6.7	5.3	11	5.7	5.9	3.8	13	9.5	5.1	3.7
1956	8.1	6.5	12	5.9	6.4	4.5	17	11	5.7	4.0
1957	9.2	6.9	14	6.7	6.9	5.0	18	12	6.0	3.6
1958	9.5	6.9	17	7.8	5.6	4.2	22	12	6.3	3.2
1959	11	6.5	17	8.5	6.3	4.6	24	14	6.1	3.4
1960	11	6.3	20	9.0	7.6	5.3	26	15	8.2	3.7
1961	11	6.0	22	9.8	9.0	5.9	29	16	6.1	2.0
1962	16	7.4	23	10	11	6.5	32	12	6.2	2.2
1963	21	8.9	23	9.7	9.6	7.4	35	13	6.6	1.1
1964	28	11	23	11	15	8.8	37	14	5.1	1.8
1965	30	9.7	26	12	17	9.9	29	17	8.7	1.4
1966	27	13	28	13	18	11	33	18	8.4	1.2
1967	29	14	30	14	20	11	33	19	11	1.3
1968	33	18	31	16	23	13	37	21	15	1.3
1969	33	18	34	17	26	14	40	23	15	1.3

F6   NORTH AMERICA: Motor Vehicles in Use (in thousands)

1925–1969

| | Honduras | | Jamaica | | Martinique | | Mexico | | New-foundland | |
	PC	CV	PC	CV	PC	CV	PC	CV	PC	CV
1925	...	...	...	...	...	...	40	13	0.9	0.1
1926	...	...	...	...	...	...	43	15	1.2	0.1
1927	...	...	...	...	...	...	44	17	1.5	0.2
1928	0.3	0.2	4.9	1.5	1.3	0.3	49	18	1.8	0.3
1929	...	...	5.6	2.0	1.5	0.5	62	22	2.1	0.4
1930	0.7	0.4	6.4	1.7	1.8	0.5	63	25	2.5	0.5
1931	...	...	6.8	1.7	...	...	62	26	2.8	0.6
1932	...	...	5.8	1.7	...	...	60	26	2.6	0.5
1933	...	...	6.5	1.6	...	...	65	31	2.7	0.5
1934	...	...	6.9	1.9	...	...	74	34	2.7	0.6
1935	...	...	7.5	2.0	...	...	65	31	3.1	0.7
1936	...	...	8.2	2.2	...	...	67	35	3.3	0.9
1937	...	...	9.0	2.7	...	...	78	42	3.7	1.0
1938	0.6	0.6	9.2	2.8	...	...	82	42	...	...
1939	0.6	0.6	9.8	2.9	...	...	89	49	...	...
1940	0.7	0.7	10	3.1	...	...	94	52	...	...
1941	...	...	9.3	2.6	...	...	106	62	...	...
1942	...	...	9.5	2.6	...	...	113	65	...	...
1943	...	...	6.8	2.0	...	...	112	66	...	...
1944	...	...	5.2	1.5	...	...	112	72	...	...
1945	...	...	7.1	1.7	...	...	113	82	...	...
1946	...	...	8.3	1.9	2.0	1.2	121	85	...	...
1947	1.5	0.6	8.6	2.5	2.4	1.6	134	101	...	...
1948	...	...	11	3.3	2.9	2.0	150	117	...	...
1949	...	...	11	3.6	...	...	163	122	9.0	4.7
1950	1.3	1.9	13	3.9	...	...	173	130	...	...
1951	1.5	2.0	12	4.2	...	...	209	152	...	...
1952	1.9	2.6	13	4.4	3.4	2.6	237	174	...	...
1953	2.3	3.2	14	4.4	...	...	253	199	...	...
1954	2.9	3.5	14	4.6	...	...	274	214	...	...
1955	3.7	4.0	17	5.4	...	...	308	243	...	...
1956	3.9	4.2	19	6.2	4.6	3.7	320	261	...	...
1957	4.2	4.3	22	7.1	...	...	366	295	...	...
1958	4.6	4.8	26	8.2	6.4	4.4	379	296	...	...
1959	5.1	5.0	31	8.9	6.9	4.6	438	327	...	...
1960	5.5	5.2	33	9.2	8.7	5.3	483	320	...	...
1961	5.7	5.3	42	11	10	5.9	550	352	...	...
1962	5.8	5.4	44	12	12	6.5	548	354	...	...
1963	7.5	6.5	53	18	11	6	618	380	...	...
1964	8.8	7.1	50	19₅ / 13	16	8.7	688	394	...	...
1965	10	8.2	46	12	18	9.7	771	419	...	...
1966	12	9.7	49	14	19	8.6	812	436	...	...
1967	12	11	54	15	22	9.3	917	468	...	...
1968	11	14	60	18	25	12	1,000	495	...	...
1969	12	15	69	20	29	13	1,133	537	...	...

F6   NORTH AMERICA: Motor Vehicles in Use (in thousands)

1925–1969

	Nicaragua		Panama[6]		Puerto Rico[2]		Trinidad & Tobago[3]		USA	
	PC	CV	PC	CV	PC	CV	PC	CV	PC	CV
1925	...	...	...	...	13		...	...	17,481	2,588
1926	...	...	...	...	15		...	...	19,268	2,932
1927	...	...	...	...	15		...	...	20,193	3,110
1928	0.7	0.1	5.8	0.7	13	3.6	4.2	1.3	21,362	3,326
1929	0.8	0.2	4.6	1.6	13	3.5	4.5	1.4	23,121	3,584
1930	1.0	0.2	6.3	1.7	10	3.2	4.5	2.0	23,035	3,715
1931	...	...	6.0	1.9	...	...	...		22,396	3,698
1932	...	...	6.4	1.7	13	3.5	...	...	20,901	3,490
1933	...	...	6.5	1.5	...	...	...	...	20,657	3,502
1934	...	...	6.8	1.6	...	...	...	...	21,544	3,717
1935	...	...	7.4	1.7	...	...	3.6	1.3	22,568	3,978
1936	...	...	8.2	1.9	...	...	4.4	1.7	24,183	4,324
1937	...	...	9.1	1.8	16	4.9	4.3	1.7	25,467	4,592
1938	0.6	0.2	9.4₆	1.9₆	17	5.3	4.3	1.8	25,250	4,563
1939	0.6	0.2	10	1.9	...	...	3.5	1.5	26,226	4,783
1940	0.6	0.2	13	2.3	...	...	4.9	1.9	27,466	4,987
1941	...	...	16	3.7	...	...	5.4	2.4	29,624	5,270
1942	...	...	15	4.6	...	...	5.3	2.3	27,973	5,031
1943	...	...	12	3.7	...	...	...	...	26,009	4,879
1944	0.7	0.6	12	3.6	...	...	...	...	25,566	4,913
1945	0.7	0.6	11	3.7	...	...	...	...	25,797	5,238
1946	0.7	0.7	13	4.2	19	11	6.2	3.5	28,217	6,156
1947	0.7	0.7	13	3.9	24	15	7.5	4.3	30,849	6,992
1948	0.8	0.8	17	4.1	26	16	8.9	3.8	33,355	7,730
1949	1.4	0.9	17	5.2	35	17	10₈ / 12	4.4₈ / 5.6	36,458	8,232
1950	1.5	1.3	20	4.3	37	19	13	6.2	40,339	8,721
1951	1.8	1.3	[8.7][7]	[3.5][7]	45	20	15	6.5	42,688	9,224
1952	2.5	1.6	[8.5][7]	[3.5][7]	50	20	16	6.7	43,823	9,439
1953	2.8	2.0	[11][7]	[4.0][7]	59₂	21₂	19	7.5	46,429	9,788
1954	4.2	2.5	[10][7]	[3.8][7]	64	24	20	7.3	48,468	10,037
1955	5.2	2.8	13	6.1	74	25	22	7.8	52,145	10,544
1956	7.0	5.3	14	7	82	30	25	8.4	54,211	10,937
1957	7.8	5.7	15	7.1	86₂	37	28	10	55,918	11,207
1958	9.3	5.6	16	7.5	101	32	28	11	56,891	11,406
1959	8.5	4.8	16	6.6	116	34	31	11	59,454₃	11,900₃
1960	8.6	5.5	18	6.6	135	37	37	12	61,682	12,186
1961	8.3	5.5	20	7.4	154	41	41	13	63,417	12,541
1962	8.1	6.3	22	8.3	171	37	46	14	66,108	13,065
1963	11	5.1	25	8.7	197	44	49	15	69,055	13,658
1964	13	5.0	27	9.5	226	48	51	15	71,983	14,318
1965	13	9.5	30	11	255	51	55	16	75,258	15,100
1966	13	9.8	34	11	305	60	59	17	78,128	15,822
1967	19	8.5	35	12	338	65	63	17	80,407	16,499
1968	20	8.9	40	13	383	78	68	19	83,604	17,294
1969	24	8.7	42	13	437	91	69	19	86,858	18,238

F6 NORTH AMERICA: Motor Vehicles in Use (in thousands).

	Bahamas		Barbados		Canada		Costa Rica		Cuba	
	PC	CV	PC	CV	PC	CV	PC	CV	PC	CV
1970	44	7.4	19	4.0	6,602	1,738	39	27	72	32
1971	40	6.2	23	4.3	6,967	1,856₅ 1,557	43	26	72	32
1972	41	6.1	22	4.1	7,407	1,682	48	30	...	...
1973	40	4.7	21	3.0	7,866	1,844	52	34	70	33
1974	40	5.5	24	3.8	8,328	2,026	55	37	...	...
1975	35	5.3	23	3.8	8,693	2,177	60	41	...	...
1976	36	5.3	25	4.0	9,016	2,319	65	42	80	40
1977	43	3.2	25	3.8	9,554	2,494	73	49	158	...
1978	42	5.6	26	2.3	9,745	2,718	80	59	160	107
1979	46	7.3	29	2.3	9,985	2,854	78	58	153	118
1980	47	8.0	...	...	10,255	2,955	88	66	159	133
1981	50	8.9	...	...	10,199	3,192	89	66	171	143
1982	58	11	...	...	10,530	3,293	91	66	182	152
1983	53	8.6	...	...	10,731	3,365	101	66	190	159
1984	48	7.1	31	4.9	10,781	3,099	106	67	200	165
1985	54	8.5	33	4.8	11,118	3,148	111	69	206	173
1986	54	9.5	35	4.7	11,477	3,212	119	76	217	184
1987	59	13	37	5.1	11,772	3,568	127	84	229	195
1988	69	14	39	4.3	12,086	3,766	135	90	241	208
1989	69	14	43	4.8	12,811	3,458	144	95	...	...
1990	69	14	39	10.0	12,622	3,931	169	95	...	...
1991	69	14	41	11.0	13,061	3,680	181	96	...	...
1992	...	...	41	11.0	13,322	3,688	204	110	...	...
1993	...	...					220	115	...	...

	Dominican Republic		El Salvador		Guadeloupe		Guatemala		Haiti	
	PC	CV	PC	CV	PC	CV	PC	CV	PC	CV
1970	39	21	28	19	28	17	43	24	12	1.4
1971	45	24	32	21	32	16	43	36	12	1.5
1972	51	24	38	22	38	16	54	37	12	1.6
1973	57	28	39	19	35	14	66	38	12	1.3
1974	65	32	41	19	...	...	71	39	16	2
1975	71	36	...	...	...	...	76	40	18	2.5
1976	77	39	...	...	61	25	83	41	19	2.4
1977	84	41	73	37	68	27	84	41	23	3.8
1978	91	46	70	46	74	28	90₅ 156	44₅ 56	24	6.5
1979	90	51	79	58	74	28	147	73	25	8.3
1980	94	47	72	71	80	31	167	81	21	10
1981	105	58	83	64	88	33	...	...	15	6.8
1982	97	61	83	64	75	24	...	...	16	7.8
1983	92	58	88	61	83	26	...	...	18	8.1
1984	109	60	85	65	89	28	...	...	25	11
1985	101	52	88	66	₅ 51	28	...	...	26	11
1986	133	77	...	...	71	28	...	...	19	13
1987	152	85	...	...	79	31	...	...	20	23
1988	...	...	...	...	79	31	...	...	21	23
1989	130	88	...	...	83	33	...	...	28	23
1990	139	90	...	...	86	34	...	...	26	10
1991	136	94	...	...	89	35	...	...	32	21
1992	127	94	...	...	95	36	...	...	32	21
1993	160	111	...	...	102	38	...	...	32	21

International Historical Statistics: The Americas 1750–1993

F6 NORTH AMERICA: Motor Vehicles in Use (in thousands, except USA)

	Honduras		Jamaica		Martinique		Mexico	
	PC	CV	PC	CV	PC	CV	PC	CV
1970	13	16	72	21	30	11	1,234	589
1971	14	17	93	22	35	18	1,338	560
1972	17	17	86	22	40	17	1,520	593
1973	16	18	110[5]	29[5]	...	...	1,767	645
1974	16	22	70	19	...	...	2,053	729
1975	18	26	59	13	...	...	2,401	888
1976	19	29	56	12	...	...	2,580	988
1977	21	34	48	14	65	22	2,829	1,057
1978	24	33	39	12	72	24	3,360	1,278
1979	24	41	40	13	78	25	3,763	1,386
1980	26	45	34	14	...	...	4,241	1,489[9]
								1,575
1981	27	45	41	17	...	...	4,727	1,792
1982	29	49	40	20	...	...	4,760	1,873
1983	29	49	35	17	...	...	4,711	1,955
1984	30	49	42	23	...	...	4,955	2,078
1985	32	57	43	26	...	...	5,260	2,183
1986	33	52	44	21	...	...	5,179	2,285
1987	36	59	53	23	...	...	5,312	2,364
1988	39	64	63	27	...	...	5,783	2,510
1989	...	...	65	25	...	...	5,942	2,590
1990	...	80	69	28	...	...	6,524	2,851
1991	44	93	78	30	...	...	6,894	3,169
1992	69	102	73	30	...	...	7,411	3,358
1993	...	...	81	36	...	...	7,832	3,438

	Nicaragua		Panama		Puerto Rico		Trinidad & Tobago		USA (in millions)	
	PC	CV	PC	CV	PC	CV	PC	CV	PC	CV
1970	34	...	46	15	490	103	75	20	89.2	19.2
1971	32	...	50	16	559	115	72	20	92.7	20.3
1972	...	...	54	18	562	104	78	20	97.1	21.7
1973	32	20	58	19	561	115	83	21	102.0	23.7
1974	32	14	63	18	608	125	89	23	104.9	25.1
1975	36	23	66	20	637	130	101	26	106.7	26.2
1976	36	30	68	21	670	137	105	29	110.2	28.4
1977	43	27	71	22	683	140	118	33	112.3	29.8
1978	41	26	75	25	807	165	131	37	116.6	31.8
1979	38	28	90	30	842	174	144	42	118.5	33.4
1980	38	28	98	32	950	160	157	49	121.6	34.2
1981	...	...	104	36	962	162	171	58	123.1	35.2
1982	...	...	110	38	993	155	188	65	123.7	35.9
1983	...	...	123	38	1,018	159	210	70	126.2	37.7
1984	...	...	129	41	1,128	171[5]	229	61	128.1	38.1
1985	...	...	129	40	1,195	148	242	79	131.9	39.8
1986	46	31	134	42	1,114	146	244	79	135.4	40.8
1987	...	...	129	45	1,227	158	360		137.3	41.7
1988	...	...	130	42	1,304	172	365		140.7	42.8
1989	...	...	121	40	1,290	173	369		143.1	53.2
1990	...	...	133	42	1,305	188	319		143.6	56.0
1991	...	...	144	47	1,322	192	272		142.6	58.2
1992	...	...	150	50	1,347	202	278		144.2	61.2
1993	...	...	161	55	1,393	240	...		146.3	82.5

F6 SOUTH AMERICA: MOTOR VEHICLES IN USE (in thousands)

1915–1949

	Argentina		Bolivia		Brazil		Chile		Colombia		Ecuador	
	PC	CV	PC	CV	PC	CV	PC	CV	PC	CV	PC	CV
1915	...	...	...	...	...	...	1.2	- -	...	...	...	...
1916	...	...	...	...	...	...	1.8	- -	...	...	...	...
1917	...	...	...	...	...	...	...	...	...	...	...	...
1918	...	...	...	...	...	...	5.7	0.2	...	...	...	...
1919	...	...	...	...	...	...	6.4	0.2	...	...	...	...
1920	48	...	...	...	...	...	7.1	0.3	...	...	...	...
1921	54	0.4	...	...	...	...	7.0	0.4	...	...	...	...
1922	68	0.9	...	...	...	...	6.9	0.5	...	...	...	...
1923	90	4.5	...	...	...	...	6.5	0.7	1.8	3.2	...	...
1924	113	11	1.1		...	...	7.5	1.0	...	...	...	...
1925	161	19	1.5		...	...	10	3.7	...	...	...	...
1926	201	28	2.0		...	...	12	5.4	...	...	...	...
1927	232	41	2.0		...		22		...	...	...	...
1928	273	61	1.4	0.9	101	52	19	8.9	9.5	5.5	1.3	0.6
1929	330	82	1.7	0.9	127	66	24	12	10	6.0	1.6	0.6
1930	344	92	1.2	1.0	133	67	28	15	8.8	5.0	1.4	1.0
1931	326	92	...	...	...	...	27	15	...	...	...	...
1932	287	85	...	...	...	...	23	11	...	...	...	...
1933	243	79	...	...	...	...	22	9.7	...	...	...	...
1934	257	82	...	...	...	...	23	9.5	...	...	...	...
1935	270	84	...	...	...	...	25	10	...	...	...	...
1936	284	87	...	...	...	...	27	11	12	8	...	...
1937	297	90	...	...	100	39	29	12	13	8.8	...	...
1938	305	101	1.9	2.8	104	62	31	13	14	9.9	1.3	1.2
1939	317	107	2.1	3.3	108	58	32	14	16	11	1.3	1.4
1940	311	117	...	...	113	64	33	16	17	13	1.8	1.8
1941	319	121	...	...	...	...	36	18	20	15	2.0	2.1
1942	319	129	...	...	...	...	35	20	17	13	2.1	2.0
1943	321	139	...	...	...	...	26	21	16	12	...	...
1944	320	146	...	...	...	...	27	22	17	13	...	...
1945	311	142	3.7	7.6	...	...	29	23	15	14	...	...
1946	283	156	2.5	5.4	114	97	32	25	19	18	...	...
1947	290	195	...	...	140	121	34	27	23	23	4.3	3.2
1948	304	204	3.7	7.9	169	160	37	32	28	25	2.7	4.8
1949	310	224	3.8	8.9	193	182	40	31	30	25	3.4	6.4

F6 SOUTH AMERICA: Motor Vehicles in Use (in thousands)

1915-1949

	Guyana*		Paraguay		Peru		Surinam†		Uruguay		Venezuela	
	PC	CV	PC	CV	PC	CV	PC	CV	PC	CV	PC	CV
1915	...	...	...	...	...	...	...	...	...	...	...	...
1916	...	...	...	...	...	...	...	...	...	...	...	...
1917	...	...	...	...	...	...	...	...	...	...	...	...
1918	...	...	...	...	...	...	...	...	...	...	...	...
1919	...	...	...	...	...	...	...	...	...	...	...	...
1920	...	...	...	...	...	...	...	...	...	...	...	...
1921	...	...	...	...	...	...	...	...	...	...	...	...
1922	...	...	...	...	...	...	...	...	...	...	...	...
1923	...	...	...	...	...	...	...	...	...	...	...	...
1924	...	...	...	...	...	...	...	...	...	...	...	...
1925	0.9	0.1	...	...	...	...	...	...	...	...	...	...
1926	0.9	0.1	...	...	...	...	...	...	...	...	...	...
1927	0.9	0.1	...	...	6.1	4.6	...	...	...	...	...	...
1928	1.1	0.1	0.7	0.5	9.3	5.9	0.2	0.1	32	8.4	11	1.0
1929	0.9	0.1	0.7	0.5	8.0	5.2	0.2	- -	36	16	12	6.0
1930	1.1	0.1	0.7	1.0	8.7	5.2	0.2		37	10	11	6.8
1931	1.1	0.2	...	...	8.0	4.6	...	...	...	...	...	...
1932	1.2	0.2	...	...	7.4	4.6	...	...	...	...	14	5.6
1933	1.1	0.2	...	...	9.2	5.2	...	...	...	...	10	4.3
1934	1.2	0.2	...	...	7.7	3.7	...	...	...	...	11	4.6
1935	1.1	0.2	...	...	9.4	6.0	...	...	...	...	12	5.0
1936	1.2	0.3	...	...	11	7.0	...	...	36	12	12	...
1937	1.4	0.3	...	...	14	10	...	...	...	...	13	8.9
1938	...	...	1.5	0.6[11]	13	10	...	...	...	...	16	11
1939	...	...	1.5	0.6[11]	14	10	...	...	49	15	18	14
1940	...	...	1.1	0.9[11]	15	11	...	...	...	...	20	17
1941	...	...	...	...	17	12	...	...	...	...	20	17
1942	...	...	...	...	17	12	...	...	...	...	19	16
1943	...	...	...	...	16	11	...	...	...	...	17	15
1944	...	...	...	...	16	12	...	...	...	...	15	14
1945	...	...	...	...	17	12	...	...	...	...	16	17
1946	...	...	...	...	17	15	...	0.4	...	...	21	25
1947	1.8	0.5	1.2	1.4	21	18	0.6	0.4	...	...	29	35
1948	2.2	0.6	0.8	1.3	23	18	0.7	0.5	...	...	41	42
1949	2.8	0.8	1.1	1.8	25	21	0.8	0.6	35	21	57	61

F6　SOUTH AMERICA: Motor Vehicles in Use (in thousands)

1950–1993

	Argentina		Bolivia		Brazil		Chile		Colombia		Ecuador	
	PC	CV	PC	CV	PC	CV	PC	CV	PC	CV	PC	CV
1950	318	239	4.0	9.0	200	198	40	32	31	27	...	...
1951	329	244	...	...	263	226	43	35	35	32	4.0	8.1
1952	336	250	6.0	14	300	262	48	41	41	39	4.9	11
1953	329	254	6.0	16	338	285	48	43	50	43	4.7	12
1954	312	251	6.3	16	368	305	49	48	66	56	5.3	14
1955	336	264	8.9	14	374	320	48	50	81	70	5.8	15
1956	347	276	10	17	423	326	52	52	...	...	6.3	16
1957	365	306	12	17	...	...	54	59	...	...	6.3	15
1958	390	326	13	22	...	...	54	62	81	68	7.3	17
1959	431	356	14	24	...	...	58	68	84	75	8.5	18
1960	473	390	15	25	...	...	58	69	90	83	9.3	19
1961	535	436	15	25	...	...	59	76	108	92	11	20
1962	624	483	14[3]	26[3]	...	...	73	95	112	93	11	20
			6.3	11								
1963	697	517	7.8	14	...	...	84	97	114	99	13	22
1964	806	570	8.7	15	1,102	471	89	99	119	105	14	18
1965	915	571	9.9	16	1,289	517	97	105	124	109	17	21
1966	1,031	619	12	19	1,449	588	108	107	135	116	19	22
1967	1,107	650	14	23	1,785	611	116	117	140[8]	117[8]	22	25
									167	98		
1968	1,184	675	15	25	1,766	619	130	124	176	107	22	28
1969	1,301	718	15	26	2,003	651	151	136	220	78	25	31
1970	1,440	755	19	29	2,324	696	176	150	239	84	27	36
1971	1,673	809	...	...	2,638	742	194	152	284	91	30	44
1972	1,860	877	25	23	3,069	809	216	158	306	104	33	52
1973	1,914	835	26	24	...	...	225	162	327	81	35	56
1974	2,140	925	29	26[5]	3,735	825	235	165	354	85	44	68
1975	2,306	970	30	34	4,834	1,150	256	164	376	88	51	77
1976	2,455	1,017	33	40	5,916	1,397	263	171	401	93	49	87
1977	2,569	1,073	36	44	6,850	905	295	181	454	104	61	115
1978	2,684[10]	1,098[10]	39	47	7,124	1,575	336	191	435	256	70	131
	2,791	1,106										
1979	2,880	1,142	43	48	7,537	1,935	386	203	478	275	65	112
1980	3,112	1,217	50	52	7,971	2,093	448	220	523	295	95	162
1981	3,319	1,293	64	52	8,251	2,063	574	259	599	328	99	159
1982	3,516	1,357	67	59	8,543	2,149	606	256	670	353	102	177
1983	3,620	1,380	71	61	9,008	2,238	619	249	723	368	120	180
1984	3,749	1,409	76	63	9,198	2,285	630	235	768	381	121	176
1985	3,863	1,432	...	...	9,527	2,410	625	258	805	391	136	185
1986	3,928	1,440	...	...	9,885	2,350	591	242	842	401	141	188
1987	4,164	1,442	...	...	10,035	2,374	618	268	...	...	146	190
1988	4,126	1,436	...	...	10,274	2,418	669	297	...	...	176	222
1989	4,302	1,446	...	...	10,475	2,451	661	333	...	...	166	207
1990	4,352	1,460	...	...	10,598	2,473	710	361	...	...	181	206
1991	4,405	1,488	...	...	12,128	1,075	766	399	...	...	195	233
1992	4,809	1,534	...	...	12,128	1,171	827	438	...	...	202	231
1993	4,856	1,589	...	...	...	...	897	480	...	...	...	...

International Historical Statistics: The Americas 1750–1993

F6 SOUTH AMERICA: Motor Vehicles in Use (in thousands)

1950–1993

	Guyana		Paraguay		Peru		Surinam		Uruguay		Venezuela	
	PC	CV	PC	CV	PC	CV	PC	CV	PC	CV	PC	CV
1950	3.2	0.8	1.2	2.1	32	28	1.0	0.7	...	23	70	61
1951	3.4	0.8	1.3	2.0	34	29	1.3	0.8	45	30	74	62
1952	3.9	0.9	1.9	2.3	38	32	1.5	0.9	47	39	94	69
1953	4.7	1.4	2.1	2.3	49	40	...	...	48	42	113	82
1954	5.3	1.5	3.4	3.4	52	45	1.3	0.6	50	46	128	93
1955	5.5	2.4	3.7	2.8	54	49	1.6	0.9	52	48	146	98
1956	6.4	2.7	3.1	4.9	55	50	1.8	1.0	52	48	160	89
1957	7.3	3.0	...	...	62	52	2.4	1.1	78	49	186	92
1958	8.2	3.3	5.8[3]	2.5[3]	70	58	3.0	1.3	79	49	186	88
1959	7.7	3.2	4.7	3.4	73	60	3.3	1.2	80	50	239	99
1960	9.8	3.3	3.8	2.5	79	65	4.2	1.5	100	76	269	101
1961	10	3.7	4.3	2.5	89	72	5.1	1.7	105	82	267	105
1962	11	3.8	5.0	3.8	100	79	5.7	1.7	107	79	280	113
1963	7.9	2.0	4.8	4.1	111	82	6.3	1.8	110	80	287	108
1964	9.1	3.0	4.8	4.9	124	97	6.8	1.9	112	81	352	132
1965	10	3.6	5.0	5.2	155	99	7.4	2.1	114	82	383	152
1966	12	4.2	5.9	6.0	178	108	8.1	2.3	118	80	426	171
1967	13	5.2	6.4	6.5	195	112	8.9	2.7	122	82	452	196
1968	14	6.8	6.9	6.6	158	78	11	3.0	126	85	498	200
1969	16	7.5	14	13	220	109	13	3.2	130	90	534	208
1970	18	8.2	15	13	230	118	15	4.5	121	88	566	198
1971	20	8.4	16	14	...	...	17	5.1	...	86	779	275
1972	21	9.2	...	...	232	121	20	5.8	...	...	769	269
1973	23	9.9	...	...	247	129	22	6.5	...	...	820	286
1974	24	11	...	...	267	140	23	8.2	...	...	876	312
1975	26	12	12	13	257	145	25	9.0	...	...	955	369
1976	27	14	18	24	278	156	29	10	127	104	1,073	428
1977	28	15	23	28	300	166	33	12	...	...	1,187	498
1978	...	...	25	31	302	167	38	14	208	41	1,277	561
1979	...	...	33[5]	31[5]	303	170	...	...	220	42	1,390	640
1980	...	...	58	18	309	177	29	...	220	43	1,506	718
1981	...	...	57	15	331	191	30	...	281	48	1,635	796
1982	...	...	63	13	360	205	32	...	298	52	1,846	853
1983	...	...	79	24	372	212	31	13	292	45	1,955	952
1984	...	...	85	24	374	213	29	12	292	45	1,559	405
1985	...	...	105	22	376	215	32	13	306	46	1,598	418
1986	...	...	112	23	377	221	32	13	318	47	1,656	430
1987	...	...	122	27	377	228	32	13	333	47	1,718	448
1988	...	...	80	19	377	233	35	13	350	50	1,740	421
1989	...	...	149	25	373	240	37	14	360	50	1,615	459
1990	...	...	165	26	368	237	36	14	380	50	1,582	464
1991	...	...	191	31	379	245	39	16	390	49	1,540	449
1992	...	...	221	35	402	271	42	18	418	45	1,566	456
1993	...	...	251	38	418	289	46	17	426	44	1,579	460

F6   Motor Vehicles in Use

NOTES

1. SOURCES: The national publications listed on pp. xiii–xv; League of Nations and UN, *Statistical Yearbooks*.
2. So far as possible, and except as indicated in footnotes, buses and taxis are included with commercial vehicles.
3. Unless otherwise indicated, statistics relate to the year-end.

FOOTNOTES

[1]   Taxis included with passenger cars. Newfoundland is included from 1949.
[2]   Buses are included with passenger cars to 1953. Government vehicles are excluded from passenger cars to 1958. Data are at 30 June.
[3]   Data for 'the early years of the century are incomplete, largely because few States required...registration.' Alaska and Hawaii are included from 1960.
     There was a rearrangement of categories. It was also subsequently stated in the source that the statistics included vehicles which are no longer in circulation.
[4]   In 1957 to 1959 (1st line) vehicles belonging to police and other security organizations are included.
[5]   The reason for this break is not given in the source.
[6]   Data to 1948 relate to the Canal Zone. Most vehicles were registered both in the state and in the Canal Zone.
[7]   Vehicles in Panama City and Colon districts only.
[8]   Vehicles licenced to 1949 (1st line), all vehicles registered subsequently.
[9]   Subsequently including buses.
[10] Subsequently including estimates of numbers of unregistered vehicles.
[11] Excluding buses.

F7 NORTH AMERICA: CIVIL AVIATION TRAFFIC

Key: Pass = passengers (in thousands); PKM = passenger-kilometres (in millions, except as otherwise indicated); TKM = metric ton-kilometres (in millions)

1920–1944

	Canada				Cuba	Guatemala	Mexico		USA			
	Pass.	PKM	Cargo TKM[2]	Mail TKM[2]	PKM	Pass.[4]	Pass.	PKM	Pass.[5]	PKM[6]	Cargo TKM[7]	Mail TKM[7]
1920	15	...	...	...	...	...	...	...	...	...	...	...
1921	9.2	...	...	...	...	...	...	...	...	...	...	...
1922	4.3	...	...	...	...	...	...	...	...	...	...	...
1923	2.3[1]	...	...	...	...	...	...	...	...	...	...	...
1924	4.3	...	...	...	...	...	...	...	...	...	...	...
1925	3.7	...	...	...	...	...	...	...	...	...	...	...
1926	4.8	...	...	...	...	...	...	...	6	...	- -	...
1927	17	...	...	...	...	...	1.5	...	9	...	- -	...
1928	55	...	...	...	...	...	11	...	49	...	0.1	...
1929	96	9.8	...	...	...	1.4	12	...	173	...	0.1	...
1930	125	8.7	...	...	...	...	21	...	418	167	0.2	...
1931	100	6.6	...	...	...	...	22	...	531	195	0.3	4.6
1932	77[1]	4.6	...	...	...	...	23	8.7	548	238	0.4	3.9
1933	69	6.1	...	...	...	...	39	12	576	322	0.6	3.7
1934	81	10	...	...	...	...	52	18	572[5]	365	0.9[7]	[3.3]
1935	157	13	...	...	...	...	60	23	790	583	1.6	6.0
1936	119	14	[1.6][2]	[0.1][2]	...	...	66	28	1,020	774[6]	2.7	8.4
1937	141	17[2] 20	2.7	0.2	...	4.3	70	26	1,097[5] 999[5]	750[6]	3.2	9.8
1938	140	18	1.4	0.4	[3.1][3]	5.0	76	29	1,186	858	3.2	11
1939	162	35	1.4	0.6	...	5.1	85	34	1,690	1,215	4.0	13
1940	149	61	1.1	0.9	...	4.3	87	41	2,686	1,854	5.1	15
1941	208	87	1.4	1.3	...	3.5	124	132	3,693	2,491	7.7	19
1942	229	114	1.6	2.2	...	4.3	184	112	3,406	2,663	17	31
1943	315	162	2.1	3.1	...	6.5	261	175	3,299	3,022	30	57
1944	404	179	2.1	3.0	[12][3]	9.7	298	213	4,387	4,006	34	79

F7 NORTH AMERICA: Civil Aviation Traffic

1945-1993

	Canada				Costa Rica				Cuba			
	Pass.[1]	PKM[2]	Cargo TKM[2]	Mail TKM[2]	Pass.	PKM	Cargo TKM	Mail TKM	Pass.	PKM	Cargo TKM	Mail TKM
1945	525	229	1.9	2.7	...	...	...	...	...	...	...	...
1946	836	322	1.8	2.2	...	...	...	...	...	32	...	...
1947	957	369	2.6	2.4	...	...	...	...	...	64	...	...
1948	1,136	498[2]	4.3[2]	4.2[2]	...	...	...	...	...	...	...	...
		596	5.1	4.4								
1949	1,308	741	7.1	6.2	...	...	...	...	...	...	...	...
1950	1,553	857	9.1	6.6	...	...	...	...	...	93	...	...
1951	1,948	1,040	10	7.3	...	...	...	...	...	118	0.9	0.1
1952	2,361	1,220	13	8.0	...	...	...	...	...	132	0.8	0.1
1953	2,796	1,425	15	9.0	...	...	...	...	...	112	1.3	0.1
1954	2,866	1,624	19	12	...	...	...	...	...	140	1.4	0.2
1955	3,303	1,864	24	13	...	...	...	...	...	142	1.8	0.2
1956	3,924	2,353	30	14	...	...	...	...	...	225	5.4	0.2
1957	4,355	2,762	33	16	...	...	...	...	...	285	12	0.5
1958	4,579	3,232	32	17	...	...	...	...	465	273	13	2.0
1959	5,348[1]	3,739	38	19	...	41	4.1	0.2	404	261	14	1.7
	5,316											
1960	5,452	4,267	46	20	155	55	5.4	0.2	321	217	11	1.4
1961	5,741	5,033	52	20	169	58	5.7	0.2	167	167	7.9	0.7
1962	6,064	5,509	62	22	153	62	8	0.3	130	122	3.6	0.3
1963	6,278	5,786	74	24	162	72	8.3	0.3	265	199	4.7	0.8
1964	6,775	6,296	95	27	155	74	9.6	0.1	432	311	5.0	0.5
1965	7,839	7,565	125	31	166	89	8.1	0.1	430	281	5.1	0.7
1966	9,024	8,976	162	35	175	97	8.7	0.1	469	290	7.4	0.7
1967	11,596	11,102	187	41	183	106	8.1	0.2	527	328	9.1	0.7
1968	11,875	12,044	252	44	199	113	6.5	0.2	529	329	6.5	0.9
1969		12,997	302	49	205	124	8.9	0.2	686	446	8.0	1.8
1970	10,180	15,397	371	54	256	168	9.3	0.2	877	502	9.1	2.1
1971	10,247	15,055	404	71	280	199	9.2	0.2	986	537	9.1	1.9
1972	11,629	18,022	433	75	307	242	8.6	0.2	934	550	10	2.2
1973	14,627	21,701	484	86	314	256	8.1	0.2	814	535	12	2.1
1974	16,368	24,605	520	93	374	299	9.2	0.2	703	528	10	1.8
1975	16,713	24,999	534	93	372	306	8.9	0.2	711	517	14	1.9
1976	16,833	26,031	568	114	390	326	13	0.3	717	663	12	1.8
1977	17,527	27,291	550	120	327	337	18	0.3	635	773	9.4	1.4
1978	18,472	29,276	609	119	321	360	19	0.2	713	1,089	9.6	1.8
1979	20,846	33,986	670	123	366	427	22	0.3	819	1,272	12	2.5
1980	22,453	36,234	689	130	431	495	22	0.4	676	932	10	1.9
1981	22,097	35,608	713	132	428	578	21	0.7	651	1,242	12	3.1
1982	19,654	32,140	747	136	459	629	21	1.1	135	1,100	13	3.2
1983	18,108	31,342	826	137	380	505	21	0.7	839	1,136	16	1.9
1984	19,383	34,122	967	125	323	546	24	0.7	839	1,289	15	3.1
1985	19,688	35,684	990	130	310	570	25	1.1	894	1,801	17	3.0
1986	20,379	39,025	977	133	335	560	25	1	913	1,856	22	3
1987	19,946	40,241	1,007	117	348	610	30	1	889	1,997	26	4
1988	22,379	46,917	1,171	121	401	786	33	1	964	2,120	28	4
1989	21,274	50,372	1,349	125	441	914	33	1	990	2,017	22	5
1990	20,601	47,115	1,385	138	467	983	39	1	1,137	1,832	19	4
1991	16,586	39,082	1,241	121 [21]	504	1,050	36	1 [21]	831	1,598	18	3 [21]
1992	16,818	41,253	5,109		589	1,204	165		733	1,370	149	
1993	17,516	40,426	5,151		719	1,432	189		624	1,321	138	

F7 NORTH AMERICA: Civil Aviation Traffic

1945-1993

	Guatemala				Honduras				Jamaica			
	Pass.[4]	PKM	Cargo TKM	Mail TKM	Pass.	PKM	Cargo TKM[9]	Mail TKM	Pass.	PKM	Cargo TKM	Mail TKM
1945	16[4] 59	...	...	...	...	...	...	...	...	...	...	...
1946	100	...	...	...	...	...	...	...	...	...	...	...
1947	116	...	...	...	...	...	...	...	...	...	...	...
1948	129	...	...	...	...	...	...	...	...	...	...	...
1949	129	...	...	...	...	...	...	...	...	...	...	...
1950	114	...			...	...	...	...	...	...	...	...
1951	101	...	...	...	...	...	...	...	...	...	...	...
1952	92	...	...	...	...	...	...	...	...	...	...	...
1953	90	...	...	...	...	...	...	...	...	...	...	...
1954	89	...	...	...	...	...	...	...	...	...	...	...
1955	105	...	...	...	...	...	...	...	...	...	...	...
1956	106	...	...	...	...	...	...	...	...	...	...	...
1957	113	18	0.8	0.1	...	35	4.6	0.1	...	...	...	...
1958	112	28	1.9	0.1	...	38	4.9	0.1	...	...	...	...
1959	107	31	2.3	0.1	...	41	5.3	0.1	...	...	...	...
1960	107	30	2.1	0.1	152	44	3.8	- -	...	...	...	...
1961	108	30	2.3	0.1	148	40	3.7	- -	...	...	...	...
1962	102	26	2.1	0.1	118	39	5.1	- -	...	...	...	...
1963	103	30	2.8	0.1	123	44	5.1	- -	25	1.9	- -	- -
1964	116	34	2.9	0.1	119	45	5.3[9]	- -	30	...	...	...
1965	136	60	3.3	0.1	135	58	5.9	- -	31	4.0	0.1	—
1966	154	73	3.4	0.1	151	79	7.7	- -	96	58	0.2	- -
1967	168	76	3.5	0.2	174	96	8.1	0.1	57	85	0.3	- -
1968	165[4] 88	77	3.4	0.2	198	109	9.7	0.1	208	144	0.5	0.1
1969	108	101	5.9	0.2	251	137	11	- -	231	253	3.3	0.1
1970	113	104	6.3	0.2	296	167	3.6	- -	279	335	2.5	- -
1971	101	85	5.3	0.2	270	169	3.7	0.1	425	457	3.3	0.3
1972	98	80	3.8	0.2	241	174	3.2	0.1	555	674	4.8	0.7
1973	43	48	3.7	—	294	205	3.4	0.1	569	737	5.8	0.5
1974	89	100	4.8	- -	326	226	2.6	0.1	743	1,235	9.7	0.6
1975	114	139	4.7	- -	299	240	3	0.1	697	1,438	11	0.8
1976	119	132	7.1	- -	289	256	5.1	0.1	643	1,379	11	0.6
1977	138	143	6.7	- -	324	276	4.2	0.1	556	1,167	12	0.9
1978	136	154	7.1	- -	320	281	5.5	0.4	657	1,352	13	0.7
1979	156	190	7.5	0.1	414	358	3.3	0.4	748	1,443	11	0.4
1980	119	159	6.4	0.1	508	387	3.8	0.6	723	1,207	9.4	0.4
1981	124	174	4.9	0.1	411	341	3	0.6	728	1,045	10	0.3
1982	115	160	5.2	0.2	377	331	2.7	0.7	873	1,230	12	0.2
1983	100	156	6.3	...	436	348	1.9	0.5	716	1,079	17	0.2
1984	124	168	8.1	...	439	408	2.2	0.8	826	1,303	20	0.2
1985	108	156	9	...	451	391	...	...	888	1,482	19	0.2
1986	103	137	10	...	320	377	...	...	1,059	1,735	19	...
1987	115	165	11	...	426	484	3	1	1,258	2,125	24	...
1988	99	165	12	...	482	466	2	2	1,189	1,941	21	...
1989	110	164	23	...	574	519	3	2	1,211	1,982	16	...
1990	156	213	9	...	610	468	4	1	1,004	1,463	19	...
1991	165	230	9	...[21]	447	336	3	1[21]	894	1,311	20	...[21]
1992	230	366	52		438	309	40		983	1,460	151	
1993	240	384	56		449	323	42		1,038	1,488	155	

F7   NORTH AMERICA: Civil Aviation Traffic

1945–1993

	Mexico				Nicaragua			
	Pass.	PKM	Cargo TKM	Mail TKM	Pass.	PKM	Cargo TKM	Mail TKM
1945	413	308	...	...	—	—	—	—
1946	707	439	...	...	...	1.7	2.9	...
1947	774	499	...	...	...	3.1	2.9	...
1948	815	552	...	...	...	3.6	2.5	- -
1949	943	562	...	...	...	4.3	2.2	- -
1950	1,033	625	...	...	...	5	...	...
1951	1,122	871	26	5.9	...	5.2	1.7	- -
1952	1,205	980	32	6.5	...	5	0.5	- -
1953	1,183	1,348	33[10]	6.8[10]	...	5.7	0.3	- -
			21	3.1				
1954	1,226	1,227	18	2.5	...	5.7	0.3	- -
1955	1,317	1,366	19	3.1	...	4.1	0.7	- -
1956	1,518	1,512	23	2.8	...	4.9	0.7	- -
1957	1,663	1,755	22	2.9	...	5.7	0.8	- -
1958	1,668	1,809	22	3.7	...	[24][11]	[4][11]	- -
1959	1,700	1,917	26	4.3	...	[14][11]	[3.3][11]	- -
1960	1,780	2,200	28	3.3	28	12	2.3	- -
1961	1,737	2,540	26	3.2	31	17	2.3	- -
1962	1,804	2,802	26	3.3	32	18	2.3	- -
1963	2,032	3,152	25	3.6	42	28	1.7	- -
1964	2,389	4,330	27	3.5	45	30	0.9	0.1
1965	3,487	4,937	32	3.9	48	34	0.7	- -
1966	3,019	4,605	32	4.1	64	45	0.8	0.1
1967	3,380	6,095	33	3.8	82	46	0.8	0.1
1968	3,859	6,085	38	4.2	100	59	0.7	0.1
1969	4,150	6,779	41	3.2	120	75	0.8	0.1
1970			37	3.7	107	77	0.8	0.1
1971			42	3.8	137	107	0.9	0.1
1972			54	3.7	144	117	0.9	0.1
1973			68	3.6	78	76	1.9	0.1
1974			72	4	81	78	1.9	0.1
1975	6,523	6,710	76	3.4	85	83	1.9	0.1
1976	7,676	8,000	87	3.9	89	86	2	0.1
1977	8,172	8,520	93	3.7	50	77	1.9	0.1
1978	9,388	10,027	106	4	110	92	2	0.1
1979	11,381	12,041	122	4.4	...	...	...	...
1980	12,890	13,870	132	4.3	...	...	...	...
1981	13,853	14,708	137	4.5	97	63	1.1	0.1
1982	13,105	13,465	112	4.3	100	120	1	0.1
1983	13,923	15,875	109	3.7	...	...	...	...
1984	14,440	17,197	146	3.8	...	...	...	...
1985	15,364	17,773	170	4.2	90	115	...	...
1986	13,825	16,885	155	4	...	...	...	...
1987	13,505	17,649	169	5	85	90	...	...
1988	11,412	14,946	122	4	87	92	...	...
1989	12,689	16,059	114	4	109	77	...	...
1990	14,341	18,290	143	8	130	111	4	...
1991	14,901	18,267	163	8	130	111	...	...
				⏟[21]				⏟[21]
1992	15,532	19,553		1,851	159	186		24
1993	14,621	18,216		1,746	34	58		4

F7 NORTH AMERICA: Civil Aviation Traffic

	Trinidad & Tobago				USA			
	Pass.	PKM	Cargo TKM	Mail TKM	Pass.	PKM	Cargo TKM	Mail TKM
1945	...	...	...	...	7,052	6,132	45	102
1946	...	...	...	...	12,254	11,344	78	60
1947	...	...	...	...	14,250	12,744	142	71
1948	...	...	...	...	14,541	12,666	216	86
1949	...	...	...	...	16,601	14,182	262	97
1950	...	...	...	...	19,020	16,449	311	108
1951	...	...	...	...	24,694	21,250	316	134
1952	...	...	...	...	27,375	25,144	347	144
1953	...	...	...	...	31,420	29,346	378	154
1954	...	...	...	...	35,218	33,172	404	184
					(million)	(thousand million)		
1955	...	...	...	...	41	39	476	219
1956	...	...	...	...	46	44	529	232
1957	...	...	...	...	53	50	550	244
1958	...	...	...	...	53	51	625	267
1959	...	...	...	...	60	59	736	295
1960	...	...	...	...	62	63	845	349
1961	...	...	...	...	63	64	980	431
1962	...	121	1.7	0.4	68	70	1,196	495
1963	319	312	4.2	0.7	77	81	1,314	519
1964	353	339	4.4	0.8	89	94	1,662	541
1965	383	355	3.1	0.6	103	111	2,249	701
1966	356	340	3.2	0.6	118	129	2,672	1,086
1967	363	381	3.6	0.5	142	159	3,083	1,410
1968	330	367	6.2	0.6	162	183	3,659	1,815
1969	338	417	8.3	0.6	172	202	4,165	1,846
1970	361	511	9.7	0.7	169	212		
1971	362	654	13	0.7	174	218		
1972	320	579	15	0.7	191	245		
1973	325	620	13	0.7	202	261		
1974	260	600	12	0.7	208	262		
1975	595	1,011	20	0.8	206	262	7,001	1,619
1976	384	1,040	23	0.9	224	288	7,440	1,644
1977	591	1,147	26	0.9	241	311	7,922	1,694
1978	428	677	15	0.4	274	364	8,409	1,711
1979	659	1,261	22	0.7	314	421	8,658	1,784
1980	877	1,505	18	0.7	295	409	8,615	1,954
1981	1,301	1,434	7.1	0.7	277	396	8,321	1,986
1982	1,381	1,540	4.9	0.7	284	409	7,972	2,038
1983	1,345	1,503	6.7	0.7	310	443	9,174	2,141
1984	1,398	1,598	7.2	0.7	330	477	10,112	2,367
1985	1,300	2,058	10	1.5	371	532	9,648	2,395
1986	1,342	2,260	11	2	411	583	10,713	2,426
1987	1,312	2,354	11	2	440	642	11,938	2,518
1988	1,296	2,507	13	2	454	679	13,847	2,639
1989	1,310	2,691	14	2	452	693	14,650	2,745
1990	1,285	2,776	15	2	464	735	14,788	2,884
1991	1,345	3,129	15	2 [21]	451	720	14,480	2,722 [21]
1992	1,354	3,077	346		466	764	87,917	
1993	1,389	3,232	364		469	772	89,846	

F7   SOUTH AMERICA: CIVIL AVIATION TRAFFIC

	Argentina	Bolivia		Brazil			
	Pass.	Pass.[12]	PKM	Pass.[13]	PKM[14]	Cargo TKM[14]	Mail TKM[14]
1920	...	...	...	...	...	...	...
1921	...	...	...	...	...	...	...
1922	...	...	...	...	...	...	...
1923	...	...	...	...	...	...	...
1924	...	...	...	...	...	...	...
1925	...	...	...	...	...	...	...
1926	...	1.0	...	...	...	...	...
1927	...	1.1	...	0.6	...	...	...
1928	...	3.0	...	2.5	...	...	...
1929	...	2.9	0.9	3.7	...	...	...
1930	...	3.7	1.1	4.7	...	...	...
1931	...	4.3	1.2	5.1	...	...	...
1932	...	5.1	1.6	8.9	...	...	...
1933	3.9	20	7.3	13	8	0.2	0.1
1934	6.2	...	4.1	18	8.4	0.2	0.1

	Chile		Colombia		Peru	Uruguay	Venezuela
	Pass.	PKM[15]	Pass.	PKM[16]	Pass.[17]	Pass.	PKM
1920	...	...	...	...	...	...	...
1921	...	...	0.4	...	...	...	...
1922	...	...	1.1	...	...	...	...
1923	...	...	1.3	...	...	...	...
1924	...	...	1.1	...	...	...	...
1925	...	...	1.1	...	...	...	...
1926	...	...	2.7	...	...	...	...
1927	...	...	3.9	...	...	...	...
1928	...	...	6.1	...	0.1	...	...
1929	0.9	...	6.6	1.6	1.6	57	0.2
1930	5.5	...	4.8	1.1	5.8	...	0.3
1931	4.8	...	5.7	1.1	5.8	...	0.3
1932	4.8	...	6.3	1.2	8.9	...	0.4
1933	3	1.2	9.4	1.3	12	...	0.4
1934	3.0	1.5	13	2.0	20	...	0.2

F7   SOUTH AMERICA: Civil Aviation Traffic

1935–1993

	Argentina				Bolivia				Brazil			
	Pass.	PKM	Cargo TKM	Mail TKM	Pass.[12]	PKM	Cargo TKM	Mail TKM	Pass.[13]	PKM[14]	Cargo TKM[14]	Mail TKM[14]
1935	6.6	0.4	...	...	...	4.8	...	...	26	12	0.3	0.1
1936	8.7	0.8	...	...	...	3.2	...	...	35	19	0.4	0.2
1937	11	1.2	...	...	...	2.5	...	...	62	31	0.6	0.2
1938	22	1.7	...	...	21	3.3	...	...	63	29	0.7	0.2
1939	36	2.3	...	...	18	4.1	...	...	71	32	0.8	0.1
1940	41	4.0	...	...	16	4.2	...	...	86	45	1.2	0.2
1941	55	6.0	...	...	15	3.4	...	...	100	53	1.5	0.2
1942	55	7.0	...	...	5.8	2.7	...	...	122	71	2.5	0.2
1943	67	10	...	...	11	4.3	...	...	172	118	5.6	0.5
1944	79	12	...	...	19	6.3	...	...	245	179	6.9	0.8
1945	89	14	...	...	25	8.4	...	...	290	207	9.0	0.6
1946	144	26	...	...	35	12	...	...	539	395	16	0.7
1947	234	89	...	...	45	16	...	...	819	566	23	0.9
1948	362	...	...	...	49	17	...	...	1,154	677	31	1.2
1949	435	198	...	...	47	17	...	...	1,327	745	...	...
1950	493	253	3.1	1.3	59	20	...	...	1,714	851	...	...
1951	462	304	3.8	1.7	58	22	...	...	2,241[13] 2,131	1,240	65[14] 46	1.8
1952	393	246	4.1	1.8	75	24	...	...	2,110	1,279	42	1.9
1953	410	317	4.5	1.9	93	29	3.3	- -	2,518	1,483	50	2.6
1954	470	342	3.7	2.0	...	39	3.7	- -	2,733	1,596	54	3.2
1955	560	371	3.6	2.0	155	47	5.1	- -	2,799	1,684	60	3.4
1956	471	439	5.2	1.8	171	54	4.8	- -	3,365	2,039[14] 1,982	71[14] 69	3.8[14] 3.7
1957	562	578	7.4	1.7	100	33	2.5	- -	3,754	2,289	80	4.4
1958	692	643	7.9	1.7	165	36	3	- -	3,947	2,438	87	4.6
1959	963	674	9.1	1.9	165	34	2.8	- -	3,890	2,599	93	5.2
1960	899	990	14	2.1	183	47	5.8	- -	3,972[13] 3,838	2,679	84	5.4
1961	955	1,131	15	3.3	176	[51][11]	[3.6][11]	- -	3,142	2,663	80	5.0
1962	825	826	8.5	2.7	167[12]	[56][11]	[3.4][11]	- -	3,310	2,764	76	7.0
1963	789	881	8.7	3.4	139	43	1.9	- -	3,106	2,868	69	5.0
1964	977	1,044	9.3	3.8	122	50	3.6	- -	2,702	2,593	71	6.2
1965	1,043	1,128	10	3.8	139	50	1.3	- -	2,524	2,592	68	6.4
1966	1,122	1,141	12	4.2	166	60	1.3	- -	2,742	3,048	72	9.1
1967	1,405	1,556	21	4.8	170	62	1.4	- -	2,940	3,210	86	8.0
1968	1,494	1,749	33	5.1	168	61	1.2	- -	3,198	3,693	96	8.5
1969	1,745	2,125	52	5.8	277	106	1.4	- -	3,167	3,933	149	9.0
1970	2,332	2,395	48	6.0	244	109	1.5	- -	3,340	4,385	164	9.3
1971	2,219	2,711	57	6.0	331	146	2.5	0.1	3,911	4,984	180	10
1972	2,359	2,963	80	7.6	379	177	2.8	0.1	4,671	5,919	254	11
1973	2,435	3,282	86	7.5	408	195	3	0.1	5,842	7,335	317	13
1974	2,943	4,080	98	7.3	430	205	3	0.1	6,856	8,559	407	13
1975	3,299	4,373	76	7.2	653	331	2.6	0.1	7,773	9,787	460	14
1976	3,294	4,222	96	7.4	745	444	4.1	0.2	8,799	10,366	472	16
1977	3,884	4,874	120	7.5	862	558	28	0.2	9,514	10,978	499	18
1978	3,949	5,370	121	8.6	1,016	700	43	0.2	10,621	12,544	571	19
1979	5,025	6,946	137	9.5	1,226	860	34	0.2	11,857	14,461	570	23
1980	5,589	8,031	195	21	1,342	944	38	0.2	13,008	15,572	588	23
1981	4,890	7,019	195	20	1,220	963	44	0.5	12,595	16,304	645	23
1982	4,596	6,083	171	19	1,160	780	28	0.8	13,168	17,229	735	24
1983	4,400	6,034	174	20	1,299	787	17	1.0	12,606	16,738	692	25
1984	5,164	7,405	180	18	1,359	877	38	1.9	12,948	17,175	832	30
1985	4,713	7,351	187	15	1,343	894	42	0.9	13,403	18,494	909	32
1986	5,035	7,942	192	14	1,301	884	28	1	17,195	23,471	1,014	31
1987	5,406	8,652	198	14	1,233	912	26	1	17,069	22,613	1,014	31
1988	5,069	8,838	194	13	1,267	955	8	1	17,011	23,712	976	37
1989	4,748	9,253	201	12	1,273	1,032	8	1	19,411	27,854	1,148	35
1990	4,353	9,431	200	10	1,238	1,068	8	1	18,941	28,500	1,082	42
1991	4,532	9,207	185	10 [21]	1,200	1,022	5	1	19,015	28,539	1,029	82 [21]
1992	5,241	10,384	1,354		1,214	1,069	107		16,210	27,827	3,796	
1993	5,095	9,221	1,117		1,117	1,092	120		16,468	29,500	4,084	

F7 SOUTH AMERICA: Civil Aviation Traffic

	Chile				Colombia				Ecuador			
	Pass.	PKM[15]	Cargo TKM[15]	Mail TKM[15]	Pass.	PKM[16]	Cargo TKM[16]	Mail TKM[16]	Pass.	PKM	Cargo TKM	Mail TKM
1935	4.0	2.4	...	...	23	4.2	...	...	...	...	...	...
1936	4.0	2.4	- -	- -	28	5.6	...	...	...	...	...	...
1937	4.0	2.4	- -	- -	47	8.3	...	...	...	...	...	...
1938	3.7	2.1	- -	- -	63	11	...	...	...	...	...	...
1939	3.2	2.0	- -	- -	60	11	...	...	...	...	...	...
1940	2.6	1.8	- -	- -	55	11	...	...	...	...	...	...
1941	7.8	5.3	- -	- -	59	13	...	...	...	...	...	...
1942	15	9.7	- -	- -	65	14	...	...	...	...	...	...
1943	15	10	- -	- -	89	31	...	...	...	...	...	...
1944	18	14	0.1	- -	103	...	...	...	...	...	...	...
1945	27	19	0.1	- -	151	56	...	...	...	...	...	...
1946	44	29	0.3	- -	223	...	...	...	...	...	...	...
1947	86	55	0.5	- -	...	...	...	...	...	...	...	...
1948	89	60	0.8	0.1	686	...	...	...	...	...	...	...
1949	67	46	0.7	0.1	776	247	...	...	...	...	...	...
1950	81	54	0.7	0.1	874	302	...	...	...	...	...	...
1951	98	66	0.9	0.1	896	321	68	0.3	...	...	...	...
1952	106	77	1.2	0.1	967	372	62	0.4	...	...	...	...
1953	134	95	1.7	0.1	1,011	415	59	2.6	...	...	...	...
1954	182	122	1.8	0.1	979	426	60	4.0	...	14	0.1	- -
1955	213	156	1.9	0.1	1,090	484	58	3.5	...	7.6	0.1	- -
1956	267	333	7.2	0.1	1,389	562	60	3.5	...	8.1	0.1	- -
1957	374	438[15]	11[15]	0.2[15]	1,490	615	53	3.3	...	9.8	0.1	- -
1958	350	377	9.3	0.2	1,436	632	49	3	...	16	0.5	0.1
1959	300	321	6.0	0.2	1,484	681[16]	50[16]	3.2[16]	...	39	0.9	0.2
1960	403	414	9.7	0.9	1,529	777	41	1.1	135	42	1.0	- -
1961	395	427	17	0.9	1,692	824	42	1.1	139	44	1.0	- -
1962	362	364	13	0.5	2,075	1,001	46	1.4	140	44	1.0	- -
1963	362	380	21	0.5	2,354	1,205	47	1.7	144	43	1.0	- -
1964	470	511	25	0.6	2,580	1,319	56	2.0	163	94	1.1	- -
1965	474	511	25	0.6	2,537	1,301	54	2.2	204	128	2.3	0.1
1966	476	529	26	0.8	2,528	1,377	53	2.6	257	161	2.6	0.2
1967	553	665	28	0.7	2,462	1,489	51	2.9	296	217	2.7	0.3
1968	498	601	24	0.6	2,386	1,562	56	3.3	385	263	4.2	0.3
1969	582	730	37	0.9	2,581	1,744	60	3.6	415	244	5.3	0.3
1970	575	839	41	1.1	3,010	2,063	75	4.1	419	256	9.3	0.3
1971	691	1,113	47	1.4	2,960	2,182	81	4.0	457	216	4.7	0.4
1972	730	1,143	54	1.4	2,964	2,284	86	4.2	438	218	4.5	0.3
1973	636	1,111	47	1.6	3,140	2,494	105	3.9	380	220	9.6	0.3
1974	505	1,159	55	1.8	3,120	2,567	118	3.7	382	189	8.1	0.3
1975	510	1,276	57	1.8	3,376	2,778	122	4.4	448	301	6.4	0.3
1976	490	1,230	76	2.0	3,730	2,976	150	4.6	463	360	6.9	0.3
1977	589	1,433	105	2.5	4,117	3,376	172	4.4	529	551	9.5	0.3
1978	533	1,472	102	3.1	4,747	3,786	206	4.4	593	676	13	0.4
1979	559	1,550	85	3	5,052	4,196	183	4.7	...	...	...	...
1980	669	1,875	145	3.7	4,808	4,198	147	5.0	701	975	40	0.6
1981	886	2,220	153	4.5	4,570	4,288	204	5.0	692	946	39	0.9
1982	822	1,824	142	2.2	6,701	5,050	249	5.1	676	862	36	1.2
1983	652	1,493	120	2	6,584	4,986	292	5.1	618	762	33	1.5
1984	731	1,624	105	2.5	5,737	4,481	381	4.5	634	893	42	2.5
1985	825	1,772	114	2.6	5,737	4,242	376	5.2	664	969	51	2.6
1986	875	1,961	137	3	5,731	4,265	392	5	697	1,073	59	2
1987	992	2,117	186	3	5,599	4,230	398	6	692	1,073	70	2
1988	1,144	2,442	243	3	5,460	4,308	403	7	684	1,051	74	1
1989	1,264	2,807	330	3	5,565	4,537	395	8	742	1,209	68	1
1990	1,364	2,987	419	3	5,267	4,384	464	8	763	1,243	63	1
1991	1,406	3,036	429	3 [21]	5,540	4,465	526	9 [21]	752	1,201	68	1 [21]
1992	1,906	3,854	879		6,232	4,875	952		756	1,188	176	
1993	2,360	4,425	1,018		6,425	5,296	1,014		769	1,255	596	

F7　SOUTH AMERICA: Civil Aviation Traffic

1935–1993

	Peru				Uruguay				Venezuela			
	Pass.[17]	PKM[19]	Cargo TKM[19]	Mail TKM[19]	Pass.	PKM[20]	Cargo TKM[20]	Mail TKM[20]	Pass.[18]	PKM	Cargo TKM	Mail TKM
1935	23	...	...	...	...	...	...	...	...	0.4	...	...
1936	30	...	...	...	...	...	...	...	...	0.7	...	...
1937	35	...	...	...	...	...	...	...	...	1.3	...	...
1938	31	...	...	...	...	...	...	...	...	1.6	...	...
1939	30	...	...	...	...	...	...	...	...	2.6	...	...
1940	28	...	...	...	...	...	...	...	...	3.5	...	...
1941	29	...	...	...	...	...	...	...	17	5	...	...
1942	39	...	...	...	...	...	...	...	21	5	...	...
1943	51	...	...	...	...	...	...	...	...	8	...	...
1944	56	...	...	...	...	...	...	...	37	10	...	...
1945	59	...	...	...	...	...	...	...	78	12	...	...
1946	75	...	...	...	...	...	...	...	181	20	...	...
1947	120	...	...	...	...	...	...	...	311	30	...	...
1948	164	63	...	...	...	...	...	...	503	40	...	...
1949	175	...	...	...	...	...	...	...	605	60	...	...
1950	169	...	...	...	...	...	...	...	565	105	...	...
1951	195	72	4.8	0.1	...	...	...	...	525	217	8.3	0.3
1952	136	69	5	0.1	...	...	...	...	545	253	8.6	0.4
1953	205	79	5	0.1	...	...	...	...	575	269	7.3	0.5
1954	237	85	5	0.1	...	28	0.1[20]	- -[20]	646[20]	291	8.6	0.7
1955	269	93	5.3	0.1	...	29	0.2	- -	662	325	11	0.8
1956	282	99	5.8	0.2	...	36	0.2	- -	648	324	12	1.5
1957	323	113	6.2	0.2	...	34	0.4	- -	715	309	13	0.7
1958	362	130	7	0.3	...	41	0.3	- -	720	360	14	0.6
1959	412	127	7.2	0.3	...	59	0.3	- -	793	408	14	0.7
1960	429	124	7.3	0.3	275	83	0.4	- -	749[18] 804	386	12	0.6
1961	488	186	7.2	0.4	269	79	0.4	- -	696	339	23	1
1962	575	183[19]	5.8[19]	0.4[19]	266	73	0.6	- -	647	432	30	1.4
1963	654	271	7.2	0.6	233	69	0.5	- -	702	461	36	1.3
1964	762	370	9.4	0.6	258	77	0.5	- -	799	544	43	1.6
1965	888	496	11	0.7	273	81	0.5	- -	885	660	50	1.5
1966	919	542	12	0.8	301	83	0.5	- -	987	740	34	1.5
1967	1,038[17]	622	12	0.9	231	73	0.3	- -	1,085	872	40	1.5
1968	326	574	14	1.2	244	75	0.2	- -	1,084	952	19	1.7
1969	362	752	18	1.7	242	66	0.1	- -	1,095	1,023	60	2
1970	391	789	22	2.2	219	63	0.3	- -	757	1,033	57	2
1971	264	224	17	0.5	221	73	0.3	- -	1,302	1,298	66	1.8
1972	525	355	16	0.2	136	27	0.1	- -	1,511	1,521	66	1.7
1973	590	404	12	0.2	145	30	0.2	- -	1,766	1,734	75	1.9
1974	745	700	20	0.4	340	80	0.1	- -	1,981	1,928	86	2.1
1975	1,335	1,222	22	0.4	334	79	0.1	- -	2,355	2,269	71	2.2
1976	1,439	1,367	25	0.8	327	83	0.2	- -	2,708	2,538	75	2.2
1977	1,425	1,353	35	0.5	293	74	0.3	- -	3,501	3,101	115	2.6
1978	1,469	1,470	36	0.6	260	64	0.2	- -	3,915	3,498	113	2.8
1979	1,686	1,795	36	0.6	448	160	1.4	0.3	4,772	4,135	107	3.1
1980	1,980	1,974	40	0.7	478	178	0.7	0.1	5,133	4,367	148	2.7
1981	1,777	1,755	48	0.5	413	198	1.1	0.1	5,147	4,645	142	2.7
1982	1,740	1,685	93	0.5	356	293	1.0	0.2	5,434	5,031	126	2.8
1983	1,698	1,699	76	0.8	310	325	1.5	0.3	5,000	3,747	103	2.4
1984	1,617	1,664	61	0.8	338	322	2.0	0.2	4,571	3,602	107	2.6
1985	1,564	1,598	47	0.8	329	389	1.9	0.2	4,967	4,370	83	3.9
1986	2,153	2,110	80	1	341	459	...	...	5,791	4,339	99	4
1987	3,009	2,670	79	1	351	459	...	...	6,454	5,040	118	5
1988	2,737	2,498	52	1	386	468	...	...	8,659	6,907	213	7
1989	1,854	2,048	30	1	313	491	...	...	10,099	6,446	161	5
1990	1,816	2,025	26	1	318	471	...	...	6,487	5,534	113	3
1991	1,491	1,759	25	1 [21]	318	471	...	...	6,626	6,010	132	7 [21]
1992	1,218	1,528	179		333	490	46		7,149	6,753	779	
1993	1,297	1,887	214		333	490	46		7,166	6,708	767	

F7   Civil Aviation Traffic

NOTES

1. SOURCES: The national publications listed on pp. xiii–xv and the League of Nations and UN, *Statistical Yearbooks*.
2. Except as otherwise indicated, the statistics relate to scheduled services (including overflow) only, by companies registered in the countries concerned.
3. Comparisons between different countries prior to the 1950s are especially difficult because of lack of uniformity in methods of collecting data.

FOOTNOTES

[1] Passengers carried under postal contracts only to 1923. From 1923 to 1932 crew other than pilots are included. Non-scheduled services are included to 1959. Statistics from 1959 (second line) exclude non-paying passengers.
[2] Domestic revenue traffic only to 1937 (1st line) or in 1936. Non-scheduled services are included to 1948 (1st line), but excluding transoceanic traffic, which amounted to 81 million PKM, 0.8 million cargo TKM, and 0.4 million mail TKM in 1947, and 162 million PKM, 1.4 million cargo TKM, and 0.5 million mail TKM in 1948.
[3] Cubana Company only.
[4] Total passenger departures, including non-scheduled services to 1968 (1st line) are for internal flights only.
[5] Including non-revenue passengers on international flights to 1937 and on domestic flights to 1934. Duplication through passengers being carried on more than one route on the same journey, whether or not by the same company, is present to 1937 (1st line).
[6] Including non-revenue passengers on international flights to 1937 and on domestic flights to 1936.
[7] Colonial Airlines Inc. and Hawaiian Airlines Ltd are not included until 1935.
[8] An additional 0.3 million TKM were flown by the US Army.
[9] Including passengers' baggage to 1964.
[10] The reason for this break is not given in the source, but is probably the earlier inclusion of non-scheduled services.
[11] Including non-scheduled services.
[12] Including non-scheduled services to 1962, but only covering the Lloyd Bolivia airline.
[13] Including foreign airlines to 1951 (1st line). Non- scheduled services are included to 1960 (1st line).
[14] Including non-scheduled services to 1956 (1st line). Baggage is included in cargo to 1951 (1st line).
[15] Including non-scheduled services to 1957. 16 Including non-scheduled services from 1943 to 1959.
[17] All passengers through Peruvian airports to 1967.
[18] Internal traffic only to 1960 (1st line).
[19] Including non-scheduled services to 1962.
[20] Including non-scheduled services in 1954.
[21] Total Freight Ton Kilometres.

F8 NORTH AMERICA: POSTAL AND TELEGRAPH TRAFFIC

Key: m = mail handled (in millions); t = telegrams sent (in millions)

	Barbados[1]	Canada	Jamaica[5]		Mexico[6]		USA	
	m	m[2]	m	t	m	t	m	t[7]
1865	...	...	...	...	...	...	...	...
1866	...	...	...	...	...	...	...	...
1867	...	...	...	...	...	...	...	5.9
1868	...	18	...	...	...	...	...	6.4
1869	...	22	...	...	...	...	...	7.9
1870	...	25	...	...	...	...	...	9.2
1871	...	27	...	...	...	...	...	11
1872	...	31	...	...	...	...	...	12
1873	...	35	...	...	...	...	...	14
1874	...	39	...	...	...	...	...	16
1875	...	42	...	...	...	...	...	17
1876	...	46	...	...	...	...	...	19
1877	...	47	...	...	...	0.2	...	21
1878	...	50	...	...	6.0	0.2	...	24
1879	...	51	...	...	5.8	0.2	...	25
1880	...	54	...	...	6.1	0.2	...	29
1881	...	58	...	...	6.7	0.2	...	33
1882	...	68	...	...	11	0.2	...	39
1883	...	76	...	...	10	0.3	...	41
1884	...	80	...	...	12	0.2	...	42
1885	...	82	...	...	13	0.2	...	42
1886	...	86	...	...	17	0.3	3,747	43
1887	...	91	...	...	27	0.4	3,495	47
1888	...	97	...	...	43	0.6	3,576	51
1889	...	112	...	...	96	0.6	3,860	54
1890	...	114	...	...	111	0.8	4,005	56
1891	1.2	118	...	...	117	0.8	4,370	59
1892	1.3	124	2.8	0.1	123	0.9	4,777	62
1893	1.3	129	3.3	0.1	36	0.9	5,022	67
1894	1.4	131	3.7	0.1	25	1	4,919	59
1895	1.6	132	4.1	0.1	30	1.1	5,134	58
1896	1.5	141	...	0.1	30	1.4	5,694	59
1897	1.5	150	5.0	0.1	113	1.5	5,781	58
1898	1.6	163	5.0	0.1	130	1.6	6,214	62
1899	1.8	178	5.0	0.1	135	2.8	6,576	61
1900	1.9	205	5.2	0.1	148	2.6	7,130	63
1901	2.1	219	5.4	0.1	157	2.8	7,424	66
1902	1.9	221	5.5	0.1	167	3.1	8,085	69
1903	2.0	262	5.7	0.1	162	3.4	8,887	70
1904	2.2	286	6.5	0.1	166	3.5	9,502	68

F8 NORTH AMERICA: Postal and Telegraph Traffic

	Barbados[1]	Canada		El Salvador	Jamaica[5]		Mexico[6]		Trinidad & Tobago[8]	USA	
	m	m[2]	t[3]	t[9]	m	t	m	t	m	m	t[7]
1905	2.3	316	...	...	7.2	0.1	140	3.8	...	10,188	67
1906	2.3	357	...	...	7.7	0.1	155	4.2	...	11,361	71
1907	2.5	[301][2]	...	...	8.6	0.1	177	4.3	...	12,256	75
1908	2.6	437	...	...	8.4	0.1	171	4.3	...	13,364	62
1909	2.8	457	...	...	10	0.1	185	4.5	3.6	14,005	68
1910	3.0	501	...	...	10	0.1	189	4.8	3.7	14,850	75[7]
1911	2.7	554	...	...	10	0.2	179	5.3	7.1	16,901	...
1912	2.9	621	10	...	10	0.2	199	5.5	7.8	17,589	...
1913	3.0	694	12	...	11	0.2	...	4.5	8.3	18,567	...
1914	2.9	737	13	...	9.5	0.2	...	2.3	4.2[8]	...	...
1915	2.6	749[2]	11	...	8.3	0.2	...	3.9	...	...	...
1916	2.5	...	12	...	9.6	0.2	...[6]	3.5[6]	4.7	...	...
1917	2.5	...	13	...	12	0.2	[48]	[2.7]	4.0	...	129
1918	2.6	...	13	...	11	0.2	86	5.7	4.0	...	134
1919	2.8	...	14[3]	...	12	0.3	91	5.9	6.1	...	139
1920	3.6	...	17	...	14	0.3	137	6.4	5.7	...	156[7] 160
1921	3.3	...	16	...	14	0.3	171	6.2	5.6	...	144
1922	3.1	...	16	...	13	0.4	213	5.5	6.3	...	155
1923	2.7	...	17	...	14	0.3	188	5.4	4.8	23,055	165
1924	3.0	...	17[3] 12	...	14	0.3	163	5.7	4.6	...	170
1925	2.9	...	12	...	14	0.3	200	6.1	5.1	...	193
1926	3.1	...	13	...	17	0.3	223	6.0	5.0	25,484	219
1927	3.2	...	14	...	17	0.4	214	6.1	5.4	26,687	219
1928	3.2	...	15	...	17	0.4	213	6.2	6.4	26,837	229
1929	3.3	...	16	...	19	0.4	200	6.2	7.0	27,952	256
1930	3.3	...	14	...	19	0.4	219	6.2	7.4	27,888	232
1931	3.1	...	12	...	17	0.4	208	5.7	6.3	26,544	201
1932	2.9	...	9.9	...	17	0.4	172	5.3	6.4	24,307	158
1933	2.9	...	9.4	...	19	0.3	182	5.8	6.6	19,868	159
1934	2.9	...	9.9	...	20	0.3	215	6.6	6.6	20,626	170
1935	3.2	...	10	...	21	0.4	255	7.8	6.4	22,332	192
1936	3.5	...	12	...	20	0.4	289	8.7	7.0	23,571	211
1937	3.5	...	12	...	21	0.4	326	9.1	7.7[8] 8.1	25,801	220
1938	3.4	...	12	...	20	0.4	348	9.0	9.6	26,042	204
1939	3.4	...	12	...	...[5]	...[5]	340	9.7	11	26,445	208
1940	...	...	12	1.3	...	...	319	10	9.2	27,749	208
1941	2.5	...	14	1.2	...	...	345	11[6] 18	9.9	29,236	227
1942	2.6	...	15	1.3	...	...	380	23	10	30,118	236
1943	2.7	...	16	1.3	...	...	390	27	9.3	32,818	248
1944	2.8	...	16	1.5	...	...	433	28	10	34,931	243

## F8	NORTH AMERICA: Postal and Telegraph Traffic

	Barbados[1]	Canada		El Salvador	Jamaica[5]		Mexico		Trinidad & Tobago[8]	USA	
	m	m	t	t[9]	m	t	m	t[6]	m	m	t[7]
1945	3.3	...	17	1.7	23	0.8	496	32	13	37,912	257
1946	3.6	...	17	1.7	24₅	...	518	27	16	36,318	234
1947	3.8	1,467	16	1.9	26	0.7	556	31	19	37,428	238
1948	4.3	...	18	2.0	26	0.8	574	32	23	40,280	213
1949	4.4	1,831	19	1.9	29	0.7	610	33	20	43,555	196
1950	4.5	2,627	19	2.1	25	0.7	506	36	20	45,064	201
1951	4.9	2,707	21	2.2	27	0.8	559	35	19	46,908	204
1952	5.4	2,830	20	2.5	29	0.9	667	37	21	49,906	176
1953	6.1	2,818	20	2.6	32	1.0	693	38	23	50,948	186
1954	6.2	2,910	19	2.5	34₅	1.0	714	39	23	52,213	177
1955	8.1	...	19	2.4	...	1.0	730	42	29	55,234	180
1956	10	3,043	19	2.8	...	1.1	813	38	29	56,441	179
1957	10	3,043	18	2.9	...	1.1	801	38	32	59,078	172
1958	10	3,175	17	2.9	78	...	881	39	34	60,130	159
1959	14	3,355	16₄	3.6	90	...	948	39	36	61,247	159
1960	13	3,419	15	3.5	92	...	925	41	37	63,675	153
1961	13	3,579	14	2.6	105	...	983	41	40	64,933	146
1962	13	3,721	14	3.8	109	...	1,073	[38][9]	39	66,493	141
1963	16	3,690	14	2.8	113	1.1	1,119	42	40	67,853	134
1964	16	3,817	14	3.7	120	1.0	1,155	36	38	69,676	127
1965	16	3,797	14	2.1	132	1.1	1,192	38	41	71,873	124
1966	18	4,574	13	1.8	138	1.2	1,242	41	41	75,607	123
1967	20	4,799	12	1.6	145	...	1,334	42	44	78,367	119
1968	23	4,893	10	1.4	152	1.2	1,367	43	46	79,517	116
1969	24	4,866	9.3	1.4	160	1.5	1,388	46	45	82,005	109
1970	26	4,729	8.4	1.4	168	1.3	1,408	48	45	84,882	102
1971	...	4,475	7.5	1.2	...	1.2	1,425	50	48	86,983	75
1972	...	4,630₂	6.8	1.3	172	1.1	1,552	54	50	87,156	69
1973	...	4,729	5.1	1.3	173	1.4	1,651	54	51	89,683	67
1974	...	5,167	5.4	1.4	176	...	1,661	55	52	90,098	71
1975	...	5,404	5.8	1.2	175	1.5	1,611	45	53	89,266	68
1976	...	5,002	4.2	1.3	119	0.9	1,668	44	54	89,768	67
1977	...	...	3.6	1.3	120	0.8	768	45	54	92,224	68
1978	...	...	3.4	1.4	121	1.6	843	47	55	96,913	72
1979	...	6,167	3.1	1.4	57	1.0	880	50	33	99,829	76
1980	...	...	2.6	1.4	56	0.7	1,029	52	34	106,311	75
1981	...	...	...	1.2	45	1.0	1,053	55	34	110,130	74
1982	...	...	...	1.2	82	...	1,005	58	33	114,049	65
1983	...	...	...	1.1	63	...	858	51	36	119,381	53
1984	...	...	...	1.1	60	...	811	...	31	131,545	48
1985	...	...	...	1.7	35	...	652	55	25	140,098	42
1986	...	...	...	...	55	...	677	58	23	147,376	29
1987	...	...	...	...	60	...	753	...	24	153,931	25
1988	...	...	...	...	71	...	751	56	23	160,491	...
1989					85		763	...	27	161,603	...
1990					76		797	...	26	166,301	...
1991					77		846	...	27	165,801	...
1992					80		883	...	28	166,443	...
1993					78		936	47	29	171,313	...

F8 SOUTH AMERICA: POSTAL AND TELEGRAPH TRAFFIC

1840–1869

	Brazil[10]			Brazil[10]		Chile		Guyana*[14]	Uruguay
	m[11]	t		m[11]	t	m[12]	t[13]	t	m[15]
1840	0.9	—	1870	9.7	- -	...	...	...	...
1841	0.8	—	1871	10	- -	...	...	...	...
1842	1.1	—	1872	12	0.1	...	...	...	...
1843	1.5	—	1873	13	0.1	...	...	...	...
1844	1.5	—	1874	14	0.1	...	...	...	...
1845	1.9	—	1875	13	0.1	...	...	...	...
1846	1.9	—	1876	15	0.1	...	...	...	...
1847	2.0	—	1877	15	0.2	...	...	...	...
1848	1.9	—	1878	16	0.2	...	...	...	...
1849	1.9	—	1879	19	0.3	...	...	...	...
1850	1.8	—	1880	20	0.3		...	...	2.2
1851	2.4	—	1881	24	0.4	...	...	...	3.0
1852	2.8	—	1882	24	0.3	...	...	...	3.6
1853	3.2	—	1883	25	0.3	...	...	...	5.5
1854	3.3	—	1884	32	0.4	...	...	0.1	12
1855	3.6	—	1885	35	0.4	...	...	0.1	12
1856	4.3	—	1886	...	...	...	...	0.1	11
1857	4.7	—	1887	[56][10]	[0.7][10]	41	0.6	0.1	17
1858	5.2	—	1888	40	0.5	44	...	0.1	20
1859	5.3	—	1889	44	0.6	43	...	0.1	21
1860	5.7	—	1890	50	0.8	48	...	0.1	22
1861	5.9	—	1891	64	1.0	39	...	0.1	20
1862	6.2	- -	1892	87	1.2	54	...	0.1	23
1863	6.5	- -	1893	72	1.1	62	...	0.1	26
1864	6.3	- -	1894	69	1.3	69[12] 25	...	0.1	27
1865	7.4	- -							
1866	7.9	- -							
1867	[9.7][10]	- -							
1868	9.2	- -							
1869	9.7	- -							

F8 SOUTH AMERICA: Postal and Telegraph Traffic

	Argentina		Brazil		Chile		Colombia	
	m	t	m[11]	t	m[12]	t[13]	m	t
1895	80	2.8	75	1.5	28	…	…	…
1896	101	3.1	105	1.7	29	…	…	…
1897	106	3.4	135	1.7	28	…	…	…
1898	120	3.4	198	1.4	30	…	…	…
1899	134	3.4	197	1.4	31	…	…	…
1900	145	3.9	278	1.4	31	1.3	…	…
1901	159	3.6	320	1.2	38	1.4	…	…
1902	191	3.9	326	1.2	39	1.4	…	…
1903	207	2.7	347	1.4	50	1.5	…	…
1904	278	3.1	380	1.5	54	1.3	…	…
1905	320	3.1	394	1.5	59	1.6	…	…
1906	337	6.2	472	1.7	77	2.0	…	…
1907	374	6.7	520	1.9	78	2.1	…	…
1908	423	6.9	567	2.3	86	2.2	…	…
1909	494	7.5	481	2.4	78	2.5	…	…
1910	521	8.8	544	2.8	65	2.3	…	…
1911	635	9.1	608	2.8	73	2.3	5.6	[1.5][1]
1912	701	10	612	3.7	73	2.5	7.0	…
1913	783	11	634	3.8	75	2.4	7.0	[1.9][1]
1914	614	10	653	4.0	66	2.5	…	…
1915	560	10	443	3.7	68	2.5	5.8	2.9
1916	543	…	479	3.9	79	2.7	…	…
1917	520	…	466	4.4	87	3.0	…	3.2
1918	510	…	514	5.4	103	3.2	…	3.4
1919	…	…	546	5.6	96	3.3	…	…
1920	…	…	642	6.6	104	3.5	…	…
1921	…	…	624	6.1	101	3.1	…	…
1922	…	…	773	6.6	97	3.2	…	…
1923	…	…	873	6.9	101	3.4	…	4.2
1924	…	11	1,225	7.2	117	3.7	…	4.2
1925	…	13	1,746	7.6	109	3.8	…	5.0
1926	…	13	1,861	7.4	105	3.6	30	…
1927	…	13	1,912	7.5	93	3.6	…	5.0
1928	…	…	2,152	6.5	101	3.8	22	7.8
1929	…	8.3	2,105	6.0	100	3.9	23	8.1
1930	477	…	1,909	5.5	101	3.9	29	7.2
1931	728	…	1,821	7.1	84	3.2	30	5.7
1932	686	11	1,403	8.1	77	3.1	25	4.7
1933	724	7.1	1,708	8.6	78	3.3	27	4.8
1934	717	7.0	1,834	8.9	75	3.6	25	5.4
1935	760	9.2	2,554	9.9	82	3.7	28	5.6
1936	825	9.7	2,555	10	92	4.2	28	5.7
1937	992	9.8	2,308	11	98	4.6	26	5.4
1938	1,100	10	3,004	11	101	4.3	38	6.2
1939	1,115	11	3,141[11]	11	110	4.4	35	6.4
			810					

F8   SOUTH AMERICA: Postal and Telegraph Traffic

	Guyana*[14]		Peru		Uruguay		Venezuela	
	m	t	m	t	m[15]	t[17]	m	t
1895	...	0.1	...	...	31	...	...	...
1896	...	0.1	...	...	35	...	...	...
1897	...	0.1	...	...	31	...	...	...
1898	...	0.1	...	...	32	...	...	...
1899	...	0.1	...	...	37	...	...	...
1900	2.2	0.1	...	...	45	...	...	...
1901	2.3	0.1	...	...	55	...	...	...
1902	2.4	0.1	...	...	63	...	...	...
1903	2.6	0.1	...	...	71	...	...	...
1904	2.8	0.1	...	...	57	...	...	...
1905	2.8	0.1	...	...	81	...	...	...
1906	2.8	0.1	...	...	91	...	...	...
1907	2.8	0.1	...	...	97[15] 46	...	...	...
1908	2.9	0.1	...	...	52	...	...	...
1909	2.9	0.1	...	0.6	53	...	...	...
1910	3.0	0.1	16	0.8	67	0.3	...	...
1911	2.9	0.1	19	0.9	63	0.4	...	...
1912	2.9	0.1	21	0.9	62	0.4	...	...
1913	2.9	0.1	18	0.9	72	0.4	...	0.7
1914	3.1[14]	0.1[14]	15	1.0	68	0.5	...	...
1915	3.0	0.1	13	0.8	59	0.5	...	...
1916	3.0	0.1	15	0.8	60	0.5	...	...
1917	3.2	0.1	15	1.0	57	0.6	...	...
1918	2.9	0.1	17	1.0	63	0.6	...	...
1919	2.8	0.1	17	1.0	65	0.7	...	...
1920	3.0	0.1	19	0.9	81	0.7	...	...
1921	3.3	0.1	17	0.9	73	0.6	...	...
1922	3.6	0.1	16	...	73	0.5	...	1.0
1923	3.6	0.1	17	0.8	73	0.6	...	...
1924	3.6	0.1	20	1.2	74	0.6	...	1.2
1925	3.5	0.1	22	1.2	74	0.6	...	1.7
1926	3.5	0.1	22	1.3	75	0.6	...	2.0
1927	3.6	0.1	26	1.4[4]	76	0.6	...	2.4
1928	3.7	0.1	29	1.6	75	0.7	42	1.9
1929	3.5	0.1	32	1.8	75	0.7	72	...
1930	3.5	0.1	28	1.8	75	0.7	67	1.8
1931	3.4	0.1	27	1.6	74	0.7	31	1.8
1932	3.4	0.1	29	1.6	67	0.6	29	...
1933	3.4	0.1	28	1.6	55	0.5	...	...
1934	3.5	0.1	25	1.7	55	0.5	...	...
1935	3.5	0.1	28	1.8	57	0.6	...	...
1936	4.0	0.1	19	1.8	59	0.6	...	...
1937	4.5	0.1	22	1.9	53	0.6	28	...
1938	4.7	0.1	25	1.9	55	0.6	42	2.7
1939	...	...	27	2.0	62	0.6	59	2.8

F8 SOUTH AMERICA: Postal and Telegraph Traffic

	Argentina		Brazil		Chile		Colombia	
	m	t[18]	m[11]	t	m[12]	t[13]	m[20]	t
1940	1,128	11	655	11	112	4.0	31	6.3
1941	1,113	12	592	13	121	4.2	31	6.6
1942	1,100	13[18] 10	546	15	119	4.5	27	7.3
1943	...	11	689	18	115	4.8	28	7.8
1944	1,190	12	932	20	121	5.1	31	8.0
1945	1,186	13	1,183	24	...	...	37	9.1
1946	1,278	15	1,280	27	134	5.9	53	9.8
1947	1,555	17	1,394	29	133	6.6	57	10
1948	1,702	19	1,850	30	137	5.6	48	10
1949	1,449	20	1,865	26	141	5.6	45	11
1950	...	21	2,017	27	...	...	52	8.9
1951	1,544	21	2,160	29	...	5.8	47	8.8
1952	1,386	18	2,300	29	...	...	45	8.7
1953	1,283	18	2,183	31	...	...	55	8.1
1954	1,352	20	2,349	29	...	...	70	9.6
1955	1,331	21	2,508	32	...	...	...	8.0
1956	1,349	21[18] 24	1,962	24	...	7.9	...	...
1957	1,391	23	3,884	21	...	5.9	...	...
1958	1,489	25	[1,687][9]	22	124	6.6	...[20]	...
1959	1,311	22	[2,734][9]	[20][19]	101	6.7	43	8.0
1960	1,423	23	4,948	26	107	5.9	37	8.6
1961	1,638	22	3,997	27	112	5.5	41	8.0
1962	1,390	19	4,398	24	131	5.1	48	8.7
1963	1,184	19	4,390	25	122[12]	5.1	50	10
1964	1,013	20	4,534	28	...	5.7	42	...
1965	964	19	2,325	18	...	[6.6][9]	42	12
1966	859	17	2,964[11] 2,455	30	...	7.1	44	12
1967	835	16	2,327	37	...	[6.2][9]	45	13
1968	881	15	2,755	22	...	...	51	13
1969	991	16	3,385[11]	18	...	5.1	...	14
1970	1,012	15	...	17	...	5.3	59	17
1971	1,067	16	622	19	...	6.3	73	17
1972	1,027	16	639	20	...	6.7	72	18
1973	1,102	18	657	21	...	7.5	...	19
1974	1,017	19	836	20	165	6.2	...	19
1975	872	17	1,246	19	170	4.9	94	21
1976	739[21] 659	13	1,692	18	185	4.7	89	20
1977	615	13	2,117	18	102	5.1	97	20
1978	641	12	2,667	17	...	4.1	135	22
1979	684	13	3,106	16	118	4.5	173	21
1980	627	14	3,524	15	180	4.2	187	20
1981	...	12	3,708	15	177	3.6	192	21
1982	...	...	3,856	16	167	3.0	...	24
1983	...	...	4,048[11] 2,054	16	122	2.7	...	21
1984	...	...	2,518	18	109	2.9	...	22
1985	...	...	2,865	21	130	3.0	...	22
1986	...	...	3,247	28	150	2.8	...	20
1987	...	...	2,952	30	161	2.1	...	18
1988	...	...	3,147	27	175	2.2	...	...
1989	455	...	3,267	27	204	2.4	...	...
1990	403	...	3,186	25	203	2.7	...	...
1991	422	...	2,939	24	215	2.2	...	...
1992	448	...	2,827	20	231	2.1	...	...
1993	529	...	3,394	19	258	1.7	...	...

F8 SOUTH AMERICA: Postal and Telegraph Traffic

	Guyana*		Peru		Uruguay		Venezuela	
	m[14]	t	m	t	m	t[17]	m	t
1940	...	...	27	2.0	78	0.6	37	2.7
1941	...	...	27	2.1	82	0.7	34	2.7
1942	...	...	30	2.3	95	0.8	26	2.9
1943	...	0.1	29	2.6	94	0.8	26	3.2
1944	...	0.2	36	3.0	95	0.9	28	3.6
1945	6.4	0.1	43	3.0	116	1.0	29	4.2
1946	6.4	0.2	33	3.3	122	1.1	32	5.0
1947	6.5	0.2	32	3.5	137	1.3	48	5.9
1948	7.3	0.2	51	3.8	...	1.3	61	5.7
1949	7.4	0.2	59	4.1	...	1.4	73	5.0
1950	7.4	0.2	51	6.0	...	1.5	67	6.8
1951	7.4	0.1	75	...	...	1.6	90	5.4
1952	6.3	0.1	88	3.8	...	1.6	117	5.4
1953	8.0	0.1	97	4.1	...	1.7	133	5.5
1954	8.8	0.1	99	4.3	...	1.7	168	6.0
1955	8.4	0.1	89	4.5	...	1.7	199	6.2
1956	11	0.1	106	4.8	...	1.8	264	6.6
1957	9.6	0.2	124	4.9	...	1.8	412	7.0
1958	12[14]	...	141	5.2	...	1.8	467	7.4
1959	114	...	230	5.3	57	1.8[17] / 1.9	215	7.6
1960	115	...	...	...	...	2.0	237	7.7
1961	...	...	...	...	...	2.0	245	5.8
1962	...	...	...	...	...	2.1	287	5.1
1963	...	...	...	...	...	2.1	223	5.0
1964	...	...	...	...	...	...	222	4.6
1965	97	...	...	...	...	...	252	4.6
1966	96	...	...	...	...	...	231	5.6
1967	101	...	...	...	...	1.6	261	4.4
1968	105	...	...	...	...	1.6	221	4.6
1969	...	...	...	3.0	...	1.8	243	4.7
1970	...	...	...	3.7	...	1.5	220[21] / 305	4.8
1971	117	...	...	3.9	...	1.2	293	4.7
1972	121	...	...	4.2	...	1.0	323	4.4
1973	127	...	...	5.3	...	0.9	371	...
1974	251	...	...	4.8	...	1.0	357	...
1975	251	...	...	5.7	...	1.0	316	4.7
1976	...	...	...	5.7[9] / 11	...	1.0	382	4.5
1977	...	...	...	11	...	1.3	...	...
1978	...	...	...	11	...	1.4	...	...
1979	...	...	...	8.8	...	...	...	...
1980	...	...	...	9.1	...	...	...	...
1981	...	...	...	8.3	...	...	...	...
1982	...	...	...	7.6	...	...	...	3.6
1983	...	...	...	6.8	...	...	...	3.3
1984	...	...	...	6.1	...	...	...	3.0
1985	...	...	...	5.9	...	...	...	3.2
1986	...	...	...	6.1	...	...	...	2.9
1987	...	...	...	6.4	...	...	...	2.9
1988	...	...	...	...	...	...	...	2.9
1989	...	...	...	...	...	...	...	2.4
1990	...	...	...	...	...	...	...	2.2
1991	...	...	...	...	...	...	...	2.1
1992	...	...	...	...	...	...	...	2.0
1993	...	...	...	...	...	...	...	...

F8 Postal and Telegraph Traffic

NOTES

1. SOURCES: The national publications listed on pp. xiii–xv, and the League of Nations and UN, *Statistical Yearbooks*.
2. So far as possible, and except as indicated in footnotes, internal mail is counted once whilst international mail is counted both on dispatch and receipt. Telegram statistics are of all telegrams sent.
3. The nature of postal, and to a lesser extent telegraph, statistics differs considerably between countries. So far as possible the classifications used here are those which give the longest possible comparable series within each country. Where there is a choice in this matter, the most comprehensive classification has been preferred.

FOOTNOTES

[1] Registered mail is excluded.
[2] First-class items only to 1915. Mail sent from 1947 to 1972. Data to 1906 are for years ending 30 June, and from 1908 they are for years ending 31 March. The 1907 figure is for the 9 months from 1 July 1906 to 31 March 1907.
[3] Telegrams and cablegrams transmitted to 1924 (1st line)—i.e. including those received from abroad. Data to 1919 are for years ending 30 June.
[4] Statistics before and after this point are not exactly comparable.
[5] Years beginning 1 April to 1938. Data for mail for 1947 to 1954 are for Kingston only.
[6] Years beginning 1 July to 1916. The 1917 figures are for the second half-year only. Telegram statistics are for the Federal network only to 1941 (1st line).
[7] Western Union Telegraph Company messages handled to 1910, for years ending 30 June. Statistics for 1917 to 1920 (1st line) are of all domestic messages handled, with international messages included subsequently.
[8] Years beginning 1 April to 1914. Data from 1937 (2nd line) include parcels and some other minor categories previously excluded.
[9] Subsequently includes international telegrams received.
[10] Statistics from 1868 to 1885 for mail and to 1885 for telegrams are for years beginning 1 July. The figure for mail in 1867 includes the first half of 1868, and the figures for 1887 are for the period 1 July 1886 to 31 December 1887.
[11] Statistics to 1939 (1st line) are of all items sent, received and in transit. Data from 1966 (2nd line) are of mail sent only. There were changes in coverage in 1970–1 and 1983.
[12] Mail sent only to 1963. All mail sent and received to 1894 (1st line), and all mail sent from them to 1963.
[13] State network only.
[14] Years beginning 1 April from 1892 to 1914. Mail statistics to 1958 are of letter mail sent.
[15] All mail sent and received to 1907 (1st line).
[16] Excluding official and press telegrams.
[17] National Telegraph Company only to 1959 (1st line).
[18] Changes in the categories included in the series occurred in 1942 and 1956.
[19] Figures from Bahia are not included, nor those from Pernambuco in the second half-year.
[20] Mail sent only from 1959.
[21] Mail sent only from 1976 (2nd line)

F9 NORTH AMERICA: NUMBER OF TELEPHONES IN USE (in thousands)

1876-1899   **1900-1944**

	USA			Barbados	Canada	Costa Rica	Cuba	Dominican Republic	El Salvador	Guadeloupe
1876	3		1900	...	...	...	...	...	...	...
1877	9		1901	...	...	...	...	...	...	...
1878	26		1902	...	...	...	...	...	...	...
1879	31		1903	...	...	...	...	...	...	...
			1904	...	95	...	...	...	...	...
1880	48									
1881	71		1905	...	...	...	...	...	0.1	...
1882	98		1906	...	...	...	...	...	...	...
1883	124		1907	...	...	...	...	...	...	...
1884	148		1908	...	...	...	...	...	...	...
			1909	...	...	...	...	...	...	...
1885	156									
1886	167		1910	...	...	...	...	...	0.1	...
1887	181		1911	...	303	...	...	...	...	...
1888	195		1912	...	371	...	...	...	...	...
1889	212		1913	0.9	464	0.9	16	0.6	0.2	...
			1914	...	521	...	...	...	...	...
1890	228									
1891	239		1915	...	533	...	...	...	...	...
1892	261		1916	...	600	...	...	...	...	...
1893	266		1917	...	657	...	...	...	...	...
1894	285		1918	...	698	1.5	...	...	...	...
			1919	...	779	1.5	...	...	...	...
1895	340									
1896	404		1920	...	856	1.6	...	...	...	...
1897	515		1921	...	902	...	...	...	...	...
1898	681		1922	1.6	944	...	...	...	...	...
1899	1,005		1923	1.6	1,009	...	48	...	2.8	...
			1924	1.7	1,072	...	...	...	...	...
			1925	1.7	1,143	...	62	...	...	...
			1926	1.8	1,201	...	64	...	...	...
			1927	1.9	1,260	...	68	...	...	...
			1928	2.0	1,335	2.9	73	2.4	3.7	0.1
			1929	2.0	1,383	...	75	2.3	...	...
			1930	2.0	1,403	...	67	...	...	...
			1931	2.0	1,364	...	54₄	...	...	...
			1932	2.0	1,261	2.6	33	...	3.8	0.2
			1933	2.1	1,192	...	...	...	...	...
			1934	2.1	1,197	...	...	...	...	...
			1935	2.3	1,209	...	...	...	...	...
			1936	2.4	1,266	...	...	2.4	...	...
			1937	2.4	1,323	...	50	2.6	...	0.3
			1938	2.6	1,359	...	53	2.9	...	...
			1939	...	1,397	2.8	55	3.0	...	...
			1940	...	1,461	...	59	3.1	4.4	...
			1941	...	1,562	...	62	3.2	4.4	...
			1942	...	1,628	...	67	2.6	4.9	...
			1943	...	1,692	...	69	2.6	5.0	...
			1944	...	1,752	...	71	2.6	5.1	...

F9   NORTH AMERICA: Number of Telephones in Use (in thousands)

1900–1944

	Guatemala	Haiti	Honduras	Jamaica	Mexico	Nicaragua	Panama	Puerto Rico	Trinidad & Tobago	USA[1]
1900	...	...	...	...	...	...	...	...	...	1,356
1901	...	...	...	...	...	...	...	...	...	1,801
1902	...	...	...	...	...	...	...	...	...	2,371
1903	...	...	...	...	...	...	...	...	...	2,809
1904	...	...	...	...	...	...	...	...	...	3,353
1905	...	...		...	...	...	...	...	...	4,127
1906	...	...	0.1	...	...	...	...	...	...	4,933
1907	...	...	...	...	...	...	...	...	...	6,119
1908	...	...	...	...	...	...	...	...	...	6,484
1909	...	...	...	...	...	...	...	...	...	6,996
1910	...	...	...	...	...	...	...	...	...	7,635
1911	...	...	...	...	...	...	...	...	...	8,349
1912	...	...	...	...	...	...	...	...	...	8,730
1913	1.8	...	0.1	...	42	0.5	2.6	...	...	9,543
1914	...	...	...	...	...	...	...	...	...	10,046
1915	...	...	...	...	...	...	...	...	...	10,524
1916	...	...	...	...	...	...	...	...	...	11,241
1917	...	...	...	...	...	...	...	...	...	11,717
1918	...	...	...	...	...	...	...	...	...	12,078
1919	...	...	...	...	...	...	...	...	...	12,669
1920	...	...	...	...	...	...	...	...	...	13,273
1921	...	...	...	...	...	...	...	...	...	13,817
1922	...	...	...	1	...	...	...	...	...	14,294
1923	...	...	...	1	...	...	...	...	...	15,316
1924	...	...	...	1	...	...	...	...	...	16,015
1925	...	...	...	1.1	...	...	...	...	...	16,875
1926	...	...	...	1.1	...	...	...	...	...	17,680
1927	...	...	...	1.4	...	...	...	...	...	18,446
1928	3.1	2.1	...	1.5	78	0.9	9.2	13	...	19,256
1929	...	...	...	1.5	58	...	...	...	...	19,970
1930	...	...	...	2	96	...	...	...	...	20,103
1931	...	...	...	2.2	99	...	...	...	...	19,602
1932	...	...	...	2.5	101	...	...	12	...	17,341
1933	...	...	...	2.7	107	1.2	...	12	...	16,628
1934	...	...	...	3.2	114	1.2	...	13	2.9	16,869
1935	...	...	3	3.5	120	...	...	14	2.9	17,424
1936	...	...	3.4	3.6	132	...	...	15	3.2	18,433
1937	...	...	...	3.9	145	1.4	...	15	3.4	19,453
1938	...	...	3.5	...	158	1.4	...	16	5.9	19,953
1939	3.5	...	...	...	175	...	...	17	6.5	20,831
1940	...	...	...		180	...	...	19	7.2	21,928
1941	...	...	...		181	...	...	21	8.5	23,521
1942	...	...	...		191	...	...	21	9.4	24,919
1943	...	...	...		200	1.9	...	22	9.2	26,381
1944	...	...	...		207	...	...	22	9.7	26,859

F9   NORTH AMERICA: Number of Telephones in Use (in thousands)

	Barbados	Canada	Costa Rica	Cuba	Dominican Republic	El Salvador	Guadeloupe	Guatemala	Haiti
1945	...	1,849	...	74	4.1	4.9		...	...
1946	3.1	2,026	7	79	4.2	5.3	0.6	4.5	2.9
1947	3.2	2,231	...	84	4.4	5.8	0.7	...	...
1948	3.6	2,452	...	93	4.7	6.0	0.7	...	3.5
1949	3.9	2,700	...	106	5.2	5.0	...	...	3.2
1950	4.3	2,912	...	113	6.6	5.2	...	...	3.1
1951	4.8	3,106	9.9	124	7.4	7.1	...	...	3.8
1952	5.0	3,342	11	...	8.0	8.9	...	5.7	4.1
1953	5.1	3,595	11	141	8.4	...	...	...	4.2
1954	5.8	3,853	11	142	8.9	9.9	1.1	9	4.3
1955	6.2	4,147	12	142	11	10	1.3	11	4.3
1956	7.0	4,500	11	144	12	10	1.9	...	4
1957	7.4	4,812	12	151	15	11	2.1	10	4
1958	8.1	5,113	13	170	17	12	2.5	12	4.2
1959	8.8	5,140	15	191	19	16	2.9	20	4
1960	9.6	5,433	16	202	20	16	3.3	18	4
1961	11	5,719	17	208	21	18	3.9	20	4
1962	12	6,340	19	218	25	20	4.7	19	4
1963	12	6,646	20	224	28	21	5.3	20	4
1964	14	7,011	22	229	30	22	6.0	23	4
1965	15	7,440	22	231	31	20	7.0	25	4
1966	18	7,893	24	234	32	30	7.7	33	4
1967	20	8,345	27	238	34	38	8.4	35	4.3
1968	25	8,821	50	242	36	37	9.7	36	4.5
1969	26	9,303	56	263	40	35	11	38	...
1970	29	9,751	61	269	47	39	14	49	...
1971	33	10,253	68	275	56	41	16	44	5
1972	36	10,979	78	278	66	43	17	54	...
1973	39	11,665	89	281	83	47	19	53	9
1974	40	12,454	99	289	95	50	22	...	...
1975	42	13,165	112	299	108	55	24	...	...
1976	44	13,885	127	311	127	60	27	...	18
1977	47	14,488	151	321	141	72	31	71	
1978	53	15,172	185	341	154	78	35	...	...
1979	54	15,839	200	362	155	83	39	...	...
1980	67	16,531	236	390	165	86	45	...	...
1981	72	16,944	256	406	175	100	50	...	...
1982	...	16,802	283	441	...	100	57	...	...
1983	75	16,618	292	...	...	116	69	...	...
1984	...	18,583	304	493	...	124	81	...	...
1985	...	19,084	315	515	...	133	96	128	...
1986	91	19,598	344	543	...	129	107	...	...
1987	94	20,126[6]	409	564	...	136[6]	100	133	...
1988	102[6]	13,796	410[6]	537[6]	...	106	103	138	...
1989	78	14,648	272	304	...	120	107	159	...
1990	83	15,296	281	337	...	125	118	190	45
1991	78	15,815	305	339	...	130	127	202	...
1992	80	16,247	327	337	...	165	139	214	...
1993	83	16,471	364	349	...	174	149	2,131	...

International Historical Statistics: The Americas 1750–1993

F9 NORTH AMERICA: Number of Telephones in Use (in thousands)

	Honduras	Jamaica	Martinique	Mexico	Nicaragua	Panama	Puerto Rico	Trinidad & Tobago	USA[1]
1945	...	...	...	216	...	...	24	10	27,867
1946	3.9	...	...	224[4]	1.9	7.0	27	10	31,611
				213					
1947	...	...	...	220	...	...	30	11	34,867
1948	4.1	...	1.5	248	2.3	10	33	12	38,205
1949	...	...	...	274	...	...	35	14	40,709
1950	...	...	...	286	...	...	37	15	43,004
1951	4.2	...	...	299	3.5	...	41	16	45,636
1952	...	15	...	312	3.5	17	43	18	48,056
1953	...	16	...	330	3.5	...	47	19	50,373
1954	...	18	...	349	3.6	18	54	21	52,806
1955	...	20	...	357	3.7	20	60	23	56,243
1956	5.5	23	4.1	383	5.7	22	65	25	60,190
1957	4.7	25	4.8	413	6.3	23	71	28	63,624
1958	5.9	27	5.2	448	7.0	24	77	30	66,645[1]
1959	...	30	5.7	492	8.0	26	82	31	70,820
1960	...	36	6.0	523	8.2	29	95	31	74,342
1961	...	39	6.5	567	9.3	33	109	32	77,422
1962	...	41	7.0	586	12	36	140	32	80,969
1963	9.3	44	7.7	659	...	39	172	35	84,453
1964	8.9	47	9.1	724	12	41	187	37	88,793
1965	8.9	50	11	823	12	47	203	39	93,656
1966	9.9	53	12	928	13	48	219	42	98,787
1967	10	57	13	1,046	13	58	241	46	103,752
1968	11	61	14	1,175	23	59	248	49	109,256
1969	13	67	16	1,327	16	62	281	52	115,222
1970	14	72	17	1,506	26	85	306	56	120,218
1971	17	76	19	1,712	26	...	356	63	125,142
1972	16	81	22	1,955	19	100	372	66	131,108
1973	15	85	25	2,223	17	...	393	66	138,286
1974	15	95	28	2,546	20	...	466	66	143,979
1975	18	101	31	2,928	36	142	474	67	149,008
1976	18	109	35	3,325	40	155	515	70	155,173
1977	19	109	39	3,737	43	155	561	75	162,072
1978	20	117	45	4,188	...	152	...	77	169,027
1979	27	117	50	4,553	58	164	651	78	175,535
1980	...	118	52	5,024	...	173	631	75	180,424
1981	32	119	...	5,537	33	185	678	77	181,892
1982	34	126	...	5,961	...	213	...	87	176,391
1983	36	133	48	6,414	...	220	...	109	...
1984	44	137	100	6,796	50	210	...	128	...
1985	46	144	112	7,329	...	223	...	166	...
1986	50	159	120	7,735	...	232	...	192	...
1987	54	164	107	8,214	...	240	...	211	...
1988	66	168	117[6]	8,665[6]	...[6]	242[6]	...	212[6]	...
1989	77	172	115	4,702	46	201	816	168	...
1990	88	178	122	5,355	50	216	.	165	...
1991	94	185	132	6,025	54	229	...	174	...
1992	105	212	141	6,754	67	243	...	180	...
1993	117	279	150	7,621	85	261	...	192	...

F9 SOUTH AMERICA: NUMBER OF TELEPHONES IN USE (in thousands)

1889-1929

	Argentina	Bolivia	Brazil	Chile	Colombia	Ecuador	Guyana	Paraguay	Peru	Surinam	Uruguay[5]	Venezuela
1889	...	...	...	...	...	...	...	...	...	...	2.7	...
1890	...	...	...	...	...	...	...	...	...	...	3.2	...
1891	...	...	...	...	...	...	...	...	...	...	2.7	...
1892	...	...	...	...	...	...	...	...	...	...	2.4	...
1893	...	...	...	...	...	...	...	...	...	...	2.8	...
1894	...	...	...	...	...	...	...	...	...	...	3.0	...
1895	...	...	...	...	...	...	...	...	...	...	3.1	
1896	...	...	...	...	...	...	...	...	...	...	3.3	
1897	...	...	...	...	...	...	...	...	...	...	3.4	
1898	...	...	...	...	...	...	...	...	...	...	3.7	...
1899	...	...	...	...	...	...	...	...	...	...	4.0	...
1900	...	...	...	5.5	...	...	...	...	...	...	4.0	
1901	...	...	...	...	...	...	...	...	...	...	4.5	
1902	...	...	...	7.2	...	...	...	...	...	...	4.6	
1903	...	...	...	7.3	...	0.3	...	...	...	...	4.8	...
1904	...	...	...	...	...	...	...	...	...	...	...	
1905	...	...	...	6.6	...	...	...	...	...	...	...	
1906	...	...	...	...	...	...	...	...	...	...	...	
1907	...	...	15	...	...	0.6	...	...	...	...	...	...
1908	...	...	...	...	...	...	...	...	...	...	6.7	...
1909	...	...	...	...	...	...	...	...	...	...	7.2	...
1910	...	...	...	...	...	1.0	...	...	...	...	8.1	...
1911	...	...	...	...	...	...	...	...	...	...	8.3	
1912	...	...	...	...	...	...	...	...	...	...	9.2	4.5
1913	74	2.5	39	15	3.2	2.9	1.3	0.5	4.0	...	10	5.0
1914	...	...	...	18	...	...	...	...	...	...	10	5.0
1915	...	...	46	18	...	2.3	...	...	...	...	11	...
1916	...	...	50	19	...	...	...	...	...	...	10	...
1917	...	...	57	19	...	...	...	...	...	...	12	
1918	...	...	58	20	...	...	...	...	...	...	13	...
1919	104	...	58	22	...	...	...	...	...	...	14	...
1920	120	...	59	22		...	...	...	...	...	15	
1921	135	...	...	24	...	...	...	...	...	...	15	...
1922	145	2.7	...	27	...	4.3	0.9	...	...	...	15	10
1923	157	...	94	27	12	...	1.7	...	...	...	16	...
1924	174	1.8	...	27	15	4.7	1.7	...	...	...	16	12
1925	189	...	...	28	17	4.5	1.7	0.5	...	...	17	12
1926	204	...	105	30	18	...	1.8	0.4	11	...	17	13
1927	225	...	108	33	19	4.4	2.0	0.4	...	...	19[5] 20	13
1928	245	2.7	130	37	22	...	1.9	1.1	14	0.7	30	15
1929	269	2.5	160	40	28	4.1	2.0	2.0	...	...	30	20

F9 SOUTH AMERICA: Number of Telephones in Use (in thousands)

1930–1974

	Argentina	Bolivia	Brazil	Chile	Colombia	Ecuador	Guyana	Paraguay	Peru	Surinam	Uruguay[5]	Venezuela
1930	291	2.3	163	44	28	...	2.0	2.1	...	...	28	22
1931	304	2.1	166	39	29	4.1	1.9	2.9	...	...	28	22
1932	307	2.0	170	44	28	6.3	1.9	...	...	...	28	23
1933	305	...	...	...	29	...	2.0	...	...	...	46	...
1934	312	...	...	...	33	...	2.0	...	...	...	30	...
1935	327	...	...	...	34	...	2.1	...	...	...	33	...
1936	349	...	...	...	37	...	2.1	3.2	...	...	34	...
1937	377	2.6	242	71	38	7.1	2.2	3.4	21	...	48	21
1938	407	2.6	...	78	39	7.1	2.4	3.5	26	...	44	22
1939	434	...	256	83	41	7.3	2.4	3.6	26	...	...	25
1940	460	...	273	90	42	7.4	2.5	3.7	26	...	47	29
1941	...	...	...	96	45	7.6	2.6	3.8	27	...	...	...
1942	...	...	380	101	47	7.8	2.7	4.0	27	...	...	...
1943	...	...	...	103	47	7.9	2.8	4.1	28	...	...	...
1944	...	...	373	107	50	8.0	2.8	4.2	28	...	...	...
1945	...	...	...	...	54	8.1	2.9	4.5	29	...	...	...
1946	573	...	...	114	56	8.3	2.9	4.7	36	...	70	43
1947	651	7.8	439	113	62	...	3.0	4.8	43	...	73	...
1948	679	8.5	492	119	68	...	3.2	5.0	44	1.5	78	...
1949	717	...	512	126	77	...	3.2	5.2	44	...	84	...
1950	798	...	550	...	90	...	3.3	5.3	47	1.6	90	...
1951	852	11	592	138	98	9.0	3.5	5.3	49	...	95	74
1952	929	11	636	141	115	12	3.5	5.5	54	...	102	82
1953	1,001	11	680	145	129	12	3.6	5.7	57	...	105	92
1954	1,080	11	746	148	144	12	4.4	5.8	61	3.2	109	98
1955	1,128	12	805	149	164	13	4.6	6.8	64	...	114	105
1956	1,155	12	843	153	198	17	4.8	7.5	69	3.9	123	112
1957	1,181	23	870	160	223	22	4.9	...	79	4.4	129	140
1958	1,224	20	928	166	247	25	5.2	9.2	91	4.8	136	159
1959	1,244	21	964	184	266	27	5.4	10	102	5.2	137	180
1960	1,296	...	1,023	193	295	29	8.2	11	109	5.5	142	202
1961	1,360	18	1,047	203	322	31	9.1	11	113	5.8	137	216
1962	1,400	19	1,152	221	344	38	9.2	12	117	6.0	178	229
1963	1,425	20	1,217	235	372	44	9.4	13	126	6.6	169	241
1964	1,472	20	1,263	250	410	43	9.9	14	132	6.9	189	260
1965	1,498	25	1,320	263	443	44	11	14	137	8.4	185	283
1966	1,527	27	1,432	270	500	44	11	14	143	9.2	192	309
1967	1,554	30	1,473	290	735	45	12	16	152	9.0	204	327
1968	1,600	32	1,561	312	817	88	13	19	165	9.6	205	346
1969	1,668	38	1,787	334	543	94	14	21	193	9.9	207	377
1970	1,748	...	2,001	357	809	130	15	24	228	...	215	406
1971	1,828	44	2,145	393	856	150	15	20	243	12	235	444
1972	1,952	...	2,190	415	1,010	120	15	21	269	12	241	474
1973	2,065	49	2,415	433	1,080	131	17	24	309	13	246	527
1974	2,177	...	2,917	427	1,186	166	19	32	336	...	248	554

F9 Number of Telephones in Use

	Argentina	Bolivia	Brazil	Chile	Colombia	Ecuador	Guyana	Paraguay	Peru	Surinam	Uruguay	Venezuela
1975	1,996	61	3,372	437	1,286	182	21	37	369	18	250	650
1976	2,302	64	4,036	451	1,296	202	23	40	389	19	258	742
1977	2,342	71	4,836	467	1,396	221	27	43	403	19	268	847
1978	2,404	104	5,525	514	1,493	240	...	48	420	20	270	678
1979	2,491	113	6,494	536	1,587	260	...	55	437	15	279	789
1980	2,588	138	7,496	551	1,718	272	...	59	458	...	287	...
1981	2,767	141	8,536	595	1,842	290	28	64	484	...	294	...
1982	3,235	151	9,126	584	1,866	312	...	71	501	...	...	1,378
1983	3,108	157	9,856	629	1,894	318	...	78	525	28	332	1,021
1984	2,954	158	10,576	680	1,978	332	...	83	563	35	338	1,311
1985	3,048	...	11,428	761	2,097	339	33	89	600	36	374	1,451
1986	3,206	182	12,193	796	2,289	352	33	93	629[6]	38	399	1,581
1987	3,655	...	13,158	815	2,438	355[6]	...	100	454	39	437	1,677[6]
1988	3,694[6]	...[6]	13,905[6]	[6]867	2,499[6]	335	...[6]	112[6]	489	41[6]	482[6]	1,402
1989	3,400	170	8,852	646	2,177	384	16	103	531	34	376	1,458
1990	3,087	184	9,409	860	2,415	491	13	112	565	37	415	1,488
1991	3,199	185	10,076	1,056	2,633	491	16	120	577	41	451	1,599
1992	3,682	193	10,872	1,283	2,822	531	28	128	614	44	492	1,832
1993	4,092	234	11,753	1,520	3,221	598	41	142	673	47	530	2,083

NOTE

SOURCES: The national publications listed on pp. xiii–xv, and League of Nations and UN, *Statistical Yearbooks*.

FOOTNOTES

[1] Including Alaska and Hawaii from 1959.
[2] At 30 June from 1911.
[3] At 31 March in the year following that shown. Connections to 1913 (1st line).
[4] The reason for this break is not clear in the sources.
[5] Montevideo only to 1927 (1st line).
[6] Main lines only.

F10   NORTH AMERICA: RADIO AND TELEVISION SETS IN USE (in thousands, except as otherwise indicated)

1920–1944   1945–1993

	Guatemala	Trinidad & Tobago[1]	USA[2]
	Radios	Radios	Radios
1920	...	...	...
1921	...	...	...
1922	...	...	60
1923	...	...	400
1924	...	...	1,250
1925	...	...	2,750
1926	...	...	4,500
1927	...	...	6,750
1928	...	...	8,000
1929	...	...	10,250
1930	...	...	13,750
1931	...	...	16,700
1932	...	...	18,450
1933	...	...	19,250
1934	...	...	20,400
1935	...	...	21,456
1936	...	...	22,869
1937	...	...	24,500
1938	...	...	26,667
1939	...	4.9	27,500
1940	22	5.6	28,500
1941	...	6.7	29,300
1942	...	7.5	30,600
1943	...	7.7	30,800
1944	...	8.4	32,500

	Barbados		Canada		Costa Rica	
	Radios	TV	Radios	TV	Radios	TV
			(millions)			
1945	...	—	...	...	...	...
1946	...	—	...	...	...	...
1947	...	—	...	...	...	...
1948	...	—	...	...	...	...
1949	6	—	...	...	...	...
1950	...	—	...	...	23	...
1951	...	—	...	...	...	...
1952	9	—	...	...	...	...
1953	13	—	...	665	...	...
1954	14	—	...	1,407	50	...
1955	...	—	...	2,000	...	...
1956	17	—	...	2,450	...	...
1957	26	—	...	2,730	75	...
1958	28	—	7	3,075	75	...
1959	31	—	7.5	3,420	75	...
1960	35	—	8.1	3,930	77	...
1961	38	—	9.2	4,100	81	7.2
1962	42	—	9.2	4,375	...	12
1963	...	—	...	4,655	100	15
1964	...	—	10	4,950	123	35
			(millions)			
1965	43	6	...	5.3	130	50
1966	45	9	12	5.7	...	65
1967	55	9	12	...	...	66
1968	57	15	14	6.1	...	...
1969	...	15	15	...	106	100
1970	89	16	16	7.1	130	100
1971	94	18	17	7.6	130	120
1972	110	32	18	7.3	135	120
1973	116	35	19	7.7	140	122
1974	...	40	20	8.2	142	150
1975	130	40	22	9.4	145	150
1976	...	48	...	...	...	155
1977	...	50	24	10.0	...	160
1978	130	50	26	11.0	160	160
1979	131	50	26	11.0	180	161
1980	135	50	27	11.3	180	162
1981	143	53	28[5]	11.9[5]	186	164
1982	190	54	19	11.3	195	200
1983	191	55	...	12	...	181
1984	...	...	...	...	...	...
1985	...	...	...	...	220	200
1986	220	66	23	14	...	210
1987	...	...	...	...	...	...
1988	223	66	25	15	740	230
1989	224	67	27	16	...	...
1990	225	70	27	17	781	420
1991	226	68	28	17	800	435
1992	227	72	28	18	823	450
1993	228	73	29	18	844	465

F10 NORTH AMERICA: Radios and Television Sets in Use (in thousands, except as otherwise indicated)

1945-1993

	Cuba		Dominican Republic		El Salvador		Guadeloupe[3]		Guatemala	
	Radios	TV	Radios	TV	Radios	TV	Radios	TV	Radios	TV
1945	...	...	...	...	...	—	...	—	...	...
1946	...	...	...	...	...	—	...	—	...	...
1947	...	...	...	...	...	—	...	—	...	...
1948	...	...	30	...	...	—	...	—	...	...
1949	700	...	...	...	...	—	...	—	30	...
1950	575	...	35	...	21	—	1.0	—	...	...
1951	...	...	...	...	...	—	1.2	—	31	...
1952	...	...	...	...	...	—	1.4	—	...	...
1953	900	150	55	1.2	...	—	...	—	...	...
1954	...	...	...	5	28	—	2.8	—	36	...
1955	...	200	...	6	...	—	...	—	...	...
1956	1,100	275	...	7	...	1	...	—	...	8.5
1957	...	300	...	...	30	...	6	—	...	11
1958	900	315	80	15	40	10	6	—	...	11
1959	1,000	365	98	16	225	16	6	—	...	20
1960	1,100	500	102	18	...	20	6	—	...	32
1961	1,300	500	...	...	353	20	6	—	210	35
1962	...	520	123	11	358	25	6	—	...	40
1963	...	525	139	19	...	30	6	—	...	50
1964	1,345	550	...	35	395	30	10	...	...	50
1965	...	...	...	50	396	35	...	0.7	...	55
1966	...	555	150	65	...	...	18	2.6	...	...
1967	...	575	150	75	396	45	24	4	...	55
1968	...	575	155	75	398	...	27	5.2	...	65
1969	1,326	...	160	100	400	75	30	5.8	...	72
1970	1,330	...	164	100	405	92	26	...	220	72
1971	1,338	...	165	...	350	125	27	7.9	...	82
1972	1,500	...	170	150	...	...	...	9	...	85
1973	1,790	525	180	155	...	110	...	10	260	105
1974	1,805	595	185	156	...	111	21	13	261	106
1975	2,100	600	190	158	1,400	135	...	...	262	110
1976	...	635	...	161	...	136	...	...	...	120
1977	...	800	211	...	1,416	148	...	...	274	150
1978	2,227	975	212	250	1,416	180	...	...	280	150
1979	2,575	1,114	215	320	1,508	276	...	...	285	160
1980	2,914	1,273	220	385	1,550	300	35	33	310	175
1981	3,000	1,500	229	...	1,600	310	37	36	320	180
1982	3,100	1,600	250	450	1,680	320	38	37	330	200
1983	...	1,658	...	...	1,900	340	39	38	340	203
1984	...	...	...	...	...	...	...	...	...	...
1985	3,282	1,977	...	500	1,900	350	...	...	370	207
1986	3,400	2,050	...	515	2,000	400	...	...	500	300
1987	...	...	...	...	...	...	...	...	...	...
1988	3,435	2,069	1,141	556	2,040	425	84	72	550	325
1989	3,608	2,140	1,180	575	2,080	450	85	100	570	400
1990	3,650	1,770	1,210	600	2,125	475	89	102	600	475
1991	3,695	1,746	1,250	615	2,175	485	91	104	625	490
1992	3,732	1,750	1,280	650	2,230	501	92	106	645	510
1993	3,768	1,880	1,300	680	2,280	520	94	108	680	530

F10 NORTH AMERICA: Radio and Television Sets in Use (in thousands, except as otherwise indicated)

1945–1993

	Haiti		Honduras		Jamaica		Martinique[5]		Mexico	
	Radios	TV	Radios	TV	Radios	TV	Radios	TV	Radios	TV
									(millions)	
1945	...	...	...	—	...	—	...	—	...	...
1946	...	...	...	—	...	—	...	—	...	...
1947	...	...	15	—	...	—	...	—	...	...
1948	4	...	...	—	...	—	...	—	0.70	...
1949	3	...	17	—	...	—	...	—	0.75	...
1950	4	...	...	—	...	—	3	—	...	...
1951	...	...	25	—	...	—	3	—	1.2	...
1952	...	...	...	—	...	—	4	—	...	...
1953	...	...	...	—	44	—	...	—	...	90
1954	14	...	26	—	50	—	7	—	2.0	100
1955	...	...	...	—	65	—	...	—	2.5	175
1956	19	...	30	—	75	—	8	—	...	250
1957	...	...	32	—	95	—	9	—	...	300
1958	20	...	...	—	137	—	17	—	3.0	400
1959	21	...	...	—	147	—	18	—	3.1	600
1960	21	1.8	125	1.3	147	—	13	—	3.3	650
1961	21	2	125	4	200	—	15	—	3.5	900
1962	50	2.5	...	4.5	210	—	17	—	5.8	930
1963	55	3.5	...	6.5	...	11	16	...	6.5	1,040
1964	60	4	128	7.2	242	20	...	...	7.3	1,300
1965	63	...	135	8	350	25	...	1.5	8.6	...
1966	64	10	...	10	365	40	30	3.5	9.9	1,516
1967	75	10	136	11	400	47	32	4.9	11	1,790
1968	80	11	140	11	425	56	35	5.9	12	2,150
1969	81	11	145	17	450	56	37	7.4	13	2,553
1970	83	11	147	22	500	70	32	9.5	14	2,993
1971	85	11	147	25	...	73	33	10	15	3,385
1972	86	12	150	...	...	105	33	12	16	3,821
1973	90	13	155	...	633	100	32	14	17	4,339
1974	91	13	158	46	...	97	31	16	18	4,885
1975	93	13	160	47	550	110	32	20	17	4,885
1976	...	14	...	48	...	111	...	...	...	...
1977	...	14	170	48	...	120	...	...	...	5,480
1978	100	14	175	48	718	120	42	30	18	5,600
1979	101	15	176	49	718	120	42	34	20	5,700
1980	105	16	176	49	800	167	49	38	19	7,500
1981	105	17	180	49	850	180	50	38	21	7,900
1982	110	18	190	50	870	190	53	42	21[5]	8,000
1983	120	19	200	52	890	200	55	42	13	8,100
1984	...	...	...	...	...	...	...	...	...	...
1985	140	20	...	...	...	...	...	...	15	8,500
1986	200	25	...	...	950	250	58	45	16	9,490
1987	...	...	...	...	...	...	...	...	...	...
1988	250	27	1,847	330	980	270	59	46	21	10,500
1989	270	29	1,910	350	995	300	71	47	21	11,000
1990	290	30	1,980	370	1,010	310	72	48	22	12,350
1991	310	31	2,045	385	1,025	320	73	49	22	12,750
1992	320	32	2,115	400	1,040	330	74	50	23	13,100
1993	330	33	2,175	415	1,045	345	75	51	23	13,500

F10 NORTH AMERICA: Radio and Television Sets in Use (in thousands, except as otherwise indicated)

1945–1993

	Nicaragua		Panama		Puerto Rico		Trinidad & Tobago[1]		USA[2]	
	Radios	TV	Radios	TV	Radios	TV	Radios	TV	Radios	TV
									(millions)	
1945	...	—	...	...	...	...	7.8	—	33	...
1946	...	—	...	...	...	...	8.2	—	34	8
1947	...	—	...	...	...	...	9.0	—	36	14
1948	...	—	...	...	...	...	11	—	38	172
1949	...	—	...	...	...	...	14	—	39	940
									(millions)	
1950	20	—	55	...	...	...	16	—	41	3.9
1951	16	—	81	...	150	...	18	—	42	10
1952	20	—	...	...	...	...	21	—	43	15
1953	...	—	95	...	...	...	24	—	45	20
1954	30	—	...	...	...	...	28	—	45	26
1955	...	—	...	...	...	65	33	—	46	31
1956	...	—	...	2	200	126	35	—	47	35
1957	35	0.5	120	3.5	270	160	38	—	48	39
1958	35	2	130	8	...	...	41	—	49[2]	42[2]
1959	75	6	163	8	...	...	47	—	49	44
1960	...	5	...	11	...	...	42	—	50	46
1961	100	5	186	30	...	...	37	—	51	47
1962	100	6.5	225	...	...	...	32	3.5	51	49
1963	...	10	...	48	...	...	28[1]	7.7[1]	52	50
1964	100	...	496	65	...	...	165	44	54	52
1965	...	16	500	70	...	...	200	...	55	53
1966	105	19	...	77	...	...	...	30	57	54
1967	105	25	...	77	...	...	169	36	58	55
1968	105	...	...	...	...	...	281	40	59	57
1969	107	45	226	125	...	...	293	43	61	58
1970	109	55	230	...	1,625	410	...	60	62[2]	60[2]
									64	63
1971	110	56	230	158	...	...	296	70	65	65
1972	115	60	250	200	...	...	...	82	67	67
1973	125	63	255	...	1,753	605	...	93	69	69
1974	126	75	260	183	1,755	625	250	100	71	70
1975	...	83	265	185	1,760	630	250	105	73	70
1976	...	...	...	186	...	...	...	110	74	71
1977	...	100	274	206	...	...	255	125	75	73
1978	175	120	280	206	1,923	670	296	140	77	74
1979	175	150	285	220	2,000	700	296	150	79	76
1980	...	175	300	220	2,000	800	300	210	81	80
1981	...	185	305	233	2,150	860	400	265	83	82
1982	...	195	325	245	2,300	940	350	300	85	83
1983	...	205	335	255	2,450	980	360	310	87	84
1984	...	...	...	...	...	...	...	...	87	85
1985	...	190	400	350	...	...	...	...	88	86
1986	...	200	410	360	2,350	865	550	305	90	87
1987	...	...	...	...	...	...	...	...	91	88
1988	...	220	515	381	2,450	900	570	370	91	89
1989	925	230	527	390	2,480	915	580	380	93	90
1990	955	240	540	400	2,505	930	600	387	94	92
1991	997	249	552	410	2,540	942	615	394	96	93
1992	1,037	260	564	420	2,565	952	625	400	97	92
1993	1,075	275	575	430	2,576	965	625	405	97	93

F10 SOUTH AMERICA: RADIO AND TELEVISION SETS IN USE (in thousands, except as otherwise indicated)

1945-1993

	Argentina		Bolivia		Brazil[4]		Chile		Colombia		Ecuador	
	Radios	TV	Radios	TV	Radios	TV	Radios	TV	Radios	TV	Radios	TV
	(millions)				(millions)							
1945	...	...	...	—	...	...	...	—	...	—	...	—
1946	...	...	...	—	...	...	...	—	...	—	...	—
1947	...	...	...	—	...	...	...	—	...	—	...	—
1948	...	...	...	—	0.8	...	...	—	...	—	30	—
1949	1.5	...	...	...	...	...	550	—	...	—	...	—
1950	2.2	...	150	—	0.8[6] / 2.5	...	...	—	500	—	50	—
1951	...	...	...	—	...	...	...	—	...	—	...	—
1952	...	...	...	—	...	...	...	—	...	—	...	—
1953	2.6	20	...	—	...	70	...	—	...	—	...	—
1954	...	...	...	—	3.5	130	650	—	...	15	...	—
1955	...	...	...	—	...	150	...	—	...	20	...	—
1956	...	75	200	—	...	200	...	—	800	50	100	—
1957	...	90	...	—	4.6	350	...	—	...	100	...	—
1958	3.2	220	...	—	...	700	700	—	...	140	120	—
1959	3.4	400	250	—	4.0	850	...	...	...	150	170	...
		(millions)										
1960	3.5	0.45	...	—	4.6	1,200	...	...	1,971	150	170	...
1961	4.0	0.7	255	—	4.7	1,621	1,016	3	2,159	200	175	5
1962	5.5	0.85	350	—	7.0	1,430	1,500	4	...	205	320	16
1963	5.8	1.2	360	—	7.2	1,800	...	35	...	210	500	17
1964	6.2	1.5	500	—	7.5	2,300	...	50	...	300	510	32
					(millions)							
1965	6.6	1.6	525	—	...	...	...	...	...	350	540	42
1966	7.0	1.8	...	—	...	2.5	...	55	2,200	400	650	55
1967	8.0	1.9	...	—	...	...	...	49	2,200	...	801	71
1968	9.0	2.5	...	—	5.6	...	...	...	2,210	500	1,200	...
1969	8.5	3.1	...	...	5.6	6.5	1,375	400	2,214	622	1,700	120
1970	9.0	3.5	402	...	5.7	6.1	1,400	500	2,217	810	1,700	150
1971	10	...	...	...	5.8	6.5	...	674	2,250	891	...	...
1972	...	3.7	...	11	6.0	6.6	1,500	865	2,255	971	...	178
1973	21	4.0	...	...	6.2	...	1,500	993	2,793	...	...	...
1974	...	4.5	425	...	6.3[4] / 15	8.7	...	1,215	2,805	...	...	250
1975	10[5]	4.5	426	45	17	11	1,700	700	2,808	1,600	...	252
1976	...	4.5	...	48	...	11	...	710	...	1,700	...	300
1977	...	4.6	...	49	...	11	2,000	...	2,859	1,850	...	340
1978	10	4.6	473	50	32	12	2,500	1,210	3,000	...	2,540	360
1979	...	4.7	500[5]	100	35	15	3,239	1,225	3,005	2,000	...	400
1980	12	5.1	2,800	300	35	15	3,250	1,225	3,300	2,250	2,350	500
1981	21	5.5	3,150	341	40	16	3,350	1,250	3,450	2,500	2,750	530
1982	...	5.9	3,380	350	45	16	3,450	1,300	3,550	2,600	2,850	550
1983	16	5.9	3,500	386	50	17	...	1,350	...	2,700	2,950	570
1984	...	...	...	...	...	...	...	...	...	...	...	...
1985	20	6.5	3,000	420	53	25	4,000	1,750	4,000	2,750	2,750	600
1986	20	6.6	3,850	500	51	26	4,100	2,000	4,500	3,000	2,850	700
1987	...	...	...	...	...	...	...	...	...	...	...	...
1988	21	6.9	3,970	535	54	28	4,308	2,330	5,200	3,350	2,987	825
1989	21	7.0	4,250	700	55	30	4,400	2,600	5,400	3,500	3,240	850
1990	22	7.1	4,380	730	57	31	4,500	2,700	5,600	3,600	3,330	880
1991	22	7.2	4,590	755	59	31	4,600	2,800	5,800	3,800	3,420	910
1992	23	7.3	4,610	775	60	32	4,680	2,850	5,900	3,900	3,510	940
1993	23	7.4	4,725	800	61	33	4,765	2,910	6,020	4,000	3,580	970

F10 SOUTH AMERICA: Radio and Television Sets in Use (in thousands, except as otherwise indicated)

1945–1993

	Guyana	Paraguay		Peru		Surinam		Uruguay		Venezuela	
	Radios	Radios	TV	Radios	TV	Radios	TV	Radios	TV	Radios	TV
1945	...	...	...	...	...	...	—	...	—	...	...
1946	...	...	...	...	...	...	—	...	—	...	...
1947	...	...	...	...	...	...	—	...	—	...	...
1948	...	...	...	...	...	...	—	300	—	150	...
1949	6	...	...	...	...	...	—	...	—	...	...
1950	...	...	...	500	...	5	—	...	—	...	...
1951	11	35	...	...	...	8	—	362	—	...	...
1952	13	...	...	...	...	...	—	...	—	218	...
1953	...	80	...	...	...	...	—	...	—	...	20
1954	21	...	...	...	...	...	—	385	—	...	...
								(millions)			
1955	27	...	...	...	...	...	—	...	...	...	65
1956	30	...	...	...	...	10	—	0.5	1	750	100
1957	33	90	...	600	...	11	—	0.7	...	750	105
1958	34	105	...	...	...	12	—	...	10	...	200
1959	35	105	...	820	28	...	—	0.8	15	...	200
				(millions)						(millions)	
1960	37	...	...	1.1	33	40	—	0.8	25	1.2	250
1961	42	150	...	...	82	40	—	0.9	60	1.3	263
1962	44	160	...	...	120	45	—	0.9	70	...	549
1963	66	...	...	2.0	150	...	—	...	158	...	573
1964	70	...	...	2.1	175	...	—	0.9	175	1.7	591
1965	80	...	...	...	210	...	7	...	200	1.7	650
1966	90	...	...	...	275	50	16	1.0	...	1.7	...
1967	...	...	...	...	275	65	...	1.0	...	1.7	...
1968	...	...	13	...	300	88	...	1.1	215	1.7	700
1969	...	165	17	1.8	390	90	25	1.1	250	1.7	700
1970	80	169	18	1.8	395	92	28	1.0	150	1.7	...
1971	90	175	...	1.8	400	95	31	1.1	200	1.8	857
1972	100	175	...	2.0	410	100	32	1.5	300	2	980
1973	150	175	53	2.0	411	108	31	1.5	305	1.6	1,095
1974	268	176	53	2.0	425	109	33	1.5	350	1.7	1,200
1975	266	180	54	2.1	610	110	34	1.5	351	2.0₅ 4.8	1,284
1976	...	...	55	...	718	...	...	...	355	...	1,431
1977	...	181	55	2.2	825	...	...	1.6	360	...	1,530
1978	301	185	56	2.4	...	120	...	1.6	361	...	...
1979	310	186	57	2.5	850	150	40	1.6	362	5.3	1,710
1980	303	224	68	2.7	850	189	40	1.6	363	5.6	1,710
1981	315	240	75	2.9	900	200	41	1.6	366	5.8	1,800
1982	325	250	80	3.0	910	215	42	1.7	370	6.0	1,850
1983	350	260	82	3.1	950	220	43	1.7	370	6.8	2,100
1984	...	...	...	...	...	...	...	...	...	...	...
1985	...	600	85	4.0	1,500	...	...	1.8	500	7.3	2,250
1986	355	624	88	5.0	1,701	246	48	1.8	520	7.5	2,500
1987	...	...	...	...	...	...	...	...	...	...	...
1988	365	668	...	5.1	1,800	255	51	1.8	535	8.0	2,760
1989	386	700	200	5.3	2,000	262	55	1.8	700	8.3	3,000
1990	387	730	300	5.4	2,080	265	55	1.9	710	8.6	3,100
1991	392	750	320	5.6	2,150	274	56	1.8	720	8.8	3,200
1992	398	775	370	5.7	2,200	280	58	1.9	725	9.0	3,300
1993	400	800	390	5.8	2,260	280	58	1.9	730	9.3	3,400

F10 Radio and Television Sets in Use

NOTES

1. SOURCES: The national publications listed on pp. xiii–xv and UN, *Statistical Yearbook*.
2. The nature of the statistics varies considerably between countries and at different times. Where it is based on licences issued, this has been indicated. Most of the figures, however, are estimates of either the number of households with sets or of the total number of sets in use.
3. So far as possible, and except as indicated in footnotes, the data relate to 31 December.
4. There are obvious breaks in the continuity of some series, which are not indicated in the sources, especially in recent years.

FOOTNOTES

[1] Licences issued to 1963.
[2] Statistics are of the number of households with sets at 30 June to 1970 and at 31 December subsequently. Alaska and Hawaii are included from 1959.
[3] Licences issued.
[4] Licences issued to 1950 (1st line). Households with sets subsequently, except for radios in 1974 (2nd line) and 1975.
[5] The reason for this break is not given in the source.

G FINANCE

Financial statistics exhibit some very great contrasts as regards availability. Some were collected and published from a very early date. Others may have been collected, but were regarded as state secrets. And yet others were not collected for a long time, either because they were regarded as private secrets, publication of which it was beyond the competence of the state to compel, or because there were no permanent financial institutions from which it was possible to require them.

The first three tables in this section, showing various monetary statistics, point some of these contrasts very well. The banknote issues of certain privileged banks are often available from their beginning, though in many Latin American countries this often did not come until relatively late in their existence. Similarly available are the figures of deposits in savings banks, at least when they came under the auspices of the state, though that was less often in Latin America than in most other parts of the world. But deposits in commercial banks were often not recorded officially until well into the twentieth century. Recently, however, such data, as well as statistics of currency, have tended to be both readily available and reasonably comparable between countries, largely thanks to the International Monetary Fund.

A new table, G3 showing measures of money supply, has been added in this edition. These are only available in a consistent form for the period since the late 1940s, and thanks to the work of the statisticians of the International Monetary Fund. Earlier national statistics have been constructed for a few countries, but too few to merit inclusion here.

Two tables are given of certain public finance statistics of central governments. Table 5 shows total expenditure so far as that can be easily ascertained, whilst table 6 shows, so far as possible, current revenue and, for the larger countries, its main tax constituents. There is, of course, a great deal of data available on the details of government expenditures, but these are so heterogeneous, are often not available in any meaningful form, and change in nature so often, that in many cases it would require considerable research effort to put the statistics of even a single country on a reasonably uniform basis. Regretfully, therefore, only the totals of expenditure are included. Tax yields, on the other hand, exhibit both less disguise and, until recently, less change in nature. These have therefore been included for some countries for the period when they are readily available. Similar data could be included for smaller countries, but in most of these, taxes on foreign trade formed much the largest part of revenue until after World War II, and it did not seem very useful to plot their exact course.

It must be stressed that the statistics of government finance tend to be subject to fairly frequent changes in accounting methods and organization, and perhaps also to occasional deliberate omissions for 'reasons of state', and it would be unwise to assume that they are always fully comprehensive, or that all their inconsistencies have been identified in footnotes. Comparisons over time, therefore, even within a single country, need to be made with caution, and this applies a *fortiori* to comparisons between countries. Perhaps an even more important reason for this than the various changes in procedures and classifications is the fact that the areas of responsibility of central and local governments differ quite a lot in different countries, especially where there are federal systems in operation, as there are in Australia and in the larger countries of the Americas.

G1   NORTH AMERICA: CURRENCY IN CIRCULATION (in millions of stated currency unit, except as otherwise indicated)

1800–1849   1850–1894

	USA			Canada[3]	USA	
	currency[1] dollars	notes[2] dollars		dollars	currency[1] dollars	notes[2] dollars
1800	26.5	10.5	1850	...	279	131
1801	...	...	1851	...	330	155
1802	...	...	1852	...	361	172
1803	...	...	1853	...	402	188
1804	...	...	1854	...	426	205
1805	...	...	1855	...	418	187
1806	...	...	1856	12.6	426	196
1807	...	...	1857	8.8	457	215
1808	...	...	1858	9.4	409	155
1809	...	...	1859	10.7	439[4]	193
1810	55	28	1860	12.5	435	207
1811	...	...	1861	13.7	484[4]	202
1812	...	...	1862	9.7	606	257
1813	...	...	1863	10.5	931[4]	551
1814	...	...	1864	8.6	1,008	626
1815	...	...	1865	12.1	1,084	668
1816	...	...	1866	9.9	940	634
1817	...	...	1867	8.1[3] 14	859	629
1818	...	...	1868	15	772	644
1819	...	...	1869	18	741	639
1820	67	45	1870	26	775	658
1821	...	...	1871	36[3] 29	794	674
1822	...	...	1872	31	829	703
1823	...	...	1873	32	838	723
1824	...	...	1874	31	864	731
1825	...	...	1875	26	834	709
1826	...	...	1876	25	807	672
1827	...	...	1877	25	814	672
1828	...	...	1878	24	820	658
1829	...	...	1879	26	819	639
1830	87	61	1880	31	973	679
1831	93	77	1881	38	1,114	733
1832	117	92	1882	42	1,174	737
1833	120	92	1883	39	1,230	804
1834	124	95	1884	37	1,244	817
1835	146	104	1885	38	1,293	868
1836	200	140	1886	36	1,253	796
1837	217	149	1887	40	1,318	837
1838	199	116	1888	41	1,372	875
1839	220	135	1889	40	1,380	898
1840	186	107	1890	41	1,429	945
1841	186	107	1891	42	1,497	973
1842	164	84	1892	43	1,601	1,073
1843	147	59	1893	41	1,597	1,066
1844	167	75	1894	38	1,661	1,054
1845	178	90				
1846	193	106				
1847	224	106				
1848	232	129				
1849	233	115				

G1 NORTH AMERICA: Currency in Circulation (in millions of stated currency unit, except as otherwise indicated)

1895–1934

	Canada[3]	Costa Rica[5]	El Salvador[9]	Guatemala[9]	Mexico[10]	Nicaragua[11]	USA currency[1]	USA notes[2]
	dollars	colones	colones	pesos	pesos	pesos	dollars	dollars
1895	39	...	...	...	...	...	1,602	1,010
1896	40	...	...	...	...	...	1,506	939
1897	45	...	...	...	...	...	1,641	1,012
1898	48	...	...	...	...	...	1,838	1,057
1899	55	...	...	...	...	...	1,904	1,094
1900	59	...	1.1	...	...	3.3	2,081	1,302
1901	63	...	1.4	...	170	5.4	2,203	1,399
1902	70	...	1.9	...	194	8.3	2,279	1,462
1903	73	...	2.2	...	210	8.1	2,400	1,585
1904	74	...	2.8	...	214	7.9	2,553	1,706
1905	81	...	2.7	...	226	7.8	2,623	1,762
1906	91	...	3.3	...	242	7.9	2,775	1,879
1907	90	...	2.8	...	261	8.9	2,814	2,008
1908	86	...	3.6	...	264	11	3,079	2,224
1909	95	...	4.0	...	274	12	3,149	2,303
1910	102	...	3.9	...	295[10]	31	3,149	2,303
1911	120	...	4.5	...	...	49	3,263	2,414
1912	131	...	4.3	...	...	...	3,335	2,458
						cordobas		
1913	129[3] / 132	...	4.5	105	...	1.6	3,419	2,529
1914	129	4.2	6.1	126	...	3.0	3,459	2,560
1915	147	5.5	7.9	155	...	2.0	3,320	2,450
1916	174	5.4	9.6	171	...	2.1	3,649	2,724
1917	219	...	11	...	...	2.1	4,066	3,066
1918	250	...	14	220	...	2.7	4,482	3,576
1919	259	...	15	245	...	3.7	4,877	4,012
1920	258	19	8.2	310	...	2.8	5,468	4,576
1921	214	18	7.0	333	...	1.9	4,911	4,085
1922	207	18	9.4	378	...	2.2	4,463	3,671
1923	210	17	10	401	...	2.6	4,823	4,021
1924	200	17[6]	15	426[6]	...	3.6	4,849	4,052
1925	199	18	16	424	353	3.8	4,815	3,996
				quetzales				
1926	213	22	16	9.4	406	4.0	4,885	4,068
1927	216	...	18	8.6	378	3.9	4,851	4,034
1928	218	22	17	9.2	478	4.0	4,797	3,984
1929	213	...	15	9.9	495	3.6	4,746	3,935
1930	188	20[7]	11	6.4	508[10]	3.0	4,522	3,727
1931	187	18[8][5]	10	6.1	188	2.3	4,822	4,034
1932	171	15	12	5.5	187	2.4	5,695	4,842
1933	177	16	14	5.6	218	2.5	5,721	5,002
1934	184	16	15	6.3	266	3.2	5,373	4,944

G1 NORTH AMERICA: Currency in Circulation (in millions of stated currency unit, except as otherwise indicated)

1935–1974

	Canada[3] dollars	Costa Rica colones	Dominican Republic[12] pesos	El Salvador colones	Guatemala quetzales	Haiti gourdes	Honduras lempiras
1935	198	19	...	13	6.2	...	...
1936	220	21	...	$\underline{16}_9$ 18	$\underline{6.8}_9$ 8.2	...	5.4
1937	237	22	2.69	18	8.8	...	5.8
1938	238	23	2.24	17	9.0	...	6.1
1939	281	24	2.46	17	9.3	...	5.9
1940	379	26	2.73	16	9.2	...	6.2
1941	492	35	4.81	21	12	...	7.0
1942	681	53	6.51	28	15	...	8.2
1943	849	69	7.99	39	19	...	11
1944	990	71	9.45	47	23	...	13
1945	1,055	70	12.8	48	27	...	16
1946	1,096	67	15.7	52	31	...	16
1947	1,112	82	$\underline{17.7}_{12}$	55	32	...	16
1948	1,185	105	13.9	60	36	...	17
1949	1,184	100	16.1	67	38	...	19
1950	1,214	95	19.4	76	39	38	20
1951	1,275	108	24.6	84	40	44	25
1952	1,377	125	29.7	96	45	55	29
1953	1,430	138	30.9	97	53	52	33
1954	1,458	155	34.5	105	54	68	39
1955	1,550	153	41.4	98	52	63	34
1956	1,605	151	42.9	110	59	75	38
1957	1,667	169	46.0	108	65	81	38
1958	1,781	181	50.2	100	62	70	37
1959	1,832	186	50.5	100	63	73	37
1960	1,876	195	48.4	98	62	73	36
1961	1,959	185	51.6	99	62	78	35
1962	1,994	207	62.4	96	63	83	39
1963	2,084	224	74	109	67	87	42
1964	2,254	229	66.7	117	72	86	46
1965	2,410	237	75.3	112	77	84	51
1966	2,580	253	64.7	115	81	79	54
1967	2,820	282	59.0	122	83	88	56
1968	3,050	306	64.8	116	83	94	61
1969	3,330	350	72.5	133	91	105	73
1970	3,560	380	81.2	136	97	115	77
1971	3,990	434	83.5	145	99	126	80
1972	4,560	521	98.9	175	114	148	90
1973	5,200	643	116	201	137	173	112
1974	5,860	734	141	241	158	183	109

G1   NORTH AMERICA: Currency in Circulation (in millions of stated currency unit, except as otherwise indicated)

1935–1974

	Jamaica	Mexico[10]	Nicaragua[11]	Trinidad & Tobago[13]	USA	
					currency[1]	notes[2]
	pounds	pesos	cordobas	dollars	thousand million dollars	
1935	...	301	3.5	...	5.6	5.1
1936	...	359	5.2	...	6.2	5.8
1937	0.4	442	6.5	0.9	6.4	5.9
1938	0.5	472[10]	10	1.3	6.5	5.9
1939	...	598	12[11]	1.3	7	6.5
1940	0.7	661	13	2.1	7.8	7.2
1941	1.1	797	16	7.1[13] 11	9.6	8.9
1942	1.6	1,021	22	20	12	12
1943	2.1	1,478	33	25	17	16
1944	2.5	1,768	41	24	23	21
1945	3	1,658	45	24	27	26
1946	3.1	1,729	43	22	28	27
1947	2.8	1,754	48	20	28	27
1948	2.8	2,118	48	19	28	26
1949	3	2,378	57	20	27	26
1950	3.2	2,915	60.	22	27	26
1951	4	3,458	80	27[13] 11	28	26
1952	4.3	3,649	91	17	29	27
1953	3.3	3,864	111	19	30	28
1954	3.9	4,635	127	22	30	28
1955	4.6	5,084	124	22	30	28
1956	4.9	5,734	131	23	31	29
1957	5.7	6,094	130	25	31	29
1958	6.1	6,615	124	27	31	29
1959	7.3	7,250	131	31	32	30
1960	7.5	7,872	135	33	32	30
1961	8.8	8,275	131	38	32	30
1962	9	9,144	167	33	34	31
1963	10	10,264	177	34	35	33
1964	11	11,923	185	37	38	35
1965	12	12,507	198	36	40	36
1966	13	13,630	227	41	43	38
1967	14	14,749	222	42	45	40
1968	16	16,674	209	49	48	42
	dollars					
1969	37	18,245	219	51	51	45
1970	47	20,144	251	57	54	48[2]
1971	58	21,824	252	58	58[1]	54
1972	72	26,777	329	81	67	59
1973	82	34,176	411	80	73	65
1974	102	42,685	452	99	80	71

G1 NORTH AMERICA: Currency in Circulation (in millions of stated currency unit, except as otherwise indicated)

	Canada	Costa Rica	Dominican Republic	El Salvador	Guatemala	Haiti	Honduras
	thousand million dollars	colones	pesos	colones	quetzales	gourdes	lempiras
1975	6.78	853	158	253	175	189	115
1976	7.32	1,117	172	380	237	243	173
1977	8.08	1,409	203	432	284	265	193
1978	8.95	1,704	224	500	325	311	215
1979	9.45	1,955	274	743	365	418	270
1980	10.40	2,255	275	719	381	487	275
1981	10.71	3,501	324	703	405	566	302
1982	11.62	5,436	358	732	405	599	314
1983	12.80	6,941	415	724	438	691	362
1984	13.50	8,588	593	836	461	763	383
1985	14.61	9,938	677	1,080	698	829	410
1986	15.59	13,241	937	1,157	805	979	426
1987	16.92	14,777	1,313	1,298	931	1,205	491
1988	18.24	24,734	1,876	1,326	1,069	1,459	570
1989	19.64	21,922	2,683	1,727	1,329	1,382	676
1990	20.05	27,506	3,733	1,856	1,897	1,545	882
1991	21.22	34,667	4,586	2,023	2,089	2,075	977
1992	23.17	47,864	5,913	2,433	2,713	2,669	1,141
1993	22.52	54,672	6,905	2,655	3,097	3,030	1,448

	Jamaica	Mexico[10]	Nicaragua	Trinidad & Tobago	USA	
					currency[1]	notes[2]
		thousand million				
	dollars	pesos	cordobas	dollars	thousand million dollars	
1975	127	52.3	445	138	87	78
1976	138	79.9	636	177	94	84
1977	182	88.6	692	231	104	94
1978	173	115	883	295	115	104
1979	220	150	1,572	412	126	114
1980	260	195	1,964	467	137	125
1981	282	283	2,375	532	146	132
1982	316	505	3,085	726	156	143
1983	375	681	5,468	758	172	158
1984	436	1,122	11,340	710	184₁ / 156	169
			thousand million			
1985	540	1,738	28.6	685	168	...
1986	729	3,067	99.1	723	180	...
1987	844	7,339	730	703	196	...
			thousand Gold Cordoba			
1988	1,288	13,201	13	672	212	...
1989	1,378	18,031	324	693	223	...
			million			
1990	1,640	24,689	29	735	247	...
1991	2,632	32,513	401	748	267	...
1992	3,741	38,116	468	698	293	...
1993	5,228	43,351	509	707	322	...

G1 SOUTH AMERICA: CURRENCY IN CIRCULATION (in millions of stated currency unit, except as otherwise indicated)

1820–1859 **1860–1899**

	Brazil[14] milreis		Argentina[15] pesos	Bolivia[17] bolivianos	Brazil[14] milreis	Chile[16] pesos
1820	...	1860	...	...	88	...
1821	...	1861	...	...	82	...
1822	9.2	1862	...	...	79	...
1823	10	1863	...	...	82	...
1824	11	1864	...	...	99	...
1825	12	1865	...	...	101	...
1826	13	1866	...	...	113	...
1827	22	1867	...	...	118	...
1828	21[14]	1868	...	...	125	...
1829	...	1869	...	0.1	183	...
1830	21	1870	...	0.1	192	...
1831	...	1871	...	0.1	192	...
1832	...	1872	...	0.4	189	...
1833	...	1873	...	0.9	185	...
1834	...	1874	...	1.5	184	...
1835	31	1875	...	1.2	182	...
1836	34	1876	...	1.4	179	...
1837	35	1877	...	0.7	179	...
1838	39	1878	...	0.7	209	...
1839	...	1879	...	1.0	217	26
1840	...	1880	...	1.3	216	34
1841	40	1881	...	1.4	212	39
1842	44	1882	...	1.8	212	29
1843	47	1883	42	1.9	211	29
1844	48	1884	48	2.7	210	29
1845	50	1885	75	2.7	208	30
1846	51	1886	89	3.4	213	34
1847	49	1887	94	4.2	202	32
1848	48	1888	130	4.5	205	36
1849	48	1889	164	5.3	197	38
1850	47	1890	248	5.3	199	39
1851	47	1891	259	6.1	514	62
1852	47	1892	282	5.5	561	45
1853	47	1893	307	5.7	632	56
1854	47[14] 63	1894	299	7.0	712	60
		1895	297	6.1	678	43
1855	68	1896	295	5.2	713	32
1856	86	1897	293	5.7	781	28
1857	96	1898	295	6.5	778	47
1858	93	1899	295	6.6	734	51
1859	96					

G1   SOUTH AMERICA: Currency in Circulation (in millions of stated currency unit, except as otherwise indicated)

	Argentina[15]	Bolivia[17]	Brazil[14] milreis or	Chile[16]	Colombia[9]	Ecuador[18]	Paraguay[19]	Peru thousand	Uruguay[21]	Venezuela
	pesos	bolivianos	cruzeiros	pesos	pesos	sucres	pesos	libras	pesos	bolivares
1900	292	7.0	670	51	...	...	...	...	5	...
1901	292	7.6	680	51	...	...	...	...	5.5	...
1902	293	7.9	676	50	...	...	...	...	6.5	...
1903	380	8.8	675	50	...	...	...	...	7	...
1904	408	8.9	674	55	...	...	...	...	7	...
1905	498	10	669	81	...	...	...	...	9.4	...
1906	527	12	702	120	...	...	...	...	11	...
1907	532	16	744	150	...	...	...	...	13	...
1908	581	17	724	150	...	...	...	...	15	3.7
1909	685	17	854	150	...	...	...	...	17	3.7
1910	716	20	925	150	...	...	...	...	18	7.4
1911	723	24	982	151	...	...	...	...	24	8.9
1912	800	26	1,004	171	...	...	...	...	28	...
1913	823	26	897	186	...	10	65	...	21	11
1914	803	23	980	225	...	11	90	675	26	11
1915	988	24	1,077	178	...	11	125	1,140	32	12
1916	1,013	26	1,217	178	...	12	125	1,115	37	14
1917	1,013	30	1,484	186	...	13	125	1,851	43	17
1918	1,154	35	1,700	228	...	12	125	3,316	56	21
1919	1,177	36	1,748	251	...	13	125	4,191	74	25
1920	1,363	42	1,848	303	...	17	150	5,383	65	27
1921	1,363	34	2,098	325	...	16	182	4,666	66	35
1922	1,363	31	2,366	302	...	16	177	4,159	64	35
1923	1,363	32	2,649	293	39	16	177	4,638	69	35
1924	1,320	35	2,964	336	50	18	216	5,088	69	42
1925	1,320	39	2,707	394	67	37	226[20]	5,693	64	49
1926	1,320	38	2,589	372	66	36	193[20]	6,052	68	71
1927	1,378	40	3,005	319	70	39[18] 41	198	6,230	72	76
1928	1,406	44	3,379	352	79	42	213	6,304	72	87
1929	1,247	43	3,391	352	61	36	206	6,209	71	88
								soles		
1930	1,261	32	2,842	306	49	31	206	70	74	96
1931	1,245	27	2,942	319	42	25	202	70	81	90
1932	1,339	38	3,238	488	44	30	197	65	85	89
1933	1,214	54	3,037	515	54	43	...	76	78	85
1934	1,171	84	3,157	516	64	57	...	83	80	91
1935	1,178	146	3,612	567	71	60	...	94	82	102
1936	1,302[15] 998	210	4,050	653[16] 565	85[9] 75	68[18] 62	1,152[6]	103	89[9] 75	117
1937	1,049	252[17] 248	4,550	630	74	74	...	108	75	111[17] 157
1938	1,038	284	4,825	719	81	73	1,240	115	83	174
1939	1,063[15]	364	4,971	862	82	78	1,230	138	81	182

G1 SOUTH AMERICA: Currency in Circulation (in millions of stated currency unit, except as otherwise indicated)

1940–1974

	Argentina[15]	Bolivia[17]	Brazil[14] thousand million cruzeiros	Chile[16]	Colombia	Ecuador	Guyana	Paraguay[19]	Peru	Uruguay[21]	Venezuela
	pesos	bolivianos	cruzeiros	pesos	pesos	sucres	dollars	pesos	soles	pesos	bolivares
1940	1,072	471	5.2	1,034	80	80	...	1,219	146	92	181
1941	1,242	634	6.6	1,310	95	120	...	1,488	208	98	194
1942	1,439	807	8.2	1,700	119	169	...	2,161	275	98	228
								guaranies			
1943	1,704	1,055	11	2,100	143	232	...	16	327	114	264
1944	2,136	1,239	14	2,390	196	295	...	21	393	128	309
1945	2,581	1,520	18[14] 14	2,682	219	321	...	24	478	147	406
1946	3,579	1,588	17	3,170	270	350	...	29	568	176	524
1947	4,772	1,727	17	3,677	306	329	...	39	653	202	620
1948	6,737	2,068	18	4,316	376	355	...	53	712	231	781
1949	9,070	2,399	19	5,208	492	373	...	84	809	251	811
1950	11,910	3,267	25	6,318	465	476	...	129	956	314	786
1951	15,360	3,866	28	7,970	519	459	...	215	1,082	315	818
1952	18,260	6,082	32	11,500	610	535	...	358[19] 344	1,216	344	896
1953	22,070	11,450	39	16,660	683	566	...	459	1,406	378	921
1954	26,740	19,870	49	22,750	764	662	...	618	1,562	418	981
	thousand million pesos	thousand million bolivianos		escudos					thousand million soles		
1955	32	39	57	40	784	627	13	817	1.66	437	1,033
1956	36	145	67	57	942	705	13	1,100	1.99	500	1,112
1957	42	213	81	70	1,178	722	16	1,225	2.10	571	1,286
1958	60	241	100	93	1,376	709	17	1,414	2.40	724	1,342
1959	84	321	127	124	1,503	758	19	1,583	2.93	903	1,374
1960	105	354	169	159	1,623	851	22	1,614	3.18	1,235	1,493
1961	119	414	256	175	1,867	879	23	2,010	3.58	1,573	1,350
1962	135	460	397	230	2,078	949	24	1,964	4.11	1,792	1,322
		million pesos									
1963	167	540	684	297	2,495	1,037	26	2,075	4.88	2,226	1,340
1964	228	658	1,156	485	3,071	1,137	26	2,624	61	3,084	1,399
1965	297	740	1,730	725	3,538	1,236	28	2,926	7.12	6,082[21] 6,674	1,545
1966	397	883	2,343	1,020	4,037	1,347	28	2,903[19]	8.13	10,332	1,654
			million new cruzeiros								
1967	509	905	2,944	1,308	4,689	1,404	30	3,048	9.18	19,611	1,788
1968	591	949	4,080	1,697	5,470	1,600	34	3,269	10.33	31,390	1,942
1969	655	1,041	5,390	2,360	6,506	1,747	36	3,454	12.17	50,573	2,031
	thousand million new pesos			thousand million escudos						thousand million pesos	
1970	7.6	1,153	6,719	4.4	7,809	2,329	37	4,021	16.56	57	2,164
1971	9.9	1,281	8,550	9	8,534	2,414	41	4,409	19.23	84	2,338
1972	13.2	1,598	11,550	28	10,729	2,890	48	5,137	22.25	121	2,584
1973	26.4	2,073	16,430	96	12,424	3,618	56	6,490	27.64	202	2,865
1974	43.2	2,746	20,810	349	15,873	4,776	64	7,553	33.96	316	3,807

G1 SOUTH AMERICA: Currency in Circulation (in millions of stated currency unit, except as otherwise indicated)

	Argentina[15] thousand million pesos	Bolivia[17] pesos	Brazil[14] thousand million cruzeiros	Chile[16] thousand million escudos	Colombia thousand million pesos	Ecuador sucres
1975	124	3,054	31.0	1,358	20.8	5,386
				million pesos		
1976	411	3,968	46.2	4,480	28.8	7,570
1977	1,073	4,864	65.2	9,340	40.5	9,126
1978	3,332	5,810	94.1	16,386	53.7	10,274
1979	7,870	7,211	167	24,894	67.3	12,338
1980	16,418	9,461	291	35,625	84.1	15,285
1981	30,207	10,852	523	44,736	102	17,414
1982	[56,190][20]	38,898	986	42,958	130	20,519
	million australes	thousand million		thousand million		thousand million
	8.7					
1983	46.3	125	1,842	51.9	168	25.4
1984	313	2,888	6,130	64.2	212	35.3
		million million	million million			
1985	2,022	174	23.5	79.5	187	42.7
1986	3,990	294	84.0	108	...	54.6
1987	9,261	397	248	136	418	74.8
			reais			
1988	43,186	529	760	182	530	124
	million pesos					
1989	182	502	14,677	222	...	176
			thousand			
1990	2,259	642	356	286	837	273
1991	5,222	754	1,314	368	1,055	384
1992	7,686	886	14,564	481	1,439	597
			million			
1993	10,067	1,034	340	582	1,804	

	Guyana dollars	Paraguay thousand million guaranies	Peru intis[22]	Uruguay thousand million pesos	Venezuela bolivares
1975	92	8.90	43	470	4,723
1976	105	10.29	50	782	5,820
1977	143	13.34	62	1,115	7,383
1978	156	18.69	92	1,814	9,012
1979	148	24.31	164	3,187	10,012
1980	167	31.18	276	5,103	12,338
1981	186	31.15	445	6,145	13,525
1982	231	33.17	631	7,880	13,094
				thousand million new pesos	
1983	269	38.47	1,140	8.41	14,728
1984	336	48.6	2,540	12.11	15,132
1985	422	62.6	8,282	23.31	16,159
1986	509	84.5	16,648	43.06	18,697
1987	726	120	42,553	76.3	24,832
1988	1,058	149	261,000	125.5	31,204
1989	1,506	216	5,372,000	219.0	40,290
			million million		
1990	2,211	300	273	420.0	56,420
1991	3,711	379	643	851.0	76,460
1992	5,095	531	1,101	1,426	108,630
1993	6,480	636	1,591	2,313	136,550

G1 Currency in Circulation

NOTES

1. SOURCES: The main sources are the national publications listed on pp. xiii–xv, with gaps filled from League of Nations, *Statistical Yearbook, Memorandum on Currency and Central Banks, Money and Banking, and Monthly Bulletin of Statistics*; and International Monetary Fund, *International Financial Statistics*.
2. Unless otherwise indicated, the statistics are of circulation at the end of each year.
3. So far as possible, statistics are of currency in the hands of the public.

FOOTNOTES

[1] Currency in circulation outside the Treasury, the Federal Reserve Banks, and, from 1984 (2nd line), the vaults of depository institutions. Data are at 30 June to 1971 and at 31 December thereafter.

[2] Banknotes, Treasury notes, gold and silver certificates in circulation at 30 June to 1970 and at 31 December thereafter.

[3] Note Issues of Ontario and Quebec banks to 1867 (1st line); Dominion notes and chartered bank notes from 1867 (2nd line) to 1913 (1st line), but excluding Dominion notes held by banks from 1871 (2nd line). From 1913 (2nd line) statistics are of currency outside banks. Figures from 1965 to 1974 are rounded to the nearest 10 million dollars.

[4] Including the total stock of silver coin in 1860–63 and of gold coin and bullion also in 1862–63.

[5] Total currency in circulation to 1931; currency in the hands of the public subsequently.

[6] In September.

[7] At 31 August.

[8] At 31 July.

[9] Note circulation to 1936 (1st line); currency in the hands of the public subsequently.

[10] Total currency in circulation. Statistics to 1910 and for 1931–38 are averages of monthly figures, those to 1910 being for the 12 months ending 30 June.

[11] Total currency in circulation to 1939; currency in the hands of the public subsequently.

[12] Currency outside banks, including US currency in circulation to 1947.

[13] Government currency in circulation to 1941 (1st line). Total currency from 1941 (2nd line) to 1951 (1st line), and currency in the hands of the public subsequently.

[14] Issues of paper money by banks to 1828, by the Treasury from 1830 to 1854 (1st line), and by the Treasury and banks subsequently, with issues of the Conversion Office, the Rediscount Department, and the Stabilization Office included as appropriate. Figures from 1971 to 1974 are rounded to the nearest 10 million cruzeiros.

[15] Total fiduciary circulation to 1936 (1st line); currency outside banks subsequently. There was an improvement in the coverage of bank holdings of currency in 1940.

[16] Total effective note circulation to 1936 (1st line); currency outside banks subsequently. The escudo (equal to one thousand pesos of the day) was introduced in 1960, but the unit is employed here from 1955 to 1975, whereafter it was replaced by a new peso, equal to 3,000 escudos. Figures from 1941 to 1944 and from 1951 to 1954 are rounded to the nearest 10 million pesos.

[17] Central Bank note circulation to 1937 (1st line); currency outside banks subsequently.

[18] Central Bank note circulation to 1927 (1st line). Total circulation from 1927 (2nd line) to 1936 (1st line) and currency in the hands of the public subsequently.

[19] Total currency in circulation to 1952 (1st line); currency in the hands of the public subsequently. Coverage was improved from 1967.

[20] At 30 November.

[21] Statistics to 1965 (1st line) are averages of weekly figures in December.

[22] The inti (equal to one thousand soles) was introduced in 1977, but the unit is employed here from 1975.

G2　NORTH AMERICA: DEPOSITS IN COMMERCIAL BANKS (in millions of stated currency unit, except as otherwise indicated)

1834–1884

	Canada[1] dollars	USA[2] dollars
1834	...	102
1835	...	122
1836	...	166
1837	...	190
1838	...	146
1839	...	143
1840	...	120
1841	...	108
1842	...	88
1843	...	78
1844	...	117
1845	...	114
1846	...	125
1847	...	120
1848	...	143
1849	...	121
1850	...	146
1851	...	175
1852	...	182
1853	...	195
1854	...	239
1855	...	236
1856	6.3	265
1857	5.8	288
1858	6.7	237
1859	8.0	328
1860	8.3	310
1861	9.7	319
1862	10	357
1863	12	504
1864	9.5	380
1865	15	689
1866	14	759
1867	14[1] / 15	744
1868	18	798
1869	19	772
1870	19[1]	775
1871	29	888
1872	30	927
1873	31	1,625
1874	37	1,740
1875	34	2,009
1876	35	1,993
1877	35	2,006
1878	35	1,921
1879	38	2,149
1880	42	2,222
1881	46	2,649
1882	47	2,777
1883	45	2,884
1884	45	2,849

1885–1929

	Canada[1] dollars	El Salvador[3] colones	Mexico[4] pesos	USA[2] dollars
1885	52	...	...	3,078
1886	49	...	...	3,186
1887	49	...	...	3,719
1888	56	...	...	3,891
1889	55	...	...	4,311
1890	54	...	...	4,576
1891	63	...	...	4,683
1892	69	...	...	5,298
1893	63	...	...	5,065
1894	69	...	...	5,268
1895	68	...	...	5,539
1896	71	...	...	5,486[2] / 2,844
1897	82	...	...	2,999
1898	91	...	...	3,431
1899	100	...	...	4,295
1900	109	...	...	4,345
1901	102	...	11	5,279
1902	116	...	14	5,541
1903	121	...	13	5,771
1904	134	...	12	6,057
1905	155	...	25	6,898
1906	192	...	41	7,403
1907	157	...	39	7,708
1908	210	...	47	7,381
1909	261	...	78	8,115
1910	281	...	86	8,566
1911	335	...	...	8,625
1912	380	...	...	9,217
1913	381	...	...	9,249
1914	350	...	...	10,306
1915	424	...	...	10,703
1916	458	3.2	...	12,917
1917	569	3.4	...	15,085
1918	711	3.3	...	15,747
1919	703	4.4	...	19,282
1920	657	...	...	21,571
1921	541	...	...	18,926
1922	538	...	...	20,106
1923	560	...	...	20,829
1924	595	5.4	...	22,069
1925	597	6.3	109	24,325
1926	609	8.0	131	24,993
1927	684	7.8	111	25,257
1928	715	8.7	150	24,857
1929	729	7.5	161	25,160

G2 NORTH AMERICA: Deposits in Commercial Banks (in millions of stated currency unit, except a otherwise indicated)

1930–1974

	Canada[1] dollars	Cost Rica colones	Cuba pesos	Dominican Republic pesos	El Salvador[3] colones	Guatemala quetzales	Haiti gourdes
1930	642	...	...	...	5.7	...	...
1931	567	...	...	...	5.4	...	...
1932	466	...	69	...	7.8	...	...
1933	502	18	56	...	7.1	...	...
1934	575	21	55	...	6.9	...	...
1935	641	24	60	...	8	...	...
1936	682	24	71	3.3	7.5[3] 6.7	5.4	...
1937	699	29	81	3.4	6.3	5.9	...
1938	734	29	80	3.9	6	5.3	...
1939	853	30	83	4.9	5.9	5.1	...
1940	1,031	35	87	5.8	5.6	5.6	...
1941	1,268	36	102	7	7.3	5.6	...
1942	1,499	69	142	10	13	9.5	...
1943	1,697	86	208	15	21	14	...
1944	1,862	89	297	17	22	15	...
1945	2,084	88[5] 77	343[5] 359	21	34[3] 29	19	...
1946	2,293	74	424	24	24	20	...
1947	2,295	78	490	22	24	19	...
1948	2,550	69	456	19	24	19	...
1949	2,483	94	453	25	30	17	...
	thousand million						
1950	2.98	106	507	22	40	20	7.6
1951	2.98	116	505	29	46	20	12
1952	3.16	139	518	32	56	18	12
1953	3.06	152	...	29	66	22	11
1954	3.36	170	...	34	79	22	13
1955	3.56	187	...	35	89	33	12
1956	3.46	191	...	34	102	43[5]	15
1957	3.62	201	...		107	50	18
1958	4.17	217[6]	...		102	44	17
1959	4.27	237	...	41	103	45	17
1960	4.50	235	...	54	92	42	15
1961	5.24	232	...	48	84	41	16
1962	5.51	269	...	51	87	45	14
1963	6.03	310	...	56	110	52	17
1964	6.64	339	...	50	115	55	21
1965	7.71	360	...	60	121	57	23
1966	8.26[1]	367	...	51	129	60	21
1967	13.93	547	...	60	129	63	29
1968	13.61	539	...	71	144	66	28
1969	12.52	606	...	75	152	69	25
1970	12.37	623	...	88	157	75	27
1971	14.20	875	...	101	167	78	34
1972	15.89	973	...	117	208	96	53
1973	16.97	1,225	...	140	263	120	76
1974	16.56	1,395	...	216	314	138	91

G2 NORTH AMERICA: Deposits in Commercial Banks (in millions of stated currency unit, except as otherwise indicated)

1930–1974

	Honduras[7] lempiras	Jamaica pounds	Mexico[4] pesos	Nicaragua cordobas	Panama balboas	Trinidad & Tobago dollars	USA[2] dollars
1930	...	...	176[4]	...	...	...	25,648
1931	...	...	128	...	...	...	22,569
1932	...	...	108	...	...	...	17,111
1933	...	...	159	...	...	...	16,019
1934	...	...	188	...	...	...	17,796
1935	...	...	204	...	...	...	21,731
1936	...	...	215	...	...	...	26,096
1937	4.3	...	245	...	...	...	27,578
1938	4.6	...	200[11]	...	...	...	26,387
1939	5.7	...	285	...	4.4	...	29,691
1940	6.0	...	399	10	9.0	...	33,646
1941	6.0	...	472	11	13	...	39,915
1942	8.6	...	729	21	22	...	44,611
1943	13	...	1,195	32	31	...	59,661
1944	18	6.4	1,542	40	38	...	64,254
1945	21[7] 20	7.1	1,882	36	42	...	72,526
1946	23	6.8	1,732	29	37	32	84,824
1947	22	7.5	1,685	34	33	26	88,030
1948	23[7] 21	7.7	1,796	41	29[8] 23	31	88,754
1949	18	7.7	1,975	55	18	42	87,999
							thousand million dollars
1950	19	9.1	3,074	63	19	37	92[2]
1951	22	10	3,342	70	19	36	98
1952	23	11	3,430	90	20	42	102
1953	26	12	3,789	119	22	45	103
1954	28	12	4,087	138	23	52	107
1955	25	12	5,433	148	23	48	110
1956	27	14	5,958	136	23	50	111
1957	23	16	6,400	129	24	69	110
1958	24	16	6,774	128	24	62	115
1959	26	18	8,184	123	26	62	116[2]
			thousand million				
1960	25	19	8.95	129	26	70	116
1961	27	15	9.53	141	29	75	120
1962	30	21	11.06	186	34	71	122
1963	34	19	13.16	220	38	‚ 88	125
1964	41	21	15.51	275	34	84	131
1965	48	20	16.56	339	38	80	137
1966	46	23	18.64	338	43	85	139
1967	56	24	19.99	318	51	87	148
1968	65	32	23.65	276	63	90	160
		dollars					
1969	73	74	27.26	293	70	89	164
1970	81	80	30.38	327	85	95	171
1971	88	102	32.65	367	88	108	182
1972	101	101	37.90	417	119	130	200
1973	125	136	45.72	733	131	133	209
1974	132	156	56.3	861	173	171	214

G2 NORTH AMERICA: Deposits in Commercial Banks (in millions of stated currency unit, except as otherwise indicated)

	Canada[1] thousand million dollars	Costa Rica colones	Dominican Republic pesos	El Salvador colones	Guatemala quetzales	Haiti gourdes
1975	19.91	1,889	210	392	169	111
1976	19.75	2,273	216	512	237	136
1977	21.86	3,065	256	550	280	156
1978	23.06	3,857	233	579	292	183
1979	22.93	4,231	323	567	320	187
1980	25.88[5]	4,862	381	693	320	224
1981	27.86	7,185	382	693[6]	327	295
1982	30.62	12,888	420	810	340	318
1983	34.77	18,401	419	785	346	357
1984	44.08	21,399	604	937	382	2,584
1985	61.81	22,367	758	1,151	614	...
1986	72.79	29,016	1,131	1,528	749	544
1987	76.87	27,624	1,453	1,370	808	659
1988	81.43	40,186	2,438	1,567	916	716
1989	88.32	41,903	2,635	1,568	1,066	767
1990	92.17	38,781	3,551	2,190	1,342	920
1991	93.36	45,039	4,760	2,288	1,753	1,063
1992	108.95	61,103	5,037	3,220	1,475	1,200
1993	123.28	62,437	6,588	3,682	1,928	1,430

	Honduras lempiras	Jamaica dollars	Mexico thousand million pesos	Nicaragua cordobas	Panama balboas	Trinidad & Tobago dollars	USA[2] thousand million dollars
1975	144	195	68.6	809	149	254	222
1976	184	200	76.9[5]	976	164	395	234
1977	214	292	106	998	185	494	251
1978	257	397	143	915	214	641	270
1979	270	410	197	...	263	735	286
1980	323	457	260	2,134	293	870	301
1981	328	492	315[5]	2,656	319	1,287	321
1982	380	560	455	3,319	330	1,772	350
				new cordobas			
1983	433	691	676	5.42	327	1,576	383
1984	447	882	1,075	9.37	334	1,500	405
1985	427	980	1,610	25.75	359	1,483	462
1986	493	1,410	2,468	90.52	394	1,260	555
1987	583	1,407	4,928	689	396	1,357	560
1988	628	1,627	7,130	...	275	1,082	590
1989	774	1,369	10,279	...	269	1,327	483
1990	903	1,881	21,487	...	380	1,704	489
1991	1,138	4,242	72,772	...	499	2,041	480
1992	1,276	6,551	82,604	...	577	1,859	541
1993	1,313	9,181	98,725	...	645	2,274	572

G2 SOUTH AMERICA: DEPOSITS IN COMMERCIAL BANKS (in millions of stated currency unit, except as otherwise indicated)

	Argentina[9]	Bolivia[10]	Brazil[11] milreis or	Chile[12]	Columbia[13]	Ecuador[14]	Paraguay	Peru[15] thousand	Uruguay	Venezuela[16]
	pesos	bolivianos	cruzeiros	pesos	pesos	sucres	pesos	libras	pesos	bolivares
1897	...	...	...	...	...	...	...	1,371	...	...
1898	...	...	...	...	...	...	...	1,480	...	...
1899	...	...	...	...	...	...	...	1,558	...	...
1900	...	...	...	...	...	...	...	1,774	...	...
1901	...	...	...	...	...	...	...	1,929	...	...
1902	...	...	...	141	...	...	...	2,249	...	...
1903	504	...	...	136	...	...	...	2,638	...	...
1904	585	...	...	171	...	...	...	2,727	...	...
1905	720	...	...	314	...	...	...	3,274	...	...
1906	755	...	...	289	...	...	...	3,759	...	...
1907	779	...	...	415	...	...	...	4,035	...	...
1908	876	...	...	415	...	...	...	4,366	...	...
1909	1,157	...	...	395	...	...	...	4,267	...	...
1910	1,332	...	...	475	...	...	...	5,630	...	...
1911	1,375	...	...	524[12] 290	...	...	...	7,368	...	...
1912	1,481	...	...	225	...	...	...	7,664	...	...
1913	1,411	12	475	222	...	3.7	...	8,108	12	10
1914	1,189	12	389	217	...	3.1	...	5,374[15] 1,906	12	8.5
1915	1,419	17	440	223	...	5.0	...	2,083	13	7.7
1916	1,596	19	575	242	...	6.2	...	2,747	18	9.4
1917	1,891	26	710	266	...	7.4	...	3,698	21	14
1918	2,666	21	1,059	407	...	8.8	...	4,663	27	17
1919	2,834	26	1,196	439	...	10	...	6,727	38	48
1920	3,294	20	1,343	529	...	12	...	7,221	30	47
1921	3,177	26	2,100	559	...	11	...	6,609	32	42
1922	3,297	35	2,519	540	...	12	...	6,161	28	37
1923	3,317	28	2,653	496	...	12	...	6,574	33	42
1924	3,320	29	2,671	530	20	12	...	7,248	26	45
1925	3,335	31	2,420	636	27	13	...	7,086	25	58
1926	3,359[9] 1,124	26	2,603	724	35	13	...	6,828	29	78
1927	1,195	27	3,088	539	45	12[14]	...	7,145	31	78
1928	1,302	28	3,688	564	54	29	38	9,402	30	118
1929	1,178	26	3,487	512	51[5] 40	25	52[6]	8,803	37	123
								soles		
1930	1,189	21	2,856	434	30	23	161	49	41	163
1931	971	19	3,490	419	27	13	114	54	43	127
1932	1,083	49	4,732	706	34	26	104	43	54	116
1933	1,171	48	4,447	893	39	44	141	61	44	115
1934	1,111	136	5,056	1,124	49	51	226	89	43	115
1935	1,065	224	4,873	1,191	49	45	426	96	39	156
1936	1,289	236[10] 149	5,245[11] 4,780	1,226[5] 1,293	58[13] 49	60[14] 64	322[6] 580	114	36	136
1937	1,402	144	5,980	1,364	54	66	837	125	44	132[16] 106
1938	1,312	168	7,590	1,393	61	71	593	142	42	114
1939	1,482	220	7,080	1,571	64	73	530	153	44	129

G2 SOUTH AMERICA: Deposits in Commercial Banks (in millions of stated currency unit, except as otherwise indicated)

	Argentina[9] thousand million pesos	Bolivia[10] bolivianos	Brazil[11] thousand million cruzeiros	Chile[12] thousand million pesos	Colombia pesos	Ecuador[14] sucres
1940	1.52[9] 1.30	301	7.1	1.93	79	103
1941	1.77	345	9.1	2.34	81	119
1942	2.12	701	11	2.79	113	176
1943	2.58	675	16	3.59	169	260
1944	3.18	734	22	4.13	210	308
1945	3.83	794[10] 726	24[11] 20	4.90	254	310
1946	4.88	718	22	6.44	313	348
1947	5.48	699	24	7.96	334	272
1948	7.03	1,086	26	8.96	373	306[14] 272
1949	8.51	1,310	32	11	421	268
1950	10.14	1,685	45	12[12] 10	488	390
1951	11.38	2,041	52	13	593	340
1952	12.16	2,788	60	18	684	439
1953	15.67	4,603	71	21	830	461
		thousand million bolivianos				
1954	17.14	7	85	31	1,059	562
1955	19.79	16	102	52	1,113	515
1956	24.09[6]	49	127	72	1,410	593
1957	26	72	176	94	1,500	608
1958	39	56	216	128	1,849	600
1959	58	62	322	169	2,093	724
				million escudos		
1960	73	61	438	225	2,324	800
1961	84	77	611	257	3,043	829
1962	84	94	1,038	327	3,836	942
		million pesos				
1963	116	122	1,704	450	4,144	1,093
1964	168	141	3,070	644	5,098	1,212
1965	201	180	5,800	1,137	5,937	1,203
1966	275	229	6,192	1,567	6,994	1,433
			thousand million new cruzeiros			
1967	363	237	9.6	1,922	8,726	1,771
1968	513	280	12.8	2,774	9,964	2,148
1969	564	307	16.8	3,698	12,080	2,496
				thousand million escudos		
1970	706	365	21.4	5.65	14,005	2,955
1971	1,010	429	28.2	12.3	15,647	3,503
1972	1,567	576	40.4	25.9	20,055	4,131
1973	2,981	849	59.4	128	28,151	5,503
1974	4,575	1,461	79.3	487	31,734	8,192

G2 SOUTH AMERICA: Deposits in Commercial Banks (in millions of stated currency unit, except as otherwise indicated)

	Guyana dollars	Paraguay guaranies	Peru[15] soles	Uruguay pesos	Venezuela bolivares
1940	...	670	209	42	161
1941	...	1,070	251	50	151
1942	...	1,430	352	55	194
		guaranies			
1943	...	24	465	79	271
1944	...	23	556	[107][17]	295
1945	...	26	588	131	350
1946	...	29	780	150	446
1947	...	26	928	134	445
1948	...	44	1,067[15]	151	572
			813		
1949	...	68	790	149	695
1950	...	101	1,008	177	
1951	...	180	1,321	174	795
1952	...	238	1,508	190	981
1953	...	403	1,668	225	1,122
1954	...	453	1,780	220	1,166
			thousand million		
1955	13	608	1.87	229	1,356
1956	13	841	2.17	261	1,616
1957	13	772	2.19	285	2,313
1958	13	970	2.24	399	2,631
1959	15	1,025	33	596	2,392
1960	16	1,060	3.80	767	2,045
1961	14	1,381	4.56	858	2,251
1962	18	1,347	4.67	669	2,182
1963	18	1,610	5.17	984	2,248
1964	21	1,849	6.22	1,388	2,933
1965	17	1,988	8	2,762	2,874
1966	19	2,132[6]	10	3,040	2,903
1967	19	2,248	11	8,820	3,396
1968	21	2,415	12	13,402	3,672
1969	23	2,484	14	16,325	4,064
				thousand million	
1970	22	2,926	28	17	4,481
1971	26	3,206	29	29	5,405
1972	37	4,041	39	57	6,735
1973	42	5,604	50	106	8,290
1974	65	7,282	76	174	11,208

G2 SOUTH AMERICA: Deposits in Commercial Banks (in millions of stated currency unit, except as otherwise indicated)

	Argentina	Bolivia	Brazil	Chile	Colombia[13]	Ecuador
			thousand million cruzeiros			
	thousand million pesos	pesos	cruzeiros	thousand million pesos	thousand million pesos	thousand million pesos
1975	13.6	1,605	114	1.62	40.9	9.9
1976	51.6	2,425	153	5.2	54.8	13.6
1977	101	2,873	215	...	69.4[13]	16.9
1978	230	2,829	307	17.6	76.5	19.5
1979	596	2,916	522	30.2	93.6	23.2
1980	1,093	4,777	907	49.7	121	31
1981	1,589	6,301	1,739	37.4	147	36
1982	6,128	17,659	2,967	49.2	181	46
	million australes	thousand million				
1983	23.6	50.7	5,798	60.3	221	59
1984	121	425	16,831	66.1	267	82
	thousand pesos					
1985	898	24,799	71,432	68.7	341	98
		million million	million million			
1986	1,650	69	282	106	...	112
1987	4,882	106	573	93	577	144
1988	22,248	158	3,468	204	723	209
	million pesos		reais			
1989	1,279	206	22,619	220	...	293
			thousand			
1990	10,702	350	550	232	1,141	431
1991	22,552	693	2,581	415	1,503	666
1992	34,564	1,037	24,073	457	2,164	953
			million			
1993	42,600	1,466	497	...	2,884	...

	Guyana	Paraguay	Peru	Uruguay	Venezuela
				thousand million new pesos	thousand million bolivares
	dollars	guaranies	intis		
1975	110	8,550	85	0.5	15
1976	111	11,033	99	0.8	20
1977	136	14,690	118	1.1	25
1978	138	20,300	169	1.7	28
1979	133	23,292	256	3.4	30
1980	136	28,566	344	4.7	35
1981	144	29,276	481	4.4[6]	39
1982	184	25,704	693	5.4	36
1983	219	34,918	1,403	6.2	46
1984	251	44,758	3,066	9.9	48
		thousand million	thousand million		
1985	286	56	13	22.2	55
1986	337	67	25	40.8	73
1987	558	114	49	57.9	95
1988	934	165	285	93.8	83[5]
					83
1989	1,165	189	4,738	155	106
1990	1,918	215	275	348	109
1991	3,126	289	656	675	151
1992	3,897	307	1,298	1,148	241
1993	4,902	367	2,142	1,735	245

G2 Deposits in Commercial Banks

NOTES

1. SOURCES: The main sources were the national publications listed on pp. xiii-xv League of Nations, *Memorandum on Commercial Banks, Money and Banking, and Statistical Yearbooks*; and International Monetary Fund, *International Financial Statistics*.
2. Except as otherwise indicated the statistics are for the end of each year.
3. So far as possible, and except as otherwise indicated, statistics relate to demand deposits in the hands of the public; i.e. they exclude interbank deposits and deposits of central government departments.

FOOTNOTES

[1]   Non-interest-bearing deposits in banks in Ontario and Quebec to 1867 (1st line) and of chartered banks in Canada to 1870. Subsequently publicly held demand deposits. From 1967 data relate to the average of all Wednesdays during the year.
[2]   Total bank deposits to 1896 (1st line), public demand deposits in commercial banks subsequently, at 30 June to 1950, at 31 December from 1951 to 1959, and on the average for December subsequently. Data for non-national banks prior to 1896 are known to be incomplete, and some are reported for dates other than 30 June. More reliable estimates of the non-national bank component are available for the period 1865-96 in David I. Fand, *Banks in the Post-Civil War Period in the United States, 1875-1896* (unpublished University of Chicago Ph.D thesis), and in Federal Deposit Insurance Corporation, *Annual Report, 1934*. The latter are adjusted for non- reporting banks, but not for under-reporting, the former are adjusted for both. Data for 1875-81 are for August. These estimates, together with the component used here, are as follows:
Non-national bank deposits according to:

	Comptroller of Currency	Fand	FDIC		Comptroller of Currency	Fand
1865	75		635	1881	1,285	1,823
1866	64		443	1882	1,412	1,844
1867	58		597	1883	1,547	2,016
1868	53		665	1884	1,616	2,057
1869	56		751	1885	1,659	2,141
1870	70		868	1886	1,727	2,395
1871	97		1,045	1887	2,069	2,528
1872	121		1,255	1888	2,175	2,569
1873	789		1,276	1889	2,391	2,694
1874	912		1,307	1890	2,598	2,971
1875	1,111	1,450	1,399	1891	2,709	3,082
1876	1,151	1,453	1,408	1892	2,970	3,409
1877	1,188	1,383		1893	3,126	3,312
1878	1,107	1,275		1894	3,039	3,311
1879	1,059	1,272		1895	3,260	3,604
1880	1,137	1,495		1896	3,345	3,545

[3]   Including the National Bank to 1945 (1st line). The reason for the break in 1936 is not clear in the sources.
[4]   Data to 1910 and for 1931-38 are annual averages, those to 1910 being for the 12 months ended 30 June.
[5]   There was a change in the coverage of the series.
[6]   There was an improvement in the collection of data subsequently.
[7]   Including central bank deposits to 1945 (1st line), and government deposits to 1948 (1st line).
[8]   Including government banks to 1948 (1st line).
[9]   Total deposits to 1926 (1st line), current account deposits from then to 1940 (1st line) and private sector monetary deposits subsequently.
[10] All sight deposits (including those of the Central Bank) to 1936 (1st line), and all such deposits other than those of the national government from 1936 (2nd line) to 1945 (1st line).
[11] All demand deposits to 1936 (1st line), those of the public subsequently. Bank of Brazil deposits are included to 1945 (1st line).
[12] Total deposits to 1911 (1st line), demand deposits of the public subsequently, with a restriction to major banks from 1950 (2nd line).
[13] All demand deposits to 1936 (1st line), those of the public subsequently, but interbank deposits are not excluded until 1978.
[14] All demand deposits to 1936 (1st line), but of the six principal banks only to 1927. Subsequent statistics are of demand deposits of the public, including those at the central bank and at development banks to 1948 (1st line).
[15] Total deposits to 1914 (1st line), current account deposits subsequently, with some government deposits included up to 1948 (1st line).
[16] Total deposits to 1937 (1st line), demand deposits of the public subsequently.
[17] At 30 June.

G3 NORTH AMERICA: SAVINGS BANK DEPOSITS (in millions of stated currency unit, except as otherwise indicated)

1820–1864

	USA[1] dollars		Barbados[2] thousand pounds	Canada[3] dollars	Jamaica[4] thousand pounds	Newfoundland dollars	Trinidad thousand pounds	USA[1] dollars
1820	1	1865	...	...	...	...	...	243
1821	...	1866	...	...	...	...	...	283
1822	...	1867	...	...	...	...	...	337
1823	...	1868	...	5.1	...	...	...	393
1824	...	1869	...	6.4	...	...	...	458
1825	3	1870	...	8.8	76	...	...	550
1826	...	1871	...	10	171	...	...	651
1827	...	1872	...	11	223	...	...	735
1828	...	1873	...	13	159	...	...	802
1829	...	1874	...	14	183	...	...	865
1830	7	1875	...	14	229	...	...	924
1831	...	1876	...	14	245	...	...	941
1832	...	1877	...	14	256	...	...	866
1833	...	1878	...	14	274	...	...	880
1834	...	1879	...	15	295	...	...	803
1835	11	1880	...	15	340	...	...	819
1836	...	1881	36	24	335	1.3	41	892
1837	...	1882	40	30	315	1.4	...	967
1838	...	1883	49	35	326	1.5	...	1,025
1839	...	1884	57	38	351	1.7	87	1,073
1840	14	1885	62	42	360	1.8	88	1,095
1841	...	1886	65	46	363	1.8	97	1,142
1842	...	1887	78	51	365	2	110	1,235
1843	...	1888	97	52	395	2	122	1,364
1844	...	1889	126	54	410[4]	2.2	128	1,425
1845	25	1890	135	52	431	2.3	145	1,525
1846	27	1891	123	50	428	2.5	144	1,623
1847	32	1892	130	52	418	3	158	1,713
1848	33	1893	153	55	458	3.1	164	1,785
1849	36	1894	158	56	454	2.8	175	1,748
1850	43	1895	181	58	465	1.2	195	1,811
1851	51	1896	182	61	471	1.4	230	1,907
1852	60	1897	211	63	470	1.4	233	1,939
1853	72	1898	219	66	494	1.2	246	2,066
1854	78	1899	226	66	469	1.1	256	2,230
1855	84	1900	221[2]	71	451	1.2	278	2,450
1856	96	1901	197	75	425	1.3	291	2,597
1857	99	1902	202	79	436	1.4	314	2,750
1858	108	1903	217	82	426	1.6	309	2,935
1859	129	1904	224	85	395	1.8	308	3,060
1860	149	1905	245	87	389	2	301	3,261
1861	147	1906	263	89[3]	399	2.2	286	3,482
1862	169	1907	293	91	403	2.4	329	3,690
1863	206	1908	306	92	390	2.6	337	3,661
1864	236	1909	348	90	364	2.6	333	3,713

G3   NORTH AMERICA: Savings Bank Deposits (in millions of stated currency unit, except as otherwise indicated)

	Barbados[2] thousand pounds	Canada[3] dollars	Jamaica[4] thousand pounds	Mexico pesos	Newfoundland dollars	Trinidad & Tobago[5] thousand pounds	USA[1] dollars
1910	426	91	334	...	2.8	361	4,071[1] 3,306
1911	436	93	333	...	3	369	3,408
1912	435	98	317	...	3.1	396	3,578
1913	426	97	320	...	2.8	427	3,749
1914	416	95	286	...	2.5	420	3,902
1915	457	92	267	...	2.4	369	3,959
1916	450	94	260	...	2.4	383	4,210
1917	475[1]	100	279[4]	...	2.5	369	4,487
1918	491	95	287	...	2.2	343	4,501
1919	524	100	417	...	2.5	353	4,895
1920	687	95	573	...	...	535	5,314
1921	612	98	534	...	2.2	499	5,655
1922	582	93	542	...	2	434	5,833
1923	592	91	560	...	1.9	382	6,334
1924	684	98	542	...	1.9	364	6,751
1925	643	99	545	...	2	358	7,203
1926	624	100	571	...	2	367	7,599
1927	604	102	574	...	2	418	8,143
1928	577	104	572	0.5	2.2	470	8,707
1929	539	99	613	3.3	2.2	468	9,038
1930	537	95	640	6.3	2	470	9,274
1931	513	95	647	5.1	1.5	458	10,257
1932	596	93	653	7.1	1.2	432	10,696
1933	658	92	745	12	1.3	457	10,793
1934	694	90	830	18	1.8	431	10,868
							thousand million dollars
1935	745	89	794	22	2.3	455	11
1936	788	92	750	28	2.7	516	11
1937	843	95	802	34	3.1	586	11
						dollars	
1938	898	100	824	33	...	3.1	11
1939	936	105	892	37	...	3.1	12
1940	997	103	...	37	...	3	12
1941	1,013	99	901	46	...	3.4	12
1942	1,151	96	1,051	57	...	4.4	12
1943	1,405	108	1,333	101	...	6.4	13
1944	1,653	132	1,853	164	13[7]	7.5	14
1945	1,989	156	2,378	249	19	8.9	18
	dollars						
1946	9.9	176	3,011	239	21	9.5	20
1947	9.6	189	2,914	276	21	9.5	21
1948	9.5	206	2,320	329	22	9.7	22
1949	9.8	222	2,275	398	22	9.7	23

G3　NORTH AMERICA: Savings Bank Deposits (in millions of stated currency unit, except as otherwise indicated)

	Barbados	Canada[3]	Jamaica	Mexico[6] thousand million	Newfoundland[7]	Trinidad & Tobago[5]	USA[1] thousand million
	thousand pounds	dollars	thousand pounds	pesos	dollars	dollars	dollars
1950	10	231	2,276	0.45	23	11	23
1951	11	232	2,368	0.60[6]	25	12	24
				1.09			
1952	12	238	2,710	1.14	25	12	25
1953	12	253	2,891	1.44	26	13	27
1954	13	257	3,107	2.75	27	14	29
1955	15	275	3,296	2.97	28	15	30
1956	16	293	3,621	3.22	29	14	32
1957	18	291	3,928	3.36	28	13	33
1958	19	301	4,515	3.63	28	13	35
1959	20	314	4,896	5.34	28	13	36
1960	20	302	4,623	79	28	13	37
1961	18	325	5,270	8.18	28	13	39
1962	17	347	5,429	10.2	...	11	42
1963	18	361	5,950	12.6	...	11	45
1964	17	390	6,742	16.3	...	10	49
1965	18	404	7,363	19	...	9.7	53
1966	17	450	7,689	20	...	9.4	55
1967	17	482[3]	8,096	18	...	9.1	60
			million dollars				
			6.0				
1968	17	510	10	17	...	8.6	65
1969	17	...[3]	12	25	...	8.5	67
1970	18	589[3]	14	37	...	8.3[5]	72
1971	20	588	21	45	...	15	82
1972	21[16]	657	53	55	...	19	92
	3.9						
1973	8.5	743	81	62	...	22	97
1974	10	837	86	70	...	29	99
1975	20	928	135	90	...	62	111
1976	24	...	133	92	...	92	124
1977	26	...	101	183[6]	...	126	135
				38			
1978	36	...	119	55	...	202	144
1979	39	...	116	73	...	238	142
1980	50	...	129	121	...	327	162
1981	68	...	158	192	...	524	164
1982	88	...	242	254	...	813	165
1983	99	...	362	470	...	992	229
1984	109	...	483	793	...	880	263
1985	115	...	771	1,241	...	...	308
1986	121	...	917	2,226	...	...	356
1987	202	...	1,403	5,732	...	...	408
1988	216	...	2,140	9,014	...	...	579

G3   SOUTH AMERICA: SAVINGS BANK DEPOSITS (in millions of stated currency unit, except as otherwise indicated)

1880-1909   1910-1949

	Chile[8]	Guyana thousand		Argentina[9]	Brazil milreis or	Chile[8]	Colombia[10]	Guyana thousand	Uruguay
	pesos	pounds		pesos	cruzeiros	pesos	pesos	pounds	pesos
1880	—	...	1910	—	...	39	...	258	...
1881	—	194	1911	—	...	53	...	242	...
1882	—	228	1912	—	242	71	...	231	...
1883	—	252	1913	—	218	93	...	247	...
1884	—	227	1914	—	189	112	...	227	...
1885	0.3	188	1915	2	189	125	...	200	...
1886	0.5	195	1916	6	214	144	...	215	...
1887	0.8	201	1917	10	222	157	...	255	...
1888	1.1	204	1918	15	267	202	...	278	...
1889	1.4	228	1919	21	303	234	...	325	...
1890	1.8	257	1920	26	327	253	...	401	17
1891	2.2	253	1921	31	350	287	...	360	21
1892	2.7	276	1922	40	397	334	...	357	25
1893	2.9	278	1923	53	435	372	...	375	27
1894	3.1	276	1924	63	443	442	1.3	392	29
1895	2.9	260	1925	67	455	465	1.5	412[11]	29
1896	2.8	265	1926	69	468	436	2.5	393	33
1897	3.0	273	1927	80	484	413	4.6	381	41
1898	3.0	295	1928	90	512	483	6.6	376	46
1899	3.2	292	1929	97	516	506	9.9	344	52
1900	3.4	286	1930	100	492	481	9.6[10]	333	53
1901	3.6	289	1931	97	535	364[8] / 164	11	311	46
1902	4.9	302	1932	94	610	199	9.6	319	44
1903	5.6	307	1933	95	777	278	9.2	361	64
1904	7.1	295	1934	99	960	338	10	431	64
1905	9.7	291	1935	106	1,170	412	11	492	67
1906	15	300	1936	114	1,400	465	13	528	76
1907	20[8] / 24	296	1937	127	1,624	547	15	578	86
								dollars	
1908	30	298	1938	134	1,858	597	17	2.9	90
1909	33	299	1939	144	2,023	693	19	2.8	90
			1940	153	2,349	819	21	2.7	103
			1941	168	2,530	935	23	3.3	...
			1942	191	2,843	1,076	28	4.6	...
			1943	227	3,524	1,322	40	6.8	...
			1944	283	4,447	1,678	56	8.8	318
			1945	341	5,306	1,991	77	9.9	360[12] / 57
			1946	454	6,778	2,359	90	11	64
			1947	607	7,898	2,562	101	11	68
			1948	841	7,997	2,932	103	12	72
			1949	1,129	9,127	3,297	90	13	78

G3 SOUTH AMERICA: Savings Bank Deposits (in millions of stated currency unit, except as otherwise indicated)

	Argentina[9]	Brazil	Chile[8]	Colombia[10]	Guyana	Uruguay[12]
		thousand million				
	pesos	cruzeiros	pesos	pesos	-dollars	pesos
1950	1,384	11	3,724	106	14	84
1951	1,617	12	4,316	137	15	91
1952	2,030	14	5,484	174	16	94
1953	2,582	16	7,108	204	16	104
1954	3,203	19	8,994	261	17	109
1955	3,659	23	11,077	306	19	110
1956	4,408	26	17,211	366	19	107
1957	5,056	31	23,123	417	19	110
1958	5,962	36	33,377	509	20	116
1959	7,118	41	47,882	587	20	114
			escudos			
1960	8,268	50	73	629	21	126
1961	9,232	64	107[8]	737	20	143
			2.5			
1962	9,253	96	13	877	17	172
1963	10,947	144	37	922	17	208
1964	14,002	243	76	1,022	16	246[12]
						615
	thousand million					
	pesos					
1965	18	...	164	1,100	14	618
1966	22	633	295	1,282	15	406
		new cruzeiros				
1967	27	898	430	1,455	15	522
1968	35	1,002	629	1,818	14	911
1969	45	1,365	...	2,365[10]	14	1,371
				2,416		
	thousand million					
	new pesos					
	0.53[9]					
1970	1.96	2,367	1,558	2,972	13	2,160
1971	2.3	3,281	2,499	3,545	12	11,900
1972	3.2	5,742	4,354	5,127	12	27,800
1973	4.8	9,482	15,912	7,408	11	43,400
1974	6.5	18,028	132,037	13,096	9.6	69,200
		thousand million	new pesos	thousand million		thousand million
1975	11	33.5	884	17	...	147
1976	120	66.2	2,444	19	...	243
1977	790	99.4	6,057	28	...	...
1978	2,270	154	8,801	42	...	...
1979	5,890	262	13,983	56	...	...
			thousand million			
1980	12,010	...	26.4	82	...	...
1981	29,690	1,349	32.2	118	...	...
1982	26,440	3,070	29.4	159	...	...
	pesos argentines					
1983	12,184	9,587	51.6	239	...	...
1984	45,000	28,313	66	317	...	...
		million million				
1985	162	104	94.2	418	...	...
1986	379	427	138	530	...	...
1987	977	...	182	667	...	...
1988	6,000	...	...	755	...	...

G3 Savings Bank Deposits

NOTES

1. SOURCES: The national publications listed on pp. xiii–xv, with gaps filled from League of Nations, *Statistical Yearbooks, Commercial Banks, and Money and Banking*; and International Monetary Fund, *International Financial Statistics*.
2. In principle, this table relates to all deposits in institutions which are described as savings banks, and excludes deposits in commercial banks, building societies, agricultural credit institutions, etc.
3. Except where otherwise indicated, the statistics are for the last working day of each year.

FOOTNOTES

[1]   Savings deposits in Savings Banks to 1910 (1st line); subsequently savings and other time deposits in Mutual Savings Banks and in the postal savings system. The figures for 1910 (2nd line) onwards are at 30 June. It is not clear whether this is also true for the earlier series.
[2]   At 30 September to 1900, and at 31 March in the year following that shown in 1901–17.
[3]   Deposits in the Post Office and Government Savings Banks, and Savings Banks in Quebec, categories which were reduced in 1968 and 1971 by closure and by absorption into ordinary commercial banks. Data are at 30 June to 1906 and at 31 March from 1907 to 1967. The 1968 figure is an aggregate of some relating to 31 March and others to 31 October, and later figures are all at 31 October.
[4]   At 30 September to 1889 and at 31 March in the year following that shown in 1890–1917.
[5]   Tobago is included from 1899. Statistics relate to the Post Office Savings Bank to 1970 (1st line), with other savings banks included subsequently.
[6]   Time deposits of financial institutions other than the central bank and commercial banks from 1951 (2nd line) to 1977 (1st line).
[7]   Statistics from 1945 are at 31 March in the year following that shown. Even after Newfoundland was incorporated in Canada the figures continue to be shown separately here for as long as they are available.
[8]   Caja Nacional de Ahorros and Caja de Ahorro de Santiago only to 1907 (1st line). From 1907 (2nd line) to 1931 (1st line) all savings accounts; from 1931 (2nd line) to 1961 (1st line) private savings accounts other than those in commercial banks; and from 1961 (2nd line) deposits in savings banks and in loans associations.
[9]   Post Office Savings Bank only to 1970 (1st line). Subsequently savings deposits of mortgage banks, with other financial institutions added from 1978 (2nd line).
[10] Time, savings, and foreign currency deposits from 1969 (2nd line). Statistics to 1930 are at 30 June.
[11] Subsequently excluding one private bank which had been included previously.
[12] All savings deposits to 1945 (1st line). Post Office Savings deposits only from 1945 (2nd line) to 1964 (1st line), and all time deposits of financial institutions other than the central bank and the commercial banks subsequently.
[13] Deposits at the end of the financial year of each bank, which was predominantly 30 June.
[14] Western Samoa accounts are included to 1960 and Cook Islands accounts to 1966. Statistics are at 31 March in the year following that shown.
[15] Government Savings Bank only to 1969 (1st line).
[16] The reason for this break is not given in the source.

G4 NORTH AMERICA: MONEY SUPPLY

	Canada		Costa Rica		Dominican Republic		El Salvador		Guatemala		Haiti	
	Canadian dollars		colones		pesos		colones		quatzales		gourdes	
	M1	M2	M1	M2	M1	M2	M1	M2	M1	M2	M1	M2
	thousand million		million		millions		million		million		million	
1948			174	192	...	...	89	101	55.6	61.2	...	...
1949	3.86	7.95	195	217	...	...	104	119	56.6	63.5	...	...
1950	4.19	8.37	204	231	41.8	54.1	129	142	58.9	65.7	60.1	72.8
1951	4.26	8.56	224	255	53.1	63.7	136	146	60.4	67.9	75.2	92.5
1952	4.54	9.14	265	303	62.1	75.2	164	174	63.6	70.6	98.3	119
1953	4.49	9.25	291	336	60.2	72.4	172	184	76.1	83.3	94.4	116
1954	4.82	10.04	325	374	68.6	94.8	190	206	77.6	84.3	117	145
1955	5.11	10.74	340	401	76.5	109	187	207	86.7	95.3	118	147
1956	5.07	11.08	342	413	76.9	114	215	241	104	118₁	127	162
1957	5.29	11.40	370	453	87.4	130	215	252	116	135	121	156
1958	5.95	12.79	399₁	502	107	144	202	257	107	129	103	135
1959	5.75	12.65	427	547	91.9	129	206	282	109	135	104	136
1960	5.98	13.19	433	561	102	129	193	276	105	137	104	138
1961	6.74	14.36	422	546	104	126	184	285	107	143	118	156
1962	7.03	14.96	480	617	114	140	183	306	109	151	122	160
1963	7.53	16.77	535	683	130	158	221	375	121	170	131	169
1964	8.25	18.51	568	734	117	147	234	423	129	194	132	171
1965	9.43	20.37	598	783	135	196	234	439	136	209	133	171
1966	10.13	22.00₁	622	808	116	165	247	479	143	234	123	161
1967	11.70₁	21.34₁	832₂	1,080	120	173	253	489	148	263	142	179
1968	15.97	28.88	849	1,069	139	211	265	509	151	277	160	201
1969	15.30	31.08	959	1,195	149	243	288	562	161	309	176	224
1970	15.57	34.05	1,006	1,277	172	290	295	595	173	344	191	249
1971	17.61	37.15	1,317	1,811	188	333	315	658	179	383	215	290
1972	19.77	42.71	1,501	2,166	222	411	390	807	214	477	271	382
1973	21.50	51.49	1,874	2,640	260	505	466	958	264	580	333	487
1974	21.83	61.36	2,146	3,446	364	726	557	1,116	305	668	342	584
1975	25.97	70.79	2,771	4,909	380	847	648	1,353	354	808	403	735
1976	26.36	84.38	3,408	6,590	390	875	917	1,770	494	1,052	550	1,015
1977	29.10	96.19	4,504	8,664	460	1,005	988	2,004	594	1,249	629	1,217
1978	31.12	112.5	5,625	11,067	458	991	1,087	2,241	664	1,424	718	1,431
1979	31.56	132.4	6,226	14,869	598	1,155	1,321	2,446	735	1,537	1,108	1,873
1980	34.75₁	144.9₁	7,271	17,235	580	1,174	1,429	2,563	753	1,692	945	1,938
			thousand million									
1981	36.75	177.4	10.8	32.3	661	1,317	1,437₁	2,834₁	776	1,907	1,166	2,175
1982	39.82	184.0	18.4	41.0	784	1,434	1,633	3,233	787	2,191	1,164	2,247
1983	44.09	182.2	25.6	56.1	842	1,654	1,596	3,575	834	2,155	1,175	2,348
1984	52.44	192.4	30.1	65.8	1,247	2,144	1,830	4,236	869	2,399	1,388	2,606
1985	68.91	205.3	32.4	76.0	1,456	2,492	2,306	5,374	1,346	3,193	1,076	1,442
1986	80.22	222.2	42.5	92.2	2,080	4,335	2,758	6,905	1,608	3,875	1,790	3,276
1987	85.20	241.6	42.6	107	2,773	5,061	2,762	7,371	1,766	4,168	2,098	3,694
1988	90.12	267.2	65.3	150	4,324	7,625	2,996	8,219	2,019	4,995	1,635	3,313
1989	95.45	303.2	64.0	175	5,374	9,954	3,370	9,130	2,438	5,801	2,633	4,559
1990	96.22	326.5	66.5	223	7,587	13,849	4,153	12,020	3,242	7,296	2,303	4,674
1991	100.45	342.4	79.8	298	9,448	19,058	4,872	14,555	3,843	10,865	2,464	5,229
1992	108.82	374.9	109.8	371	11,047	24,368	6,284	18,881	4,193	14,248	3,150	6,822
1993	114.40	415.7	117.1	427	13,549	30,775	7,353	23,853	5,048	16,403	3,866	8,811

G4 NORTH AMERICA: Money Supply

	Honduras		Jamaica		Mexico		Nicaragua		Panama		Trinidad & Tobago		USA	
	lempiras		pounds		pesos		cordobas		balboas		T&T dollars		US dollars	
	M1	M2	M1	M2	M1	M2	M1	M2	M1	M2	M1	M2	M1	M2
	million		million		thousand million		million		million		million		thousand million	
1948	38	43	...	...	4.04	5.06	89	93	29	48	...	...		
1949	37	43	...	...	4.50	5.79	112	113	24	43	...	...	110	145
1950	38	44	...	...	6.24	7.45	122	125	24	42	...	...	115	150
1951	47	54	...	...	6.97	8.46	150	152	25	42	46	90	123	159
1952	52	60	...	...	7.26	9.13	180	182	27	44	58	102	129	169
1953	59	68	15	26	8.05	10.10	230	239	30	49	64	112	131	173
1954	69	79	16	29	9.01	12.03	264	272	33	51	74	127	135	181
1955	61	72	17	30	10.77	14.13	272	291	33	52	70	133	138	185
1956	67	83	19	35	11.98	15.69	267	285	34	66	73	143	139	189
1957	64	77	22	41	12.78	17.43	260	279	38	61	94	163	138	193
1958	63	75	22	43	13.72	19.17	252	274	40	65	89	173	144	207
1959	66	81	25	48	15.87	21.13	253	282	42	69	93	189	146	210
1960	64	85	26	51	17.35	22.75	264	297	42	70	103	199	146	217
1961	66	89	23	47	18.49	24.51	273	305	44	75	113	225	151	340
1962	73	102	30	62	20.9	27.6	353	384	49	87	104	225	153	367
1963	79	114	29	71	24.3	32.4	397	449	60	111	122	263	159	398
1964	90	129	32	78	28.6	37.8	460	545	51	105	121	255	167	430
1965	105	151	32	84	30.2	40.6	537	672	56	125	116	263	174	465
1966	107	166	36	97	33.9	45.7	565	751	62	149	126	295	179	486
1967	114	183	38	106	37.0	50.1	541	760	70	181	129	315	190	530
1968	127	213	47	135	42.3	57.0	485	682	81	206[2]	130	362	204	572
1969	148	252	56	162	48.6	65.4	513	721	85	196	140	415	211	592

million dollars[5]

	Honduras		Jamaica		Mexico		Nicaragua		Panama		Trinidad & Tobago		USA	
1970	159	288	127	379	54	72	578	829	100	256	151	489	222	631
1971	169	321	160	471	58	77	619	949	105	302	177	606	237	714
1972	193	366	173[3]	528[3]	68	91	749	1,226	154	393	211	723	259	806
1973	238	445	218	578	84	115	1,146	1,734	161	444	213	823	272	859
1974	242	460	258	687	101	139	1,313	2,016	196	530	270	1,073	284	905
1975	263	507	322	828	122	164	1,256	2,030	173	548	392	1,388	298	1,020
1976	361	672	339	897	158[1]	243[1]	1,615	2,699	190	578	572	1,863	318	1,160
1977	411	796	474	1,044	208	525	1,699	2,855	213	672	725	2,360	344	1,282
1978	480	962	570	1,235	270	699	1,579	2,652	246	833	936	2,941	372	1,381
1979	546	1,040	629	1,422	361	949	2,654	3,427	301	1,043	1,147	3,816	397	1,467
1980	610	1,128	717	1,712	477	1,297	4,102	5,747	335	1,316	1,337	4,298	424	1,570
1981	637	1,226	775	2,197	635[2]	1,933[2]	5,206	7,926	360	1,561	1,855	5,492	451	1,644
1982	717	1,478	876	2,773	1,031	3,055	6,545	9,895	379	1,749	2,547	7,395	491	1,787

million new cordobas[6]

	Honduras		Jamaica		Mexico		Nicaragua		Panama		Trinidad & Tobago		USA	
1983	815	1,731	1,066	3,527	1,447	4,945	10.94	17.24	373	1,748	2,434	7,934	538	2,078
1984	846	1,911	1,319	4,197	2,315	8,332	20.84	30.7	381	1,863	2,294	8,342	570	2,267
1985	856	1,871	1,520	5,238	3,462	11,936	54.8	74.4	409	1,952	2,260	8,444	641	2,483
1986	955	2,050	2,140	6,687	5,790	21,299	193	249	449	2,360	2,073	8,198	746	2,707
1987	1,119	2,497	2,252	7,527	12,627	52,656	1,422	1,622	442	2,278	2,170	8,493	767	2,929
1988	1,253	2,869	3,445	9,958	21,191	43,448	...	...	304	1,648	1,875	8,549	804	3,090
1989	1,524	3,301	3,153	10,612	29,087	93,818	...	...	307	1,600	2,133	9,094	812	3,245

million gold cordobas

	Honduras		Jamaica		Mexico		Nicaragua		Panama		Trinidad & Tobago		USA	
1990	1,968	4,014	4,016	12,891	47,439	164,952	53	90	433	2,185	2,576	9,662	844	3,357
1991	2,277	4,738	7,818	19,516	106,227	246,335	758	1,450	557	2,862	2,922	9,906	916	3,458
1992	2,582	5,810	13,391	34,299	122,220	302,593	845	1,741	639	3,577	2,696	9,222	1,047	3,528
1993	2,876	6,572	16,903	46,628	143,902	346,468	806	2,179	708	4,191	3,137	10,629	1,154	3,591

G4 SOUTH AMERICA: MONEY SUPPLY

	Argentina		Bolivia		Brazil		Chile		Colombia		Ecuador	
	pesos		bolivianos		cruzeiros		pesos		pesos		sucres	
	M1	M2	M1	M2	M1	M2	M1	M2	M1	M2	M1	M2
	thousand million		thousand million				thousand million		million		million	
1948	16.9	24.2	...	...	48	62	32	...	760	861	651	765
1949	20.4	30.1	...	...	57	73	41	...	927	1,029	709	850
1950	24.7	35.4	5.0	5.8	76	94	20	...	974	1,113	913	1,093
1951	30.4	41.7	5.9	7.0	88	108	21	...	1,127	1,316	845	1,005
1952	34.3	46.7	9.0	10.0	101	122	29	...	1,318	1,522	1,051	1,233
1953	43.1	58.0	16.3	17.5	123	145	40	...	1,550	1,757	1,088	1,318
1954	51.9	69.6	26.9	27.9	150	175	55	...	1,843	2,223	1,273	1,543
1955	61.2	81.4	56	59	178	201	92	108	1,911	2,411	1,193	1,545
1956	71.3	96.4	197	203	219	243	129	154	2,377	3,215	1,358	1,746
1957	82.8	113	291	301	290	318	165	193	2,698	3,351	1,412	1,881
1958	119	160	301	310	354	385	222	277	3,263	3,905	1,400	1,791
1959	170	215	386	401	500	535	294	456	3,633	4,400	1,577	2,017
							million escudos[14]					
1960	218	279	419	435	691	735	384	595	3,985	4,750	1,732	2,201
1961	243[2]	318[2]	496	513	1,043	1,104	432	698	4,961	5,881	1,778	2,376
	202	277										
1962	220	305	556	585	1,689	1,762	557	896	5,927	7,474	2,000	2,678
			million pesos[10]									
1963	283	406	665	702	2,777	2,887	747	1,206	6,693	8,206	2,241	2,850
1964	396	574	803	853	5,126	5,308	1,129	1,849	8,246	9,700	2,626	3,195
									thousand million			
1965	497	729	943	995	9,050	9,347	1,367	2,364	9.6	11.8	2,670	3,285
					million new cruzeiros[12]							
1966	671	959	1,153	1,253	10.5	11.4	2,594	4,118	11.2	13.0	3,016	3,847
1967	1,092	1,475	1,192	1,343	14.9	16.6	3,240	5,389	13.7	15.8	3,439	4,460
1968	1,364	1,889	1,287	1,513	21.3	24.0	4,471	7,565	15.9	18.1	4,172	5,563
1969	1,655	2,279	1,361	1,667	27.4	31.8	6,058	10,605	19.4	22.1	4,751	6,298
	thousand million new pesos[7]						*thousand million escudos*				*thousand million*	
1970	18	26	1,532	1,913	34.7	40.8	10	16	22.4	25.8	5.99	7.73
1971	20	30	1,766	2,259	42	45	21	32	25.1	29.2	6.72	8.89
1972	33	53	2,210	2,844	59	65	54	80	31.9	37.7	8.38	10.97
1973	57	97	2,969	3,776	87	94	229	441	41.6[1]	50.9[1]	11.3	14.4
1974	90	150	4,257	5,449	117	125	838	2,025	49.1	63.7	16.9	21.0
			thousand million pesos				*thousand million pesos[15]*					
1975	280	360	4.8	6.7	169	181	2.99	7.49	58.9	78.5	18.3	23.1
	million million pesos											
1976	1.05	1.59	6.5	9.9	231	250	9.72	25.89	79.4	105	22.8	28.8
1977	2.26	5.17	7.9	12.8	319[1]	363[1]	34.2	45.9	103[4]	141[4]	29.9	36.0
1978	5.87	14.65	8.8	14.4	434	529	33.9	104	133	180	32.9	39.7
1979	14.0	43.5	10.3	16.6	759	913	55.1	180	166	221	42.0	52.2
1980	27.5	82.3	14.7	23.1	1,288	1,473	85.3	307	212	320	53.6	66.2
1981	46.7	175.0	17.6	29.4	2,352	2,861	81.9	412	256	435	61.8	75.7
1982	162.3	459.3	57.8	97.2	3,964	5,299	92.2	577	321	526	73.1	93.6
	thousand million pesos argentinos[8]											
1983	75	230	178	265	8,036	12,806	112	702	397	659	95.1	118
					thousand million							
1984	451	1,638	3,370	4,053	24.4	46.3	130	720	492	817	129	169
	thousand million australes[9]		*million million pesos*									
1985	3.03	8.43	198	287	106	203	148	1,061	545	982	153	217
					reals							
1986	5.60	17.76	369	817	166	266	215	1,329	...	...	183	268
			million bolivianos[11]									
1987	12.58	48.42	516	1,576	524	834	229	1,794	1,020	1,815	246	384
1988	55	260	698	2,028	2,623	13,440	385	2,280	1,282	2,198	373	622
	million pesos											
1989	273	652	715	2,477	37,697	210,019	441	2,991	...	...	540	882
					thousand							
1990	3,068	7,913	997	3,784	917	2,918	518	3,696	2,116	3,897	853	1,357
1991	7,626	19,097	1,447	5,696	4,856	21,404	784	4,733	2,786	4,707	1,334	2,048
1992	11,364	31,030	1,923	7,660	52,539	365,286	937	5,838	4,020	6,827	1,860	3,231
					million							
1993	15,119	45,453	2,499	10,242	1,113	11,092	1,186	7,202	5,136	9,386	3,051	6,827

G4 SOUTH AMERICA: Money Supply

	Guyana		Paraguay		Peru		Uruguay		Venezuela	
	Guyanese dollars		guaranies		soles		pesos		bolivares	
	M1	M2	M1	M2	M1	M2	M1	M2	M1	M2
	million		million		thousand million		million		million	
1948	...	...	97	...	1.61	2.25	442	828	1,380	1,506
1949	...	...	153	...	1.68	2.54	500	...	1,537	1,684
1950	...	...	229	...	1.97	3.14	588	1,084	1,576	1,741
1951	...	...	395	...	2.41	3.65	577	1,137	1,646	1,849
1952	...	...	582	632	2.73	4.28	630	1,220	1,909	2,182
1953	...	...	861	943	3.10	4.86	712	1,393	2,085	3,457
1954	...	...	1,070	1,172	3.37	5.40	763	1,518	2,169	2,663
1955	26	39	1,426	1,601	3.58	6.12	807	1,602	2,414	3,083
1956	26	42	1,941	2,036	4.21	7.21	904	1,796	2,756	3,678
1957	28	47	1,997	2,177	4.37	7.85	980	2,094	3,649	5,150
1958	30	52	2,384	2,760	4.68	8.45	1,248	2,527	4,017	5,877
1959	35	57	2,609	2,874	6.05	10.1	1,771	3,193	3,823	5,906
1960	38	62	2,674	3,031	7.10	11.7	2,394	4,045	3,574	5,265
1961	36	61	3,391	3,933	8.30	13.7	2,924	4,828	3,684	5,327
1962	42	72	3,311	4,136	8.87	15.6	2,832	5,117	3,604	5,410
1963	43	84	3,685	4,929	10.3	18.1	3,652	7,839	3,840	6,240
1964	47	96	4,473	6,234	13.2	22.7	5,185[2]	10,876[2]	4,390	7,290
							thousand million		thousand million	
1965	45	102	4,913	7,278	15.8	28	10.5	18.5	4.79	7.78
1966	47	109	5,034[1]	7,856[1]	18.2	31.9	14.7	23.9	5.02	7.93
1967	51	122	6,691	10,339	20.7	34.7	30.9	46.7	5.57	9.01
1968	56	138	5,786	10,111	22.8	37.1	47.6	71.4	6.09	9.87
1969	61	152	6,557	11,587	27.5	42	76.7	108	6.64	10.95
			thousand million							
1970	61	164	7.3	13.5	43.3	57.4	87.8	130	7.07	11.8
1971	69	191	7.8	15.2	46.6	62.1	135	197	8.19	13.8
1972	88	233	9.4	18.8	60.3	77.0	198	316	9.65	16.6
1973	101	274	12.5	24.3	75.7	94.8	357	540	11.5	19.9
1974	133	317	15.1	29.4	105	127	586	921	16.9	26.9
							million new pesos[17]			
1975	207	448	17.8	37.1	123	147	834	1,637	25.6	41.5
1976	221	487	21.6	45.7	155	182	1,380	3,260	29.0	50.7
1977	285	599	28.6	60.1	185	225	1,938	5,922	37.4	64.1
1978	300	663	39.8	78.5	270	362	3,588	11,339	44.0	73.3
1979	288	710	49.5	97.5	461	695	6,160	21,038	46.5	78.7
							thousand million new pesos			
1980	328	846	62.4	131	730	1,276	9.1	36.4	54.5	92.3
1981	351	982	62.4	157	1,075	2,152	9.8[1]	54.2[1]	58.3	105
1982	436	1,254	60.2	166	1,509	3,701	13.7	72.5	60.8	114
1983	509	1,518	75.6	193	2,965	7,525	14.9	81.9	76.2	140
1984	619	1,795	97.8	226	6,060	17,098	22.1	133	96.7	168
					thousand million intis[16]					
1985	740	2,140	125	273	23	44	46	260	105	188
1986	881	2,489	159	348	43	68	84	478	110[2]	211[2]
1987	1,333	3,820	244	469	96	139	135	702	123	260
1988	1,999	4,732	328	523	593	1,006	222	1,370	145	299
1989	2,677	7,164	435	841	10,403	20,286	383	2,773	170	436
					million million					
1990	4,136	10,930	558	1,282	708	1,316	770	5,984	269	743
1991	6,844	18,956	739	1,897	1,608	4,349	1,528	10,715	348	1,030
1992	8,999	30,760	905	2,584	2,884	8,184	2,583	16,385	375	1,207
1993	11,881	37,351	1,054	3,300	4,343	14,060	4,074	22,164	416	1,514

G4 Money Supply

NOTES

1. SOURCES: International Monetary Fund, *International Financial Statistics*.
2. M1 is defined as notes and coin in the hands of the public plus demand deposits of residents. M2 additionally includes time and savings deposits. Non-residents, and banks, deposits are not always excluded in practice, especially in earlier years.
3. Breaks in continuity through changes in coverage or sectorization are indicated in footnotes where possible, it should be noted that these improvements do not necessarily imply an increase in the figures for later years, since they may include the elimination of double-counting and the exclusion of non-residents deposits or other funds which should not have been counted as part of the money supply.

FOOTNOTES

[1] There was a change in the coverage or sectorization of accounts.
[2] No reason is given for this break in the source.
[3] Subsequently excluding non-residents deposits.
[4] Subsequently excluding the Agricultural Bank.
[5] Two Jamaican dollars equalled one pound.
[6] One new equalled 1,000 old cordobas.
[7] One new (1970) pesos equalled 100 old pesos.
[8] One peso argentino equalled 10,000 old (1970) pesos.
[9] One austral equalled 1,000 pesos argentinos.
[10] One peso equalled 1,000 bolivianos.
[11] One (1987) boliviano equalled 1 million pesos.
[12] One new (1966) cruzeiro equalled 1,000 old pesos.
[13] One cruzado equalled 1,000 (1966) cruzeiros.
[14] One escudo equalled 1,000 pesos.
[15] One (1975) peso equalled 1,000 escudos.
[16] One inti equalled 1,000 soles.
[17] One new equalled 1,000 old pesos.

G5 NORTH AMERICA: TOTAL CENTRAL GOVERNMENT EXPENDITURE (in millions of stated currency unit, except as otherwise indicated)

1789–1824 **1825–1864**

	USA[1]		Barbados	Jamaica[2]	Mexico[3]	Trinidad	USA[1]
	dollars		thousand pounds	thousand pounds	pesos	thousand pounds	dollars
1789	⎫	1825	...	...	17	...	16
1790	⎬ 4.3	1826	...	...	17	...	17
1791	⎭	1827	...	...	16	...	16
1792	5.1	1828	...	...	16	...	16
1793	4.5	1829	...	...	16	...	15
1794	7.0						
		1830	...	...	14	...	15
1795	7.5	1831	...	...	17	...	15
1796	5.7	1832	...	...	20	...	17
1797	6.1	1833	...	...	22	...	23
1798	7.7	1834	...	...	17	...	19
1799	9.7						
		1835	27	...	13	...	18
1800	11	1836	...	...	14	...	31
1801	9.4	1837	...	...	17	...	37
1802	7.9	1838	...	...	41	...	34
1803	7.9	1839	...	...	20	...	27
1804	8.7						
		1840	54	225	19	...	24
1805	11	1841	...	269	22	...	27
1806	9.8	1842	...	303	19	...	25
1807	8.4	1843	...	325	21	...	[12][1]
1808	9.9	1844	...	294	20	...	22
1809	10						
		1845	52	277	25	...	23
1810	8.2	1846	...	277	24	...	28
1811	8.1	1847	...	305	27	...	57
1812	20	1848	...	236	25	...	45
1813	32	1849	...	193	17	...	45
1814	35						
		1850	47	219	20	77	40
1815	33	1851	50	260	26	106	48
1816	31	1852	59	240	16	111	44
1817	22	1853	70	153	32	119	48
1818	20	1854	72	216	18	101	58
1819	21						
		1855	63	240	14	81	60
1820	18	1856	71	213	14	80	70
1821	16	1857	81	207	15	108	68
1822	15	1858	88	191	14	174	74
1823	15	1859	80	262	15	187	63
1824	20						
		1860	111	255	16	187	63
		1861	116	275	8.3	189	67
		1862	93	292	10	196	475
		1863	105	285	8.5	189	715
		1864	99	364	7.2	193	865

G5 NORTH AMERICA: Total Central Government Expenditure (in millions of stated currency unit, except as otherwise indicated)

1865–1899

	Barbados[4] thousand pounds	Canada[5] dollars	Costa Rica[6] pesos	Cuba[7] paper pesos	El Salvador[8] silver pesos	Guatemala[9] paper	pesos	Honduras[10] pesos	Jamaica[2] thousand pounds	Mexico[3] pesos	Trinidad[11] thousand pounds	USA[1] dollars
1865	90	—	...	...	...		...	...	370	6.1	222	1,298
1866	90	—	...	28	...		...	...	388	9.8	184	521
1867	100	—	...	25	...		...	...	372	14	196	358
1868	99	14	...	31	...		...	...	354	17	177	377
1869	105	15	...	...	...		...	...	375	14	214	323
1870	106	18	...	...	...		...	...	418	15	226	310
1871	122	19	...	...	...		...	...	455	15	229	292
1872	124	25	...	...	...		...	...	478	16	277	278
1873	122	39	...	...	...		...	...	523	16	315	290
1874	124	33	...	...	...		...	...	537	17	364	303
1875	127	32	...	...	...		...	...	587	18	352	275
1876	124	31	...	...	...		...	...	537	18	318	265
1877	120	32	...	...	...		...	...	536	19	306	241
1878	124	30	...	...	...		...	...	505	18	354	237
1879	124	30	...	...	...		...	0.9	561	21	456	267
1880	130	33	...	...	...		...	1.0	687	24	571	268
1881	133	33	...	44	...		...	0.7	699	33	557	261
1882	141	33	...	...	...		7.3	1.4	701	41	468	258
1883	143	42	2.0	36	4.0		6.6	1.1	728	48	510	265
1884	144	56	3.1	34	4.1		5.8	...	704	51	501	244
1885	146	48	3.2	32	3.6		8.1	...	781	34	457	260
1886	137	60	2.8	32	4.3		8.4	} 2.8 {	622	36	453	242
1887	155	40	3.4	32	2.8		...		647	61	431	268
1888	150	43	3.9	24[7]	2.9		...	1.4	634	88	471	268
1889	146	42	5.0	26[7]	4.0		...	...	684[2]	78	464	299
1890	182	40	5.5	...	5.4		...	...	711	63	483	318
1891	177	39	5.4	25	7.4		8.3	...	897	43	536	366
1892	199	40	...	...	6.8		...	3.0	802	49	516	345
1893	165	39	4.7	23	7.2		9.7	2.6	812	46	513	383
1894	161	41	6.1	...	8.6		11	1.2	822	46	508[11] 560	368
1895	414	41	6.2	...	7.9		14	2.3	850	46	661	356
1896	197	42	6.7	26	9.4		16	2.4	853	49	768	352
1897	174	41	8.3	26	8.6		17	...	823	53	775	366
1898	179	43	8.1	26	5.3		21	2.4	755	55	705[11]	443
1899	210	49	7.4	26	5.2		10	2.6	815	63	749	605

G5 NORTH AMERICA: Total Central Government Expenditure (in millions of stated currency unit, except as otherwise indicated)

1900-1944

	Barbados[4] thousand pounds	Canada[5] dollars	Costa Rica[6] colones	Cuba[7] paper pesos	Dominican Republic pesos	El Salvador[8] silver pesos	Guatemala[9] paper pesos	Haiti[12] gourdes
1900	183[4]	50	9.3	...	...	6.8	...	...
1901	181	56	5.9	...	...	7.6	12	...
1902	199	61	5.5	...	...	8.6	16	...
1903	183	59	6.4	14	...	7.7	19	...
1904	180	70	4.1	17	...	8.8	17	...
1905	183	77	5.9	17	1.7	10	23	...
1906	186	81[5]	7.1	19	2.1	12	20[9] / 45	...
1907	188	110	9.2	24	2.4	11	46	...
1908	201	131	[6.1][6]	23	4.4	12	45	...
1909	209	114	7.2	24	4.0	11	50	...
						colones[17]		
1910	216	122	8.9	...	4.6	10	71	...
1911	223	136	10	31	4.8	13	46	...
1912	236	143	9.3	34	5.8	13	69	...
1913	224	185	10	34	3.2	15	46	...
1914	239	246	9.7	40	5.3	15	49	...
1915	230	338	9.2	40	4.4	12	68	...
1916	270	497	9.5	40	4.1	12	92	...
1917	521	574	13	44	5.0	14	131	15
1918	348	696	13	63	5.0	15	78	16
1919	359	740	21	63	7.9	14	101	23
1920	531	529	19	63	12	16	196	21
1921	419	476	19	63	9.0	14	387	33
1922	360	441	17	55	11	14	348	40
1923	352	372	18	63	7.2	14	396	31
							quetzales[17]	
1924	365	352	20	70	8.0	16	8.1	34
1925	394	356	24	84	11	18	9.7	39
1926	419	359	23	86[7]	13	20	12	41
1927	481	380	28	81	15	22[8]	12	40
1928	460	394	27	84	16	27	15	41
1929	451	405	36	85	16	26	16	43
1930	422	442	33	77	11	...	14	45
1931	424	449	28	60	8.4	19	13	37
1932	412	532	25	52	7.4	18	9.9	34
1933	451	458	24	42	8.3	18	8.3	34
1934	413	478	26	55	9.2	19	8.2	37
1935	462	533	32	65	11	20	8.8	42
1936	543	532	35	73	11	23	10	37
1937	558	534	35	70[7]	12	22	10	35
1938	560	553	36	...	12	20	11	29
1939	628	681	40	76	12	[11][8]	14	38
1940	819	1,250	44	79	12	22	11	37
1941	661	1,885	53	78	13	21	11	33
1942	755	4,387	49	102	15	22	11	30
1943	874	5,322	72	112	19	23	13	28
1944	1,008	5,246	67	133	26	25	18	32

G5 NORTH AMERICA: Total Central Government Expenditure (in millions of stated currency unit, except as otherwise indicated)

1900–1944

	Honduras[10]	Jamaica[2] thousand	Mexico[3]	Nicaragua[13]	Panama[14]	Puerto Rico[15]	Trinidad & Tobago[11] thousand	USA[1]
	pesos	pounds	pesos	pesos	balboas	dollars	pounds	dollars
1900	2.8	1,004	62	5.3	...	...	697[11]	521
1901	2.6	924	68	5.6	...	...	788	525
1902	1.9	942	74	5.2	...	...	773	485
1903	...	949	120	10	...	...	847	517
1904	3.0	943	109	11	...	...	833	584
1905	3.3	914	99	...	...	...	898	567
1906	4.7	920	102	...	...	3.6	835	570
1907	4.2	1,053	105	...	...	...	803	579
1908	3.5	1,031	104	...	...	...	918	659
1909	3.7	1,175	107	...	2.8	...	928	694
1910	3.3	1,135	113	38	6.7	5.5	927	694
1911	4.7	1,263	120	47	3.3	3.9	960	691
1912	4.4	1,459	153	...	3.3	8.7	947	690
				cordobas[17]				
1913	5.0	1,289	111	1.9	3.3	9.5	952	715
1914	5.5	1,230	...	4.8	4.4	11	1,208	726
1915	6.5	1,282	...	2.3	3.1	13	[756][11]	746
1916	5.5	1,274	...	1.8	5.7	8.9	1,033	713
1917	5.4	1,292	126	2	3.6	9.7	1,098	1,954
1918	5.5	1,450	166	1.8	3.4	12	1,124	12,677
1919	7.8	1,809	168	1.6	4.3	13	1,309	18,493
1920	7.7	2,485	213	2.1	4.4	16	1,864	6,358
1921	7.1	2,322	258	3.4	7.3	12	2,301	5,062
1922	16	1,950	228	1.9	6.1	13	2,175	3,289
1923	14	2,559	236	1.9	} 16 {	11	1,735	3,140
1924	14	2,153	211	2		12	1,657	2,908
1925	12	2,120	298	2.2	} 12 {	14	1,724	2,924
1926	11	2,164	325	2.4		14	1,616	2,930
1927	15	2,103	310	2.5	} 14[14] / 17 {	14	1,515	2,857
1928	13	2,458	288	2.5		15	1,576	2,961
1929	14	2,670	276	4.2	} 17 {	15	1,659	3,127
1930	14	2,446	279	3.8		14	1,756	3,320
1931	12	2,320	226	4.9	} [19][14] {	16	2,075[16]	3,577
1932	11	2,485	212	4.8		12	1,740	4,659
	lempiras[17]							
1933	12	2,312	245	4.1	} 15 {	11	2,452	4,598
1934	12	2,403	265	4.7		16	1,976	6,648
1935	13	2,310	301	4.9	} 14 {	15	2,084	6,497
							dollars[17]	
1936	12	2,303	406	5.5		15	9.2	8,422
1937	12	2,436	479	6.9	9.7	18	10	7,733
1938	[12][10]	2,854	504	8.7	13	20	12	6,765
1939	12	3,164	571	14	13	19	13	8,841
1940	11	3,781	610	23	18	19	21	9,055
1941	12	3,823	689	28	17	17	17	13,255
1942	11	4,045	845	38	21	24	21	34,037
1943	14	5,949	1,085	36	23	41	29	79,368
1944	17	7,408	1,505	43	25	51	31	94,986

G5 NORTH AMERICA: Total Central Government Expenditure (in millions of stated currency unit, except as otherwise indicated)

	Barbados[4]	Canada[5]	Costa Rica[6]	Cuba[7]	Dominican Republic[19]	El Salvador	Guatemala[9]	Haiti[12]
	thousand pounds	dollars	colones	paper pesos	pesos	colones	quetzales	gourdes
1945	1,145	5,136	74	145	30	29	20	35
	dollars							
1946	5.8	2,634	79	174	43	45	29	37
1947	7.5	2,196	97	199	73	52	32	49
1948	8.8	2,176	115	289[7]	89	64	46	76
1949	11	2,449	125	229	80	67	49	85
1950	11	2,945	127	271	91	89	47	98
1951	12	3,990	141	325	102	121	48	120
1952	12	4,688	165	341	128	131	59	159
1953	13	4,221	197	304	104	140	61	152
1954	14	4,289	219	329	104	152	63	175
1955	17	4,424	249[6]	325	125	157	79	174
			290					
1956	20	4,851	290	355	145	183	100	195
1957	23	5,039	300	386	153	197	114	146
1958	28	5,364	311	458[7]	164	198	114[9]	189
1959	30	5,703	324	...	154	186	104	192
1960	29	5,958[5]	356	411	147	184	93	...
		6,521						
1961	32	7,004	386	1,143	139	221	101	[114][20]
1962	35	6,931	445	1,657	185	201	93	153
1963	37	7,112	454	2,904	190	196	107	144
1964	39	7,903	488	2,399	214	203	116	...
1965	45	8,109	541	2,536	149	251	128	143
1966	54	9,108	612	...	194	280	139	141
1967	54	10,461	683	...	201[18]	260	150	140[21]
								179
1968	66	11,672	710	...	203	242	146	200
1969	75	12,889[5]	810	...	231	288	167	207
		14,270						
1970	98	15,990	975	...	254	283	178	239
1971	114	18,420	1,247	...	296[19]	328	203[9]	273
1972	124	21,320	1,414	...	359	351	204	284
1973	168	24,670	1,865[6]	...	413	391	245	307
			1,846					
1974	198[4]	31,460	2,415	...	548	542	318	367
		thousand million						
1975	234	37.47[5]	3,217	...	632	605	348	600
		36.00						
1976	288	39.69	4,148	...	633	827	438	729
1977	328	45.06	5,085	...	669	1,077	594	973
1978	325	50.51	7,000	...	745	1,184	667	1,116
1979	396	55.54	8,601	...	969	1,280	785[9]	865
			thousand million					
1980	532	65.52	10.37	...	1,122	1,422	1,128	1,332
1981	625[4]	76.15	11.99	...	1,174	1,581	1,387	1,482
1982	608	89.36	17.94	...	1,077	1,695	1,278	1,832
1983	636	98.81	30.49	...	1,205	1,571	1,169[9]	2,082
1984	707	111.4	37.2	...	...	1,821	1,015	1,785
1985	797	117.2	43.1	...	...	2,150	1,053	2,035
1986	824	119.3	65.1	...	...	2,723	1,512	1,968
1987	1,008	127.1	77.4	...	...	3,023	1,979	2,075
1988	1,071	133.3	85.7	...	5,368	3,096	2,455	...
1989	1,136	149.0	111.1	...	6,161	3,307	2,775	...
1990	...	159.5	133.9	...	7,029	3,855	3,444	1,800
1991	...	166.7	171.1	...	10,677	4,928	4,272	...
1992	...	174.1	216.4	...	15,041	7,254	5,607	...
1993	...	178.9	280.7	...	21,123	8,314	6,229	...

G5 NORTH AMERICA: Total Central Government Expenditure (in millions of stated currency unit, except as otherwise indicated)

	Honduras[10] lempiras	Jamaica[2] pounds	Mexico[3] pesos	Nicaragua[13] cordobas	Panama[14] balboas	Puerto Rico[15] dollars	Trinidad & Tobago dollars	USA[1] dollars
								thousand million dollars
1945	18	7.6	1,633	60	34	62	34	98
1946	22	7.9	1,829	58	39	113	32	60
1947	29	8.4	2,343	66	39	97	37	39
1948	26	10.1	2,773	70	35	109	39	33
1949	38	9.9	3,741	77	33	132	42	39
1950	39	10	3,700	... [13]	37	136	50	40
1951	46	14	5,075	112	34	141	53	44
1952	59	14	6,063	135	39	141	62	65
1953	62	15	5,825	166	42	168[17] / 160	67	74
1954	63	17	8,471	166	44	171	74	71
1955	72	20	9,255	220	47	179	79	69
1956	[43][10]	22	10,567	246	55	185	86	70
1957	87	29	11,815	252	52	227	90	77
1958	89	34	13,841	262	64	236	128	83
1959	83	37	14,777	263	56	254	169	92
1960	89	38	20,778	263	65	279	169	92
1961	88	42	20,946	251	78	307	196	98
1962	93[10] / 84	46	21,421	296	73	315	212	107
1963	85	47	21,371	323	85	378	229	111
1964	100	55	29,660	366	78[14]	425	265	119
			thousand million					
1965	108	64	37.7	432	90	479	251	118
1966	125	67	34.5[3] / 31.9	520	107	541	267	135
1967	133	74	33.9	583	126	586	271	158
1968	153	86	39.4	529	128	719	305	178
		dollars[17]						
1969	183	191	46.9	581	195	766	327	184
1970	217	236	48.6	718	209	891	390	196
1971	226	287	52[3]	871	213	1,133	465	210
1972	238	333	67	918	303[14]	1,263[15] / 1,549	539	231
1973	235	417	88	972	387	1,797	574	246
1974	263	627	124	1,631	504	1,957	1,301	269
1975	320	823	162	1,916	582	2,405	1,681[21]	332
1976	384	1,013	212	2,040	626	2,646	1,600	372[1]
1977	554	1,428	286	2,936	650	2,840	1,913	409
1978	579	1,724	367	2,526	737	3,020	2,680	459
1979	735	2,165	505	2,999	1,066	3,297	3,655	503
1980	897	2,488	750	6,332	1,163	3,696	4,622	591
1981	883	2,417	1,182	9,620	1,322	4,033	5,061[22]	678
1982	1,150	2,806	2,829	13,993	1,612	4,018	9,464	746
1983	1,382	3,643	4,468	22,274	1,512	4,111	8,780	808
1984	1,630	4,727	6,747	28,775	1,653	...	8,276	852
			million million	*thousand million*				
1985	1,718	4,671	11.8	69	1,504	...	7,684	946
1986	1,644	5,674	22.8	228	1,621	...	6,570	990
1987	1,589	6,012	59.7	...	1,702	...	6,387	1,084
1988	1,652	8,733	107.3	155	1,237	...	6,061	1,118
1989	1,873	9,546	115.4	...	1,178	...	5,855	1,195
				million gold cordobas				
1990	2,484	9,424	134.1	113	1,264	...	...	1,305
1991	2,726	17,510	144.8	2,035	1,390	...	...	1,429
1992	3,106	26,871	165.6	2,762	1,661	...	...	1,445
1993	3,821	41,757	188.1	3,322	1,779	...	...	1,492

G5 SOUTH AMERICA: TOTAL CENTRAL GOVERNMENT EXPENDITURE (in millions of stated currency unit, except as otherwise indicated)

1823–1864

	Argentina[23] gold pesos	Brazil[24] milreis	Chile[25] pesos	Guyana[26] thousand dollars	Peru[27] pesos	Venezuala[28] pesos
1823	...	4.7	...	...	...	...
1824	...	9.6	...	...	...	...
1825	...	8.4	...	...	...	...
1826	...	9.4	...	...	...	...
1827	...	12	...	...	...	...
1828	...	11[24]	...	...	...	...
1829		14				
1830	...	18	...	...	...	5.1
1831	...	20	...	...	...	5.7
1832	...	12	...	...	...	5.6
1833	...	14	...	...	...	6.2
1834	...	11	...	...	...	5.8
1835	...	13	...	...	...	6.0
1836	...	14	...	...	...	8.2
1837	...	14	...	...	...	7.3
1838	...	19	...	605	...	7.2
1839	...	18	...	638	...	9.7
1840	...	25	...	584	...	7.2
1841	...	23	...	1,066	...	7.7
1842	...	27	...	862	...	14
1843	...	29	...	810	...	9.4
1844	...	26	...	680	...	15
1845	...	26	...	867	...	12
1846	...	24	...	1,207	} 12 {	18
1847	...	27	...	1,364		12
1848	...	26	...		} 11 {	14
1849	...	28	...	632		17
1850	...	29	...	875	} 11 {	17
1851	...	33	...	926		19
1852	...	43	...	1,090	} 14 {	14
1853	...	32	...	1,138		24
1854	...	36	...	1,099	} 20 {	23
1855	...	39	...	1,152		32
1856	...	40	...	1,128	...	25
1857	...	40	17	1,349	...	23
1858	...	52	19	1,306	...	20
1859	...	53	20	1,262	...	11
1860	...	53	19	1,512	...	29
1861	...	52	16	1,560	} 33 {	34
1862	...	53	16	1,493		24
1863	...	57	18	1,282	} 44 {	11
1864	7.1	56	20	1,210		24

G5 SOUTH AMERICA: Total Central Government Expenditure (in millions of stated currency unit, except as otherwies indicated)

1865–1804

	Argentina[23]	Bolivia[29]	Brazil[24]	Chile[25]	Ecuador	Guyana[26] thousand	Paraguay[31]	Peru[27]	Surinam	Uruguay[32]	Venezuela[28]
	gold pesos	bolivianos	milreis	pesos	sucres	dollars	gold pesos	soles	guilders	pesos	bolivares
1865	13	...	83	25	...	1,306	...	...	...	...	25
1866	14	...	122	35	...	1,363	...	...	...	...	21
1867	14	...	121	36	...	1,392	...	...	...	...	15
1868	17	...	166	31	...	1,344	...	...	...	...	20
1869	15	...	151	30	...	1,435	...	} 62 {	...	6.5	22
1870	19	...	142	32	...	1,464	...		...	...	10
1871	21	...	100	33	...	1,493	...	} 59 {	...	6.3	9.9
1872	26	...	102	36	...	1,584	...		...	...	15
1873	31	...	122	40	...	1,752	...	} 47 {	...	6.7	17
1874	30	...	121	50	...	1,733	...		...	8.7	25
1875	29	...	126	48	...	1,709	...	} 74 {	...	13	22
1876	22	...	127	42	...	1,651	...		...	5.0	24
1877	20	...	136	43	...	1,829	...	} 43 {	...	...	21
1878	21	...	151	32	...	2,006	...		...	...	9.8
1879	23	...	181	44	...	2,414	...	} 30 {	...	8.7	24
1880	27	...	150	44	...	2,290	...		...	...	23
1881	28	...	139	55	...	3,163	0.8	...	...	...	30
	paper pesos										
1882	58	...	139	76	...	3,269	0.8	...	...	...	25
1883	45	...	153	84	...	2,621	0.8	...	...	9.9	36
1884	56	...	154	73	...	2,712	1.1	...	...	12	35
1885	56	...	158	50	3.9	2,837	1.3	...	...	13	31
1886	54	...	154	67	4.7	2,549	3.0	...	...	13	29
1887	65	...	[227][24]	74	4.4	3,283	0.8	} 14 {	1.5	14	42
1888	76	4.6	147	60	[4.4][30]	[2,520][26]	1.4		1.6	14	37
1889	107	3.6	186	77	3.1	2,530	2.1	} 13 {	1.5	...	46
1890	95	3.6	221	91	3.8	2,707	0.9		1.5	...	49
1891	129	3.6	221	98	3.9	2,809	0.5	6.6	1.7	...	45
1892	129	5.9	279	68	4.1	2,678	0.7	7.1	1.7	15	33
1893	123	5.7	301	50	4.4	2,894	0.9	8	1.9	...	52
1894	143	6.1	373	48	...	2,904	0.8	7.3	2.1	16	44
1895	167	6.7[24]	345	74	...	2,990	0.9	...	2	...	66
1896	230	4.3	369	103	...	2,957	1.1	9.3	2.3	...	47
1897	179	...	379	72	5.7	2,765	1.0	11	2.3	...	46
1898	311	5.7	668	88	5.4	2,606	1.1	11[27] 12	2.2	16	36
1899	174	8.1	295	82	6.7	2,587	1.1	12	2.2	16	24
1900	159	7.9	434	92[25] 277	7.4	2,438	1.5	13	2.2	...	38
1901	163	7.8	335	310	9.3	2,530	...	14	2.5	...	32
1902	203	9.3	298	309	13	2,410	...	14	2.4	15	24
1903	183	7.5	363	272	12	2,549	...	15	4.4	...	38
1904	195	6.1	463	331	11	2,453	...	19	5	16	51

G5 SOUTH AMERICA: Total Central Government Expenditure (in millions of stated currency unit, except as otherwise indicated)

1905–1949

	Argentina[23] paper pesos	Bolivia bolivianos	Brazil[24] milreis or cruzeiros	Chile[25] pesos	Colombia[33] pesos	Ecuador sucres
1905	322	7.5	375	312	7.0	10
1906	270	12	423	357	...	13
1907	253	15	522	363	16	15
1908	252	17	511	322	[17][30]	13
1909	392	17	518	377	[17][30]	16
1910	411	13	624	490	12	15
1911	417	18	682	460	12	16
1912	404	16	789	558	14	20
1913	403	22	763	496	16	22
1914	420	23	767	519	15	23
1915	391	21	689	462	13	[21][30]
1916	375	23	687	486	[20][33]	[18][30]
1917	390	17	801	577	15	[18][30]
1918	421	33	867	665	18	17
1919	428	31	932	549	[17][33]	14
1920	488	54	1,227	793	23	23
1921	560	47	1,189	629[25] 605	24	22
1922	614	40	1,428	566	...	27
1923	632	38	1,569	618	39	29
1924	671	45	1,630	677	40	35
1925	713	45	1,760	825	50	44
1926	746	48	1,868	1,122	67	44
1927	1,049	50	2,026	906	84	70
1928	919	61	2,350	1,484	115	57
1929	988	53	2,422	1,596	83	63
1930	1,092	49	2,511	1,663	61	60
1931	908	31	2,047	1,223	52	45
1932	850	34	2,860	992	46	42
1933	880	104	2,392	944	63	42
1934	934	129	3,050	975	75	48
1935	981	193	2,872	1,291	61	65
1936	1,052	...	3,226	1,383	72	76
1937	1,221	...	4,144	1,545	86	80
1938	1,278	339	4,735	1,745	88	132
1939	1,460	400	4,850	1,839	97	117
1940	1,322	564	5,189	2,282	129	114
1941	1,371	1,018	5,436	2,811	110	128
1942	1,554	1,162	6,343	3,069	154	128
1943	1,786	1,200	6,512	4,386	177	176
1944	2,491	1,170	8,399	4,534	174	231
1945	2,815	1,183	10,839	6,327	194	293
1946	3,321	1,183	14,203	7,264	276	336
1947	4,220	1,307	13,393	10,112	356	403
1948	7,076	1,667	15,696	12,509	403	391
1949	7,783	1,813	20,727	14,860	402	396

G5 SOUTH AMERICA: Total Central Government Expenditure (in millions of stated currency unit, except as otherwise indicated)

1905–1949

	Guyana[26] thousand dollars	Paraguay[31] gold pesos	Peru[27] soles	Surinam guilders	Uruguay[32] pesos	Venezuela[28] bolivares
1905	2,429	...	21	4.3	17	50
1906	2,467	...	24	4.8	19	61
1907	2,496	...	27	4.3	19	49
1908	2,587	...	30	5.1	21	48
1909	2,635	...	27	5.1	26	52
1910	2,621	...	27	6.7	32	62
1911	2,827	...	30	7.3	32	64
1912	2,837	...:31	37	7.0	38	62
1913	3,082	4.9	54	7.3	35	65
1914	3,331	3.8	41	7.1	35	45
1915	[2,150][26]	4.2	34	7.3	32	58
1916	3,254	3.4	36	4.2	28	58
1917	3,552	...	48	4.9	30	53
1918	6,062	...	54	5.1	30	58
1919	5,453	5.4[31]	66	5.2	...	68
		paper pesos				
1920	5,294	70	89	9.8	42	103
1921	6,883	114	88	...	43	81
1922	6,125	145	88	9.6	42	72
1923	6,370	151	91	9.1	61	87
1924	6,293	161	118	8.7	59	115
1925	7,277	178	128	8.1	59	163
1926	7,642	235	189	8.2	56	179
1927	6,485	219	185	7.7	59	156
1928	7,882	248	257	8.2	66	245
1929	6,648	281	205	7.8	59	264
1930	5,885	287	149	7.6	63	261
1931	5,309	231	136	7.8	62	166
1932	5,395	233	99	7.7	[30][32]	162
1933	5,189	...	132	6.8	61	154
1934	5,462	...	169	6.8	61	179
1935	6,427	323	139	6.7	81	233
1936	5,765	762	195	6.7	86	285
1937	6,206[26] 6,051	1,889	198	6.3	86	313
1938	6,153	345	265	6.5	92	361
1939	6,425	256	236	6.9	97	382
	million	**guaranies[17]**				
1940	6.8	17[31]	210	7.5	101	347
1941	7.1	20	328	5.8	107	320
1942	8.0	20	409	11	113	307
1943	11	25	423	17	122	363
1944	13	26	503	16	134	488
1945	14	31	536	12	143	755
1946	14	36	699	12	167	1,065
1947	17	57	970	18	190	1,438
1948	20	45	1,094	20	232	1,946
1949	21	53	1,143	25	257	1,928

G5   SOUTH AMERICA: Total Central Government Expenditure (in millions of stated currency unit, except as otherwise indicated)

	Argentina[23] thousand million paper pesos	Bolivia thousand million bolivianos	Brazil[24] thousand million cruzeiros	Chile[25] thousand million pesos	Colombia[33] pesos	Ecuador[34] sucres
1950	8.7	2.36	24	20	520	426[34] 488
1951	13.4	3.71	27	26	691[33] 615	533
1952	15.4	4.19	30	42	646	587
1953	16.4	9.00	52	54	855	776
1954	18.1	15	54	83	1,043	1,072
				escudos[17]		
1955	20	26	65	156	1,588	1,237
1956	26	77	98	231	1,220	1,240
1957	[28][23]	273	138	351	1,243	1,237
1958	67	331	162	457	1,573	1,217
1959	109[23]	453	222	647	1,718[33] 1,574	1,333
1960	126	454	324	903	2,191	1,740
1961	165	520	509	1,030	3,188	2,081
1962	197	544	847	1,273	2,583	1,878
		pesos[17]				
1963	226	619	1,556	1,728	4,011	1,905
1964	349	701	2,857	2,378	4,263	2,462
1965	395	928	4,500	3,992	4,629	2,624
1966	598	1,023	6,497	5,693	6,094	2,831
	[23]		new cruzeiros[17]	thousand million	thousand million	
1967	551	1,177	8.0	6.9	7.1	3,027
1968	577	1,440	12	9.7	10.4	3,785
1969	660	1,360	15	13.7	13.5	4,200
	thousand million new pesos[17]					thousand million
1970	7.6	1,399	20[24] 34	22	16.9	5.3
1971	11.6	1,708	46	36	20.8	6.2
1972	18.4	2,019	60	65	22.0	6.4[34]
1973	38.7	3,370	80	305	27.2	7.8
1974	59.5	…	117	2,985[25] 3,042	33.1	11.4
	202 [23]	thousand million		thousand million pesos[17]		
1975	280	6.8	184	12.2	46.8	13.1
1976	1,340	8.8	291	38.8	52.8	16.8
1977	3,250	11	464	92.1	72.8	21.8
1978	9,260	12	716	155	101	21.4
	million million					
1979	24.8	15	1,094	222	156	24.6
1980	53.8	22	2,507	301	195	41.7
1981	123	24	4,988	375	237	56.1
1982	305	130	10,561	423	331	64.5
	australes[17]					
1983	149[35]	356	24,939	497	402	74.2
1984	885[35]	8,221	79,723	617	541	107
	thousand million	million million	thousand million cruzados[17]			
1985	9.4	1,384	351	806	698	168
1986	16.0	1,010	1,021	969	924	218
1987	35.5	1,110[36]	2,871	1,218	1,209	279
1988	120	1,515[36]	27,094	1,620[21]	1,608	413
	million pesos		reais			
1989	305.6	1,929	160,561	1,571	2,158	735
			thousand reais			
1990	7,282.6	2,530	4,027	1,884	2,343	1,190
1991	20,648.6	3,221	14,685	2,542	3,011	1,739
1992	27,271.7	4,461	187,241	3,152	5,094	3,145
			million reais			
1993	…	5,877	5,250	3,843	6,309	4,166

G5 SOUTH AMERICA: Total Central Government Expenditure (in millions of stated currency unit, except as otherwise indicated)

	Guyana[26] dollars	Paraguay[31] guaranies	Peru[27] soles	Surinam guilders	Uruguay[32] pesos	Venezuela[28] bolivares
1950	24	[124][31]	1,716	29	307	2,156
1951	25	...	2,037	27	365	2,375
1952	28	171[31]	2,200	29	376	2,377
1953	31	382	2,692[27] 3,525	37	431	2,430
1954	35	...	3,819	42	503	2,798
1955	40	...	4,770	43	505	3,052
1956	40	...	5,773	46	516	3,804
1957	43	...	6,027	55	709	5,442
1958	46	2,231	6,226	65	791	6,248
1959	46	2,312	6,858	69	843	6,484
1960	50	2,451	7,120	85	1,347	6,718
1961	57	2,805	9,427	93	2,253	[3,400][28]
1962	62	3,339	10,718	97	3,009	6,258
1963	62	4,240	12,761	96	3,261	6,590
1964	71	4,090	16,341	101	4,646	7,100
		thousand million	thousand million		thousand million	thousand million
1965	82	4.5	21.5	108	8.2	7.4
1966	84	6.7	25.4	124	14	7.8
1967	88	7.8[31] 6.9	29.9[27]	131	25	8.2[28]
1968	98	7.6	34.1	144	53	9.0
1969	107[26]	8.4	34.3	167	74	9.6[28]
1970	169	8.7	42.3	190	91	9.8
1971	173	9.3	49.5	200	145[32]	11.1
1972	202	12.4	56.5	223	306	12.7
1973	280	13.3	67.4	218	580	14.2
1974	340	16.3	82.6	237	1,084	22.8
					new pesos	
1975	560	21.2	118	318	1,877	27.5
1976	685	25.3	160	424	3,054	32.7
1977	513	29.2	233	541	4,677	42.2
1978	533	37.7	344	537	7,068	46.3
1979	689	45.5	570	542	11,615	44.8
					thousand million	
1980	906	56.8	1,159	581	20.1	55.8
1981	1,154	75.6	1,928	714	30.5	84.5
1982	1,508	86.7	3,050	788	38.1	84.5[28]
1983	1,141	87.3	6,083	801	46.3	73.4
1984	1,457	115	12,496	768	69.4	82.6
			thousand million intis[17]			
1985	1,913	127	32.3	803	118	94.6
1986	2,353	148	58	926	223	105
1987	2,715	225	108	...	406	175
1988	3,098	295	558	...	708	235
1989	5,017	412	13,455	...	1,792	327
			new soles			
1990	11,237	609	831	...	2,539	510
1991	15,430	991	3,496	...	5,550	723
1992	21,332	1,307	6,765	...	10,165	824
1993	24,940	1,560	11,187	...	18,103	1,015

G5A   TOTAL EXPENDITURE OF CANADIAN COLONIES BEFORE CONFEDERATION CANADA (in thousand pounds)[37]

1805–1839

	Lower Canada*	Upper Canada†
1805	...	...
1806	35	...
1807	42	...
1808	43	...
1809	39	...
1810	47	...
1811	47	...
1812	98	...
1813	181	...
1814	161	...
1815	91	...
1816	50	...
1817	109	...
1818	121	...
1819	72	...
1820	54	...
1821	79	...
1822	74	...
1823	106	...
1824	84	44
1825	80	35
1826	80	72
1827	101	90
1828	62	42
1829	170	49
1830	161	98
1831	164	100
1832	166	80
1833	126	125
1834	124	310
1835	71	221
1836	2.3	} 636 {
1837	0.3	
1838	223	260
1839	166	196

*later Quebec †later Ontario

1840–1866

	British Columbia[36]	Lower Canada*	Upper Canada†	New Brunswick	Nova Scotia[40]	Prince Edward Island
1840	—	[197][38]	[252][38]	...	...	...
1841	—	...	...	...	...	...
		Province of Canada[39]				
1842	—	476		...	...	...
1843	—	771I		...	...	...
1844	—	957		...	...	...
1845	—	906		...	...	...
1846	—	770		...	...	...
1847	—	716		...	...	...
1848	—	[390][39]		...	...	...
1849	—	[371][39]		...	...	...
1850	—	673		85	92	9
1851	—	722		89	101	16
1852		927		129	114	15
1853	—	1,384		105	107	20
1854	—	1,737		136	169	35
1855	—	1,217		138	...	30
1856	—	[946][39]		...	34	
		142		——[40]		
1857	—	2,359		135	159	32
1858	—	2,212		133	148	29
1859	13	1,932		154	138	30
1860	70	2,989		174	117	41
1861	99	2,467		176	130	33
1862	170	2,284		167	119	34
1863	181	2,207[39]		185	139	36
1864	179	3,143		176	137	39
1865	206	2,685		190	220	51
1866	94	2,587		281	279	103

G5 Total Central Government Expenditure

NOTES

1. SOURCES:- The national publications listed on pp. xiii–xv, with gaps filled from League of Nations, *Public Finance Statistics and Statistical Yearbooks*, and U.N. *Statistical Yearbooks*. From the 1960s, International Monetary Fund, *International Financial Statistics* is the main source.
2. So far as possible, all kinds of central government budgetary expenditure, other than debt redemption, are included in this table. However, in many cases extra-budgetary expenditures are included, and the types of outlay included within the budget have varied very much from country to country and from time to time. So far as possible, changes and the reasons for them are indicated in footnotes.
3. It must be recalled that in some countries, especially those with federal systems of government, central government expenditures may be no more important than the outlays of 'local' governments.
4. Except where otherwise indicated, statistics are taken from closed accounts, not budgets.

FOOTNOTES

[1] Federal government expenditure exclusive of debt repayment. Prior to 1913, expenditures are on a gross basis, but subsequently various refunds are treated as reductions. Certain inter-fund transactions are not excluded until 1932, but the amounts involved were insignificant. From 1844 to 1976 data apply to years ended 30 June. Subsequently they are for years ended 30 September. The 1843 figure is for the first half-year only. Expenditure in July–September 1976 was $96 thousand million.

[2] Statistics to 1889 are for years ended 30 September. Subsequently they are for years beginning 1 April.

[3] Federal government ordinary expenditure to 1971, but with a narrower definition from 1966 (2nd line). Consolidated central government expenditure subsequently.

[4] Statistics from 1901 are for years beginning 1 April. Some extra-budgetary funds are included from 1975 and more from 1982.

[5] Federal government expenditure exclusive of debt repayment. Some extra-budgetary items are included from 1960 and more from 1969, but from 1970 (2nd line) figures are of consolidated central government expenditure. Data to 1906 are for years ended 30 June. Subsequently they are for years beginning 1 April. Expenditure in the period 1 July 1906 to 31 March 1907 was $65 million.

[6] Ordinary budget expenditure only to 1955 (1st line), and consolidated central government expenditure from 1973 (2nd line). Data to 1907 are for years beginning 1 April. The 1908 figure is for the period 1 April to 31 December.

[7] Budget estimates to 1926, except for 1888, which is a provisional result, and 1889, which is actual expenditure. Outlays under special laws are not included. Data to 1937 and from 1947 to 1958 are for years beginning 1 July.

[8] Statistics for 1910 to 1927 are of estimates rather than actual expenditure. Data to 1938 are for years beginning 1 July. The 1939 figure is for the second half-year only.

[9] Ordinary budget expenditure only to 1906 (1st line), and budgetary central government expenditure from 1972, except in 1980–1983 when various extra-budgetary expenditures are included. Data from 1927 to 958 are for years ended 30 June.

[10] Statistics to 1962 (1st line) are of ordinary budget expenditure. Subsequently they are of consolidated central government expenditure. Data to 1937 are for years beginning 1 August, and those for 1939–55 are for years beginning 1 July. The 1938 figures is for the period 1 August 1938 to 30 June 1939, and the 1956 figure is for the second half-year only.

[11] There was a change in the treatment of Immigration Fund expenditure in 1894. Tobago is included from 1899. Statistics from 1901 to 1914 are for years beginning 1 April. The 1915 figure is for the period 1 April tp 31 December.

[12] Years ended 30 September.

[13] Years beginning 1 July to 1949.

[14] Ordinary budget expenditure only to 1927–8 (1st line). Data to 1929–30 are for one- or two-year periods beginning 1 July. The 1931–2 figure is for the period 1 March 1931 to 28 February 1933. Subsequent statistics are for one or two calendar years. Expenditure on floating debt is excluded from 1965, and from 1973 the figures are of consolidated central government expenditure.

[15] Statistics to 1953 (1st line) include certain refund payments. Coverage is wider from 1972 (2nd line). They are for years ended 30 June throughout.

[16] Including £300 thousand transferred to a 'Special Reserve Fund'.

[17] See p. xi for conversion rates between old and new currencies.

[18] On a cash basis subsequently.

[19] Including social security and extra-budgetary expenditures from 1972.

[20] Ten months only, the first two months of the fiscal year being omitted.

[21] The reason for this break is not given in the sources.

[22] Subsequently budgetary central government expenditure only.

[23] Budgetary central government expenditure exclusive of debt repayment to 1975 (1st line) and consolidated central government expenditure subsequently. The 1957 figure is for the ten months ended 31 October, and the 1958 and 1959 figures are for years ended 31 October.

[24] Federal government expenditure exclusive of debt repayment to 1970 (1st line) and consolidated central government expenditure subsequently. Statistics from 1829 to 1886 are for years ended 30 June. The 1887 figure is for the 18 months from 1 July 1886 to 31 December 1887.

[25] Fiscal expenditure only to 1900 (1st line). There was a reorganisation of the system of accounts in 1921. Some extra-budgetary expenditures are included from 1974 (2nd line).

[26] Budgetary expenditure to 1969 and consolidated central government expenditure subsequently. From 1937 to 1949 (1st line) only current expenditure is covered.

[27] Budgeted expenditures of the ordinary and extraordinary budgets to 1898 (1st line) and realised expenditure from 1898 (2nd line) to 1953 (1st line). Consolidated central government exoenditure subsequently, with wider coverage of government agencies and some other outlays from 1968.

[28] Statistics to 1960 are for years beginning 1 July. The 1961 figure is for the second half-year only. There was a widening of coverage to include various extra-budgetary expenditures in 1968, 1970, and 1984.

[29] Statistics to 1895 are estimates.

[30] Budget estimates.

[31] Statistics to 1900 are for years ended 30 June, and from 1920 to 1940 they are for years ended 31 August. The 1950 figure is for the 18 months ended 30 June 1951, and the 1952 figure is for the year ended 30 June. Debt amortisation and extra-budgetary expenditures are included to 1967 (1st line).

G5 Total Central Government Expenditure

[32] Statistics to 1899 are estimates. They are for years beginning 1 July to 1931. The 1932 figure is for the second half-year only. Extra-budgetary expenditure is included from 1972.

[33] There was change in the treatment of debt charges in 1951, and a narrowing of the coverage of budget expenditure in 1959. The figure for 1916 is for 14 months ended 28 February 1917, and those for 1917 and 1918 are for years beginning 1 March, and that for 1919 is for ten months from 1 March to 31 December.

[34] Coverage was widened in 1951, but from 1973 it was confined to budgetary central government expenditure.

[35] In 1983 and 1984 the peso argentino was the currency actually in use, but the figures have been converted here to the austral, which was introduced in 1985.

[36] In 1987 and 1988 the boliviano was the currency actually in use, but for the sake of continuity, the figures have been converted here to the previous currency. For the conversion ratio see p. xii.

[37] Local currency to 1841. This was often converted to sterling on the conventional basis that '1 local was equal to 18 shillings sterling.

[38] From 1 January 1840 to 9 February 1841.

[39] Statistics for 1848, 1849, and 1856 are net. The equivalent figure for 1850 is 437. A new system of accounts was adopted in 1857. Data for 1864–66 are for years ended 30 June.

[40] Statistics from 1857 are for years ended 30 September.

G6 NORTH AMERICA: CENTRAL GOVERNMENT REVENUE, WITH SOME MAIN TAX YIELDS (in millions of stated currency unit, except as otherwise indicated)

1759-1784

	Cuba[1]
	Total
	thousand pesos
1759	164
1760	164
1761	316
1762	...
1763	...
1764	316
1765	...
1766	...
1767	...
1768	...
1769	...
1770	...
1771	...
1772	...
1773	...
1774	...
1775	561
1776	726
1777	1,027
1778	885
1779	956
1780	1,001
1781	1,066
1782	1,424
1783	1,211
1784	1,203

1785-1824

	Cuba[1]	USA[2]		
	Total	**Customs**	**Internal Revenue[3]**	**Total**
	thousand pesos	dollars		
1785	1,203	...	...	...
1786	498	...	...	...
1787	865	...	...	...
1788	892	...	...	...
1789	740		—	4.4
1790	974	4.4		
1791	825			
1792	1,118	3.4	0.2	3.7
1793	1,085	4.3	0.3	4.7
1794	1,137	4.8	0.3	5.4
1795	...	5.6	0.3	6.1
1796	...	6.6	0.5	8.4
1797	...	7.6	0.6	8.7
1798	...	7.1	0.6	7.9
1799	...	6.6	0.8	7.5
1800	...	9.1	0.8	11
1801	...	11	1.0	13
1802	...	12	0.6	15
1803	...	10	0.2	11
1804	...	11	0.1	12
1805	...	13	- -	14
1806	...	15	- -	16
1807	...	16	- -	16
1808	3,168	16	- -	17
1809	4,873	7.3	- -	7.8
1810	4,115	8.6	- -	9.4
1811	2,558	13	- -	14
1812	2,379	9.0	- -	9.8
1813	...	13	- -	14
1814	2,431	6.0	1.7	11
	pesos			
1815	3.4	7.3	4.7	16
1816	2.8	36	5.1	48
1817	3.1	26	2.7	33
1818	3.8	17	1.0	22
1819	4.1	20	0.2	25
1820	3.5	15	0.1	18
1821	3.3	13	0.1	15
1822	4.4	18	0.1	20
1823	4.2	19	- -	21
1824	5.0	18	- -	19

G6 NORTH AMERICA: Central Government Revenue, with some Main Tax Yields (in millions of stated currency unit, except as otherwise indicated)

1825–1864

	Barbados	Cuba[1]	Jamaica[4]	Mexico[5]	Trinidad[6]	USA[2]		
	Total	Total	Total	Total	Total	Customs	Internal Revenue[3]	Total
	thousand pounds	pesos	thousand pounds	pesos	thousand pounds		dollars	
1825	...	5.7	...	15	...	20	- -	22
1826	...	7.1	...	15	...	23	- -	25
1827	...	8.5	...	17	...	20	- -	23
1828	...	9.1	...	14	...	23	- -	25
1829	...	9.1	...	15	...	23	- -	25
1830	...	9.0	...	14	...	22	- -	25
1831	...	8.3	...	18	...	24	- -	29
1832	...	8.4	...	18	...	28	- -	32
1833	...	8.9	...	21	...	29	- -	34
1834	...	8.9	...	21	...	16	- -	22
1835	41	8.8	...	18	...	19	- -	35
1836	...	9.3	...	26	...	23	- -	51
1837	...	8.8	...	17	...	11	- -	25
1838	...	9.7	...	25	...	16	- -	26
1839	...	11	...	29	...	23	- -	31
1840	54	12	161	21	...	14	- -	19
1841	...	11	271	24	...	14	- -	17
1842	...	12	322	31	...	18	- -	20
1843	...	10	388	34	...	[7.0][2]	[- -][2]	[8.3][2]
1844	...	10	290	32	...	26	- -	29
1845	51	9.2	280	24	...	28	- -	30
1846	...	11	261	24	...	27	- -	30
1847	...	13	240	26	...	24	- -	26
1848	...	13	191	26	...	32	- -	36
1849	...	13	176	18	...	28	—	31
1850	54	10	181	15	89	40	—	44
1851	56	13	209	11	96	49	—	53
1852	59	12	237	10	107	47	—	50
1853	62	12	156	19	143	59	—	62
1854	60	13	118	26	101	64	—	74
1855	59	14	206	16	72	53	—	65
1856	82	15	210	16	93	64	—	74
1857	83	17	210	16	137	64	—	69
1858	97	18	178	15	145	42	—	47
1859	88	19	280	14	167	50	—	53
1860	95	19	262	13	175	53	—	56
1861	98	...	274	16	172	40	—	42
1862	94	...	291	18	199	49	—	52
1863	103	18	286	7.0	184	69	38	113
1864	107	22	308	6.0	207	102	110	265

G6 NORTH AMERICA: Central Government Revenue, with some Main Tax Yields (in millions of state currency unit, except as otherwise indicated)

1865–1904

	Barbados[12]	Canada[7]			Costa Rica[9]	Cuba[1]	El Salvador[10]	Guatemala
	Total	Customs	Excises[8]	Total	Total	Total	Total	Total
	thousand pounds		dollars		paper pesos	pesos	silver pesos	pesos
1865	99	...	...	...	...	...[1]	...	...
1866	104	...	...	...	...	...	...	...
1867	98	8.6	3.0	14	...	31	...	...
1868	106	8.4	2.7	14	...	31	...	...
1869	103	9.3	3.6	16	...	...	...	...
1870	105	12	4.3	19	...	...	...	...
1871	119	13	4.7	21	...	...	...	...
1872	118	13	4.5	21	...	...	...	...
1873	124	14	5.6	25	...	...	...	...
1874	124	15	5.1	25	...	...	...	...
1875	132	13	5.6	23	...	...	...	...
1876	117	13	4.9	23	...	...	...	...
1877	121	13	4.8	22	...	...	...	...
1878	139	13	5.4	27	...	...	...	...
1879	121	14	4.2	23	...	...	...	...
1880	136	18	5.3	30	...	...	...	...
1881	132	22	5.9	35	...	44	...	...
1882	140	23	6.3	37	...	...	...	7.5
1883	139	20	5.5	33	...	36	4.1	6.6
1884	144	19	6.5	33	2.0	35	4.1	5.9
1885	144	19	5.8	34	2.4	35	3.6	8.3
1886	135	22	6.3	36	2.4	32	4.5	8.5
1887	152	22	6.1	36	3.1	32	3.0	...
1888	162	24	6.9	39	4.3	24[1]	3.8	...
1889	173	24	7.6	40	5.2	26[1]	4.1	...
1890	186	23	6.9	39	5.6	...	4.2	6.2
1891	163	21	7.9	37	5.8	26	7.5	7.3
1892	163	21	8.4	38	...	...	6.9	8.7
1893	162	19	8.4	36	4.8	23	7.1	8.7
1894	161	18	7.8	34	6.1	...	8.8	9.4
1895	146	20	7.9	37	6.5	...	8.4	12
1896	177	19	9.2	38	7.4	25	8.7	14
1897	185	22	7.9	41	8.4	25	7.7	15
1898	183	25	9.6	47	8.4	25	4.6	12
1899	176	28	9.9	51	8.2	26[1]	5.3	9.7
1900	185[12]	28	10	53	8.7	...	6.7	8.6
1901	180	32	11	58	5.6	...	7.7	9.1
1902	162	37	12	69	5.5	16	8.6	14
1903	182	41	13	71	6.4	22	6.8	18
1904	185	42	13	71	5.3	29	8.1	18

G6   NORTH AMERICA: Central Government Revenue, with some Main Tax Yields (in millions of stated currency unit, except as otherwise indicated)

1865–1904

	Haiti[14]	Honduras[11]	Jamaica[4]	Mexico[5]	Nicaragua[15]	Trinidad[6]	USA[2]		
	Total	Total	Total	Total	Total	Total	Customs	Internal Revenue[3]	Total
	gourdes	pesos	thousand pounds	pesos	pesos	thousand pounds		dollars	
1865	...	...	333	5.1	...	220	85	209	334
1866	...	...	334	8.1	...	218	179	309	558
1867	...	...	383	17	...	216	176	266	491
1868	...	...	372	14	...	211	164	191	406
1869	...	...	446	14	...	244	180	158	371
1870	...	...	447	18	...	234	195	185	411
1871	...	...	439	19	...	272	206	143	383
1872	...	...	495	20	...	296	216	131	374
1873	...	...	515	23	...	282	188	114	334
1874	...	...	542	22	...	385	163	102	305
1875	...	...	591	16	...	342	157	110	288
1876	...	...	573	17	...	316	148	117	294
1877	...	...	533	29	...	310	131	119	281
1878	...	...	539	29	...	369	130	111	258
1879	...	1.0	547	21	...	425	137	114	274
1880	...	1.1	599	26	...	431	187	124	334
1881	...	1.3	563	33	...	434	198	135	361
1882	...	1.4	586	37	...	437	220	146	404
1883	...	1.3	594	41	...	473	215	145	398
1884	...	2.6	580	34	...	487	195	122	349
1885	...	} 2.6	612	32	...	440	181	112	324
1886	...		578	50	...	462	193	117	336
1887	...	} 2.8	606	76	...	466	217	119	371
1888	...	1.4	691	77	...	491	219	124	379
1889	...	...	695[4]	78	...	469	224	131	387
1890	...	...	789	68	...	477	230	143	403
1891	...	...	779	39	...	487	220	146	393
1892	...	1.9	714	43	...	518	177	154	355
1893	...	1.8	759	50	...	519	203	161	386
1894	...	2.2	786	44	...	549[6] / 595	132	147	306
1895	...	1.9	819	51	...	600	152	143	325
1896	...	2.4	754	53	...	628	160	147	338
1897	...	3	697	56	...	620	177	147	348
1898	19	2.4	749	65	...	624	150	171	405
1899	19	2.8	788	71	...	681	206	273	516
1900	17	3.0	883	72	5.6	699[6]	233	295	567
1901	21	2.8	917	79	5.6	712	239	307	588
1902	18	2.6	1,008	81	6.3	788	254	272	562
1903	14	...	1,076	191	8.8	804	284	231	562
1904	16	3.3	891	129	8.7	812	261	233	541

G6 NORTH AMERICA: Central Government Revenue, with some MainTax Yields (in millions of stated currency unit, except as otherwise indicated)

	Barbados[12]	Canada[7]					Costa Rica[9]	Cuba[1]
	Total	Customs	Excises[8]	Sales Tax	Income Tax	Total	Total	Total
	thousand pounds			dollars			colones	pesos
1905	192	46	14	—	—	80	6.2	33
1906	205	[40][7]	[12][7]	—	—	[68][7]	6.9	31
1907	210	57	16	—	—	96	7.9	33
1908	190	47	15	—	—	86	[5.2][9]	28
1909	196	60	15	—	—	102	7.3	35
1910	213	72	17	—	—	118	8.1	36
1911	222	85	19	—	—	136	9.7	38
1912	234	112	21	—	—	169	10	40
1913	215	105	21	—	—	163	9.6	31
1914	223	76	22	—	—	133	8.6	58
1915	212	99	24	—	—	172	6.3	41
1916	311	134	27	—	—	233	7.3	52
1917	400	144	29	—	—	261	6.9	65
1918	347	147	42	—	9.4	313	7.3	70
1919	420	169	58	—	20	350	12	93
1920	454	163	78	38	46	437	18	108
1921	341	106	49	61	79	395	18	57
1922	401	118	53	90	60	410	19	73
1923	427	122	61	98	54	408	21	91
1924	502	108	61	63	56	353	23	94
1925	391	127	68	73	56	383	26	87
1926	379	142	73	81	47	401	27	80
1927	413	157	77	71	57	431	31	82
1928	420	187	84	63	59	462	33	79
1929	407	179	84	44	69	453	35	77
1930	390	131	72	20	71	358	28	60
1931	378	104	67	42	61	335	25	47
1932	444	70	63	57	62	312	23	44
1933	468	66	81	61	61	325	24	46
1934	472	77	83	72	67	362	26	65
1935	468	74	80	78	83	373	27	65
1936	482	84	86	113	102	454	35	78
1937	527	94	95	138	120	517	38	76[1]
1938	559	79	91	122	142	502	38	...
1939	612	104	90	137	134	562	43	74
1940	690	131	193	180	248	872	42	78.
1941	819	142	327	236	510	1,489	43	80
1942	804	119	395	232	860	2,250	37	106
1943	942	168	476	305	1,037	2,765	50	125
1944	1,147	115	486	209	978	2,687	53	148
1945	1,530	129	471	212	933	3,013	61	158
	dollars							
1946	7.5	237	477	298	939	3,008	63	201
1947	8.5	293	465	372	1,060	2,872	88	277
1948	8.5	223	463	377	1,298	2,771	90	242[1]
1949	8.6	226	389	403	1,273	2,580	125	230

G6   NORTH AMERICA: Central Government Revenue, with some Main Tax Yields (in millions of stated currency unit, except as otherwise indicated)

| | Dominican Republic | El Salvador[10] | Guatemala[13] | Haiti[14] | Honduras[11] | Jamaica | Mexico[5] | | |
| | Total | Total | Total | Total | Total | Total | Customs | Income Tax[17] | Total |
	pesos	silver pesos	pesos	gourdes	pesos	thousand pounds		pesos	
1905	1.7	8.5	30	19	3.5	999	...	...	107
1906	3.8	8.5	34	15	3.2	1,041	...	...	118
1907	4.0	8.7	31	19	3.9	1,162	...	...	115
1908	4.2	13	35	24	3.5	1,083	...	...	102
1909	3.9	12	37	21	3.5	1,158	...	...	111
		colones							
1910	4.7	6.3	49	20	3.8	1,165	...	...	116
1911	4.6	5.6	52	24	4.6	1,348	...	...	110
1912	4.8	5.4	62	28	5.2	1,379	...	...	126
1913	5.1	5.5	84	27	5.4	1,241	...	...	121
1914	4.4	5.0	82	29	6.0	1,651	...	...	...
1915	4.5	4.3	85	30	4.7	1,147	...	...	...
1916	4.7	4.5	135	23	5.6	1,340	...	...	...
1917	6.7	10	135	19	4.8	1,228	...	...	154
1918	7.1	6.9	111	15	5.3	1,347	...	...	157
1919	8.7	9.1	127	29	6.7	2,029	...	...	188
1920	9.5	15	168	34	7.6	2,347	...	...	260
1921	9.3	10	256	20	7.4	1,927	...	...	293
1922	12	12	307	25	16	2,057	...	...	280
1923	6.2	14	386	32	14	2,061	...	...	287
			quetzales						
1924	8.7	18	8.1	33	8.6	1,923	...	...	273
1925	11	20	10	40	9.2	2,021	95	52	322
1926	14	21	12[13]	45	9.7	2,147	98	43	309
1927	15	26	12	39	12	2,275	85	30	295
1928	15	27	14	50	14	2,213	93	36	300
1929	15	25	15	50	14	2,293	96	34	322
1930	10	21	13	43	12	2,198	112	32	289
1931	7.2	15	11	32	11	2,086	60	23	256
1932	7.2	19	9.2	28	9.0	2,169	55	21	212
					lempiras				
1933	8.5	17	8.3	37	10	2,037	54	22	223
1934	9.3	22	8.6	37	11	2,260	66	50	295
1935	11	22	9.6	30	10	2,121	73	64	313
1936	11	23	11	35	[12][16]	2,212	92	63	385
1937	12	21	12	35	[12][16]	2,476	134	73	451
1938	12	20	13	28	[11][11]	2,840	119	76	438
1939	12	[9.7][10]	12	31	11	3,082	187	77	566
1940	12	20	12	27	11	3,622	170	93	577
1941	13	20	12	27	12	4,167	243	92	665
1942	16	20	12	26	11	4,372	223	126	746
1943	19	25	14	33	13	5,655	314	278	1,092
1944	24	28	17	42	15	8,009	334	376	1,295
1945	27	29	17	42	18	7,748	383	372	1,404
1946	41	40	29	45	23	8,391	486	466	2,012
1947	57	44	41	65	26	9,300	482	619	2,055
1948	65	59	40	79	28	9,713	549	623	2,268
1949	64	69	45	83	30	10,003	882	748	3,891

G6 NORTH AMERICA: Central Government Revenue, with some Main Tax Yields (in millions of state currency unit, except as otherwise indicated)

	Nicaragua[15] Total	Panama[19] Total	Puerto Rico[20] Total	Trinidad & Tobago[6] Total	USA[2] Customs	USA[2] Internal Revenue[3] Excises	USA[2] Internal Revenue[3] Income Tax	USA[2] Internal Revenue[3] Social Security Tax	USA[2] Total
	pesos	balboas	dollars	thousand pounds	dollars		dollars		dollars
1905	...	...	...	848	262		234		544
1906	...	...	3.5	765	300		249		595
1907	...	...	...	871	332		270		666
1908	...	...	...	835	286		252		602
1909	...	2.8	...	854	301		246		604
1910	19	5.9	5.4	948	334		290		676
1911	22	3.3	4.4	951	314		323		702
1912	...	3.4	7.8	933	311		322		693[2]
	cordobas								
1913	1.7	4.0	8.8	971	319		344		714
1914	3.4	3.8	10	935	292		480		725
1915	2.2	3.3	12	[782][6]	210		416		633
1916	2.1	3.5	9.1	1,065	213	340	125	—	761
1917	2.3	3.9	11	1,098	226	388	387	—	1,101
1918	2.4	3.1	12	1,173	180	669	...	—	3,645
1919	3.0	6.3	14	1,343	184	837	...	—	5,130
1920	4.3	5.8	17	1,918	323	808	...	—	6,649
1921	3.4	5.4	12	1,868	309	685	...	—	5,571
1922	2.3	5.3	12	1,662	356	593	...	—	4,026
1923	2.7	} 16 {	10	1,664	562	625	...	—	3,853
1924	3.5		13	1,587	546	716	...	—	3,871
1925	3.7	} 12 {	14	1,663	548	543	1,762	—	3,641
1926	4.4		14	1,737	579	571	1,974	—	3,795
1927	4.5	} 14[19] {	14	1,686	606	482	2,220	—	4,013
1928	5.7	17	15	1,764	569	483	2,175	—	3,900
1929	6.0	} 17 {	15	1,871	602	459[3] / 540	2,331	—	3,862
1930	5.9		13	1,801	587	565	2,410	—	4,058
1931	5.4	} [19][19] {	16	1,641	378	520	1,910	—	3,116
1932	4.7		13	1,694	328	454	1,057	—	1,924
1933	3.8	} 16 {	11	1,687	251	839	747	—	1,997
1934	4.2		15	1,710	313	1,288	820	—	3,015
1935	5.0	} 14 {	15	1,811	343	1,364	1,106	—	3,706
				dollars					
1936	5.3		16	13	387	1,547	1,427	- -	3,997
1937	7.5	9.7	19	12	486	1,765	2,280	266	4,956
1938	10	9.9	20	13	359	1,731	2,629	743	5,588
1939	17	13	18	13	319[2]	1,768	2,185	740	4,979
1940	28	13	21	16	331	1,885[3] / 1,844	2,130[3] / 2,088	834[21] / 1,715	6,879
1941	33	17	21	19	365	2,386	3,438	2,004	9,202
1942	40	21	38	23	369	3,121	7,978	2,429	15,104
1943	35	26	44	29	308	3,769	16,060	3,013	25,097
1944	49	26	108	29	417	4,379	35,434	3,428	47,818
1945	48	26	79	31	341	5,893	34,756	3,438	50,162
1946	53	31	82	42	424	6,646	28,367	3,078	43,537
1947	77	34	88	37	477	7,182	26,544	3,333	43,531
1948	59	32	100	45	403	7,356	28,988	3,966	45,357
1949	78[15]	32	109	51	367	7,502	26,736	3,809	41,576

G6 NORTH AMERICA: Central Government Revenue, with some Main Tax Yields (in millions of stated currency unit, except as otherwise indicated)

	Barbados[12]	Canada[7]					Costa Rica[22]	Cuba[1]
	Total	Customs	Excises[8]	Sales Tax	Income Tax	Total	Total	Total
				dollars			colones	pesos
1950	10	296	468	460	1,513	3,113	138	286
1951	13	346	530	598	2,164	4,007	160	328
1952	13	389	517	708	2,556	4,585	190	309
1953	14	407	523	734	2,579	4,689	216	270
1954	16	397	479	715	2,412	4,414	234	303
1955	16	481	510	802	2,435	4,716	262	329
1956	18	549	538	896	2,938	5,478	272	371
1957	20	498	549	879	2,995	5,420	312	387
1958	22	487	558	868	2,637	5,130	334	415[1]
1959	21	526	622	1,003	3,059	5,837	337	…
1960	24	499	636	991	3,409	6,221	351	411
1961	25	535	626	1,045	3,466	6,374	366	1,143
1962	27	645	642	1,108	3,445	6,570	381	1,657
1963	32	581	666	1,278	3,668	7,003	386	2,904
1964	37	622	680	1,588	4,348	8,141	433	2,399
1965	40	686	742	1,917	4,566	8,865	474	2,536
1966	43	778	777	2,073	4,997	9,662	522	…
1967	48	747	826	2,146	5,692	10,571	542	…
1968	62	762	887	2,098	6,753	11,817	622	…
1969	76	818	897	2,294	8,676	14,155	720	…
1970	90	815	964	2,281	9,079	14,717	883	…
1971	102	989	995	2,653	9,911	13,345	910	…
1972	111	1,182	1,039	3,052	11,589	18,821[7]	1,041[22]	…
						21,426	1,260	…
1973	129	1,385	1,091	3,590	13,260	25,102	1,620	…
1974	164[12]	1,809	1,159	3,866	16,974	32,192	2,449	…
	177							
1975	214	1,887	1,523	3,515	18,938	34,703	3,027	…
1976	230	2,097	1,946	3,929	20,579	38,313	3,648	…
1977	266	2,312	1,939	4,427	19,883	38,237	4,393	…
1978	328	2,747	2,181	4,729	21,005	41,638	5,755	…
1979	377	3,000	3,850	4,698	25,624	48,219	6,317	…
1980	474	3,199	9,276	5,429	30,208	57,491	7,373	…
1981	512[12]	3,449	9,794	6,185	34,306	72,280	10,199	…
1982	571	2,846	7,841	5,894	35,433	73,238	17,027	…
1983	634	3,394	8,526	6,660	37,336	77,327	28,115	…
1984	662	3,811	7,068	7,729	41,366	85,298	36,382	…
							thousand million	
1985	747	3,989	[3,409][8]	9,383	44,908	91,100	41.0	…
1986	773	4,205	5,179	12,022	50,640	99,206	54.6[22]	…
1987	842	4,402	6,410	12,984	58,967	111,549	70.1	…
1988	1,034	4,540	6,093	15,744	61,224	119,311	87.7	…
1989	1,120	4,638	6,397	17,768	69,505	132,537	104.5	…
1990	…	4,033	6,370	17,061	73,707	138,785	120.7	…
1991	…	4,108	7,472	17,055	75,060	142,404	162.5	…
1992	…	4,098	7,842	17,264	71,639	144,298	225.2	…
1993	…	3,652	7,964	18,306	68,695	147,559	277.9	…

G6 NORTH AMERICA: Central Government Revenue, with some Main Tax Yields (in millions of state currency unit, except as otherwise indicated)

	Dominican Republic[23]	El Salvador[10]	Guatemala[13]	Haiti[14]	Honduras[11]	Jamaica[24]	Mexico[5]		
								Income	
	Total	Total	Total	Total	Total	Total	Customs	Tax[17]	Total
	pesos	colones	quetzales	gourdes	lempiras	pounds		pesos	
1950	76	88	43	109	37	11	991	914	3,614
1951	90	118	47	125	41	14	1,397	1,408	4,935
1952	96	128	57	146	43	14	1,475	1,627	6,318
1953	119	140	65	136	46	15	1,317	1,280	5,147
1954	112	167	66	161	48	17	1,875	1,393	6,405
1955	130	166	72	162	46	19	2,519	2,261	7,819
1956	137	171	86	161	[17][11]	22	2,555	2,740	9,201
1957	155	191	92	150	61	26	2,259	2,853	9,666
1958	154	169	92	154	66	28	2,702	3,124	11,872
1959	152	157	90	176	69	31	2,925	3,238	10,184
1960	143	171	86	...	72	33	3,084	3,866	12,992
1961	118	161	87	[97][14]	72	36	2,944	4,227	12,225
1962	151	172	88	153	74	39	3,041	4,839	14,148
1963	174	181[10] 192	84	144	80	40	2,816	5,579	14,845
1964	192	223	98[13]	...	93	48	3,282	7,411	18,023
								thousand million pesos	
1965	120	276	121	143	109	54	4.6	6.0	22
1966	163	251	121	141	120	56	4.8	8.7	25
1967	174	258	124	140[14] 158	129	63	6.0	10	27
1968	189	229	137	191	148	73	5.8	13	32
							dollars		
1969	214	258	150	199	155	176	6.3	15	36
1970	240	284	165	235	178	213	7.4	16	41
1971	276	298	173	271	181	244	7.8	18	45
1972	315[23] 361	326	183	290	193	281	7.5	21	54
1973	397	403	212	308	220	345	7.5	27	69
1974	513	488	280	376	257	507[24]	10	36	94[5] 95
1975	695	581	327	519	272	634	13	49	133
1976	622	805	410	666	353	616	15	66	169
1977	678	1,257	589	807	457	733	26	93	241
1978	695	1,048	661	925	549	854	35	132	323
1979	739	1,171	667[13]	719	656	1,129	50	173	439
1980	954	1,029	885	893	757	1,222	189	246	675
1981	988	1,068	899	1,109	739	1,662	258	332	894
1982	823	1,091	882	1,484	770	1,576	500	464	1,520
1983	999	1,258	874[13]	1,538	778	1,844	218	716	3,222
1984	1,263	1,574	665	1,414	951	2,334	122	1,177	4,774
1985	1,727	1,902	862	1,921	1,064	2,708	309	1,899	7,820
1986	2,249	2,688	1,462	1,786	1,152	3,700	662	3,344	12,643
1987	3,019	2,815	1,852	1,759	1,290	5,064	1,687	7,794	33,683
1988	4,659	2,677	2,291	...	1,378	6,028	2,194	20,103	67,476
1989	6,112	2,677	2,427	...	1,534	8,308	4,409	25,909	86,858
1990	7,334	3,350	2,788	...	2,059	9,630	6,998	34,668	113,289
1991	10,809	4,271	4,305	...	2,838	14,549	10,771	44,204	141,373
1992	18,430	5,339	5,734	...	3,271	21,029	14,037	57,945	173,530
1993	20,871	6,550	5,781	...	3,770	34,243	12,684	69,221	187,282

G6   NORTH AMERICA: Central Government Revenue, with some Main Tax Yields (in millions of stated currency unit, except as otherwise indicated)

	Nicaragua[25]	Panama[19]	Puerto Rico[20]	Trinidad & Tobago[6]	USA[2]				
	Total	Total	Total	Total	Customs	Excises	Income Tax	Social Security Taxes[21]	Total
	cordobas	balboas	dollars	dollars			dollars		
1950	...	31	122	51	407	7,550	26,196	4,386	40,940
1951	96	32	135	59	609	8,648	35,705	5,714	53,390
1952	125	36	128	67	533	8,852	49,144	6,496	68,011
1953	155	41	140[20]	68	596[2]	9,878[2]	51,018[2]	6,821[2]	71,495
1954	182	43	148	76	542	9,945	50,643	7,210	71,630[2]
									69,719
1955	197	45	152	85	585	9,131	46,608	7,866	65,469
1956	282	49	164	92	682	9,929	53,068	9,323	74,547
1957	249	51	182	106	735	10,534	56,787	9,997	79,990
1958	255	53	187	130	782	10,638	54,798	11,239	79,636
1959	233	51	206	141	925	10,578	54,085	11,722	79,249
							thousand million dollars		
1960	233	58	233	154	1.1	12	62	15	92
1961	252	63	252	156	1.0	12	62	16	94
1962	288	68	285	181	1.1	13	66	17	100
1963	346	69	329	186	1.2	13	69	20	107
1964	373	76[19]	372	205	1.3	14	72	22	113
1965	444	87	416	233	1.4	15	74	22	117
1966	476	100	488	235	1.8	13	86	26	131
1967	486	113	546	263	1.9	14	95	33	149
1968	470	119	605	285	2.0	14	97	35	153
1969	499	133	710	315	2.3	15	124	40	187
1970	572[25]	160	772	318	2.4	16	123	45	193
	667								
1971	736	181	902	352	2.6	17	113	49	187
1972	760	198	1,074	403	3.3	16	127	54	207
1973	1,064	226[19]	1,185	480	3.2	16	139	65	231
		306							
1974	1,481	391	1,188[20]	1,301	3.3	17	158	77	263
			1,102						
1975	1,530	452	1,294	1,715	3.7	17	163	85	279
1976	1,763	440	1,605	2,125	4.1	17	173	91	298[2]
1977	2,065	546	1,723	2,749	5.2	18	212	106	356
1978	1,893	598	1,812	2,770	6.6	18	241	121	400
1979	2,145	696	1,973	3,644	7.4	19	283	139	463
1980	4,974	966	2,118	5,995	7.2	24	309	158	517
1981	7,017	1,030	2,307	6,629	8.1	41	347	183	599
1982	8,257	1,204	2,491	6,687	8.9	36	347	201	618
1983	11,971	1,324	2,628	6,323	8.7	35	326	209	601
1984	18,166	1,374	...	6,419	11	37	355	239	666
	thousand million								
1985	43	1,383	...	6,266	12	36	396	265	734
1986	164	1,485	...	5,169	13	33	412	284	769
	thousand gold cordobas								
1987	...	1,537	...	5,133	15	32	476	303	854
1988	15	1,205	...	4,670	16	35	496	334	909
1989	812	1,079	...	4,965	16	34	549	359	991
	million								
1990	52	1,365	...	...	17	35	561	380	1,031
1991	1,617	1,661	...	...	16	42	566	396	1,054
1992	2,191	1,696	...	...	17	46	577	414	1,090
1993	2,483	1,961	...	...	19	48	627	428	1,153

G6 SOUTH AMERICA: CENTRAL GOVERNMENT REVENUE, WITH SOME MAIN TAX YIELDS (in millions of stated currency unit, except as otherwise indicated)

1830–1864

	Argentina	Brazil[26]	Chile[27]	Ecuador	Guyana[29]	Peru[30]	Venezuala[31]
	Total	Total	Total	Total	Total	Total	Total
					thousand		
	gold pesos	milreis	gold pesos[28]	sucres	dollars	pesos	bolivares
1823	...	3.8	...	...	...	...	...
1824	...	6	...	...	...	...	...
1825	...	4.7	...	...	...	...	...
1826	...	4.4	...	...	...	...	...
1827	...	6.9	...	...	...	...	...
1828	...	7.2[26]	...	...	...	...	...
1829	...	9.9	...	...	...	...	...
1830	...	17	...	...	...	...	5.8
1831	...	17	...	...	...	...	6.1
1832	...	12	...	...	...	...	7.0
1833	...	16	...	...	...	...	7.5
1834	...	12	...	...	...	...	7.2
1835	...	15	...	...	...	...	6.6
1836	...	14	...	...	...	...	8.6
1837	...	14	...	...	...	...	8.0
1838	...	13	...	...	674	...	9.3
1839	...	15	...	...	1,188	...	11
1840	...	16	...	...	409	...	13
1841	...	16	...	...	1,092	...	9.7
1842	...	16	...	...	839	...	11
1843	...	19	...	...	830	...	11
1844	...	21	...	...	832	...	11
1845	...	25	...	...	825	...	12
1846	...	26	...	...	901	} 8.4 {	13
1847	...	28	...	...	1,022		11
1848	...	25	...	...		} 11 {	14
1849		26	...	...	494		18
1850	...	28	...	...	883	} 11 {	21
1851	...	33	...	...	974		21
1852	...	38	...	...	1,046	} 14 {	14
1853	...	38	...	...	1,200		18
1854	...	35	...	...	1,171	} 20 {	18
1855	...	36	...	...	1,224		20
1856	...	39	...	...	1,109		19
1857	...	49	51	...	1,282	...	24
1858	...	50	51	...	1,310	...	22
1859	...	47	72	...	1,325	...	14
1860	...	44	63	...	1,344	...	21
1861	...	50	54	...	1,450	} 42 {	20
1862	...	52	66	...	1,358		24
1863	...	48	69	} 3.7 {	1,277	} 46 {	...
1864	7.0	55	81		1,498		32

G6 SOUTH AMERICA: Central Government Revenue, with some Main Tax Yields (in millions of stated currency unit, except as otherwise indicated)

1865–1894

	Argentina	Bolivia	Brazil[26]	Chile[27]	Ecuador	Guyana[29]	Paraguay[32]	Surinam[33]	Peru[30]	Uruguay[34]	Venezuela[31]
	Total	Total	Total	Total	Total	Total	Total	Total	Total	Total	Total
				gold		thousand					
	gold pesos	bolivianos	milreis	pesos[28]	sucres	dollars	gold pesos	guilders	pesos	pesos	bolivares
1865	8.3	...	57	92	} 3.9 {	1,483	...	...	...	...	30
1866	9.6	...	59	75		1,464	...	...	...	...	22
1867	12	...	65	81	} 3.7 {	1,320	...	...	...	...	14
1868	12	...	71	87		1,397	...	...	soles	...	19
1869	13	...	88	99	} 3.1 {	1,493	...	...	} 45 {	...	22
1870	15	...	95	102		1,699	...	...		5.3	...
1871	13	...	96	87	} 4.3 {	1,824	...	...	} 59 {	...	...
1872	18	...	102	90		1,814	...	...		5.1	24
1873	20	...	111	93	} 4.8 {	1,738	...	...	} 34 {	...	27
1874	16	...	103	90		1,752	...	...		3.8	25
1875	17	...	105	99	...	1,690	...	...	} 66 {	5.9	33
1876	14	...	101	99	...	1,747	...	...		7.4	26
1877	15	...	99	84	...	1,872	...	...	} 44 {	4.6	24
1878	18	...	109	84	} 6.4 {	1,963	...	...		...	...
1879	21	...	112	135		1,901	...	...	} 35 {	...	29
1880	20	...	120	198	...	1,939	...	...		7.7	30
1881	21	...	128	165	...	1,934	0.8	...	...	...	29
1882	27	...	130	186	...	2,203	0.8	...	...	...	29
1883	31	...	130	219	...	2,294	0.6	...	...	...	34
1884	38	...	133	171	3.2	2,208	0.8	...	...	11	33
1885	27	3.2	122	129	2.5	2,088	1.4	...	...	12	27
1886	30	4.1	127	123	2.9	2,141	2.9	...	...	12	34
1887	38	4.3	[219][26]	162	4.5	2,227	1.5	1.4	} 16 {	13	41
1888	35	4.3	151	201	4.2	2,218[29]	1.7	1.3		14	40
1889	38	5.0	161	207	3.1	2,510	2.1	1.4	} 13 {	16	45
1890	29	3.6	195	225	4.2	2,688	0.5	1.5		17	54
1891	19	3.3	229	276	3.9	2,674	0.3	1.5	6.7	15	44
1892	33	3.9	228	204	3.8	2,717	0.5	1.6	7.1	14	37
1893	38	4.2	260	186	4.3	2,846	0.9	1.8	7.9	14	51
1894	34	4.2	265	189	...	2,779	0.7	1.7	7.3	15	49

G6 SOUTH AMERICA: Central Government Revenue, with some MainTax Yields (in millions of state currency unit, except as otherwise indicated)

1895–1944

	Argentina[34]			Bolivia	Brazil[26]			
	Customs[36]	Income & Wealth Taxes	Total	Total	Customs	Excises	Income & Wealth Taxes	Total
		paper pesos		bolivianos			milreis or cruzeiros	
1895	94	4.2	132	4.1	...	...	—	308
1896	86	3.6	124	4.4	...	...	—	346
1897	82	6.2	151	5.6	...	...	—	303
1898	75	5.4	136	5.2	...	...	—	324
1899	89	4.9	166	5.9	...	...	—	321
1900	73	5.1	151	6.0	165	37	—	308
1901	72	5.2	151	6.4	162	32	—	305
1902	67	5.5	156	6.0	186	34	—	344
1903	91	5.4	172	5.3	189	35	—	415
1904	97	5.5	199	6.8	198	35	—	443
1905	105	5.8	212	7.9	224	35	—	401
1906	121	5.0	232	10	248	43	—	432
1907	129	8.7	246	14	287	48	—	536
1908	137	8.7	263	16	237	45	—	441
1909	150	9.0	285	13	233	46	—	450
1910	173	9.3	308	13	289	55	—	525
1911	177	9.6	316	17	318	60	—	564
1912	188	12[18] / 5.5	363	20	348	63	—	615
1913	199	10	370	22	344	65	—	654
1914	118	10	273	23	195	52	—	423
1915	95	...	252	17	153	68	—	404
1916	105	...	255	16	184	84	—	478
1917	97	...	254	19	158	118	—	537
1918	139	...	322	30	171	120	—	619
1919	180	14	401	25	213	132	—	626
1920	297	15	509	31	349	176	—	922
1921	203	...	470	24	319	154	—	891
1922	206	16	453	23	309	165	—	972
1923	268	16	542	29	468	258	45	1,258
1924	296	22	597	41	567	299	24	1,588
1925	350	23	663	42	722	312	34	1,742
1926	304	24	640	43	578	364	36	1,648
1927	313	25	681	46	812	403	61	2,040
1928	358	26	739	45	939	440	68	2,217
1929	356	27	748	49	928	427	76	2,201
1930	290	27	663	36	626	352	62	1,678
1931	257	28	686	22	605	378	93	1,753
1932	241	81	742	20	527	389	94	1,751
1933	257	92	754	26	757	445	123	2,078
1934	248	93	764	43	837	512	153	2,520
1935	272	117	847	56	975	558	167	2,723
1936	261	143	873	80	1,012	606	199	3,127
1937	285	145	991	200	1,173	667	232	3,462
1938	329	155	991	274	1,053	854	287	3,880
1939	...	...	1,015	426	1,031	1,030	324	4,353
1940	239	173	969	565	978	1,054	411	4,645
1941	189	180	914	824	1,059	1,185	537	4,765
1942	168	256	1,030	976	674	1,254	988	4,988
1943	108	277	1,050	1,096	596	1,554	1,498	6,011
1944	96	471	1,484	1,095	902	1,947	2,038	8,311

G6   SOUTH AMERICA: Central Government Revenue, with some Main Tax Yields (in millions of stated currency unit, except as otherwise indicated)

	Chile[27]			Colombia[33]			Ecuador	Guyana[29]	Paraguay[32]
	Customs	Income & Wealth Taxes[37]	Total	Customs	Income & Wealth Taxes	Total	Total	Total	Total
	gold pesos[28]			pesos			sucres	dollars	gold pesos
1895	186	1.4	252	...	...	...	...	2.7	0.9
1896	189	1.5	297	...	...	...	...	2.6	1.0
1897	184	1.5	216	...	...	...	6.8	2.4	0.7
1898	172	1.2	327	...	...	...	7.8	2.5	1.2
1899	206	1.3	294	...	...	...	6.6	2.5	1.2
1900	236	1.6	330[27] 267	...	...	...	8.1	2.4	1.2
1901	216	1.6	237	...	...	...	11	2.5	1.3
1902	215	3.4	231	...	...	...	13	2.6	1.3[32]
1903	239	3.2	284	...	...	...	11	2.6	...
1904	247	2.7	271	...	...	...	10	2.4	...
1905	272	2.7	304	...	...	9.2	12	2.5	...
1906	310	3.1	349	...	...	...	12	2.5	...
1907	336	3.0	379	...	...	16	13	2.6	...
1908	324	2.2	363	...	...	[17][16]	13	2.6	...
1909	340	2.6	377	...	...	[17][16]	16	2.6	...
1910	388	7.1	437	...	...	11	15	2.7	...
1911	409	7.9	465	...	...	12	13	2.8	...
1912	424	8.6	490	...	...	13	20	2.8	...
1913	441	9.3	515	...	...	17	20	2.9	4.4
1914	324	9.6	405	...	...	13	16	2.8	4.1
1915	272	41	374	...	...	12	[21][16]	[2.3][29]	3.1
1916	419	27	508	...	...	[20][38]	[18][16]	3.2	3.0
1917	502	38	639	...	...	13	[19][16]	3.5	...
1918	550	40	738	...	...	11	18	4.1	...
1919	223	31	374	...	...	[14][38]	15	4.1	5.5[32]
									paper pesos
1920	448	38	638	...	...	26	21	6.1	57
1921	237	23	375[27] 346	...	...	16	21	4.6	122
1922	234	22	366	...	...	21	25	4.3	116
1923	414	23	551	...	...	34	25	5.3	123
1924	405	55	609	...	...	33	31	5.1	192
1925	448	86	701	...	...	46	39	5.2	235
1926	428	127	735	...	...	56	48	5.0	233
1927	511	162[37]	909	...	...	63	65	5.1	256
1928	592	170	1,021	42	4.0	75	62	5.7	265
1929	670	219	1,234	41	3.7	75	61	6.0	256
1930	505	226	1,069	22	4.1	49	61	4.9	269
1931	221	151	792	20	2.8	44	45	4.4	213
1932	148	101	515	19	2.1	36	35	4.9	186
1933	378	148	950	23	2.4	43	39	5.1	...
1934	383	168	1,043	26	2.9	55	48	5.5	...
1935	543	160	1,341	29	5.3	62	66	5.2	343
1936	644	178	1,351	32	14	73	72	5.5	458
1937	721	212	1,437	36	17	86	80	5.9	1,889
1938	810	255	1,635	32	20	83	121	6.1	555
1939	782	374	1,793	42	21	96	121	6.2	411
									guaranies[35]
1940	844	487	2,052	29	24	79	115	7.0	16[32]
1941	946	640	2,496	32	25	105	118	8.5	16
1942	842	664	2,954	20	31	111	139	10	19
1943	771	1,112	3,648	23	31	129	178	12	22
1944	853	1,363	4,089	27	53	122	233	14	21

G6 SOUTH AMERICA: Central Government Revenue, with some Main Tax Yields (in millions of state currency unit, except as otherwise indicated)

	Peru[30]			Surinam[33]	Uruguay[34]			Venezuela[31]			
	Customs	Direct Taxes[39]	Total	Total	Customs	Direct Taxes	Total	Customs[38]	Direct Taxes	Oil Royalties	Total
	soles			guilders	pesos			bolivares			
1895	...	...	...	1.8	10	...	15	38	—	...	51
1896	...	...	8.4	3.0	8.6	...	17	35	—	...	48
1897	...	...	11	2.0	9.9	...	16	23	—	...	33
1898	...	...	11$_{30}$	2.2	10	...	16	28	—	...	41
1899	6.5	0.4	11	2.1	9.4	...	17	18	—	...	27
1900	7.4	0.4	13	2.2	9.4	...	19	...	—	...	45
1901	8.6	0.5	15	2.2	9.7$_{34}$	...	18	...	—	...	32
1902	8.2	0.6	15	2.2	9.5	...	19	...	—	...	26
1903	8.6	0.7	16	4.1	9.9	...	19	...	—	...	57
1904	10	0.8	20	4.5	9.2	...	18	...	—	...	47
1905	11	0.9	22	3.7	10	...	17	...	—	...	49
1906	13	1.9	26	4.0	13	...	21	...	—	...	50
1907	14	2.1	28	3.6	13	...	22	...	—	...	51
1908	13	3.3	29	4.1	13	...	23	...	—	...	50
1909	11	2.4	25	4.3	14	...	24	...	—	...	49
1910	13	2.5	28	5.8	15	...	25	22	—	...	70
1911	15	2.6	32	5.5	15	...	26	20	—	...	83
1912	16	2.6	34	6.1	17	...	29	22	—	...	65
1913	15	3.0	35	6.4	18	...	32	22	—	...	60
1914	11	3.1	31	6.3	15	...	28	35	—	...	51
1915	7.0	3.0	28	6.5	11	...	23	44	—	...	66
1916	15	3.2	39	3.1	12	...	27	35	—	...	72
1917	18	3.4	45	3.2	11	...	25	20	—	...	53
1918	20	3.9	49	3.5	11	...	27	34	—	...	57
1919	26	4.1	62	3.9	13	...	31	64	—	...	101
1920	42	4.9	81	5.3	17	...	36	24	—	...	82
1921	24	5.2	62	...	14	...	31	33	—	...	71
1922	22	5.3	66	4.5	13	...	31	46	—	...	88
1923	33	6.7	76	6.6	16	...	37	56	—	...	102
1924	41	6.7	92	5.2	18	...	41	76	—	...	120
1925	38	8.0	92	4.7	14	...	45	96	—	...	172
1926	39	8.6	102	5.2	15	...	48	93	—	...	182
1927	40	12	107	4.9	16	...	52	92	—	...	187
1928	43	14	122	4.6	18	...	60	118	—	46	230
1929	48	15	140	4.4	19	11	59	139	—	54	255
1930	37	11	119	4.6	23	12	58	100	—	48	210
1931	25	13	100	4.8	19	11	56	81	—	51	185
1932	18	8.9	87	4.7	16$_{34}$	17$_{34}$	58$_{34}$	70	—	45	172
1933	30	11	103	3.9	20	14	58	70	—	48	172
1934	43	14	126	4.0	19	15	61	77	—	55	203
1935	48	15	140	4.1	38	17	87	76	—	62	189
1936	55	18	160	4.0	42	15	87	76	—	58	274
1937	57	23	173	3.7	43	13	88	117	1.4	108	331
1938	55	25	185	3.7	42	14	94	125	0.9	82	341
1939	50	27	180	4.0	41	14	93	139	1.1	90	354
1940	49	34	185	4.2	40	14	100	104	1.8	121	346
1941	59	35	229	4.3$_{33}$	36	15	100	97	1.4	100	325
1942	88	52	275	19	30	18	103	77	3.2	68	306
1943	105	89	346	17	23	20	106	83	41	149	446
1944	120	98	386	16	28	18	117	110	55	277	614

G6   SOUTH AMERICA: Central Government Revenue, with some Main Tax Yields (in millions of stated currency unit, except as otherwise indicated)

	Argentina[40]				Bolivia[42]	Brazil[26]			
	Customs[36]	Income & Wealth Taxes	VAT	Total	Total	Customs	Excises	Income & Wealth Taxes	Total
	pesos				bolivianos	cruzeiros			
1945	113	483	—	1,547	1,159	1,026	2,832	2,350	9,845
1946	248	619	—	1,972	1,038	1,404	4,009	2,751	11,570
1947	519	1,085	—	3,502	1,070	1,876	4,463	3,902	13,853
1948	471	1,443	—	4,327	1,385	1,650	4,854	4,195	15,699
1949	279	1,630	—	5,159	1,382	1,701	5,639	4,785	17,917
1950	291	2,238	—	6,096	1,824	1,695	6,410	5,582	19,373
1951	691	3,170	—	9,465	3,377	2,801	8,216	8,104	27,428
1952	457	4,074	—	11,492	3,182	2,589	9,124	9,994	30,740
1953	264	4,131	—	11,781	7,437	1,385	10,775	11,639	37,057
1954	388	4,414	—	12,782	15,037	2,281	14,542	15,340	46,539
	thousand million pesos				thousand million bolivianos	thousand million cruzeiros			
1955	0.53	4.68	—	12.6	31	2.2	17	19	56
1956	0.88	5.44	—	16.0	74	2.0	23	25	74
1957	[14][40]	[6.24][40]	—	[18.6][40]	240	2.8	30	27	86
1958	1.37	8.99	—	36.6	232	13	40	32	118
1959	20.5[40]	12.6[40]	—	66.5[40]	286	19	54	46	158
1960	29	21	—	103	304	22	83	62	233 / 208
1961	38	27	—	145	383	36	123	84	300
1962	32	21	—	143	395	58	204	116	475
					pesos[35]				
1963	29	26	—	163	446	87	408	243	876
1964	47	29	—	229	528	124	880	482	1,811
1965	64	51	—	322	632	209	1,308	1,023	3,231
1966	71	72	—	421	741	416	2,215	1,339	4,974
						million new cruzeiros[35]			
1967	136	138	—	476	792	370	2,840	1,550	5,493
1968	121	124	—	505	862	816	5,075	2,173	10,380
1969	140	143	—	572	901	1,078	6,752	3,764	14,766
	thousand million new pesos[35]					thousand million new cruzeiros			
1970	1.7	1.8	—	6.8	1,131	...	8.5	4.9	19
1971	2.2	2.0	—	8.6	1,151	1.8	11	6.5	26
1972	4.8	2.8	—	14	1,389	2.6	15	10	39
1973	7.3	3.8	—	19	2,479	3.8	20	14	50
1974	6.7	5.8	—	30 / 76	5,070	6.8	35	19	76
					thousand million pesos				
1975	20	6	9	160	5.7	9.6	44	26	101
1976	183	48	81	928	8.2[42] / 3.8	15	75	41	172
1977	380	270	280	2,950	4.4	17	99	71	253
1978	690	670	720	8,350	5.1	23	138	92	358
	million million new pesos								
1979	1.96	1.30	2.12	23.4	5.7	36	190	170	544
1980	4.29	3.12	5.26	49	5.0	108	320	320	1,230
1981	8.74	7.24	16.2	92	6.2	152	585	674	2,352
1982	25.3	21	44.7	232	9.3	241	1,175	1,457	4,775
1983	160[41]	80[41]	140[41]	1,060[41]	28.2	703	2,492	4,044	11,780
1984	960[41]	450[41]	930[41]	7,830[41]	257	1,951	5,316	14,733	36,414
	thousand million australes				bolivianos	thousand million cruzados[35]			
1985	1.10	0.61	1.14	8.3	232	8.1	25	58	135
1986	1.62	1.97	2.31	15.2	1,000	18	79	149	563
1987	2.83	4.94	4.77	32.6	1,164	48	298	398	1,692
1988	9.85	10.4	6.36	103	1,354	365	1,968	3,511	15,950
	million pesos					reals			
1989	12.5	17.5	21.1	314	1,619	2,121	10,027	20,505	102,300
						thousand reals			
1990	166	171	689	7,159	2,112	54	286	539	3,628
1991	599	452	2,494	20,192	2,842	291	1,327	2,150	15,553
1992	1,449	841	5,497	27,832	3,378	2,620	15,480	24,910	173,586
						million reals			
1993	...	...	...	...	3,993	64	351	549	4,272

G6 SOUTH AMERICA: Central Government Revenue, with some Main Tax Yields (in millions of stated currency unit, except as otherwise indicated)

	Chile[27]			Colombia				Ecuador[45]	Guyana	Paraguay[32]
	Customs	Income & Wealth Taxes[37]	Total	Customs	Income & Wealth Taxes	General Sales Tax	Total	Total	Total	Total
	gold pesos[28]			pesos				sucres	dollars	
1945	1,204	1,954	5,531	43	64	...	157	251	13	24
1946	1,542	1,979	6,198	50	84	...	209	299	14	33
1947	2,007	2,960	9,979	67	125	...	285	396	18	42
1948	2,573	5,165	14,379	60	138	...	311	373	21	46
1949	3,690	5,247	15,823	44	177	...	358	391	22	64
	thousand million pesos									
1950	2.7	5.3	17	99	231	...	514	389[45] 473	22	[153][32]
1951	5.4	7.4	26	217	285	...	668	556	25	148[32]
1952	7.0	9.7[37] 14	36	198	328	...	694	587	30	...
1953	7.1	15	44	259	384	...	840	732	32	433[32]
1954	8.1	28	75	386	460	...	1,043	998	36	...
	escudos[35]									
1955	18	45	138	395	556	...	1,329	1,092	41	...
1956	32	84	197	243	605	...	1,138	1,050	42	...
1957	53	111	296	206	601	...	1,227	1,254	46	...
1958	53	133	366	609	762	...	1,637	1,288	49	2,831
1959	90	206	582	582	974	...	1,916	1,256	49	2,696
1960	138	242	708	709	1,112	...	2,132	1,363	56	3,233
1961	169	271	796	695	1,140	...	3,095	1,565	60	3,632
1962	188	333	957	550	1,201	...	2,149	1,623	63	4,328
1963	257	472	1,354	601	1,683	...	3,236	1,639	64	4,220
1964	206	792	1,959	1,320	2,001	...	4,163	2,094	68	4,375
1965	347	1,364	3,209	1,047	2,371	...	4,412	1,998	79	5,710
1966	549	2,118	4,898	2,319	2,689	...	6,456	2,205	86	6,241
1967	664	2,712	6,312	1,517	3,650	...	7,295	2,649	99	6,632
1968	986	3,435	8,758	2,014	4,430	...	9,737	2,923	104	7,284
1969	1,452	5,068	13,069	2,462	5,910	...	11,249	3,356	113	8,567
	thousand million escudos									
1970	2.0	7.7	16	3,523	6,395	...	13,156	4,235	134 144	8,819
1971	2.3	7.9	23	3,838	8,553	1,615	17,166	5,097	141	8,970[23]
1972	3.8	10	71	3,932	8,376	1,839	18,625	6,331	163	11,039
1973	12	60	326	3,747	8,804	2,232	25,064	7,973	180	13,494
1974	176	512	2,610	4,965	10,586	3,428	32,459	11,390	323	18,442
	thousand million new pesos[35]			thousand million pesos				thousand million		thousand million
1975	1.04	2.42	12.5	5.3	17.8	7.0	48.2	12.4	503	21.2
1976	2.92	5.94	41	6.9	20.7	9.2	62	14.7	399	23.9
1977	6.79	12.9	91	9.5	24.3	12.6	82	16.5	380	31.4
1978	9.64	21.5	157	13.6	30.9	17.5	106	19.1	405	40.9
1979	11.2	40.9	241	16.9	37.7	22.8	139	23.1	481	51
1980	14.9	62	344	25.0	47.6	30.3	189	37.5	540	62
1981	21.4	67	388	29.9	54	40.0	229	39.3	647	73
1982	13.1	71	360	38.4	66	60	283	46.0	627	86
1983	25.6	85	429	42.9	79	62	347	60	631	84
1984	49.1	84	544	44.8	99	97	428	100	651	103
1985	76	85	746	82	158	124	586	189	781	136
1986	75	111	914	132	216	178	827	187	1,022	179
1987	119	119	1,144	203	310	250	1,136	237	1,221	253
1988	...	164	1,317	273	402	332	1,492	411	1,730	323
1989	...	203	1,595	320	532	427	1,918	832	3,248	524
1990	...	238	1,903	466	754	629	2,557	1,490	5,642	796
1991	...	494	2,679	424	1,526	901	3,654	1,907	13,392	980
1992	...	632	3,476	399	1,997	1,389	4,537	3,096	17,192	1,392
1993	...	759	4,161	543	2,395	2,341	6,430	4,371	23,191	1,688

International Historical Statistics: The Americas 1750–1993

G6 SOUTH AMERICA: Central Government Revenue, with some Main Tax Yields (in millions of stated currency unit, except as otherwise indicated)

	Peru[30]			Surinam	Uruguay				Venezuela[31]			
	Customs	Direct Taxes[39]	Total	Total	Customs	Direct Taxes	VAT	Total	Customs[47]	Direct Taxes	Oil Royalties	Total
	soles			guilders	pesos				bolivares			
1945	126	119	431	12	34	27	—	132	148	99	244	713
1946	213	161	609	13	54	40	—	169	203	237	364	1,100
1947	285	196	930	17	75	64	—	193	265	346	562	1,562
1948	235	272	1,021	21	52	80	—	232	343	485	702	1,963
1949	340	313	1,175	27	43	87	—	245	335	472	601	1,896
1950	702	403	1,728	27	63	95	—	280	363	460	784	2,126
1951	1,064	484	2,151	27	85	115	—	358	360	585	811	2,298
1952	956	460	2,209	33	54	120	—	372	375	665	764	2,371
1953	863	639[39] 1,071	2,160[30] 3,248	35	54	138	—	397	387	759	905	2,758
1954	1,001	1,367	3,654	39	86	174	—	454	436[47] 737	739	948	2,826
1955	1,083	1,598	4,787	43	75	182	—	448	758	915	1,104	3,201
1956	1,188	1,868	5,478	48	65	229	—	518	812	1,117	3,104	5,527
1957	1,319	2,004	5,274	56	77	263	—	665	1,141	1,310	1,870	4,881
1958	690	2,050	5,255	68	39	283	—	700	1,120	2,031	1,566	5,324
1959	599	2,558	6,240	71	63	367	—	900	1,144	1,820	1,520	5,863
1960	730	2,714	8,892	77	164	574	—	1,455	1,010	2,244	1,646	6,813
1961	880	2,970	10,999	90	228	726	—	2,105	[673]	[823][31]	[807][31]	[3,291][31]
1962	960	3,173	12,304	86	196	732	—	2,065	1,391	2,197	1,603	6,589
1963	1,493	3,510	11,298	94	155	752	—	2,276	1,639	2,504	1,715	6,619
1964	3,208	3,734	13,078	104	210	1,252	—	3,468	832	2,982	2,499	7,217
	thousand million soles				thousand million pesos							
1965	4.6	3.8	16	111	1.3	...	—	5.5	563	3,245	2,532	7,367
1966	5.1	4.3	18	122	4.1	...	—	12	559	3,673	2,557	7,952
1967	6.6	7.5	24	130	5.6	...	—	18	528	4,192	2,737	8,679
1968	8.6	8.7	28	146	12	...	—	42	542	4,364	2,746	8,964
1969	8.0	11	32	164	...	...	—	62	576	4,140	2,749	9,576
1970	8.8	13	39	169	...	...	—	83	706[47] 630	4,626	2,864	10,137
1971	9.7	12	41	165	...	...	—	103[23]	657	6,666	2,873	12,362
1972	8.1	13	46	196	9	24	—	278	712	7,151	2,794	13,297
1973	9.6	16	53	200	15	53	62	552	722	10,231	3,280	17,027
1974	13	25	69	229	29	91	144	914	1,209	29,531	9,287	44,325
					new pesos[35]				thousand million bolivares			
1975	24	28	88	318	96	154	324	1,519	1.9	26	8.4	42
1976	25	29	111	403	228	302	602	2,800	2.2	25	6.5	40
1977	36	39	154	474	450	583	900	4,539	2.9	26	7.7	43
1978	71	54	264	512	573	865	1,352	6,923	3.6	24	7.2	43
1979	156	136	552	562	1,652	1,511	2,358	12,188	3.8	31	7.4	51
					thousand million new pesos							
1980	281	331	1,019	609	2.9	3.0	5.2	20.5	4.5	45	7	67
1981	437	364	1,523	657	3.4	3.2	7.5	29.1	5.5	74	7.2	98
1982	594	576	2,485	690	2.8	2.8	6.9	27.5	7.0[48]	52[48]	6.3[48]	84[48]
1983	812	784	3,738	491	2.8	5.3	8.5	40.1	3.6	43	6.1	77
1984	1,860	1,703	9,554	519	5.3	5.5	14	56	4.4	62	8.7	105
	thousand million intis[35]											
1985	6.2	4.1	28	492	9.7	13	30	109	6.2	79	8.3	127
1986	9.4	12	45	498	22	28	56	220	8.8	48	9.7	109
1987	14.3	16	66	...	36	50	107	395	15.6	71	...	123
	thousand new soles											
1988	55	109	403	...	55	86	199	668	21.1	97	...	168
1989	1,265	1,589	7,499	...	84	190	337	1,157	22.7	183	...	288
	millions new soles											
1990	63	85	673	...	700	372	582	2,598	...	345	...	526
1991	321	427	3,665	...	393	781	1,274	5,769	56.9	453	6.2	842
1992	623	951	6,977	...	586	1,373	2,321	10,421	84.3	402	27.7	772
1993	1,175	1,661	10,643	...	673	1,961	3,189	17,799	...	483	...	975

G6a TOTAL REVENUE OF CANADIAN COLONIES BEFORE CONFEDERATION CANADA (in thousands pounds)[49]

1806-1839

	Lower Canada*	Upper Canada†
1806	29	...
1807	28	...
1808	30	...
1809	55	...
1810	57	...
1811	61	...
1812	50	...
1813	82	...
1814	145	...
1815	104	...
1816	94	...
1817	80	...
1818	56	...
1819	94	...
1820	99	...
1821	73	...
1822	40	...
1823	90	...
1824	83	62
1825	110	32
1826	89	62
1827	111	95
1828	109	49
1829	118	40
1830	144	76
1831	130	102
1832	163	92
1833	163	121
1834	82	329
1835	163	189
1836	2.3 }	648
1837	2.3 }	
1838	126	259
1839	147	158

* later Quebec † later Ontario

1840-1866

	British Columbia[50]	Lower Canada*	Upper Canada†	New Brunswick	Nova Scotia[54]	Prince Edward Island
1840	—	[196][51]	[222][51]	...	...	...
1841	—	...		...	...	...

Province of Canada[52]

1842	—	465		...	...	...
1843	—	895		...	...	...
1844	—	1,108		...	...	...
1845	—	846		...	...	...
1846	—	645		...	...	...
1847	—	720		...	...	...
1848	—	[312][52]		...	...	...
1849	—	[422]		...	...	...
1850	—	875		84	99	17
1851	—	899		95	104	15
1852	—	1,103		111	114	21
1853	—	1,349		152	119	24
1854	—	1,591		163	167	31
1855	—	1,153		[94][53]	...	28
1856	—	[1,115][52]		119	...[54]	27
1857	—	1,471		135	146	28
1858	—	1,708		107	143	22
1859	15	1,723		160	140	27
1860	75	1,889		179	155	29
1861	88	2,034		146	146	28
1862	112	1,728		149	206	26
1863	142	2,006[52]		175	213	41
1864	139	3,261		214	178	44
1865	172	2,442		170	261	45
1866	91	2,640		298	307	64

G6   Central Government Revenue, with some Main Tax Yields

NOTES

1. SOURCES: As for table G5.
2. Total revenue, unless otherwise indicated, means total ordinary revenue exclusive of loan receipts. Whether or not receipts from public enterprises are included (and, if so, whether net or gross) varies from country to country. Changes in composition are indicated in footnotes where this is possible.
3. It must be recalled that in some countries, especially those with federal systems of government, central government revenues may be no more important than the receipts of 'local' governments.
4. Except where otherwise indicated, statistics are from the closed accounts.

FOOTNOTES

[1]   Statistics are budget estimates to 1899, except for 1888 which is a provisional result, and 1889, which is an actual result. Data from 1866 to 1937 and from 1949 to 1958 are for years beginning 1 July.
[2]   Except as indicated in footnotes 3 and 21, statistics to 1939 relate to the administrative budget. From 1940 to 1953 (or 1954 (1st line) for total revenue) they are of consolidated federal government cash receipts, and subsequently the receipts of the unified budget. The difference between total administrative budget receipts and consolidated cash receipts in 1934–39 varied from 26.2 to 30.3 thousand million dollars. From 1913 to 1939, refunds and transfers etc. are excluded from total revenue. The amounts excluded are as follows (in million dollars):

1913	10	1920	46	1927	117	1934	101
1914	10	1921	54	1928	142	1935	95
1915	14	1922	83	1929	172	1936	119
1916	21	1923	154	1930	120	1937	338
1917	24	1924	141	1931	74	1938	654
1918	19	1925	139	1932	82	1939	689
1919	22	1926	168	1933	83		

Statistics from 1844 to 1976 are for years ended 30 June and subsequently they are for years ended 30 September. The 1843 figures are for the first half-year only. Total revenue for July–September 1976 was $81 thousand million.

[3]   Total internal revenue receipts to 1915, the majority of which came from excises except in 1863–73. Income tax collections during that period were as follows (in million dollars):

1863	2.7	1866	73	1869	35	1872	14
1864	20	1867	66	1870	38	1873	5.1
1865	61	1868	41	1871	19		

From 1916 to 1940 (1st line) statistics are of revenue collections, which are not exactly comparable with earlier and later figures owing to differences in the time or stage of operations when the receipts were recorded.
[4]   Statistics to 1889 are for years ended 30 September. Subsequently they are for years beginning 1 April.
[5]   Federal government ordinary revenue to 1974 (1st line), consolidated central government revenue subsequently.
[6]   Tobago is included from 1899. Statistics from 1901 to 1914 are for years beginning 1 April. The 1915 figure is for the period 1 April to 31 December. There was a change in the treatment of the Immigration Fund in 1894.
[7]   Statistics to 1972 (1st line) are of budgetary revenues, exclusive of earmarked funds such as unemployment insurance, but including tax credits to the Old Age Security Fund. Subsequently they are of gross federal government receipts. Data to 1905 are for years beginning 1 July, and from 1907 they are for years beginning 1 April. The 1906 figures are for nine months from 1 July 1906 to 31 March 1907.
[8]   Excise duties plus 'other excise taxes' except sales tax. "Other consumption taxes" are not included in 1985.
[9]   Statistics to 1907 are for years beginning 1 April. The 1908 figure is for nine months from 1 April to 31 December.
[10]   Statistics to 1963 (1st line) are for the general budget only. Subsequently they are of consolidated government current revenue. Data to 1938 are for years beginning 1 July. The 1939 figure is for the second half-year only.
[11]   Statistics to 1937 are for years beginning 1 August and from 1939 to 1956 they are for years beginning 1 July. The 1938 figure is for the period 1 August 1938 to 30 June 1939, and the 1956 figure is for the second half-year only.
[12]   Statistics from 1901 are for years beginning 1 April. There are changes in the coverage of extrabudgetary revenues in 1974 and 1982.
[13]   Statistics from 1927 to 1964 are for years ended 30 June. Extra-budgetary receipts are included in 1980–83.
[14]   Years ended 30 September. The figure for 1961 is for 10 months only, October and November 1960 being omitted. Coverage was widened from 1967 (2nd line).
[15]   Years beginning 1 July to 1949.
[16]   Budget estimates.
[17]   Including the tax on the exploitation of natural resources.
[18]   Subsequent coverage is narrower than before.
[19]   Ordinary budget revenue to 1927/8 (1st line); all fiscal receipts from 1927/8 (2nd line) to 1973 (1st line), but excluding floating debt receipts from 1965; and consolidated central government revenue from 1973 (2nd line).
[20]   Statistics to 1953 are of total receipts other than those of special funds. Subsequently all loans are excluded. There is no break in 1953. From 1974 (2nd line) statistics are of tax revenues and social security contributions only. Data are for years ended 30 June.
[21]   Statistics to 1940 (1st line) are of employment taxes collections. Subsequently they are of receipts from social insurance taxes and contributions.

G6 Central Government Revenue, with some Main Tax Yields

22 There was a widening of the coverage of extra-budgetary receipts in 1972 and 1987.
23 There was a widening of the coverage of extra-budgetary receipts in 1972.
24 Capital Development Fund revenue is included from 1975.
25 Consolidated central government revenue from 1970 (2nd line).
26 Ordinary and extraordinary revenues to 1960 (1st line), but ordinary revenue only thereafter. Data from 1829 to 1886 are for years ended 30 June. The 1887 figure is for the 18 months ended 31 December 1887.
27 Total fiscal receipts to 1900 (1st line), ordinary budget revenue subsequently. The reason for the break in 1921 is not given in the source.
28 The 'peso de 6p.oro'.
29 Statistics from 1889 to 1914 are for years beginning 1 April. The 1915 figure is for the period 1 April to 31 December.
30 Budget estimates to 1898, ordinary budget revenue from 1899 to 1953 (1st line), and consolidated budget receipts subsequently. Export taxes levied directly on companies are included with Customs, not with Direct Taxes. The export duty on rubber, which was of some importance for a time, before 1910, is not included here.
31 Statistics to 1960 are for years beginning 1 July. The 1961 figures are for the second half-year only.
32 Statistics to 1902 are for years ended 30 June. For 1913–19 they are for calendar years, and from 1920 to 1940 they are for years ending 31 August. 1941–49 figures are again for calendar years as are those for 1958 onwards, whilst those for 1951 and 1953 are for years beginning 1 July. The 1950 figure for the 18 months ended 30 June 1951.
33 Local revenues only to 1941.
34 Statistics to 1932 are for years ending 30 June, except for customs receipts to 1901, which are for calendar years.
35 For conversion rates between old and new currencies see p. xi.
36 Including other taxes on foreign trade.
37 Akl direct taxes to 1927, and income tax only from 1928 to 1952 (1st line).
38 The figure for 1916 is for the 14 months ended 28 February 1917. The 1917 and 1918 figures are for years beginning 1 March, and the 1919 figure is for the 10 months from 1 March to 31 December.
39 All taxes on income and property from 1953 (2nd line).
40 Statistics for 1957 are for the 10 months ended 31 October, and those for 1958 and 1959 are for years ended 31 October. Coverage of extra-budgetary receipts was increased in 1974.
41 In 1983 and 1984 the peso argentino was the currency actually in use, but the figures here have been left in the old currency.
42 Data are for budgetary central government only from 1976 (2nd line).
43 The revenues covered by the Customs Administration were much enlarged from 1934.
44 There was a widening of the coverage from 1971.
45 There was a widening of the coverage from 1950 (2nd line).
46 There was a widening of the coverage from 1970 (2nd line).
47 All importa and export taxes from 1954 (2nd line) to 1970 (1st line).
48 There was a widening of the coverage of social security revenue in 1983.
49 Local currency to 1841. This was often converted to sterling on the conventional basis that £1 local was equal to 18 shillings sterling.
50 Including Vancouver Island.
51 From 1 January 1840 to 9 February 1841.
52 Statistics for 1848, 1849 and 1856 are net. The equivalent figure for 1850 is 579. A new system of accounts was adopted in 1857. Data for 1864–66 are for years ended 30 June.
53 For ten months only.
54 Statistics from 1857 are for years ended 30 September.

H PRICES

There is a considerable array of material on prices available for most countries for a comparatively long way back in time. Most of this, however, is intractable in the extreme, and it has been decided to include none of it in this work. Instead, there are two sets of indices, based on this material but reducing it to some sort of readily comprehensible order. It was felt that annual average prices, in local currency, of (say) a kilogram of wheat were unlikely to be of use except to the specialist, and that a general indication of overall price levels would be more widely useful. Of course, there is over-simplification and distortion in the process, and like all index numbers, those presented here require careful interpretation. In order to achieve exact comparability of an index over long periods of time the commodities and their weightings must remain unchanged. However, in a changing economy first the weightings and then possibly the commodities themselves will cease to be appropriate representations of the quantities and things actually used. All indices, therefore, must compromise between continuity and relevance, and the more rapid is economic change the more frequent must be the breaks in continuity. In the period since World War II, the official indices in some countries have been changed very frequently indeed. In other countries and periods where commodity consumption patterns have changed very little, the indices have not changed either. In this way the danger of lack of representativeness has generally been avoided.

It is perhaps worth pointing out that until recently in many Latin American countries, the underlying data for price indices were derived from only a few cities, often only the capital. There may well have been quite wide regional variations in the larger countries of which the indices take no account.

In order to facilitate comparisons between countries—though it must be understood that these are necessarily inexact owing to the nature of indices and the variety of consumption patterns—many of the indices shown here have been converted to common base years. Anyone wanting to use these indices for further calculations should bear in mind this shifting of the base year, and also the fact that different indices have, when necessary, been crudely spliced together.

H1 NORTH AMERICA: WHOLESALE PRICE INDICES

1749–1794

Year	USA[1] (1910–14 = 100)
1749	68
1750	60
1751	65
1752	66
1753	65
1754	65
1755	66
1756	66
1757	65
1758	70
1759	79
1760	79
1761	77
1762	87
1763	79
1764	74
1765	72
1766	73
1767	77
1768	74
1769	77
1770	77
1771	79
1772	89
1773	84
1774	76
1775	75
1776	86
1777	123
1778	140
1779	226
1780	225
1781	216
1782	...
1783	...
1784	...
1785	92
1786	90
1787	90
1788	...
1789	86
1790	90
1791	85
1792	...
1793	102
1794	108

1795–1839

Year	USA[1] (1910–14 = 100)
1795	131
1796	146
1797	131
1798	122
1799	126
1800	129
1801	142
1802	117
1803	118
1804	126
1805	141
1806	134
1807	130
1808	115
1809	130
1810	131
1811	126
1812	131
1813	162
1814	182
1815	170
1816	151
1817	151
1818	147
1819	125
1820	106
1821	102
1822	106
1823	103
1824	98
1825	103
1826	99
1827	98
1828	97
1829	96
1830	91
1831	94
1832	95
1833	95
1834	90
1835	100
1836	114
1837	115
1838	110
1839	112

1840–1884

Year	Canada[2] (1900 = 100)	USA[1] (1910–4 = 100)
1840	...	95
1841	...	92
1842	...	82
1843	...	75
1844	...	77
1845	...	83
1846	...	83
1847	...	90
1848	91	82
1849	80	82
1850	87	84
1851	85	83
1852	91	88
1853	108	97
1854	134	108
1855	155	110
1856	150	105
1857	154	111
1858	108	93
1859	124	95
1860	112	93
1861	98	89
1862	94	104
1863	101	193
1864	108	193
1865	124	185
1866	122	174
1867	124$_2$	162
	129	
1868	128	158
1869	129	151
1870	128	135
1871	130	130
1872	145	136
1873	146	133
1874	138	126
1875	133	118
1876	124	110
1877	118	106
1878	109	91
1879	105	90
1880	115	100
1881	116	103
1882	116	108
1883	113	101
1884	107	93

1885–1924

Year	Canada[2] (1900 = 100)	USA[1] (1910–14 = 100)
1885	101	85
1886	100	82
1887	102	85
1888	106	86
1889	...	106
1890	108	82
1891	108	82
1892	100	76
1893	101	78
1894	95	70
1895	93	71
1896	90	68
1897	91	68
1898	95	71
1899	97	76
1900	100	82
1901	102	81
1902	107	86
1903	108	87
1904	109	87
1905	113	88
1906	113	90
1907	122	95
1908	122	92
1909	124	99
1910	126	103
1911	130	95
1912	137	101
1913	134	102
1914	137	99
1915	147	102
1916	176	125
1917	239	172
1918	266	192
1919	280	202
1920	326	226
1921	230	143
1922	203	141
1923	205	147
1924	208	143

H1 NORTH AMERICA: Wholesale Price Indices

	Canada[2]	Costa Rica[5]	Dominican Republic[6]	El Salvador	Guatemala[3]	Mexico[4]	USA[1]
	1900 = 100	1938 = 100	1953 = 100	1939 = 100	1938 = 100	1938 = 100	1910-14 = 100
1925	214	...	...	...	...	89	151
1926	209	...	...	...	...	86	146
1927	204	...	...	...	...	84	139
1928	201	...	...	...	...	81	141
1929	200	...	...	...	...	81	139
1930	181	...	...	...	...	81	126
1931	151	...	...	...	...	71	107
1932	139	...	...	...	...	66	95
1933	140	...	...	...	...	71	96
1934	150	...	...	...	...	75	109
1935	151	...	...	...	...	75	117
1936	155	98	...	...	...	79	118
1937	174	104	...	...	106	94	126
1938	163	100	...	...	100	100	115
	1938 = 100						1938 = 100
1939	97	102	...	100	99	99	98
1940	106	100	...	88	96	102	100
1941	114	105	37	110	86	110	111
1942	121	137	46	130	102	119	126
1943	125	172	62	156	130	144	132
1944	128	179	76	176	149	178	132
1945	130	198	76	203	185	195	135
1946	137	198	88	239	230[3]	225	154
1947	163	228	106	291	248	237	189
1948	194	233	106	327	261	256	204
1949	198	230	91	331	266	280	194
1950	211	260	88	445	279	309	202
1951	242	267	98	471	295	381	225
1952	228	242	100	445	292	395[4]	219
1953	222	230	100	471	293	389	216
1954	219	239	94	570	307	425	216
1955	222	246	95	491	297	483	217
1956	229	249	94	487	296	506	224
1957	230	249	103	469	294	528	230
1958	231	249	102	444	297	552	234
1959	234	246	96	417	300	558	234

H1 NORTH AMERICA: Wholesale Price Indices

	Canada[2]	Costa Rica[5]	Dominican Republic[6]	El Salvador	Guatemala	Mexico	USA[1]
	1938 = 100	1938 = 100	1953 = 100	1939 = 100	1938 = 100	1938 = 100	1938 = 100
1960	234	244	99	419	296	585	234
1961	237	252	93	407	292	590	233
1962	243	249	102	405	297	601	234
1963	248	257	110	412	295	604	233
1964	249	262	111	440	306	630	234
1965	254	259	120	432	300	642	239
1966	264	259	114	432	298	650	246
1967	270	269	117	431	299	669	247
1968	276	281	125	433	312	681	253
1969	289	294	120	431	322	699	263
1970	295	312	120	469	330	740	273
1971	297	331	120	443	335	768	282
1972	317	350	123	469	335	790	294
1973	385	406	140	568	382	914	333
1974	471	568	169	712	535	1,120	395
1975	501	693	211	725	527	1,237	432
	1980 = 100	1980 = 100	1980 = 100	1980 = 100	1980 = 100	1980 = 100	1980 = 100
1975	62	58	73	54	60	34	65
1976	65	60	69	73	67	41	68
1977	70	65	77	107	75	59	72
1978	77	70	77	86	78	68	78
1979	88	81	88	97	86	80	88
1980	100	100	100	100	100	100	100
1981	110	165	101	106	112	125	109
1982	118	344	108	119	105	194	111
1983	122	434	113	127	106	403	113
1984	127	468	143	135	112	686	115
1985	131	516	202	154	...	1,001	115
1986	132	560	...	203	...	1,797	112
1987	136	...	284	206	...	4,407	114
1988	141	734	...	216	...	8,784	119
1989	144	841	...	237	...	10,198	125
1990	144	966	...	282	...	12,574	130
1991	143	1,237	...	301	...	15,152	130
1992	144	1,462	...	308	...	17,182	131
1993	149	1,556	...	331	...	18,711	133

H1 SOUTH AMERICA: WHOLESALE PRICE INDICES

	Argentina	Brazil	Chile	Colombia	Ecuador	Paraguay[8]	Peru[9]	Venezuela[11]
	1938 = 100	1938 = 100	1938 = 100	1953 = 100	1953 = 100	1938 = 100	1938 = 100	1938 = 100
1913	71	...	37	...	...	...	49	109
1914	72	...	...	...	...	...	51	...
1915	77	...	...	...	...	...	59	...
1916	88	...	...	...	...	...	71	...
1917	109	...	...	...	...	...	86	...
1918	119	...	...	...	...	...	104	...
1919	123	...	...	...	...	...	107	...
1920	129	...	...	...	...	...	117	173
1921	102	...	...	...	...	...	100	137
1922	93	...	...	...	...	...	93	126
1923	96	...	...	...	...	...	92	124
1924	104	...	...	...	...	...	94	133
1925	105	...	...	...	...	...	99	139
1926	94	...	...	...	...	...	99	145
1927	92	...	...	...	...	...	99	139
1928	93	...	44	...	...	...	94	139
1929	91	...	45	...	...	...	91	132
1930	87	...	39	...	...	...	87	124
1931	84	...	35	...	...	...	85	119
1932	85	...	53	...	...	...	83	112
1933	81	...	80	...	...	...	88	101
1934	92	...	80	...	...	...	92	95
1935	92	...	79	...	...	...	92	89
1936	93	...	88	...	...	...	94	95
1937	107	107	105	...	...	...	100	104
1938	100	100	100	...	...	100	100	100[11]
1939	102	104	100	...	...	104	104	106
1940	109	107	107	...	...	104	115	105
1941	119	133	125	...	...	123	135	101
1942	150	159	171	...	...	169	169	105
1943	164	181	189	...	...	200	196	113
1944	178	193	196	...	...	200	204	120
1945	194	226	207	...	...	223	212	125
1946	224	263	243[7]	...	...	281	227	136
1947	232	319	311	...	...	319	308	100
1948	268	370	357	74	...	385	385	173
1949	330	405	415	79	...	504	542	172
1950	397	461	483	88	...	754	628	173
1951	592	552	637	96	...	1,173	706	180
1952	776	613	782	95	97	2,555	761	178
1953	867	699	965	100	100	4,188	785	172
1954	894	908	1,515	107	99	5,109	879	175

H1 SOUTH AMERICA: Wholesale Price Indices

	Argentina	Brazil	Chile	Colombia	Ecuador	Paraguay[8]	Peru[9]	Uruguay[10]	Venezuela[11]
	1938 = 100	1938 = 100	1938 = 100	1953 = 100	1953 = 100	1938 = 100	1938 = 100	1970 = 100	1938 = 100
1955	974	1,027	2,674	108	98	6,031	950	...	177
1956	1,227	1,230	4,382	117	97	8,031	1,089	...	176
1957	1,523	1,382	6,236	145	100	9,740	1,112	...	172
1958	1,995	1,544	7,828	171	100	10,502	1,158	...	175
1959	4,665	2,131	10,177	187	99	12,357	1,425	...	176
			1959 = 100			1959 = 100			
1960	5,402	2,795	105	195	98	113	1,679	...	174
1961	5,831	3,861	105	207	102	127	1,679	...	176
1962	7,611	5,915	114	213	104	134	1,703	...	185
1963	9,821	10,255	175	269	108	137	...	4.3	191
1964	12,399	19,586	265	316	112	142	...	6.4	199
	1964 = 100	1964 = 100					1970 = 100		
1965	124	152	328	342	113	155	...	10	206
1966	149	210	404	402	116	162	...	20	208
1967	186	262	481	429	118	158	...	33	211
1968	204	324	633	456	119	155	76	76	215
1969	217	390	856	486	125	157	88	88	218
1970	248	476	1,172	524	...	151	100	100	221
1971	345	576	1,383	584	...	171	121	121	229
1972	610	686	2,357	691	...	202	229	229	237
			1972 = 100						
1973	917	786	610	883	...	279	492	492	252
1974	1,100	1,019	6,886	1,202	...	364	879	879	294
1975	3,218	1,148	40,067	1,507	...	419	1,515	1,515	333
	1975 = 100	1975 = 100	1975 = 100					1975 = 100	
1976	599	140	321	2,065	117	423	2,091	151	356
1977	1,494	197	598	2,471	126	423	3,075	226	393
1978	3,676	274	855	2,999	147	457	5,409	336	423
1979	9,164	426	1,277	3,873	163	515	8,257	607	463
1980	16,075	891	1,782	4,853	175	649	9,211	860	556
	1980 = 100	1980 = 100	1980 = 100	1980 = 100			1980 = 100	1980 = 100	1980 = 100
1981	210	213	109	124	191	704	168	123	114
1982	750	413	117	154	224	...	263	139	123
1983	3,408	1,116	170	181	...	...	560	242	132
1984	23,002	3,617	212	199	...	...	1,233	429	155
	1984 = 100	1984 = 100							
1985	852	333	303	255	...	...	3,376	757	178
1986	1,250	794	363	304	...	...	5,412	1,266	208
1987	2,787	2,489	433	385	...	...	8,198	2,066	303
1988	14,283	19,809	459	495	...	...	58,001	3,253	362
1989	504,476	270,987	528	635	...	...	1,513,826	5,634	715
							1989 = 100		
1990	8,611,405	7,595,765	643	804	...	...	6,737	11,702	909
	1990 = 100	1990 = 100							
1991	110	401	781	1,026	...	...	27,352	21,953	1,112
1992	117	4,363	872	1,232	...	...	42,997	34,752	1,373
1993	119	93,804	939	1,407	...	...	63,464	46,359	1,832

H1 Wholesale Price Indices

NOTES

1. SOURCES: The national publications listed on pp. xiii–xv; UN and League of Nations, *Statistical Yearbooks*; International Monetary Fund, *International Financial Statistics*.
2. Various indices have been crudely spliced together in a number of cases to give a rough indicator of the long-term movement of prices. The differences in the construction of these indices should be borne in mind if they are used in further calculations.

FOOTNOTES

[1] Warren & Pearson's index to 1889, Bureau of Labour Statistics index subsequently.
[2] H. Michell's index of prices of 15 foodstuffs in Toronto to 1867 (1st line), the general wholesale price index (excluding gold) from then to 1975 (1st line), and the index of industrial products prices subsequently.
[3] Foodstuffs only to 1946.
[4] Mexico City only to 1951.
[5] San José only.
[6] Santa Domingo only.
[7] Home-consumed goods subsequently.
[8] Asunción only to 1955.
[9] Lima-Callao only.
[10] Montevideo only.
[11] Caracas only to 1938.

H2 NORTH AMERICA: CONSUMER PRICE INDICES

1800–1844			1845–1889				1890–1934
	USA			USA		Canada[1]	Honduras[3]	USA
	1913 = 100			1913 = 100		1913 = 100	1938 = 100	1913 = 100
1800	172	1845	94	1890	...	...	91
1801	168	1846	91	1891	...	...	91
1802	145	1847	94	1892	...	...	91
1803	152	1848	88	1893	...	...	91
1804	152	1849	84	1894	...	...	88
1805	152	1850	84	1895	...	...	84
1806	158	1851	84	1896	...	...	84
1807	148	1852	84	1897	...	...	84
1808	162	1853	84	1898	...	...	84
1809	158	1854	91	1899	...	...	84
1810	158	1855	94	1900	70[2]	...	84
1811	168	1856	91	1901	...	...	84
1812	172	1857	94	1902	...	...	88
1813	195	1858	88	1903	...	...	91
1814	212	1859	91	1904	...	...	91
1815	185	1860	91	1905	78[2]	...	91
1816	172	1861	91	1906	...	...	91
1817	162	1862	101	1907	...	...	94
1818	155	1863	125	1908	...	...	91
1819	155	1864	158	1909	...	...	91
1820	141	1865	155	1910	91	...	94
1821	135	1866	148	1911	93	...	94
1822	135	1867	141	1912	98	...	98
1823	121	1868	135	1913	100₁	...	100
1824	111	1869	135	1914	101	...	101
1825	114	1870	128	1915	102	...	102
1826	114	1871	121	1916	111	...	110
1827	114	1872	121	1917	131	...	129
1828	111	1873	121	1918	148	...	152
1829	108	1874	114	1919	163	...	174
1830	108	1875	111	1920	189	...	202
1831	108	1876	108	1921	166	...	180
1832	101	1877	108	1922	152	...	169
1833	98	1878	98	1923	153	...	172
1834	101	1879	94	1924	150	...	172
1835	104	1880	98	1925	152	...	177
1836	111	1881	98	1926	153	...	178
1837	114	1882	98	1927	151	...	175
1838	108	1883	94	1928	151	...	173
1839	108	1884	91	1929	153	122	173
1840	101	1885	91	1930	152	...	168
1841	104	1886	91	1931	137	...	154
1842	98	1887	91	1932	124	105	138
1843	94	1888	91	1933	119	...	131
1844	94	1889	91	1934	120	...	135

H2 NORTH AMERICA: Consumer Price Indices

	Canada	Costa Rica[4]	Cuba	Dominican Republic[5]	El Salvador[6]	Guatemala[7]	Haiti[8]
	1913 = 100	1938 = 100	1938 = 100	1941 = 100	1938 = 100	1937 = 100	1948 = 100
1935	121	...	...	...	...	...	...
1936	123	93	...	...	...	...	...
1937	127	99	...	...	113	100	...
1938	129	100	100	...	100	...	...
	1938 = 100						
1939	99	100	94	...	94	92	...
1940	103	98	92	...	97	91	...
1941	109	101	100	100	109	87	...
1942	114	122	132	120	111	...	...
1943	116	156	151	150	123	111	...
1944	117	165	172	174	160	130	...
1945	118	175	194	181	180	163	...
1946	122	182	210	202	177	194	...
1947	133	207	248	227	189	198	...
1948	152	214	269	229	191	223	100
1949	157	232	234	219	200	240	...
1950	162	256	226	219	234	247	...
1951	178	274	251	239	271[6]	269	[102][10]
1952	183	266	253	241	265	263	109
1953	181	268	245	238	284	271	101
1954	182	275	238	233	301	278	106
1955	183	285	238	233	314	283	107
1956	186	287	238	236	319	285	111
1957	192	296	238	248	304	282	114
1958	197	304	...	242	322	285	111
1959	199	305	...	242	320	284	108
1960	201	307	...	234	319	281	103
1961	203	315	...	224	310	279	106
1962	205	323	...	244	311	285	106
1963	209	333	...	266	316	285	110
1964	213	344	...	272	321	285	121
1965	218	341	...	266	323	283	123
1966	226	342	...	267	319	284	133
1967	234	346	...	271	324	286	130
1968	244	360	...	271	332	291	131
1969	255	370	...	273	331	297	133
1970	263	387	...	284	341	304	134
1971	271	399	...	296	342	303	148
1972	284	417	...	319	347	305	153
1973	305	[481]	...	367	369	346	187
1974	339	[625]	...	416	432	404	216
1975	375	733	...	476	515		252

H2 NORTH AMERICA: Consumer Price Indices

1935–1975

	Honduras[3]	Jamaica[9]	Mexico	Nicaragua[11]	Panama[12]	Puerto Rico	Trinidad & Tobago	USA
	1938 = 100	1940 = 100	1938 = 100	1938 = 100	1939–40 = 100	1943 = 100	1952 = 100	1913 = 100
1935	105	...	70	...	...	...	...	138
1936	98	...	75	...	...	...	...	140
1937	100	...	88	66	...	...	...	145
1938	100	...	100	100	...	...	...	142
								1938 = 100
1939	102	[84][10]	102	148	100	...	...	99
1940	107	100	103	181	...	...	...	100
1941	108	114	106	178	...	[71][10]	...	105
1942	117	127	123	240	153	[95][10]	...	116
1943	133	131	161	317	156	100	...	123
1944	145	133	202	538	159	101	...	125
1945	158	133	217	632	162	104	...	128
1946	162	137	272	508	175	113	...	139
1947	163	163	304	549	194	125	...	159
1948	167	196	323	518[11]	196	127	...	171
1949	173	204	340	489	184	116	...	169
1950	182	214	362	585	178	114	...	171
1951	200	243	407	700	186	125	...	184
1952	196	269	466	710	192[12]	133	100	188
1953	200	269	458	796	194	137	102	190
1954	211	269	481	863	192	141	102	191
1955	227	272	558	978	191	140	107	190
1956	220	277	583	949	191	141	108	193
1957	215	283	614	911	190	147	111	200
1958	221	298	689	959	190	150	116	205
1959	223	307	708	930	189	153	119	207
1960	219	316	742	911	190	158	121	210
1961	223	338	754	911	190	162	123	212
1962	225	343	762	916	192	165	126	215
1963	232	348	767	921	193	168	131	217
1964	243	356	786	959	198	172	132	220
1965	250	365	814	988	199	177	135	224
1966	251	373	848	1,015	199	182	140	230
1967	254	383	873	1,033	202	189	143	237
1968	260	406	893	...	205	195	155	247
1969	265	431	927	...	209	200	159	260
1970	273	473	975	...	215	207	163	276
1971	279	498	1,028	...	220	216	169	287
1972	289	525	1,079	...	231	216	184	297
				1980 = 100				
1973	302	617	1,209	[35][10]	247	239	212	315
1974	341	786	1,490	39	289	286	258	350
1975	369	923	1,724	42	304	311	302	383

H2 NORTH AMERICA: Consumer Price Indices

1980 = 100

	Canada	Costa Rica[4]	Dominican Republic[5]	El Salvador	Guatemala[7]	Haiti[8]	Honduras[3]
1975	66	68	62	54	60	64	64
1976	71	70	67	58	67	68	67
1977	76	73	76	65	75	73	73
1978	83	77	79	73	81	71	77
1979	91	85	86	85	90	80	85
1980	100	100	100	100	100	100	100
1981	112	137	107	115	111	111	109
1982	124	260	116	128	112	119	120
1983	132	346	124	145	[99][10]	131	130
1984	138	387	154	162	100	139	137
1985	143	443	212	198	120	154	139
1986	149	498	232	262	158	160	144
1987	155	582	269	327	175	141	148
1988	162	703	389	391	205	147	156
1989	170	819	565	460	228	157	171
1990	178	954	870	570	321	190	211
1991	188	1,228	1,339	652	428	219	283
1992	191	1,496	1,401	725	471	261	308
1993	194	1,643	1,474	860	527	320	341

	Jamaica[9]	Mexico	Nicaragua[11]	Panama[12]	Puerto Rico	Trinidad & Tobago	USA
1975	37	38	42	72	76	55	65
1976	40	45	43	75	78	60	69
1977	45	57	48	78	81	67	73
1978	60	67	50	81	85	74	79
1979	78	79	74	88	91	85	88
1980	100	100	100	100	100	100	100
1981	112	128	124	107	110	114	110
1982	119	203	155	112	114	127	117
1983	133	410	203	114	115	148	121
1984	170	679	274	116	117	168	126
1985	214	1,071	877	117	117	181	131
1986	246	1,995	6,852	117	117	195	133
1987	262	4,626	69,256	118	120	216	138
1988	284	9,907	7 million	119	124	233	144
			1988 = 100				
1989	325	11,888	4,770	119	128	260	151
1990	397	15,062	361,804	120	130	289	159
1991	599	18,376	1,065,512	122	133	300	166
1992	1,062	21,224	2,557,230	124	136	320	171
1993	1,297	23,303	3,078,904	125	141	354	176

H2 SOUTH AMERICA: CONSUMER PRICE INDICES

1863–1899			1900–1934						
	Colombia[13]		Argentina[14]	Brazil[15]	Chile[16]	Colombia[13]	Peru[17]	Uruguay[18]	Venezuela[23]
	1864 = 100		1913 = 100	1913 = 100	1913 = 100	1864 = 100	1913 = 100	1938 = 100	1938 = 100
1863	...	1900	...	...	...	...	...	...	...
1864	100	1901	...	...	...	2,416	...	...	...
		1902	...	...	...	...	...	...	...
1865	...	1903	...	...	...	...	...	...	...
1866	...	1904	...	...	...	7,888	...	...	...
1867	...								
1868	...	1905	...	...	...	9,532	...	...	...
1869	...	1906	...	...	...	...	...	...	...
		1907	...	...	...	9,750	...	...	...
1870	...	1908	...	...	...	...	...	...	...
1871	...	1909	...	...	...	10,510	...	...	...
1872	...								
1873	...	1910	...	...	...	10,942	...	...	...
1874	...	1911	...	...	...	16,974	...	...	...
		1912	...	99	...	25,882	...	...	...
1875	...	1913	100	100	100	...	100	...	...
1876	...	1914	100	100	108	...	104	...	...
1877	...								
1878	131	1915	107	109	120	...	112	...	...
1879	117	1916	115	117	117	28,426	123	...	...
		1917	135	129	118	29,910	142	...	...
1880	...	1918	169	144	121	...	164	...	...
1881	143								
1882	139					*1938 = 100*			
1883	126								
1884	134	1919	160	149	143	58	188	...	...
1885	...	1920	186	164	168	72	210	...	...
1886	127	1921	167	169	169	53	199	...	...
1887	...	1922	139	185	173	...	190	...	...
1888	...	1923	137	203	176	78	180	...	...
1889	...	1924	139	237	186	78	187	...	...
1890	...	1925	136	253	202	79	200	...	...
1891	275	1926	132	261	199	97	201	...	...
1892	276	1927	131	268	196	87	193	...	...
1893	...								
1894	353					*1938 = 100*			
1895	...	1928	117	264	58	89	181	...	...
1896	...	1929	131	262	59	87	176	103	...
1897	410	1930	133	238	59	72	169	103	...
1898	...	1931	114	230	58	66	158	103	...
1899	...	1932	102	231	62	56	151	101	...
		1933	108	229	77	57	147	96	104
		1934	102	246	77	79	150	96	94

H2 SOUTH AMERICA: Consumer Price Indices

1935-1975

	Argentina[14]	Bolivia[19]	Brazil[15]	Chile[16]	Colombia[13]	Ecuador[20]	Guyana	Paraguay	Peru[17]	Uruguay[18]	Venezuela[23]
	1913=100	1938=100	1913=100	1938=100	1938=100	1938=100	1938[21]=100	1938=100	1913=100	1938=100	1938=100
1935	108	...	262	78	82	...	...	...	152	99	92
1936	118	45	299	85	87	...	...	...	159	98	95
1937	121	76	321	96	88	...	...	...	170	101	98
1938	120	100	355	100	100	100	[100][21]	100	172	100	100
	1938=100		1938=100						1938=100		
1939	102	124	103	101	104	153	...	109	99	106	106
1940	104	166	107	114	101	165	...	113	106	111	101
1941	107	212	119	132	99	153	...	128	115	110	99
1942	113	276	132	165	108	176	[159][10]	144	130	113	109
1943	114	337	146	192	125	188	[163][10]	176	142	119	120
1944	114	359	164	215	150	224	159	193	162	122	138
1945	136	379	191	234	167	259	159	214	180	140	138
1946	161	431	223	271	180	318	173	235	197	155	147
1947	182	547	272	362	212	524	184	309	254	179	169
1948	207[14]	526	281	427	247	588	196	412	334	182	204
1949	266	578	294	507	264	576	206	556	378	191	199
1950	354	784	321	584[16]	316	571	224	951	430	184	197
1951	472	994[19]	359	714	346	638	239	1,300	474	210	202
1952	667	1,235	421	868	337	659	267	2,827	507	239	199
1953	694	2,485	482	1,095	362	662	267	4,478	554	255	198
1954	722	5,566	590	1,711	394	686	275	5,795	583	285	201
								1954=100			
1955	806	10,010	726	3,017	390	696	283	124	610	312	199
1956	917	27,928	878	5,003	415	663	288	150	643	335	197
		1956=100									
1957	1,139	215	1,047	6,439	478	668	292	174	692	382	191
1958	1,500	222	1,203[15]	8,109	549	679	294	185	747	448	197
1959	3,167	267	1,504	11,238	588	680	302	204	841	624	206
	1959=100		1959=100	1959=100					1959=100		
1960	128	298	120	112	611	690	304	220	109	869	207
1961	146	320	180	120	664	719	307	261	115	1,068	202
1962	187	339	260	137	679	739	318	265	123	1,184	201
1963	231	337	440	197	898	783	324	270	130	1,433	203
1964	282	371	860	278	1,055	809	326	274	143	2,020	207
										1964=100	
1965	362	381	1,420	360	1,092	836	334	285	166	157	211
1966	477	408	2,001	441	1,309	869	341	293	181	272	214
1967	618	454	2,601	534	1,417	903	351	297	199	517	215
1968	718	479	3,181	673	1,500	941	362	299	237	1,163	217
1969	773	485	3,881	870	1,652	1,002	367	305	252	1,400	222
	1969=100		1969=100	1969=100	1969=100						
1970	107	508	123	133	107	1,052	379	303	265	1,642	228
1971	109	527	147	159	117	1,141	383	318	283	1,239	236
1972	113	561	172	285	132	1,230	402	348	303	2,187	242
1973	120	738	194	1,288	159	1,391	433	392	332	4,309	252
1974	126	1,201	247	7,811	197	1,715	508	490	388	7,635	273
1975	137	1,297	319	37,037	242	1,978	548	523	479	13,849	301

H2 SOUTH AMERICA: Consumer Price Indices

1980 = 100	Argentina	Bolivia	Brazil	Chile	Colombia[13]	Ecuador[20]
1975	0.49	46	14	6.6	35	57
1976	2.58	48	19	21	41	64
1977	7.04	51	27	40	54	72
1978	19	57	37	55	63	80
1979	50	68	56	74	78	88
1980	100	100	100	100	100	100
1981	204	132	196	120	129	112
1982	541	295	370	132	160	130
1983	2,403	1,109	874	167	192	193
1984	17,462	15,325	2,380	201	223	254
	1984 = 100	1984 = 100	1984 = 100			
1985	772	11,848	302	262	279	325
1986	1,468	44,591	693	313	330	399
1987	3,395	51,092	2,227	376	404	517
1988	15,041	59,268	15,286	431	526	818
1989	463,112	68,277	212,017	504	662	
1990	10,716,641	79,952	6,438,956	635	834	
	1990 = 100					
1991	271	97,062	34,828,313	773	1,088	
			1991 = 100			
1992	339	108,807	1,009	892	1,382	
1993	369	118,056	22,682	1,005	1,694	

	Guyana	Paraguay[22]	Peru[17]	Uruguay[18]	Venezuela[23]
1975	55	50	13	11	59
1976	60	53	17	16	63
1977	65	58	24	25	68
1978	74	64	37	37	73
1979	88	82	63	61	82
1980	100	100	100	100	100
1981	122	114	175	134	116
1982	148	122	288	159	127
1983	170	138	609	238	135
1984	[209][10]	166	1,280	370	152
			1984 = 100		
1985	245	208	263	637	169
1986	252	274	460	1,123	189
1987	340	334	871	1,836	242
1988	476	410	6,680	2,978	313
1989	495	518	233,666	5,372	577
1990	513	716	17,723,566	11,416	812
			1990 = 100		
1991	525	890	410	23,060	1,090
1992	539	1,024	711	38,856	1,432
1993	...	1,211	1,057	59,877	1,978

H2 Consumer Price Indices

NOTES

1. SOURCES: As for table H1, with Colombia to 1917 from Miguel Urrutia and Mario Arrubla (eds.), *Compendio de Estadisticas Historicas de Colombia* (Bogota, 1970).
2. Various indices have been crudely spliced together in some cases to give a rough indicator of the long-term movement of the cost of living. The differences in the construction of these indices should be borne in mind if they are used in further calculations.

FOOTNOTES

[1] Family budget price index to 1913, consumer price index subsequently.
[2] December only.
[3] In Tegucigalpa.
[4] In San José.
[5] In Santo Domingo to 1978.
[6] In San Salvador to 1951.
[7] In Guatemala City to 1975 (1st line).
[8] In Port-au-Prince to 1979.
[9] In Kingston.
[10] The figure applies to less than the full 12 months.
[11] Cost of food in Managua to 1948, consumer price index subsequently (but in Managua only to 1979).
[12] Cost of food in Panama City to 1952, consumer price index there subsequently.
[13] In Bogota. The index to 1864–1917 relates to food prices only.
[14] In Buenos Aires to 1948.
[15] In Rio de Janeiro to 1953.
[16] In Santiago to 1950.
[17] In Lima-Callao.
[18] In Montevideo.
[19] In La Paz to 1951.
[20] In Quito.
[21] March–December only.
[22] In Asunción.
[23] In Caracas.

I EDUCATION

Of all the subjects on which statistical material exists, probably none shows less uniformity, both over time and between countries, than education. There is no universal definition of what constitutes a primary school, or a general secondary school, and even that of a university has shown considerable flexibility in the recent past. Moreover, there have been several major reorganizations of school systems in practically every country, and minor changes have been very frequent. Furthermore, the statistics of pupils and teachers have not always been collected in a consistent manner, even within the same school system. In addition, the date in the school year to which the statistics relate has been altered on various occasions; the exact meaning of the data has changed, sometimes referring to all pupils on the register, sometimes to those in regular attendance, sometimes to those present on a particular day, and sometimes to those present when an inspector visited. Moreover, private schools have not always been included in the data collection process, and in some cases statistics for tertiary education have not distinguished between different types of institution, teacher-training even being included quite frequently with secondary education. Nevertheless, for all the impossibility of making precise comparisons over long periods of time, and, even more, between many countries, when used with care these statistics do provide useful comparative material, even if only of a very rough nature.

I1 NORTH AMERICA: PUPILS AND TEACHERS IN SCHOOLS (in thousands, except as otherwise indicated)

Key: a = primary schools; b = secondary schools

1854–1884

	Barbados	Canada[2]	Guatemala	Jamaica	Newfoundland	Nicaragua	Trinidad	USA[4]		Teachers[5]
	Pupils	Pupils	Pupils	Pupils	Pupils	Pupils	Pupils	Pupils		All Schools
	a[1]	All Schools	a	All Schools	All Schools	a	a	a	b	
1854	...	...	...	...	...	...	1.8	...	...	...
1855	8.1	...	...	...	...	...	1.8	...	...	...
1856	11	...	...	...	...	...	2.2	...	...	...
1857	13	...	...	...	...	...	2.3	...	...	...
1858	...	...	...	...	...	...	2.3	...	...	...
1859	11	...	...	...	...	...	3.5	...	...	...
1860	11	...	...	...	...	...	3.4	...	...	...
1861	9.7	...	...	...	...	...	3.7	...	...	...
1862	13	...	...	...	...	...	3.7	...	...	...
1863	12	...	...	...	...	...	3.6	...	...	...
1864	10	...	...	...	...	...	3.1	...	...	...
1865	11	...	...	...	...	...	3.5	...	...	...
1866	11	...	...	...	...	...	3.1	...	...	...
1867	13	...	...	...	...	...	2.9	...	...	...
1868	13	720	...	20	...	...	3.2	...	...	...
1869	12	739	...	20	...	...	2.9	...	...	...
1870	13	749	...	26	...	...	3.5	...	...	201
1871	15	767	...	33	19	...	4.1	7,481	80	220
1872	16	784	...	38	20	...	5.1	...	...	230
1873	17	810	...	37	20	...	5.7	...	...	238
1874	18₁	825₂	...	43	19	...	6.2	...	...	248
1875	...	837	...	41	...	...	7.6	...	...	258
1876	11	[837]	...	47	19	...	6.5	...	...	260
1877	12	864	...	50	19	...	6.5	...	...	267
1878	12	...	...	51	20	...	7.2	...	...	277
1879	11	866	...	52	18	...	8.1	...	...	280
1880	12	852₂	...	56	18	...	9.4	9,757	110	287
1881	12	852₂	...	49	...	...	9.1	...	...	294
1882	11	[804]³	...	53	...	...	9.0	...	...	299
1883	11	[851]³	41	56	25	15	10	...	...	304
1884	12	[868]³	...	58	26	14	11	...	...	314

I1 NORTH AMERICA: Pupils and Teachers in Schools (in thousands, except as otherwise indicated) (a: primary schools; b: secondary schools)

1885–1914

Year	Barbados Pupils a[1]	Barbados Pupils b	Canada[2] All Schools Pupils	Canada[2] All Schools Teachers	Costa Rica Pupils a[8]	Costa Rica Pupils b[9]	Costa Rica Teachers a[8]	Cuba All Schools[10] Pupils	Cuba All Schools[10] Teachers[11]	Cuba Pupils a	Cuba Pupils b	El Salvador Pupils a	El Salvador Pupils b	Guatemala Pupils a[13]	Honduras Pupils b
1885	11	…	964	…	13		…	…	…	…	…	39	…	…	…
1886	11	…	911	…	14		…	…	…	…	…	…	…	…	…
1887	13	0.5	968	…	11		…	…	…	…	…	…	…	…	…
1888	14	0.4	998	…	13		…	…	…	27	1.3	45	…	…	…
1889	13	…	[936][3]	…	…		…	…	…	…	…	…	…	…	…
1890	14	0.5	961	21	9		…	…	…	…	…	…	…	…	…
1891	13	0.5	[943][6]	…	…	…	…	…	…	…	…	65	…	…	…
1892	16	0.5	[889][6]	…	17	…	0.5	…	…	…	…	…	…	…	…
1893	18	0.5	998	…	20	…	0.6	…	…	29	1.2	…	…	…	…
1894	16	0.6	1,018	…	19	…	0.6	…	…	…	…	…	…	…	…
1895	14	0.6	1,040	26	22	…	0.7	…	…	…	…	75	…	…	…
1896	15	0.5	1,049	…	22	…	0.8	…	…	…	…	…	…	…	…
1897	16	0.6	1,108	…	23	…	0.9	…	…	…	…	…	…	…	…
1898	15	0.6	1,082	…	23	…	0.9	…	…	…	…	…	…	…	…
1899	15	0.5	1,085	…	21	…	0.9	85	2.7	…	…	47[12]	…	…	…
1900	14 / 24	0.5	1,079	28	19	…	0.9	172	3.6	…	…	…	…	…	…
1901	24	0.5	1,093	27	19	…	0.8	163[10]	3.6[10]	…	…	…	…	…	…
1902	23	0.5	1,104	28	19	…	0.7	163	3.6	…	…	…	…	30	0.6
1903	25	0.6	1,114	29	23	…	0.8	…	…	30	…	…	…	…	…
1904	26	0.6	1,121	29	23	…	0.9	143	3.6	…	…	…	…	…	…
1905	25	0.5	1,150	29	22	0.4	1.0	135	…	…	…	…	…	…	…
1906	25	0.5	1,164	32	24	…	1.0	142	…	32	…	…	…	…	…
1907	25	0.6	1,196	33	26	…	0.7	131	…	…	…	…	…	…	…
1908	26	0.6	1,230	35	24	…	0.8	…	…	…	…	…	…	26	…
1909	27	0.6	1,272	36	28	0.5	0.8	143	3.6	…	…	…	…	…	…
1910	28	0.6	1,311	38	27	0.4	1.0	153	3.9	…	…	54	…	…	…
1911	28	0.6	1,357	41	30	0.5	1.1	…	…	32	…	56	…	30	0.3
1912	26	0.6	[1,322][7]	[39][7]	31	0.6	1.2	235	4.1	…	…	60	…	30	…
1913	26	0.6	1,471	44	33	0.6	1.3	277	4.3	44	…	61	…	36	…
1914	25	0.6	1,555	46	35	0.6	1.4	290	4.9	41	…	64	…	41	…

Note: For Costa Rica 1885–1890 the figures (13, 14, 11, 13, 9) are bracketed together as combined figures.

I1   NORTH AMERICA: Pupils and Teachers in Schools (in thousands, except as otherwise indicated) (a: primary schools; b: secondary schools)

1885-1914

	Jamaica	Mexico			Newfoundland	Nicaragua	Puerto Rico[15]	Trinidad[16]		USA[4]		
	Pupils	Pupils		Teachers	Pupils	Pupils	Pupils	Pupils		Pupils		Teachers
	All Schools[14]	a	b	All Schools	All Schools	a	All Schools	a	b	a	b	All Schools
1885	62				27			11				326
1886	62				29			12				331
1887	62				29	12		14				339
1888	72							16				347
1889	76				32			17				357
1890	80				32			20		12,520	203	364
1891	84				33					12,839	212	368
1892	92				35			18		13,016	240	374
1893	97				35			18		13,229	254	383
1894	104				34			21		13,706	289	389
1895	100[14]	561			33			22		13,894	350	398
1896	93				31			22		14,118	380	400
1897	98				34			24		14,414	409	405
1898	96				35			25		14,654	450	411
1899	99				37			25[15]		14,700	476	414
1900					38	18	34	30		14,984	519	423
1901							56	31		15,161	542	432
1902							63	38		15,367	551	442
1903							65	38		15,417	592	449
1904							57	39		15,620	636	455
1905							49	41		15,789	680	460
1906			5.8	40			52	41		15,919	723	466
1907		658					63	44		16,140	751	481
1908						18	83	45		16,292	770	495
1909					42		95	45		16,665	841	506
1910					44		114	48		16,899	915	523
1911					44		125	49	0.8	17,050	985	534
1912							132	49	0.8	17,078	1,105	547
1913						31	183	52	0.8	17,474	1,135	565
1914							160	51	0.8	17,935	1,219	580

I1 NORTH AMERICA: Pupils and Teachers in Schools (in thousands, except as otherwise indicated)

1915–1944

	Barbados Pupils		Canada[2] All Schools		Costa Rica Pupils		Costa Rica Teachers		Cuba All Schools[10]		Dominican Republic Pupils		Dominican Republic Teachers
	a[1]	b	Pupils	Teachers	a[8]	b[9]	a[8]	b[9]	Pupils	Teachers[11]	a	b	a
					(numbers)								
1915	23	0.6	1,604	48	35	0.5	1.3	...	290	4.9	...	...	...
1916	23	0.6	1,626	50	37	...	1.5	...	...	...	...	...	...
1917	22	0.7	1,651	52	35	...	1.5	...	...	...	...	...	...
1918	20	0.7	1,675	53	...	0.9	...	...	335	...	...	...	...
1919	19	0.8	1,750	51	30	...	1.1	...	...	...	...	...	...
1920	19	0.9	1,827	56	35	1.2	1.3	...	...	...	...	...	...
1921	19	0.9	1,881	58	38	...	1.3	...	358[10]	6.1[10]	...	...	...
1922	20	0.8	1,965	61	39	1.0	1.3	...	386	7.6	...	...	...
1923	21	0.8	1,940	...	41	1.1	1.4	...	301	8.9	...	...	...
1924	22	0.8	1,967	62	39	0.9	1.4	...	426	...	...	...	...
1925	22	0.8	1,993	62	40	...	1.4	...	346	8.4	...	...	...
1926	23	0.8	2,026	64	42	1.0	1.5	...	352	8.7	...	...	...
1927	23	0.9	2,049	66	42	1.0	1.4	...	...	...	...	...	...
1928	23	1.0	2,081	68	47	1.2	1.7	...	373	9.2	...	...	...
1929	23	1.0	2,121[2]	69	47	1.1	1.7	62	374	9.0	...	...	...
1930	23	1.0	2,151[17]	70	49	1.1	1.9	81	484	9.2	...	...	...
1931	24	1.1	2,189	71	51	1.1	1.9	86	451	9.1	...	...	...
1932	24	1.1	2,230	...	53	1.0	1.9	70	...	...	...	...	...
1933	24	1.1	2,243	73	54	1.2	2.3	79	428	9.3	68	...	...
1934	25	1.2	2,241[17]	73	59	1.4	2.3	78	...	...	...	...	...
1935	25	1.2	2,222	74	59	1.4	2.3	82	...	...	104	...	...
1936	26	1.3	2,223	73	60	...	2.3	...	493	11	113	...	1.9
1937	26	1.4	2,215	73	62	1.4	2.6	78	...	...	114	1.8	2.0
1938	27	1.5	2,222	74	63	1.3	2.6	77	455	11	116	...	2.1
1939	28	1.6	2,233	75	65	1.2	2.7	78	[446][10]	[9.4][10]	117	...	2.3
1940	28	1.6	2,202	76	67	1.5	2.8	78	...	...	132	...	2.3
1941	28	1.7	2,167	76	70	...	...	...	...	...	130	...	2.3
1942	29	1.8	2,109	75	72	...	...	...	...	...	128	...	2.3
1943	30	2.3	2,070	74	77	1.7	3.8	122	...	...	128	3.1	2.4
1944	29	2.4	2,075	75	79	...	...	...	...	...	213	...	3.7

I1 NORTH AMERICA: Pupils and Teachers in Schools (in thousands, except as otherwise indicated)

1915–1944

	El Salvador			Guatemala				Haiti		Honduras		
	Pupils		Teachers	Pupils		Teachers		Pupils		Pupils[18]		Teachers
	a	b	a	a	b	a	b	a	b	a[13]	b	a[13]
1915	...	...	...	66	...	...	...	...	...	...	...	...
1916	58	2.3	...	67	...	...	...	...	...	...	...	...
1917	...	...	...	54	...	...	...	...	...	33[18]	...	...
1918	...	...	...	...	...	...	...	62	4.8	...	...	...
1919	51	...	1.6	...	...	...	...	...	...	...	...	...
1920	49	...	...	55[12]	...	...	...	...	...	36	...	...
1921	58	...	1.5	77	...	...	...	...	...	39	...	...
1922	42	...	...	83	...	...	...	...	...	33	0.2	1.1
1923	37	...	1.1	89	...	...	...	...	...	31	...	0.8
1924	45	...	...	94	...	...	...	...	...	...	...	...
1925	50	...	...	103	...	3.2	...	79	4.3	28	...	...
1926	52	...	...	104	...	3.4	...	...	...	35	...	...
1927	48	...	...	115	...	3.6	...	...	...	39	...	1.4
1928	...	...	...	...	...	...	...	...	...	35	...	...
1929	41	...	...	...	...	...	...	87	...	42[18]	...	2.0
1930	...	...	...	...	...	...	...	...	...	...	...	...
1931	47	...	...	...	...	...	...	...	...	...	...	...
1932	51	...	...	88	3.2	...	...	...	...	30	...	1.4
1933	64	...	...	...	...	...	...	...	...	35	...	1.2
1934	...	...	...	104	3.6	4.1	1.1	...	...	38	...	1.4
1935	71	...	...	112	5.4	4.6	1.2	[66]¹	...	31	...	1.2
1936	77	...	...	...	...	...	...	...	...	41	...	1.2
1937	83	...	...	123	5.7	5.1	1.3	...	...	37	...	1.3
1938	85	...	...	123	5.7	5.1	1.3	...	...	40	...	1.5
1939	94	...	...	130	...	...	...	...	...	46	...	1.5
1940	96	...	...	137	...	...	...	[72]¹ 83	...	50	...	1.6
1941	86	...	...	132	...	...	...	87	...	52	...	1.7
1942	91	1.7	...	133	5.6	...	...	98	...	48	...	1.7
1943	80	...	...	132	...	...	...	...	...	48	...	1.8
1944	99	1.9	...	135	7	5.5	1.1	...	51	...	...	1.9

I1 NORTH AMERICA: Pupils and Teachers in Schools (in thousands, except as otherwise indicated)

1915–1944

| | Jamaica | | Mexico | | | Newfoundland | Nicaragua | | | |
| | Pupils | | Pupils | | Teachers | Pupils | Pupils | | Teachers | |
	a	b	a	b	a	All Schools	a	b	a	b
1915	97	..	..	..	..		..	..	..	..
1916	97	..	..	..	..		..	..	..	..
1917	100	..	..	..	..		..	..	..	..
1918	94	..	..	..	..		..	..	..	..
1919	90	..	..	..	..		..	..	..	..
1920	92	..	..	..	..	54	..	..	..	..
1921	100	..	..	..	..	56	..	..	..	..
1922	112	..	..	..	..	55	30	0.4	..	..
1923	115	..	..	..	..	56	..	0.5	..	..
1924	113	..	..	..	..	58	30	..	..	..
1925	118	..	..	..	..	59	..	..	..	..
1926	122	..	..	17	..	59	..	..	..	..
1927	126	..	887	16	..	60	..	..	..	..
1928	128	..	1,002	16	..	61	..	..	..	..
1929	133	..	1,212	..	..	61	..	..	..	..
1930	132	..	1,300	17	..	61	..	..	..	..
1931	134	..	1,396	22	..	61	..	..	..	..
1932	136	..	1,479	..	..	59	..	..	..	..
1933	142	..	1,486	..	..	55	..	..	..	..
1934	148	..	1,419	..	..	55	..	..	..	..
1935	151	..	1,511	26	..	57	..	..	..	..
1936	152	..	1,683	..	..	59	..	..	..	..
1937	158	..	1,810	..	..	63	..	..	..	..
1938	164	..	1,916	..	..	63	54	1.0	1.7	0.1
1939	164	..	1,964	..	..	64	..	..	..	..
1940	163	..	1,961	..	..	66	..	..	..	..
1941	164	..	2,017	..	..	67	..	..	..	..
1942	163	3.6	2,154	..	44	67	..	..	..	..
1943	164	4.0	1,819	..	49	66	..	..	..	..
1944	171	4.3	1,882	..	52	69	..	..	..	..

I1 NORTH AMERICA: Pupils and Teachers in Schools (in thousands, except as otherwise indicated)

1915–1944

	Panama	Puerto Rico		Trinidad and Tobago[21]				USA[4]		Teachers[5]
	Pupils	All Schools		Pupils		Teachers		Pupils		All Schools
	a	Pupils	Teachers	a	b	a	b	a	b	
1915	...	150	...	49	0.6	...	...	18,375	1,329	604
1916	...	146	...	49	0.8	...	...	18,896	1,456	622
1917	...	138	...	47	0.9	...	...	...	...	...
1918	...	157	...	46	0.9	...	...	18,920	1,934	651
1919	...	178	...	48	0.9	...	...	...	...	...
1920	...	186	...	50	1.1	...	...	18,897	2,200	680
1921	34	214	...	55	1.1	...	...	...	...	...
1922	...	213	...	58	1.0	...	...	19,837	2,873	723
1923	...	213	...	58	1.1	...	...	...	...	...
1924	...	215	...	57	1.1	...	...	20,289	3,390	761
1925	...	213	...	58	1.3	...	...	20,311	3,757	...
1926	...	212	...	59	1.5	...	...	...	...	814
1927	...	221	...	62	1.4	...	...	...	...	832
1928	...	220	...	63	1.5	...	...	20,573[4]	3,911[4] / 22,808	4,252
1929	...	221	...	63	1.7	...	...	...	...	...
1930	51	226	...	64	1.8	...	...	22,811	4,740	854
1931	49	229	...	66	1.8	...	...	...[4]	5,543	...
1932	48	233	...	68	1.7	...	...	22,818		872
1933	46	239	...	71	1.8	...	...	...	...	...
1934	47	246	...	73	1.6	...	...	22,534	6,029	847
1935	54	256	...	71	1.7	...	0.1	22,039	6,362	...
1936	55	247	...	72	2.0	...	0.1	...	...	871
1937	61	262	...	73	2.1	1.8	0.1	...	...	...[5]
1938	64	281	...	75	2.3	1.4	...	21,393[4]	6,664	877
1939	63	286	...	77	2.4	0.9	...	...	...	...
1940	61	282	6.2	79	2.6	0.9	...	20,333	7,059	875
1941	62	293	6.8	81	2.8	0.9	...	...	...	...
1942	61	303	6.7	79	3.0	0.9	...	19,634	6,871	859
1943	67	310	7.3	82	3.6	...	...	...	...	...
1944	71	330	8.1	86	3.8	...	...	19,038	5,975	828

I1 NORTH AMERICA: Pupils and Teachers in Schools (in thousands, except as otherwise indicated)

1945–1974

	Barbados		Canada[2]		Costa Rica				Cuba			
	Pupils		All Schools		Pupils		Teachers		Pupils		Teachers	
	a[1]	b	Pupils	Teachers	a[8]	b[9]	a[8]	b[9]	a	b	a[11]	b
1945	29	2.5	2,090	75	81	5.2	...	...	512	...	16	...
1946	29	2.6	[2,060][2]	...	84	[2.0][9]	3.9	[0.1][9]	...	...	...	...
1947	29	2.7	[2,092][2]	77[2]	96	...	...	...	...	...	...	...
1948	30	2.4	2,191[2]	...	89	...	...	...	...	...	...	...
1949	30	2.6	2,452	...	96	[4.4][9]	4.3	[0.3][9]	...	...	...	...
1950	30	2.5	2,532[2][22]	89	107	6.0	3.7	...	593	21	21	1.2
1951	31	2.7	2,667	90	101	6.6[9]	...	...	...	21	...	1.2
1952	32	3.0	2,810	94	103	...	...	...	...	26	...	2.0
1953	33	3.1	2,972	98	124	12	...	...	697	35	18	2.0
1954	36	3.2	3,135	108	125[8] / 138	13	...[8] / 5.5	...	669	28	...	...
1955	36	3.2	3,336[2][22]	113	154	15	5.8	...	702	35	20	2.0
1956	37	3.4	3,497	120	155	17	...	1.1	747	36	21	2.0
1957	38	3.6	3,633	127	168	19	6.7	1.4	756	...	...	...
1958	39	3.8	3,827	133[2] / 148	174	23	...	...	783	...	...	...
1959	41	4.0	4,010	154	184	26	7.5	1.2	962	63	22	3.7
1960	43	4.1	4,202	164	198	27	7.6	1.3	1,030	90	25	5.2
1961	44	4.3	4,410	174	208	29	8.3	1.4	1,087	108	29	6.6
1962	46	4.4	4,610	185	226	31	9.1	1.7	1,121	123	34	7.4
1963	48[19]	4.7	4,802	194	244	34	9.6	2.1	1,194	138	35	7.7
1964	46	4.8	4,994	206	258	37	9.7	1.4	1,206	136	36	8.4
1965	50	4.8	5,160	211	277	41	10	1.9	1,232	149	42[11]	9.6
1966	51	4.9	5,312	225	292	48	11	2.6	1,253	170		10
1967	52	5.2	5,471	243	308	54	11	2.4	1,274	177		11
1968	52	5.3	5,647	256	313	56	11	2.4	1,333	187		11
1969	52	5.3	5,771	269	340	64	11	2.9	1,428	175		13
1970	52	5.2	5,832	272	349	68	12	3.3	1,530	187		15
1971	...	5.2	5,823	272	356	75	12	...	1,631	202		16
1972	50	5.3	5,768	274	365	81	12	3.5	1,733	222		17
1973	46[19] / 34	5.4[19] / 21	5,680	273	374	104	13	...	1,779	266		21
1974	31	22	5,632	274	368	114	13	...	1,800	338		27

I1 NORTH AMERICA: Pupils and Teachers in Schools (in thousands, except as otherwise indicated)

1945–1974

	Dominican Republic				El Salvador				Guatemala			
	Pupils		Teachers		Pupils		Teachers		Pupils		Teachers	
	a	b	a	b	a	b	a	b	a	b	a	b
1945	213	...	4.0	...	106	...	3.7		141	7.3	5.4	...
1946	220	...	4.2	...	121	2.1	4.0		175	8.9	6.1	1.3
1947	220	...	4.2	...	134	...	...		161	9.9	6.3	1.6
1948	226	...	4.7	...	144	3.4	...		167	12	7.2	1.7
1949	231	6.7	4.8	0.4	144	...	4.6		166	13	7.2	1.9
1950	230	8.3	4.9	0.4	149	6.9	4.8		165	15	7.3	2.2
1951	240	...	4.9	...	155	6.8	5.2		173	17	7.4	2.2
1952	252	8.5	4.9	0.5	164	8.5	...		183	17	7.5	2.3
1953	252	...	5.3	...	176	11	6.1		191	17	7.8	2.2
1954	399	9.6	7.7	...	197	11	6.0		208	18	7.9	2.4
1955	386	9.5	8.3	...	207	13	6.8		216	19	8.1	2.5
1956	445	...	...	...	220	14	7.1		229	...	8.6	2.8
1957	461	...	...	...	245	17	7.9		245	20	8.8	2.7
1958	480	...	...	...	262	19	9.0		260	21	9.4	3.2
1959	497	26	8.6	1.2	288	20	8.7		282	21	9.4	3.4
1960	507	31	8.8	1.2	307[20] / 321	21	8.7		297	27	9.7	4.0
1961	508	34	8.9	1.4	341	25	9.5		313	31	10	4.7
1962	488	38	9.3	1.8	354	26	11		339	37	11	5.2
1963	451	43	...	...	358	29	9.4		361	40	11	5.8
1964	516	51	...	...	379	34	11		386	44	11	5.8
1965	557	56	10	2.3	398	38	12		405	49	12	6.4
1966	585	67	11	2.7	434	42	...		407	53	12	4.6
1967	649	76	12	3.3	475	50	13		457	60	12	4.9
1968	686	88	12	3.6	462	55	13		493	63	13	5.1
1969	726	98	13	4.2	517	59	13		518	68	14	5.1
1970	765	114	14	4.4	531	62	14		506	74	14	5.5
1971	820	127	15	5.4	595	76	15		531	81	15	5.6
1972	833	147	15	...	618	87	16		556	87	15	6.2
1973	837	159	16	...	667	125	15		571	105	16	5.9
1974	868	171	17	...	704	154	15		601	111	17	7.1

I1 NORTH AMERICA: Pupils and Teachers in Schools (in thousands, except as otherwise indicated)

1945–1974

Year	Haiti Pupils a[23]	Haiti Pupils b[23]	Haiti Teachers a	Haiti Teachers b[23]	Honduras Pupils a[13]	Honduras Pupils b	Honduras Teachers a[13]	Honduras Teachers b	Jamaica Pupils a	Jamaica Pupils b	Jamaica Teachers a	Jamaica Teachers b
1945	...		...	...	61		2.1		178	4.5	...	0.3
1946	...		...	...	65	2	2.1		186	4.8	...	0.3
1947	...		...	...	68	3	2.3	0.7	186		...	
1948	...		...	...	88	...	2.7	...	191	5.3	3.5	0.3
1949	129		...	...	97	...	3.1	...	200	7.1	4.1	0.3
1950	119	3.4	...	0.5	105[13] / 104	4	3.3	0.9	211	7.9	4.2	0.3
1951	144	4.0	2.3	0.4	104	5	3.8	...	211	8.4	4.2	0.4
1952	173	4.7[23] / 6.8	...	...[23]	114	6	4.1	0.9	214	9.0	4.3	0.4
1953	186	7.8	4.1	0.6	116	6.5	4.1	0.9	219	10	4.2	0.4
1954	179	7.2	6.0	0.6	125	6.6	4.5	1.0	220	10	4.3	0.5
1955	212	12	4.4	0.9	128	9.3	...	1.2	228	9.0	4.4	
1956	201	...	...	...	134	10	4.4	1.3	233	9.6	4.7	
1957	203	...	...	...	147	12	4.6	1.3	241	11	4.7	
1958	...	...	...	...	172	13	...	1.6	246	13	4.8	0.6
1959	238	14	5.4	1.1	192	14	6.1	1.4	255	13	4.9	...
1960	239	15	5.6	1.2	209	14	6.5	1.6	285	16	5.0	...
1961	231	...	5.5	...	228	15	7.2	1.7	306	17	5.0	1.0
1962	233	17	5.4	1.1	244	16	7.9	1.9	329	18	5.2	1.0
1963	...	...	...	...	252	18	8.6	2.1	338[19]	20[19]	5.4[19]	...[19]
1964	276	19	6.1	1.2	267	21	9.3	2.1	321	34	5.7	1.3
1965	284	20	6.2	1.3	284	24	9.9	2.0	324	36	6.0	1.5
1966	286	21	6.5	1.3	331	26	11	2.1	333	39	6.2	1.4
1967	289	26	6.6	1.6	367	30	10	2.3	352	39	6.5	1.7
1968	291	28	6.7	1.7	377	33	10	2.5	372	41	6.9	1.8
1969	...	...	...	...	393	34	11	...	374	57	7.3	2.2
1970	...	...	...	...	382	...	11	...	366	69	8.1	2.5
1971	337	27	7.5	1.5	393	39	11	2.7	382	71	9.5	2.9
1972	376	...	...	...	412	43	11	2.8	395	76	9.6	3.3
1973	391[20]	51	11	3.2	421	49	12	2.5	413	85	10	3.6
1974	451	52	12	...	443	58	12	3.1	422	107	10	4.5

I1 NORTH AMERICA: Pupils and Teachers in Schools (in thousands, except as otherwise indicated)

1945–1974

	Mexico[24]				Newfoundland	Nicaragua				Panama			
	Pupils		Teachers		Pupils	Pupils		Teachers		Pupils		Teachers	
	a	b[25]	a	b[25]	All Schools	a	b[25]	a	b[25]	a	b	a	b
1945	2,074	54	54	7.5	70	...	...	...	...	84	10	...	...
1946	2,428	55	61	7.7	71	...	...	...	...	94	12	2.9	0.6
1947	2,464	61	62	7.8	72	...	...	...	...	98	13	3.0	0.7
1948	2,539	63	64	7.8	73	...	...	...	...	101	15	3.2	0.8
1949	2,666	62_{25} / 113	66	8.6_{25} / 12	...	...	...	...	...	106	16	3.5	0.8
1950	2,785	118	69	...	...	91	...	3.0	...	110	18	3.4	0.9
1951	2,926	132	76	15	...	83	3.7	3.0	0.6	114	19	3.6	0.9
1952	3,098	143	78	13	...	84	5.2	2.7	0.5	...	...	...	...
1953	3,340	179	87	...	...	116	3.8	4.1	0.5	125	22	3.9	1.0
1954	3,527	153	86	11	...	...	...	...	...	133	24	4.1	1.1
1955	3,680	195	87	...	...	119	4.3	3.8	0.4	138	25	4.3	1.2
1956	3,880	242	103	14	...	146	...	...	...	141	27	4.4	...
1957	3,920	237	101	...	...	137	...	3.7	...	143	...	4.6	...
1958	4,390	270	103	18	...	129	5.7	...	...	...	36	...	1.6
1959	4,913	331	111	22	...	153	5.9	4.7	...	156	...	4.9	...
1960	5,247	471	117	29	...	168	6.9_{25} / 12	...	0.5_{25} / 0.9	162	39	5.3	1.7
1961	5,516	552	127	33	...	182	13	4.9	1.1	171	42	5.6	1.9
1962	5,929	572	132	...	...	198	15	5.1	1.3	180	45	5.6	2.0
1963	6,279	675	142	...	...	212	19	5.2	1.4	187	47	5.9	2.2
1964	6,610	832	148	51	...	217	23	5.6	1.6	196	51	6.1	2.5
1965	7,073	869	157	59	...	216	27	5.9	1.7	203	55	6.4	2.6
1966	7,495	950	159	67	...	235	30	6.5	1.9	211	59	6.7	2.8
1967	7,812	1,082	175	80	...	257	34	7.4	1.7	218	63	7.1	3.0
1968	8,179	1,188	183	108	...	266	40	7.4	2.0	223	67	7.4	3.3
1969	8,530	1,239	201	109	...	279	46	7.5	2.0	239	71	8.0	3.4
1970	8,905	1,370	208	...	...	295	51	7.6	2.0	255	78	9.4	3.8
1971	9,338	1,673	221	...	...	310	55	8.1	2.1	288	87	11	4.5
1972	10,113	1,818	231	$\dots_{25}$	...	314	61	8.1	1.9	306	99	12	5.1
1973	10,510	2,013	242	139	...	327	63	7.9	1.8	319	112	12	5.4
1974	10,954	2,166	254	142	...	333	71	8.5	2.0	328	123	12	5.8

I1 NORTH AMERICA: Pupils and Teachers in Schools (in thousands, except as otherwise indicated)

1945–1974

	Puerto Rico			Trinidad and Tobago[21]				USA		
	Pupils		Teachers	Pupils		Teachers		Pupils		Teachers[5]
	a	b	All Schools	a	b	a	b	a	b	All Schools
1945	350		8.9	91	4.2	1.3	...	...	...	...
1946	367		9.2	94	4.8	1.3	...	19,118	6,187	831
1947	305	95	9.1	100	4.9	1.5	...	...	...	...
1948	313	94	9.4	103	5.0	2.8	...	19,571	6,255	861
1949	331	99	9.5	111	5.3	2.9	0.2	...	...	...
1950	355	108	9.7	115	5.6	3.0	0.2	20,928	6,397	914
1951	365	113	9.9	121	5.9	2.9	0.2	...	...	...
1952	385	121	10	124	6.2	3.1[21] / 2.9	0.3	22,331	6,538	963
1953	410	130	11	132	6.5	3.4	0.3	...	...	...
1954	426	142	12	138	6.8	3.7	0.3	24,347	7,037	1,042
1955	434	154	13	146	7.2	3.9	0.3	...	...	...
1956	435	164	...	154	7.5	4.2	0.3	26,349	7,696	1,149
1957	439	175	14	160	9.1	4.4	0.4	...	...	...
1958	434	188	...	177	10	4.7	0.5	27,841	8,791	1,261
1959	428	199	15	174	11	5.0	0.6	...[4]	...[4]	...[4]
1960	426	207	...	180	12	5.4	0.6	29,965	9,520	1,387
1961	429	217	16	191	13	5.8	0.6	31,143	10,686	1,504
1962	434	226	...	196	15	6.0	...	...	...	...
1963	438	233	18	204	17	6.1	0.8	...	...	...
1964	445	238	18	209	20	6.3	...	31,968	12,070	1,625
1965	454	245	20	216	22	6.3	1.0	...	...	...
1966	462	253	22	220	26	6.3	1.2	33,078	12,926	1,786
1967	464	257	25	223	27	6.3	1.2	...	...	...
1968	464	266	23	224	27	6.3	1.2	34,375	13,888	1,957
1969	455	269	25	227	28	6.4	1.3	...[19]	...[19]	...
1970	459	281	26	228	28	6.5	1.3	31,553	19,208	2,131[5] / 2,288
1971	460	290	27	228	28	6.7	1.3	31,588	19,698	2,305
1972	462	302	28	223	35	6.7	1.4	31,023	19,721	2,338
1973	453	311	...	214	46	6.7	...	30,135	20,295	2,376
1974	808[20] / 807		28	204	55	6.6	...	30,087	19,971	2,404

I1   NORTH AMERICA: Pupils and Teachers in Schools (in thousands except as otherwise indicated)

	Barbados		Canada		Costa Rica				Cuba			
	Pupils		All Schools		Pupils		Teachers		Pupils		Teachers	
	a	b	Pupils	Teachers	a	b[27]	a[8]	b	a	b	a	b
1975	32	29	5,594	275	361	121	12	4.9	1,796	420	77	33
1976	34	29	5,514	275[20]	368	130[27]	13	5.9	1,748	535	82	45
1977	34	30	5,410	267	367	122	...	7.7	1,694	646	86	51
1978	35	29	5,294	263	362	130	...	...	1,626	759	87	58
1979	31	30	5,185	258	356	137	13	7.3	1,550	816	87	62
1980	31	29	5,106	...	349	142	13	7.2	1,469	837	84	64
1981	31	28	5,030	...	349	141	12	7.0	1,410	826	83	65
1982	30	28	4,994	272	342	131	13[8] / 11	...	1,363	774	83	65
1983	31	28	4,975	273	344	123	10	...	1,283	774	83	65
1984	30	29	4,946	295	351	117	10	7.1	1,174	794	80	64
1985	...	...	4,928[39]	299	363	113	12	6.6	1,077	808	77	66
1986	...	...	4,506	302	380	115	12	...	1,001	801	75	67
1987	...	25	4,533	307	393	117	12	...	937	775	74	68
1988	30	25	4,568	316	409	118	13	...	900	770	73	70
1989	29	24	4,789	312	412	125	13	...	886	728	72	70
1990	27	...	4,845	307	435	130	14	6.9	888	672	71	64
1991	...	...	4,915	303	453	139	14	7.2	918	598	74	62
1992	...	...	4,968	303	471	151	15	7.6	942	520	76	57
1993	...	...	5,022	306	485	160	15	8.3	983	459	76	53

I1 NORTH AMERICA: Pupils and Teachers in Schools (in thousands except as otherwise indicated)

	Dominican Republic				El Salvador				Guatemala			
	Pupils		Teachers		Pupils		Teachers		Pupils		Teachers	
	a	b	a	b	a	b	a	b	a	b	a	b
1975	912	188	18	8.5	759	171	17		627	122	18	7.3
1976	935	207	:	:	796	188	17		640	:	19	7.7
1977	947	249	:	:	795	198	17		673	146	19	8.3
1978	1,033	319	:	:	830	213	:		740	159	21	8.6
1979	1,069	338	:	:	901	230	17		740	156	22	9.0
1980	1,106	356	:	:	834	211	17		827	157	24	9.6
1981	1,150	379	:	:	710	188	17		899	162	24	13
1982	1,092	:	24	:	811	219	18		867	178	25	13
1983	1,122	380	:	:	852	234	18		873	174	27	14
1984	1,206	431	28	12	853	220	21		980	176	27	14
1985	1,220	439	28	12	852	246	:		1,016	183	28	15
1986	1,296	427	31	10	:	:	22		1,041	223	30	17
1987	1,271	:	31	:	996	:	22		1,098	241	31	16
1988	:	:	:	:	1,029	:	23		1,121	:	32	:
1989	1,032	:	21	:	1,016	:	25		:	:	:	:
1990	:	:	:	:	964	:	24		:	:	:	:
1991	:	:	:	:	1,000	:	23		1,249	294	37	21
1992	:	:	:	:	1,028	:	23		1,340	322	38	21
1993	1,336	232	39	11	1,042	:	23		1,393	334	44	21

I1 NORTH AMERICA: Pupils and Teachers in Schools (in thousands except as otherwise indicated).

	Haiti				Honduras				Jamaica			
	Pupils		Teachers		Pupils		Teachers		Pupils		Teachers	
	a	b	a	b	a	b	a	b	a	b	a	b
1975	487	55	13	3.4	461	56	13	3.1	432	135	10	5.3
1976	511	56	13	3.3	483	61	14	...	418	123	11	6.4
1977	518	73	13	3.8	493	72	13	3.4	426	137	11	6.8
1978	529	81	13	3.8	525	81	14	3.5	432	155	11	6.6
1979	580	88	13	3.6	575	...	13	4.4	428	152	11	7.1
1980	642	97	15	4.0	601	...	16	4.5	425	154	11	7.1
1981	658	99	15	4.2	614	81	16	5.1	427	155	11	7.5
1982	723	117	17	5.7	672	106	18	5.2	423	156	11	7.4
1983	783	134	18	5.8	705	113	19	5.9	416	158	10	7.8
1984	820	154	20	6.1	737	112	20	6.3	414	160	10	7.5
1985	872	139	23	7.0	774	113	22	6.5	407	154	9.6	7.4
1986	763	155	21	7.9	810	122	22	7.0	394	161	9.5	7.8
1987	781	...	22	...	840	121	24	7.6	391	160	9.6	7.8
1988	553	...	23	...	863	125	26	8.1	387	161	9.9	7.9
1989	554	...	25	...	...	...	...	...	382	163	10.1	7.7
1990	555	...	26	...	...	...	...	...	382	166	9.7	8.0
1991	...	...	...	...	908	194	24	8.5	373	165	9.8	8.1
1992	...	...	...	...	...	...	...	...	...	...	9.9	8.2
1993	...	...	...	...	990	203	27	10.2	...	...	...	...

I1 NORTH AMERICA: Pupils and Teachers in Schools (in thousands except as otherwise indicated)

| | Mexico | | | | Nicaragua | | | | Panama | | | |
| | Pupils | | Teachers | | Pupils | | Teachers | | Pupils | | Teachers | |
	a	b	a	b	a	b	a	b	a	b	a	b
1975	11,461	2,506	286	167	351	80	8.8	2.5	342	126	12	5.7
1976	12,572	2,823	...	174	362	95	9.3	2.8	354	132	12	5.7
1977	...	...	319	187	371	105	9.7	3.0	358	137	15	5.9
1978	13,536	3,328	347	209	379	99	10	2.7	369	139	15	6.0
1979	14,126	3,713	375	229	449	111[20]	12	3.5	373[19]	138[19]	16[19]	6.2[19]
1980	14,666	4,042	400	252	472	140	13	4.2	338	171	12	8.1
1981	14,981	4,513	415	263	509	137	15	4.2	335	174	13	8.6
1982	15,223	4,811	428	279	513	140	15	4.1	337	175	13	8.9
1983	15,376	5,153	437	296	537	158	17	5.0	336	176	13	9.2
1984	15,219	5,397	450	321	534	162	18	6.1	339	182	13	9.5
1985	15,124	5,718	457	327	562	151	17	...	340	185	13	9.7
1986	14,995	5,822	463	332	557	167	17	5.8	344	187	14	9.8
1987	14,768	5,933	468	339	584	177	18	6.7	346	190	14	10
1988	14,656	5,998	463	388	600	182	18	...	345	190	13	9.8
1989	14,494	5,945	466	341	596	187	19	...	350	190	15	9.9
1990	14,401	5,911	472	344	633	190	19	...	351	195	15	9.7
1991	14,397	5,885	480	348	674	186	18	...	350	198	...	10.0
1992	14,426	5,970	486	353	704	189	19	...	353	201	...	10.5
1993	14,469	6,179	496	366	737	199	20	...	357	207	...	11.0

I1   **NORTH AMERICA: Pupils and Teachers in Schools** (in thousands except as otherwise indicated)

	Puerto Rico		Trinidad & Tobago				USA		
	All Schools		Pupils		Teachers		Pupils		Teachers
	Pupils	Teachers	a	b	a	b	a	b	All Schools
1975	800	28	200	64	6.5	1.6	29,340	20,451	2,451
1976	813	...	190	76	6.5	...	29,255	20,229	2,471
1977	817	27	182	84	6.4	...	28,751	19,960	2,478
1978	825	30	172	82	6.1	...	28,749	18,887	2,480
1979	815	...	167	82	6.4	...	28,243	18,402	2,458
1980	815	32	167	87	7.0	1.7	28,148	18,170	2,422
1981	811	...	167	91	7.3	1.7	27,919	17,680	2,403
1982	814	...	170	91	7.5	1.7 [20]	28,075	17,177	2,401
1983	816	...	167	92	7.3	4.7	28,325	16,742	...
1984	805	...	169	90	7.6	4.7	28,447	16,546	...
1985	800	...	172	91	7.6	...	28,485	16,581	...
1986	817	32	177	92	7.7	4.9	28,317	16,972	2,554
1987	801	...	183	93	7.7	4.9	28,433	16,938	2,592
1988	790	...	186	97	7.5	4.9	29,242	16,196	2,627
1989	798	...	190	99	6.8	4.9	30,494	15,327	2,679
1990	796	33	194	96	7.5	4.9	31,080	15,344	2,753
1991	802	...	196	97	7.5	4.8	31,691	15,573	2,787
1992	800	...	197	100	7.6	4.9	32,227	15,969	2,821
1993	728	38	195	101	7.2	4.9	32,586	16,830	2,871

I1 SOUTH AMERICA: PUPILS AND TEACHERS IN SCHOOLS (in thousands, except as otherwise indicated)

1855–1884

	Argentina Pupils		Bolivia Pupils	Brazil Pupils	Chile[29] Pupils		Guyana Pupils	Uruguay[30] Pupils	Teachers
	a	b	a	a	a	b	a	a	a
1855	...	...	...	...	...	...	2.2	...	...
1856	...	...	...	...	...	...	3.0	...	...
1857	...	...	...	...	...	...	3.4	...	...
1858	...	...	...	...	...	...	4.0	...	...
1859	...	...	...	...	...	...	4.5	...	...
1860	...	...	...	...	...	...	4.8	...	...
1861	...	...	...	...	...	...	4.9	...	...
1862	...	...	...	...	...	...	5.0	...	...
1863	...	...	...	...	...	...	5.3	...	...
1864	...	...	...	...	...	...	5.6	...	...
1865	...	...	...	...	...	...	5.8	...	...
1866	...	...	...	...	...	...	6.6	...	...
1867	...	...	...	...	...	...	7.3	...	...
1868	...	...	...	...	...	...	16	...	...
1869	...	...	...	...	...	...	15	...	...
1870	...	...	...	138	...	...	16	...	...
1871	...	...	...	139	...	...	16	...	...
1872	...	...	...	164	...	...	16	...	...
1873	...	...	...	173	...	...	16	...	...
1874	...	...	...		...	...	17	...	...
1875	...	...	...	173	...	...	17	17	0.3
1876	...	...	...	134	...	...	17	17	0.3
1877	...	...	...	...	...	...	...	20	0.4
1878	...	...	...	...	...	...	...	...	...
1879	...	...	...	...	...	...	20	23	...
1880	...	...	...	...	66	3.1	21	25	0.5
1881	...	1.6	...	...	...	...	21	26	0.5
1882	98	2.3	10	209	63	4.3	23	...	...
1883	108	...	...	222	...	...	19	26	0.5
1884	...	...	...	233	64	4.3	18	27	0.6

I1   SOUTH AMERICA: Pupils and Teachers in Schools (in thousands, except as otherwise indicated)

1885–1914

	Argentina			Bolivia			Brazil				Chile[24]			
	Pupils		Teachers	Pupils		Teachers	Pupils		Teachers		Pupils		Teachers	
	a	b	a	a	b	All Schools	a	b	a	b	a	b	a	b
1885	168													
1886											79			
1887							259				108			
1888				24	2.3	0.7					117			
1889				25	2.2									
1890				24	2.1	0.8					119	4.7		
1891	228	3.2										4.6		
1892	250										138	6.6	2.0	
1893	248										131	6.8	2.1	
1894			8.0	25	2.1	0.8					145	7.7		
1895	202		6.9	27	2.1	0.9					140	8.6	2.1	
1896	283	4.4	8.9	33							140	9.1	2.2	
1897	298		9.3		2.1						132	8.8	2.3	
1898	318	6.1	9.6	33	3.0						141	7.5	2.3	
1899	381		11	36	2.3	1.1					149	7.8	2.3	
1900	387		11								157	8.7	2.7	
1901	393		11	33	2.6	1.2					166	9.5	3.1	
1902	412		12								187	11	3.4	
1903	427		13								212	12	3.6	
1904	478		13								201	12	4.0	
1905	541		14	49	2.5	1.3					201	14	4.5	
1906	[503][31]		15				638	30	16	2.3	217	15	4.5	
1907	570		16								219	14	4.0	
1908	592		17								262	17	4.1	
1909	671		19	62							278	17[29] / 32	4.7	1.0
1910	694		20		1.6	1.4					317	34	4.8	1.1
1911	735		22								328	40	5.4[29] / 6.8	1.5[29] / 2.6
1912	780 / 784		24		2.2						356	41	7.4	2.8
1913	843		23		2.6						390	44	7.5	2.8
1914	863	19	25		2.8						393	44	7.8	2.7

I1 SOUTH AMERICA: Pupils and Teachers in Schools (in thousands, except as otherwise indicated). 1885–1914

	Colombia Pupils		Ecuador Pupils	Guyana Pupils	Paraguay Pupils		Peru[33] Pupils		Teachers		Uruguay[30] Pupils		Teachers
	a	b	a	a	a	b[32]	a	b	a	b	a	b	a
1885				18							30		0.6
1886				19							28		0.6
1887	75			21							31		0.7
1888				21			[53]1				33		0.7
1889	93			24							33		0.7
1890			58	27							39		0.8
1891				26	19						44		0.9
1892	114			26							46		0.9
1893		[5.1]1		27							46		0.9
1894				28							47		1.0
1895		[4.5]1		28							50		1.0
1896	[137]1			28	23		86	2.0			51		1.0
1897		[6.0]1		29			92	2.2			46		1.0
1898				29							50		1.1
1899				29							53		1.1
1900				28		0.4					52		1.1
1901				27	25	0.4	105				55		1.2
1902				28	28	0.4					56		1.2
1903				29		0.4					54		1.2
1904			68	29	32	0.4					50[30] / 73		1.2[30] / 2.0
1905				30	30	0.4	154			0.4	71		2.0
1906				29	37	0.4	162	2.6		0.4	75		1.9
1907				31	38	0.4[32] / 0.6		2.8			79		1.9
1908	[201]1			34	41	0.8	168	3.0	3.1	0.4	90		2.2
1909	235		94	34	40	0.8	154	3.9		0.4	92		2.2
1910	240			35	52	0.7	146	3.8	2.8	0.3	95		2.3
1911	273			35	49	0.7	148	4.7		0.3	102	1.9	2.5
1912	292		98	36	45	0.6	168	4.9	3.1	0.3	112	2.3	2.7
1913	280	26	66	37	69	0.7	178	5.1		0.3	112	2.8	2.7
1914	306			37	71	0.8	171	5.1		0.3	114	3.5	2.7

I1 SOUTH AMERICA: Pupils and Teachers in Schools (in thousands, except as otherwise indicated)

1915–1944

	Argentina				Bolivia			Brazil			
	Pupils		Teachers		Pupils		Teachers	Pupils		Teachers	
	a	b[34]	a	b[34]	a	b	All Schools	a	b	a	b
1915	914	27	27								
1916	938										
1917	1,003		35								
1918	1,020		33								
1919	1,058		37								
1920	1,121		36					1,251			
1921	1,164										
1922	1,230		40								
1923	1,261										
1924	1,267				81	4.1	2.9				
1925	1,273										
1926	1,279				80	4.2	3.2				
1927	1,312	41	45					1,784	52	47	
1928	1,350		50					2,052	68		6.2
1929	1,407	45	49					2,058	83	50	8.1
1930	1,445		57					2,085	73	53	7.4
1931	1,524		55				1.6	2,021	48	54	4.5
1932	1,545		56					2,071	56	56[20]	5.2
1933	1,644	60		7.2			1.5	2,108	66	53	5.9
1934	1,703			7.8				2,265	79	55	6.8
1935	1,766	64	74	8.7	94			2,414	94	60	7.5
1936	1,799	69	76	9.7			2.9	2,563	108	62	8.1
1937	1,867	78	77	10				2,702	124	67	9.3
1938	1,916[19] / 40	84[34]		11[34] / 5.9				2,902	143	69	10
1939	1,905	41	79	6.2	104			2,986	156	70	11
1940	1,930	42		6.2				3,068	176	73	12
1941	1,946	43		6.6				3,097	182	75	13
1942	1,928	47	80	7.4	131			3,095	199	78	14
1943	1,936	50		8.0	162			3,075	211	78	18
1944	1,957	53		8.3	136		11	3,133	233	80	18

I1 SOUTH AMERICA: Pupils and Teachers in Schools (in thousands, except as otherwise indicated)

1915–1944

	Chile[29]				Colombia				Ecuador			
	Pupils		Teachers		Pupils		Teachers		Pupils		Teachers	
	a	b	a	b	a	b	a	b	a	b	a	b
1915	376	44	7.5	2.8	326	29	...	...	...	...	...	...
1916	414	47	7.7	2.8	348	33	5.7	...	...	...	...	...
1917	406	48	7.9	2.9	365	33	...	...	...	...	...	...
1918	396	55	8.4	3.1	...	...	...	...	...	...	...	...
1919	...	54	8.5	...	322	...	...	...	93	...	...	...
1920	401	53	8.6	3.0	334	...	...	...	103	...	...	...
1921	...	58	9.7	...	...	...	...	...	109	...	2.5	...
1922	507	60	10	3.4	373	...	...	...	101	...	...	...
1923	487	59	11	3.3	361	...	...	...	...	...	...	...
1924	512	62	11	3.3	396	...	...	...	...	...	...	...
1925	507	62	11	...	...	...	...	...	...	...	...	...
1926	506[29]	63[29]	11	...	427	...	...	...	...	...	...	...
	527	47										
1927	571	46	11	2.6	441	...	...	...	129	2.8	...	...
1928	594	49	11[29]	2.4	470	...	...	...	...	...	...	...
			9.4									
1929	594	47	9.9	...	...	...	...	...	114	...	...	...
1930	559	52	9.6	2.4	...	...	...	...	147	2.5	...	...
1931	554	59	9.7	3.5	...	...	...	...	153	2.6	...	...
1932	514	36	9.9	...	...	...	...	...	161	3.2	...	...
1933	488	41	10	3.3	...	...	...	...	169	3.6	...	...
1934	496	41	11	...	548	31	12	2.9	179	3.7	...	...
1935	542	42	11	3.7	546	29	12	2.8	190	5.7	...	...
1936	569	43	11	...	588	32	12	3.1	198	5.9	...	...
1937	587	44	11	3.6	574	33	12	3.4	...	5.9	...	...
1938	611	46	11	...	628	34	14	3.4	133	5.8	5.3	0.4
1939	602	44	11	...	606	35	13	3.7	221	6.2	5.6	0.5
1940	591	47	12	...	606	37	13	3.4	223	6.3	5.9	0.7
1941	600	50	12	...	664	35	14	3.8	249	6.6	6.1	0.8
1942	603	54	13	...	647	36	14	3.9	244	6.8	6.4	0.8
1943	671	59	13	...	679	40	15	4.2	...	...	...	...
1944	685	62	13	...	699	40	17	4.2	...	...	...	...

I1 SOUTH AMERICA: Pupils and Teachers in Schools (in thousands, except as otherwise indicated)

1915-1944

	Guyana		Paraguay				Peru[33]			
			Pupils		Teachers		Pupils		Teachers	
	Pupils	Teachers a	a	b	a	b[35]	a	b	a	b
1915	34	...	74	0.8	...	...	166	5.0	...	0.4
1916	34	...	80	0.8	...	...	166	5.2	3.3	0.4
1917	33	...	...	0.8	...	...	170	5.7	...	0.4
1918	32	...	...	0.8	...	...	177	6.2	4.3	0.4
1919	34	...	82	0.7	...	...	181	6.4	4.4	0.4
1920	35	1.1	71	0.7	...	...	196	6.9	5.1	0.4
1921	37	1.1	...	0.8	...	...	203	7.0	...	0.4
1922	39	1.1	78	1.0	...	...	210	7.4	...	0.4
1923	40	1.2	73	1.0	...	...	221	7.1	4.7	0.4
1924	41	1.2	91	1.0	...	...	228	7.6	4.7	0.4
1925	43	1.3	79	0.9	...	...	236	7.8	...	0.5
1926	43	1.3	93	0.9	...	...	262	8.6	5.5	0.6
1927	44	1.4	100	0.9	...	...	293	9.2	5.8	0.6
1928	43	1.4	102	1.1	...	...	308	9.8	6.1	0.6
1929	45	1.3	104	1.2	2.3	...	319	11	6.2	0.6
1930	43	0.9	108	1.3	2.5	...	342	12	6.5	0.7
1931	41	0.9	109	1.4	2.4	...	350	10	...	...
1932	43	1.0	105	1.7	2.3	...	367	13	...	...
1933	44	1.0	95	—	2.3	...	380	13	...	...
1934	45	1.0	97	1.0	2.3	...	424	15	...	...
1935	50	1.1	101	1.1	2.5	...	465	...	...	...
1936	51	1.1	115	1.7	2.8	...	484	...	...	...
1937	52	1.2	139	2.0	3.1	0.2	469	...	...	...
1938	53	1.3	156	2.4	3.8	0.2	493	14	...	...
1939	55	1.3	167	2.1	3.9	0.1	...	...	...	...
1940	56	1.3	171	1.8	3.9	0.2	566	25	...	...
1941	58	1.4	168	2.0	3.8	0.3	630	21	...	...
1942	60	1.4	177	2.0	3.2	0.3	646	23	...	...
1943	60	1.6	173	2.0	3.7	0.3[35] / 0.7	664	28	...	...
1944	60	1.5	180	2.1	4.0	0.7	...	...	...	...

I1 SOUTH AMERICA: Pupils and Teachers in Schools (in thousands, except as otherwise indicated)

1915–1944

	Uruguay			Venezuela			
	Pupils		Teachers	Pupils		Teachers	
	a	b	a	a	b	a	b
1915	117	4.0	2.8	...	...	...	...
1916	120	5.0	2.8	...	...	...	...
1917	125	5.2	2.8	...	...	...	...
1918	125	5.8	2.9	...	...	...	...
1919	126	6.1	2.8	...	...	...	...
1920	124	6.0	3.2	...	...	...	...
1921	131	6.2	3.4	...	...	...	...
1922	132	6.2	3.4	...	...	...	...
1923	135	6.6	3.4	...	...	...	...
1924	139	6.9	3.5	...	...	...	...
1925	144	6.9	3.7	...	...	...	...
1926	148	7.5	3.9	89	...	...	...
1927	160	8.2	4.4	...	...	...	...
1928	170	...	4.6	112	...	...	...
1929	175	9.8	4.8	...	...	...	...
1930	178	9.7[19] 8.9	4.8	...	...	...	...
1931	178	16	4.8	114	...	...	...
1932	180	15	4.8	...	...	...	...
1933	182	16	4.9	121	...	...	...
1934	184	12	4.8	...	...	...	...
1935	192	12	4.9	...	...	...	...
1936	195	13	4.9	...	...	...	...
1937	204	14	5.2	234	3.3	...	...
1938	210	14	5.3	244	3.5	6.0	0.4
1939	214	18	5.4	235	4.7	7.2	...
1940	219	18	5.9	266	6.4	8.0	0.8
1941	221	...	5.9	276	6.9	8.1	0.8
1942	218	19	6.0	276	7.6	8.1	0.9
1943	218	22	6.0	292	9.5	8.6	1.3
1944	221	24	6.6	298	12	9.1	1.6

I1 SOUTH AMERICA: Pupils and Teachers in Schools (in thousands, except as otherwise indicated)

1945–1974

Year	Argentina Pupils a	Argentina Pupils b	Argentina Teachers a	Argentina Teachers b	Bolivia Pupils a	Bolivia Pupils b	Bolivia Teachers All Schools	Brazil Pupils a	Brazil Pupils b	Brazil Teachers a	Brazil Teachers b
1945	1,977	55	80	8.9	155	...	...	3,239	256	84	19
1946	1,993	60	...	9.6	170	...	...	3,416	282	88	20
1947	2,036	60	...	10	162	...	...	3,616	312	93	22
1948	2,074	62	...	11	176	...	...	3,913	336	101	24
1949	2,120	66	93	12	176	...	...	4,098	366	107	25
1950	2,212	67	93	12	185[19]	26	9.1	4,352	437	112	29
1951	2,286	70	102	12	131	26	10	4,546	439	122	31
1952	2,376	74	...	13	137	27	12	4,713	467	128	33
1953	2,473	85	...	14	143	28	12	4,902	514	136	35
1954	2,565	91	110	15	155	29	14	5,257	557	148	38
1955	2,642	102	114	15	166	31	15	5,611	604	159	41
1956	2,724	113	120	16	172	32	16	6,094	648	173	43
1957	2,783	125	...	19	176	34	16	6,466	695	183	46
1958	2,860	...	126	...	192	38	17	6,776	761	197	51
1959	2,821	140	125	21	208	43	18	7,129	795	212	53
1960	2,849	147	130	23	182	45	18	7,477[19]	868[19]	226[19]	58[19]
1960								8,368	267	284	36
1961	2,871	150	132	24	244	48	19	8,806	301	309	38
1962	2,933	156	124	26	283[20]	53	20	9,664	336	340	38
1962					497						
1963	2,990	164	128	27	475	66	...	10,622	397	380	43
1964	3,074	171	152	27	495	74	21	11,671	439	423	46
1965	3,125	179	154	29	527	83	22	11,569	509	446	50
1966	3,192	183	158	28	560	92	...	12,585	593	496	55
1967	3,207	190	159	29	556	101	25	13,384	688	499	66
1968	3,239	198	165	30	568[19]	114[19]	27	14,348	801	556	79
1969	3,355	212[20]	172	32[20]	664	62	29	15,014	910	608	96
1970	3,386	405	176	58	679	92	30	15,895	1,003	654	112
1971	3,444	405	181	58	694	100	33	17,066	1,119	724	123
1972	3,464	413	185	59	731	111	38	18,371	1,300	770	127
1973	3,485	424	184	60	770	115	39	18,573	1,478	699	143
1974	3,545	443	186	61	810	121	41	19,287	1,682	887	156

I1   SOUTH AMERICA: Pupils and Teachers in Schools (in thousands, except as otherwise indicated)

1945–1974

	Chile				Colombia				Ecuador			
	Pupils		Teachers		Pupils		Teachers		Pupils		Teachers	
	a	b	a	b	a	b	a	b	a	b[36]	a	b[36]
1945	682	64	13	...	678	36	15	3.3	258	14	6.8	1.1
1946	699	67	14	...	712	46	17	4.1	...	...	...	...
1947	713	71	14	...	739	47	18	4.2	284	16	7.0	1.5
1948	746	75	14	...	765	42	18	3.8	309	16	7.5	1.0
1949	776	78	14	...	766	48	18	4.1	321	17	...	...
1950	798	81	...	...	808	56	19	5.0	342	18	8.2	1.8
1951	803	87	...	...	875	64	22	5.9	352	19	...	...
1952	849	94	...	...	923	65	23	6.0	357	21	8.9	2.2
1953	903	104	...	...	1,055	66	25	6.4	397	23	9.5	2.3
1954	943	116	...	...	1,125	70	29	6.6	...	...	...	...
1955	976	127	23	...	1,236	77	32	7.0	461	27	10	2.7
1956	1,007	138	25	7.8	1,312	93	34	8.1	490	30	11	2.9
1957	1,059	151	25	...	1,381	108	35	8.8	502	33	12	3.1
1958	1,095	...	...	...	1,493	115	38	9.6	529	36	...	...
1959	1,155	155	...	...	1,569	128	40	11	567	37	14	3.7
1960	1,176	229	...	...	1,690	140	45	13	596	40	15	4.1
1961	1,228	248	...	...	1,792	156	49	13	609	46	16	4.6
1962	1,318	259	...	...	1,949	175	53	14	654	49	17	5.0
1963	1,370	274	...	...	2,096	202	58	16	698	54	19	5.4
1964	1,398	293	27	11	2,213	229	62	16	752	57	20	5.6
1965	1,517	320	29	11	2,274	266	63	20	797	63[36] / 117	21	6.0[36] / 9.2
1966	1,560	341	—[19]	10[19] / 10	2,402	320	68	21	842	134	22	10
1967	1,835	185	34	...	2,586	377	70	25	845	151	22	11
1968	1,933	231	34	...	2,802	447	76	27	929	174	24	12
1969	1,976	272	36	12	3,108	523	82	30	980	198	26	14
1970	2,045	308	41	...	3,286	589	86	34	1,024	219	27	15
1971	2,202	373	46	...	3,466	652	90	36	1,057	242	27	16
1972	2,265	415	60	...	3,604	734	100	40	1,102	268	28	18
1973	2,317	446	61	...	3,752	812	110	45	1,167	299	30	20
1974	2,333	456	68	18	3,844	903	123	47	1,164	337	31	21

I1   SOUTH AMERICA: Pupils and Teachers in Schools (in thousands, except as otherwise indicated)

1945–1974

	Guyana[37]				Paraguay				Peru			
	Pupils		Teachers		Pupils		Teachers		Pupils		Teachers	
	a	b	a	b	a	b	a	b	a	b	a	b
1945	62	...	1.5	...	178	1.6[35] / 7.3	4.4	0.5	695	...	14	...
1946	63	...	1.5	...	185	6.1	4.4	0.4	777	37	16	1.9
1947	66	...	1.6	...	149	9.6	5.5	0.8[20]	857	55	19	4.6
1948	69	0.8	1.6	--	180	10	5.5	1.2	990	61	22	4.7
1949	71	1.2	1.7	--	189	11	5.7	1.4	993	61	23	4.7
1950	77	0.9	1.8	--	196	11	6.2	1.5	1,010	63	24	4.1
1951	78	0.9	1.8	--	222	12	6.5	1.7	1,035	63	25	4.4
1952	79	...	1.9	...	231	13	6.9	1.8	1,038	78	26	5.1
1953	84	1.7	2.1	0.1	239	13	7.5	1.9	1,047	83	27	5.8
1954	89	1.6	2.4	0.1	254	14	8.3	2.0	1,086	87	29	6.0
1955	95	1.7	2.5	0.1	268	13	9.1	2.1	1,128	92	30	6.4
1956	102	...	2.7	...	275	17[35] / 10	9.5	2.3	1,203	98	31	6.7
1957	106	4.6	2.8	0.2	287	13	9.9	2.6	1,234	117	32	7.0
1958	112	...	3.0	...	290	16	10	2.7	1,308	122	35	8.3
1959	118	7.0	3.2	0.3	297	18	10	3.0	1,392	141	38	8.7
1960	125	7.2	3.2	0.3	302	17	11	3.2	1,440	159	42	11
1961	130	8.8	3.4	0.4	312	15	11	3.4	1,495	...	45	...
1962	135	8.4	3.3	0.3	323	17	11	3.6	1,554	...	...	...
1963	148	...	4.4	...	335	24	11	3.4	...	...	...	...
1964	157	14	4.3	0.6	349	28	12	4.1	1,877	261	53	16
1965	163	15	5.1	0.7	362	30	12	4.5	1,901	311	57	19
1966	168[37]	16[37]	5.2[37]	0.7[37]	373	34	12	4.7	2,151	369	62	22
1966	135	49	...	1.6								
1967	139	49	4.4	1.7	385	36	12	5.0	2,236	424	65	25
1968	131	50	4.4	1.8	406	41	13	5.2	2,335	471	68	27
1969	130	53	4.3	1.9	416	45	13	5.6	...	490	69	26
1970	130	57	4.5	2.3	432	49	13	...	2,341	547	64	28
1971	131	62	...	...	437	52	14	6.7	2,488	570	68	25
1972	132	63	...	...	440	58	14	6.9	2,649	609	73	26
1973	132	64	4.1	...	452	63	15	6.7	2,641	623	71	27
1974	132	...	4.1	2.8	455	68	16	7	2,761	681	73	29

I1 SOUTH AMERICA: Pupils and Teachers in Schools (in thousands, except as otherwise indicated)

1945–1974

	Uruguay			Venezuela			
	Pupils		Teachers	Pupils		Teachers	
	a	b	a	a	b	a	b
1945	222	27	6.8	339	13	9.8	1.5
1946	221	29	6.8	361	16	12	1.9
1947	223	31	6.9	326	17	12	2.0
1948	227	31	6.8	442	22	12	1.7
1949	239	33	7.8	497	23	13	1.7
1950	257	34	9.2	503	27	14	2.2
1951	256	37	9.1	536	28	15	2.5
1952	261	38	8.3	570	27	16 ·	2.5
1953	273	42	8.3	596	32	17	2.8
1954	275	46	8.4	623	· 36	18	3.1
1955	283	49	8.6	647	44	19	3.9
1956	295	55	8.6	694	52	20	4.2
1957	302	58	8.8	752	55	21	4.5
1958	310	63	9.5	917	71	25	5.3
1959	314	66	9.7	1,155	88	31	6.5
1960	320	71	10	1,244	105	35	7.7
1961	332	73	10	1,298	122	36	8.3
1962	323	76	10	1,340	139	38	10
1963	320	79	...	1,371	155	...	11
1964	350	85	11	1,422	173	41	13
1965	335	91	11	1,481	190	43	14
1966	366	...	12	1,541	210[20] 256	45	15[20]
1967	368	109	12	1,557	283	46	16
1968	370	118	13	1,609	316	48	18
1969	...	123	...	1,690	360	50	20
1970	354	132	12	1,776	417	52	22
1971	360	138	13	1,838	476	54	26
1972	352	147	14	1,894	534	56	28
1973	354	152	14	1,924	584	58	31
1974	331	152	14	1,990	631	63	36

I1   SOUTH AMERICA: Pupils and Teachers in Schools (in thousands, except as otherwise indicated)

	Argentina				Bolivia			Brazil			
	Pupils		Teachers		Pupils		Teachers	Pupils		Teachers	
	a	b	a	b	a	b	All Schools	a	b	a	b
1975	3,579[20] / 3,802	452	196[20] / 217	62	859	130	46	19,549	1,936	897	133
1976	3,832	442	220	60	923	128	...	19,523	2,213	861	151
1977	3,884	439	218	60	949	143	...	20,368	2,438	893	168
1978	3,937	442	208	59	...	...	...	21,473	2,519	855	181
1979	4,004	441	225	60	...	...	...	21,887	2,658	863	183
1980	4,111	510	217	...	978	171	48	22,149[38]	2,824[38]	883[38]	198[38]
1981	4,218	528	218	78	1,023	166	57	22,473	2,821	943	206
1982	4,382	594	225	...	1,049	176	52	23,564	2,875	961	204
1983	4,511	615	233	80	1,106	183	54	24,556	2,944	1,033	180
1984	4,631	657	219	87	1,181	200	56	24,826	2,947	1,016	215
1985	4,589	716	230	94	1,205	...	60	24,770	3,016	1,041	206
1986	4,778	762	239	96	1,300	209	61	25,608	3,143	1,068	217
1987	4,907	774	252	111	...	218	63	26,208	3,242	1,094	223
1988	4,999	811	260	118	1,187	207	67	26,821	3,340	1,120	229
1989	...	...	...	...	1,286	208	58	27,397	3,441	1,201	238
1990	4,965	...	...	...	1,279	219	63	28,943	3,499	1,260	243
1991	5,041	...	306	...	...	...	...	29,204	3,770	1,295	259
1992	...	...	...	...	...	...	...	30,106	4,085	1,329	265
1993	4,990	...	286	...	...	...	...	30,549	4,183	1,344	274

I1 SOUTH AMERICA: Pupils and Teachers in Schools (in thousands, except as otherwise indicated)

	Chile				Colombia				Ecuador			
	Pupils		Teachers		Pupils		Teachers		Pupils		Teachers	
	a	b	a	b	a	b	a	b	a	b	a	b
1975	2,299	449	66	30	3,953	978	131	51	1,255	384	33	23
1976	2,243	466	57	31	4,224	1,075	143	54	1,256	431	35	…
1977	2,242	487	71	28	4,165[19]	1,154[19]	134[19]	55[19]	1,307	470	37	28
1978	2,233	510	72	29	3,609	1,459	111	70	1,367	487	38	30
1979	2,236	536	66	27	3,612	1,474	114	72	1,450	535	40	31
1980	2,185	538	…	…	3,597	1,434	116	70	1,534	587	44	35
1981	2,139	555	…	…	3,676	1,677	120	81	1,573	627	45	37
1982	2,093	566	63	…	3,714	1,718	124	85	1,611	673	45	41
1983	…	…	…	…	3,750	1,817	125	90	1,677	655	50	41
1984	…	…	…	…	3,412	1,652	115	81	1,673	706	51	45
1985	2,062	668	78	37	3,385	1,742	113	84	1,742	701	52	48
1986	2,048	680	…	…	3,740	1,685	123	83	1,775	744	56	50
1987	2,056	696	69	42	3,902	1,973	130	85	1,843	765	57	54
1988	2,028	736	…	…	4,029	2,069	136	99	1,898	743	60	54
1989	1,988	742	67	…	4,206	2,282	140	115	1,843	792	60	58
1990	1,991	720	…	…	4,247		142		1,846	785	61	60
1991	2,034	699	81	49	4,310	2,378	143	120	2,020	811	64	61
1992	2,035	675	…	…	4,525	2,686	162	131	1,987	814	63	…
1993	2,066	652	78	…	4,599	2,796	166	134	…	…	…	…

I1   **SOUTH AMERICA: Pupils and Teachers in Schools** (in thousands, except as otherwise indicated)

	Guyana				Paraguay				Peru			
	Pupils		Teachers		Pupils		Teachers		Pupils		Teachers	
	a	b	a	b	a	b	a	b	a	b	a	b
1975	130	71	4.1	3.2	452	75	16	7.5	2,841	813	73	34
1976	140	77	4.3	...	468	82	16	...	2,961	890	74	35
1977	138	...	4.5	...	477	92	17	8.0	3,020	969	75	35
1978	137	...	4.2	...	493	101	18	...	3,093	1,050	78	38
1979	132	...	4.3	...	504	110	18	...	3,117	1,095	80	41
1980	131	75	3.9	4.2	519	118	19	...	3,161	1,152	84	45
1981	130	74	3.5	3.8	530	124	20	...	3,319	1,226	90	50
1982	126	69	3.5	3.5	540	137	21	...	3,454	1,286	96	55
1983	122	67	3.3	3.5	550	144	21	...	3,515	1,322	98	58
1984	117	71	3.3	3.5	559	151	22	...	3,559	1,375	101	63
1985	114	77	3.9	...	571	151	23	...	3,712	1,421	106	68
1986	113	76	3.9	...	580	150	23	...	3,679	1,474	111	74
1987	115	...	3.9	...	600	151	24	...	3,764	1,523	120	76
1988	118	...	4.0	...	627	153	25	...	3,728	1,578	126	80
1989	...	...	...	...	657	163	26	...	3,793	1,652	130	83
1990	...	...	...	...	687	164	28	...	3,855	1,698	133	86
1991	...	...	...	...	721	169	29	12	3,857	1,710	134	87
1992	...	...	...	...	749	193	33	...	3,853	1,704	136	88
1993	...	...	...	...	799	214	33	21	3,914	1,720	133	85

I1 SOUTH AMERICA: Pupils and Teachers in Schools (in thousands, except as otherwise indicated)

	Uruguay			Venezuela			
	Pupils		Teachers	Pupils		Teachers	
	a	b	a	a	b	a	b
1975	323	144	14	2,103	669	69	40
1976	323	142	14	2,204	720	75	41
1977	324	137	14	2,309	751	80	42
1978	325	131	14	2,379	787	82	44
1979	327	129	15	2,457	821	88	46
1980	331	125	16	2,530	850	93	49
1981	336	162	16	2,591	884	97	50
1982	344	164	17	2,620	930	99	54
1983	350	171	17	2,641	963	100	55
1984	350	177	15	2,710	1,008	104	58
1985	356	188	15	2,770	1,038	108	60
1986	355	183	16	2,880[19]	1,058[19]	112[19]	62[19]
1987	354	176	17	3,663	275	167	32
1988	352	209	17	3,721	281	166	29
1989	350	215	16	3,778	278	171	30
1990	346	224	16	3,871	280	177	31
1991	341	231	16	4,053	281	183	32
1992	338	227	16	4,190	289	184	34
1993	338	221	16	...	...	...	...

I1 Pupils and Teachers in Schools (in thousands, except as otherwise indicated)

NOTES

1. SOURCES: The national publications listed on pp. xiv–xvi; UNESCO, *Yearbook of Educational Statistics.*
2. The definition of the different sorts of schools varies from country to country, sometimes from province to province, and from time to time, and it is not always unambiguous. Nor is it always clear to exactly what time of year the statistics relate, and which pupils are covered by them. So far as possible, changes in the scope and nature of the statistics are indicated in the footnotes, but there are believed to be many which are not recorded in the sources.
3. Only general secondary schools are normally covered in this table, not vocational, technical, or teacher-training institutions.

FOOTNOTES

[1] State schools only.
[2] Publicly-controlled schools only to 1948, except in Quebec to 1929. Excluding Prince Edward Island to 1874 and in 1876; excluding Manitoba in 1875–80; and excluding private schools in Quebec from 1875 to 1881 and in 1946 and 1947. Newfoundland is included from 1949, and additional schools, with 36 thousand pupils, from 1951. The teachers series relates to state schools only to 1958 (1st line). Figures from 1972 (2nd line) are later revisions or recategorizations.
[3] The only pupils in Quebec who are included are those in controlled Roman Catholic schools in these years.
[4] Public day schools only to 1928 (1st line). Earlier data are available for total pupils in private schools as follows (in thousands):

1889	1,269	1897	1,317	1905	1,338	1913	1,739
1890	1,757*	1898	1,355	1906	1,414	1914	1,781
1891	1,491	1899	1,298	1907	1,309	1915	1,770
1892	1,300	1900	1,382	1908	1,547	1916	1,820
1893	1,343	1901	1,370	1909	1,489	1918	1,662
1894	1,319	1902	1,209	1910	1,558	1920	1,669
1895	1,211	1903	1,196	1911	1,601	1922	1,727
1896	1,335	1904	1,304	1912	1,647	1924	1,727
						1926	2,439

*Excluding kindergartens, which are included in private school data in all other years except 1932–38. These statistics are broken down by grade in census years, as follows:

	Primary	Secondary		Primary	Secondary
1890	1,662	95	1910	1,440	117
1900	1,147	111	1920	1,456	214

'Other' schools (e.g. Federal schools on military bases and on Indian reservations, residential schools for handicapped children, etc.) are excluded throughout. The following figures at ten-year intervals indicate the numbers involved (in thousands):

	Primary	Secondary		Primary	Secondary
1890	...	60	1940	113	71
1900	37	69	1950	105	56
1910	71	83	1960	154	80
1920	99	86	1970	195	97
1930	143	71			

[5] In public day schools only to 1970 (1st line). Prior to 1938, statistics are of numbers employed rather than numbers of posts. Librarian, guidance, and some other non-supervisory posts are included, but school principals are not.
[6] Excluding Nova Scotia.
[7] Excluding Manitoba.
[8] State schools only to 1954 (1st line) and form 1982 (2nd line).
[9] Schools in San José only to 1943 and in 1947 and 1949. State schools throughout the country in 1945, 1950, and 1951.
[10] State schools only from 1902 and 1922 (2nd line) and in 1939.
[11] Including pre-primary school teachers to 1965.
[12] No break is indicated in the source, but it is very likely that there is one, and the probable cause is a change from enrolment to attendance. This change was reversed in 1921.
[13] Including pre-primary school to 1950 (1st line). There is no break in the teachers series.
[14] Primary schools only from 1896.
[15] State schools only to 1947.
[16] Tobago is included from 1900.
[17] An element of double-counting in Manitoba and Ontario was eliminated between 1931 and 1934.
[18] Statistics from 1918 to 1929 are of attendance rather than enrolment.
[19] There was a change in the categorization of schools.
[20] The reason for this break is not clear from the sources.

I2 NORTH AMERICA: STUDENTS IN UNIVERSITIES

1870-1899

	USA (thousands)
1870	52
1871	...
1872	...
1873	...
1874	...
1875	...
1876	...
1877	...
1878	...
1879	...
1880	116
1881	...
1882	...
1883	...
1884	...
1885	...
1886	...
1887	...
1888	...
1889	...
1890	157
1891	...
1892	...
1893	...
1894	...
1895	...
1896	...
1897	...
1898	...
1899	...

1900-1934

	Canada[1] (thousands)	Cuba	El Salvador	Guatemala[2]	Honduras	Maxico (thousands)	USA (thousands)
1900	...	600	...	...	...	...	238
1901	...	534	...	...	...	...	...
1902	...	638	...	...	135	...	...
1903	...	...	...	...	...	...	...
1904	...	503	...	...	...	...	...
1905	...	524	...	...	...	...	264
1906	...	581	...	...	...	...	...
1907	...	521	...	...	...	...	...
1908	...	634	...	...	...	...	...
1909	...	1,017	...	...	...	...	...
1910	...	1,070	...	...	...	...	355
1911	...	...	...	...	...	...	354
1912	...	1,176	...	...	...	...	356
1913	...	...	...	...	...	...	361
1914	...	1,273	...	...	...	...	379
1915	...	1,432	...	...	...	...	404
1916	...	...	...	...	...	...	441
1917	...	...	...	...	...	...	...
1918	...	...	...	...	...	...	441
1919	...	2,272	...	...	...	...	...
1920	22	...	...	...	...	...	598
1921	23	...	...	...	98	...	...
1922	24	...	...	...	107	...	681
1923	25	4,006	...	...	...	...	...
1924	25	...	...	...	...	9.6	823
1925	25	4,068	...	...	72	11	...
1926	25	5,473	...	...	...	10	941
1927	26	4,148	368	...	70	8.7	...
1928	27	3,932	...	...	...	9.4	1,054
1929	28	4,795	409	...	...	8.2	...
1930	30	...	411	...	179	9.6	1,101
1931	32	...	...	714	...	9.7	...
1932	33	...	491	...	...	11	1,154
1933	33	...	...	...	308	9.2	...
1934	33	...	...	694	299	8.2	1,055

I2 NORTH AMERICA: Students in Universities

	Barbados[3]	Canada[1] (thousands)	Costa Rica (thousands)	Cuba (thousands)	Dominican Republic	El Salvador	Guatemala[2] (thousands)	Honduras
1935	—	33	...	—	...	...	...	312
1936	—	34	...	...	328	...	...	298
1937	—	34	...	...	450	...	...	298
1938	—	34	...	...	498	...	...	...
1939	—	35	...	...	702	...	...	...
1940	—	36	...	...	754	...	...	357
1941	—	35	...	...	898	...	...	...
1942	—	35	...	...	1,040	468	...	...
1943	—	36	...	...	1,134	...	...	368
1944	—	35	...	8.2	1,218	633	...	467
					(thousands)			
1945	—	38	...	...	1.4	916	...	433
1946	—	62	...	...	1.6	...	...	462
1947	—	76	...	...	1.7	...	...	496
1948	...	79	...	...	1.9	...	...	653
1949	...	76	...	...	2.1	1,120	...	653
						(thousands)		
1950	...	69	...	17	2.3	1.2	2.3	716
1951	...	64	1.4	17	2.4	1.3	...	894
1952	...	60	1.9		2.8	0.7	...	843
1953	...	60	...	21	3.0	1.0	...	831
1954	...	61	...	23	3.1	1.0	3.4	...
1955	...	65	2.2	24	3.2	1.1	3.2	...
1956	...	69	...	17	3.8	1.5	...	1,137
1957	...	75	2.5	...	4.0	1.3	...	1,185
1958	...	82[1] 95	3.1	1.9	3.9	1.9	...	1,306
1959	...	102	3.7	18	3.8	2.1	...	1,310
								(thousands)
1960	...	114	3.8	20	3.4	2.2	5.2	1.4
1961	...	129	4.2	18	4.0	2.5	5.5	1.5
1962	...	141[1] 185	...	17	5.3	2.9	5.9	1.7
1963	...	215	4.4	20	...	3.2	6.2	1.7
1964	...	231	5.1	26	5.5	3.5	7.0	1.8
1965	226	277	5.8	26	6.6	3.8	7.7	2.1
1966	245	315	6.0	28	6.9	5.0	...	2.5
1967	293	351	7.2	29	10	6.1	9.4[2]	2.5
1968	385	368	9.3	30	15	7.1	12	2.9
1969	429	416	11	31	18	7.8	14	...
1970	459	477	13	26	23	9.2	16	3.3
1971	615	478	15	37	29	12	17	4.7
1972	881	475	18	49	33	13	19	8.1
1973	942	491	24	55	35	16[4]	22[2]	9.3
1974	991	502	28	68	39	21	20	9.2

I2 NORTH AMERICA: Students in Universities

1935–1974

	Jamaica[3]	Mexico[5] (thousands)	Nicaragua (thousands)	Panama[6] (thousands)	Puerto Rico (thousands)	Trinidad & Tobago[3]	USA[7] (thousands)
1935	—	10	...	...	...	—	...
1936	—	12	...	...	...	—	1,208
1937	—	13	...	...	...	—	...
1938	—	17	...	...	...	—	1,351
1939	—	16	...	...	...	—	...
1940	—	17	...	...	...	—	1,494
1941	—	18	...	...	...	—	...
1942	—	19	...	...	...	—	1,404
1943	—	22	...	...	...	—	...
1944	—	22	0.7	...	...	—	1,155
1945	—	23	0.7	0.8	...	—	...
1946	—	22	0.6	1.0	10	—	1,677
1947	—	21	...	1.0	11	—	...
1948	35	24	...	1.3	12	...	2,616
1949	70	25₅ / 29	...	1.4	13	...	...
1950	145	17	...	1.5	14	...	2,659
1951	205	31	...	1.7	13	...	...
1952	254	27	...	...	13	...	2,302
1953	302	21	1.1	1.7	15	...	...
1954	384	26	...	2.0	16	...	2,515
1955	444	19	...	2.0	18	...	...
1956	494	18	...	2.3	19	...	2,619
1957	555	16	0.9	2.8	21	...	...
1958	622	19	1.0	3.3	22	...	2,900
1959	695	23	1.2	3.4	25	...	...₆
1960	977	83	1.3	3.9	26	...	3,216
1961	1,268	95	2.0	4.2	30	...	...
1962	1,422	100	2.1	5.1	31	...	3,726
1963	2,187	102	2.4	5.4₆ / 6.2	33	...	...
1964	2,523₃	130	2.8	7.0	37	692	4,296
1965	1,923	135	3.3	8.9	40	910	...
1966	2,073	143	4.1	9.9	42	964	...
1967	2,234	141	5.1	11	45	1,087	...
1968	2,564	166	6.4	12	51	1,267	6,659
1969	2,687	215	8.0	7.9	53	1,511	...
1970	2,886	248	9.4	8.9	59	1,671	7,545₇ / 7,920
1971	3,301	291₅	9.4	15	65	...	8,116
1972	3,576	369	12	18	71	1,966	8,265
1973	3,608	453	12	22	79	2,089	8,518
1974	3,735	520	15	24	84	2,202	9,023

I2 NORTH AMERICA: Students in Universities

	Barbados	Canada[1] (thousands)	Costa Rica (thousands)	Cuba (thousands)	Dominican Republic (thousands)	El Salvador (thousands)	Guatemala (thousands)	Honduras (thousands)
1975	1,065	547	33	85	29	27	23	11
1976	1,140	567	36	107	...	...	26	13
1977	1,235	586	39	123	45	28	29	15
1978	1,362	584	45	133	42	29	34	19
1979	1,497	601	47	146	...	9	48	21
1980	1,587	628	47	152	...	13	51	24
1981	1,601	649	47	165	...	18	47	27
1982	1,564	692	46	173	...	34	47	28
1983	1,641	729	47	193	...	47	44	29
1984	1,790	739	47	212	...	53	46	30
1985	1,902	752	50	235	124	57	48	29
1986	2,007	763	50	257	...	61	52	30
1987	2,103	781	52	263	...	...	...	31
1988	...	806	53	251	...	72	...	33
1989	...	819	58	242	...	75	...	36
1990	2,408	841	58	242	...	67	...	39
1991	2,580	867	61	224	...	56	...	38
1992	2,572	890	65	198	...	...	...	40
1993	...	875	...	176	...	...	...	

	Jamaica	Mexico (thousands)	Nicaragua (thousands)	Panama (thousands)	Puerto Rico (thousands)	Trinidad & Tobago	USA (thousands)
1975	3,963	525	16	26	91	2,229	9,731
1976	4,091	622	20	30	69	2,310	9,589
1977	4,361	655	20	35	85	2,489	9,807
1978	4,496	731	...	35	...	2,661	11,260
1979	4,574	818	27	38	97	2,915	11,570
1980	4,548	840	33	40	...	2,923	12,097
1981	4,798	910	...	43	...	3,144	12,372
1982	4,884	973[15]	28	46	...	3,125	12,426
1983	5,157	1,233	30	45	...	3,197	12,465
1984	5,325	1,310	26	52	...	3,428	12,242
1985	5,057	1,427	24	53	...	3,728	12,247
1986	4,979	1,538	24	60	...	3,803	12,505
1987	5,235	1,527	24	55	...	4,156	12,768
1988	5,209	1,586	...	51	...	4,252	12,849
1989	5,426	1,643	...	50	...	...	13,358
1990	5,857	1,678	30	53	...	4,090	13,710
1991	6,093	1,722	30	58	...	4,529	14,361
1992	6,333	1,723	35	63	...	4,947	14,423
1993	...	1,767	...	69	...	5,191	14,473

I2 SOUTH AMERICA: STUDENTS IN UNIVERSITIES

1885–1924

	Argentina	Bolivia	Brazil (thousands)	Chile	Colombia	Ecuador	Paraguay	Peru (thousands)	Uruguay
1885	880	...	...	...	...	...	...	...	...
1886	...	...	...	968	...	...	...	...	193
1887	743	...	...	1,014	...	...	...	...	208
1888	...	774	...	1,074	...	...	...	...	251
1889	963	...	...	...	...	...	...	...	232
1890	1,007	...	...	...	...	...	...	...	282
1891	900	...	...	1,245	...	...	...	...	291
1892	...	...	...	1,179	...	...	...	...	262
1893	...	...	...	...	...	216	...	...	281
1894	...	...	...	1,181	...	...	...	...	279
1895	...	506	...	1,190	...	...	...	...	271
1896	...	...	...	1,317	...	...	...	...	317
1897	...	...	...	1,275	1,519	...	...	0.8	398
1898	2,553	...	...	1,181	...	...	...	0.9	378
1899	...	...	...	1,251	...	...	...	...	396
	(thousands)								
1900	...	...	...	1,228	1,558	...	...	...	401
1901	...	613	...	1,242	...	...	...	...	415
1902	3.0	...	...	1,392	...	...	...	...	412
1903	...	...	...	1,775	...	...	...	...	426
1904	3.7	...	...	1,829	...	...	...	...	...
1905	...	...	...	1,960	...	...	...	...	...
1906	...	680	...	1,948	...	...	...	...	851
1907	...	...	6.4	2,121	...	...	...	...	730
1908	...	...	7.7	2,234	...	...	...	...	...
1909	10	...	8.7	2,378	...	...	...	...	1,366
1910	...	...	8.8	2,425	...	...	...	...	1,039
1911	...	...	10	2,874	...	...	...	...	1,081
1912	...	780	11	3,129	...	437	...	1.7	1,139
1913	7.5	...	...	3,813	...	...	...	1.7	1,084
1914	...	...	...	4,024	1,576	474	192	1.8	1,077
				(thousands)					
1915	7.1	...	...	4.5	...	465	214	1.6	...
1916	...	...	...	4.7	...	...	...	1.8	...
					(thousands)				
1917	14	...	...	4.7	2.5	...	...	2.0	...
1918	15	...	...	4.9	...	...	252	2.0	...
1919	14	...	...	4.7	...	744	247	1.8	...
1920	15	...	...	5.1	...	...	247	1.7	...
1921	...	...	...	5.4	...	680	279	0.5	...
									(thousands)
1922	...	...	...	6.5	...	670	...	1.5	1.6
1923	...	...	...	6.5	...	...	...	1.7	...
1924	...	...	...	6.1	...	...	...	2.1	2.0

I2   SOUTH AMERICA: Students in Universities

	Argentina[8] (thousands)	Bolivia	Brazil[9] (thousands)	Chile (thousands)	Colombia (thousands)	Ecuador	Paraguay	Peru (thousands)	Uruguay (thousands)	Venezuela (thousands)
1925	...	...	...	6.3	...	...	364	2.3	2.1	...
1926	...	802	...	5.0	...	...	347	2.2	2.1	0.7
1927	...	...	13	5.1	...	...	334	2.2	2.3	...
1928	17	...	14	5.8	...	776	414	2.3	2.1	...
1929	...	...	15	6.6	...	...	435	2.7	1.8	...
1930	23	...	...	...	...	...	467	2.9	1.9	...
1931	25	...	...	5.2	...	...	449	0.6	2.0	...
1932	23	1,745	21	5.8	...	958	490	0.5	1.7	...
1933	26	1,682	23	...	...	1,064	—	1.4	2.3	...
1934	26	...	25[9] 24	...	3.0	1,051	381	2.8	2.5	...
1935	27	...	26	6.0	4.1	1,230	445	2.4	2.3	...
1936	30	1,482	26	6.4	3.3	1,426	673	2.9	2.5	...
1937	30	...	25	6.3	3.3	1,476	871	3.4	2.7	2.0
1938	32	...	22	6.2	3.1	1,493	1,125	4.8	...	1.8
1939	34	...	19	6.4	3.8	1,505	1,293	4.0	...	1.9
1940	42	...	18	...	3.0	1,588	1,203	3.8	...	2.4
1941	44	...	18	[5.5][10]	3.7	1,755	1,208	5.5	...	2.5
1942	48	...	20	6.3	4.1	1,885	1,344	5.3	...	3.1
1943	48	...	23	6.4	5.1	...	1,358	7.2	...	2.9
1944	52	...	26	6.8	5.8	...	1,581	8.6	...	3.2
						(thousands)	(thousands)			
1945	53	...	27	7.1	6.5	2.6	1.5	10	...	3.3
1946	57	...	29	7.2	7.3	...	1.7	14	...	4.6
1947	56	...	31	8.2	8.0	3.4	1.2	13	...	5.4
1948	62	...	34	8.1	8.3	4.1	1.5	15	...	5.8
1949	69	...	38	9.5	9.4	4.1	1.9	16	...	6.3
		(thousands)								
1950	85	4.6	43	11	11	4.1	1.8	16	...	6.9
1951	95	...	46	11	11	4.6	2.0	15	12	2.0
1952	103	...	50	...	12	4.8	2.2	15	...	5.1
1953	128	...	55	...	12	5.1	2.3	16	11	7.5
1954	145	...	60	14	12	...	...	17	12	7.4
1955	152	...	63	17	13	5.9	...	18	15	7.7
1956	149	...	67	17	15	5.2	2.4	19	...	9.2
1957	159	...	71	11	16	6.5	2.9	21	15	11
1958	153	...	74	19	19	7.3	3.0	22	...	17
1959	167	...	87	22	21	7.6	3.1	25	15	23

I2 SOUTH AMERICA: Students in Universities

1960–1993

	Argentina[8] (thousands)	Bolivia	Brazil[9] (thousands)	Chile (thousands)	Colombia (thousands)	Ecuador	Guyana[3]	Paraguay	Peru (thousands)	Uruguay (thousands)	Venezuela[13] (thousands)
1960	181	7.5	93	25	23	...	...	3.4	31	15	26
1961	190	...	99	29	27	10	...	3.7	35	...	32
1962	193	7.6	107	33	30	11	...	3.8	41	15	34
1963	217	...	124	35	34	12	169	3.8	46	...	38
1964	254	...	142	37	37	...	268	3.9	54	16	41
1965	247[8] 222	14	156	44	43	14	319	4.1	65	17	46
1966	226	...	180	53	52	16	449	4.6	74	...	54
1967	240	17	213	56	59	19	579	5.0	81	17	59
1968	234	19	278	53	67	22	775	5.3	94	19	46
1969	238	22	343	73	74	32	1,030	5.5	98	20	35
1970	253	29	425	78	86	39	1,112	6.0	108	...	47
1971	290	...	561	101	95	44	1,232	6.7	116	...	50[13] 89
1972	333	...	688	127	111	58	1,385	7.3	128	...	108
1973	378	25	773	140	124	98	1,509	7.9	149	...	145
1974	441	31	938	144	141	137	...	9.2[12] 14	170	26	165
1975	537	34	1,073	147	168	170	1,749	17	182	33	186
1976	533	35	1,096	134	197	181	...	18	197	...	201
1977	465	41	1,159	131	229	...	...	20	199	39	216
1978	402	45	1,226	130	244	231	1,527	20	209	32	228
1979	389	49	1,312	126	257	252	1,582	22	222	38	232
1980	398	61	1,378	119	235	264	1,681	25	258	36	243
1981	402	[53][11]	1,393	119	283	258	1,995	27	279	37	259
1982	411	[57][11]	1,203	119	296	252	1,567	28	294	48	269
1983	417	89	1,439	126	312	264	1,580	31	317	50	282
1984	508	80	1,400	186	332	278	1,544	30	336	64	286
1985	604	95	1,368	197	318	265	1,598	...	355	77	321
1986	707	...	1,418	214	320	...	...	...	388	92	314
1987	755	97	1,471	224	331	265	2,245	28	410	61	[467][14]
1988	...	107	1,504	235	319	239	...	28	431	62	[500][14]
1989	...	128	1,518	241	403	186	2,192	29	445	62	530
1990	...	140	1,540	255	...	...	...	29	443	62	542
1991	817	...	1,565	286	430	...	...	...	476	63	551
1992	700	...	1,536	317	...	...	...	...	463	57	...
1993	...	...	1,595	327	...	...	3,607	37	450		...

I2   Students in Universities

NOTES

1. SOURCES: As for table I1. Uruguay figures to 1899 are from E. Acevedo, *Anales Historicas del Uruguay*.
2. Institutions of higher education other than universities and equivalent institutions are covered in some of the statistics in this table. Where this has been identified it is indicated in footnotes.
3. Most sources do not distinguish between undergraduates and graduate students. It is presumed that both are included normally.
4. Unless otherwise indicated, the statistics refer to the academic year beginning in the one shown.

FOOTNOTES

[1] Full-time undergraduates to 1958 (1st line), all full-time students subsequently, with part-time students included from 1962 (2nd line).
[2] San Carlos University only to 1967 and from 1974. The total for 1965 was 8.5 thousand.
[3] All students at the University of British West Indies are shown under Jamaica to 1964.
[4] State universities only to 1973. There were 3 thousand students in private universities in that year.
[5] All higher education from 1950 (2nd line). Coverage was widened in 1972.
[6] Including extension courses from 1962 (2nd line).
[7] Including Alaska and Hawaii from 1960. Coverage was widened in 1970.
[8] All higher education to 1965 (1st line). The figure for universities only in 1960 is 168 thousand.
[9] Numbers at the beginning of the academic year to 1933 (1st line), numbers still registered at the end of the year subsequently. Statistics relate to all undergraduates in higher education.
[10] Excluding Concepción University.
[11] Excluding the Catholic University.
[12] All higher education from 1974 (2nd line).
[13] Coverage was widened in 1971.
[14] All higher education
[15] Change in source.

J NATIONAL ACCOUNTS

Whilst it has been the general principle in most sections of this work to prefer raw data to those which have been processed, there are no such things as raw national accounts statistics, and everything in this section is 'synthetic', the result of elaborate calculations by sophisticated statisticians. It is really impossible to summarize briefly all the complex operations involved, and the user who requires descriptions of them is advised to consult the latest United Nations *Yearbook of National Accounts Statistics*, or, for more detail, their *National Accounting Practices in Sixty Countries*, and the International Monetary Fund *Balance of Payments Yearbook*.

Whilst interest in the nation's wealth and income can be traced in a number of European countries as far back as the later middle ages, and in some of the countries of America back far into the 19th century, the modern national accounts concepts date from the period of World War II (though what is essentially one of the component concepts, the balance of payments, became operational during the inter-war years for most of the larger countries in the region). Since then a great deal of work has been done in many countries not only to improve the concepts and the collection of current statistical material with which to clothe them, but also to produce retrospective estimates, going back to its foundations in the case of the United States, and well into the 19th century for Canada. There are also reasonably lengthy retrospective series for Argentina, Chile, Cuba, and Mexico.

Two main concepts of overall product were used for table J1. Net National Product (or National Income) was the first concept to be much used, and is characteristic of most estimates made before 1948, though not of more recent retrospective exercises. It relates to the disposable income of individuals, institutions, and governments, after providing for the maintenance and depreciation of capital stocks. Gross Domestic Product (or, occasionally, Gross National Product, which takes into account net factor income to or from aboard) is the other main concept used, and includes depreciation and maintenance outlays. It has been preferred where a choice exists. Both concepts can be expressed in terms of either market prices or factor costs, the latter excluding the excess of indirect taxes over subsidies. In most cases market prices have been preferred here. In the case of Cuba since 1962 the concept of Gross Material Product is used. Unlike most centrally-planned economies in Europe, the Cubans have included in this so-called 'unproductive' services, so that their concept is not so very far removed from the Gross Domestic Product of market economies.

It is worth remembering, in making comparisons both over time and between countries, that few national product concepts include 'income in kind', amongst which are the rental value of owner-occupied buildings and the consumption of home-produced goods (including farmers' consumption of their own products). These have tended to be proportionally more important the less developed is a country's economy and the more dependent it is on agriculture, and as development occurs they become increasingly less significant, and in so doing may give an exaggerated picture of rising economic growth. Another warning is in order in relation to the constant price series. Aside from technical problems associated with price index numbers, it is impossible in practice to reflect completely the changes which take place in the quality of goods having the same designation. These changes may be either improvements or deteriorations, but it seems to be generally accepted that the former predominate on balance.

Table J2 takes Gross Domestic Product as its base, where possible, and shows estimates of the proportion contributed by each of the major sectors of the different economies. Once again, it is necessary to be cautious in making comparisons between countries, owing to differences in definitions and sometimes in concept.

The modern balance of payments concepts grew out of the disruptions of international trading relations that became evident quite early in the inter-war years. However, it was only the more developed countries for which more than occasional benchmark estimates were made during these years, and it is the United States for which long retrospective series have been estimated subsequently. For the great majority of the smaller economies, balance of payments statistics begin on a continuous basis only in 1946.

Table J3 shows rather more of the components of these estimates than in the first edition, in particular including some detail on invisibles, net movements of capital, and international reserves. For the last four decades, balances of payments are available in a uniform basis for most countries thanks to the work of International Monetary Fund statisticians, and these have been preferred generally in the second part of the table to national statistics because they facilitate comparisons. Statistics on national definitions, continuing those in the first part of the table, are generally available in national sources.

J1 NORTH AMERICA: NATIONAL ACCOUNTS TOTALS (in millions of stated unit, except as otherwise indicated)

Key:- GDP = gross domestic product; GNP = gross national product; NNP = net national product (national income); G(PF)CF = gross (private fixed) capital formation; NMP = net material product

1789-1824

	USA (dollars)	
	Current Prices	1929 Prices
	GNP	GNP
1789	158	307
1790	188	347
1791	199	373
1792	227	405
1793	239	409
1794	291	454
1795	352	469
1796	404	502
1797	397	539
1798	381	529
1799	421	575
1800	459	632
1801	528	683
1802	490	728
1803	488	727
1804	534	757
1805	592	778
1806	609	844
1807	564	803
1808	461	717
1809	502	720
1810	588	830
1811	580	841
1812	569	802
1813	623	761
1814	701	760
1815	812	888
1816	854	960
1817	847	972
1818	816	958
1819	754	1,036
1820	656	1,063
1821	607	1,059
1822	704	1,181
1823	699	1,232
1824	751	1,356

1825-1864

	USA (dollars)	
	Current Prices	1929 Prices
	GNP	GNP
1825	850	1,425
1826	884	1,633
1827	868	1,648
1828	881	1,685
1829	905	1,744
1830	933	1,861
1831	1,073	2,121
1832	1,155	2,231
1833	1,298	2,431
1834	1,333	2,568
1835	1,633	2,796
1836	1,896	2,949
1837	1,830	3,025
1838	1,758	2,990
1839	1,932	3,167
1840	1,672	3,215
1841	1,658	3,254
1842	1,517	3,319
1843	1,468	3,406
1844	1,629	3,669
1845	1,786	3,874
1846	1,911	4,119
1847	2,180	4,283
1848	2,139	4,796
1849	2,205	4,793
1850	2,586	5,162
1851	2,674	5,548
1852	2,864	5,881
1853	3,363	6,418
1854	3,625	6,532
1855	3,891	6,640
1856	4,022	6,863
1857	3,977	6,353
1858	3,716	6,946
1859	3,972	7,235
1860	3,839	7,096
1861	3,677	6,613
1862	4,012	6,368
1863	5,096	6,542
1864	6,479	5,960

J1   NORTH AMERICA: National Accounts Totals (in millions of stated unit, except as otherwise indicated)

	Canada (dollars)				Cuba (pesos)		Mexico (pesos)	USA (thousand million dollars)	
	Current prices		1935–39 Prices		Current Prices	1926 Prices	1950 Prices	Current Prices	1929 Prices
	GNP	GPFCF[1]	GNP[2]	GPFCF[1]	NNP	NNP	GNP	GNP	GNP
1865	...	...	...	...	...	...	...	6.56	6.30
1866	...	...	...	...	...	...	...	6.88	7.02
1867	419	...	695	...	...	...	...	6.84	7.47
1868	...	...	...	...	...	...	...	7.06	7.93
1869	...	...	...	...	...	...	...	7.41	8.71
1870	458	54	747[2]	100	...	...	...	7.35	9.63
1871	...	...	769	...	...	...	...	7.55	10.29
1872	...	...	645	...	...	...	...	8.52	11.00
1873	...	...	710	...	...	...	...	8.79	11.74
1874	...	...	855	...	...	...	...	8.54	11.97
1875	...	...	827	...	...	...	...	8.22	12.07
1876	...	...	833	...	...	...	...	7.91	12.47
1877	...	...	855	...	...	...	...	8.08	13.01
1878	...	...	843	...	...	...	...	8.02	14.77
1879	...	...	985	...	...	...	...	8.81	16.43
1880	612	...	1,096[2]	...	...	...	...	10.51	17.94
1881	...	...	1,247	...	...	...	...	11.27	18.97
1882	...	...	1,238	...	...	...	...	12.16	17.72
1883	...	...	1,216	...	...	...	...	11.55	20.02
1884	...	...	1,337	...	...	...	...	10.97	20.24
1885	...	...	1,482	...	...	...	...	10.64	20.95
1886	...	...	1,337	...	...	...	...	10.93	22.17
1887	...	...	1,340	...	...	...	...	12.00	23.58
1888	...	...	1,408	...	...	...	...	12.42	24.02
1889	...	...	1,374	...	...	...	...	12.97[3]	26.10[3]
								12.5	1958 prices 49.1
1890	815	113	1,408[2]	210	...	...	...	13.1	52.7
1891	...	...	1,642	...	...	...	...	13.5	55.1
1892	...	...	1,605	...	...	...	...	14.3	60.4
1893	...	...	1,562	...	...	...	...	13.8	57.5
1894	...	...	1,553	...	...	...	...	12.6	55.9
1895	...	...	1,636	...	...	...	8,863	13.9	62.6
1896	...	...	1,794	...	...	...	9,137	13.3	61.3
1897	...	...	1,559	...	...	...	9,750	14.6	67.1
1898	...	...	1,846	...	...	...	10,318	15.4	68.6
1899	...	...	1,769	...	...	...	9,814	17.4	74.8
1900	1,032	126	1,849[2]	227	...	...	9,891	18.7	76.9
1901	...	...	2,031	...	...	...	10,741	20.7	85.7
1902	...	...	2,179	...	...	...	9,975	21.6	86.5
1903	...	...	2,244	...	193	324	11,092	22.9	90.8
1904	...	...	2,284	...	222	372	11,287	22.9	89.7
1905	...	...	2,457	...	264	439	12,460	25.1	96.3
1906	...	...	2,599	...	249	403	12,319	28.7	107.5
1907	...	...	2,612	...	250	383	13,042	30.4	109.2
1908	...	...	2,723	...	238	378	13,022	27.7	100.2
1909	...	...	3,031	...	300	444	13,405	33.4	116.8

J1   NORTH AMERICA: National Accounts Totals (in millions of stated unit, except as otherwise indicated)

| | Canada (dollars) | | | | | | Cuba (pesos) | | El Salvador (colones) | Guatemala[5] (quetzales) | | | |
| | Current Prices | | | 1935/1971 Prices[4] | | | Current Prices | 1926 Prices | Current Prices | Current Prices | | 1946 Prices | |
	GNP	GPFCF[1]	Stocks	GNP[2]	GPFCF[1]	Stocks	NNP	NNP	GNP	GNP	GCF[5]	GNP	GCF[5]
1910	2,138	389	...	3,087[2]	610	...	347	493	...	...	...	...	...
1911	...	...	...	3,355	...	...	295	455	...	...	...	...	...
1912	...	...	...	3,413	...	...	397	575	...	...	...	...	...
1913	...	...	...	3,708	...	...	379	543	...	...	...	...	...
1914	...	...	...	3,483	...	...	400	587	...	...	...	...	...
1915				3,591	...	...	519	747	...	...	...	...	...
1916	...	...	...	3,749	...	...	644	753	...	...	...	...	...
1917	...	...	...	3,831	...	...	678	577	...	...	...	...	...
1918	...	...	...	3,864	...	...	734	577	...	...	...	...	...
1919	...	...	...	4,046	...	...	862	622	...	...	...	...	...
1920	5,543	1,008	...	3,844[2]	651	...	1,191	771	...	...	...	...	...
1921	...	...	...	3,495	...	...	588	602	...	...	...	...	...
1922	...	...	...	3,780	...	...	656	678	...	...	...	...	...
1923	...	...	...	4,015	...	...	761	756	...	93	...	...	...
1924	...	...	...	4,010	...	...	783	798	...	127	...	...	...
1925	...	...[1]	...	4,182	...	...	708	684	...	162	...	...	...
1926	5,146	814	135	4,548[4]	...[4]	...[4]	604	604	...	179	...	...	...
				14,086	2,619	399							
1927	5,561	994	253	15,423	3,235	533	648	679	...	174	...	...	...
1928	6,050	1,195	159	16,831	3,845	390	604	...	...	201	...	...	...
1929	6,139	1,361	52	16,894	4,254	311	...	...	...	194	...	...	...
1930	5,720	1,150	77	16,174	3,722	221	598	...	...	122	...	...	...
1931	4,693	809	−95	14,118	2,762	−253	...	...	...	100	...	...	...
1932	3,814	432	−100	12,654	1,532	−306	...	...	...	63	...	...	...
1933	3,492	299	−91	11,811	1,094	−236	446	...	...	51	...	...	...
1934	3,969	380	32	13,245	1,379	81	...	...	...	65	...	...	...
1935	4,301	458	39	14,279	1,645	152	...	...	...	70	...	...	...
1936	4,634	531	−72	14,912	1,870	2	631	...	...	83	...	...	...
1937	5,241	755	9	16,410	2,483	246	...	...	...	104	...	...	...
1938	5,272	717	57	16,545	2,371	154	468	...	...	127	12	...	...
1939	5,621	687	282	17,774	2,295	604	488	...	244	120	10	...	...
1940	6,713	833	264	20,277	2,619	573	548	...	229	103	6	...	...
1941	8,282	1,096	85	23,194	3,206	245	678	...	232	108	6	...	...
1942	10,265	1,055	145	27,497	2,923	−21	710	...	279	111	6	...	...
1943	11,053	902	−142	28,604	2,371	−45	933	...	398	132	4	...	...
1944	11,848	964	−134	29,736	2,486	−70	1,212	...	435	153	6	...	...
1945	11,863	1,230	−340	29,071	3,182	−122	1,069	...	...	168	9	...	...
1946	11,885	1,682	195	28,292	4,207	420	1,247	...	...	254	16[5]	254	...[5]
											25		25
1947	13,473	2,350	343	29,498	5,316	672	1,649	...	...	299	44	284	37
1948	15,509	3,057	97	30,231	6,103	109	1,602	...	...	429	51	376	30
1949	16,800	3,439	78	31,388	6,553	215	1,509	...	...	420	45	337	25

J1 NORTH AMERICA: National Accounts Totals (in millions of stated unit, except as otherwise indicated).

	Haiti (gourdes) 1970 prices[6]	Honduras (lempiras)						Jamaica (pounds) Current prices	Mexico (pesos)		1950 prices	1960 prices
		Current prices			1948 prices				Current prices			
	GDP	GDP	GFCF	Stocks	GDP	GFCF	Stocks	NNP	GDP	GFCF	GNP	GDP
1910	...	...	...	...	...	...	...	...	...	...	13,524	...
1911	...	...	...	...	...	...	...	...	...	...	...	...
1912	...	...	...	...	...	...	...	...	...	...	...	...
1913	...	...	...	...	...	...	...	...	...	...	...	...
1914	...	...	...	...	...	...	...	...	...	...	...	...
1915	...	...	...	...	...	...	...	...	...	...	...	...
1916	...	...	...	...	...	...	...	...	...	...	...	...
1917	...	...	...	...	...	...	...	...	...	...	...	...
1918	...	...	...	...	...	...	...	...	...	...	...	...
1919	...	...	...	...	...	...	...	...	...	...	...	...
1920	...	...	...	...	...	...	...	...	...	...	...	...
1921	...	...	...	...	...	...	...	...	...	...	14,560	...
1922	...	...	...	...	...	...	...	...	...	...	14,899	...
1923	...	...	...	...	...	...	...	...	...	...	15,411	...
1924	...	...	...	...	...	...	...	...	...	...	15,159	...
1925	...	150	8.4	1.6	240	12	2.2	...	4,937	...	16,102	37,402
1926	...	154	8.8	1.6	242	12	2.2	...	5,154	...	17,335	39,646
1927	...	164	9.7	1.2	265	14	1.8	...	4,700	...	16,932	37,902
1928	...	181	12	1.5	298	17	2.5	...	4,729	...	17,240	38,137
1929	...	185	16	2.2	297	22	3.6	18.7	4,583	...	16,666	36,662
1930	...	182	15	2.3	315	22	4.1	18.6	4,399	...	15,538	34,364
1931	...	170	10	0.8	318	15	1.7	17.9	3,976	...	16,106	35,503
1932	...	155	7.1	−0.4	285	11	−1.1	16.7	3,021	...	13,494	30,207
1933	...	160	6.8	1.6	269	12	3.6	16.4	3,564	...	14,943	33,620
1934	...	165	9.0	0.1	262	14	—	16.1	3,912	...	15,927	35,889
1935	...	165	13	2.8	250	21	5.7	16.7	4,279	...	17,039	38,549
1936	...	157	12	0.8	255	18	1.4	16.9	5,038	...	18,491	41,663
1937	...	153	13	2.2	244	20	4.0	18.7	6,409	...	19,120	43,011
1938	...	162	13	1.3	257	20	2.5	19.6	6,862	...	19,473	43,708
1939	...	173	...	1.5	265	20	2.9	...	7,337	649	20,505	46,058
1940	...	187	15	0.9	281	22	1.5	...	7,774	773	20,721	46,693
1941	...	189	16	2.8	281	22	4.5	...	8,701	970	23,289	51,241
1942	...	205	10	2.6	257	14	3.8	33.3	10,066	1,005	26,373	54,116
1943	...	209	14	0.9	257	18	1.4	40.5	12,285	1,277	27,358	56,120
1944	...	244	16	3.8	295	20	4.9	...	17,719	1,730	29,690	60,701
1945	1,503	274	22	3.6	323	29	5.2	...	19,382	2,276	31,959	62,608
1946	1,516	315	34	9.0	350	40	11	64	26,322	3,261	34,064	66,722
1947	1,541	362	41	11	375	43	12	...	29,237	4,104	34,517	69,020
1948	1,557	384	42	6.2	384	42	6.2	...	31,196	4,552	36,080	71,864
1949	1,573	416	47	8.7	390	47	9.0	...	34,316	5,117	37,627	75,803

J1   NORTH AMERICA: National Accounts Totals (in millions of stated unit, except as otherwise indicated)

	Nicaragua (cordobas) 1958 Prices		Panama (balboas) Current Prices			Panama 1950 Prices		Puerto Rico[8] (dollars) Current Prices		
	GDP	GFCF	GDP	GFCF	Stocks	GDP	GFCF	NNP/GNP[9]	GFCF	Stocks
1929	...	...	...	...	...	...	...	189	...	...
1930	...	...	...	...	...	...	...	169	...	...
1931	...	...	...	...	...	...	...	156	...	...
1932	...	...	...	...	...	...	...	140	...	...
1933	...	...	...	...	...	...	...	179	...	...
1934	...	...	...	...	...	...	...	177	...	...
1935	...	...	...	...	...	...	...	199	...	...
1936	...	...	...	...	...	...	...	210	...	...
1937	...	...	...	...	...	...	...	217	...	...
1938	...	...	...	...	...	...	...	207	...	...
1939	...	...	...	...	...	...	...	228	24	6
1940	...	...	...	...	...	...	...	278	34	
1941	...	...	...	...	...	...	...	359	59	
1942	...	...	...	...	...	...	...	435	22	
1943	...	...	...	...	...	...	...	477	18	
1944	...	...	...	...	...	...	...	564	46	
1945	1,128	143	...	...	...	265	36	587	43	
1946	1,225	179	229	28	−8	269$_7$ / 254	42$_7$ / 39	612$_9$ / 733	68	31
1947	1,229	218	258	44	14	265	47	743	102	5
1948	1,336	184	257	35	−5	249	33	771	110	2
1949	1,312	205	260$_7$	32$_7$	4$_7$	255$_7$	30$_7$	773	100	−8

J1 NORTH AMERICA: National Accounts Totals (in millions of stated unit, except as otherwise indicated)

	USA					
	(thousand million dollars)					
	Current Prices			1958/1982 Prices[11]		
	GNP	GPFCF	Stocks	GNP	GPFCF	Stocks
1910	35.3	...	...	120.1	...	...
1911	35.8	...	...	123.2	...	...
1912	39.4	...	...	130.2	...	...
1913	39.6	...	...	131.4	...	...
1914	38.6	...	...	125.6	...	...
1915	40.0	...	...	124.5	...	...
1916	48.3	...	...	134.3	...	...
1917	60.4	...	...	135.2	...	...
1918	76.4	...	...	151.8	...	...
1919	84.0	...	...	146.4	...	...
1920	91.5	...	...	140.0	...	...
1921	69.6	...	...	127.8	...	...
1922	74.1	...	...	148.0	...	...
1923	85.1	...	...	165.9	...	...
1924	84.7	...	...	165.5	...	...
1925	93.1	...	...	179.4	...	...
1926	97.0	...	...	190.0	...	...
1927	94.9	...	...	189.8	...	...
1928	97.0[10]	...	...	190.9	...	...
1929	103.9	15.0	1.7	203.6	...	...
				709.6	128.4	10.8
1930	91.2	11.0	−0.4	643.5	98.4	−0.9
1931	76.4	7.0	−1.1	588.1	67.3	−7.1
1932	58.5	3.6	−2.5	509.2	39.0	−16.4
1933	56.0	3.2	−1.6	498.5	33.4	−10.7
1934	65.6	4.2	−0.7	536.7	42.9	−7.6
1935	72.8	5.5	1.1	580.2	54.7	6.2
1936	83.1	7.4	1.3	662.2	73.1	9.0
1937	91.3	9.6	2.5	695.3	85.8	14.1
1938	85.4	7.6	−0.9	664.2	69.1	−6.0
1939	91.3	9.1	0.4	716.6	82.1	3.9
1940	100.4	11.2	2.2	772.9	97.4	14.4
1941	125.5	13.8	4.5	909.4	111.0	27.8
1942	159.0	8.5	1.8	1,080.3	69.0	12.0
1943	192.7	6.8	−0.6	1,276.2	49.7	0.7
1944	211.4	8.7	−1.0	1,380.6	61.6	−5.2
1945	213.4	12.3	−1.0	1,354.8	84.9	−8.4
1946	212.4	25.1	6.4	1,096.9	150.2	27.9
1947	235.2	34.5	−0.5	1,066.7	178.9	−1.0
1948	261.6	42.4	4.7	1,108.7	195.9	12.3
1949	260.4	39.6	−3.1	1,109.0	178.5	−9.7

J1 NORTH AMERICA: National Accounts Totals (in millions of stated unit, except as otherwise indicated)

	Canada						Costa Rica					
	(thousand million dollars)						(colones)					
	Current Prices			1971/1981 Prices[12]			Current Prices			1966 Prices		
	GNP	GFCF	Stocks	GNP	GFCF	Stocks	GDP	GFCF	Stocks	GDP	GFCF	Stocks
1950	18.49	3.86	0.55	33.76	7.04	0.79	1,348	222	12	...	...	...
1951	21.64	4.42	0.87	35.45	7.07	1.02	1,462	243	14	...	...	...
1952	24.59	5.10	0.55	38.62	7.89	0.48	1,709	297	21	...	...	...
1953	25.83	5.73	0.60	40.60	8.86	0.75	1,877	318	14	...	...	...
1954	25.92	5.71	−0.06	40.11	8.86	−0.24	2,039	314	15	...	...	...
1955	28.53	6.42	0.29	43.89	9.68	0.41	2,225	362	22	...	...	...
1956	32.06	8.00	0.98	47.60	11.45	1.14	2,292	403[7]	22[7]	...	...	...
1957	33.51	8.69	0.17	48.72	12.26	0.25	2,500	409	61	...	...	...
1958	34.78	8.54	−0.30	49.84	12.13	−0.28	2,609	431	6	...	...	...
1959	36.85	8.65	0.41	51.74	12.19	0.47	2,679	450	52	...	...	...
1960	38.36	8.47	0.41	53.23	11.79	0.52	2,861	460	40	3,096	...	...
1961	40.16	8.39[10] 8.76	0.11	54.74[10] 55.45	11.75[10] 12.26	0.25	2,929	504	49	3,067	...	...
1962	43.64	9.26	0.67	59.45	12.80	0.76	3,187	591	29	3,317	...	...
1963	46.83	9.95	0.72	62.63	13.37	0.76	3,404	621	19	3,476	...	...
1964	51.28	11.67	0.59	66.89	15.15	0.65	3,608	591	−14	3,620	...	...
1965	56.53	13.67	1.30	71.45	16.86	1.44	3,929	730	37	3,976	...	...
1966	63.27	15.92	1.28	76.59	18.67	1.38	4,288	736	81	4,288	736	81
1967	67.82	16.25	0.21	78.99	18.66	0.25	4,634	834	63	4,531	810	62
1968	74.20	16.49	0.74	83.68	18.80	0.77	5,127	882	42	4,915	822	36
1969	81.82	18.14	1.48	88.39	19.84	1.52	5,565	1,024	109	5,184	899	91
1970	87.77	19.01	0.24	90.54	19.95	0.08	6,525	1,270	70	5,574	1,078	51
1971	95.78	21.57	0.37	95.78	21.57	0.37	7,137	1,579	158	5,951	1,254	145
1972	107.2	23.88	0.78	102.1	22.74	0.74	8,216	1,800	10	6,438	1,313	−16
1973	125.6	28.86	1.86	109.6	25.27	1.58	10,162	2,252	187	6,934	1,424	115
1974	149.9	35.78	3.59	113.5	26.83	2.75	13,216	3,175	359	7,319	1,563	108
1975	169.0	41.85	1.37	115.5[12] 279.4	27.86[12] 59.04	0.68[12] 2.50	16,805	3,695	−58	7,473	1,544	−21
1976	194.4	46.71	2.33	295.6	61.64	4.23	20,676	4,846	46	7,885	1,910	17
1977	213.3	50.23	1.86	305.2	62.91	3.16	26,331	5,889	502	8,587	2,147	218
1978	235.6	54.58	1.05	317.9	64.79	1.82	30,194	6,952	132	9,125	2,322	34
1979	268.9	63.44	4.99	329.5	70.14	6.90	34,584	9,050	−295	9,576	2,677	−104
							(thousand million colones)					
1980	302.1	72.29	0.34	334.6	77.13	0.33	41.41	9.89	1.11	9.65	2.42	0.33
1981	344.7	86.12	1.19	344.7	86.12	1.19	57.10	13.74	2.84	9.43	1.82	−0.11
1982	361.8	81.33	−9.75	332.9	76.65	−9.14	97.50	19.81	4.26	8.74	1.31	−0.04
1983	394.1	81.23	−2.85	345.9	76.11	−2.49	126.3	23.06	8.00	8.99	1.42	0.28
1984	431.2	84.70	4.75	366.9	77.73	3.90	163.0	32.68	4.32	9.71	1.79	0.09
1985	463.7	94.20	2.28	384.5	85.08	2.59	197.9	38.24	13.00	9.78	1.89	0.14
1986	501.4	101.6	2.55	501.4	101.6	2.55	246.6	46.02	16.14	10.33	2.12	0.54
1987	546.8	116.2	3.07	522.1	112.5	3.22	284.5	56.31	20.85	10.83	2.33	0.41
1988	600.8	132.8	3.80	548.1	124.1	2.52	349.7	66.21	19.35	11.20	2.25	0.31
1989	645.1	146.1	3.62	561.1	131.6	3.78	425.9	87.22	25.51	12.82	2.60	0.26
1990	662.8	141.4	−2.84	559.4	126.9	−1.74	522.8	117.07	25.67	12.25	2.97	−0.05
1991	667.4	132.0	−3.24	548.9	124.2	−2.91	690.1	136.09	36.54	12.52	2.59	−0.03
1992	681.3	129.0	−3.70	552.5	120.7	−3.47	906.3	188.31	75.80	13.49	3.16	0.21
1993	704.8	129.1	1.10	565.1	120.4	0.9	1068.5	248.53	70.98	14.36	3.88	−0.13

J1 NORTH AMERICA: National Accounts Totals (in millions of stated unit, except as otherwise indicated)

	Cuba						Dominican Republic					
	(pesos)						(pesos)					
	Current Prices			1965/1981 Prices[15]			Current Prices			1970 Prices		
	NNP/GDP/ NMP[13]	GFCF/ NFCF[14]	Stocks	GDP/ GMP[13]	CF	Stocks	GDP	GFCF	Stocks	GDP	GFCF	Stocks
1950	1,692[13] 1,992	...	...	...	...	...	399	37	...	538	61	...
1951	2,392	308	−1	...	...	...	485	51	...	602	69	...
1952	2,474	310	138	...	...	...	522	100	...	650	125	...
1953	2,131	240	−49	...	...	...	519	87	...	642	106	...
1954	2,170	274	61	...	...	...	546	83	...	679	100	...
1955	2,269	372	−24		...	...	564	104	...	721	128	...
1956	2,478	469	−69	...	...	...	633	124	...	794	139	...
1957	2,835	506	8	...	...	...	714	129	...	844	148	...
1958	2,604	461	4	...	...	...	746	142	...	888	156	...
1959	...	...	...	...	...	...	696	116	...	894	116	...
1960	...	...	...	...	...	...	732	75	20	915	75	33
1961	...[13]	...[14]	...[7]	...	...	...	694	60	3	872	64	6
1962	3,021	572	220	...	...	...	880	97	7	1,028	110	14
1963	3,450	696	231	3,737	733	249	1,009	139	18	1,010	147	27
1964	4,075	210	419	...	...	...	1,123	188	17	1,140	197	24
1965	4,138	842	105	4,138	842	105	954	87	−2	1,031	92	−5
1966	3,986	935	113	...	...	...	1,074	156	15	1,184	164	18
1967	4,083	1,032	103	...	...	...	1,122	161	7	1,217	167	13
1968	4,377	918	102	...	...	...	1,149	166	−5	1,201	169	−10
1969	4,181	896	158	...	...	...	1,345	220	31	1,384	223	46
1970	4,204	668[14]	...	...	...	...	1,486	245	38	1,486	245	38
1971	4,617	...	...	...	...	...	1,667	294	4	1,647	329	4
1972	5,472	261	−190	...	...	...	1,987	427	−35	1,818	391	−17
1973	6,565	621	241	...	...	...	2,345	498	20	2,053	464	11
1974	7,302	774	392	...[15]	...[15]	...[15]	2,931	644	39	2,176	509	57
1975	8,113	1,348	734	8,204	1,439	791	3,599	803	79	2,289	572	40
1976	8,356	1,600	578	8,618	1,686	623	3,952	780	101	2,443	526	46
1977	8,413	1,716	613	9,336	1,804	661	4,587	939	60	2,564	578	41
1978	9,466	1,463	695	9,986	1,537	749	4,734	1,032	98	2,619	575	61
1979	9,621	1,432	484	10,051	1,507	522	5,499	1,335	59	2,738	653	34
1980	9,853	1,529	577	9,523	1,615	622	6,631	1,584	82	2,904	683	52
1981	11,503	2,247	711	11,503	2,247	711	7,267	1,655	61	3,022	624	31
1982	12,175	1,812	601	12,087	1,812	573	7,964	1,491	99	3,069	543	51
1983	12,926	2,243	553	12,745	2,243	536	8,623	1,754	62	3,280	560	35
1984	13,695	2,895	590	13,696	2,895	560	10,355	2,169	33	3,322	608	15
1985	13,952	3,098	663	14,261	3,098	616	13,972	2,747	52	3,251	571	22
1986	12,857	2,729	−247	13,944	2,771	−179	15,780	3,492	85	3,366	591	26
1987	12,284	1,994	−260	13,273	2,119	−187	19,536	5,319	118	3,706	743	40
1988	12,764	2,054	−78	13,565	2,225	−56	28,353	8,034	89	3,786	833	25
1989	12,791	2,223	137	13,496	2,417	−99	42,393	11,505	100	3,953	927	20
1990	...	...	...	...	...	...	64,867	15,041	120	3,755	766	17
1991	...	...	...	...	...	...	100,070	20,821	127	3,784	670	33
1992	...	...	...	...	...	...	112,368	25,068	150	4,077	907	36
1993	...	...	...	...	...	...	120,752	27,869	158	4,199	959	45

J1 NORTH AMERICA: National Accounts Totals (in millions of stated unit, except as otherwise indicated)

| | El Salvador (colones) | | | | | | Guatemala[5] (quetzales) | | | | | |
| | Current Prices | | | 1962 Prices | | | Current Prices | | | 1946/1958 Prices[18] | | |
	GDP	GFCF	Stocks	GDP	GFCF	Stocks	GNP/GDP[17]	GFCF	Stocks	GNP/GDP	GFCF	Stocks
1950	...	...	...	...	...	...	468[5,17]	40[5]		340[5,17,18]	26[5,18]	
							645	67	−1	721	87	−1
1951	1,064	105	...	950[16]	...	...	687	72	−1	731	84	−1
1952	1,097	106	...	1,020[16]	...	...	689	63	−7	746	76	−8
1953	1,167	115	...	1,043	...	...	738	60	1	775	68	1
1954	1,259	112	...	1,070	...	...	784	60	—	789	63	—
1955	1,303	116	...	1,120	...		813	80	14	809	90	14
1956	1,353	158	...	1,172	...		901	134	7	883	142	7
1957	1,405	177	...	1,230	...		940	150	4	932	154	4
1958	1,401	166	10	1,243	...		976	136	−1	976	136	−1
1959	1,422	160	41	1,266	...		1,037	112	−3	1,018	126	−1
1960	1,397	204	−8	1,372			1,044	102	5	1,049	108	5
1961	1,405	168	−16	1,419			1,077	109	−13	1,094	113	−13
1962	1,590	173	9	1,590			1,144	107	−6	1,133	109	−6
1963	1,694	203	12	1,672			1,263	125	8	1,241	129	9
1964	1,867	263	55	1,828			1,294	159	7	1,299	158	7
1965	1,992	296	11	1,926			1,331	175	2	1,355	159	8
1966	2,110	326	36	2,064			1,391	167	−18	1,430	166	−17
1967	2,216	324	3	2,176			1,454	192	−4	1,489	184	−4
1968	2,292	248	7	2,246	...	...	1,611	221	23	1,619	209	23
1969	2,382	274	30	2,324	...	...	1,715	231	−35	1,696	213	−35
1970	2,571	308	33	2,394	259	29	1,904	239	6	1,793	210	5
1971	2,704	359	62	2,509	302	56	1,985	264	22	1,893	227	21
1972	2,882	474	−66	2,646	386	−58	2,102	273	−18	2,032	226	−17
1973	3,332	521	88	2,780	351	74	2,569	357	−5	2,169	252	−4
1974	3,944	719	174	2,959	401	134	3,162	468	120	2,308	247	88
1975	4,478	1,031	−40	3,124	519	−38	3,646	571	16	2,353	271	10
1976	5,706	1,145	−26	3,247	535	−3	4,365	900	34	2,526	371	20
1977	7,167	1,521	158	3,443	677	86	5,481	1,039	60	2,724	406	30
1978	7,692	1,652	182	3,665	695	91	6,071	1,218	95	2,860	436	45
1979	8,607	1,512	44	3,602	587	19	6,903	1,286	8	2,995	413	3
1980	8,917	1,210	−27	3,289	422	−10	7,879	1,295	−43	3,107	373	−17
1981	8,647	1,173	58	3,017	377	19	8,608	1,443	23	3,127	401	8
1982	8,966	1,130	56	2,848	339	17	8,871	1,310	−76	3,017	358	−26
1983	10,152	1,180	44	2,870	314	12	9,050	950	52	2,940	258	17
1984	11,657	1,336	58	2,936	321	14	9,470	912	183	2,954	235	57
1985	14,331	1,723	−169	2,994	354	−37	11,180	1,225	60	2,936	220	16
1986	19,763	2,594	26	3,013	380	5	15,838	1,593	43	2,940	228	8
1987	23,141	3,158	−297	3,094	415	−46	17,711	2,188	275	3,044	266	47
1988	27,366	3,456	45	3,144	430	16	20,545	2,747	67	3,163	299	10
1989	32,230	4,293	646	3,177	469	81	23,685	3,255	−54	3,288	319	−8
1990	36,487	5,004	54	3,285	388	2	34,317	4,455	213	3,390	286	21
1991	42,594	6,456	107	3,401	461	16	47,302	5,760	1,002	3,514	297	80
1992	49,841	6,561	673	3,576	572	27	53,982	8,445	1,448	3,682	381	110
1993	60,522	10,818	452	...	...	...	63,737	10,308	753	3,829	423	94

J1   NORTH AMERICA: National Accounts Totals (in millions of stated unit, except as otherwise indicated)

	Haiti[6] (gourdes)						Honduras (lempiras)					
	Current Prices			1970/1976 Prices[19]			Current Prices			1948/1970/1978 Prices[20]		
	GDP	GFCF	Stocks	GDP	GFCF	Stocks	GDP	GFCF	Stocks	GDP	GFCF	Stocks
1950	...	...		1,599 / 1,656	...	...	452	49	5	403[20] / 670	47[20] / 82	7.5[20] / 9
1951	...	...		1,633	...	...	480	62	7	700	99	11
1952	...	...		1,751	...	...	499	76	6	715	129	10
1953	...	...		1,695	...	...	541	85	4	758	143	9
1954	...	...		1,833	...	...	512	69	3	712	105	5
1955	1,386	83		1,760	...	...	549	78	6	754	115	11
1956	1,462	112		1,913	...	...	575	80	5	787	117	8
1957	1,450	78		1,800	...	...	596	88	6	820	129	10
1958	1,529	91		1,942	...	...	635	82	4	866	116	6
1959	1,358	87		1,851	...	...	658	79	5	886	112	8
1960	1,366	106		1,898	...	...	671	84	9	907	119	14
1961	1,355	105		1,853	...	...	712	77	10	925	110	16
1962	1,410	114		2,008	...	...	775	106	9	974	142	18
1963	1,474	109	8	1,949	99	10	820	122	9	1,008	169	13
1964	1,626	106	9	1,918	90	10	914	123	11	1,066	168	15
1965	1,766	112	10	1,959	90	10	1,017	132	16	1,158	177	21
1966	1,845	96	10	1,947	78	11	1,100	159	17	1,221	204	21
1967	1,846	96	11	1,906	79	11	1,196	213	22	1,287	265	26
1968	1,840	93	11	1,967	87	11	1,299	226	13	1,373	277	15
1969	1,959	124	11	2,042[19]	105[19]	11[19]	1,348	244	14	1,392	279	16
1970	2,055	161	12	3,364	307		1,446	268	34	1,446	268	34
1971	2,262	186	13	3,582	314		1,551	253	−3	1,514	265	−3
1972	2,312	207	13	3,617	370		1,683	245	11	1,587	251	11
1973	3,129	258	17	3,789	457		1,895	325	23	1,658	323	23
1974	2,828	410	19	4,008	564		2,114	433	109	1,686	331	87
1975	3,408	533	23	4,053	595		2,248	476	−50	1,728[20] / 2,876	373[20] / 637	−57[20] / −64
1976	4,395	678		4,395	678		2,696	550	−32	3,150[16]	670[16]	−37
1977	4,897	748		4,416	736		3,339	711	59	3,508	763	62
1978	5,060	857		4,631	771		3,798	941	93	3,796	941	93
1979	5,600	938		4,983	921		4,425	1,004	170	4,038	920	154
1980	7,183	1,238		5,349	934		5,088	1,235	13	4,090	1,011	10
1981	7,397	1,252		5,196	941		5,553	1,051	100	4,153	781	75
1982	7,425	1,230		5,018	877		5,762	966	−190	4,072	645	−134
1983	8,148	1,331		5,056	924		6,154	1,028	−176	4,073	660	−103
1984	9,082	1,442		5,071	967		6,638	1,251	−95	4,250	750	−53
1985	10,047	1,673		5,101	1,078		7,279	1,234	27	4,428	726	14
1986	11,177	1,614		5,075	987		7,619	1,045	10	4,460	591	5
1987	10,042	1,546		5,037	997		8,305	1,132	314	4,729	630	147
1988	9,907	1,501		5,076	955		9,251	1,429	513	4,947	764	230
1989	10,496	1,692		5,132	901		10,334	1,884	94	5,161	920	37
1990	11,742	1,161		5,125	841		12,537	2,533	348	5,166	877	111
1991	13,363	1,156		5,160	916		16,314	3,096	926	5,334	879	286
1992	13,564	776		4,714	495		18,800	4,202	679	5,634	1,116	194
1993	15,715	817		4,648	467		22,444	5,672	823	5,980	1,322	216

J1 NORTH AMERICA: National Accounts Totals (in millions of stated unit, except as otherwise indicated)

	Jamaica						Mexico					
	(dollars)						(thousand million pesos[24])					
	Current Prices			Prices[22]			Current Prices			1960/1970/1980 Prices[26]		
	NNP/GDP[21]	GFCF	Stocks	GDP	GFCF	Stocks	GDP	GFCF	Stocks	GDP	GFCF	Stocks
1950	170[21] 155	... 14	... 2	...	...	...	41.1	4.8	...	84	...	...
1951	180	24	1	...	...	...	53.0	6.9	...	93	...	...
1952	206	27	2	...	...	...	59.3	8.2	...	96	...	...
1953	231	28	2	254	56	2	58.9	8.1	...	97	...	...
1954	258	35	3	282	65	3	72.2	10.1	...	106	...	...
1955	294	43	6	310	67	7	88.2	12.6	...	116	...	...
1956	343	78	6	343	78	6	101	16.8	...	124	...	...
1957	413	104	10	384	96	9	115	19.1	...	134	...	...
1958	427	95	7	396[22]	95[22]	7[22]	129	18.9	...	141	...	...
1959	433	91	9	442	84	11	138	19.6	...	145	...	...
1960	474	99	5	471	99	5	156	23.2	2.9	156	23	3
1961	508	98	8	483	90	7	166	24.1	2.9	161	23	3
1962	528	98	6	489	85	5	180	24.8	3.0	169	23	3
1963	558	92	8	506	82	7	195	32.6	5.2	178	30	5
1964	589	112	9	549	98	7	221	41.0[10]	5.3[10]	190	37[10]	5[10]
1965	636	124	5	592	109	4	252	44.2	—	212	39	—
1966	691	146	6	615	117	5	283	50.2	3.0	229	44	3
1967	745	170	7	631	133	2	306	59.6	—	241	49	—
1968	820	221	9	669	167	2	339	65.7	4.9	261	53	4
1969	993	315	34	713	172	32	375	72.8	6.4	277	57	5
1970	1,171	367	2	840[22] 1,982	246[22]	2[22]	444	88.7	12[26]	315[26]	67[26]	10
1971	1,282	356	56	2,042	...	...	490	88.1	11	463	87	9
1972	1,439	367	27	2,231	...	...	565	107	8	502	98	8
1973	1,720	448	94	2,263	...	...	691	133	14	544	112	10
1974	2,159	478	47	2,170	...	...	900	179	30	578	121	23
1975	2,600	610	60	2,153	525	50	1,100	236	25	610	132	19
1976	2,702	451	40	2,014	...	...	1,371[25]	288[25]	17[25]	636[25]	133[25]	14[25]
1977	2,960	349	12	1,966	263	8	1,849	363	59	658	124	23
1978	3,749	499	63	1,976	281	33	2,337	492	59	712	143	22
1979	4,293	748	74	1,940	268	34	3,068	719	78	777	172	22
1980	4,773	690	69	1,829	207	26	4,276	1,033	170	842[26]	197[26]	39[26]
1981	5,307	954	123	1,875	241	44	5,874	1,509	193	4,862	1,286	339
1982	5,867	1,168	57	1,899	282	18	9,417	2,099	−98	4,832	1,070	−392
1983	6,993	1,436	120	1,942	278	33	17,142	2,972	500	4,629	768	2
1984	9,358	1,981	183	1,926	243	38	28,749[24]	5,287[24]	566[24]	4,796[24]	817[24]	—[24]
1985	11,203	2,581	256	1,836	240	42	47.4	9.05	0.99	4.92	0.88	0.02
1986	13,389	2,432	142	1,870	217	21	79.5	15.4	−0.70	4.73	0.78	−0.07
1987	16,629	3,540	160	1,983	281	20	194	35.7	1.5	4.82	0.77	−0.03
1988	19,436	4,865	133	2,013	336	15	390	75.2	4.5	4.88	0.82	0.01
1989	23,354	6,538	188	2,104	399	18	508	92.2	16.4	5.05	0.87	0.25
1990	30,514	8,362	171	...	...	...	686	127.7	22.5	5.27	0.99	0.07
1991	44,128	11,870	260	...	...	...	865	168.4	25.3	5.46	1.07	−0.01
1992	72,539	20,494	200	...	...	...	1,019	211.9	25.3	5.62	1.19	0.37
1993	95,785	32,813	454	...	...	...	1,127	229.5	18.3	5.65	1.17	0.15

J1 NORTH AMERICA: National Accounts Totals (in millions of stated unit, except as otherwise indicated)

	Nicaragua (cordobas[27])						Panama (balboas)					
	Current Prices			1958/1985 Prices[28]			Current Prices			1960/1970 Prices[29]		
	GDP	GFCF	Stocks	GDP	GFCF	Stocks	GDP	GFCF	Stocks	GDP	GFCF	Stocks
1950	...	...	...	1,482	143		257	31	5	259	36	...
1951	...	...	...	1,582	201		264	29	2	257	30	...
1952	...	...	...	1,850	274		276	30	3	271	31	...
1953	...	...	...	1,895	306		293	34	14	287	36	...
1954	...	...	...	2,071	377		307	33	4	297	37	...
1955	...	...	...	2,211	376		332	39	4	315	43	...
1956	...	...	...	2,209	348		347	50	4	331	53	...
1957	...	...	...	2,396	346		383	49	7	366	52	...
1958	...	...	...	2,404	334		382	53	11	369	55	...
1959	...	...	...	2,440	358		404	65	7	392	68	...
1960	2,348	300	52	2,393	296	53	416	61	6	416	61	...
1961	2,527	319	55	2,571	326	56	464	80	8	461	78	...
1962	2,783	422	61	2,851	426	62	505	85	14	499	83	...
1963	3,076	470	67	3,162	465	70	559	97	13	541	96	...
1964	3,590	628	78	3,532	639	79	601	88	14	565	85	...
1965	3,966	746	84	3,868	743	85	660	100	16	617	97	...
1966	4,247	887	90	3,996	828	88	719	142	15	664	135	...
1967	4,600	868	98	4,274	834	94	801	153	16	721	143	...
1968	4,871	762	102	4,332	700	95	861	173	18	771	161	...
1969	5,236	883	110	4,602	815	101	945	201	22	836	183	...
1970	5,436	891	120	4,664	825	103	1,021	262	20	894[29]	222[29]	...[29]
1971	5,786	898	127	4,894	851	108	1,152	306	21	1,132	289	20
1972	6,060	930	−138	5,050	756	−112	1,265	372	30	1,171	373	26
1973	7,578	1,476	360	5,307	1,037	249	1,447	435	51	1,233	374	41
1974	10,646	2,498	855	5,981	1,268	481	1,654	465	91	1,264	334	59
1975	10,950	2,510	−200	6,113	1,151	−101	1,841	535	32	1,286	361	19
1976	12,590	2,610	−300	6,421	1,215	−128	1,956	609	10	1,307	368	8
1977	14,740	3,620	300	6,824	1,557	343	2,070	446	45	1,321	245	17
1978	14,270[27]	2,180[27]	−300[27]	6,336[27,28] 145	868	−96	2,452	606	45	1,451	303	23
1979	14.51	0.97	−1.8	107	...	...	2,800	661	124	1,516	300	52
1980	20.80	3.03	0.5	112	...	...	3,559	866	120	1,746	365	46
1981	24.48	5.24	0.5	118	...	...	3,878	1,080	88	1,819	426	37
1982	28.35	4.70	0.6	117	...	...	4,279	1,185	−1	1,919	430	1
1983	32.92	6.39	1.0	122	...	...	4,428	918	16	1,918	333	8
1984	45.03	8.74	1.3	120	...	...	4,610	780	−19	1,910	310	−7
1985	115	23.9	2.8	115	...	...	4,948	773	−20	2,000	331	−7
1986	436	60.3	13.3	114	...	...	5,191	897	−37	2,067	363	−12
1987	42,696	188	71.4	113	...	...	5,363	937	−9	2,117	364	−4
1988	330,970	97	7.9	104	...	...	4,605	408	−94	1,787	166	−35
	thousand gold cordobas			1990 prices								
1989	3,176	881	−16.8	311.9	...	...	4,639	320	−161	1,779	135	−61
		million										
1990	312	60	—	312	...	...	5,009	473	386	1,862	178	132
1991	7,429	1,359	139.1	312	...	...	5,496	924	69	2,039	321	24
1992	9,226	1,777	−23.1	313	...	...	6,015	1,270	103	2,213	451	36
1993	11,067	2,238	−55.6	312	...	...	6,565	1,604	35	2,332	594	14

J1 NORTH AMERICA: National Accounts Totals (in millions of stated units, except as otherwise indicated)

	Puerto Rico[8]						Trinidad & Tobago				
	(dollars)						(dollars)				
	Current Prices			1954 Prices			Current Prices			1975/1985 Prices[30]	
	GDP[7]	GFCF	Stocks	GDP	GFCF	Stocks	GDP	GFCF	Stocks	GDP	GCF
1950	779	127	20	884	...	...	...	...	...	...	...
1951	881	150	42	925	...	...	331	70	16	...	...
1952	933	159	−1	959	...	...	364	75	20	...	...
1953	1,006	173	13	989	...	...	408	79	7	...	...
1954	1,062	203	14	1,062	203	14	436	84	7	...	...
1955	1,148	217	12	1,123	...	...	505	109	7	...	...
1956	1,241	260	15	1,186	235	13	589	121	5	...	...
1957	1,342	279	23	1,245	245	19	695	161	11	...	...
1958	1,501	302	56	1,318	261	51	763	196	11	...	...
1959	1,693	355	42	1,466	302	36	846	243	7	...	...
1960	1,865	377	22	1,568	309	20	918	268	18	3,293	...
1961	2,078	448	85	1,645	358	75	1,003	259	−2	3,546	...
1962	2,311	489	77	1,762	382	67	1,062	295	3	3,648	...
1963	2,570	584	77	1,994	449	61	1,145	276	−4	3,826	...
1964	2,881	720	128	2,083	531	111	1,220	274	5	4,039	...
1965	3,170	745	131	2,329	540	110	1,263	327		4,152	...
1966	3,552	902	35	2,482	645	33	1,241	286		3,803	...
1967	3,936	964	71	2,616	665	58	1,324	233		4,215	...
1968	4,461	1,102	108	2,692	727	83	1,518	301		4,367	...
1969	5,035	1,402	50	3,068	870	32	1,558	268		4,345	...
1970	5,659	1,594	114	3,268	941	72	1,644	425		4,582	425
1971	6,333	1,761	101	3,501	975	63	1,771	602		4,538	...
1972	7,023	1,601	192	3,723	849	127	2,082	652		4,886	...
1973	7,710	1,696	104	3,724	797	2	2,564	666		4,994	...
1974	8,226[10]	2,079	139	3,634[10]	836	46	4,193	915		5,247[30]	...
1975	8,996	1,836	138	3,830	723	54	5,300	1,085	364	14,086	927
1976	9,930	1,560	−61	4,111	601	−9	6,091	1,398	98	14,989	1,061
1977	11,172	1,746	125	4,408	618	65	7,533	1,735	272	16,356	1,095
1978	12,786	1,888	176	4,677	617	42	8,550	2,323	261	17,994	1,402
1979	14,436	2,067	407	4,662	614	114	11,046	2,952	261	18,642	1,447
1980	15,956	2,162	125	4,712	576	53	14,966	4,204	376	20,579	1,774
1981	16,764	1,851	−336	4,569	453	−55	16,438	4,342	199	21,521	1,479
1982	17,276	1,722	24	4,590	412	21	19,176	5,189	228	22,389	1,558
1983	19,163	2,100	535	4,926	492	141	18,719	5,038	30	20,329	1,389[30]
1984	20,289	2,346	155	5,027	545	46	18,615	4,514		18,850	4,394
1985	21,969	2,327	−69	5,438	540	2	18,071	3,656		18,071	3,451
1986	23,878	3,030	245	5,705	688	70	17,260	3,593		17,478	3,031
1987	26,178	3,894	186	6,077	853	62	17,272	3,200		16,681	2,449
1988	28,267	4,411	473	6,377	918	121	17,285	2,186		16,027	2,023
1989	30,604	4,771	418	6,618	943	110	18,373	2,714		15,895	...
1990	32,287	5,006	30	6,770	959	13	21,539	2,970		16,134	1,787
1991	34,630	5,042	309	7,079	947	91	22,559	3,565		16,567	1,817
1992	36,847	5,545	430	7,356	1,025	110	23,118	3,152		16,287	1,386
1993	39,765	5,870	346	7,616	1,054	84	24,883	3,168		16,062	1,358

J1   NORTH AMERICA: National Accounts Totals (in millions of stated units, except as otherwise indicated)

	USA[32]					
	(thousand million dollars)					
	Current Prices			1982 Prices		
	GNP	GPFCF[31]	Stocks	GNP	GPFCF[31]	Stocks
1950	288.3	48.3	6.8	1,204	210.7	24.2
1951	333.4	50.3	10.2	1,328	204.4	30.8
1952	351.6	50.4	3.1	1,381	201.8	10.0
1953	371.6	54.5	0.4	1,435	213.8	2.8
1954	372.5	55.7	−1.6	1,416	217.4	−4.8
1955	405.9	64.0	5.7	1,495	243.5	16.3
1956	428.2	68.1	4.6	1,526	244.9	12.9
1957	451.0	69.7	1.4	1,551	240.4	3.0
1958	456.8	65.1	−1.5	1,539	224.8	−3.4
1959	495.8[32]	74.4[32]	5.8[32]	1,629[32]	253.8[32]	16.5[32]
1960	515.3	75.1	3.1	1,665	252.8	7.7
1961	533.8	74.7	2.4	1,709	251.8	7.3
1962	574.6	81.5	6.1	1,799	272.4	16.2
1963	606.9	87.3	5.8	1,873	290.5	16.6
1964	649.8	94.2	5.4	1,973	310.2	15.7
1965	705.1	106.3	9.9	2,088	341.8	25.2
1966	772.0	114.4	14.2	2,208	353.5	36.9
1967	816.4	115.4	10.3	2,271	344.6	28.8
1968	892.7	129.1	7.9	2,366	370.8	21.0
1969	963.9	143.4	9.8	2,423	385.2	25.1
1970	1,015.5	145.7	3.1	2,416	373.3	8.2
1971	1,103	164.7	7.8	2,485	399.7	19.6
1972	1,213	191.5	10.5	2,608	443.6	21.8
1973	1,359	219.2	19.6	2,744	480.8	40.0
1974	1,473	225.4	15.4	2,729	448.0	33.3
1975	1,598	225.2	−5.6	2,695	396.1	−12.8
1976	1,783	261.7	16.0	2,827	431.4	22.1
1977	1,991	322.8	21.3	2,959	492.2	29.1
1978	2,250	388.2	28.6	3,115	540.1	36.8
1979	2,508	441.9	13.0	3,192	560.2	15.0
1980	2,732	445.3	−8.3	3,187	516.2	−6.9
1981	3,053	491.5	24.0	3,249	521.7	23.9
1982	3,166	471.8	−24.5	3,166	471.8	−24.5
1983	3,406	509.4	−7.1	3,279	510.4	−6.4
1984	3,772	597.1	67.7	3,501	596.1	62.3
1985	4,015	631.8	11.3	3,619	627.9	9.1
1986	4,232	652.5	6.9	3,718	634.1	5.6
1987	4,524	670.6	29.3	3,854	650.3	23.7
1988	4,881	777.4	30.6	4,024	687.9	27.9
1989	5,453	798.9	33.3	4,283	694.4	31.4
1990	5,765	793.2	6.3	4,973	692.7	9.8
1991	5,932	736.9	−.1	5,342	675.8	4.8
1992	6,256	788.3	3.0	6,059	691.2	7.0
1993	6,560	882.0	15.4	6,196	719.3	16.9

J1 SOUTH AMERICA: NATIONAL ACCOUNTS TOTALS (in millions of stated unit, except as otherwise indicated)

1860–1899

	Brazil	
	(milreis)	
	Current Prices	1949 Prices
	GDP	GDP
1860	...	...
1861	0.27	11
1862	0.30	12
1863	0.31	12
1864	0.25	12
1865	0.38	13
1866	0.40	13
1867	0.39	12
1868	0.51	12
1869	0.52	13
1870	0.49	15
1871	0.50	15
1872	0.51	15
1873	0.53	15
1874	0.57	18
1875	0.53	18
1876	0.57	18
1877	0.54	17
1878	0.54	17
1879	0.56	17
1880	0.62	18
1881	0.58	18
1882	0.57	16
1883	0.69	15
1884	0.54	15
1885	0.63	16
1886	0.71	19
1887	0.66	21
1888	0.64	21
1889	0.66	22
1890	0.86	22
1891	1.57	22
1892	1.96	21
1893	2.31	22
1894	2.63	21
1895	2.79	20
1896	2.91	19
1897	3.19	17
1898	3.26	16
1899	3.13	16

1900–1934

	Argentina (thousand million pesos)		Brazil (milreis or cruzeiros)		Chile (thousand million pesos)	Colombia (pesos)		
	1950 Prices		Current Prices	1949 Prices	1960 Prices	1950 Prices		
	GDP	GFCF	GDP	GDP	GDP	GDP	GFC	Stocks
1900	8.87		3.1	19	...	...	...	...
1901	9.62		2.7	21	...	...	...	...
1902	9.43	12.65	2.9	23	...	...	...	...
1903	10.77		2.9	24	...	...	...	...
1904	11.92		3.2	26	...	...	...	...
1905	13.50		2.7	29	...	...	...	...
1906	14.18		3.2	32	...	...	...	...
1907	14.48	36.03	3.7	33	...	...	...	...
1908	15.90		3.7	37	675	...	...	...
1909	16.69		4.2	41	688	...	...	...
1910	17.90		4.8	47	744	...	...	...
1911	18.22		5.5	55	738	...	...	...
1912	19.71	39.49	5.7	62	819	...	...	...
1913	19.91		5.7	60	830	...	...	...
1914	17.85		4.7	53	772	...	...	...
1915	17.95	3.19	4.5	48	718	...	...	...
1916	17.43	2.88	4.8	48	851	...	...	...
1917	16.01	2.25	5.5	50	919	...	...	...
1918	18.95	2.28	5.5	57	921	...	...	...
1919	19.65	2.58	8.3	65	729	...	...	...
1920	21.08	4.81	9.8	70	832	...	...	...
1921	21.62	5.39	10.0	72	716	...	...	...
1922	23.35	6.31	12.0	78	765	...	...	...
1923	25.92	8.65	16.0	90	954	...	...	...
1924	27.94	9.28	20.0	100	1,039	...	...	...
1925	27.82	9.31	22.0	100	1,052[33] 1,242	2,189	480	70
1926	29.16	9.22	23.0	103	1,322	2,398	599	85
1927	31.23	10.56	25.0	109	1,118	2,614	723	87
1928	33.17	12.53	28.0	125	1,328	2,806	857	133
1929	34.70	14.31	25.0	121	1,494	2,907	740	95
1930	33.26	12.07	22.0	110	1,388	2,882	482	64
1931	30.96	6.93	18.0	91	1,106	2,836	397	49
1932	29.93	4.78	18.0	91	1,089	3,024	469	62
1933	31.33	5.40	19.0	98	1,231	3,194	459	61
1934	33.81	7.29	25.0	118	1,437	3,395	468	56

J1   SOUTH AMERICA: National Accounts Totals (in millions of stated unit, except as otherwise indicated)

1935–1969

	Argentina (thousand million pesos)[34]						Bolivia (pesos)					
	Current Prices			1950/1960 Prices[35]			Current Prices			1958 Prices		
	GDP	GFCF	Stocks	GDP	GFCF	Stocks	GDP	GFCF	Stocks	GDP	GFCF	Stocks
1935	9.3	0.8	0.1	35.30[35] 453	. . .[35] 7.0	. . .[35] 0.8	...	...	...	...	...	...
1936	9.8	1.0	0.1	458	7.5	0.2	...	...	...	...	...	...
1937	11.3	1.4	−0.1	495	10.2	−0.7	...	...	...	...	...	...
1938	11.0	1.5	0.4	502	10.9	1.0	...	...	...	...	...	...
1939	11.6	1.4	—	520	9.3	0.1	...	...	...	...	...	...
1940	12.0	1.4	—	509	8.3	0.1	...	...	...	...	...	...
1941	12.9	1.5	0.4	534	7.9	1.4	...	...	...	...	...	...
1942	14.6	1.7	0.1	559	7.4	0.7	...	...	...	...	...	...
1943	15.3	1.8	0.1	563	7.3	0.2	...	...	...	...	...	...
1944	17.5	2.2	−0.3	618	8.4	−0.3	...	...	...	...	...	...
1945	19.3	2.6	−0.3	588	8.4	−1.2	...	...	...	...	...	...
1946	26.2	3.9	0.4	637	10.9	0.7	...	...	...	...	...	...
1947	35.9	6.9	1.5	725	16.5	2.3	...	...	...	...	...	...
1948	43.8	10.3	1.6	733	17.0	2.1	...	...	...	...	...	...
1949	52.6	11.9	−0.5	700	14.6	−0.7	...	...	...	...	...	...
1950	62.2[10] 68	14	−0.7	710	114	−13	46	5	0.2	3,363	389	13
1951	96	19	1.7	739	140	8	80	12	0.4	3,600	561	19
1952	112	21	2.2	692	125	1	107	17	0.5	3,709	589	19
1953	129	23	2.0	741	123	12	327	33	1.1	3,358	332	11
1954	145	24	1.8	769	120	10	632	85	2.8	3,428	444	15
1955	171	30	0.5	822	140	7	1,501	308	10	3,609	729	24
1956	218	40	−1.4	835	148	−10	2,757	551	—	3,395	675	—
1957	271	54	−1.0	881	158	−8	2,960	558	—	3,263	619	—
1958	387	77	−0.6	945	171	−7	3,361	489	76	3,361	489	76
1959	741	126	9.2	890	139	10	3,862	526	−49	3,350	506	−47
1960	1,006	208	10	1,006	208	10	4,479	637	38	3,494	590	35
1961	1,200	268	−5	1,078	242	−4	4,872	532	14	3,567	493	13
1962	1,485	318	- -	1,060	221	−1	5,327	835	41	3,766	782	38
1963	1,855	328	−13	1,034	187	−7	5,736	924	−15	4,008	816	−13
1964	2,580[34]	424[34]	59[34]	1,142[34]	208[34]	19[32]	6,463	958	51	4,201	832	44
1965	36.2	6.2	0.8	13	2.2	0.3	7,180	1,051	167	4,491	899	143
1966	45.2	7.9	0.1	13	2.2	- -	7,950	949	342	4,806	801	284
1967	59.1	10.7	—	13	2.4	—	8,979	1,155	129	5,110	912	104
1968	68.8	13.0	—	14	2.6	—	10,192	1,574	65	5,477	1,204	50
1969	80.4	15.7	−0.1	15	3.0	—	11,044	1,741	162	5,722	1,290	119

J1 SOUTH AMERICA: National Accounts Totals (in millions of stated unit, except as otherwise indicated)

1935-1969

	Brazil (cruzeiros)[36]						Chile (thousand million pesos/escudos)[38]					
	Current Prices			1949/1953/1970 Prices[37]			Current Prices			1960/1961/1965 Prices		
	GDP	GFCF	Stocks	GDP	GFCF	Stocks	GDP	GFCF	Stocks	GDP	GFCF	Stocks
1935	30	...	...	133	...	...	...	...	...	1,438	...	...
1936	37	...	...	147	...	...	...	...	...	1,505	...	...
1937	42	...	...	153	...	...	...	...	...	1,522	...	...
1938	45	...	...	158	...	...	...	...	...	1,518	...	...
1939	45	...	...	155	...	...	...	...	...	1,634	...	...
1940	48	...	...	155	...	...	22	2.4	0.2	1,631[31.39]	...[39]	...[39]
										2,676	241	10
1941	51	...	...	150	...	...	27	2.7	0.1	2,657	238	6
1942	58	...	...	152	...	...	32	2.7	0.3	2,710	189	19
1943	67	...	...	152	...	...	40	3.4	0.4	2,333	203	22
1944	88	...	...	157	...	...	47	4.5	1.1	2,376	228	62
1945	112	...	...	172	...	...	54	4.7	1.3	3,125	241	66
1946	148	...	...	194	...	...	68	7.8	3.2	3,320	334	140
1947	186	...	...	201[37]	...[37]	...[37]	79	9.1	-4.1	3,110	367	-143
1948	195	31	-0.2	350	55	-0.4	109	10	3.2	3,501	326	93
1949	230	36	-1.7	373	60	-2.9	130	13	1.5	3,138	373	39
1950	272	41	-1.3	398	64	-2.0	156	14	3.3	3,690	344	73
1951	323	60	-2.1	421	79	-2.7	191	19	1.3	3,881	392	23
1952	397	66	1.5	458	85	1.7	259	24	-2.0	4,139	410	-27
1953	470	72	-2.3	470	72	-2.3	351	32	12	4,391	414	132
1954	627	105	6.1	517	78	4.7	571	47	-10	4,369	401	-69
1955	783	106	14	552	73	9.6	1,041	87	-2	4,431	464	-8
1956	996	141	-0.3	570	79	-0.2	1,668	138	28	4,484	443	70
1957	1,218	125	29	616	90	15	2,309	247	-18	4,834	506	-31
1958	1,458	237	18	663	95	8.3	2,995	310	-9	4,973	498	-13
1959	1,989[34]	368[34]	60[34]	700	107	20	4,227[38]	405[38]	21[38]	5,000[38]	429[38]	22[38]
1960	2.8	0.5	0.04	768	112	10	4,974	513	81	5,364[39]	556[39]	87[39]
1961	4.1	0.7	0.09	847	117	17	5,538	720	65	17,565	2,312	207
1962	6.6[10]	1.2	0.16	892[10]	121	19	6,699	812	17	18,493	2,443	53
1963	14.1	2.1	0.13	1,057	118	9	9,993[10]	1,275[10]	106[10]	19,501[10]	2,508[10]	193[10]
1964	27.3	3.8[10]	0.49	1,099[36.37]	121[10.36.37]	17[10.36.37]	13,227	2,111[36]	111[38]	17,615[38]	2,735[38]	149[38]
1965	44	8	2	146	26	6	18.8	2.9	0.4	18.8	2.9	0.4
1966	64	13	2	153	31	5	26.2	3.8	0.7	20.6	2.9	0.5
1967	86	17	- -	160	32	0.4	34.4	4.8	0.3	20.9	2.9	0.2
1968	122	26	3	174	38	3	46.3	6.7	0.4	21.6	3.2	0.2
1969	162	36	4	191	43	5	67.4	9.7	1.1	22.8	3.3	0.4

J1 SOUTH AMERICA: National Accounts Totals (in millions of stated unit, except as otherwise indicated)

1935–1969

	Colombia						Ecuador					
	(pesos)						(thousand million sucres)					
	Current Prices			1950/1970 Prices[40]			Current Prices			1960/1965 Prices[41]		
	GDP	GFCF	Stocks	GDP	GFCF	Stocks	GDP[42]	GFCF	Stocks	GDP[42]	GFCF	Stocks
1935	...	...	...	3,478	535	87	...	...	...	...	...	...
1936	...	...	...	3,662	589	81	...	...	...	...	...	...
1937	...	...	...	3,719	684	87	...	...	...	...	...	...
1938	...	...	...	3,964	699	90	...	...	...	...	...	...
1939	...	...	...	4,204	798	105	0.9	...	...	3.3	...	...
1940	...	...	...	4,295	767	137	1.0	...	...	3.5	...	...
1941	...	...	...	4,367	735	159	1.0	...	...	3.5	...	...
1942	...	...	...	4,376	646	168	1.3	...	...	3.7	...	...
1943	...	...	...	4,394	685	266	1.8	...	...	4.2	...	...
1944	...	...	...	4,691	746	−27	2.3	...	...	4.2	...	...
1945	2.55	0.19	0.03	4,911[10] / 5,126	930	248	3.0	...	...	4.2	...	...
1946	3.10	0.32	0.04	5,590	1,099	−86	3.8	...	...	4.7	...	...
1947	3.78	0.41	0.07	5,810	1,326	241	4.8	...	...	5.3	...	...
1948	4.45	0.42	0.01	5,990	1,297	214	6.2	...	...	6.0	...	...
1949	5.30[10]	0.45[10]	0.05[10]	6,321[10,40]	990[10,40]	−238[10,40]	6.2[42]	...	...	6.1[42]	...	...
1950	7.86	1.11	0.21	50	...	...	7.2	0.6	0.2	8.7	...	...
1951	8.94	1.19	0.17	51	...	...	7.8	0.9	0.1	8.9	...	...
1952	9.65	1.33	0.16	55	...	...	8.9	0.8	0.1	9.9	0.9	0.1
1953	10.7	1.78	−0.14	58	15	−0.63	9.3	1.0	0.3	10	1.1	0.3
1954	12.8	2.16	−0.02	62	18	−0.05	10	1.4	0.2	11	1.5	0.3
1955	13	2.38	—	64	19	—	11	1.5	0.3	11	1.6	0.3
1956	15	2.53	0.18	67	18	0.7	11	1.6	0.2	12	1.6	0.2
1957	18	2.64	0.89	68	13	2.6	12	1.6	0.3	12	1.6	0.3
1958	21	3.34	0.52	70	13	1.5	12	1.5	0.3	13	1.5	0.3
1959	24	3.91	0.49	75	14	1.4	13	1.7	0.2	13	1.8	0.2
1960	27	4.8	0.7	78	16	1.5	14	1.9	0.3	14	1.9	0.3
1961	30	5.6	0.8	82	18	1.9	15	2.0	0.3	14	1.9	0.3
1962	34	6.1	0.3	87	18	0.6	16	2.0	0.3	15	1.8	0.3
1963	44	7.2	0.7	90	16	1.4	18	2.1	0.3	16	1.9	0.3
1964	54	8.7	0.9	95	18	1.6	19	2.3	0.4	17[25,41]	2.0[25,41]	0.3[25,41]
1965	61	9.5	1.2	99	17	2.0	21	2.3	0.6	21	2.3	0.6
1966	74	12	2.7	94	19	3.9	23	2.6	0.8	22	2.5	0.7
1967	83	15	0.6	108	20	0.9	25	3.4	0.9	23	2.8	0.8
1968	96	19	1.6	115	23	1.8	27	3.9	1.0	24	2.8	0.7
1969	111	21	1.5	122	23	1.6	30	4.8	0.5	25	3.4	0.3

J1 SOUTH AMERICA: National Accounts Totals (in millions of stated unit, except as otherwise indicated)

1935-1969

	Guyana (dollars)						Paraguay (thousand million guaranies)					
	Current Prices			1970 Prices			Current Prices			1970 Prices		
	GDP	GFCF	Stocks	GDP	GFCF	Stocks	GDP	GFCF	Stocks	GDP[43]	GFCF	Stocks
1935	...	...	...	...	...	...	...	...		...		
1936	...	...	...	...	...	...	...	...		...		
1937	...	...	...	...	...	...	...	...		...		
1938	...	...	...	...	...	...	...	...		26		
1939	...	...	...	...	...	...	...	...		31		
1940	...	...	...	...	...	...	...	...		26		
1941	...	...	...	...	...	...	...	...		30		
1942	...	...	...	...	...	...	...	...		31		
1943	...	...	...	...	...	...	...	...		32		
1944	...	...	...	...	...	...	...	...		33		
1945	...	...	...	...	...	...	...	...		32		
1946	...	...	...	...	...	...	...	...		35		
1947	...	...	...	...	...	...	...	...		30		
1948	...	...	...	...	...	...	...	...		30		
1949	...	...	...	...	...	...	...	...		36		
1950	...	...	...	...	...	...	... 1.41	...		35[43] 36	...	
1951	...	...	...	...	...	...	2.38	...		36	...	
1952	178	26	0.6	...	...	...	4.39	...		36	...	
1953	195	27	−2.4	...	...	...	7.88	1.4		38	5.9	
1954	211	36	2.3	...	...	...	10.8	1.6		39	5.8	
1955	216	46	0.5	...	...	...	14	1.7		41	4.2	
1956	232	48	0.1	...	...	...	18	2.0		42	3.9	
1957	247	63	0.3	...	...	...	23	4.1		45	6.8	
1958	235	63	5.0	...	...	...	26	4.4		48	6.7	
1959	241	59	−0.8	...	...	...	29	4.3		47	5.9	
1960	293	80	2.8	389	104	4	35	5.8		47	6.9	
1961	321	77	−0.9	419	...	...	40	6.7		50	7.3	
1962	336	57	−1.6	425	...	...	45	5.2	0.5	53	5.9	0.6
1963	301	40	11.0	351	75	13	48	4.9	0.5	55	5.3	0.5
1964	334	53	0.8	411	...	...	51	5.6	0.5	58	6.0	0.5
1965	362	70	10.6	456	86	12	56	8.0	0.4	61	8.5	0.5
1966	389	86	6.5	456	...	...	59	9.1	0.2	62	9.1	0.2
1967	425	105	4.8	501	...	...	62	10	0.2	66	10	0.2
1968	459	96	6.3	495	...	...	65	10	0.3	68	10	0.3
1969	499	98	5.8	518	...	...	70	11	0.4	71	10	0.4

J1 SOUTH AMERICA: National Accounts Totals (in millions of stated unit, except as otherwise indicated)

1935–1969

	Peru (million soles)[44]						Uruguay (peses)[47]					
	Current Prices			1973 Prices			Current Prices			1961 Prices		
	GNP/GDP[45]	GFCF[46]	Stocks	GDP	GFCF	Stocks	GDP	GFCF	Stocks	GDP	GFCF	Stocks
1935	...	...	...	...	...	...	...	...	...	8,015	...	...
1936	...	...	...	...	...	...	...	...	...	8,300	...	...
1937	...	...	...	...	...	...	...	...	...	9,020	...	...
1938	...	...	...	...	...	...	...	...	...	8,581	...	...
1939	...	...	...	...	...	...	...	...	...	8,508	...	...
1940	...	...	...	...	...	...	...	...	...	8,324	...	...
1941	...	...	...	...	...	...	...	...	...	8,813	...	...
1942	2,960	236	−36	...	...	...	...	...	...	8,015	...	...
1943	3,241	504	−34	...	...	...	...	...	...	8,135	...	...
1944	3,829	627	−101	...	...	...	...	...	...	9,184	...	...
1945	4,455	697	−176	...	...	...	...	...	...	9,392	...	...
1946	5,291	1,098[46]	−12	...	...	...	...	...	...	10,432	...	...
1947	6,816	1,284	332	...	...	...	...	...	...	11,135	...	...
1948	8,624	1,106	199	...	...	...	...	...	...	11,422	...	...
1949	12,190[44]	1,645[44]	721[44]	...	...	...	...	...	...	11,844	...	...
1950	15.1[45]	2.7[25]	0.4	...	...		...	...	...	12,208	...	...
	15.9	2.3		110	14	3						
1951	19.9	3.5	1.0	121	18	6	...	...	...	13,214	...	...
1952	21.2	4.4	1.1	125	22	6	...	...	...	13,161	...	...
1953	22.9	5.4	0.6	127	24	3	...	...	...	14,011	...	...
1954	26.9	4.5	0.7	142	18	4	...	...	...	14,813	...	...
1955	29.6	5.5	1.2	150	21	6	...	...	...	15,045[25]	...	...
							4,602	624	4	16,838	3,135	9
1956	33.0	7.7	0.9	154	27	4	5,163	692	−15	17,131	2,895	−34
1957	36.1	8.9	1.2	154	28	5	6,118	961	90	17,304	2,970	21.3
1958	40.3	9.2	1.0	162	26	4	6,616	711	11	16,681	2,152	44
1959	47.4	8.4	0.5	170	20	2	8,865[47]	1,008[47]	159[47]	16,214[47]	2,261[47]	243[47]
1960	55.6	9.5	2.8	182	21	9	13.6	2.0	0.3	17	2.5	0.3
1961	63.9	12.3	1.9	202	27	6	17.3	2.8	0.1	17	2.8	0.1
1962	73.4	15.1	1.6	221	32	5	18.8	2.9	−0.1	17	2.8	−0.1
1963	78.7	15.1	1.3	222	30	4	22.4	2.9	0.1	17	2.3	0.1
1964	96.7	15.4	2.7	245	28	7	32.6	3.4	0.2	17	2.0	0.1
1965	115	19.2	2.2	258	35	5	52.5	5.7	—	18	2.0	- -
1966	137	22.6	4.9	274	39	10	99.6	10.9	1.1	18	1.9	0.2
1967	157	23.4	7.6	285	37	14	170	22.8	0.6	17	2.2	0.1
1968	186	24.1	1.7	285	31	3	375	38.3	−0.3	18	2.0	- -
1969	209	25.9	2.0	296	33	3	506	56.0	−0.8	19	2.6	- -

J1 SOUTH AMERICA: National Accounts Totals (in millions of stated unit, except as otherwise indicated)

1935–1969

	Venezuela (thousand million bolivares)					
	Current Prices			1957 Princes		
	GDP	GFCF	Stocks	GDP	GFCF	Stocks
1935	...	...	...	...	...	...
1936	...	...	...	...	...	...
1937	...	...	...	...	...	...
1938	...	...	...	...	...	...
1939	...	...	...	...	...	...
1940	...	...	...	...	...	...
1941	...	...	...	...	...	...
1942	...	...	...	...	...	...
1943	...	...	...	...	...	...
1944	...	...	...	...	...	...
1945	...	...	...	...	...	...
1946	...	...	...	...	...	...
1947	...	...	...	...	...	...
1948	...	...	...	...	...	...
1949	...	...	...	...	...	...
1950	12	2.8	0.1	...	...	...
1951	13	3.2	0.1	...	...	...
1952	14	4.0	0.4	...	...	...
1953	15	4.3	- -	16	4.7	...
1954	16	5.0	0.1	18	5.4	...
1955	18	4.4	0.2	19	5.1	...
1956	20	5.1	0.2	21	5.5	...
1957	24	6.0	0.3	24	6.0	0.4
1958	25	6.0	0.4	24	5.7	...
1959	26	6.1	0.3	26	5.9	0.4
1960	26	4.8	−0.3	27	4.7	−0.3
1961	27	4.3	0.3	28	4.0	0.3
1962	30	4.6	0.6	31	4.2	0.5
1963	32	5.0	0.5	33	4.3	0.4
1964	36		1.3	36	5.2	1.1
1965	38	7.0	0.9	39	5.6	0.7
1966	40	7.4	0.5	39	5.7	0.4
1967	42	7.9	0.5	41	5.9	0.4
1968	45	9.4[48]	1.2[48]	43	6.7[48]	1.0[48]
		10	2.7		7.5	2.1
1969	46	11	1.0	45	7.9	0.8

J1   SOUTH AMERICA: National Accounts Totals (in millions of stated unit, except as otherwise indicated).

	Argentina (thousand million new (1970) pesos)[49]						Bolivia (thousand million pesos)[50]					
	Current Prices			1960/1970 Prices[33]			Current prices			1970/1980/1990 Prices[51]		
	GDP	GFCF	Stocks	GDP	GFCF	Stocks	GDP	GFCF	Stocks	GDP	GFCF	Stocks
1970	95	19	0.4	15[33]	3.3[33]	0.1[33]	12.4	1.8	0.3	12.4	1.8	0.3
1971	133	26	1.2	96	20	0.5	13.5	2.0	0.4	13.0	2.0	0.4
1972	220	44	2.0	98	21	0.5	17.2	2.6	0.8	13.7	2.2	0.7
1973	365	70	4.1	99	21	1.0	26.1	4.5	0.9	14.6	2.2	0.4
1974	497[49]	100[49]	10.4[49]	103	22	2.0	43.3	6.5	0.6	15.4	2.3	0.2
1975	1.35	0.29	- -	95	15	- -	49.2	9.1	3.0	16.4	2.8	0.8
1976	7.59	2.04	0.02	101	22	- -	56.4	10.7	1.3	17.4	2.9	0.3
1977	20.93	5.69	—	107	26	—	65.2	12.4	1.1	18.2	3.1	0.2
1978	52.34	12.76	−0.27	104	23	...	75.2	16.4	2.2	18.8[51]	3.4[51]	0.4[51]
										124	25	4.1
1979	142.5[49]	32.35[49]	−0.18[49]	111	24	- -	90.2	17.4	1.4	125	23	2.1
1980	28.3	6.3	0.16	113	26	1.0	123	17.5	0.5	123	18	0.5
1981	54.8	10.3	−0.27	105	21	−0.7	155	22	—	124	17	—
1982	148	23.4	−1.61	100	15	1.1	402	52	—	119	12	—
1983	683	118	−0.45	103	15	0.1	1,387	163	10	113	10	- -
1984	5,281[49]	813[49]	−47[49]	106	13	−0.2	20,900[50]	2,260[50]	−50[50]	113	11	0.4
1985	39.6	5.3	−0.4	101	12	−1.3	2,867	336	148	112	14	0.7
	1986 Prices											
1986	9,984	1,743	...	9,884	...	...	8,924	959	234	109	15	0.4
			million pesos									
1987	23	5	...	10,242	...	...	10,180	1,146	368	112	15	0.5
1988	111	21	...	10,049	...	...	11,361	1,812	186	115	16	- -
1989	3,244	503	...	9,424	...	...	14,749	1,694	−243	118	16	−0.2
1990	68,922	9,647	...	9,430	...	...	16,937	2,278	−16	121	15	−0.3
										16,937	2,227	−16
1991	180,898	26,478	...	10,270	...	...	20,916	2,732	414	17,721	2,343	349
1992	226,638	37,854	...	11,159	...	...	23,520	3,520	772	18,214	2,618	599
1993	...	...	...	...	...	...	26,057	4,264	911	18,962	2,756	485

	Brazil (thousand million cruzeiros/cruzados)[36]						Chile (pesos)					
	Current Prices			1970/1980/1986 Prices[51]			Current Prices			1965/1977/1986 Prices		
	GDP	GFCF	Stocks	GDP	GFCF	Stocks	GDP	GFCF	Stocks	GDP	GFCF	Stocks
1970	196	45	3	196	45	3	97	13	2.0	23.6	3.4	0.5
1971	261	61	7	223	52	6	129	17	2.0	24.4	3.4	0.3
1972	345	81	9	251	59	7	239	29	5.0	24.4	2.9	0.5
1973	483	114	21	291	69	13	1,213	162	6.0	23.5	2.8	0.2
1974	708	177	53	304	83	25	9,661	1,202	39	24.9	3.2	0.1
										291	50	1.6
1975	1,005	245	...	347[36] [51]	89[36] [51]	...	36	6.3	−1.6	253	39	−3.5
				9.0	2.3							
1976	1,629	366	...	9.9	2.4	...	129	17	−0.6	262	33	−2.3
1977	2,491	532	...	10.3	2.4	...	288	38	3.2	288	38	3.2
1978	3,627	805	...	10.8	2.5	...	487	72	15	311	45	6.2
1979	6,059[36]	1,393[36]	−35[36]	11.6	2.6	- -	772	115	22	337	53	14
1980	12.6	2.8	—	12.6	2.8	- -	1,075	179	47	363	64	23
1981	24.6	5.2	—	12.2	2.1	—	1,273	237	52	384	75	31
1982	50.5	10.8	−0.2	12.3	2.3	- -	1,239	181	−42	330	49	−13
1983	117	21.3	−1.7	12.0	1.8	- -	1,558	186	−34	327	42	−12
1984	386	65.2	−4.4	12	2.0	- -	1,893	234	24	348	46	7.3
1985	1,383	234	...	13	2.1	...	2,652	447	9	356	53	−3.0
1986	3,662	699	...	14	2.6	...	3,419	586	60	377	56	0.3
										3,419	586	60
1987	11,537	2,573	...	15	2.6	...	4,541	882	128	3,643	713	106
1988	86,198	19,666	...	15	2.8	...	5,918	1,202	146	3,911	814	100
1989	1,266,348	314,869	...	15	3.0	...	7,529	1,733	187	4,297	1,008	111
	million cruzeiros reais											
1990	32,646	7,037	...	...	...	...	9,270	2,159	276	4,437	1,026	137
1991	164,486	31,272	...	...	...	...	12,017	2,510	435	4,759	1,004	178
1992	1,846,813	352,288	...	...	...	...	18,454	3,517	636	5,284	1,265	225
1993	...	...	...	...	...	...	21,918	4,715	591	5,616	1,490	186

J1   SOUTH AMERICA: National Accounts Totals (in millions of stated unit, except as otherwise indicated)

	Colombia (thousand million pesos)						Ecuador (thousand million sucres)					
	Current Prices			1975 Prices			Current Prices			1965/1975 Prices[52]		
	GDP	GFCF	Stocks	GDP	GFCF	Stocks	GDP	GFCF	Stocks	GDP	GFCF	Stocks
1970	133	21	2.9	307	47	6.8	35	5.8	0.5	27[52]	4.8[52]	0.4[52]
										65	8.2	1.0
1971	156	24	3.0	326	50	6.2	40	8.7	0.6	67	14	1.0
1972	190	27	3.9	351	48	7.2	47	8.4	0.9	77	11	1.5
1973	243	32	6.0	374	50	9.3	62	11	1.2	96	14	1.8
1974	322	37	16	396	45	19	93	17	4.0	102	19	4.4
1975	405	55	6.7	405	55	6.7	108	25	3.9	108	25	3.9
1976	532	85	8.9	424	68	7.2	133	29	2.1	118	25	2.0
1977	716	104	30	442	69	19	166	39	4.9	125	29	4.0
1978	909	140	26	479	75	19	191	50	4.3	134	33	4.0
1979	1,189	183	32	505	78	15	234	59	3.9	141	33	3.1
1980	1,579	265	36	526	88	15	293	65	7.3	148	35	4.2
1981	1,983	350	59	538	94	23	349	78	3.2	153	32	1.5
1982	2,497	436	76	543	96	27	416	94	11	155	33	5.6
1983	3,054	525	83	551	88	23	560	93	5.4	151	24	2.2
1984	3,857	654	77	570	99	15	813	125	15	157	23	2.9
1985	4,966	870	75	588	94	9.1	1,110	178	23	164	25	3.4
1986	6,788	1,204	18	622	101	6.4	1,383	260	28	169	26	3.1
1987	8,824	1,537	227	655	101	15	1,794	407	—	159	27	1.1
1988	11,731	2,288	292	682	112	14	3,020	643	6	175	25	1.4
1989	15,127	2,733	288	705	107	10	5,171	1,071	−1	176	25	2.4
1990	20,228	3,365	387	735	103	13	8,204	1,513	−77	181	24	−0.5
1991	26,107	3,810	354	750	97	9	12,296	2,417	309	191	27	3.9
1992	33,144	5,214	493	779	113	34	19,414	3,784	333	197	28	1.7
1993	41,932	8,027	...	...	...	...	27,451	5,457	303	201	29	0.01

	Guyana (dollars)						Paraguay (thousand million guaranies)					
	Current Prices			1970/1985 Prices[58]			Current Prices			1970/1982 Prices[59]		
	GDP	GFCF	Stocks	GDP	GFCF	Stocks	GDP	GFCF	Stocks	GDP	GFCF	Stocks
1970	533	113	9.2	533	113	9	75	11	0.2	75	11	0.2
1971	561	103	2.3	544	102	2	84	12	0.4	78	12	0.2
1972	599	108	11	586	79	8	97	13	1.3	82	12	0.2
1973	645	155	21	549	112	18	125	20	3.5	89	17	0.5
1974	955	198	54	588	84	33	168	31	4.4	96	19	0.5
1975	1,188	350	42	651[58]	175	29	190	40	6.4	101[59]	23[59]	0.8[59]
				2,719						416	63	15
1976	1,136	381	44	2,798	...	...	214	49	4	447	87	9
1977	1,125	290	...	2,664	...	...	264	63	2.2	495	104	5
1978	1,268	242	...	2,618	...	...	322	81	6.5	552	126	12
1979	1,326	325	...	2,312	...	...	430	116	6.8	614	151	10
1980	1,508	404	...	2,350	...	...	560	153	8.6	685	184	11
1981	1,597	500	...	2,343	...	...	709	194	10	744	217	11
1982	1,446	380	...	2,099	...	...	737	177	12	737	177	12
1983	1,468	395	...	1,905	...	...	818	164	11	715	145	9
1984	1,700	390	...	1,945	...	...	1,070	231	14	740	146	10
1985	1,964	410	...	1,964	...	...	1,394	288	18	766	147	12
1986	2,219	586	...	1,969	...	...	1,834	432	27	766	152	13
1987	3,382	1,123	...	1,981	...	...	2,494	591	34	799	161	14
1988	4,138	890	...	1,921	...	...	3,319	768	41	850	167	15
1989	10,330	3,536	...	...	...	...	4,608	1,045	53	899	185	16
1990	15,665	6,624	...	...	...	...	6,474	1,425	55	927	203	16
1991	38,966	13,746	...	...	...	...	8,280	1,962	94	950	215	23
1992	46,734	25,113	...	...	...	...	9,671	2,117	98	967	202	21
1993	56,647	30,118	...	...	...	...	11,992	2,642	109	...	...	...

J1   SOUTH AMERICA: National Accounts Totals (in millions of stated unit, except as otherwise indicated)

Peru[53]
(intis)

	Current Prices			1973/1979 Prices[54]		
	GDP	GFCF	Stocks	GDP	GFCF	Stocks
1970	241	29.9	1.2	319	36	2
1971	264	33.3	6.4	331	38	9
1972	295	37.8	·4.0	340[54]	41[54]	8[54]
1973	359	45.4	10.8	2,465	386	74
1974	448	68.0	16.5	2,666	499	98
1975	550	96.8	12.4	2,656	604	35
1976	765	128	9.2	2,862	557	34
1977	1,058	154	5	2,917	451	11
1978	1,678	235	9	2,911	411	−16
1979	3,490[53]	724[53]	33[53]	3,490[53]	724[53]	33[53]
1980	5.99	1.50	0.24	3.66	1.06	0.15
1981	10.6	3.04	0.58	3.81	1.12	0.22
1982	17.4	5.1	0.66	3.70	1.03	0.15
1983	31.4	7.4	0.17	3.33	0.70	- -
1984	68.8	14.4	−0.22	3.49	0.66	−0.02
1985	189	34.3	0.41	3.57	0.58	−0.02
1986	360	73.6	3.2	3.90	0.69	0.06
1987	722	143	16.3	4.24	0.82	0.14
1988	4,431	880	150	3.88	0.70	0.17

million
New Soles

	Current Prices			1973/1979 Prices		
1989	115	24	- -	3.43	0.56	0.02
1990	6,791	1,423	12	3.24	0.57	0.10
1991	32,936	5,933	707	3.36	0.59	0.16
1992	52,062	9,971	775	3.25	0.61	0.08
1993	80,529	16,483	2,261	3.46	0.68	0.11

Uruguay
(thousand million pesos[55])

	Current Prices			1961/1978/1983 Prices[56]		
	GDP	GFCF	Stocks	GDP	GFCF	Stocks
1970	601	69	0.4	20	2.7	- -
1971	722	83	8.4	19	2.9	0.2
1972	1,242	121	26	19	2.3	0.2
1973	2,561	229	93	19[56]	2.0[56]	0.4[56]
				25,579	2,021	298
1974	4,546	465	60	26,383	2,238	171
1975	8,166	1,090	12	27,930	3,141	−84
1976	12,638	1,952	−81	29,043	4,031	−333
1977	19,915	3,030	−2	29,384	4,321	14
1978	30,930	4,943	8	30,930	4,943	8
1979	57,630[55]	9,310[55]	660[55]	32,838	5,882	250
1980	92.2	15.4	0.6	34,808	6,255	206
1981	122	19.2	−0.4	35,469	6,067	−179
1982	129	19.4	−0.8	32,138	5,165	−350
1983	175	24.0	0.1	175,417	24,042	953
1984	271	30.0	0.3	173,501	18,531	2,339
1985	479	46.0	0.8	176,061	14,847	3,828
1986	890	88.0	1.1	191,654	16,751	5,122
1987	1,661	189	4.8	206,858	21,329	4,570
1988	2,726	325	3.4	206,840	22,272	1,774
1989	4,839	560	−1.4	209,499	22,158	−313
1990	9,784	1,055	1.8	211,418	20,848	2,211
1991	20,271	2,418	31.8	215,357	23,880	3,374
1992	35,346	4,634	23.8	…	…	…
1993	…	…	…	…	…	…

J1 SOUTH AMERICA: National Accounts Totals (in millions of stated unit, except as otherwise indicated)

	Venezuela (thousand million bolivares)					
	Current Prices			**1968/1984 Prices**[57]		
	GDP	GFCF	Stocks	GDP	GFCF	Stocks
1970	52	12	3.9	51	11	3.8
1971	57	13	3.7	54	12	...
1972	61	16	3.4	54	14	...
1973	73	19	2.8	57	15	...
1974	112	21	5.9	61	15	...
1975	118	31	5.8	64	19	...
1976	135	43	3.7	70	24	...
1977	156	60	4.2	75	31	...
1978	169	72	0.6	76	33	...
1979	208	66	0.1	77	26	...
1980	254	64	−1.3	76	22	...
1981	285	70	−4.4	76	23	...
1982	291	70	5.2	76	22	...
1983	290	55	−21	72	16	...
	<u>348</u>	<u>50</u>	<u>−1.7</u>	83[57]	18[57]	...
1984	420	67	6.2			
1985	465	81	5.4	420	72	4.9
1986	489	100	2.6	421	78	2.1
1987	696	148	23	448	78	13
1988	873	199	44	464	85	20
1989	1,510	255	−63.2	491	64	−14
1990	2,279	322	−89	449	60	−14
1991	3,037	552	15	478	81	1.9
1992	4,131	871	109	525	103	11
1993	5,449	1,063	−41	557	97	−3.4

J1 National Accounts Totals (in millions of stated units, except as otherwise indicated)

NOTES

1. SOURCES: The national publications referred to on pp. xiii–xv; IMF, *International Financial Statistics*; UN, *Yearbook of National Accounts Statistics* and *Statistics of National Income and Expenditure*; and Economic Commission for Latin America, *Statistical Abstract of Latin America*, together with the following:
Canada to 1926 (1st line)—O.J. Firestone, *Canada's Economic Development, 1867–1953* (*Income and Wealth*, Series VII, London, 1958).
Cuba to 1927—Julian Alienes, *Caracteristicas Fundamentales de la Economia Cubana* (Havana, 1950).
Mexico, capital Formation to 1950, from Combined Mexican Working Party, *The Economic Development of Mexico* (Baltimore, 1953) USA to 1889 (1st line)—Thomas S. Berry, *Estimated Annual Variations in Gross National Product, 1789 to 1909* (Richmond, 1968).
USA from 1929 to 1980—U.S. Department of Commerce, *Survey of Current Business* vol 66, no 2. (February 1986).
Argentina, Capital formation to 1934, based on Alexander Ganz and on Manuel Balboa and Alberto Fracchia in *Income and Wealth*, Series VIII (London, 1959).
Brazil to 1947, from or based on Claudio R. Contador & Claudio L. Haddad, 'Produto Real, Moeda e Preços: A Experiênca Brasileira no Período 1861–1970', *Revista Brasileira de Estatística* (XXXVI, 143, July-Sept 1975).
Chile to 1925 (1st line), from or based on Marto A. Ballasteros and Tom E. Davis, 'The Growth of Output and Employment in Basic Sectors of the Chilean Economy, 1908–1957', *Economic Development and Cultural Change* (January 1963).
Chile 1925 (2nd line) to 1940 (1st line), based on or from the Economic Commission for Latin America sources as modified in Markos Mamalakis and Clark W. Reynolds, *Essays on the Chilean Economy* (Homewood, III., 1965), p. 384.
2. For definitions of concepts see the UN publications on national accounts.

FOOTNOTES

[1] Excluding government capital formation to 1920.
[2] The annual estimates shown in table 87 of the source are given here, but they are said by the author to be less reliable than those which he made for benchmark years in current as well as constant prices, and it is the latter figures which correspond to the current prices statistics given here. They are as follows (in 1935–39 prices):

1870	762	1900	1,833
1880	1,034	1910	3,087
1890	1,386	1920	3,844

[3] This break occurs on a change of source. The estimates in the source of the earlier figures are continued there to 1909.
[4] 1935–39 prices to 1920 and 1971 prices from 1926.
[5] The series to 1950 (1st line) are presumably less complete than later revised figures. Government capital formation is not included in the GCF series to 1946 (1st line).
[6] Years ended 30 September. Figures to 1950 (1st line) are at factor cost.
[7] Later revisions to the GDP series were not carried so far back in the component series.
[8] Years beginning 1 July.
[9] NNP to 1946 (1st line), GNP from 1946 (2nd line) to 1949, and GDP subsequently. The 1950 figure for GNP is $864 million.
[10] Later revisions to were not carried back further and there may be a break in the continuity of the series.
[11] 1958 prices to 1929 (1st line) and 1982 prices subsequently.
[12] 1971 prices to 1975 (1st line) and 1981 prices subsequently.
[13] NNP to 1950 (1st line), GDP from 1950 (2nd line) to 1958, and NMP from 1962 (though the same series was described as gross until 1981).
[14] GFCF to 1970 and NFCF subsequently. There was a change in concept from 1962.
[15] 1965 prices to 1965, 1981 prices from 1975.
[16] These figures are approximate estimates.
[17] GNP to 1950 (1st line) and GDP subsequently.
[18] 1946 prices to 1950 (1st line) and 1958 prices subsequently.
[19] 1970 prices to 1969 and 1976 prices subsequently.
[20] 1948 prices to 1950 (1st line), 1970 prices from then to 1975 (1st line), and 1978 prices subsequently.
[21] NNP to 1950 (1st line) and GDP subsequently.
[22] 1956 prices to 1958, 1960 prices from 1959 to 1970 (1st line), and 1974 prices subsequently.
[23] *footnote suppressed*
[24] Million million pesos from 1985.
[25] There was a change in the concept employed.
[26] 1960 prices to 1970, 1970 prices from 1971 to 1980, and 1980 prices subsequently.
[27] Thousand million cordobas from 1978 (2nd line) or 1979.
[28] 1958 prices to 1978 (1st line) and 1985 prices subsequently.
[29] 1960 prices to 1970 and 1970 prices subsequently.
[30] 1975 prices to 1974 and 1985 prices subsequently for GDP, and 1970 prices to 1983 and 1985 prices subsequently for GCF

J1 National Accounts Totals (in millions of stated units, except as otherwise indicated)

31 For recent decades a consistent series of total GFCF in current prices is given in IMF sources as follows (in thousand million dollars):-

1959	90.1	1969	174.6	1979	502.4
1960	91.6	1970	177.5	1980	516.8
1961	92.3	1971	198.6	1981	564.6
1962	99.9	1972	225.2	1982	549.0
1963	108.2	1973	254.3	1983	563.5
1964	116.8	1974	268.3	1984	674.9
1965	131.2	1975	273.7	1985	731.1
1966	142.0	1976	277.7	1986	752.8
1967	144.7	1977	374.3	1987	770.6
1968	160.6	1978	444.9	1988	814.1

32 Including Alaska and Hawaii from 1960.
33 This break occurs on a change of source.
34 Million million pesos from 1965.
35 1950 prices to 1936 (1st line), 1960 prices to 1970, and 1070 prices subsequently.
36 Thousand million cruzeiros from 1960 for current prices and 1965 for constant prices. From 1980 for current and 1975 for constant prices, figures are in cruzados.
37 1949 prices to 1947, 1953 prices from 1948 to 1964, and 1970 prices subsequently.
38 Million escudoes from 1960 to 1964 and thousand million escudos from 1965 to 1969.
39 1960 prices to 1940 (1st line), 1961 prices from 1940 (2nd line) to 1960, and 1965 prices subsequently.
40 1950 prices to 1949 and 1970 prices subsequently.
41 1960 prices to 1964 and 1965 prices subsequently.
42 At factor cost to 1949.
43 At factor cost to 1950 (1st line).
44 Thousand million soles from 1950.
45 GNP to 1950 (1st line) and GDP subsequently.
46 Not including government capital formation to 1946.
47 Thousand million pesos from 1960.
48 New concepts were employed from 1968 (2nd line). There is no break in the GDP series at this level of rounding.
49 For current prices series, million million pesos from 1975 to 1979, million australes from 1980 to 1984, and thousand million australes subsequently.
50 Million bolivianos from1985.
51 1970 prices to 1975 (1st line) and 1980 prices subsequently.
52 1965 prices to 1970 (1st line) and 1975 prices subsequently.
53 Thousand million intis from 1980.
54 1973 prices to 1972 and 1979 prices subsequently.
55 Thousand million pesos from 1980.
56 1961 prices to 1973 (1st line) and 1978 prices subsequently.
57 1968 prices to 1984 and 1984 prices subsequently.
58 1970 prices to 1975 (1st line) and 1985 prices subsequently.
59 1970 prices to 1975 (1st line) and 1952 prices subsequently.

J2 NORTH AMERICA: PROPORTIONS OF GDP BY SECTOR OF ORIGIN (percentages)

Key: A = agriculture, forestry and fishing; I = manufacturing, mining and public utilities; B = construction; T = transport   and   communications; C & F = commerce and finance.

	Canada						Honduras					
	A	I	B	T	C&F	Other	A	I	B	T	C&F	Other
1925–29	17.8[1]	25.8[1,2]	4.5[1]	12.9[1,3]	22.0[1]	16.7[1]	55	7	3	...	11	14
1930–34	11.4	25.7[2]	3.7	13.4[2]	25.3	20.5	57	7	3	...	11	14
1935–39	12.7	30.3[2]	3.0	12.8[2]	22.9	18.3	50	10	4	...	14	17

	Mexico						Puerto Rico					
1895–99	32	15	...	2	...	50	...	...	...	...	...	...
1900–04	28	19	...	2	...	50	...	...	...	...	...	...
1905–10	28	19	...	2	...	50	...	...	...	...	...	...
1921–24	24	21	...	2	...	55	...	...	...	...	...	...
1925–29	22	21	...	2	...	55	...	...	...	...	...	...
1930–34	22	20	...	3	...	...	...	...	...	...	...	...
1935–39	20	22	...	3	...	55	30[2]	13[3]		7[3]	10[3]	39[3]

	USA[2,4]					
1869&1879	20.5	15.7[2]	5.3	11.9[2]	27.4	19.1
1879&1889	16.1	18.7[2]	5.5	11.9[2]	29.2	18.5
1889&1899	17.1	20.7[2]	4.9	10.7[2]	28.8	17.8
1899&1908	16.7	21.5[2]	4.5	10.7[2]	31.3	15.2
1904–13	17.0	22.2[2]	4.3	11.0[2]	31.2	14.3
1909–18	17.7	24.1[2]	3.2	10.7[2]	29.9	14.5
1914–23	15.2	25.5[2]	3.0	11.0[2]	29.0	16.2
1919–28	12.2	25.3[2]	3.9	11.3[2]	29.4	18.0
1929	9.8	27.6[2]	4.4	10.8[2]	32.6	16.9
1930–34	8.7	22.6[2]	2.9	11.9[2]	30.0	23.7
1935–39	9.6	26.8[2]	2.9	10.2[2]	27.7	22.9

J2   NORTH AMERICA: Proportions of GDP by Sector of Origin (percentages)

	Canada						Costa Rica					
	A	I	B	T	C&F	Other	A	I	B	T	C&F	Other
1940–44	13	34[2]	3	12[2]	16	20	...	...	...	...	...	...
1945–49	14	34	5	10	20	17	37[7]	12[7]	6[7]	3[7]	15[7,8]	26[7,8]
1950–54	12	35	6	9	22	16	38	13	5	3	16[8]	25[8]
1955–59	7	35	6	10	24	18	31	14	5	4	17[8]	28[8]
1960–64	6	33	6	9	24	21	29	14	5	4	20	28
1965–69	5	32	6	9	23	24	27	16	5	5	21	27
1970–74	5	29	7	8	24[6]	28[6]	24	18	5	5	22[6]	25[6]
1975–79	4	27	8	7	31	22	20	20	6	6	25	19
1980–84	3	28	7	7	31	23	20	21	5	8	...	...
1985–88[5]	3	28	6	7	33	24	19	22	4	4	...	...
1989–93	2	28	6	6	31	25	16	23	3	5	...	...

	Dominican Republic						El Salvador					
1945–49	...	...	...	...	...	...	45	13	2	3	17	20
1950–54	33	14	5	6	13	28	39	14	3	4	18	22
1955–59	31	14	6	7	14	27	37	15	3	4	19	22
1960–64	29	17	4	7	13	31	36	16	3	5	19	20
1965–69	26	17	5	8	12	33	30	19	3	5	22	21
1970–74	23	22	7	8	13[6]	26[6]	29	20	3	5	20	22
1975–79	20	23	7	6	26	17	27	21	5	6	21	21
1980–84	18	21	8	5	29	19	28	19	4	6	20	23
1985–88[5]	19	20	8	6	28	20	27	19	3	4	24	23
1989–93	14	23	8	9	29	18	24	22	3	6	21	25

	Guatemala						Haiti					
1950–54	36	12	4	2	25	24	51	12		2	12	22
1955–59	33	12	4	3	25	25	49	12		2	11	24
1960–64	33	13	3	3	25	24	50	13		2	11	23
1965–69	31	15	2	3	22	22	53	10	2	2	11	21
1970–74	31	16	2	4	27[6]	20[6]	49	12	3	3	11	21
1975–79	29	16	3	4	30	16	44	15	4	3	12	21
1980–84	28	17	4	4	30	17	39	17	5	3	15	21
1985–88[5]	27	19	3	4	29	18	34	17	6	2	16	23
1989–93	25	18	2	8	33	15	34	14	6	2	23	22

	Honduras						Jamaica					
1940–44	49	10	4	...	14	18	...	...	...	...	...	...
1945–49	47	10	5	...	14	16	...	...	...	...	...	...
1950–54	42	13	6	5	15	18	21[9]	18[9]	9[9]	7[9]	25[9]	20[9]
1955–59	39	14	5	6	16	20	15[10]	21[10]	12[10]	7[10]	25[10]	20[10]
1960–64	34	17	5	8	15	22	12	25	11	8	24	19
1965–69	36	17	5	7	16	20	11[10]	28[10]	11[10]	7[10]	23[10]	20[10]
1970–74	34	19	4	7	16	20	7	27	11	6	34	15
1975–79	29	20	6	8	17	21	8	30	7	6	31	18
1980–84	28	19	5	8	17	22	7	27	7	6	36	17
1985–88[5]	25	20	5	8	20	22	6	29	9	8	36	12
1989–93	25	17	5	8	22	24	7	33	10	10	38	3

J2 NORTH AMERICA: Proportions of GDP by Sector of Origin (percentages)

	Mexico						Nicaragua					
	A	I	B	T	C&F	Other	A	I	B	T	C&F	Other
1940–44	19	23	4	3	25	26	...	...	...	...	...	...
1945–49	17	23	4	3	27	26	35	14	1	4	18	29
1950–54	18	23	4	3	29	24	34	13	1	4	21	29
1955–59	17	23	4	3	29	24	32	14	2	6	21	29
1960–64	15	25	5	3	29	24	30	17	3	6	20	27
1965–69	13	27	5	3	29	23	30	19	4	6	21	22
1970–74	11	29	6	3	29	23	28	22	4	6	21	20
1975–79	9	31[6]	6	3[6]	27[6]	23[6]	29	22	4	6	20	20
1980–84	9	27	6	8	36	16	27	23	2	6	...	...
1985–88[5]	9[11]	28[11]	5[11]	7[11]	35[11]	16[11]	23[11]	29[11]	3[11]	5[11]	...	...
1989–93	8	28	5	7	37	16	...	...	...	...	...	...

	Panama						Puerto Rico[2,12]					
1940–44	...	...	...	...	...	...	26	13		7	11	44
1945–49	30	8	6	3	11	47	24[12]	13[7][12]	2[12]	5[12]	19[12]	38[12]
1950–54	31	10	5	3	11	42	21	21	5	6	28	19
1955–59	29	12	5	4	12	41	14	24	6	7	28	21
1960–64	25	15	6	4	13	38	10[6]	26[6]	7[6]	7[6]	28[6]	22[6]
1965–69	23	17	6	5	13	36	4	27	7	6	35	19
1970–74	19	18	7	6	14	35	3	31	7	5	33	21
1975–79	19	16	5	9	14	36	3	38	3	6	31	20
1980–84	13	14	7	19	...	...	2	43	2	5	30	18
1985–88[5]	9	13	5	23	...	...	2	43	2	5	31	18
1989–93	13	12	4	13	...	...	3	46	2	7	37	7

	Trinidad & Tobago						USA[2,4,16]					
1940–44	...	...	...	...	...	...	8	34	3	9	24	22
1945–49	...	...	...	...	...	...	9[4]	31[4]	4[4]	8[4]	26[4]	21[4]
1950–54	18[14]	46[6][14]	3[14]	5[6][14]	11[6][14]	18[6][14]	6	34	5	8	26	21
1955–59	14	48	4	3	15	16	4[16]	33[16]	5[16]	8[16]	26[16]	23[16]
1960–64	11	46	5	20		18	4	31	5	8	26	27
1965–69	8[6][15]	46[6]	4[6]	21[6]		20[6]	3	31	5	8	26	25
1970–74	4	36	7	12	23	15	3	29	5	6	31	25
1975–79	3	44	11	8	20	13	3	29	5	6	31	25
1980–84	2	36	14	9	22	15	3	28	4	6	31	26
1985–88[5]	2	30	9	9	28	22	2[11]	25[11]	5[11]	6[11]	33[11]	29[11]
1989–93	3	33	9	10	23	23	3	26	4	7	34	27

J2 SOUTH AMERICA: PROPORTIONS OF GDP BY SECTOR OF ORIGIN (percentages)

	Argentina						Bolivia					
	A	I	B	T	C&F	Other	A	I	B	T	C&F	Other
1900–04	33	16	5	4	20	21	...	...	...	...	...	...
1905–09	29	16	8	5	23	18	...	...	...	...	...	...
1910–14	26	18	8	6	23	18	...	...	...	...	...	...
1915–19	31	17	2	7	20	22	...	...	...	...	...	...
1920–24	28	19	4	7	22	20	...	...	...	...	...	...
1925–29	26	20	5	9	23	18	...	...	...	...	...	...
1930–34	24	21	4	10	21	21	...	...	...	...	...	...
1935–39	24	23	4	9	20	20	...	...	...	...	...	...
1940–44	24	25	4	9	17	21	...	...	...	...	...	...
1945–49	19	26	4	10	18	23	...	...	...	...	...	...
1950–54	16	25	5	11	17	26	23	34	2	7	11	22
1955–59	16	28	5	11	17	24	23	30	3	9	11	24
1960–64	15	30	4	10	17	23	24	26	4	10	11	26
1965–69	14	33	4	10	16	22	20	29	5	9	11	26
1970–74	12	36	5	10	16[6]	20[6]	16	29	4	9	12	26
1975–79	13	35	6	10	19	13	17	24	4	10	17	29
1980–84	15	33	6	11	21	14	19	22	3	12	19	24
1985–88	14	34	4	10	21	13	21	23	3	8	18	26
1989–93	8	31	5	5	31	20	16	25	4	11	24	21

	Brazil						Chile					
1920–24	24	13[17]	...	3	21	...	...	...	...	...	...	...
1925–29	22	13[17]	...	4	22	...	...	...	...	...	...	...
1930–34	24	13[17]	...	3	19	...	...	...	...	...	...	...
1935–39	23	14[17]	...	3	20	...	...	...	...	...	...	...
1940–44	21	18	8	4	20	28	12	38	4	20		26
1945–49	18	21	9	4	22	26	12	37	5	20		27
1950–54	16	23	10	5	22	24	11	36	5	3	16	29
1955–59	15	26	10	5	21	23	11	37	4	4	16	29
1960–64	13	29	8	5	20	24	9	39	5	4	16	27
1965–69	12	28	6	6	20	26	8	41	4	6	16	25
1970–74	9	33	6	6	21	25	7	42	4	6	17	24
1975–79	8	33	7	6	21	25	9	39	3	5	17	27
1980–84	8	33	6	7	...	...	8	37	4	7	...	...
1985–89	10	31	7	5	...	...	8	33	6	6	...	...
1989–93	9	30	7	6	...	...	9	29	5	7	...	...

J2   SOUTH AMERICA: Proportions of GDP by Sector of Origin (percentages)

	Colombia						Ecuador					
	A	I	B	T	C&F	Other	A	I	B	T	C&F	Other
1925–29	52	8[11]	4	2[18]	...	...	...	...	...	...	...	...
1930–34	51	9[17]	3	2[18]	...	...	...	...	...	...	...	...
1935–39	47	10[17]	4	2[18]	...	...	...	...	...	...	...	...
1940–44	45	12[17]	5	3[18]	...	...	...	...	...	...	...	...
1945–49	42	14[17]	5	4[18]	14	20	37[14]	12[14]	6[14]	3[14]	15[14]	27[14,19]
1950–54	36	18	4	6	16	20	38	13	5	3	16	25[19]
1955–59	34	19	5	7	15	20	31	14	5	4	17	28[19]
1960–64	32	20	5	7	16	20	29	14	5	4	20	28
1965–69	30	21	5	7	17	21	27	16	5	5	21	27
1970–74	27	22	5	8	18	20	24[20]	18[20]	5	5[20]	22[20]	25[20]
							22	16		6	26	14
1975–79	26	22	4	9	19	20	16	29	7	7	27	14
1980–84	24	20	5	8	20	23	13	33	7	9	26	14
1985–88	18	29	6	8	19	20	15	32	5	9	27	12
1989–93	22	27	3	9	26	14	13	33	5	9	28	12

	Guyana						Paraguay					
1938–39	...	...	...	...	...	...	44	16	1	4	20	16
1940–44	...	...	...	...	...	...	45	15	1	4	21	17
1945–49	...	...	...	...	...	...	41	15	1	4	20	19
1950–54	30[21]	25[21]	7[21]	6[21]	16[21]	16[21]	41	17	1	4	17	18
1955–59	26	23	10	24 {		17	40[20][23]	16[20][23]	2[20][23]	4[20][23]	19[20][23]	19[20][23]
1960–64	26	26	7	7	18	17	38[24]	16[24]	2[24]	4[24]	26[24]	14[24]
1965–69	21	31	7	7	16	19	34	17	3	4	27	15
1970–74	22	29	8	6	16	20	35	18	3	4	26	14
1975–79	25	27	7	5	15	21	34	18	4	4	27	12
1980–84	24	21	8	7	18	23	28	19	6	4	29	13
1985–88	26[22]	20[22]	7[22]	8[22]	16[22]	25[22]	28	19	6	4	29	13
1989–93	40	16	3	5	12	26	...	...	...	...	...	...

J2   SOUTH AMERICA: Proportions of GDP by Sector of Origin (percentages)

	Peru						Uruguay					
	A	I	B	T	C&F	Other	A	I	B	T	C&F	Other
1935-39	...	...	...	...	...	...	15	19	3	11	...	...
1940-44	...	...	...	...	...	...	14	19	3	10	...	...
1945-49	26	21[17]	6	...	...	...	14	19	5	10	...	...
1950-54	26	22[17]	8	...	...	...	13	22	5	10	...	...
1955-59	24	24[17]	8	...	...	...	12	25	5	9	15[19]	32
1960-64	23	29	6	20		25	12	25	4	9	20	30
1965-69	19	30	5	20		27	12	25	4	9	17	33
1970-74	17[20]	30[20]	5[20]	17[20]		30[20]	12	26	4	9	16	33
	15	32	3	6	26	18						
1975-79	13	33	4	7	27	14	11	28	5	9	17	32
1980-84	10	32	7	6	29	15	11	24	5	8	...	...
1985-88	10	30	7	5	28	17	12[11]	29[11]	3[11]	6[11]	...	...
1989-93	14	34	6	7	30	10	11	29	4	6	...	...

	Venezuela					
1936-39	22	33	3	...	...	...
1940-44	18	34	3	...	...	...
1945-49	11	38	6	11	13	34
1950-54	9	39	7	14	13	36
1955-59	8	42	7	12	14	30
1960-64	8	41	4	10	12	29
1965-69	7	38	4	10	13	28
1970-74	7	34	5	12	13	30
1975-79	6	27	7	13	12	35
1980-84	7	23	6	13[25]	...	...
1985-88	7[11]	21[11]	3[11]	10[11]	...	...
1989-93	5	41	5	5	...	...

J2 Proportions of GDP by Sector of Origin

NOTES

1. SOURCES: Canada to 1969, Mexico to 1910, and USA throughout are based on national publications listed on pp. xiii–xv. Guyana, Jamaica, Puerto Rico and Trinidad & Tobago are based on UN, *Yearbook of National Accounts Statistics* (issues to the 1988 volume). This source has also been used as a supplement for recent years for other countries, though most of the figures are based on James W. Wilkie (ed.), *Statistical Abstract of Latin America* vol. 20 (Los Angeles, 1980) with some updating from later volumes.
2. Totals do not always add up to 100%, partly owing to rounding, but mainly because the methodology employed (especially by the Economic Commission for Latin America) is based on extrapolation over time for each sector separately. For the same reason statistics for the category "other" have not been inserted as a residual: Figures only appear where they have been separately estimated.

FOOTNOTES

[1] 1926–29 only.
[2] Gas, water, and electricity supply is included with transport not industry.
[3] 1939 only.
[4] Proportions of aggregate payments to 1919–28, based on Robert F. Martin, *National Income in the United States, 1799–1938* (New York, 1939). Proportions of national income from 1929 to 1949, and of GNP subsequently.
[5] Provisional and approximate figures.
[6] There as a rearrangement of components of the categories.
[7] 1946–49 only.
[8] Financial services are included in "Other" to 1959.
[9] 1953 and 1954 only.
[10] The definition of GDP and the composition of the categories was changed.
[11] 1985–87 only.
[12] Data are for years beginning 1 July, and relate to proportions of national income to 1949.
[13] *footnote suppressed*
[14] 1951–54 only.
[15] 1965–68 only.
[16] Including Alaska andHawaii from 1960.
[17] Excluding gas, water, and electricity supply.
[18] Transport only.
[19] Excluding financial services.
[20] This break occurs on the change from ECLA to UN sources.
[21] 1952–54 only.
[22] 1986–86 only.
[23] 1955 and 1958 only.
[24] 1963–65 only.
[25] 1980–82 only.

J3 NORTH AMERICA: BALANCE OF PAYMENTS (in millions of stated currency)

Key:- VB = visible balance; IB = invisible balance; TTB = tourism & travel balance; IIB = investment income balance; GSIB = balance on goods, services, and requited income; OCB = overall current balance; (LT)CB = (long term)capital balance; CR = change in reserves.

PART A. to 1950 in national currencies

	VB	IB	TTB	IIB	GSIB	OCB	LTCB	CR[2]
				Canada[1] (dollars)				
1900	−20.5	−32.1	+1.2	−32.0	...	−52.6	+6.4	+16.0
1901	−12.4	−33.9	+1.6	−33.5	...	−46.3	+11.3	+23.2
1902	−13.0	−30.6	+3.5	−34.4	...	−43.6	+15.8	+11.6
1903	−49.9	−30.7	+3.1	−35.5	...	−80.6	+27.5	+6.5
1904	−73.1	−32.3	+3.9	−38.5	...	−105.4	+33.6	+7.9
1905	−58.4	−42.9	+1.9	−42.1	...	−101.3	+69.5	+14.0
1906	−58.3	−49.8	+1.4	−45.7	...	−108.1	+62.6	+6.1
1907	−109.2	−61.5	+0.4	−51.1	...	−170.7	+51.7	+3.8
1908	−133.3	−87.2	+1.1	−71.3	...	−120.5	+173.3	−13.9
1909	−70.6	−86.6	—	−75.6	...	−157.2	+209.0	−1.1
1910	−148.2	−97.0	−0.3	−82.5	...	−245.2	+202.0	−6.1
1911	−222.2	−122.1	−2.4	−92.9	...	−344.3	+255.5	−19.4
1912	−274.3	−159.8	−3.6	−108.8	...	−434.1	+236.1	+12.8
1913	−212.0	−191.4	−6.7	−128.5	...	−403.3	+463.2	−4.8
1914	−101.7	−209.5	−7.0	−164.3	...	311.2	+295.1	+23.0
1915	+166.7	−209.4	+8.0	−160.2	...	−42.7	+174.0	−14.6
1916	+310.0	−298.7	+16.5	−166.9	...	+11.3	+246.2	+11.6
1917	+558.7	−381.8	+23.6	−175.8	...	+176.9	+116.9	−0.9
1918	+287.0	−384.8	+32.1	−181.6	...	−97.8	−22.8	+16.0
1919	+310.3	−273.9	+23.5	−171.9	...	+36.4	−14.9	+13.9
1920	−161.6	−196.8	+28.9	−166.1	...	−358.4	+98.7	+35.0
1921	−27.4	−171.8	+40.7	−187.0	...	−199.2	+83.6	+42.0
1922	+139.5	−140.9	+55.7	−190.4	...	−1.4	+190.3	−46.0
1923	+118.8	−149.0	+68.9	−213.5	...	−30.2	+69.6	+80.3
1924	+242.7	−112.2	+81.1	−202.0	...	+130.5	+93.0	+7.0
1925	+368.7	−115.4	+100.7	−210.5	...	+253.3	−67.0	+19.9
1926	+277.4₁	−104.2₁	+103.1₁	−218.1₁	...	+173.2₁	+26.0₁	+38.0₁
	+329	−169	+53	−208	+160	+127		
1927	+190	−168	+63	−216	+22	−10	+14	+7
1928	+172	−172	+79	−229	—	−32	−94	−49
1929	−57	−220	+90	−261	−277	−311	+212	−37
1930	−54	−253	+88	−289	−307	−337	+392	−36
1931	+78	−239	+82	−282	−161	−174	+87	−33
1932	+167	−252	+21	−265	−85	−96	+33	−3
1933	+236	−233	+38	−226	+3	−2	−37	−6
1934	+278	−204	+64	−211	+74	+68	−91	+4
1935	+325	−196	+55	−206	+129	+125	−151	+6
1936	+474	−226	+57	−236	+248	+244	−237	+5
1937	+410	−223	+58	−226	+187	+180	−157	+6
1938	+356	−246	+75	−241	+110	+99	−97	+17
1939	+377	−245	+103	−249	+132	+128	−104	+37

J3   NORTH AMERICA: Balance of Payments (in millions of stated currency)

	VB	IB	TTB	IIB	GSIB	OCB	(LT)CB	CR[2]
				Canada				
				(dollars)				
1940	+399	−256	+160	−261	+143	+151	−102	+3
1941	+672	−185	+183	−226	+487	+501	+53	+568
1942	+1,293	−205	+158	−203	+1,088	+106	−787	−674
1943	+1,613	−411	+106	−202	+1,202	+690	−315	+364
1944	+2,302	−1,297	+52	−193	+1,005	+60	+224	+274
1945	+2,128	−615	+13	−171	+1,513	+689	−46	+668
1946	+667	−247	−39	−242	+420	+363	−715	−266
1947	+287	−217	−68	−273	+70	+49	−721	−668
1948	+551	−126	−15	−255	+425	+451	+43	+492
1949	+432	−281	−54	−307	+151	+177	−29	+128
1950	+200	−534	−63	−381	−334	−319	+610	+722
				Costa Rica				
				(colones)				
1938	+13.1	−8.3	−0.6	−10.5	+4.8	−0.6	+3.3[3]	−0.9[4]
1946	−57.3	−5.6	+2.8	−9.0	−65.7	−62.9	−33.7[3]	+22.5[4]
1947	−29.2	−49.4	+1.1	−27.5	−78.6	−77.5	+106.1[3]	—
1948	+75.2	−69.6	−1.7	−46.0	+5.6	+6.7	−42.1[3]	—
1949	+78.0	−96.5	−5.6	−85.9	−18.5	+16.3	+44.9[3]	—
1950	+84.1	−75.8	−5.3	−79.9	+8.3	+9.5	−52.7[3]	—
				Cuba[5]				
				(pesos)				
1919	+218	−83	—	−39	...	+135	+2	+38
1920	+237	−103	—	−42	...	+134	+27	+13
1921	−75	−69	+5	−25	...	−144	+11	+72
1922	+147	−65	+2	−34	...	+83	+59	−2
1923	+154	−76	+1	−39	...	+78	+83	+6
1924	+145	−83	+2	−47	...	+62	+25	+3
1925	+57	−88	+3	−53	...	−32	+14	+17
1926	+41	−95	+3	−60	...	−54	+55	+1
1927	+67	−93	+5	−55	...	−26	+38	+23
1928	+65	−79	+7	−45	...	−14	+12	+12
1929	+56	−63	+7	−41	...	−7	+13	+5
1930	+5	−45	+9	−31	...	−40	+25	+36
1931	+39	−39	+9	−27	...	—	−11	+18
1932	+30	−30	+6	−20	...	−1	−15	+9
1933	+42	−26	+2	−17	...	+16	−6	—
1934	+34	−16	—	−7	...	+19	−1	−2

J3   NORTH AMERICA: Balance of Payments (in millions of stated currency)

Cuba[5]
(pesos)

	VB	IB	TTB	IIB	GSIB	OCB	(LT)CB	CR
1935	+33	−17	+1	−8	...	+16	−2	−8
1936	+52	−16	+5	−13	...	+35	−2	−28
1937	+57	−20	+5	−19	...	+37	−3	+4
1938	+37	−23	+6	−21	...	+14	−2	+12
1939	+42	−23	+5	−21	...	+19	−1	+15
1940	+23	−14	+11	−19	+9	+4	−6	−12
1941	+78	−30	...	−31	+47	+47	−13	−39
1942	+36	−49	...	−30	−13	−14	+16	−86
1943	+173	−38	...	−22	+135	+139	+4	−104
1944	+219	−58	...	−27	+160	+169	−15	−202
1945	+171	−53	...	−21	+118	+120	−5	−102
1946	+198	−96	−18	—	+103	+95	+17	+69
1947	+185	−143	−31	—	+41	+32	−48	+84
1948	+177	−125	−33	—	+52	+44	−2	−24
1949	+124	−95	−12	—	+29	+24	−6	−1
1950	+91	−113	−15	—	−22	−23	−9	+1

Dominican Republic
(pesos)

	VB	IB	TTB	IIB	GSIB	OCB	(LT)CB	CR
1939	+7.6	−8.2	−0.2	−4.0	−0.6	−1.2	+1.6[3]	−0.3[4]
1946	+39.7	−20.1	−1.6	−5.3	+19.6	+18.8	−2.9[3]	+2.0[4]
1947	+29.7	−25.8	−1.8	−18.1	+3.9	+2.9	−0.1[3]	—
1948	+17.0	−23.9	−1.6	−15.9	−6.9	−7.4	+9.4[3]	−2.0[4]
1949	+27.7	−21.0	−1.0	−12.4	+6.7	+6.1	−0.3[3]	—
1950	+43.9	−23.7	−1.1	−11.8	+20.2	+19.2	−6.6[3]	—

El Salvador
(colones)

	VB	IB	TTB	IIB	GSIB	OCB	(LT)CB	CR
1938	+4.6	−3.0	+0.1	−0.8	+1.6	+1.7	+1.3[3]	—
1946	+12.9	−5.0	−1.8	−1.6	+7.9	+8.5	+10.0[3]	−1.9[4]
1947	+7.7	−1.3	−2.2	−2.5	+6.4	+6.9	−6.6[5]	+5.2
1948	+9.4	−6.2	−2.3	−3.1	+3.2	+3.2	−2.1[5]	−0.7
1949	+38.6	−5.5	−1.7	−2.8	+33.1	+33.0	−6.6[5]	−25.7
1950	+48.3	−14.1	−7.4	−3.9	+34.2	+34.6	—	−5.4

Guatemala[5]
(quetzales)

	VB	IB	TTB	IIB	GSIB	OCB	(LT)CB	CR
1946	+19.6	−12.0	+0.5	−8.0	+7.6	+8.5	−1.0	+5.8
1947	+17.9	−7.9	+1.3	−2.2	+10.0	+12.1	−6.3	−0.5
1948	+7.8	−13.6	+2.0	−7.1	−5.8	−3.7	−0.6	+5.9
1949	+1.5	−14.9	+1.5	−7.2	−13.4	−11.7	−11.3	+10.3
1950	+10.4	−10.4	+0.7	−2.8	—	—	+2.0	−1.3

Honduras
(lempiras)

	VB	IB	TTB	IIB	GSIB	OCB	(LT)CB	CR
1947	+23.8	−43.9	−0.5	−44.8	−20.1	−21.7	+21.1[3]	—
1948	+36.7	−43.3	−0.7	−45.1	−6.6	−8.3	+6.7[3]	—
1949	+39.3	−46.4	−0.6	−36.8	−7.1	−8.6	+7.5[3]	—
1950	+51.1	−50.4	−0.7	−41.4	+0.7	−0.9	−2.2[3]	—

J3　NORTH AMERICA: Balance of Payments (in millions of stated currency)

	Mexico (US dollars)							
	VB	**IB**	**TTB**	**IIB**	**GSIB**	**OCB**	**CB**	**CR**
1910	+20	−159	...	...	...	−139	...	...
1926	+283[18]	−315[18]	...	...	...[18]	−32[18]	...	...
1938	+80.5[18]	−31.4[18]	+8.2	−40.7	+49.1[18]	+51.1[18]	+4.2	−4.8
1939	+27.7	+2.2	...		+29.9	+32.8	...	...
1940	+15.2	−7.8	...	...	+7.4	+11.1	...	...
1941	−50.5	−7.9	...	...	−58.4	−56.4	...	...
1942	+22.9	−10.6[18]	...	...	+12.3[18]	+13.0	...	...
1943	+27.5	−15.5	...	...	+12.0	+48.2	...	...
1944	−72.6	−2.9	...	...	−75.5	−23.8	...	...
1945	−42.2[18]	+1.3[18]	...	...	−90.9[18]	−32.7[18]	...	...
1946	−234.8	+48.2	+87.5	−46.6	−186.6	−167.5	−46.7	+120.5
1947	−245.8	+23.8	+82.8	−92.6	−222.0	−186.8	+84.7	+218.6
1948	−137.1	+49.6	+104.1	−77.0	−87.5	−77.9	+65.6	+64.5
1949	−65.2	+96.1	+133.3	−56.8	+30.9	+55.6	−40.1	−49.6
1950	−64.2	+32.5	+155.6	−76.4	−31.7	−47.0	−129.5	−195.7

	Nicaragua[5] (cordobas)							
1938	+4.0	−5.1	...	...	−1.1	−1.1	...	...
1946	−20.0	+4.8	...	−20.5	−15.2	−3.8	...	...
1947	+6.5	−33.0	—	−22.0	−26.5	−23.5	+3.4	+2.5
1948	+21.0	−42.0	−3.5	−23.5	−21.0	−15.5	−1.5	+2.2
1949	+21.5	−39.5	−3.0	−23.5	−18.0	−17.0	+1.2	−1.6
1950	+66.9	−64.8	−8.9	−41.6	+2.1	+3.4	−0.7	+0.9

J3 NORTH AMERICA: Balance of Payments (in millions of stated currency)

	USA (dollars)						
	VB	IB	TTB	IIB	GSIB	OCB[6]	CB[5,7]
1790	−3	—	...	−4	−1	−1	...
1791	−10	+1	...	−4	−8	−8	...
1792	−10	+1	...	−4	−8	−8	...
1793	−5	+6	...	−5	+2	+2	...
1794	—	+9	...	−5	+10	+9	...
1795	−25	+12	...	−4	−12	−13	...
1796	−17	+14	...	−5	−3	−4	...
1797	−20	+9	...	−5	−11	−11	...
1798	−10	+8	...	−6	−2	−2	...
1799	−1	+15	...	−6	+15	+15	...
1800	−19	+17	...	−5	−2	−2	...
1801	−19	+21	...	−5	+2	+2	...
1802	−3	+10	...	−5	+7	+7	...
1803	−8	+17	...	−4	+8	−3	...
1804	−6	+18	...	−5	+12	+12	...
1805	−31	+21	...	−4	−10	−10	...
1806	−32	+24	...	−4	−7	−7	...
1807	−37	+31	...	−5	−5	−5	...
1808	−32	+16	...	−5	−17	−17	...
1809	−6	+18	...	−6	+12	+12	...
1810	−23	+29	...	−6	+7	+7	...
1811	+2	+34	...	−5	+35	+35	...
1812	−44	+23	...	−3	−21	−21	...
1813	+10	+6	...	−4	+15	+15	...
1814	−8	−1	...	−3	−9	−9	...
1815	−30	+15	...	−4	−15	−15	...
1816	−67	+9	...	−5	−58	−58	...
1817	−13	+2	...	−7	−11	−11	...
1818	−33	+7	...	−6	−25	−25	...
1819	−22	+7	...	−6	−15	−15 [6]	...
1820	−5	+4	−2	−5	+1	+2	−1
1821	+3	+1	−2	−5	+4	+5	−5
1822	−10	+1	−1	−5	−9	−9	+8
1823	−3	+5	−1	−5	+2	+2	−2
1824	−4	+5	−1	−5	—	+1	−1
1825	+4	+2	−2	−5	+6	+7	−7
1826	−7	+3	−2	−5	−4	−3	+3
1827	+3	+4	−2	−5	+8	+10	−10
1828	−12	+2	−1	−4	−14	−12	+11
1829	−2	—	−2	−5	—	+2	−2

International Historical Statistics: The Americas 1750–1993

J3 NORTH AMERICA: Balance of Payments (in millions of stated currency)

	USA (dollars)						
	VB	IB	TTB	IIB	GSIB	OCB	CB[5,7]
1830	+3	+3	—	−5	+6	+8	−8
1831	−21	+6	—	−4	−15	−14	+14
1832	−15	+3	—	−5	−12	−7	+7
1833	−20	+1	—	−5	−19	−14	+14
1834	−24	—	−1	−6	−24	−18	+19
1835	−31	−3	−2	−7	−33	−30	+30
1836	−65	−4	−2	−9	−68	−58	+59
1837	−26	−2	−2	−9	−28	−21	+22
1838	−7	—	−4	−10	−7	−4	+3
1839	−44	−10	−4	−14	−53	−49	+49
1840	+24	+3	−5	−12	+26	+30	−31
1841	−8	−4	−5	−8	−12	−8	+8
1842	+3	−3	−4	−8	+1	+7	−6
1843	+19	—	−2	−7	+20	+22	−22
1844	+1	−1	−4	−7	—	+4	−4
1845	−5	+2	−3	−9	−2	+4	−4
1846	−12	+2	−1	−9	−10	+1	−1
1847	+9	−7	−2	−9	+3	+19	−19
1848	−6	−9	—	−12	−15	−2	+2
1849	−8	−1	+1	−12	−8	+8	−3
1850	−32	−12	−4	−12	−44	−24	+29
1851	−6	−14	−19	−13	−20	−5	+6
1852	−10	−23	−16	−15	−33	−16	+16
1853	−48	−27	−21	−16	−75	−56	+56
1854	−35	−28	−21	−20	−63	−42	+42
1855	+7	−29	−21	−22	−22	−14	+15
1856	+2	−22	−17	−23	−20	−12	+12
1857	−9	−21	−14	−15	−30	−16	+17
1858	+33	−15	−15	−15	+17	+24	−23
1859	+6	−37	−25	−23	−32	−26	+26
1860	+25	−25	−18	−25	−1	+7	−7
1861	−83	−20	−14	−24	−103	−104	+103
1862	+37	−35	−13	−30	—	—	—
1863	+27	−41	−14	−31	−15	−12	+13
1864	−51	−63	−17	−34	−114	−111	+111
1865	+5	−69	−22	−45	−64	−59	+59
1866	−13	−78	−24	−51	−91	−95	+95
1867	−61	−89	−24	−58	−149	−145	+145
1868	+13	−89	−24	−67	−77	−73	+73
1869	−85	−89	−15	−69	−172	−175	+176

J3   NORTH AMERICA: Balance of Payments (in millions of stated currency)

	USA (dollars)							
	VB	**IB**	**TTB**	**IIB**	**GSIB**	**OCB**	**CB**[5,7]	**CR**
1870	−2	−99	−19	−80	−101	−100	+100	...
1871	+7	−108	−22	−84	−101	−101	+101	...
1872	−123	−122	−28	−86	−246	−242	+242	...
1873	−52	−128	−23	−99	−181	−183	+167	...
1874	+76	−138	−27	−102	−61	−72	+82	−11
1875	+34	−134	−27	−99	−99	−113	+87	+27
1876	+142	−123	−25	−96	+20	+9	+2	−10
1877	+212	−109	−20	−86	+102	+89	−57	−33
1878	+318	−96	−25	−76	+218	+207	−162	−44
1879	+315	−113	−31	−78	+202	+194	−160	−34
1880	+235	−121	−28	−79	+114	+110	+30	−140
1881	+264	−127	−28	−88	+137	+132	−41	−91
1882	+77	−132	−32	−84	−55	−68	+110	−42
1883	+127	−139	−32	−89	−12	−34	+51	−17
1884	+92	−151	−41	−90	−59	−83	+105	−23
1885	+157	−145	−41	−86	+12	−15	+34	−19
1886	+83	−160	−45	−93	−77	−105	+137	−32
1887	+15	−172	−51	−98	−157	−185	+231	−46
1888	−41	−185	−53	−107	−226	−256	+287	−30
1889	+24	−191	−48	−118	−166	−210	+202	+8
1890	+56	−205	−53	−125	−150	−195	+194	+1
1891	+122	−211	−56	−134	−90	−140	+136	+4
1892	+196	−216	−55	−143	−20	−74	+41	+33
1893	+76	−195	−36	−139	−119	−163	+146	+17
1894	+251	−152	−25	−113	+98	+44	−66	+22
1895	+81	−208	−61	−126	−127	−182	+137	+44
1896	+232	−198	−56	−122	+34	−15	+40	−25
1897	+333	−201	−54	−127	+132	+91	−23	−68
1898	+651	−208	−60	−133	+444	+400	−279	−121
1899	+628	−201	−60	−124	+427	+379	−229	−130
1900	+640$_8$	−212$_8$	−79$_8$	−114$_8$	+429$_8$	+375$_8$	−296$_8$	−78$_8$
	+774	−247	−112	−99	+507	+412	−218	−91
1901	+673	−235	−122	−88	+438	+334	−245	−61
1902	+477	−219	−115	−80	+258	+153	−135	−71
1903	+556	−216	−118	−72	+340	+225	−21	−71
1904	+501	−222	−127	−71	+279	+152	−10	−25
1905	+536	−238	−142	−69	+298	+165	−83	−71
1906	+556	−260	−164	−62	+296	+149	+68	−171
1907	+582	−286	−189	−66	+296	+119	+23	−154
1908	+721	−294	−193	−71	+427	+235	−46	−44
1909	+335	−309	−210	−64	+26	−161	+59	+18

International Historical Statistics: The Americas 1750–1993

J3 NORTH AMERICA: Balance of Payments (in millions of stated currency)

	USA (dollars)							
	VB	IB	TTB	IIB	GSIB	OCB	(LT)CB[5,7]	CR
1910	+386	−340	−227	−64	+46	−158	+255	−71
1911	+652	−378	−248	−76	+274	+50	+48	−90
1912	+666	−409	−257	−74	+257	+45	+23	−81
1913	+771	−397	−261	−73	+374	+167	+77	−25
1914	+415	−359	−233	−55	+56	−114	−522	+100
1915	+1,873	−125	−136	+64	+1,748	+1,598	−1,579	−499
1916	+3,137	−35	−101	+132	+3,102	+2,952	−1,455	−531
1917	+3,392	+83	−66	+250	+3,475	+3,270	−630	−312
1918	+3,329	−871	−39	+350	+2,458	+2,190	−396	−5
1919	+4,896	−28	−67	+489	+4,868	+3,824	−384	+166
1920	+3,097	+426	−123	+476	+3,523	+2,844	−832	+68
1921	+2,014	+108	−124	+340	+2,122	+1,613	−592	−735
1922	+745	+252	−182	+565	+997	+645	−815[5]	−269
1923	+400	+442	−189	+710	+842	+277	−45	−315
1924	+1,057	+294	−226	+722	+1,351	+987	−700	−256
1925	+720	+367	−264	+732	+1,087	+684	−570	+100
1926	+422	+404	−262	+753	+826	+445	−716	−93
1927	+742	+331	−286	+741	+1,073	+716	−1,037	+133
1928	+1,090	+287	−327	+805	+1,377	+1,012	647[9]	+238
1929	+884	+264	−344	+809	+1,148	+771	−278	−143
1930	+825	+207	−334	+745	+1,032	+690	−298	−310
1931	+374	+142	−247	+546	+516	+197	+194	+133
1932	+324	+83	−194	+392	+407	+169	+225	−53
1933	+226	+132	−133	+322	+358	+150	+77	+131
1934	+475	+126	−137	+302	+601	+229	+200	−1,266
1935	−58	+186	−144	+366	+128	−54	+436	−1,822
1936	+44	+71	−180	+299	+115	−93	+777	−1,272
1937	+270	+27	−213	+282	+297	+62	+521	−1,364
1938	+1,070	+221	−173	+385	+1,291	+1,109	+97	−1,799
1939	+938	+128	−155	+311	+1,066	+888	+27	−3,174
1940	+1,426	+292	−95	+354	+1,719	+1,509	−22	−4,243
1941	+1,927	+484	−142	+357	+2,410	+1,274	−261	−719
1942	+5,688	+725	−73	+356	+6,413	+77	−149	+23
1943	+10,516	+522	−89	+354	+11,038	−1,869	−23	+757
1944	+11,926	+526	−108	+412	+12,452	−1,691	+284	+1,350
1945	+7,228	−1,187	−147	+358	+6,041	−1,072	−300	+548
1946	+6,697	+1,110	−191	+756	+7,807	+5,515	−887	−623
1947	+10,124	+1,493	−209	+1,047	+11,617	+8,992	−896	−3,315
1948	+5,708	+810	−297	+1,262	+6,518	+1,993	−962	−1,736
1949	+5,339	+879	−308	+1,273	+6,218	+780	−621	−266
1950	+1,122	+770	−335	+1,460	+1,892	−2,125	−702	+1,758

J3 SOUTH AMERICA: BALANCE OF PAYMENTS (in millions of stated currency)

				Argentina[10] (pesos)				
	VB	IB	TTB	IIB	GSIB	OCB	CB	CR
1919	+302	−215	...		...	+87	+64	—
1920	+328	−211	...		...	+117	−123	−78
1921–22	−111	−363	...		...	−474	+185	+19
1923	−79	−202	...		...	−123	+40	+2
1924–25	+178	−421	...		...	−243	+208	+31
1926	−52[10]	−190[10]	...		...	−242[10]	+34[10]	−2[10]
	+255	−523		−416	...	−268	+271	−5
1927	+656	−605	...	—	...	+51	+170	−196
1928	+526	−638	...	−468	...	−112	+259	−197
1929	+237	−616	...	−48	...	−379	−16	+403
1930	−266	−585	...	−468	...	−319	+635	+71
1931	+301	−561	...	−483	...	−260	−302	+562
1932	+469	−526	...	−459	...	−57	−80	+18
1933	+230	−477	...	−426	...	−247	+236	—
1934	+508	−535	...	−482	...	−27	+114	+61
1935	+551	−537	...	−472	...	+14	+36	+12
1936	+668[11]	−551[11]	...	−469[11]	...	+117[11]	+310[11]	−2[11]
1937	+869	−475	...	−432	...	+394	−430	+77
1938	−109	−391	...	−366	...	−500	+53	+456
1939	+350	−406	...	−431	...	−56	+66	−165
1940	+167	−321	...	−375	...	−154	+63	+63
1941	+447	−275	...	−405	...	+171	+304	−481
1942	+627	−324	...	−480	...	+303	+100	−507
1943	+1,246	−154	...	−372	...	+1,092	−115	−1,099
1944	+1,409	−319	...	−483	...	+1,090	−227	−1,008
1945	+1,459[3]	−204[3]	...	−383[3]	...	+1,255[3]	−100[3]	−1,198[3]
1946	+1,679	−251	...	−451	...	+1,428	−1,102	−239
1947	+100	−198	...	−276	...	−98	−511	+989
1948	+122	+60	...	−34	...	+182	−2,052	−1,650
1949	−694	+4	...	−49	...	−690	+44	+198
1950	+611	−43	...	−14	...	+568	+35	+48

				Bolivia (U.S. dollars)			
1938	−0.8	−3.4	...	−5.1	...	−4.2	
1939	+7.7	−9.5	...	−9.7	...	−1.8	
1940	+14.0	−11.6	...	−11.7	...	+2.4	
1947	+10.6	−19.8	−1.4	−9.2	−9.2	−8.8	
1948	+28.3	−32.2	−1.5	−17.2	−3.9	−3.6	
1949	+9.3	−19.9	−1.8	−1.2	−10.6	−10.3	
1950	−20.4	−20.9	−1.3	−3.6	−0.5	−0.1	

J3　SOUTH AMERICA: Balance of Payments (in millions of stated currency)

	Brazil[5] (cruzeiros)							
	VB	**IB**	**TTB**	**IIB**	**GSIB**	**OCB**	**(LT)CB**	**CR**
1947	+2,410	−5,094	−597	−1,013	−2,684	−3,120	−598	+763
1948	+5,151	−5,641	−94	−1,943	−490	−817	+477	−1,495
1949	+2,830	−5,009	−28	−1,881	−2,179	−2,232	−138	+866
1950	−7,859	−5,867	−55	−2,034	+1,992	+1,947	−598	+4,913

	Chile (US dollars)							
1938	+37.9	−51.8	+2.1	−59.3	...	−13.9	+1.5	...
1942	+20.2	−4.8	+1.1	−13.5	+15.4	+15.4	+14.4	+2.9
1943	+42	−3	+3.5	−12.2	...	+40	+4.5	−37.5
1944	+52	−25	+3.6	−30.6	...	+26	−6.7	−21.8
1945	+44[7]	−16[7]	...	...	...[7]	+28[7]	...[7]	...
1946	+11.0	−40.1	+0.8	−37.6	−29.2	−29.2	...	+14.8
1947	+7.0	−54.9	+0.9	−57.5	−47.9	−47.3	−31.8	+19.5
1948	+62.3	−70.8	+1.2	−73.0	−8.5	−6.5	+14.6	+1.9
1949	−34.2	−50.9	+1.0	−57.8	−85.1	−83.4	+74.5	+0.2
1950	+149.6	−61.9	+0.1	−58.1	+87.7	+87.7	+9.1	−0.3

	Colombia (pesos)							
1938	+17.7	−31.5	−8.8	...	...	−13.8	+10.0	−13.8
1946	−34.5	−40.6	−13.0	−16.6	...	−75.1	+129.1	−32.9
1947	−178.6	−44.0	−16.5	−14.9	...	−222.6	+58.2	+108.7
1948	−61.3	−26.9	−4.8	−11.4	...	−88.2	+27.5	+54.4
1949	+121.7	−94.3	−9.0	−27.0	...	+27.4	−70.6	−0.6
1950	+140.3	−115.4	−12.9	−77.0	+24.9	−26.5	+104.1	−43.7

	Ecuador (US dollars)							
1939	+7.6	−8.2	...	...	−0.6	−1.2	...	...
1946	+9.5	−11.4	−3.6	−1.2	−1.9	−1.5	+3.5	−0.1
1947	+4.3	−11.0	−2.7	−3.3	−6.7	−6.3	+15	+1.1
1948	+3.2	−14.2	−1.8	−5.6	−11.4	−10.9	+8.1	−0.2
1949	−4.0	−15.9	−2.1	−7.3	−19.9	−18.0	+18.9	−0.1
1950	+36.4	−17.0	−2.6	−7.8	+19.4	+20.7	−19.8	+1.9

	Paraguay (US dollars)							
1948	+2.5	−7.1	−0.1	−1.0	−4.6	−3.9	+1.6	+2.9
1949	+3.0	−5.5	−0.8	−0.4	−2.6	−2.1	−1.1	+3.1
1950	+14.8	−6.2	−0.7	−0.5	+8.6	+9.0	−0.6	−9.4

J3   SOUTH AMERICA: Balance of Payments (in millions of stated currency)

Peru
(soles)

	VB	IB	TTB	IIB	GSIB	OCB	LTCB	CR
1938	+63.5	−110.3	−2	−118	−46.8	−42.3	−3.5	+19.5
1939	+114.8	−107.3	...	−111	+7.5	+14.0	−8.5	+7.8
1940	+82.0	−98.6	...	−101	−16.6	−9.6	+13.8	−4.1
1941	+130.2	−121.2	...	−103	+9.1	+10.2	−5.2	+10.6
1942	+218.6	−123.9	...	−107	+94.7	+100.9	+4.7	−63.1
1943	+124.6[7]	−115.1[7]	...[7]	−99[7]	+9.5[7]	+15.9[7]	+28.8[7]	−26.0[7]
1946	+150	−299	−24	−120	−149	−124	−391	+231
1947	+99	−260	−7	−73	−161	−145	−81	+165
1948	+182	−247	−10	−88	−65	−42	+79	−64
1949	+305	−468	+21	−167	−163	−98	+151	−93
1950	+818	−928	−61	−144	−111	−54	−135	−3

Uruguay
(US dollars)

	VB	IB	TTB	IIB	GSIB	OCB	LTCB	CR
1930	+4.6	−22.2	...	−20.5	...	−17.6	+2.5[5]	+6.7
1931	−22.1	−14.2	...	−12.8	...	−26.3	+4.85[5]	+4.9
1940	+18.9	−3.3	+0.8	−7.0	+15.6	+18.8	−0.8	−15.2[4]
1941	+9.8	−5.0	+0.9	−8.2	+4.8	+6.2	+1.8	−9.6[4]
1942	−8.6	−5.5	+0.2	−7.3	−14.1	−13.6	−2.1	+10.5[4]
1943	+38.1	−3.9	+1.5	−8.5	+34.2	+34.1	−1.7	−31.4[4]
1944	+27.1	−2.7	+3.0	−8.2	...	+24.4	−1.6	−36.0[4]
1946	+8.9	+4.2	+9.2	−9.1	+13.1	+11.6	+7.9	−23.9
1947	−47.6	+9.4	+14.8	−6.6	−38.2	−39.1	+16.8	+20.5
1948	−20.2	+8.1	+14.5	−6.0	−12.1	−13.1	+6.2	+11.3
1949	+7.4	+2.5	+8.1	−4.9	+9.9	+8.6	−22.3	−41.2
1950	+49.4	−0.1	+6.1	−4.5	+49.3	+47.8	+5.5	−51.3

Venezuela
(US dollars)

	VB	IB	TTB	IIB	GSIB	OCB	LTCB	CR
1938	+83	−73	...	...	+10	+10	...	...
1942	+16	−3	−1.7	−1.5	...	+13	+3.7	−21.6
1943	+26	−2	−1.1	−1.5	...	+24	+2.7	−26.9
1944	+47	−1	−0.6	−1.3	...	+46	+1.7	−49.6
1946	+201	−206	...	−158	−5	−17	...	...
1947	+136	−327	...	−250	−191	−202	+222	+11
1948	+373	−513	...	−435	−140	−156	+343	−128
1949	+266	−424	−23	−288	−158	−176	+270	−60
1950	+655	−528	−34	−392	+127	+112	−2	+80

J3   NORTH AMERICA: BALANCE OF PAYMENTS (in million US dollars)

PART B. 1950-88 in US dollars.

	Canada							
	VB	IB	TTB	IIB	GSIB	OCB	LTCB	CR[2]
1950	+200	−534	−63	−381	−334	−319	+610	+722
1951	−1	−527[12]	−6	−337	−528[12]	−512	+666	+56
1952	+635	−479	−66	−261	+186	+187	+455	+37
1953	+84	−522	−63	−242	−438	−448	+649	−38
1954	+173	−591	−84	−277	−418	−424	+599	+124
1955	−56	−597	−121	−331	−653	−687	+414	−44
1956	−581	−746	−161	−382	−1,327	−1,372	+1,490	+48
1957	−450	−950	−162	−441	−1,400	−1,451	+1,320	—
1958	−19	−993	−193	−447	−1,012	−1,137	+1,153	−109
1959	−273	−1,101	−208	−491	−1,374	−1,487	+1,179	−11
1960	+12[13]	−1,121[13]	−207	−485[13]	−1,107[13]	−1,233[13]	+929[13]	−39[2]
	−224	−893		−522	−1,117	−1,338		−41
1961	+186	−812	−160	−617	−998	−936	+451	+279
1962	+215	−571	−43	−652	−786	−774	+374	+562
1963	+500	−1,001	+24	−720	−501	−480	+134	+54
1964	+717	−1,105	−50	−768	−388	−382	+162	+282
1965	+148	−869	−49	−853	−1,017	−1,012	+379	+22
1966	+250	−1,304	−56	−873	−1,054	−1,027	+726	−230
1967	+590	−1,088	+391	−1,174	−498	−455	+523	+46
1968	+1,446	−1,674	−26	−1,157	−228	−80	+338	+481
1969	+973	−1,958	−197	−1,148	−985	−888	+324	+51
1970	+3,047	−2,167	−197	−1,323	+880	−1,008	+1,034	+1,654
1971	+2,672	−2,543	−201	−1,569	+129	+363	+1,028	+951
1972	+2,172	−2,672	−233	−1,565	−500	−278	+1,955	+377
1973	+3,181	−3,172	−283	−1,669	+9	+305	+519	−374
1974	+2,087	−3,920	−286	−2,404	−1,833	−1,324	+1,885	+43
1975	−271	−4,609	−713	−2,638	−4,880	−4,571	+4,247	−500
1976	+1,884	−6,573	−1,195	−3,733	−4,689	−4,152	+7,711	+495
1977	+3,137	−7,535	−1,566	−4,446	−4,398	−4,101	+4,606	−1,262
1978	+4,180	−8,411	−1,529	−5,331	−4,231	−4,285	+989	−118
1979	+4,178	−8,739	−906	−6,088	−4,561	−4,138	+1,628	−731
1980	+8,001	−9,865	−1,054	−6,695	−1,864	−967	+916	−555
1981	+6,584	−12,799	−886	−9,483	−6,215	−5,110	+74	+214
1982	+14,996	−13,934	−1,062	−10,272	+1,062	+2,231	+5,680	−576
1983	+14,989	−16,516	−1,790	−9,412	+1,527	+2,487	−690	+425
1984	+15,984	−16,527	−1,672	−10,419	−543	+1,995	+3,307	−986
1985	+12,587	−16,927	−1,544	−10,498	−4,340	−1,470	+1,534	+1
1986	+7,677	−17,980	−829	−11,800	−10,303	−10,107	+10,356	+591
1987	+8,961	−20,721	−1,898	−12,204	−11,760	−11,801	+10,646	+3,491
1988	+8,157	−25,520	−2,268	−19,810	−17,363	−17,106	+12,965	+7,521
1989	+5,985	−28,975	−3,503	−21,152	−22,990	−22,728	+21,497	−264
1990	+8,334	−29,844	−5,613	−19,571	−21,510	−21,548	+14,788	−1,276
1991	+3,871	−27,565	−6,430	−16,741	−23,694	−24,052	+13,505	+2,231
1992	+5,699	−27,399	−6,616	−16,607	−21,700	−27,060	+10,272	+5,843
1993	+7,927	−31,796	−5,985	−20,199	−22,690	−23,869	+19,975	+347

J3   NORTH AMERICA: Balance of Payments (in million US dollars)

	VB	IB	TTB	IIB	GSIB	OCB	LTCB	CR
					Costa Rica			
1950	+15.2	−12.7	−0.9	−13.5	+2.5	+2.6	+0.5	+1.1
1951	+13.2	−13.4	−1.5	−12.1	−0.2	+0.8	+2.4	−4.7
1952	+12.7	−18.7	−2.0	−14.7	−5.8	−4.4	+1.0	−6.2
1953	+14.5	−16.2	−2.0	−11.9	−1.6	−0.5	−0.1	−0.2
1954	+14.8	−14.9	−0.4	−11.7	−0.3	+2.0	−0.1	−7.3
1955	+3.0	−11.3	+0.2	−7.6	−8.2	−5.3	+10.5	−3.9
1956	−16.9	−2.5	+0.6	−1.2	−19.4	−16.4	+1.3	+7.8
1957	−9.3	−10.6	+1.0	−6.9	−19.9	−12.7	+2.3	—
1958	+4.2	−13.1	+1.4	−8.9	−8.9	+0.6	+7.3	−7.8
1959	−17.5	−8.3	+1.0	−3.7	−25.8	−19.2	+9.0₁₄	+6.2
1960	−11.9	−8.2	+1.7	−3.7	−20.1	−16.0	+1.9	+1.2
1961	−12.7	−7.0	+1.9	−2.7	−19.7	−12.6	+7.8	+7.1
1962	−9.7	−12.1	+1.0	−8.2	−21.8	−17.2	+21.2	−6.2
1963	−17.8	−12.6	+2.0	−8.3	−30.4	−21.5	+34.8	−2.8
1964	−11.4	−17.5	+1.7	−10.8	−28.9	−19.4	+24.8	−2.7
1965	−49.2	−27.0	+0.4	−13.4	−76.2	−67.8	+33.0	−2.7
1966	−26.4	−26.1	+2.3	−14.9	−52.5	−44.0	+41.7	+2.7
1967	−30.4	−28.6	+1.9	−17.0	−59.0	−50.2	+19.2	−4.8
1968	−23.7	−27.8	+3.4	−18.6	−51.5	−42.9	+22.9	−4.7
1969	−31.9	−26.8	+5.5	−16.4	−58.7	−50.3	+31.6	−7.7
1970	−55.8	−24.2	+9.4	−13.6	−80.0	−74.1	+43.8	+11.6
1971	−92.0	−29.8	+7.2	−14.6	−121.8	−114.4	+57.1	−13.0
1972	−58.3	−48.3	+10.9	−34.9	−106.6	−100.0	+80.1	−19.9
1973	−67.4	−51.7	+14.4	−38.0	−119.1	−112.2	+92.4	−16.5
1974	−208.8	−67.0	+21.2	−38.6	−275.8	−266.1	+135.9	+10.0
1975	−134.2	−93.1	+16.8	−64.2	−227.3	−217.7	+221.6	+4.6
1976	−103.0	−111.7	+12.9	−73.1	−214.7	−201.5	+203.2	−66.5
1977	−97.3	−144.1	+11.0	−79.7	−241.4	−225.6	+292.1	−107.6
1978	−185.5	−194.3	+10.8	−113.3	−379.8	−363.2	+334.4	−21.7
1979	−315.1	−255.3	+10.3	−149.6	−570.4	−558.2	+347.6	+87.5
1980	−374.3	−304.1	+24.5	−218.5	−678.4	−663.9	+387.5	−98.1
1981	−88.0	−348.2	+47.2	−307.3	−436.2	−409.1	+188.5	+20.9
1982	+64.1	−366.7	+89.0	−378.8	−302.6	−271.7	−73.9	−127.4
1983	−41.8	−307.1	+80.6	−342.5	−348.9	−312.6	−65.9	−160.0
1984	+4.6	−296.6	+66.2	−323.7	−292.0	−251.1	−182.8	+93.4
1985	−61.9	−282.8	+64.5	−294.5	−344.7	−291.1	−131.8	−83.5
1986	+39.6	−271.5	+71.4	−288.8	−231.9	−160.6	−252.2	−78.2
1987	−138.5	−343.9	+67.6	−309.7	−482.4	−376.4	−411.1	−11.4
1988	−97.9	−336.0	+105.3	−359.7	−433.9	−303.5	−227.0	−225.9
1989	−238.6	−304.1	+94.0	−380.0	−542.7	−479.9	−222.0	−149.6
1990	−442.5	−173.4	+129.0	−245.0	−615.9	−494.9	−71.0	+197.2
1991	−199.5	−17.3	+186.0	−187.0	−216.8	−99.2	+80.0	−352.0
1992	−497.6	−46.1	+213.0	−216.0	−543.7	−371.2	+134.0	−146.8
1993	−663.0	+40.1	+318.0	−242.0	−622.9	−470.0	+191.0	+61.2

J3   NORTH AMERICA: Balance of Payments (in million US dollars)

	Dominican Republic							
	VB	IB	TTB	IIB	GSIB	OCB	LTCB	CR
1950	+43.9	−23.7	−1.1	−11.8	+20.2	+19.2	−2.0	−4.6
1951	+42.6	−35.4	−0.3	−26.5	+7.2	+6.3	+0.6	−10.3
1952	+19.6	−23.8	−1.5	−14.4	−4.2	−5.3	+2.0	−2.5
1953	+18.3	−14.4	−1.7	−5.4	+3.9	+3.1	−8.0	+4.0
1954	+37.6	−14.5	−1.7	−4.1	+23.1	+21.6	+6.4	−7.6
1955	+14.8	−23.6	−2.6	−12.3	−8.8	−10.7	−5.1	−1.4
1956	+11.8	−16.3	+2.3	−5.5	−4.5	−6.5	+5.4	−2.3
1957	+44.0	−20.9	−0.5	−11.6	+23.1	+20.2	−8.6	−8.2
1958	−8.0	−14.1	−1.4	−3.3	−22.1	−25.1	+34.1	+0.7
1959	+20.3	−21.9	−1.0	−14.2	−1.6	−1.7	+6.3	+5.7
1960	+67.1	−21.5	−2.1	−9.6	+45.6	+42.5	−0.3	+21.1
1961	+66.8	−31.8	−1.7	−18.4	+35.0	+33.0	−24.8	+16.8
1962	+37.3	−21.0	−13.7	−21.3	−16.3	−10.4	+14.7	−11.7
1963	+9.7	−58.3	−16.0	−19.9	−48.6	−19.4	+28.6	−21.3
1964	−23.0	−57.4	−16.9	−16.1	−80.4	−61.8	+56.0	+0.5
1965	+4.8	−38.5	−15.5	−12.0	−33.7		+4.8	+1.8
1966	−30.2	−61.2	−18.0	−20.0	−91.4	−74.9	+66.0	+7.2
1967	−18.5	−54.7	−20.5	−19.7	−73.2	−66.2	+61.6	+11.3
1968	−33.3	−51.9	−17.0	−19.0	−85.2	−75.2	+53.1	−3.2
1969	−33.8	−59.3	−18.3	−23.4	−93.1	−84.7	+82.7	−4.2
1970	−64.0	−69.1	−20.6	−25.9	−133.1	−101.9	+109.5	+7.7
1971	−69.0	−77.4	−15.1	−28.9	−146.4	−129.4	+81.5	−24.0
1972	+9.9	−87.5	−4.6	−46.9	−77.6	−47.0	+82.2	−2.5
1973	+20.2	−147.4	−13.7	−76.8	−127.2	−96.6	+69.6	−29.3
1974	−36.2	−239.8	−22.1	−89.7	−276.0	−241.0	+161.3	−2.8
1975	+121.1	−232.9	−16.4	−61.2	−111.8	−72.8	+159.2	−25.3
1976	−47.2	−208.6	−17.9	−55.6	−255.8	−129.2	+174.9	−10.5
1977	−68.8	−199.4	−9.8	−98.4	−268.2	−128.6	+173.2	−69.6
1978	−186.9	−274.8	−34.1	−135.7	−461.7	−311.9	+146.5	+38.1
1979	−268.9	−268.2	−34.2	−187.7	−537.1	−331.3	+260.3	−84.5
1980	−557.8	−367.6	+6.8	−210.2	−925.4	−719.9	+287.8	+31.4
1981	−263.7	−318.7	+78.5	−276.6	−582.4	−389.4	+150.5	−28.6
1982	−489.6	−158.0	+179.1	−254.8	−647.6	−442.6	+199.3	+112.7
1983	−493.8	−139.1	+232.6	−297.1	−632.9	−417.9	+62.6	−29.8
1984	−389.0	−39.4	+281.5	−241.4	−428.4	−163.4	+294.1	−57.7
1985	−547.4	+83.5	+367.5	−226.3	−463.9	−107.6	+185.5	−89.4
1986	−629.6	+153.1	+417.1	−249.7	−476.5	−185.5	+141.8	−11.1
1987	−880.2	+181.8	+475.8	−306.1	−698.4	−363.5	+69.0	+188.9
1988	−718.3	+345.8	+641.1	−270.6	−372.5	−18.9	+133.0	−124.7
1989	−1,039.4	+439.3	+682.0	−249.0	−600.1	−215.7	+100.0	−5.1
1990	−1,058.3	+581.5	+756.0	−249.0	−476.8	−106.2	−126.0	−1.8
1991	−1,070.5	+648.3	+723.0	−193.0	−422.2	−35.7	+102.0	−340.0
1992	−1,612.0	+735.0	+844.0	−218.0	−877.0	−445.2	+42.0	−46.0
1993	−1,588.0	+985.4	+1,068	−258.0	−602.6	−161.0	+94.0	−89.2

J3 NORTH AMERICA: Balance of Payments (in million US dollars)

	El Salvador							
	VB	IB	TTB	IIB	GSIB	OCB	LTCB	CR
1950	+19.3	−5.6	−5.4	−7.4	+13.7	+13.8	−2.3	−1.9
1951	+16.6	−8.2	−3.8	−1.6	+8.4	+8.7	+4.1	−1.6
1952	+18.2	−10.2	−4.1	−2.2	+8.0	+8.2	−0.1	−1.0
1953	+19.2	−11.2	−6.2	−2.4	+8.0	+8.7	+11.5	+0.2
1954	+17.9	−9.5	−6.6	−2.6	+8.4	+9.0	−17.7	−0.8
1955	+14.6	−13.0	−8.6	−2.6	+1.6	+2.1	−12.5	+5.5
1956	+18.0	−12.2	−7.8	−2.7	+5.8	+6.1	+3.0	+2.6
1957	+11.9	−9.7	−7.0	−2.5	+2.2	+3.1	+4.7	−5.0
1958	+9.7	−8.1	−3.6	−3.3	+1.6	+1.9	+4.7	+2.0
1959	+12.1	−11.7	−5.2	−3.6	+0.4	+0.6	−11.1₁₄	+4.7
1960	−20.0	−8.7	−4.0	−3.9	−28.7	−27.7	+7.4	+10.5
1961	+9.8	−12.4	−4.9	−4.3	−2.6	−0.4	+2.6	+8.1
1962	+14.0	−15.8	−6.0	−5.1	−1.8	+2.4	+6.3	−1.8
1963	−2.0	−15.3	−6.5	−5.8	−17.3	−10.1	+14.9	−15.9
1964	−16.3	−15.8	−7.2	−6.2	−32.1	−23.3	+16.4	−10.9
1965	+4.3	−30.2	−8.2	−7.7	−25.9	−12.6	+22.1	−5.2
1966	−12.0	−38.8	−8.6	−7.6	−50.8	−41.0	+33.9	+0.8
1967	+2.4	−37.7	−5.8	−8.6	−35.3	−23.4	+25.4	+2.1
1968	+13.5	−37.0	−6.6	−8.2	−23.5	−15.1	+19.0	−7.2
1969	+9.1	−42.1	−10.4	−8.4	−33.3	−19.8	+12.3	−1.8
1970	+41.4	−47.0	−11.9	−8.8	−5.6	+8.7	+4.9	+1.1
1971	+18.0	−49.2	−10.3	−6.5	−31.2	−14.2	+13.5	−0.7
1972	+52.0	−51.6	−9.6	−8.0	+0.4	+12.4	+62.2	−17.5
1973	+18.6	−76.1	−24.4	−8.6	−57.5	−43.9	+35.0	+22.6
1974	−57.7	−94.8	−21.3	−26.6	−152.5	−134.2	+94.9	−36.3
1975	−17.7	−102.6	−15.4	−40.8	−120.3	−92.9	+113.6	−29.4
1976	+63.7	−69.3	−13.4	−18.2	−5.6	+23.6	+72.9	−78.4
1977	+112.5	−121.3	−26.2	−37.7	−8.8	+30.8	+38.2	−26.1
1978	−149.4	−187.8	−66.6	−60.6	−337.2	−285.8	+165.8	−56.9
1979	+177.6	−207.6	−92.1	−49.0	−30.0	+21.4	+68.3	+125.2
1980	+178.4	−196.8	−92.7	−94.5	−18.4	+30.6	+109.5	+64.6
1981	−100.3	−210.5	−55.1	−100.8	−310.8	−250.4	+170.5	+5.8
1982	−100.2	−227.0	−71.6	−121.6	−327.2	−119.8	+151.8	−36.6
1983	−74.3	−225.1	−61.9	−135.2	−299.4	−148.0	+211.7	−49.7
1984	−188.6	−172.5	−43.7	−136.6	−361.1	−188.5	+33.9	−5.6
1985	−216.0	−156.3	−45.9	−118.5	−372.3	−188.7	+57.6	—
1986	−124.4	−142.0	−32.0	−122.4	−266.4	−17.1	+18.6	−34.8
1987	−349.1	−54.0	−32.4	−112.3	−403.1	−68.2	−36.7	−76.7
1988	−355.9	−118.8	−19.7	−121.6	−474.7	−129.2	+29.2	+18.5
1989	−591.7	−127.2	−46.0	−107.0	−718.9	−330.1	+139.0	−161.2
1990	−599.8	−105.5	+15.0	−137.0	−705.3	−235.0	+2.0	−154.0
1991	−706.1	−133.0	+14.0	−127.0	−839.1	−212.8	+22.0	+127.4
1992	−1,000.1	−45.9	+15.0	−104.0	−1,046.0	−194.9	−36.0	−134.9
1993	−1,053.0	−69.5	+17.0	−117.0	−1,122.5	−118.3	+100.0	−114.1

J3   NORTH AMERICA: Balance of Payments (in million US dollars)

				Guatemala				
	VB	IB	TTB	IIB	GSIB	OCB	LTCB	CR
1950	+10.4	−10.4	+0.7	−2.8	—	+0.3	+1.4	−1.3
1951	+3.6	−9.2	+0.1	+0.2	−5.6	−5.3	−0.5	−2.3
1952	+15.4	−3.2	−0.9	+6.9	+12.2	+12.2	−1.6	−3.2
1953	+21.0	−26.8	−0.1	+4.5	−5.8	+11.6	−0.9	+0.1
1954	+19.0	−24.0	−0.9	−2.5	−5.0	+1.5	+0.2	+2.5
1955	+8.2	−13.2	+2.3	−0.3	−5.0	+5.0	+7.6	−15.5
1956	−4.4	−3.4	+2.1	−2.4	−7.8	−7.8	+15.2	−15.7
1957	−20.2	−1.8	+2.4	−2.1	−18.4	−18.4	+23.6	−3.9
1958	−30.2	−19.8	+2.9	−3.4	−50.0	−38.2	+19.7	+26.0
1959	−20.6	−19.6	+3.3	−4.7	−40.2	−28.6	+25.5[14]	+5.1
1960	−8.9	−16.7	+2.3	−5.0	−25.6	−11.0	+21.5	−10.0
1961	−6.6	−17.6	+2.1	−6.7	−24.2	−7.9	+10.3	−1.1
1962	−3.9	−19.1	+1.8	−8.6	−23.0	−15.7	+6.2	+9.5
1963	+3.0	−23.8	−7.1	−4.7	−20.8	−17.3	+24.4	−12.5
1964	−6.2	−39.5	−7.6	−11.9	−45.7	−37.9	+23.0	−3.4
1965	−14.0	−28.1	−10.6	−11.2	−42.1	−34.6	+43.4	−8.9
1966	+30.1	−51.7	−18.2	−17.4	−21.6	−12.2	+24.0	+7.4
1967	−22.6	−48.7	−4.4	−19.4	−71.3	−62	+50.4	−5.2
1968	−4.1	−57.3	−3.4	−31.4	−61.4	−50.7	+51.4	−0.8
1969	+21.6	−54.0	+0.3	−35.7	−32.4	−19.0	+43.1	−10.0
1970	+30.5	−25.9	−2.4	−38.2	−25.4	−7.9	+55.0	−3.5
1971	−3.1	−71.4	−7.9	−41.9	−74.5	−49.2	+46.5	−13.4
1972	+41.1	−82.6	−7.4	−45.6	−41.5	−11.5	+33.0	−42.9
1973	+50.7	−85.4	−1.4	−45.9	−34.7	+7.7	+60.0	−77.3
1974	−49.2	−109.3	+4.9	−48.0	−158.5	−103.1	+100.1	+6.2
1975	−31.4	−111.1	+23.3	−66.0	−143.5	−65.7	+138.3	−102.6
1976	−190.3	−86.1	−16.0	−46.8	−276.4	−77.5	+76.3	−219.2
1977	+73.2	−54.4	−33.4	−19.0	−127.6	−35.3	+178.1	−183.1
1978	−191.4	−188.6	−39.8	−10.0	−380.0	−270.5	+247.6	−70.2
1979	−180.3	−151.5	−38.4	+5.2	−331.8	−205.6	+238.7	+18.2
1980	+47.2	−320.7	−102.6	−60.0	−273.5	−163.3	+229.1	+252.5
1981	−248.7	−414.9	−102.6	−45.7	−663.6	−572.7	+291.2	+199.3
1982	−113.9	−347.9	−88.3	−97.9	−461.8	−399.1	+269.1	+29.0
1983	+35.7	−290.2	−82.6	−95.2	−254.5	−223.9	+28.8	−9.0
1984	−50.0	−356.1	−50.1	−164.4	−406.1	−377.4	−48.1	−30.9
1985	−17.0	−249.0	−10.2	−159.8	−266.0	−246.3	−71.3	−62.3
1986	+168.1	−260.8	+14.0	−204.5	−92.7	−17.6	−302.2	−101.9
1987	−355.3	−300.5	+18.2	−171.6	−635.8	−442.5	−152.5	+62.2
1988	−339.9	−298.4	−33.1	−173.1	−638.3	−414.0	−89.0	+139.7
1989	−358.3	−258.6	−15.0	−191.0	−616.9	−367.1	−3.0	−84.4
1990	−216.6	−223.3	−18.0	−204.0	−439.9	−232.9	−55.0	+35.4
1991	−443.0	−0.4	−45.0	−140.0	−443.4	−183.7	+197.0	−553.9
1992	−1,044.0	−52.4	−83.0	−179.0	−1,096.4	−705.9	+132.0	+18.5
1993	−1,025.0	−39.9	−88.0	−151.0	−1,064.9	−687.4	+373.0	−143.8

J3 NORTH AMERICA: Balance of Payments (in million US dollars)

	VB	IB	TTB	IIB	GSIB	OCB	LTCB	CR
				Haiti[15]				
1950	+2.2	−4.0	+0.8	−4.6	−1.8	+1.3	+3.4	−2.2
1951	+5.7	−5.1	+0.1	−5.5	+0.6	+1.6	+5.9	−1.6
1952	+2.6	−3.0	−0.2	−3.8	−0.4	−1.0	+4.5	−2.8
1953	−6.7	−5.7	−0.1	−5.8	−12.4	−11.4	+9.3	+5.8
1954	+8.0	−13.4	−0.1	−2.6	−5.4	+6.0	+7.0	−4.5
1955	−17.1	—	+1.8	−1.7	−17.1	−15.3	+13.2	+2.7
1956	−6.7	+4.4	+3.9	−2.7	−2.3	+1.9	+8.6	+1.2
1957	−13.3	−1.2	+4.5	−1.9	−14.1	−10.1	−3.1	+3.2
1958	−5.4	−3.8	+4.2	−2.9	−9.2	−4.2	+8.4	+2.9
1959	−9.5	−0.9	+5.2	−3.3	−10.4	+4.2	+5.5	+1.6
1960	−5.3	−2.5	+4.3	−4.1	−7.8	+1.3	+6.8	−2.2
1961	−21.4	−3.1	+6.0	−3.4	−24.5	−10.1	+15.5	−2.8
1962	−7.1	−7.1	+3.3	−6.1	−14.2	−7.3	+8.9	+4.1
1963	+4.1	−14.2	−1.6	−4.7	−10.1	−3.2	−9.9	+2.5
1964	+0.8	−15.0	−3.5	−6.2	−14.2	−7.7	+18.8	+0.3
1965	−4.8	−17.7	−4.2	−5.2	−22.5	−13.7	+2.2[14]	+0.9
1966	−8.9	−14.3	−3.3	−3.7	−23.2	−6.2	+0.1	+0.3
1967	−8.0	−9.8	−1.2	−2.9	−17.8	−0.7	+0.3	+0.4
1968	−2.4	−8.1	+0.9	−3.1	−10.5	+2.3	+0.2	−0.6
1969	+4.4	−7.0	+1.6	−3.6	−2.6	+13.1	+2.1	−1.3
1970	−2.8	−8.0	+2.3	−3.6	−10.8	+11.1	+2.8	−0.6
1971	−17.5	−7.3	+5.8	−4.0	−24.8	−21.2	+2.7	−6.1
1972	−25.3	−7.1	+9.2	−4.5	−32.4	−22.7	+15.3	−7.5
1973	−27.5	−12.4	+11.8	−4.4	−39.9	−35.5	+1.3	+0.8
1974	−50.1	−20.7	+13.1	−5.9	−70.8	−64.2	+10.3	−2.7
1975	−69.9	−19.4	+17.7	−7.2	−89.3	−109.2	+36.1	+7.3
1976	−64.5	−35.1	+19.9	−7.0	−99.6	−102.3	+33.9	−15.5
1977	−62.3	−38.6	+23.9	−12.3	−100.9	−37.7	+68.0	−6.1
1978	−57.5	−55.0	+25.4	−15.0	−112.5	−44.9	+40.1	−5.0
1979	−82.1	−46.3	+32.2	−13.6	−128.4	−55.0	+61.2	−21.7
1980	−103.2	−86.4	+35.8	−14.2	−189.6	−101.1	+80.3	+35.2
1981	−209.0	−79.2	+42.7	−12.7	−288.2	−148.8	+111.1	−5.6
1982	−124.8	−75.5	+39.5	−14.1	−210.3	−98.6	+84.6	+20.7
1983	−139.3	−82.2	+46.1	−14.1	−221.5	−111.1	+85.3	−4.7
1984	−123.3	−102.7	+44.7	−18.1	−226.0	−103.0	+90.4	−4.0
1985	−121.7	−118.0	+55.3	−19.8	−239.7	−94.7	+53.8	+6.6
1986	−112.5	−84.3	+45.5	−15.3	−196.8	−44.9	+39.2	−8.2
1987	−101.1	−101.1	+48.3	−20.9	−202.2	−31.2	+58.0	−1.1
1988	−103.5	−129.7	+39.6	−27.1	−233.2	−40.3	+23.0	+3.6
1989	−110.0	−126.9	+37.0	−25.0	−236.9	−62.7	+30.0	−13.5
1990	−87.0	−194.2	−3.0	−18.0	−281.2	−21.9	+35.0	−22.0
1991	−137.5	−220.0	+5.0	−18.0	−357.5	−56.1	+57.0	+47.9
1992	−124.0	−72.4	+19.0	−12.0	−196.4	+7.9	...	−19.0
1993	−144.0	−107.3	+13.0	−11.0	−251.3	−16.6	...	−16.7

International Historical Statistics: The Americas 1750–1993

J3 NORTH AMERICA: Balance of Payments (in million US dollars)

	Honduras							
	VB	IB	TTB	IIB	GSIB	OCB	LTCB	CR
1950	+25.5	−25.2	−0.3	−20.7	+0.3	−0.4	+0.1	−4.2
1951	+20.1	−22.4	−0.1	−18.7	−2.3	−2.8	+9.0	−9.7
1952	+6.5	−15.6	—	−13.0	−9.1	−9.1	+13.6	−2.1
1953	+15.3	−20.2	—	−13.7	−4.9	−5.2	+6.9	−0.6
1954	+4.1	−3.4	−0.2	+4.2	+0.7	+1.0	+0.7	−1.2
1955	−1.6	−5.9	−0.2	+1.1	−7.5	−6.6	−0.8	+4.1
1956	+15.2	−21.4	−0.2	−12.1	−6.2	−5.6	−0.2	+2.0
1957	−3.8	−10.0	−0.6	−3.5	−13.8	−12.7	+8.6	+4.1
1958	+3.8	−13.0	−0.6	−5.8	−9.2	−7.9	−4.3	+4.3
1959	+6.9	−8.5	−0.4	−2.6	−1.6	+0.9	+4.3[14]	−0.8
1960	−1.1	+4.1	−0.4	+8.5	+3.0	+5.7	−4.8	−0.4
1961	+7.7	−7.2	−0.4	−1.0	+0.5	+5.1	−6.9	+0.7
1962	+8.7	−11.5	−0.5	−4.3	−2.8	+0.2	+5.8	−1.1
1963	−3.9	−12.9	−0.5	−6.0	−16.8	−13.8	+15.7	+0.8
1964	+0.4	−17.8	−2.9	−7.0	−17.4	−11.2	+12.9	−7.2
1965	+15.0	−25.7	−2.2	−13.0	−10.7	−7.0	+10.8	−3.7
1966	+6.4	−29.9	−4.0	−15.5	−23.5	−19.2	+10.8	−4.0
1967	+3.9	−37.2	−4.5	−21.2	−33.3	−28.6	+15.4	+2.3
1968	+11.6	−42.5	−6.3	−23.1	−30.9	−24.7	+28.5	−6.5
1969	+1.2	−39.1	−7.4	−18.6	−37.9	−30.6	+29.9	+0.6
1970	−25.2	−45.2	−7.8	−22.6	−70.4	−63.8	+40.1	+9.7
1971	+16.5	−46.0	−7.9	−24.8	−29.5	−22.7	+35.3	−2.6
1972	+35.6	−54.9	−9.0	−27.4	−19.3	−12.7	+23.4	−13.3
1973	+23.1	−64.7	−6.3	−33.1	−41.6	−34.6	+32.4	−6.9
1974	−87.2	−39.3	−5.2	−13.3	−126.5	−103.9	+63.2	−3.1
1975	−62.7	−67.1	−4.6	−28.9	−129.8	−112.1	+84.4	−53.2
1976	−20.8	−97.3	−4.5	−58.6	−118.1	−104.8	+95.2	−37.9
1977	−20.3	−122.6	−7.1	−69.8	−142.9	−128.7	+132.2	−51.9
1978	−28.4	−146.2	−6.4	−86.5	−174.6	−157.2	+158.0	−4.7
1979	−27.0	−185.6	−7.6	−121.8	−212.6	−192.1	+157.3	−25.0
1980	−103.8	−234.5	−6.5	−155.0	−338.3	−316.8	+225.4	+58.0
1981	−114.8	−215.4	+3.8	−154.8	−330.2	−302.7	+200.3	+46.3
1982	−4.2	−256.1	+2.1	−203.7	−258.3	−228.3	+134.1	−13.3
1983	−57.6	−206.1	+2.0	−154.2	−263.7	−232.0	+129.9	−3.4
1984	−147.8	−248.7	−1.2	−179.8	−396.5	−374.3	+247.3	−15.9
1985	−89.6	−260.1	−2.0	−192.5	−349.7	−292.6	+209.9	+20.6
1986	+17.2	−322.7	−4.0	−255.3	−305.5	−254.6	+53.7	−7.1
1987	−49.5	−306.6	−7.7	−240.9	−356.1	−306.9	+68.0	+4.1
1988	−34.0	−398.0	−9.5	−264.3	−364.0	−181.0	+46.0	+54.7
1989	−44.5	−407.4	−10.0	−251.0	−362.9	206.3	−53.0	−7.4
1990	−11.8	−319.3	−9.0	−250.0	−331.1	−227.9	+89.0	+49.1
1991	−71.9	−297.8	−6.0	−277.0	−369.7	−258.4	−78.0	+46.8
1992	−150.9	−323.2	−6.0	−334.0	−474.1	−351.0	+76.0	+25.1
1993	−203.5	−269.5	−7.0	−321.0	−473.0	−308.7	...	−191.6

J3 NORTH AMERICA: Balance of Payments (in million US dollars)

	Jamaica							
	VB	**IB**	**TTB**	**IIB**	**GSIB**	**OCB**	**LTCB**	**CR**
1960	−23.0	−20.4	+17.1	−15.6	−43.4	−26.6	+19.4	+1.6
1961	−12.9	−12.9	+17.1	−17.9	−25.8	−12.4	+18.5	−13.4
1962	−9.0	−18.2	+14.4	−18.0	−27.2	−8.4	+3.8₁₄	+3.4
1963	+9.5	−19.9	+28.6	−37.0	−10.4	+9.8	+38.6	−24.6
1964	−36.1	−25.8	+31.9	−40.0	−61.9	−43.7	+7.5	−10.6
1965	−38.1	−9.5	+52.9	−42.8	−47.6	−30.5	+22.7	+1.6
1966	−8.0	−48.5	+67.2	−90.8	−56.5	−42.0	+91.8	+20.0
1967	−23.2	−52.9	+68.1	−92.3	−76.1	−81.4	+96.3	+0.3
1968	−81.8	−34.8	+65.3	−73.6	−116.6	−91.9	+136.2	−31.4
1969	−89.9	−48.6	+78.5	−87.0	−138.5	−123.6	+113.4	+2.6
1970	−107.6	−67.8	+80.0	−98.2	−175.4	−152.9	+160.7	−24.9
1971	−131.9	−61.9	+93.0	−103.1	−193.8	−172.2	+188.4	−39.4
1972	−151.9	−73.6	+114.1	−126.5	−225.5	−196.7	+126.7	+22.0
1973	−178.3	−96.7	+107.4	−132.9	−275.0	−247.6	+176.2	+31.9
1974	−59.2	−57.6	+112.6	−67.6	−116.8	−91.9	+211.8	−67.2
1975	−161.0	−149.5	+76.2	−107.6	−310.5	−282.8	+181.3	+34.3
1976	−135.2	−173.3	+46.9	−116.7	−308.5	−302.6	+85.1	+124.1
1977	+71.1	−133.2	+93.6	−129.8	−62.1	−42.1	+42.7	−12.5
1978	+81.0	−156.8	+136.5	−183.2	−75.8	−50.0	−132.2	−11.0
1979	−64.3	−154.7	+184.5	−207.2	−219.0	−138.9	−25.3	−5.0
1980	−75.5	−181.2	+228.9	−252.6	−256.7	−166.0	+140.3	−40.9
1981	−322.7	−138.4	+270.6	−202.5	−461.1	−336.8	+39.6	+27.9
1982	−441.5	−112.2	+306.1	−214.0	−553.7	−408.5	+224.4	−19.7
1983	−438.5	−18.1	+374.3	−186.4	−456.6	−358.6	+70.8	+73.1
1984	−334.7	−118.0	+386.6	−302.7	−452.7	−335.2	+390.0	−75.6
1985	−435.6	−87.2	+375.3	−314.4	−522.8	−304.4	+107.7	−60.3
1986	−247.9	+61.4	+480.9	−324.3	−186.5	−40.2	−192.7	+40.9
1987	−351.7	+38.8	+551.2	−391.5	−312.9	−136.7	+255.3	−72.8
1988	−356.9	−117.5	+470.6	−354.3	−474.4	+54.1	+12.4	−167.7
1989	−589.8	−194.8	+490.0	−435.0	−784.6	−291.5	+249.0	−59.9
1990	−502.1	−100.9	+637.0	−517.0	−603.0	−320.6	+284.0	−87.1
1991	−391.6	−117.0	+703.0	−479.0	−508.6	−190.8	+198.0	+97.2
1992	−424.6	+95.7	+777.0	−348.0	−328.9	+117.0	+4.0	−225.9
1993	−815.1	+241.3	+858.0	−240.0	−573.8	−181.5	+79.0	−117.9

J3 NORTH AMERICA: Balance of Payments (in million US dollars)

	Mexico							
	VB	**IB**	**TTB**	**IIB**	**GSIB**	**OCB**	**LTCB**	**CR**
1950	−74	+106	+156	−76	+32	+47	+84	−196
1951	−221	+96	+173	−100	−125	−118	+117	+15
1952	−175₈	+71₈	+162	−123	−104₈	−99₈	+77₈	+12₈
1953	−169	+47	+162	−94	−122	−117	+37	+32
1954	−92	+69	+172	−86	−23	−29	+127	+40
1955	+21	+133	+252	−93	+154	+149	+119	−231
1956	−174	+60	+280	−134	−114	−116	+142	−72
1957	−362	+66	+304	−134	−296	−293	+170	+36
1958	−338	+73	+241	−143	−265	−264	+197	+80
1959	−220	+59	+254	−154	−161	−162	+98₁₄	−62
1960	−354	+35	+260	−190	−319	−324	+90	+16
1961	−260	+32	+269	−204	−228	−241	+253	+30
1962	−167	—	+275	−237	−167	−182	+246	−14
1963	−201	—	+308	−266	−201	−218	+305	−116
1964	−370	−42	+327	−324	−412	−423	+519	−46
1965	−352	−35	+361	−339	−387	−392	+169	+78
1966	−337	−5	+396	−394	−342	−343	+313	+24
1967	−608	−84	+441	−473	−692	−685	+510	−22
1968	−634	−122	+501	−559	−756	−743	+547	−71
1969	−529	−98	+528	−617	−627	−592	+800	−5
1970	−888	−235	+416	−695	−1,123	−1,068	+626	−83
1971	−749	−143	+533	−603	−892	−835	+766	−192
1972	−894	−86	+623	−700	−980	−916	+828	−212
1973	−1,515	+26	+839	−997	−1,489	−1,415	+1,819	−171
1974	−2,791	−207	+902	−1,447	−2,998	−2,876	+3,046	−37
1975	−3,272	−910	+812	−1,818	−4,182	−4,042	+4,667	−146
1976	−2,295	−1,270	+615	−2,355	−3,565	−3,409	+4,994	+279
1977	−1,021	−1,003	+939	−2,517	−2,024	−1,854	+4,611	−467
1978	−1,745	−1,618	+1,059	−3,044	−3,363	−3,171	+5,121	−199
1979	−2,830	−1,854	+1,257	−4,288	−4,684	−5,459	+5,178	−233
1980	−3,385	−7,871	+1,072	−6,359	−11,256	−10,750	+10,530	−943
1981	−3,846	−13,412	+771	−10,546	−17,258	−16,061	+18,938	−1,333
1982	+6,795	−13,727	+433	−12,636	−6,932	−6,307	+8,349	+3,320
1983	+13,762	−9,071	+1,145	−9,418	+4,691	+5,403	−259	−3,222
1984	+12,941	−10,118	+1,116	−10,304	+2,823	+4,194	−324	−3,454
1985	+8,451	−9,635	+640	−9,197	−1,184	+1,130	−1,289	+2,363
1986	+4,599	−7,550	+810	−8,031	−2,951	−1,377	+70	+112
1987	+8,433	−6,105	+1,134	−7,427	+2,328	+4,247	+1,984	−5,759
1988	+1,668	−6,297	+798	−7,533	−4,629	−2,374	−5,316	+6,789
1989	−645	−7,723	+574	−8,681	−8,368	−5,825	+2,046	−121
1990	−4,433	−6,993	+7	−8,922	−11,426	−7,451	+5,594	−2,018
1991	−11,329	−6,305	+147	−8,881	−17,634	−14,888	+21,796	−7,619
1992	−20,677	−7,150	−23	−9,839	−27,827	−24,806	+20,160	−1,935
1993	−18,891	−8,149	+605	−11,227	−27,040	−23,391	+31,450	−7,291

J3 NORTH AMERICA: Balance of Payments (in million US dollars)

				Nicaragua				
	VB	IB	TTB	IIB	GSIB	OCB	LTCB	CR
1950	+10.8	−10.5	−1.3	−6.1	+0.3	+0.5	+0.4	+0.9
1951	+16.8	−10.8	−0.9	−6.5	+6.0	+6.4	+0.4	−6.2
1952	+12.1	−12.2	−0.8	−5.4	−0.1	+0.9	+5.3	−6.1
1953	+11.2	−14.9	−1.8	−6.7	−3.7	−2.8	+6.5	−
1954	+4.4	−16.7	−2.0	−5.6	−12.3	−11.3	+5.0	+3.5
1955	+20.5	−20.1	−2.2	−8.0	+0.4	+2.6	+1.3	−0.9₁₄
1956	+7.9	−18.0	−4.2	−4.4	−9.1	−6.9	+2.8	+7.3
1957	+2.2	−13.1	−4.2	−1.4	−10.9	−8.1	+10.3	−2.4
1958	+5.1	−18.5	−4.6	−4.0	−13.4	−9.3	+5.8	+1.9
1959	+22.3	−17.7	−5.0	−2.4	+4.6	+7.8	+0.8₁₄	−4.6
1960	+7.5	−18.8	−3.3	−2.8	−11.3	−8.4	+4.4	+0.1
1961	+11.2	−18.4	−4.6	−3.0	−7.2	−3.4	+4.6	−1.6
1962	+11.7	−25.0	−4.7	−3.1	−13.3	−9.8	+10.5	−3.9
1963	+15.6	−24.6	−6.5	−2.7	−9.0	−4.9	+15.1	−14.5
1964	+15.7	−30.3	−7.7	−5.5	−14.6	−9.2	+22.2	−6.9
1965	+15.3	−45.0	−8.6	−12.8	−29.7	−23.2	+16.5	−18.2
1966	−9.8	−47.5	−6.4	−15.7	−57.3	−50.2	+32.1	−0.7
1967	−24.3	−45.7	−6.1	−18.7	−70.0	−64.2	+31.0	+29.0
1968	−4.2	−41.9	−1.6	−24.7	−46.1	−39.8	+55.5	−18.3
1969	−0.6	−42.7	−2.1	−25.2	−43.0	−36.0	+28.3	+5.7
1970	−	−45.5	−1.9	−29.3	−45.5	−39.5	+45.9	−6.1
1971	−2.9	−46.6	−2.9	−31.9	−49.5	−44.5	+51.3	−12.0
1972	+43.9	−29.3	−2.8	−37.0	+14.6	+21.7	+50.5	−24.5
1973	−49.1	−74.2	−4.2	−49.8	−123.3	−65.9	+112.0	−73.6
1974	−160.8	−111.9	−7.5	−65.7	−272.7	−257.2	+173.5	+37.7
1975	−107.2	−94.4	−5.9	−60.7	−201.6	−185.0	+152.3	−47.1
1976	+56.8	−105.4	−6.9	−67.2	−48.6	−39.3	+22.3	+5.1
1977	−68.0	−125.1	−12.4	−68.2	−193.1	−181.9	+208.4	−1.6
1978	+92.7	−127.1	−34.6	−81.5	−34.4	−24.9	+79.9	+82.7
1979	+227.0	−138.4	−29.2	−73.4	+88.6	+180.2	+122.5	−89.7
1980	−352.5	−182.8	−9.4	−122.5	−535.3	−411.4	+184.9	+204.9
1981	−414.2	−247.7	−7.5	−167.7	−661.9	−591.6	+340.4	−62.6
1982	−317.5	−247.9	−	−174.0	−565.4	−513.9	+297.0	−31.3
1983	−290.4	−296.3	−2.3	−212.1	−586.7	−507.4	+67.3	−13.6
1984	−322.9	−364.0	+1.6	−263.4	−686.9	−597.1	+204.4	−244.4
1985	−489.0	−363.6	+1.2	−273.3	−852.6	−725.7	+515.2	−7.8
1986	−419.6	−383.2	+3.8	−253.6	−802.8	−687.7	+126.9	+211.3
1987	−439.3	−374.9	+3.0	−243.9	−814.2	−678.8	+56.0	−6.2
1988	−482.6	−362.6	+3.6	−262.1	−845.2	−715.2	+105.0	−43.9
1989	−228.6	−302.0	+3.0	−205.0	−530.6	−361.7	−99.0	−70.6
1990	−237.3	−269.5	−3.0	−217.0	−506.8	−305.2	−168.0	40.2
1991	−419.9	−429.3	−11.0	−363.0	−849.2	−4.8	−518.0	−82.6
1992	−547.7	−556.9	−7.0	−494.0	−1,104.6	−695.4	−476.0	16.1
1993	−392.4	−485.5	+10.0	−430.0	−877.9	−456.6	−493.0	95.3

J3 NORTH AMERICA: Balance of Payments (in million US dollars)

	Panama							
	VB	IB	TTB	IIB	GSIB	OCB	LTCB	CR
1950	−36.3	+25.1	+26.6	−11.6	−11.2	−16.9	+6	−2.4
1951	−38.2	+20.5	+20.4	−12.0	−17.7	−21.4	+11	+2.2
1952	−46.4	+24.5	+21.3	−11.3	−21.9	−22.5	+3	−3.2
1953	−38.9	+27.1	+22.9	−11.8	−11.8	−14.3	+8	−1.6
1954	−32.3	+20.8	+24.9	−17.2	−11.5	−17.1	−1	+1.2
1955	−21.4	+17.0	+25.1	−17.8	−4.4	−10.9	−2	—
1956	−34.2	+12.3	+26.5	−17.8	−21.9	−20.3	+18	−2
1957	−51.7	+20.6	+26.7	−18.9	−31.0	−34.8	+9	+4
1958	−53.7	+20.2	+18.8	−12.1	−33.5	−28.7	+21	−4
1959	−54.1	+19.7	+18.4	−13.3	−34.4	−31.6	+15	+5
1960	−70	+38	+18	−10	−32	−31	+22	−3
1961	−83	+55	+22	−7	−28	−24	+35	+3
1962	−85	+66	+28	−7	−19	−19	+23	—
1963	−91	+65	+27	−9	−26	−25	+33	−3
1964	−86	+64	+21	−9	−22	−21	+9	+2
1965	−99	+66	+31	−20	−33	−29	+22	−1
1966	−115	+73	+34	−23	−42	−40	+25	—
1967	−123	+95	+40	−23	−28	−26	+15	−1
1968	−129	+114	+43	−24	−15	−15	+27	−4
1969	−153	+122	+49	−25	−31	−29	+60	−3
1970	201	+133	+55	−29	−68	−64	+119	−1
1971	−226	+148	+55	−30	−78	−73	+87	−3
1972	−263	+161	+61	−35	−102	−98	+128	−22
1973	−296	+190	+80	−42	−106	−111	+148	+2
1974	−510	+290	+95	−57	−220	−224	+114	+2
1975	−492	+328	+105	−23	−164	−169	+186	+5
1976	−514	+342	+121	−37	−172	−176	+723	−44
1977	−502	+349	+142	−68	−153	−155	−113	+8
1978	−558	+347	+164	−59	−211	−208	+451	−80
1979	−730	+406	+166	−106	−324	−311	+314	+32
1980	−727	+401	+115	−65	−326	−311	−720	+1
1981	−775	+800	+109	+362	+25	+56	+570	−3
1982	−634	+537	+93	+26	−97	−51	+1,200	+19
1983	−645	+1,016	+101	+115	+371	+416	+367	−106
1984	−823	+929	+121	+63	+106	+218	+228	−9
1985	−757	+930	+135	+36	+173	+286	−263	+118
1986	−541	+801	+122	−5	+260	+355	−10	−30
1987	−465	+720	+98	−106	+255	+318	−434	+85
1988	−79	+618	+80	−358	+539	+611	−539	−12
1989	−403	+488	+75	−1,129	+85	+155	−476	−56
1990	−488	+537	+73	−668	−49	+47	−386	−272
1991	−815	+548	+94	−882	−267	−192	−40	−212
1992	−882	+680	+95	−902	−202	−43	−329	−111
1993	−986	+876	+103	−712	−110	−55	−246	−90

J3 NORTH AMERICA: Balance of Payments (in million US dollars)

	Trinidad & Tobago							
	VB	IB	TTB	IIB	GSIB	OCB	LTCB	CR
1960	−26.4	−73.1	−1.7	−93.1	−99.5	−59	+40.2	+2.8
1961	+13.8	−78.4	−4.1	−119.3	−64.6	−41.2	+31.8	−2.0
1962	+2.5	−96.4	−5.1	−117.4	−93.9	−57.0	+46.4	+6.6
1963	+1.0	−59.1	+0.1	−67.5	−58.1	−59.7	+78.1	−3.4
1964	+11.4	−61.3	+0.2	−70.9	−49.9	−49.3	+34.4	−9.8
1965	−27.7	−52.4	0.1	−60.0	−80.1	−68.3	+63.3	+1.4
1966	+17.9	−73.9	+1.9	−63.1	−56.0	−30.3	+26.1	−1.2
1967	+37.6	−55.6	−0.4	−65.2	−18.0	−35.6	+26.6	+1.1
1968	+32.8	−15.1	+8.3	−63.4	+17.7	−6.3	+27.7	−20.2
1969	+0.6	−24.8	+10.6	−68.5	−24.2	−53.8	+64.8	+4.8
1970	−50.9	−26.6	+1.0	−61.2	−77.5	−108.6	+83.3	+12.0
1971	−138.3	+5.2	+10.9	−61.8	−133.1	−168.9	+126.7	−20.1
1972	−129.7	+9.1	+23.7	−69.7	−120.6	−123.9	+103.2	+8.8
1973	−38.1	+11.4	+35.5	−88.2	−26.7	−29.9	+60.5	+9.8
1974	+445.8	−162.1	+28.7	−208.5	+283.7	+274.1	+69.6	−342.8
1975	+329.2	+23.8	+44.9	−80.1	+353.0	+331.8	+43.2	−364.9
1976	+288.3	+2.9	+40.8	−102.9	+285.4	+255.4	+14.2	−265.4
1977	+307.4	−102.1	+42.3	−187.7	+205.3	+174.1	+230.7	−461.7
1978	+164.4	−83.8	+44.8	−72.1	+80.6	+42.7	+270.5	−333.4
1979	+314.7	−302.9	+23.3	−249.9	+11.8	−33.9	+434.1	−336.2
1980	+752.6	−353.7	+13.4	−306.5	+398.9	+334.7	+335.9	−640.8
1981	+848.8	−381.9	−12.0	−195.5	+466.9	+374.5	+327.1	−566.7
1982	−258.1	−246.7	−28.0	+78.6	−504.8	−644.9	+540.6	+267.0
1983	−206.8	−715.5	−174.4	−133.9	−922.3	−1,002.9	+283.0	+976.0
1984	+405.9	−845.2	−177.7	−314.1	−439.3	−522.5	+13.2	+747.9
1985	+756.1	−787.0	−121.6	−346.3	−30.9	−83.1	+32.3	+228.2
1986	+153.6	−545.4	−82.0	−210.7	−391.8	−433.5	−59.8	+654.4
1987	+339.3	−544.7	−63.8	−276.3	−205.4	−239.2	+8.2	+284.0
1988	+405.3	−484.7	−76.5	−336.7	−79.4	−88.6	−65.0	+191.6
1989	+505.5	−881.5	−34.0	−376.0	−31.1	−38.5	−97.0	−29.5
1990	+1,012.5	−547.3	−27.0	−394.0	+465.2	+459.0	−521.0	−120.8
1991	+564.2	−571.2	−9.0	−439.0	−7.0	−4.7	−237.0	+208.6
1992	+695.7	−557.2	−4.0	−444.0	+138.5	+138.9	−165.0	+63.0
1993	+547.2	−438.8	−25.0	−325.0	+108.4	+113.1	...	+263.0

J3   NORTH AMERICA: Balance of Payments (in million US dollars)

	USA							
	VB	**IB**	**TTB**	**IIB**	**GSIB**	**OCB**	**LTCB**	**CR**
1950	+1,122	+770	−335	+1,460	+1,892	−2,125	−702	+1,758
1951	+3,067	+750	−284	+1,720	+3,817	+302	−740	−33
1952	+2,611	−255	−290	+1,675	+2,356	−175	−900	−415
1953	+1,437	−905	−355	+1,732	+532	−1,949	−322	+1,256
1954	+2,576	−617	−414	+2,112	+1,959	−321	−713	+480
1955	+2,897	−744	−499	+2,297	+2,153	−345	−674	+182
1956	+4,753	−608	−570	+2,494	+4,145	+1,722	−1,961	−869
1957	+6,271	−370	−587	+2,588	+5,901	+3,556	−2,902	−1,165
1958	+3,462	−1,106	−835	+2,584	+2,356	−5	−2,552	+2,292
1959	+1,148	−838	−708	+2,726	+310	−2,138	−1,589	+1,035
1960	+4,906[13]	−798[13]	−831[13]	+2,841[13]	+4,107[13]	+1,815[13]	−2,100[13]	+2,145[13]
	+4.89	+0.30	−0.86	+3.24	+5.19	+2.82	−3.01	+2.14
1961	+5.57	+1.00	−0.85	+3.82	+6.57	+3.82	−2.78	+0.61
1962	+4.52	+1.60	−1.01	+4.35	+6.12	+3.38	−3.34	+1.53
1963	+5.22	+2.02	−1.10	+4.59	+7.24	+4.40	−4.07	+0.38
1964	+6.80	+2.92	−1.00	+5.03	+9.72	+6.82	−4.19	+0.17
1965	+4.95	+3.41	−1.06	+5.35	+8.36	+5.41	−5.72	+1.22
1966	+3.82	+2.27	−1.07	+5.51	+6.09	+3.03	−4.81	+0.57
1967	+3.80	+2.05	−1.56	+5.06	+5.85	+2.59	−4.40	+0.05
1968	+0.64	+3.04	−1.25	+5.73	+3.68	+0.59	−1.63	−0.88
1969	+0.60	+2.95	−1.33	+5.82	+3.55	+0.42	−3.12	−1.26
1970	+2.59	+3.19	−1.65	+6.23	+5.78	+2.33	−4.93	+2.47
1971	−2.27	+4.66	−1.85	+9.59	+2.39	−1.45	−6.06	+2.18
1972	−6.42	+16.26	−2.21	+10.68	+9.84	−5.78	−2.87	−0.01
1973	+0.91	+10.28	−2.09	+14.95	+11.19	+7.07	−5.35	−0.06
1974	−5.51	+14.89	−1.95	+18.99	+9.38	+1.94	−5.69	−1.46
1975	+8.90	+14.04	−1.74	+16.68	+22.94	+18.06	−15.00	−0.20
1976	−9.47	+18.97	−1.13	+19.85	+9.50	+4.18	−12.21	−2.52
1977	−31.11	+21.61	−1.30	+22.37	−9.50	−14.49	−8.67	−0.56
1978	−33.94	+24.11	−1.28	+25.72	−9.83	−15.40	−8.52	+1.06
1979	−27.54	+33.72	−0.98	+36.47	+6.18	+0.20	−15.53	+2.76
1980	−25.50	+34.92	+0.18	+78.57	+9.42	+1.20	+0.55	−7.64
1981	−27.99	+43.22	+1.40	+69.37	+15.23	+7.26	+18.25	−3.21
1982	−36.44	+40.35	—	+32.82	+3.91	−5.86	+11.94	−3.86
1983	−67.08	+37.87	−1.21	+31.97	−29.21	−40.18	+9.98	+0.45
1984	−112.51	+26.13	−6.24	+49.22	−86.38	−98.99	+42.73	−0.97
1985	−122.16	+15.39	−8.48	+21.24	−106.77	−122.25	+102.34	−8.21
1986	−145.05	+15.52	−6.48	+17.15	−129.53	−151.14	+80.39	−5.11
1987	−159.49	+15.44	−6.66	+12.99	−144.05	−167.06	+61.49	+2.58
1988	−126.97	+23.71	+9.03	+13.23	−103.26	−128.28	+93.78	−1.79
1989	−115.25	+38.29	+67.66	+13.65	−76.96	−102.85	+77.61	−26.80
1990	−109.02	+50.97	+10.13	+20.69	−58.05	−91.74	+7.51	−8.71
1991	−74.06	+60.47	+18.04	+15.13	−13.59	−6.91	+17.03	+5.62
1992	−96.10	+60.27	+21.66	+10.05	−35.83	−67.85	−14.04	+6.41
1993	−132.57	+60.80	+24.16	+8.99	−71.77	−103.94	−49.73	−2.10

J3 SOUTH AMERICA: BALANCE OF PAYMENTS (in millions US dollars)

	Argentina							
	VB	IB	TTB	IIB	GSIB	OCB	LTCB	CR
1950	+26[14]	+88[14]	...	−3	+114[14]	+114[14]	...	+19[14]
1951	−142	+69	...	−33	−73	−224	+99	+25
1952	−367	+25	...	−10	−342	−412	+11	+49
1953	+398	−66	...	−11	+332	+344	+8	−86
1954	+161	−75	...	−15	+86	+83	+5	−30
1955	−109	−130	—	−21	−239	−242	+29	+68
1956	−54	−77	+4	−17	−131	−131	+111	+38
1957	−186	−114	+1	−13	−300	−303	+57	+175
1958	−97	−159	−6	−31	−256	−259	+46	+154
1959	+130	−116[14]	−6	−40	+14[14]	+11[14]	+266[14]	−178[14]
1960	−27	−29	−15	−57	−56	−60	+332	−258
1961	−328	−90	−16	−102	−418	−417	+120	+232
1962	+16	−130	−32	−72	−114	−117	+74	+297
1963	+497	−153	−17	−68	+344	+346	+78	−141
1964	+457	−295	−49	−103	+162	+162	+27	+74
1965	+431	−207	−49	−53	+224	+222	+48	−127
1966	+598	−332	−34	−151	+266	+259	+65	−26
1967	+494	−361	−77	−194	+133	+130	+20	−541
1968	+333	−382	−69	−205	−49	−53	+60	−33
1969	+217	−443	−64	−219	−226	−230	+34	+222
1970	+274	−434	−56	−223	−160	−163	+95	−135
1971	+87	−474	−21	−331	−387	−390	+146	+390
1972	+256	−479	+1	−383	−223	−227	+51	+14
1973	+1,289	−589	+2	−467	+700	+711	−151	−814
1974	+714	−596	+5	−423	+118	+118	−109	−127
1975	−549	−733	+61	−446	−1,282	−1,287	−56	+1,071
1976	+1,153	−484	+65	−508	+669	+651	−66	−921
1977	+1,852	−695	−25	−780	+1,157	+1,126	+144	−1,828
1978	+2,913	−989	−307	−745	+1,924	+1,856	+374	−2,297
1979	+1,782	−1,234	−996	−990	−548	−513	+487	−4,381
1980	−1,373	−3,424	1,449	−1,632	−4,797	−4,774	+942	+2,749
1981	+712	−5,402	−1021	−3,354	−4,690	−4,712	+2,049	+3,437
1982	+2,764	−5,151	+45	−5,068	−2,387	−2,353	+556	+758
1983	+3,716	−6,168	−54	−5,930	−2,452	−2,436	+832	+1,254
1984	+3,982	−6,479	−160	−6,153	−2,497	−2,495	+640	+59
1985	+4,878	−5,830	−148	−5,715	−952	−952	+302	−2,030
1986	+2,446	−5,307	−326	−4,820	−2,861	−2,859	+32	+984
1987	+1,017	−5,244	−275	−4,751	−4,227	−4,235	+168	+2,213
1988	+4,242	−5,814	−261	−5,346	−1,572	−1,572	+346	−1,922
1989	+5,709	−7,022	−224	−6,422	−1,313	−1,305	−615	+1,322
1990	+8,628	−5,074	−268	−4,400	+3,554	+4,552	+261	−3,092
1991	+4,419	−5,859	−957	−5,830	−1,440	−672	+2,288	−1,977
1992	−1,450	−5,845	−1,429	−3,656	−7,295	−6,677	+2,521	−4,250
1993	−2,455	−5,443	−1,608	−2,989	−7,898	−7,568	+1,183	−2,596

J3   SOUTH AMERICA: Balance of Payments (in million US dollars)

	Bolivia							
	VB	**IB**	**TTB**	**IIB**	**GSIB**	**OCB**	**LTCB**	**CR**
1950	+20.4	−20.9	−1.3	−3.6	−0.5	−0.1	+15.5	−3.7
1951	+34.8	−31.4	−1.9	−3.3	+3.4	+3.8	+4.5	−5.5
1952	−2.2	−6.8	−1.6	−18.8	−9.0	−8.0	−2.3	+4.0
1953	−6.3	−18.4	−1.1	−1.9	−24.7	−22.1	+11.1	+6.9
1954	+1.1	−18.3	−0.6	−1.1	−17.2	−2.5	−6.3	+12.1
1955	+6.0	−29.9	−0.4	−4.1	−23.9	−3.3	+12.3	+3.3
1956	+5.5	−26.6	−0.7	−3.1	−21.1	−0.8	+17.6	+9.9
1957	−9.0	−24.3	0.7	−3.0	−33.3	−5.2	+3.3	−3.8
1958	−22.8	−21.3	−0.6	−6.5	−44.1	−15.2	+13.4	+1.5
1959	−0.8[14]	−24.3[14]	−0.8	+1.9	−25.1[14]	−2.4[14]	+20.1[14]	−6.7[14]
1960	−15.6	−16.9	−0.7	+1.2	−32.5	−19.5	+17.1	−1.5
1961	−13.2	−17.7	−0.5	−0.7	−30.9	−8.7	+11.7	−0.5
1962	−30.8	−20.8	−0.6	−2.8	−51.6	−31.2	+28.9	+3.4
1963	−25.3	−22.9	−0.9	−2.6	−48.2	−18.8	+28.3	−6.5
1964	−9.3	−25.6	−1.5	−2.8	−34.9	−9.1	+19.7	−12.0
1965	−11.5	−28.4	−1.7	−3.6	−39.9	−23.9	+24.2	−14.0
1966	−7.9	−25.9	−1.4	−0.8	−33.8	−12.5	+22.6	−4.6
1967	+1.4	−43.8	−1.2	−18.0	−42.4	−29.5	+25.2	+3.3
1968	−6.0	−51.2	−0.6	−23.1	−57.2	−50.5	+53.7	−1.6
1969	+4.4	−60.1	−0.8	−30.5	−55.7	−47.9	+52.7	−2.5
1970	+55.2	−54.9	−1.4	−25.0	+0.3	+4.2	+33.2	−3.5
1971	+37.3	−46.8	−2.0	−17.1	−9.5	−2.4	+69.1	−7.6
1972	+48.1	−65.2	−2.0	−21.7	−17.1	−3.6	+92.9	−5.5
1973	+67.6	−70.5	−1.9	−23.0	−2.9	+12.5	+36.9	−10.7
1974	+232.4	−95.4	−8.1	−25.3	+150.6	+137.0	+100.1	−123.0
1975	−25.1	−118.2	−6.6	−9.0	−143.3	−130.2	+158.9	+34.7
1976	+50.7	−118.2	−6.0	−32.4	−67.5	−53.5	+226.0	−30.8
1977	+55.3	−188.2	−9.0	−68.8	−132.9	−117.9	+337.8	−75.8
1978	−96.6	−261.9	−5.9	−119.1	−350.5	−331.5	+273.5	+61.5
1979	+21.4	−469.6	−26.5	−183.1	−448.2	−397.0	+254.0	−25.6
1980	+367.8	−433.7	−19.0	−264.1	−65.9	−6.4	+79.6	+87.7
1981	+84.7	−589.0	−14.0	−364.2	−504.3	−465.7	+160.4	−8.8
1982	+331.7	−550.1	−10.0	−413.9	−218.4	−173.7	−94.5	−48.4
1983	+259.1	−503.4	+22.0	−361.3	−244.3	−138.9	−216.1	−50.1
1984	+312.2	−574.9	+2.5	−418.4	−262.7	−174.9	−144.2	−95.9
1985	+160.6	−522.5	—	−375.9	−361.9	−282.4	−229.8	+34.3
1986	−51.0	−535.2	+8.8	−308.3	−484.2	−384.2	−154.0	−104.4
1987	−127.6	−416.4	−1.7	−280.9	−544.0	−426.8	−37.8	+75.2
1988	−48.4	−391.3	−2.2	−267.8	−439.7	−303.1	+86.0	+36.0
1989	−6.0	−414.0	−2.0	−255.0	−420.0	−264.2	+78.0	+100.1
1990	+55.2	−413.2	−2.0	−244.0	−358.1	−198.1	+100.0	+0.2
1991	−43.9	−401.2	−1.0	−243.0	−445.1	−262.1	−106.0	−20.7
1992	−432.4	−344.1	−3.0	−193.0	−776.5	−533.3	+329.0	−36.8
1993	−396.2	−346.3	+1.0	−201.0	−742.4	−505.5	. . .	+168.6

J3 SOUTH AMERICA: Balance of Payments (in millions US dollars)

	Brazil							
	VB	IB	TTB	IIB	GSIB	OCB	LTCB	CR
1950	+425	−317	−3	−110	+108	+106	−30	+87
1951	+67	−526	−16	−157	−459	−471	+39	+137
1952	−286	−422	−4	−121	−708	−710	+96	−32
1953	+423	−393	−26	−165	+30	+18	+385	+63
1954	+150	−380	−14	−137	−230	−235	+203	+38
1955	+320	−347	−12	−117	−27	−35	+276	−15
1956	+437	−430	−34	−140	+7	+2	+249	−148
1957	+107	−411	−40	−137	−304	−308	+302	+173
1958	+65	−332	−26	−114	−267	−273	+213	+49
1959	+72	−409	−31	−150	−337	−342	+281₁₄	+8₁₄
1960	−23	−498	−48	−194	−521	−517	+75	+36
1961	+113	−389	−19	−184	−276	−261	+587	−80
1962	−89	−402	−25	−199	−491	−452	+265	+108
1963	+112	−326	−14	−144	−214	−171	+124	+45
1964	+344	−370	−3	−190	−26	+81	+86	−28
1965	+655	−447	−1	−259	+208	+284	+375	−219
1966	+438	−548	−31	−282	−110	−31	+287	+14
1967	+213	−566	−34	−296	−353	−276	+168	+193
1968	+26	−574	−41	−302	−548	−526	+217	−70
1969	+318	−685	−49	−344	−367	−336	+555	−399
1970	+232	−1,090	−130	−353	−858	−837	+1,217	−530
1971	−365	−1,286	−135	−743	−1,651	−1,638	+1,668	−556
1972	−252	−1,444	−178	−722	−1,696	−1,690	+3,543	−2,437
1973	−61	−2,125	−206	−1,112	−2,186	−2,158	+4,100	−2,227
1974	−4,748	−2,816	−249	−1,284	−7,564	−7,562	+6,231	+1,144
1975	−3,550	−3,461	−352	−2,360	−7,011	−7,008	+4,936	+1,235
1976	−2,386	−4,172	−304	−2,730	−6,558	−6,554	+6,108	−2,508
1977	−100	−5,012	−174	−3,475	−5,112	−5,112	+6,040	−712
1978	−1,158	−5,950	−187	−4,283	−7,108	−7,036	+10,088	−4,638
1979	−2,717	−7,778	−234	−6,008	−10,495	−10,478	+6,466	+2,860
1980	−2,823	−10,152	−241	−7,058	−12,975	−12,806	+7,105	+3,321
1981	+1,185	−13,135	−165	−10,283	−11,950	−11,751	+11,663	−750
1982	+778	−17,082	−846	−13,510	−16,304	−16,312	+8,011	+4,354
1983	+6,469	−13,414	−392	−11,023	−6,945	−6,837	−1,366	−817
1984	+13,086	−13,215	−153	−11,476	−129	+42	−2,802	−7,474
1985	+12,466	−12,894	−375	−11,215	−428	−273	−6,677	+492
1986	+8,304	−13,695	−509	−11,157	−5,391	−5,304	−9,432	+5,372
1987	+11,158	−12,678	−184	−10,355	−1,520	−1,450	−10,566	−1,800
1988	+19,168	−15,103	−588	−12,126	+4,065	+4,159	−11,783	−2,115
1989	+16,112	−15,331	+474	−12,547	+781	+1,025	−11,957	−1,585
1990	+10,747	−15,369	−122	−11,613	−4,622	−3,788	−5,171	−1,139
1991	+10,578	−13,722	−212	−9,652	−2,964	−1,408	−1,343	−209
1992	+15,525	−11,625	−319	−8,002	+3,900	+6,275	+3,914	−15,001
1993	+13,072	−15,362	−801	−10,211	−2,290	−637	+8,921	−8,811

J3   SOUTH AMERICA: Balance of Payments (in million US dollars)

					Chile			
	VB	IB	TTB	IIB	GSIB	OCB	LTCB	CR
1950	+50	−61	—	−58	−11	−28	+9	−5
1951	+70	−115	−1	−67	−45	−45	+35	−2
1952	+131	−115	−1	−67	+16	+16	+46	−19
1953	+35	−95	−1	−44	−60	−59	+60	+10
1954	+108	−107	−1	−52	+1	—	−43	+15
1955	+160	−136	—	−78	+24	+24	+6	−21
1956	+157	−181	−6	−98	−24	−13	+28	+3
1957	+19	−128	−9	−53	109	−93	+34	+51
1958	+1	−108	−8	−55	−107	−82	+72	−1
1959	+90	−132₁₄	−7	−58	−42₁₄	−19₁₄	+45₁₄	−73₁₄
1960	+6	−108	−23	−65	−102	−55	+28	+4
1961	−88	−118	−26	−82	−206	−182	+151	+33
1962	−28	−106	−7	−94	−134	−119	+175	−5
1963	+3	−123	−20	−90	−120	−114	+134	+2
1964	+63	−111	−1	−103	−48	−38	+155	−12
1965	+162	−212	+15	−126	−50	−43	+119	−49
1966	+199	−307	+11	−201	−108	−93	+89	−34
1967	+232	−302	+5	−198	−70	−62	+61	+45
1968	+182	−327	+8	−210	−145	−138	+246	−82
1969	+386	−301	−30	−172	+85	+89	+273	−135
1970	+246	−343	−37	−194	−97	−91	+140	−44
1971	+73	−277	−34	−118	−204	−198	−164	+174
1972	−161	−317	−54	−148	−478	−471	−258	+73
1973	−13	−281	−36	−110	−294	−279	−412	−16
1974	+250	−556	−25	−271	−306	−292	−543	−80
1975	+70	−572	−45	−285	−502	−490	−82	+79
1976	+643	−543	−1	−333	+100	+148	+46	−413
1977	+35	−682	−124	−378	−647	−551	+49	−54
1978	−426	−759	−21	−505	−1,185	−1,088	+1,510	−707
1979	−355	−939	−16	−696	−1,294	−1,189	+1,685	−960
1980	−764	−1,320	−22	−958	−2,084	−1,971	+2,242	−1,346
1981	−2,677	−2,164	−24	−1,502	−4,841	−4,733	+3,579	−4
1982	+63	−2,476	−70	−1,954	−2,413	−2,304	+1,681	+1,416
1983	+986	−2,200	−145	−1,780	−1,214	−1,117	−1,269	−101
1984	+362	−2,580	−167	−2,050	−2,218	−2,111	−733	−367
1985	+850	−2,239	−153	−1,924	−1,389	−1,328	−1,652	−136
1986	+1,100	−2,376	−174	−1,913	−1,276	−1,137	−2,069	+255
1987	+1,230	−2,103	−168	−1,730	−873	−808	−906	−79
1988	+2,219	−2,635	−221	−1,955	−416	−234	+800	−867
1989	+1,578	−2,498	+12	−1,925	−920	−705	+45	−581
1990	+1,273	−2,009	+105	−1,810	−736	−536	+1,599	−2,323
1991	+1,574	−1,803	+243	−1,810	−229	+109	+339	−1,342
1992	+748	−1,807	+174	−1,860	−1,139	−703	+942	−2,442
1993	−979	−1,503	+275	−1,505	−2,482	−2,073	+1,682	−559

J3   SOUTH AMERICA: Balance of Payments (in million US dollars)

	Colombia							
	VB	IB	TTB	IIB	GSIB	OCB	LTCB	CR
1950	+72	−84	−7	−39	−13	−14	−4	+25
1951	+84	−93	−7	−36	−9	+5	+20	+26
1952	+103	−134	−11	−19	−31	+29	+65	−28
1953	+98	−82	−9	−23	+16	+15	+21	−10
1954	+48	−89	−10	−15	−41	−43	+60	−
1955	−27	−100	−10	−23	−128	−125	+12	−
1956	+40	−54	−13	−16	−14	−42	+32	+8
1957	+139	−72	−17	−26	+67	+70	−14	−7
1958	+143	−96	−6	−62	+47	+52	−6	−9
1959	+112₁₄	−60₁₄	−5	−36	+52₁₄	+49₁₄	+17₁₄	−7₁₄
1960	−8	−84	−6	−40	−92	−87	−7	+43
1961	−66	−88	−2	−50	−154	−145	+35	+69
1962	−61	−115	−10	−57	−176	−162	+67	+63
1963	−16	−134	−6	−81	−150	−132	+176	+47
1964	+54	−197	−30	−73	−143	−129	+218	−29
1965	+161	−184	−22	−79	−23	−11	+67	−16
1966	−113	−185	−22	−86	−298	−288	+123	+17
1967	+88	−183	−12	−105	−95	−73	+32	+28
1968	−10	−185	−15	−113	−195	−164	+158	−69
1969	+24	−237	−14	−144	−213	−175	+228	−55
1970	−14	−315	−12	−176	−329	−293	+227	−36
1971	−148	−340	−3	−182	−488	−454	+194	+7
1972	+129	−356	−9	−195	−227	−191	+263	−180
1973	+280	−370	−13	−190	−90	−55	+286	−207
1974	−17	−385	−19	−260	−402	−352	+228	+85
1975	+268	−488	+22	−329	−220	−172	+302	−73
1976	+548	−436	+14	−319	+112	+163	+79	−632
1977	+690	−362	+99	−280	+328	+375	+225	−668
1978	+603	−408	+93	−305	+195	+258	+108	−669
1979	+463	−127	+173	−296	+336	+438	+755	−1,615
1980	−297	−74	+238	−243	−371	−206	+815	−1,237
1981	−1,572	−631	+151	−486	−2,203	−1,961	+1,642	−218
1982	−2,244	−979	+225	−933	−3,223	−3,054	+1,615	+722
1983	−1,494	−1,673	−80	−1,168	−3,167	−3,003	+1,528	+1,753
1984	+246	−1,946	−84	−1,487	−1,700	−1,401	+1,822	+1,166
1985	−23	−2,247	−121	−1,560	−2,270	−1,809	+2,350	−285
1986	+1,922	−2,324	−193	−1,728	−402	+383	+2,469	−1,354
1987	+1,868	−2,533	−317	−1,967	−665	+336	−906	+106
1988	+827	−2,007	−77	−1,787	−1,180	−216	+800	−348
1989	+1,474	−2,573	−159	−2,291	−1,099	−201	+45	−220
1990	+1,971	−2,455	−48	−2,269	−484	+542	+1,599	−667
1991	+2,959	−2,308	−41	−1,810	+651	+2,349	+339	−1,891
1992	+1,233	−2,066	+64	−1,860	−833	+901	+942	−1,225
1993	−1,656	−446	…	−1,505	−3,240	−2,102	+1,682	−941

International Historical Statistics: The Americas 1750–1993

J3 SOUTH AMERICA: Balance of Payments (in million US dollars).

				Ecuador				
	VB	IB	TTB	IIB	GSIB	OCB	LTCB	CR
1950	+36	−17	−3	−8	+19	+21	+3	−20
1951	+18	−18	−2	−7	—	—	+3	+50
1952	+44	−25	−1	−14	+19	+20	+3	−11
1953	+30	−32	−2	−14	−2	−1	+3	+3
1954	+25	−42	−2	−17	−17	−15	+11	+2
1955	+20	−42	−1	−19	−22	−20	+11	+6
1956	+22	−47	—	−20	−25	−21	+23	—
1957	+39	−45	−1	−22	−6	−3	+8	−2
1958	+35	−48	—	−22	−13	−8	+6	−1
1959	+48	−53	−1	−23	−5	−1	+13[14]	−6[14]
1960	+36	−56	—	−23	−20	−13	+22	—
1961	+23	−51	+1	−23	−28	−21	+18	−3
1962	+37	−47	+1	−20	−10	−1	+11	−9
1963	+32	−41	+2	−17	−9	−3	+5	−10
1964	+22	−53	+1	−19	−31	−19	+14	—
1965	+29	−57	—	−25	−28	−19	+17	+6
1966	+27	−60	−1	−25	−33	−24	+35	−15
1967	+3	−44	—	−25	−41	−54	+40	−8
1968	−21	−83	−1	−27	−104	−91	+60	+12
1969	−25	−83	−1	−28	−108	−95	+66	−8
1970	−15	−115	−1	−29	−130	−113	+110	−9
1971	−69	−103	−3	−36	−172	−156	+181	+18
1972	+39	−132	−4	−66	−93	−77	+159	−77
1973	+187	−207	−5	−138	−20	+7	+77	−91
1974	+350	−344	−2	−201	+6	+38	+105	−108
1975	+7	−259	−7	−67	−252	−220	+200	+65
1976	+259	−296	−19	−121	−37	−7	+157	−224
1977	+40	−420	−33	−193	−380	−343	+591	−146
1978	−175	−569	−32	−267	−744	−703	+782	−13
1979	+5	−665	−76	−374	−660	−630	+689	−86
1980	+278	−950	−97	−573	−672	−641	+763	−291
1981	+174	−1,197	−129	−723	−1,023	−998	+1,077	+381
1982	+140	−1,342	−114	−895	−1,202	−1,182	−503	+328
1983	+927	−1,066	−32	−857	−139	−115	−1,150	−340
1984	+1,055	−1,348	−24	−1,011	−293	−273	−846	+33
1985	+1,294	−1,298	−63	−987	−4	+76	−690	−117
1986	+555	−1,196	+14	−929	−641	−585	−269	+247
1987	−33	−1,271	+3	−956	−1,304	−1,124	−292	+169
1988	+619	−1,327	+6	−1,034	−708	−536	−784	−45
1989	+661	−1,175	+18	−1,190	−691	−514	−317	−199
1990	+1,003	−1,169	+13	−1,209	−317	−166	−649	−252
1991	+644	−1,111	+12	−1,115	−652	−467	−513	−168
1992	+960	−1,153	+14	−947	−193	+10	−794	−107
1993	+578	−1,238	+40	−925	−660	−360	−270	−528

J3 SOUTH AMERICA: Balance of Payments (in million US dollars)

	Guyana							
	VB	IB	TTB	IIB	GSIB	OCB	LTCB	CR
1961	+2.0	−27.8	−2.0	−21.9	−25.8	−19.2	+15.9	...
1962	+37.3[14]	−34.1[14]	−1.5	−35.9	+3.2[14]	+9.1[14]	+6.1[14]	...
1963	+37.9	−22.4	−1.0	−16.1	+13.5	+15.3	+8.0	−3.7
1964	+18.7	−28.5	−2.3	−16.8	−9.8	−6.8	+6.5	+1.3
1965	+8.1	−28.6	−2.3	−18.4	−20.5	−15.5	+9.2	−3.6
1966	+7.0	−37.7	−2.2	−19.9	−30.7	−22.3	+17.6	+3.2
1967	+8.4	−33.1	−3.2	−17.3	−24.8	−21.5	+22.2	−2.0
1968	+16.6	−32.7	−2.7	−21.0	−16.1	−17.2	+19.8	−4.7
1969	+18.3	−32.1	−0.6	−20.5	−13.8	−12.0	+16.9	+2.2
1970	+9.1	−29.7	+0.4	−15.9	−20.6	−21.8	+17.1	+0.2
1971	+25.6	−32.2	—	−18.2	−6.6	−6.6	+16.1	−5.5
1972	+14.8	−29.2	−1.8	−10.6	−14.4	−16.3	+15.3	−10.8
1973	−23.7	−40.1	−4.5	−12.0	−63.8	−64.5	+28.7	+22.8
1974	+39.8	−40.7	+1.1	−18.9	−7.2	−10.7	+30.2	−49.3
1975	+45.5	−64.3	−2.7	−18.9	−18.6	−24.6	+81.4	−39.5
1976	−51.4	−85.3	−3.3	−23.9	−136.7	−142.8	+18.7	+70.9
1977	−27.4	−66.2	—	−21.7	−93.6	−97.5	+28.0	+11.2
1978	+42.1	−65.1	−1.8	−23.3	−23.0	−29.6	+32.5	−33.1
1979	+3.9	−87.2	−3.1	−34.4	−83.3	−82.9	+28.2	+40.5
1980	+2.4	−130.1	−4.6	−42.7	−127.7	−128.5	+34.0	+4.8
1981	−53.2	−130.5	−7.1	−54.6	−183.7	−184.5	+38.7	+9.0
1982	−12.7	−120.9	−9.4	−48.9	−133.6	−142.3	−39.9	−3.6
1983	−32.4	−134.1	−9.8	−57.5	−156.5	−157.5	−57.0	+4.1
1984	+15.2	−114.4	−14.2	−44.6	−99.2	−96.4	−27.7	−14.3
1985	+4.9	−96.3	−2.7	−40.3	−91.4	−96.6	−36.0	−2.5

J3 SOUTH AMERICA: Balance of Payments (in million US dollars)

				Paraguay			
	VB	IB	TTB	IIB	GSIB	OCB	LTCB	CR
1950	+14.8	−6.2	−0.7	−0.5	+8.6	+9	−0.9	−9.4
1951	+11.4	−3.4	−2.6	−0.7	+8	+8.5	+1.1	−6.2
1952	−0.9	−5.4	−0.9	−1.6	−6.3	−5.7	−1.6	+1.9
1953	−5.5	−0.2	−0.7	−1.3	−5.7	−3.9	+1.5	+1.5
1954	+0.4	−5.7[16]	−0.5	−0.6	−5.3[16]	−4.3[16]	+0.4[16]	+5.8
1955	+4.8	−6.8	−0.5	−1.0	−2.0	+0.1	—	+2.3
1956	−0.3	−7.2	−0.5	−1.0	−7.5	−5.2	+3.1	−2.1
1957	−2.3	−7.3	−0.9	−0.8	−9.6	−7.5	+9.7	+4.0
1958	−10.9	−5.3	−0.6	−0.2	−16.2	−14.7	+7.3	−0.3
1959	−1.1	−4.6	−0.3	−1.0	−5.7	−3.0	+4.2[14]	+1.6[14]
1960	−7.4	−5.8	+0.8	−0.8	−13.2	−9.7	+5.7	+2.2
1961	−4.8	−8.4	−0.3	−1.8	−13.2	−8.2	+3.9	−3.9
1962	−0.7	−8.7	−0.7	−1.9	−9.4	−5.1	+5.9	−0.1
1963	−1.9	−9.6	−1.0	−2.0	−11.5	−5.2	+7.6	−1.1
1964	+1.1	−12.5	−1.2	−2.5	−11.4	−6.6	+8.3	−2.2
1965	+4.1	−17.6	−1.6	−3.0	−13.5	−9.3	+10.0	−4.8
1966	−9.7	−11.9	−0.2	−4.1	−22.6	−18.2	+17.9	−1.2
1967	−15.3	−14.5	+0.4	−5.5	−29.8	−24.8	+22.7	−0.5
1968	−23.5	−12.8	+3.3	−5.1	−36.3	−31.7	+26.3	+0.1
1969	−26.0	−12.0	+8.4	−7.0	−38	−32.5	+30.7	+1.9
1970	−11.3	−10.3	+9.1	−9.8	−21.6	−16.4	+18.8	−7.3
1971	−16.4	−13.7	+8.7	−10.0	−30.1	−22.5	+24.6	−3.4
1972	+6.8	−18.6	+3.3	−12.1	−11.8	−5.3	+20.4	−10.4
1973	+0.7	−22.5	+1.3	−12.0	−21.8	−16.0	+29.6	−25.6
1974	−25.1	−31.4	+1.9	−20.3	−56.5	−52.7	+52.9	−30.1
1975	−39.3	−46.9	−1.6	−36.9	−86.2	−72.2	+85.9	−27.9
1976	−34.3	−38.4	+1.0	−27.0	−72.7	−68.5	+117.3	−42.5
1977	−33.0	−26.9	+18.9	−34.0	−59.9	−58.7	+85.2	−112.4
1978	−75.9	−42.7	+20.8	−61.2	−118.6	−112.9	+156.4	−179.5
1979	−192.6	−20.7	+38.0	−28.4	−213.3	−205.9	+135.5	−165.1
1980	−275.0	−5.8	+56.1	−58.7	−280.8	−276.2	+192.2	−152.6
1981	−373.9	−6.4	+42.2	−17.8	−380.3	−373.5	+168.4	−43.4
1982	−315.1	−64.7	+16.6	+26.1	−379.8	−374.8	+265.4	+64.8
1983	−225.4	−28.7	+4.7	−73.0	−254.1	−247.9	+289.2	+56.1
1984	−287.8	−38.9	+52.1	−56.6	−326.7	−317.4	+219.4	+18.1
1985	−191.5	−41.5	+58.5	−6.0	−233.0	−225.5	+121.3	+100.8
1986	−162.4	−207.5	+100.3	−167.2	−369.9	−358.9	+212.0	+119.7
1987	−97.2	−63.2	+70.1	−174.1	−160.4	−133.4	−434.0	−50.3
1988	−159.1	−86.0	+54.8	−122.3	−245.3	−210.2	−539.0	+173.3
1989	+164.1	+68.0	+52.0	−62.0	+232.1	+255.6	−130.0	+313.4
1990	−253.5	+25.6	+25.0	−48.0	−227.9	−172.3	−66.0	+74.1
1991	−746.8	+350.4	+366.0	−49.0	−396.4	−324.1	+44.0	+79.6
1992	−869.1	+235.1	+338.0	−112.0	−634.0	−600.1	+1.0	−645.8
1993	−1,210.7	+334.7	+412.0	−92.0	−876.0	−834.0	+200.0	−433.2

J3   SOUTH AMERICA: Balance of Payments (in million US dollars)

	Peru							
	VB	IB	TTB	IIB	GSIB	OCB	LTCB	CR
1950	+55	−62	−4	−10	−7	−4	−9	−9
1951	+43	−82	−4	−21	−39	−34	+26	−1
1952	−5	−51	+1	−21	−56	−48	+54	+3
1953	−21	−51	−1	−20	−71	−64	+55	+7
1954	+37	−58	−3	−22	−21	−11	+26	−8
1955	+20	−65	−3	−23	−45	−37	+39	+3
1956	−20	−80	−3	−32	−100	−87	+75	−15
1957	−65	−91	−3	−33	−156	−130	+102	+33
1958	−39	−78	+1	−32	−117	−99	+95	+13
1959	+50	−89	—	−51	−39	−25	+52[14]	−32
1960	+118	−116	−2	−66	+2	+8	−2	−17
1961	+101	−117	−2	−63	−16	−9	+3	−34
1962	+88	−133	−2	−66	−45	−37	+33	−6
1963	+46	−139	—	−73	−93	−81	+55	−19
1964	+174	−169	−12	−72	+5	+14	+71	−25
1965	+32	−196	−14	−91	−164	−148	+124	−15
1966	−14	−239	−12	−128	−253	−233	+203	+17
1967	−68	−243	−4	−147	−311	−282	+134	+30
1968	+177	−236	−4	−149	−59	−22	+92	+18
1969	+222	−252	−4	−185	−30	+3	+128	−31
1970	+335	−215	−4	−133	+120	+202	−17	−187
1971	+159	−232	−8	−125	−73	−34	+9	−90
1972	+132	−203	+15	−121	−71	−31	+107	−30
1973	+15	−319	+14	−163	−304	−262	+408	−94
1974	−403	−370	+32	−172	−773	−725	+721	−413
1975	−1,099	−492	+7	−242	−1,591	−1,541	+1,293	+499
1976	−740	−511	+43	−371	−1,251	−1,193	+642	+312
1977	−438	−541	+75	−424	−979	−922	+675	−59
1978	+340	−588	+108	−573	−248	−192	+11	−5
1979	+1,540	−689	+143	−964	+851	+729	+2	−1,066
1980	+826	−1,074	+186	−908	−248	−101	−96	−609
1981	−553	−1,336	+86	−1,114	−1,889	−1,733	+276	+632
1982	−428	−1,348	+46	−1,034	−1,776	−1,612	+1,027	+65
1983	+293	−1,384	+19	−1,130	−1,091	−875	+213	−2
1984	+1,007	−1,398	+27	−1,165	−391	−235	−618	−297
1985	+1,172	−1,214	+35	−999	−42	+90	−820	−124
1986	−65	−1,257	+4	−819	−1,322	−1,173	−1,187	+411
1987	−521	−1,299	−20	−718	−1,820	−1,640	−1,226	+835
1988	−99	−1,358	+65	−783	−1,457	−1,246	−1,271	−54
1989	+1,197	−1,357	−16	−984	−160	+94	−917	−613
1990	+340	−1,516	−37	−1,054	−1,176	−840	−886	−226
1991	−165	−1,484	+5	−807	−1,649	−1,331	−792	−413
1992	−565	−1,578	−67	−987	−2,143	−1,710	−367	−594
1993	−580	−1,637	−3	−1,006	−2,217	−1,800	+270	−447

J3 SOUTH AMERICA: Balance of Payments (in million US dollars)

	Uruguay							
	VB	IB	TTB	IIB	GSIB	OCB	LTCB	CR
1950	+48	+1	+6	−4	+49	+48	+5	−61
1951	−76	−1	+5	−4	−77	−79	+11	+64
1952	−31	−3	+4	−5	−34	−36	+42	−34
1953	+76	−5	+2	−5	+71	+68	[+7][17]	−65
1954	−25	−8	+1	−5	−33	−35	[+7][17]	+42
1955	−45	−5	+1	−5	−51	−53	−14	+78
1956	−2	−4	+2	−5	−6	−8	+19	−27
1957	−127	+4	+10	−5	−123	−124	+2	+65
1958	−13	+3	+8	−4	−10	−11	+2	+4
1959	−43	−6	+25	−3	−50	−47	+4[14]	+3
1960	−58	−17	+20	−7	−75	−74	+6	−6
1961	−8	−15	+20	−6	−23	−18	+9	−6
1962	−54	−18	+17	−7	−72	−68	+14	−1
1963	+15	−19	+10	−10	−4	—	+30	−17
1964	+15	−21	+15	−16	−6	−1	−2	−1
1965	+73	−4	+26	−15	+69	+72	−16	+8
1966	+58	−8	+27	−19	+50	+59	−3	+2
1967	+13	−30	+27	−26	−16	−4	−16	+15
1968	+43	−27	+27	−24	+16	+23	−19	−5
1969	+29	−56	+6	−22	−27	−19	−6	−17
1970	+21	−75	−2	−25	−54	−45	−4	+8
1971	−6	−65	+5	−22	−72	−64	+27	−1
1972	+103	−56	+4	−24	+47	+59	−8	−24
1973	+79	−61	−1	−33	+18	+37	−57	−23
1974	−52	−83	+14	−43	−135	−118	+28	+2
1975	−109	−87	+37	−71	−196	−189	+106	+18
1976	+28	−109	+8	−72	−81	−74	+56	−102
1977	−75	−99	+22	−68	−174	−167	+101	−149
1978	−24	−110	+29	−77	−134	−127	+152	−33
1979	−378	+14	+133	−58	−364	−357	+359	−123
1980	−610	−108	+95	−100	−718	−709	+404	−114
1981	−362	−109	+80	−74	−471	−461	+346	−20
1982	+218	−463	−198	−197	−245	−235	+515	+409
1983	+417	−491	−169	−288	−74	−60	+643	−31
1984	+192	−331	+56	−362	−139	−133	+42	+79
1985	+178	−286	+73	−351	−108	−99	+60	−170
1986	+273	−257	+84	−301	+16	−42	+137	−244
1987	+102	−250	+79	−308	−148	−152	+90	−39
1988	+292	−291	+64	−331	+1	+2	−18	−35
1989	+463	−337	+61	−376	+126	+121	+12	−104
1990	+426	−248	+127	−394	+178	+170	−10	−142
1991	+61	−59	+223	−439	+2	+42	−183	−156
1992	−238	+201	+277	−444	−37	−17	+274	−93
1993	−545	+293	+318	−325	−252	−227	+376	−106

J3   SOUTH AMERICA: Balance of Payments (in million dollars)

	Venezuela							
	VB	**IB**	**TTB**	**IIB**	**GSIB**	**OCB**	**LTCB**	**CR**
1950	+555	−528	−33	−392	+27	+12	+17	+80
1951	+648	−576	−41	−423	+72	+55	+1	−4
1952	+871	−812	−42	−447	+59	+40	+159	−70
1953	+659	−622	−36	−446	+37	+16	+169	−45
1954	+720	−702	−43	−493	+18	−4	+36	+7
1955	+897	−826	−51	−501	+71	+48	−6	−46
1956	+1,051	−1,096	−64	−761	−45	−69	+590	−417
1957	+989	−1,494	−134	−971	−505	−569	+982	−505
1958	+996	−1,042	−95	−600	−46	−117	+83	+395
1959	+806	−883	−85	−513	−77	−164	+19[14]	+338
1960	+1,239	−757	−72	−522	+482	+395	−135	+115
1961	+1,398	−841	−61	−581	+557	+473	−388	+29
1962	+1,383	−920	−68	−631	+463	+385	−449	−2
1963	+1,427	−872	−69	−607	+555	+476	−209	−163
1964	+1,288	−1,012	−73	−671	+276	+193	−48	−86
1965	+1,128	−1,023	−69	−706	+105	+35	−52	−11
1966	+1,088	−981	−80	−696	+107	+26	+85	+67
1967	+1,129	−907	−71	−662	+222	+147	+42	−95
1968	+958	−1,072	−82	−782	−114	−194	+263	−50
1969	+855	−978	−65	−665	−123	−220	+335	−11
1970	+889	−901	−93	−553	−12	−104	+91	−87
1971	+1,207	−1,135	−81	−740	+72	−11	+374	−469
1972	+930	−936	−110	−481	−6	−101	−261	−208
1973	+2,095	−1,107	−79	−689	+988	+877	−53	−637
1974	+7,209	−1,250	−114	−637	+5,959	+5,760	−810	−4,480
1975	+3,391	−1,047	−237	+101	+2,344	+2,171	+396	−2,669
1976	+1,916	−1,630	−508	+208	+286	+254	+1,466	−2,377
1977	−638	−2,258	−893	+89	−2,896	−3,179	+2,109	−847
1978	−2,150	−3,178	−1,444	+38	−5,328	−5,735	+3,716	+977
1979	+4,155	−3,398	−1,559	−4	+757	+350	+1,443	−4,234
1980	+8,174	−2,997	−1,756	+331	+5,177	+4,728	+2,060	−3,823
1981	+7,840	−3,431	−2,185	+574	+4,409	+4,000	+810	+12
1982	+2,748	−6,355	−2,616	−1,530	−3,607	−4,246	+3,157	+8,215
1983	+8,162	−3,524	−763	−2,113	+4,636	+4,427	+284	−28
1984	+8,632	−3,809	−705	−2,058	+4,823	+4,651	−1,301	−1,355
1985	+6,782	−3,284	−181	−2,230	+3,498	+3,327	−1,204	−1,438
1986	+669	−2,793	−99	−1,597	−2,124	−2,245	−1,422	+4,176
1987	+1,567	−2,866	−93	−1,612	−1,299	−1,390	−1,732	+1,096
1988	−1,998	−3,664	−218	−1,763	−5,662	−5,809	−491	+3,871
1989	+5,632	−3,288	−251	−2,368	+2,344	+2,161	−1,318	−96
1990	+10,637	−2,056	−527	−765	+8,581	+8,279	−3,159	−2,825
1991	+4,837	−2,737	−717	−592	+2,100	+1,736	+2,195	−2,259
1992	+1,274	−4,653	−984	−1,745	−3,379	−3,753	+2,606	+1,032
1993	+3,209	−5,085	−1,521	−1,714	−1,876	−2,223	+2,380	+230

J3 Balance of Payments

NOTES

1. SOURCES: The volumes of national historical statistics listed on pp. xiii–xv for Canada and USA to 1960 (1st line), and Susan Schroeder, Cuba: *A Handbook of Historical Statistics* (Boston, 1982) for Cuba. Other statistics are derived from League of Nations (or United Nations), *Balance of Payments* (the last one being published in 1948), and from IMF *Balance of Payments Yearbook* and *International Financial Statistics*. The latest available revisions for each series have been used.
2. Except as indicated in footnotes, both exports and imports are valued f.o.b., and, where possible, non-monetary gold is included in the visible balance
3. In principle, the visible balance and the invisible balance sum to the balance on goods, services and requited income. The overall current balance includes, additionally, unrequited transfers. If no figure is given under the heading GSIB, unrequited transfers and errors and omissions are included in the invisible balance.
4. In the Change in Reserves column, a plus sign indicates financing from reserves (i.e. a decrease in reserves) and a minus sign indicates an addition to reserves.

FOOTNOTES

[1] All gold movements are included in the visible and overall current balances to 1926 (1st line), not merely non-monetary gold. Other changes which occur on the change in original source in 1926 include a shift from a.c.i.f. to f.o.b. basis for imports.
[2] The gold balance only to 1926, and net official monetary movements subsequently to 1926 (1st line).
[3] All financial movements except gold.
[4] Gold movements only.
[5] Short-term capital is included in the Capital Balance column (to 1922 in the case of USA).
[6] Unilateral transfers by private individuals are not separately covered to 1819.
[7] Excluding borrowing and lending by government to 1960 (1st line).
[8] There is a change in the basis of accounts, including a shift from a c.i.f. to f.o.b. basis for imports.
[9] Subsequently excludes the reinvested earnings of subsidiary businesses.
[10] Statistics to 1926 (1st line) are for years ended 30 September.
[11] There was a change in the system of conversion to dollars in 1937 from official selling to official buying rates.
[12] Receipts of pensions are included in the invisible and goods, services and requited income balance to 1951, but are treated as unrequited transfers thereafter.
[13] This break occurs on a change in source and consequent change in the definition of certain concepts.
[14] Later revisions were not carried back to earlier years.
[15] Statistics are for years ended 30 September.
[16] Repatriation of capital is treated as a current invisible item to 1954.
[17] Excluding private sector capital movements.
[18] Figures to 1910 are for the year ending 30 June. Figures for 1938 are on the same basis as those for 1946–50 and are not exactly comparable with those for 1939–1945. Amongst other things, the latter value imports c.i.f. and personal unrequited transfers are included with invisibles.